COLLECTED WORKS OF JOHN STUART MILL

VOLUME VII

The Collected Edition of the works of John Stuart Mill was planned and directed by an editorial committee appointed from the Faculty of Arts and Science of the University of Toronto, and from the University of Toronto Press. The primary aim of the edition is to present fully collated texts of those works which exist in a number of versions, both printed and manuscript, and to provide accurate texts of works previously unpublished or which had become relatively inaccessible.

A System of Logic Ratiocinative and Inductive

Being a Connected View of the Principles of Evidence and the Methods of Scientific Investigation

by JOHN STUART MILL

Volume 7

BOOKS I–III

Editor of the Text

J. M. ROBSON

Professor of English and Principal
Victoria College, University of Toronto

Introduction by

R. F. McRAE

Professor of Philosophy
University of Toronto

Liberty Fund
Indianapolis

This book is published by Liberty Fund, Inc., a foundation established to encourage study of the ideal of a society of free and responsible individuals.

The cuneiform inscription that serves as our logo and as the design motif for our endpapers is the earliest-known written appearance of the word "freedom" (*amagi*), or "liberty." It is taken from a clay document written about 2300 B.C. in the Sumerian city-state of Lagash.

This Liberty Fund paperback edition of 2006 is a reprint from the original edition published by The University of Toronto Press in 1973.
© 1973 The University of Toronto Press.

06 07 08 09 10 P 5 4 3 2 1

Library of Congress Cataloging-in-Publication Data
Mill, John Stuart, 1806–1873.
[Works. 2006]
The collected works / of John Stuart Mill
p. cm.
Reprint. Originally published: Toronto, Ont.; Buffalo, N.Y.: University of Toronto Press, 1965–1981.
Includes bibliographical references and index.
ISBN-13: 978-0-86597-658-0 (8-vol. set: alk. paper: pbk.) ISBN-10: 0-86597-658-9
ISBN-13: 978-0-86597-655-9 (vol. 7: alk. paper: pbk.) ISBN-10: 0-86597-655-4
ISBN-13: 978-0-86597-692-4 (2-vol. pbk. set, vols. 7–8) ISBN-10: 0-86597-692-9
1. Philosophy. 2. Political science. 3. Economics. I. Title.
B1602 .A2 2006
192—dc22   2005044313

The original, hardcover edition of this volume was published with the assistance of a grant from the Canada Council

The text of this book was set in Times Roman, a typeface designed by Stanley Morison for the *Times* of London and introduced by that newspaper in 1932. Also used for book work throughout the world, Times Roman is among the most important type designs of the twentieth century.

Printed on paper that is acid-free and meets the requirements of the American National Standard for Permanence of Paper for Printed Library Materials, Z39.48-1992. ♾

Cover design by Erin Kirk New, Watkinsville, Georgia
Printed and bound by The University of Toronto Press Inc.

Liberty Fund, Inc.
8335 Allison Pointe Trail, Suite 300
Indianapolis, Indiana 46250-1684

Contents

Volume 7

*a–a*MS defining

BOOK II: OF REASONING

^bMS, 43, 46 § 1. Definition, why treated of in this place [*in* MS, 43, 46 *subsequent section numbers consequently altered,* § 1 *being* § 2, *and so on*]
^{c-c}+62, 65, 68, 72
^{d-d}+65, 68, 72

*e–e*MS, 43, 46 —and why
*f–f*MS, 43 only necessary truths   *g–g*+56, 62, 65, 68, 72
*h*MS, 43, 46, 51 , and of logical necessity   *i–i*+56, 62, 65, 68, 72
j–j+72   *k–k*56, 62, 65, 68 § 4.

l–l+51, 56, 62, 65, 68, 72   *m–m*+72
*n–n*MS, 43, 46, 51, 56, 62, 65, 68   § 5.   *o–o*MS, 43, 46, 51, 56, 62, 65, 68   § 6.
*p–p*MS, 43, 46, 51, 56, 62, 65, 68   § 7.   *q–q*MS, 43, 46, 51, 56, 62, 65, 68   § 8.
*r*MS, 43   § 9. M. Comte's objections to the word cause]   46   § 9. Laws of causation, and so-called laws of phenomena
s–s+72   *t–t*+51, 56, 62, 65, 68, 72
*u–u*51, 56, 62, 65, 68   § 9.

^{v}MS, 43, 46   § 2. —how far a perfect example

$^{w-w}$MS, 43, 46   § 3. ^{x}MS , by Mr. Alexander Bain

$^{y-y}$MS, 43, 46   § 4. $^{z-z}$+65, 68, 72

$^{a-a}$51, 56, 62   § 4. $^{b-b}$+62, 65, 68, 72

$^{c-c}$62   § 5. $^{d-d}$MS, 43, 46, 51   to [*slip of the pen?*]

*e–e*MS, 43, 46, 51, 56, 62   Liebig's theory of the contagiousness of chemical action
*f–f*MS, 43, 46, 51, 56, 62   His theory of respiration
*g–g*MS, 43   Other speculations of Liebig]   46, 51, 56, 62   Other chemical speculations
*h–h*MS, 43, 46   The deductive method henceforth the main instrument of scientific
inquiry
*i–i*56, 62, 65   On
*j–j*MS, 43, 46, 51, 56, 62, 65, 68   Legitimate, how distinguished from illegitimate
hypotheses

^{k-k}MS, 43, 46   And hence

^lMS, 43, 46   § 7. Most, if not all, cases of sequence from very complex antecedents, are resolvable

  ^{m-m}MS, 43, 46   § 8.   ⁿ⁻ⁿMS, 43 The foundation

  ^{o-o}MS, 43   Laplace, defective]   46, 51, 56, 62, 65   mathematicians

^{p-p}+46, 51, 56, 62, 65, 68, 72   ^{q-q}MS, 43   § 2. The real foundation, what

^{r-r}+51, 56, 62, 65, 68, 72   ^{s-s}MS, 43   § 3.]   46   § 4.

^tMS, 43   § 4. In what cases the doctrine is practically applicable]   46   § 5.... as MS

  ^{u-u}MS, 43   § 5.

*v–v*MS, 43, 46   rests upon an induction by simple enumeration
w–w+51, 56, 62, 65, 68, 72   *x–x*MS, 43, 46   § 2.
*y–y*MS, 43, 46   § 3.
*z–z*MS, 43, 46   may once have been doubtful
*a*MS, 43   § 4. Ground of its present certainty   § 5. Limits of the reliance due to it]
46   § 4. Grounds of . . . *as* MS
*b–b*MS, 43, 46   The uniformities   *c–c*MS, 43, 46   must

$^{d-d}$+46, 51, 56, 62, 65, 68, 72
$^{e-e}$MS, 43   § 5.

Volume 8

BOOK IV: OF OPERATIONS SUBSIDIARY TO INDUCTION

$^{d-d}$+46, 51, 56, 62, 65, 68, 72 $^{e-e}$MS, 43   § 5.
$^{f-f}$+ 43, 46, 51, 56, 62, 65, 68, 72
$^{g-g}$MS, 43, 46, 51, 56   Cases in which the conception must pre-exist

h–hMS, 43, 46, 51   Of

ⁱ⁻ⁱMS, 43, 46   other

*j*MS   which
*k–k*MS, 43, 46   radically different phenomena

l–l+51, 56, 62, 65, 68, 72

ᵐ⁻ᵐ+62, 65, 68, 72
ⁿ⁻ⁿMS, 43, 46, 51, 56   XI.
ᵒ⁻ᵒMS,43, 46   Art consists of the
ᵖ⁻ᵖ+51, 56, 62, 65, 68, 72
ᑫ⁻ᑫMS, 43, 46   Application of the preceding principles to Morality
ʳ⁻ʳ+51, 56, 62, 65, 68, 72
ˢ⁻ˢMS, 43, 46   § 7.

APPENDICES

Introduction

R. F. McRAE

JOHN STUART MILL'S *System of Logic* is his principal philosophical work. Its subject matters cost him more effort and time to think through than those of his other writings, including the *Political Economy*, which, though of comparable scope, was, he says, far more rapidly executed. He believed that the *System of Logic* was destined to survive longer than anything else he had written, than even, perhaps, the essay *On Liberty*. In so far as it introduces technical material, it has contributed the Four Experimental Methods—though usually criticised in one way or another—to almost every later textbook on logic which treats of induction. Mill would appear, therefore, to have succeeded in his intention of doing for inductive arguments what Aristotle, in originating the rules of syllogism, did for ratiocination or deduction. The survival of Mill's *System of Logic* as a philosophical work is a consequence of other features. It was conceived in controversy, and on many subjects it still remains pertinent to controversy because of the classic formulation it gives to one of a set of alternative theses, whether at the very beginning of the book in the theory of meaning, or at the end in the idea of a social science. It consequently has a survival value greatly extending beyond any that can be estimated by the number of adherents to its doctrines. The *System of Logic* has survived also in a third, and ghostly, fashion under the labels "empiricism" and "psychologism," with the varying connotations which these have. Mill himself was not in the least averse to labels. He saw himself as protagonist in a conflict of "schools." If, however, some general, undistorted, view is to be taken of his *System of Logic*, it becomes necessary to give precision to the applicability of these two labels, often interconnected as they are, as, for example, in a recent description of it as an "attempt to expound a psychological system of logic within empiricist principles."[1]

R. P. Anschutz has forcefully drawn attention to the fact that Mill did not regard himself as an empiricist but as in fundamental opposition to empiri-

[1]*Philosophy of Recent Times*, ed. J. B. Hartmann (New York: McGraw-Hill, 1967), I, 14.

cism.[2] By empiricism Mill meant "bad generalization" and "unscientific surmise." His own position he identified with "the School of Experience." It may have been natural enough for Mill to have retained the term "empiricism" in its ordinary, as well as in its older philosophical use, and in any case, it aptly covered the type of political theory associated with Mackintosh and Macaulay. The latter's attack on his father's *Essay on Government* caused Mill to see that Macaulay "stood up for the empirical mode of treating political phenomena, against the philosophical; that even in physical science, his notion of philosophizing . . . would have excluded Newton and Laplace."[3] However, the members of what Mill called "the School of Experience" are today more generally called the British empiricists, and he is counted among them. To speak of Mill's empiricism is to speak of his adherence to what he described as "the prevailing theory in the eighteenth century," a theory which had its starting point, as he believed every system of philosophy should, with two questions, one about the sources of human knowledge, and the other about the objects which the mind is capable of knowing. With regard to the first question, the answer of this school was that "all knowledge consists of generalizations from experience. . . . There is no knowledge *à priori*; no truths cognizable by the mind's inward light, and grounded on intuitive evidence. Sensation, and the mind's consciousness of its own acts, are not only the exclusive sources, but the sole materials of our knowledge." With regard to the second question their answer was, "Of nature, or anything whatever external to ourselves, we know . . . nothing, except the facts which present themselves to our senses, and such other facts as may, by analogy, be inferred from these."[4] This means that the "nature and laws of Things in themselves, or of the hidden causes of the phenomena which are the objects of experience," are "radically inaccessible to the human faculties." Nothing "can be the object of our knowledge except our experience, and what can be inferred from our experience by the analogies of experience itself. . . ."[5]

In general, the term "experience" refers in the *System of Logic* to observation that something is the case and to experimentation as an adjunct of such observation. When Mill states the empirical thesis that "all knowledge consists in generalization from experience," he is using the term in this sense. For example, he asks about the proposition, All men are mortal, "whence do we derive our knowledge of that general truth? Of course from observation. Now all that man can observe are individual cases. From these all general truths are drawn, and into these they may again be resolved." But Mill also uses "experience" to refer to the undergoing of sensations and feelings, or

[2]*The Philosophy of J. S. Mill* (Oxford: Oxford University Press, 1953), 73–7.
[3]*Autobiography*, ed. Jack Stillinger (Boston: Houghton Mifflin, 1969), 95.
[4]"Coleridge," in *Essays on Ethics, Religion, and Society*, ed. J. M. Robson, *Collected Works*, X (Toronto: University of Toronto Press, 1969), 125.
[5]*Ibid.*, 128–9.

having what he calls collectively "states of consciousness." It is this sense of "experience" which is indicated when he says that "sensation and the mind's consciousness of its own acts are . . . the sole materials of our knowledge." This too is a familiar empirical thesis, but by virtue of the kind of experience to which it refers, it is different from the first thesis, and it constitutes the basis of Mill's phenomenalism. Both senses of the term "experience" are common and philosophically neutral, but the first of them, observation that something is the case, ceases to be taken in neutral fashion when it is reduced to, or considered to mean the same in the end as the second, namely, having sensations. While acknowledging in the *System of Logic* that he is here on disputed philosophical territory, Mill does perform this reduction, as in the following example which he gives of something which can be observed to be the case.

Let us take, then, as our example, one of what are termed the sensible qualities of objects, and let the example be whiteness. When we ascribe whiteness to any substance, as, for instance, snow; when we say that snow has the quality white-ness, what do we really assert? Simply, that when snow is present to our organs, we have a particular sensation, which we are accustomed to call the sensation of white. But how do I know that snow is present? Obviously from the sensations which I derive from it, and not otherwise. I infer that the object is present, be-cause it gives me a certain assemblage or series of sensations. And when I ascribe to it the attribute whiteness, my meaning is only, that, of the sensations composing this group or series, that which I call the sensation of white colour is one.[6]

We must then distinguish two levels of empiricism in Mill, one in which "ex-perience" refers to observation of what is the case and to experimentation as related to it, and the other more radical level, that of his phenomenalism, in which all experience is reduced to one kind, namely, undergoing sensations, feelings, and other "states of consciousness." On which of these levels of empiricism are Mill's logical doctrines constructed?

On the relation of logic to experience Mill appears to take two contradic-tory positions, one in his *Autobiography* and the other in the Introduction to the *System of Logic*. In the *Autobiography* he says, "The German, or *à priori* view of human knowledge, and of the knowing faculties, is likely for some time longer (though it may be hoped in a diminishing degree) to pre-dominate among those who occupy themselves with such inquiries, both here and on the Continent. But the 'System of Logic' supplies what was much wanted, a text-book of the opposite doctrine—that which derives all knowl-edge from experience, and all moral and intellectual qualities principally from the direction given to the associations."[7] In the Introduction to the

[6]*Logic*, 65 below. Henceforth references to the present edition of the *Logic* are given in parentheses in the text.
[7]*Autobiography*, 134.

System of Logic, however, Mill proclaims the philosophical neutrality of logic. "Logic is common ground on which the partisans of Hartley and of Reid, of Locke and Kant, may meet and join hands. Particular and detached opinions of all these thinkers will no doubt occasionally be controverted, since all of them were logicians as well as metaphysicians; but the field on which their principal battles have been fought, lies beyond the boundaries of our science"(14). Mill concludes the Introduction with this remark: ". . . I can conscientiously affirm that no one proposition laid down in this work has been adopted for the sake of establishing, or with any reference to its fitness for being employed in establishing, preconceived opinions in any department of knowledge or of inquiry on which the speculative world is still undecided" (14–15).

Mill's claim for the neutrality of logic derives from a distinction which he makes between two ways in which truths may be known. Some are known directly, that is, by intuition; some are known by means of other truths, that is, are inferred. Logic has no concern with the former kind of truths, nor with the question whether they are part of the original furniture of the mind or given through the senses. It is concerned only with inferred truths. Moreover, while there is much in our knowledge which may seem to be intuited, but which may actually be inferred, the decision as to what part of our knowledge is intuitive and what inferential is something which also falls outside the scope of logic. It belongs to what Mill calls Metaphysics, a term he uses in such a way as to include psychology and theory of knowledge. It is clear from his description of metaphysics in the Introduction that it is this science, not logic, which decides the issue which separates "the German, or *à priori* view of human knowledge" from that which "derives all knowledge from experience." In the *Autobiography*, however, Mill looked to his *Logic* to settle the issue.

The notion that truths external to the mind may be known by intuition or consciousness, independently of observation and experience, is, I am persuaded, in these times, the great intellectual support of false doctrines and bad institutions. . . . And the chief strength of this false philosophy in morals, politics, and religion, lies in the appeal which it is accustomed to make to the evidence of mathematics and of the cognate branches of physical science. To expel it from these, is to drive it from its stronghold. . . . In attempting to clear up the real nature of the evidence of mathematical and physical truths, the "System of Logic" met the intuitive philosophers on ground on which they had previously been deemed unassailable. . . .[8]

The apparent contradiction dissolves, however, as the course of Mill's argument reveals that it rests on no assumptions about the nature of direct knowledge, and reaches a conclusion which, if valid, would subvert the *à*

[8]*Ibid.*, 134–5.

priori school. The argument also reveals the nature and extent of Mill's empiricism.

Because twentieth-century empiricists, with their predominantly Viennese background, express their doctrine in the language, not of the British empiricists, but of Leibniz and Kant, it will be useful to state Mill's argument in this latter, more familiar language. Leibniz distinguished between two kinds of propositions, truths of reason and truths of fact. Truths of reason are necessary and their opposites are impossible, that is, contain a contradiction. A necessary truth can be shown to be so by a mere analysis of its terms; the analysis will reveal the concept of the predicate to be contained within the concept of the subject. A truth of fact, on the other hand, is not necessary but contingent. By this Leibniz means, not that the predicate is not contained within the concept of the subject, but that no finite analysis, however far it is pursued, can ever show the concept of the predicate to be contained within that of the subject, for the required analysis is infinite. Only by experience can it be known that the subject and predicate are connected. Kant modified Leibniz's division in an important way by introducing a further distinction, one between analytic and synthetic judgments. Analytic judgments, like Leibniz's truths of reason, are those in which the concept of the predicate is contained within that of the subject. Synthetic judgments, a type not recognized by Leibniz, are, on the other hand, those in which the concept of the predicate is *not* contained within that of the subject. No analysis of the concept of the subject can extract it. Where an analytic judgment is merely explicative of the concept of the subject, a synthetic judgment is ampliative; it extends our knowledge of the subject. Kant now enlarged Leibniz's class of necessary truths so that it should include not only propositions which were analytical, but also some which were synthetic, that is, some whose negation did not contain a contradiction. These synthetic propositions, being necessary, could only be known to be true independently of sense experience. Modern empiricists have adopted the Kantian distinction between the analytic and the synthetic as so basic that it has been labelled one of the "dogmas of empiricism."[9] But while accepting Kant's distinction, they of course rule out the possibility of the class of synthetic propositions which are necessary. Like Leibniz they hold that all necessary truths are analytical.

Mill makes a distinction which, he says, corresponds to "that which is drawn by Kant and other metaphysicians between what they term *analytic*, and *synthetic*, judgments; the former being those which can be evolved from the meaning of the terms used" (116n). Mill's distinction is between propositions which are merely verbal or relate to the meaning of terms, and propositions which assert matters of fact. Verbal propositions, those "(. . . in

[9]W. V. Quine, "Two Dogmas of Empiricism," *From a Logical Point of View* (New York: Harper and Row, 1963), 20ff.

which the predicate connotes the whole or part of what the subject connotes, but nothing besides) answer no purpose but that of unfolding the whole or some part of the meaning of the name, to those who did not previously know it" (113). Every man is a corporeal being, or Every man is rational, would be examples. Real propositions, on the other hand, "predicate of a thing some fact not involved in the signification of the name by which the proposition speaks of it. . . . Such are . . . all general or particular propositions in which the predicate connotes any attribute not connoted by the subject. All these, if true, add to our knowledge: they convey information, not already involved in the names employed" (115–16).

But while Mill accepts the distinction between analytic and synthetic propositions, this is not for him one between two kinds of truths. Verbal propositions are "not, strictly speaking, susceptible of truth or falsity, but only of conformity or disconformity to usage or convention; and all the proof they are capable of, is proof of usage . . ." (109). Analytic propositions are not, then, as they are for Leibniz, Kant, and modern empiricists, necessary truths, for they are not truths at all. Some examples of what Mill considered to be true propositions, that is, propositions asserting matters of fact, would be: All men are mortal, Two straight lines cannot enclose a space, Two and one is equal to three, Every fact which has a beginning has a cause, The same proposition cannot at the same time be false and true. All these assert something about what is the case in *this* world. They do not assert what would be, in the language of Leibniz, true in all possible worlds. In the case of two of these propositions, the arithmetical one and the principle of contradiction, Mill considered, and rejected, the possibility that they were not assertions of matters of fact, and therefore neither true nor false, but were merely verbal or analytical. Indeed, he acknowledged great plausibility in the view that the "proposition, Two and one is equal to three . . . is not a truth, is not the assertion of a really existing fact, but a definition of the word three; a statement that mankind have agreed to use the name three as a sign exactly equivalent to two and one; to call by the former name whatever is called by the other more clumsy phrase" (253). Mill did not, however, consider the possibility of looking at geometry in this way; "that science cannot be supposed to be conversant about non-entities" (225). Geometrical theorems add to our knowledge of the world. Consequently he thought it fatal to the view that the science of numbers is merely a succession of changes in terminology, that it is impossible to explain by it how, when a new geometrical theorem is demonstrated by algebra, the series of translations brings out new facts. Mill takes note also—again with some degree of sympathy—of those who regard the principle of contradiction as "an identical proposition; an assertion involved in the meaning of terms; a mode of defining Negation, and the word Not" (277), and indeed he is willing to go part way with this. "If the negative is true the affirmative is false," is merely an identical proposition, for what the negative means is only the falsity of the affirmative. But the statement that the same proposition cannot at the same time be false and true, is not a merely verbal one but a generalization about facts in the world. The principle of contradiction states a truth.

The distinction between verbal, or analytic, and real, or synthetic, propositions has an important bearing on Mill's conception of the nature of logic. For him logic is primarily concerned with real propositions, that is, assertions of matters of fact, or propositions which are either true or false. It is, in his words, a "logic of truth." But there are two ways in which truths are known. Some are known directly, some are known by inference from other truths. Logic is concerned only with the second of these two ways. This means that Mill's logic is concerned with the way in which we infer from some truths other truths which are quite distinct from them. Such inference Mill calls "real," in order to contrast it with merely "apparent" inference. The latter kind occurs in instances of equivalence or implication, for in these the conclusion asserts no new truth, but only what is already asserted in the premises: "the conclusion is either the very same fact, or part of the fact asserted in the original proposition." Moreover, the logic of truth requires an interpretation of the syllogism different from any it has traditionally received. Mill finds it unanimously admitted that a syllogism is invalid if there is anything in the conclusion which is not contained in the premises. This being so, syllogism cannot, then, be inference at all, though it may perform some important function in relation to inference. This function Mill sought to determine. In short, formal logic, which some have taken to be the whole of logic, is not concerned with inference, and must be sharply contrasted with the logic of truth. Its sole aim is consistency. As a logic of consistency it performs a subordinate, but indispensable, role in relation to the logic of truth, for consistency is a condition for truth.

If thought be anything more than a sportive exercise of the mind, its purpose is to enable us to know what can be known respecting the facts of the universe: its judgments and conclusions express, or are intended to express, some of those facts: and the connexion which Formal Logic, by its analysis of the reasoning process, points out between one proposition and another, exists only because there is a connexion between one objective truth and another, which makes it possible for us to know objective truths which have never been observed, in virtue of others which have. This possibility is an eternal mystery and stumbling-block to Formal Logic. The bare idea that any new truth can be brought out of a Concept—that analysis can ever find in it anything which synthesis has not first put in—is absurd on the face of it: yet this is all the explanation that Formal Logic, as viewed by Sir W. Hamilton, is able to give of the phænomenon; and Mr. Mansel expressly limits the province of Logic to analytic judgments—to such as are merely identical. But what the Logic of mere consistency cannot do, the Logic of the ascertainment of truth, the Philosophy of Evidence in its larger acceptation, can. It can explain the function of the Ratiocinative process as an instrument of the human intellect in the discovery of truth, and can place it in its true correlation with the other instruments.[10]

But Mill's logic is not only a logic of truth; it is intended to be a "logic of experience," and as such to subvert the doctrines of the German or *à priori* school.[11] Its single most important thesis, that on which the whole conception of the logic of experience rests, is that all inference is from particulars to particulars. This is by no means advanced by Mill as a dogma. It is given as the conclusion of an argument in which he examines the nature of the syllogism. It is to be observed that in doing so, Mill adopts as his example of the syllogism, one in which the major premise, All men are mortal, is obviously a generalization from observation. The minor premise asserts that the Duke of Wellington is a man, and the conclusion is drawn that the Duke, who was alive at the time, is mortal. Mill points out that the conclusion is not inferred from the generalization stated in the major premise, for it is already included in that generalization. The evidence for the mortality of the Duke of Wellington is the same as that for all men, namely John and Thomas and other known individual cases. It is on the basis of this instance of the syllogism that Mill maintains his general principle that all inference is from particulars to particulars. But what the argument presupposes is that all universal propositions are empirical generalizations, as in his example, All men are mortal. This, however, is just the issue which separated Mill from the German or *à priori* school. The latter maintained that there are some propositions which are necessary, and that necessary propositions cannot be got by empirical generalization. They must therefore be *à priori*. Of the five examples which were cited earlier of propositions which Mill regarded as truly asserting matters of fact, four would have been regarded by Kant as necessary, namely, the arithmetical and geometrical propositions, the causal axiom, and the principle of contradiction, although he would not, as Mill did, have considered this last to be an assertion of fact.[12] As necessary, they cannot be derived from experience. But Mill is not only opposing the German or *à priori* school. In the case of mathematics he felt that he was opposing almost everyone. "Why," he asks, "are mathematics by almost all philosophers, and (by some) even those branches of natural philosophy which, through the medium of mathematics, have been converted into deductive

[10]*An Examination of Sir William Hamilton's Philosophy*, 4th ed. (London: Longmans, 1872), 477–8.

[11]"But mine professes to be a logic of *experience* only, & to throw no further light upon the existence of truths not experimental, than is thrown by shewing to what extent reasoning from experience will carry us." Letter to John Sterling, 4 Nov., 1839, in *Earlier Letters*, ed. F. E. Mineka, *Collected Works*, XIII (Toronto: University of Toronto Press, 1963), 412. Hereafter cited as *EL, CW*.

[12]The principle of contradiction belongs for Kant to logic, and he does not speak of logical principles as true.

sciences, considered to be independent of the evidence of experience and observation, and characterized as systems of Necessary Truth?" (224.)

Because it is the deductive sciences which give rise to the illusion that there are systems of necessary truth, an important part of Mill's defence of the main thesis of his logic of experience is to consider the nature of deduction and of the deductive sciences, in order to get rid altogether of the distinction between induction and deduction as two opposed types of inference. There is only one kind of inference. Mill's account of deduction is clear in spite of the fact that his key word in the account, "reasoning," is sometimes used in a broad sense, sometimes in a more narrow and technical sense, without notice of change from one to the other being given. In what Mill calls "the most extensive sense of the term," reasoning is a synonym of inference, and he frequently couples the words "reasoning or inference." In its narrower sense it is the process which is exemplified in the syllogism, and is alternatively called by him ratiocination or deduction. But syllogism or ratiocination or deduction is not inference; it is rather what in theology and law is called interpretation. "All inference is from particulars to particulars: General propositions are merely registers of such inferences already made, and short formulae for making more: The major premise of a syllogism, consequently, is a formula of this description: and the conclusion is not an inference drawn *from* the formula, but an inference drawn *according to* the formula: the real logical antecedent, or premise, being the particular facts from which the general proposition was collected by induction" (193). Just as in a case of law or of theological dogma, the

only point to be determined is, whether the authority which declared the general proposition, intended to include this case in it; and whether the legislator intended his command to apply to the present case among others, or not. This is ascertained by examining whether the case possesses the marks by which, as those authorities have signified, the cases which they meant to certify or to influence may be known. The object of the inquiry is to make out the witness's or the legislator's intention, through the indication given by their words. This is a question, as the Germans express it, of hermeneutics. The operation is not a process of inference, but a process of interpretation.

In this last phrase we have obtained an expression which appears to me to characterize, more aptly than any other, the functions of the syllogism in all cases. (194.)

The term induction applies equally to inference from particulars to a general proposition or formula, and to inference from particulars to particulars according to the formula. Usage, however, tends to limit the term induction to the former, and to call the interpretation of the formula deduction. Hence, Mill will speak of an inference to an unobserved case as consisting of "an Induction followed by a Deduction; because, although the process needs not necessarily be carried on in this form, it is always susceptible of the form, and must be thrown into it when assurance of scientific accuracy is needed and desired" (203).

The task of determining whether Socrates or the Duke of Wellington have the marks which justify bringing them under the general formula, All men are mortal, is easily accomplished by observation, and the result stated in the minor premise. But not all cases are so simple. The minor premise may by itself have to be established by an induction followed by a deduction or interpretation, that is, by a syllogism. The succession of deductions or interpretations may, as required, be extended indefinitely, and this is pre-eminently the case in the mathematical sciences, where the inductions themselves may be obvious, while yet it may be far from obvious whether particular cases come under these inductions. Geometry rests on a very few simple inductions, the formulae of which are expressed in the axioms and a few of the so-called definitions.

The remainder of the science is made up of the processes employed for bringing unforeseen cases within these inductions; or (in syllogistic language) for proving the minors necessary to complete the syllogisms; the majors being the definitions and axioms. In those definitions and axioms are laid down the whole of the marks, by an artful combination of which it has been found possible to discover and prove all that is proved in geometry. The marks being so few, and the inductions which furnish them being so obvious and familiar; the connecting of several of them together, which constitutes Deductions, or Trains of Reasoning, forms the whole difficulty of the science, and with a trifling exception, its whole bulk; and hence Geometry is a Deductive Science. (218.)

Every science aspires to the condition of mathematics, that is, to be a deductive science, resting on a small number of inductions of the highest generality.[13] A science begins as almost wholly observational and experimental, each of its generalizations resting on its own special set of observations and experiments. Some sciences, however, by being rendered mathematical, have already advanced to the stage of becoming almost entirely "sciences of pure reasoning; whereby multitudes of truths, already known by induction from as many different sets of experiments, have come to be exhibited as deductions or corollaries from inductive propositions of a simpler and more universal character" (218). But they are not, says Mill, to be regarded as less inductive by virtue of having become more deductive.

A deductive science is, then, one which is distinguished from an experimental science, not as being independent of observation and experiment,

---

[13]In the physical sciences these inductions would not be of uniform coexistences, as they are in the mathematical sciences, but of uniform successions, that is, causal laws. The "whole problem of the investigation of nature" consists in this: "What are the fewest assumptions, which being granted, the order of nature as it exists would be the result? What are the fewest general propositions from which all the uniformities existing in nature could be deduced?" (472.)

thereby constituting a system of necessary truth, but one whose conclusions are arrived at by successive interpretations of inductions of great generality, instead of resting directly on observation and experiment. Whewell, who was for Mill the chief spokesman for the *à priori* school in matters of science, found him to be much too optimistic—in the light of the history of the sciences—about the efficacy of deduction in their progress. Whewell was, however, prepared to accept Mill's account of the nature of deduction as being the interpretation of the formula contained in the major premise.

I say then that Mr. Mill appears to me especially instructive in his discussion of the nature of the proof which is conveyed by the syllogism; and that his doctrine, that the force of the syllogism consists in an *inductive assertion, with an interpretation added to it,* solves very happily the difficulties which baffle other theories of this subject. I think that this doctrine of his is made still more instructive, by his excepting from it the cases of Scriptural Theology and of Positive Law, as cases in which general propositions, not particular facts, are our original data.[14]

Thus, while the main thesis of Mill's logic of experience, that all inference is from particulars to particulars, is derived from an analysis of the syllogism, that analysis is inconclusive for Mill's purpose; Whewell is quite happy to accept the analysis, since it allows that the general proposition expressed in the major premise may be an original datum not derivative from particular facts. In this class Whewell would put the axioms of geometry, which he would say are necessary truths and hence incapable of being inductively arrived at. To complete the case for his main thesis Mill must dispose of the doctrine that there are necessary truths, such as, Two straight lines cannot enclose a space. Because we cannot, according to Mill, look at any two straight lines which intersect without seeing that they continue to diverge, he asks what reason there is for maintaining that our knowledge of the axiom is grounded in any other way than through that evidence of the senses by which we know other things. This experiential evidence is quite sufficient. "The burden of proof lies on the advocates of the contrary opinion: it is for them to point out some fact, inconsistent with the supposition that this part of our knowledge of nature is derived from the same sources as every other part" (232). Mill finds that the *à priori* case is made to rest on two arguments, both of which he takes from Whewell.

The first argument is that we are able to perceive in intuition that two straight lines cannot enclose a space. Whewell calls it "imaginary looking," and maintains that by means of it alone, and without any real looking, that is independently of, and prior to, visual perception, we can "see" that the two straight lines cannot enclose a space. But for Mill this is easily explainable by the abundantly experienced fact that spatial forms in the imagination can exactly resemble those given to visual perception. Hence it is possible to con-

[14]*On the Philosophy of Discovery* (London: Parker, 1860), 289–90.

duct experiments with lines and angles in the imagination, and to know that the conclusions hold for observable lines and angles in the external world. Whether we work with mental diagrams or real figures, the conclusions are inductions.[15] Mill must be counted among those philosophers who believe that geometry rests on intuition, if we include under this heading what he calls "inspection" or "contemplation," whether in imagination or visually. He sees no reason for maintaining that such intuition has any *à priori* form. Against such a position as Kant's, who maintains that there must be *à priori* forms of intuition if the necessity which characterizes mathematical propositions is to be accounted for, Mill would simply deny that there is any necessity in the mathematical propositions to be accounted for.

This brings us to the second argument for the apriority of certain truths, namely that they are necessary, and must, therefore, be know independently of experience. Whatever force this argument has depends on what is meant by the term "necessary," and in particular what meaning it has for those who use it to qualify the term "truth."

Mill recognized that in popular usage there were two kinds of necessity which were referred to, logical necessity and causal necessity. The latter he variously calls philosophical or metaphysical or physical necessity. He remarks in one of his letters, "You are probably, however, right in thinking that the notion of physical necessity is partly indebted for the particular shape it assumes in our minds to an assimilation of it with logical necessity."[16] In his *Autobiography* Mill writes:

during the later returns of my dejection, the doctrine of what is called Philosophical Necessity weighed on my existence like an incubus. I felt as if I was scientifically proved to be the helpless slave of antecedent circumstances; as if my character and that of all others had been formed for us by agencies beyond our control, and was wholly out of our own power. . . . I pondered painfully on the subject, till gradually I saw light through it. I perceived, that the word Necessity, as a name for the doctrine of Cause and Effect applied to human action, carried with it a misleading association; and that this association was the operative force in the depressing and paralysing influence which I had experienced.[17]

Thereafter, Mill says, he discarded altogether "the misleading word Necessity." The theory which released him from his dilemma is contained in the chapter of the *Logic* entitled "Of Liberty and Necessity," and which he de-

---

[15]For Mill it is merely a fact of our experience that space in our part of the universe is uniformly the same. He believed that there was ample evidence that it was the same also in the region of the fixed stars, but he accepts the possibility of space being differently constituted elsewhere. It would appear that, if the notion of non-Euclidean geometries were to make sense for Mill, it would have to be in terms of the possibility of experiencing elsewhere alternative kinds of actual space.

[16]To Thomas Squire Barrett (6/5/72), in *Later Letters*, ed. F. E. Mineka and D. Lindley, *Collected Works*, XVII (Toronto: University of Toronto Press, 1972), 1890.

[17]*Autobiography*, 101–2.

scribed to de Tocqueville as "the most important chapter" in that work. There he writes, "The application of so improper a term as Necessity to the doctrine of cause and effect in the matter of human character, seems to me one of the most signal instances in philosophy of the abuse of terms, and its practical consequences one of the most striking examples of the power of language over our associations. The subject will never be generally understood, until that objectionable term is dropped." (841.)

Hume had maintained that necessity, or necessary connection, is an essential part of our idea of cause and effect. He claimed to have shown just what our idea of necessity is, or what we mean when we use the term. Mill does not at all agree with Hume as to what the term means, but he agrees that the term is used with meaning.[18] He himself, however, uses an expression which he regards as less objectionable. He points out that when we define the cause of a thing as the antecedent which the thing invariably follows, we do not mean that which the thing invariably *has* followed in our past experience, but that which it invariably *will* follow. Thus we would not call night the cause of day. The sun could cease to rise without, for all we know, any violation of the laws of nature. "Invariable sequence . . . is not synonymous with causation, unless the sequence, besides being invariable, is unconditional." "This is what writers mean when they say that the notion of cause involves the idea of necessity. If there be any meaning which confessedly belongs to the term necessity, it is *unconditionalness*. That which is necessary, that which *must* be, means that which will be, whatever supposition we may make in regard to all other things." (339.)

Thus the word necessity is eliminated from the treatment of causation, and a synonym will also be found for the word when used in its logical sense, namely certainty.[19] The conclusions of a deductive science are said to be necessary as following certainly or correctly or legitimately from the axioms and definitions of the science, whether these latter, either as inductions or as assumptions, are true or false. But the *à priori* school refers to the axioms or principles of a science themselves as necessary truths. In what sense are they said to be necessary? For this sense Mill turns to Whewell as representative of the school. According to Whewell the necessity of a necessary truth lies

---

[18]Hume says, "Necessity may be defined two ways, conformably to the two definitions of *cause*, of which it makes an essential part. It consists in the constant conjunction of like objects, or in the inference of the understanding from one object to another." (*An Enquiry concerning Human Understanding* [Oxford: Clarendon Press, 1894], 97.) By the latter Hume means the psychological compulsion to make the inference. Mill would reject both these definitions. He would reject the first on the grounds that causation is not mere uniformity, but unconditional uniformity, unconditional being for Mill a synonym of necessary; and the second on the ground that it has no relevance to facts in the external world.

[19]See the Textual Introduction, xci below, for references to successive revisions involving "necessity."

in the impossibility of conceiving the reverse. "Now I cannot but wonder," says Mill, "that so much stress should be laid on the circumstance of inconceivableness, when there is such ample experience to show, that our capacity or incapacity of conceiving a thing has very little to do with the possibility of the thing in itself; but is in truth very much an affair of accident, and depends on the past history and habits of our own minds" (238). Psychological impossibilities are contingent facts with a fluctuating history, and Mill points out that the history of science has abounded with "inconceivabilities" which have become actualities.

It has been noted that Mill denies that there are two kinds of inference, inductive and deductive. All inference is inductive. In this regard he stands in direct contrast with those who hold that all inference is deductive, an inference being valid by virtue of the relation of implication which holds between propositions. If the latter view of the nature of inference is taken, then according to some, Hume included, induction could be justified only if every induction could be put in deductive form with one supreme premise, such as the principle of the uniformity of nature or the causal axiom. Only then would inductive conclusions be implied, and hence logically valid.

It is sometimes said that not only did Mill share this view as to what is required to make inductions valid, but he also undertook to justify the one supreme premise by induction. To assert that the principle which justifies induction is itself an induction from experience is, of course, to argue in a circle. Hume's conclusion was, therefore, that inductive inference cannot be justified, that is to say, converted into a deductive inference. But Mill, it is widely thought, happily committed himself to the circle. Let us consider, then, Mill's position in relation to what is variously called the problem of induction, or Hume's problem, or the justification of induction. Mill says:

the proposition that the course of nature is uniform, is the fundamental principle, or general axiom, of Induction. . . . I hold it to be itself an instance of induction. . . . Far from being the first induction we make, it is one of the last, or at all events one of those which are latest in attaining strict philosophical accuracy. . . . The truth is, that this great generalization is itself founded on prior generalizations. The obscurer laws of nature were discovered by means of it, but the more obvious ones must have been understood and assented to as general truths before it was ever heard of. . . . In what sense, then, can a principle, which is so far from being our earliest induction, be regarded as our warrant for all the others? In the only sense, in which . . . the general propositions which we place at the head of our reasonings when we throw them into syllogisms, ever really contribute to their validity. As Archbishop Whately remarks, every induction is a syllogism with the major premise suppressed; or (as I prefer expressing it) every induction may be thrown into the form of a syllogism, by supplying a major premise. If this be actually done, the principle which we are now considering, that of the uniformity of the course of nature, will appear as the ultimate major premise of all inductions, and will, therefore, stand to all inductions in the relation in which . . . the major

proposition of a syllogism always stands to the conclusion; not contributing at all
to prove it, but being a necessary condition of its being proved; since no conclusion is proved, for which there cannot be found a true major premise. (307–8.)

This makes it clear that Mill is not seeking to solve Hume's problem, for the
latter rests on the assumption that inductive inference is justified only if it can
be shown to be a deductive inference. But since for Mill there is no such
thing as deductive inference, and since the major premise of the syllogism
into which any induction can be formulated, forms no part of the proof for
the inductive conclusion, he cannot be considered to mean by "the warrant"
for induction, what those who have concerned themselves with Hume's
problem have called the "justification" of induction. The formulation of an
induction syllogistically or deductively does not, for Mill, relate an inference
to the evidence for it. It is rather the interpretation of an induction, in which
the major premise, as we have seen, is a formula, not *from which* the conclusion is inferred, but in *accordance with which* the conclusion is inferred. It
is, in Mill's language, a warrant or authorization for inferring the conclusion
from the particulars which constitute the evidence for it. It warrants the inference because it states in, for example, the proposition, All men are mortal,
that having the attributes of a man is satisfactory evidence for the inference
to the attribute mortality. The function of the minor premise in turn is to
state that in the particular case in question, that of the Duke of Wellington,
this evidence does exist for the inference that he will die. According to this
account of the syllogism it is not necessary that inductions or inferences in
order to be sound should be warranted. It is the evidence from the particular
facts alone, and not they together with a general warrant, which makes an
induction or inference valid, and this will be no less true for the induction
to the principle of the uniformity of nature than for any other induction. Of
course, as the ultimate warrant for all other inductions, the principle cannot
itself as an induction be warranted by a formula. But its validity, like that of
other inductions, is independent of any general warrant. Contrary to a common misunderstanding there is no circle in Mill's account of "the ground of
induction."

This throws some light on the way in which Mill conceived the nature of
scientific explanation. Although in the deductively ordered sciences major
premises state general matters of fact (either the uniformities of coexistence
in the case of the axioms of mathematics, or of succession in the case of the
laws of physical science), they nevertheless function as formulae or rules for
making inferences from particular facts to particular facts, as well as providing security that the inferences have been correctly made. To explain a
particular fact is, for Mill, to show that the way in which it came about is an
instance of a causal law. The fact is *explained* when its mode of production
is deduced from a law or laws. To explain a law is in turn to deduce it from

another law or laws more general than itself, and the ultimate goal of the sciences is to find "the fewest general propositions from which all the uniformities existing in nature could be deduced" (472). Viewed in terms of the directional function for inference which Mill assigns to major premises in deductions, this means that scientific explanation consists not in dispelling the mysteries of nature, but in bringing the formulae for inferring particulars from particulars under the fewest and most general formulae for inferring. So far as laws are viewed in their character as statements of general matters of fact, Mill says, "What is called explaining one law of nature by another, is but substituting one mystery for another; and does nothing to render the general course of nature other than mysterious; we can no more assign a *why* for the more extensive laws than for the partial ones" (471).

The case against the *à priori* school is for Mill complete when he has established that all inference is from particulars to particulars. It is this which makes his logic a logic of experience, for he could consider himself to be on philosophically neutral ground in asserting that *particular* facts, not known inferentially, can be known only by observation. The empiricism of Mill's logic is solely of that kind in which "experience" refers to observation that something is the case. So far as the more radical type of empiricism is concerned, in which "experience" refers to feelings and states of consciousness, and on which his phenomenalism is built, Mill scrupulously seeks to avoid resting his logical theory on it, in order that the partisans of Hartley and of Reid, of Locke and of Kant, can meet on common ground. However conspicuous the appearance of Mill's phenomenalism in the *System of Logic*, it is never used for grounding his logical theory, nor on the other hand is it in any respect the outcome of his argument. When Mill introduces phenomenalist doctrines they are accompanied by expressions of the following sort:

here the question merges in the fundamental problem of metaphysics properly so called: to which science we leave it (59).

For the purposes of logic it is not of material importance which of these opinions we adopt (65).

But, as the difficulties which may be felt in adopting this view of the subject cannot be removed without discussions transcending the bounds of our science, I content myself with a passing indication, and shall, for the purposes of logic, adopt a language compatible with either view of the nature of qualities (67).

Among nameable things are:

. . . Bodies, or external objects which excite certain of those feelings, together with the powers or properties whereby they excite them; these latter (at least) being included rather in compliance with common opinion, and because their existence is taken for granted in the common language from which I cannot prudently deviate, than because the recognition of such powers or properties as real existences appears to be warranted by a sound philosophy (77).

As a logic of truth whose concern is with propositions asserting observable matters of fact in a world of things denoted by names, Mill's logic rests on a certain ontology which is reflected in "common language," and which as such provides neutral ground for metaphysicians of different schools. For Mill as a phenomenalist metaphysician the only constituents of matters of fact are individual sensations and permanent groups of possible individual sensations, some of which on occasion become actual. However, common language, he observes, allows for no designation of sensations other than by circumlocution. It cannot designate them by attribute-words. On the other hand for Mill, author of the logic of experience, the constituents of the observed matters of fact from which inferences are made are of quite a different nature, and they are of two kinds, either substances or the attributes by which substances are designated. The substances are individuals, and the attributes are universals. While a sensation is always individual, "a quality, indeed, in the custom of the language, does not admit of individuality; it is supposed to be one thing common to many."

In his various discussions of universals Mills rejects each of realism, conceptualism, and nominalism. Of realism he has this to say,

Modern philosophers have not been sparing in their contempt for the scholastic dogma that genera and species are a peculiar kind of substances, which general substances being the only permanent things, while the individual substances comprehended under them are in a perpetual flux, knowledge, which necessarily imports stability, can only have relation to those general substances or universals, and not to the facts or particulars included under them. Yet, though nominally rejected, this very doctrine . . . has never ceased to poison philosophy. (175.)

It is, however, important to take note of the kind of realism which Mill was rejecting. In order to do so we must look first at his distinction between general names and individual or singular names, and also at his distinction between concrete and abstract names. A general name is one which can be affirmed of an indefinite number of things because they possess the attributes expressed by that name; an individual name is one which can be truly affirmed, in the same sense, of only one thing. A concrete name is one which stands for a thing or things. Thus "white" is a concrete name, for it is *the name of all things which are white*. "Whiteness" on the other hand is an abstract name, for it is the name of the attribute possessed by those things. By realism Mill means the doctrine according to which "concrete general terms were supposed to be, not names of indefinite numbers of individual substances, but names of a peculiar kind of entities termed Universal Substances" (757). But, while Mill's concrete general names do not refer to real universals, but only to individual things, the attributes to which his abstract names refer perform the functions of real universals in his theory of inference. He warns the reader that in using the term "abstract name" he is not following the unfortunate practice initiated by Locke of applying it to names which are the result of abstraction or generalization. He is retaining the sounder scholastic usage, according to which an abstract name refers to an attribute as opposed to a thing or object. A concrete general name denotes many different objects, but in the case of an abstract name, "though it denotes an attribute of many different objects, the attribute itself is always conceived as one, not many" (30). And so it is in Mill's account of the import of propositions and of the syllogism:

Every proposition which conveys real information asserts a matter of fact. . . . It asserts that a given object does or does not possess a given attribute; or it asserts that two attributes, or sets of attribues, do or do not (constantly or occasionally) co-exist. . . .
Applying this view of propositions to the two premises of a syllogism, we obtain the following results. The major premise, which . . . is always universal, asserts, that all things which have a certain attribute (or attributes) have or have not along with it, a certain other attribute (or attributes). The minor premise asserts that the thing or set of things which are the subject of that premise, have the first-mentioned attribute; and the conclusion is, that they have (or that they have not), the second. (177.)

The realism involved in this did not escape Herbert Spencer. Mill's reply to his criticism is instructive:

Mr. Herbert Spencer . . . maintains, that we ought not to say that Socrates possesses *the same* attributes which are connoted by the word Man, but only that he possesses attributes *exactly like* them. . . .
The question between Mr. Spencer and me is merely one of language; for neither of us . . . believes an attribute to be a real thing, possessed of objective existence; we believe it to be a particular mode of naming our sensations, or our expectations of sensation, when looked at in their relation to an external object which excites them. (178n–179n.)

But Mill says that he has chosen to use the phraseology "commonly used by philosophers" because it seems best. As he goes on, however, he indicates the unavoidability of regarding attributes as real universals if there is to be any such thing as language at all:

Mr. Spencer is of opinion that because Socrates and Alcibiades are not the same man, the attribute which constitutes them men should not be called the same attribute; that because the humanity of one man and that of another express themselves to our senses not by the same individual sensations but by sensations exactly alike, humanity ought to be regarded as a different attribute in every different man. But on this showing, the humanity even of any one man should be considered as different attributes now and half-an-hour hence; for the sensations by which it will then manifest itself to my organs will not be a continuation of my present sensations, but a repetition of them; fresh sensations, not identical with, but only exactly like the present. If every general conception, instead of being "the One in the Many," were considered to be as many different conceptions as there are things to which it is applicable, there would be no such thing as general language. A name would have no general meaning if *man* connoted one thing when predicated of John, and another, though closely resembling, thing when predicated of William. (179n.)

Thus language prohibits Mill from basing his theory of inference on phenomenalism.

The principal characteristics of Mill's empiricism, so far as it is related to his logical doctrines, can be summed up. It is observational, not sensational as in his phenomenalism. It is metaphysically neutral, in the sense of being based on an ontology embedded in "common language," even though the terms it uses, like attributes, powers, states, are for Mill, as a phenomenalist, "not real things existing in objects" but "logical fictions."[20] Mill's empiricism differs from that of Hume and modern empiricists in general in that in his all inference is inductive, while in theirs all valid inference is deductive. It is more radical than theirs in that it includes mathematics within its scope, and that on the ground, which they reject, that mathematical propositions assert matters of fact. They prefer to regard them as necessary, or, in Mill's language, as merely "verbal." Finally, it is an empiricism in which the ideal of any science is to become deductive instead of directly experimental, or "empirical" in the old sense of the term. It achieves this ideal to the extent that less general warrants to infer (or major premises) can be brought under more general warrants.

We come now to the second way in which Mill's logic has been characterized. It has been said, for example, that "Mill is the one great logician of the

[20]While there would seem to be no escape from the ontology embedded in "common language" so long as we are compelled to speak, Mill is completely hostile to the conception of language as a reflection of, and a clue to, the nature of things. He considered this notion to be a very extended and ancient prejudice: "scientific investigation among the Greek schools of speculation and their followers in the middle ages, was little more than a mere sifting and analysing of the notions attached to common language. They thought that by determining the meaning of words, they could become acquainted with facts." (760.) According to Whewell, whom Mill here quotes with approval, it was Thales who was the founder of this method of doing philosophy. "When he was asked," says Whewell, "'What is the *greatest* thing?' he replied '*Place*; for all other things are *in* the world, but the world is *in* it.' In Aristotle we have the consummation of this mode of speculation. The usual point from which he starts in his inquiries is, that *we say* thus or thus in common language." (Quoted by Mill, 761.) Mill's case against this use of common language is the same as his case against conceptualism. "The propensity to assume that the same relations obtain between objects themselves, which obtain between our ideas of them, is here seen [with language] in the extreme stage of its development" (762).

school which, following Hume, tried to rest logic upon psychology."[21] Mill's own often quoted words appear to give ample justification for taking this view. He says of logic, "It is not a Science distinct from, and coordinate with, Psychology. So far as it is a science at all, it is a part, or branch, of Psychology; differing from it, on the one hand as a part differs from the whole, and on the other, as an Art differs from a Science. Its theoretic grounds are wholly borrowed from Psychology, and include as much of that science as is required to justify the rules of the art."[22]

There are four distinct views which are, or might be, taken as to the sense in which Mill's logic is grounded in psychology. First, we may consider a statement by Ernest Nagel: "What is characteristic of Mill is his conception of what the *basic facts* are to which beliefs should be subjected for testing, and what are the essential requirements for the process of testing them. The theoretical grounds of logic, he explicitly argued, are 'wholly borrowed from Psychology'; and it is the psychological assumptions of sensationalistic empiricism that are made to support the principles of evidence which emerge in the *Logic*."[23] Mill's sensationalistic empiricism is given in the important chapter of *The System of Logic*, "Of the Things denoted by Names," which incorporated much of what he was later to say in "The Psychological Theory of the Belief in an External World."[24] It is a chapter which is decisive for his account of the import of propositions and for his theory of syllogism. But while "the psychological theory" is incorporated in the chapter, it does not exhaust it. Moreover, as we have already observed, not only does Mill maintain that "for the purposes of logic it is not of material importance" whether we adopt the psychological theory or not, but his logic is also, in fact, entirely independent of the psychological theory. The *basic facts* to which beliefs should be subjected for testing are those of an observational, not a sensationalistic, empiricism.

Secondly, we can consider Husserl's reference to "the misled followers of British empiricism," according to whose point of view "concepts, judgments, arguments, proofs, theories, would be psychic occurrences; and logic would be, as John Stuart Mill said it is, a 'part or branch of psychology.' This highly plausible conception is *logical psychologism*."[25] But does this cover Mill's own case? It would at first appear so. "Our object," he says, "will be, to attempt a correct analysis of the intellectual process called Reasoning or In-

---

[21]Brand Blanshard, *The Nature of Thought* (London: Allen and Unwin, 1948), I, 468.

[22]*An Examination of Sir William Hamilton's Philosophy*, 461–2.

[23]*John Stuart Mill's Philosophy of Scientific Method*, ed. Ernest Nagel (New York: Hafner, 1950), xxxii.

[24]Chapter xi of *An Examination of Sir William Hamilton's Philosophy*.

[25]Edmund Husserl, *Formal and Transcendental Logic*, tr. Dorion Cairns (The Hague: Martinus Nijhoff, 1969), 153–4.

ference, and of such other mental operations as are intended to facilitate this. . . ." (12). In turning to the subject of inference in Book II, Mill says, "The proper subject, however, of Logic is Proof" (157). To understand what proof is, it is necessary first to understand the nature of what is proved, namely, propositions, for it is propositions which are believed or disbelieved, affirmed or denied, as true or false. In inquiring into the nature of propositions we must, says Mill, distinguish, as all language recognizes, between "the state of mind called Belief" and "what is believed"; between "an opinion" and "the fact of entertaining the opinion"; between "assent" and "what is assented to":

> Logic . . . has no concern with the nature of the act of judging or believing; the consideration of that act, as a phenomenon of the mind, belongs to another science. Philosophers, however, from Descartes downward, and especially from the era of Leibnitz and Locke, have by no means observed this distinction and would have treated with great disrespect any attempt to analyse the import of Propositions, unless founded on an analysis of the act of Judgment. A proposition, they would have said, is but the expression in words of a Judgment. The thing expressed, not the mere verbal expression, is the important matter. When the mind assents to a proposition, it judges. Let us find out what the mind does when it judges, and we shall know what propositions mean, and not otherwise. (87.)

Mill observed that almost every writer on logic in the two previous centuries had treated the proposition as a judgment in which one idea or conception is affirmed or denied of another, as a comparison of two ideas, or, in the language of Locke, as perception of the agreement or disagreement of ideas. But, Mill points out, an account of the process occurring in the mind is irrelevant to determining the nature of propositions, for propositions are not about our ideas but about things. "The notion that what is of primary importance to the logician in a proposition, is the relation between the two *ideas* corresponding to the subject and predicate, (instead of the relation between the two *phenomena* which they respectively express), seems to me one of the most fatal errors ever introduced into the philosophy of Logic; and the principal cause why the theory of the science has made such inconsiderable progress during the last two centuries" (89).

Mill has said that to understand the nature of proof it is necessary to understand the nature of propositions, for it is these which are proved. But, in turn, to understand the nature of propositions, or the meaning of what is asserted, it is necessary to consider the nature of the meanings of names, for in every proposition one name is asserted of another name, the predicate of the proposition being the name which denotes what is affirmed or denied, and the subject being the name which denotes the person or thing of which something is affirmed or denied. It is because the import of propositions is determined by the import of names that the consideration of the latter becomes the starting point for the analysis of reasoning or inference. In treating of the import of names one of Mill's principal intentions is to depsychologize the theory of meaning in radical fashion. A meaning of a name is not an idea in the mind; it is not a mental phenomenon. This forms the basis of his attack on conceptualism. Mill says, ". . . I consider it nothing less than a misfortune, that the words Concept, General Notion, or any other phrase to express the supposed mental modification corresponding to a class name, should ever have been invented. Above all, I hold that nothing but confusion ever results from introducing the term Concept into Logic, and that instead of the Concept of a class, we should always speak of the signification of a class name."[26] Nor is the meaning of a name the thing or things *denoted* by the name. Its meaning is what the name *connotes*—that attribute or set of attributes by the possession of which things can be said to be denoted by that name. A meaning is a real universal. So far as concepts and judgments are concerned, Mill's logic is not an exemplification of what Husserl calls psychologism, but, rather, a forceful condemnation of it.[27]

Thirdly, it has been said of Mill that "In his view logical and mathematical necessity is psychological; we are unable to conceive any other possibilities than those which logical and mathematical propositions assert."[28] Mill denied that logical principles (the so-called laws of thought) and mathematical axioms possessed necessity. It was those whom he opposed who attributed necessity to them, and the necessity which they attributed was, according to Mill, nothing but the psychological inability to conceive their negation. Such psychological inability could be fully accounted for by the laws of association, and it had no bearing on the truth or falsehood of the logical or mathematical propositions asserted. These are true only as they

[26]*An Examination of Sir William Hamilton's Philosophy*, 1st ed. (London: Longman, Green, Longman, Roberts, and Green, 1865), 331–2. In the 3rd ed. (London: Longmans, Green, Reader, and Dyer, 1867), the first of the two sentences quoted was revised to read: ". . . I think that the words Concept, General Notion, and other phrases of like import, convenient as they are for the lighter and every-day uses of philosophical discussion, should be abstained from where precision is required" (388).

[27]Mill's criticism is less harsh in the *Examination of Sir William Hamilton's Philosophy* than in the *System of Logic*. "Many writers have given good and valuable expositions of the principles and rules of Logic, from the Conceptualist point of view. The doctrines which they have laid down respecting Conception, Judgment, and Reasoning, have been capable of being rendered into equivalent statements respecting Terms, Propositions, and Arguments; these, indeed, were what the writers really had in their thoughts, and there was little amiss except a mode of expression which attempted to be more philosophical than it knew how to be. To say nothing of less illustrious examples, this is true of all the properly logical part of Locke's Essay. His admirable Third Book requires hardly any other alteration to bring it up to the scientific level of the present time, than to be corrected by blotting out everywhere the words Abstract Idea, and replacing them by 'the connotation of the class-name.' " (414.)

[28]D. W. Hamlyn, "Empiricism," *Encyclopaedia of Philosophy* (New York: Macmillan, 1967), II, 503.

are generalizations from the facts of experience. When Sir William Hamilton says of the laws of identity, contradiction, and excluded middle, "To deny the universal application of the three laws is, in fact, to subvert the reality of thought; and as this subversion is itself an act of thought, it in fact annihilates itself. When, for example, I say that A is, and then say that A is not, by the second assertion I sublate or take away what, by the first assertion, I posited or laid down; thought, in the one case, undoing by negation what, in the other, it had by affirmation done," Mill simply comments, "This proves only that a contradiction is unthinkable, not that it is impossible in point of fact."[29] This third version of psychologism attributed to Mill's conception of logic is repudiated by him in his criticisms of Spencer in Book II, Chapter vii. In Book V, "On Fallacies" it appears among the first in the five classes of fallacies.

Fourthly, it might be said that Mill's statement that logic is a branch of psychology confuses questions of validity with questions of fact. This is perhaps what is most often meant by the term psychologism as applied to a theory of logic. Mill's statement occurs in his analysis of Sir William Hamilton's conception of logic as a science, and it is important to consider it within that context. Hamilton had said that logic is both a science and an art, without, however, in Mill's view finding any satisfactory basis for distinguishing between the science and the art. As science its subject matter is stated to be "the laws of thought as thought." Mill finds that by this Hamilton means that the laws are "the conditions subject to which by the constitution of our nature we cannot but think." But it soon turns out that this is "an entire mistake"; that they are not laws which by its nature the mind cannot violate, but laws which it ought not to violate if it is to think validly. Laws now mean precepts or rules.

So that, after all, the real theory of Thought—the laws, in the scientific sense of the term, of Thought as Thought—do not belong to Logic, but to Psychology: and it is only the *validity* of thought which Logic takes cognisance of. It is not with Thought as Thought, but only as Valid thought, that Logic is concerned. There is nothing to prevent us thinking contrary to the laws of Logic: only, if we do, we shall not think rightly, or well, or conformably to the ends of thinking, but falsely, or inconsistently, or confusedly. This doctrine is at complete variance with the saying of our author in his controversy with Whately, that Logic is, and never could have been doubted to be, in Whately's sense of the terms, both a Science and an Art. For the present definition reduces it to the narrowest conception of an Art—that of a mere system of rules. It leaves Science to Psychology, and represents Logic as merely offering to thinkers a collection of precepts, which they are enjoined to observe, not in order that they may think, but that they may think correctly, or validly.[30]

[29]*An Examination of Sir William Hamilton's Philosophy*, 492–3.
[30]*Ibid.*, 460–1.

Nevertheless Mill thinks that with this Hamilton is nearer the mark. Logic is not the theory of thought as thought, but the theory of valid thought, not of thinking, but of valid thinking. At the same time he does not agree with Hamilton's final position, or that into which Mill drives him, in so far as it implies that logic is merely an art. The art, the set of rules, does have theoretical grounds, and these belong to psychology, though constituting a very limited part of it; that is, it "includes as much of that science as is required to justify the rules of art." Here Mill is using the term psychology in the broadest sense, to include everything that comes under the heading of thinking; it includes not only what, by the definition of psychology given in the *System of Logic*, would be an inquiry into the laws or uniformities according to which one mental phenomenon succeeds another; it also includes "a scientific investigation into the requisites of valid thinking," or the conditions for distinguishing between good and bad thinking. The first kind of inquiry, concerned as it is with what is common to all thinking, good or bad, valid or invalid, "is irrelevant to logic, unless by the light it indirectly throws on something besides itself." Logic for Mill borrows nothing from it. Logic is concerned only with the second kind of inquiry. If Mill calls this latter a branch of psychology, it is solely because "the investigation into the requisites of valid thinking" is *theory of* valid *thinking*, a type of theory which is essential for the grounding of rules, or of logic as an art. Not only does Mill's statement that logic is "a part or branch of Psychology" not imply a confusion of questions of *justification* or *validity* with questions of *fact*, the statement occurs within a discussion dominated by the great importance which he attaches to keeping separate the two kinds of questions.

For Mill there were in logic two sets of rules: the rules of the syllogism for deduction, and the four experimental methods for induction. The former he considered to be available in "the common manuals of logic." The latter he considered himself to be formulating explicitly for the first time. The question as to how these rules of art can be viewed as grounded in the science of valid thinking must be brought under the larger question as to how rules of art in general are grounded in science. For Mill, the way in which they are grounded is universally the same for all arts in which there are rules. He distinguishes two kinds of practical reasoning. One is typified in the reasoning of a judge, the other in that of a legislator. The judge's problem is to interpret the law, or to determine whether the particular case before him comes under the intention of the legislator who made the law. Thus the reasoning of the judge is syllogistic, for syllogism or deduction consists in the interpretation of a formula. The legislator's problem, on the other hand, is to find rules. This depends on determining the best means of achieving certain desired ends. It is science alone which can determine these means, for the relation between means and ends is the relation between causes and effects.

In this second kind of practical reasoning, art prescribes the end, science provides the theorem which shows how it is to be brought about, and art then converts the theorem into a rule. In this way propositions which assert only what ought to be, or should be done, are grounded on propositions which assert only matters of fact.

The task of finding the rules of logic, whether of deduction or of induction, is of the same type as the legislator's. Knowledge of what ought to be done, as expressed in the rules of art, must be grounded on knowledge of what is the case, as expressed in the theorems of science. The rules of the syllogism are the rules for interpreting an induction; the rules of induction are the rules for "discovering and proving general propositions." What then are the theoretical foundations of these two classes of rules? So far as the rules for interpreting inductions are concerned Mill has nothing to say, for he is not concerned with the task of finding them. They exist already in the manuals of logic as the rules of the syllogism. But he sees himself as confronted with the task of stating in "precise" terms or, "systematically and accurately," the rules or canons of induction for the first time, and the problem of their derivation does concern him, for he had both to find them and to justify them.[31] In accordance with his own account of the logic of practice Mill looks to matter of fact to ground his rules for "discovering and proving general propositions." "Principles of Evidence and Theories of Method are not to be constructed à priori. The laws of our rational faculty, like those of every other natural agency, are only learnt by seeing the agent at work." (833.) In the Preface to the 1st edition, in which he describes what he had undertaken to do in the *System of Logic*, Mill says, "On the subject of In-

[31]The extent of the novelty which Mill attributed to his formulation of the canons is indicated in a letter to Sir John Herschel, 1 May, 1843: "You will find that the most important chapter of the book, that on the four Experimental Methods, is little more than an expansion & a more scientific statement of what you had previously stated in the more popular manner suited to the purpose of your 'Introduction'" *EL, CW,* XIII, 583). As for Bacon, it was he who recognized *elimination* as "the foundation of experimental inquiry." For his criticism of the ancients' *inductio per enumerationem simplicem* he "merited the title . . . of Founder of the Inductive Philosophy. The value of his own contributions to a more philosophical theory of the subject has certainly been exaggerated." (Below, 392, 313.) "A revolution is peaceably and progressively effecting itself in philosophy, the reverse of that to which Bacon has attached his name. That great man changed the method of the sciences from deductive to experimental, and it is now rapidly reverting from experimental to deductive." (482.) On the failure of Bacon's inductive logic to produce any actual scientific results, Mill says, "But this, though not unfrequently remarked, has scarcely received any plausible explanation; and some, indeed, have preferred to assert that all rules of induction are useless, rather than suppose that Bacon's rules are grounded on an insufficient analysis of the inductive process. Such, however, will be seen to be the fact, as soon as it is considered, that Bacon entirely overlooked Plurality of Causes." (763.) It is not uncommon to link Mill's conception of induction not only with Bacon's but also with Hume's, as given in the section of his *Treatise of Human Nature* entitled, "Rules by which to judge of causes and effects." However, Mill makes no mention of Hume in this regard.

duction, the task to be performed was that of generalizing the modes of investigating truth and estimating evidence, by which so many important and recondite laws of nature have, in the various sciences, been aggregated to the stock of human knowledge" (cxii). He found that what metaphysicians had written on the subject of logic had suffered from want of sufficient acquaintance with the processes by which science had actually succeeded in establishing general truths, and even when correct they had not been specific enough to provide rules. On the other hand scientists, who had only to generalize the methods which they themselves use to get at the theoretical basis for the rules, had not thought it worthwhile to reflect on their procedures.

This suggests that Mill considered that the rules of induction are to be got by generalizing or reconstructing the procedures which the history of science reveals scientists actually to have used. It would appear as though Mill shared exactly Whewell's conception of how we arrive at a theory of scientific method. Whewell says:

We may best hope to understand the nature and conditions of real knowledge by studying the nature and conditions of the most certain and stable portions of knowledge which we already possess: and we are most likely to learn the best methods of discovering truth, by examining how truths, now universally recognized, have really been discovered. Now there do exist among us doctrines of solid and acknowledged certainty, and truths of which the discovery has been received with universal applause. These constitute what we commonly term *Sciences* and of these bodies of exact and enduring knowledge, we have within our reach so large and varied a collection, that we may examine them, and the history of their formation, with a good prospect of deriving from their study such instruction as we seek.[32]

Whewell criticized Mill's four experimental methods on the ground that they were not derived from the actual procedures of scientists as revealed in the history of science. "Who will tell us," he asks, "which of the methods of inquiry those historically real and successful inquiries exemplify? Who will carry these formulæ through the history of the sciences, as they have really grown up; and show us that these four methods have been operative in their formation; or that any light is thrown upon the steps of their progress by reference to these formulæ?" (Quoted by Mill, 430.)

If Mill found his canons of induction by generalizing and reconstructing the procedures successfully followed by natural scientists, their derivation from this source does not appear in the *System of Logic* itself. Illustrations are given, but it is evidently not on these that the generalizations are based, for the illustrations were sought after the canons were formulated. When his publisher's referee had suggested that more of these be added to the text, Mill replied, "I fear I am nearly at the end of my stock of apt illustrations. I

[32]*The Philosophy of the Inductive Sciences* (London: Parker, 1847), I, 1.

had to read a great deal for those I have given. . . ."[33] His debt to Bain for producing examples was considerable.[34] How Mill actually arrived at his rules indicates, however, that he means by "generalization" something other than Whewell's induction from the history of science. The groundwork for Mill's rules is to be found in the chapters on causation which precede the enunciation of the rules, for he says, "The notion of Cause being the root of the whole theory of Induction, it is indispensable that this idea should, at the very outset of our inquiry be, with the utmost practicable degree of precision, fixed and determined" (326).

In the means-end relation, with which the rules of induction are concerned, the desired end is the solution of a problem—"the discovering and proving general propositions"—the means consists in the way in which the problem is solved. The generalizing which Mill performs lies not in generalizing the means used by scientists, but in generalizing and reconstructing what he considered to be the nature of their problem, or of reducing their inquiries to one fundamental type. The problem in its full generality having in his view been ascertained, Mill then proceeds to solve it. Indeed the very statement of the problem dictates the solution; there is no need to consult the history of science for its solution. The method of solution once found can then be formulated in canons; or in the language of Mill's logic of practice, "Art . . . converts the theorem into a rule or precept."[35] In so far as the "Four Methods" can be said to be a generalization of scientists' actual modes of investigation, it is not because Mill has taken those modes of investigation themselves as his data, but because the scientist must, in successfully solving his problem as subsumed under the general form given by Mill, have used the method of solution dictated by that general problem. Nor is Mill's generalization of the *problem* of scientific investigation in any direct sense an induction from the history of science, but rests on a conception of the whole course of nature as one in which the general uniformity is made up out of separate threads of uniformity holding between single phenomena. The course of nature is a web composed of separate fibres, a "collective order . . . made up of particular sequences, obtaining invariably among the separate parts" (327). These separate threads are the laws of nature or the laws of causation. The task of the scientist, and the main business of induction, is to discover these separate threads, or "to resolve this complex uniformity

[33]*EL, CW*, XIII, 514.

[34]For examples of Bain's assistance, see the Textual Introduction, lxviii and lxxiff. below.

[35]*Logic*, 945. Mill provides five canons, with the titles, the Method of Agreement, the Method of Difference, the Joint Method of Agreement and Difference, the Method of Residues, and the Method of Concomitant Variations, but he calls them collectively "the Four Methods of Experimental Inquiry" without giving any direct explanation of this anomaly. For an explanation, see the Textual Introduction, n49 on lxviii below.

into the simpler uniformities which compose it, and assign to each portion of the vast antecedent the portion of the consequent which is attendant on it" (379). The antecedents in the complex having been discriminated from one another, and the consequents also, it remains to be determined which antecedents and consequents are invariably connected. That being the nature of the problem, it is solved by methods of elimination, which are described by Mill as "the successive exclusion of the various circumstances which are found to accompany a phenomenon in a given instance, in order to ascertain what are those among them which can be absent consistently with the existence of the phenomenon. . . . [W]hatever can be eliminated, is not connected with the phenomenon by any law. . . . [W]hatever cannot be eliminated, is connected with the phenomenon by a law." (392.)

To return now to the definition of logic as the science as well as the art of reasoning, in which the science consists of an analysis of the mental process which takes place when we reason, and the art consists of the rules grounded on that science, it can be said that in the case of induction the mental process consists in the solving of a problem stated in its full generality. Mill discovers what this mental process is by directly solving the problem himself. The account of this process constitutes the theoretical part of the logic of induction and is found in the chapters on causation; it reveals the means-end relation which provides the foundation for the rules of discovering the solution for any particular problem which can be subsumed under the general problem of induction. In basing the rules of art on the theoretical relation between means and end no more confusion arises here between questions of validity and questions of fact than in any other sphere of practice concerned with the means to a desired end.

In conclusion it may be remarked that any logic which deals with inference, as well as any which deals with scientific method, is concerned with a psychological process. Only persons with mental capacities infer or are governed by methods. In so far as Mill considered the principal subject matter of logic to be inference, and not implication, he was quite correct in asserting it to be a branch of psychology. This, and no more, constitutes the psychologism of his *System of Logic*. But Mill, in taking inference to be his subject, is in so numerous a company—one, moreover, composed of such varied types of logical theorists—that one wonders why he should have been so singled out in this regard, if not for merely having called a spade a spade.

Textual Introduction

JOHN M. ROBSON

I. THE WRITING OF THE *LOGIC*

IN 1831, when he was twenty-five years old, John Stuart Mill made a significant analysis of his intellectual and active powers in a letter to his friend
John Sterling:

the only thing that I believe I am really fit for, is the investigation of abstract
truth, & the more abstract the better. If there is any science which I am capable
of promoting, I think it is the science of science itself, the science of investigation
—of method. I once heard Maurice say . . . that almost all differences of opinion
when analysed, were differences of method. But if so, he who can throw most
light upon the subject of method, will do most to forward that alliance among the
most advanced intellects & characters of the age, which is the only definite object
I ever have in literature or philosophy so far as I have any *general* object at all.
Argal, I have put down upon paper a great many of my ideas on logic, & shall in
time bring forth a treatise: but whether it will see the light until the Treaty of
Westphalia is signed at the close of another cycle of reformation & antagonism,
no one can tell except Messrs. Drummond, M'Niel, Irving, & others, who possess
the hidden key to the Interpretation of the Prophecies.[1]

Though the "cycle of reformation & antagonism" has not yet come to a close,
the key of history is ours; the treatise did see the light, as *A System of Logic,
Ratiocinative and Inductive*, in 1843, not quite twelve years after this letter.

As the obituaries of Mill demonstrate, his contemporaries judged the
Logic to be his most important work. The significance he himself attached
to it may be inferred from the lengthy discussions of its composition and
content in his *Autobiography*. In particular, one may note his linking it with
his best-loved work: "The 'Liberty' is likely to survive longer than anything
else that I have written (with the possible exception of the 'Logic'). . . ."[2] As
Professor McRae, also citing this passage, suggests in his Introduction above,

---

[1]*Earlier Letters*, ed. Francis E. Mineka, *Collected Works*, XII (Toronto: University
of Toronto Press, 1963), 78–9 (20–22/10/31). Hereafter cited as *EL, CW*, with volume and page numbers.
[2]*Autobiography*, ed. Jack Stillinger (Boston: Houghton Mifflin, 1969), 150. Hereafter references to this edition (which supersedes the Columbia edition of 1924) are
usually given in parentheses in the text.

the formal discipline of logic has altered vastly since Mill's day, and so, although the *Logic* had a very long life as a textbook, it now is seen not as definitive, but as an important document in the history of logical speculation. It remains, moreover, central to an understanding of Mill's thought, for the approaches and doctrines contained in it throw light on almost every aspect of his writings. Furthermore, as his first published book, it played a major role in determining the course of his career, for its wide reception gave him prominence and confidence. There is more than technical interest, then, in tracing the course of his logical studies, and the history of the composition of the *Logic*.[3]

MILL'S EARLY STUDIES OF LOGIC, 1818–30

Mill was first introduced to logic in 1818, when he was twelve, and of all his precocities, it was here, as Bain says, that he was "most markedly in advance of his years."[4] His own account deserves quotation:

. . . I began at once with the Organon, and read it to the Analytics inclusive, but profited little by the Posterior Analytics, which belong to a branch of speculation I was not yet ripe for. Contemporaneously with the Organon, my father made me read the whole or parts of several of the Latin treatises on the scholastic logic; giving each day to him, in our walks, a minute account of what I had read, and answering his numerous and searching questions. After this, I went, in a similar manner, through the "Computatio sive Logica" of Hobbes, a work of a much higher order of thought than the books of the school logicians, and which he estimated very highly; in my own opinion beyond its merits, great as these are. It was his invariable practice, whatever studies he exacted from me, to make me as far as possible understand and feel the utility of them: and this he deemed peculiarly fitting in the case of the syllogistic logic, the usefulness of which had been impugned by so many writers of authority. I well remember how, and in what particular walk, in the neighbourhood of Bagshot Heath (where we were on a visit to his old friend Mr. Wallace, then one of the Mathematical Professors at Sandhurst) he first attempted by questions to make me think on the subject, and frame some conception of what constituted the utility of the syllogistic logic, and when I had failed in this, to make me understand it by explanations. The explanations did not make the matter at all clear to me at the time; but they were not therefore useless; they remained as a nucleus for my observations and reflections

[3]There has been only one serious study of the composition of the *Logic*, Oskar A. Kubitz's *Development of John Stuart Mill's System of Logic*, Illinois Studies in the Social Sciences, XVIII, No. 1 (Urbana, March, 1932), 1–310. Though much evidence was not then available, this is a very useful examination of "the gradual metamorphosis" of Mill's ideas on methodology from 1825 to 1843 (beyond which Kubitz does not go), with illuminating comments on influences.

[4]Alexander Bain, *John Stuart Mill* (London: Longmans, 1882), 26. Apart from Mill himself, Bain, his closest and most important disciple, is the best source for information about the *Logic*, and so is frequently cited below.

to crystallize upon; the import of his general remarks being interpreted to me, by the particular instances which came under my notice afterwards. My own consciousness and experience ultimately led me to appreciate quite as highly as he did, the value of an early practical familiarity with the school logic. I know of nothing, in my education, to which I think myself more indebted for whatever capacity of thinking I have attained. (*Autobiography*, 12–13.)

He goes on to mention the practice this gave him in dissecting arguments, and to outline his reading of the classical rhetoricians and Plato, which reinforced the practice.

At the same time he became interested in experimental science, the foundation of the inductive portion of his *Logic*. "I never remember being so wrapt up in any book," he says, "as I was in Joyce's Scientific Dialogues; and I was rather recalcitrant to my father's criticisms of the bad reasoning respecting the first principles of physics which abounds in the early part of that work" (*ibid.*, 12). He also "devoured" chemical treatises, especially Thomson's *System of Chemistry*, which he first read in 1816, and again in 1818,[5] and which provided an important clue in his later speculations. During the same visit to Sandhurst in which the utility of syllogistic logic was brought home to him, he attended chemistry lectures given to the cadets by Phillips, and won fame by his notes and general performance.[6]

The most important element in Mill's logical training in these years was, of course, his father's constant supervision of his studies. Though James Mill never wrote a treatise on logic, the analysis of meaning and the dissection of arguments were his great polemical instruments. Bain, who had a high opinion of his logical powers, notes, "a considerable portion" of his *Analysis of the Phenomena of the Human Mind* "should have gone to make up a treatise on Logic."[7] His direct influence on his son's studies did not stop when, in 1819, James Mill began his career in the East India Company, nor even when in the following, aged fourteen, John Mill went to France to live with the family of Sir Samuel Bentham, Jeremy's younger brother.

In response to a letter from his father concerning the study of Political Economy and Logic, Mill wrote from France (11 July, 1820): "The best exercise in both these branches of knowledge would perhaps be to write treatises on particular subjects appertaining to both. This I have not yet

[5]Bain, *James Mill* (London: Longmans, 1882), 157, 168, quoting letters from James Mill to Thomson. In the latter (22/2/18) James Mill says: "John has fastened with great greediness upon your book, and gives me an account of the new knowledge he gets out of it. He would have a great passion for the science, if he had the opportunity of seeing a course of experiments."

[6]BM Add. MSS 35153, f.50; *Works of David Ricardo*, ed. P. Sraffa (Cambridge: Cambridge University Press, 1952), VII, 313–14, 324n.

[7]Bain, *James Mill*, 413; cf. *ibid.*, 209, where, before saying much the same, he quotes from a letter of James Mill to Macvey Napier (11/9/23): "As to Logic, we must talk of that another time: but you must not expect the book too soon: though my expositions are pretty well down upon paper."

commenced doing, but I shall certainly do so."[8] In the next few days, he worked on classification tables for insects and chemicals, and began a "Treatise on Value" (in French), and a "treatise on the definition of political economy" (the latter at Lady Bentham's suggestion). Having already been at work on Sanderson's *Logic*, he notes on 24 August, "Je commençai à me faire des tables Logiques," and on 24 October began his "court Traité de Logique." In November he began to attend courses of lectures in the Faculty of Sciences of the Academy of Montpellier in Chemistry, Zoology, and Logic, the last offered by Joseph-Diez Gorgonne, Dean of the Faculty, "comme servant d'introduction à la Philosophie des Sciences."[9] His grasp of the material, as well as his diligence, is revealed in two extant documents, one containing Mill's notes of the eighteenth through thirty-second of Gorgonne's lectures, and the other the "Traité de Logique" started before the lectures began, but clearly incorporating material from them.[10]

On his return to England in the summer of 1821, Mill began his intensive reading of Bentham in Dumont's French version. The most important result of this reading, as he indicates in an oft-cited passage in the *Autobiography* (42), was his adoption of utilitarianism as "in one among the best senses of the word, a religion," but one should also note his delight in Bentham's method of classification, which appealed to him not only because of his previous intellectual training, but also because of his new interest in botany, his life-long avocation.[11]

[8]Anna J. Mill, *John Mill's Boyhood Visit to France* (Toronto: University of Toronto Press, 1960), 43.

[9]*Ibid.*, 44–84, *passim*, esp. 45 (13/7/20), 53 (23/7/20), 64 (24/8/20), 80 (24/10/20), and 84 (16/11/20).

[10]These manuscripts, which are respectively in the London School of Economics and the Pierpont Morgan Library, will be found in Vol. XX of the *Collected Works*.

[11]*Autobiography*, 41–2. Henry Trimen, in discussing Mill's botanical studies, says: "It may be safely stated, that the chapters on classification in the 'Logic' would not have taken the form they have, had not the writer been a naturalist as well as a logician" (H. R. Fox Bourne, *et al. John Stuart Mill: His Life and Works* [New York: Holt, 1873], 47). It is interesting to note that Mill's first instructor in botany, who was also responsible for correcting the French in his "Traité," was George Bentham (Sir Samuel's son). George Bentham published *An Outline of a New System of Logic* in 1827, a work highly critical of Whately; Mill was quite severe about Bentham's book (*EL, CW*, XII, 23 [10/3/28]), just after his own appreciative review of Whately and the beginning of the discussions of logic in Threadneedle Street. Curiously, Mill, like the few others who read Bentham's *Outline* (only about sixty copies were sold before the publisher went bankrupt), paid no attention to Bentham's treatment of what was later called the "Quantification of the Predicate," which both Augustus De Morgan and Sir William Hamilton claimed to have first developed; Hamilton's claim led to a considerable controversy, involving (as well as De Morgan), Spencer, Baines, and Jevons, during which Bentham's work was rediscovered. See B. Dayton Jackson, *George Bentham* (London: Dent, 1906), 57, 215–16, 227; and *Later Letters*, ed. Francis E. Mineka and Dwight Lindley, *Collected Works*, XVII (Toronto: University of Toronto Press, 1972), 2004, for Mill's reading of De Morgan's claim as against Hamilton's. (*Later Letters* hereafter cited as *LL, CW*, with volume and page numbers.) See also the text below, 170*p*.

The next few years saw his first articles in newspapers and in the newly founded *Westminster Review*. His imitation of his father's and Bentham's methods may be seen in these published writings, and in his speeches in the London Debating Society; his continued interest in logic may be inferred from what little is known of his continuing education, which included John Austin's tutoring and lectures in law. (He also began his professional career in these years, entering the East India Company as a clerk in the Examiner's Office the day after his seventeenth birthday, on 23 May 1823.)[12]

In 1825 Mill joined several other young men in a "Society of Students of Mental Philosophy" that met in George Grote's house in Threadneedle Street.[13] Their discussions, which led to the writing of Mill's first complete book, *Essays on Some Unsettled Questions in Political Economy* (written 1830–31, published 1844), and also to the *Logic*, were a very effective educational instrument, as Mill indicates in his *Autobiography* (72–3):

We chose some systematic treatise as our textbook. . . . One of us read aloud a chapter, or some smaller portion, of the book. The discussion was then opened, and any one who had an objection or other remark to make, made it. Our rule was to discuss thoroughly every point raised, whether great or small, prolonging the discussion until all who took part were satisfied with the conclusion they had individually arrived at; and to follow up every topic of collateral speculation which the chapter or the conversation suggested, never leaving it until we had untied every knot which we found. We repeatedly kept up the discussion of some one point for several weeks, thinking intently on it during the intervals of our meetings, and contriving solutions of the new difficulties which had risen up in the last morning's discussion.

[12]The choice of occupation, though of course not fortuitous, as Mill was joining his father, was in accord with the belief of both father and son that, in Bain's words (*John Stuart Mill*, 147), "literature and philosophy should not be resorted to as a means of livelihood; that people should derive their subsistence from some of the common vocations, and work at the higher themes in leisure hours." Bain comments: "[John] Mill himself was nominally engaged six hours a-day; but probably never gave more than the half of that time to his office routine. His two great works—the *Logic* and the *Political Economy*—were, I may say, written during his office hours"—and, one may add, undoubtedly on India Office stationery.

[13]The name of the group is given in Ethel E. Ellis, *Memoir of William Ellis and an Account of his Conduct-Teaching* (London: Longmans, Green, 1888); Mill never identifies it by name. The group, which met twice a week, from 8:30 to 10 a.m., before the members took up their "daily occupations," consisted of "a dozen or more," according to Mill, who mentions as members, in addition to himself, Grote (who joined for the discussions of logic), Prescott (Grote's banking partner), Roebuck, Ellis, and Graham. H. R. Fox Bourne, in his sketch of Mill's life (*John Stuart Mill: His Life and Works*, 12–13), quoting from Grote's obituary in the *Examiner*, lists the same members (giving "Ellice" for "Ellis"), adding "two brothers Whitmore," and comments: "The mentor of their studies was the elder Mr. Mill." Henry Cole joined the group in 1827; he notes in his diary that the discussions had ended by 30 January, 1828, and were resumed late in 1829 for the discussion of James Mill's *Analysis*, at which time Bulwer and Wilson also joined (Anna J. Mill, "Some Notes on Mill's Early Friendship with Henry Cole," *Mill News Letter*, IV [Spring, 1969], 2).

Having begun with political economy, they turned to scholastic logic in 1827.

Our first textbook was Aldrich [*Artis logicæ compendium*], but being disgusted with its superficiality, we reprinted [by subscription] one of the most finished among the many manuals of the school logic, which my father, a great collector of such books, possessed, the Manuductio ad Logicam of the Jesuit Du Trieu. After finishing this, we took up Whately's Logic, then first republished from the Encyclopædia Metropolitana, and finally the "Computatio sive Logica" of Hobbes. These books, dealt with in our manner, afforded a wide range for original metaphysical speculation: and most of what has been done in the First Book of my System of Logic, to rationalize and correct the principles and distinctions of the school logicians, and to improve the theory of the Import of Propositions, had its origin in these discussions; Graham and I originating most of the novelties, while Grote and others furnished an excellent tribunal or test. From this time I formed the project of writing a book on Logic, though on a much humbler scale than the one I ultimately executed.[14]

Mill "always dated" his "own real inauguration as an original and independent thinker" from these meetings, which bore their first fruits in his review of Whately's *Logic*, one of their texts. This important article, which includes discussion of the utility of logic, the analysis of arguments, the Predicables, the relation of Induction and Syllogism, and the problem of assenting to general propositions without knowing all that they contain, concludes with Mill's assessment of what important tasks remained for Whately and other logicians in 1828:

A large portion of the philosophy of General Terms still remains undiscovered; the philosophical analysis of Predication, the explanation of what is the immediate object of belief when we assent to a proposition, is yet to be performed: and though the important assistance rendered by general language, not only in what are termed the exact sciences, but even in the discovery of physical facts, is known and admitted, the nature of the means by which it performs this service is a problem still to a great extent unsolved.[15]

The next important step in Mill's logical speculations resulted from the attacks in 1829 by Macaulay on James Mill's essay *On Government* and on utilitarianism in general.[16] These shook his faith in his father's methodology in political philosophy, without converting him to Macaulay's posi-

---

[14]*Autobiography*, 73–4. The words "by subscription" in square brackets derive from the *Early Draft* of the *Autobiography*, ed. Jack Stillinger (Urbana: University of Illinois Press, 1961), 109. Henceforth referred to as Stillinger, to avoid confusion with the "Early Draft" of the *Logic*, discussed below.

[15]"Whately's Elements of Logic," *Westminster Review*, IX (Jan., 1828), 171–2; this article will be found in Vol. XI of the *Collected Works*. For the discussion, cf. Bain, *John Stuart Mill*, 36–7.

[16]T. B. Macaulay, "Mr. Mill's Essay on Government," "Bentham's Defence of Mill," and "Utilitarian Theory of Government, and the 'Greatest Happiness Principle,'" *Edinburgh Review*, XLIX (1829), 159–89, 273–99, and L (1829), 99–125.

tion, which he thought shallow. The source of James Mill's and Macaulay's errors "flashed" upon him "in the course of other [i.e., logical] studies" (*Autobiography*, 95). James Mill had appropriately chosen a deductive method in politics, but had wrongly used a geometrical model, while Macaulay had mistakenly advocated an experimental method, that of chemistry (*ibid.*, 96).

FIRST VERSIONS OF THE *Logic*, 1830–40

The result of all these activities was the first step towards the composition of the *Logic*, as described by Mill in the *Autobiography* (95–7):

In the early part of 1830 I had begun to put on paper the ideas on Logic (chiefly on the distinctions among Terms, and the import of Propositions) which had been suggested and in part worked out in the morning conversations already spoken of. Having secured these thoughts from being lost, I pushed on into the other parts of the subject, to try whether I could do anything further towards clearing up the theory of Logic generally. I grappled at once with the problem of Induction, postponing that of Reasoning, on the ground that it is necessary to obtain premises before we can reason from them. Now, Induction is mainly a process for finding the causes of effects: and in attempting to fathom the mode of tracing causes and effects in physical science, I soon saw that in the more perfect of the sciences, we ascend, by generalization from particulars, to the tendencies of causes considered singly, and then reason downward from those separate tendencies, to the effect of the same causes when combined. I then asked myself, what is the ultimate analysis of this deductive process; the common theory of the syllogism evidently throwing no light upon it. My practice (learnt from Hobbes and my father) being to study abstract principles by means of the best concrete instances I could find, the Composition of Forces, in dynamics, occurred to me as the most complete example of the logical process I was investigating. On examining, accordingly, what the mind does when it applies the principle of the Composition of Forces, I found that it performs a simple act of addition. It adds the separate effect of the one force to the separate effect of the other, and puts down the sum of these separate effects as the joint effect. But is this a legitimate process? In dynamics, and in all the mathematical branches of physics, it is; but in some other cases, as in chemistry, it is not; and I then recollected that something not unlike this was pointed out as one of the distinctions between chemical and mechanical phenomena, in the introduction to that favorite of my boyhood, Thomson's System of Chemistry. This distinction at once made my mind clear as to what was perplexing me in respect to the philosophy of politics. I now saw, that a science is either deductive or experimental, according as, in the province it deals with, the effects of causes when conjoined, are or are not the sums of the effects which the same causes produce when separate. It followed that politics must be a deductive science. . . . A foundation was thus laid in my thoughts for the principal chapters of what I afterwards published on the Logic of the Moral Sciences; and my new position in respect to my old political creed, now became perfectly definite.

One cannot give an exact date to the speculations here described, but they evidently preceded by some months at least the letter to Sterling of 20–22 October, 1831. In the portion of that letter already quoted, Mill says he has put down upon paper a great many of his ideas on logic; these would seem to include not the speculations on method mentioned in the section of the *Autobiography* just quoted, which he says laid a "foundation" in his "thoughts" for what became Book VI of the *Logic*, but rather his "ideas . . . on the distinctions among Terms, and the import of Propositions," which he dates in the early part of 1830. In any event, the letter to Sterling provides an instructive guide to his work in the following years, for it continues, after an account of his having finished his part of the work on political economy in which Graham was intending to collaborate,[17] with the following sentence: "The next thing I shall do will be to complete my speculations on Logic: very likely I shall not get to the end of the subject yet, viewed as I understand it; but I shall at least gather in another harvest of ideas, & then let the ground lie fallow a while longer."[18]

Once again the *Autobiography* provides a full and interesting account. In 1830 and 1831, he says, he resumed[19] his logical inquiries, puzzling himself "with the great paradox of the discovery of new truths by general reasoning." He continues:

As to the fact, there could be no doubt. As little could it be doubted, that all reasoning is resolvable into syllogisms, and that in every syllogism the conclusion is actually contained and implied in the premises. How, being so contained and implied, it could be new truth, and how the theorems of geometry, so different, in appearance, from the definitions and axioms, could be all contained in these, was a difficulty which no one, I thought, had sufficiently felt, and which at all events no one had succeeded in clearing up. The explanations offered by Whately and others, though they might give a temporary satisfaction, always, in my mind, left a mist still hanging over the subject. At last, when [sitting in the garden at Mickleham] reading a second or third time the chapters on Reasoning in the second volume of Dugald Stewart, interrogating myself on every point, and following out as far as I knew how, every topic of thought which the book suggested, I came upon an idea of his respecting the use of axioms in ratiocination, which I did not remember to have before noticed, but which now, in meditating on it, seemed to me not only true of axioms, but of all general propositions whatever,

---

[17]Graham never did complete his part, and Mill eventually published his contributions as *Essays on Some Unsettled Questions of Political Economy* (see *Collected Works*, IV, 230).

[18]*EL, CW*, XII, 80.

[19]As has already been suggested, and will be mentioned again, Mill in the *Autobiography* is somewhat vague about dates. If he actually resumed his logical speculations in 1830, it would have been after only a few months; it is much more likely that he had started to think again on the subject just before he wrote to Sterling in late October, 1831, and the account in the next quotation from the *Autobiography* refers mainly to 1832.

and to be the key of the whole perplexity. From this germ grew the theory of the Syllogism propounded in the second Book of the Logic; which I immediately fixed by writing it out. And now, with greatly increased hope of being able to produce a work on Logic, of some originality and value, I proceeded to write the First Book, from the rough and imperfect draft I had already made. What I now wrote became the basis of that part of the subsequent Treatise; except that it did not contain the Theory of Kinds, which was a later addition, suggested by otherwise inextricable difficulties which met me in my first attempt to work out the subject of some of the concluding chapters of the Third Book.[20]

What Mill began to put on paper at this time led to the manuscript henceforth referred to as the "Early Draft," which is here printed for the first time in Appendix A. In the headnote to that Appendix, the manuscript is described, and the evidence about its dating is given. In reconstructing the process of composition, the following are the most significant facts: the manuscript is a scribal copy, in three different hands, with corrections, additions, and some footnotes in Mill's hand. The paper is of various makes, and three different dates, 1833, 1834, and 1836. Mill collected his folios into "gatherings," rough equivalents of printed signatures, normally of 20ff., which he lettered alphabetically, in the top right corner, A through P, with a second N for the final gathering. The most important external evidence is in a series of letters from Mill to John Pringle Nichol in 1834. In the first of these (17 January), he mentions that he would like to have Nichol's comments not only on articles, but also on "a much more elaborate work on Logic" which he has "made some progress in." On 14 October

---

[20]*Autobiography*, 108–9; the bracketed words appear in Stillinger, 150, as a cancelled reading. It is surely not fanciful to argue that, like the earlier strong recollection of the walk near Bagshot Heath, when his father explained the importance of syllogistic reasoning, this reference to a specific moment, at Mickleham, indicates the great importance that logical speculations had in Mill's development. (James Mill rented a cottage at Mickleham from 1828 till 1835, the year before his death; the family stayed there six months of the year, with John Mill and his father coming down for their holidays—six weeks in James Mill's case—and for weekends. There are two other excised references to Mickleham in Stillinger.)

In the *Logic* itself there are some exceptional passages that may be called personal. The most important of these is, of course, Book VI, Chap. ii, "Of Liberty and Necessity," which, he says in the *Autobiography* (101–2), grew out of "later returns" of his dejection in the winter of 1826–27 (his famed "mental crisis"). Writing to James Martineau (21/5/41), when revising the *Logic*, he says: "I shall never forget the time when I was myself under that awful shadow [of Necessity] you speak of [in your "Introductory Lecture"], nor how I got from under it, but it is all written down in my book" (*EL, CW*, XIII, 476–7). Years later, in a cancelled draft passage in a letter to Florence Nightingale (10/9/60), Mill says: "It is very agreeable to me that you should have found my Logic of so much use to you, & particularly the chapter on Free Will & Necessity, to which I have always attached much value as being the writing down of a train of thought which had been very important to myself many years before, & even (if I may use the expression) critical in my own development" (*LL, CW*, XV, 706n).

For other personal references, see also below, 681 (which suggests parts of *On Liberty*), 839[l], and (in the Early Draft), 1046.

he asks whether he may send Nichol "as much as is written of my book on *Logic*; if book it can be called, which is but the raw material out of which I shall some time or other make a book." And finally, on 26 November, he says: "I will send the Logic very soon. I anticipate the greatest help in it, both from your general powers of thought and from your peculiar acquaintance with the philosophy of algebra, in which I am myself far from profound, but yet have found the little I do know to be of the utmost possible use."[21] As a note by Nichol's son in the Early Draft indicates, the manuscript was sent to Nichol, though we know not when.

This evidence does not permit an exact reconstruction of the process of composition, but the general pattern may be set out as follows. The manuscript reveals three stages of composition: the first consists of Gatherings A–F and K–M (K–M having been relettered over the original G–I), and contains the equivalent of what became, in the published version of 1843, the Introduction, Book I, Chapters i–vi, and Book II, Chapters i–iii. This material would appear to have been copied by a scribe in 1834 from the draft Mill wrote after his re-reading of Stewart (perhaps as early as the autumn of 1831).

The next stage consists of Gatherings G–J and the second Gathering N, and contains an expanded re-writing of the conclusion of Gathering F equivalent to the end of the final Book I, Chapter vi, plus material equivalent to the final Book I, Chapters vii and viii, and (in the second Gathering N) Mill's first attempt to deal with Induction, in three chapters containing material that contributed to Chapters ii and iii of Book III. The second scribe, in copying this material, presumably not long after the first scribe had finished copying the material of the first stage (i.e., in 1834), relettered the original Gatherings G–I (the material of Book II, Chapters i–iii) as K–M, to follow on the new conclusion of Book I, and then a third scribe continued with N (i.e., what finally was the second Gathering N).[22]

Stage three consists of Gatherings N–P, and contains material equivalent to what became Book II, Chapters iv–vi of the published version. The third scribe, who also copied this material, did not reletter the old Gathering N, which should have become Q to accommodate the added material. Scribe C made his copy sometime after the beginning of 1836, as the watermarks

---

[21]*EL*, *CW*, XII, 211–12, 235, 238. The reference to algebra is repeated in a later letter to Nichol of 21 December, 1837, that implies some now lost intermediate communication: "as to the 'great subject', I will read Peacock's Algebra" (*ibid.*, 363); he did, as references in the published version of the *Logic* (but not in the Early Draft) confirm.

[22]The intrusion of a third scribe at this point may suggest yet another stage, but the paper is the same as that in Gatherings H–J. Another anomaly is that the paper of Gathering G is different in make from that in H–J, and reappears mixed with 1836 paper in Gatherings O–P. See the headnote to Appendix A for a table giving paper makes and dates.

establish, and undoubtedly before Mill began, in 1837, the version of the *Logic* that appears in the Press-copy Manuscript.[23]

In view of the rewritings that occurred from 1837 to 1843, it is surprising to see how closely the Early Draft corresponds to the Introduction[24] and Books I and II in the Press-copy Manuscript, and even to the subsequent editions through Mill's lifetime. Table 1, which includes the tentative chapter headings of the Early Draft, gives the equivalents,[25] and summarizes the three-stage composition.

[23]The missing piece in the puzzle, which prevents full articulation, is the time of Nichol's possession of the Early Draft. If Mill did not send the manuscript to Nichol until the third scribe had copied his portion, that is, until after the beginning of 1836, then one may assume that it never was returned to Mill; Nichol made his comments by letter (perhaps as late as the fall of 1837—see note 21 above), and retained the manuscript, which passed to his son. Mill then must have used a holograph version of the Early Draft for his rewriting of 1837, the parallels in wording and order being too great to assume that he began afresh.

If, on the other hand, as the letter of 26 November, 1834 would seem to indicate, he sent a version of the Early Draft to Nichol *before* the third scribe had copied his portion, Nichol must have returned the manuscript before the conclusion of Book II was written, and then at an indeterminable later date received it back, in its present form, and retained it. Again one may assume a Mill holograph, but in this case the assumption would be that the Early Draft itself, which contains corrections and additions in Mill's hand, was used for the rewriting that began in 1837.

[24]The closeness of the Early Draft's Introductory Matter to the final Introduction, especially since Mill had not formulated his theory of induction in the Early Draft, points to the problem of defining the purpose of the *Logic*. In the Introduction logic is seen as the science of proof or evidence, while the work as a whole is entitled *A System of Logic, Ratiocinative and Inductive, Being a Connected View of the Principles of Evidence and the Methods of Scientific Investigation* (the Early Draft has no title). Kubitz (*Mill's Logic*, 22–3) argues, not in this context, that one of the most important influences on Mill's early logical thought was his editing of Bentham's *Rationale*, which explains his concentration on logic as the science of evidence. Bain (*John Stuart Mill*, 68), commenting on "the seeming incompatibility" between the definition in the Introduction and the subtitle, says: "But the title, although larger than the definition, is not larger than the work; he did discuss the methods of Investigation, as aids to Discovery, as well as means of Proof; only, he never explained the mutual bearings of the two. Any one that tries, will find this not an easy matter."

One may also mention Caroline Fox's note of Mill's conversation (*Memories of Old Friends*, 2nd ed., 2 vols. [London: Smith, Elder, 1882], I, 152; entry for 27/3/40): "John Mill considers it the duty of life to endeavour to reconcile the two, the active and the speculative; and from his own experience and observation the former gives vigour and system and effectiveness to the latter." This gives added point to what many readers of the *Logic* have noted, as expressed in a letter from Mill to Pasquale Villari (*LL, CW*, XIV, 239–40; 22/8/54): "Vous avez vu, avec raison, dans ce sixième livre, le but principal de l'ouvrage tout entier, qui a été surtout destiné à répandre sur la méthode des sciences morales, les lumières qu'on peut trouver dans les procédés des sciences physiques. Je ne m'exagère pas la portée de ce que j'ai fait, ni même de ce qui peut se faire dans ce genre."

See also the brief comments, lxxxv below, on the polemical nature of the *Logic*.

[25]The equivalence is, of course, of varying degrees of closeness; full collation is aided by the paragraph-by-paragraph comparison indicated in the text of Appendix A. There are no Book or Section divisions in the Early Draft. As will be noted, because the gatherings normally do not coincide with divisions in the text, there is overlap in the section divisions in the table.

TABLE 1: THE EARLY DRAFT

	GATHERING	SCRIBE	EARLY DRAFT CHAPTER	EQUIVALENT IN PRESS-COPY MS
Stage 1	A	A	"Introductory Matter"	"Introduction," §§1–7
	B	A	"Statement of the Problem"	Book I, "Of Names and Propositions," Chap. i, "Of the Necessity of commencing with an Analysis of Language," §§1–2
				I, ii, "Of Names," §§2–5
	C	A	"Of Names"	" (cont.), §§5–8
			" (cont.)	I, iii, "Of the Things denoted by Names," §§1–2
	D	A	"Classification of Things"	" (cont.), §§2,6,7,9,10,14, plus some other parts
	E	A	" (cont.)	" (cont.), some isolated parts
			" (cont.)	I, iv, "Of Propositions," §§1–4, and I, v, "Of the Import of Propositions," §§1–3, and some isolated parts
	F	A	"Of Predication"	" (cont.), §4, and some isolated parts; and
			" (cont.)	I, vi, "Of Propositions merely Verbal," §§1–4 (the last part being cancelled, and replaced by the opening of Gathering G below)
	K (formerly G)	A	"Of Inference, or Reasoning"	Book II, "Of Reasoning," i, "Of Inference, or Reasoning, in general," §§1–3
			"Of Ratiocination, or Syllogism"	II, ii, "Of Ratiocination, or Syllogism," §§1–3; and II, iii, "Of the Functions and Logical Value of the Syllogism," §1
	L (formerly H)	A	" (cont.)	" (cont.), §§1–5
	M (formerly I)	A	" (cont.)	" (cont.), §§5–7

	GATHERING	SCRIBE	EARLY DRAFT CHAPTER	EQUIVALENT IN PRESS-COPY MS
Stage 2	G	B	"Of Predication" (cont. from Gathering F)	I, vi (cont.), §4, and some isolated parts
	H	B	"Of the Predicables or Universals"	I, vii, "Of the Nature of Classification, and the Five Predicables," §2–5
			" (cont.)	" (cont.), §§5–8
	I	B	"Of Definition"	I, viii, "Of Definition," §§1–2
	J	B	" (cont.)	" (cont.), §§2–5, 7
			" (cont.)	" (cont.), §7
	N (should be Q)	C	"Of Induction in General"	Book III, no close chapter equivalence
			"Of the Various Grounds of Induction"	III, ii, "Of Inductions improperly so called," §§1–2
			"Of the Uniformity in the Course of Nature"	iii, "On the Ground of Induction," §§1, 3
Stage 3	N	C	"Of Trains of Reasoning"	II, iv, "Of Trains of Reasoning, and Deductive Sciences," §§ 1–3
			"Of Deductive Sciences"	" (cont.), §§4–6
	O	C	"Of Demonstration and Necessary Truths"	v, "Of Demonstration, and Necessary Truths," §§1–3, plus some isolated parts; and vi, "The same Subject continued," §§2–3
	P	C	" (cont.)	" (cont.), §§3–5

As a guide to Mill's rewriting between 1837 and 1843, when the *Logic* was published, the major differences between the Early Draft and the Press-copy Manuscript may be described as follows:

The most noticeable difference is the absence in the Early Draft of Books IV, V, and VI, and the embryonic form of Book III. As finally published, the Introduction and Books I and II follow quite closely the organization of the equivalent material in the Early Draft. In comparing the versions one finds the following:

The "Introductory Matter" is closest in wording to the final version, and has relatively few gaps when compared with the Press-copy Manuscript.

Book I is somewhat closer in bulk than Book II to the final version, but varies more, especially in two important places, in wording and organization. These two places, equivalent to parts of the final Book I, Chapters iii and vi, are significant for a study of the composition of the *Logic,* and also for its doctrine. The first of these reflects Mill's problems in laying out the chapter on the Classification of Things. As indicated in the notes to the text of the Early Draft, §§1–2, and much of 6–10 are generally covered in the Early Draft, with the other sections being either absent, or so different in organization as to prevent direct collation. Mill's dissatisfaction with the account may be inferred from his insertion, at the end of this chapter in the Early Draft, of the "Linea Prædicamentalis" (see 1004 below), which does not, as might appear, summarize the preceding account, but seems to indicate his second thoughts on the proper ordering of the argument. This chapter continued to give Mill trouble, for, as will be shown later, Alexander Bain found it difficult, and so Mill made changes in the final stages of revision of the Press-copy Manuscript to clarify the argument.

The second place in Book I where there is a major departure from the final version reflects, in part, Mill's recasting of Chapter iii, and in part his development, after the Early Draft was completed, of the theory of Natural Kinds, which led to extensive changes in the conclusion of Chapter vi and in Chapter vii, as well as minor changes elsewhere.

The sections of the Early Draft that correspond to Book II are, as mentioned above, generally closer in wording and order to the final version than those corresponding to Book I. The equivalents of Chapters iv, v, and vi were in fact, as the preceding table indicates, the last part of the Early Draft to be composed. (Book II, Chapter vii, it should be noted, first appeared only in the 4th edition, 1856.) The most extensive rewriting between the Early Draft and the Press-copy Manuscript occurred in the discussion of the syllogism (the end of Chapter ii, and throughout Chapter iii), and in those parts of Chapters iv and v affected by Mill's fuller development of the theory of induction after 1837.

Given all these differences, the Early Draft and the Press-copy Manuscript provide a striking exemplification of Mill's comment in the *Auto-biography* (132–3) on his methods of composition. His books, he says,

were always written at least twice over; a first draft of the entire work was completed to the very end of the subject, then the whole begun again *de novo*; but incorporating, in the second writing, all sentences and parts of sentences of the old draft, which appeared as suitable to my purpose as anything which I could write in lieu of them. I have found great advantages in this system of double redaction. It combines, better than any other mode of composition, the freshness and vigour of the first conception, with the superior precision and completeness resulting from prolonged thought. In my own case, moreover, I have found that the patience necessary for a careful elaboration of the details of exposition and expression, costs much less effort after the entire subject has been once gone through, and the substance of all that I find to say has in some manner, however imperfect, been got upon paper. The only thing which I am careful, in the first draft, to make as perfect as I am able, is the arrangement. If that is bad, the whole thread on which the ideas string themselves becomes twisted; thoughts placed in a wrong connexion are not expounded in a manner that suits the right, and a first draft with this original vice is next to useless as a foundation for the final treatment.

This admirable method, it may be noted, while more coherently followed by Mill than by Bentham, from whom he may have borrowed it, still makes for great editorial problems in dating as well as in text.

His inability to resolve the difficulties in inductive theory, Mill says in the *Autobiography* (109), brought him to a halt, which lasted until 1837. "I had come to the end of my tether; I could make nothing satisfactory of Induction, at this time. I continued to read any book which seemed to promise light on the subject, and appropriated, as well as I could, the results; but for a long time I found nothing which seemed to open to me any very important vein of meditation." Early in 1837, having become convinced that a "comprehensive and . . . accurate view of the whole circle of physical science," which it would take him long to acquire, was necessary before he could continue with Induction, he read Whewell's recently published *History of the Inductive Sciences*. Stimulated by this reading, he returned to Herschel's *Discourse on the Study of Natural Philosophy*, which he had reviewed favourably in 1831 on its first appearance.[26] Setting "vigorously to work out the subject" of Induction, he wrote, during two months of the summer of 1837, what he later estimated at about one-third, "the most difficult third," of the whole work (what he had written earlier, i.e., the major part of the Early Draft, comprised another third).[27] "What

[26]*Examiner*, 20 March, 1831, 179–80.
[27]*Autobiography*, 124–5; *EL, CW*, XII, 340–1, 345. In the former of these letters (30/6/37) Mill characteristically deprecates his work to Carlyle: "I am using this interval [of leisure, resulting from a lull in India House duties] to get on with my book —a book I have done little to since the review began, & which you will think very little worth doing—a treatise on Logic. I hope I do not overrate the value of anything I can

I wrote at this time," he says in the *Autobiography* (125), "consisted of the remainder of the doctrine of Reasoning (the theory of Trains of Reasoning, and Demonstrative Science), and the greater part of the Book on Induction."[28] If his memory is accurate, the third stage of the composition of the Early Draft (Gatherings N, O, and P) occurred in the summer of 1837 and, following one (though the less likely) hypothesis suggested above (see n23), he may have sent the Early Draft to Nichol at that time, keeping before him a holograph to which he then added "the greater part" of Book III.[29]

Noting that Mill considered the time necessary for this writing as having been "stolen from occupations more urgent" (*Autobiography*, 125), one is reminded that his major avocation during these years was the editing of the *London and Westminster Review*, and that he had become the head of the family after his father's death in mid-1836. His role as teacher included initiating his youngest brother, Henry, into the mysteries of logic; he undoubtedly profitted himself from this instruction, for during 1837, when engaged in the writing just described, he "carried [Henry] through the Aristotelian logic," and started him on Hobbes.[30]

Mill interrupted his work on logic to compose two articles for the *London and Westminster*,[31] and then, after reading for the first time Volumes I and

do of that kind but it so happens that this, whatever be its value, is the only thing which I am sure I can do & do not believe can be so well done by anybody else whom I know of. In regard to all things which are not merely for the day, that seems to be the best rule for chusing one's work.—Further, I do it in order to deliver myself of various things which I have in my head on the subject. As for its being read, it will be so by fewer people than even yours [*The French Revolution*], but it may be of use to some of those few."

[28]Stillinger (162) reads "Deductive Science" where the final reading is "Demonstrative Science."

[29]The great difficulty in reconciling Mill's account with the other evidence is that he twice refers, in the *Autobiography*, to a five-year gap in his writing of the *Logic*, dating back from 1837 (he never clearly gives the earlier date). Excluding Gatherings N-P, the *terminus ab quo* of the *copying* of the Early Draft (admittedly not of its *composition*) is established as 1834 by the watermarks; the epistolary evidence would tend to support the argument that he was in fact, if perhaps sporadically, setting down his thoughts as late as 1834. (His quotation from his own review of Lewis's *Use and Abuse*, which appeared in April, 1832, dates the composition of at least Gathering J as after that time; see 1050 below.) The gap would seem, then, to have been under three years, rather than about five.

[30]*EL, CW*, XII, 366 (21/12/37). Bain, mentioning that James Mill intended, before his death, to start Henry on logic at the age of fourteen, compares John's beginning at twelve as evidence of his precocity (*John Stuart Mill*, 26n).

[31]"Parties and the Ministry," and "Armand Carrel," *London and Westminster Review*, 28 (Oct. 1837), 1–26, 66–111. In the years when he was most actively engaged on the *Logic* (1835–42), Mill's contributions to newspapers and short pieces for other periodicals dropped in volume (the early 1830's saw his greatest activity of this kind), only some forty appearing. His thirty-odd periodical articles in the period, however, are of great importance, including, among others, his reviews of Tennyson's *Poems* and Carlyle's *French Revolution*, his two articles on de Tocqueville, and his essays on Bentham and Coleridge.

II of Comte's *Cours de philosophie positive*,[32] he wrote three more chapters of Book III in the autumn, and "did not return to the subject until the middle of the next year: the review engrossing all the time [he] could devote to authorship, or to thinking with authorship in view."[33]

In July and August of 1838 he completed the first draft of Book III and, as a result, was led to "recognize Kinds as realities in nature," and so to "modify and enlarge several chapters" of Book I (i.e., v and vi, and, in part, iii).[34] On 2 October, while on holiday, he wrote to John Robertson that he had planned "the concluding portion" since leaving London (in the middle of September), had written a "large piece" of it, and hoped to do more before returning to London. During this holiday he read the third volume of Comte's *Cours*.[35] In the *Autobiography* (132) he identifies the work done that autumn as the "Book on Language and Classification [Book IV], and the chapter on the Classification of Fallacies [Book V, Chap. ii]." With so much done, he then hoped to finish, except for rewriting, during the winter of 1838–39.[36] But a severe illness interrupted his plans, and he went to Italy on a six-month leave, returning to London in the early summer. Resuming work on the *Logic* on his return, he told Sterling that he could hardly fail to finish during the next year,[37] and, after a month in Falmouth during which his brother Henry died, he completed the draft of the whole work during the summer and autumn of 1840.[38]

It seems safe to assume that what Mill had written up to this time was gathered in a holograph manuscript not now extant (except for a few folios that appear in the Press-copy Manuscript), consisting of the Early Draft, rewritten in parts, and its continuation through the rest of Book III, Books IV and V, and probably Book VI. He therefore felt himself near the end of his task, and so, though he had to rewrite the work completely, and Sterling had advised him to read the German logicians,[39] he was looking forward to publication in 1841.

[32]*Autobiography*, 125. The first two volumes of Comte's *Cours* were *Les Preliminaires généraux et la philosophie mathematique* (1830) and *La Philosophie astronomique et la philosophie de la physique* (1835).

[33]Stillinger, 163 (this passage is not in the *Autobiography*).

[34]*Autobiography*, 132. The difficulties arose presumably in Book III, Chap. xxii; see also Book IV, Chaps. vii and viii.

[35]*EL, CW*, XIII, 388–9. The third volume of Comte's *Cours* was *La Philosophie chimique et la philosophie biologique* (1838).

[36]*EL, CW*, XIII, 390.

[37]*Ibid.*, 406.

[38]*Autobiography*, 132; *EL, CW*, XIII, 448 (to R. B. Fox, 25/11/40): ". . . I put the last hand to [the draft] a few weeks ago"; cf. *ibid.*, 474. In a letter to Thornton cited by Bain (*John Stuart Mill*, 159; *LL, CW*, XV, 718), who dates it in 1860, Mill says that he finished the draft twenty years earlier, during a holiday in which he visited Oxford.

[39]*EL, CW*, XIII, 412, 450, 455. As always when Mill's knowledge of German philosophy, or of the German language, is in question, there is conflicting evidence. His first acquaintance with Kantian thought evidently came in 1828–29, through Thomas Wirgman (see *LL, CW*, XVII, 1954–5, 1956), at the time when he was presumably

FINAL MANUSCRIPT VERSION, 1841–43

The rewriting of the *Logic* beginning in 1841 produced the Press-copy Manuscript and, finally, the 1st edition, published in March, 1843. The main pattern of composition in these years may be traced, before the details are discussed.

In April, 1841, Mill began the final draft, and worked steadily on the revision until the end of January, 1842,[40] having finished Book I by 6 May, and "about half of it, & the most difficult half" towards the end of September.[41] During the rewriting he read Whewell's *Philosophy of the Inductive Sciences*,[42] and introduced many references to the work. His intention was to finish the *Logic* in time for publication in April, 1842,[43] and to that end submitted it (not complete) to John Murray on 20 December, 1841, sending what he thought was the final revision of the last three Books at the beginning of February, 1842. In early March, Murray, who had been ill in the interval, turned down the manuscript for reasons, now unknown, that in Mill's opinion could have been given much sooner.[44] Annoyed at what he thought an unreasonable delay[45] (it will hardly seem so to modern authors), Mill sent the manuscript to John Parker—or rather, sent such portions as

---

learning German "on the Hamiltonian method" (*Autobiography*, 72). Michael St. J. Packe, in his *Life of John Stuart Mill* (London: Secker and Warburg, 1954, 271), says that Mill read the German logicians at Sterling's suggestion for the *Logic*, but in a letter to Comte of 13 March, 1843 (*EL, CW*, XIII, 576), after the *Logic* was printed, Mill says: "Je ne suis pas peutêtre en droit de donner là-dessus [la philosophie allemande] une opinion très décidée, n'ayant moi-même lu ni Kant ni Hegel ni aucun autre des chefs de cette école, que je n'ai d'abord connue que par ses interprètes anglais et français" (presumably mainly Cousin's). But later in his life he commented, after reading J. H. Stirling's *Secret of Hegel* in 1867, that certain words, such as "reflexion, development, evolution, &c.," gave him "a sort of sickening feeling" because they reminded him of his reading of Hegel; he had "found by actual experience of Hegel that conversancy with him tends to deprave one's intellect" (*LL, CW*, XVI, 1324).

[40]*Autobiography*, 132, says, with reasonable accuracy, "the end of 1841," but see *EL, CW*, XIII, 946–8. See also *ibid.*, 474, 476–7, 478, 481, 485, 506.

[41]*EL, CW*, XIII, 474, 485, 485–6. In the last of these, to Sarah Austin (4/10/41) he says: "I find the rewriting harder work still than I had anticipated. I knew that the whole business of arranging it & of making it readable was yet to come, but the thoughts themselves I find were much more crude & imperfect than I fancied, & those only who have tried to write a systematic treatise on anything, know what the difficulty is of keeping the whole of a subject before one at once."

[42]*Autobiography*, 133.

[43]Bain, *John Stuart Mill*, 65; *EL, CW*, XIII, 506.

[44]*EL, CW*, XIII, 493–4 (20/12/41), 497–8 (31/1/42), 500 (24/2/42), 506 (11/3/42). In returning the manuscript, Murray forgot to include the Preface and Table of Contents, and Mill had to write asking for them (*LL, CW*, XVII, 1996). John Sterling had written to Murray on 16 Dec., 1841, saying that Mill had finished, to encourage acceptance of the manuscript (*EL, CW*, XIII, 493n).

[45]*Autobiography*, 133; *EL, CW*, XIII, 513 (5/4/42).

Parker's reader (William Cooke Taylor) wished to see, saying that he had to include "some other chapters or portions of chapters which from the manner in which the papers are stitched together [i.e., in Gatherings], cannot conveniently be separated from them." He continues: "I fear some parts are by no means so legible as I could wish, owing to the number of interlineations & erasures. The portions moreover of the Third Book, will scarcely perhaps be intelligible without the chapters which are intended to precede them."[46]

Parker accepted the manuscript early in April, suggesting an edition of 750 copies at his own risk, and half-profit; Mill was delighted:

I am very much indebted to your referee for so favorable an opinion, expressed in such complimentary terms, & am much gratified by the result. I will keep his observations in view in finally reading through the manuscript before it goes to press, but I fear I am nearly at the end of my stock of apt illustrations. I had to read a great deal for those I have given, & I believe that the chapters on Fallacies which preceded those that were submitted to your friend's judgment, are considerably richer than those he has seen, in examples selected as he recommends from eminent writers.

With respect to your very handsome offer of half profit, my feeling is that if I were to take advantage of your liberality in any manner, the shape in which I should most like to do so would be by a certain latitude in giving away copies—chiefly to foreigners or persons who would not be likely to buy the book. . . . I have not in view any alarming number, some 25 or 30 copies being as far as I can now judge, the extreme limit.

In reference to the contingency of a future edition, it is I think very unlikely that I should be inclined to change my publisher, especially when he is as I believe you to be, the most desirable one in England for the kind of book.[47]

By this time it was too late to think of spring publication, and Parker suggested the end of the year, with printing to begin in July. But the rewriting was far from completed, even at this late stage, and though Mill was somewhat annoyed that printing did not begin until September, and had reached only Vol. I, p. 160 by 19 December,[48] this delay enabled him to make significant revisions in the manuscript before the proof stage. (And, as will be shown, there were many changes in the proofs as well.) A major insight into these late revisions is given by comparing the final Table of Contents with the Table of Contents Mill enclosed in a letter to John

[46]*EL, CW*, XIII, 505–6 (March, 1842).

[47]*Ibid.*, 514. In later years Mill was less happy about this contract; see *ibid.*, 723–4 (27/10/47), and Mill's letter to Harriet (*LL, CW*, XIV, 17; cf *ibid.*, 83–4), both referring to improvements in the contract for the *Principles of Political Economy*. Mill continued, however, to publish through Parker until Longmans took over the firm in 1863, and remained with Longmans thereafter.

[48]*EL, CW*, XIII, 505–6, 514, 527, 541, 547, 564. Vol. I, p. 160 of the 1st edition comes at the end of Signature L, in Book I, Chapter vii.

Austin on 7 July, 1842, the implications of which will be dealt with in the detailed discussion below.[49]

Two events were largely responsible for these late revisions. The first was Mill's meeting Alexander Bain, with whom he had previously corresponded, in London in April, 1842. Impressed by Bain's abilities, and in particular by his scientific knowledge, Mill asked him in the middle of July "to revise the MS. of his *Logic*, now nearly ready for the press."[50] Bain immediately set to work, especially looking for inductive examples. He remained in London for the purpose until 10 September (just at the time printing was beginning), and continued his work in Aberdeen, with the assistance of John Shier, the assistant to Thomas Clark, Professor of Natural History at Aberdeen. He finished what he could do in November; however, as he had contracted to write a review of the *Logic* for the *Westminster Review*, he immediately began to receive proof sheets as they were worked off,[51] and there can be little doubt that some of the proof changes also resulted from his comments. Mill's due appreciation is seen in the *Autobiography* (147n):

> The only person from whom I received any direct assistance in the preparation of the "System of Logic" was Mr. Bain, since so justly celebrated for his philosophical writings. He went carefully through the manuscript before it was sent to press, and enriched it with a great number of additional examples and illustrations from science; many of which, as well as some detached remarks of his own in confirmation of my logical views, I inserted nearly in his own words.

The second event was the publication in 1842 of the sixth and final volume of Comte's *Cours, Le Complément de la philosophie sociale, et les conclusions générales*. Mill, having in the interval read Comte's fourth and fifth volumes, was immensely impressed by the sixth, which led him, in

---

[49]One may mention here that the letter clears up one matter that has caused some discussion among commentators on Mill's Experimental Methods. In the *Logic*, having said there are four methods, Mill goes on to treat five, and a question has arisen as to which of the five is included among the other four. The letter to Austin has a marginal note against the relevant chapter title (III, viii, "Of the Four Methods of Experimental Enquiry"), which reads: "1. Method of Agreement. 2. Method of Difference. 3. Method of Residues. 4. Method of Concomitant Variations" (BM Add. MSS 36878, ff.66v). The Joint Method of Agreement and Difference, as might be expected, is subsumed under the first two. Moreover, it is the Joint Method that is not included when Mill lists the four inductive methods in "Theism" (*CW*, X, 448).

The letter to Herschel (*EL, CW*, XIII, 583 [1/5/43]), cited by Professor McRae above, should also be recalled: "You will find that the most important chapter of the book, that on the four Experimental Methods, is little more than an expansion & a more scientific statement of what you had previously stated in the more popular manner suited to the purpose of your 'Introduction' [*A Preliminary Discourse on the Study of Natural Philosophy*]." *Inter alia*, Herschel had adduced Well's researches on dew, used by Mill in Book III, Chap. ix.

[50]Bain, *Autobiography* (London: Longmans, Green, 1904), 137.
[51]*Ibid.*, 141–2.

January, 1843, into a "remaniement complet" of the concluding chapters of Book VI.[52]

At last, however, though he was ill in the autumn of 1842 and again in December, and although he was greatly troubled by the American repudiations of that year. Mill managed to get the work through the press in about five months,[53] and sent off a large number of complimentary copies on its publication in March, 1843.[54]

With the major pattern in mind, one may turn to important particular revisions in the period 1841–43, relying for the most part on internal evidence in the Press-copy Manuscript.[55] In doing so, it should be remembered that the first full draft (that completed in 1840) is not now extant, except for a few intercalated folios in the Press-copy Manuscript, and so cannot be used for comparison.[56] The account is based on the divisions into Books, rather than on the exact times of various revisions, which cannot be determined.

Book I. As mentioned above, Bain felt, on first reading the manuscript, that the chapter on "Things denoted by Names" (I, iii) was not fully intelligible; he also had doubts about its place in the total scheme, though he did not press this objection. "The result was that [Mill] revised the chapter, and introduced the subordinate headings, which very much lightened the burden of its natural abstruseness."[57] The manuscript evidence confirms this

[52] *EL, CW*, XIII, 567 (28/1/43). See also *ibid.*, 517, and Bain, *John Stuart Mill*, 68. The fourth and fifth volumes of Comte's *Cours* were *La Philosophie sociale et les conclusions générales: première partie* (1839) and *La partie historique de la philosophie sociale, en tout ce qui concerne l'état théologique et l'état métaphysique* (1841).

Having mentioned these major influences, one may note that, although Mill met Harriet Taylor, his future wife, in 1830, just about the time he began to put his thoughts about logic on paper, there is, for once, little need to consider her part in one of his works. "The 'System of Logic,'" Mills says in his *Autobiography* (147), "owed little to her except in the minuter matters of composition, in which respect my writings, both great and small, have largely benefited by her accurate and clear-sighted criticism." In Stillinger (177), in a passage not found in the *Autobiography* as finally published, he explicitly rules out the *Logic* from among those works in which what "deserves remembrance" is owing mainly to her "intellect & character." See also Bain, *John Stuart Mill*, 172. For some comments on her part "in the minuter matters of composition" in the *Logic*, see John M. Robson, "'Joint Authorship' Again: The Evidence in the Third Edition of Mill's *Logic*," *Mill News Letter*, VI (Spring, 1971), 15–20.

[53] Bain, *John Stuart Mill*, 68, 77; *EL, CW*, XIII, 577.

[54] Complimentary copies were sent to, among others, R. B. Fox, Comte, George Bentham, Bulwer, Austin, Herschel, and de Tocqueville; see *EL, CW*, XIII, 569, 574, 577, 578, 579, 583, 612.

[55] For further details concerning the internal evidence, see Appendix J below, where the Press-copy Manuscript is described.

[56] For example, the changes in Book I resulting from Mill's development of his doctrine of Natural Kinds in 1838 are not seen in the Press-copy Manuscript, which they antedate, but presumably were evident in the earlier manuscript.

[57] Bain, *John Stuart Mill*, 66. As the following account dwells on Bain's objections, it should be noted that he was, in general, overwhelmingly impressed by Mill's *Logic*.

account. The grossest evidence is that while Mill's normal "gatherings" (except for those concluding the Books) contain twenty folios, Gatherings D and E, which include all but the first two folios of Chap. iii, contain, respectively, 24 and 25 folios, and indications of revision are seen where both would have ended had they contained 20 folios: e.g., f.77, which would be the first folio of the original Gathering E, is a relatively clean copy, as is f.81, on which the final Gathering E begins; also, f.101 is headed "(Supplement to E)", and ff.99–105 are clean copies. (Less obviously, the paper's colour changes slightly between ff.80 and 81, and between ff.82 and 83, and f.82, like f.81, is a clean copy.) The insertion of the "subordinate headings" is also plainly indicated, as at f.62v, where, along with the concluding sentence of §2, the title, "I. Feelings, or States of Consciousness," is added. Throughout the chapter there are cancellations, interlineations, and additions on the versos, all relevant to the changes prompted by Bain's criticism.[58]

All the paper in Book I is watermarked 1839, and so, since Bain met Mill only in April 1842, it may be assumed that Mill was using 1839 paper as late as the autumn of 1842; this assumption leads to the conclusion that the latest paper in the manuscript, that of 1841, was used solely for very late revisions (all in Book VI).

Only one other slight change need be mentioned here, as again helping to date the revisions. In his letter to Austin of 7 July, 1842, Mill gives the title of Chapter vii as "Of the five Predicables, & the nature of Classification"; the final title reversed the elements, reading, "Of the Nature of Classification, & the Five Predicables." This change, in conjunction with others cited below, enables one to date portions of the manuscript as pre-July, 1842, and many changes involving cancellations and interlineations as post-July, 1842. In other words, Mill, after rewriting the whole of the manuscript by February, 1842, went through it again, making not only the major changes prompted by Bain's advice and his rereading of Comte, but also altering and tidying up throughout.

In addition, one may mention (treating the "Introduction" as similar to Book I in history) the unquestionably late addition of the reference to Mill's review of Bailey on Berkeley's theory of vision, which appeared in the *Westminster* for October 1842 (see 8 below).

Book II. There is comparatively little evidence of manuscript revision of Book II. Three gatherings, M, O, and P, are of anomalous length, O having an extra folio because Mill's diagram on f.283 was cut out and pasted on

---

[58]There is also, as mentioned below, evidence of such rewriting throughout the manuscript. As an example in Book I, one may cite the addition of the opening sentences of Chapter v, §5, to replace the cancelled bottom half of MS Vol. I, f.138 and the first sentence of f.139. This addition probably came at the time that the section indications were added (see Appendix J, 1164 below).

a separate sheet. The other two anomalies are more interesting. Bain remarks, in his *John Stuart Mill* (67): "I was so much struck with the view
of Induction that regarded it as reasoning from particulars to particulars,
that I suggested a farther exemplification of it in detail, and [Mill] inserted
two pages of instances that I gave him." These "pages" were added to
Gathering M, which grew to 24 folios by the addition of ff.251–4, comprising paragraphs 7–9 of Chapter iii, §3, and including, among other examples, the anecdote about Lord Mansfield (190 below).

Gathering P has an extra folio because the long note that concludes
Chapter v was added, running from f.320v to the bottom of f.321r (on
which the text ends), and onto an extra part folio (f.322r, unnumbered by
Mill). This note deals with Herschel's review of Whewell in the *Quarterly
Review* for June, 1841; in the note Mill says: "the whole of the present
chapter was written before I had seen the article (the greater part indeed
before it was published) . . ." (cf. 248 below). Since Bain refers to letters
to and from Mill late in 1841, in which mention is made of Whewell and
Herschel,[59] one may reasonably assume that this note (plus another in
Chapter vi, §2, later deleted)[60] was added in the autumn of 1841.

One other addition merits mention, that of the reference to the Dutens
edition of Leibniz, in Chapter v, §6. (The reference to Leibniz's *Oeuvres*,
1842 ed., in Book V, Chapter iii, §3, is also added, apparently at the same
time.)

Book III. Here the importance of Bain's contributions is most clearly
apparent.[61] Being familiar with "the Experimental Physics, Chemistry and

[59]Bain, *John Stuart Mill*, 67.

[60]See 257r below.

[61]Once again the absence of the first draft of the complete work makes the extent of
an influence impossible to ascertain. Mill, admitting that he derived from Comte "many
valuable thoughts, conspicuously in the chapter on Hypotheses [see III, xiv] and in the
view taken of the logic of algebra [see II, vi, and III, xxiv]," adds that his main debt
was in Book VI, and asserts that the "first volume, which contains all the fundamental
doctrines of the book, was substantially complete before I had seen Comte's treatise"
(*Autobiography*, 147n). Bain twice refers to this question, once saying that "Mill got
wind of the [first] two volumes [of Comte's *Cours*] in the end of 1837, after he had completed the draft of his Book on Induction"; and later, with perhaps excusable enthusi-
asm in view of his own contribution, remarking, "To my mind, the best piece of work
that [Mill] ever did, was the Third Book of the *Logic*—Induction. Now, he tells us
how fortunate he was in having finished this Book before reading Comte." (*John Stuart
Mill*, 70, 146.) Bain had himself no knowledge of Comte's writings during the time he
was working on Mill's manuscript, though he began to learn French in order to read the
copy of Comte that Mill lent him in June, 1843, and he "steadily" talked about Comte
to Mill during that summer (Bain, *Autobiography*, 145). Later in life, when the question of posthumous publication of the Mill-Comte correspondence first arose, Bain insisted that passages referring to him be deleted, evidently fearing damage to his reputation (see his unpublished correspondence with Helen Taylor in 1874 in the Mill-Taylor
Collection). In any case, the Press-copy Manuscript shows no evidence of revisions of
Book III because of Comte's influence.

Physiology of that day,"[62] he saw, on first reading Mill's manuscript, that the main defect was in the experimental examples, which were "too few and not unfrequently incorrect." Therefore, with the help of Shier, who "went carefully over all the chemical examples with [Bain], and struck out various erroneous statements," he gave Mill "a large stock of examples to choose from, as he revised the Third Book for press."[63]

This aid is most markedly seen in the addition of Chapters ix and xiii after the letter to Austin of 7 July, 1842, in which these chapters are not mentioned. Both chapters contain inductive examples: Chapter ix is entitled "Miscellaneous Examples of the Four Methods," and Chapter xiii, "Miscellaneous Examples of the Explanation of Laws of Nature." The first folio of each of these chapters has a note in Mill's hand, requesting duplicate proofs of the chapter; these were undoubtedly for Bain, who, though he was receiving proofs of the whole work for his review, probably marked up these duplicate sheets and returned them to Mill. As the variants in the text below show, there were important changes in the proof stage, probably resulting from Bain's further reflection on these matters; he comments that he spent some time from November, 1842, to April, 1843, on "the final contribution of scientific examples to Mill. . . ."[64]

Chapters ix and xiii were evidently both added at the same time, as the numbers of the chapters from Chapter x on are altered by current cancel-

[62]Some evidence of this familiarity may be found in Bain's *Autobiography*. For example, he made "a minute analysis" of Faraday's collected papers on electricity in 1840, a portion of which he later shaped "into an example of Mill's four methods" (92–3; see 410ff. below). He heard an abstract of Gregory's lectures on the animal chemistry of Liebig in the winter of 1841–42; in October of 1842 Mill asked him, on Hickson's behalf, to review Liebig's two books. Bain did not write the review, but Mill, "seeing by [his] extracts the importance of the works," read them and "was exceedingly struck with their bold originality" (115, 142; cf. *John Stuart Mill*, 66–7). Bain also met, in the summer of 1842, Thomas Graham, Faraday, and Carpenter. One anecdote, concerning the references to Liebig, is worth repetition from Bain: ". . . Liebig, in a reprint of his *Animal Chemistry*, handsomely repaid the notice taken of his researches in the *Logic*: saying of his amended views that 'he feels that he can claim no other merit than that of having applied so [*sic*] some special cases, and carried out farther than had previously been done, those principles of research in natural science which have been laid down' in Mill's work. Mill exultingly remarked—'The tree may be known by its fruits. Schelling and Hegel have done nothing of the kind.'" (*John Stuart Mill*, 88.)

[63]Bain, *John Stuart Mill*, 66–7. Mill acknowledged this help in a passage quoted above (lxviii) from the *Autobiography*. To list all the definite and possible additions made in the Press-copy Manuscript through Bain's aid is here not practicable, but one may note the example cited in the previous note (III, ix, 2), that of the "electrical machine" (III, vii, 3), a corrected chemical example (III, vii, 4), and the heavily revised opening of III, viii. Also worth mentioning is Bain's comment on one of his examples from Faraday: ". . . I extracted one generalization, somewhat modified by myself, and this Mill prized very highly; nevertheless, it was afterwards carped at by Whewell, as going beyond what Faraday would have allowed" (*John Stuart Mill*, 67).

[64]Bain, *Autobiography*, 145. Examples of proof revisions may be seen at 412[i–i] and [k].

Chapter IX. [The printer is requested to send proof of this chapter in duplicate]

Miscellaneous Examples of the Four Methods.

(running title)
Examples of the Four Methods

I shall select as my first example an interesting speculation of one of the most eminent theoretical chemists of the present or any age, Dr Liebig. The object in view is to ascertain the immediate cause of the death produced by metallic poisons. Arsenious acid, & the salts of lead, bismuth, copper, & mercury, if introduced into the animal organism, except in the smallest doses, destroy life. These facts have long been known as insulated truths, of the lowest order of generalization; but it was reserved for Liebig, by an apt employment of the first two of our methods of experimental enquiry, to connect these truths together by a higher induction, pointing out what property, common to all these deleterious substances, is the really operating cause of their fatal effect.

When solutions of these substances are placed in sufficiently close contact with many animal products, albumen, milk, muscular fibre, & animal membranes, the acid or salt leaves the water in which it was dissolved & enters into combination with the animal substance; the substance, being thus acted upon, is found to have lost

The opening folio of Book III, Chapter ix, of the Press-copy Manuscript
British Museum

lations and additions, so that x–xiii are altered from ix–xii, and xiv–xxv from xii–xxiii.[65] The other internal evidence confirms these conclusions.[66]

One interesting change in title occurred before the letter to Austin: in the MS, Chapter xvii was originally entitled "Of the Evidence of Empirical Laws"; this was changed (when it was still Chapter xv, i.e., before ix and xiii were added) to the final "Of Chance and its Elimination."[67]

There are a few other noteworthy additions in Book III at this stage. The reference to Carpenter's *Physiology* was almost certainly added to Chapter vi, §2: Mill's notice of the 2nd edition appeared in the *Westminster Review*, XXXVII (Jan., 1842), 254. Bain, who met Carpenter in the summer of 1842, mentions that George Bentham Mill, John's second youngest brother, was living at this time in Carpenter's house as a pupil, and comments that John Mill was "very much impressed from the outset by [Carpenter's] writings on Physiology."[68] A reference (deleted in a later edition) to Vol. VI of Comte's *Cours* was added to Chapter xxiv, §6 (see 615^{g-g} below), and the latter part of the note to Chapter xviii, §5 (543n below), concerning a quotation from Laplace, was also evidently added.

A light on the types of examples used by Mill in Book III is thrown by the text of Mill's letter to Austin, where, evidently encouraging Austin to review the *Logic* for the *Edinburgh*, Mill admits that "the part relating to Induction is *not* 'more occupied with the mental & social than with the

---

[65]Other evidence of these changes appears on MS Vol. II, f.29v, where there is a reference to "Infra, chap. 19"; the printed text refers, correctly, to Chapter xxi (see 311n below).

[66]The addition of Chapter ix shows in the number of folios in Gathering X. Chapter ix occupies 29 folios (124–52) of the total 33 folios, but the matter of ff.137–52 was originally part of Chapter viii. Mill evidently decided first simply to divide Chapter viii into two, writing the new heading on f.123v, and under it the first nine words of what became §4 of Chapter ix. He also cancelled the final words of f.123, "will be mostly extracted from Sir John", substituting "accordingly, will form the subject of the succeeding Chapter." At this time f.123 was followed directly by what became f.137, which begins, "Herschel's Discourse. . . ." Then Mill cancelled f.123v, and began Chapter ix anew on f.124, adding §§1–3 (with examples from Liebig, Bain, and Faraday), and ending f.136 (a short folio) with "§4. Our third example shall be extracted from Sir John", again matching the opening of f.137.

The 24 folios of Chapter xiii are included in the 38 folios of Gathering Aa, the last in MS Vol. II, and in Vol. I of the published work. There were more than 14 folios in the original form of Aa, however, for a cancelled "Bb" appears on MS Vol. III, f.56, indicating that ff.50–5 (the first 49 folios of MS Vol. III being misbound or nontextual) completed the original 20 folios. The final Gathering Bb, then, includes these extra 6 folios, plus one (MS Vol. III, f.62) clearly added in revision, in its 27 folios.

[67]On MS Vol. II, f.87, the opening folio of Chapter vii, the title, "Of Observation and Experiment," is added to replace the cancelled title of what became Chapter viii, "Of the Four Methods of Experimental Inquiry." Two slight differences in chapter titles between the MS and the letter to Austin are probably slips of the pen in the latter ("Grounds" in the title of Chapter iii is given as "Ground" in the letter; "of" appears in the title of Chapter xv in the MS, but not in the letter).

[68]Bain, *Autobiography*, 132–3.

mathematical & physical sciences' because it was more convenient to illustrate inductive methods from those subjects on which the conclusions elicited by them are undisputed."[69] Bain's comment may be compared: "For the Deductive Method, and the allied subjects of Explanation and Empirical and Derivative Laws, the examples that we found were abundant. When, however, I suggested his adopting some from Psychology, he steadily, and I believe wisely, resisted; and, if he took any of these it was in the Deductive department."[70]

Book IV. This Book was little revised in 1841–43, as the regularity of the gatherings shows.[71] There were two minor changes in chapter titles, one before the letter to Austin (the title of Chapter vii, "Of Classification, as subsidiary to Induction," replaces the cancelled "Of the Principles of Classification"), and the other before and perhaps again after that letter (in the letter the title of Chapter v, "On the Natural History of the Variations in the Meaning of Terms," is given without the first two words; originally in the MS the title was "On the Natural History of the Variations in Language").

There are some brief additions, mainly on the versos, such as the reference to Chalmers (of whom Bain had a high opinion), coupled with a reference to electrical terminology (see 703^f), and the quotations from Paris's *Pharmacologia* (see 692^k and 693–4); the first section of Chapter iii was also added. These additions, like similar ones in Book V, may reflect the desire of Parker's reader for more examples (see lxvii above).[72]

Book V. One gathering, Ww, is anomalous in length, having 24 folios, but the internal evidence of revision is inconclusive, and there are no significant changes in chapter titles.[73] The most interesting additions are the

[69]*EL, CW*, XIII, 527.

[70]Bain, *John Stuart Mill*, 67. See III, xiii, 6 below.

[71]Gathering P, which has 19 folios, would have the normal 20 if the folio between 338 and 339 (Mill's f.93) were not missing from the MS.

[72]The catch-all quality of Book IV is mentioned by Bain in his *John Stuart Mill* (67): "I remember [Mill's] saying at a later period [than 1842], that the Fourth Book (which I have always regarded as the crude materials of a Logic of Definition and Classification) was made up of a number of subjects that he did not know where to place."

[73]The most likely explanation of the anomaly is that MS Vol. III, ff.108–11 are added, as there is a definite change of pen indicated; these include paragraphs 11–15 of Chapter vii, §1, with the illustrations drawn from Descartes, Coleridge, "the free-will controversy," Whately, Plato, and Aristotle. But pen evidence is very weak, and the bottom of f.111 has four lines that, if the above inference is correct, must have been copied from another folio not now extant, so that one would still have to account for one folio. The section numbers in this chapter, it may be mentioned, were altered during revision; §1 contains what were originally eleven sections, and §2 (running into the next gathering) contains what were originally four sections.

Concerning the chapter titles, one may mention that a difference between the MS and the letter to Austin reflects Mill's uncertainty in other works as well as in the *Logic*

references to Malebranche and to Coleridge's borrowing from Spinoza (770-1), to Paris's *Pharmacologia* (750, 766, 778-80, 783^e, 793n, the last with some additional text), and the probable addition of §6 to Chapter v.

Book VI. The final Book of the *Logic* was the last and most heavily revised in this period. Bain says:

The first letter I had from Mill this year (19th January [1843]) was to the effect that he had recomposed nearly the whole of the Sixth Book of the *Logic*, thinking it the weakest part of the work, but [was] now satisfied that it was put on a level with the others.

Comte's sixth volume, a very bulky one, had not been long out, and he had made a point of completing its perusal before giving the finishing touch to his treatment of the logic of politics.[74]

The internal evidence strongly establishes the outlines of the extensive late revision. None of the gatherings has 20ff.; in revision Mill adapted the gatherings to the lengths of the chapters, so that each gathering contains all of at least one chapter (Yy contains i and ii; Zz, iii and iv; 3A, v; 3B, vi, vii, and viii; 3C, ix; 3D, x; and 3E, xi). The major revisions are revealed by differences between the chapters as indicated in the letter to Austin and as they finally appear in the MS.

In the letter, the final Chapters ii and iii are listed in reverse order, with the final ii being entitled "Digression concerning Liberty & Necessity," rather than "Of Liberty and Necessity" (the change is revealed, through cancellation and interlineation, in the MS). Chapter iv, "Of the Laws of Mind," does not appear in the letter to Austin; consequently, all the subsequent equivalent chapters have altered numbers.[75] Chapter ix, "Of the Physical, or Concrete Deductive Method," appears in the letter as Chapter viii, "Of the Mathematico-Physical, or Analytic Method." The letter has as Chapter ix "Of the Verification of the Social Science," and as Chapter x "Of the Progressiveness of Human Nature in connexion with the Social

---

about the propriety of "Of" or "On": in the MS Chapter i is "Of Fallacies . . . ," and in the letter "On Fallacies. . . ." Also, the letter to Austin, like the MS, includes the word "Bad" in the titles of Chapters iv–vi; the word was cancelled in proof.

[74]Bain, *Autobiography*, 145-6.

[75]Interesting minor changes are seen in the title of Chapter v, finally entitled "Of Ethology, or the Science of the Formation of Character." An earlier, cancelled MS reading is "Of Ethology, or the Philosophy of Character"; in the letter to Austin (which must predate the cancelled MS reading), the title is "Of Ethology; or the Philosophy of Human Character, considered as an Exact Science."

Mill, it will be recalled, long "cherished" the subject of Ethology, intending to write a full work on it "as the foundation and cornerstone of Sociology" (Bain, *John Stuart Mill*, 78). Bain, who disapproved of Mill's insistence (shared by his father) on environmental rather than hereditary differences, pursued his own line of thought on the question in his *Study of Character* (1860), though he does not assert any connection between his work and Mill's abortive plans (Bain, *Autobiography*, 259).

Science; & of the new Historical Method founded thereupon"; in place of these the MS has only Chapter x, "Of the Inverse Deductive, or Historical Method."

The evidence suggests the following line of argument. Unhappy about the placing of the chapter on Liberty and Necessity (as "Digression" indicates), Mill retitled and renumbered it, and then divided the original Chapter ii into Chapters iii and iv, adding material to both.[76] The numbers of the succeeding chapters were then changed, so that Chapters v–ix became vi–x. Such evidence as cancellations at the bottom of folios that are not continued on the following folios, short folios, and paper dates (alternation between 1839 and 1841 papers begins with MS Vol. IV, f.218), indicates revisions and additions in Chapters v–x, evidently resulting in the main from Mill's reading of Vol. VI of Comte's *Cours*. The changes are most evident in Chapters ix and x where, as noted above, the titles in the letter to Austin are not matched in the MS. Apparently Mill first added Chapter x ("Of the Inverse Deductive, or Historical Method"), retaining both the original Chapter ix ("Of the Verification of the Social Science") and Chapter x ("Of the Progressiveness of Human Nature in connexion with the Social Science; & of the modern Historical Method founded thereupon"), renumbering x and xi as xii and xiii (iv also having been added).[77] He then amalgamated four chapters (ix–xii) into two, deleting the titles of ix and xi, and rewrote to produce the final MS form.[78]

The extent of the rewriting obscures some of the details, because the discarded sheets are not found in the MS. One may mention, however, that Chapter i, which was not completely rewritten, shows extensive revision, and an added reference to Vol. VI of Comte's *Cours* shows in §6 of the final chapter (see 948[i–i]), which also was not completely rewritten in January, 1843.

[76]That the move preceded the division is indicated by a late revision of the last sentence in the final Chapter iii (MS Vol. IV, f.160), where "the succeeding chapter" is changed to "the two succeeding chapters". An indication of the rewriting of Chapter iii is seen in the cancellation of the opening of §3 (f.156, with the cancellation not continued on f.157), and a new §2 beginning on f.157 (the original §2 not appearing in the MS).

[77]The number of Chapter xi in the MS shows evidence of having been changed from xi to xiii and then back to xi. Also the heading of the original Chapter x (the chapter that disappeared in the final rewriting) appears cancelled at the head of f.259, with x having evidently been altered to xii, and then back to x; its title shows, through cancellation and interlineation, a change from the title in the letter to Austin, "modern" being substituted for "New".

It is in Chapter x, as Bain notes (*John Stuart Mill*, 72), that Mill adopted Comte's law of "the Three Stages" as an essential methodological tool.

[78]Under the cancelled title on f.259 (see preceding note), "§3" has been added at the beginning of the first paragraph, indicating that that chapter as originally conceived was spliced onto the first three folios (ff.256–8) of the final Chapter x (f.258 is short).

REVISIONS, PROOF TO 8TH EDITION, 1843–72

As will by now be amply evident, the *Logic* was the most carefully composed and revised of all Mill's works. Comparison of the variants with
those in his other major systematic work, the *Principles of Political Economy*, demonstrates, of course, the dependence of revisions on the subject
matter. That is, Mill's economic treatise, while containing a great deal of
analysis, also involves much description and some normative comment,
and so was more open to alterations of attitudes (towards socialism and
labour, for example) than was his logical treatise. The passage of time
(nearly thirty years between the final manuscript and the 8th edition of the
Logic) did not introduce any new logical "facts," and the major changes
in logical analysis that have almost totally altered logic in the twentieth
century were only beginning to be introduced towards the end of Mill's life,
and did not influence his thought in any marked degree. In the *Logic*,
therefore, the most extensive changes reflecting the passage of time do not,
as they often do in the *Principles*, reveal a shift in attitudes; rather, they
typically consist of answers to opponents, or new illustrations of methods.

This is not to suggest that the *Logic* of 1872 is not different in important ways from the Press-copy Manuscript. Most obviously, the work increased in length. The number of pages of text (1st ed., 1204; 2nd ed.,
1210; 3rd ed., 1029; 4th ed., 1059; 5th ed., 1086; 6th ed., 1096; 7th ed.,
1096; 8th ed., 1120) is misleading, because the number of words per page
was significantly increased in the 3rd edition, so that, taking the amount of
material in the 1st edition as 1.00, the other editions contain approximately
the following amounts: 2nd edition, 1.005; 3rd edition, 1.04; 4th edition,
1.07; 5th edition, 1.10; 6th edition, 1.11; 7th edition, 1.11; 8th edition,
1.13. This comparison partly indicates the extent of the revisions, although
it disguises substitutions and deletions. In fact, there were over 4800 substantive alterations in the text,[79] and many of these, singly or in groups,
cast new light on various aspects of Mill's thought and life, and on attitudes
to logic and science in the nineteenth century. Because the *Logic*, unlike
the *Principles*, is not complemented over a long period by many other of

---

[79]This count, like all subsequent ones, excludes typographical errors, changes between italic and roman type, variations in punctuation, spelling, capitalization, and
word division, and alterations in footnote references. My figures are based on the form
of the variants as recorded in this edition (including variants within variants) and
should not be taken as numerically precise, because changes entailed by other changes
are counted as one if they are sufficiently close together to be included in one variant
note, but otherwise are counted separately. The intention is merely to suggest the
scope of the changes, and their comparative frequency and distribution.

Mill's writings (the *Hamilton* is of course important), his revisions have a special significance for an understanding of his speculative development.

The variants have until now received no critical attention beyond allusions to isolated changes, there being wide awareness only that complimentary references to Comte were excised at some point.[80] Mill's Prefaces have perhaps contributed to this neglect because, though they call attention to the fact of revision, and indicate many of the major changes, they do not indicate the scope and nature of the rewriting. The first seven paragraphs of the Preface to the 1st edition remained, with minor alterations, in all editions; the Preface to the 3rd edition, again with minor alterations, was retained, under a separate heading, in all subsequent editions; and in each edition a concluding paragraph or paragraphs (deleted or substantially altered in the next subsequent edition) described the current edition. (The exact changes are shown in the text below.)

Just how carefully Mill revised and reconsidered, and just how seriously he took the duties of an author to his public, are demonstrated clearly by a full collation, which yields the results seen in Table 2.

What immediately strikes the eye is the large number of changes—almost 40 per cent of the total—made in the 3rd edition. Almost equally striking to the twentieth-century author is the very considerable number of proof changes. While nineteenth-century authors had considerably more leeway than our contemporaries in running up printing costs, it should be remembered that Mill, while not unknown, was not an established author, this being his first published book. It will also be noted that, compared to the other editions, the final three, like the final two of Mill's *Principles*, were lightly rewritten. But even in these editions his careful revision is evident: the pattern of changes in the various portions of the *Logic* is surprisingly similar in all editions, with the minor variants sufficiently outnumbering the major ones to give this consistency. The table shows that Book III was the most heavily revised (as will be demonstrated, it also contains many of the

[80]The fullest listing of the changed references to Comte is in W. M. Simon, *European Positivism in the Nineteenth Century* (Ithaca, N.Y.: Cornell University Press, 1963), 275–9, where most of the differences between the 1st and 8th editions are identified, though not traced to the editions in which they first occurred; changes among editions, including reinstatement of views, are not indicated. For other comments on the references to Comte, see Bain, *John Stuart Mill*, 72, and Packe, 280. See also lxxxii–lxxxiii and xc–xci below.

Of the very few explicit references to other variants, one may cite those of Maurice Mandelbaum, who calls attention to the changes in §§5–7 of Book VI, Chapter xii, in his "Two Moot Issues in Mill's *Utilitarianism*," in J. B. Schneewind, ed., *Mill: A Collection of Critical Essays* (Garden City, N.Y.: Doubleday, 1968), 206–33. And in an essay reprinted in the same volume, Reginald Jackson refers ("Mill's Treatment of Geometry—A Reply to Jevons," 90n) to Jevons' mention of an alteration of "false" to "not strictly true" (225^{d-d} below), and describes (105n) the change from "makes" to "make" (234^{c-c} below) as careless (the syntax is ambiguous).

TABLE 2: CHANGES INTRODUCED IN EACH EDITION

	PREFACE	INTRODUCTION	BOOK I	BOOK II	BOOK III	BOOK IV	BOOK V	BOOK VI	TOTAL
1843[81]	14	6	132	53	284	133	131	135	888
1846	3	1	30	39	196	70	52	74	465
1851	8	51	277	160	701	141	231	310	1879
1856	1	4	60	58	158	41	28	24	374
1862	2	16	70	67	156	60	35	40	446
1865	2	4	46	38	106	22	21	16	255
1868	1	2	34	31	75	21	28	45	237
1872	1	1	50	48	111	26	20	21	278
Total	32	85	699	494	1787	514	546	665	4822

[81]Changes between the MS and the 1st ed., that is, proof changes.

major variants); it should be remembered, however, that it is much the longest Book, and when the number of variants per page is calculated, the order of frequency of changes is seen to be: Introduction, Book V, Book VI, Book IV, Book I, Book III, Book II.[82]

Such calculations are of course less meaningful than a study of individual variants in context, not here practicable. Only as prolegomena to more detailed study, therefore, the following comments are offered, beginning with a discussion of the longer variants,[83] and those of special interest, edition by edition, and then moving to an outline of the shorter variants of diverse kinds. As there are no long variants between the Press-copy Manuscript and the 1st edition, one may begin with the 2nd edition.

2nd Edition, 1846. In the Preface to the 2nd edition Mill says that the text has been "carefully revised, and all errors corrected which have been either discovered by the author himself, or pointed out by others." He also calls attention to the "materially changed" chapter on the Calculation of Chances (III, xviii), and the revision of the latter part of that on the Grounds of Disbelief (III, xxv).[84] The changes in these chapters are, indeed, the most significant in the edition. As Mill indicates in the Preface, his revised opinion was largely the result of Sir John Herschel's objections in correspondence.[85] On 10 July, 1845, replying to Mill's thanks for the complimentary remarks he had made in his Presidential Address to the British Association, Herschel mentioned some problems in the treatment of physical science and mathematics in the *Logic*, and said he would, on request, specify particular passages that needed correction. In December, when he was beginning to prepare the 2nd edition, Mill wrote asking for specific objections, which Herschel supplied on 22 December, discussing at some length the treatment of Laplace in the chapters on probability.

---

[82]On the basis of the pagination of the 8th edition, the number of variants per page is: Introduction, 6.09; Book V, 4.79; Book VI, 4.75; Book IV, 4.66; Book I, 4.39; Book III, 4.31; Book II, 3.43. The overall average (excluding the Prefaces) is 4.37.

[83]I have arbitrarily selected as long variants those involving one page or more of the original text. Using this measure, there are about fifty passages qualifying as major: of these, over half appear in Book III, and over twenty percent in Book II, with four examples in each of Books I and VI, only two in Book IV, and none in Book V. Of the total number, seventeen involve the addition or rewriting of a full section or more (two of these being added chapters, and one an almost complete rewriting of a chapter); of the total, twelve are referred to in Mill's Prefaces. Two of these latter do not involve the addition or rewriting of full sections or more, so there are seven places where the addition or rewriting of at least one full section is not signalled by Mill in his Prefaces.

[84]In a letter to John Austin of 22 April, 1848, thanking him for his approbation of the *Logic*, and sending him, at that late date, a copy of the offprint of Chapters xviii and xxv of Book III mentioned below, Mill says the offprint contains "the only alterations *in opinion* in the 2^d edition of the Logic. Whatever other alterations were made, are little more than verbal." (*EL, CW,* XIII, 730.)

[85]In this context he also thanks J. M. Macleod, whom he may have known through the East India Company. What Macleod's contribution was is not now known.

Other criticisms, Mill replied, had already convinced him that Laplace was not so wrong as he had accused him of being in Book III, Chapter xviii, and he would rectify the matter (see Appendix F); he was not yet convinced that Herschel's comments on the treatment of probability in Book III, Chapter xxv, were justified. As the revision progressed, Mill wrote on 2 February, 1846, asking whether Herschel had found anything objectionable in the 1st volume. As a result of Herschel's reply, Mill made further changes in Book III (see 456^{p-p}, 469^{o-o}, 469^{d-d}, 501n). And finally, after a further exchange concerning Book III, Chapter xxv, Mill said, in April, 1846, that he was convinced that Herschel was right, and so had written a new conclusion to the chapter (see Appendix G).[86]

The changes in Book III, Chapters xviii and xxv led to a bibliographic rarity. Not foreseeing how much revision lay in the years ahead, Mill had the two chapters offprinted from the 2nd edition, probably with a view to sending copies to those who had received complimentary sets of the 1st edition.[87]

Although, in Bain's word's, the *Logic* was "about the best attacked book of the time,"[88] it was not extensively reviewed on its first appearance. This fact is worthy of notice here because so many of the major revisions introduced in later editions contain Mill's responses to his critics. Mill was understandably disappointed that prospective reviews in the *Edinburgh Review* by Austin and in the *Quarterly Review* by Herschel never materialized,[89] and that Whewell did not reply at this time. He may have been later consoled by the comment of R. H. Hutton in the *Prospective Review* in

---

[86]For Mill's side of the correspondence, see *EL, CW*, XIII, 673, 676, 688–9, 694–5, 698–9, 700; Herschel's drafts are in the Library of the Royal Society. (It may be noted that Mill's great opponent, Whewell, praised Mill for the revised estimate of Laplace in his *Of Induction* [London: Parker, 1849], 85–6, reprinted in his *Philosophy of Discovery* [London: Parker, 1860], 290.) The timing of the revisions is indicated in these letters: having begun the process in December, 1845, Mill sent Vol. I to press about the end of February, 1846, and it was set by 30 March, at which time he began sending Vol. II.

[87]The offprint, a copy of which is in the library of Somerville College, Oxford, has, on its title page, "[*Two chapters of "A System of Logic, Inductive and Ratiocinative, by JOHN STUART MILL," as altered in the Second Edition.*]" It is repaged, with added signatures, so that the two chapters are numbered seriatum, Al–C39. The last lines of four pages (2nd ed., II, 70, 71, 74, 75; offprint, 1, 2, 5, 6) are carried over to the next page in the offprint, but the line settings are not altered, and there are no variants in the text. Because Chapter xviii begins recto in the offprint instead of verso, as it does in the 2nd edition, the running titles of the chapter are reversed in the offprint.

For one recipient of the offprint, see note 84 above.

[88]*John Stuart Mill*, 67.

[89]See *EL, CW*, XIII, 527–8 (7/7/42), in which he expresses pleasure that Austin, rather than Hamilton or Brewster, is to do the *Edinburgh* review, and hopes that Herschel will do the *Quarterly* one; see also *ibid.*, 683 (20/10/45), by which time he knew that neither the *Edinburgh* nor *Quarterly* would review the 1st edition. Herschel, in a letter of 10 July, 1845 (MS draft, Royal Society), which Mill must have received after he wrote to Austin on the 7th, says want of time prevented him from reviewing Mill's book in the same spirit that he had Whewell's.

1850: "The prolonged silence with which his book has been received by English critics seems to imply a surrender without terms; and in fact the qualities of Mr. Mill's mind are eminently calculated to impress and frighten our countrymen into silence, even when unconvinced."[90]

The "prolonged silence" was not in fact total; two important reviews appeared, that of Bain in the *Westminster Review*,[91] and that of W. G. Ward in the *British Critic*.[92]

Two other sets of changes that, though most of the individual variants are brief, are of cumulative significance, began in the 2nd edition. These are alterations in passages referring to Whewell and Comte. Even though Whewell's first reply to Mill did not appear until 1849 in his *On Induction*, Mill removed twenty-eight references to him in the 2nd edition, three in the 3rd, and three more in the 5th.[93]

The alterations reflecting Mill's revised view of Comte are even more extensive, and demonstrate, more than those concerning Whewell, extra-logical considerations. Mill had an extensive correspondence with Comte from 1842, when he was engaged in the final revisions of the manuscript of the *Logic*, and the final volumes of Comte's *Cours* were appearing, until 1845, when his reservations about Comte's social and political views (and

[90]"Mill and Whewell on the Logic of Induction," *Prospective Review*, VI (Feb., 1850), 110. Mill certainly would have green gratified had he seen a letter from James Stephen to MacVey Napier of 14 May, 1845 (BM Add. MSS 34625, ff.210–13), in which he tries to persuade Napier himself to review the *Logic*. Before mentioning certain "exceedingly debateable" tenets, such as those of "the last two or three chapters," and Mill's objectionable anti-religious views, Stephen says: "My more immediate object in writing is to remind you of John Mill's Book of which I have been lately reading a considerable part, and I have done so with the conviction that it is one of the most remarkable productions of this 19th Century. . . . I . . . wish Mill to be treated respectfully and handsomely. I wish it the more because I have a great personal liking for him, and an high esteem for his knowledge and powers. A good stiff job in the thinking way would do you good also; and would animate your long vacation. Add to all this, that it is many a day since you have had any speculation on subjects of this kind in the E. R."

[91]*Westminster Review*, XXXIX (1843), 412–56. This can hardly be considered a disinterested review: Mill read it in manuscript, recommended some cuts as too complimentary, and "gave the article the benefit of verbal revision, by which it was otherwise improved. After all, it was referred to by different criticis as a eulogy rather than a review." (Bain, *Autobiography*, 147–8.)

[92]"Mill's *Logic*," *British Critic*, XXXIV (Oct., 1843), 349–427. Ward returned again and again to the *Logic* in reviews, coupling the successive editions with other works by Mill (see the reprinted reviews in Vol. I of his *Philosophy of Theism*, 1884). He also corresponded with Mill on the subject, never quite, one judges, giving up hope of curing Mill's "miserable moral and religious deficiencies" (see xc below).

[93]This count excludes simple changes such as those from "Mr. Whewell" to "he". Some of the deletions (see, e.g., 798^{x-x}), like some of those concerning Comte, could even leave Mill open to a charge of plagiarism.

For a full appreciation of the controversy with Whewell, the individual variants should be consulted in conjunction with the information in the Bibliographic Appendix under Whewell, where the complex publishing history of his works is outlined.

financial affairs) resulted in a complete break. While a large number of quotations from and references to Comte remain in all editions, Mill's disillusionment is adequately demonstrated in his revision or deletion in the 2nd edition, just after their correspondence ended, of nearly fifty generally laudatory references. In the 3rd edition of 1851, probably at the urging of Harriet Taylor, who took profound exception to Comte's attitude to women, and who married Mill in that year, some ten similar changes were made, including the deletion of an epigraph to Book VI that had survived the cutting away of 1846. A few changes also appear in the 4th edition (1856), but one of these involves the deletion of a new criticism introduced in 1851. In the 5th edition (1862), presumably as a result of time's balancing power and Comte's death (though it should be noted that Harriet also had died in the interval), a few complimentary changes were made, and finally, in the 8th edition (1872), two of the deletions of 1846 were reinstated.[94]

3rd Edition, 1851. The 3rd edition of the *Logic*, like the 3rd edition of the *Principles*, which appeared in the next year, is the most heavily revised of all, introducing, as already mentioned, nearly 40 per cent of the total number of variants. In the Preface, noting the necessity of replying to criticisms, especially those of Whewell, Mill says he has "carefully reconsidered" all points on which he had been assailed, and "in general silently" corrected such "minor oversights" as were detected by himself and his critics, adding, "it is not to be inferred that I agree with the objections which have been made to a passage, in every instance in which I have altered or cancelled it." This generalized statement covers nearly 1900 variants, including twenty-one long ones. Five of these are of considerable importance: four in Book III involve the addition of a whole section (ii, §5; v, §11; ix, §6 [in 51, 56, this appeared as a footnote]; and xviii, §4); the fifth, in the final chapter of Book VI, involved the significant rewriting and expansion of §§5–6 into §§5–7.

In addition to Whewell's strictures (see, e.g., 287n, 300n), Mill replied to those of Francis Bowen in his *Lowell Lectures, on the Application of Metaphysics and Ethical Science to the Evidences of Religion* (see 354, 356n),[95] and of R.H. Hutton in his "Mill and Whewell on the Logic of Induction" (see, e.g., 331n). He also incorporated references to De Morgan's work on logic (see 170n),[96] and received from Bain some suggestions for "alterations and additional examples," of which Bain says in 1882, "I scarcely remember what they were."[97]

---

[94]Some of these variants are discussed below, xc–xci.

[95]See also Mill's subsequent comment on Bowen's rejoinder, in a letter to Harriet, *LL, CW,* XIV, 149 (4/2/54).

[96]See *ibid.,* XVII, 2003–4 (10/5/47), 2005 (13/9/47), and XIV, 48 (21/7/50).

[97]*John Stuart Mill,* 92. Bain considered the overall revision for the 3rd edition the first important one, and thought that "no revision of anything like the same extent was

4th Edition, 1856. The sale of the *Logic* remaining steady, probably because of its use in "colleges & other places of education,"[98] Mill was again called on for revisions, resulting, as he says in the Preface to the 4th edition, in "a considerable number of additions," the "most important" relating to the "doctrine of Causation" (see, e.g., 340^{k-k}, 363^{a-a}) and to his controversy with Spencer (II, vii being added). This disagreement between two generally allied philosophers was sparked by criticisms of the *Logic* in Spencer's "Universal Postulate" (first published 1853), and was continued through various works and editions by both.[99]

In addition to these long variants mentioned in the Preface, there are six others in the 4th edition, one of them being the deletion of a passage added in the 3rd edition (see 950^e), and another the addition of a passage subsequently rewritten and then deleted in the 8th edition (see Appendix D).

5th Edition, 1862. In 1861, concurrently with his revision of the *Principles* for its 5th edition, Mill again went through the *Logic*, finishing early in 1862.[100] Though this edition (like its companion edition of the *Principles*) is the most heavily revised after the 3rd, there are only six long variants,[101] one being the addition of a section (II, iii, §8), and another the addition of a whole chapter (VI, xi); the latter, referred to in the Preface (along with "many minor improvements") shows the influence on Mill of Buckle's *History of Civilization in England*.[102] Another interesting addition is the reference to Darwin (498n–499n), foreshadowed in his letter to Bain of 11 April, 1860.[103]

---

undertaken till the eighth edition came out in 1872" (*ibid.*). Bain was, of course, impressed not by the total number of changes, but by their significance; the 8th edition, it may be mentioned, contains a large number of references to his own *Logic*, which was published in 1870.

[98]Mill to Harriet, 29/1/54, in *LL, CW,* XIV, 142. Its use as a text gradually grew, partly as a result of Bain's Examinership in Logic at the University of London (1857 to the late 1860s) and his Professorship at Aberdeen (after 1860); see his *Autobiography*, 248, 271ff..

[99]See the Bibliographic Appendix, under Spencer. See also references in *LL, CW,* XV, 540, 648.

[100]*LL, CW,* XV, 738 (8/8/61) and 775 (29/1/62). In the latter, Mill's worries about accuracy surface: "I hope the remaining sheets of the Logic and Political Economy will be looked through carefully. The reader who examines them is evidently a painstaking and careful man, but it nevertheless happens at times that one word is put instead of another with a very awkward effect."

[101]Two of these (205n, 308n) are related to variants introduced in the 3rd edition.

[102]As no detailed study of the influence of Mill's *Logic* on his contemporaries has been made, it is worth mentioning that Buckle's heavily annotated copy of the 5th edition (in which he is first mentioned) is in the collection of Dr. Gordon N. Ray; also, Leslie Stephen's copy of the 4th edition, probably used for Vol. III of his *English Utilitarians*, is in the British Museum.

[103]*LL, CW,* XV, 695.

6th Edition, 1865. Mill's candidacy for Westminster in 1865 led to his "cheap volumes," the People's Editions, going off "like wildfire, while there was an increased demand for the *Logic*."[104] So again Mill was faced with "an unusual amount of revision,"[105] once more for both the *Logic* and the *Principles*, which also went into a sixth edition in 1865.

Four long variants were introduced into the *Logic*, three of them involving at least a full section (II, iii, §9; III, ix, §4; and III, xiii, §§1–3). The final two of these are covered by the Preface's reference to "new and apt examples of inductive and deductive investigation," for which Mill was again indebted to Bain, who comments: "I referred him to Brown Séquard's interesting research on Cadaveric Rigidity, and induced him to read the same author's volume of Researches on the Nervous System. I also obtained from Thomas Graham a complete set of his researches on Gases and Liquids; pointing his attention to what I thought most available."[106]

Mill also mentions in the extensive Preface his introduction of material previously excluded, indicating that he supports the "experiential" epistemology in its battle with the "*à priori* or intuitional" school. This comment points to the first of the long variants mentioned above, and also to many other changes, none of them reaching a page in length, but all contributing to a different tone (certainly not a different opinion) concerning the relation between logic and epistemology. In fact the difference in tone would be more marked if Mill had not silently introduced similar qualifications and explanations into the 3rd and 4th editions.[107] Perhaps the most noticeable changes in the 6th edition are found in the footnoted references, eleven in total, to the matter of Mill's *Examination of Sir William Hamilton's Philosophy*, which was first published in 1865 after some years of preparatory study of Hamilton and his allies.[108]

---

[104]Bain, *John Stuart Mill*, 124. Inexpensive People's Editions of the *Principles, Representative Government*, and *On Liberty* were published in 1865. In April only 137 copies of the *Logic* were unsold. (See *LL, CW*, XVI, 1040n2, 1041nn3,5.) For the People's Edition of the *Logic*, see lxxxvi and n111 below.

[105]*LL, CW*, XVI, 1041 (30/4/65).

[106]*John Stuart Mill*, 126.

[107]Book II, Chapter vii, controverting Spencer, which Mill added in the 4th edition (Bain, *John Stuart Mill*, 126, mistakenly says it was introduced in the 6th), begins somewhat disingenuously: "Polemical discussion is foreign to the plan of this work. But . . ." (262 below).

[108]The main weight of the argument against the intuitionists is of course carried in the *Hamilton*, but Mill was fully aware of the close dependence of the two works on one another. See, for example, his comments to Bain, in 1861 and 1863: "The great recommendation of this project [writing the *Hamilton*] is, that it will enable me to supply what was prudently left deficient in the *Logic*, and to do the kind of service which I am capable of to rational psychology, namely, to its *Polemik*"; and: "I mean in this book to do what the nature & scope of the Logic forbade me to do there, to face the ultimate metaphysical difficulties of every question on which I touch." (*LL, CW*, XV, 752, 816.) Mill's prudence may be seen as early as the concluding paragraphs of

Another interesting change (further altered in the 8th edition) resulted from criticisms of the argument in Book III, Chapter xxiii, §6 by De Morgan and his son (599^n).[109]

7th Edition, 1868. Mill's parliamentary prominence, and the increasing use of the *Logic* as a textbook, quickly exhausted the 6th edition, and late in 1867 Longmans reported the need for a new edition.[110] The wide sales of the People's Editions of his other works suggested that the *Logic* should appear in a cheaper format, but Mill was by this time fully aware that the People's Editions were cutting into the sales of the Library Editions (the *Principles* did not go into a seventh edition until 1871), and so refused the suggestion, as he did again in 1870, and the People's Edition of the *Logic* (still very much in use in reprints) appeared only posthumously in 1884, with Helen Taylor's agreement.[111]

Comparatively lightly revised, perhaps because of Mill's very busy schedule at this time, the 7th edition was quickly prepared.[112] The Preface refers unspecifically to "a few further corrections . . . , but no material additions," and there is only one long variant, in Book I, Chapter vi, §2. This correction of the interpretation of Porphyry's *Isagoge* has special interest as arising from a criticism by George Grote, Mill's lifelong friend, who had a

---

the "Introductory Matter" in the Early Draft (967 below), which should be compared with the conclusion of the Introduction and its variants (13ff. below). Even so, he knew from the beginning that his loyalties would be evident; see, for example, his letter to Maurice of 9 Sept., 1842 (*LL, CW*, XVII, 1998), where he says: ". . . I am afraid you will not be able to look upon [the *Logic*] or its tendency with any favour, as though I do not concern myself with ontological questions directly the whole effect of the book where it produces any, must be anti-ontological."

One of the footnotes (62n) referring to the *Hamilton* may be specially mentioned, as it also contains a reference to a work by George Grote's brother, John, the *Exploratio Philosophica* (see also Mill's letter to George Grote, *LL, CW*, XVI, 1095–6), and to Ferrier's *Institutes of Metaphysic.*

[109]See *LL, CW*, XV, 808–9; XVI, 1084, 1088, 1107.

[110]In a letter of 12 Dec., 1867, Longmans reported that 271 copies had sold since 1 June, and that only 193 were on hand (see *LL, CW*, XVI, 1336n).

[111]The number of copies of the two-volume Library Edition of the *Logic* had risen to 1500 by the time of the 6th edition from the original 750. Longmans proposed a People's Edition of 10,000 copies, to sell at 7s. 6d. Mill refused on 9 Jan., 1868 (*LL, CW*, XVI, 1351). The suggestion in 1870 came from William Trant, one of Mill's working-class correspondents; in refusing it, Mill referred to the potential financial loss, with little useful effect to offset it, and sent complimentary copies for distribution by Trant to Workingmen's Clubs and Institutes (*ibid.*, XVII, 1756, 1765–6, 1773). Helen Taylor's agreement to the publication of a People's Edition in 1884 is noted on a letter to her from Longmans (22/3/84), Mill-Taylor Collection, British Library of Political and Economic Science, V, 218. On the verso there is a list apparently giving her understanding of the dates of the various Library Editions, as follows: "1st ed. Feb. 1843. 2. May 46. 3. Nov. 50. 4. Aug. 56. 5. Mch. 62. 6. Sep. 65. 7. Mch. 68. 8. July 72. 9. Dec. 75. 10. Ap. 79."

[112]See *LL, CW*, XVI, 1357, 1374–5, to Gomperz (21/1/68 and 18/3/68).

very high opinion of the *Logic*.[113] Grote wrote to Mill on 12 January, 1867 concerning this passage, enclosing a memorandum giving the authorities, and commenting that "So excellent a book ought to be cleared even from small reproaches of *incurie*."[114]

De Morgan also contributed a correction, in this case not a mathematical but a literary one. In a letter of 3 September, 1868, referring to Book V, Chapter vii, §2 (822 below), he comments: "you say that a pedantic physician in Molière accounts for the fact that 'l'opium endormit' by the maxim 'parcequ'il a une vertu soporifique.' From whom do you get your quotation marks? Not from Molière." And he goes on to quote the passage correctly. Mill replied, on 13 September, "I had marked the humourous doggrel from Molière to be quoted correctly, instead of incorrectly, as I had done on the authority of Whewell. The words I used in p. 71 [66 in this edition] were probably also quoted at secondhand from some writer who retained the pith of the satire without remembering its words."[115]

John Venn, another important figure in the history of logic, also influenced the 7th edition, through his *Logic of Chance* (1866), a copy of which he sent to Mill. Though not accepting all Venn's views, Mill made some alterations, and acknowledged his indebtedness in the concluding footnote to Book III, Chapter xviii.[116]

One other variant, the introduction of Bishop Butler's name into the discussion of miracles in Book III, Chapter xxv, §4, though very slight, may

---

[113]Bain, who was an intimate and admirer of Grote, says of him: "I doubt if any living man conned and thumbed the book as he did. 'John Mill's *Logic*,' I remember his saying, 'is the best book in my library'; he had not the same high opinion of any of Mill's other books." (*John Stuart Mill*, 83.)

[114]A.l.s. in the collection of Dr. Gordon Ray. The memorandum has a note by Mill: "Grote on Aristotle & Porphyry (used in 7th ed.)." (Grote, who was using the 5th edition, also notes a typographical error in the Greek that had, in fact, been corrected in the 6th edition, after persisting from the 2nd through the 5th.) In sending the sheets of the 7th edition to Gomperz for the German translation, Mill says that this change is the only one worth a translator's attention, and attributes it to Grote (*LL, CW*, XVI, 1375).

[115]See *LL, CW*, XVI, 1437, where De Morgan's letter, with its other criticisms (not acted upon), is quoted by Professor Mineka in notes.

[116]*Ibid.*, 1360–1; see also *ibid.*, 1376–7, and XVII, 1574, 1881. Concerning other philosophers whose writings began to alter logical thought at this time, but did little to modify Mill's views, one should see Mill's letter to Cairnes of 5 December 1871, where, saying he has not yet seen Jevon's *Theory of Political Economy* (1871), he comments that Jevons "seems to me to have a mania for encumbering questions with useless complications, and with a notation implying the existence of greater precision in the data than the questions admit of. His speculations on Logic, like those of Boole and De Morgan, and some of those of Hamilton, are infected in an extraordinary degree with this vice. It is one preeminently at variance with the wants of the time, which demand that scientific deductions should be made as simple and as easily intelligible as they can be made without ceasing to be scientific." (*Ibid.*, 1862–3.)

be cited as an example of private criticism leading to reconsideration over time, for the question was raised in a letter from Joseph Napier of 22 December, 1861, though the variant was not introduced until the 7th edition.[117] It is also interesting because the passage as a whole relates to similar discussions in one of Mill's earliest publications, his edition of Bentham's *Rationale of Judicial Evidence* (1827), and in one of his latest writings, "Theism" (written 1868–70, published posthumously, 1874).[118]

8th Edition, 1872. The final edition of the *Logic* in Mill's lifetime included several important revisions.[119] There are nine long variants, the most significant being the addition of two sections (5 and 10) to Book III, Chapter v, "Of the Law of Universal Causation," the deletion of part of Book III, Chapter x, §4, and the addition of §4 to Book II. Chapter vii in further response to Spencer.

It is fitting that Bain, the most important contemporary influence on Mill's *Logic*, should be noticed in the Preface, although once again the extent of the revisions is disguised by the wording: "The additions and corrections in the present (eighth) edition, which are not very considerable, are chiefly such as have been suggested by Professor Bain's *Logic*, a book of great merit and value." Most of the direct debts are indicated not in the text, but in footnotes, twenty-eight of those added in this edition referring to Bain's book.[120] Furthermore, two of the long variants mentioned above, the deletion of part of Book III, Chapter x, §4, and (in effect) its replacement by Book III, Chapter v, §10, as is only hinted in the Preface, also show the importance of Bain's views. These sections, dealing with the Conservation of Force, reveal more than almost any other parts of the *Logic* the growth of physical knowledge in the middle of the nineteenth century, and Mill's hesitation about speculation in areas beyond his special competence. The complexities of the matter justify its separate

---

[117]*Ibid.*, XV, 813; cf. 831.

[118]See Bentham, *Rationale of Judicial Evidence*, 5 vols., ed. J. S. Mill (London: Hunt and Clarke, 1827), I, 137, and "Theism," *CW*, X, 470ff.

[119]Mill was actively revising the *Logic*, this time in conjunction with the *Hamilton* (for its 4th edition, also 1872), from late 1871 through the spring of 1872: see *LL*, *CW*, XVII, 1862, 1879, to Cairnes, in the former of which he responds to Cairnes' comments on the Laws of Coexistence. Some of the variants, however, especially those concerning the Conservation of Force, are based on long consideration (see, e.g., *ibid.*, XV, 871, to Glennie, of 23/7/63).

[120]Some of the footnotes deal with disagreements: see, e.g., 76n, 166n. But one should end with a tribute; writing to Cliffe Leslie on 8 Feb., 1869, Mill says: "The physical illustrations in my Logic were all reviewed & many of them suggested by Bain, who has a very extensive & accurate knowledge of physical science. He has promised me to revise them thoroughly for the next edition [the 8th], & to put them sufficiently in harmony with the progress of science, which I am quite aware that they have fallen behind." (*LL*, *CW*, XVII, 1558.)

treatment in Appendix D below, where, along with the excised passage and its variants, the relevant exchanges between Bain and Mill are printed.

Other Variants, 1843–72. After this outline of the long variants, all of which merit more detailed examination, one may return to a general description of the different types of substantive variants. Choosing Book IV as most typical,[121] and categorizing the variants as (1) alterations in opinion or fact, including major amplifications and corrections of information; (2) alterations resulting from the time between writings, including changes in statement of fact resulting from the passage of time and new publications; (3) alterations which qualify, emphasize, or give technical clarity; and (4) alterations which are verbal, give semantic clarity, or result from changes in usage, one obtains the following results:

TABLE 3: SUBSTANTIVE CHANGES IN BOOK IV

	OPINION, FACT, ETC.	TIME, ETC.	QUALIFICATION, ETC.	VERBAL, ETC.	TOTAL
1843	1	0	30	102	133
1846	6	0	31	33	70
1851	12	2	56	71	141
1856	4	1	12	24	41
1862	9	3	16	32	60
1865	0	2	4	16	22
1868	0	2	8	11	21
1872	6	5	8	7	26
Total	38	15	165	296	514

Table 3 shows again that the more significant alterations (those in the first two categories) are most frequent in the 3rd, 5th, and 8th editions; it also demonstrates that the numerous proof alterations for the 1st edition were of a minor kind, and that minor changes play a comparatively small role in the 8th edition. (It can be argued, of course, that the relative infrequency of minor changes in the last three editions indicates not that Mill was less concerned with the revision but that he was more satisfied with the general texture of the work; this argument would support the contention that the revision for the 8th edition was especially important to Mill, for the number of long changes increased over those of the two previous editions.)

[121]While the Books are surprisingly consistent in the frequency and distribution of variants, Book IV most closely approximates the overall pattern, having the same order of frequency (3rd, 1st, 2nd, 5th, 4th, 8th, 6th, and 7th editions), and also less variation from the norm, in percentage of variants, from edition to edition (there is a relatively higher percentage in the 1st and 2nd editions, and a lower in the 3rd).

Of the first type of variant, that reflecting an alteration in opinion or fact, the longest in Book IV is that at 659^{b-b}, where five paragraphs on classification were added in 1862 to Chapter ii, §6, and a long concluding sentence referring to Whewell was deleted at the same time (662^i), with a consequent change in section title (659^{a-a}). An interesting deletion is found at 695°, where two long paragraphs deal with the tendency, "which grows as civilization advances," to speak "of disagreeable things with the least possible suggestion of their disagreeable details, and of agreeable things with as little obtrusion as possible of the mere mechanism of their production. . . ." The passage contains an anecdote that may, in 1851, when it was deleted, have seemed to Mill to suggest too much for Victorian civilized taste. Indeed, it probably was the one referred to in Ward's review of 1843, where, alluding to Mill's "miserable moral and religious deficiencies" in the *Logic*, he says: "We cannot however conclude our notice of these [deficiencies], without severely condemning his utterly gratuitous introduction of a most objectionable anecdote. We trust he will be advised to omit it, should his work reach another edition."[122]

One other passage (690–1) may be mentioned as involving a series of connected changes concerning examples of misapplication of terms through generalization; one of the changes (691n), an addition in the 4th edition, relates to a letter Mill wrote to the *Times*, printed on 7 April, 1847, on the spelling of "sanitary."

The changes resulting from Mill's altered attitude to Comte, mentioned above in connection with the 2nd edition, may be illustrated from Book IV.[123] The deletions made in the 2nd edition are often of the sort found at 730^{e-e} and $^{h-h}$ where Comte's judgments are retained without his name, in a rather unfair manner. In the first of these, the reading in the manuscript and 1st edition is: "M. Comte, for example, blames Cuvier for having formed his natural groups with an undue degree of reference to the mode of alimentation . . ."; in the 2nd edition the sentence is altered to begin: "Cuvier, for example, has been justly criticised for having . . . ." An instance of a deletion for the 3rd edition may be seen at 713^h, which involves also the deletion of a reference to Whewell. The reintroduction, in 1862, of deletions made in 1846 is instanced in one of the epigraphs to Book IV

[122]"Mill's *Logic*," *British Critic*, XXIV (Oct., 1843), 427n. Bain says (*John Stuart Mill*, 69) that at Ward's "instigation, Mill expunged from his second edition an objectionable anecdote"; there seems to be no deletion in 1846 that meets this description, and it is most likely that Bain has simply mistaken the edition, though there is no apparent reason why Mill should have overlooked the criticism in 1846 and heeded it in 1851, except again that Harriet played a large part in the revisions for the 3rd edition.

[123]Actually these changes, more than sixty in all, are most frequent in Books III and VI (nearly a quarter of them appearing in Chapters ix and x of Book VI, the last part of the *Logic* to be written, and under the immediate influence of Vol. VI of Comte's *Cours*).

(640^{b-b}). And, finally, an alteration of 1846, further changed in 1872, is seen at 715^{i-i}, where the earlier reading, "as M. Comte justly remarks", was altered in 1846 to read, "as has been justly remarked", and in 1872 to "as M. Comte remarks". Here credit for the comment is finally restored, but without the laudatory adverb; a glance at other variants involving Comte shows that they often turn either on a deleted complimentary phrase if the reference is retained, or on a deleted reference if the complimentary phrase is retained. (The same observation is only slightly less applicable to the variants, mentioned above, involving Whewell.)

The second type of variant, that reflecting the passage of time, is seen most obviously in such footnotes as those at 649n, 650n, 676n, and 726n, where publications by Bailey, Mill himself (the *Hamilton*), Bain, and Whewell are cited. The first of these, added in 1862, also involved a change in the text, with Bailey's authority being substituted for Dugald Stewart's. In the same sentence another change of this type, found in several places in the *Logic*, was introduced in 1868, when Mill altered "Mr. Mill" to "Mr. James Mill" to make what was by then a necessary distinction between his father and himself. A minor example of Mill's awareness of the growth of scientific knowledge is signalled at 673^{b-b}, where until the final edition he had said that questions concerning definitions of Specific Heat, Latent Heat, Chemical Combination, and Solution, "are still open"; in 1872 the passage was altered (Bain's influence may be assumed) to read, "were long open and are not yet completely closed". (Cf. 716^{m-m}, where the reference to "the secondary" and "tertiary" geological periods was altered to "the palæozoic, mesozoic, and tertiary" in 1872; and 721^{s-s}, where the "azote" of earlier editions became "nitrogen" in 1862.) Changes directly revealing the passage of time between editions, more necessary and frequent in the *Principles* than here, but made vaguely and erratically in both, are illustrated at 679^{a-a}, where "a few thinkers of the present generation" was altered in 1868 to "a few thinkers of the present century".

Of the third type of variants, those that qualify, emphasize, or give technical clarity, one of the most interesting is indicated at 686^{b-b} and ^{d}, where in the first case "*necessarily*" was changed to "*certainly*", and in the second "necessarily" was deleted, both changes being made in 1868. In his *Principles of Psychology* (1st ed., 1855), Spencer had criticized Mill's use of the term "necessity," and in a note added to the *Logic* in 1856 (267n), Mill, without conceding his ground, says that he has "corrected the expressions" which led Spencer to misapprehend his meaning. The point is further discussed in a letter to W. G. Ward of 28 November, 1859. The kind of change referred to in the note of 1856 will be seen at 252^{c-c} and $^{d-d}$, 257^{t-t}, 260^a, and 261^e, in the fourth of which Mill deleted, from the title of Book II, Chapter vi, §5, the words "*and of logical necessity*"; but Mill continued, as the cited variants in Book IV indicate, to make related changes in later editions.[124]

The most common variants of this third type involve qualification, as Mill typically tries to be as precise as his information and experience, and the vagaries of language, allow. See, for example, 722^{a-a}, where "possibly" replaced "probably" in 1868, and in the next sentence (722^b) where the manuscript reading "perhaps" was deleted in proof. Other examples are the change from "utterly lost" to "in danger of being totally lost" in 1851 (682^{o-o}), and the deletion of "so far as I am aware" in 1856 (707^h) and of "(what appears to be the truest opinion)" in 1872 (650^j). Attempts to give philosophical clarity to phrases may be seen in the change in 1865 (within a passage added in 1862) of "predicated" to "affirmed" (660^{d-d}), and, in a passage relating to perception, the change in 1851 from "seem to see" to "see what seems" (642^{d-d}; cf. 642^{e-e}). A change of a similar sort, perhaps reflecting a friend's criticism, is seen at 688^{c-c}, where the term "*villain* or *villein*" is applied to those subject to "the less onerous forms of feudal bondage"; until 1846 this read "the least onerous form of feudal bondage, those serfs who were *adscripti glebæ*". And one further variant may be cited, to illustrate the difficulty of precisely accounting for some of these changes: in illustrating the folly of ignoring habitual associations when applying terms, Mill cites (671^{b-b}) the imaginary case of calling "the higher classes in Europe savages"; until 1872 "France or England" appeared in the place of "Europe".[125]

The fourth type of variant, that which is verbal, or gives semantic clarity, or reflects changing word usage, is the most common, and is not without importance, especially in cumulative effect. A few, of varying kinds, may be cited in illustration. A frequent change (see, e.g., 670^{l-l}) is of "men" to "people" or "mankind" (and "a man" or "he" to "a person") in 1851,

---

[124]For changes in 1862, see 391^{j-j}, 396^{k-k}; in 1865, 166^{g-g}, 227^{i-i}, $^{j-j}$, 252^{d-d}; in 1868, 686^{b-b}, ^{d} (cited above); and in 1872 (in a passage added in 1856, concerning Spencer), 271^{i-i}. The student interested in these changes should also see Professor McRae's comments, xxxiiff., the discussion in the text on 338ff., the change in 1851 at 620^e, the letter to Ward (*LL*, *CW*, XV, 647–8), and the following places in *CW*, X: 123^{u-u} (a change of 1859 in "Coleridge"), 258n (an addition in 1863 to *Utilitarianism* concerning Spencer's use of "necessarily"), and 269^g (a change of 1865 in *Auguste Comte and Positivism*).

[125]Was Mill influenced in part by the events of the Franco-Prussian War, and the English sympathy—which he shared—for the German cause?

For a series of variants that illustrate how a large number of this third type may add up to a significant change, see 681^{n-n}ff., where the relation between the revisions of the *Logic* and the composition of other of Mill's writings ("Coleridge" and *On Liberty*), and his revised view of Benthamism, may be perceived.

There being so many variants of this third type, a selection of "interesting" ones from outside Book IV would principally reveal the editor's bias; attentive readers will find significances of their own.

a change also found in the 3rd edition of the *Principles* in the next year.[126] A hint that the term "philosopher" was being more strictly applied by Mill, and perhaps generally, at mid-century, is seen in the frequent substitution of another term: in 1851 at 657^{e-e} "philosophers" became "inquirers", at 664^{a-a} "thinkers", at 709^{s-s} "writers", at 680^{d-d} "metaphysicians", and at 428^{f-f} "astronomers". There are many similar changes (not all in the 3rd edition): for example, at 666^{a-a} "metaphysicians" became "thinkers" in 1868. The meaning of "scientific" is also involved, as "philosophic" became "scientific" inquirers, writers, or thinkers, in various places at various times.

Mill's desire for semantic clarity, simply illustrated at 644^{k-k} (the introduction of "that" in 1862), often, though not so often as in the *Principles*, led him into double and triple revision: on 655^{p-p}, where the final reading is "This is the tentative process which Dr. Whewell speaks of; and which has not unnaturally suggested the theory . . .", the manuscript reading of the second clause is "and this it is which suggests the theory . . ."; in the 1st edition it reads "and this it is which suggested the theory"; and in the 2nd edition the final version is introduced. Mill's sharing of the common infirmities of mankind may be seen in his frequent uncertainty over verbal forms and agreement with collective nouns; see, e.g., 644^{i-i}, where he cancelled the "s" on "remains" in the manuscript, and returned to the singular form in 1865; and 647^{d-d}, where "corresponds" became "correspond" in 1846. Sometimes this verbal hesitation also led to multiple changes, as at 697^{q-q} and $^{r-r}$, where the manuscript reading of the passage is "mankind now see the meaning which before they only felt, and will . . ."; in the 1st and 2nd editions the reading is "mankind shall see the meaning which before they only felt, and shall . . ."; in the 3rd edition the first "shall" became "can", but in the 4th "shall" was restored.[127]

As Table 3 shows, most of the changes between the manuscript and the 1st edition are of a minor kind. Two special types may be mentioned, as indicating the printers' difficulty in reading Mill's hand, and Mill's return in later editions to a manuscript reading, sometimes to a cancelled reading. Both are seen at 646^{e-e}, where the manuscript's "those" was printed as "these" in 1843 and 1846, with "those" appearing again in 1851. (Cf. 670^{m-m}.) The second type is seen at 664^{b-b}, where in the manuscript "the

---

[126]One should remember, in this context, Mill's proposed amendment to the Second Reform Bill in 1867, to replace "man" with "person." For an interpretation, see Robson, "'Joint Authorship' Again," *Mill News Letter*, VI (Spring, 1971), 15–20, which undoubtedly shows that bias may be revealed in discussions of the fourth type of variant; again readers will find their own favourites.

[127]Actually in the manuscript Mill first wrote "mankind shall see & recognize their mea" [*sic*] and then cancelled the words after "mankind" and substituted "now" to give the final manuscript reading.

sole" replaced the cancelled *"the"* which was, however, restored for the 1st edition, and at 689^{g-g}, where in the manuscript Mill wrote "the two" and then cancelled "two", "the" appearing in all editions until 1862, when it was replaced by "two".

When one turns from the substantive variants to the accidentals, exceedingly complex problems emerge, without dominant patterns to guide interpretation or editorial practice.[128] There are a bewildering number of changes in punctuation, the great majority being between the manuscript and the 1st edition. Again taking Book IV as typical, one finds some 940 changes, over 700 of them between the manuscript and the 1st edition. Most of these (696 overall; 528 in the 1st edition) involve the addition or deletion of a comma (or two enclosing commas), with the additions outnumbering the deletions about five to three. The most frequent changes apart from comma addition and deletion are the replacement of a comma with a semi-colon and the reverse, and a colon with a semi-colon and the reverse, in those orders. With the exception of the 1st edition, the frequency of punctuation changes approximates that of the substantive changes, with more occurring in the heavily revised 3rd edition, though there are, compared with substantive variants, relatively more in the 6th edition and relatively fewer in the 4th.[129]

[128]As the dominant practice of analytical bibliographers is to present an "eclectic" text, incorporating the earliest form of the accidentals with later forms of authorial substantives, a few comments on the departure from that practice here are necessary. The painstaking and productive biblographic analysis that has made it possible in many circumstances to determine the responsibility for accidentals grew out of concern with early printed works, especially literary texts, in which printing-house corruption was manifest, for which the author seldom read proof, and in which the current technology and working habits led to texts of a mixed and unreliable kind. Most of the applications of analytical techniques to later, machine-set works have dealt with literary texts in which there are comparatively few substantive variants, and these generally short ones, and in which, because of the importance of slight shades of meaning to literary scholars, the accidentals are more significant than in non-imaginative works.

In the text here printed the "conservative" position is adopted of accepting the accidental as well as the substantive readings of the last edition in Mill's lifetime, returning to earlier readings only when there is demonstrable corruption. The rationale is that (a) none of the conditions mentioned above applies with great force to Mill's *Logic*; (b) we know he was concerned over accidentals; (c) the manuscript does not give adequate readings (for example, the end of a line serves for punctuation in some places, essential commas are omitted in interlineations and elsewhere, and many points are ambiguous in form) where later editions do; and (d) a vast number of the substantives include accidentals, to accept the form of which, in conjunction with those of the manuscript, would be to introduce an obviously inconsistent kind of eclecticism. Even those who accept this reasoning might argue for standardization of spelling and word division, but since Mill (in the manuscript and elsewhere) and the printers (who are undoubtedly responsible for some changes) were not consistent, it has been thought best to give these inconsistencies as they passed, repeatedly, through Mill's detailed proofreading.

[129]In view of the influence of printing-house practice on accidentals, it should be noted that Harrison and Co. were the printers for the 1st edition; Woodfall and Son for

The largest number of changes in initial capitalization also was made in the proof revisions for the 1st edition, which is far less heavily capitalized than the manuscript, seventy-three single or linked words having their initial letters reduced in the Preface and Introduction alone. In subsequent editions there was a slight tendency to reduce capitals, most marked in the 3rd edition, where twenty-seven capitals are reduced, and ten introduced. No consistent practice is discernible, however, and in some cases (especially A/a, K/k, M/m)[130] difficulty in reading Mill's hand is probably responsible for some changes and some inconsistencies.

Similarly, a comparison of the manuscript with the 1st edition reveals the largest number of changes in word division and hyphenation, in the work as a whole 148 hyphens being added (of just over 200 added in all editions) and nine (of fifty-four) being removed. Nearly one-third of the total additions occur after the prefixes "co", "pre", and "re"; "to-day" and "to-morrow" become the standard forms in the 1st edition; and hyphens are introduced into numbers such as "ninety-nine" and fractions such as "one-half." Here too, though printing-house practice was undoubtedly responsible for many, if not most, of the changes (in the 1st edition especially), there are many inconsistencies, and again Mill's intentions in the manuscript are not always clear.

Like comments are appropriate on the spelling changes, which also are most frequent between the manuscript and the 1st edition. Some of these, however, are made with such regularity that they seem to reflect house practice: in 1843, changes from "enquire" to "inquire", "shew" to "show", "chuse" to "choose"; in 1856, "premiss" to "premise".[131] The most common (though not always consistent) alterations that suggest house practice are from "z" to "s" and the reverse (usually in participles): "analyse" becomes "analyze" in 1843, and "analyse" again in 1851; the manuscript "characterize" is spelled with an "s" in 1843, and returns to "z" in 1851; and "recognize" normally becomes "recognise" in 1843 and remains in that form. These of course reflect, as do most of the other changes, uncertainties and alterations in common nineteenth-century spelling, and the later and earlier forms of all these words appear in other Mill holographs.

Other less frequent and less consistent changes (with late forms some-

---

the 2nd; Savill and Edwards for the 3rd through the 8th. Parker published the first five editions; Longmans, after taking over Parker's business, the final three (and the posthumous 9th and People's).

[130]The K/k confusion is particularly annoying because of the different meanings of "Kind" and "kind." As the list of typographical errors in Appendix I shows, some corrections are here necessary. In a few places in the manuscript Mill, evidently aware of the problem, used proof-reader's underlinings to indicate majuscule K's.

[131]All these examples include cognate forms. Both "shew" and "enquire" occur in passages added in 1851, but were altered in 1856 to the standard form.

times appearing as early as the manuscript, and early forms persisting in late editions) include "develope" to "develop", "decypher" to "decipher", "favor" and "honor" to "favour" and "honour" (all these usually made in 1843; the last example shows a tendency to consistency, for the usual manuscript form is "our"). While "mixt", "dropt", and "stopt" all took "ed" forms in 1843, "learnt" was not altered in 1843, though it was in five cases in later editions, but both "learnt" and "learned" are found in the manuscript and in all editions.[132] A few changes have minor separate interest: "Houyhnhms" (which also appears in the Early Draft) was corrected to "Houyhnhnms" in 1851 and 1856; "Spinosa" altered to "Spinoza" in 1862 and 1868; "Majendie" to "Magendie" in 1865; and "schirrus" to "scirrhus" (both, surprisingly, acceptable) in 1862.

As a final comment on the accidentals, one may note the tendency to reduce italicization: there are over two hundred cases where roman replaced italic, as against a handful of reverse cases. Here the reduction is most marked in the 5th and 6th editions.

SUMMARY OF THE COMPOSITION OF THE LOGIC

This lengthy treatment of the details, great and small, of the history of Mill's *Logic* has perhaps obscured the main pattern. Table 4, which isolates the most salient points in that history, is an attempt to re-establish the broader perspective. As the account above indicates, the dates for the manuscripts are not certain, though the *termini ad quos* are generally reliable, and two manuscript versions are not now extant (Mill's holograph of the Early Draft and the complete draft preceding the Press-copy Manuscript).

MILL'S SOURCES

One matter not covered in Table 4 is the debt Mill owed to others. Kubitz, in his *Development of John Stuart Mill's System of Logic*, gives an instructive, if somewhat outdated, account up to 1843, and the text of the *Logic* itself gives important evidence, which can here only be summarized. In his Preface, Mill characteristically remarks that the *Logic* is "an attempt not to supersede, but to embody and systematize, the best ideas . . . promulgated on its subject by speculative thinkers, or conformed to by accurate

---

[132]Though affected in many ways by Whewell's views, it is not likely that Mill knew of his strong opinions on "t," "d," and "ed" forms: see Mrs. Stair Douglas, *The Life and Selections from the Correspondence of William Whewell* (London: Kegan Paul, 1881), 202–3.

thinkers in their scientific inquiries." Somewhat more strongly, he goes on to say that the subject has never yet been "treated as a whole," and his originality lies only in trying to "cement" and "harmonize."

Whatever one's view of the justice of these remarks, they point to the use Mill makes of other thinkers. As Appendix K, the Bibliographic Appendix, shows, this use was extensive: some 250 individuals and 200 works being referred to, and 125 quoted from. Most frequently cited are Whewell (nine works referred to, and six quoted from, often at length), Comte, Bain, Spencer and Whately.[133] The British empiricists are often mentioned (Hume is slighted) but seldom quoted (except Bain); similarly with the Scottish Common-Sense school. There are quite a few references to, and a few quotations from, the Continental Rationalists, but the Idealists (five mentions of Kant, and three of Hegel) are really not used to any extent. Aristotle and (vaguely) the "scholastic logicians" or "Aristotelians" are quite widely cited, and (in Book III) a variety of scientific monographs is quoted or summarized. Mill refers to ten of his own writings, and quotes, at considerable length, from six of them.

Mill's notes to his sources are typical of nineteenth-century practice, often too slight for immediate and precise identification; his quotations are fairly accurate (more so, on the whole, than in the *Principles*), but there is considerable departure from his originals in accidentals, and there are some errors in transcription.

Some of the points brought out by a study of Mill's sources (which Appendix K is intended to facilitate) may be mentioned here. Evidence of the help given by Mill's friends is seen, for example, in Grote's marginal markings in his copies of Brandis's *Handbuch* and Preller and Ritter's *Historia*, of passages cited by Mill. Variant readings sometimes establish which form of a particular source Mill was using (see, for example, the entries under Whewell and Herschel).

Hints towards the interpretation of other of Mill's writings may be drawn from some of the references: for example, his treatment of James Martineau's "On the Life, Character, and Works of Dr. Priestley" points to the influence of that essay on Mill's theory of poetry.[134] The variants in his

---

[133]With the exception of Comte (whose importance is referred to frequently in the text), all these are mentioned in one Preface or another, with some indication of debts and disagreements. The strongest references, apart from that to Bain in the 8th edition, are in the 1st (retained through the 8th), where Mill says that without Whewell's *History of the Inductive Sciences* "the corresponding portion of this work would probably not have been written," and in the 1st (retained in the 2nd), where he recommends Whately's *Logic*, the earlier portion of Brown's *Lectures on the Philosophy of the Human Mind*, and his *Inquiry into the Relation of Cause and Effect*.

[134]Martineau's essay appeared in the *Monthly Repository* in the same year (1833) as Mill's "What is Poetry?" and "The Two Kinds of Poetry." Mill wrote to Martineau on 26 May, 1835 (*LL, CW*, XVII, 1961), saying that the last two pages of Martineau's

TABLE 4

Date	INTRODUCTION	BOOK I	BOOK II	BOOK III	BOOK IV	BOOK V	BOOK VI
1830		Notes on Terms and Propositions (i–v)	(see Book VI)				Notes (?) on method of Political Philosophy (vii; related to II, iv–vi)
1830–32		Draft of i–vi (?)	Draft of theory of Syllogism (i–iii)				Working out of doctrine of Liberty and Necessity (ii) (date indeterminate)
1834	Early Draft	Early Draft (1st stage), i–vi Early Draft (2nd stage), vii–viii	Early Draft (1st stage), i–iii	Early Draft (2nd stage), ii–iii (roughly)			
1836–37			Early Draft (3rd stage), iv–vi				
1837 autumn				Draft of early chaps. Draft of three chaps.			
1838 summer		Theory of Kinds, v–vi, and iii revised		Complete draft			
autumn					Complete Draft		
1839–40						Draft of ii	
1841 MS to Murray, December	Press-copy MS	Press-copy MS	Press-copy MS	Press-copy MS		Complete draft	Complete draft
1842 MS to Murray, February MS to Parker, March					Press-copy MS	Press-copy MS	Final draft (see below)

DATE	BOOK I	BOOK II	BOOK III	BOOK IV	BOOK V	BOOK VI	ENTIRE WORK
1842 (cont.) July–Dec	iii revised		ix and xiii added				Revision of Press-copy MS
1843 January						iv added, ix–x rewritten	Proof revision
January to March							
1846			xviii and latter part of xxv rewritten				2nd edition, revised
1851	Sectioning of viii altered	Supplementary note to iii added	ii, 5, v, 11 (as 9), and xviii, 4 added; v, 9 rewritten; note added to ix, 5; xxi partly rewritten and sectioning altered			xi (became xii after 5th ed.), 5–6 rewritten as 5–7	3rd edition, revised
1856		vii added	x, 4 rewritten				4th edition, revised
1862		iii, 8 added, and supplementary note to iii rewritten and redisposed	note added to ix, 5 in 51 became ix, 6			xi added (former xi became xii)	5th edition, revised
1865		iii, 9 added	ix, 4 added; and xiii, 1–3 revised				6th edition, revised
1868							7th edition, revised
1872		vii, 4 added	v, 5 and 10 added; part of x, 4 deleted				8th edition, revised

quotations from his "Coleridge" and *Essays on Some Unsettled Questions of Political Economy* are useful in dating composition and revision, and a comparison of his quotation from his "On Miss Martineau's Summary of Political Economy" with the original gives variant readings for that essay.

The revision of an example (that of the sentinel off his post, 331n–332n) is explained when one sees the full passage from Hutton's "Mill and Whewell on the Logic of Induction," from which Mill quotes only a part. Somewhat more complicated is the case of Mill's citations from Prout's *Chemistry, Meteorology, and the Function of Digestion* (identified by Mill simply as a "Bridgewater Treatise"): he twice quotes from it in exemplifying fallacies; Prout, in his 3rd edition (1845, after the publication of the *Logic*) rewrote the first passage (having already altered it in the 2nd edition before Mill's work appeared), and deleted the second (also rewritten in the 2nd edition); in 1846, perhaps having looked at Prout's 3rd edition, Mill deleted the second quotation.

Finally, a few examples of departures from the source readings may be mentioned: the printers' difficulty in reading Mill's hand is probably shown at 885^{b-b}, where "whenever" appears rather than "wherever"; this may also be the case at 101.n10 where "concrete form" rather than "correcter form" appears. Some of these are treated below as typographical errors, when the sense requires the change, as in the last example, or when there is supporting evidence, as at 640.11 and 12, where "que ceux" rather than "que de ceux" appears in the final two editions, with the correct form earlier; and at 357.28, where the omission of closing quotation marks in the 5th and subsequent editions cloaks the omission of a paragraph from Reid's *Essay on the Active Powers of Man*. And at 577.24, in a passage added in 1872, where Mill cites Bain as saying that induction involves a "leap in the dark," Bain says "leap to the future" and "the leap, the hazard of Induction": was Mill recalling Lord Derby's famous reference to the Reform Bill of 1867?

II. THE PRESENT TEXT

THE NARRATIVE and analytical complexities, and the bias inherent in any selective treatment of Mill's revisions make apparent the value of a text giving full variant readings. In the text below, therefore, the 8th edition,

---

paper (from which he quotes in the *Logic*) "made an impression upon [him] which will never be effaced," and that in "The Two Kinds of Poetry" he had "attempted to follow out [Martineau's] speculation into some of those ulterior consequences w^h [he] had rather indicated than stated."

the last in Mill's lifetime,[135] is printed with the substantive textual changes found in a complete collation of the eight editions and the Press-copy Manuscript. "Substantive" here means all changes in text except spelling, capitalization, word division, punctuation, italicization, demonstrable typographical errors, alterations in footnote references and style, such printing-house concerns as type size and orthographic changes between the manuscript and the printed text (such as "&" for "and" and superscripts in abbreviations).[136]

A glance at any of the heavily revised pages in this edition will reveal the difficulties in providing variant readings without making the text difficult to follow. Mill's own recognition of the desirability and the difficulty of recording variants is seen in a letter to De Morgan, where he says: "I have sometimes thought I ought to have some mark for alterations and additions. But one could scarcely give distinctive marks to all the successive strata of new matter, and a mere note of distinction from the edition immediately previous would not answer the [purposes of] those readers who only possess a still earlier one."[137] No one has yet done anything for the

---

[135]For arguments supporting the choice of this edition as copy-text, see n123 above, the Textual Introduction to Mill's *Principles* (*CW*, II, lxxixff.), and my "Principles and Methods in the Collected Edition of John Stuart Mill," in John M. Robson, ed., *Editing Nineteenth-Century Texts* (Toronto: University of Toronto Press, 1967), 96–122.

[136]To avoid annoyance, some slight and easily described changes are not reproduced. Of these the most frequent are changes from "upon" to "on" (most commonly after "grounded," "founded," "dependent," and "rest," but also after other words, the changes being made in 1851; there is only one case of the reverse change, at 514.3), and of "although" to "though" (occurring in the 3rd, 4th, 5th, and 6th editions); both forms of each are however found in all editions. Two other non-recorded changes are from "Sir William Hamilton" to "Sir W. Hamilton" (173.n21, changed in 1865), and "viz." to "namely" (102.38, in 1843). Four other changes are recorded only on their first appearance (and so noted): (i) the consistent and frequent change of "Mr. Whewell" to "Dr. Whewell" in 1851 (see cxiii^{p-p}); this matter gave Mill some trouble, for in the Press-copy Manuscript "Dr." is often cancelled for "Mr.", occasionally "Professor" is also cancelled, and in a few places both "Professor" and "Mr." are cancelled for "Dr." which became always "Mr." in 1843; Whewell actually took the degree of Doctor of Divinity in 1844, and having been Professor of Mineralogy at Cambridge from 1828 to 1832, he became Professor of Moral Theology in 1838 (similar changes in the text of "Mr." to "Professor" Bain are too infrequent to justify an exception); (ii) "necessarian" to "necessitarian" in 1872 (see 838^{h-h}); (iii) "mode" (of a syllogistic figure) to "mood" in 1856 (see 165^{d-d}); and (iv) "A," "B," "C," to "As," "Bs," "Cs" in 1865 (see 598^{g-g})—the final three appear only in limited contexts. And finally, eight changes from "a" to "an" (before "universe" and "universal" in 1851, 52.26 and 132.13; before "hypothetical" in 1843, 84.1, and in 1862, 710.10; and before "historical" in 1851, 724.25), or from "an" to "a" (before "hundred" in 1846, 515.11, and twice on 610.24 and 25) are not recorded.

[137]*LL*, *CW*, XVI, 1108 (25/10/65). Occasionally in late works, especially the *Hamilton* (the editions coming after this letter, it may be noted), Mill put square brackets around added matter in footnotes, sometimes giving some verbal indication of when the matter was added; in other footnotes he simply indicates why the matter did not appear earlier.

unfortunate owners of "still earlier" editions (though they may of course own valuable first editions and so be comforted), but our hope is that the method here adopted will meet the needs of all other readers. It is intended to provide a text as little interrupted by editorial apparatus as possible, variant readings that allow reconstruction of the earlier texts without separate instructions for each variant, and the minimum number of levels of text on each page consistent with accuracy and the above objectives. The method is harder to describe than to apply, as testing a few examples will indicate; one may well bear in mind, however, the note found in some construction kits: if all else fails, follow the instructions.

On a typical page, there will be three levels of text: the text of the 8th edition; in slightly smaller type, Mill's own footnotes; in smaller type again, footnotes containing the variant readings. In the text itself, the usual indicators (*, †, etc.) call attention to Mill's footnotes; where editorial notes of reference are added, they (and the indicators) appear in square brackets; small italic superscript letters, in alphabetical sequence (beginning anew in each section) call attention to variant readings. These variants are of three kinds: addition of a word or words, substitution of a word or words, deletion of a word or words. Illustrative examples will be drawn mainly from the early pages of the text.

Addition of a word or words: see 11^{b-b}. In the text, the words "consciously or unconsciously" appear as "^{b}consciously or unconsciously^b"; the variant note reads "$^{b-b}$+51, 56, 62, 65, 68, 72". Here the plus sign indicates that the words "consciously or unconsciously" were added; the following numbers (51, 56, 62, 65, 68, 72) indicate the editions in which they appear. The editions are always indicated by the last two numbers of the year of publication, as follows: 43 = 1843 (1st edition) 46 = 1846 (2nd edition), 51 = 1851 (3rd edition), 56 = 1856 (4th edition). 62 = 1862 (5th edition), 65 = 1865 (6th edition), 68 = 1868 (7th edition), 72 = 1872 (8th edition). The Press-copy Manuscript is indicated by MS. If the variant occurs within a quotation, and the earlier version (i.e., that in the variant note) is the reading of the source from which Mill is quoting, the word "Source" precedes the manuscript and edition indicators in the variant note (see, e.g., 885^{b-b}). (If the reading in the text, as opposed to that in the variant note, were the same as that of the source, "Source" would not appear.) If the text varies from the source, but not among editions, there is no variant note (the variant reading is given, however, in the Bibliographic Appendix; see, e.g., the entry for 250.19 under Herschel's "Whewell on the Inductive Sciences").

Placing the example (11^{b-b}) in context, then, the interpretation is that from the manuscript through the 2nd edition, the reading is "every mind conforms"; in the 3rd edition (51) this was altered to "every mind consciously or unconsciously conforms", and the reading of the 3rd edition was retained (as is clear in the text) in all subsequent editions through the 8th.

It should be noted that when the variant is a long one, the second enclosing superscript may appear on the next page, or even several pages after the first; when necessary, to make reference easier, the superscript notation in the footnote (which appears on the same page as the first superscript) will give the page number on which the variant passage concludes (see, e.g., 147^{w-w148}).

Substitution of a word or words: see 12^{b-b}. In the text the word "advancing" appears as "^{b}advancing^b"; the variant note reads "$^{b-b}$MS, 43, 46, 51, 56 proceeding". Here the word following the edition indicators is that for which "advancing" was substituted; again applying the rules and putting the variant in context, the interpretation is that from the manuscript through the 4th edition (56) the reading is "of proceeding from known truths"; in the 5th edition this was altered to "of advancing from known truths", and the reading of the 5th edition was retained (as is clear in the text) through the 8th edition.

In a few places, to reduce the number of superscripts and to indicate linked changes, the procedure exemplified at 145^{l-l} is followed. Here the passage in the text begins "^{l}to which" and concludes "appeals^l"; the note reads "$^{l-l}$MS which . . . appeals to". The interpretation is that in 1843 Mill moved "to" from the end of the sentence to before "which" without altering the rest of the passage, the unrecorded words being indicated in the note by the marks of ellipsis.

Deletion of a word or words: see 11^e. In the text, a *single* superscript ^{e} appears *centred* between "often" and "correctly"; the variant note reads "^{e}MS, 43, 46 very". Here the word following the edition indicators is that deleted; applying the rules and putting the variant in context, the interpretation is that the reading through the 2nd edition (46) was "often very correctly"; the word "very" was deleted in the 3rd edition and the reading of the 3rd edition was retained (as is clear in the text) through the 8th.

Variants within variants. As mentioned above, Mill often altered a passage more than once. Such rewritings require different treatments. In most cases, the procedure exemplified at 28^{a-a} is followed. Here the text reads "^{a}George, Mary^a", and the variant note reads "$^{a-a}$MS, 43, 46 Peter, George] 51 Peter, George, Mary". The different readings are given in chronological order, separated by a square bracket; the interpretation is that in the manuscript and 1st and 2nd editions the reading was "truly affirmed of John, Peter, George, and other persons"; in the 3rd edition this was altered to "truly affirmed of John, Peter, George, Mary, and other persons"; and the final reading, "truly affirmed of John, George, and Mary", first appeared in the 4th edition.[138]

In longer variants of this sort, it seems unnecessary to repeat the whole passage, and so such variant notes as that at 25^{c-c} appear, where the note reads "$^{c-c}$MS   but that the physical object, the sun himself, is the cause from which the outward phenomenon, day, follows as an effect]   43, 46 *as* MS . . . the sun itself . . . *as* MS"; the interpretation is that the 1st and 2nd editions have the same reading as the manuscript, except for the word "itself" which is substituted for "himself", and that the final reading was reached in the 3rd edition.

A similar procedure is adopted for some contiguous variants, to reduce the number of superscripts. At 3^{c-c}, for example, the note reads "$^{c-c}$MS, 43, 46   There cannot be agreement about the definition of a thing]   51, 56   *as* 72 . . . of a thing"; this procedure avoids the placing of another pair of superscripts around the word "anything" in the text, "a thing" (the only retention in 51, 56 from the earlier reading) being the only departure in 51, 56 from the 72 text. In other words, the interpretation is that the final reading appeared in the 3rd and 4th editions, except for the final two words ("a thing") in which they agree with the MS and 1st and 2nd editions; "anything" replaced "a thing" in the 5th edition and was retained through the 8th. (Cf. 5^{e-e} for similar treatment of a slightly different kind of variant.)

In other places, for the reader's convenience, especially where a substitution or deletion appears in the middle of an earlier and lengthy substitution, the variants within variants are indicated in the text by superscripts placed within other superscripts: see, e.g., 14^{n-n} and $^{o-o}$. Here the passage indicated by $^{n-n}$ was given its final form in the 3rd edition, except for the words indicated by $^{o-o}$, which appeared only in the 7th and 8th editions.

In all cases, variants within variants conclude as indicated. For example, at 614^{g-g616} there is no footnote in 46, 51, 56, 62; and at 625^{q-q626} the version in 46 ends "Disbelief."

Variants in Mill's footnotes. These are treated in the same manner as other variants, the alphabetical superscripts (and consequently the placing

---

[138]One could wish for a definite explanation of these apparently unnecessary changes, of which there are other examples. It will be noticed that a female name is introduced in 1851 (and retained thereafter), and that apart from Peter (who disappeared in 1856) the names derive from Mill's immediate family, though Mill objected strenuously to his brother George's and his sister Mary's responses to his marriage in 1851.

There are not many related changes in the wording of logical examples; one stands out sufficiently for comment. At 26^{f-f} Mill, in 1851, substituted the opening of Johnson's *Rasselas* for a passage from *Paradise Lost*. The reason may well be inferred from his description of Milton, in a letter to John Lalor (27/6/52), as having "with all his republicanism . . . the soul of a fanatic a despot & tyrant" (*LL, CW*, XIV, 91).

of the variant notes at the foot of the page) following the order dictated by a reading of Mill's footnotes where they appear in the text. Again for convenience exceptional treatment is accorded footnotes added subsequent to the manuscript and retained throughout (sometimes with altered wording): here, in the footnote after the indicator, a square-bracketed edition indicator shows when the footnote first appeared. At 6n, for example, the note begins: "*[62] I use . . . ", indicating that it was added in the 5th edition, and was retained in the 6th, 7th, and 8th. If no such indicator appears, the note is in the manuscript as well as all subsequent editions (see, e.g., 8n).

The same practice is used for the epigraphs to the several Books; see, e.g., 18.

Accidental variants. For reasons given earlier, these are not normally indicated in this edition. If, however, they occur within a variant, the earlier form is given (e.g., "&" appears in readings that occur *only* in manuscript), and the superscripts are placed exactly with reference to punctuation. Changes *within* variants, however, like changes in non-variant passages, are not indicated, so that if a reference is, say, to "MS, 43, 46", the accidentals derive from the 2nd edition, the last cited.

Prefaces. To indicate clearly the special matters to which Mill wished to call attention in the successive editions, the additional prefatory matter in each edition is given in chronological order; variant notes indicate in the usual way changes in the material that appeared in all editions.

Other textual liberties. Typographical errors in the 8th edition have been silently corrected; a full list is given in Appendix I. (Where the authority for alternate readings is inconclusive, the final reading is retained, and the variant note concludes with "[*printer's error?*]".) Mill's section titles in the Table of Contents have been introduced, in square brackets and italics, after each section number, so that the argumentative transitions can be followed without constant reference to the Table of Contents. (The wording of these titles has been slightly altered in a few cases to suit the different provenance.) Long quotations have been set in smaller type; this restyling leads to apparent anomalies between the variant notes and the text where, as at 761[e], quotation marks appear in the variant, while restyling has removed them from the text. When necessary, Mill's references to sources have been amplified and corrected,[139] with all added information being

---

[139]The following list gives the corrected references, in this form: page and line reference to the present text. JSM's reference] The corrected reference in the present text.
72.n26 p.298] pp.298–300
85.n2 81] 81–2
86.n4 82] 82–3
101.n15 407] 107
104.n1 103–105] 103, 105

placed in square brackets; internal references to the *Logic* have been altered to apply to the present edition. References to sources not identified by Mill have been added, with both indicators and footnotes in square brackets. Indications of ellipsis in quotations have been standardized to three dots plus, when required, terminal punctuation. A few trivial alterations in printing style have been made, such as the removal of periods after section titles and of dashes when combined with other punctuation as introducing quotations and references, and the restyling of chapter titles. The running heads have been modified to suit this edition's format. Finally, in a few places where Mill removed italics from words used as examples, the italics have been returned for clarity.

III. APPENDICES

Appendix A consists of the Early Draft of the *Logic*, with a headnote describing the manuscript, and setting out the editorial apparatus. The Early Draft has been printed in full, rather than in variant notes, because, though it closely parallels in many places the Press-copy Manuscript, there are more, and more complicated, variants than can intelligibly be accommodated in our method.

Appendices B–H contain variant passages of the *Logic* so lengthy or so heavily revised that they too require special treatment. Appendix B consists of the Supplementary Note to Book II, Chapter iii, in the 3rd and 4th editions, with the text taken from the 4th edition and variant notes giving the readings of the 3rd edition and those of later editions that incorporated parts of the Note. Appendix C consists of Book III, Chapter v, §9, in the MS, 1st and 2nd editions, with the text taken from the 2nd edition, and variant notes giving the readings of the MS and 1st edition. Appendix D consists

---

167.n16 148] 48
181.n1 157] 157–8
203n.1 367] 366–7
228.n7 pp.149 *et seqq.*] p.149
236.n11 222] 222–3
241.26–7 *Philosophy of the Inductive Sciences*] *Novum Organon Renovatum* [*altered because JSM altered his footnote reference; in subsequent references to Whewell's* Novum Organon *corrections have been made, as necessary (often JSM abbreviated the title), from the erroneous* Novum Organum Renovatum *(presumably on the Baconian rather than the Aristotelian model)*]
242.n1 32, 33] 33, 32–3
251.6 *Discourses*] *Discussions*
300.n4 p.231] pp. 251–2
304.n1 p. 256] pp. 256–7
364.24 211] 211n
426.nn4, 5; 427.n1 pp. 156–8, and 171] pp. 156–7, 171–2, 158 [*placed after separate passages, the first two in square brackets, the third where the original note occurs*]

of the complicated variant in Book III, Chapter x, §4 (at the end of the penultimate paragraph) in the 56, 62, 65, 68 versions, with the text taken from the 7th edition, and variant notes giving the readings of the 4th, 5th, and 6th; to this are added the papers written by Mill and Bain on the Conservation of Force, and supporting correspondence between them. Appendix E consists of Book III, Chapter xiii, §§1–3 in the MS, 43, 46, 51, 56, 62 versions, with the text taken from the 5th edition, and variant notes giving the readings of the MS, 1st, 2nd, 3rd, and 4th editions. Appendix F consists of Book III, Chapter xviii in the MS and 43 versions, with the text taken from the 1st edition, and variant notes giving the manuscript readings. Appendix G consists of Book III, Chapter xxv, §6, in the MS and 43 versions, with the text taken from the 1st edition, and variant notes giving the readings of the manuscript. Appendix H consists of Book VI, Chapter xii, §6, in the MS, 43, 46 versions, with the text taken from the 2nd edition, and variant notes giving the readings of the manuscript and 1st edition.

Appendix I lists the typographical errors in the 8th edition that are silently corrected in the text, and the manuscript slips of the pen that are not recorded in variant notes.

Appendix J gives an account of the Press-copy Manuscript, with examples of cancelled readings.

Appendix K, the Bibliographic Appendix, which lists all the persons and works quoted or referred to in the *Logic*, is designed to give a guide to logical writings and references in the nineteenth century, and also to Mill's reading and to influences on him. Substantive variants between Mill's quotations and his sources are given, both to correct misquotations and to provide contexts for partial quotations. Because this appendix includes all references to persons and books, it is in effect also an index of names and titles, which are therefore omitted from the Index proper.

The Index, a most essential doorway into a work so long and complicated as the *Logic*, has been prepared by R. F. McRae.

442.n1 Chap. vii, §1] Chap. vi, §2
475.n3 1862] 1861
489.n1 656] 655–7
497.n1 434–437] 437–8, 434
518.n1 §7] §8 [*JSM did not change when another section was added to* III, v]
598.n2 224] 224n
672.n2 35–37] 35–6 [*JSM includes the following quotations, which are here footnoted separately to avoid confusion*]
676.n21 173–4] 173, 174
725.n1 274] 274–5
725.n2 i] Vol. II [*as in* 62]
766.n3 43–5] 43
778.n1 21] 21n
779.n1 23–4] 22–4
783.n5 76–7] 76n–77n
885.n1 214 214–15

ACKNOWLEDGEMENTS

For permission to publish manuscript material, we are greatly indebted to the National Provincial Bank (literary executors and residual legatees of Mary Taylor, Mill's step-grand-daughter), to the Pierpont Morgan Library (the Early Draft), the British Museum (the Press-copy Manuscript), and the Milton S. Eisenhower Library, Johns Hopkins University (the Bain-Mill material in Appendix D). I should like to express my deep gratitude to the staffs of the British Museum Reading Room and Manuscript Room, the University of London Library, the Library of Political and Economic Science, the Somerville College Library, and the University of Toronto Library. To Professors McRae and Priestley, and the other members of the Editorial Committee of the *Collected Works*, to the copy-editor of the *Logic*, Rosemary Shipton, and the editorial and printing staff of the University of Toronto Press, my warm gratitude for long-suffering and guidance. My debts to others, incurred over the long years while this edition was in preparation, are numerous and varied; omissions from the following list should be attributed not to ingratitude but to failing memory or embarrassment: Francis E. Mineka (first and affectionately foremost), Pauline Adams, Peter and Caroline Allen, J. H. Burns, Kathleen Coburn, Daniel de Montmollin, Walter Houghton, J. R. de J. Jackson, Patricia Kennedy, Elizabeth Korotash, Dennis Lee, Judith Le Goff, John McClelland, Anne McWhir, Penelope Nettlefold, Gordon N. Ray, Francis Sparshott, the late Adelaide Weinberg, Ian Willison, and Elizabeth Zymans. And to my wife, the only one who can understand why it took me as long to edit this work as it took Mill to write it, my loving thanks for material aid and shared experience.

PREFACES

Preface

[To all editions]

THIS BOOK MAKES NO PRETENCE of giving to the world a new theory of ᵃtheᵃ
intellectual operations. Its claim to attention, if it possess any, is grounded
on the fact that it is an attempt not to supersede, but to embody and systematize, the best ideas which have been either promulgated on its subject by
speculative writers, or conformed to by accurate thinkers in their scientific
inquiries.

To cement together the detached fragments of a subject, never yet treated
as a whole; to harmonize the true portions of discordant theories, by supplying the links of thought necessary to connect them, and ᵇbyᵇ disentangling
them from the errors with which they are always more or less interwoven;
must necessarily require a considerable amount of original speculation. To
other originality than this, the present work lays no claim. In the existing
state of the cultivation of the sciences, there would be a very strong presumption against any one who should imagine ᶜthat he hadᶜ effected a revolution in the theory of the investigation of truth, or ᵈ added any fundamentally
new ᵉprocessᵉ to the practice of it. The improvement which remains to be
effected in ᶠtheᶠ methods of philosophizing (and the ᵍ author believes that
they have much need of improvement) can only consist in performing, more
systematically and accurately, operations with which, at least in their elementary form, the human intellect in some one or other of its employments
is already familiar.

In the portion of the work which treats of Ratiocination, the author has
not deemed it necessary to enter into technical details which may be obtained
in so perfect a shape from the existing treatises on what is termed the Logic
of the Schools. In the contempt entertained by many modern philosophers
for the syllogistic art, it will be seen that he by no means participates; though
the scientific theory on which its defence is usually rested appears to him

ᵃ⁻ᵃMS, 43, 46   our
ᶜ⁻ᶜMS   himself to have
ᵉ⁻ᵉMS   processes
ᵍMS   present

ᵇ⁻ᵇ+43, 46, 51, 56, 62, 65, 68, 72
ᵈMS   to have
ᶠ⁻ᶠ+46, 51, 56, 62, 65, 68, 72

erroneous: and the view which he has suggested of the nature and functions of the Syllogism may, perhaps, afford the means of conciliating the principles of the art with as much as is well grounded in the doctrines and objections of its assailants.

The same abstinence from details could not be observed in the First Book, on Names and Propositions; because many useful principles and distinctions which were contained in the old Logic, have been gradually omitted from the writings of its later teachers; and it appeared desirable both to revive these, and to reform and rationalize the philosophical foundation on which they stood. The earlier chapters of this preliminary Book will consequently appear, to some readers, needlessly elementary and scholastic. But those who know in what darkness the nature of our knowledge, and of the *h*processes by which it is obtained*h*, is often involved by a confused apprehension of the import of the different classes of Words and Assertions, will not regard these discussions as either frivolous, or irrelevant to the topics considered in the later Books.

On the subject of Induction, the *i*task*i* to be performed was that of generalizing the modes of investigating truth and estimating evidence, by which so many important and recondite laws of nature have, in the various sciences, been aggregated to the stock of human knowledge. That this *j*is*j* not a task free from difficulty may be presumed from the fact, that even at a very recent period, eminent writers (among whom it is sufficient to name Archbishop Whately, and the author of a celebrated article on Bacon in the *Edinburgh Review*)[*] have not scrupled to pronounce it impossible.* The

[*See Thomas Babington Macaulay, "Lord Bacon," *Edinburgh Review,* LXV (July, 1837), pp. 87ff.]

*[51] In the later editions of Archbishop Whately's *Logic* *k*, he states his meaning to be, not that "rules" for the ascertainment of truths by inductive investigation cannot be laid down, or that they may not be "of eminent service," but that they "must always be comparatively vague and general, and incapable of being built up into a regular demonstrative theory like that of the Syllogism." (Bk. IV, Chap. iv, § 3. [9th ed. London: Parker, 1848, p. 268.]) And he observes, that to devise a system for this purpose, capable of being "brought into a scientific form," would be an achievement which "he must be more sanguine than scientific who expects." (Bk. IV, Chap. ii, § 4. [p. 256.]) To effect this, however, being the express object of the portion of the present work which treats of Induction, the words in the text are no overstatement of the difference of opinion between Archbishop Whately and me on the subject*k*.

*h–h*MS   modes of arriving at it
*i–i*MS   business
*j–j*MS   was
*k–k*51   and *Rhetoric* [London: Murray, 1828] there are some expressions, which, though indefinite, resemble a disclaimer of the opinion here ascribed to him. If I have imputed that opinion to him erroneously, I am glad to find myself mistaken; but he has not altered the passages in which the opinion appeared to me to be conveyed, and which

author has endeavoured to combat their theory in the manner in which Diogenes confuted the sceptical reasonings against the possibility of motion; remembering that Diogenes' argument would have been equally conclusive, though his individual perambulations might not have extended beyond the circuit of his own tub.

*l*Whatever may be the value of what the author has*l* succeeded in effecting on this branch of his subject, it is a duty to acknowledge that for *m*much of it*m* he has been indebted to several important treatises, partly historical and partly philosophical, on the generalities and processes of physical science, which have been published within the last few years. To *n*these*n* treatises, and to their authors, he has endeavoured to do *o* justice in the body of the work. But as with one of these writers, *p*Dr.*p* Whewell, he has occasion frequently to express differences of opinion, it is more particularly incumbent on him in this place to declare, that without the aid derived from the facts and ideas contained in that gentleman's *History of the Inductive Sciences*,[*] the corresponding portion of this work would probably *q*not*q* have been written.

The concluding Book is an attempt to contribute towards the solution of a question, which the decay of old opinions, and the agitation *r*that*r* disturbs European society to its inmost depths, render as important in the present day to the practical interests of human life, as it must at all times be to the completeness of our speculative knowledge: viz. Whether moral and social phenomena are really exceptions to the general certainty and uniformity of the course of nature; and how far the methods, by which so many of the laws of the physical world have been numbered among truths irrevocably acquired and universally assented to, can be made instrumental to the *s* formation of a similar body of received doctrine in moral and political science.

[Additional paragraph in MS, 1st (1843), and 2nd (1846) editions only]

While the views promulgated in these volumes still await the verdict of competent judges, it would have been useless to attempt to make the exposition of them so elementary, as to be suited to readers wholly unacquainted with the subject. It can scarcely be hoped that the Second Book will be

[*3 vols. London: Parker, 1837.]

I still think inconsistent with the belief that Induction can be reduced to strict rules]
56   *as* 51 . . . mistaken; but the passages in which the opinion appeared to me to be conveyed, still seem to me inconsistent . . . *as* 51
   *l–l*MS   However little the author may have
   *m–m*MS   a great portion even of that little
   *n–n*MS   those [*printer's error?*]
   *o*MS, 43, 46   full
   *p–p*MS, 43, 46   Mr. [*this change, which was made throughout the work in 51, is not henceforth recorded*]
   *q–q*MS   never   *r–r*MS   which   *s*MS, 43, 46   gradual

throughout intelligible to any one who has not gone carefully through some one of the common treatises on Logic; [t] among which that of Archbishop Whately is, on every account, to be preferred. And the Third Book presupposes some degree of acquaintance with the most general truths of mathematics, as well as of the principal branches of physical science, and with the evidence on which those doctrines rest. Among books professedly treating of the mental phenomena, a previous familiarity with the earlier portion of Dr. Brown's *Lectures* or with his treatise on Cause and Effect,[*] would, though not indispensable, be advantageous; that philosopher having, in the author's judgment, taken a more correct view than any other English writer on the subject, of the ultimate intellectual laws of scientific inquiry; while his unusual powers of popularly stating and felicitously illustrating whatever he understood, [u] render his works the best preparation which can be suggested, for speculations similar to those contained in this Treatise.

[Concluding paragraph in the 2nd edition (1846) only]

The present edition has been carefully revised, and all errors corrected which have been either discovered by the author himself, or pointed out by others. The only portions which have been materially changed are the chapter on the Calculation of Chances,[†] and the latter part of that on the Grounds of Disbelief;[‡] on both which topics the author has been indebted to Sir John Herschel, and to Mr. J. M. Macleod, for some important rectifications of his original conclusions.

[Additional Preface to the 3rd (1851) and subsequent editions[§]]

Several criticisms, of a more or less controversial character, on this work, have appeared since the publication of the second edition; and Dr. Whewell has lately published a reply to those parts of it in which some of his opinions were controverted.*

I have carefully reconsidered all the points on which my conclusions have been assailed. But I have not to announce a change of opinion on any matter

[*Thomas Brown. *Lectures on the Philosophy of the Human Mind.* 4 vols. Edinburgh: Tait, 1820; and *Inquiry into the Relation of Cause and Effect.* 3rd ed. Edinburgh: Constable, 1818.]

[†Bk. III, Chap. xviii.]

[‡Bk. III, Chap. xxv.]

[§Headed in the 8th edition: "Preface to the Third and Fourth Editions." This heading was added in the 3rd edition (1851), expanded by the alteration of "Third Edition" to "Third and Fourth Editions" in the 5th edition (1862), and subsequently retained.]

*[65] [*Of Induction: with especial reference to Mr. J. Stuart Mill's System of Logic.* London: Parker, 1849.] Now forming a chapter in his volume on *The Philosophy of Discovery* [London: Parker, 1860, Chap. xxii, pp. 238–91].

[t]MS &

[u]MS, 43 powers which it would be in vain for the present writer to attempt to rival,

of importance. Such minor oversights as have been detected, either by my-self or by my critics, I have, in general silently, corrected: but it is not to be inferred that I agree with the objections which have been made to a passage, in every instance in which I have altered or cancelled it. I have often done so, merely that it might not remain a stumbling-block, when the amount of discussion necessary to place the matter in its true light would have exceeded what was suitable to the occasion.

To several of the arguments which have been urged against me, I have thought it useful to reply with some degree of minuteness; not from any taste for controversy, but because the opportunity was favourable for placing my own conclusions, and the grounds of them, more clearly and completely before the reader. Truth on these subjects is militant, and can only establish itself by means of conflict. The most opposite opinions can make a plausible show of evidence while each has the statement of its own case; and it is only possible to ascertain which of them is in the right, after hearing and com-paring what each can say against the other, and what the other can urge in its defence.

Even the criticisms from which I most dissent have been of great service to me, by showing in what places the exposition most needed to be improved, or the *argument* strengthened. And I should have been well pleased if the book had undergone a much greater amount of attack; as in that case I should probably have been enabled to improve it still more than I believe I have now done.

[Concluding paragraph in the 4th edition (1856) only]

The wish expressed in the preceding paragraph has subsequently been fulfilled, and a considerable number of additions have consequently been made in the present fourth edition. The most important of these relate to the doctrine of Causation, and to the incessantly renewed attempt to make human conceptions, and supposed incapacities of conception, the test of objective truth. On the latter subject I have thought it useful to discuss, in some detail, the opinions promulgated by a writer, the great value of some of whose con-tributions to analytic psychology makes me sincerely regret that the only part of his speculations which falls within the scope of the present treatise, is a part which I am compelled to controvert.

[Concluding paragraph in the 5th edition (1862) only]

In the present fifth edition, many minor improvements have been made, and an entire chapter[*] has been added to the concluding Book, for the pur-pose of further clearing up the idea of the Science of History, and removing some of the misconceptions by which it is obscured.

[*Bk. VI, Chap. xi.]

*v-v*51   arguments

[Concluding paragraphs in the 6th edition (1865) only]

In the present (sixth) edition a cause of complaint has been removed, which could hardly have arisen at a much earlier period. The main doctrines of this treatise are on the whole compatible with either of the conflicting theories respecting the ultimate structure of the human mind—the *à priori* or intuitional theory, and the experiential theory: though they may require from the former, or rather from certain forms of it, the sacrifice of some of its outworks. I had, therefore, as announced in the Introduction, abstained as much as possible from carrying the inquiry beyond the peculiar field of Logic, into the remoter metaphysical regions of thought, and have been content to express the doctrines and reasonings of Logic in terms which are the common property of both the contending schools of metaphysicians. This reserve was probably favourable, in the first instance, to the reception of the work; but a time came when some readers became impatient of it. Finding that the investigations continually stopped short because they could not have been carried further without entering on the higher metaphysics, some were disposed to conclude that the author had not himself ventured to pursue his speculations into that province, and that if he had done so he might probably have brought back from that region different conclusions from those arrived at in the work. The reader has now the means of satisfying himself whether this is the case or not. I have indeed maintained the same abstinence as in the former editions from the actual discussion of any but a few outlying questions of metaphysics, since no other plan seems to me appropriate to a treatise on Logic; but the place of such discussion has been supplied by references to a work recently published, *An Examination of Sir William Hamilton's Philosophy*,[*] in which will be found the remainder of the investigations which have necessarily been cut short in these pages. In a few cases in which it appeared possible and appropriate, as in the concluding section of chap. iii of the Second Book, a place has been made for the substance of what has been set forth and explained with greater fulness in the separate work.

Of the numerous minor improvements in this edition, the only one which is worth special notice is the addition of some new and apt examples of inductive and deductive investigation, in the room of others which the progress of science has superseded, or failed to confirm.

[Concluding paragraph in the 7th edition (1868) only]

In the subsequent editions,[†] the attempt to improve the work by additions and corrections, suggested by criticism or by thought, has been con-

[*London: Longmans, 1865.]
[†I.e., subsequent to the 4th ed.; this paragraph appeared in the 7th ed. at the end of the "Preface to the Third and Fourth Editions."]

tinued. In the present (seventh) edition, a few further corrections have been made, but no material additions.

[Concluding paragraphs in the 8th edition (1872) only]

In the subsequent editions,[*] the attempt to improve the work by additions and corrections, suggested by criticism or by thought, has been continued. The additions and corrections in the present (eighth) edition, which are not very considerable, are chiefly such as have been suggested by Professor Bain's *Logic*,[†] a book of great merit and value. Mr. Bain's view of the science is essentially the same with that taken in the present treatise, the differences of opinion being few and unimportant compared with the agreements; and he has not only enriched the exposition by many applications and illustrative details, but has appended to it a minute and very valuable discussion of the logical principles specially applicable to each of the sciences; a task for which the encyclopedical character of his knowledge peculiarly qualified him. I have in several instances made use of his exposition to improve my own, by adopting, and occasionally by controverting, matter contained in his treatise.

The longest of the additions belongs to the chapter on Causation, and is a discussion of the question, how far, if at all, the ordinary mode of stating the law of Cause and Effect requires modification to adapt it to the new doctrine of the Conservation of Force: a point still more fully and elaborately treated in Mr. Bain's work.[‡]

[*I.e., again subsequent to the 4th ed.; these paragraphs appeared in the 8th ed. at the end of the "Preface to the Third and Fourth Editions."]
[†Alexander Bain. *Logic*. 2 Parts. London: Longmans, 1870.]
[‡*Ibid*., Part II, pp. 20ff.]

A SYSTEM OF LOGIC
RATIOCINATIVE AND INDUCTIVE

Introduction

§ 1. [*A definition at the commencement of a subject must be provisional*]
There is as great *ᵃ* diversity among authors in the modes which they have adopted of defining logic, as in their treatment of the details of it. This is what might naturally be expected on any subject on which writers have availed themselves of the same language as a means of delivering different ideas. Ethics and jurisprudence are liable to the remark in common with logic. Almost every *ᵇ*writer*ᵇ* having taken a different view of some of the particulars which these branches of knowledge are usually understood to include; each has so framed his definition as to indicate beforehand his own peculiar tenets, and sometimes to beg the question in their favour.

This diversity is not so much an evil to be complained of, as an inevitable and in some degree a proper result of the imperfect state of those sciences. *ᶜ*It is not to be expected that there should be agreement about the definition of anything*ᶜ*, until there is agreement about the thing itself. To define *ᵈ*, is to select from among all the properties of a thing,*ᵈ* those which shall be understood to be designated and declared by its name; and the properties must be *ᵉ* well known to us before we can be competent to determine which of them are fittest to be chosen for this purpose. Accordingly, in the case of so complex an aggregation of particulars as are comprehended in anything which can be called a science, the definition we set out with is seldom that which a more extensive knowledge of the subject shows to be the most appropriate. Until we know the particulars themselves, we cannot fix upon the most correct and compact mode of circumscribing them by a general description. It was not *ᶠ*until*ᶠ* after an extensive and accurate acquaintance with the details of chemical phenomena, that it was found possible to frame a rational definition of chemistry; and the definition of the science of life and organization is still a matter of dispute. So long as the sciences are imperfect, the definitions must partake of their *ᵍ*imperfection*ᵍ*; and if the former are progressive, the

*ᵃ*MS a   *ᵇ⁻ᵇ*MS, 43, 46   philosopher
*ᶜ⁻ᶜ*MS, 43, 46   There cannot be agreement about the definition of a thing] 51, 56 *as* 72 . . . of a thing
*ᵈ⁻ᵈ*MS, 43, 46, 51, 56   a thing, is to select from among the whole of its properties
*ᵉ*MS, 43, 46   very   *ᶠ⁻ᶠ*MS, 43, 46, 51   till
*ᵍ⁻ᵍ*MS, 43, 46, 51, 56, 62   imperfections

latter ought to be so too. As much, therefore, as is to be expected from a definition placed at the commencement of a subject, is that it should define the scope of our inquiries: and the definition which I am about to offer of the science of logic, pretends to nothing more, than to be a statement of the question which I have put to myself, and which this book is an attempt to resolve. The reader is at liberty to object to it as a definition of logic; but it is at all events a correct definition of the subject of these volumes.

§ 2. [*Is logic the art and science of reasoning?*] Logic has often been called the Art of Reasoning. A writer* who has done more than any other *a* person to restore this study to the rank from which it had fallen in the estimation of the cultivated *b*class*b* in our own country, has adopted the above definition with an amendment; he has defined Logic to be the Science, as well as the Art, of reasoning; meaning by the former term, the analysis of the mental process which takes place whenever we reason, and by the latter, the rules, grounded on that analysis, for conducting the process correctly. There can be no doubt as to the propriety of the emendation. A right understanding of the mental process itself, of the conditions it depends on, and the steps of which it consists, is the only basis on which a system of rules, fitted for the direction of the process, can possibly be founded. Art necessarily presupposes knowledge; art, in any but its infant state, presupposes scientific knowledge: and if every art does not bear the name of *c*a science*c*, it is only because several sciences are often necessary to form the groundwork of a single art. *d*So complicated are the conditions which govern our practical agency*d*, that to enable one thing to be *done*, it is often requisite to *know* the nature and properties of many things.

Logic, then, comprises the science of reasoning, as well as an art, founded on that science. But the word Reasoning, again, like most other scientific terms in popular use, abounds in ambiguities. In one of its acceptations, it means syllogizing; or the mode of inference which may be called (with sufficient accuracy for the present purpose) concluding from generals to particulars. In another of its senses, to reason is simply to infer any assertion, from assertions already admitted: and in this sense induction is as much entitled to be called reasoning as the demonstrations of geometry.

Writers on logic have generally preferred the former acceptation of the term: the latter, and more extensive signification is that in which I mean to use it. I do this by virtue of the right I claim for every author, to give what-

*Archbishop Whately [*Elements of Logic*, p. 1].

*a*MS, 43, 46, 51, 56 living
*b–b*MS, 43, 46 classes
*c–c*MS, 43, 46, 51, 56 the science on which it rests
*d–d*MS, 43, 46, 51, 56 Such is the complication of human affairs

ever provisional definition he pleases of his own subject. But sufficient reasons will, I believe, unfold themselves as we advance, why this should be not only the provisional but the final definition. It involves, at all events, no arbitrary change in the meaning of the word; for, with the general usage of the English language, the wider signification, I believe, accords better than the more restricted one.

§ 3. [*Or is logic the art and science of the pursuit of truth?*] But Reasoning, even in the widest sense of which the word is susceptible, does not seem to *ª*comprehend*ª* all that is included, either in the best, or even in the most current, conception of the scope and province of our science. The employment of the word Logic to denote the theory of Argumentation, is derived from the Aristotelian, or, as they are commonly termed, the scholastic, logicians. Yet even with them, in their systematic treatises, Argumentation was the subject only of the third part: the two former treated of Terms, and of Propositions; under one or other of which heads were *ᵇ*also*ᵇ* included Definition and Division. *ᶜ*By some, indeed, these previous topics were professedly*ᶜ* introduced only on account of their connexion with reasoning, and as a preparation for the doctrine and rules of the syllogism. Yet they were treated with greater minuteness, and dwelt on at greater length, than was required for that purpose alone. More recent writers on logic have generally understood the term as it was employed by the able *ᵈ*author*ᵈ* of the Port Royal Logic;[*] viz. as equivalent to the Art of Thinking. Nor is this acceptation confined to *ᵉ*books, and scientific inquiries*ᵉ*. Even in *ᶠ*ordinary*ᶠ* conversation, the ideas *ᵍ* connected with the word Logic include at least precision of language, and accuracy of classification: and we perhaps oftener hear persons speak of a logical arrangement, or *ʰ*of*ʰ* expressions logically defined, than of conclusions logically deduced from premises. *ⁱ*Again,*ⁱ* a man is often called a great logician, or a man of powerful logic, not for the accuracy of his deductions, but for the extent of his command over premises; because the general propositions required for explaining a difficulty or refuting a sophism, copiously and promptly occur to him *ʲ*: because, in short, his knowledge, besides being

[*Arnauld, Antoine, and Pierre Nicole. *La Logique ou l'Art de penser: contenant outre des règles communes, plusieurs observations nouvelles, propres à former le jugement*. Amsterdam: Wolfgank, 1775.]

*ª–ª*MS, 43, 46   include
*ᵇ–ᵇ*MS, 43, 46   , moreover,
*ᶜ–ᶜ*MS, 43, 46, 51   Professedly, indeed, these previous topics were
*ᵈ–ᵈ*MS, 43   authors
*ᵉ–ᵉ*MS, 43, 46   philosophers, and works of science]   51, 56, 62   *as* 72 . . . scientific inquirers
ᶠ–ᶠ+51, 56, 62, 65, 68, 72   *ᵍ*MS, 43, 46   usually
ʰ–ʰ+51, 56, 62, 65, 68, 72   *ⁱ–ⁱ*MS, 43, 46   Moreover
*ʲ–ʲ*MS, 43, 46   ; as in the case of Chillingworth, or Samuel Johnson

ample, is well under his command for argumentative use[j]. Whether, therefore, we conform to the practice of those who have made the subject their
particular study, or to that of popular writers and common discourse, the
province of logic will include several operations of the intellect not usually
considered to fall within the meaning of the terms Reasoning and Argumentation.

These various operations might be brought within the compass of the
science, and the additional advantage be obtained of a very simple definition,
if, by an extension of the term, sanctioned by high authorities, we were to
define logic as the science which treats of the operations of the human understanding in the pursuit of truth. For to this ultimate end, naming, classification, definition, and all [k] other operations over which logic has ever claimed
jurisdiction, are essentially subsidiary. They may all be regarded as contrivances for enabling a person to know the truths which are needful to him, and
to know them at the precise moment at which they are needful. Other purposes, indeed, are also served by these operations; for instance, that of imparting our knowledge to others. But, viewed with regard to this purpose,
they have never been considered as within the province of the logician. The
sole object of Logic is the guidance of one's own thoughts: the communication of those thoughts to others falls under the consideration of Rhetoric, in
the large sense in which that art was conceived by the ancients; or of the still
more extensive art of Education. Logic takes cognizance of [l]our[l] intellectual
operations, only as they conduce to our own knowledge, and to our command
over that knowledge for our own uses. If there were but one rational being
in the universe, that being might be a perfect logician; and the science and
art of logic would be the same for that one person as for the whole human
race.

§ 4. [*Logic is concerned with inferences, not with intuitive truths*] But, if
the definition which we formerly examined included too little, that which is
now suggested has the opposite fault of including too much.

Truths are known to us in two ways: some are known directly, and of
themselves; some through the medium of other truths. The former are the
subject of Intuition, or Consciousness;* the latter, of Inference. The truths
known by intuition are the original premises from which all others are in-

---

*[62] I use these terms indiscriminately, because, for the purpose in view, there
is no need for making any distinction between them. But metaphysicians usually
restrict the name Intuition to the direct knowledge we are supposed to have of
things external to our minds, and Consciousness to our knowledge of our own
mental phenomena.

[k]MS, 43, 46   the   [l-l]43, 46   all

ferred. Our assent to the conclusion being grounded on the truth of the premises, we never could arrive at any knowledge by reasoning, unless something could be known antecedently to all reasoning.

Examples of truths known to us by immediate consciousness, are our own bodily sensations and mental feelings. I know directly, and of my own knowledge, that I was *a*vexed*a* yesterday, or that I am hungry to-day. Examples of truths which we know only by way of inference, are occurrences which took place while we were absent, the events recorded in history, or the theorems of mathematics. The two former we infer from the testimony adduced, or from the traces of those past occurrences which still *b*exist;*b* the latter, from the premises laid down in books of geometry, under the title of definitions and axioms. Whatever we are capable of knowing must belong to the one class or to the other; must be in the number of the primitive data, or of the conclusions which can be drawn *c*from these*c*.

With the original data, or ultimate premises of our knowledge; with their number or nature, the mode in which they are obtained, or the tests by which they may be distinguished; logic, in a direct way at least, has, in the sense in which I conceive the science, nothing to do. These questions are partly not a subject of science at all, partly that of a very different science.

Whatever is known to us by consciousness, is known beyond possibility of question. What one sees or feels, whether bodily or mentally, one cannot but be sure that one sees or feels. No science is required for the purpose of establishing such truths; no rules of art can render our knowledge of them more certain than it is in itself. There is no logic for this portion of our knowledge.

But we may fancy that we see or feel what we in reality infer. *d* A truth, or supposed truth, which is really the result of a very rapid inference, may seem to be apprehended intuitively. It has long been agreed by *e*thinkers*e* of the most opposite schools, that this mistake is actually made in so familiar an instance as that of the eyesight. There is nothing *f*of which we appear to ourselves to be more directly conscious*f*, than the distance of an object from us. Yet it has long been ascertained, that what is perceived by the eye, is at most nothing more than a variously coloured surface; that when we fancy we see distance, all we really see is certain variations of apparent size, and *g*degrees of*g* faintness of colour; *h* that our estimate of the object's distance from us

*a–a*MS grieved   *b–b*MS subsist:
*c–c*MS, 43, 46 therefrom
*d*MS, 43, 46, 51, 56 Newton saw the truth of many propositions of geometry without reading the demonstrations, but not, we may be sure, without their flashing through his mind.
*e–e*MS, 43, 46 philosophers   *f–f*MS, 43, 46 which . . . conscious of
*g–g*MS, 43, 46 more or less   *h*MS, 43, 46, 51, 56 and

is the result *i*partly of a rapid inference from the muscular sensations accompanying the adjustment of the focal distance of the eye to objects unequally remote from us, and partly*i* of a comparison (made with so much rapidity that we are unconscious of making it) between the size and colour of the object as they appear at the time, and the size and colour of the same or of similar objects as they appeared when close at hand, or when their degree of remoteness was known by other evidence. The perception of distance by the eye, which seems so like intuition, is thus, in reality, an inference grounded on experience; an inference, too, which we learn to make; and which we make with more and more correctness as our experience increases; though in familiar cases it takes place so rapidly as to appear exactly on a par with those perceptions of sight which are really intuitive, our perceptions of colour.*

Of the science, therefore, which expounds the operations of the human understanding in the pursuit of truth, one essential part is the inquiry: What are the *o*facts*o* which are the objects of intuition or consciousness, and what are those which we merely infer? But this inquiry has never been considered a portion of logic. Its place is in another and a perfectly distinct department of science, *p*to which the name metaphysics more particularly belongs:*p* that portion of mental philosophy which attempts to determine what part of the furniture of the mind belongs to it originally, and what part is constructed *q*out of materials furnished to it*q* from without. To this science appertain the great and much debated questions of the existence of matter; *r*the existence of spirit, and of a distinction between it and matter;*r* the reality of time and space, as things without the mind, and distinguishable from the objects which are said to exist *in* them. For in the present state of the discussion on these

*This *j*important*j* theory has *k*of late*k* been called in question by a writer of deserved reputation, Mr. Samuel Bailey [*A Review of Berkeley's Theory of Vision.* London: Ridgway, 1842]; but I do not conceive that the grounds on which it has been *l*admitted as an established doctrine*l* for a century past, have been at all shaken by that gentleman's objections. I have elsewhere said what appeared to me necessary in reply to his arguments. (*Westminster Review* [XXXVIII] for October 1842 [pp. 318–36] *m*; reprinted in *Dissertations and Discussions* [London: Parker, 1859], Vol. II [pp. 84–114])*m. n*

i-i+62, 65, 68, 72   *j-j*MS, 43, 46   celebrated
*k-k*MS, 43, 46, 51, 56, 62   recently   *l-l*MS, 43, 46   received by philosophers
m-m+62, 65, 68, 72
*n*51, 56   It may be necessary to add, that some other processes of comparison than those described in the text (but equally the result of experience) appear occasionally to enter into our judgment of distances by the eye.
*o-o*MS, 43, 46   truths
*p-p*MS, 43, 46   which may be called the higher or transcendental metaphysics. For such is the title which has been given to
*q-q*MS, 43, 46   by itself out of materials furnished
*r-r*MS, 43, 46   of the existence of spirit, and the distinction between it and matter; of

topics, it is *almost* universally allowed that the existence of matter or of spirit, of space or of time, is in its nature unsusceptible of being proved; and that *if anything is known of them, it must be* by immediate intuition. To the same science belong the inquiries into the nature of Conception, Perception, Memory, and Belief; all of which are operations of the understanding in the pursuit of truth; but with which, as phenomena of the mind, or with the possibility which may or may not exist of analysing any of them into simpler phenomena, the logician as such has no concern. To this science must also be referred the following, and all analogous questions: To what extent our intellectual faculties and our emotions are innate—to what extent the result of association: Whether God, and duty, are realities, the existence of which is manifest to us *à priori* by the constitution of our rational faculty; or whether our ideas of them are acquired notions, the origin of which we are able to trace and explain; and the reality of the objects themselves a question not of consciousness or intuition, but of evidence and reasoning.

The province of logic must be restricted to that portion of our knowledge which consists of inferences from truths previously known; whether those antecedent data be general propositions, or particular observations and perceptions. Logic is not the science of Belief, but the science of Proof, or Evidence. *In so far* as belief professes to be founded on proof, the office of logic is to supply a test for ascertaining whether or not the belief is well grounded. With the claims which any proposition has to belief on *the evidence of consciousness*, that is, without evidence in the proper sense of the word, logic has nothing to do.

§ 5. [*Relation of logic to the other sciences*] *By far the greatest portion of our knowledge, whether of general truths or of particular facts, being* avowedly matter of inference, nearly the whole, not only of science, but of human conduct, is amenable to the authority of logic. To draw inferences has been said to be the great business of life. Every one has daily, hourly, and momentary need of ascertaining facts which he has not directly observed; not from any general purpose of adding to his stock of knowledge, but because the facts themselves are of importance to his interests or to his occupations. The business of the magistrate, of the military commander, of the navigator, of the physician, of the agriculturist, is merely to judge of evidence, and to act accordingly. They all have to ascertain certain facts, in order that they may afterwards apply certain rules, either devised by themselves, or prescribed for their guidance by others; and as they do this well or ill, so they

⁻+51, 56, 62, 65, 68, 72
*⁻*MS, 43, 46   whatever is known of them, is known
*⁻*MS, 43, 46   So far forth
*⁻*MS, 43, 46   its own intrinsic evidence
*⁻*MS, 43, 46   As the far greatest . . . facts is

discharge well or ill the duties of their several callings. It is the only occupation in which the mind never ceases to be engaged; and is the subject, not of
logic, but of knowledge in general.

*b*Logic, however, is not the same thing with knowledge, though the field
of logic is coextensive with the field of knowledge. Logic is the common judge
and arbiter of all particular investigations. It does not undertake to find evidence, but to determine whether it has been found. Logic neither observes,
nor invents, nor discovers; but judges. It is no part of the business of logic to
inform the surgeon what appearances are found to accompany*b* a violent
death. This he must learn from his own experience and observation, or from
that of others, his predecessors in his peculiar *c*pursuit*c*. But logic sits in judgment on the sufficiency of that observation and experience to justify his rules,
and on the sufficiency of his rules to justify his conduct. It does not give him
proofs, but teaches him what makes them proofs, and how he is to judge of
them. *d*It does not teach that any particular fact proves any other, but points*d*
out to what conditions all facts must conform, in order that they may prove
other facts. To decide whether any given fact fulfils these conditions, or
whether facts can be found which fulfil them in *e*a*e* given case, belongs exclusively to the particular art or science, or to our knowledge of the particular subject.

It is in this sense that logic is, what *f*it was so expressively called by the
schoolmen and by Bacon*f*, *ars artium*;[*] the science of science itself. All
science consists of data and conclusions from those data, of proofs and what
they prove: now logic points out what relations must subsist between data
and whatever can be concluded from them, between proof and everything
which it can prove. If there be any such indispensable relations, and if these
can be precisely determined, every particular branch of science, as well as
every individual in the guidance of his conduct, is bound to conform to those
relations, under the penalty of making false inferences—of drawing conclu-

[*See Francis Bacon, *De Augmentis Scientiarum*. In *Works*. Ed. J. Spedding,
et al. London: Longman, 1857–74, Vol. I, p. 616.]

*b–b*MS, 43, 46 [*no paragraph*] Our definition of logic, therefore, will be in danger
of including the whole field of knowledge, unless we qualify it by some further limitation, showing distinctly where the domain of the other arts and sciences and of common
prudence ends, and that of logic begins.
The distinction is, that the science or knowledge of the particular subject-matter
furnishes the evidence, while logic furnishes the principles and rules of the estimation
of evidence. Logic does not pretend to teach the surgeon what are the symptoms which
indicate
*c–c*MS, 43, 46   science
*d–d*MS, 43, 46   Logic alone can never show that the fact A proves the fact B; but it
can point
*e–e*MS, 43, 46   any
*f–f*MS, 43, 46, 51, 56, 62, 65, 68   Bacon so expressively called it

sions which are not grounded in the realities of things. Whatever has at any time been concluded justly, whatever knowledge has been acquired otherwise than by immediate intuition, depended on the observance of the laws which it is the province of logic to investigate. If the conclusions are just, and the knowledge *g*real, those laws, whether known or not, have*g* been observed.

a§ 6.*a* [*The utility of logic, how shown*] We need not, therefore, seek any farther for a solution of the question, so often agitated, respecting the utility of logic. If a science of logic exists, or is capable of existing, it must be useful. If there be rules to which every mind *b*consciously or unconsciously*b* conforms in every instance in which it *c*infers*c* rightly, there seems little necessity for discussing whether a person is more likely to observe those rules, when he knows the rules, than when he is unacquainted with them.

A science may undoubtedly be brought to a certain, not inconsiderable, stage of advancement, without the application of any other logic to it than what all persons, who are said to have a sound understanding, acquire empirically in the course of their studies. *d*Mankind*d* judged of evidence, and often *e* correctly, before logic was a science, or they never could have made it one. And they executed great mechanical works before they understood the laws of mechanics. But there are limits both to what mechanicians can do without principles of mechanics, and to what thinkers can do without principles of logic. *f*A few individuals, *g*by extraordinary genius, or by the accidental acquisition of a good set of intellectual habits, may work without principles in the same way, *h*or nearly the same way,*h* in which they would have worked if they had been in possession of principles. But*g* the bulk of mankind require either to understand the theory of what they are doing, or to have rules laid down for them by those who have understood the theory. In*f* the progress of science from its easiest to its more difficult problems, *i*each great step in advance has usually*i* had either as its precursor, or as its accompaniment and necessary condition, a corresponding improvement in the notions and principles of logic received among the most advanced

*g–g*MS, 43, 46   sound, those laws have actually
*a–a*MS   [*no section division*]
b–b+51, 56, 62, 65, 68, 72
*c–c*MS, 43, 46   judges
*d–d*MS, 43, 46   Men
*e*MS, 43, 46   very
*f–f*MS, 43, 46   And the limits, in the two cases, are of the same kind. The extent of what man can do without understanding the theory of what he is doing, is in all cases much the same: he can do whatever is very easy; what requires only time, and patient industry. But in
*g–g*51   may, by extraordinary genius, anticipate the results of science; but
h–h+62, 65, 68, 72
*i–i*MS, 43, 46   every great step in advance has

thinkers. And if several of the more difficult sciences are still in so defective a state; if not only so little is proved, but disputation has not terminated even about the little which seemed to be so; the reason perhaps is, that men's logical notions have not yet acquired the degree of extension, or of accuracy, requisite for the estimation of the evidence proper to those particular departments of knowledge.

  § 7. [*Definition of logic stated and illustrated*] Logic, then, is the science of the operations of the understanding which are subservient to the estimation of evidence: both the process itself of *advancing* from known truths to unknown, and all *other intellectual operations in so far as* auxiliary to this. It includes, therefore, the operation of Naming; for language is an instrument of thought, as well as a means of communicating our thoughts. It includes, also, Definition, and Classification. For, the use of these operations (putting all other minds than one's own out of consideration) is to serve not only for keeping our evidences and the conclusions from them permanent and readily accessible in the memory, but for so marshalling the facts which we may at any time be engaged in investigating, as to enable us to perceive more clearly what evidence there is, and to judge with fewer chances of error whether it be sufficient. *These, therefore, are operations specially instrumental to the estimation of evidence, and, as such, are within the province of Logic. There are other more elementary processes, concerned in all thinking, such as Conception, Memory, and the like; but of these it is not necessary that Logic should take any peculiar cognizance, since they have no special connexion with the problem of Evidence, further than that, like all other problems addressed to the understanding, it presupposes them.*

  Our object, *then*, will be, to attempt a correct analysis of the intellectual process called Reasoning or Inference, and of such other mental operations as are intended to facilitate this: as well as, on the foundation of this analysis, and *pari passu* with it, to bring together or frame a set of rules or canons for testing the sufficiency of any given evidence to prove any given proposition.

  With respect to the first part of this undertaking, I do not attempt to decompose the mental operations in question into their ultimate elements. It is enough if the analysis as far as it goes is correct, and if it goes far enough for the practical purposes of logic considered as an art. The separation of a com-

---

  *a–a*MS §6.   *b–b*MS, 43, 46, 51, 56   proceeding
  *c–c*MS, 43, 46   intellectual operations
  *d–d*MS, 43, 46   The analysis of the instruments we employ in the investigation of truth, is part of the analysis of the investigation itself; since no art is complete, unless another art, that of constructing the tools and fitting them for the purposes of the art, is embodied in it.
  *e–e*MS, 43, 46   therefore

plicated phenomenon into its component parts is not like a connected and interdependent chain of proof. If one link of an argument breaks, the whole drops to the ground; but one step towards an analysis holds good and has an independent value, though we should never be able to make a second. The results *which have been obtained by* analytical chemistry are not the less valuable, though it should be discovered that all which we now call simple substances are really compounds. All other things are at any rate compounded of those elements: whether the elements themselves admit of decomposition, is an important inquiry, but does not affect the certainty of the science up to that point.

g I shall, accordingly, attempt to analyse the process of inference, and the processes subordinate to inference, so far only as may be requisite for ascertaining the difference between a correct and an incorrect performance of those processes. The reason for thus limiting our design, is evident. It has been said by objectors to logic, that we do not learn to use our muscles by studying their anatomy.[*] The fact is not quite fairly stated; for if the action of any of our muscles were vitiated by local weakness, or other physical defect, a knowledge of their anatomy might be very necessary for effecting a cure. But we should be justly liable to the criticism involved in this objection, were we, in a treatise on logic, to carry the analysis of the reasoning process beyond the point at which any inaccuracy which may have crept into it must become visible. In learning bodily exercises (to carry on the same illustration) we do, and must, analyse the bodily motions so far as is necessary for distinguishing those which ought to be performed from those which ought not. To a similar extent, and no further, it is necessary that the logician should analyse the mental processes with which Logic is concerned. *ʰLogic has no interest in carrying the analysis beyond the point at which it becomes apparent whether the operations have in any individual case been rightly or wrongly performed: in the same manner as the science of music teaches us to discriminate between musical notes, and to know the combinations of which they are susceptible, but not what number of vibrations in a second correspond to each; which, though useful to be known, is useful for totally different purposes. The extension of Logic as a Science is determined by its necessities as an Art: whatever it does not need for its practical ends, it leaves to the larger science which may be said to correspond, not to any particular

[*See, e.g., Thomas Carlyle, "Characteristics," *Edinburgh Review*, LIV (Dec., 1831), p. 355.]

*f–f*MS, 43, 46, 51, 56 of
*g*MS [*no paragraph*]
*h–h*MS, 43, 46 Any ulterior and minuter analysis must be left to transcendental metaphysics; which in this, as in other parts of our mental nature, decides] 51, 56, 62 *as* MS . . . to metaphysics . . . *as* MS [*cf.* 15n]

art, but to art in general; the science which deals with the constitution of the human faculties; and to which, in the part of our mental nature which concerns Logic, as well as in all other parts, it belongs to decide[h] what are ultimate facts, and what are resolvable into other facts. And I believe it will be found that [i]most of[i] the conclusions arrived at in this work have no necessary connexion with any particular views respecting the ulterior analysis. Logic is common ground on which the partisans of Hartley and of Reid, of Locke and of Kant, may meet and join hands. Particular and detached opinions of all these [j]thinkers[j] will no doubt occasionally be controverted, since all of them were logicians as well as metaphysicians; but the field on which their [k]principal[k] battles have been fought, lies beyond the boundaries of our science [l].

It cannot, indeed, be pretended that logical principles can be altogether irrelevant to those more abstruse discussions; nor is it possible but that the view we are led to take of the problem which logic proposes, must have a tendency favourable to the adoption of some one opinion, on these controverted subjects, rather than another. [m] For metaphysics, in endeavouring to solve its own peculiar problem, must employ means, the validity of which falls under the cognizance of logic. It proceeds, no doubt, as far as possible, merely by a closer and more attentive interrogation of our consciousness, or more properly speaking, of our memory; and so far is not amenable to logic. But wherever this method is insufficient to attain the end of its inquiries, it must proceed, like other sciences, by means of evidence. Now, the moment this science begins to draw inferences from evidence, logic becomes the sovereign judge whether its inferences are well grounded, or what other inferences would be so.

[n]This, however, constitutes no nearer or other relation between logic and metaphysics, than that which exists between logic and [o]every other science[o]. And[n] I can conscientiously affirm, that no one proposition laid down in this work has been adopted for the sake of establishing, or with any reference to its fitness for being employed in establishing, preconceived opinions in any

[i-i]+56, 62, 65, 68, 72
[j-j]MS, 43, 46   philosophers
[k-k]MS, 43, 46   great
[l]MS, 43, 46   ; and the views which will be here promulgated, may, I believe, be held in conjunction with the principal conclusions of any one of their systems of philosophy
[m]MS, 43, 46   Logic, although differing from the higher metaphysics like the other half of a great whole, (the one being the science of the appreciation of evidence, the other having for its main object to determine what are the propositions for the establishment of which evidence is not required,) yet when viewed under another of its aspects, stands in the same relation to this, its sister science, as it does to all the other sciences.
[n-n]MS, 43, 46   This influence, however, of logic over the questions which have divided philosophers in the higher regions of metaphysics, is indirect and remote; and
[o-o]51, 56, 62, 65   all the other sciences

department of knowledge or of inquiry on which the speculative world is still undecided.*

*[65] *p*The view taken in the text, of the definition and purpose of Logic, stands in marked opposition to that of the school of philosophy which, in this country, is represented by the writings of Sir William Hamilton and of his numerous pupils. Logic, as this school conceives it, is "the Science of the Formal Laws of Thought" [William Hamilton, *Lectures on Metaphysics and Logic*. 4 vols. Edinburgh: Blackwood, 1859–60, Vol. III, p. 25]; a definition framed for the express purpose of excluding, as irrelevant to Logic, whatever relates to Belief and Disbelief, or to the pursuit of truth as such, and restricting the science to that very limited portion of its total province, which has reference to the conditions, not of Truth, but of Consistency. What I have thought it useful to say in opposition to this limitation

*p–p*56   *It is perhaps requisite that something should here be said of a definition of Logic, different from any of those which have been discussed in the text, and belonging essentially to the school of philosophy of which Sir William Hamilton is in this country the most eminent representative. Logic, as conceived by these philosophers, is "the Science of the Formal Laws of Thought." If it be objected to this definition that the laws of thought, as of every other operation of the mind, are the subject not of Logic, but of Psychology, it might be answered, that Logic as a Science, is, and cannot but be, a *portion* of Psychology; consisting of the scientific analysis of those mental operations which it is the purpose of Logic, so far as it is an Art, to enable us to perform correctly. But (as I have already pointed out) Logic has no interest in carrying this analysis beyond the point at which it becomes apparent whether the operations have in any individual case been rightly or wrongly performed: in the same manner as the science of music teaches us to discriminate between musical notes, and to know the combinations of which they are susceptible, but not what number of vibrations in a second corresponds to each, which, though useful to be known, is useful for totally different purposes. The extension of Logic as a Science is determined by its necessity as an Art: whatever it does not need for its practical ends, it leaves to the larger science, which corresponds not to any particular art, but to art in general; the science which deals with the constitution of the human faculties.

The definition, therefore, of Logic as "the science of the formal laws of thought" requires, as it seems to me, in order to be tenable, limitation in one direction, as well as extension in another. It requires, on the one hand, that the meaning of the word Thought should be limited to Reasoning, and to the intellectual operations auxiliary to Reasoning, in so far as they are auxiliary; and that the "laws of thought" should be understood to mean the immediate, not the ultimate, laws; a sufficient, but not a complete, analysis of the operations. But again, on the other hand, this sufficient analysis must be extended to *all* the processes which the mind goes through when it proves a proposition, or judges correctly of proof. Thus corrected, the definition would accord with that which we ultimately arrived at in the text. This, however, is not what the authors of the definition intend by it. By the expression "*formal* laws," they mean, among other things, to intimate that the province of Logic is not coextensive with Proof, but extends only to one species of proof, namely, that in which the conclusion follows from the mere form of the expression; or (to say the same thing in other words) when what is asserted explicitly in the conclusion, has been already, by implication, asserted in the premises. Now I am aware of no good reason for confining the name of Logic to the theory and rules of the interpretation of old generalizations, and refusing it to those of the formation of new. Both processes equally admit of, and equally require, a strictly scientific theory. Whether Logic shall be said to be the theory of both, or only of one, is a question of naming. But most questions of naming have questions of fact lying underneath them; and the question lying under this, is the fundamental

of the field of Logic, has been said at some length in a separate work, *q*first*q* published in 1865, and entitled *An Examination of Sir William Hamilton's Philosophy, and of the Principal Philosophical Questions discussed in his Writings.* For the purposes of the present Treatise, I am content that the justification of the larger extension which I give to the domain of the science, should rest on the sequel of the Treatise itself. Some remarks on the relation which the Logic of Consistency bears to the Logic of Truth, and on the place which that particular part occupies in the whole to which it belongs, will be found in the present volume (Book II, Chap. iii, § 9).*p*

identity of the theories of Induction and of Deduction; operations which cannot, in my opinion, be rightly understood, except as parts of one and the same process. The grounds of this opinion cannot be entered on in this early stage of our inquiry, but will be found fully set forth in the second Book.]   62   *as* 56 . . . faculties. [*paragraph*] Any definition, therefore, which treats Logic as the science of the laws of thought, requires . . . *as* 56 [*cf.* 13*h–h*] [*This footnote was replaced in 65 by the footnote printed above.*] *q–q*+68, 72

The opening folio of Book I, Chapter i, of the Press-copy Manuscript
British Museum

BOOK I

OF NAMES AND PROPOSITIONS

"La scolastique, qui produisit dans la logique, comme dans la morale, et dans une partie de la métaphysique, une subtilité, une précision d'idées, dont l'habitude inconnue aux anciens, a contribué plus qu'on ne croit au progrès de la bonne philosophie." [Marie Jean Caritat, marquis de] Condorcet, *Vie de Turgot* [London: n.p., 1786, p. 9.]

[56] "To the schoolmen the vulgar languages are principally indebted for what precision and analytic subtlety they possess." Sir William Hamilton, *Discussions in Philosophy* [2nd ed. London: Longman, 1853, p. 5n].

CHAPTER I

Of the Necessity of Commencing with an Analysis of Language

§ 1. [*Theory of names, why a necessary part of logic*] It is so much the established practice of writers on logic to commence their treatises by a few general observations (in most cases, it is true, rather meagre) on Terms and their varieties, that it will, perhaps, scarcely be required from me in merely following the common usage, to be as particular in assigning my reasons, as it is usually expected that those should be who deviate from it.

The practice, indeed, is recommended by considerations far too obvious to require a formal justification. Logic is a portion of the Art of Thinking: Language is evidently, and by the admission of all philosophers, one of the principal instruments or helps of thought; and any imperfection in the instrument, or in the mode of employing it, is confessedly liable, still more than in almost any other art, to confuse and impede the process, and destroy all ground of confidence in the result. For a mind not previously versed in the meaning and right use of the various kinds of words, to attempt the study of methods of philosophizing, would be as if some one should attempt to *become* an astronomical observer, having never learned to adjust the focal distance of his optical instruments so as to see distinctly.

Since Reasoning, or Inference, the principal subject of logic, is an operation which usually takes place by means of words, and in *b* complicated cases can take place in no other way; those who have not a thorough insight into the signification and purposes of words, will be under *c*chances, amounting almost to certainty,*c* of reasoning or inferring incorrectly. And logicians have generally felt that unless, in the very first stage, they removed this *d* source of error; unless they taught their pupil to put away the glasses which distort the object, and to use those which are adapted to his purpose in such a manner as to assist, not perplex, his vision; he would not be in a condition to practise the remaining part of their discipline with any prospect of advantage. Therefore it is that an inquiry into language, so far as is needful to guard

*a–a*MS, 43, 46, 51, 56   make himself   *b*+43, 46   all
*c–c*MS, 43, 46   almost a necessity   *d*MS, 43, 46, 51, 56   fertile

against the errors to which it gives rise, has at all times been deemed a necessary preliminary to the *study* of logic.

But there is another reason, of a still more fundamental nature, why the
import of words should be the earliest subject of the logician's consideration:
because without it he cannot examine into the import of Propositions. Now
this is a subject which stands on the very threshold of the science of logic.

The object of logic, as defined in the Introductory Chapter, is to ascertain
how we come by that portion of our knowledge (much the greatest portion)
which is not intuitive: and by what criterion we can, in matters not self-
evident, distinguish between things proved and things not proved, between
what is worthy and what is unworthy of belief. Of the various questions
which *present themselves to our inquiring faculties, some receive an answer
from direct consciousness, others, if resolved at all, can only be resolved* by
means of evidence. Logic is concerned with these last. *g* But before inquiring
into the mode of resolving questions, it is necessary to inquire what are
those which offer themselves; what questions are conceivable; what inquiries are there, to which *mankind* have either obtained, or been able to
imagine it possible that they should obtain, an answer. This point is best
ascertained by a survey and analysis of Propositions.

§ 2. [*First step in the analysis of Propositions*] The answer to every question which it is possible to frame, *must be* contained in a Proposition, or
Assertion. Whatever can be an object of belief, or even of disbelief, must,
when put into words, assume the form of a proposition. All truth and all error
lie in propositions. What, by a convenient misapplication of an abstract term,
we call a Truth, *means* simply a True Proposition; and errors are false propositions. To know the import of all possible propositions, would be to know
all questions which can be raised, all matters which are susceptible of being
either believed or disbelieved. How many kinds of inquiries can be propounded; how many kinds of judgments can be *made*; and how many kinds
of propositions it is possible to frame with a meaning; are but different forms
of one and the same question. Since, then, the objects of all Belief and of all
Inquiry express themselves in propositions; a sufficient scrutiny of Propositions and of their varieties will apprize us what questions mankind have
actually asked *of* themselves, and what, in the nature of answers to those
questions, they have actually thought they had grounds to believe.

*e–e*MS, 43, 46   science
*f–f*MS, 43, 46   the universe presents to our inquiring faculties, some are soluble by
direct consciousness, others only
*g*MS, 43, 46   The solution, by means of evidence, of questions respecting the universe and the things contained in it, is the purpose of logic.
*h–h*MS, 43, 46   the questions which present
*i–i*MS, 43, 46   men   *a–a*MS, 43, 46, 51   is
*b–b*MS, 43, 46   is   *c–c*MS   passed
d–d+51, 56, 62, 65, 68, 72

Now the first glance at a proposition shows that it is formed by putting together two names. A proposition, according to the common simple definition, which is sufficient for our purpose, is, *discourse, in which something is affirmed or denied of something.* Thus, in the proposition, Gold is yellow, the quality *yellow* is affirmed of the substance *gold.* In the proposition, Franklin was not born in England, the fact expressed by the words *born in England* is denied of the man Franklin.

Every proposition consists of three parts: the Subject, the Predicate, and the Copula. The predicate is the name denoting that which is affirmed or denied. The subject is the name denoting the person or thing which something is affirmed or denied of. The copula is the sign denoting that there is an affirmation or denial; and thereby enabling the hearer or reader to distinguish a proposition from any other kind of discourse. Thus, in the proposition, The earth is round, the Predicate is the word *round*, which denotes the quality affirmed, or (as the phrase is) predicated: *the earth*, words denoting the object which that quality is affirmed of, compose the Subject; the word *is*, which serves as the connecting mark between the subject and predicate, to show that one of them is affirmed of the other, is called the Copula.

Dismissing, for the present, the copula, of which more will be said hereafter, every proposition, then, consists of at least two names; brings together two names, in a particular manner. This is already a first step towards what we are in quest of. It appears from this, that for an act of belief, *one* object is not sufficient; the simplest act of belief supposes, and has something to do with, *two* objects: two names, to say the least; and (since the names must be names of something) two *nameable things.* A large class of thinkers would cut the matter short by saying, two *ideas.* They would say, that the subject and predicate are both of them names of ideas; the idea of gold, for instance, and the idea of yellow; and that what takes place (or [e] part of what takes place) in the act of belief, consists in bringing (as it is often expressed) one of these ideas under the other. But this we are not yet in a condition to say: whether such be the correct mode of describing the phenomenon, is an after consideration. The result with which for the present we must be contented, is, that in every act of belief *two* objects are in some manner taken cognizance of; that there can be no belief claimed, or question propounded, which does not embrace two distinct (either material or intellectual) subjects of thought; each of them capable, or not, of being conceived by itself, but incapable of being believed by itself.

I may say, for instance, "the sun." The word has a meaning, and suggests that meaning to the mind of any one who is listening to me. But suppose I ask him, Whether it is true: whether he believes it? He can give no answer. There is as yet nothing to believe, or to disbelieve. Now, however, let me make, of all possible assertions respecting the sun, the one which involves

[e]MS, 43, 46, 51   a

the least of reference to any object besides itself; let me say, "the sun exists." Here, at once, is something which a person can say he believes. But here, instead of only one, we find two distinct objects of conception: the sun is one object; existence is another. Let it not be said that this second conception, existence, is involved in the first; for the sun may be conceived as no longer existing. "The sun" does not convey all the meaning that is conveyed by "the sun exists:" "my father" does not include all the meaning of "my father exists," for he may be dead; "a round square" does not include the meaning of "a round square exists," for it does not and cannot exist. When I say "the sun," "my father," or a "round square," I *do not call upon the hearer for any* belief or disbelief, nor can either the one or the other be afforded me; but if I say, "the sun exists," "my father exists," or "a round square exists," I call for belief; and should, in the first of the three instances, meet with it; in the second, with belief or disbelief, as the case might be; in the third, with disbelief.

§ 3. [*Names must be studied before things*] This first step in the analysis of the object of belief, which, though so obvious, will be found to be not unimportant, is the only one which we shall find it practicable to make without a preliminary survey of language. If we attempt to proceed further in the same path, that is, to analyse any further the import of Propositions; we find forced upon us, as a subject of previous consideration, the import of Names. For every proposition consists of two names; and every proposition affirms or denies one of these names, of the other. Now what we do, what passes in our mind, when we affirm or deny two names of one another, must depend on what they are names of; since it is with reference to that, and not to the mere names themselves, that we make the affirmation or denial. Here, therefore, we find a new reason why the signification of names, and the relation generally between names and the things signified by them, must occupy the preliminary stage of the inquiry we are engaged in.

It may be objected that the meaning of names can guide us at most only to the opinions, possibly the foolish and groundless opinions, which mankind have formed concerning things, and that as the object of philosophy is truth, not opinion, the philosopher should dismiss words and look into things themselves, to ascertain what questions can be asked and answered in regard to them. This advice (which *a* no one has it in his power to follow) is in reality an exhortation to discard the whole fruits of the labours of his predecessors, and *b*conduct*b* himself as if he were the first person who had ever turned an inquiring eye upon nature. What does any one's personal knowledge of

*f–f*MS, 43, 46, 51, 56, 62, 65   call upon the hearer for no
*a*MS, 43, 46   fortunately
*b–b*MS, 43, 46   demean

Things amount to, after subtracting all which he has acquired by means of the words of other people? Even after he has learned as much as °people° usually do learn from others, will the notions of things contained in his individual mind afford as sufficient a basis for a *catalogue raisonné* as the notions which are in the minds of all mankind?

d In any enumeration and classification of Things, which does not set out from their names, no varieties of things will of course be comprehended but those recognised by the particular inquirer; and it will still remain °to be established°, by a subsequent examination of names, that *'the'* enumeration has omitted nothing which ought to have been included. But if we begin with names, and use them as our clue to the things, we bring at once before us all the distinctions which have been recognised, not by a single inquirer *ᵍ*, but by all inquirers taken together*ᵍ*. It doubtless may, and I believe it will, be found, that mankind have multiplied the varieties unnecessarily, and have imagined distinctions among things, where there were only distinctions in the manner of naming them. But we are not entitled to assume this in the commencement. We must begin by recognising the distinctions made by ordinary language. If some of these appear, on a close examination, not to be fundamental, *ʰtheʰ* enumeration of the different kinds of realities may be abridged accordingly. But to impose upon the facts in the first instance the yoke of a theory, while the grounds of the theory are reserved for discussion in a subsequent stage, is *ⁱ* not a course which a logician can reasonably adopt.

*c–c*MS, 43, 46   men
*d*MS   [*no paragraph*]
*e–e*MS, 43, 46   for him to establish
*f–f*MS, 43, 46   his
*g–g*MS, 43, 46   of perhaps limited views, but by the collective intelligence of mankind
*h–h*MS, 43, 46   our
*ⁱ*MS, 43, 46   evidently

CHAPTER II

Of Names

§ 1. [*Names are names of things, not of our ideas*] "A name," says Hobbes,* "is a word taken at pleasure to serve for a mark which may raise in our mind a thought like to some thought we had before, and which being pronounced to others, may be to them a sign of what thought the speaker had† before in his mind." This simple definition of a name, as a word (or set of words) serving the double purpose of a mark to recall to ourselves the likeness of a former thought, and a sign to make it known to others, appears unexceptionable. Names, indeed, do much more than this; but whatever else they do, grows out of, and is the result of this: as will appear in its proper place.

Are names more properly said to be the names of things, or of our ideas of things? The first is the expression in common use; the last is that of some ^ametaphysicians^a, who conceived that in adopting it they were introducing a highly important distinction. The eminent thinker, just quoted, seems to countenance the latter opinion. "But seeing," he continues, "names ordered in speech (as is defined) are signs of our conceptions, it is manifest they are not signs of the things themselves; for that the sound of this word *stone* should be the sign of a stone, cannot be understood in any sense but this, that he that hears it collects that he that pronounces it thinks of a stone."[*]

If it be merely meant that the conception alone, and not the thing itself, is recalled by the name, or imparted to the hearer, this of course cannot be denied. Nevertheless, there seems good reason for adhering to the common usage, and calling ^b(as indeed Hobbes himself does in other places)^b the word *sun* the name of the sun, and not the name of our idea of the sun. For names are not intended only to make the hearer conceive what we conceive, but also to inform him what we believe. Now, when I use a name for the purpose of expressing a belief, it is a belief concerning the thing itself, not

*"Computation or Logic," [in *The English Works of Thomas Hobbes*, Vol. I. Ed. William Molesworth. London: Bohn, 1839,] Chap. ii [p. 16].

†In the original "had, *or had not*." These last words, as involving a subtlety foreign to our present purpose, I have forborne to quote.

[*Ibid., p. 17.]

^{a–a}MS, 43, 46 philosophers   ^{b–b}+72

concerning my idea of it. When I say, "the sun is the cause of day," I do not mean that my idea of the sun causes or excites in me the idea of day; °or in other words, that thinking of the sun makes me think of day. I mean, that a certain physical fact, which is called the sun's presence (and which, in the ultimate analysis, resolves itself into sensations, not ideas) causes another physical fact, which is called day°. It seems proper to consider a word as the *name* of that which we intend to be understood by it when we use it; of that which any fact that we assert of it is to be understood of; that, in short, concerning which, when we employ the word, we intend to give information. Names, therefore, shall always be spoken of in this work as the names of things themselves, and not merely of our ideas of things.

But the question now arises, of what things? and to answer this it is necessary to take into consideration the different kinds of names.

§ 2. [*Words which are not names, but parts of names*] It is usual, before examining the various classes into which names are commonly divided, to begin by distinguishing from names of ªevery^a description, those words which are not names, but only parts of names. Among such are reckoned particles, as *of, to, truly, often*; the inflected cases of nouns substantive, as *me, him, John's*; ^b and even adjectives, as *large, heavy*. These words do not express things of which anything can be affirmed or denied. We cannot say, Heavy fell, or A heavy fell; Truly, or A truly, was asserted; Of, or An of, was in the room. Unless, indeed, we are speaking of the mere words themselves, as when we say, Truly is an English word, or, Heavy is an adjective. In that case they are complete names, viz. names of those particular sounds, or of those particular collections of written characters. This employment of a word to denote the mere letters and syllables of which it is composed, was termed by the schoolmen the *suppositio materialis* of the word. In any other sense we cannot introduce one of these words into the subject of a proposition, unless in combination with other words; as, A heavy *body* fell, A truly *important fact* was asserted, A *member* of *parliament* was in the room.

An adjective, however, is capable of standing by itself as the predicate of a proposition; as when we say, Snow is white; and occasionally even as the subject, for we may say, White is an agreeable colour. The adjective is often said to be so used by a grammatical ellipsis: Snow is white, instead of Snow

---

ᶜ⁻ᶜMS but that the physical object, the sun himself, is the cause from which the outward phenomenon, day, follows as an effect]   43, 46   *as* MS . . . the sun itself . . . *as* MS

ª⁻ªMS any

ᵇMS, 43, 46, 51, 56   [*footnote:*] *It would, perhaps, be more correct to say that inflected cases are names and something more; and that this addition prevents them from being used as the subjects of propositions. But the purposes of our inquiry do not demand that we should enter with scrupulous accuracy into similar minutiae.

is a white object; White is an agreeable colour, instead of, A white colour, or, The colour *c* white, is agreeable. The Greeks and Romans were *d*allowed*d*, by the rules of their language, to employ this ellipsis universally in the subject as well as in the predicate of a proposition. In English this cannot, generally speaking, be done. We may say, The earth is round; but we cannot say, Round is easily moved; we must say, A round object. *e*This*e* distinction, however, is rather grammatical than logical. Since there is no difference of meaning between *round*, and *a round object*, it is only custom which prescribes that on any given occasion one shall be used, and not the other. We shall, there-fore, without scruple, speak of adjectives as names, whether in their own right, or as representative of the more circuitous forms of expression above exemplified. The other classes of subsidiary words have no title whatever to be considered as names. An adverb, or an accusative case, cannot under any circumstances (except when their mere letters and syllables are spoken of) figure as one of the terms of a proposition.

Words which are not capable of being used as names, but only as parts of names, were called by some of the schoolmen Syncategorematic terms: from σὺν, with, and κατηγορέω, to predicate, because it was only *with* some other word that they could be predicated. A word which could be used either as the subject or predicate of a proposition without being accompanied by any other word, was termed by the same authorities a Categorematic term. A combination of one or more Categorematic, and one or more Syncategore-matic words, as A heavy body, or A court of justice, they sometimes called a *mixed* term; but this seems a needless multiplication of technical expressions. A mixed term is, in the only useful sense of the word, Categorematic. It belongs to the class of what have been called many-worded names.

For, as one word is frequently not a name, but only part of a name, so a number of words often compose one single name, and no more. *f*These words, "The place which the wisdom or policy of antiquity had destined for the residence of the Abyssinian princes,"*f*[*] form in the estimation of the logician only one name; one Categorematic *g*term*g*. A mode of determining whether any set of words makes only one name, or more than one, is by

[*Samuel Johnson, *The History of Rasselas*. In *Works*. London: Buckland, 1787, Vol. XI, pp. 1–2.]

*c*MS, 43, 46 of
*d–d*MS, 43, 46 permitted
*e–e*MS The [?]
*f–f*MS, 43, 46 Thus, in the opening of the *Paradise Lost* [Bk. I, ll. 1–5] these lines,
           . . . the fruit
       Of that forbidden tree, whose mortal taste
       Brought death into the world, and all our woe,
       With loss of Eden, till one greater Man
       Restore us, and regain the blissful seat, . . .

*g–g*MS word

predicating something of it, and observing whether, by this predication, we make only one assertion or several. Thus, when we say, John Nokes, who was the mayor of the town, died yesterday—by this predication we make but one assertion; whence it appears that "John Nokes, who was the mayor of the town," is no more than one name. It is true that in this proposition, besides the assertion that John Nokes died yesterday, there is included another assertion, namely, that John Nokes was [h] mayor of the town. But this last assertion was already made: we did not make it by adding the predicate, "died yesterday." Suppose, however, that the words had been, John Nokes *and* the mayor of the town, they would have formed two names instead of one. For when we say, John Nokes and the mayor of the town died yesterday, we make two assertions: one, that John Nokes died yesterday; the other, that the mayor of the town died yesterday.

It being needless to illustrate at any greater length the subject of many-worded names, we proceed to the distinctions which have been established among names, not according to the words they are composed of, but according to their signification.

§ 3. [*General and Singular names*] All names are names of something, real or imaginary; but all things have not names appropriated to them individually. For some individual objects we require, and consequently have, separate distinguishing names; there is a name for every person, and for every remarkable place. Other objects, of which we have not occasion to speak so frequently, we do not designate by a name of their own; but when the necessity arises for naming them, we do so by putting together several words, each of which, by itself, might be and is used for an indefinite number of other objects; as when I say, *this stone*: "this" and "stone" being, each of them, names that may be used of many other objects besides the particular one meant, though the only object of which they can both be used at the given moment, consistently with their signification, may be the one of which I wish to speak.

Were this the sole purpose for which names, that are common to more things than one, could be employed; if they only served, by mutually limiting each other, to afford a designation for such individual objects as have no names of their own: they could only be ranked among contrivances for economizing the use of language. But it is evident that this is not their sole function. It is by their means that we are enabled to assert *general* propositions; to affirm or deny any predicate of an indefinite number of things at once. The distinction, therefore, between *general* names, and *individual* or *singular* names, is fundamental; and may be considered as the first grand division of names.

[h]MS the

A general name is familiarly defined, a name which is capable of being truly affirmed, in the same sense, of each of an indefinite number of things. An individual or singular name is a name which is only capable of being truly affirmed, in the same sense, of one thing.

Thus, *man* is capable of being truly affirmed of John, *a*George, Mary*a*, and other persons without assignable *b*limit*b*; and it is affirmed of all of them in the same sense; for the word man expresses certain qualities, and when we predicate it of those persons, we assert that they all possess those qualities. But *John* is only capable of being truly affirmed of one single person, at least in the same sense. For, though there are many persons who bear that name, it is not conferred upon them to indicate any qualities, or anything which belongs to them in common; and cannot be said to be affirmed of them in any *sense* at all, consequently not in the same sense. *c*"The king who succeeded William the Conqueror,"*c* is also an individual name. For, that there *d*cannot be more than one person*d* of whom it can be truly affirmed, is implied in the meaning of the words. *e*Even "*the* king," when the occasion or the context defines the individual of whom it is to be understood, may justly be regarded as an individual name.*e*

It is not unusual, by way of explaining what is meant by a general name, to say that it is the name of a *class*. But this, though a convenient mode of expression for some purposes, is objectionable as a definition, since it explains the clearer of two things by the more obscure. It would be more logical to reverse the proposition, and turn it into a definition of the word *class*: "A class is the indefinite multitude of individuals denoted by a general name."

It is necessary to distinguish *general* from *collective* names. A general name is one which can be predicated of *each* individual of a multitude; a collective name cannot be predicated of each separately, but only of all taken together. "The 76th regiment of foot *f*in the British army*f*," which is a collective name, is not a general but an individual name; for though it can be predicated of a multitude of individual soldiers taken jointly, it cannot be predicated of them severally. We may say, Jones is a soldier, and Thompson is a soldier, and Smith is a soldier, but we cannot say, Jones is the 76th regiment, and Thompson is the 76th regiment, and Smith is the 76th regiment. We can only say, Jones, and Thompson, and Smith, and Brown, and so forth (enumerating all the soldiers), are the 76th regiment.

"The 76th regiment" is a collective name, but not a general one: "a

---

*a–a*MS, 43, 46   Peter, George]   51   Peter, George, Mary

*b–b*MS, 43, 46   limits

*c–c*MS, 43, 46, 56   "The present king of England"]   51   "The present queen of England"

*d–d*MS, 43, 46, 51, 56   never can be more than one person at a time

e–e+62, 65, 68, 72

f–f+62, 65, 68, 72

regiment" is both a collective and a general name. General with respect to all individual regiments, of each of which separately it can be affirmed: collective with respect to the individual soldiers of whom any regiment is composed.

§ 4. [*Concrete and Abstract names*] The second general division of names is into *concrete* and *abstract*. A concrete name is a name which stands for a thing; an abstract name is a name which stands for an attribute of a thing. Thus *John, the sea, this table*, are names of things. *White*, also, is a name of a thing, or rather of things. Whiteness, again, is the name of a quality or attribute of those things. Man is a name of many things; humanity is a name of an attribute of those things. *Old* is a name of things; *old age* is a name of one of their attributes.

I have used the words concrete and abstract in the sense annexed to them by the schoolmen, who, notwithstanding the imperfections of their philosophy, were unrivalled in the construction of technical language, and whose definitions, in logic at least, though they never went more than a little way into the subject, have seldom, I think, been altered but to be spoiled. A practice, however, has grown up in more modern times, which, if not introduced by Locke, has gained currency chiefly from his example, of applying the expression "abstract name" to all names which are the result of abstraction or generalization, and consequently to all general names, instead of confining it to the names of attributes. The metaphysicians of the Condillac school,—whose admiration of Locke, passing over the profoundest speculations of that truly original genius, usually fastens with peculiar eagerness upon his weakest points,—have gone on imitating him in this abuse of language, until there is now some difficulty in restoring the word to its original signification. A more wanton alteration in the meaning of a word is rarely to be met with; for the expression *general name*, the exact equivalent of which exists in all languages I am acquainted with, was already available for the purpose to which *abstract* has been misappropriated, while the misappropriation leaves that important class of words, the names of attributes, without any compact distinctive appellation. The old acceptation, however, has not gone so completely out of use, as to deprive those who still adhere to it of all chance of being understood. By *abstract*, then, I shall *always, in Logic proper, mean* the opposite of *concrete*; by an abstract name, the name of an attribute; by a concrete name, the name of an object.

Do abstract names belong to the class of general, or to that of singular names? Some of them are certainly general. I mean those which are names not of one single and definite attribute, but of a class of attributes. Such is the word *colour*, which is a name common to whiteness, redness, &c. Such is

---

*a–a*MS, 43, 46, 51, 56, 62, 65   always mean]   68   always, in Logic, mean

even the word whiteness, in respect of the different shades of whiteness to which it is applied in common; the word magnitude, in respect of the various degrees of magnitude and the various dimensions of space; the word weight, in respect of the various degrees of weight. Such also is the word *attribute* itself, the common name of all particular attributes. But when only one attribute, neither variable in degree nor in kind, is designated by the name; as visibleness; tangibleness; equality; squareness; milkwhiteness; then the name can hardly be considered general; for though it denotes an attribute of many different objects, the attribute itself is always conceived as one, not many.* *b*To avoid needless logomachies, the best course would probably*b* be to consider these names as neither general nor individual, *c*and*c* to place them in a class apart.

It may be objected to our definition of an abstract name, that not only the names which we have called abstract, but adjectives, which we have placed in the concrete class, are names of attributes; that *white*, for example, is as much the name of the colour as *whiteness* is. But (as before remarked) a word ought to be considered as the name of that which we intend to be understood by it when we put it to its principal use, that is, when we employ it in predication. When we say snow is white, milk is white, linen is white, we do not mean it to be understood that snow, or linen, or milk, is a colour. We mean that they are things having the colour. The reverse is the case with the word whiteness; what we affirm to *be* whiteness is not snow, but the colour of snow. Whiteness, therefore, is the name of the colour exclusively: white is a name of all things whatever having the colour; a name, not of the quality whiteness, but of every white object. It is true, this name was given to all those various objects on account of the quality; and we may therefore say, without impropriety, that the quality forms part of its signification; but a name can only be said to stand for, or to be a name of, the things of which it can be predicated. We shall presently see that all names which can be said to have any signification, *d*all names*d* by applying which to an individual we give any information respecting that individual, may be said to *imply* an attribute of some sort; but they are not names of the attribute; it has its own proper abstract name.

§ 5. [*Connotative and Non-connotative names*] This leads *a*to the consideration of a*a* third great division of names, into *connotative* and *non-*

*[62] Vide infra, note at the end of §3, Bk. II, Chap. ii. [p. 178n.]

*b–b*MS, 43, 46, 51, 56   The question is, however, of no moment, and perhaps the best way of deciding it would
   *c–c*MS, 43, 46, 51, 56, 62, 65   but
   *d–d*MS   or
   *a–a*MS, 43, 46   us to the consideration of the

connotative, the latter sometimes, but improperly, called *absolute*. This is one of the most important distinctions which we shall have occasion to point out, and one of those which go deepest into the nature of language.

A non-connotative term is one which signifies a subject only, or an attribute only. A connotative term is one which denotes a subject, and implies an attribute. By a subject is here meant anything which possesses attributes. Thus John, or London, or England, are names which signify a subject only. Whiteness, length, virtue, signify an attribute only. None of these names, therefore, are connotative. But *white, long, virtuous*, are connotative. The word white, denotes all white things, as snow, paper, the foam of the sea, &c., and implies, or *ᵇin the language ofᵇ* the schoolmen, *connotes*,* the attribute *whiteness*. The word white is not predicated of the attribute, but of the subjects, snow, &c.; but when we predicate it of them, we *ᶜconvey the meaningᶜ* that the attribute whiteness belongs to them. The same may be said of the other words above cited. Virtuous, for example, is the name of a class, which includes Socrates, Howard, the Man of Ross, and an *ᵈundefinableᵈ* number of other individuals, past, present, and to come. *ᵉTheseᵉ* individuals, collectively and severally, can alone be said with propriety to be denoted by the word: of them alone can it properly be said to be a name. But it is a name applied to *ᶠall of themᶠ* in consequence of an attribute which they *ᵍare supposed toᵍ* possess in common, the attribute which *ʰhas received the name ofʰ* virtue. It is applied to all beings that are considered to possess this attribute; and to none which are not so considered.

All concrete general names are connotative. The word *man*, for example, denotes Peter, *ⁱJaneⁱ*, John, and an indefinite number of other individuals, of whom, taken as a class, it is the name. But it is applied to them, because they possess, and to signify that they possess, certain attributes. These seem to be, corporeity, animal life, rationality, and a certain external form, which for distinction we call the human. Every existing thing, which possessed all these attributes, would be called a man; and anything which possessed none of them, or only one, or two, or even three of them without the fourth, would not be so called. For example, if in the interior of Africa there were to be discovered a race of animals possessing reason equal to that of human beings,

---

*Notare, to mark; *connotare*, to mark *along with*; to mark one thing *with* or *in addition to* another.

ᵇ⁻ᵇMS, 43, 46, 51, 56, 62, 65, 68   as it was termed by
ᶜ⁻ᶜMS, 43, 46, 51, 56, 62, 65, 68   imply, or connote,
ᵈ⁻ᵈMS, 43, 46, 51, 56, 62   undefined
ᵉ⁻ᵉMS   Those [*printer's error?*]
ᶠ⁻ᶠMS   them all
ᵍ⁻ᵍ+51, 56, 62, 65, 68, 72
ʰ⁻ʰMS, 43, 46   men have agreed to call
ⁱ⁻ⁱMS, 43, 46   Paul

but with the form of an elephant, they would not be called men. Swift's Houyhnhnms[*] *would not be* so called. Or if such newly-discovered beings possessed the form of man without any vestige of reason, it is probable that some other name than that of man would be found for them. How it happens that there can be any doubt about the matter, will appear hereafter. The word *man*, therefore, signifies all these attributes, and all subjects which possess these attributes. But it can be predicated only of the subjects. What we call men, are the subjects, the individual Stiles and Nokes; not the qualities by which their humanity is constituted. The name, therefore, is said to signify the subjects *directly*, the attributes *indirectly*; it *denotes* the subjects, and implies, or involves, or indicates, or as we shall say henceforth *connotes*, the attributes. It is a connotative name.

Connotative names have hence been also called *denominative*, because the subject which they denote is denominated by, or receives a name from the attribute which they connote. Snow, and other objects, receive the name white, because they possess the attribute which is called whiteness; *Peter, James, and others* receive the name man because they possess the attributes which are considered to constitute humanity. The attribute, or attributes, may therefore be said to denominate those objects, or to give them a common name.*

It has been seen that all concrete general names are connotative. Even abstract names, though the names only of attributes, may in some instances be justly considered as connotative; for attributes themselves may have attributes ascribed to them; and a word which denotes attributes may connote an attribute of those attributes. *Of this description, for example, is* such a word as *fault*; equivalent to *bad* or *hurtful quality*. This word is a name common to many attributes, and connotes hurtfulness, an attribute of those various attributes. When, for example, we say that slowness, in a horse, is a fault, we do not mean that the slow movement, the actual change of place of the slow horse, *is a bad thing*, but that the property or peculiarity of the horse, from which it derives that name, the quality of being a slow mover, is an undesirable peculiarity.

[*See *Gulliver's Travels*, Bk. IV.]

*[51] Archbishop Whately, who, in the *later editions of his *Elements of Logic*, aided in reviving the important distinction treated of in the text, proposes the term "Attributive" as a substitute for "Connotative" (p. 122, 9th ed.). The expression is, in itself, appropriate; but as it has not the advantage of being connected with any verb, of so markedly distinctive a character as "to connote," it is not, I think, fitted to supply the place of the word Connotative in scientific use.

*ᶨ⁻ᶨMS, 43, 46, 51, 56, 62, 65   were not
ᵏ⁻ᵏMS, 43, 46   James and Robert]   51, 56   James, Mary and others
ˡ⁻ˡ51, 56, 62   more recent editions of his *Elements of Logic*, has
ᵐ⁻ᵐMS, 43, 46, 51   It is thus, for example, with
ⁿ⁻ⁿMS, 43, 46   has any mischievous effects]   51, 56   is a thing to be avoided

In regard to those concrete names which are not general but individual, a distinction must be made.

Proper names are not connotative: they denote the individuals who are called by them; but they do not indicate or imply any attributes as belonging to those individuals. When we name a child by the name *Paul*, or a dog by the name Cæsar, these names are simply marks used to enable those individuals to be made subjects of discourse. It may be said, indeed, that we must have had some reason for giving them those names rather than any others; and this is true; but the name, once given, *is* independent of the reason. A man may have been named John, because that was the name of his father; a town may have been named Dartmouth, because it is situated at the mouth of the Dart. But it is no part of the signification of the word John, that the father of the person so called bore the same name; nor even of the word Dartmouth, to be situated at the mouth of the Dart. If sand should choke up the mouth of the river, or an earthquake change its course, and remove it to a distance from the town, *the name of the town would not necessarily* be changed. That fact, therefore, can form no part of the signification of the word; for otherwise, when the fact *confessedly ceased to be true, no one would any longer think of applying the name*. Proper names are attached to the objects themselves, and are not dependent on the continuance of any attribute of the object.

But there is another kind of names, which, although they are individual names, that is, predicable only of one object, are really connotative. For, though we may give to an individual a name utterly unmeaning, which we call a proper name,—a word which answers the purpose of showing what thing it is we are talking about, but not of telling anything about it; yet a name peculiar to an individual is not necessarily of this description. It may be significant of some attribute, or some union of attributes, which, being possessed by no object but one, determines the name exclusively to that individual. "The sun" is a name of this description; "God," when used by a *monotheist*, is another. These, however, are scarcely examples of what we are now attempting to illustrate, being, in strictness of language, general, *not individual names: for, however they may be *in fact* predicable only of one object, there is nothing in the meaning of the words themselves which implies this: and, accordingly, when we are imagining and not affirming, we may speak of many suns; and the majority of mankind have believed, and still believe, that there are many gods. But it is easy to produce words which

o–oMS, 43, 46   Mary
p–pMS, 43, 46, 51, 56   becomes
q–qMS, 43, 46   there is no reason to think that the name of the town would
r–rMS, 43, 46   ceased to be true, the name would cease to be applied
s–sMS, 43, 46   Christian
tMS, 43, 46, 51, 56   and

are real instances of connotative individual names. It may be part of the meaning of the connotative name itself, that there "can exist" but one individual possessing the attribute which it connotes: as, for instance, "the *only* son of John Stiles;" "the *first* emperor of Rome." Or the attribute connoted may be a connexion with some determinate event, and the connexion may be of such a kind as only one individual could have; or may at least be such as only one individual actually had; and this may be implied in the form of the expression. "The father of Socrates" is an example of the one kind (since Socrates could not have had two fathers); "the author of the Iliad," "the murderer of Henri Quatre," of the second. For, though it is conceivable that more persons than one might have participated in the authorship of the Iliad, or in the murder of Henri Quatre, the employment of the article *the* implies that, in fact, this was not the case. What is here done by the word *the*, is done in other cases by the context: thus, "Cæsar's army" is an individual name, if it appears from the context that the army meant is that which Cæsar commanded in a particular battle. The still more general expressions, "the Roman army," or "the Christian army," may be individualized in a similar manner. Another case of frequent occurrence has already been noticed; it is the following. The name, being a many-worded one, may consist, in the first place, of a *general* name, capable therefore in itself of being affirmed of more things than one, but which is, in the second place, so limited by other words joined with it, that the entire expression can only be predicated of one object, consistently with the meaning of the general term. This is exemplified in such an instance as the following: "the present prime minister of England." Prime Minister of England is a general name; the attributes which it connotes may be possessed by an indefinite number of persons: in succession however, not simultaneously; since the meaning of the "name" itself imports (among other things) that there can be only one such person at a time. This being the case, and the application of the name being afterwards limited by "the article and" the word *present*, to such individuals as possess the attributes at one indivisible point of time, it becomes applicable only to one individual. And as this appears from the meaning of the name, without any extrinsic proof, it is strictly an individual name.

From the preceding observations it will easily be collected, that whenever the names given to objects convey any information, that is, whenever they have properly any meaning, the meaning resides not in what they *denote*, but in what they *connote*. The only names of objects which connote nothing are *proper* names; and these have, strictly speaking, no signification.*

*[62] A writer who entitles his book *Philosophy; or, the Science of Truth*,

ᵘ⁻ᵘMS, 43, 46, 51, 56   exists
ᵛ⁻ᵛMS, 43, 46, 51, 56, 62, 65   word
ʷ⁻ʷ+62, 65, 68, 72

If, like the robber in the *Arabian Nights*,[*] we make a mark with chalk on a house to enable us to know it again, the mark has a purpose, but it has not properly any meaning. The chalk does not declare anything about the house; it does not mean, This is such a person's house, or This is a house which contains booty. The object of making the mark is merely distinction. I say to myself, All these houses are so nearly alike that if I lose sight of them I shall not again be able to distinguish that which I am now looking at, from any of the others; I must therefore contrive to make the appearance of this one house unlike that of the others, that I may hereafter know when I see the mark—not indeed any attribute of the house—but simply that it is the same house which I am now looking at. Morgiana chalked all the other houses in a similar manner, and defeated the scheme: how? simply by obliterating the difference of appearance between that house and the others. The chalk was still there, but it no longer served the purpose of a distinctive mark.

When we impose a proper name, we perform an operation in some degree analogous to what the robber intended in chalking the house. We put a mark, not indeed upon the object itself, but, *so to* speak, upon the idea of the object. A proper name is but an unmeaning mark which we connect in our minds with the idea of the object, in order that whenever the mark meets our eyes or occurs to our thoughts, we may think of that individual object. Not being attached to the thing itself, it does not *y*, like the chalk, enable us*y* to distinguish the object when we see it; but it enables us to distinguish it when it is spoken of, either in the records of our own experience, or in the discourse of others; to know that what we find asserted in any proposition of which it is the subject, is asserted of the individual thing with which we were previously acquainted.

When we predicate of anything its proper name; when we say, pointing to a man, this is Brown or Smith, or pointing to a city, that it is York, we do not, merely by so doing, convey to the hearer any information about them,

---

charges me in his very first page (referring at the foot of it to this passage) with asserting that *general* names have properly no signification. And he repeats this statement many times in the course of his volume, with comments, not at all flattering, thereon. It is well to be now and then reminded to how great a length perverse misquotation (for, strange as it appears, I do not believe that the writer is dishonest) can sometimes go. It is a warning to readers when they see an author accused, with volume and page referred to, and the apparent guarantee of inverted commas, of maintaining something more than commonly absurd, not to give implicit credence to the assertion without verifying the reference.

[*"The History of Ali Baba, and of the Forty Robbers, Killed by One Slave," *The Arabian Nights*. Tr. Edward Forster. 5 vols. London: Miller, 1802, Vol. V, pp. 168 70.]

*x–x*MS, 43, 46   if I may so
*y–y*MS, 43, 46   enable us, as the chalk did,

except that those are their names. By enabling him to identify the individuals, we may connect them with information previously possessed by him; by saying, This is York, we may tell him that it contains the Minster. But this is in virtue of what he has previously heard concerning York; not by anything implied in the name. It is otherwise when objects are spoken of by connotative names. When we say, The town is built of marble, we give the hearer what may be entirely new information, and this merely by the signification of the many-worded connotative name, "built of marble." Such names are not signs of the mere objects, invented because we have occasion to think and speak of those objects individually; but signs which accompany an attribute: a kind of livery in which the attribute clothes all objects which are recognised as possessing it. They are not mere marks, but more, that is to say, significant marks; and the connotation is what constitutes their significance.

As a proper name is said to be the name of the one individual which it is predicated of, so (as well from the importance of adhering to analogy, as for the other reasons formerly assigned) a connotative name ought to be considered a name of all the various individuals which it is predicable of, or in other words *denotes*, and not of what it connotes. But by learning what things it is a name of, we do not learn the meaning of the name: for to the same thing we may, with equal propriety, apply many names, not equivalent in meaning. Thus, I call a certain man by the name Sophroniscus: I call him by another name, The father of Socrates. Both these are names of the same individual, but their meaning is altogether different; they are applied to that individual for two different purposes: the one, merely to distinguish him from other persons who are spoken of; the other to indicate a fact relating to him, the fact that Socrates was his son. I further apply to him these other expressions: a man, a Greek, an Athenian, a sculptor, an old man, an honest man, a brave man. All these are *, or may be,* names of Sophroniscus, not indeed of him alone, but of him and each of an indefinite number of other human beings. Each of these names is applied to Sophroniscus for a different reason, and by each whoever understands its meaning is apprised of a distinct fact or number of facts concerning him; but those who knew nothing about the names except that they were applicable to Sophroniscus, would be altogether ignorant of their meaning. It is even *possible* that I might know every single individual of whom a given name could be with truth affirmed, and yet could not be said to know the meaning of the name. A child knows who are its brothers and sisters, long before it has any definite conception of the nature of the facts which are involved in the signification of those words.

In some cases it is not easy to decide precisely how much a particular word does or does not connote; that is, we do not exactly know (the case not having arisen) what degree of difference in the object would occasion a difference in the name. Thus, it is clear that the word *man*, besides animal life and rationality, connotes also a certain external form; but it would be impossible to say precisely what form; that is, to decide how great a deviation from the form ordinarily found in the beings whom we are accustomed to call men, would suffice in a newly-discovered race to make us refuse them the name of man. Rationality, also, being a quality which admits of degrees, it has never been settled what is the lowest degree of that quality which would entitle any creature to be considered a human being. In all such cases, the meaning of the general name is so far unsettled and vague; mankind have not come to any positive agreement about the matter. When we come to treat of Classification, we shall have occasion to show under what conditions this vagueness may exist without practical inconvenience; and cases will appear in which the ends of language are better promoted by it than by complete precision; in order that, in natural history for instance, individuals or species of no very marked character may be ranged with those more strongly characterized individuals or species to which, in all their properties taken together, they bear the nearest resemblance.

But this partial uncertainty in the connotation of names can only be free from mischief when guarded by strict precautions. One of the chief sources, indeed, of lax habits of thought, is the custom of using connotative terms without a distinctly ascertained connotation, and *b*with no*b* more precise notion of their meaning than can be loosely collected from observing what objects they are used to *c*denote*c*. It is in this manner that we all acquire, and inevitably so, our first knowledge of our vernacular language. A child learns the meaning of the words *man*, or *white*, by hearing them applied to a variety of individual objects, and finding out, by a process of generalization and analysis *d*which he could not himself describe*d*, what those different objects have in common. In the case of these two words the process is so easy as to require no assistance from culture; the objects called human beings, and the objects called white, differing from all others by qualities of a peculiarly definite and obvious character. But in many other cases, objects bear a general resemblance to one another, which *e* leads to their being familiarly classed together under a common name, while, without more analytic habits than the generality of mankind possess, it is not immediately apparent what are the particular attributes, upon the possession of which in common by them all, their general resemblance depends. When this is the case, *f*people*f* use the name without any recognised connotation, that is, without any precise

---

*b–b*MS without any
*c–c*MS *denote*
*d–d*MS, 43, 46, 51, 56, 62 of which he is but imperfectly conscious
*e*MS resemblance
*f–f*MS, 43, 46 men

meaning; they talk, and consequently think, vaguely, and remain contented to attach only the same degree of significance to their own words, which a child *g* three years old attaches to the words brother and sister. The child at least is seldom puzzled by the starting up of new individuals, on whom he is ignorant whether or not to confer the title; because there is usually an authority close at hand competent to solve all doubts. But a similar resource does not exist in the generality of cases; and new objects are continually presenting themselves to men, women, and children, which they are called upon to class *proprio motu*. They, accordingly, do this on no other principle than that of superficial similarity, giving to each new object the name of that familiar object, the idea of which it most readily recalls, or which, on a cursory inspection, it seems to them most to resemble: as an unknown substance found in the ground will be called, according to its texture, earth, sand, or a stone. In this manner, names creep on from subject to subject, until all traces of a common meaning sometimes disappear, and the word comes to denote a number of things not only independently of any common attribute, but which have actually no attribute in common; or none but what is shared by other things to which the name is capriciously refused.* Even *ᶦscientific writersᶦ* have aided in this perversion of general language from its

---

ʰ[72] "Take the familiar term Stone. It is applied to mineral and rocky materials, to the kernels of fruit, to the accumulations in the gall-bladder and in the kidney; while it is refused to polished minerals (called gems), to rocks that have the cleavage suited for roofing (slates), and to baked clay (bricks). It occurs in the designation of the magnetic oxide of iron (loadstone) and not in speaking of other metallic ores. Such a term is wholly unfit for accurate reasoning, unless hedged round on every occasion by other phrases; as building stone, precious stone, gall stone, &c. Moreover, the methods of definition are baffled for want of sufficient community to ground upon. There is no quality uniformly present in the cases where it is applied, and uniformly absent where it is not applied; hence the definer would have to employ largely the licence of striking off existing applications, and taking in new ones." Bain, *Logic*, Vol. II, p. 172.*ʰ*

*g*MS of
*ʰ⁻ʰ*MS, 43, 46   *It would be well if this natural degeneracy of language took place only in the hands of the ignorant vulgar; but some of the most remarkable instances are to be found in terms of art, and among technically educated persons, such as English lawyers. *Felony*, for example, is a law term, with the sound of which all ears are familiar; but there is no lawyer who would undertake to tell what a felony is, otherwise than by enumerating the various kinds of offences which are so called. Originally the word felony had a meaning; it denoted all offences, the penalty of which included forfeiture of goods; but subsequent acts of parliament have declared various offences to be felonies without enjoining that penalty, and have taken away the penalty from others which continue nevertheless to be called felonies, insomuch that the acts so called have now no property whatever in common, save that of being unlawful and punishable.]   51, 56, 62   *It would be well if this degeneracy . . . *as MS* . . . the untaught vulgar . . . *as MS* . . . sound of which all are . . . *as MS* . . . various offences . . . *as MS* . . . forfeiture of lands or goods . . . *as MS*]   65, 68   [*no footnote*]
*ᶦ⁻ᶦ*MS, 43, 46   philosophers

purpose; sometimes because, like the vulgar, they knew no better; and sometimes in deference to that aversion to admit new words, which induces mankind, on all subjects not considered technical, to attempt to make the original *j* stock of names serve with but little augmentation to express a constantly increasing number of objects and distinctions, and, consequently, to express them in a manner progressively more and more imperfect.

To what *k*a*k* degree this loose mode of classing and denominating objects has rendered the vocabulary of mental and moral philosophy unfit for the purposes of accurate thinking, is best known to whoever has most *l*meditated*l* on the present condition of those branches of knowledge. Since, however, the introduction of a new technical language as the vehicle of speculations on *m*subjects belonging to the domain of daily discussion, is extremely difficult to effect, and would not be free from inconvenience even if effected,*m* the problem for the philosopher, and one of the most difficult which he has to resolve, is, in retaining the existing phraseology, how best to alleviate its imperfections. This can only be accomplished by giving to every general concrete name which *n*there is*n* frequent occasion to predicate, a definite and fixed connotation; in order that it may be known what attributes, when we call an object by that name, we really mean to predicate of the object. And the question of most nicety is, how to give this fixed connotation to a name, with the least possible change in the objects which the name is habitually employed to *o*denote*o*; with the least possible disarrangement, either by adding or subtraction, of the group of objects which *p*, in however imperfect a manner, it serves*p* to circumscribe and hold together; and with the least vitiation of the truth of any propositions which are commonly received as true.

This desirable purpose, of giving a fixed connotation where it is wanting, is the end aimed at whenever any one attempts to give a definition of a general name already in use; every definition of a connotative name being an attempt either merely to declare, or to declare and analyse, the connotation of the name. And the fact, that no questions which have arisen in the moral sciences have been subjects of keener controversy than the definitions of almost all the leading expressions, is a proof how great an extent the evil to which we have adverted has attained.

*j*MS, 43, 46, 51   small

k–k+62, 65, 68, 72

*l–l*MS, 43, 46, 51   reflected

*m–m*MS, 43, 46   moral subjects would not, in this country at least, be tolerated, and if tolerated, would deprive those subjects of the benefit of the habitual feelings, which have grown round the established phrases and the recognised groups, and which would not for a long time take an equally strong hold of new ones;

*n–n*MS, 43, 46   he has

*o–o*MS   *de*note

*p–p*MS, 43, 46   it serves, in however imperfect a manner,

Names with indeterminate connotation are not to be confounded with names which have more than one connotation, that is to say, [q] ambiguous words. A word may have several meanings, but all of them fixed and recognised ones; as the word *post*, for example, [r]or the word *box*,[r] the various senses of which it would be endless to enumerate. And the paucity of existing names, in comparison with the demand for them, may often render it advisable and even necessary to retain a name in this multiplicity of acceptations, distinguishing these so clearly as to prevent their being confounded with one another. Such a word may be considered as two or more names, accidentally written and spoken alike.*

*Before quitting the subject of connotative names, it is proper to observe, that the [s]first writer who, in our [t] times[s], has adopted from the schoolmen the word *to connote*, [u]Mr. [v]James[v] Mill, in his *Analysis of the Phenomena of the Human Mind*,[u] [2 vols. London: Baldwin and Cradock, 1829, Vol. II, p. 67,] employs it in a signification different from that in which it is here used. [w] He uses the word in a sense coextensive with its etymology, applying it to every case in which a name, while pointing directly to one thing, (which is consequently termed its signification,) includes also a tacit reference to some other thing. In the case [x] considered in the text, that of concrete general names, [y]his language and mine are the converse of one another[y]. Considering (very justly) the signification of the name to lie in the attribute, he speaks of the word as *noting* the attribute, and [z]connoting[z] the things possessing the attribute. And he describes abstract names as being properly concrete names with their connotation dropped: whereas, in my view, it is the *de*notation which would be said to be dropped, what was previously connoted becoming the whole signification.

In adopting a phraseology at variance with that which so high an authority, and one which [a]I am less likely than[a] any other person to undervalue, has deliberately sanctioned, I have been influenced by the urgent necessity for a term exclusively appropriated to express the manner in which a concrete general name serves to mark the attributes which are involved in its signification. This necessity can scarcely be felt in its full force by any one who has not found by experience how vain is the attempt to communicate clear ideas on the philosophy of language without such a word. It is hardly an exaggeration to say, that some of the most prevalent of the errors with which logic has been infected, and a large part of the cloudiness and confusion of ideas which have enveloped it, would, in all probability, have been avoided, if a term had been in common use to express exactly what I have

[q]MS, 43, 46   with
[r-r]+43, 46, 51, 56, 62, 65, 68, 72
[s-s]MS, 43, 46   only recent writer who, to my knowledge
[t]51   own
[u-u]+43, 46, 51, 56, 62, 65, 68, 72
[v-v]+68, 72
[w]MS   The writer to whom I allude is the late Mr. James Mill, in his *Analysis of the Phenomena of the Human Mind.*
[x]MS   which we have
[y-y]MS   Mr. Mill's language is the direct converse of mine
[z-z]MS   *con*noting
[a-a]MS   it would be more unpardonable in me than in

§ 6. [*Positive and Negative names*] The fourth principal division of names, is into *positive* and *negative*. Positive, as *man*, *ᵃtreeᵃ*, *good*; negative, as *not-man*, *ᵇnot-treeᵇ*, *not-good*. To every positive concrete name, a corresponding negative one might be framed. After giving a name to any one thing, or to any plurality of things, we might create a second name which should be a name of all things whatever, except that particular thing or things. These negative names are employed whenever we have occasion to speak collectively of all things other than some thing or class of things. When the positive name is connotative, the corresponding negative name is connotative likewise; but in a peculiar way, connoting not the presence but the absence of an attribute. Thus, *not-white* denotes all things whatever except white things; and connotes the attribute of not possessing whiteness. For the non-possession of any given attribute is also an attribute, and may receive a name as such; and thus negative concrete names may obtain negative abstract names to correspond to them.*

Names which are positive in form are often negative in reality, and others

---

signified by the term *to connote*. And the schoolmen, to whom we are indebted for the greater part of our logical language, gave us this also, and in this very sense. For though some of their general expressions countenance the use of the word in the more extensive and *ᵇvagueᵇ* acceptation in which it is taken by Mr. Mill, yet when they had to define it specifically as a technical term, and to fix its meaning as such, with that admirable precision which always *ᶜcharacterizesᶜ* their definitions, they clearly explained that nothing was said to be connoted except *forms*, which word may generally, in their writings, be understood as synonymous with *attributes*.

Now, if the word *to connote*, so well suited to the purpose to which they applied it, be diverted from that purpose by being taken to fulfil another, for which it does not seem to me to be at all required; I am unable to find any expression to replace it, but *ᵈsuch asᵈ* are commonly employed in a sense so much more general, that it would be useless attempting to associate them peculiarly with this precise idea. Such are the words, to involve, to imply, &c. By employing these, I should fail of attaining the object for which alone the name is needed, namely, to distinguish this particular kind of involving and implying from all other kinds, and to assure to it the degree of habitual attention which its importance demands.

*[72] Professor Bain (*Logic*, Vol. I, p. 56) thinks that negative names are not names of all things whatever except those denoted by the correlative positive name, but only for all things of some particular class: *not-white*, for instance, he deems not to be a name for everything in nature except white things, but only for every *coloured* thing other than white. In this case, however, as in all others, the test of what a name denotes is what it can be predicated of: and we can certainly predicate of a sound, or a smell, that it is not white. The affirmation and the negation of the same attribute cannot but divide the whole field of predication between them.

ᵇ⁻ᵇMS vaguer   ᶜ⁻ᶜMS, 43, 46 characterized
ᵈ⁻ᵈMS what
ᵃ⁻ᵃMS *stone*   ᵇ⁻ᵇMS *not-stone*

are really positive though their form is negative. The word *inconvenient*, for example, does not express the mere absence of convenience; it expresses a positive attribute, that of being the cause of discomfort or annoyance. So the word *unpleasant*, notwithstanding its negative form, does not connote the mere absence of pleasantness, but a less degree of what is signified by the word *painful*, which, it is hardly necessary to say, is positive. *Idle*, on the other hand, is a word which, though positive in form, expresses nothing but what would be signified either by the phrase *not working*, or by the phrase *not disposed to work*; and *sober*, either by *not drunk* or by *not drunken*.

There is a class of names called *privative*. A privative name is equivalent in its signification to a positive and a negative name taken together; being the name of something which has once had a particular attribute, or for some other reason might have been expected to have it, but which has it not. Such is the word *blind*, which is not equivalent to *not seeing*, or to *not capable of seeing*, for it would not, except by a poetical or rhetorical figure, be applied to stocks and stones. A thing is not usually said to be blind, unless the class to which it is most familiarly referred, or to which it is referred on the particular occasion, be chiefly composed of things which can see, as in the case of a blind man, or a blind horse; or unless it is supposed for any reason that it ought to see; as in saying of a man, that he rushed blindly into an abyss, or of philosophers or the clergy that the greater part of them are blind guides. The names called privative, therefore, connote two things; the absence of certain attributes, and the presence of others, from which the presence also of the former might naturally have been expected.

§ 7. [*Relative and Absolute names*] The fifth leading division of names is into *relative* and *absolute*, or let us rather say, *relative* and *non-relative*; for the word absolute is put upon much too hard duty in metaphysics, not to be willingly spared when its services can be dispensed with. It resembles the word *civil* in the language of jurisprudence, which stands for the opposite of criminal, the opposite of ecclesiastical, the opposite of military, the opposite of political—in short, the opposite of any positive word which wants a negative.

Relative names are such as father, son; ruler, subject; like; equal; unlike; unequal; longer, shorter; cause, effect. Their characteristic property is, that they are always given in pairs. Every relative name which is predicated of an object, supposes another object (or objects), of which we may predicate either that same name or another relative name which is said to be the *correlative* of the former. Thus, when we call any person a son, we suppose other persons who must be called parents. When we call any event a cause, we suppose another event which is an effect. When we say of any distance that it is longer, we suppose another distance which is shorter. When we say of any object that it is like, we mean that it is like some other object, which is also said to be like the first. In this *last* case both objects receive the same name; the relative term is its own correlative.

It is evident that these words, when concrete, are, like other concrete general names, connotative; they denote a subject, and connote an attribute; and each of them has or might have a corresponding abstract name, to denote the attribute connoted by the concrete. Thus the concrete *like* has its abstract *likeness*; the concretes, father and son, have *b*, or might have,*b* the abstracts, paternity, and *filiety, or sonship*. The concrete name connotes an attribute, and the abstract name which answers to it denotes that attribute. But of what nature is the attribute? Wherein consists the peculiarity in the connotation of a relative name?

The attribute signified by a relative name, say some, is a relation; and this they give, if not as a sufficient explanation, at least as the only one attainable. If they are asked, What then is a relation? they do not profess to be able to tell. It is generally regarded as something peculiarly recondite and mysterious. I cannot, however, perceive in what respect it is more so than any other attribute; indeed, it appears to me to be so in a somewhat less degree. I conceive rather, that it is by examining into the signification of relative names, or, in other words, into the nature of the attribute which they connote, that a clear insight may best be obtained into the nature of all attributes: of all that is meant by an attribute.

It is obvious, in fact, that if we take any two correlative names, *father* and *son* for instance, though the objects *de*noted by the names are different, they both, in a certain sense, connote the same thing. They cannot, indeed, be said to connote the same *attribute*: to be a father, is not the same thing as to be a son. But when we call one man a father, another *a* son, what we mean to affirm is a set of facts, which are exactly the same in both cases. To predicate of A that he is the father of B, and of B that he is the son of A, is to assert one and the same fact in different words. The two propositions are exactly equivalent: neither of them asserts more or asserts less than the other. The paternity of A and the *filiety* of B are not two facts, but two modes of expressing the same fact. That fact, when analysed, consists of a series of physical events or phenomena, in which both A and B are parties concerned, and from which they both derive names. What those names really connote, is *this* series of events: that is the meaning, and the whole meaning, which either of them is intended to convey. The series of events may be said to

a–a+51, 56, 62, 65, 68, 72
b–b+51, 56, 62, 65, 68, 72
*c–c*MS, 43, 46   filiation]   51, 56   filiety, or filiation
*d–d*MS, 43, 46, 51, 56, 62   his
*e–e*MS, 43, 46   filiation
*f–f*MS   the

constitute the relation; the schoolmen called it the foundation of the relation, *fundamentum relationis*.

In this manner any fact, or series of facts, in which two different objects are implicated, and which is therefore predicable of both of them, may be either considered as constituting an attribute of the one, or an attribute of the other. According as we consider it in the former, or in the latter aspect, it is connoted by the one or the other of the two correlative names. *Father* connotes the fact, regarded as constituting an attribute of A; *son* connotes the same fact, as constituting an attribute of B. It may evidently be regarded with equal propriety in either light. And all that appears necessary to account for the existence of relative names, is, that whenever there is a fact in which two individuals are *g* concerned, an attribute grounded on that fact may be ascribed to either of these individuals.

A name, therefore, is said to be relative, when, over and above the object which it denotes, it implies in its signification the existence of another object, also deriving a denomination from the same fact which is the ground of the first name. Or (to express the same meaning in other words) a name is relative, when, being the name of one thing, its signification cannot be explained but by mentioning another. Or we may state it thus—when the name cannot be employed in discourse so as to have a meaning, unless the name of some other thing than what it is itself the name of, be either expressed or understood. *h*These definitions*h* are all, at bottom, equivalent, being modes of variously expressing this one distinctive circumstance—that every other attribute of an object might, without any contradiction, be conceived still to exist if *i*no object besides that one had ever existed*i*;* but those of its attributes which are expressed by relative names, would on that supposition be swept away.

§ 8. [*Univocal and Æquivocal names*] Names have been further distinguished into *univocal* and *æquivocal*: these, however, are not two kinds of names, but two different modes of employing names. A name is univocal, or

---

*Or rather, all objects except itself and the percipient mind; for, as we shall see hereafter, to ascribe any attribute to an object, necessarily implies a mind to perceive it.

*j*The simple and clear explanation given in the text, of relation and relative names, a subject so long the opprobrium of metaphysics, was given (as far as I know) for the first time, by Mr. James Mill, in his *Analysis of the Phenomena of the Human Mind* [Vol. II, pp. 6ff.].*j*

*g*MS, 43, 46   alike
*h–h*MS, 43, 46   We may take our choice among these definitions. They
*i–i*MS 43, 46, 51, 56   all objects besides that one were annihilated
j–j+68, 72

applied univocally, with respect to all things of which it can be predicated *in the same sense*; [a] it is æquivocal, or applied æquivocally, as respects those things of which it is predicated in different senses. It is scarcely necessary to give instances of a fact so familiar as the double meaning of a word. In reality, as has been already observed, an æquivocal or ambiguous word is not one name, but two names, accidentally coinciding in sound. *File* [b]meaning a steel[b] instrument, and *file* [c]meaning[c] a line of soldiers, have no more title to be considered one word, because written alike, than *grease* and *Greece* have, because they are pronounced alike. They are one sound, appropriated to form two different words.

An intermediate case is that of a name used *analogically* or metaphorically; that is, a name which is predicated of two things, not univocally, or exactly in the same signification, but in significations somewhat similar, and which being derived one from the other, one of them may be considered the primary, and the other a secondary signification. As when we speak of a brilliant light and a brilliant achievement. The word is not applied in the same sense to the light and to the achievement; but having been applied to the light in its original sense, that of brightness to the eye, it is transferred to the achievement in a derivative signification, supposed to be somewhat like the primitive one. The word, however, is just as properly two names instead of one, in this case, as in that of the most perfect ambiguity. And one of the commonest forms of fallacious reasoning arising from ambiguity, is that of arguing from a metaphorical expression as if it were literal; that is, as if a word, when applied metaphorically, were the same name as when taken in its original sense: which will be seen more particularly in its place.

[a]MS, 43, 46, 51, 56   but
[b–b]MS, 43, 46, 51   standing for an iron
[c–c]MS, 43, 46, 51   standing for

CHAPTER III

Of the Things Denoted by Names

§ 1. [*Necessity of an enumeration of Nameable Things. The Categories of Aristotle*] Looking back now to the commencement of our inquiry, let us attempt to measure how far it has advanced. Logic, we found, is the Theory of Proof. But proof supposes something provable, which must be a Proposition or Assertion; since nothing but a Proposition can be an object of belief, *or* therefore of proof. A Proposition is, discourse which affirms or denies something of some other thing. This is one step: there must, it seems, be two things concerned in every act of belief. But what are these Things? They can be no other than those signified by the two names, which being joined together by a copula constitute the Proposition. If, therefore, we knew what all names signify, we should know everything which *b*, in the existing state of human knowledge,*b* is capable either of being made a subject of affirmation or denial, or of being itself affirmed or denied of a subject. We have accordingly, in the preceding chapter, reviewed the various kinds of Names, in order to ascertain what is signified by each of them. And we have now carried this survey far enough to be able to take an account of its results, and to exhibit an enumeration of all *c* kinds of Things which are capable of being made predicates, or of having anything predicated of them: after which to determine the import of Predication, that is, of Propositions, can be no arduous task.

The necessity of an enumeration of Existences, as the basis of Logic, did not escape the attention of the schoolmen, and of their master Aristotle, the most comprehensive, if not *d*also*d* the most sagacious, of the ancient philosophers.[*] The Categories, or Predicaments—the former a Greek word, the latter its literal translation in the Latin language—were *e*believed to be*e* an enumeration of all things capable of being named; an enumeration by the *summa genera, i.e.* the most extensive classes into which things could be distributed; which, therefore, were so many highest Predicates, one or other

[*See Aristotle. *The Categories*, in his *Organon*. Ed. Harold P. Cooke and Hugh Tredennick. London: Heinemann, 1938.]

*a–a*MS nor
*c*MS, 43, 46, 51, 56 the
*e–e*MS, 43, 46, 51, 56, 62, 65, 68

b–b+68, 72
d–d+56, 62, 65, 68, 72
intended by him and his followers as

of which was supposed capable of being affirmed with truth of every name-able thing whatsoever. The following are the classes into which, according to this school of philosophy, Things in general might be reduced:

Οὐσία,	Substantia.
Ποσόν,	Quantitas.
Ποιόν,	Qualitas.
Πρός τι,	Relatio.
Ποιεῖν,	Actio.
Πάσχειν,	Passio.
Ποῦ,	Ubi.
Πότε,	Quando.
Κεῖσθαι,	Situs.
Ἔχειν,	Habitus.

The imperfections of this classification are too obvious to require, and its merits are not sufficient to reward, a minute examination. It is a mere cata-logue of the distinctions rudely marked out by the language of familiar life, with little or no attempt to penetrate, by philosophic analysis, to the *rationale* even of those common distinctions. Such an analysis, however superficially conducted, would have shown the enumeration to be both redundant and defective. Some objects are omitted, and others repeated several times under different heads. It is like a division of animals into men, quadrupeds, horses, asses, and ponies. That, for instance, could not be a very comprehensive view of the nature of Relation which could exclude action, passivity, and local situation from that category. The same observation applies to the categories Quando (or position in time), and Ubi (or position in space); while the distinction between the latter and Situs is merely verbal. The in-congruity of erecting into a *summum genus* the class which forms the tenth category is manifest. On the other hand, the enumeration takes no notice of anything besides substances and attributes. In what category are we to place sensations, or any other feelings and states of mind; as hope, joy, fear; sound, smell, taste; pain, pleasure; thought, judgment, conception, and the like? Probably all these would have been placed by the Aristotelian school in the categories of *actio* and *passio*; and the relation of such of them as are active, to their objects, and of such of them as are passive, to their causes, would rightly be so placed; but the things themselves, the feelings or states of mind, wrongly. Feelings, or states of consciousness, are assuredly to be ʲaccountedʲ among realities, but they cannot be reckoned either among substances or attributes.*

*[72] On the preceding passage Professor Bain remarks (*Logic*, Vol. I, p. 265): "The Categories do not seem to have been intended as a classification of Name-

ʲ⁻ʲMS, 43, 46, 51, 56, 62, 65, 68 counted

§ 2. [*Ambiguity of the most general names*] Before recommencing, under better auspices, the attempt made with such imperfect success by the *early logicians*, we must take notice of an unfortunate ambiguity in all the concrete names which correspond to the most general of all abstract terms, the word Existence. When we have occasion for a name which shall be capable of denoting whatever exists, as contradistinguished from non-entity or Nothing, there is hardly a word applicable to the purpose which is not also, and even more familiarly, taken in a sense in which it denotes only substances. But substances are not all that *exists*; attributes, if such things are to be spoken of, must be said to exist; feelings *certainly* exist. Yet when we speak of an *object*, or of a *thing*, we are almost always supposed to mean a substance. There seems a kind of contradiction in using such an expression as that one *thing* is merely an attribute of another thing. And the announcement of a Classification of Things would, I believe, prepare most readers for an enumeration like those in natural history, beginning with the great divisions of animal, vegetable, and mineral, and subdividing them into classes and

---

able Things, in the sense of 'an enumeration of all kinds of Things which are capable of being made predicates, or of having anything predicated of them.' They seem to have been rather intended as a generalization of *predicates*; an analysis of the final import of predication. Viewed in this light, they are not open to the objections offered by Mr. Mill. The proper question to ask is not—In what Category are we to place sensations or other feelings or states of mind? but, Under what Categories can we predicate regarding states of mind? Take, for example, Hope. When we say that it is a state of mind, we predicate Substance: we may also describe how great it is (Quantity), what is the quality of it, pleasurable or painful (Quality), what it has reference to (Relation). Aristotle seems to have framed the Categories on the plan—Here is an individual; what is the final analysis of all that we can predicate about him?"

This is doubtless a true statement of the leading idea in the classification. The Category Οὐσία was certainly understood by Aristotle to be a general name for all possible answers to the question Quid sit? when asked respecting a concrete individual; as the other Categories are names comprehending all possible answers to the questions Quantum sit? Quale sit? &c. In Aristotle's conception, therefore, the Categories may not have been a classification of Things; but they were soon converted into one by his Scholastic followers, who certainly regarded and treated them as a classification of Things, and carried them out as such, dividing down the Category Substance as a naturalist might do, into the different classes of physical or metaphysical objects as distinguished from attributes, and the other Categories into the principal varieties of quantity, quality, relation, &c. It is, therefore, a just subject of complaint against them, that they had no Category of Feeling. Feeling is assuredly predicable as a summum genus, of every particular kind of feeling, for instance, as in Mr. Bain's example, of Hope: but it cannot be brought within any of the Categories as interpreted either by Aristotle or by his followers.

a–aMS, 43, 46, 51, 56, 62, 65, 68   great founder of the science of logic
b–bMS, 43, 46, 51, 56, 62   exist   c–cMS, 43, 46, 51, 56   also

orders. If, rejecting the word Thing, we endeavour to find another of a more general import, or at least more exclusively confined to that general import, a word denoting all that exists, and connoting only simple existence; no word might be presumed fitter for such a purpose than *being*: originally the present participle of a verb which in one of its meanings is exactly equivalent to the verb *d exists d*; and therefore suitable, even by its grammatical formation, to be the concrete of the abstract *existence*. But this word, strange as the fact may appear, is still more completely spoiled for the purpose which it seemed expressly made for, than the word Thing. *Being* is, by custom, exactly synonymous with substance; except that it is free from a slight taint of a second ambiguity; being applied impartially to matter and to mind, while substance, though originally and in strictness applicable to both, is apt to suggest in preference the idea of matter. Attributes are never called Beings; nor are feelings. A Being is that which excites feelings, and which possesses attributes. The soul is called a Being; God and angels are called Beings; but if we were to say, extension, colour, wisdom, virtue, are beings, we should perhaps be suspected of thinking with some of the ancients, that the cardinal virtues are animals; or, at the least, of holding with the Platonic school the doctrine of self-existent Ideas, or with the followers of Epicurus that of Sensible Forms, which detach themselves in every direction from bodies, and by coming in contact with our organs, cause our perceptions. We should be supposed, in short, to believe that Attributes are Substances.

In consequence of this perversion of the word Being, philosophers looking about for something to supply its place, laid their hands upon the word Entity, a piece of barbarous Latin, invented by the schoolmen to be used as an abstract name, in which class its grammatical form would seem to place it; but being seized by logicians in distress to stop a leak in their terminology, it has ever since been used as a concrete name. The kindred word *essence*, born at the same time and of the same parents, scarcely underwent a more complete transformation when, from being the abstract of the verb *to be*, it came to denote something sufficiently concrete to be enclosed in a glass bottle. The word Entity, since it settled down into a concrete name, has retained its universality of signification somewhat less *e impaired e* than any of the names before mentioned. Yet the same gradual decay to which, after a certain age, all the language of psychology seems liable, has been at work even here. If you call virtue an *entity*, you are indeed somewhat less strongly suspected of believing it to be a substance than if you called it a *being*; but you are by no means free from the suspicion. Every word which was originally intended to connote mere existence, seems, after a *f* time, to enlarge its connotation to *separate* existence, or existence freed from the condition of

*d–d*MS, 43, 46, 51, 56, 62   *exist*
*e–e*MS, 43, 46   unimpaired   *f*62, 65, 68   long

belonging to a substance; which condition being precisely what constitutes an attribute, attributes are gradually shut out; and along with them feelings, which in ninety-nine cases out of a hundred have no other name than that of the attribute which is grounded on them. Strange that when the greatest embarrassment *felt by* all who have any considerable number of thoughts to express, is to find a sufficient variety of *precise* words *fitted* to express them, there should be no practice to which even *scientific thinkers* are more addicted than that of taking valuable words to express ideas which are sufficiently expressed by other words already appropriated to them.

When it is impossible to obtain good tools, the next best thing is to understand thoroughly the defects of those we have. I have therefore warned the reader of the ambiguity of the *k* names which, for want of better, I am necessitated to employ. It must now be the writer's endeavour so to employ them as in no case to leave *the* meaning doubtful or obscure. No one of the above terms being altogether unambiguous, I shall not confine myself to any one, but shall employ on each occasion the word which seems least likely in the particular case to lead to *misunderstanding*; nor do I pretend to use either these or any other words with a rigorous adherence to one single sense. To do so would often leave us without a word to express what is signified by a known word in some one or other of its senses: unless authors had an unlimited licence to coin new words, together with (what it would be more difficult to assume) unlimited power of making *readers understand* them. Nor would it be wise in a writer, on a subject involving so much of abstraction, to deny himself the advantage derived from even an improper use of a term, when, by means of it, some familiar association is called up which brings the meaning home to the mind, as it were by a flash.

The difficulty both to the writer and reader, of the attempt which must be made to use vague words so as to convey a precise meaning, is not wholly a matter of regret. It is not unfitting that logical treatises should afford an example of that, to facilitate which is among the most important uses of logic. Philosophical language will for a long time, and popular language *still longer*, retain so much of vagueness and ambiguity, that logic would be of little value if it did not, among its other advantages, exercise the understanding in doing its work neatly and correctly with these imperfect tools.

*g–g*MS of
h–h+51, 56, 62, 65, 68, 72
*i–i*MS wherewith
*j–j*MS, 43, 46 philosophers
*k*MS, 43, 46, 51, 56, 62 very
*l–l*MS, 43, 46 his
*m–m*MS, 43, 46 a misunderstanding of my meaning
*n–n*MS their readers receive] 43, 46, 51, 56 their readers adopt] 62, 65 their readers understand
*o–o*MS, 43, 46 perhaps always

After this preamble it is time to proceed to our enumeration. We shall commence with Feelings, the simplest class of nameable things; the term Feeling being of course understood in its most enlarged sense.

I. FEELINGS, OR STATES OF CONSCIOUSNESS

§ 3. [*Feelings, or states of consciousness*] A Feeling and a State of Consciousness are, in the language of philosophy, equivalent expressions: everything is a feeling of which the mind is conscious; everything which it *feels*, or, in other words, which forms a part of its own sentient existence. In popular language Feeling is not always synonymous with State of Consciousness; being often taken more peculiarly for those states which are conceived as belonging to the sensitive, or to the emotional, phasis of our nature, and sometimes, with a still narrower restriction, to the emotional alone, as distinguished from what are conceived as belonging to the percipient or *ᵃto theᵃ* intellectual phasis. But this is an admitted departure from correctness of language; just as, by a popular perversion the exact converse of this, the word Mind is withdrawn from its rightful generality of signification, and restricted to the intellect. The still greater perversion by which Feeling is sometimes confined not only to bodily sensations, but to the sensations of a single sense, that of touch, needs not be more particularly adverted to.

Feeling, in the proper sense of the term, is a genus, of which Sensation, Emotion, and Thought, are subordinate species. Under the word Thought is here to be included whatever we are internally conscious of when we are said to think; from the consciousness we have when we think of a red colour without having it before our eyes, to the most recondite thoughts of a philosopher or poet. Be it remembered, however, that by a thought is to be understood what passes in the mind itself, and not any object external to the mind, which the person is commonly said to be thinking of. He may be thinking of the sun, or of God, but the sun and God are not thoughts; his mental image, however, of the sun, and his idea of God, are thoughts; states of his mind, not of the objects themselves; and so also is his belief of the existence of the sun, or of God; or his disbelief, if the case be so. Even imaginary objects (which are said to exist only in our ideas) are to be distinguished from our ideas of them. I may think of a hobgoblin, as I may think of the loaf which was eaten yesterday, or of the flower which will bloom to-morrow. But the hobgoblin which never existed is not the same thing with my idea of a hobgoblin, any more than the loaf which once existed is the same thing with my idea of a loaf, or the flower which does not yet exist, but which will exist, is the same with my idea of a flower. They are all, not thoughts, but

ᵃ⁻ᵃ+51, 56, 62, 65, 68, 72

objects of thought; though at the present time all the objects are alike non-existent.

In like manner, a Sensation is to be carefully distinguished from the object which causes the sensation; our sensation of white from a white object: nor is it less to be distinguished from the attribute whiteness, which we ascribe to the object in consequence of its exciting the sensation. Unfortunately for clearness and due discrimination in considering these subjects, our sensations seldom receive separate names. We have a name for the objects which produce in us a certain sensation: the word *white*. We have a name for the quality in those objects, to which we ascribe the sensation: the name *whiteness*. But when we speak of the sensation itself (as we have not occasion to do this often except in our *b*scientific*b* speculations), language, which adapts itself for the most part only to the common uses of life, has provided us with no single-worded or immediate designation; we must employ a circumlocution, and say, The sensation of white, or The sensation of whiteness; we must denominate the sensation either from the object, or from the attribute, by which it is excited. Yet the sensation, though it never *does*, might very well be *conceived* to exist, without anything whatever to excite it. We can conceive it as arising spontaneously in the mind. But if it so arose, we should have no name to denote it which would not be a misnomer. In the case of our sensations of hearing we are better provided; we have the word Sound, and a whole vocabulary of words to denote the various kinds of sounds. For as we are often conscious of these sensations in the absence of any perceptible object, we can more easily conceive having them in the absence of any object whatever. We need only shut our eyes and listen to music, to have a conception of an universe with nothing in it except sounds, and ourselves hearing them: and what is easily conceived separately, easily obtains a separate name. But in general our names of sensations denote indiscriminately the sensation and the attribute. Thus, *colour* stands for the sensations of white, red, &c., but also for the quality in the coloured object. We talk of the colours of things as among their *properties*.

§ 4. [*Feelings must be distinguished from their physical antecedents. Perceptions, what*] In the case of sensations, another distinction has also to be kept in view, which is often confounded, and never without mischievous consequences. This is, the distinction between the sensation itself, and the state of the bodily organs which precedes the sensation, and which constitutes the physical agency by which it is produced. One of the sources of confusion on this subject is the division commonly made of feelings into Bodily and Mental. Philosophically speaking, there is no foundation at all for this distinction: even sensations are states of the sentient mind, not states of the

---

*b–b*MS, 43, 46   philosophical

body, as distinguished from it. What I am conscious of when I see the colour blue, is a feeling of blue colour, which is one thing; the picture on my retina, or the phenomenon of hitherto mysterious nature which takes place in my optic nerve or in my brain, is another thing, of which I am not at all conscious, and which scientific investigation alone could have apprised me of. These are states of my body; but the sensation of blue, which is the consequence of these states of body, is not a state of body: that which perceives and is conscious is called Mind. When sensations are called bodily feelings, it is only as being the class of feelings which are immediately occasioned by bodily states; whereas the other kinds of feelings, thoughts, for instance, or emotions, are immediately excited not by anything acting upon the bodily organs, but by sensations, or by previous thoughts. This, however, is a distinction not in our feelings, but in the agency which produces our feelings: all of them when actually produced are states of mind.

Besides the affection of our bodily organs from without, and the sensation thereby produced in our minds, many writers admit a third link in the chain of phenomena, which they *call* a Perception, and which consists in the recognition of an external object as the exciting cause of the sensation. This perception, they say, is an *act* of the mind, proceeding from its own spontaneous activity; while in *a* sensation the mind is passive, being merely acted upon by the outward object. And according to some *metaphysicians,* it is by an act of the mind, similar to perception, except in not being preceded by any sensation, that *the existence of God, the soul, and other hyperphysical objects is recognised*.

These acts of *what is termed* perception, whatever be the conclusion ultimately come to respecting their nature, must, I conceive, take their place among the varieties of feelings or states of mind. In so classing them, I have not the smallest intention of declaring or insinuating any theory as to the law of mind in which these mental processes may be supposed to originate, or the conditions under which they may be legitimate or the reverse. Far less do I mean (as Dr. Whewell seems to suppose must be meant in an analogous case*) to indicate that as they are "*merely* states of mind," it is superfluous to inquire into their distinguishing peculiarities. I abstain from the inquiry as irrelevant to the science of logic. In these so-called perceptions, or direct recognitions by the mind, of objects, whether physical or spiritual, which are external to itself, I can see only cases of belief; but of belief which claims to

Philosophy of the Inductive Sciences, Vol. I, p. 40.

*a-a*MS, 43, 46   term
b-b+56, 62, 65, 68, 72
*c-c*MS, 43, 46   philosophers
*d-d*MS, 43, 46   we recognise the existence of God, of the soul, and other hyperphysical realities
e-e+51, 56, 62, 65, 68, 72

be intuitive, or independent of external evidence. When a stone lies before me, I am conscious of certain sensations which I receive from it; but *if* I say that these sensations come to me from an external object which I *perceive*, the meaning of these words is, that receiving the sensations, I intuitively *believe* that an external cause of those sensations exists. The laws of intuitive belief, and the conditions under which it is legitimate, are a subject which, as we have already so often remarked, belongs not to logic, but to the *science of the ultimate laws of the human mind*.

h To the same region of speculation belongs all that can be said respecting the distinction which the German metaphysicians and their French and English followers *i* so elaborately draw between the *acts* of the mind and its merely passive *states*; between what it receives from, and what it gives to, the crude materials of its experience. I am aware that with reference to the view which those writers take of the primary elements of thought and knowledge, this distinction is fundamental. But for *the present* purpose, which is to examine, not the original groundwork of our knowledge, but how we come by that portion of it which is not original; the difference between active and passive states of mind is of secondary importance. For us, they are all states of mind, they all are feelings; by which, let it be said once more, I mean to imply nothing of passivity, but simply that they are psychological facts, facts which take place in the mind, and *are* to be carefully distinguished from the external or physical facts with which they may be connected either as effects or as causes.

§ 5. [*Volitions, and Actions, what*] Among active states of mind, there is, however, one species which merits particular attention, because it forms a principal part of the connotation of some important classes of names. I mean *volitions*, or acts of the will. When we speak of sentient beings by relative names, a large portion of the connotation of the name usually consists of the actions of those beings; actions past, present, and possible or probable future. Take, for instance, the words Sovereign and Subject. What meaning do these words convey, but that of innumerable actions, done or to be done by the sovereign and the subjects, to or in regard to one another reciprocally? So with the words physician and patient, leader and follower, *tutor and pupil*. In many cases the words also connote actions which would be done under certain contingencies by persons other than those denoted: as the words mortgagor and mortgagee, obligor and obligee, and many other words ex-

*f–f*MS, 43, 46, 51   when
*g–g*MS, 43, 46   higher or transcendental branch of metaphysics
*h*MS   §5.
*i*MS, 43   (among whom Mr. Whewell is one of the most distinguished,)
*j–j*MS, 43, 46   our   *k–k*+51, 56, 62, 65, 68, 72
*a–a*MS   [*no section division*]   *b–b*MS, 43, 46   master and servant

pressive of legal relation, which connote what a court of justice would do to enforce the legal obligation if not fulfilled. There are also words which connote actions previously done by persons other than those denoted either by the name itself or by its correlative; as the word brother. From these instances, it may be seen how large a portion of the connotation of names consists of actions. Now what is an action? Not one thing, but a series of two things: the state of mind called a volition, followed by an effect. The volition or intention to produce the effect, is one thing; the effect produced in consequence of the intention, is another thing; the two together constitute the action. I form the purpose of instantly moving my arm; that is a state of my mind: my arm (not being tied ᶜorᶜ paralytic) moves in obedience to my purpose; that is a physical fact, consequent on a state of mind. The intention, ᵈ followed by the fact, or (if we prefer the expression) the fact when preceded and caused by the intention, is called the action of moving my arm.

§ 6. [*Substance and Attribute*] Of the first leading division of nameable things, viz. Feelings or States of Consciousness, we began by recognising three sub-divisions; Sensations, Thoughts, and Emotions. The first two of these we have illustrated at considerable length; the third, Emotions, not being perplexed by similar ambiguities, does not require similar exemplification. And, finally, we have found it necessary to add to these three a fourth species, commonly known by the name Volitions. ᵃ We shall ᵇnowᵇ proceed to the two remaining classes of nameable things; all things which are ᶜregarded asᶜ external to the mind being considered as belonging either to the class of Substances or to that of Attributes.

II. SUBSTANCES

Logicians have endeavoured to define Substance and Attribute; but their definitions are not so much attempts to draw a distinction between the things themselves, as instructions what difference it is customary to make in the grammatical structure of the sentence, according as ᵈweᵈ are speaking of substances or of attributes. Such definitions are rather lessons of English, or of Greek, Latin, or German, than of mental philosophy. An attribute, say the school logicians, must be the attribute *of* something; colour, for example,

ᶜ⁻ᶜMS, 43, 46 nor
ᵈMS, 43, 46 when
ᵃMS, 43, 46, 51, 56, 62, 65, 68 Without seeking to prejudge the metaphysical question whether any mental state or phenomenon can be found which is not included in one or other of these four species, it appears to me that the amount of illustration bestowed upon these may, so far as we are concerned, suffice for the whole genus.
ᵇ⁻ᵇMS, 43, 46, 51, 56, 62, 65, 68 , therefore,
ᶜ⁻ᶜ+72
ᵈ⁻ᵈMS, 43, 46 you

must be the colour *of* something; goodness must be the goodness *of* something: and if this something should cease to exist, or should cease to be connected with the attribute, the existence of the attribute would be at an end. A substance, on the contrary, is self-existent; in speaking about it, we need not put *of* after its name. A stone is not the stone *of* anything; the moon is not the moon *of* anything, but simply the moon. Unless, indeed, the name which we choose to give to the substance be a relative name; if so, it must be followed either by *of*, or by some other particle, implying, as that preposition does, a reference to something else: but then the other characteristic peculiarity of an attribute would fail; the *something* might be destroyed, and the substance might still subsist. Thus, a father must be the father *of* something, and so far resembles an attribute, in being referred to something besides himself: if there were no child, there would be no father: but this, when we look into the matter, only means that we should not call him father. The man called father might still exist though *there were no child, as he existed before there was a child:* and there would be no contradiction in supposing him to exist, though the whole universe except himself were destroyed. But destroy all white substances, and where would be the attribute whiteness? Whiteness, without any white thing, is a contradiction in terms.

This is the nearest approach to a solution of the difficulty, that will be found in the common treatises on logic. It will scarcely be thought to be a satisfactory one. If an attribute is distinguished from a substance by being the attribute *of* something, it seems highly necessary to understand what is meant by *of*; a particle which needs explanation too much itself, to be placed in front of the explanation of anything else. And as for the self-existence of *substance*, it is very true that a substance may be conceived to exist without any other substance, but so also may an attribute without any other attribute: and we can no more imagine a substance without attributes than we can imagine attributes without a substance.

Metaphysicians, however, have probed the question deeper, and given an account of Substance considerably more satisfactory than this. Substances are usually distinguished as Bodies or Minds. Of *each* of these, philosophers have at length provided us with a definition which seems unexceptionable.

§ 7. [*Body*] A body, according to the received doctrine of modern metaphysicians, may be defined, the external cause to which we ascribe our sensations. When I see and touch a piece of gold, I am conscious of a sensation of yellow colour, and sensations of hardness and weight; and by varying the mode of handling, I may add to these sensations many others completely distinct from them. The sensations are all of which I am directly conscious;

*e–e*MS, 43, 46   the child were annihilated;
*f–f*MS, 43, 46, 51   substances   *g–g*MS   the former

but I consider them as produced by something not only existing independently of my will, but external to my bodily organs and to my mind. This external something I call a body.

It may be asked, how come we to ascribe our sensations to any external cause? And is there sufficient ground for so ascribing them? It is known, that there are metaphysicians who have raised a controversy on the point; maintaining ^a that we are not warranted in referring our sensations to a cause such as we understand by the word Body, or to any ^bexternal cause whatever^b. Though we have no concern here with this controversy, nor with the metaphysical niceties on which it turns, one of the best ways of showing what is meant by Substance is, to consider what position it is necessary to take up, in order to maintain its existence against opponents.

It is certain, then, that a part of our notion of a body consists of the notion of a number of sensations of our own, or of other sentient beings, habitually occurring simultaneously. My conception of the table at which I am writing is compounded of its visible form and size, which are complex sensations of sight; its tangible form and size, which are complex sensations of our ^corgans^c of touch and of our muscles; its weight, which is also a sensation of touch and of the muscles; its colour, which is a sensation of sight; its hardness, which is a sensation of the muscles; its composition, which is another word for all the varieties of sensation which we receive under various circumstances from the wood of which it is made, and so forth. All or most of these various sensations frequently are, and, as we learn by experience, always might be, experienced simultaneously, or in many different orders of succession at our own choice: and hence the thought of any one of them makes us think of the others, and the whole ^dbecomes^d mentally amalgamated into one mixed state of consciousness, which, in the language of the school of Locke and Hartley, is termed a Complex Idea.

Now, there are philosophers who have argued as follows. If we ^econceive an orange^e to be divested of its natural colour without acquiring any new one; to lose its softness without becoming hard, its roundness without becoming square or pentagonal, or of any other regular or irregular figure whatever; to be deprived of size, of weight, of taste, of smell; to lose all its mechanical and all its chemical properties, and acquire no new ones; to become, in short, invisible, intangible, ^f imperceptible not only by all our senses, but by the senses of all other sentient beings, real or possible; nothing,

---

^aMS, 43, 46   the paradox,

^{b–b}MS, 43, 46   cause whatever, unless, indeed, the First Cause]   51   *as* MS . . . a First Cause

^{c–c}MS, 43, 46   organ

^{d–d}MS, 43, 46   become

^{e–e}MS, 43, 46, 51   take an orange, and conceive it

^fMS, 43, 46   and

say these *thinkers*, would remain. For of what nature, they ask, could be the residuum? and by what token could it manifest its presence? To the un-reflecting its existence seems to rest on the evidence of the senses. But to the senses nothing is apparent except the sensations. We know, indeed, that these sensations are bound together by some law; they do not come together at random, but according to a systematic order, which is part of the order established in the universe. When we experience one of these sensations, we usually experience the others also, or know that we have it in our power to experience them. But a fixed law of connexion, making the sensations occur together, does not, say these philosophers, necessarily require what is called a substratum to support them. The conception of a substratum is but one of many possible forms in which that connexion presents itself to our imagina-tion; a mode of, as it were, realizing the idea. If there be such a substratum, suppose it *at* this instant *miraculously annihilated*, and let the sensations continue to occur in the same order, and how would the substratum be missed? By what signs should we be able to discover that its existence had terminated? Should we not have as much reason to believe that it still existed as we now have? And if we should not then be warranted in believing it, how can we be so now? A body, therefore, according to these metaphysicians, is not anything intrinsically different from the sensations which the body is said to produce in us; it is, in short, a set of sensations *j*, or rather, of possibilities of sensation,*j* joined together according to a fixed law.

*k*The controversies to which these speculations*k* have given rise, and the doctrines which have been developed in the attempt to find a conclusive answer to them, have been fruitful of important consequences to the Science of Mind. The sensations (it was answered) which we are conscious of, and which we receive, not at random, but joined together in a certain uniform manner, imply not only a law or laws of connexion, but a cause external to our mind, which cause, by its own laws, determines the laws according to which the sensations are connected and experienced. The schoolmen used to call this external cause by the name we have already employed, a *substratum*; and its attributes (as they expressed themselves) *inhered*, literally *stuck*, in it. To this substratum the name Matter is usually given in philosophical dis-cussions. It was soon, however, acknowledged by all who reflected on the subject, that the existence of matter *cannot* be proved by extrinsic evidence. The answer, therefore, now usually made to Berkeley and his followers, is,

---

*g–g*MS, 43, 46   philosophers
h–h+72
*i–i*MS, 43, 46   annihilated by the fiat of Omnipotence
j–j+65, 68, 72
*k–k*MS, 43, 46   These ingenious speculations have at no time in the history of philosophy made many proselytes; but the controversies to which they
*l–l*MS, 43, 46, 51, 56, 62   could not

that the belief is intuitive; that mankind, in all ages, have felt themselves compelled, by a necessity of their nature, to refer their sensations to an external cause: that even those who deny it in theory, yield to the necessity in practice, and both in speech, thought, and feeling, do, equally with the vulgar, acknowledge their sensations to be the effects of something external to them: this knowledge, therefore, *m*it is affirmed,*m* is as evidently intuitive as our knowledge of our sensations themselves is intuitive. And here the question merges in the fundamental problem of *n*metaphysics properly so called:*n* to which science we leave it.

But although the extreme doctrine of the Idealist metaphysicians, that objects are nothing but our sensations and the laws which connect them, has *o*not been generally adopted by subsequent thinkers; the point of most*o* real importance is one on which those metaphysicians are now very generally considered to have made out their case: viz., that *all we know* of objects is the sensations which they give us, and the order of the occurrence of those sensations. Kant himself, on this point, is as explicit as Berkeley or Locke. However firmly convinced that there exists an universe of "Things in themselves," totally distinct from the universe of phenomena, or of things as they appear to our senses; and even when bringing into use *p*a*p* technical expression (*Noumenon*) to denote what the thing is in itself, as contrasted with the *representation* of it in our minds; he allows that this representation (the matter of which, he says, consists of our sensations, though the form is given by the laws of the mind itself) is all we know of the object: and that the real nature of the Thing is, and by the constitution of our faculties ever must remain, at least in *q*the present state of*q* existence, an impenetrable mystery to us.

*r*Of things absolutely or in themselves, [says Sir William Hamilton,*] be they external, be they internal, we know nothing, or know them only as incognisable; and become aware of their incomprehensible existence, only as this is indirectly and accidentally revealed to us, through certain qualities related to our faculties of knowledge, and which qualities, again, we cannot think as unconditioned, irrelative, existent in and of themselves. All that we know is therefore phænomenal,—phænomenal of the unknown.†

*[56] *Discussions on Philosophy*, &c. [2nd ed. London: Longman, 1853,] App. I, pp. 643–4.
†[56] *s*It is to be regretted that Sir William Hamilton, though he often strenuously insists on this doctrine, and though, in the passage quoted, he states it with a

m–m+51, 56, 62, 65, 68, 72
*n–n*MS, 43, 46 transcendental metaphysics;
*o–o*MS, 43, 46 appeared to few subsequent thinkers to be worthy of assent; the only point of much
*p–p*MS, 43 the
*q–q*MS, 43, 46 this sublunary   *r–r*+56, 62, 65, 68, 72
*s–s*56, 62 †Sir William Hamilton even goes so far as to assert that this opinion not

The same doctrine is laid down in the clearest and strongest terms by M. Cousin, whose observations on the subject are the more worthy of attention, as, in consequence of the ultra-German and ontological character of his philosophy in other respects, they may be regarded as the admissions of an opponent.^r*

---

comprehensiveness and force which leave nothing to be desired, did not consistently adhere to his own doctrine, but maintained along with it opinions with which it is utterly irreconcilable. See the third and other chapters of *An Examination of Sir William Hamilton's Philosophy*.[8]

* ^t "Nous savons qu'il existe quelque chose hors de nous, parceque nous ne pouvons expliquer nos perceptions sans les rattacher à des causes distinctes de nous-mêmes; nous savons de plus que ces causes, dont nous ne connaissons pas d'ailleurs l'essence, produisent les effets les plus variables, les plus divers, et même les plus contraires, selon qu'elles rencontrent telle nature ou telle disposition du

---

only now is, but always has been, held by nearly all philosophers. "It has been commonly confessed, that, as substances, we know not what is Matter, and are ignorant of what is Mind. With the exception, in fact, of a few late Absolutist theorisers in Germany, this is, perhaps, the truth of all others most harmoniously re-echoed by every philosopher of every school." And he supports his assertion by quotations from seventeen thinkers of eminence, beginning with Protagoras and Aristotle, and ending with Kant. [*Discussions*, pp. 644–7.] Gladly, however, as I should learn that a philosophical truth destructive of so great a mass of baseless and misleading speculation had been universally recognised by philosophers of all past time, and that Ontology, instead of being, as I had hitherto believed, the oldest form of philosophy, was a recent invention of Schelling and Hegel; I am obliged to confess, that none of the passages extracted by Sir William Hamilton, except one from the elder Scaliger and another from Newton, convey to my mind the conclusion that the writers had ever come within sight of the great truth which he supposes them to have intended to express. Almost all the passages seem to me perfectly compatible with the rejection of it; and in most I cannot, by any legitimate interpretation, find anything more than a recognition of the far more obvious principle, that our knowledge of external things is necessarily conditioned by the laws of our knowing faculty: a very different thing from the assertion that the laws of that faculty are such as to deny us all knowledge of outward things, except that of their mere existence.

Whether Sir William Hamilton has or has not antedated this latter doctrine, as an historical fact; philosophically, at least, the exposition of it, and refutation of the Ontologists from their own premises and in their own language, which he has furnished in the first paper of his *Discussions* ["On the Philosophy of the Unconditioned"], leaves nothing to be desired.

^tMS, 43 I have much pleasure in quoting a passage in which this doctrine is laid down in the clearest and strongest terms by M. Cousin, the most distinguished living teacher of German philosophy out of Germany, whose authority on this side of the question is the more valuable, as his philosophical views are generally those of the post-Kantian movement represented by Schelling and Hegel, whose tendencies are much more objective and ontological than those of their master, Kant.] 46 This doctrine is laid . . . *as* MS] 51 *as* 46 . . . Cousin, whose observations on the subject are the more worthy of attention, as, in consequence of the ultra-German and ontological character of his philosophy considered generally, they may be regarded as the admissions of an opponent.

u There is not the slightest reason for believing that what we call the sensible qualities of the object are a type of anything inherent in itself, or bear any affinity to its own nature. A cause does not, as such, resemble its effects; an east wind is not like the feeling of cold, nor *v* heat like the steam of boiling water. Why then should matter resemble our sensations? Why should the inmost nature of fire or water resemble the impressions made by *w*those*w* objects upon our senses?* *d*Or on what principle are we authorized

---

sujet. Mais savons-nous quelque chose de plus? et même, vu le caractère indéterminé des causes que nous concevons dans les corps, y a-t-il quelque chose de plus à savoir? Y a-t-il lieu de nous enquérir si nous percevons les choses telles qu'elles sont? Non évidemment. . . . Je ne dis pas que le problème est insoluble, *je dis qu'il est absurde et enferme une contradiction.* Nous *ne savons pas ce que ces causes sont en elles-mêmes,* et la raison nous défend de chercher à le connaître: mais il est bien évident *à priori,* qu'*elles ne sont pas en elles-mêmes ce qu'elles sont par rapport à nous,* puisque la présence du sujet modifie nécessairement leur action. Supprimez tout sujet sentant, il est certain que ces causes agiraient encore puisqu'elles continueraient d'exister; mais elles agiraient autrement; elles seraient encore des qualités et des propriétés, mais qui ne ressembleraient à rien de ce que nous connaissons. Le feu ne manifesterait plus aucune des propriétés que nous lui connaissons: que serait-il? C'est ce que nous ne saurons jamais. *C'est d'ailleurs peut-être un problème qui ne répugne pas seulement à la nature de notre esprit, mais à l'essence même des choses.* Quand même en effet on supprimerait par la pensée tous les sujets sentants, il faudrait encore admettre que nul corps ne manifesterait ses propriétés autrement qu'en relation avec un sujet quelconque, et dans ce cas *ses propriétés ne seraient encore que relatives:* en sorte qu'il me paraît fort raisonnable d'admettre que les propriétés déterminées des corps n'existent pas indépendamment d'un sujet quelconque, et que quand on demande si les propriétés de la matière sont telles que nous les percevons, il faudrait voir auparavant si elles sont en tant que déterminées, et dans quel sens il est vrai de dire qu'elles sont." *Cours d'Histoire de la Philosophie Morale au 18me siècle* [*Seconde Partie: Ecole ecossaise.* Paris: Ladrange, 1840], 8me leçon [pp. 230–2; *JSM's italics*].
*An attempt, indeed, has been made by Reid and others, to establish that although some of the properties we ascribe to objects exist only in our sensations, others exist in the things themselves, being such as cannot possibly be copies of any impression upon the senses; and they ask, from what *x*sensations*x* our notions of extension and figure have been derived? The gauntlet thrown down by Reid was taken up by Brown, who, applying greater powers of analysis than had previously been applied to the notions of extension and figure, *y*pointed out that the sensations from which those notions are derived, are*y* sensations of touch, combined with sensations of a class previously too little adverted to by metaphysi-

---

*u*MS, 43, 46, 51 [*no paragraph*]
*v*MS, 43, 46 is
*w–w*MS, 43, 46, 51 these
*x–x*MS, 43, 46 sensation
*y–y*MS showed clearly what are the sensations from which those notions were derived, viz.,] 43, 46, 51, 56, 62 *as* MS . . . notions are derived, viz.

to deduce from the effects, anything concerning the cause, except that it is a cause adequate to produce those effects?^{d} It may, therefore, safely be laid down as a truth both obvious in itself, and admitted by all whom it is at present necessary to take into consideration, that, of the outward world, we know and can know absolutely nothing, except the sensations which we experience from it.* ^{f}

---

cians, those which have their seat in our muscular frame. ^{z}His analysis, which was adopted and followed up by James Mill, has been further and greatly improved upon in Professor Bain's profound work, *The Senses and the Intellect* [London: Parker, 1855], and in the chapters on "Perception" of a work of eminent analytic power, Mr. Herbert Spencer's *Principles of Psychology* [London: Longman, 1855].

On this point M. Cousin may again be cited in favour of the better doctrine.^{z} M. Cousin recognises, in opposition to Reid, the essential subjectivity of our conceptions of ^{a}what are called^a the primary qualities of matter, ^{b}as^b extension, solidity, &c., equally with those of colour, heat, and the remainder of ^{c}the so-called^c secondary qualities. *Cours*, ut supra, 9me leçon [pp. 252–81].

^{e}*[65] This doctrine, which is the most complete form of the philosophical theory known as the Relativity of Human Knowledge, has, since the recent revival

$^{z-z}$MS, 43, 46   Whoever wishes to be more particularly acquainted with this admirable specimen of metaphysical analysis, may consult the first volume of Brown's *Lectures*, or Mill's *Analysis of the Mind*.
On this subject also, the authority of M. Cousin may be quoted in favour of conclusions rejected by some of the most eminent thinkers of the school to which he belongs.]   51   *as* MS . . . this excellent specimen . . . *as* MS . . . subject also, M. Cousin . . . *as* MS]   56   Any student who is not yet acquainted with . . . *as* 51 . . . *Analysis of the Mind*, or *The Senses and the Intellect*, by Mr. Alexander Bain, or the chapters on Perception in Mr. Herbert Spencer's *Principles of Psychology*: though the last writer, after tracing with great analytic power the generation of the very complex mental impressions of extension and figure from the sensation of physical resistance and other muscular sensations, nevertheless, with singular inconsistency, regards those impressions as direct perceptions of inherent qualities of the world without [see *Principles of Psychology*, pp. 190ff.].
On this point . . . *as* 72]   62   *as* 56 . . . though the last-mentioned thinker, after tracing with great analytical power . . . *as* 56

$^{a-a}$+56, 62, 65, 68, 72

$^{b-b}$+43, 46, 51, 56, 62, 65, 68, 72

$^{c-c}$MS, 43, 46, 51   what are called

$^{d-d}$MS, 43, 46, 51   And if not on the principle of resemblance, on what other principle can the manner in which objects affect us through our senses afford us any insight into the inherent nature of those objects?

$^{e-e}$MS, 43, 46, 51, 56   [*no footnote*]]   62   *Since the sentence in the text was first published, two important exceptions to the unanimity there spoken of have declared themselves. Mr. Herbert Spencer (see the preceding note) and Mr. Bailey, whose *Letters on the Philosophy of the Human Mind* have since appeared. This is not the place for examining Mr. Bailey's opinions; but it would be uncandid to repeat the statement made in the text, without qualifying it by the express mention of so distinguished a dissentient. And I am the more bound to do so, as the work in question is one, to nearly the whole of which, except the part relating to this subject, I attach real and great value.

^{f}MS, 43, 46   Those, however, who still look upon Ontology as a possible science,

§ 8. [*Mind*] Body having now been defined the external cause, and (according to the more reasonable opinion) the *a*unknown*a* external cause, to which we refer our sensations; it remains to frame a definition of Mind. Nor, after the preceding observations, will this be difficult. For, as our conception of a body is that of an unknown exciting cause of sensations, so our conception of a mind is that of an unknown recipient, or percipient, of them; and not of them alone, but of all our other feelings. As body is *b*understood to be*b* the mysterious something which excites the mind to feel, so mind is the mysterious something which feels and thinks. It is unnecessary to give in the

---

in this country of an active interest in metaphysical speculation, been the subject of a greatly increased amount of discussion and controversy; and dissentients have manifested themselves in considerably greater number than I had any knowledge of when the passage in the text was written. The doctrine has been attacked from two sides. Some thinkers, among whom are the late Professor Ferrier, in his *Institutes of Metaphysic* [Edinburgh: Blackwood, 1854], and Professor John Grote, in his *Exploratio Philosophica* [Pt. I. Cambridge: Deighton, Bell, 1865], appear to deny altogether the reality of Noumena, or Things in themselves—of an unknowable substratum or support for the sensations which we experience, and which, according to the theory, constitute all our knowledge of an external world. It seems to me, however, that in Professor Grote's case at least, the denial of Noumena is only apparent, and that he does not essentially differ from the other class of objectors, including Mr. Bailey in his valuable *Letters on the Philosophy of the Human Mind* [First Series. London: Longman, 1855], and (in spite of the striking passage quoted in the text) also Sir William Hamilton, who contend for a direct knowledge by the human mind of more than the sensations—of certain attributes or properties as they exist not in us, but in the Things themselves.

With the first of these opinions, that which denies Noumena, I have, as a metaphysician, no quarrel; but, whether it be true or false, it is irrelevant to Logic. And since all the forms of language are in contradiction to it, nothing but confusion could result from its unnecessary introduction into a treatise, every essential doctrine of which could stand equally well with the opposite and accredited opinion. The other and rival doctrine, that of a direct perception or intuitive knowledge of the outward object as it is in itself, considered as distinct from the sensations we receive from it, is of far greater practical moment. But even this question, depending on the nature and laws of Intuitive Knowledge, is not within the province of Logic. For the grounds of my own opinion concerning it, I must content myself with referring to a work already mentioned—*An Examination of Sir William Hamilton's Philosophy*; several chapters of which are devoted to a full discussion of the questions and theories relating to the supposed direct perception of external objects.*e*

---

and think, not only that bodies have an essential constitution of their own, lying deeper than our perceptions, but that this essence or nature is not altogether inaccessible to human investigation, cannot expect to find their refutation here. The question depends on the nature and laws of Intuitive Knowledge, and is not within the province of logic.] 51, 56, 62   *as* MS . . . or nature is accessible to . . . *as* MS

*a–a*MS, 43, 46, 51, 56, 62   *hidden*
b–b+65, 68, 72

case of mind, as we gave in the case of matter, a particular statement of the sceptical system by which its existence as a Thing in itself, distinct from the series of what are denominated its states, is called in question. But it is necessary to remark, that on the inmost nature *(whatever be meant by inmost nature)* of the thinking principle, as well as on the inmost nature of matter, we are, and with our *d* faculties must always remain, entirely in the dark. All which we are aware of, even in our own minds, is (in the words of *James* Mill) a certain "thread of consciousness;"[*] a series of feelings, that is, of sensations, thoughts, emotions, and volitions, more or less numerous and complicated. There is a something I call Myself, or, by another form of expression, my mind, which I consider as distinct from these sensations, thoughts, &c.; a something which I conceive to be not the thoughts, but the being that has the thoughts, and which I can conceive as existing for ever in a state of quiescence, without any thoughts at all. But what this being is, though it is myself, I have no knowledge, *other* than the series of its states of consciousness. As bodies manifest themselves to me only through the sensations of which I regard them as the causes, so the thinking principle, or mind, in my own nature, makes itself known to me only by the feelings of which it is conscious. I know nothing about myself, save my capacities of feeling or being conscious (including, of course, thinking and willing): and were I to learn anything new concerning *my own nature*, I cannot with my present faculties conceive this new information to be anything else, than that I have some additional capacities, *as yet* unknown to me, of feeling, thinking, or willing.

Thus, then, as body is the unsentient cause to which we are naturally prompted to refer a certain portion of our feelings, so mind may be described as the sentient *subject* (in the *scholastic* sense of the term) of all feelings; that which has or feels them. But of the nature of either body or mind, further than the feelings which the former excites, and which the latter experiences, we do not, according to the best existing doctrine, know anything; and if anything, logic has nothing to do with it, or with the manner in which *the knowledge* is acquired. With this result we may conclude this portion of our subject, and pass to the third and only remaining class or division of Nameable Things.

[*See *Analysis*, Vol. I, p. 274; Vol. II, p. 134.]

c–c+65, 68, 72
*d*MS, 43, 46   human
e–eMS   the late Mr. James] 43, 46, 51, 56, 62, 65   Mr.]   68   Mr. James
f–fMS, 43, 46   further
g–gMS, 43, 46   myself
h–hMS, 43, 46   before
i–iMS, 43, 46, 51, 56, 62, 65   German
j–jMS   it

III. ATTRIBUTES: AND, FIRST, QUALITIES

§ 9. [*Qualities*] From what has already been said of Substance, what is to be said of Attribute is easily deducible. For if we know not, and cannot know, anything of bodies but the sensations which they excite in us or *a*in*a* others, those sensations must be all that we can, at bottom, mean by their attributes; and the distinction which we verbally make between the properties of things and the sensations we receive from them, must originate in the convenience of discourse rather than in the nature of what is *b*signified*b* by the terms.

Attributes are usually distributed under the three heads of Quality, Quantity, and Relation. We shall come to the two latter presently: in *c*the first*c* place we shall confine ourselves to the former.

Let us take, then, as our example, one of what are termed the sensible qualities of objects, and let that example be whiteness. When we ascribe whiteness to any substance, as, for instance, snow; when we say that snow has the quality whiteness, what do we really assert? Simply, that when snow is present to our organs, we have a particular sensation, which we are accustomed to call the sensation of white. But how do I know that snow is present? Obviously by the sensations which I derive from it, and not otherwise. I infer that the object is present, because it gives me a certain assemblage or series of sensations. And when I ascribe to it the attribute whiteness, my meaning is only, that, of the sensations composing this group or series, that which I call the sensation of white colour is one.

This is one view which may be taken of the subject. But there is also another and a different view. It may be said, that it is true we *know* nothing of sensible objects, except the sensations they excite in us; that the fact of our receiving from snow the particular sensation which is called a sensation of white, is the *ground* on which we ascribe to that substance the quality whiteness; the sole proof of its possessing that quality. But because one thing may be the sole evidence of the existence of another thing, it does not follow that the two are one and the same. The attribute whiteness (it may be said) is not the fact of *d* receiving the sensation, but something in the object itself; a *power* inherent in it; something *in virtue* of which the object produces the sensation. And when we affirm that snow possesses the attribute whiteness, we do not merely assert that the presence of snow produces in us that sensation, but that it does so through, and by reason of, that power or quality.

For the purposes of logic it is not of material importance which of these *e*opinions*e* we adopt. The full discussion of the subject belongs to the *f*other

a–a+56, 62, 65, 68, 72
c–cMS   this
e–eMS, 43, 46   views

b–bMS, 43, 46, 51, 56   denoted
dMS, 43, 46, 51   our
f–fMS, 43, 46   department of

department of scientific^f inquiry, so often alluded to under the name of ^{g} metaphysics; but it may be said here, that for the doctrine of the existence of a peculiar species of entities called qualities, I can see no foundation except in a tendency of the human mind which is the cause of many delusions. I mean, the disposition, wherever we meet with two names which are not precisely synonymous, to suppose that they must be the names of two different things; whereas in reality they may be names of the same thing viewed in two different lights, ^{h}or^h under different suppositions as to surrounding circumstances. Because *quality* and *sensation* cannot be put indiscriminately one for the other, it is supposed that they cannot both signify the same thing, namely, the impression or feeling with which we are affected through our senses by the presence of an object; though there is at least no absurdity in supposing that this identical impression or feeling may be called a sensation when considered merely in itself, and a quality when ^{i}looked at in relation to^i any one of the numerous objects, the presence of which to our organs excites in our minds that among various other sensations or feelings. And if this be admissible as a supposition, it rests with those who contend for an entity *per se* called a quality, to show that their opinion is preferable, or is anything in fact but a lingering remnant of the ^{j}old^j doctrine of occult causes; the very absurdity which Molière so happily ridiculed when he made one of his pedantic physicians account for the fact that ^{k}opium produces sleep by the maxim, Because it has a soporific virtue.^{k}[*]

It is evident that when the physician stated that opium ^{l}has a soporific virtue,^{l} he did not account for, but merely asserted over again, the fact that it ^{m}produces sleep^m. In like manner, when we say that snow is white because it has the quality of whiteness, we are only re-asserting in more technical language the fact that it excites in us the sensation of white. If it be said that the sensation must have some cause, I answer, its cause is the presence of the ^{n}assemblage of phenomena which is termed the^n object. When we have asserted that as often as the object is present, and our organs in their normal state, the sensation takes place, we have stated all that we know about the matter. There is no need, after assigning a certain and intelligible cause, to suppose an occult cause besides, for the purpose of enabling the real cause

[*See Jean-Baptiste Molière. "Troisième Intermède," *Le Malade imaginaire*.]

^{g}MS, 43, 46   the higher
$^{h-h}$MS, 43, 46, 51   which is as much as to say
$^{i-i}$MS, 43, 46, 51, 56, 62   regarded as emanating from
$^{j-j}$MS, 43, 46, 51, 56, 62, 65, 68   scholastic
$^{k-k}$MS, 43, 46, 51, 56, 62, 65, 68   "l'opium endormit," by the maxim "parcequ'il a une vertu soporifique."
$^{l-l}$MS, 43, 46, 51, 56, 62, 65, 68   had "une vertu soporifique,"
$^{m-m}$MS, 43, 46, 51, 56, 62, 65, 68   *endormit*
$^{n-n}$+51, 56, 62, 65, 68, 72

to produce its effect. If I am asked, why does the presence of the object cause this sensation in me, I cannot tell: I can only say that such is my nature, and the nature of the object; °that the fact forms a part of the constitution of things°. And to this we must at last come, even after interpolating the imaginary entity. Whatever number of links the chain of causes and effects may consist of, how any one link produces the one which is next to it, remains equally inexplicable to us. It is as easy to comprehend that the object should produce the sensation directly and at once, as that it should produce the same sensation by the aid of something else called the *power* of producing it.

But, as the difficulties which may be felt in adopting this view of the subject cannot be removed without discussions transcending the bounds of our science, I content myself with a passing indication, and shall, for the purposes of logic, adopt a language compatible with either view of the nature of qualities. I shall say,—what at least admits of no dispute,—that the quality of whiteness ascribed to the object snow, is *grounded* on its exciting in us the sensation of white; and adopting the language already used by the school logicians in the case of ᵖtheᵖ kind of attributes called Relations, I shall term the sensation of white the *foundation* of the quality whiteness. For logical purposes the sensation is the only essential part of what is meant by the word; the only part which we ever can be concerned in proving. When that is proved, the quality is proved; if an object excites a sensation, it has, of course, the power of exciting it.

IV. RELATIONS

§ 10. [*Relations*] The *qualities* of a body, we have said, are the attributes grounded on the sensations which the presence of that particular body to our organs excites in our minds. But when we ascribe to any object the kind of attribute called a Relation, the foundation of the attribute must be something in which other objects are concerned besides itself and the percipient.

As there may with propriety be said to be a relation between any two things to which two correlative names are or may be given, we may expect to discover what constitutes a relation in general, if we enumerate the principal cases in which mankind have imposed correlative names, and observe what ᵃ these cases have in common.

What, then, is the character which is possessed in common by states of circumstances so heterogeneous and discordant as these: one thing *like* another; one thing *unlike* another; one thing *near* another; one thing *far from* another; one thing *before, after, along with* another; one thing *greater, equal,*

o–oMS, 43, 46   the constitution of things, the scheme of the universe, will have it so
p–pMS   that
ªMS, 43, 46   all

less, than another; one thing the *cause* of another, the *effect* of another; one person the *master, servant, child, parent, ᵇdebtor, creditorᵇ, sovereign, subject, attorney, client,* of another, and so on?

Omitting, for the present, the case of Resemblance, (a relation which requires to be considered separately,) there seems to be one thing common to all these cases, and only one; that in each of them there exists or occurs, or has existed or occurred, ᶜor may be expected to exist or occur,ᶜ some fact or phenomenon, into which the two things which are said to be related to each other, both enter as parties concerned. This fact, or phenomenon, is what the Aristotelian logicians called the *fundamentum relationis.* Thus in the relation of greater and less between two magnitudes, the *fundamentum relationis* is the fact that ᵈone of the two magnitudes could, under certain conditions, be included in, without entirely filling, the space occupied by the other magnitudeᵈ. ᵉIn the relation of master and servant, the *fundamentum relationis* is the fact that the one has undertaken, or is compelled, to perform certain services for the benefit and at the bidding of the other.ᵉ ᶠ Examples might be indefinitely multiplied; but it is already obvious that whenever two things are said to be related, there is some fact, or series of facts, into which they both enter; and that whenever any two things are involved in some one fact, or series of facts, we may ascribe to those two things a mutual relation grounded on the fact. Even if they have nothing in common but what is common to all things, that they are members of the universe, we call that a relation, and denominate them fellow-creatures, fellow-beings, or fellow-denizens of the universe. But in proportion as the fact into which the two objects enter as parts is of a more special and peculiar, or of a more complicated nature, so also is the relation grounded upon it. And there are as many conceivable relations as there are conceivable kinds of fact in which two things can be jointly concerned.

In the same manner, therefore, as a quality is an attribute grounded on the fact that a certain sensation or sensations are produced in us by the object, so an attribute grounded on some fact into which the object enters jointly with another object, is a relation between it and that other object. But the fact in the latter case consists of the very same kind of elements as the

---

ᵇ⁻ᵇMS, 43, 46   *husband, wife*

ᶜ⁻ᶜ+51, 56, 62, 65, 68, 72

ᵈ⁻ᵈMS, 43, 46   when one of the two magnitudes is applied to the other, it more than covers it; and cannot, by any new arrangement of parts, be entirely brought within the boundaries of the other object

ᵉ⁻ᵉ+43, 46, 51, 56, 62, 65, 68, 72

ᶠMS   In the relation of husband and wife, the *fundamentum relationis* is the fact that the parties are a man and a woman, that they have promised certain things with certain formalities, and are in consequence invested by the law with certain rights, and subjected to certain duties.]   43, 46   In that of . . . *as MS* . . . *relationis* consists of the facts that . . . *as MS*

fact in the former; namely, states of consciousness. In the case ^{g}, for example, of any legal relation, as debtor and creditor, principal and agent, guardian and ward,^{g} the *fundamentum relationis* consists entirely of thoughts, ^{h}feelings^h, and volitions (actual or contingent), either of the ^{i}persons themselves or of other persons^i concerned in the same series of transactions; as, for instance, the intentions which would be formed by a judge, in case a complaint were made to his tribunal of the infringement of any of the legal ^{j}obligations imposed^j by ^{k}the relation^k; and the acts which the judge would perform in consequence; acts being (as we have already seen) another word for intentions followed by an effect, and that effect ^{l} being but another word for sensations, or some other feelings, occasioned either to ^{m}the agent himself^m or to somebody else. There is no part ^{n} of what the names expressive of the relation imply, that is not resolvable into states of consciousness; outward objects being, no doubt, supposed throughout as the causes by which some of those states of consciousness are excited, and minds as the subjects by which all of them are experienced, but neither the external objects nor the minds making their existence known otherwise than by the states of consciousness.

Cases of relation are not always so complicated as ^{o}those^o to which we last alluded. The simplest of all cases of relation are those expressed by the words antecedent and consequent, ^{p}and^p by the word simultaneous. If we say, for instance, that dawn preceded sunrise, the fact in which the two things, dawn and sunrise, were jointly concerned, consisted only of the two things themselves; no third thing entered into the fact or phenomenon at all. Unless, indeed, we choose to call the succession of the two objects a third thing; but their succession is not something added to the things themselves; it is something involved in them. Dawn and sunrise announce themselves to our consciousness by two successive sensations. Our consciousness of the succession of these sensations is not a third sensation or feeling added to them; we have not first the two feelings, and then a feeling of their succession. To have two feelings at all, implies having them either successively, or else simultaneously. Sensations, or other feelings, being given, succession and simultaneousness are the two conditions, to the alternative of which they are subjected by the nature of our faculties; and no one has been able, or needs expect, to analyse the matter any farther.

$g-g$MS, 43, 46   last cited, for example, the relation of husband and wife;
$h-h$MS, 43, 46   emotions, sensations
$i-i$MS, 43, 46   parties themselves or of other parties
$j-j$MS   rights conferred
$k-k$MS, 43, 46   marriage
lMS, 43, 46   (again)
$m-m$MS, 43, 46, 51, 56   oneself nMS, 43, 46   whatever
$o-o$MS, 43, 46   that $p-p$MS   or

§ 11. [*Resemblance*] In a somewhat similar position are two other sorts of *a*relations*a*, Likeness and Unlikeness. I have two sensations; we will suppose them to be simple ones; two sensations of white, or one sensation of white and another of black. I call the first two sensations *like*; the last two *unlike*. What is the fact or phenomenon constituting the *fundamentum* of this relation? The two sensations first, and then what *b*we*b* call a feeling of resemblance, or *c* of want of resemblance. Let us confine ourselves to the former case. Resemblance is evidently a feeling; a state of the consciousness of the observer. Whether the feeling of the resemblance of the two colours be a third state of consciousness, which I have *after* having the two sensations of colour, or whether (like the feeling of their succession) it is involved in the sensations themselves, may be a matter of discussion. But in either case, these feelings of resemblance, and of its opposite dissimilarity, are parts of our nature; and parts so far from being capable of analysis, that they are presupposed in every attempt to analyse any of our other feelings. Likeness and unlikeness, therefore, as well as antecedence, sequence, and simultaneousness, must stand apart among relations, as things *sui generis*. They are attributes grounded on facts, that is, on states of consciousness, but on states which are peculiar, unresolvable, and inexplicable.

But, though likeness or unlikeness cannot be resolved into anything else, complex cases of likeness or unlikeness can be resolved into simpler ones. When we say of two things which consist of parts, that they are like one another, the likeness of the wholes does admit of analysis; it is compounded of likenesses between the various parts respectively *d*, and of likeness in their arrangement*d*. Of how vast a variety of resemblances of parts must that resemblance be composed, which induces us to say that a portrait, or a landscape, is like its original. If one person mimics another with any success, of how many simple likenesses must the general or complex likeness be compounded: likeness in a succession of bodily postures; likeness in voice, or in the accents and intonations of the voice; likeness in the choice of words, and in the thoughts or sentiments expressed, whether by word, countenance, or gesture.

All likeness and unlikeness of which we have any cognizance, resolve themselves into likeness and unlikeness between states of our own, or some other, mind. When we say that one body is like another, (since we know nothing of bodies but the sensations which they excite,) we mean really that there is a resemblance between the sensations excited by the two bodies, or between some *e*portions*e* at least of *f*those*f* sensations. If we say that two attributes are like one another, (since we know nothing of attributes except

*a–a*MS, 43, 46, 51, 56, 62   relation
*c*MS, 43, 46   a feeling
*e–e*MS, 43, 46, 51, 56, 62, 65   portion
*b–b*MS   I
d–d+62, 65, 68, 72
*f–f*43, 46, 51, 56   these [*printer's error?*]

the sensations or states of feeling on which they are grounded,) we mean really that those sensations, or states of feeling, resemble each other. We may also say that two relations are alike. The fact of resemblance between relations is sometimes called *analogy*, forming one of the numerous meanings of that word. The relation in which Priam stood to Hector, namely, that of father and son, resembles the relation in which Philip stood to Alexander; resembles it so closely that they are called the same relation. The relation in which Cromwell stood to England resembles the relation in which Napoleon stood to France, though not so closely as to be called the same relation. The meaning in both these instances must be, that a resemblance existed between the facts which constituted the *fundamentum relationis*.

This resemblance may exist in all conceivable gradations, from perfect undistinguishableness to something *ᵍextremely slightᵍ*. When we say, that a thought suggested to the mind of a person of genius is like a seed cast into the ground, because the former produces a multitude of other thoughts, and the latter a multitude of other seeds, this is saying that between the relation of an inventive mind to a thought contained in it, and the relation of a fertile soil to a seed contained in it, there exists a resemblance: the real resemblance being in the two *fundamenta relationis*, in each of which there occurs a germ, producing by its development a multitude of other things similar to itself. And as, whenever two objects are jointly concerned in a phenomenon, this constitutes a relation between those objects, so, if we suppose a second pair of objects concerned in a second phenomenon, the slightest resemblance between the two phenomena is sufficient to admit of its being said that the two relations resemble; provided, of course, the points of resemblance are found in those portions of the two phenomena respectively which are connoted by the relative names.

While speaking of resemblance, it is necessary to take notice of an ambiguity of language, against which scarcely any one is sufficiently on his guard. Resemblance, when it exists in the highest degree of all, amounting to undistinguishableness, is often called identity, and the two similar things are said to be the same. I say often, not always; for we do not say that two visible objects, two persons for instance, are the same, because they are so much alike that one might be mistaken for the other: but we constantly use this mode of expression when speaking of feelings; as when I say that the sight of any object gives me the *same* sensation or emotion to-day that it did yesterday, or the *same* which it gives to some other person. This is evidently an incorrect application of the word *same*; for the feeling which I had yesterday is gone, never to return; *ʰ* what I have to-day is another feeling, exactly like the former perhaps, but distinct from it; and it is evident that two different

ᵍ⁻ᵍMS, 43, 46   very slight indeed   ʰMS &

persons cannot be experiencing the same feeling, in the sense in which we say that they are both sitting at the same table. By a similar ambiguity we say, that two persons are ill of the *same* disease; that two *persons* hold the *same* office; not in the sense in which we say that they are engaged in the same adventure, or sailing in the same ship, but in the sense that they fill offices exactly similar, though, perhaps, in distant places. Great confusion of ideas is often produced, and many fallacies engendered, in otherwise enlightened understandings, by not being sufficiently alive to the fact (in itself not always to be avoided), that they use the same name to express ideas so different as those of identity and undistinguishable resemblance. Among modern writers, Archbishop Whately stands almost alone in having drawn attention to this distinction, and to the ambiguity connected with it. *j*

Several relations, generally called by other names, are really cases of resemblance. As, for example, equality; which is but another word for *k*the exact resemblance*k* commonly called identity, considered as subsisting between things in respect of their *quantity*. And this example forms a suitable transition to the third and last of the three heads under which, as already remarked, Attributes are commonly arranged.

*i–i*MS, 43, 46   people

*j*MS, 43, 46   [*footnote:*] *"Same (as well as 'One,' 'Identical,' and other words derived from them) is used frequently in a sense very different from its primary one, as applicable to a *single* object, being employed to denote great *similarity*. When several objects are undistinguishably alike, *one single description* will apply equally to any of them; and thence they are said to be all of *one and the same* nature, appearance, &c., as *e.g.* when we say, 'this house is built of the *same* stone with such another,' we only mean that the stones are undistinguishable in their qualities; not that the one building was pulled down, and the other constructed with the materials. Whereas sameness, in the primary sense, does not even necessarily imply similarity; for if we say of any man, that he is greatly altered since such a time, we understand, and, indeed, imply by the very expression, that he is *one person*, though different in several qualities. It is worth observing also, that Same, in the secondary sense, admits, according to popular usage, of *degree*. We speak of two things being *nearly* the same, but not entirely; personal identity does not admit of degrees. Nothing, perhaps, has contributed more to the error of Realism than inattention to this ambiguity. When several persons are said to have *One and the Same* opinion, thought, or idea, men, overlooking the true simple statement of the case, which is, that they *are all thinking alike*, look for something more abstruse and mystical, and imagine there must be some *One Thing*, in the primary sense, though not an individual, which is present at once in the mind of each of these persons; and thence readily sprung Plato's Theory of Ideas, each of which was, according to him, one real, eternal object, existing entire and complete in each of the individual objects that are known by one name. . . . The Hindoos of the present day, from observing the similar symptoms which are known by the name of small-pox, and the communication of the like from one patient to another, do not merely call it (as we do) *one* disease, but believe (if we may credit the accounts given) that the small-pox is a goddess who becomes incarnate in each infected patient." *Logic*; Appendix on Ambiguous Terms, pp. 298–300 [9th ed., pp. 339–40]. My references to this work are always to the first edition. [MS *gives reference and final sentence at the beginning of the footnote.*]

*k–k*MS   that exact resemblance which is

V. QUANTITY

§ 12. [*Quantity*] Let us imagine two things, between which there is no difference (that is, no dissimilarity), except in quantity alone: for instance, a gallon of water, and more than a gallon of water. A gallon of water, like any other external object, makes its presence known to us by a set of sensations which it excites. Ten gallons of water are also an external object, making its presence known to us in a similar manner; and as we do not mistake ten gallons of water for a gallon of water, it is plain that the set of sensations is more or less different in the two cases. In like manner, a gallon of water, and a gallon of *a*wine*a*, are two external objects, making their presence known by two sets of sensations, which sensations are different from each other. In the first case, however, we say that the difference is in quantity; in the last there is a difference in quality, while the quantity of the water and of the *b*wine*b* is the same. What is the real distinction between the two cases? It is not *c*within*c* the province of Logic to analyse it; nor to decide whether it is susceptible of analysis or not. For us the following considerations are sufficient. It is evident that the sensations I receive from the gallon of water, and those I receive from the gallon of *d*wine*d*, are not the same, that is, not precisely alike; neither are they altogether unlike: they are partly similar, partly dissimilar; and that in which they resemble is precisely that in which alone the gallon of water and the ten gallons do not resemble. That in which the gallon of water and the gallon of wine are like each other, and in which the gallon and the ten gallons of water are unlike each other, is called their quantity. This likeness and unlikeness I do not pretend to explain, no more than any other kind of likeness or unlikeness. But my object is to show, that when we say of two things that they differ in quantity, just as when we say that they differ in quality, the assertion is always grounded on a difference in the sensations which they excite. Nobody, I presume, will say, that to see, or to lift, or to drink, ten gallons of water, does not include in itself a different set of sensations from those of seeing, lifting, or drinking one gallon; or that to see or handle a foot-rule, and to see or handle a yard-measure made exactly like it, are the same sensations. I do not undertake to say what the difference in the sensations is. Everybody knows, and nobody can tell; no more than any one could tell what white is to a person who had never had the sensation. But the difference, so far as cognizable by our faculties, lies in the sensations. Whatever difference we say there is in the things themselves, is *e*, in this as in all other cases, grounded*e*, and grounded exclusively, on a difference in the sensations excited by them.

*a–a*MS, 43, 46 Madeira   *b–b*MS, 43, 46 Madeira
c–c+72   *d–d*MS, 43, 46 Madeira
*e–e*MS grounded, in this as in all other cases

VI. Attributes Concluded

§ 13. [*All attributes of bodies are grounded on states of consciousness*] Thus, then, all the attributes of bodies which are classed under Quality or Quantity, are grounded on the sensations which we receive from those bodies, and may be defined, the powers which the bodies have of exciting those sensations. And the same general explanation has been found to apply to most of the attributes usually classed under the head of Relation. They, too, are grounded on some fact or phenomenon into which the related objects enter as parts; that fact or phenomenon having no meaning and no existence to us, except the series of sensations or other states of consciousness by which it makes itself known; and the relation being simply the power or capacity which the object possesses of taking part along with the correlated object in the production of that series of sensations or states of consciousness. We have been obliged, indeed, to recognise a somewhat different character in certain peculiar relations, those of succession and simultaneity, of likeness and unlikeness. These, not being grounded on any fact or phenomenon distinct from the related objects themselves, do not admit of the same kind of analysis. But these relations, though not, like other relations, grounded on states of consciousness, are themselves states of consciousness: resemblance is nothing but our feeling of resemblance; succession is nothing but our feeling of succession. Or, if this be disputed (and we cannot, without transgressing the bounds of our science, discuss it here), at least our knowledge of these relations, and even our possibility of knowledge, is confined to those which subsist between sensations, or other states of consciousness; for, though we ascribe resemblance, or succession, or simultaneity, to objects and to attributes, it is always in virtue of resemblance or succession or simultaneity in the sensations or states of consciousness which those objects excite, and on which those attributes are grounded.

§ 14. [*So also are all attributes of minds grounded on states of consciousness*] In the preceding investigation we have, for the sake of simplicity, considered bodies only, and omitted minds. But what we have said, is applicable, *mutatis mutandis*, to the latter. The attributes of minds, as well as those of bodies, are grounded on states of feeling or consciousness. But in the case of a mind, we have to consider its own states, as well as those which it produces in other minds. Every attribute of a mind consists either in being itself affected in a certain way, or affecting other minds in a certain way. Considered in itself, we can predicate nothing of it but the series of its own feelings. When we say of any mind, that it is devout, or superstitious, or meditative, or cheerful, we mean that the ideas, emotions, ᵃorᵃ volitions implied in

ᵃ⁻ᵃMS　& [*printer's error?*]

those words, form a frequently recurring part of the series of feelings, or states of consciousness, which fill up the sentient existence of that mind.

In addition, however, to those attributes of a mind which are grounded on its own states of feeling, attributes may also be ascribed to it, in the same manner as to a body, grounded on the feelings which it excites in other minds. A mind does not, indeed, like a body, excite sensations, but it may excite thoughts or emotions. The most important example of attributes ascribed on this ground, is the employment of terms expressive of approbation or blame. When, for example, we say of any character, or (in other words) of any mind, that it is admirable, we mean that the contemplation of it excites the sentiment of admiration; and indeed somewhat more, for the word implies that we not only feel admiration, but approve that sentiment in ourselves. In some cases, under the semblance of a single attribute, two are really predicated: one of them, a state of the mind itself; the other, a state with which other minds are affected by thinking of it. As when we say of any one that he is generous. The word generosity expresses a certain state of mind, but being a term of praise, it also expresses that this state of mind excites in us another mental state, called approbation. The assertion made, therefore, is twofold, and of the following purport: Certain feelings form habitually a part of this person's sentient existence; and *b* the idea of those feelings of his, excites the sentiment of approbation in ourselves or others.

As we thus ascribe attributes to minds on the ground of ideas and emotions, so may we to bodies on similar grounds, and not solely on the ground of sensations: as in speaking of the beauty of a statue; since this attribute is grounded on the peculiar feeling of pleasure which the statue produces in our minds; *c* which is not a sensation, but an emotion.

VII. GENERAL *a*RESULTS*a*

§ 15. [*Recapitulation*] Our survey of the varieties of Things which have been, or which are capable of being, named—which have been, or are capable of being, either predicated of other Things, or *b*themselves made*b* the subject of predications—is now *c*concluded*c*.

Our enumeration commenced with Feelings. These we scrupulously distinguished from the objects which excite them, and from the organs by which they are, or may be supposed to be, conveyed. Feelings are of four sorts: Sensations, Thoughts, Emotions, and Volitions. What are called Perceptions are merely a particular case of Belief, and belief is a kind of thought. Actions are merely volitions followed by an effect. *d*

*b*MS, 43, 46 , moreover,
*a–a*MS, 43, 46 RESULT
*c–c*MS, 43, 46 complete
*c*MS, 43, 46 and
*b–b*MS, 43, 46, 51 made themselves
*d*MS, 43, 46, 51, 56, 62, 65, 68 If there be any other kind of mental state not in-

After Feelings we proceeded to Substances. These are either Bodies or Minds. Without entering into the grounds of the metaphysical doubts which have been raised concerning the existence of Matter and Mind as objective realities, we stated as sufficient for us the conclusion in which the best thinkers are now *for the most part* agreed, that all we can know of Matter is the sensations which it gives us, and the order of occurrence of those sensations; and that while the substance Body is the unknown cause of our sensations, the substance Mind is the unknown *recipient*.

The only remaining class of Nameable Things is Attributes; and these are of three kinds, Quality, Relation, and Quantity. Qualities, like substances, are known to us no otherwise than by the sensations or other states of consciousness which they excite: and while, in compliance with common usage, we have continued to speak of them as a distinct class of Things, we showed that in predicating them no one means to predicate anything but those sensations or states of consciousness, on which they may be said to be grounded, and by which alone they can be defined *or described*. Relations, except the simple cases of likeness and unlikeness, succession and simultaneity, are similarly grounded on some fact or phenomenon, that is, on some series of sensations or states of consciousness, more or less complicated. The third species of Attribute, Quantity, is also manifestly grounded on something in our sensations or states of feeling, since there is an indubitable difference in the sensations excited by a larger and a smaller bulk, or by a greater or a less degree of intensity, in any object of sense or of consciousness. All attributes, therefore, are to us nothing but either our sensations and other states of feeling, or something inextricably involved therein; and to this even the peculiar and simple relations just adverted to are not exceptions. Those peculiar relations, however, are so important, and, even if they might in strictness be classed among *h* states of consciousness, are so fundamentally distinct from any other of those states, that it would be a vain subtlety to *bring them under that common description*, and it is necessary that they should be classed apart.*

*[72] Professor Bain (*Logic*, Vol. I, p. 49) defines attributes as "points of community among classes." This definition expresses well one point of view, but is liable to the objection that it applies only to the attributes of classes; though an object, unique in its kind, may be said to have attributes. Moreover, the definition is not ultimate, since the points of community themselves admit of, and require, further analysis; and Mr. Bain does analyse them into resemblances in the sensations, or other states of consciousness excited by the object.

---

cluded under these subdivisions, we did not think it necessary or proper in this place to discuss its existence, or the rank which ought to be assigned to it.
*e-e*MS, 43, 46, 51, 56   very generally   *f-f*MS, 43, 46   percipient
g-g+51, 56, 62, 65, 68, 72   *h*MS, 43, 46   our
*i-i*MS, 43, 46, 51, 56, 62, 65   confound them under that common head

As the result, therefore, of our analysis, we obtain the following as an enumeration and classification of all Nameable Things:

1st. Feelings, or States of Consciousness.

2nd. The Minds which experience those feelings.

3rd. The *j*Bodies, or*j* external objects which excite certain of those feelings, together with the powers or properties whereby they excite them; *k*these latter (at least)*k* being included rather in compliance with common opinion, and because their existence is taken for granted in the common language from which I cannot prudently deviate, than because the recognition of such powers or properties as real existences appears to *l*be*l* warranted by a sound philosophy.

4th, and last. The Successions and Co-existences, the Likenesses and Unlikenesses, between feelings or states of consciousness. Those relations, when considered as subsisting between other things, *m*exist*m* in reality only between the states of consciousness which those things, if bodies, excite, if minds, either excite or experience.

This, until a better can be suggested, *n*may serve*n* as a substitute for the *o*Categories of Aristotle considered as a Classification of Existences*o*. The practical application of it will appear when we commence the inquiry into the Import of Propositions; in other words, when we inquire what it is which the mind actually believes, when it gives what is called its assent to a proposition.

These four classes comprising, if the classification be correct, all Nameable Things, these or some of them must of course compose the signification of all names; and of these, or some of them, is made up whatever we call a fact.

For distinction's sake, every fact which is solely composed of feelings or states of consciousness considered as such, is often called a Psychological or Subjective fact; while every fact which is composed, either wholly or in part, of something different from these, that is, of substances and attributes, is called an Objective fact. We may say, then, that every objective fact is grounded on a corresponding subjective one; and has no meaning to us, (apart from the subjective fact which corresponds to it,) except as a name for the unknown and inscrutable process by which that subjective or psychological fact is brought to pass.

j–j+43, 46, 51, 56, 62, 65, 68, 72
*k–k*MS, 43, 46, 62, 65, 68   these last]   51, 56   these
*l–l*MS, 43, 46, 51   me
*m–m*MS   existing [*slip of the pen?*]
*n–n*MS, 43, 46   must serve us
*o–o*MS, 43, 46, 51, 56, 62, 65, 68   abortive Classification of Existences, termed the Categories of Aristotle

CHAPTER IV

Of Propositions

§ 1. [*Nature and office of the copula*] In treating of Propositions, as already in treating of Names, some considerations of a comparatively elementary nature respecting their form and varieties must be premised, before entering upon that analysis of the import conveyed by them, which is the real subject and purpose of this preliminary book.

A proposition, we have before said, is a portion of discourse in which a predicate is affirmed or denied of a subject. A predicate and a subject are all that is necessarily required to make up a proposition: but as we cannot conclude from merely seeing two names put together, that they are a predicate and a subject, that is, that one of them is intended to be affirmed or denied of the other, it is necessary that there should be some mode or form of indicating that such is the intention; some sign to distinguish a predication from any other kind of discourse. This is sometimes done by a slight alteration of one of the words, called an *inflection*; as when we say, Fire burns; the change of the second word from *burn* to *burns* showing that we mean to affirm the predicate burn of the subject fire. But this function is more commonly fulfilled by the word *is*, when an affirmation is intended, *is not*, when a negation; or by some other part of the verb *to be*. The word which thus serves the purpose of a sign of predication is called, as we formerly observed, the *copula*. It is ᵃimportantᵃ that there should be no indistinctness in our conception of the nature and office of the copula; for confused notions respecting it are among the causes which have spread mysticism over the field of logic, and perverted its speculations into logomachies.

It is apt to be supposed that the copula is ᵇsomethingᵇ more than a mere sign of predication; that it also signifies existence. In the proposition, Socrates is just, it may seem to be implied not only that the quality *just* can be affirmed of Socrates, but moreover that Socrates *is*, that is to say, exists. This, however, only shows that there is an ambiguity in the word *is*; a word which not only performs the function of the copula in affirmations, but has also a meaning of its own, in virtue of which it may itself be made the predicate of a proposition. That the employment of it as a copula does not necessarily

ᵃ–ᵃMS, 43, 46   of the utmost importance
ᵇ–ᵇMS, 43, 46   much

include the affirmation of existence, appears from such a proposition as this, A centaur is a fiction of the poets; where it cannot possibly be implied that a centaur exists, since the proposition itself expressly asserts that the thing has no real existence.

Many volumes might be filled with the frivolous speculations concerning the nature of Being, (τὸ ὄν, οὐσία, Ens, Entitas, Essentia, and the like) which have risen from overlooking this double meaning of the ᶜwordᶜ *to be*; from supposing that when it signifies *to exist,* and when it signifies to *be* some specified thing, as to *be* a man, to *be* Socrates, to *be* seen or spoken of, to *be* a phantom, even to *be* a nonentity, it must still, at bottom, answer to the same idea; and that a meaning must be found for it which shall suit all these cases. The fog which rose from this narrow spot diffused itself at an early period over the whole surface of metaphysics. Yet it becomes us not to triumph over the ᵈgreatᵈ intellects of Plato and Aristotle because we are now able to preserve ourselves from many errors into which they, perhaps inevitably, fell. The fire-teazer of a modern steam-engine produces by his exertions far greater effects than Milo of Crotona could, but he is not therefore a stronger man. The Greeks seldom knew any language but their own. This rendered it far more difficult for them than it is for us, to acquire a readiness in detecting ambiguities. One of the advantages of having ᵉaccuratelyᵉ studied a plurality of languages, especially of those languages which ᶠeminent thinkersᶠ have used as the vehicle of their thoughts, is the practical lesson we learn respecting the ambiguities of words, by finding that the same word in one language corresponds, on different occasions, to different words in another. When not thus exercised, even the strongest understandings find it difficult to believe that things which have a common name, have not in some respect or other a common nature; and often expend much labour ᵍvery unprofitablyᵍ (as was frequently done by the two philosophers just mentioned) ʰinʰ vain attempts to discover in what this common nature consists. But, the habit once formed, intellects much inferior are capable of detecting even ambiguities which are common to many languages: and it is surprising that the one now under consideration, though it exists in the modern languages as well as in the ancient, should have been overlooked by almost all authors. The quantity of futile speculation which had been caused by a misapprehension of the nature of the copula, was hinted at by Hobbes;[*]

[*See "Computation or Logic," pp. 30-1, 60-1.]

ᶜ⁻ᶜ43, 46, 51, 56   words [*printer's error?*]
ᵈ⁻ᵈMS, 43, 46   gigantic
ᵉ⁻ᵉMS, 43, 46   systematically
ᶠ⁻ᶠMS, 43, 46   philosophers
ᵍ⁻ᵍMS, 43, 46, 51, 56, 62   not only unprofitably but mischievously
ʰ⁻ʰMS, 43, 46, 51   on

but *Mr. James* Mill* was, I believe, the first who distinctly characterized the ambiguity, and pointed out how many errors in the received systems of philosophy it has had to answer for. It has indeed misled the moderns scarcely less than the ancients, though their mistakes, because our understandings are not yet so completely emancipated from their influence, do not appear equally *irrational*.

We shall now briefly review the principal distinctions which exist among propositions, and the technical terms most commonly in use to express those distinctions.

§ 2. [*Affirmative and Negative propositions*] A proposition being a portion of discourse in which something is affirmed or denied of something, the first division of propositions is into affirmative and negative. An affirmative proposition is that in which the predicate is *affirmed* of the subject; as, Cæsar is dead. A negative proposition is that in which the predicate is *denied* of the subject; as, Cæsar is not dead. The copula, in this last species of proposition, consists of the words *is not*, which are the sign of negation; *is* being the sign of affirmation.

Some logicians, among whom may be mentioned Hobbes,[*] state this distinction differently; they recognise only one form of copula, *is*, and attach the negative sign to the predicate. "Cæsar is dead," and "Cæsar is not dead," according to these writers, are propositions agreeing not in the subject and predicate, but in the subject only. They do not consider "dead," but "not dead," to be the predicate of the second proposition, and they accordingly define a negative proposition to be one in which the predicate is a negative name. The point, though not of much practical moment, deserves notice as an example (not unfrequent in logic) where by means of an apparent simplification, but which is merely verbal, matters are made more complex than before. The *notion* of these writers was, that they could get rid of the distinction between affirming and denying, by treating every case of denying as the affirming *of* a negative name. But what is meant by a negative name? A name expressive of the *absence* of an attribute. So that when we affirm a negative name, what we are really predicating is absence and not presence; we are asserting not that anything is, but that something is not; to express which operation no word seems so proper as the word denying. The fundamental distinction is between a fact and the non-existence of that fact; be-

---

Analysis of the Human Mind, Vol. I, pp. 126 et seq.
[*See, e.g., "Computation or Logic," pp. 18, 27, 35, 40.]

*i-i*MS   the late Mr. James]   43, 46, 51, 56, 62, 65   Mr.
*j-j*MS, 43, 46   ridiculous
*a-a*MS, 43, 46   idea
b-b+43, 46, 51, 56, 62, 65, 68, 72

tween seeing something and not seeing it, between Cæsar's being dead and his not being dead; and if this were a merely verbal distinction, the generalization which brings both within the same form of assertion would be a real simplification: the distinction, however, being real, and in the facts, it is the generalization confounding the distinction that is merely verbal; and tends to obscure the subject, by treating the difference between two kinds of *ctruths*c as if it were only a difference between two kinds of words. To put things together, and to put them or keep them asunder, will remain different operations, whatever tricks we may play with language.

A remark of a similar nature may be applied to most of those distinctions among propositions which are said to have reference to their *modality*; as, difference of tense or time; the sun *did* rise, the sun *is* rising, the sun *will* rise. *dThesed* differences, like that between affirmation and negation, might be glossed over by considering the incident of time as a mere modification of the predicate: thus, The sun is *an object having risen*, The sun is *an object now rising*, The sun is *an object to rise hereafter*. But the simplification would be merely verbal. Past, present, *eande* future, do not constitute so many different kinds of rising; they are *f* designations belonging to the event asserted, to the *sun's* rising to-day. They affect, not the predicate, but the applicability of the predicate to the particular subject. That which we affirm to be past, present, or future, is not what the subject signifies, nor what the predicate signifies, but specifically and expressly what the predication signifies; what is expressed only by the proposition as such, and not by either or both of the terms. Therefore the circumstance of time is properly considered as attaching to the copula, which is the sign of predication, and not to the predicate. If the same cannot be said of such modifications as these, Cæsar *may* be dead; Cæsar is *perhaps* dead; it is *possible* that Cæsar is dead; it is only because these fall altogether under another head, being properly assertions not of anything relating to the fact itself, but of the state of our own mind in regard to it; namely, our absence of disbelief of it. Thus "Cæsar may be dead" means "I am not sure that Cæsar is alive."

§ 3. [*Simple and Complex propositions*] The next division of propositions is into Simple and Complex *a*; more aptly (by Professor Bain*) termed Compound*a*. A simple proposition is that in which one predicate is affirmed or denied of one subject. A *bcompoundb* proposition is that in which there is more than one predicate, or more than one subject, or both.

*[72] *Logic*, Pt. I, p. 85.

c–c51, 56   truth [*printer's error?*]   d–dMS, 43, 46   All these
e–eMS, 43   or   f51   the
a–a+72
b–bMS, 43, 46, 51, 56, 62, 65, 68   complex

At first sight this division has the air of an absurdity; a solemn distinction of things into one and more than one; as if we were to divide horses into single horses and teams of horses. And it is true that what is called a complex ^c(or compound)^c proposition is often not a proposition at all, but several propositions, held together by a conjunction. Such, for example, is this: Cæsar is dead, and Brutus is alive: or even this, Cæsar is dead, *but* Brutus is alive. There are here two distinct assertions; and we might as well call a street a complex house, as these two propositions a complex proposition. It is true that the syncategorematic words *and* and *but* have a meaning; but that meaning is so far from making the two propositions one, that it adds a third proposition to them. All particles are abbreviations, and generally abbreviations of propositions; a kind of short-hand, whereby ^dsomething^d which, to be expressed fully, would have required a proposition or a series of propositions, is suggested to the mind at once. Thus the words, Cæsar is dead and Brutus is alive, are equivalent to these: Cæsar is dead; Brutus is alive; it is ^edesired^e that the two preceding propositions should be thought of together. If the words were, Cæsar is dead, *but* Brutus is alive, the sense would be equivalent to the same three propositions together with a fourth; "between the two preceding propositions there exists a contrast:" viz. either between the two facts themselves, or between the feelings with which it is ^fdesired^f that they should be regarded.

In the instances cited the two propositions are kept visibly distinct, each subject having its separate predicate, and each predicate its separate subject. For brevity, however, and to avoid repetition, the propositions are often blended together: as in this, "Peter and James preached at Jerusalem and in Galilee," which contains four propositions: Peter preached at Jerusalem, Peter preached in Galilee, James preached at Jerusalem, James preached in Galilee.

We have seen that when the two or more propositions ^gcomprised in^g what is called a complex proposition are stated absolutely, and not under any condition or proviso, it is not a proposition at all, but a plurality of propositions; since what it expresses is not a single assertion, but several assertions, which, if true when joined, are true also when separated. But there is a kind of proposition which, though it contains a plurality of subjects and of predicates, and may be said in one sense of the ^hword^h to consist of several propositions, contains but one assertion; and its truth does not at all imply that of the simple propositions which compose it. An example of this is, when the simple propositions are connected by the particle *or*; as, either A is B or C is D; or by the particle *if*; as, A is B if C is D. In the former case,

^{c−c}+72
^{e−e}MS, 43, 46   my wish
^{g−g}MS, 43, 46   comprising

^{d−d}MS, 43, 46, 51, 56, 62, 65   that
^{f−f}MS, 43, 46   my wish
^{h−h}MS   words

the proposition is called *disjunctive*, in the latter, *conditional*: the name *hypothetical* was originally common to both. As has been well remarked by Archbishop Whately[*] and others, the disjunctive form is resolvable into the conditional; every disjunctive proposition being equivalent to two or more conditional ones. "Either A is B or C is D," means, "if A is not B, C is D; and if C is not D, A is B." All hypothetical propositions, therefore, though disjunctive in form, are conditional in meaning; and the words hypothetical and conditional may be, as indeed they generally are, used synonymously. Propositions in which the assertion is not dependent on a condition, are said, in the language of logicians, to be *categorical*.

An hypothetical proposition is not, like the pretended complex propositions which we previously considered, a mere aggregation of simple propositions. The simple propositions which form part of the words in which it is couched, form no part of the assertion which it conveys. When we say, If the Koran comes from God, Mahomet is the prophet of God, we do not intend to affirm either that the Koran does come from God, or that Mahomet is really his prophet. Neither of these simple propositions may be true, and yet the truth of the hypothetical proposition may be indisputable. What is asserted is not the truth of either of the propositions, but the inferribility of the one from the other. What, then, is the subject, and what the predicate of the hypothetical proposition? "The Koran" is not the subject of it, nor is "Mahomet:" for nothing is affirmed or denied either of the Koran or of Mahomet. The real subject of the predication is the entire proposition, "Mahomet is the prophet of God;" and the affirmation is, that this is a legitimate inference from the proposition, "The Koran comes from God." The subject and predicate, therefore, of an hypothetical proposition are names of propositions. The subject is some one proposition. The predicate is a general relative name applicable to propositions; of this form—"an inference from so and so." A fresh instance is here afforded of the remark, that [i] particles are abbreviations; since "*If* A is B, C is D," is found to be an abbreviation of the following: "The proposition C is D, is a legitimate inference from the proposition A is B."

The distinction, therefore, between hypothetical and categorical propositions, is not so great as it at first appears. In the conditional, as well as in the categorical form, one predicate is affirmed of one subject, and no more: but a conditional proposition is a proposition concerning a proposition; the subject of the assertion is itself an assertion. Nor is this a property peculiar to hypothetical propositions. There are other classes of assertions concerning propositions. Like other things, a proposition has attributes which may be

[*Elements of Logic, p. 106.]

[i]MS, 43, 46, 51, 56 all

predicated of it. The attribute predicated of it in an hypothetical proposition, is that of being an inference from a certain other proposition. But this is only one of many attributes that might be predicated. We may say, That the whole is greater than its part, is an axiom in mathematics: That the Holy Ghost proceeds from the Father alone, is a tenet of the Greek Church: The doctrine of the divine right of kings was renounced by Parliament at the Revolution: The infallibility of the Pope has no countenance from Scripture. In all these cases the subject of the predication is an entire proposition. That which these different predicates are affirmed of, is *the proposition*, "the whole is greater than its part;" *the proposition*, "the Holy Ghost proceeds from the Father alone;" *the proposition*, "kings have a divine right;" *the proposition*, "the Pope is infallible."

Seeing, then, that there is much less difference between hypothetical propositions and any others, than one might be led to imagine from their form, we should be at a loss to account for the conspicuous position which they have been selected to fill in treatises on logic, if we did not remember that what they predicate of a proposition, namely, its being an inference from something else, is precisely that one of its attributes with which most of all a logician is concerned.

§4. [*Universal, Particular, and Singular propositions*] The next of the common divisions of Propositions is into Universal, Particular, Indefinite, and Singular: a distinction founded on the degree of generality in which the name, which is the subject of the proposition, is to be understood. The following are examples:

All men are mortal	Universal.
Some men are mortal	Particular.
Man is mortal	Indefinite.
Julius Cæsar is mortal	Singular.

The proposition is Singular, when the subject is an individual name. The individual name needs not be a proper name. "The Founder of Christianity was crucified," is as much a singular proposition as "Christ was crucified."

When the name which is the subject of the proposition is a general name, we may intend to affirm or deny the predicate, either of all the things that the subject denotes, or only of some. When the predicate is affirmed or denied of all and each of the things denoted by the subject, the proposition is universal; when of some ᵃundefinedᵃ portion of them only, it is particular. Thus, All men are mortal; Every man is mortal; are universal propositions. No man is immortal, is also an universal proposition, since the predicate, immortal, is denied of each and every individual denoted by the term man; the negative proposition being exactly equivalent to the following, Every man

ᵃ⁻ᵃMS, 43, 46, 51, 56   non-assignable

is not-immortal. But "some men are wise," "some men are not wise," are particular propositions; the predicate *wise* being in the one case affirmed and in the other denied not of each and every individual denoted by the term man, but only of each and every one of some portion of those individuals, without specifying what portion; for if this were specified, the proposition would be changed either into a singular proposition, or into an universal proposition with a different subject; as, for instance, "all *bproperlyb* instructed men are wise." There are other forms of particular propositions; *cas,c* "*Most* men are *dimperfectly educated:d*" it being immaterial how large a portion of the subject the predicate is asserted of, as long as it is left uncertain how that portion is to be distinguished from the rest.*

When the form of the expression does not clearly show whether the general name which is the subject of the proposition is meant to stand for all the individuals denoted by it, or only for some of them, the proposition is *e*, by some logicians,*e* called Indefinite; but this, as Archbishop Whately observes, is a solecism, of the same nature as that committed by some grammarians when in their list of genders they enumerate the *doubtful* gender.[*] The speaker must mean to assert the proposition either as an universal or as a particular proposition, though he has failed to declare which: and it often happens that though the words do not show which of the two he intends, the context, or the custom of speech, supplies the deficiency. Thus, when it is affirmed that "Man is mortal," nobody doubts that the assertion is intended of all human beings; and the word indicative of universality is commonly omitted, only because the meaning is evident without it. *f*In the proposition, "Wine is good," it is understood with equal readiness, though for somewhat different reasons, that the assertion is not intended to be universal, but

---

*[72] Instead of Universal and Particular as applied to propositions, Professor Bain proposes (*Logic*, Pt. I, pp. 81–2) the terms Total and Partial; reserving the former pair of terms for their inductive meaning, "the contrast between a general proposition and the particulars or individuals that we derive it from." This change in nomenclature would be attended with the further advantage, that Singular propositions, which in the Syllogism follow the same rules as Universal, would be included along with them in the same class, that of Total predications. It is not the Subject's denoting many things or only one, that is of importance in reasoning, it is that the assertion is made of the whole or a part only of what the Subject denotes. The words Universal and Particular, however, are so familiar and so well understood in both the senses mentioned by Mr. Bain, that the double meaning does not produce any material inconvenience.

[*Whately, *Elements of Logic*, p. 66 (Bk. II, Chap. ii, § 2).]

b–b+51, 56, 62, 65, 68, 72
c–cMS   instead of "Some men," we may say [*printer's error? MS alteration on verso of folio*]
d–dMS, 43, 46   incapable of self-government,
e–eMS, 43, 46, 51   commonly   f–f+51, 56, 62, 65, 68, 72

particular.*[f] *[g]As is observed by Professor Bain,† the chief examples of Indefinite propositions occur "with names of material, which are the subjects sometimes of universal, and at other times of particular predication. 'Food is chemically constituted by carbon, oxygen, &c.,' is a proposition of universal quantity; the meaning is all food—all kinds of food. 'Food is necessary to animal life' is a case of particular quantity; the meaning is some sort of food, not necessarily all sorts. 'Metal is requisite in order to strength' does not mean all kinds of metal. 'Gold will make a way,' means a portion of gold."[g]

When a general name stands for each and every individual which it is a name of, or in other words, which it denotes, it is said by logicians to be *distributed*, or taken distributively. Thus, in the proposition, All men are mortal, the subject, Man, is distributed, because mortality is affirmed of each and every man. The predicate, Mortal, is not distributed, because the only mortals who are spoken of in the proposition are those who happen to be men; while the word may, for aught that appears, and in fact does, comprehend [h]within[h] it an indefinite number of objects besides men. In the proposition, Some men are mortal, both the predicate and the subject are undistributed. In the following, No men [i]have wings[i], both the predicate and [j]the[j] subject are distributed. Not only [k]is the attribute of having wings[k] denied of the entire class Man, but that class is severed and cast out from the whole of the class [l]Winged[l], and not merely from some part of that class.

This phraseology, which is of great service in stating and demonstrating the rules of the syllogism, enables us to express very concisely the definitions of an universal and a particular proposition. An universal proposition is that of which the subject is distributed; a particular proposition is that of which the subject is undistributed.

There are many more distinctions among propositions than those we have here stated, some of them of considerable importance. But, for explaining and illustrating these, more suitable opportunities will occur in the sequel.

---

*[62] It may, however, be considered as equivalent to an universal proposition with a different predicate, viz. "All wine is good *quâ* wine," or "is good in respect of the qualities which constitute it wine."

†[72] *Logic*, Pt. I, pp. 82–3.

[g]–[g]+72
[h]–[h]MS, 43, 46   under
[i]–[i]MS   are gods]   43, 46   are perfect
[j]–[j]+51, 56, 62, 65, 68, 72
[k]–[k]MS   are the attributes of a god]   43, 46   is the attribute perfection
[l]–[l]MS   Gods]   43, 46   Perfect

CHAPTER V

Of the Import of Propositions

§ 1. [*Doctrine that a proposition is the expression of a relation between two ideas*] An inquiry into the nature of propositions must have one of two objects: to analyse the state of mind called Belief, or to analyse what is believed. All language recognises a difference between a doctrine or opinion, and the *ᵃfactᵃ* of entertaining the opinion; between assent, and what is assented to.

Logic, according to the conception here formed of it, has no concern with the nature of the act of judging or believing; the consideration of that act, as a phenomenon of the mind, belongs to another science. Philosophers, however, from Descartes downwards, and especially from the era of Leibnitz and Locke, have by no means observed this distinction; and ᵇ would have treated with great disrespect any attempt to analyse the import of Propositions, unless founded on an analysis of the act of Judgment. A proposition, they would have said, is but the expression in words of a Judgment. The thing expressed, not the mere verbal expression, is the important matter. When the mind assents to a proposition, it judges. Let us find out what the mind does when it judges, and we shall know what propositions mean, and not otherwise.

Conformably to these views, almost all the writers on Logic in the last two centuries, whether English, German, or French, have made their theory of Propositions, from one end to the other, a theory of Judgments. They considered a Proposition, or a Judgment, for they used the two words indiscriminately, to consist in affirming or denying one *idea* of another. To judge, was to put two ideas together, or to bring one idea under another, or to compare two ideas, or to perceive the agreement or disagreement between two ideas: and the whole doctrine of Propositions, together with the theory of Reasoning, (always necessarily founded on the theory of Propositions,) was stated as if Ideas, or Conceptions, or whatever other term the writer preferred as a name for mental representations generally, constituted essentially the subject matter and substance of those operations.

It is, of course, true, that in any case of judgment, as for instance when we judge that gold is yellow, a process takes place in our minds, of which some

ᵃ⁻ᵃMS, 43, 46, 51, 56   act   ᵇ⁻ᵇMS   they

one or other of these theories is a partially correct account. We must have the idea of gold and the idea of yellow, and these two ideas must be brought together in our mind. But in the first place, it is evident that this is only a part of what takes place; for we may put two ideas together without any act of belief; as when we merely imagine something, such as a golden mountain; or when we actually disbelieve: for in order even to disbelieve that Mahomet was an apostle of God, we must put the idea of Mahomet and that of an apostle of God together. To determine what it is that happens in the case of assent or dissent besides putting two ideas together, is one of the most intricate of metaphysical problems. But whatever the solution may be, we may venture to assert that it can have nothing whatever to do with the import of propositions; for *this* reason, that propositions (except *sometimes when* the mind itself is the subject treated of) are not assertions respecting our ideas of things, but assertions respecting the things themselves. In order to believe that gold is yellow, I must, indeed, have the idea of gold, and the idea of yellow, and something having reference to those ideas must take place in my mind; but my belief has not reference to the ideas, it has reference to the things. What I believe, is a fact relating to the outward thing, gold, and to the impression made by that outward thing upon the human organs; not a fact relating to my conception of gold, which would be a fact in my mental history, not a fact of external nature. It is true, that in order to believe this fact in external nature, another fact must take place in my mind, a process must be performed upon my ideas; but so it must in everything else that I do. I cannot dig the ground unless I have the idea of the ground, and of a spade, and of all the other things I am operating upon, and unless I put those ideas together.* But it would be a very ridiculous description of digging the ground to say that it is putting one idea into another. Digging is an operation which is performed upon the things themselves, though it cannot be performed unless I have in my mind the ideas of them. And *ᶠ* in like manner, believing is an act which has for its subject the facts themselves, though a previous mental conception of the facts is an indispensable condition. When I say that

---

*[51] Dr. Whewell (*Philosophy of Discovery*, p. 242) questions this statement, and asks, "Are we to say that a mole cannot dig the ground, except he has an idea of the ground, and of the snout and paws with which he digs it?" *ᵉI do not know what passes in a mole's mind, nor what amount of mental apprehension may or may not accompany his instinctive actions. But a human being does not use a spade by instinct; and he certainly could not use it unless he had knowledge of a spade, and of the earth which he uses it upon.ᵉ*

ᶜ⁻ᶜMS the
ᵈ⁻ᵈMS, 43, 46, 51, 56, 62, 65 where
ᵉ⁻ᵉ51, 56 I thought it had been evident that I was here speaking of rational digging, and not of digging by instinct.
ᶠMS, 43, 46, 51, 56, 62 so,

fire causes heat, do I mean that my idea of fire causes my idea of heat? No: I mean that the natural phenomenon, fire, causes the natural phenomenon, heat. When I mean to assert anything respecting the ideas, I give them their proper name, I call them ideas: as when I say, that a child's idea of a battle is unlike the reality, or that the ideas entertained of the Deity have a great effect on the characters of mankind.

The notion that what is of primary importance to the logician in a proposition, is the relation between the two *ideas* corresponding to the subject and predicate, (instead of the relation between the two *phenomena* which they respectively express,) seems to me one of the most fatal errors ever introduced into the philosophy of Logic; and the principal cause why the theory of the science has made such inconsiderable progress during the last two centuries. The treatises on Logic, and on the branches of Mental Philosophy connected with Logic, which have been produced since the intrusion of this cardinal error, though sometimes written by men of extraordinary abilities and attainments, almost always tacitly imply a theory that the investigation of truth consists in contemplating and handling our ideas, or conceptions of things, instead of the things themselves: a *g*doctrine tantamount to the assertion, that the only mode of acquiring knowledge of nature is to study it at second hand, as represented in our own minds*g*. Meanwhile, inquiries into every kind of natural phenomena were incessantly establishing great and fruitful truths on *h* most important subjects, by processes upon which these views of the nature of Judgment and Reasoning threw no light, and in which they afforded no assistance whatever. No wonder that those who knew by practical experience how truths are *i*arrived*i* at, should deem a science futile, which consisted chiefly of such speculations. What has been done for the advancement of Logic since these doctrines came into vogue, has been done not by professed logicians, but by discoverers in the other sciences; in whose methods of investigation many *j* principles of logic, not previously thought of, have successively come forth into light, but who have generally committed the error of supposing that nothing whatever was known of the art of philosophizing by the old logicians, because their modern interpreters have written to so little purpose respecting it.

We have to inquire, then, on the present occasion, not into Judgment, but judgments; not into the act of believing, but into the thing believed. What is the immediate object of belief in a Proposition? What is the matter of fact signified by it? What is it to which, when I assert the proposition, I give my

---

*g–g*MS, 43, 46   process by which, I will venture to affirm, not a single truth ever was arrived at, except truths of psychology, a science of which Ideas or Conceptions are avowedly (along with other mental phenomena) the subject-matter
*h*43, 46, 51   the
*i–i*MS, 43, 46, 51, 56   come   *j*MS, 43, 46   great

assent, and call upon others to give theirs? What is that which is expressed by the form of discourse called a Proposition, and the conformity of which to fact constitutes the truth of the proposition?

§ 2. [*Doctrine that a proposition is the expression of a relation between the meaning of two names*] One of the clearest and most consecutive thinkers whom this country or the world has produced, I mean Hobbes, has given the following answer to this question. In every proposition (says he)[*] what is signified is, the belief of the speaker that the predicate is a name of the same thing of which the subject is a name; and if it really is so, the proposition is true. Thus the proposition, All men are living beings (he would say) is true, because *living being* is a name of everything of which *man* is a name. All men are six feet high, is not true, because *six feet high* is not a name of everything (though it is of some things) of which *man* is a name.

What is stated *a*in this theory*a* as the definition of a true proposition, must be allowed to be a property which all true propositions possess. The subject and predicate being both of them names of things, if they were names of quite different things the one name could not, consistently with its signification, be predicated of the other. If it be true that some men are copper-coloured, it must be true—and the proposition does really assert—that among the individuals denoted by the name man, there are some who are also among those denoted by the name copper-coloured. If it be true that all oxen ruminate, it must be true that all the individuals denoted by the name ox are also among those denoted by the name ruminating; and whoever asserts that all oxen ruminate, undoubtedly does assert that this relation subsists between the two names.

The assertion, therefore, which, according to Hobbes, is the only one made in any proposition, really is made in every proposition: and his analysis has consequently one of the requisites for being the true one. We may go a step farther; it is the only analysis that is rigorously true of all propositions without exception. What he gives as the meaning of propositions, is part of the meaning of all propositions, and the whole meaning of some. This, however, only shows what an extremely minute fragment of meaning it is quite possible to include within the logical formula of a proposition. It does not show that no proposition means more. To warrant us in putting together two words with a copula between them, it is really enough that the thing or things denoted by one of the names should be capable, without violation of usage, of being called by the other name also. If, then, this be all the meaning necessarily implied in the form of discourse called a Proposition, why do *b*I*b*

[*See "Computation or Logic," p. 30.]

*a–a*MS, 43   by Hobbes   *b–b*MS   we

object to it as the scientific definition of what a proposition means? Because, though the mere collocation which makes the proposition a proposition, conveys no more *than this scanty amount of meaning*, that same collocation combined with other circumstances, that *form* combined with other *matter*, does convey more, and *the proposition in those other circumstances does assert more, than merely that relation between the two names*.

The only propositions of which Hobbes' principle is a sufficient account, are that limited and unimportant class in which both the predicate and the subject are proper names. For, as has already been remarked, proper names have strictly no meaning; they are mere marks for individual objects: and when a proper name is predicated of another proper name, all the signification conveyed is, that both the names are marks for the same object. But this is precisely what Hobbes produces as a theory of predication in general. His doctrine is a full explanation of such predications as these: Hyde was Clarendon, or, Tully is Cicero. It exhausts the meaning of those propositions. But it is a sadly inadequate theory of any others. That it should ever have been thought of as such, can be accounted for only by the fact, that Hobbes, in common with the other Nominalists, bestowed little or no attention upon the *connotation* of words; and sought for their meaning exclusively in what they *denote*: as if all names had been (what none but proper names really are) marks put upon individuals; and as if there were no difference between a proper and a general name, except that the first denotes only one individual, and the last a greater number.

It has been seen, however, that the meaning of all names, except proper names and that portion of the class of abstract names which are not connotative, resides in the connotation. When, therefore, we are analysing the meaning of any proposition in which the predicate and the subject, or either of them, are connotative names, it is to the connotation of those terms that we must exclusively look, and not to what they *denote*, or in the language of Hobbes (language so far correct) are names of.

In asserting that the truth of a proposition depends on the conformity of *import between* its terms, as, for instance, that the proposition, Socrates is wise, is a true proposition, because Socrates and wise are names *applicable to, or, as he expresses it, names of, the same person*; it is very remarkable that so powerful a thinker should not have asked himself the question, But how came they to be names of the same *person*?[*] Surely not because such

[*See "Computation or Logic," p. 35.]

c–cMS, 43   meaning than Hobbes contends for
d–dMS, 43, 46, 51, 56, 62, 65, 68   much more
e–eMS   denote
f–fMS   denote   g–gMS   meaning of
h–hMS   for the same thing   i–iMS   thing

was the intention of those who invented the words. When mankind fixed the meaning of the word wise, they were not thinking of Socrates, nor, when his parents gave him the name *of* Socrates, were they thinking of wisdom. The names *happen* to fit the same *person* because of a certain *fact*, which fact was not known, nor in being, when the names were invented. If we want to know what the fact is, we shall find the clue to it in the *connotation* of the names.

A bird, or a stone, a man, or a wise man, means simply, an object having such and such attributes. The real meaning of the word man, is those attributes, and not *Smith, Brown, and the remainder of the individuals*. The word *mortal*, in like manner connotes a certain attribute or attributes; and when we say, All men are mortal, the meaning of the proposition is, that all beings which possess the one set of attributes, possess also the other. If, in our experience, the attributes connoted by *man* are always accompanied by the attribute connoted by *mortal*, it will follow as a consequence, that the class *man* will be wholly included in the class *mortal*, and that *mortal* will be a name of all things of which *man* is a name: but why? Those objects are brought under the name, by possessing the attributes connoted by it: but their possession of the attributes is the real condition on which the truth of the proposition depends; not their being called by the name. Connotative names do not precede, but follow, the attributes which they connote. If one attribute happens to be always found in conjunction with another attribute, the concrete names which answer to those attributes will of course be predicable of the same subjects, and may be said, in Hobbes' language, (in the propriety of which on this *occasion* I fully concur,) to be two names for the same things. But the possibility of a concurrent application of the two names, is a mere consequence of the conjunction between the two attributes, and was, in most cases, never thought of when the names were *introduced* and their signification fixed. That the diamond is combustible, was a proposition certainly not dreamt of when the words Diamond and Combustible *first received their* meaning; and could not have been discovered by the most ingenious and refined analysis of the signification of those words. It was found out by a very different process, namely, by exerting the *p* senses, and learning from them, that the attribute of combustibility existed in *the* diamonds upon which the experiment was tried; *the number *or* character

j-j+65, 68, 72   *k-k*MS thing
*l-l*MS, 43, 46 John, Peter, Thomas, &c.] 51, 56, 62 John, Jane, and the remainder of the individuals
  *m-m*MS point   *n-n*MS, 43, 46, 51, 56, 62 invented
*o-o*MS, 43, 46 received their present   *p*MS, 43, 46 five
*q-q*MS, 43, 46, 51, 56 all those
  *r-r*MS these being so numerous, and the circumstances of the experiments being]
43, 46 *as* MS . . . experiments
  *s-s*51, 56 and

of the experiments being^r such, that what was true of those individuals might be concluded to be true of all substances "^{t}called by^t the name," that is, of all substances possessing the attributes which the name connotes. The assertion, therefore, when analysed, is, that ^{u}wherever we find certain attributes, there will be found a certain other attribute: which^u is not a question of the signification of names, but of ^{v} laws of nature; the order existing among phenomena.

§ 3. [*Doctrine that a proposition consists in referring something to, or excluding something from, a class*] Although Hobbes' theory of Predication has not, in the terms in which he stated it, met with a very favourable reception from ^{a}subsequent thinkers^a, a theory virtually identical with it, and not by any means so perspicuously expressed, may almost be said to have taken the rank of an established opinion. The most generally received notion of Predication decidedly is that it consists in referring something to a class, *i.e.*, either placing an individual under a class, or placing one class under another class. Thus, the proposition, Man is mortal, asserts, according to this view of it, that the class man is included in the class mortal. "Plato is a philosopher," asserts that the individual Plato is one of those who compose the class philosopher. If the proposition is negative, then instead of placing something in a class, it is said to exclude something from a class. Thus, if the following be the proposition, The elephant is not carnivorous; what is asserted (according to this theory) is, that the elephant is excluded from the class carnivorous, or is not numbered among the things comprising that class. There is no real difference, except in language, between this theory of Predication and the theory of Hobbes. For a class *is* absolutely nothing but an indefinite number of individuals denoted by a general name. The name given to them in common, is what makes them a class. To refer anything to a class, therefore, is to look upon it as one of the things which are to be called by that common name. To exclude it from a class, is to say that the common name is not applicable to it.

How widely these views of predication have prevailed, is evident from this, that they are the basis of the celebrated *dictum de omni et nullo*. When the syllogism is resolved, by all who treat of it, into an inference that what is true of a class is true of all things whatever that belong to the class; and when this is laid down by almost all professed logicians as the ultimate principle to which all reasoning owes its validity; it is clear that in the general estimation of logicians, the propositions of which reasonings are composed

$^{t-t}$MS, 43, 46   coming within
$^{u-u}$MS   wheresoever we find certain attributes, there, also, will be found a certain other attribute. And this
^{v}MS, 43, 46   the
$^{a-a}$MS, 43, 46   philosophers

can be the expression of nothing but the process of dividing things into classes, and referring everything to its proper class.

This theory appears to me a signal example of a logical error very often committed in logic, that of ὕστερον πρότερον, or explaining a thing by something which presupposes it. When I say that snow is white, I may and ought to be thinking of snow as a class, because I am asserting a proposition as true of all snow: but I am certainly not thinking of white objects as a class; I am thinking of no white object whatever except snow, but only of that, and of the sensation of white which it gives me. When, indeed, I have judged, or assented to the propositions, that snow is white, and that several other things *are also* white, I gradually begin to think of white objects as a class, including snow and those other things. But this is a conception which followed, not preceded, those judgments, and therefore cannot be given as an explanation of them. Instead of explaining the effect by the cause, this doctrine explains the cause by the effect, and is, I conceive, founded on a latent misconception of the nature of classification.

There is a sort of language very generally prevalent in these discussions, which seems to suppose that classification is an arrangement and grouping of definite and known individuals: that when names were imposed, mankind took into consideration all the individual objects in the universe, *distributed them* into parcels or lists, and gave to the objects of each list a common name, repeating this operation *toties quoties* until they had invented all the general names of which language consists; which having been once done, if a question subsequently arises whether a certain general name can be truly predicated of a certain particular object, we have only (as it were) to read the roll of the objects upon which that name was conferred, and see whether the object about which the question arises is to be found among them. The framers of language (it would seem to be supposed) have predetermined all the objects that are to compose each class, and we have only to refer to the record of an antecedent decision.

So absurd a doctrine will be owned by nobody when thus nakedly stated; but if the commonly received explanations of classification and naming do not imply this theory, it requires to be shown how they admit of being reconciled with any other.

General names are not marks put upon definite objects; classes are not made by drawing a line round a given number of assignable individuals. The objects which compose any given class are perpetually fluctuating. We may frame a class without knowing the individuals, or even any of the individuals, of which it *may* be composed; we may do so while believing that no such individuals exist. If by the *meaning* of a general name are to be understood

---

^{b–b}MS, 43, 46, 51   also are
^{c–c}MS, 43, 46, 51   made them up   ^{d–d}MS, 43, 46, 51, 56, 62, 65   will

the things which it is the name of, no general name, except by accident, has a fixed meaning at all, or ever long retains the same meaning. The only mode in which any general name has a definite meaning, is by being a name of an *indefinite* variety of things; namely, of all things, known or unknown, past, present, or future, which possess certain definite attributes. When, by studying not the meaning of words, but the phenomena of nature, we discover that *these* attributes are possessed by some object not previously known to possess them, (as when chemists found that the diamond was combustible), we include this new object in the class; but it did not already belong to the class. We place the individual in the class because the proposition is true; the proposition is not true because the object is placed in the class.*

It will appear hereafter, in treating of reasoning, how much the theory of that intellectual process has been vitiated by the influence of these erroneous *notions*, and by the habit which they exemplify of assimilating all the operations of the human understanding which have truth for their object, to processes of mere classification and naming. Unfortunately, the minds which have been entangled in this net are precisely those which have escaped the other cardinal error commented upon in the beginning of the present chapter. Since the revolution which dislodged Aristotle from the schools, logicians may almost be divided into those who have looked upon reasoning as essentially an affair of Ideas, and those who have looked upon it as essentially an affair of Names.

Although, however, Hobbes' theory of Predication, according to the well-known remark of Leibnitz, and the avowal of Hobbes himself,† renders

---

*[72] Professor Bain remarks, in qualification of the statement in the text (*Logic*, Pt. I, p. 50), that the word Class has two meanings; "the class definite, and the class indefinite. The class definite is an enumeration of actual individuals, as the Peers of the Realm, the oceans of the globe, the known planets. . . . The class indefinite is unenumerated. Such classes are stars, planets, gold-bearing rocks, men, poets, virtuous. . . . In this last acceptation of the word, class name and general name are identical. The class name denotes an indefinite number of individuals, and connotes the points of community or likeness."

The theory controverted in the text, tacitly supposes all classes to be *definite*. I have assumed them to be indefinite; because, for the purposes of Logic, definite classes, as such, are almost useless; though often serviceable as means of abridged expression. (Vide infra, Bk. III, Chap. ii.)

†"From hence also this may be deduced, that the first truths were arbitrarily made by those that first of all imposed names upon things, or received them from the imposition of others. For it is true (for example) that *man is a living creature*, but it is for this reason, that it pleased men to impose both these names on the same thing." "Computation or Logic," Chap. iii, § 8 [p. 36].

*e–e*MS   *indefinite*
*f–f*MS   those [*printer's error?*]
*g–g*MS, 43, 46   views
*h–h*MS, 43, 46   One thing it is but just to remark. Although

truth and falsity completely arbitrary, with no standard but the will of men, it must not be concluded that either Hobbes, or any of the other *thinkers* who have in the main agreed with him, did in fact consider the distinction between truth and error as less real, or attached *less* importance to it, than other people. To suppose that they did so would argue total unacquaintance with their other speculations. But this shows how little hold their doctrine possessed over their own minds. No person, at bottom, ever imagined that there was nothing more in truth than propriety of expression; than using language in conformity to a previous convention. *k* When the inquiry was brought down from generals to a particular case, it has always been acknowledged that there is a distinction between verbal and real questions; that some false propositions are uttered from ignorance of the meaning of words, but that in others the source of the error is a misapprehension of things; that a person who has not the use of language at all may form propositions mentally, and that they may be untrue, that is, he may believe as matters of fact what are not really so. This last admission cannot be made in stronger terms than it is by Hobbes himself,* though he will not allow such erroneous belief to be called falsity, but only error. And *l* he has himself laid down, in other places, doctrines in which the true theory of predication is by implication contained. He distinctly says that general names are given to things on account of their attributes, and that abstract names are the names of those attributes. "Abstract is that which in any subject denotes the cause of the concrete name. . . . And these causes of names are the same with the causes of our conceptions, namely, some power of action, or affection, of the thing conceived, which some call the manner by which anything works upon our

*"Men are subject to err not only in affirming and denying, but also in perception, and in silent cogitation. . . . Tacit errors, or the errors of sense and cogitation, are made by passing from one imagination to the imagination of another different thing; or by feigning that to be past, or future, which never was, nor ever shall be; as when by seeing the image of the sun in water, we imagine the sun itself to be there; or by seeing swords, that there has been, or shall be, fighting, because it uses to be so for the most part; or when from promises we feign the mind of the promiser to be such and such; or, lastly, when from any sign we vainly imagine something to be signified which is not. And errors of this sort are common to all things that have sense." "Computation or Logic," Chap. v, § 1 [pp. 55–6].

*i–i*MS, 43, 46   philosophers
*j–j*MS, 43, 46   one jot less of
*k*MS, 43, 46   With whatever illusions even profound thinkers may have satisfied themselves when engaged in finding a general solution for a metaphysical problem; when they came to the practical application of their doctrines, they were always prepared with some means of explaining the solution away.
*l*MS, 43, 46   moreover,

senses, but by most men they are called *accidents*."* It is strange that having gone so far, he should not have gone one step *m*farther*m*, and seen that what he calls the cause of the concrete name, is in reality the meaning of it; and that when we predicate of any subject a name which is given *because* of an attribute (or, as he calls it, an accident), our object is not to affirm the name, but, by means of the name, to affirm the attribute.

§ 4. [*What a proposition really is*] Let the predicate be, as we have said, a connotative term; and to take the simplest case first, let the subject be a proper name: "The summit of Chimborazo is white." The word white connotes an attribute which is possessed by the individual object designated by the words "summit of Chimborazo;" which attribute consists in the physical fact, of its exciting in human beings the sensation which we call a sensation of white. It will be admitted that, by asserting the proposition, we wish to communicate information of that physical fact, and are not thinking of the names, except as the necessary means of making that communication. The meaning of the proposition, therefore, is, that the individual thing denoted by the subject, has the attributes connoted by the predicate.

If we now suppose the subject also to be a connotative name, the meaning expressed by the proposition has advanced a step farther in complication. Let us first suppose the proposition to be universal, as well as affirmative: "All men are mortal." In this case, as in the last, what the proposition asserts (or expresses a belief *a*of*a*) is, of course, that the objects *b*denoted*b* by the subject (man) possess the attributes connoted by the predicate (mortal). But the characteristic of this case is, that the objects are no longer *individually* designated. They are pointed out only by some of their attributes: they are the objects called men, that is, *c* possessing the attributes connoted by the name man; and the only thing known of them may be those attributes: indeed, as the proposition is general, and the objects denoted by the subject are therefore indefinite in number, most of them are not known individually at all. The assertion, therefore, is not, as before, that the attributes which the predicate connotes are possessed by any given individual, or by any number of individuals previously known as John, Thomas, *d* &c., but that those attributes are possessed by each and every individual possessing certain other attributes; that whatever has the attributes connoted by the subject, has also those connoted by the predicate; that the latter set of attributes *constantly*

Ibid., Chap. iii, § 3 [pp. 32–3].

*m–m*MS further
*a–a*MS, 43, 46 in *b–b*MS denoted
*c*MS, 43, 46 the beings *d*MS, 43, 46 Richard,

accompany the former set. Whatever has the attributes of man has the attribute of mortality; mortality constantly accompanies the attributes of man.*

If it be remembered that every attribute is *grounded* on some fact or phenomenon, either of outward sense or of inward consciousness, and that to *possess* an attribute is another phrase for *being the cause of, or forming* part of, the fact or phenomenon upon which the attribute is grounded; we may add one more step to complete the analysis. The proposition which asserts that one attribute always accompanies another attribute, *really asserts* thereby no other thing than this, that one phenomenon always accompanies another phenomenon; insomuch that where we find the *latter*, we have assurance of the existence of the former*. Thus, in the proposition, All men are mortal, the word man connotes the attributes which we ascribe to a certain kind of living creatures, on the ground of certain phenomena which they exhibit, and which are partly physical phenomena, namely the impressions made on our senses by their bodily form and structure, and partly mental phenomena, namely the sentient and intellectual life which they have of their own. All this is understood when we utter the word man, by any one to whom the meaning of the word is known. Now, when we say, Man is mortal, we mean that wherever these various physical and mental phenomena are all found, there we have assurance that the other physical and mental phenomenon, called death, will not fail to take place. The proposition does not affirm *when*; for the connotation of the word *mortal* goes no

---

*[62] To the preceding statement it has been objected, that "we naturally construe the subject of a proposition in its extension, and the predicate (which therefore may be an adjective) in its intension, (connotation): and that consequently coexistence of attributes does not, any more than the opposite theory of equation of groups, correspond with the living processes of thought and language." I acknowledge the distinction here drawn, which, indeed, I had myself laid down and exemplified a few pages back (pp. 93–4). But though it is true that we naturally "construe the subject of a proposition in its extension," this extension, or in other words, the extent of the class denoted by the name, is not apprehended or indicated directly. It is both apprehended and indicated solely through the attributes. In the "living processes of thought and language" the extension, though in this case really thought of (which in the case of the predicate it is not), is thought of only through the medium of what my acute and courteous critic terms the "intension."

*For further illustrations of this subject, see *Examination of Sir William Hamilton's Philosophy*, Chap. xxii.*

e–e+65, 68, 72
*f–f*MS   to be the cause of, or to form a
*g–g*MS, 43, 46   does really assert
*h–h*MS, 43, 46, 51, 56, 62, 65, 68   one, we have assurance of the existence of the other

farther than to the occurrence of the phenomenon at some time or other, leaving the *particular* time undecided.

§ 5. [*A proposition asserts (or denies) a sequence, a coexistence, a simple existence, a causation*] We have already proceeded far enough, not only to demonstrate the error of Hobbes, but to ascertain the real import of by far the most numerous class of propositions. The object of belief in a proposition, when it asserts anything more than the meaning of words, is generally, as in the cases which we have examined, either the co-existence or the sequence of two phenomena. At the very commencement of our inquiry, we found that every act of belief implied two Things: we have now ascertained what, in the most frequent case, these two things are, namely two Phenomena, in other words, two states of consciousness; and what it is which the proposition affirms (or denies) to subsist between them, namely either succession or co-existence. And this case includes innumerable instances which no one, previous to reflection, would think of referring to it. Take the following example: A generous person is worthy of honour. Who would expect to recognise here a case of co-existence between phenomena? But so it is. The attribute which causes a person to be termed generous, is ascribed to him on the ground of states of his mind, and particulars of his conduct: both are phenomena: the former are facts of internal consciousness; the latter, so far as distinct from the former, are physical facts, or perceptions of the senses. Worthy of honour admits of a similar analysis. Honour, as here used, means a state of approving and admiring emotion, followed on occasion by corresponding outward acts. "Worthy of honour" connotes all this, together with our approval of the act of showing honour. All these are phenomena; states of internal consciousness, accompanied or followed by physical facts. When we say, A generous person is worthy of honour, we affirm co-existence between the two complicated phenomena connoted by the two terms respectively. We affirm, that wherever and whenever the inward feelings and outward facts implied in the word generosity have place, then and there the existence and manifestation of an inward feeling, honour, would be followed in our minds by another inward feeling, approval.

After the analysis, in a former chapter, of the import of names, many examples are not needed to illustrate the import of propositions. When there is any obscurity, or difficulty, it does not lie in the meaning of the proposition, but in the meaning of the names which compose it; in the *a*extremely complicated*a* connotation of many words; the immense multitude and prolonged series of facts which often constitute the phenomenon connoted by a name.

*i–i*MS further   *j–j*MS, 43, 46, 51, 56, 62, 65, 68 precise
*a–a*MS, 43 complicated nature of the] 46, 51, 56, 62 very complicated

But [b]where[b] it is seen what the phenomenon is, there is seldom any difficulty in seeing that the assertion conveyed by the proposition is, the co-existence of one such phenomenon with another; or the succession of one such phenomenon to another: [c]so that where the one is found, we may calculate on finding the other, though perhaps not conversely[c].

This, however, though the most common, is not the only meaning which propositions are ever intended to convey. In the first place, sequences and co-existences are not only asserted respecting Phenomena; we make propositions also respecting those hidden causes of phenomena, which are named substances and attributes. A substance, however, being to us nothing but either that which causes, or that which is conscious of, phenomena; and the same being true, *mutatis mutandis*, of attributes; no assertion can be made, at least with a meaning, concerning these unknown and unknowable entities, [d] except in virtue of the Phenomena by which alone they manifest themselves to our faculties. When we say, Socrates was [e]cotemporary[e] with the Peloponnesian war, the foundation of this assertion, as of all assertions concerning substances, is an assertion concerning the phenomena which they exhibit,— namely, that the series of facts by which Socrates manifested himself to mankind, and the series of mental states which constituted his [f]sentient[f] existence, went on simultaneously with the series of facts known by the name of the Peloponnesian war. Still, the proposition [g]as commonly understood[g] does not assert that alone; it asserts that the Thing in itself, the *noumenon* Socrates, was existing, and doing or experiencing those various facts during the same time. Co-existence and sequence, therefore, may be affirmed or denied not only between phenomena, but between noumena, or between a noumenon and phenomena. And [h]both of noumena and of phenomena we may affirm[h] simple existence. But what is a noumenon? An unknown cause. In affirming, therefore, the existence of a noumenon, we affirm causation. Here, therefore, are two additional kinds of fact, capable of being asserted in a proposition. Besides the propositions which assert Sequence or Coexistence, there are some which assert simple Existence;* and others assert Causation, which,

---

*[72] Professor Bain, in his *Logic* (Pt. I, p. 256), excludes Existence from the list, considering it as a mere name. All propositions, he says, which predicate

[b-b]MS   when [*printer's error?*]
[c-c]MS, 43, 46, 51, 56, 62, 65, 68   their *conjunction*, in short, so that where the one is found, we may calculate on finding both
[d]MS, 43, 46   (beyond their mere existence,)
[e-e]MS, 43, 46   contemporary
[f-f]MS, 43, 46   earthly
[g-g]+72
[h-h]MS, 43, 46   there is one kind of assertion which may be made respecting noumena, independently of the phenomena which are their sensible manifestation; the assertion of their

subject to the explanations which will follow in the Third Book, must be considered provisionally as a distinct and peculiar kind of assertion.

---

mere existence "are more or less abbreviated, or elliptical: when fully expressed they fall under either coexistence or succession. When we say there *exists* a conspiracy for a particular purpose, we mean that at the present time a body of men have formed themselves into a society for a particular object; which is a complex affirmation, resolvable into propositions of coexistence and succession (as causation). The assertion that the dodo does not exist, points to the fact that this animal, once known in a certain place, has disappeared or become extinct; is no longer associated with the locality: all which may be better stated without the use of the verb 'exist.' There is a debated question—Does an ether exist? but the correcter form would be this—'Are heat and light and other radiant influences propagated by an ethereal medium diffused in space;' which is a proposition of causation. In like manner the question of the Existence of a Deity cannot be discussed in that form. It is properly a question as to the First *Cause* of the Universe, and as to the continued exertion of that Cause in providential superintendence." (*Ibid.*, p. 107.)

Mr. Bain thinks it "fictitious and unmeaning language" [*ibid.*, p. 255] to carry up the classification of Nature to one *summum genus*, Being, or that which Exists; since nothing can be perceived or apprehended but by way of contrast with something else (of which important truth, under the name of Law of Relativity, he has been in our time the principal expounder and champion), and we have no other class to oppose to Being, or fact to contrast with Existence.

I accept fully Mr. Bain's Law of Relativity, but I do not understand by it that to enable us to apprehend or be conscious of any fact, it is necessary that we should contrast it with some other positive fact. The antithesis necessary to consciousness need not, I conceive, be an antithesis between two positives; it may be between one positive and its negative. Hobbes was undoubtedly right when he said that a single sensation indefinitely prolonged would cease to be felt at all [*see* "Physics, or the Phenomena of Nature," Part IV of *Elements of Philosophy*, *English Works*, Vol. I, p. 394]; but simple intermission, without other change, would restore it to consciousness. In order to be conscious of heat, it is not necessary that we should pass to it from cold; it suffices that we should pass to it from a state of no sensation, or from a sensation of some other kind. The relative opposite of Being, considered as a summum genus, is Non-entity, or Nothing; and we have, now and then, occasion to consider and discuss things merely in contrast with Non-entity.

I grant that the *decision* of questions of Existence usually if not always depends on a previous question of either Causation or Coexistence. But Existence is nevertheless a different thing from Causation or Coexistence, and can be predicated apart from them. The meaning of the abstract name Existence, and the connotation of the concrete name Being, consist, like the meaning of all other names, in sensations or states of consciousness: their peculiarity is that to exist, is to excite, or be capable of exciting, *any* sensations or states of consciousness: no matter what, but it is indispensable that there should be some. It was from overlooking this that Hegel, finding that Being is an abstraction reached by thinking away all particular attributes, arrived at the self-contradictory proposition on which he founded all his philosophy, that Being is the same as Nothing. It is really the name of Something, taken in the most comprehensive sense of the word.

§ 6. [*Or it asserts (or denies) a resemblance*] To these four kinds of matter-of-fact or assertion, must be added a fifth, Resemblance. This was a species of attribute which we found it impossible to analyse; for which no *fundamentum*, distinct from the objects themselves, could be assigned. *Besides* propositions which assert a sequence or coexistence between two phenomena, there are therefore also propositions which assert resemblance between them; as, This colour is like that colour;—The heat of to-day is *equal* to the heat of yesterday. It is true that such an assertion might with some plausibility be brought within the description of an affirmation of sequence, by considering it as an assertion that the simultaneous contemplation of the two colours is *followed* by a specific feeling termed the feeling of resemblance. But there would be nothing gained by encumbering ourselves, especially in this place, with a generalization which may be looked upon as strained. Logic does not undertake to analyse *mental facts* into their ultimate elements. Resemblance between two phenomena is more intelligible in itself than any explanation could make it, and under any classification must remain specifically distinct from the ordinary cases of sequence and coexistence.

It is sometimes said, that all propositions whatever, of which the predicate is a general name, do, in point of fact, affirm or deny resemblance. All such propositions affirm that a thing belongs to a class; but things being classed together according to their resemblance, everything is of course classed with the things which it *is supposed to resemble* most; and thence, it may be said, when we affirm that Gold is a metal, or that Socrates is a man, the affirmation intended is, that gold resembles other metals, and Socrates other men, more nearly than they resemble the objects contained in any other of the classes co-ordinate with these.

There is some slight degree of foundation for this remark, but no more than a slight degree. The arrangement of things into classes, such as the class *metal*, or the class *man*, is grounded indeed on a resemblance among the things which are placed in the same class, but not on a mere general resemblance: the resemblance it is grounded on consists in the possession by all those things, of certain common peculiarities; and those peculiarities it is which the terms connote, and which the propositions consequently assert; not the resemblance. For though when I say, Gold is a metal, I say by implication that if there be any other metals it must resemble them, yet if there were no other metals I might still assert the proposition with the same meaning as at present, namely, that gold has the various properties implied in the word metal; just as it might be said, Christians are men, even if there were no

---

*a–a*MS, 43   In addition to
*b–b*MS, 43, 46   things
*c–c*MS, 43, 46   resembles

men who were not Christians [d]. Propositions, therefore, in which objects are referred to a class because they possess the attributes constituting the class, are so far from asserting nothing but resemblance, that they do not, properly speaking, assert resemblance at all.

But we remarked some time ago (and the reasons of the remark will be more fully entered into in a subsequent Book*) that there is sometimes a convenience in extending the boundaries of a class so as to include things which possess in a very inferior degree, if in any, [e]some of[e] the characteristic properties of the class,—provided they resemble that class more than any other, insomuch that the general propositions which are true of the class, will be nearer to being true of those things than any other equally general propositions. [f]For[f] instance, there are substances called metals which have very few of the properties by which metals are commonly recognised; and almost every great family of plants or animals has a few anomalous [g]genera or[g] species on its borders, which are admitted into it by a sort of courtesy, and concerning which it has been matter of discussion to what family they properly belonged. Now when the class-name is predicated of any object of this description, we do, by so predicating it, affirm resemblance and nothing more. And in order to be scrupulously correct it ought to be said, that in every case in which we predicate a general name, we affirm, not absolutely that the object possesses the properties designated by the name, but that it *either* possesses those properties, or if it does not, at any rate resembles the things which do so, more than it resembles any other things. [h]In most cases, however,[h] it is unnecessary to suppose any such alternative, the latter of the two grounds being very seldom that on which the assertion is made: and when it is, there is generally some slight difference in the form of the expression, as, This species (or genus) is *considered*, or *may be ranked*, as belonging to such and such a family: we should hardly say positively that it does belong to it, unless it possessed unequivocally the properties of which the class-name is scientifically significant.

There is still another exceptional case, in which, though the predicate is [i]the[i] name of a class, yet in predicating it we affirm nothing but resemblance, the class being founded not on resemblance in any [j]given particular[j], but on general unanalysable resemblance. The classes in question are those into which our simple sensations, or other simple feelings, are divided. Sensations of white, for instance, are classed together, not because we can take them to pieces, and say they are alike in this, and not alike in that, but because we

*[51] Bk. IV, Chap. vii [pp. 712ff.].

[d]MS, 43, 46   ; or as the expression, Jehovah is God, might be used by the firmest believer in the Unity of the godhead

[e-e]+51, 56, 62, 65, 68, 72   [f-f]MS, 43, 46, 51, 56   As, for
[g-g]+43, 46, 51, 56, 62, 65, 68, 72   [h-h]MS   But in most cases
[i-i]MS, 43, 46, 51, 56   a   [j-j]MS, 43, 46   particular *respect*

feel them to be alike altogether, though in different degrees. When, therefore, I say, The colour I saw yesterday was a white colour, *or,* The sensation I feel is one of tightness, in both *l* cases the attribute I affirm of the colour or of the other sensation is mere resemblance—simple *likeness* to sensations which I have had before, and which have had those names bestowed upon them. The names of feelings, like other concrete general names, are connotative; but they connote a mere resemblance. When predicated of any individual feeling, the information they convey is that of its likeness to the other feelings which we have been accustomed to call by the same name. *Thus much* may suffice in illustration of the kind of propositions in which the matter-of-fact asserted (or denied) is simple Resemblance.

Existence, Coexistence, Sequence, Causation, Resemblance: one or other of these is asserted (or denied) in every proposition *which is not merely verbal*. This five-fold division is an exhaustive classification of matters-of-fact; of all things that can be believed, or tendered for belief; of all questions that can be propounded, and all answers that can be returned to them.

Professor Bain distinguishes two kinds of Propositions of Coexistence. "In the one kind, account is taken of Place; they may be described as propositions of Order in Place." In the other kind, the coexistence which is predicated is termed by Mr. Bain Co-inherence of Attributes.

This is a distinct variety of Propositions of Coexistence. Instead of an arrangement in place with numerical intervals, we have the concurrence of two or more attributes or powers in the same part or locality. A mass of gold contains, in every atom, the concurring attributes that mark the substance—weight, hardness, colour, lustre, incorrosibility, &c. An animal, besides having parts situated in place, has co-inhering functions in the same parts, exerted by the very same masses and molecules of its substance. . . . The Mind, which affords no Propositions of Order in Place, has co-inhering functions. We affirm mind to contain Feeling, Will, and Thought, not in local separation, but in commingling exercise. The concurring properties of minerals, of plants, and of the bodily and the mental structure of animals, are united in affirmations of co-inherence.

The distinction is real and important. But, as has been seen, an Attribute, when it is anything but a simple unanalysable Resemblance between the subject and some other things, consists in causing impressions of some sort on consciousness. Consequently, the co-inherence of two attributes is but the coexistence of the two states of consciousness implied in their meaning: with the difference, however, that this coexistence is sometimes potential only, the attribute being considered as in existence though the fact on which it is

---

*[72] *Logic*, Pt. I, pp. 103, 105.

k–k+43, 46, 51, 56, 62, 65, 68, 72   *l*MS   these
*m–m*MS   And this]   43, 46   And thus much
*n–n*MS, 43, 46, 51   , without exception   *o–o*+72

grounded may not be actually, but only potentially present. Snow, for instance, is, with great convenience, said to be white even in a state of total darkness, because, though we are not now conscious of the colour, we shall be conscious of it as soon as morning breaks. Coinherence of attributes is therefore still a case, though a complex one, of coexistence of states of consciousness: a totally different thing, however, from Order in Place. Being a part of simultaneity, it belongs not to Place but to Time.[o]

[p]We may therefore (and we shall sometimes find it a convenience) instead of Coexistence and Sequence,[p] say, for greater particularity, Order in Place and Order in Time: Order in Place being [q]a specific mode[q] of coexistence, not necessary to be more particularly analysed here; while the mere fact of coexistence, [r]whether between actual sensations, or between the potentialities of causing them, known by the name of attributes[r], may be classed, together with Sequence, under the head of Order in Time.

§ 7. [*Propositions of which the terms are abstract*] In the foregoing inquiry into the import of Propositions, we have thought it necessary to analyse directly those alone, in which the terms of the proposition (or the predicate at least) are concrete terms. But, in doing so, we have indirectly analysed those in which the terms are abstract. The distinction between an abstract term and its corresponding concrete, [a]does not turn upon any[a] difference in what they are appointed to signify; for the real signification of a concrete general name is, as we have so often said, its connotation; and what the concrete term connotes, forms the entire meaning of the abstract name. Since there is nothing in the import of an abstract name which is not in the import of the corresponding concrete, it is natural to suppose that neither can there be anything in the import of a proposition of which the terms are abstract, but what there is in some proposition which can be framed of concrete terms.

And this presumption a closer examination will confirm. An abstract name is the name of an attribute, or combination of attributes. The corresponding concrete is a name given to things, because of, and in order to express, their possessing that attribute, or that combination of attributes. When, therefore, we predicate of anything a concrete name, the attribute is what we in reality predicate of it. But [b]it has now been[b] shown that in all propositions of which the predicate is a concrete name, what is really predicated is one of five things: Existence, Coexistence, Causation, Sequence, or Resemblance. An attribute, therefore, is necessarily either an existence, a coexistence, a causa-

---

[p-p]MS, 43, 46, 51, 56, 62, 65, 68 [*no paragraph*] Instead of Coexistence and Sequence, we shall sometimes
[q-q]MS, 43, 46, 51, 56 one of the modes] 62, 65, 68 the specific mode
[r-r]MS, 43, 46, 51, 56, 62, 65, 68 or simultaneousness
[a-a]MS, 43, 46 is no
[b-b]MS we have now

tion, a sequence, or a resemblance. When a proposition consists of a subject and predicate which are abstract terms, it consists of terms which must necessarily signify one or other of these things. When we predicate of anything an abstract name, we affirm of the thing that it is one or other of these five things; that it is a case of Existence, or of Coexistence, or of Causation, or of Sequence, or of Resemblance.

It is impossible to imagine any proposition expressed in abstract terms, which cannot be transformed into a precisely equivalent proposition in which the terms are concrete; namely, either the concrete names which connote the attributes themselves, or the names of the *fundamenta* of those attributes; the facts or phenomena on which they are grounded. To illustrate the latter case, let us take this proposition, of which *c*the subject only is*c* an abstract name, "Thoughtlessness is dangerous." Thoughtlessness is an attribute, grounded on the facts which we call thoughtless actions; and the proposition is equivalent to this, Thoughtless actions are dangerous. In the next example the predicate as well as the subject are abstract names: "Whiteness is a colour;" or "The colour of snow is a whiteness." These attributes being grounded on sensations, the equivalent propositions in the concrete would be, The sensation of white is one of the sensations called those of colour,— The sensation of sight, caused by looking at snow, is one of the sensations called sensations of white. In these propositions, as we have before seen, the matter-of-fact asserted is a Resemblance. In the following examples, the concrete terms are those *d*which directly correspond*d* to the abstract names; connoting the attribute which these denote. "Prudence is a virtue:" this may be rendered, "All prudent persons, *in so far as* prudent, are virtuous:" "Courage is deserving of honour," thus, "All courageous persons are deserving of honour *e*in so far*e* as they are courageous:" which is equivalent to this —"All courageous persons deserve an addition to the honour, or a diminution of the disgrace, which would attach to them on other grounds."

In order to throw still further light upon the import of propositions of which the terms are abstract, we will subject one of the examples given above to a minuter analysis. The proposition we shall select is the following: "Prudence is a virtue." Let us substitute for the word virtue an equivalent but more definite expression, *f*such*f* as "a mental quality beneficial to society," or "a mental quality pleasing to God," or *g*whatever else we adopt as the definition of virtue*g*. What the proposition asserts is a sequence, accompanied with causation; namely, that benefit to society, or that the approval of God,

*c–c*MS, 43, 46   only the subject is]   56   the subject is only
*d–d*MS   directly corresponding
*e–e*MS, 43, 46   *so far forth*
f–f+43, 46, 51, 56, 62, 65, 68, 72
*g–g*MS, 43   whichever other of the definitions of virtue we prefer]   46   whichever of the other definitions of virtue we prefer

is consequent on, and caused by, prudence. Here is a sequence; but between what? We understand the consequent of the sequence, but we have yet to analyse the antecedent. Prudence is an attribute; and, in connexion with it, two things besides itself are to be considered; prudent persons, who are the *subjects* of the attribute, and prudential conduct, which may be called the *foundation* of it. Now is either of these the antecedent? and, first, is *h*it meant, that the approval of God, or benefit to society, is*h* attendant upon all prudent *persons*? No; except *i*in so far*i* as they are prudent; for prudent persons who are scoundrels can seldom on the whole be beneficial to society, *j*nor can they be acceptable to a good being*j*. Is it upon prudential *conduct*, then, that divine approbation and benefit to mankind are *k*supposed to be*k* invariably consequent? Neither is this the assertion meant, when *l*it is said*l* that prudence is a virtue; except with the same reservation as before, and for the same reason, namely, that prudential conduct, although in *so far as* it is prudential it is beneficial to society, may yet, by reason of some other of its qualities, be productive of an injury outweighing the benefit, and *m*deserve a displeasure*m* exceeding the approbation which would be due to the prudence. Neither the substance, therefore, (viz. the person,) nor the phenomenon, (*n* the conduct,) is an antecedent on which the other term of the sequence is universally consequent. But the proposition, "Prudence is a virtue," is an universal proposition. What is it, then, upon which the proposition affirms the effects in question to be universally consequent? Upon that in the person, and in the conduct, which causes them to be called prudent, and which is equally in them when the action, though prudent, is wicked; namely, a correct foresight of consequences, *o*a*o* just estimation of their importance to the object in view, and repression of any unreflecting impulse at variance with the deliberate purpose. These, which are states of the person's mind, are the real antecedent in the sequence, the real cause in the causation, *p* asserted by the proposition. But these are also the real ground, or foundation, of the attribute Prudence; since wherever these states of mind exist we may predicate prudence, even before we know whether any conduct has followed. And in this manner every assertion respecting an attribute, may be transformed into an assertion exactly equivalent respecting the fact or phenomenon which

*h–h*MS the approval of God or the benefit to society
*i–i*MS, 43, 46 *so far forth*
*j–j*MS nor can they be acceptable to infinite wisdom] 43, 46 nor acceptable to even finite wisdom] 51 nor acceptable to any good being] 56 or acceptable to any good being
k–k+51, 56, 62, 65, 68, 72
*l–l*MS we say
*m–m*MS of a displeasure to the Almighty] 43, 46 of a divine displeasure
*n*MS viz.
o–o+43, 46, 51, 56, 62, 65, 68, 72
*p*43, 46 which are

is the ground of the attribute. And no case can be assigned, where that which is predicated of the fact or phenomenon, does not belong to one or other of the five species formerly enumerated: it is either simple Existence, or it is some Sequence, Coexistence, Causation, or Resemblance.

And as these five are the only things which can be affirmed, so are they the only things which can be denied. "No horses are web-footed" denies that the attributes of a horse ever co-exist with web-feet. It is scarcely necessary to apply the same analysis to Particular affirmations and negations. "Some birds are web-footed," affirms that, with the attributes connoted by *bird*, the phenomenon web-feet is sometimes co-existent: "Some birds are not web-footed," asserts that there are other instances in which this co-existence does not have place. Any *q*further*q* explanation of a thing which, if the previous exposition has been assented to, is so obvious, may *r*here*r* be spared.

*q–q*43, 46   farther
*r–r*MS, 43, 46   well

CHAPTER VI

Of Propositions Merely Verbal

§ 1. [*Essential and Accidental propositions*] As a preparation for the inquiry which is the proper object of Logic, namely, in what manner propositions are to be proved, we have found it necessary to inquire what they contain which requires, or is susceptible of, proof; or (which is the same thing) what they assert. In the course of this preliminary investigation into the import of Propositions, we examined the opinion of the Conceptualists, that a proposition is the expression of a relation between two ideas; and the doctrine of the *ªextremeª* Nominalists, that it is the expression of an agreement or disagreement between the meanings of two names. We decided that, as general theories, both of these are erroneous; and that, though propositions may be made both respecting names and respecting ideas, neither the one nor the other are the subject-matter of Propositions considered generally. We then examined the different kinds of Propositions, and *ᵇ* found that, with the exception of those which are merely verbal, they assert five different kinds of matters of fact, namely, Existence, Order in Place, Order in Time, Causation, and Resemblance; that in every proposition one of these five is either affirmed, or denied, of some fact or phenomenon, or of some object the unknown source of a fact or phenomenon.

In distinguishing, however, the different kinds of matters of fact asserted in propositions, we reserved one class of propositions, which do not relate to any matter of fact, in the proper sense of the term, at all, but to the meaning of names. Since names and their signification are entirely arbitrary, such propositions are not, strictly speaking, susceptible of truth or falsity, but only of conformity or disconformity to usage or convention; and all the proof they are capable of, is proof of usage; proof that the words have been employed by others in the acceptation in which the speaker or writer desires to use them. These propositions occupy, however, a conspicuous place in philosophy; and their nature and characteristics are of as much importance in logic, as those of any *ᶜof the otherᶜ* classes of propositions previously adverted to.

If all propositions respecting the signification of words were as simple and unimportant as those which served us for examples when examining Hobbes'

ª–ª+72   *ᵇ*MS, 43, 46 we   *ᶜ–ᶜ*MS other of the

theory of predication, viz. those of which the subject and predicate are proper names, and which assert only that those names have, or that they have not, been conventionally assigned to the same individual, there would be little to attract to such propositions the attention of philosophers. But the class of merely verbal propositions embraces not only much more than these, but much more than any propositions which at first sight present themselves as verbal; comprehending a kind of assertions which have been regarded not only as relating to things, but as having actually a more intimate relation with them than any other propositions whatever. The student in philosophy will perceive that I allude to the distinction on which so much stress was laid by the schoolmen, and which has been retained either under the same or under other names by most metaphysicians to the present day, viz. between what were called *essential*, and what were called *accidental*, propositions, and between essential and accidental properties or attributes.

§ 2. [*All essential propositions are identical propositions*] Almost all metaphysicians prior to Locke, as well as many since his time, have made a great mystery of Essential Predication, and of predicates which *are* said to be of the *essence* of the subject. The essence of a thing, they said, was that without which the thing could neither be, nor be conceived to be. Thus, rationality was of the essence of man, because without rationality, man could not be conceived to exist. The different attributes which made up the essence of the thing were called its essential properties; and a proposition in which any of these were predicated of it was called an Essential Proposition, and was considered to go deeper into the nature of the thing, and to convey more important information respecting it, than any other proposition could do. All properties, not of the essence of the thing, were called its accidents; were supposed to have nothing at all, or nothing comparatively, to do with its in-most nature; and the propositions in which any of these were predicated of it were called Accidental Propositions. A connexion may be traced between this distinction, which originated with the schoolmen, and the well-known dogmas of *substantiæ secundæ* or general substances, and *substantial forms*, doctrines which under varieties of language pervaded alike the Aristotelian and the Platonic schools, and of which more of the spirit has come down to modern times than might be conjectured from the disuse of the phraseology. The false views of the nature of classification and generalization which pre-vailed among the schoolmen, and of which these dogmas were the technical expression, afford the only explanation which can be given of their having misunderstood the real nature of those Essences which held so conspicuous a place in their philosophy. They said, truly, that *man* cannot be conceived

*a–a*MS, 43, 46, 51   were

without rationality. But though *man* cannot, a being may be conceived exactly like a man in all points except that one quality, and those others which are the conditions or consequences of it. All therefore which is really true in the assertion that man cannot be conceived without rationality, is only, that if he had not rationality, he would not be reputed a man. There is no impossibility in conceiving the *thing*, nor, for aught we know, in its existing: the impossibility is in the conventions of language, which will not allow the thing, even if it exist, to be called by the name which is reserved for rational beings. Rationality, in short, is involved in the meaning of the word man: *b* is one of the attributes connoted by the name. The essence of man, simply means the whole of the attributes connoted by the word; and any one of those attributes taken singly, is an essential property of man.

c But these reflections, so easy to us, would have been difficult to persons who thought, as most of the *d*later*d* Aristotelians did, that objects were made what they were called, that *e*gold (for instance) was made gold*e*, not by the possession of certain properties to which mankind have chosen to attach that name, but by participation in the nature of a certain general substance, called *f*gold*f* in general, which substance, together with all the properties that be-

---

*b*MS, 43   it

*c*MS, 43, 46   The doctrines which prevented the real meaning of Essences from being understood, not having assumed so settled a shape in the time of Aristotle and his immediate followers as was afterwards given to them by the Realists of the middle ages, we find a nearer approach to true views of the subject in the writings of the ancient Aristotelians than in their more modern followers. Porphyry, in his *Isagoge*, approached so near to the true conception of essences, that only one step remained to be taken, but this step, so easy in appearance, was reserved for the Nominalists of modern times. By altering any property, not of the essence of the thing, you merely, according to Porphyry, made a difference in it; you made it ἀλλοῖον: but by altering any property which was of its essence, you made it *another thing*, ἄλλο.* To a modern it is obvious that between the change which only makes a thing different, and the change which makes it another thing, the only distinction is that in the one case, though changed, it is still called by the same name. Thus, pound ice in a mortar, and being still called ice, it is only made ἀλλοῖον: melt it, and it becomes ἄλλο, another thing, namely, water. Now it is really the same thing, *i.e.* the same particles of matter, in both cases; and you cannot so change anything that it shall cease to be the same thing in this sense. The identity which it can be deprived of is merely that of the name: when the thing ceases to be called ice, it becomes *another thing*; its essence, what constitutes it ice, is gone; while, so long as it continues to be so called, nothing is gone except some of its accidents. [*no paragraph*]]   51, 56   *as* MS . . . nearer approach to a rational view of the subject . . . *as* MS . . . what constituted it ice, is gone; while, as long . . . *as* MS]   62, 65   *as* 51 . . . distinction is that in the former case . . . *as* 51 [*footnote:*] *Καθόλου μὲν οὖν πᾶσα διαφορὰ προσγινομένη τινὶ ἐτεροῖον ποιεῖ· ἀλλ' αἱ μὲν κοινῶς τε καὶ ἰδίως (differences in the accidental properties) ἀλλοῖον ποιοῦσιν· αἱ δὲ ἰδιαίτατα, (differences in the essential properties) ἄλλο. Porphyry, *Isagoge*, cap. iii [in Aristotle, *Organon* Ed. J. Pacius. 3rd ed. 3 vols. Geneva: Vignonianis, 1605, Vol. I, p. 14].

d–d+68, 72

*e–e*MS, 43, 46, 51, 56, 62, 65   ice (for instance) was made ice

*f–f*MS, 43, 46, 51, 56, 62, 65   Ice

longed to it, *inhered* in every individual piece of *g*gold*g*.* As they did not consider these universal substances to be attached to all general names, but only to some, they thought that an object borrowed only a part of its properties from an universal substance, and that the rest belonged to it individually: the former they called its essence, and the latter its accidents. The scholastic doctrine of essences long survived the theory on which it rested, that of the existence of real entities corresponding to general terms; and it was reserved for Locke at the end of the seventeenth century, to convince philosophers that the supposed essences of classes were merely the signification of their names; nor, among the signal services which *h*his writings*h* rendered to philosophy, was there one more needful or more valuable. *i*

Now, as the most familiar of the general names *j*by which an object is designated*j* usually connotes not one only, but several attributes of the object, each of which attributes separately forms also the bond of union of some class, and the meaning of some general name; we may predicate of a name which connotes a variety of attributes, another name which connotes only one of these attributes, or some smaller number of them than all. In such cases, the universal affirmative proposition will be true; since whatever pos-

---

*[68] The doctrines which prevented the real meaning of Essences from being understood, had not assumed so settled a shape in the time of Aristotle and his immediate followers, as was afterwards given to them by the Realists of the middle ages. Aristotle himself (in his Treatise on the Categories [*see* Chap. v]) expressly denies that the δεύτεραι οὐσίαι, or Substantiæ Secundæ, inhere in a subject. They are only, he says, predicated of it.

*g–g*MS, 43, 46, 51, 56, 62, 65   ice
*h–h*MS, 43, 46   that great man
*i*MS, 43, 46 [*footnote:*]   *Few among the great names in philosophy have met with a harder measure of justice from the present generation than Locke; the unquestioned founder of the analytic philosophy of mind, but whose doctrines were first caricatured, then, when the reaction arrived, cast off by the prevailing school even with contumely, and who is now regarded by one of the conflicting parties in philosophy as an apostle of heresy and sophistry, while among those who still adhere to the standard which he raised, there has been a disposition in later times to sacrifice his reputation in favour of Hobbes; a great writer, and a great thinker for his time, but inferior to Locke not only in sober judgment but even in profundity and original genius. Locke, the most candid of philosophers, and one whose speculations bear on every subject the strongest marks of having been wrought out from the materials of his own mind, has been mistaken for an unworthy plagiarist, while Hobbes has been extolled as having anticipated many of his leading doctrines. He did anticipate many of them, and the present is an instance in what manner it was generally done. They both rejected the scholastic doctrine of essences; but Locke understood and explained what these supposed essences really were; Hobbes, instead of explaining the distinction between essential and accidental properties, and between essential and accidental propositions, jumped over it, and gave a definition which suits at most only essential propositions, and scarcely those, as the definition of Proposition in general.]   51, 56   *as* MS . . . names in mental science have . . . *as* MS]   62   *as* 51 . . . Propositions in general.
*j–j*MS, 43, 46   predicable of an object

sesses the whole of any set of attributes, must possess any part of that same set. A proposition of this sort, however, conveys no information to any one who previously understood the whole meaning of the terms. The propositions, Every man is a corporeal being, Every man is a living creature, Every man is rational, convey no knowledge to any one who was already aware of the entire meaning of the word *man*, for the meaning of the word includes all this: and that every *man* has the attributes connoted by all these predicates, is already asserted when he is called a man. Now, of this nature are all the propositions which have been called essential. They are, in fact, identical propositions.

It is true that a proposition which predicates any attribute, even though it be one implied in the name, is in most cases understood to involve a tacit assertion that there *exists* a thing corresponding to the name, and possessing the attributes connoted by it; and this implied assertion may convey information, even to those who understood the meaning of the name. But all information of this sort, conveyed by all the essential propositions of which man can be made the subject, is included in the assertion, Men exist. And this assumption of real existence is, after all, [k] the result of an imperfection of language. It arises from the ambiguity of the copula, which, in addition to its proper office of a mark to show that an assertion is made, is also, as [l] formerly remarked, a concrete word connoting existence. The actual existence of the subject of the proposition is therefore only apparently, not really, implied in the predication, if an essential one: we may say, A ghost is a disembodied spirit, without believing in ghosts. But an accidental, or non-essential, affirmation, does imply the real existence of the subject, because in the case of a non-existent subject there is nothing for the proposition to assert. Such a proposition as, The ghost of a murdered person haunts the couch of the murderer, can only have a meaning if understood as implying a belief in ghosts; for since the signification of the word ghost implies nothing of the kind, the speaker either means nothing, or means to assert a thing which he wishes to be believed [m]to have really[m] taken place.

It will be hereafter seen that when any important consequences seem to follow, as in mathematics, from an essential proposition, or, in other words, from a proposition involved in the meaning of a name, what they really flow from is the tacit assumption of the real existence of the [n]objects[n] so named. Apart from this assumption of real existence, the class of propositions in which the predicate is of the essence of the subject (that is, in which the predicate connotes the whole or part of what the subject connotes, but nothing besides) answer no purpose but that of unfolding the whole or some part of the meaning of the name, to those who did not previously know it. Ac-

---

[k]MS, 43, 46, 51, 56, 62   only
[m]-[m]MS, 43, 46   really to have

[l]MS, 43, 46, 51, 56   we have]   62   we
[n]-[n]MS, 43, 46, 51, 56, 62   object

cordingly, the most useful, and in strictness the only useful kind of essential propositions, are Definitions: which, to be complete, should unfold the whole of what is involved in the meaning of the word defined; that is, (when it is a connotative word,) the whole of what it connotes. In defining a name, however, it is not usual to specify its entire connotation, but so much only as is sufficient to mark out the objects usually denoted by it from all other known objects. And sometimes a merely accidental property, not involved in the meaning of the name, answers this purpose equally well. The various kinds of definition which these distinctions give rise to, and the purposes to which they are respectively subservient, will be minutely considered in the proper place.

§ 3. [*Individuals have no essences*] According to the above view of essential propositions, no proposition can be reckoned such which relates to an individual by name, that is, in which the subject is a proper name. Individuals have no essences. When the schoolmen talked of the essence of an individual, they did not mean the properties implied in its name, for the names of individuals imply no properties. They regarded as of the essence of an individual, whatever was of the essence of the species in which they were accustomed to place that individual; *i.e.* of the class to which it was most familiarly referred, and to which, therefore, they conceived that it by nature belonged. Thus, because the proposition Man is a rational being, was an essential proposition, they affirmed the same thing of the proposition, Julius Cæsar is a rational being. This followed very naturally if genera and species were to be considered as entities, distinct from, but *inhering* in, the individuals composing them. If *man* was a substance inhering in each individual man, the *essence* of man (whatever that might mean) was naturally supposed to accompany it; to inhere in John Thompson, and *a*to*a* form the *common essence* of Thompson and Julius Cæsar. It might then be fairly said, that rationality, being of the essence of Man, was of the essence also of Thompson. But if Man altogether be only the individual men and a name bestowed upon them in consequence of certain common properties, what becomes of John Thompson's essence?

A fundamental error is seldom expelled from philosophy by a single victory. It retreats slowly, defends every inch of ground, and often *b*, after it has been driven from the open country, retains a footing in some remote fastness*b*. The essences of individuals were an unmeaning figment arising from a misapprehension of the essences of classes, yet even Locke, when he extirpated the parent error, could not shake himself free from that which was its fruit.

He distinguished two sorts of essences, Real and Nominal. His nominal essences were the essences of classes, explained nearly as we have now explained them. Nor is anything wanting to render the third book of Locke's *Essay*[*] a nearly *unexceptionable* treatise on the connotation of names, except to free its language from the assumption of what are called Abstract Ideas, which unfortunately is involved in the phraseology, though not necessarily connected with the thoughts contained in that immortal Third Book.* But besides nominal essences, he admitted real essences, or essences of individual objects, which he supposed to be the causes of the sensible properties of those objects. We know not (said he) what these are; (and this acknowledgment rendered the fiction comparatively innocuous;) but if we did, we could, from them alone, demonstrate the sensible properties of the object, as the properties of the triangle are demonstrated from the definition of the triangle. *I* shall have occasion to revert to this theory in treating of Demonstration, and of the conditions under which one property of a thing admits of being demonstrated from another property. It is enough here to remark that, according to this definition, the real essence of an object has, in the progress of physics, come to be conceived as nearly equivalent, in the case of bodies, to their corpuscular structure: what it is now supposed to mean in the case of any other entities, I would not take upon myself to define.

§ 4. [*Real propositions, how distinguished from verbal*] An essential proposition, then, is one which is purely verbal; which asserts of a thing under a particular name, only what is asserted of it in the fact of calling it by that name; and which therefore either gives no information, or gives it respecting the name, not the thing. Non-essential, or accidental propositions, on the contrary, may be called Real Propositions, in opposition to Verbal. They predicate of a thing some fact not involved in the signification of the name by

[*Of Human Understanding. In *Works*. New ed. London: Tegg, 1823, Vol. I.]
*The always acute and often profound author of *An Outline of Sematology* [London: Richardson, 1831] (Mr. B. H. Smart) justly says, "Locke will be much more intelligible, if, in the majority of places, we substitute 'the knowledge of' for what he calls 'the Idea of'" (p. 10). Among the many criticisms on Locke's use of the word Idea, this is the *d* one which, as it appears to me, *most nearly* hits the mark; and I quote it for the additional reason that it precisely expresses the point of difference respecting the import of Propositions, between my view and what I have *spoken of as* the Conceptualist view of them. Where a Conceptualist says that a name or a proposition expresses our Idea of a thing, I should generally say (instead of our Idea) our Knowledge, or Belief, concerning the thing itself.

c–cMS, 43, 46   perfect
dMS, 43, 46, 51, 56, 62   only
e–eMS, 43, 46, 51   precisely]   56, 62   exactly
f–fMS, 43, 46   called   g–gMS   We

which the proposition speaks of it; some attribute not connoted by that name. Such are all propositions concerning things individually designated, and all general or particular propositions in which the predicate connotes any attribute not connoted by the subject. All these, if true, add to our knowledge: they convey information, not already involved in the names employed. When I am told that all, or even that some objects, which have certain qualities, or which stand in certain relations, have also certain other qualities, or stand in certain other relations, I learn from this proposition a new fact; a fact not included in my knowledge of the meaning of the words, nor even of the existence of Things answering to the signification of those words. It is this class of propositions only which are in themselves instructive, or from which any instructive propositions can be inferred.*

Nothing has probably contributed more to the opinion so *long* prevalent of the futility of the school logic, than the circumstance that almost all the examples used in the common school books to illustrate the *doctrine* of predication and *that* of the syllogism, consist of essential propositions. They were usually taken either from the branches or from the main trunk of the Predicamental Tree, which included nothing but what was of the *essence* of the species: *Omne corpus est substantia, Omne animal est corpus, Omnis homo est corpus, Omnis homo est animal, Omnis homo est rationalis*, and so forth. It is far from wonderful that the syllogistic art should have been thought to be of no use in assisting correct reasoning, when almost the only propositions which, in the hands of its professed teachers, it was employed to prove, were such as every one assented to without proof the moment he comprehended the meaning of the words; and stood exactly on a level, in point of evidence, with the premises from which they were drawn. I have, therefore, throughout this work, *d* avoided the employment of essential propositions as examples, except where the nature of the principle to be illustrated specifically required them.

§ 5. [*Two modes of *representing* the import of a Real proposition*] With respect to propositions which do convey information—which assert something of a Thing, under a name that does not already presuppose what is about to be asserted; there are two different aspects in which these, or rather such of them as are general propositions, may be considered: we may either look at them as portions of speculative truth, or as memoranda for practical

*[62] This distinction corresponds to that which is drawn by Kant and other metaphysicians between what they term *analytic*, and *synthetic*, judgments; the former being those which can be evolved from the meaning of the terms used.

*a–a*MS, 43, 46, 51   commonly   *b–b*MS, 43, 46   doctrines
c–c+62, 65, 68, 72   *d*MS, 43, 46   studiously
*a–a*MS *defining*

use. According as we consider propositions in one or the other of these lights, their import may be conveniently expressed in one or in the other of two formulas.

According to the formula which we have hitherto employed, and which is best adapted to express the import of the proposition as a portion of our theoretical knowledge, All men are mortal, means that the attributes of man are always accompanied by the attribute mortality: No men are gods, means that the attributes of man are never accompanied by the attributes, or at least never by all the attributes, *signified by the word* god. But when the proposition is considered as a memorandum for practical use, we shall find a different mode of expressing the same meaning better adapted to indicate the office which the proposition performs. The practical use of a proposition is, to apprise or remind us what we have to expect, in any individual case which comes within the assertion contained in the proposition. In reference to this purpose, the proposition, All men are mortal, means that the attributes of man are *evidence of*, are a *mark of*, mortality; an indication by which the presence of that attribute is made manifest. No men are gods, means that the attributes of man are a mark or evidence that some or all of the attributes *understood to belong to* a god are not there; that where the former are, we need not expect to find the latter.

These two forms of expression are at bottom equivalent; but the one points the attention more directly to what a proposition means, the latter to the manner in which it is to be used.

Now it is to be observed that Reasoning (the subject to which we are next to proceed) is a process into which propositions enter not as ultimate results, but as means to the establishment of other propositions. We may expect, therefore, that the mode of exhibiting the import of a general proposition which shows it in its application to practical use, will best express the function which propositions perform in Reasoning. And accordingly, in the theory of Reasoning, the mode of viewing the subject which considers a Proposition as asserting *that one fact or phenomenon is* a *mark* or *evidence* of another fact or phenomenon, will be found almost indispensable. For the purposes of that Theory, the best mode of defining the import of a proposition is not the mode which shows *f* most clearly what it is in itself, but that which most distinctly suggests the manner in which it may be made available for advancing from it to other propositions.

b–bMS, 43, 46 of a
c cMS, 43, 46 of] 51, 56 supposed to belong to
d–dMS [*no paragraph*] The
e–eMS one fact or phenomenon to be
fMS, 43, 46 the

CHAPTER VII

Of the Nature of Classification, and the Five Predicables

§ 1. [*Classification, how connected with Naming*] In examining into the nature of general propositions, we have adverted much less than is usual with logicians to the ideas of a Class, and Classification; ideas which, since the Realist doctrine of General Substances went out of vogue, have formed the basis of almost every attempt at a philosophical theory of general terms and general propositions. We have considered general names as having a meaning, quite independently of their being the names of classes. That circumstance is in truth accidental, it being wholly immaterial to the signification of the name whether there are many objects, or only one, to which it happens to be applicable, or whether there be any at all. God is as much a general term to the Christian or *a* Jew as to the Polytheist; and dragon, hippogriff, chimera, mermaid, ghost, are as much so as if real objects existed, corresponding to those names. Every name the signification of which is constituted by attributes, is potentially a name of an indefinite number of objects; but it needs not be actually the name of any; and if of any, it may be the name of only one. As soon as we employ a name to connote attributes, the things, be they more or fewer, which happen to possess those attributes, are constituted *ipso facto* a class. But in predicating the name we predicate only the attributes; and the fact of belonging to a class does not, in *b*many*b* cases, come into view at all.

Although, however, Predication does not presuppose Classification, and though the theory of Names and of Propositions is not cleared up, but only encumbered, by intruding the idea of classification into it, there is nevertheless a close connexion between Classification and the employment of General Names. By every general name which we introduce, we create a class, if there be any *c*things, real or imaginary,*c* to compose it; that is, any Things corresponding to the signification of the name. Classes, therefore, mostly owe their existence to general language. But general language, also, though that is not the most common case, sometimes owes its existence to classes. A general, which is as much as to say a significant, name, is indeed mostly

*a*MS, 43, 46, 51, 56, 62   the
*b–b*MS, 43, 46, 51, 56   ordinary   *c–c*MS, 43, 46   existing things

introduced because we have a signification to express by it; because we need a word by means of which to predicate the attributes which it connotes. But it is also true that a name is sometimes introduced because we have found it convenient to create a class; because we have thought it useful for the regulation of our mental operations, that a certain group of objects should be thought of together. A naturalist, for purposes connected with his particular science, sees reason to distribute the animal or vegetable creation into certain groups rather than into any others, and he requires a name to bind, as it were, each of his groups together. It must not however be supposed that such names, when introduced, differ in any respect, as to their mode of signification, from other connotative names. The classes which they denote are, as much as any other classes, constituted by certain common attributes, and their names are significant of those attributes, and of nothing else. The names of Cuvier's classes and orders, *Plantigrades*, *Digitigrades*, &c., are as much the expression of attributes as if those names had preceded, instead of *d*grown*d* out of, his classification of animals. The only peculiarity of the case is, that the convenience of classification was here the primary motive for introducing the names; while in other cases the name is introduced as a means of predication, and the formation of a class denoted by it is only an indirect consequence.

The principles which ought to regulate Classification as a logical process subservient to the investigation of truth, cannot be discussed to any purpose until a much later stage of our inquiry. But, of Classification as resulting from, and implied in, the fact of employing general language, we cannot forbear to treat here, without leaving the theory of general names, and of their employment in predication, mutilated and formless.

§ 2. [*The Predicables, what*] This portion of the theory of general language is the subject of what is termed the doctrine of the Predicables; a set of distinctions handed down from Aristotle, and his follower Porphyry, many of which have taken a firm root in scientific, and some of them even in popular, phraseology. The predicables are a five-fold division of General Names, not grounded as usual on a difference in their meaning, that is, in the attribute which they connote, but on a difference in the kind of class which they *a*denote*a*. We may predicate of a thing five different varieties of class-name:

A *genus* of the thing	(γένος).
A *species*	(εἶδος).
A *differentia*	(διαφορά).
A *proprium*	(ἴδιον).
An *accidens*	(συμβεβηκός).

*d–d*MS, 43, 46, 51, 56, 62, 65   growing
*a–a*MS, 43   denote

It is to be remarked of these distinctions, that they express, not what the predicate is in its own meaning, but what relation it bears to the subject of which it happens on the particular occasion to be predicated. There are not some names which are exclusively genera, and others which are exclusively species, or differentiæ; but the same name is referred to one or another predicable, according to the subject of which it is predicated on the particular occasion. *Animal*, for instance, is a genus with respect to man, or John; a species with respect to Substance, or Being. *Rectangular* is one of the Differentiæ of a geometrical square; it is merely one of the Accidentia of the table *b*at*b* which I am writing. The words genus, species, &c. are therefore relative terms; they are names applied to certain predicates, to express the relation between them and some given subject: a relation grounded, as we shall see, not on what the predicate connotes, but on the class which it *c*denotes*c*, and on the place which, in some given classification, that class occupies relatively to the particular subject.

§ 3. [*Genus and Species*] Of these five names, two, Genus and Species, are not only used by naturalists in a technical acceptation not precisely agreeing with their philosophical meaning, but have also acquired a popular acceptation, much more general than either. In this popular sense any two classes, one of which includes the whole of the other and more, may be called a Genus and a Species. Such, for instance, are Animal and Man; Man and Mathematician. Animal is a Genus; Man and Brute are its two species; or we may divide it into a greater number of species, as man, horse, dog, &c. *Biped*, or *two-footed animal*, may also be considered a genus, of which man and bird are two species. *Taste* is a genus, of which sweet taste, sour taste, salt taste, &c. are species. *Virtue* is a genus; justice, prudence, courage, fortitude, generosity, &c. are its species.

The same class which is a genus with reference to the sub-classes or species included in it, may be itself a species with reference to a more comprehensive, or, as it is often called, a superior genus. Man is a species with reference to animal, but a genus with reference to the species Mathematician. Animal is a genus, divided into two species, man and brute; but animal is also a species, which, with another species, vegetable, makes up the genus, organized being. Biped is a genus with reference to man and bird, but a species with respect to the superior genus, animal. Taste is a genus divided into species, but also a species of the genus sensation. Virtue, a genus with reference to justice, temperance, &c., is one of the species of the genus, mental quality.

In this popular sense the words Genus and Species have passed into common discourse. And it should be observed that in ordinary parlance, not the

*b–b*MS, 43, 46   on
*c–c*MS, 43, 46, 51, 56   *denotes*

name of the class, but the class itself, is said to be the genus or species; not, of course, the class in the sense of each individual of *the* class, but the individuals collectively, considered as an aggregate whole; the name by which the class is designated being then called not the genus or species, but the generic or specific name. And this is an admissible form of expression; nor is it of any importance which of the two modes of speaking we adopt, provided the rest of our language is consistent with it; but, if we call the class itself the genus, we must not talk of predicating the genus. We predicate of man the *name* mortal; and by predicating the name, we may be said, in an intelligible sense, to predicate what the name expresses, the *attribute* mortality; but in no allowable sense of the word predication do we predicate of man the *class* mortal. We predicate of him the fact of belonging to the class.

By the Aristotelian logicians, the terms genus and species were used in a more restricted sense. They did not admit every class which could be divided into other classes to be a genus, or every class which could be included in a larger class to be a species. Animal was by them considered a genus; *b* man and brute co-ordinate species under that genus: *biped* *c*, however,*c* would not have been admitted to be a genus with reference to man, but a *proprium* or *accidens* only. It was requisite, according to their theory, that genus and species should be of the *essence* of the subject. *Animal* was of the essence of man; *biped* was not. And in every classification they considered some one class as the lowest or *infima* species. Man, for instance, was a lowest species. Any further divisions into which the class might be capable of being broken down, as man into white, black, and red man, or into priest and layman, they did not admit to be species.

It has been seen, however, in the preceding chapter, that the distinction between the essence of a class, and the attributes or properties which are not of its essence—a distinction which has given occasion to so much abstruse speculation, and to which so mysterious a character was formerly, and by many writers is still, attached,—amounts to nothing more than the difference between those attributes of the class which are, and those which are not, involved in the signification of the class-name. As applied to individuals, the word Essence, we found, has no meaning, except in connexion with the exploded tenets of the Realists; and what the schoolmen chose to call the essence of an individual, was simply the essence of the class to which that individual was most familiarly referred.

Is there no difference, then, *d*save*d* this merely verbal one, between the classes which the schoolmen admitted to be genera or species, and those to which they refused the title? Is it an error to regard some of the differences which exist among objects as differences *in kind* (*genere* or *specie*), and

*a–a*43, 46, 51, 56   that   *b*MS, 43, 46, 51, 56   and
c–c+62, 65, 68, 72   *d–d*MS, 43, 46   except

others only as differences in the accidents? Were the schoolmen right or wrong in giving to some of the classes into which things may be divided, the name of *kinds*, and considering others as secondary divisions, grounded on differences of a comparatively superficial nature? Examination will show that the Aristotelians did mean something by this distinction, and something important; but which, being but indistinctly conceived, was inadequately expressed by the phraseology of essences, and *e* the various other modes of speech to which they had recourse.

§ 4. [*Kinds have a real existence in nature*] It is a fundamental principle in logic, that the power of framing classes is unlimited, as long as there is any (even the smallest) difference to found a distinction upon. Take any attribute whatever, and if some things have it, and others have *a* not, we may ground on the attribute a division of all things into two classes; and we actually do so, the moment we create a name which connotes the attribute. The number of possible classes, therefore, is boundless; and there are as many actual classes (either of real or of imaginary things) as there are *b* general names, positive and negative together.

But if we contemplate any one of the classes so formed, such as the class animal or plant, or the class sulphur or phosphorus, or the class white or red, and consider in what particulars the individuals included in the class differ from those which do not come within it, we find a very remarkable diversity in this respect between some classes and others. There are some classes, the things contained in which differ from other things only in certain particulars which may be numbered, while others differ in more than can be numbered, more even than we need ever expect to know. Some classes have little or nothing in common to characterize them by, except precisely what is connoted by the name: white things, for example, are not distinguished by any common properties except whiteness; or if they are, it is only by such as are in some way dependent on, or connected with, whiteness. But a hundred generations have not exhausted the common properties of animals or of plants, of sulphur or of phosphorus; nor do we suppose them to be exhaustible, but proceed to new observations and experiments, in the full confidence of discovering new properties which were by no means implied in those we previously knew. While, if any one were to propose for investigation the common properties of all things which are of the same colour, the same shape, or the same specific gravity, the absurdity would be palpable. We have no ground to believe that any such common properties exist, except such as may be shown to be involved in the supposition itself, or to be derivable from it by some law of causation. It appears, therefore, that the

*e*MS, 43, 46, 51, 56, 62   by
*a*MS   it   *b*51   of

properties, on which we ground our classes, sometimes exhaust all that the class has in common, or contain it all by some mode of implication; but in other instances we make a selection of a few properties from among not only a greater number, but a number inexhaustible by us, and to which as we know no bounds, they may, so far as we are concerned, be regarded as infinite.

There is no impropriety in saying that, of these two classifications, the one answers to a much more radical distinction in the things themselves, than the other does. And if any one even chooses to say that the one classification is made by nature, the other by us for our convenience, he will be right; provided he means no more than this: *cWherec* a certain apparent difference between things (though perhaps in itself of little moment) answers to we know not what number of other differences, pervading not only their known properties, but properties yet undiscovered, it is not optional but imperative to recognise this difference as the foundation of a specific distinction; while, on the contrary, differences that are merely finite and determinate, like those designated by the words white, black, or red, may be disregarded if the purpose for which the classification is made does not require attention to those particular properties. The differences, however, are made by nature, in both cases; while the recognition of those differences as grounds of classification and of naming, is, equally in both cases, the act of man: only in the one case, the ends of language and of classification would be subverted if no notice were taken of the difference, while in the other case, the necessity of taking notice of it depends on the importance or unimportance of the particular qualities in which the difference happens to consist.

Now, these classes, distinguished by unknown multitudes of properties, and not solely by a few determinate ones*d*—which are parted off from one another by an unfathomable chasm, instead of a mere ordinary ditch with a visible bottom—*d*are the only classes which, by the Aristotelian logicians, were considered as genera or species. Differences which extended *eonlye* to a certain property or properties, and there terminated, they considered as differences only in the *accidents* of things; but where any class differed from other things by an infinite series of differences, known and unknown, they considered the distinction as one of *kind*, and spoke of it as being an *essential* difference, which is also one of the *fcurrentf* meanings of that vague expression at the present day.

Conceiving the schoolmen to have been justified in drawing a broad line of separation between these two kinds of classes and of class-distinctions, I shall not only retain the division itself, but continue to express it in their language. According to that language, the proximate (or lowest) Kind to

*c-c*MS, 43   that where   *d-d*+56, 62, 65, 68, 72
e-e+46, 51, 56, 62, 65, 68, 72   *f-f*MS, 43, 46, 51   usual

which any individual is referrible, is called its species. Conformably to this, *g* Isaac Newton would be said to be of the species man. There are indeed numerous sub-classes included in the class man, to which *h* Newton also belongs; *i* for example, Christian, and Englishman, and Mathematician. But these, though distinct classes, are not, in our sense of the term, distinct Kinds of men. A Christian, for example, differs from other human beings; but he differs only in the attribute which the word expresses, namely, belief in Christianity, and whatever else that implies, either as involved in the fact itself, or connected with it through some law of cause and effect. We should never think of inquiring what properties, unconnected with Christianity, *j*either as cause or effect,*j* are common to all Christians and peculiar to them; while in regard to all Men, physiologists are perpetually carrying on such an inquiry; nor is the answer ever likely to be completed. Man, therefore, we may *k* call a species; Christian, or Mathematician, we cannot.

Note here, that it is by no means intended to imply that there may not be different Kinds, or logical species, of man. The various races and temperaments, the two sexes, and even the various ages, may be differences of kind, within our meaning of the term. *l*I do not say that they are so.*l* For in the progress of physiology it may *m*almost be said to be made out, that the differences which really exist between different races, sexes, &c.,*m* follow as consequences, under laws of nature, from *n*a small number of*n* primary differences which can be precisely determined, and which, as the phrase is, *account for* all the rest. If this be so, these are not distinctions in kind; no more than Christian, Jew, Mussulman, and Pagan, a difference which also carries many consequences along with it. And in this way classes are often mistaken for real Kinds, which are afterwards proved not to be so. But if it *o*turned out that the differences were not capable of being thus*o* accounted for, then *p*Caucasian, Mongolian,*p* Negro, &c. *q*would be*q* really different Kinds of human beings, and entitled to be ranked as species by the logician; though not by the naturalist. For (as already *r*noticed*r*) the word species is used in a *s* different signification in logic and in natural history. By the naturalist,

*g*MS, 43, 46, 51, 56, 62, 65, 68   Sir
*h*MS, 43, 46   Sir Isaac
*i*MS, 43, 46, 51   as,
j-j+51, 56, 62, 65, 68, 72
*k*MS, 43, 46   be permitted to
*l-l*MS, 43   I say, they may be; I do not say, they are.
*m-m*MS, 43   be made out, that the differences which distinguish different races, sexes, &c., from one another
*n-n*MS, 43   some one or a few
*o-o*MS, 43   shall turn out that the differences are not capable of being
*p-p*MS, 43, 46   man and woman, Caucasian, Mongolian, and
*q-q*MS, 43   are
*r-r*MS, 43, 46   hinted   *s-s*MS, 43, 46, 51   very

organized beings are *not usually* said to be of different species, if it is sup-posed that they *u* have descended from the same stock. That, however, is a sense artificially given to the word, for the technical purposes of a particular science. To the logician, if a negro and a white man differ in the same manner (however less in degree) as a horse and a camel do, that is, if their differences are inexhaustible, and not referrible to any common cause, they are different species, whether they are *v*descended from common ancestors*v* or not. But if their differences can all be traced to climate and habits, *w*or to some one *x*or a few special differences*x* in structure,*w* they are not, in the logician's view, *y*specifically*y* distinct.

When the *infima species*, or proximate Kind, to which an individual be-longs, has been ascertained, the properties common to that Kind include necessarily the whole of the common properties of every other real Kind to which the individual can be referrible. Let the individual, for example, be Socrates, and the proximate Kind, man. Animal, or living creature, is also a real Kind, and includes Socrates; but, since it likewise includes man, or in other words, since all men are animals, the properties common to animals form a portion of the common properties of the sub-class, man. And if there be any class which includes Socrates without including man, that class is not a real Kind. Let the class, for example, be *flat-nosed*; that being a class which includes Socrates, without including all men. To determine whether it is a real Kind, we must ask ourselves this question: Have all flat-nosed animals, in addition to whatever is implied in their flat noses, any common properties, other than those which are common to all animals whatever? If they had; if a flat nose were a mark or index to an indefinite number of other peculiarities, not deducible from the former by *z*an*z* ascertainable law, then out of the class man we might cut another class, flat-nosed man, which according to our definition, would be a Kind. But if we could do this, man would not be, as it was assumed to be, the proximate Kind. Therefore, the properties of the proximate Kind do comprehend those (whether known or unknown) of all other Kinds to which the individual belongs; which was the point we under-took to prove. And hence, every other Kind which is predicable of the in-dividual, will be to the proximate Kind in the relation of a genus, according to even the popular acceptation of the terms genus and species; that is, it will be a larger class, including it and more.

*t–t*MS, 43, 46, 51, 56, 62, 65   never
*u*MS, 43, 46, 51, 56, 62, 65, 68   could possibly
*v–v*MS, 43, 46   both descended from Noah
w–w+46, 51, 56, 62, 65, 68, 72
*x–x*46, 51, 56, 62, 65   special difference
*y–y*65, 68   specially [*printer's error?*]
*z–z*MS, 43, 46, 51, 56, 62   any

We are now able to fix [a] the logical meaning of [b]these[b] terms. Every class which is a real Kind, that is, which is distinguished from all other classes by an indeterminate multitude of properties not derivable from [c]one[c] another, is either a genus or a species. A Kind which is not divisible into other Kinds, cannot be a genus, because it has no species under it; but it is itself a species, both with reference to the individuals below and to the genera above (Species Prædicabilis and Species Subjicibilis.) But every Kind which admits of division into real Kinds (as animal into [d]mammal, bird, fish, &c., or bird into various species of birds[d]) is a genus to all below it, a species to all genera in which it is itself included. And here we may close this part of the discussion, and pass to the three remaining predicables, Differentia, Proprium, and Accidens.

§ 5. [*Differentia*] To begin with Differentia. This word is correlative with the words genus and species, and as all [a]admit[a], it signifies the attribute which distinguishes a given species from every other species of the same genus. This is so far clear: but [b]we may still ask, which of the distinguishing attributes it signifies.[b] For we have seen that every Kind (and a species must be a Kind) is distinguished from other Kinds, not by any one attribute, but by an indefinite number. Man, for instance, is a species of the genus animal: Rational (or rationality, for it is of no consequence [c]here[c] whether we use the concrete or the abstract form) is generally assigned by logicians as the Differentia; and doubtless this attribute serves the purpose of distinction: but it has also been remarked of man, that he is a cooking animal; the only animal that dresses its food. This, therefore, is another of the attributes by which the species man is distinguished from other species of the same genus: would this attribute serve equally well for a differentia? The Aristotelians say No; having laid it down that the differentia must, like the genus and species, be of the *essence* of the subject.

And here we lose even that vestige of a meaning grounded in the nature of the things themselves, which may be supposed to be attached to the word essence when it is said that genus and species must be of the essence of the thing. There can be no doubt that when the schoolmen talked of the essences of things as opposed to their accidents, they had confusedly in view the distinction between differences of kind, and the differences which are not of

[a]MS, 43, 46 also
[b-b]MS those
[c-c]+MS, 51, 56, 62, 65, 68, 72 [*printer's error?*]
[d-d]MS quadruped, bird, &c., or quadruped into the various species of quadrupeds]
43, 46, 51, 56, 62 *as* MS . . . into various . . . *as* MS
[a-a]MS, 43 agree
[b-b]MS, 43, 46 *which of the distinguishing attributes does it signify?*
[c-c]+68, 72

kind; they meant to intimate that genera and species must be Kinds. Their notion of the essence of a thing was a vague notion of a something which makes it what it is, *i.e.* which makes it the Kind of thing that it is—which causes it to have all that variety of properties which distinguish its Kind. But when the matter came to be looked at more closely, nobody could discover what caused the thing to have all those properties, nor even that there was anything which caused it to have them. Logicians, however, not liking to admit this, and being unable to detect what made the thing to be what it was, satisfied themselves with what made it to be what it was called. Of the innumerable properties, known and unknown, that are common to the class man, a portion only, and of course a very small portion, are connoted by its name; these few, however, will naturally have been thus distinguished from the rest either for their greater obviousness, or for greater supposed importance. These properties, then, which were connoted by the name, logicians seized upon, and called them the essence of the species; and not stopping there, they affirmed them, in the case of the *infima species*, to be the essence of the individual too; for it was their maxim, that the species contained the "whole essence" of the thing. Metaphysics, that fertile field of delusion propagated by language, does not afford a more signal instance of such delusion. On this account it was that rationality, being connoted by the name man, was allowed to be a differentia of the class; but the peculiarity of cooking their food, not being connoted, was relegated to the class of accidental properties.

The distinction, therefore, between Differentia, Proprium, and Accidens, is not *d*grounded*d* in the nature of things, but in the connotation of names; and we must seek it there, if we wish to find what it is.

From the fact that the genus includes the species, in other words *de*notes more than the species, or is predicable of a greater number of individuals, it follows that the species must connote more than the genus. It must connote all the attributes which the genus connotes, or there would be nothing to prevent it from denoting individuals not included in the genus. And it must connote something besides, otherwise it would include the whole genus. Animal denotes all the individuals denoted by man, and many more. Man, therefore, must connote all that animal connotes, otherwise there might be men who *e*are*e* not animals; and it must connote something more than animal connotes, otherwise all animals would be men. This surplus of connotation— this which the species connotes over and above the connotation of the genus —is the Differentia, or specific difference; or, to state the same proposition in other words, the Differentia is that which must be added to the connotation of the genus, to complete the connotation of the species.

*d–d*MS, 43, 46, 51, 56, 62   founded
*e–e*MS, 43   were

The word man, for instance, exclusively of what it connotes in common with animal, also connotes rationality, and at least some approximation to that external form which we all know, but which as we have no name for it considered in itself, we are content to call the human. The Differentia, or specific difference, therefore, of man, as referred to the genus animal, is that outward form and the possession of reason. The Aristotelians said, the possession of reason, without the outward form. But if they adhered to this, they would have been obliged to call the Houyhnhnms men. The question never arose, and they were never called upon to decide how such a case would have affected their notion of essentiality. *However this may be, they* were satisfied with taking such a portion of the differentia as sufficed to distinguish the species from all other *existing* things, though by so doing they might not exhaust the connotation of the name.

§ 6. [*Differentia for general purposes, and differentia for special or technical purposes*] And here, to prevent the notion of differentia from being restricted within too narrow limits, it is necessary to remark, that a species, even as referred to the same genus, will not always have the same differentia, but a different one, according to the principle and purpose which *ᵃpresideᵃ* over the particular classification. For example, a naturalist surveys the various kinds of animals, and looks out for the classification of them most in accordance with the order in which, for zoological purposes, *ᵇhe considers it desirable that we should think of themᵇ*. With this view he finds it advisable that one of his fundamental divisions should be into warm-blooded and cold-blooded animals; or into animals which breathe with lungs and those which breathe with gills; or into carnivorous, and frugivorous or graminivorous; or into those which walk on the flat part and those which walk on the extremity of the foot, a distinction on which *ᶜtwoᶜ* of Cuvier's families are founded. In doing this, the naturalist creates *ᵈasᵈ* many new classes; which are by no means those to which the individual animal is familiarly and spontaneously referred; nor should we ever think of assigning to them so prominent a position in our arrangement of the animal kingdom, unless for a *ᵉpreconceivedᵉ* purpose of scientific convenience. And to the liberty of doing this there is no limit. In the examples we have given, *ᶠmost of theᶠ* classes are real

---

*ᶠ⁻ᶠ*MS, 43, 46   But, so far as it is possible to determine how language would be used in a case which is purely imaginary, we may say that the Houyhnhms [*sic*] would not be called men, and that the term man, therefore, requires other conditions besides rationality. The schoolmen, however,
    *ᵃ⁻ᵃ*43, 46   presides [*printer's error?*]
    *ᵇ⁻ᵇ*MS, 43   it is desirable that his ideas should arrange themselves]   46   he thinks it desirable that his ideas should arrange themselves]   51, 56   he thinks it desirable that our ideas should arrange themselves
    *ᶜ⁻ᶜ*MS, 43, 46, 51, 56, 62   some   *ᵈ⁻ᵈ*51, 56   so
    *ᵉ⁻ᵉ*MS, 43, 46   preconcerted   *ᶠ⁻ᶠ*MS, 43, 46   the new

Kinds, since each of the peculiarities is an index to a multitude of properties belonging to the class which it characterizes: but even if the case were otherwise—if the other properties of those classes could all be derived, by any process known to us, from the one peculiarity on which the class is founded—even then, if *these* derivative properties were of primary importance for the purposes of the naturalist, he would be warranted in founding his primary *divisions* on them.

If, however, practical convenience is a sufficient warrant for making the main demarcations in our arrangement of objects run in lines not coinciding with any distinction of Kind, and so creating genera and species in the popular sense which are not genera or species in the rigorous sense at all; *à fortiori* must we be warranted, when our genera and species *are* real genera and species, in marking the distinction between them by those of their properties which considerations of practical convenience most strongly recommend. If we cut a species out of a given genus—the species man, for instance, out of the genus animal—with an intention on our part that the peculiarity by which we are to be guided in the application of the name man should be rationality, then rationality is the differentia of the species man. Suppose, however, that being naturalists, we, for the purposes of our particular study, cut out of the genus animal the same species man, but with an intention that the distinction between man and all other species of animal should be, not rationality, but the possession of "four incisors in each jaw, tusks solitary, and erect posture." It is evident that the word man, when used by us as naturalists, no longer connotes rationality, but connotes the three other properties specified; for that which we have expressly in view when we impose a name, assuredly forms part of the meaning of that name. We may, therefore, lay it down as a maxim, that wherever there is a Genus, and a Species marked out from that genus by an assignable differentia, the name of the species must be connotative, and must connote the differentia; but the connotation may be special—not involved in the signification of the term as ordinarily used, but given to it when employed as a term of art or science. The word Man in common use, connotes rationality and a certain form, but does not connote the number or character of the teeth; in the Linnæan system it connotes the number of incisor and canine teeth, but does not connote rationality nor any particular form. The word *man* has, therefore, two different meanings; though not commonly considered as ambiguous, because it happens in both cases to *de*note the same individual objects. But a case is conceivable in which the ambiguity would become evident: we have only to imagine that some new kind of animal were discovered, having Linnæus's three characteristics of humanity, but not rational, or not of the human form.

*g–g*MS, 43, 46, 51, 56, 62   those
*h–h*MS, 43, 46   division

In ordinary parlance, these animals would not be called men; but in natural history they must still be called so by those, if any there ⁱshouldⁱ be, who adhere to the Linnæan classification; and the question would arise, whether the word should continue to be used in two senses, or the classification be given up, and the technical sense of the term be abandoned along with it.

Words not otherwise connotative may, in the mode just adverted to, acquire a special or technical connotation. Thus the word whiteness, as we have so often remarked, connotes nothing; it merely ʲdenotesʲ the attribute corresponding to a certain sensation: but if we are making a classification of colours, and desire to justify, or even merely to point out, the particular place assigned to whiteness in our arrangement, we may define it "the colour produced by the mixture of all the simple rays;" and this fact, though by no means implied in the meaning of the word whiteness as ordinarily used, but only known by subsequent scientific investigation, ᵏisᵏ part of its meaning in the particular essay or treatise, and becomes the differentia of the species.*

The differentia, therefore, of a species may be defined to be, that part of the connotation of the specific name, whether ordinary or special and technical, which distinguishes the species in question from all other species of the genus to which on the particular occasion we are referring it.

§ 7. [*Proprium*] Having disposed of Genus, Species, and Differentia, we shall not find much difficulty in attaining a clear conception of the distinction between the other two predicables ᵃ, as well as between them and the first threeᵃ.

In the Aristotelian phraseology, Genus and Differentia are of the *essence* of the subject; by which, as we have seen, is really meant that the properties signified by the genus and those signified by the differentia, form part of the connotation of the name denoting the species. Proprium and Accidens, on the other hand, form no part of the essence, but are predicated of the species only *accidentally*. Both are Accidents, in the wider sense in which the accidents of a thing are opposed to its essence; though, in the doctrine of the Predicables, Accidens is used for one sort of accident only, Proprium being another sort. Proprium, continue the schoolmen, is predicated *accidentally*, indeed, but *necessarily*; or, as they further explain it, signifies an attribute which is not indeed part of the essence, but which flows from, or is a consequence of,

---

*If we allow a differentia to what is not really a species. For the distinction of Kinds, in the sense explained by us, not being in any way applicable to attributes, it of course follows that although attributes may be put into classes, those classes can be admitted to be genera or species only by courtesy.

ⁱ⁻ⁱ+72   ʲ⁻ʲMS *denotes*   ᵏ⁻ᵏMS becomes
ᵃ⁻ᵃ+51, 56, 62, 65, 68, 72

the essence, and is, therefore, inseparably attached to the species; *e.g.* the various properties of a triangle, which, though no part of its definition, must necessarily be possessed by whatever comes under that definition. Accidens, on the contrary, has no connexion whatever with the essence, but may come and go, and the species still remain what it was before. If a species could exist without its Propria, it must be capable of existing without that on which its Propria are necessarily consequent, and therefore without its essence, without that which constitutes it a species. But an Accidens, whether separable or inseparable from the species in actual experience, may be supposed separated, without the necessity of supposing any other alteration; or at least, without supposing any of the essential properties of the species *b*to be*b* altered, since with them an Accidens has no connexion.

A Proprium, therefore, of the species, may be defined, any attribute which belongs to all the individuals included in the species, and which, though not connoted by the specific name, *c*(either ordinarily if the classification we are considering be for ordinary purposes, or specially if it be for a special purpose,)*c* yet follows from some attribute which the name either ordinarily or specially connotes.

One attribute may follow from another in two ways; and there are consequently two kinds of Proprium. It may follow as a conclusion follows premises, or it may follow as an effect follows a cause. Thus, the attribute of having the opposite sides equal, which is not one of those connoted by the word Parallelogram, nevertheless follows from those connoted by it, namely, from having the opposite sides straight lines and parallel, and the number of sides four. The attribute, therefore, of having the opposite sides equal, is a Proprium of the class parallelogram; and a Proprium of the first kind, which follows from the connoted attributes by way of *demonstration*. The attribute of being capable of understanding language, is a Proprium of the species man, since without being connoted by the word, it follows from an attribute which the word does connote, viz., from the attribute of rationality. But this is a Proprium of the second kind, which follows by way of *causation*. How it is that one property of a thing follows, or can be inferred, from another; under what conditions this is possible, and what is the exact meaning of the phrase; are among the questions which will occupy us in the two succeeding Books. At present it needs only be said, that whether a Proprium follows by demonstration or by causation, it follows *necessarily*; that is to say, *d*its not following would be inconsistent*d* with some law which we regard as a part of the constitution either of our thinking faculty or of the universe.

b–b+51, 56, 62, 65, 68, 72
*c–c*MS   either ordinarily (if . . . purposes) or specially (if . . . purpose)
*d–d*MS, 43, 46, 51, 56, 62   it *cannot but* follow, consistently

§ 8. [*Accidens*] Under the remaining predicable, Accidens, are included all attributes of a thing which are neither involved in the signification of the name (whether ordinarily or as a term of art), nor have, so far as we know, any necessary connexion with attributes which are so involved. They are commonly divided into Separable and Inseparable Accidents. Inseparable accidents are those which—although we know of no connexion between them and the attributes constitutive of the species, and although, therefore, so far as we are aware, they might be absent without making the name inapplicable and the species a different species—are yet never in fact known to be absent. A concise mode of expressing the same meaning is, that inseparable accidents are properties which are universal to the species, but not necessary to it. Thus, blackness is an attribute of a crow, and, as far as we know, an universal one. But if we were to discover a race of white birds, in other respects resembling crows, we should not say, These are not crows; we should say, These are white crows. Crow, therefore, does not connote blackness; nor, from any of the attributes which it does connote, whether as a word in popular use or as a term of art, could blackness be inferred. Not only, therefore, can we conceive a white crow, but we know of no reason why such an animal should not exist. Since, however, none but black crows are known to exist, blackness, in the present state of our knowledge, ranks as an accident, but an inseparable accident, of the species crow.

Separable Accidents are those which are found, in point of fact, to be sometimes absent from the species; which are not only not necessary, but not even universal. They are such as do not belong to every individual of the species, but only to some individuals; or if to all, not at all times. Thus the colour of an European is one of the separable accidents of the species man, because it is not an attribute of all human creatures. Being born, is also ᵃ(speaking in the logical sense)ᵃ a separable accident of the species man, because, though an attribute of all human beings, it is so only at one particular time. *A fortiori* those attributes which are not constant even in the same individual, as, to be in one or in another place, to be hot or cold, sitting or walking, must be ranked as separable accidents.

ᵃ⁻ᵃ+51, 56, 62, 65, 68, 72

CHAPTER VIII

Of Definition

§ 1. *[A definition, what]* One necessary part of the theory of Names and of Propositions remains to be treated of in this place: the theory of Definitions. As being the most important of the class of propositions which we have characterized as purely verbal, they have already received some notice in the chapter preceding the last. But their fuller treatment was at that time postponed, because definition is so closely connected with classification, that, until the nature of the latter process is in some measure understood, the former cannot be discussed to much purpose.

b The simplest and most correct notion of a Definition is, a proposition declaratory of the meaning of a word; namely, either the meaning which it bears in common acceptation, or that which the speaker or writer, for the particular purposes of his discourse, intends to annex to it.

The definition of a word being the proposition which enunciates its meaning, words which have no meaning are unsusceptible of definition. Proper names, therefore, cannot be defined. A proper name being a mere mark put upon an individual, and of which it is the characteristic property to be destitute of meaning, its meaning cannot of course be declared; though we may indicate by language, as we might indicate still more conveniently by pointing with the finger, upon what individual that particular mark has been, or is intended to be, put. It is no definition of "John Thomson" to say he is "the son of General Thomson;" for the name John Thomson does not express this. Neither is it any definition of "John Thomson" to say he is "the man now crossing the street." These propositions may serve to make known who is the particular man to whom the name belongs, but that may be done still more unambiguously by pointing to him, which, however, has not *c* been esteemed one of the modes of definition.

In the case of connotative names, the meaning, as has been so often observed, is the connotation; and the definition of a connotative name, is *d*the*d* proposition which declares its connotation. This *e*might*e* be done either directly or indirectly. The direct mode would be by a proposition in this

*a–a*MS, 43, 46 [*Definition, why treated of in this place*]
*b*MS, 43, 46 §2. [*A definition, what*] *c*MS, 43, 46, 51, 56 usually
*d–d*MS a *e–e*MS, 43, 46, 51, 56, 62, 65 may

form: "Man" (or whatsoever the word may be) "is a name connoting such and such attributes," or "is a name which, when predicated of anything, signifies the possession of such and such attributes by that thing." Or thus: Man is everything which possesses such and such attributes: Man is everything which possesses corporeity, organization, life, rationality, and *certain peculiarities of external form*.

This form of definition is the most precise and least equivocal of any; but it is not brief enough, and is besides too technical *g* for common discourse. The more usual mode of declaring the connotation of a name, is to predicate of it another name or names of known signification, which connote the same aggregation of attributes. This may be done either by predicating of the name intended to be defined, another connotative name exactly synonymous, as, "Man is a human being," which is not commonly accounted a definition at all; or by predicating two or more connotative names, which make up among them the whole connotation of the name to be defined. In this last case, again, we may either compose our definition of as many connotative names as there are attributes, each attribute being connoted by one, as, Man is a corporeal, organized, animated, rational being, shaped so and so; or we may employ names which connote several of the attributes at once, as, Man is a rational *animal*, shaped so and so.

The definition of a name, according to this view of it, is the sum total of all the *essential* propositions which can be framed with that name for their subject. All propositions the truth of which is implied in the name, all *ʰthoseʰ* which we are made aware of by merely hearing the name, are included in the definition, if complete, and may be evolved from it without the aid of any other premises; whether the definition expresses them in two or three words, or in a larger number. It is, therefore, not without reason that Condillac and other writers have affirmed a definition to be an *analysis*.[*] To resolve any complex whole into the elements of which it is compounded, is the meaning of analysis: and this we do when we replace one word which connotes a set of attributes collectively, by two or more which connote the same attributes singly, or in smaller groups.

ᵃ§ 2.ᵃ [*Every name can be defined, whose meaning is susceptible of analysis*] From this, however, the question naturally arises, in what manner are we to define a name which connotes only a single attribute: for instance,

[*See Etienne Bonnot de Condillac. *La Logique.* In *Oeuvres complètes.* 31 vols. Paris: Dufart, 1803, Vol. XXX, pp. 141ff. (Part II, Chap. vi).]

*f–f*MS, 43, 46   a form resembling that of the descendants of Adam
*g*MS, 43, 46, 51   and pedantic
h–h+43, 46, 51, 56, 62, 65, 68, 72
*a–a*MS, 43, 46   §3.

"white," which connotes nothing but whiteness; "rational," which connotes nothing but the possession of reason. It might seem that the meaning of such names could only be declared in two ways; by a synonymous term, if any such can be found; or in the direct way already alluded to: "White is a name connoting the attribute whiteness." Let us see, however, whether the analysis of the meaning of the name, that is, the breaking down of that meaning into *several* parts, admits of being carried farther. Without at present deciding this question as to the word *white*, it is obvious that in the case of *rational* some further explanation may be given of its meaning than is contained in the proposition, "Rational is that which possesses the attribute of reason;" since the attribute reason itself admits of being defined. And here we must turn our attention to the definitions of attributes, or rather of the names of attributes, that is, of abstract names.

In regard to such names of attributes as are connotative, and express attributes of those attributes, there is no difficulty: like other connotative names they are defined by declaring their connotation. Thus the word *fault* may be defined, "a quality productive of evil or inconvenience." Sometimes, again, the attribute to be defined is not one attribute, but an union of several: we have only, therefore, to put together the names of all the attributes taken separately, and we obtain the definition of the *name which belongs* to them all taken together; a definition which will correspond exactly to that of the corresponding concrete name. For, as we define a concrete name by enumerating the attributes which it connotes, and as the attributes connoted by a concrete name form the entire signification of the corresponding abstract *name*, the same enumeration will serve for the definition of both. Thus, if the definition of *a human being* be this, "a being, corporeal, animated, rational, *shaped so and so," the definition of *humanity* will be corporeity and animal life, combined with rationality, and with such and such a shape.

When, on the other hand, the abstract name does not express a complication of attributes, but a single attribute, we must remember that every attribute is grounded on some fact or phenomenon, from which, and which alone, it derives its meaning. To that fact or phenomenon, called in a former chapter the foundation of the attribute, we must, therefore, have recourse for its definition. Now, the foundation of the attribute may be a phenomenon of any degree of complexity, consisting of many different parts, either coexistent or in succession. To obtain a definition of the attribute, we must analyse the phenomenon into these parts. Eloquence, for example, is the name of one attribute only; but this attribute is grounded on external effects of a compli-

*b–b*MS, 43, 46   separate
*c–c*MS   name belonging]   43, 46   names which belong
*d–d*MS, 43, 46, 51   one
*e*MS, 43, 46, 51   and

cated nature, flowing from acts of the person to whom we ascribe the attribute; and by resolving this phenomenon of causation into its two parts, the cause and the effect, we obtain a definition of eloquence, viz. the power of influencing the *feelings by* speech or writing.

A name, therefore, whether concrete or abstract, admits of definition, provided we are able to analyse, that is, to distinguish into parts, the attribute or set of attributes which constitute the meaning both of the concrete name and of the corresponding abstract: if a set of attributes, by enumerating them; if a single attribute, by dissecting the fact or phenomenon (whether of perception or of internal consciousness) which is the foundation of the attribute. But, further, even when the fact is one of our simple feelings or states of consciousness, and therefore unsusceptible of analysis, the names both of the object and of the attribute still admit of definition: or rather, would do so if all our simple feelings had names. Whiteness may be defined, the property or power of exciting the sensation of white. A white object may be defined, an object which excites the sensation of white. The only names which are unsusceptible of definition, because their meaning is unsusceptible of analysis, are the names of the simple feelings themselves. These are in the same condition as proper names. They are not indeed, like proper names, unmeaning; for the words *sensation of white* signify, that the sensation which I so denominate resembles other sensations which I remember to have had before, and to have called by that name. But as we have no words by which to recal those former sensations, except the very word which we seek to define, or some other which, being exactly synonymous with it, requires definition as much, words cannot unfold the signification of this class of names; and we are obliged to make a direct appeal to the personal experience of the individual whom we address.

§ 3. [*Complete, how distinguished from incomplete definitions*] Having stated what seems to be the true idea of a Definition, *I* proceed to examine some opinions of philosophers, and some popular conceptions on the subject, which conflict more or less with *that idea*.

The only adequate definition of a name is, as already remarked, one which declares the facts, and the whole of the facts, which the name involves in its signification. But with most persons the object of a definition does not embrace so much; they look for nothing more, in a definition, than a guide to the correct use of the term—a protection against applying it in a manner inconsistent with custom and convention. Anything, therefore, is to them a

---

*f–f*MS, 43, 46   affections of human beings by means of
*a–a*MS, 43, 46   §4.
*b–b*MS, 43, 46, 51, 56, 62, 65, 68   we
*c–c*MS, 43, 46   the above

sufficient definition of a term, which will serve as a correct index to what the term *de*notes; though not embracing the whole, and sometimes, perhaps, not even any part, of what it connotes. This gives rise to two sorts of imperfect, or unscientific definition; *d* Essential but incomplete Definitions, and Accidental Definitions, or Descriptions. In the former, a connotative name is defined by a part only of its connotation; in the latter, by something which forms no part of the connotation at all.

An example of the first kind of imperfect definitions is the following:— Man is a rational animal. It is impossible to consider this as a complete definition of the word Man, since (as before remarked) if we adhered to it we should be obliged to call the Houyhnhnms men; but as there happen to be no Houyhnhnms, this imperfect definition is sufficient to mark out and distinguish from all other things, the objects at present *e*denoted*e* by "man;" all the beings actually known to exist, of whom the name is predicable. Though the word is defined by some only among the attributes which it connotes, not by all, it happens that all known objects which possess the enumerated attributes, possess also those which are omitted; so that the field of predication which the word covers, and the employment of it which is conformable to usage, are as well indicated by the inadequate definition as by an adequate one. Such definitions, however, are always liable to be overthrown by the discovery of new objects in nature.

Definitions of this kind are what logicians have had in view, when they laid down the rule, that the definition of a species should be *per genus et differentiam*. Differentia being seldom taken to mean the whole of the peculiarities constitutive of the species, but some one of those peculiarities only, a complete definition would be *per genus et differentias*, rather than *differentiam*. It would include, with the name of the superior genus, not merely *some* attribute which distinguishes the species intended to be defined from all other species of the same genus, but *all* the attributes implied in the name of the species, which the name of the superior genus has not already implied. The assertion, however, that a definition must of necessity consist of a genus and differentiæ, is not tenable. It was early remarked by logicians, that the *summum genus* in any classification, having no genus superior to itself, could not be defined in this manner. Yet we have seen that all names, except those of our elementary feelings, are susceptible of definition in the strictest sense; by setting forth in words the constituent parts of the fact or phenomenon, of which the connotation of every word is ultimately composed.

a§ 4.*a* [*And how complete definitions are distinguished from descriptions*] Although the first kind of imperfect definition, (which defines a connotative

---

*d*MS, 43, 46, 51, 56, 62   namely,   *e–e*MS   *de*noted
*a–a*MS, 43, 46   §5.

term by a part only of what it connotes, but a part sufficient to mark out correctly the boundaries of its denotation,) has been considered by the ancients, and by logicians in general, as a complete definition; it has always been deemed necessary that the attributes employed should really form part of the connotation; for the rule was that the definition must be drawn from the *essence* of the class; and this would not have been the case if it had been in any degree made up of attributes not connoted by the name. The second kind of imperfect definition, therefore, in which the name of a class is defined by any of its accidents,—that is, by attributes which are not included in its connotation,—has been rejected from the rank of genuine Definition by all *b*logicians*b*, and has been termed Description.

This kind of imperfect definition, however, takes its rise from the same cause as the other, namely, the willingness to accept as a definition anything which, whether it expounds the meaning of the name or not, enables us to discriminate the things denoted by the name from all other things, and consequently to employ the term in predication without deviating from established usage. This purpose is duly answered by stating any (no matter what) of the attributes which are common to the whole of the class, and peculiar to it; or any combination of attributes which *c*happens*c* to be peculiar to it, though separately each of those attributes may be common to it with some other things. It is only necessary that the definition (or description) thus formed, should be *convertible* with the name which it professes to define; that is, should be exactly co-extensive with it, being predicable of everything of which it is predicable, and of nothing of which it is not predicable; though the attributes specified may have no connexion with those which *d*mankind*d* had in view when they formed or recognised the class, and gave it a name. The following are correct definitions of Man, according to this test: Man is a mammiferous animal, having (by nature) two hands (for the human species answers to this description, and no other animal does): Man is an animal who cooks his food: Man is a featherless biped.

What would otherwise be a mere description, may be raised to the rank of a real definition by the peculiar purpose which the speaker or writer has in view. As was seen in the preceding chapter, it may, for the ends of a particular art or science, or for the more convenient statement of an author's particular *e*doctrines*e*, be advisable to give to some general name, without altering its denotation, a special connotation, different from its ordinary one. When this is done, a definition of the name by means of the attributes which make up the special connotation, though in general a mere accidental definition or description, becomes on the particular occasion and for the particular purpose a complete and genuine definition. This actually occurs with respect

---

to one of the preceding examples, "Man is a mammiferous animal having two hands," which is the scientific definition of man, considered as one of the species in Cuvier's distribution of the animal kingdom.[*]

In cases of this sort, though the definition is still a declaration of the meaning which in the particular instance the name is appointed to convey, it cannot be said that to state the meaning of the word is the purpose of the definition. The purpose is not to expound a name, but *f* a classification. The special meaning which Cuvier assigned to the word Man, (quite foreign to its ordinary meaning, though involving no change in the *g*denotation*g* of the word,) was incidental to a plan of arranging animals into classes on a certain principle, that is, according to a certain set of distinctions. And since the definition of Man according to the ordinary connotation of the word, though it would have answered every other purpose of a definition, would not have pointed out the place which the species ought to occupy in that particular classification; he gave the word a special connotation, that he might be able to define it by the kind of attributes on which, for reasons of scientific convenience, he had resolved to found his division of animated nature.

Scientific definitions, whether they are definitions of scientific terms, or of common terms used in a scientific sense, are almost always of the kind last spoken of: their main purpose is to serve as the landmarks of scientific classification. And since the classifications in any science are continually modified as scientific knowledge advances, the definitions in the sciences are also constantly varying. A striking instance is afforded by the words Acid and Alkali, especially the former. As experimental discovery advanced, the substances classed with acids have been constantly multiplying, and by a natural consequence the attributes connoted by the word have receded and become fewer. At first it connoted the attributes, of combining with an alkali to form a neutral substance (called a salt); being compounded of a base and oxygen; causticity to the taste and touch; fluidity, &c. The true analysis of muriatic acid, into chlorine and hydrogen, caused the second property, composition from a base and oxygen, to be excluded from the connotation. The same discovery fixed the attention of chemists upon hydrogen as an important element in acids; and more recent discoveries having led to the recognition of its presence in sulphuric, nitric, and many other acids, where its existence was not previously suspected, there is now a tendency to include the presence of this element in the connotation of the word. But carbonic acid, silica, sulphurous acid, have no hydrogen in their composition; that property cannot therefore be connoted by the term, unless those substances

[*See Georges Cuvier. *Le Règne animal*. 4 vols. Paris: Deterville, 1817, Vol. I, p. 81.]

*f*MS, 43, 46, 51 to help to expound
*g–g*MS *de*notation

are no longer to be considered acids. Causticity and fluidity have long since been excluded from the characteristics of the class, by the inclusion of silica and many other substances in it; and the formation of neutral bodies by combination with alkalis, together with such electro-chemical peculiarities as this is supposed to imply, are now the only *differentiæ* which form the fixed connotation of the word Acid, as a term of chemical science. [h]

What is true of the definition of any term of science, is of course true of the definition of a science itself; and accordingly, [i](as observed in the Introductory Chapter of this work,)[i] the definition of a science must necessarily be progressive and provisional [j]. Any[j] extension of knowledge or alteration in the current opinions respecting the subject matter, may lead to a change more or less extensive in the particulars included in the science; and its composition being thus altered, it may easily happen that a different set of characteristics will be [k]found[k] better adapted as differentiæ for defining its name.

In the same manner in which [l] a special or technical definition has for its object to expound the artificial classification out of which it grows; the Aristotelian logicians seem to have imagined that it [m]was[m] also the business of ordinary definition to expound the ordinary, and what they deemed the natural, classification of things, namely, the division of them into Kinds; and to show the place which each Kind occupies, as superior, collateral, or subordinate, among other Kinds. This notion would account for the rule that all definition must necessarily be *per genus et differentiam*, and would also explain why [n]a single[n] differentia was deemed sufficient. But to expound, or express in words, a distinction of Kind, has already been shown to be an

[h]MS *[paragraph]* Scientific men are still seeking, and may be long ere they find, a suitable definition of one of the earliest words in the vocabulary of the human race, and one of those of which the popular sense is plainest and best understood. The word I mean is Heat; and the source of the difficulty is the imperfect state of our scientific knowledge, which has shewn us multitudes of phenomena certainly connected with the same power which is the cause of what our senses recognise as heat, but has not yet taught us the laws of those phenomena with sufficient accuracy to admit of our determining under what characteristics the whole of those phenomena shall ultimately be embodied as a class: which characteristics would of course be so many differentiæ for the definition of the power itself. We have advanced far enough to know that one of the attributes connoted must be that of operating as a repulsive force; but this is certainly not all which must ultimately be included in the scientific definition of heat.] 43 *as* MS . . . which has shown to us . . . *as* MS] 46, 51 *as* 43 . . . same power which causes what . . . *as* MS] 56 *as* 46 . . . attributes connoted must be that of exercising a repulsive . . . *as* MS] 62 *as* 46 . . . laws of those phenomena sufficiently to admit of our determining under what characteristics the whole of the phenomena . . . *as* 56
[i-i]MS, 43, 46 we showed in the Introductory Chapter of this work, that
[j-j]MS , since any
[k-k]+43, 46, 51, 56, 62, 65, 68, 72
[l]MS, 43, 46 , as we have now shown,
[m-m]MS is
[n-n]MS, 43, 46, 51, 56, 62, 65 any one

impossibility: the very meaning of a Kind is, that the properties which distinguish it do not grow out of one another, and cannot therefore be set forth in words, even by implication, otherwise than by enumerating them all: and all are not known, nor *are ever likely to be so*. It is idle, therefore, to look to this as one of the purposes of a definition: while, if it be only required that the definition of a Kind should indicate what kinds include it or are included by it, any definitions which expound the connotation of the names will do this: for the name of each class must *necessarily* connote enough of its properties to fix the boundaries of the class. If the definition, therefore, be a full statement of the connotation, it is all that a definition can be required to be.*

*[72] Professor Bain, in his *Logic*, takes a peculiar view of Definition. He holds (Pt. I, p. 71) with the present work, that "the definition in its full import, is the sum of all the properties connoted by the name; it exhausts the meaning of a word." But he regards the meaning of a general name as including, not indeed all the common properties of the class named, but all of them that are ultimate properties, not resolvable into one another. "The enumeration of the attributes of oxygen, of gold, of man, should be an enumeration of the final (so far as can be made out,) the underivable, powers or functions of each," and nothing less than this is a complete Definition (*ibid.*, p. 75). An independent property, not derivable from other properties, even if previously unknown, yet as soon as discovered becomes, according to him, part of the meaning of the term, and should be included in the definition. "When we are told that diamond, which we know to be a transparent, glittering, hard, and high-priced substance, is composed of carbon, and is combustible, we must put these additional properties on the same level as the rest; to us they are henceforth connoted by the name" (*ibid.*, p. 73). Consequently the propositions that diamond is composed of carbon, and that it is combustible, are regarded by Mr. Bain as merely verbal propositions. He carries this doctrine so far as to say that unless mortality can be shown to be a consequence of the ultimate laws of animal organization, mortality is connoted by man, and "Man is Mortal" is a merely verbal proposition. And one of the peculiarities (I think a disadvantageous peculiarity) of his able and valuable treatise, is the large number of propositions requiring proof, and learnt by experience, which, in conformity with this doctrine, he considers as not real, but verbal, propositions.

The objection I have to this language is that it confounds, or at least confuses, a much more important distinction than that which it draws. The only reason for dividing Propositions into real and verbal, is in order to discriminate propositions which convey information about facts, from those which do not. A proposition which affirms that an object has a given attribute, while designating the object by a name which already signifies the attribute, adds no information to that which was already possessed by all who understood the name. But when this is said, it is implied that, by the signification of a name, is meant the signification attached to it in the common usage of life. I cannot think we ought to say that the meaning of a word includes matters of fact which are unknown to every person who uses the word unless he has learnt them by special study of a particular department of

*o–o*MS ever will be] 43, 46, 51 ever will be so
p–p+43, 46, 51, 56, 62, 65, 68, 72

§ 5. [*What are called definitions of Things, are definitions of Names with an implied assumption of the existence of Things corresponding to them*] Of the two incomplete *and popular modes* of definition, and in what they differ from the complete or *philosophical mode*, enough has now been said. We shall next examine an ancient doctrine, once generally prevalent and still by no means exploded, which I regard as the source of a great part of the obscurity hanging over some of the most important processes of the understanding in the pursuit of truth. According to this, the definitions of which we have now treated are only one of two sorts into which definitions may be divided, viz. definitions of names, and definitions of things. The former are intended to explain the meaning of a term; the latter, the nature of a thing; the last being incomparably the most important.

This opinion was held by the ancient philosophers, and by their followers, with the exception of the Nominalists; but as the spirit of modern metaphysics, until a recent period, has been on the whole a Nominalist spirit, the notion of definitions of things has been to a certain extent in abeyance, still continuing, however, to breed confusion in logic, by its consequences indeed rather than by itself. Yet the doctrine in its own proper form now and then breaks out, and has appeared (among other places) where it was scarcely to be expected, in a *justly admired* work, Archbishop Whately's *Logic*.* In a

---

Nature; or that because a few persons are aware of these matters of fact, the affirmation of them is a proposition conveying no information. I hold that (special scientific connotation apart) a name means, or connotes, only the properties which it is a mark of in the general mind; and that in the case of any additional properties, however uniformly found to accompany these, it remains possible that a thing which did not possess the properties might still be thought entitled to the name. Ruminant, according to Mr. Bain's use of language, connotes cloven hoofed, since the two properties are always found together, and no connexion has ever been discovered between them: but ruminant does not mean cloven-hoofed; and were an animal to be discovered which chews the cud, but has its feet undivided, I venture to say that it would still be called ruminant.

*[51] In the fuller discussion which Archbishop Whately has given to this subject in his later editions, he almost ceases to regard the definitions of names and those of things as, in any important sense, distinct. He seems (9th ed., p. 145) to limit the notion of a Real Definition to one which "explains anything *more* of the nature of the thing than is implied in the name;" (including under the word "implied," not only what the name connotes, but everything which can be deduced by reasoning from the attributes connoted). Even this, as he adds, is usually called, not a Definition, but a Description; and (as it seems to me) rightly so called. A Description, I conceive, can only be ranked among Definitions, when taken (as in the case of the zoological definition of man) to fulfil the true office

*a–a*MS, 43, 46   §6.
*b–b*MS   or unscientific kinds]   43, 46, 51, 56   or unscientific modes
*c–c*MS   scientific kind]   43, 46, 51, 56   scientific mode
*d–d*MS, 43, 46, 51, 56   deservedly popular

review of that work published by me in the *Westminster Review* for January 1828,[*] and containing some opinions which I no longer entertain, I find the following observations on the question now before us; observations with which my present *ᵉview of that question isᵉ* still sufficiently in accordance.

The distinction between nominal and real definitions, between definitions of words and what are called definitions of things, though conformable to the ideas of most of the Aristotelian logicians, cannot, as it appears to us, be maintained. We apprehend that no definition is ever intended to 'explain and unfold the nature of *ᶠaᶠ* thing.' It is some confirmation of our opinion, that none of those writers who have thought that there were definitions of things, have ever succeeded in discovering any criterion by which the definition of a thing can be distinguished from any other proposition relating to the thing. The definition, they say, unfolds the nature of the thing: but no definition can unfold its whole nature; and every proposition in which any quality whatever is predicated of the thing, unfolds some part of its nature. The true state of the case we take to be this. All definitions are of names, and of names only; but, in some definitions, it is clearly apparent, that nothing is intended except to explain the meaning of the word; while in others, besides explaining the meaning of the word, it is intended to be implied that there exists a thing, corresponding to the word. Whether this be or be not implied in any given case, cannot be collected from the mere form of the expression. 'A centaur is an animal with the upper parts of a man and the lower parts of a horse,' and 'A triangle is a rectilineal figure with three sides,' are, in form, expressions precisely similar; although in the former it is not implied that any *thing*, conformable to the term, really exists, while in the latter it is; as may be seen by substituting, in both definitions, the word *means* for *is*. In the first expression, 'A centaur means an animal,' &c., the sense would remain unchanged: in the second, 'A triangle means,' &c., the meaning would be altered, since it would be obviously impossible to deduce any of the truths of geometry from a

---

of a Definition, by declaring the connotation given to a word in some special use, as a term of science or art: which special connotation of course would not be expressed by the proper definition of the word in its ordinary employment.

Mr. De Morgan, exactly reversing the doctrine of Archbishop Whately, understands by a Real Definition one which contains *less* than the Nominal Definition, provided only that what it contains is sufficient for distinction. "By *real* definition I mean such an explanation of the word, be it the whole of the meaning or only part, as will be sufficient to separate the things contained under that word from all others. Thus the following, I believe, is a complete definition of an elephant: An animal which naturally drinks by drawing the water into its nose, and then spurting it into its mouth." [Augustus De Morgan,] *Formal Logic* [London: Taylor and Walton, 1847], p. 36. Mr. De Morgan's general proposition and his example are at variance; for the peculiar mode of drinking of the elephant certainly forms no part of the meaning of the word elephant. It could not be said, because a person happened to be ignorant of this property, that he did not know what an elephant means.

[*"Whately's *Elements of Logic*," *Westminster Review*, IX (Jan., 1828), pp. 164–5.]

ᵉ⁻ᵉMS, 43, 46 views on that question are
ᶠ⁻ᶠSource, MS, 43, 46, 51 the

proposition expressive only of the manner in which we intend to employ a particular sign.

There are, therefore, expressions, commonly passing for definitions, which include in themselves more than the mere explanation of the meaning of a term. But it is not correct to call an expression of this sort a peculiar kind of definition. Its difference from the other kind consists in this, that it is not a definition, but a definition and something more. The definition above given of a triangle, obviously comprises not one, but two propositions, perfectly distinguishable. The one is, 'There may exist a figure, bounded by three straight lines;' the other, 'And this figure may be termed a triangle.' The former of these propositions is not a definition at all: the latter is a mere nominal definition, or explanation of the use and application of a term. The first is susceptible of truth or falsehood, and may therefore be made the foundation of a train of reasoning. The latter can neither be true nor false; the only character it is susceptible of is that of conformity or discomformity to the ordinary usage of language.

There is a real distinction, then, between definitions of names, and what are erroneously called definitions of things; but it is, that the latter, along with the meaning of a name, covertly *asserts* a matter of fact. This covert assertion is not a definition, but a postulate. The definition is a mere identical proposition, which gives information only about the use of language, and from which no conclusions affecting matters of fact can possibly be drawn. The accompanying postulate on the other hand, affirms a fact, which may lead to consequences of every degree of importance. It affirms the *actual or possible* existence of Things possessing the combination of attributes set forth in the definition; and this *, if true, may be* foundation sufficient on which to build a whole fabric of scientific truth.

We have already made, and shall often have to repeat, the remark, that the philosophers who overthrew Realism by no means got rid of the consequences of Realism, but retained long afterwards, in their own philosophy, numerous propositions which could only have a rational meaning as part of a Realistic system. It had been handed down from Aristotle, and probably from earlier times, as an obvious truth, that the science of Geometry is deduced from definitions. This, so long as a definition was considered to be a proposition "unfolding the nature of the thing," did well enough. But Hobbes *followed*, and rejected utterly the notion that a definition declares the nature of the thing, or does anything but state the meaning of a name; yet he continued to affirm as broadly as any of his predecessors, that the ἀρχαί, *principia*, or original premises of mathematics, and even of all science, are definitions;[*] producing the singular paradox, that systems of scientific truth, nay, all truths whatever at which we arrive by reasoning, are deduced

[*See, e.g., "Computation or Logic," pp. 17, 81ff.]

*g–g*MS   assert   *h–h*MS, 43, 46, 51, 56   real
*i–i*MS   is often   *j–j*MS, 43, 46   came

from the arbitrary conventions of mankind concerning the signification of words.

To save the credit of the doctrine that definitions are the premises of scientific knowledge, the proviso is sometimes added, that they are so only under a certain condition, namely, that they be framed conformably to the phenomena of nature; that is, that they ascribe such meanings to terms as shall suit objects actually existing. But this is only an instance of the attempt [k]so[k] often made, to escape from the necessity of abandoning old language after the ideas which it expresses have been exchanged for contrary ones. From the meaning of a name (we are told) it is possible to infer physical facts, provided the name has corresponding to it an existing thing. But if this proviso be necessary, from which of the two is the inference really drawn? From the existence of a thing having the properties, or from the existence of a name meaning them?

Take, for instance, any of the definitions laid down as premises in Euclid's *Elements*; the definition, let us say, of a circle. This, being analysed, consists of two propositions; the one an assumption with respect to a matter of fact, the other a genuine definition. "A figure may exist, having all the points in the line which bounds it equally distant from a single point within it:" "Any figure possessing this property is called a circle."[*] Let us look at one of the demonstrations which are said to depend on this definition, and observe [l]to which of the two propositions contained in it the demonstration really appeals[l]. "About the centre A, describe the circle B C D."[†] Here is an assumption that a figure, such as the definition expresses, *may* be described; which is no other than the postulate, or covert assumption, involved in the so-called definition. But whether that figure be called a circle or not is quite immaterial. The purpose would be as well answered, in all respects except brevity, were we to say, "Through the point B, draw a line returning into itself, of which every point shall be at an equal distance from the point A." By this the definition of a circle would be got rid of, and rendered needless; but not the postulate implied in it; without that the demonstration could not stand. The circle being now described, let us proceed to the consequence. "Since B C D is a circle, the radius B A is equal to the radius C A." B A is equal to C A, not because B C D is a circle, but because B C D is a figure with the radii equal. Our warrant for assuming that such a figure about the centre A, with the radius B A, may be made to exist, is the postulate.

[*See Euclid, Bk. I, Definition 11; in John Playfair. *Elements of Geometry; containing the first six books of Euclid.* 9th ed. Edinburgh: Bell and Bradfute, 1836, p. 19.]

[†See *ibid.*, Proposition 1; Playfair, *Elements of Geometry*, p. 23.]

[k]–[k]MS, 43 , too
[l]–[l]MS which . . . appeals to

[m]Whether the admissibility of these postulates rests on intuition, or on proof, may be a matter of dispute[m]; but in either case they are the premises on which the [n]theorems depend[n]; and while these are retained it would make no difference in the certainty of geometrical truths, though every definition in Euclid, and every technical term therein defined, were laid aside.

It is, perhaps, superfluous to dwell at so much length on what is so nearly self-evident; but when a distinction, obvious as it may appear, has been confounded, and by [o]powerful intellects[o], it is better to say too much than too little for the purpose of rendering such mistakes impossible in future. [p]I will, therefore, detain the reader while I[p] point out one of the absurd consequences flowing from the supposition that definitions, as such, are the premises in any of our reasonings, except such as relate to words only. If this supposition were true, we might argue correctly from true premises, and arrive at a false conclusion. We should only have to assume as a premise the definition of a nonentity; or rather of a name which has no entity corresponding to it. Let this, for instance, be our definition:

A dragon is a serpent breathing flame.

This proposition, considered only as a definition, is indisputably correct. A dragon *is* a serpent breathing flame: the word *means* that. The tacit assumption, indeed, (if there were any such understood assertion), of the existence of an object with properties corresponding to the definition, would, in the present instance, be false. Out of this definition we may carve the premises of the following syllogism:

A dragon is a thing which breathes flame:

[q]A[q] dragon is a serpent:

From which the conclusion is,

Therefore some serpent or serpents breathe flame:

an unexceptionable syllogism in the first mode of the third figure, in which both premises are true and yet the conclusion false; which every logician knows to be an absurdity. The conclusion being false and the syllogism correct, the premises cannot be true. But the premises, considered as parts of a definition, are true [r] . Therefore, the premises considered as parts of a definition cannot be the real ones. The real premises must be—

A dragon is a *really existing* thing which breathes flame:

A dragon is a *really existing* serpent:

which implied premises being false, the falsity of the conclusion presents no absurdity.

[m-m]MS, 43, 46 —The admissiblity of these assumptions may be intuitive, or may admit of proof
   [n-n]MS theorem depends
   [o-o]MS, 43, 46 men of the most powerful intellect
   [p-p]MS, 43 We will, therefore, detain the reader while we
   [q-q]MS, 43, 46 But a
   [r]MS, 43, 46 : there is no possibility of controverting them

[s] If we would determine what conclusion follows from the same ostensible premises when the tacit assumption of real existence is left out, let us, according to the recommendation in [t]a previous page[t], substitute *means* for *is*.[*] We then have—

[u]Dragon[u] is *a word meaning* a thing which breathes flame:

[v]Dragon[v] is *a word meaning* a serpent:

From which the conclusion is,

Some *word or words which mean* a serpent, also mean a thing which breathes flame:

where the conclusion (as well as the premises) is true, and is the only kind of conclusion which can ever follow from a definition, namely, a proposition relating to the meaning of words.

[w]There is still another shape into which we may transform this syllogism. We may suppose the middle term to be the designation neither of a thing nor of a name, but of an idea. We then have—

The *idea of* a dragon is *an idea of* a thing which breathes flame:

The *idea of* a dragon is *an idea of* a serpent:

Therefore, there is *an idea of* a serpent, which is *an idea of* a thing breathing flame.

Here the conclusion is true, and also the premises; but the premises are not definitions. They are propositions affirming that an idea existing in the mind, includes certain ideal elements. The truth of the conclusion follows from the existence of the psychological phenomenon called the idea of a dragon; and therefore still from the tacit assumption of a matter of fact.*

[*See p. 143 above.]

*[51] In the only attempt which, so far as I know, has been made to refute the preceding argumentation, it is maintained that in the first form of the syllogism,

A dragon is a thing which breathes flame,

A dragon is a serpent,

Therefore some serpent or serpents breathe flame,

"there is just as much truth in the conclusion as there is in the premises, or rather, no more in the latter than in the former. If the general name serpent includes both real and imaginary serpents, there is no falsity in the conclusion; if not, there is falsity in the minor premise." [Anon., "Mill's System of Logic," *British Quarterly Review*, IV (Aug., 1846), p. 16.]

Let us, then, try to set out the syllogism on the hypothesis that the name ser-

[s]MS, 43, 46 [*no paragraph*]
[t-t]MS, 43, 46, 51, 56 the *Westminster Review*
[u] [u]MS, 43, 46 A dragon   [v-v]MS, 43, 46 A dragon
[w-w]148MS, 43, 46 [*no paragraph*] If it relate to anything else, we may know that it does not follow from the definition, but from the tacit assumption of a matter of fact.

It is only necessary further to enquire, in what cases that tacit assumption is really made, and in what cases not. Unless we declare the contrary, we always convey the impression that we intend to make the assumption

When, as in this last syllogism, the conclusion is a proposition respecting an idea, the assumption on which it depends may be merely that of the existence of an idea. But when the conclusion is a proposition concerning a Thing, the postulate involved in the definition which stands as the apparent premise, is the existence of a thing conformable to the definition, and not merely of an idea conformable to it. This assumption of real existence *we* always convey the impression that we intend to make*, when we profess to define any name which is already known to be a name of really existing objects. On this account it is, that the assumption was not necessarily implied in the definition of a dragon, while there was no doubt of its being included in the definition of a circle.

§ 6. [*What are called definitions of Things are definitions of Names even when such Things do not in reality exist*] One of the circumstances which have contributed to keep up the notion, that demonstrative truths follow from definitions rather than from the postulates implied in those definitions, is, that the postulates, even in those sciences which are considered to surpass all others in demonstrative certainty, are not always exactly true. It is not true that a circle exists, or can be described, which has all its radii *exactly* equal. Such accuracy is ideal only; it is not found in nature, still less can it be realized by art. People had a difficulty, therefore, in conceiving that the most certain of all conclusions could rest on premises which, instead of being certainly true, are certainly not true to the *full* extent asserted. This apparent paradox will be examined when we come to treat of Demonstration; where we shall be able to show that as much of the postulate is true, as is required to support as much as is true of the conclusion. Philosophers, how-

---

pent includes imaginary serpents. We shall find that it is now necessary to alter the predicates; for it cannot be asserted that an imaginary creature breathes flame; in predicating of it such a fact, we assert by the most positive implication that it is real and not imaginary. The conclusion must run thus, "Some serpent or serpents either do or are *imagined* to breathe flame." And to prove this conclusion by the instance of dragons, the premises must be, A dragon is *imagined* as breathing flame, A dragon is a (real or imaginary) serpent: from which it undoubtedly follows, that there are serpents which are imagined to breathe flame; but the major premise is not a definition, nor part of a definition; which is all that I am concerned to prove.

Let us now examine the other assertion—that if the word serpent stands for none but real serpents, the minor premise (a dragon is a serpent) is false. This is exactly what I have myself said of the premise, considered as a statement of fact: but it is not false as part of the definition of a dragon; and since the premises, or one of them, must be false, (the conclusion being so,) the real premise cannot be the definition, which is true, but the statement of fact, which is false.

*–*68   will [*printer's error?*]
*–*MS, 43, 46   §7.   *–*MS, 43, 46   whole

ever, to whom this view had not occurred, or whom it did not satisfy, have thought it indispensable that there should be found in definitions something *more* certain, or at least more accurately true, than the implied postulate of the real existence of a corresponding object. And this something they flattered themselves they had found, when they laid it down that a definition is a statement and analysis not of the mere meaning of a word, nor yet of the nature of a thing, but of an idea. Thus, the proposition, "A circle is a plane figure bounded by a line all the points of which are at an equal distance from a given point within it," was considered by them, not as an assertion that any real circle has that property, (which would not be exactly true,) but that we *conceive* a circle as having it; that our abstract idea of a circle is an idea of a figure with its radii exactly equal.

Conformably to this it is said, that the subject-matter of mathematics, and of every other demonstrative science, is not things as they really exist, but abstractions of the mind. A geometrical line is a line without breadth; but no such line exists in nature; it is a *c*notion merely suggested to the mind by its experience of*c* nature. The definition (it is said) is a definition of this mental line, not of any actual line: and it is only of the mental line, not of any line existing in nature, that the theorems of geometry are accurately true.

Allowing this doctrine respecting the nature of demonstrative truth to be correct (which, in a subsequent place, I shall endeavour to prove that it is not;) even on that supposition, the conclusions which seem to follow from a definition, do not follow from the definition as such, but from an implied postulate. Even if it be true that there is no object in nature answering to the definition of a line, and that the geometrical properties of lines are not true of any lines in nature, but only of the idea of a line; the definition, at all events, postulates the real existence of such an idea: it assumes that the mind can frame, or rather has framed, the notion of length without breadth, and without any other sensible property whatever. *d*To me, indeed, it appears that*d* the mind cannot form any such notion; it cannot conceive length without breadth; it can only, in contemplating objects, attend to their length, exclusively of their other sensible qualities, and so determine what properties may be predicated of them in virtue of their length alone. If this be true, the postulate involved in the geometrical definition of a line, is the real existence, not of length without breadth, but merely of length, that is, of long objects. This is quite enough to support all the truths of geometry, since every property of a geometrical line is really a property of all physical objects *e*in so far as*e* possessing length. But even what I hold to be the false doctrine on

---

*c–c*MS, 43, 46   mere notion made up by the mind, out of the materials in]   51, 56, 62, 65   notion . . . *as* MS
   *d–d*MS, 43, 46   According to what appears to me the sounder opinion,
   e–e+68, 72

the subject, leaves the conclusion that our reasonings are grounded on the matters of fact postulated in definitions, and not on the definitions themselves, entirely unaffected; and accordingly *f*this conclusion is one which I have in common with Dr. Whewell, in his*f* *Philosophy of the Inductive* *g*Sciences: though, on*g* the nature of demonstrative truth, Dr. Whewell's opinions are greatly at variance with mine *h* . And here, as in many other instances, *i*I gladly acknowledge that*i* his writings are eminently serviceable in clearing from confusion the initial steps in the analysis of the mental processes, even where his views respecting the ultimate analysis *j* are such as (though with unfeigned respect) I cannot but regard as fundamentally erroneous.

a§ 7.*a* [*Definitions, though of names only, must be grounded on knowledge of the corresponding things*] Although, according to the *b*opinion*b* here presented, Definitions are properly of names only, and not of things, it does not follow *c*from this that definitions are arbitrary*c*. How to define a name, may not only be an inquiry of considerable difficulty and intricacy, but may *d*involve*d* considerations going deep into the nature of the things which are denoted by the name. Such, for instance, are the inquiries which form the subjects of the most important of Plato's Dialogues; as, "What is rhetoric?" the topic of the "Gorgias," or "What is justice?" that of the "Republic." Such, also, is the question scornfully asked by Pilate, "What is truth?"[*] and the fundamental question with speculative moralists in all ages, "What is virtue?"

It would be a mistake to represent these difficult and noble inquiries as having nothing in view beyond ascertaining the conventional meaning of a name. They are inquiries not so much to determine what is, as what should be, the meaning of a name; which, like other practical questions of terminology, requires for its solution that we should enter, and sometimes enter very deeply, into the properties not merely of names but of the things named.

Although the meaning of every concrete general name resides in the attri-

[*St. John, 18:38.]

*f–f*MS, 43   I am able to appeal in confirmation of this conclusion, to the authority of Mr. Whewell, in his recent treatise on *The*]   46   I am able to refer in . . . *as* MS
*g–g*MS, 43, 46   *Sciences.* On
*h*MS, 43   , but on the particular point in question it gives me great pleasure to observe, that there is a complete agreement between us]   46   *as* MS . . . question there . . . *as* MS
*i–i*MS   as I gladly acknowledge,
*j*MS, 43, 46   (a matter generally of far less importance)
*a–a*MS, 43, 46   §8.
*b–b*MS, 43, 46   views
*c–c*MS, 43, 46   that definition is an easy matter
*d–d*MS, 43, 46   turn upon

butes which it connotes, the objects were named before the attributes; as appears from the fact that in all languages, abstract names are mostly compounds or *other* derivatives of the concrete names which correspond to them. Connotative names, therefore, were, after proper names, the first which were used: and in the simpler cases, no doubt, a distinct connotation was present to the minds of those who first used the name, and was distinctly intended by them to be conveyed by it. The first person who used the word *white*, as applied to snow or to any other object, knew, no doubt, very well what quality he intended to predicate, and had a perfectly distinct conception in his mind of the attribute signified by the name.

But where the resemblances and differences on which our classifications are founded are not of this palpable and easily determinable kind; especially where they consist not in any one quality but in a number of qualities, the effects of which, being blended together, are not very easily discriminated, and referred each to its true source; it often happens that names are applied to nameable objects, with no distinct connotation present to the minds of those who apply them. They are only influenced by a general resemblance between the new object and all or some of the old familiar objects which they have been accustomed to call by that name. This, as we have seen, is the law which even the mind of the philosopher must follow, in giving names to the simple elementary feelings of our nature: but, where the things to be named are complex wholes, a philosopher is not content with noticing a general resemblance; he examines what the resemblance consists in: and he only gives the same name to things which resemble one another in the same definite particulars. The philosopher, therefore, habitually employs his general names with a definite connotation. But language was not made, and can only in some small degree be mended, by philosophers. In the minds of the real arbiters of language, general names, especially where the classes they denote cannot be brought before the tribunal of the outward senses to be identified and discriminated, connote little more than a vague gross resemblance to the things which they were earliest, or have been most, accustomed to call by those names. When, for instance, ordinary persons predicate the words *just* or *unjust* of any action, *noble* or *mean* of any sentiment, expression, or demeanour, *statesman* or *charlatan* of any personage figuring in politics, do they mean to affirm of those various subjects any determinate attributes, of whatever kind? No: they merely recognise, as they think, some likeness, more or less vague and loose, between *these* and some other things which they have been accustomed to denominate or to hear denominated by those appellations.

Language, as Sir James Mackintosh used to say of governments, "is not

e–e+46, 51, 56, 62, 65, 68, 72
f–fMS   *refined* or *vulgar*   g–gMS, 43   them

made, but grows."[*] A name is not imposed at once and by previous purpose upon a *class* of objects, but is first applied to one thing, and then extended by a series of transitions to another and another. By this process (as has been remarked by several writers, and illustrated with great force and clearness by Dugald Stewart in his *Philosophical Essays*)[†] a name not unfrequently passes by successive links of resemblance from one object to another, until it becomes applied to things having nothing in common with the first things to which the name was given; which, however, do not, for that reason, drop the name; so that it at last denotes a confused huddle of objects, having nothing whatever in common; and connotes nothing, not even a vague and general resemblance. When a name has fallen into this state, in which by predicating it of any object we assert literally nothing about the object, it has become unfit for the purposes either of thought or of the communication of thought; and can only be made serviceable by stripping it of some part of its multifarious denotation, and confining it to objects possessed of some attributes in common, which it may be made to connote. Such are the inconveniences of a language which "is not made, but grows." Like *h*the governments which are in a similar case, it may be compared to*h* a road which is not made but has made itself: it requires continual mending in order to be passable.

From this it is already evident, why the question respecting the definition of an abstract name is often one of so much difficulty. The question, What is justice? is, in other words, What is the attribute which mankind mean to predicate when they call an action just? To which the first answer is, that having come to no precise agreement on the point, they do not mean to predicate distinctly any attribute at all. Nevertheless, all believe that there is some common attribute belonging to all the actions which they are in the habit of calling just. The question then must be, whether there is any such common attribute? and, in the first place, whether mankind agree sufficiently with one another as to the particular actions which they do or do not call just, to render the inquiry, what quality those actions have in common, a possible one: if so, whether the actions really have any quality in common; and if they have, what it is. Of these three, the first alone is an inquiry into usage and convention; the other two are inquiries into matters of fact. And if the second question (whether the actions form a class at all) has been answered negatively, there remains a fourth, often more arduous than all the rest, namely, how best to form a class artificially, which the name may denote.

[*See, e.g., *History of England*. 10 vols. London: Longman, 1830–40, Vol. I, p. 72.]

[†Edinburgh: Creech and Constable, 1810, pp. 216ff.]

h–h+51, 56, 62, 65, 68, 72

And here it is fitting to remark, that the study of the spontaneous growth of languages is of the utmost importance to [i]those[i] who would logically remodel them. The classifications rudely made by established language, when retouched, as they almost [j]all[j] require to be, by the hands of the logician, are often in themselves excellently suited to [k] his purposes. [l]As[l] compared with the classifications of a philosopher, they are like the customary law of a country, which has grown up as it were spontaneously, compared with laws methodized and digested into a code: the former are a far less perfect instrument than the latter; but being the result of a long, though unscientific, course of experience, they contain [m]a mass of materials which may be made very usefully available in the formation of the systematic body of written law[m]. In like manner, the established grouping of objects under a common name, [n]even when[n] founded only on a gross and general resemblance, is evidence, in the first place, that the resemblance is obvious, and therefore considerable; and, in the next place, that it is a resemblance which has struck great numbers of persons during a series of years and ages. Even when a name, by successive extensions, has come to be applied to things among which there does not exist [o]this[o] gross resemblance common to them all, still at every step in its progress we shall find such a resemblance. And these transitions of the meaning of words are often an index to real connexions between the things denoted by them, which might otherwise escape the notice [p]of thinkers[p]; of those at least who, from using a different language, or from any difference in their habitual associations, have fixed their attention in preference on some other aspect of the things. The history of philosophy abounds in examples of such oversights, [q]committed for want of perceiving[q] the hidden link that connected together the seemingly disparate meanings of some ambiguous word.*

*"Few people" (I have said in another place) "have reflected how great a knowledge of Things is required to enable a man to affirm that any given argument turns wholly upon words. There is, perhaps, not one of the leading terms of philosophy which is not used in almost innumerable shades of meaning, to express ideas more or less widely different from one another. Between two of these ideas a sagacious and penetrating mind will discern, as it were intuitively, an unobvious link of connexion, upon which, though perhaps unable to give a logical account of it, he will found a perfectly valid argument, which his critic, not having so keen

[i-i]MS, 43, 46 the philosopher
[j-j]MS, 43, 46, 51 always
[k]MS, 43, 46 many of
[l-l]MS, 43, 46, 51, 56 When
[m-m]MS, 43, 46 the greater part of the materials out of which the systematic body of written law may and ought to be formed
[n-n]MS, 43, 46, 51, 56, 62, 65 though it may be
[o-o]MS, 43 even a
[p-p]MS, 43, 46 even of philosophers
[q-q]MS, 43, 46 which would not have been committed if a philosopher had seen

Whenever the inquiry into the definition of the name of any real object consists of anything else than a mere comparison of authorities, we tacitly assume that a meaning must be found for the name, compatible with its continuing to denote, if possible all, but at any rate the greater or the more important part, of the things of which it is commonly predicated. The inquiry, therefore, into the definition, is an inquiry into the resemblances and differences among those things: whether there be any resemblance running through them all; if not, through what portion of them such a general resemblance can be traced: and finally, what are the common attributes, the possession of which gives to them all, or to that portion of them, the character of resemblance which has led to their being classed together. When these common attributes have been ascertained and specified, the name which belongs in common to the resembling objects acquires a distinct instead of a vague connotation; and by possessing this distinct connotation, becomes susceptible of definition.

In giving a distinct connotation to the general name, the philosopher will endeavour to fix upon such attributes as, while they are common to all the things usually denoted by the name, are also of greatest importance in themselves; either directly, or from the number, the conspicuousness, or the interesting character, of the consequences to which they lead. He will select, as far as possible, such *differentiæ* as lead to the greatest number of interesting *propria*. For these, rather than the more obscure and recondite qualities on which they often depend, give that general character and aspect to a set of objects, which determine the groups into which they naturally fall. But to ᴿpenetrateᴿ to the more hidden agreement on which these obvious and superficial agreements depend, is often one of the most difficult of scientific problems. As it is among the most difficult, so it seldom fails to be among the most important. And since upon the result of this inquiry respecting the causes of the properties of a class of things, there incidentally depends the question what shall be the meaning of a word; some of the most profound and most valuable investigations which philosophy presents to us, have been introduced by, and have offered themselves under the guise of, inquiries into the definition of a name.

---

an insight into the Things, will mistake for a fallacy turning on the double meaning of a term. And the greater the genius of him who thus safely leaps over the chasm, the greater will probably be the crowing and vain-glory of the mere logician, who, hobbling after him, evinces his own superior wisdom by pausing on its brink, and giving up as desperate his proper business of bridging it over." [Review of George Cornewall Lewis's *Remarks on the Use and Abuse of some Political Terms, Examiner,* 22 April, 1832, p. 259.]

ᴿ⁻ᴿMS, 43, 46   mount up

BOOK II

OF REASONING

Διωρισμένων δὲ τούτων λέγωμεν ἤδη, διὰ τίνων, καὶ πότε, καὶ πῶς γίνεται πᾶς συλλογισμός· ὕστερον δὲ λεκτέον περὶ ἀποδείξεως. πρότερον γὰρ περὶ συλλογισμοῦ λεκτέον, ἢ περὶ ἀποδείξεως. διὰ τὸ καθόλου μᾶλλον εἶναι τὸν συλλογισμόν. ἡ μὲν γὰρ ἀπόδειξις συλλογισμός τις· ὁ συλλογισμός δὲ οὐ πᾶς, ἀπόδειξις.

Aristotle, *Analytica Priora*, Bk. I,
Chap. iv [(25ᵇ26–31). In *Organon*, p. 208].

CHAPTER I

Of Inference, or Reasoning, in General

§ 1. [*Retrospect of the preceding book*] In the preceding Book, we have been occupied not with the nature of Proof, but with the nature of Assertion: the import conveyed by a Proposition, whether that Proposition be true or false; not the means by which to discriminate true from false Propositions. The proper subject, however, of Logic is Proof. Before we could understand what Proof is, it was necessary to understand what that is to which proof is applicable; what that is which can be a subject of belief or disbelief, of affirmation or denial; what, in short, the different kinds of Propositions assert.

This preliminary inquiry we have prosecuted to a definite result. Assertion, in the first place, relates either to the meaning of words, or to some property of the things which words signify. Assertions respecting the meaning of words, among which definitions are the most important, hold a place, and an indispensable one, in philosophy; but as the meaning of words is essentially arbitrary, this class of assertions are not susceptible of truth or falsity, nor therefore of proof or disproof. Assertions respecting Things, or what may be called Real Propositions, in contradistinction to verbal ones, are of various sorts. We have analysed the import of each sort, and have ascertained the nature of the things they relate to, and the nature of what they severally assert respecting those things. We found that whatever be the form of the proposition, and whatever its nominal subject or predicate, the real subject of every proposition is some one or more facts or phenomena of consciousness, or some one or more of the hidden causes or powers to which we ascribe those facts; and that what is predicated or asserted, either in the affirmative or negative, of those phenomena or *those* powers, is always either Existence, Order in Place, Order in Time, Causation, or Resemblance. This, then, is the theory of the Import of Propositions, reduced to its ultimate elements: but there is another and a less abstruse expression for it, which, though stopping short in an earlier stage of the analysis, is sufficiently scien-

a–a+43, 46, 51, 56, 62, 65, 68, 72

tific for many of the purposes for which such a general expression is required. This expression recognises the commonly received distinction between Subject and Attribute, and gives the following as the analysis of the meaning of propositions:—Every Proposition asserts, that some given subject does or does not possess some attribute; or that some attribute is or is not (either in *all*[b] or in some portion of the subjects in which it is met with) conjoined with some other attribute.

We shall now for the present take our leave of this portion of our inquiry, and proceed to the peculiar problem of the Science of Logic, namely, how the assertions, of which we have analysed the import, are proved or disproved; such of them, at least, as, not being amenable to direct consciousness or intuition, are appropriate subjects of proof.

We say of a fact or statement, that it is proved, when we believe its truth by reason of some other fact or statement from which it is said to *follow*. Most of the propositions, whether affirmative or negative, universal, particular, or singular, which we believe, are not believed on their own evidence, but on the ground of something previously assented to, [c] from which they are said to be *inferred*. To infer a proposition from a previous proposition or propositions; to give credence to it, or claim credence for it, as a conclusion from something else; is to *reason*, in the most extensive sense of the term. There is a narrower sense, in which the name reasoning is confined to the form of inference which is termed ratiocination, and of which the syllogism is the general type. The reasons for not conforming to this restricted use of the term were stated in an [d]earlier[d] stage of our inquiry, and additional motives will be suggested by the considerations on which we are now about to enter.

§ 2. [*Inferences improperly so called*] In proceeding to take into consideration the cases in which inferences can legitimately be drawn, we shall first mention some cases in which the inference is apparent, not real; and which require notice chiefly that they may not be confounded with cases of inference properly so called. This occurs when the proposition ostensibly inferred from another, appears on analysis to be merely a repetition of the same, or part of the same, assertion, which was contained in the first. All the cases mentioned in books of Logic as examples of æquipollency or equivalence of propositions, are of this nature. Thus, if we were to argue, No man is incapable of reason, for every man is rational; or, All men are mortal, for no man is exempt from death; it would be plain that we were not proving the proposition, but only appealing to another mode of wording it, which may or

[b]–[b]MS   the whole
[c]MS, 43, 46, 51, 56, 62   and
[d]–[d]MS, 43, 46, 51, 56, 62, 65   early

may not be more readily comprehensible by the hearer, or better adapted to suggest the real proof, but which contains in itself no shadow of proof.

Another case is where, from an universal proposition, we affect to infer another which differs from it only in being particular: as All A is B, therefore Some A is B: No A is B, therefore Some A is not B. This, too, is not to conclude one proposition from another, but to repeat a second time something which had been asserted at first; with the difference, that we do not here repeat the whole of the previous assertion, but only an indefinite part of it.

A third case is where, the antecedent having affirmed a predicate of a given subject, the consequent affirms of the same subject something already connoted by the former predicate: as, Socrates is a man, therefore Socrates is a living creature; where all that is connoted by living creature was affirmed of Socrates when he was asserted to be a man. If the propositions are negative, we must invert their order, thus: Socrates is not a living creature, therefore he is not a man; for if we deny the less, the greater, which includes it, is already denied by implication. These, therefore, are not really cases of inference; and yet the trivial examples by which, in manuals of Logic, the rules of the syllogism are illustrated, are often of this ill-chosen kind; *a*formal demonstrations*a* of conclusions to which whoever understands the terms used in the statement of the data, has already, and consciously, assented.*

The most complex case of this sort of apparent inference is what is called the Conversion of propositions; which consists in *b*turning the predicate into a subject, and the subject into*b* a predicate, and framing out of the same terms thus reversed, another proposition, which must be true if the former is true. Thus, from the particular affirmative proposition, Some A is B, we may infer that Some B is A. From the universal negative, No A is B, we may conclude that No B is A. From the universal affirmative proposition, All A is B, it cannot be inferred that All B is A; though all water is liquid, it is not implied that all liquid is water; but it is implied that some liquid is so; and hence the proposition, All A is B, is legitimately convertible into Some B is A. This process, which converts an universal proposition into a particular, is termed conversion *per accidens*. From the proposition, Some A is not B, we cannot even infer that some B is not A; though some men are not Englishmen, it does not follow that some Englishmen are not men. The only *c*mode usually

*[72] The different cases of Æquipollency, or "Equivalent Propositional Forms," are set forth with some fulness in Professor Bain's *Logic* [Pt. I, p. 107]. One of the commonest of these changes of expression, that from affirming a proposition to denying its negative, or *vice versâ*, Mr. Bain designates, very happily, by the name Obversion.

*a–a*MS, 43, 46, 51, 56   demonstrations in form,
*b–b*MS, 43, 46   making the predicate become a subject, and the subject become
*c–c*MS, 43, 46, 51   legitimate conversion, if such it can be called, of

recognised of converting[c] a particular negative proposition, is in the form, Some A is not B, therefore, something which is not B is A; and this is termed conversion by contraposition. In this case, however, the predicate and subject are not merely reversed, but one of them is [d]changed[d]. Instead of [A] and [B], the terms of the new proposition are [a thing which is not B], and [A]. The original proposition, Some A *is not* B, is first changed into a proposition æquipollent with it, Some A *is* "a thing which is not B;" and the proposition, being now no longer a particular negative, but a particular affirmative, admits of conversion in the first mode, or as it is called, *simple* conversion.*

In all these cases there is not really any inference; there is in the conclusion no new truth, nothing but what was already asserted in the premises, and obvious to whoever apprehends them. The fact asserted in the conclusion is either the very same fact, or part of the fact, asserted in the original proposition. This follows from our previous analysis of the Import of Propositions. When we say, for example, that some lawful sovereigns are tyrants, what is the meaning of the assertion? That the attributes connoted by the term "lawful sovereign," and the attributes connoted by the term "tyrant," sometimes coexist in the same individual. Now this is also precisely what we mean, when we say that some tyrants are lawful sovereigns; which, therefore, is not a second proposition inferred from the first, any more than the English translation of Euclid's *Elements* is a collection of theorems different from, and consequences of, those contained in the Greek original. Again, if we assert that no great general is a [e]rash man[e], we mean that the attributes connoted by "great general," and those connoted by "[f]rash[f]," never coexist in the same subject; which is also the exact meaning which [g]would be expressed by saying, that no rash man[g] is a great general. When we say that all quadrupeds are warm-blooded, we assert, not only that the attributes connoted by "quadruped" and those connoted by "warm-blooded" sometimes coexist, but that the former never exist without the latter: now the proposition, Some warm-blooded creatures are quadrupeds, expresses the first half of this meaning, dropping the latter half; and therefore has been already affirmed in the antecedent proposition, All quadrupeds are warm-blooded. But that *all* warm-blooded creatures are quadrupeds, or, in other words, that the [h]attributes connoted by "warm-blooded" never exist[h] without those connoted by "quadruped," has not been asserted, and cannot be inferred. In order to re-

*[56] As Sir William Hamilton has pointed out, "Some A is not B" may also be converted in the following form: "No B is *some* A." Some men are not negroes; therefore, No negroes are *some* men (*e.g.* Europeans). [See Hamilton, *Discussions*, p. 664.]

[d–d]MS, 43, 46, 51, 56   altered
[e–e]MS, 43, 46   fool
[f–f]MS, 43, 46   fool
[g–g]MS, 43, 46   we express when we say, that no fool
[h–h]MS   attribute . . . exists

assert, in an inverted form, the whole of what was affirmed in the proposition, All quadrupeds are warm-blooded, we must convert it by contraposition, thus, Nothing which is not warm-blooded is a quadruped. This proposition, and the one from which it is derived, are exactly equivalent, and either of them may be substituted for the other; for, to say that when the attributes of a quadruped are present, those of a warm-blooded creature are present, is to say that when the latter are absent the former are absent.

In a manual for young students, it would be proper to dwell at greater length on the conversion and æquipollency of propositions. For though that cannot be called reasoning or inference which is a mere reassertion in different words of what had been asserted before, there is no more important intellectual habit, nor any the cultivation of which falls more strictly within the province of the art of logic, than that of discerning rapidly and surely the identity of an assertion when disguised under diversity of language. That important chapter in logical treatises which relates to the Opposition of Propositions, and the excellent technical language which logic provides for distinguishing the different kinds or modes of opposition, are of use chiefly for this purpose. Such considerations as these, that contrary propositions may both be false, but cannot both be true; that subcontrary propositions may both be true, but cannot both be false; that of two contradictory propositions one must be true and the other false; that of two subalternate propositions the truth of the universal proves the truth of the particular, and the falsity of the particular proves the falsity of the universal, but not *vice versâ*;* are apt to appear, at first sight, very technical and mysterious, but when explained, seem almost too obvious to require so formal a statement, since the same amount of explanation which is necessary to make the principles intelligible, would enable the truths which they convey to be apprehended in any particular case which can occur. In this respect, however, these axioms of logic are on a level with those of mathematics. That things which are equal to the same thing are equal to one another, is as obvious in any particular case as it is in the general statement: and if no such general maxim had ever been laid down, the demonstrations in Euclid would never have halted for any difficulty in stepping across the gap which this axiom at present

*All A is B ⎱ contraries.
 No   A is B ⎰

Some A is B   ⎱ subcontraries.
Some A is not B ⎰

All   A is B   ⎱ contradictories.
Some A is not B ⎰

No   A is B ⎱ also contradictories.
Some A is B ⎰

All   A is B ⎱ and No   A is B   ⎱ respectively subalternate.
Some A is B ⎰   Some A is not B ⎰

serves to bridge over. Yet no one has ever censured [i]writers[i] on geometry, for placing a list of these elementary generalizations at the head of [j]their treatises[j], as a first exercise to the learner of the faculty which will be required in him at every step, that of apprehending a *general* truth. And the student of logic, in the discussion even of such truths as we have cited above, acquires habits of circumspect interpretation of words, and of exactly measuring the length and breadth of his assertions, which are among the most indispensable conditions of any considerable [k]mental attainment[k], and which it is one of the primary objects of logical discipline to cultivate.

§ 3. [*Inferences proper, distinguished into inductions and ratiocinations*] Having noticed, in order to exclude from the province of Reasoning or Inference properly so called, the cases in which the [a]progression[a] from one truth to another is only apparent, the logical consequent being a mere repetition of the logical antecedent; we now pass to those which are cases of inference in the proper acceptation of the term, those in which we set out from known truths, to arrive at others really distinct from them.

Reasoning, in the extended sense in which I use the term, and in which it is synonymous with Inference, is popularly said to be of two kinds: reasoning from particulars to generals, and reasoning from generals to particulars; the former being called Induction, the latter Ratiocination or Syllogism. It will presently be shown that there is a third species of reasoning, which falls under neither of these descriptions, and which, nevertheless, is not only valid, but [b]is[b] the foundation of both the others.

[c]It[c] is necessary to observe, that the expressions, reasoning from particulars to generals, and reasoning from generals to particulars, are recommended by brevity rather than by precision, and do not adequately mark, without the aid of a commentary, the distinction between Induction [d](in the sense now adverted to)[d] and Ratiocination. The meaning intended by these expressions is, that Induction is inferring a proposition from propositions *less general* than itself, and Ratiocination is inferring a proposition from propositions *equally* or *more* general. When, from the observation of a number of individual instances, we ascend to a general proposition, or when, by combining a number of general propositions, we conclude from them [e] another proposition still more general, the process, which is substantially the same in both instances, is called Induction. When from a general proposition, not alone (for from a single proposition nothing can be concluded which is not involved in the terms), but by combining it with other propositions, we

---

[i–i]MS a writer   [j–j]MS his treatise
[k–k]MS, 43, 46 attainment in science
[a–a]MS, 43, 46 progress   [b–b]+51, 56, 62, 65, 68, 72
[c–c]MS [*no paragraph*] At present it   [d–d]+51, 56, 62, 65, 68, 72
[e]MS to

infer a proposition of the same degree of generality with itself, or a less general proposition, or a proposition merely individual, the process is Ratiocination. When, in short, the conclusion is more general than the largest of the premises, the argument is *commonly called* Induction; when less general, or equally general, it is Ratiocination.

As all experience begins with individual cases, and proceeds from them to generals, it might seem most conformable to the natural order of thought that Induction should be treated of before we touch upon Ratiocination. It will, however, be advantageous, in a science which aims at tracing our acquired knowledge to its sources, that the inquirer should commence with the *latter* rather than with the earlier stages of the process of constructing our knowledge; and should trace derivative truths backward to the truths from which they are deduced, and on which they depend for their evidence, before attempting to point out the original spring from which both ultimately take their rise. The advantages of this order of proceeding in the present instance will manifest themselves as we advance, in a manner superseding the necessity of any further justification or explanation.

Of Induction, therefore, we shall say no more at present, than that it at least is, without doubt, a process of real inference. The conclusion in an induction embraces more than is contained in the premises. The principle or law collected from particular instances, the general proposition in which we embody the result of our experience, covers a much larger extent of ground than the individual experiments which *h* form its basis. A principle ascertained by experience, is more than a mere summing up of what *has been specifically observed in the individual cases which have been* examined; it is a generalization grounded on those cases, and expressive of our belief, that what we there found true is true in an indefinite number of cases which we have not examined, and are never likely to examine. The nature and grounds of this inference, and the conditions necessary to make it legitimate, will be the subject of discussion in the Third Book: but that such inference really takes place is not susceptible of question. In every induction we proceed from truths which we knew, to truths which we did not know; from facts certified by observation, to facts which we have not observed, and even to facts not capable of being now observed; future facts, for example; but which we do not hesitate to believe on the sole evidence of the induction itself.

Induction, then, is a real process of Reasoning or Inference. Whether, and in what sense, *as* much can be said of the Syllogism, remains to be determined by the examination into which we are about to enter.

f–f+43, 46, 51, 56, 62, 65, 68, 72
*g–g*MS, 43, 46   later
*h*MS, 43, 46, 51, 56   are said to
*i–i*MS, 43, 46   we have specifically observed in the individual cases that we have
*j–j*MS, 43, 46, 51   so

CHAPTER II

Of Ratiocination, or Syllogism

§ 1. [*Analysis of the Syllogism*] The analysis of the Syllogism has been so accurately and fully performed in the common manuals of Logic, that in the present work, which is not designed as a manual, it is sufficient to recapitulate, *memoriæ causâ*, the leading results of that analysis, as a foundation for the remarks to be afterwards made on the functions of the Syllogism, and the place which it holds in ᵃscienceᵃ.

To a legitimate syllogism it is essential that there should be three, and no more than three, propositions, namely, the conclusion, or proposition to be proved, and two other propositions which together prove it, and which are called the premises. It is essential that there should be three, and no more than three, terms, namely, the subject and predicate of the conclusion, and another called the middleterm, which must be found in both premises, since it is by means of it that the other two terms are to be connected together. The predicate of the conclusion is called the major term of the syllogism; the subject of the conclusion is called the minor term. As there can be but three terms, the major and minor terms must each be found in one, and only one, of the premises, together with the middleterm which is in them both. The premise which contains the middleterm and the major term is called the major premise; that which contains the middleterm and the minor term is called the minor premise ᵇ .

Syllogisms are divided by some logicians into three *figures*, by others into four, according to the position of the middleterm, which may either be the subject in both premises, the predicate in both, or the subject in one and the predicate in the other. The most common case is that in which the middleterm is the subject of the major premise and the predicate of the minor. This is reckoned as the first figure. When the middleterm is the predicate in both premises, the syllogism belongs to the second figure; when it is the subject in both, to the third. In the fourth figure the middleterm is the subject of the minor premise and the predicate of the major. Those writers who reckon no more than three figures, include this case in the first.

ᵃ⁻ᵃMS, 43, 46   philosophy
ᵇMS, 43, 46   of the syllogism

Each figure is *divided* into *moods*, according to what are called the *quantity* and *quality* of the propositions, that is, according as they are universal or particular, affirmative or negative. The following are examples of all the legitimate moods, that is, all those in which the conclusion correctly follows from the premises. A is the minor term, C the major, B the middle-term.

FIRST FIGURE

All B is C	No B is C	All B is C	No B is C
All A is B	All A is B	Some A is B	Some A is B
therefore	therefore	therefore	therefore
All A is C	No A is C	Some A is C	Some A is not C

SECOND FIGURE

No C is B	All C is B	No C is B	All C is B
All A is B	No A is B	Some A is B	Some A is not B
therefore	therefore	therefore	therefore
No A is C	No A is C	Some A is not C	Some A is not C

THIRD FIGURE

All B is C	No B is C	Some B is C	All B is C	Some B is not C	No B is C
All B is A	All B is A	All B is A	Some B is A	All B is A	Some B is A
therefore	therefore	therefore	therefore	therefore	therefore
Some A is C	Some A is not C	Some A is C	Some A is C	Some A is not C	Some A is not C

FOURTH FIGURE

All C is B	All C is B	Some C is B	No C is B	No C is B
All B is A	No B is A	All B is A	All B is A	Some B is A
therefore	therefore	therefore	therefore	therefore
Some A is C	Some A is *not* C	Some A is C	Some A is not C	Some A is not C

In these exemplars, or blank forms for making syllogisms, no place is assigned to *singular* propositions; not, of course, because such propositions are not used in ratiocination, but because, their predicate being affirmed or denied of the whole of the subject, they are ranked, for the purposes of the syllogism, with universal propositions. Thus, these two syllogisms—

All men are mortal,	All men are mortal,
All kings are men,	Socrates is a man,
therefore	therefore
All kings are mortal,	Socrates is mortal,

c–cMS, 43, 46 subdivided
d–dMS, 43, 46, 51 *modes* [*the changes of* "mode(s)" *to* "mood(s)" *that were made in* 56 *throughout this section are not henceforth recorded*]
e–e+46, 51, 56, 62, 65, 68, 72

are arguments precisely similar, and are both ranked in the first mood of the first figure.*

The reasons why syllogisms in any of the above forms are legitimate, that is, why, if the premises *are* true, the conclusion must *inevitably* be so, and why this is not the case in any other possible mood, (that is, in any other combination of universal and particular, affirmative and negative propositions,) any person taking interest in these inquiries may be presumed to have either learned from the common school books of the syllogistic logic, or to be capable of *discovering* for himself. The reader may, however, be referred, for every needful explanation, to Archbishop Whately's *Elements of Logic*, where he will find stated with philosophical precision, and explained with *remarkable* perspicuity, the whole of the common doctrine of the syllogism.

All valid ratiocination; all reasoning by which, from general propositions previously admitted, other propositions equally or less general are inferred; may be exhibited in some of the above forms. The whole of Euclid, for example, might be thrown without difficulty into a series of syllogisms, regular in mood and figure.

*[72] Professor Bain denies the claim of Singular Propositions to be classed, for the purposes of ratiocination, with Universal; though they come within the designation which he himself proposes as an equivalent for Universal, that of Total. He would even, to use his own expression, banish them entirely from the syllogism. He takes as an example,

> Socrates is wise,
> Socrates is poor, therefore
> Some poor men are wise,

or more properly (as he observes) "one poor man is wise." "Now, if wise, poor, and a man, are attributes belonging to the meaning of the word Socrates, there is then no march of reasoning at all. We have given in Socrates, *inter alia*, the facts wise, poor, and a man, and we merely repeat the concurrence which is selected from the whole aggregate of properties making up the whole, Socrates. The case is one under the head 'Greater and Less Connotation' in Equivalent Propositional Forms, or Immediate Inference.

But the example in this form does not do justice to the syllogism of singulars. We must suppose both propositions to be real, the predicates being in no way involved in the subject. Thus

> Socrates was the master of Plato,
> Socrates fought at Delium,
> The master of Plato fought at Delium.

It may fairly be doubted whether the transitions, in this instance, are anything more than equivalent forms. For the proposition 'Socrates was the master of Plato and fought at Delium,' compounded out of the two premises, is obviously nothing more than a grammatical abbreviation. No one can say that there is here any change of meaning, or anything beyond a verbal modification of the original form. The next step is, 'The master of Plato fought at Delium,' which is the pre-

Though a syllogism framed according to any of these formulæ is a valid argument, all correct ratiocination admits of being stated in syllogisms of the first figure alone. The rules for throwing an argument in any of the other figures into the first figure, are called rules for the *reduction* of syllogisms. It is done by the *conversion* of one or other, or both, of the premises. Thus an argument in the first mood of the second figure, as—

> No C is B
> All A is B
> therefore
> No A is C,

---

vious statement cut down by the omission of Socrates. It contents itself with reproducing a part of the meaning, or saying less than had been previously said. The full equivalent of the affirmation is, 'The master of Plato fought at Delium, and the master of Plato was Socrates:' the new form omits the last piece of information, and gives only the first. Now, we never consider that we have made a real inference, a step in advance, when we repeat *less* than we are entitled to say, or drop from a complex statement some portion not desired at the moment. Such an operation keeps strictly within the domain of equivalence, or Immediate Inference. In no way, therefore, can a syllogism with two singular premises be viewed as a genuine syllogistic or deductive inference." (*Logic*, Pt. I, p. 159.)

The first argument, as will have been seen, rests upon the supposition that the name Socrates has a meaning; that man, wise, and poor, are parts of this meaning; and that by predicating them of Socrates we convey no information; a view of the signification of names which, for reasons already given,* I cannot admit, and which, as applied to the class of names which Socrates belongs to, is at war with Mr. Bain's own definition of a Proper Name (Pt. I, p. 48) "a single *meaningless* mark or designation appropriated to the thing." Such names, Mr. Bain proceeded to say, do not necessarily indicate even human beings: much less then does the name Socrates include the meaning of wise or poor. Otherwise it would follow that if Socrates had grown rich, or had lost his mental faculties by illness, he would no longer have been called Socrates.

The second part of Mr. Bain's argument, in which he contends that even when the premises convey real information, the conclusion is merely the premises with a part left out, is applicable, if at all, as much to universal propositions as to singular. In every syllogism the conclusion contains less than is asserted in the two premises taken together. Suppose the syllogism to be

> All bees are intelligent,
> All bees are insects, therefore
> Some insects are intelligent:

one might use the same liberty taken by Mr. Bain, of joining together the two premises as if they were one—"All bees are insects and intelligent"—and might say that in omitting the middle term *bees* we make no real inference, but merely reproduce part of what had been previously said. Mr. Bain's is really an objection to the syllogism itself, or at all events to the third figure: it has no special applicability to singular propositions.

---

*Note to § 4 of the chapter on Definition, *supra*, p. 141n.

may be reduced as follows. The proposition, No C is B, being an universal negative, admits of simple conversion, and may be changed into No B is C, which, as we showed, is the very same assertion in other words—the same fact differently expressed. This transformation having been effected, the argument assumes the following form:

> No B is C
> All A is B
> therefore
> No A is C,

which is a good syllogism in the second mood of the first figure. Again, an argument in the first mood of the third figure must resemble the following:

> All B is C
> All B is A
> therefore
> Some A is C,

where the minor premise, All B is A, conformably to what was laid down in the last chapter respecting universal affirmatives, does not admit of simple conversion, but may be converted *per accidens*, thus, Some A is B; which, though it does not express the whole of what is asserted in the proposition All B is A, expresses, as was formerly shown, part of it, and must therefore be true if the whole is true. We have, then, as the result of the reduction, the following syllogism in the third mood of the first figure:

> All B is C
> Some A is B,

from which it obviously follows, that

> Some A is C.

In the same manner, or in a manner on which after these examples it is not necessary to enlarge, every mood of the second, third, and fourth figures may be reduced to some one of the four moods of the first. In other words, every conclusion which can be proved in any of the last three figures, may be proved in the first figure from the same premises, with a slight alteration in the mere manner of expressing them. Every valid ratiocination, therefore, may be stated in the first figure, that is, in one of the following forms:

> Every B is C   No B is C
> All A ⎫   All A ⎫
> Some A ⎬ is B,   Some A ⎬ is B,
>   ⎭   ⎭
> therefore   therefore
> All A ⎫   No A is ⎫
> Some A ⎬ is C.   Some A is not ⎬ C.
>   ⎭   ⎭

Or if more significant symbols are preferred:

To prove an affirmative, the argument must admit of being stated in this form:

All animals are mortal;

All men ⎫
Some men ⎬ are animals;
Socrates ⎭

therefore

All men ⎫
Some men ⎬ are mortal.
Socrates ⎭

To prove a negative, the argument must be capable of being expressed in this form:

No one who is capable of self-control is necessarily vicious;

All negroes ⎫
Some negroes ⎬ are capable of self-control;
Mr. A's negro ⎭

therefore

No negroes are ⎫
Some negroes are not ⎬ necessarily vicious.
Mr. A's negro is not ⎭

Though all ratiocination admits of being thrown into one or the other of these forms, and sometimes gains considerably by the transformation, both in clearness and in the obviousness of its consequence; there are, no doubt, cases in which the argument falls more naturally into one of the other three figures, and in which its conclusiveness is more apparent at the first glance in those figures, than when reduced ʲtoʲ the first. Thus, if the proposition were that pagans may be virtuous, and the evidence to prove it were the example of Aristides; a syllogism in the third figure,

Aristides was virtuous,
Aristides was a pagan,
therefore
Some pagan was virtuous,

would be a more natural mode of stating the argument, and would carry conviction more instantly home, than the same ratiocination strained into the first figure, thus—

Aristides was virtuous,
Some pagan was Aristides,
therefore
Some pagan was virtuous.

ʲ⁻ʲMS, 43, 46   into

A German philosopher, Lambert, whose *Neues Organon* (published in the year 1764) contains among other things [k]one of the most elaborate and complete expositions [l]which had ever been[l] made of the syllogistic doctrine[k], has expressly examined what [m]sort[m] of arguments fall most naturally and suitably into each of the four figures; and his [n]investigation[n] is characterized by great ingenuity and clearness of thought.* The argument, however, is one and the same, in whichever figure it is expressed; since, as we have already seen, the premises of a syllogism in the second, third, or fourth figure, and those of the syllogism in the first figure to which it may be reduced, are the

*His conclusions are, "The first figure is suited to the discovery or proof of the properties of a thing; the second to the discovery or proof of the distinctions between things; the third to the discovery or proof of instances and exceptions; the fourth to the discovery, or exclusion, of the different species of a genus." The reference of syllogisms in the last three figures to the *dictum de omni et nullo* is, in Lambert's [o]opinion[o], strained and unnatural: to each of the three belongs, according to him, a separate axiom, co-ordinate and of equal authority with that *dictum*, and to which he gives the names of *dictum de diverso* for the second figure, *dictum de exemplo* for the third, and *dictum de reciproco* for the fourth. See Part I or "Dianoiologie," [of *Neues Organon*,] Chap. iv, § 229 *et seqq.* [pp. 138–9, 142]. [p] [q]Mr. Bailey, (*Theory of Reasoning*, 2nd ed. [London: Longmans, 1852,] pp. 70–4) takes a similar view of the subject.[q]

[k–k]MS, 43, 46   the most elaborate and complete exposition of the syllogistic doctrine which I have happened to meet with
[l–l]51, 56   ever yet
[m–m]MS, 43, 46, 51, 56, 62   sorts   [n–n]MS, 43, 46, 51   solution
[o–o]MS, 43, 46   view
[p]MS, 43, 46   [*paragraph*] Were it not that the views I am about to propound on the functions and ultimate foundation of the syllogism render such distinctions as these of very subordinate importance, I should have availed myself largely of this and other speculations of Lambert; who has displayed, within the limits of the received theory of the syllogism, an originality for which it was scarcely to be supposed that there could still have been room on so exhausted a subject, and whose book may be strongly recommended to those who may attempt still further to improve the excellent manuals we already possess of this elementary portion of the Art of Reasoning.]   51   [*paragraph*] Mr. De Morgan's *Formal Logic, or the Calculus of Inference, Necessary and Probable*, (a work published since the statement in the text was made,) far exceeds in elaborate minuteness Lambert's treatise on the syllogism. Mr. De Morgan's principal object is to bring within strict technical rules the cases in which a conclusion can be drawn from premises of a form usually classed as particular. He observes, very justly, . . . *as* 171.n12–172.n9 . . . can be formidable. The "quantification of the predicate," an invention to which Sir William Hamilton attaches so much importance as to have raised an angry dispute with Mr. De Morgan respecting its authorship, appears to me, I confess, as an accession to the art of Logic, of singularly small value. It is of course true, that "All men are mortal" is equivalent to "Every man is *some* mortal." But as mankind certainly will not be persuaded to "quantify" their predicates in common discourse, they want a logic which will teach them to reason correctly with propositions in the usual form, by furnishing them with a type of ratiocination to which propositions can be referred, retaining that form. Not to mention that the quantification of the predicate, instead . . . *as* 173.n28–35 . . . something more.
[q–q]+62, 65, 68, 72

same premises in everything except language, or, at least, as much of them as contributes to the proof of the conclusion is the same. We are therefore at liberty, in conformity with the general opinion of logicians, to consider the two elementary forms of the first figure as the universal types of all correct ratiocination; the one, when the conclusion to be proved is affirmative, the other, when it is negative; even though certain arguments may have a tendency to clothe themselves in the forms of the second, third, and fourth figures; which, however, cannot possibly happen with the only class of arguments which are of first-rate scientific importance, those in which the conclusion is an universal affirmative, such conclusions being susceptible of proof in the first figure alone.*

*[56] Since this chapter was written, two treatises have appeared (or rather a treatise and a fragment of a treatise), which aim at a further improvement in the theory of the forms of ratiocination: Mr. De Morgan's *Formal Logic; or, the Calculus of Inference, Necessary and Probable*; and the "New Analytic of Logical Forms," attached as an Appendix to Sir William Hamilton's *Discussions on Philosophy* [App. II(A), pp. 614–20], and ʳat greater length, to his posthumous *Lectures on [Metaphysics and] Logic* [Vol. IV, pp. 249–317]ʳ.

In Mr. De Morgan's volume—abounding, in its more popular parts, with valuable observations felicitously expressed—the principal feature of originality is an attempt to bring within strict technical rules the cases in which a conclusion can be drawn from premises of a form usually classed as particular. Mr. De Morgan observes, [*Formal Logic*, p. 139,] very justly, that from the premises Most Bs are Cs, most Bs are As, it may be concluded with certainty that some As are Cs, since two portions of the class B, each of them comprising more than half, must necessarily in part consist of the same individuals. Following out this line of thought, it is equally evident that if we knew exactly what proportion the "most" in each of the premises bear to the entire class B, we could increase in a corresponding degree the definiteness of the conclusion. Thus if 60 per cent of B are included in C, and 70 per cent in A, 30 per cent at least must be common to both; in other words, the number of As which are Cs, and of Cs which are As, must be at least equal to 30 per cent of the class B. Proceeding on this conception of "numerically definite propositions," and extending it to such forms as these:— "45 Xs (or more) are each of them one of 70 Ys," or "45 Xs (or more) are no one of them to be found among 70 Ys," [*Formal Logic*, p. 142,] and examining what inferences admit of being drawn from the various combinations which may be made of premises of this description, Mr. De Morgan establishes universal formulæ for such inferences; creating for that purpose not only a new technical language, but a formidable array of symbols analogous to those of algebra.

Since it is undeniable that inferences, in the cases examined by Mr. De Morgan, can legitimately be drawn, and that the ordinary theory takes no account of them, I will not say that it was not worth while to show in detail how these also could be reduced to formulæ as rigorous as those of Aristotle. What

ʳ⁻ʳ56 which, together with some partial notices that have found their way to the public through his pupils, form the only exposition yet extant of a rather elaborate theory

§ 2. [*The* dictum de omni *not the foundation of reasoning, but a mere identical proposition*] On examining, then, these two general formulæ, we

––––––––

Mr. De Morgan has done was worth doing once (perhaps more than once, as a school exercise); but I question if its results are worth studying and mastering for any practical purpose. The practical use of technical forms of reasoning is to bar out fallacies: but the fallacies which require to be guarded against in ratiocination properly so called, arise from the incautious use of the common forms of language; and the logician must track the fallacy into that territory, instead of waiting for it on a territory of his own. While he remains among propositions which have acquired the numerical precision of the Calculus of Probabilities, the enemy is left in possession of the only ground on which he can be formidable. And since the propositions (short of universal) on which a thinker has to depend, either for purposes of speculation or of practice, do not, except in a few peculiar cases, admit of any numerical precision; common reasoning cannot be translated into Mr. De Morgan's forms, which therefore cannot serve any purpose as a test of it.

Sir William Hamilton's theory of the "quantification of the predicate" [s] may be [t] described as follows:

"Logically" (I quote his [u] words) "we ought to take into account the quantity, always understood in thought, but usually, for manifest reasons, elided in its expression, not only of the subject, but also of the predicate of a judgment." [*Discussions,* p. 650.] All A is B, is equivalent to all A is *some* B. No A is B, to No A is *any* B. Some A is B, is tantamount to some A is *some* B. Some A is not B, to Some A is *not any* B. As in these forms of assertion the predicate is exactly coextensive with the subject, they all admit of simple conversion; and by this we obtain two additional forms–Some B is *all* A, and No B is *some* A. We may also make the assertion All A is all B, which will be true if the classes A and B are exactly coextensive. The last three forms, though conveying real assertions, have no place in the ordinary classification of Propositions. All propositions, then, being supposed to be translated into this language, and written each in that one of the preceding forms which answers to its signification, there emerges a new set of syllogistic rules, materially different from the common ones. A general view of the points of difference may be given in the words of Sir W. Hamilton (*ibid.,* p. 651):

"The revocation of the two terms of a Proposition to their true relation; a proposition being always an *equation* of its subject and its predicate.

The consequent reduction of the Conversion of Propositions from three species to one—that of Simple Conversion.

The reduction of all the *General Laws* of Categorical Syllogisms to a single Canon.

The evolution from that one canon of all the Species and varieties of Syllogisms.

The abrogation of all the *Special Laws* of Syllogism.

A demonstration of the exclusive possibility of Three Syllogistic Figures; and (on new grounds) the scientific and final abolition of the Fourth.

A manifestation that Figure is an unessential variation in syllogistic form; and

––––––––

[s] 56, 62, 65, 68 (concerning the originality of which in his case there can be no doubt, however Mr. De Morgan may have also, and independently, originated an equivalent doctrine)
[t] 56, 62, 65, 68   briefly   [u] 56, 62, 65, 68   own

find that in both of them, one premise, the major, is an universal proposition; and according as this is affirmative or negative, the conclusion is so too. All

the consequent absurdity of Reducing the syllogisms of the other figures to the first.

An enouncement of *one Organic Principle* for each Figure.

A determination of the true number of the Legitimate Moods; with

Their amplification in number (thirty-six);

Their numerical equality under all the figures; and

Their relative equivalence, or virtual identity, throughout every schematic difference.

That, in the second and third figures, the extremes holding both the same relation to the middle term, there is not, as in the first, an opposition and subordination between a term major and a term minor, mutually containing and contained, in the counter wholes of Extension and Comprehension.

Consequently, in the second and third figures, there is no determinate major and minor premise, and there are two indifferent conclusions: whereas in the first the premises are determinate, and there is a single proximate conclusion."

This doctrine, like that of Mr. De Morgan previously noticed, is a real addition to the syllogistic theory; *v*and*v* has moreover this advantage over Mr. De Morgan's "numerically definite Syllogism," that the forms it supplies are really available as a test of the correctness of ratiocination; since propositions in the common form may always have their predicates quantified, and so be made amendable to Sir W. Hamilton's *w*rules*w*. *x* Considered however as a contribution to the *Science* of Logic, that is, to the analysis of the mental processes concerned in reasoning, the new doctrine appears to me, I confess, not merely superfluous, but erroneous; since the form in which it clothes propositions does not, like the ordinary form, express what is in the mind of the speaker when he enunciates the proposition. I cannot think Sir William Hamilton right in maintaining that the quantity of the predicate is "always understood in thought." It is implied, but is not present to the mind of the person who asserts the proposition. The quantification of the predicate, instead of being a means of bringing out more clearly the meaning of the proposition, actually leads the mind out of the proposition, into another order of ideas. For when we say, All men are mortal, we simply mean to affirm the attribute mortality of all men; without thinking at all of the *class* mortal in the concrete, or troubling ourselves about whether it contains any other beings or not. It is only for some artificial purpose that we ever look at the proposition in the aspect in which the predicate also is thought of as a class name, either including the subject only, or the subject and something more. (See above, p. 93.) [Parts of this note appear in the previous note in 51; see above, p. 170*p*.]

*y*For a fuller discussion of this subject, see the twenty-second chapter of a work already referred to, *An Examination of Sir William Hamilton's Philosophy.*y

*v–v*56, 62 for by writing the premises in the more definitely quantitative forms which Sir William Hamilton has provided, conclusions become possible (though, I apprehend, of very small importance) in moods in which nothing could be concluded in the common forms of syllogistic notation. The doctrine of the quantification of the predicate

*w–w*56 rule

*x*56, 62 If therefore I do not consider the doctrine of the quantification of the predicate a valuable accession to the Art of Logic, it is only because I consider the ordinary rules of the syllogism to be an adequate test, and perfectly sufficient to exclude all inferences which do not follow from the premises.

y–y+65, 68, 72

ratiocination, therefore, starts from a *general* proposition, principle, or assumption: a proposition in which a predicate is affirmed or denied of an entire class; that is, in which some attribute, or the negation of some attribute, is asserted of an indefinite number of objects distinguished by a common characteristic, and designated in consequence, by a common name.

The other premise is always affirmative, and asserts that something (which may be either an individual, a class, or part of a class) belongs to, or is included in, the class respecting which something was affirmed or denied in the major premise. It follows that the attribute affirmed or denied of the entire class may (if *ᵃ*that affirmation or denial was correct*ᵃ*) be affirmed or denied of the object or objects alleged to be included in the class: and this is precisely the assertion made in the conclusion.

Whether or not the foregoing is an adequate account of the constituent parts of the syllogism, will be presently considered; but as far as it goes it is a true account. It has accordingly been generalized, and erected into a logical maxim, on which all ratiocination is said to be founded, insomuch that to reason, and to apply the maxim, are supposed to be one and the same thing. The maxim is, That whatever can be affirmed (or denied) of a class, may be affirmed (or denied) of everything included in the class. This axiom, supposed to be the basis of the syllogistic theory, is termed by logicians the *dictum de omni et nullo.*

This maxim, however, when considered as a principle of reasoning, appears suited to a system of metaphysics once indeed generally received, but which for the last two centuries has been considered as finally abandoned, though there have not been wanting in our own day attempts at its revival. So long as what *ᵇ*are*ᵇ* termed Universals were regarded as a peculiar kind of substances, having an objective existence distinct from the individual objects classed under them, the *dictum de omni* conveyed an important meaning; because it expressed the intercommunity of nature, which it was necessary on that theory that we should suppose to exist between those general substances and the particular substances which were subordinated to them. That everything predicable of the universal was predicable of the various individuals contained under it, was then no identical proposition, but a statement of what was conceived as a fundamental law of the universe. The assertion that the entire nature and properties of the *substantia secunda* formed part of the *ᶜ*nature and*ᶜ* properties of each of the individual substances called by the same name; that the properties of Man, for example, were properties of all men; was a proposition of real significance when man did not *mean* all men, but something inherent in men, and vastly superior to them in dignity. Now,

---

*ᵃ⁻ᵃ*MS, 43, 46, 51, 56, 62, 65   there was truth in that affirmation or denial
*ᵇ⁻ᵇ*MS, 43, 46, 51, 56   were
ᶜ⁻ᶜ+56, 62, 65, 68, 72

however, when it is known that a class, an universal, a genus or species, is not an entity *per se*, but neither more nor less than the individual substances themselves which are placed in the class, and that there is nothing real in the matter except those objects, a common name given to them, and common attributes indicated by the name; what, I should be glad to know, do we learn by being told, that whatever can be affirmed of a class, may be affirmed of every object contained in the class? The class *is* nothing but the objects contained in it: and the *dictum de omni* merely amounts to the identical proposition, that whatever is true of certain objects, is true of each of those objects. If all ratiocination were no more than the application of this maxim to particular cases, the syllogism would indeed be, what it has so often been declared to be, solemn trifling. The *dictum de omni* is on a par with another truth, which in its time was also reckoned of great importance, "Whatever is, *d*is."*d* To give any real meaning to the *dictum de omni*, we must consider it not as an axiom, but as a definition; we must look upon it as intended to explain, in a circuitous and paraphrastic manner, the meaning of the word *class*.

An error which seemed finally refuted and dislodged from *e*thought*e*, often needs only put on a new suit of phrases, to be welcomed back to its old quarters, and allowed to repose unquestioned for another cycle of ages. Modern philosophers have not been sparing in their contempt for the scholastic dogma that genera and species are a peculiar kind of substances, which general substances being the only permanent things, while the individual substances comprehended under them are in a perpetual flux, knowledge, which necessarily imports stability, can only have relation to those general substances or universals, and not to the facts or particulars included under them. Yet, though nominally rejected, this very doctrine, whether disguised under the Abstract Ideas of Locke (whose speculations, however, it has less vitiated than those of perhaps any other writer who has been infected with it), under the ultra-nominalism of Hobbes and Condillac, or the ontology of the later *f*German schools*f*, has never ceased to poison philosophy. Once accustomed to consider scientific investigation as essentially consisting in the study of universals, men did not drop this habit of thought when they ceased to regard universals as possessing an independent existence: and even those who went the length of considering them as mere names, could not free themselves from the notion that the investigation of

---

*d–d*MS, 43, 46, 51 is;" and not to be compared in point of significance to the cognate aphorism, "It is impossible for the same thing to be and not to be;" since this is, at the lowest, equivalent to the logical axiom that contradictory propositions cannot both be true.

*e–e*MS, 43, 46 science

*f–f*MS, 43, 46, 51, 56, 62, 65, 68 Kantians

truth consisted entirely or partly in some kind of conjuration or juggle with those names. When a philosopher adopted fully the Nominalist view of the signification of general language, retaining along with it the *dictum de omni* as the foundation of all reasoning, two such premises fairly put together were likely, if he was a consistent thinker, to land him in rather startling conclusions. Accordingly it has been seriously held, by writers of deserved celebrity, that the process of arriving at new truths by reasoning consists in the mere substitution of one set of arbitrary signs for another; a doctrine which they *g*suppose*g* to derive irresistible confirmation from the example of algebra. If there were any process in sorcery or necromancy more preternatural than this, I should be much surprised. The culminating point of this philosophy is the noted aphorism of Condillac, that a science is nothing, or scarcely anything, but *une langue bien faite*;[*] in other words that the one sufficient rule for discovering the nature and properties of objects is to name them properly: as if the reverse were not the truth, that it is impossible to name them properly except in proportion as we are already acquainted with their nature and properties. Can it be necessary to say, that none, not even the most trivial knowledge with respect to Things, ever was or could be originally got at by any conceivable manipulation of mere names *h*, as such*h*; and that what can be learned from names, is only what somebody who used the names knew before? Philosophical analysis confirms the indication of common sense, that the function of names is but that of enabling us to *remember* and to *communicate* our thoughts. That they also strengthen, even to an incalculable extent, the power of thought itself, is most true: but they do this by no intrinsic and peculiar virtue; they do it by the power inherent in an artificial memory, an instrument of which few have adequately considered the immense potency. As an artificial memory, language truly is, what it has so often been called, an instrument of thought; but it is one thing to be the instrument, and another to be the exclusive subject upon which the instrument is exercised. We think, indeed, to a considerable extent, by means of names, but what we think of, are the things called by those names; and there cannot be a greater error than to imagine that thought can be carried on with nothing in our mind but names, or that we can make the names think for us.

§ 3. [*What is the really fundamental axiom of Ratiocination*] Those who considered the *dictum de omni* as the foundation of the syllogism, looked upon arguments in a manner corresponding to the erroneous view which Hobbes took of propositions. Because there are some propositions which are

[*See *La Logique*, pp. 131ff. (Part II, Chap. v).]

*g-g*MS, 43, 46, 51, 56   supposed
h-h+51, 56, 62, 65, 68, 72

merely verbal, Hobbes, in order apparently that his definition might be rigorously universal, defined a proposition as if no propositions declared anything except the meaning of words.[*] If Hobbes was right; if no further account than this could be given of the import of propositions; no theory could be given but the commonly received one, of the combination of propositions in a syllogism. If the minor premise asserted nothing more than that something belongs to a class, and if *a* the major premise asserted nothing of that class except that it is included in another class, the conclusion would only be that what was included in the lower class is included in the higher, and the result, therefore, nothing except that the classification is consistent with itself. But we have seen that it is no sufficient account of the meaning of a proposition, to say that it refers something to, or excludes something from, a class. Every proposition which conveys real information asserts a matter of fact, dependent on the laws of nature, and not on *b* classification. It asserts that a given object does or does not possess a given attribute; or it asserts that two attributes, or sets of attributes, do or do not (constantly or occasionally) coexist. Since such is the purport of all propositions which convey any real knowledge, and since ratiocination is a mode of acquiring real knowledge, any theory of ratiocination which does not recognise this import of propositions, cannot, we may be sure, be the true one.

Applying this view of propositions to the two premises of a syllogism, we obtain the following results. The major premise, which, as already remarked, is always universal, asserts, that all things which have a certain attribute (or attributes) have or have not along with it, a certain other attribute (or attributes). The minor premise asserts that the thing or set of things which are the subject of that premise, have the first-mentioned attribute; and the conclusion is, that they have (or that they have not), the second. Thus in our former example,

> All men are mortal,
> Socrates is a man,
> therefore
> Socrates is mortal,

the subject and predicate of the major premise are connotative terms, denoting objects and connoting attributes. The assertion in the major premise is, that along with one of the two sets of attributes, we always find the other: that the attributes connoted by "man" never exist unless conjoined with the attribute called mortality. The assertion in the minor premise is that the

[*See "Computation or Logic," p. 30.]

*a*MS, 43, 46 , as consistency would require us to suppose,
*b*MS, 43, 46, 51, 56, 62, 65   artificial

individual named Socrates possesses the former attributes; and it is concluded that he possesses also the attribute mortality. Or if both the premises are general propositions, as

All men are mortal,
All kings are men,
therefore
All kings are mortal,

the minor premise asserts that the attributes denoted by kingship only exist in conjunction with those signified by the word man. The major asserts as before, that the last-mentioned attributes are never found without the attribute of mortality. The conclusion is, that wherever the attributes of kingship are found, that of mortality ^{c}is^c found also.

If the major premise were negative, as, No men are ^{d}omnipotent^d, it would assert, not that the attributes connoted by "man" never exist without, but that they never exist with, those connoted by "^{e}omnipotent^e:" from which, together with the minor premise, it is concluded, that the same incompatibility exists between the ^{f}attribute omnipotence^f and those constituting a king. In a similar manner we might analyse any other example of the syllogism.

If we generalize this process, and look out for the principle or law involved in every such inference, and presupposed in every syllogism, the propositions of which are anything more than merely verbal; we find, not the unmeaning *dictum de omni et nullo*, but a fundamental principle, or rather two principles, strikingly resembling the axioms of mathematics. The first, which is the principle of affirmative syllogisms, is, that things which coexist with the same thing, coexist with one another ^{g}: or (still more precisely) a thing which coexists with another thing, which other coexists with a third thing, also coexists with that third thing^g. The second is the principle of negative syllogisms, and is to this effect: that a thing which coexists with another thing, with which other a third thing does not coexist, is not coexistent with that third thing. These axioms manifestly relate to facts, and not to conventions; and one or other of them is the ground of the legitimacy of every argument in which facts and not conventions are the matter treated of.*

*[56] Mr. Herbert Spencer (*Principles of Psychology*, pp. 125–7) though his theory of the syllogism coincides with all that is essential of mine, thinks it a logical fallacy to present the two axioms in the text, as the regulating principles of syllogism. He charges me with falling into the error pointed out by Archbishop Whately and myself, of confounding exact likeness with literal identity; and

$^{c-c}$MS   will be
$^{d-d}$MS, 43, 46   gods
$^{e-e}$MS, 43, 46   God
$^{f-f}$MS, 43, 46   attributes constituting a god
$^{g-g}$+72

§ 4. [*The other form of the fundamental axiom*] It [a] remains to translate this exposition of the syllogism from the one into the other of the two

---

maintains, that we ought not to say that Socrates possesses *the same* attributes which are connoted by the word Man, but only that he possesses attributes *exactly like* them: according to which phraseology, Socrates, and the attribute mortality, are not two things coexisting with the same thing, as the axiom asserts, but two things coexisting with two different things.

[h]The question between Mr. Spencer and me is merely one of language; for neither of us (if I understand Mr. Spencer's opinions rightly) believes an attribute to be a real thing, possessed of objective existence; we believe it to be a particular mode of naming our sensations, or our expectations of sensation, when looked at in their relation to an external object which excites them. The question raised by Mr. Spencer does not, therefore, concern the properties of any really existing thing, but the comparative appropriateness, for philosophical purposes, of two different modes of using a name. Considered in this point of view, the phraseology I have employed, which is that commonly used by philosophers, seems to me to be the best. Mr. Spencer is[h] of opinion that because Socrates and Alcibiades are not the same man, the attribute which constitutes them men [i]should not be called[i] the same attribute; that because the humanity of one man and that of another express themselves to our senses not by the same individual sensations but by sensations exactly alike, humanity ought to be regarded as a different attribute in every different man. But on this showing, the humanity even of any one man should be considered as different attributes now and half-an-hour hence; for the sensations by which it will then manifest itself to my organs will not be a continuation of my present sensations, but a repetition of them; fresh sensations, not identical with, but only exactly like the present. If every general conception, instead of being "the One in the Many," were considered to be as many different conceptions as there are things to which it is applicable, there would be no such thing as general language. A name would have no general meaning if *man* connoted one thing when predicated of John, and another, though closely resembling, thing when predicated of [j]William[j]. [k]Accordingly a recent pamphlet asserts the impossibility of general knowledge on this precise ground.[k]

The meaning of any general name is some outward or inward phenomenon, consisting, in the last resort, of feelings; and these feelings, if their continuity is for an instant broken, are no longer the same feelings, in the sense of individual identity. What, then, is the common something which gives a meaning to the general name? Mr. Spencer can only say, it is the similarity of the feelings; and I rejoin, the attribute is precisely that similarity. The names of attributes are [l]in their ultimate analysis[l] names for the resemblances of our sensations (or other feelings). Every general name, [m]whether[m] abstract or concrete, denotes or connotes one or more of those resemblances. It will not, probably, be denied, that if a hundred sensations are undistinguishably alike, their resemblance ought to be spoken of as one resemblance, and not a hundred resemblances which merely *resemble* one another. The things compared are many, but the something com-

---

[h–h]56, 62   I think it is Mr. Spencer's phraseology and not mine which is faulty. Mr. Spencer appears to be
[i–i]56   is not   [j–j]56   Tom
[k–k]+68, 72   [l–l]+65, 68, 72
[m–m]56   either   [a]MS, 43, 46   only

languages in which we formerly remarked* that all propositions, and of course therefore all combinations of propositions, might be expressed. We observed that a proposition might be considered in two different lights; as a portion of our knowledge of nature, or as a memorandum for our guidance. Under the former, or speculative aspect, an affirmative general proposition is an assertion of a speculative truth, viz. that whatever has a certain attribute has a certain other attribute. Under the other aspect, it is to be regarded not as a part of our knowledge, but as an aid for our practical exigencies, by enabling us, when we see or learn that an object possesses one of the two attributes, to infer that it possesses the other; thus employing the first attribute as a mark or evidence of the second. Thus regarded, every syllogism comes within the following general formula:

Attribute A is a mark of attribute B,
The given object has the mark A,
therefore
The given object has the attribute B.

c Referred to this type, the arguments which we have lately cited as specimens of the syllogism, will express themselves in the following manner:

The attributes of man are a mark of the attribute mortality,
Socrates has the attributes of man,
therefore
Socrates has the attribute mortality.

---

mon to all of them must be conceived as one, just as the name is conceived as one, though corresponding to numerically different sensations of sound each time it is pronounced. The general term *man* does not connote the sensations derived once from one man, which, once gone, can no more occur again than the same flash of lightning. It connotes the general type of the sensations derived always from all men, and the power (always thought of as one) of producing sensations of that type. And the axiom might be thus worded: Two *types of sensation* each of which coexists with a third type, coexist with one another; or Two *powers* each of which coexists with a third power coexist with one another.

Mr. Spencer has misunderstood me in another particular. He supposes that the coexistence spoken of in the axiom, of two things with the same third thing, means simultaneousness in time. The coexistence meant is that of being jointly attributes of the same subject. The attribute of being born without teeth, and the attribute of having thirty-two teeth in mature age, are in this sense coexistent, both being attributes of man, though *ex vi termini* never of the same man at the same time.

*Supra, pp. 116–17.

b–bMS, 43, 46, 51   A
cMS   [no paragraph]

d And again,

> The attributes of man are a mark of the attribute mortality,
> The attributes of a king are a mark of the attributes of man,
> therefore
> The attributes of a king are a mark of the attribute mortality.

e And, lastly,

> The attributes of man are a mark of the absence of the
> *f*attribute omnipotence*f*,
> The attributes of a king are a mark of the attributes of man,
> therefore
> The attributes of a king are a mark of the absence of the
> *g*attribute signified by the word omnipotent*g*
> (or, are evidence of the absence of *h*that attribute*h*).

To correspond with this alteration in the form of the syllogisms, the axioms on which the syllogistic process is founded must undergo a corresponding transformation. In this altered phraseology, both those axioms may be brought under one general expression; namely, that whatever *i*has any mark, has*i* that which it is a mark of. Or, when the minor premise as well as the major is universal, we may state it thus: Whatever is a mark of any mark, is a mark of that which this last is a mark of. To trace the identity of these axioms with those previously laid down, may be *j* left to the intelligent reader. We shall find, as we proceed, the great convenience of the phraseology into which we have last thrown them, and which is better adapted than any I am acquainted with, to express with precision and force what is aimed at, and actually accomplished, in every case of the ascertainment of a truth by ratiocination.*

*[72] Professor Bain (*Logic*, Pt. I, pp. 157–8) considers the axiom (or rather axioms) here proposed as a substitute for the *dictum de omni*, to possess certain advantages, but to be "unworkable as a basis of the syllogism. The fatal defect consists in this, that it is ill-adapted to bring out the difference between total and partial coincidence of terms, the observation of which is the essential precaution in syllogizing correctly. If all the terms were coextensive, the axiom would flow on admirably; A carries B, all B and none but B; B carries C in the same manner; whence A carries C, without limitation or reserve. But in point of fact, we know that while A carries B, other things carry B also; whence a process of limitation is

*d*MS, 43, 46 [*no paragraph*]
*e*MS, 43, 46 [*no paragraph*]
*f–f*MS, 43, 46 attributes of a god
*g–g*MS, 43, 46 attributes signified by the word god
*h–h*MS, 43, 46 those attributes
*i–i*MS, 43, 46, 51, 56, 62 possesses any mark, possesses
*j*MS, 43, 46 safely

required, in transferring A to C through B. A (in common with other things) carries B; B (in common with other things) carries C; whence A (in common with other things) carries C. The axiom provides no means of making this limitation; if we were to follow A literally, we should be led to suppose A and C coextensive: for such is the only obvious meaning of 'the attribute A coincides with the attribute C.' "

It is certainly possible that a careless learner here and there may suppose that if A carries B, it follows that B carries A. But if any one is so incautious as to commit this mistake, the very earliest lesson in the logic of inference, the Conversion of propositions, will correct it. The first of the two forms in which I have stated the axiom, is in some degree open to Mr. Bain's criticism: when B is said to coexist with A, (it must be by a *lapsus calami* that Mr. Bain uses the word *coincide*) it is possible, in the absence of warning, to suppose the meaning to be that the two things are only found together. But this misinterpretation is excluded by the other, or practical, form of the maxim; *Nota notæ est nota rei ipsius.* No one would be in any danger of inferring that because *a* is a mark of *b*, *b* can never exist without *a*; that because being in a confirmed consumption is a mark of being about to die, no one dies who is not in a consumption; that because being coal is a mark of having come out of the earth, nothing can come out of the earth except coal. Ordinary knowledge of English seems a sufficient protection against these mistakes, since in speaking of a mark of anything we are never understood as implying reciprocity.

A more fundamental objection is stated by Mr. Bain in a subsequent passage (p. 158). "The axiom does not accommodate itself to the type of Deductive Reasoning as contrasted with Induction—the application of a general principle to a special case. Anything that fails to make prominent this circumstance is not adapted as a foundation for the syllogism." But though it may be proper to limit the term Deduction to the application of a general principle to a special case, it has never been held that Ratiocination or Syllogism is subject to the same limitation; and the adoption of it would exclude a great amount of valid and conclusive syllogistic reasoning. Moreover if the *dictum de omni* makes prominent the fact of the application of a general principle to a particular case, the axiom I propose makes prominent the condition which alone makes that application a real inference.

I conclude, therefore, that both forms have their value, and their place in Logic. The *dictum de omni* should be retained as the fundamental axiom of the logic of mere consistency, often called Formal Logic; nor have I ever quarrelled with the use of it in that character, nor proposed to banish it from treatises on Formal Logic. But the other is the proper axiom for the logic of the pursuit of truth by way of Deduction; and the recognition of it can alone show how it is possible that deductive reasoning can be a road to truth.

CHAPTER III

Of the Functions and Logical Value of the Syllogism

§ 1. [*Is the syllogism a* petitio principii?] We have shown what is the real nature of the truths with which the Syllogism is conversant, in contradistinction to the more superficial manner in which their import is conceived in the common theory; and what are the fundamental axioms on which its probative force or conclusiveness depends. We have now to inquire, whether the syllogistic process, that of reasoning from generals to particulars, is, or is not, a process of inference; a progress from the known to the unknown: a means of coming to a knowledge of something which we did not know before.

Logicians have been remarkably unanimous in their mode of answering this question. It is universally allowed that a syllogism is vicious if there be anything more in the conclusion than was assumed in the premises. But this is, in fact, to say, that nothing ever was, or can be, proved by syllogism, which was not known, or *a*assumed*a* to be known, before. Is ratiocination, then, not a process of inference? And is the syllogism, to which the word reasoning has so often been represented to be exclusively appropriate, not really entitled to be called reasoning at all? This seems an inevitable consequence of the doctrine, admitted by all writers on the subject, that a syllogism can prove no more than is involved in the premises. Yet the acknowledgment so explicitly made, has not prevented one set of writers from continuing to represent the syllogism as the correct analysis of what the mind actually performs in discovering and proving the larger half of the truths, whether of science or of daily life, which we believe; while those who have avoided this inconsistency, and followed out the general theorem respecting the logical value of the syllogism to its legitimate corollary, have been led to impute uselessness and frivolity to the syllogistic theory itself, on the ground of the *petitio principii* which they allege to be inherent in every syllogism. As I believe both these opinions to be fundamentally erroneous, I must request the attention of the reader to certain considerations, without which any just appreciation of the true character of the syllogism, and the functions it per-

*a–a*MS supposed

forms in philosophy, appears to me impossible; but which seem to have been either overlooked, or insufficiently adverted to, both by the defenders of the syllogistic theory and by its assailants.

§ 2. [*Insufficiency of the common theory*] It must be granted that in every syllogism, considered as an argument to prove the conclusion, there is a *petitio principii*. When we say,

> All men are mortal,
> Socrates is a man,
>   therefore
> Socrates is mortal;

it is unanswerably urged by the adversaries of the syllogistic theory, that the proposition, Socrates is mortal, is presupposed in the more general assumption, All men are mortal: that we cannot be assured of the mortality of all men, unless we *are already* certain of the mortality of every individual man: that if it be still doubtful whether Socrates, or any other individual *we* choose to name, be mortal or not, the same degree of uncertainty must hang over the assertion, All men are mortal: that the general principle, instead of being given as evidence of the particular case, cannot itself be taken for true without exception, until every shadow of doubt which could affect any case comprised with it, is dispelled by evidence *aliundè*; and then what remains for the syllogism to prove? That, in short, no reasoning from generals to particulars can, as such, prove anything: since from a general principle *we* cannot infer any particulars, but those which the principle itself assumes as *known*.

This doctrine *appears to me* irrefragable; and if logicians, though unable to dispute it, have usually exhibited a strong disposition to explain it away, this was not because they could discover any flaw in the argument itself, but because the contrary opinion seemed to rest on arguments equally indisputable. In the syllogism last referred to, for example, or in any of those which we previously constructed, is it not evident that the conclusion may, to the person to whom the syllogism is presented, be actually and *bonâ fide* a new truth? Is it not matter of daily experience that truths previously *unthought* of, facts which have not been, and cannot be, directly observed, are arrived at by way of general reasoning? We believe that the Duke of Wellington is mortal. We do not know this by direct observation, *so long as he is not yet*

*a–a*MS   are previously]   43, 46   were previously
*b–b*MS, 43, 46, 51, 56, 62   you
*c–c*MS, 43, 46, 51   you   *d–d*MS, 43, 46   foreknown
*e–e*MS, 43, 46   is   *f–f*MS, 43, 46, 51, 56   undreamt
*g–g*MS, 43, 46   since he is not yet]   51   since he is not

dead. If we were asked how, this being the case, we know the duke to be mortal, we should probably answer, Because all men are so. Here, therefore, we arrive at the knowledge of a truth not (as yet) susceptible of observation, by a reasoning which admits of being exhibited in the following syllogism:

All men are mortal,
The Duke of Wellington is a man,
therefore
The Duke of Wellington is mortal.

And since a large portion of our knowledge is thus acquired, logicians have persisted in representing the syllogism as a process of inference or proof; though none of them has cleared up the difficulty which arises from the inconsistency between that assertion, and the principle, that if there be anything in the conclusion which was not already asserted in the premises, the argument is vicious. For it is impossible to attach any serious scientific value to such a mere salvo, as the distinction drawn between being involved *by implication* in the premises, and being directly asserted in them. When Archbishop Whately *h* says* that the object of reasoning *i*is "merely*i* to expand and unfold the assertions wrapt up, as it were, and implied in those with which we set out, and to bring a person to perceive and acknowledge the full force of that which he has admitted," he does not, I think, meet the real difficulty requiring to be explained, namely, how it happens that a science, like geometry, *can* be all "wrapt up" in a few definitions and axioms. Nor does this defence of the syllogism differ much from what its assailants urge against it as an accusation, when they charge it with being of no use except to those who seek to press the consequences of an admission into which a *j*person*j* has been entrapped without having considered and understood its full force. When you admitted the major premise, you asserted the conclusion; but, says Archbishop Whately, you asserted it by implication merely: this, however, can here only mean that you asserted it unconsciously; that you did not know you were asserting it; but, if so, the difficulty revives in this shape—Ought you not to have known? Were you warranted in asserting the general proposition without having satisfied yourself of the truth of everything which it fairly includes? And if not, *k*is not the syllogistic art *primâ facie* what its assailants affirm it to be,*k* a contrivance for catching you in a trap, and holding you fast in it?†

Logic, p. 239 (9th ed.).
†[51] It is hardly necessary to say, that I am not contending for any such

*h*MS, 43, 46, 51, 56   , for example,
*i–i*MS "is merely
*j–j*MS, 43, 46   man
*k–k*MS, 43, 46, 51, 56   what then is the syllogistic art but

§ 3. [*All inference is from particulars to particulars*] From this difficulty
there appears to be but one issue. The proposition that the Duke of Wellington is mortal, is evidently an inference; it is got at as a conclusion from
something else; but do we, in reality, conclude it from the proposition, All
men are mortal? I answer, no.

The error committed is, I conceive, that of overlooking the distinction
between *ᵃ* two parts of the process of philosophizing, the inferring part, and
the registering part; and ascribing to the latter the functions of the former.
The mistake is that of referring a *ᵇperson to his own notes for the origin of
his knowledge. If a personᵇ* is asked a question, and is at the moment unable
to answer it, he may refresh his memory by turning to a memorandum which
he carries about with him. But if he were asked, how the fact came to his
knowledge, he would scarcely answer, because it was set down in his note-
book: unless the book was written, like the Koran, with a quill from the wing
of the angel Gabriel.

Assuming that the proposition, The Duke of Wellington is mortal, is immediately an inference from the proposition, All men are mortal; whence do
we derive our knowledge of that general truth? *ᶜOf course fromᶜ* observation.
Now, all which man can observe are individual cases. From these all general
truths must be drawn, and into these they may be again resolved; for a
general truth is but an aggregate of particular truths; a comprehensive expression, by which an indefinite number of individual facts are affirmed or
denied at once. But a general proposition is not merely a compendious form
for recording and preserving in the memory a number of particular facts, all
of which have been observed. Generalization is not a process of mere naming,
it is also a process of inference. From instances which we have observed, we
feel warranted in concluding, that what we found true in those instances,
holds in all similar ones, past, present, and future, however numerous they

---

absurdity as that we *actually* "ought to have known" and considered the case of
every individual man, past, present, and future, before affirming that all men are
mortal: although this interpretation has been, strangely enough, put upon the
preceding observations. There is no difference between me and Archbishop
Whately, or any other defender of the syllogism, on the practical part of the
matter; I am only pointing out an inconsistency in the logical theory of it, as
conceived by almost all writers. I do not say that a person who affirmed, before
the Duke of Wellington was born, that all men are mortal, *knew* that the Duke
of Wellington was mortal; but I do say that he *asserted* it; and I ask for an explanation of the apparent logical fallacy, of adducing in proof of the Duke of
Wellington's mortality, a general statement which presupposes it. Finding no
sufficient resolution of this difficulty in any of the writers on Logic, I have attempted to supply one.

ᵃMS, 43, 46, 51, 56   the
ᵇ⁻ᵇMS, 43, 46   man to . . . a man
ᶜ⁻ᶜMS, 43, 46   No supernatural aid being supposed, the answer must be, by

may be. We then, by that valuable contrivance of language which enables us to speak of many as if they were one, record all that we have observed, together with all that we infer from our observations, in one concise expression; and have thus only one proposition, instead of an endless number, to remember or to communicate. The results of many observations and inferences, and instructions for making innumerable inferences in unforeseen cases, are compressed into one short sentence.

When, therefore, we conclude from the death of John and Thomas, and every other person we ever heard of in whose case the experiment had been fairly tried, that the Duke of Wellington is mortal like the rest; we may, indeed, pass through the generalization, All men are mortal, as an intermediate stage; but it is not in the latter half of the process, the descent from all men to the Duke of Wellington, that the *inference* resides. The inference is finished when we have asserted that all men are mortal. What remains to be performed afterwards is merely deciphering our own notes.

Archbishop Whately has contended that syllogizing, or reasoning from generals to particulars, is not, agreeably to the vulgar idea, a peculiar *mode* of reasoning, but the philosophical analysis of *the* mode in which all men reason, and must do so if they reason at all.[*] With the deference due to so high an authority, I cannot help thinking that the vulgar notion is, in this case, the more correct. If, from our experience of John, Thomas, &c., who once were living, but are now dead, we are entitled to conclude that all human beings are mortal, we might surely without any logical inconsequence have concluded at once from those instances, that the Duke of Wellington is mortal. The mortality of John, Thomas, and ᵈothersᵈ is, after all, the whole evidence we have for the mortality of the Duke of Wellington. Not one iota is added to the proof by interpolating a general proposition. Since the individual cases are all the evidence we can possess, evidence which no logical form into which we choose to throw it can make greater than it is; and since that evidence is either sufficient in itself, or, if insufficient for ᵉtheᵉ one purpose, cannot be sufficient for the other; I am unable to see why we should be forbidden to take the shortest cut from these sufficient premises to the conclusion, and constrained to travel the "high priori road," by the arbitrary fiat of logicians. I cannot perceive why it should be impossible to journey from one place to another unless we "march up a hill, and then march down again." It may be the safest road, and there may be a resting-place at the top of the hill, affording a commanding view of the surrounding country; but for the mere purpose of arriving at our journey's end, our taking that road is perfectly optional; it is a question of time, trouble, and danger.

[*Elements of Logic, p. 12.]

ᵈ⁻ᵈMS, 43, 46, 51, 56, 62, 65, 68   company
ᵉ⁻ᵉ+46, 51, 56, 62, 65, 68, 72

Not only *may* we reason from particulars to particulars without passing through generals, but we perpetually do so reason. All our earliest inferences are of this nature. From the first dawn of intelligence we draw inferences, but years elapse before we learn the use of general language. The child, who, having burnt his fingers, avoids to thrust them again into the fire, has reasoned or inferred, though he has never thought of the general maxim, Fire burns. He knows from memory that he has been burnt, and on this evidence believes, when he sees a candle, that if he puts his finger into the flame of it, he will be burnt again. He believes this in every case which happens to arise; but without looking, in each instance, beyond the present case. He is not generalizing; he is inferring a particular from particulars. In the same way, also, brutes reason. There is *no ground for attributing to any of the lower animals the use of signs, of such a nature as to render general propositions possible*. But those animals profit by experience, and avoid what they have found to cause them pain, in the same manner, though not always with the same skill, as a human creature. Not only the burnt child, but the burnt dog, dreads the fire.

I believe that, in point of fact, when drawing inferences from our personal experience, and not from maxims handed down to us by books or tradition, we much oftener conclude from particulars to particulars directly, than through the intermediate agency of any general proposition. We are constantly reasoning from ourselves to other people, or from one person to another, without giving ourselves the trouble to erect our observations into general maxims of human or external nature. When we conclude that some person will, on some given occasion, feel or act so and so, we sometimes judge from an enlarged consideration of the manner in which *human beings in general, or persons* of some particular character, are accustomed to feel and act; but much oftener from *merely recollecting* the feelings and conduct of the same *person* in some previous instance, or from considering how we should feel or act ourselves. It is not only the village matron, who, when called to a consultation upon the case of a neighbour's child, pronounces on the evil and its remedy simply on the recollection and authority of what she accounts the similar case of her Lucy. We all, where we have no definite maxims to steer by, guide ourselves in the same way: and if we have an extensive experience, and retain its impressions strongly, we may acquire in this manner a very considerable power of accurate judgment, which we may be utterly incapable of justifying or of communicating to others. Among the higher order of practical intellects there have been many of whom it was

---

*f–f*MS, 43, 46   little or no ground for attributing to any of the lower animals the use of conventional signs, without which general propositions are impossible
*g–g*MS, 43, 46   men in general, or men
*h–h*MS, 43, 46, 51, 56   having known
*i–i*MS, 43, 46   man

remarked how admirably they suited their means to their ends, without being able to give any sufficient reasons for what they did; and applied, or seemed to apply, recondite principles which they were wholly unable to state. This is a natural consequence of having a mind stored with appropriate particulars, and having been long accustomed to reason at once from these to fresh particulars, without practising the habit of stating to oneself or *j*to*j* others the corresponding general propositions. An old warrior, on a rapid glance at the outlines of the ground, is able at once to give the necessary orders for a skilful arrangement of his troops; though if he has received little theoretical instruction, and has seldom been called upon to answer to other people for his conduct, he may never have had in his mind a single general theorem respecting the relation between ground and array. But his experience of encampments, *k*in*k* circumstances more or less similar, has left a number of vivid, unexpressed, ungeneralized analogies in his mind, the most appropriate of which, instantly suggesting itself, determines him to a judicious arrangement.

The skill of an uneducated person in the use of weapons, or of tools, is of a precisely similar nature. The savage who executes unerringly the exact throw which brings down his game, or his enemy, in the manner most suited to his purpose, under the operation of all the conditions necessarily involved, the weight and form of the weapon, the direction and distance of the object, the action of the wind, &c., owes this power to a long series of previous experiments, the results of which he certainly never framed into any verbal theorems or rules. *l*The same thing may generally be said of any other*l* extra-ordinary manual dexterity. Not long ago a Scotch manufacturer procured from England, at a high rate of wages, a working dyer, famous for producing very fine colours, with the view of teaching to his other workmen the same skill. The workman came; but his mode of proportioning the ingredients, in which lay the secret of the effects he produced, was by taking them up in handfuls, while the common method was to weigh them. The manufacturer sought to make him turn his handling system into an equivalent weighing system, that the general principle of his peculiar mode of proceeding might be ascertained. This, however, the man found himself quite unable to do, and therefore could impart his skill to nobody. He had, from the individual cases of his own experience, established a connexion in his mind between fine effects of colour, and tactual perceptions in handling his dyeing materials; and from these perceptions he could, in any particular *m*case*m*, infer the means to be employed, and the effects which would be produced, but could not put others in possession of the grounds on which he proceeded, from having never generalized them in his own mind, or expressed them in language.

j–j+43, 46, 51, 56, 62, 65, 68, 72
*l–l*MS, 43, 46   It is the same in all

*k–k*MS, 43, 46   under
*m–m*43, 46   cases [*printer's error?*]

Almost every one knows Lord Mansfield's advice to a man of practical good sense, who, being appointed governor of a colony, had to preside in its court of justice, without previous judicial practice or legal education.[*] The advice was to give his decision boldly, for it would probably be right; but never to venture on assigning reasons, for they would almost infallibly be wrong. In cases like this, which are of no uncommon occurrence, it would be absurd to suppose that the bad reason was the source of the good decision. Lord Mansfield knew that if any reason were assigned it would be necessarily an afterthought, the judge being *in fact* guided by impressions from past experience, without the circuitous process of framing general principles from them, and that if he attempted to frame any such he would assuredly fail. Lord Mansfield, however, would not have doubted that a man of equal experience who had also a mind stored with general propositions derived by legitimate induction from that experience, would have been greatly preferable as a judge, to one, however sagacious, who could not be trusted with the explanation and justification of his own judgments. The cases of [n]men of talent[n] performing wonderful things they know not how, are examples of the [o]rudest[o] and most spontaneous form of the operations of superior minds. It is a defect in them, and often a source of errors, not to have generalized as they went on; but generalization [p], though[p] a help, the most important indeed of all helps, [q]is[q] not an essential.

Even [r]the scientifically instructed[r], who possess, in the form of general propositions, a systematic record of the results of the experience of mankind, need not always revert to those general propositions in order to apply that experience to a new case. It is justly remarked by Dugald Stewart,[†] that though [s]the[s] reasonings in mathematics depend entirely on the axioms, it is by no means necessary to our seeing the conclusiveness of the proof, that the axioms should be expressly adverted to. When it is inferred that AB is equal to CD because each of them is equal to EF, the most uncultivated understanding, as soon as the propositions were understood, would assent to the inference, without having ever heard of the general truth that "things which are equal to the same thing are equal to one another." This remark of Stewart, consistently followed out, goes to the root, as I conceive, of the philosophy of ratiocination; and it is to be regretted that he himself stopt short at a much more limited application of it. He saw that the general propositions on which a reasoning is said to depend, may, in certain cases, be

[*See John, Lord Campbell. *Lives of the Chief Justices of England.* 2nd ed. London, 1849, Vol. II, p. 572.]

[†*Elements of the Philosophy of the Human Mind.* 3 vols. London: Strahan and Cadell, *et al.*, 1792, 1814, 1827, Vol. II, pp. 28ff., Chap. i, sect. 1.]

[n-n]MS, 43, 46 able men
[o-o]MS, 43, 46 less civilized
[p-p]MS, 43, 46 is
[q-q]MS but] 43, 46 yet
[r-r]MS, 43, 46 philosophers
[s-s]MS, 43, 46, 51 our

altogether omitted, without impairing its probative force. But he imagined this to be a peculiarity belonging to axioms; and argued from it, that axioms are not the foundations or first principles of geometry, from which all the other truths of the science are synthetically deduced (as the laws of motion and of the composition of forces in *dynamics*, the equal mobility of fluids in hydrostatics, the laws of reflection and refraction in optics, are the first principles of those sciences); but are merely necessary assumptions, self-evident indeed, and the denial of which would annihilate all demonstration, but from which, as premises, nothing can be demonstrated. *In the present, as* in many other instances, this thoughtful and elegant writer has perceived an important truth, but only by halves. Finding, in the case of geometrical axioms, that general names have not any talismanic virtue for conjuring new truths out of the *well where they lie hid*, and not seeing that this is equally true in every other case of generalization, he contended that axioms are in their nature barren of consequences, and that the really fruitful truths, the real first principles of geometry, are the definitions; that the definition, for example, of the circle is to the properties of the circle, what the laws of equilibrium and of the pressure of the atmosphere are to the rise of the mercury in the Torricellian tube. Yet all that he had asserted respecting the function to which the axioms are confined in the demonstrations of geometry, holds equally true of the definitions. Every demonstration in Euclid might be carried on without them. This is apparent from the ordinary process of proving a proposition of geometry by means of a diagram. What assumption, in fact, do we set out from, to demonstrate by a diagram any of the properties of the circle? Not that in all circles the radii are equal, but only that they are so in the circle ABC. As our warrant for assuming this, we appeal, it is true, to the definition of a circle in general; but it is only necessary that *the assumption be granted* in the case of the particular circle supposed. From this, which is not a general but a singular proposition, combined with other propositions of a similar kind, some of which *when generalized* are called definitions, and others axioms, we prove that a certain conclusion is true, not of all circles, but of the particular circle ABC; or at least would be so, if the facts precisely accorded with our assumptions. The enunciation, as it is called, that is, the general theorem which stands at the head of the demonstration, is not the proposition actually demonstrated. One instance only is demonstrated: but the process by which this is done, is a process which, when we consider its nature, we perceive might be exactly copied in an indefinite number of other instances; in every instance which conforms to certain conditions. The contrivance of general language furnishing us with terms

---

*t–t*MS, 43, 46   mechanics
*u–u*MS   As
*v–v*MS, 43, 46, 51, 56, 62, 65   pit of darkness
*w–w*MS, 43   you should grant the assumption

which connote these conditions, we are able to assert this indefinite multitude of truths in a single expression, and this expression is the general theorem. By dropping the use of diagrams, and substituting, in the demonstrations, general phrases for the letters of the alphabet, we might prove the general theorem directly, that is, we might demonstrate all the cases at once; and to do this we must, of course, employ as our premises, the axioms and definitions in their general form. But this only means, that if we can prove an individual conclusion by assuming an individual fact, then in whatever case we are warranted in making an exactly similar assumption, we may draw an exactly similar conclusion. The definition is a sort of notice to ourselves and others, what assumptions we think ourselves entitled to make. And so in all cases, the general propositions, whether called definitions, axioms, or laws of nature, which we lay down at the beginning of our reasonings, are merely abridged statements, in a kind of short-hand, of the particular facts, which, as occasion arises, we either think we may proceed on as proved, or intend to assume. In any one demonstration it is enough if we assume for a particular case suitably selected, what by the statement of the definition or principle we announce that we intend to assume in all cases which may arise. The definition of the circle, therefore, is to one of Euclid's demonstrations, exactly what, according to Stewart, the axioms are; that is, the demonstration does not depend on it, but yet if we deny it the demonstration fails. The proof does not rest on the general assumption, but on a similar assumption confined to the particular case: that case, however, being chosen as a specimen or paradigm of the whole class of cases included in the theorem, there can be no ground for making the assumption in that case which does not exist in every other; and *to deny the assumption as a general truth, is to* deny the right *of making* it in the particular instance.

There are, undoubtedly, the most ample reasons for stating both the principles and the theorems in their general form, and these will be explained presently, so far as explanation is requisite. But, that *unpractised learners, even in making use of one theorem to demonstrate another, reason* rather from particular to particular than from the general proposition, is manifest from the difficulty *they find* in applying a theorem to a case in which the configuration of the diagram is extremely unlike that of the diagram by which the original theorem was demonstrated. A difficulty which, except in cases of unusual mental power, long practice can alone remove, and removes chiefly by rendering us familiar with all the configurations consistent with the general conditions of the theorem.

$x-x$MS, 43, 46, 51   if you deny . . . truth, you
$y-y$MS, 43, 46, 51   to make
$z-z$MS, 43, 46   an unpractised learner, even . . . another, reasons
$a-a$MS, 43, 46   he finds

§ 4. [*General propositions are a record of such inferences from particulars to particulars, and the rules of the syllogism are rules for the interpretation of the record*] From the considerations now adduced, the following conclusions seem to be established. All inference is from particulars to particulars: General propositions are merely registers of such inferences already made, and short formulæ for making more: The major premise of a syllogism, consequently, is a formula of this description: and the conclusion is not an inference drawn *from* the formula, but an inference drawn *according to* the formula: the real logical antecedent, or *ªpremiseª*, being the particular facts from which the general proposition was collected by induction. Those facts, and the individual instances which supplied them, may have been forgotten: but a record remains, not indeed descriptive of the facts themselves, but showing how those cases may be distinguished, respecting which, the facts, when known, were considered to warrant a given inference. According to the indications of this record we draw our conclusion: which is, to all intents and purposes, a conclusion from the forgotten facts. For this it is essential that we should read the record correctly: and the rules of the syllogism are a set of precautions to ensure our doing so.

This view of the functions of the syllogism is confirmed by the consideration of precisely those cases which might be expected to be least favourable to it, namely, those in which ratiocination is independent of any previous induction. We have already observed that the syllogism, in the ordinary course of our reasoning, is only the latter half of the process of travelling from premises to a conclusion. There are, however, some peculiar cases in which it is the whole process. Particulars alone are capable of being subjected to observation; and all knowledge which is derived from observation, begins, therefore, of necessity, in particulars; but our knowledge may, in cases of *ᵇcertain descriptionsᵇ*, be conceived as coming to us from other sources than observation. It may present itself as coming from *ᶜtestimony*, which, on the occasion and for the purpose in hand, is accepted as of an authoritative character: and the information thus*ᶜ* communicated, may be conceived to comprise not only particular facts but general propositions, *ᵈas when a scientific doctrine is accepted without examination on the authority of writers ᵉ, or a theological doctrine on that of Scriptureᵉᵈ*. Or the generalization may not be, in the ordinary sense, an assertion at all, but a command; a law, not in the philosophical, but in the moral and political sense of the term: an expression of the desire of a superior, that we, or any number of other per-

---

*ª–ª*MS, 43, 46, 51   premisses

*ᵇ–ᵇ*MS, 43, 46, 51, 56   a certain description

*ᶜ–ᶜ*MS, 43, 46   revelation; and the knowledge, thus supernaturally

*ᵈ–ᵈ*MS, 43, 46   such as occur so abundantly in the writings of Solomon and in the apostolic epistles

ᵉ–ᵉ+62, 65, 68, 72

sons, shall conform our conduct to certain general instructions. So far as this asserts a fact, namely, a volition of the legislator, that fact is an individual fact, and the proposition, therefore, ᶠisᶠ not a general proposition. But the description therein contained of the conduct which it is the will of the legislator that his subjects should observe, is general. The proposition asserts, not that all men *are* anything, but that all men *shall* do something. ᵍ

In both these cases the generalities are ʰthe original dataʰ, and the particulars are elicited from them by a process which correctly resolves itself into a series of syllogisms. The real nature, however, of the supposed deductive process, is evident enough. ⁱ The only point to be determined is, whether the authority which declared the general proposition, intended to include this case in it; and whether the legislator intended his command to apply to the present case among others, or not. ʲThis is ascertained by examining whether the case possesses the marks by which, as those authorities have signified, the cases which they meant to certify or to influence may be known. The object of the inquiry is to make out the witness's or the legislator's intention, through the indication given by their words.ʲ This is a question, as the Germans express it, of hermeneutics ᵏ. The operation is not a process of inference, but a process of interpretation.

In this last phrase we have obtained an expression which appears to me to characterize, more aptly than any other, the functions of the syllogism in all cases. When the premises are given by authority, the function of Reasoning is to ascertain the testimony of a witness, or the will of a legislator, by interpreting the signs in which the one has intimated his assertion and the other his command. In like manner, when the premises are derived from observation, the function of Reasoning is to ascertain what we (or our predecessors) formerly thought might be inferred from the observed facts, and to do this by interpreting a memorandum of ours, or of theirs. The memorandum reminds us, that from evidence, more or less carefully weighed, it formerly appeared that a certain attribute might be inferred wherever we perceive a certain mark. The proposition, All men are mortal (for instance) shows that we have had experience from which we thought it followed that the attributes

---

ᶠ⁻ᶠ+43, 46, 51, 56, 62, 65, 68; 72

ᵍMS, 43, 46   These two cases, of a truth revealed in general terms, and a command intimated in the like manner, might be exchanged for the more extensive cases, of any general statement received upon testimony, and any general practical precept. But the more limited illustrations suit us better, being drawn from subjects where long and complicated trains of ratiocination have actually been grounded upon premisses which came to mankind from the first in a general form, the subjects of Scriptural Theology and of positive Law.

ʰ⁻ʰMS, 43, 46   given to us

ⁱMS, 43, 46   It is a search for truth, no doubt, but through the medium of an inquiry into the meaning of a form of words.

ʲ⁻ʲ+51, 56, 62, 65, 68, 72

ᵏMS, 43, 46   ; it relates to the meaning of a certain form of discourse

connoted by the term man, are a mark of mortality. But when we conclude that the Duke of Wellington is mortal, we do not infer this from the memorandum, but from the former experience. All that we infer from the memorandum is our own previous belief, (or that of those who transmitted to us the proposition), concerning the inferences which that former experience would warrant.

This view of the nature of the syllogism renders consistent and intelligible what otherwise remains obscure and confused in the theory of Archbishop Whately and other enlightened defenders of the syllogistic doctrine, respecting the limits to which its functions are confined. They [l] affirm in as explicit terms as can be used, that the sole office of general reasoning is to prevent inconsistency in our opinions; to prevent us from assenting to anything, the truth of which would contradict something to which we had previously on good grounds given our assent. And they tell us, that the sole ground which a syllogism affords for assenting to the conclusion, is that the supposition of its being false, combined with the supposition that the premises are true, would lead to a contradiction in terms. Now this would be but a lame account of the real grounds which we have for believing the facts which we learn from reasoning, in contradistinction to observation. The true reason why we believe that the Duke of Wellington will die, is that his fathers, and our fathers, and all other persons who were [m]cotemporary[m] with them, have died. Those facts are the real premises of the reasoning. But we are not led to infer the conclusion from those premises, by the necessity of avoiding any verbal inconsistency. There is no contradiction in supposing that all those persons have died, and that the Duke of Wellington may, notwithstanding, live for ever. But there would be a contradiction if we first, on the ground of those same premises, made a general assertion including and covering the case of the Duke of Wellington, and then refused to stand to it in the individual case. There is an inconsistency to be avoided between the memorandum we make of the inferences which may be justly drawn in future cases, and the inferences we actually draw in those cases when they arise. With this view we interpret our own formula, precisely as a judge interprets a law: in order that we may avoid drawing any inferences not conformable to our former intention, as a judge avoids giving any decision not conformable to the legislator's intention. The rules for this interpretation are the rules of the syllogism: and its sole purpose is to maintain consistency between the conclusions we draw in every particular case, and the previous general directions for drawing them; whether those general directions were framed by ourselves as the result of induction, or were received by us from an authority competent to give them.

[l]MS, 43   all
[m]–[m]MS, 43, 46   contemporary

§ 5. [*The syllogism not the type of reasoning, but a test of it*] In the above observations it has, I think, been *a* shown, that, though there is always a process of reasoning or inference where a syllogism is used, the syllogism is not a correct analysis of that process of reasoning or inference; which is, on the contrary, (when not a mere inference from testimony) an inference from particulars to particulars; authorized by a previous inference from particulars to generals, and substantially the same with it; of the nature, therefore, of Induction. But while these conclusions appear to me undeniable, I must yet enter a protest, as strong as that of Archbishop Whately himself, against the doctrine that the syllogistic art is useless for the purposes of reasoning. The reasoning lies in the act of generalization, not in interpreting the record of that act; but the syllogistic form is an indispensable collateral security for the correctness of the generalization itself.

It has already been seen, that if we have a collection of particulars sufficient for grounding an induction, we need not frame a general proposition; we may reason at once from those particulars to other particulars. But it is to be remarked withal, that whenever, from a set of particular cases, we can legitimately draw any inference, we may legitimately make our inference a general one. If, from observation and experiment, we can conclude to one new case, so may we to an indefinite number. If that which has held true in our past experience will therefore hold in time to come, it will hold not merely in some individual case, but in all cases of *b*some*b* given description. Every induction, therefore, which suffices to prove one fact, proves an indefinite multitude of facts: the experience which justifies a single prediction must be such as will suffice to bear out a general theorem. This theorem it is extremely important to ascertain and declare, in its broadest form of generality; and thus to place before our minds, in its full extent, the whole of what our evidence must prove if it proves anything.

This throwing of the whole body of possible inferences from a given set of particulars, into one general expression, operates as a security for their being just inferences, in more ways than one. First, the general principle presents a larger object to the imagination than any of the singular propositions which it contains. A process of thought which leads to a comprehensive generality, is felt as of greater importance than one which terminates in an insulated fact; and the mind is, even unconsciously, led to bestow greater attention upon the process, and to weigh more carefully the sufficiency of the experience appealed to, for supporting the inference grounded upon it. There is another, and a more important, advantage. In reasoning from a course of individual observations to some new and unobserved case, which we are but imperfectly acquainted with (or we should not be inquiring into it), and in

*a*MS, 43, 46, 51   clearly
b–*b*MS, 43, 46, 51, 56   a

which, since we are inquiring into it, we probably feel a peculiar interest; there is very little to prevent us from giving way to negligence, or to any bias which may affect our wishes or our imagination, and, under that influence, accepting insufficient evidence as sufficient. But if, instead of concluding straight to the particular case, we place before ourselves an entire class of facts—the whole contents of a general proposition, every tittle of which is legitimately inferrible from our premises, if that one particular conclusion is so; there is then a considerable likelihood that if the premises are insufficient, and the general inference, therefore, groundless, it will comprise within it some fact or facts the reverse of which we already know to be true; and we shall thus discover the error in our generalization by ^{c} a *reductio ad impossibile*.

Thus if, during the reign of Marcus Aurelius, a subject of the Roman empire, under the bias naturally given to the imagination and expectations by the lives and characters of the Antonines, had been disposed to ^{d}expect^d that Commodus would be a just ruler; supposing him to stop there, he might only have been undeceived by sad experience. But if he reflected that this ^{e}expectation^e could not be justifiable unless from the same evidence he was ^{f} warranted in concluding some general proposition, as, for instance, that all Roman emperors are just rulers; he would immediately have thought of Nero, Domitian, and other instances, which, showing the falsity of the general conclusion, and therefore the insufficiency of the premises, would have warned him that those premises could not prove in the instance of Commodus, what they were inadequate to prove in any collection of cases in which his was included.

The advantage, in judging whether any controverted inference is legitimate, of referring to a parallel case, is universally acknowledged. But by ascending to the general proposition, we bring under our view not one parallel case only, but all possible parallel cases at once; all cases to which the same set of evidentiary considerations are applicable.

When, therefore, we argue from a number of known cases to another case supposed to be analogous, it is always possible, and generally advantageous, to divert our argument into the circuitous channel of an induction from those known cases to a general proposition, and a subsequent application of that general proposition to the unknown case. This second part of the operation, which, as before observed, is essentially a process of interpretation, will be resolvable into a syllogism or a series of syllogisms, the majors of which will be general propositions embracing whole classes of cases; every

^{c}MS, 43, 46, 51, 56   what the schoolmen termed
$^{d-d}$MS, 43, 46, 51, 56, 62   conclude
$^{e-e}$MS, 43, 46, 51, 56, 62   conclusion
^{f}MS, 43, 46, 51, 56, 62   also

one of which propositions must be true in all its extent, if *the* argument is maintainable. If, therefore, any fact fairly coming within the range of one of these general propositions, and consequently asserted by it, is known or suspected to be other than the proposition asserts it to be, this mode of stating the argument causes us to know or to suspect that the original observations, which are the real grounds of our conclusion, are not sufficient to support it. And in proportion to the greater chance of our detecting the inconclusiveness of our evidence, will be the increased reliance we are entitled to place in it if no such evidence of defect shall appear.

The value, therefore, of the syllogistic form, and of the rules for using it correctly, does not consist in their being the form and the rules according to which our reasonings are necessarily, or even usually, made; but in their furnishing us with a mode in which those reasonings may always be represented, and which is admirably calculated, if they are inconclusive, to bring their inconclusiveness to light. An induction from particulars to generals, followed by a syllogistic process from those generals to other particulars, is a form in which we may always state our *reasonings* if we please. It is not a form in which we *must* reason, but it is a form in which we *may* reason, and into which it is indispensable to throw our reasoning, when there is any doubt of its validity: though when the case is familiar and little complicated, and there is no suspicion of error, we may, and do, reason at once from the known particular cases to unknown ones.*

These are the uses of *i* syllogism, as a mode of verifying any given argument. Its ulterior uses, as respects the general course of our intellectual operations, hardly require illustration, being in fact the acknowledged uses of general language. They amount substantially to this, that the inductions may be made once for all: a single careful interrogation of experience may suffice, and the result may be registered in the form of a general proposition, which is committed to memory or to writing, and from which afterwards we have only to syllogize. The particulars of our experiments may then be dismissed from the memory, in which it would be impossible to retain so great a multitude of details; while the knowledge which those details afforded for

*[62] The language of ratiocination would, I think, be brought into closer agreement with the real nature of the process, if the general propositions employed in reasoning, instead of being in the form All men are mortal, or Every man is mortal, were expressed in the form Any man is mortal. This mode of expression, exhibiting as the type of all reasoning from experience "The men A, B, C, &c. are so and so, therefore *any* man is so and so," would much better manifest the true idea—that inductive reasoning is always, at bottom, inference from particulars to particulars, and that the whole function of general propositions in reasoning, is to vouch for the legitimacy of such inferences.

*g–g*MS, 43, 46   our   *h–h*MS   reasoning
*i*MS, 43, 46   the

future use, and which would otherwise be lost as soon as the observations were forgotten, or as their record became too bulky for reference, is retained in a commodious and immediately available shape by means of general language.

Against this advantage is to be set the countervailing inconvenience, that inferences originally made on insufficient evidence, become consecrated, and, as it were, hardened into general maxims; and the mind cleaves to them from habit, after it has outgrown any liability to be misled by similar fallacious appearances if they were now for the first time presented; but having forgotten the particulars, it does not think of revising its own former decision. An inevitable drawback, which, however considerable in itself, forms evidently but a *small set-off against* the immense *benefits* of general language.

The use of the syllogism is in truth no other than the use of general propositions in reasoning. We *can* reason without them; in simple and obvious cases we habitually do so; minds of great sagacity can do it in cases not simple and obvious, provided their experience supplies them with instances essentially similar to every combination of circumstances likely to arise. But other *minds, and the same minds where they have not* the same pre-eminent advantages of personal experience, are quite helpless without the aid of general propositions, wherever the case presents the smallest complication; and if we made no general propositions, few *persons* would get much beyond those simple inferences which are drawn by the more intelligent of the brutes. Though not necessary to reasoning, *general propositions* are necessary to any considerable progress in reasoning. It is, therefore, natural and indispensable to separate the process of investigation into two parts; and obtain general formulæ for determining what inferences may be drawn, before the occasion arises for drawing the inferences. The work of drawing them is then that of applying the formulæ; and the rules of *o* syllogism are a system of securities for the correctness of the application.

§ 6. [*The true type of reasoning, what*] To complete the series of considerations connected with the philosophical character of the syllogism, it is requisite to consider, since the syllogism is not the universal type of the reasoning process, what is the real type. This resolves itself into the question, what is the nature of the minor premise, and in what manner it contributes to establish the conclusion: for as to the major, we now fully understand,

*j–j*MS, 43, 46   trifling deduction from]   51, 56, 62, 65   small deduction from
*k–k*MS, 43, 46, 51, 56   advantages
*l–l*MS, 43, 46   men, or the same men when without]   51, 56   minds, or the same minds without]   62   minds, and the same minds without
*m–m*MS, 43, 46   of us
*n–n*MS   they
*o*MS, 43, 46   the

that the place which it nominally occupies in our reasonings, properly belongs to the individual facts or observations of which it expresses the general result; the major itself being no real part of the argument, but an intermediate halting-place for the mind, interposed by an artifice of language between the real premises and the conclusion, by way of a security, which it is in a most material degree, for the correctness of the process. The minor, however, being an indispensable part of the syllogistic expression of an argument, without doubt either is, or corresponds to, an equally indispensable part of the argument itself, and we have only to inquire what part.

It is perhaps worth while to notice here a speculation of *a philosopher to whom mental science is much*[a] indebted, but who, though a very penetrating, was a very hasty thinker, and whose want of due circumspection rendered him fully as remarkable for what he did not see, as for what he saw. I allude to Dr. Thomas Brown, whose theory of ratiocination is peculiar.[*] He saw the *petitio principii* which is inherent in every syllogism, if we consider the major to be itself the evidence by which the conclusion is proved, instead of being, what in fact it is, an assertion of the existence of evidence sufficient to prove any conclusion of a given description. Seeing this, Dr. Brown not only failed to see the immense advantage, in point of security for correctness, which is gained by interposing this step between the real evidence and the conclusion; but he thought it incumbent on him to strike out the major altogether from the reasoning process, without substituting anything else, and maintained that our reasonings consist only of the minor premise and the conclusion, Socrates is a man, therefore Socrates is mortal: thus actually suppressing, as an unnecessary step in the argument, the appeal to former experience. The absurdity of this was disguised from him by the opinion he adopted, that reasoning is merely analysing our own general notions, or abstract ideas; and that the proposition, Socrates is mortal, is evolved from the proposition, Socrates is a man, simply by recognising the notion of mortality as already contained in the notion we form of a man.

After the explanations so fully entered into on the subject of propositions, much further discussion cannot be necessary to make the radical error of this view of ratiocination apparent. If the word man connoted mortality; if the meaning of "mortal" were involved in the meaning of "man;" we might, undoubtedly, evolve the conclusion from the minor alone, because the minor would have *already*[b] asserted it. But if, as is in fact the case, the word man does not connote mortality, how does it appear that in the mind of every person who admits Socrates to be a man, the idea of man must include the idea of mortality? Dr. Brown could not help seeing this difficulty, and in

[*See *Lectures on the Philosophy of the Human Mind*, Vol. II, pp. 575ff.]

*[a–a]*MS, 43, 46, 51, 56   one of the philosophers to whom mental science is most
*[b–b]*MS, 43, 46, 51, 56, 62, 65   distinctly

order to avoid it, was led, contrary to his intention, to re-establish, under another name, that step in the argument which corresponds to the major, by affirming the necessity of *previously perceiving* the relation between the idea of man and the idea of mortal. If the reasoner has not previously perceived this relation, he will not, says Dr. Brown, infer because Socrates is a man, that Socrates is mortal. But even this admission, though amounting to a surrender of the doctrine that an argument consists of the minor and the conclusion alone, will not save the remainder of Dr. Brown's theory. The failure of assent to the argument does not take place merely because the reasoner, for want of due analysis, does not perceive that his idea of man includes the idea of mortality; it takes place, much more commonly, because in his mind that relation between the two ideas has never existed. And in truth it never does exist, except as the result of experience. Consenting, for the sake of the argument, to discuss the question on a supposition of which we have recognised the radical incorrectness, namely, that the meaning of a proposition relates to the ideas of the things spoken of, and not to the things themselves; *c* I must yet observe, that the idea of man, as an universal idea, the common property of all rational creatures, cannot involve anything but what is strictly implied in the name. If any one includes in his own private idea of man, as no doubt is *d* always the case, some other attributes, such for instance as mortality, he does so only as the consequence of experience, after having satisfied himself that all men possess that attribute: so that whatever the idea contains, in any person's mind, beyond what is included in the conventional signification of the word, has been added to it as the result of assent to a proposition; while Dr. Brown's theory requires us to suppose, on the contrary, that assent to the proposition is produced by evolving, through an analytic process, this very element out of the idea. This theory, therefore, may be considered as sufficiently refuted; and the minor premise must be regarded as totally insufficient to prove the conclusion, except with the assistance of the major, or of that which the major represents, namely, the various singular propositions expressive of the series of observations, of which the generalization called the major premise is the result.

In the argument, then, which proves that Socrates is mortal, one indispensable part of the premises will be as follows: "My father, and my father's father, A, B, C, and an indefinite number of other persons, were mortal;" which is only an expression in different words of the observed fact that they have died. This is the major premise divested of the *petitio principii*, and cut down to as much as is really known by direct evidence.

In order to connect this proposition with the conclusion Socrates is mortal, the additional link necessary is such a proposition as the following: "Socrates

*c*MS, 43, 46   and conceding for a moment the existence of abstract ideas,
*d*MS, 43, 46, 51   almost

resembles my father, and my father's father, and the other individuals specified." This proposition we assert when we say that Socrates is a man. By saying so we likewise assert in what respect he resembles them, namely, in the attributes connoted by the word man. And [e] we conclude that he further resembles them in the attribute mortality.

§ 7. [*Relation between Induction and Deduction*] We have thus obtained what we were seeking, an universal type of the reasoning process. We find it resolvable in all cases into the following elements: Certain individuals have a given attribute; an individual or individuals resemble the former in certain other attributes; therefore they resemble them also in the given attribute. This type of ratiocination does not claim, like the syllogism, to be conclusive from the mere form of the expression; nor can it possibly be so. That one proposition does or does not assert the very fact which was already asserted in another, may appear from the form of the expression, that is, from a comparison of the language; but when the two propositions assert facts which are *bonâ fide* different, whether the one fact proves the other or not can never appear from the language, but must depend on other considerations. Whether, from the attributes in which Socrates resembles those [a]men[a] who have heretofore died, it is allowable to infer that he resembles them also in being mortal, is a question of Induction; and is to be decided by the principles or canons which we shall hereafter recognise as tests of the correct performance of that great mental operation.

Meanwhile, however, it is certain, as before remarked, that if this inference can be drawn as to Socrates, it can be drawn as to all others who resemble the observed individuals in the same attributes in which he resembles them; that is (to express the thing concisely) of all [b]mankind[b]. If, therefore, the argument be [c]admissible[c] in the case of Socrates, we are at liberty, once for all, to treat the possession of the attributes of man as a mark, or satisfactory evidence, of the attribute of mortality. This we do by laying down the universal proposition, All men are mortal, and interpreting this, as occasion arises, in its application to Socrates and others. By this means we establish a very convenient division of the entire logical operation into two steps; first, that of ascertaining what attributes are marks of mortality; and, secondly, whether any given individuals possess those marks. And it will generally be advisable, in our speculations on the reasoning process, to consider this double operation as in fact taking place, and all reasoning as [d] carried on in the form into which it must necessarily be thrown to enable us to apply to it any test of its correct performance.

[e]MS, 43, 46, 51, 56   from this
[a–a]+43, 46, 51, 56, 62, 65, 68, 72   [b–b]MS, 43, 46   men
[c–c]MS, 43, 46, 51, 56   conclusive   [d]MS   being

Although, therefore, all processes of thought in which the ultimate premises are particulars, whether we conclude from particulars to a general formula, or from particulars to other particulars according to that formula, are equally Induction; we shall yet, conformably to usage, consider the name Induction as more peculiarly belonging to the process of establishing the general proposition, and the remaining operation, which is substantially that of interpreting the general proposition, we shall call by its usual name, Deduction. And we shall consider every process by which anything is inferred respecting an unobserved case, as consisting of an Induction followed by a Deduction; because, although the process needs not necessarily be carried on in this form, it is always susceptible of the form, and must be thrown into it when assurance of scientific accuracy is needed and desired. *e*

a§ 8. [*Objections answered*] The theory of the syllogism laid down in the preceding pages, has obtained, among other important adhesions, three of peculiar value; those of Sir John Herschel,* Dr. Whewell,† and Mr. Bailey;‡ Sir John Herschel considering the doctrine, though not strictly "a discovery," *b*having been anticipated by Berkeley,*b*§ to be "one of the greatest steps which have yet been made in the philosophy of Logic." "When we consider" (to quote the further words of the same authority) "the inveteracy of the habits and prejudices which it has cast to the winds," there is no cause for misgiving in the fact that other thinkers, no less entitled to consideration, have formed a very different estimate of it. Their principal objection cannot be better or more succinctly stated than by borrowing a sentence from Archbishop Whately.‖ "In every case where an inference is drawn from Induction (un-

*[62] Review of Quetelet on Probabilities, *Essays* [London: Longman, 1857], pp. 366–7.

†[62] *Philosophy of Discovery*, p. 289.

‡[62] *Theory of Reasoning*, Chap. iv, to which I may refer for an able statement and enforcement of the grounds of the doctrine.

§[62] *c*On a recent careful reperusal of Berkeley's whole works, I have been unable to find this doctrine in them. Sir John Herschel probably meant that it is implied in Berkeley's argument against abstract ideas. But I cannot find that Berkeley saw the implication, or had ever asked himself what bearing his argument had on the theory of the syllogism. Still less can I admit that the doctrine*c* is (as has been affirmed by one of my ablest and most candid critics) "among the standing marks of what is called the empirical philosophy."

‖[62] *Logic*, Bk. IV, Chap. i, § 1 [p. 234].

*e*51, 56 Note Supplementary to the Preceding Chapter [*see* Appendix B *and* p. 205n *below*]

*a–a*205+62, 65, 68, 72

b b+72

*c–c*62, 65, 68 It is very probable that the doctrine is not new, and that it was, as Sir John Herschel thinks, substantially anticipated by Berkeley. But I certainly am not aware that it

less that name is to be given to a mere random guess without any grounds at all) we must form a judgment that the instance or instances adduced are *sufficient* to authorize the conclusion; that it is *allowable* to take these instances as a sample warranting an inference respecting the whole class;" and the expression of this judgment in words (it has been said by several of my critics) *is* the major premise.

I quite admit that the major is an affirmation of the sufficiency of the evidence on which the conclusion rests. That it is so, is the very essence of my own theory. And whoever admits that the major premise is *only* this, adopts the theory in its essentials.

But I cannot concede that this recognition of the sufficiency of the evidence—that is, of the correctness of the induction—is a part of the induction itself; unless we ought to say that it is a part of everything we do, to satisfy ourselves that it has been done rightly. We conclude from known instances to unknown by the impulse of the generalizing propensity; and (until after a considerable amount of practice and mental discipline) the question of the sufficiency of the evidence is only raised by a retrospective act, turning back upon our own footsteps, and examining whether we were warranted in doing what we have *d*provisionally*d* done. To speak of this reflex operation as part of the original one, requiring to be expressed in words in order that the verbal formula may correctly represent the psychological process, appears to me false psychology.* We review our syllogistic as well as our inductive processes, and recognise that they have been correctly performed; but logicians do not add a third premise to the syllogism, to express this act of recognition. A careful copyist verifies his transcript by collating it with the original; and if no error appears, he recognises that the transcript has been correctly made. But we do not call the examination of the copy a part of the act of copying.

The conclusion in an induction is inferred from the evidence itself, and not from a recognition of the sufficiency of the evidence; as I infer that my friend is walking towards me because I see him, and not because I recognise that my eyes are open, and that eyesight is a means of knowledge. In all operations which require care, it is good to assure ourselves that the process has been performed accurately; but the testing of the process is not the process itself; and, besides, may have been omitted altogether, and yet the process be correct. It is precisely because that operation is omitted in ordinary unscientific reasoning, that there is anything gained in certainty by throwing reasoning into the syllogistic form. To make sure, as far as possible, that it

---

*[62] See the important chapter on Belief, in *e*Professor*e* Bain's great treatise, *The Emotions and the Will* [London: Parker, 1859], pp. 581–4.

d–*d*62, 65, 68   already
e–*e*62   Mr.

shall not be omitted, we make the testing operation a part of the reasoning process itself. We insist that the inference from particulars to particulars shall pass through a general proposition. But this is a security for good reasoning, not a condition of all reasoning; and in some cases not even a security. Our most familiar inferences are all made before we learn the use of general propositions; and a person of untutored sagacity will skilfully apply his acquired experience to adjacent cases, though he would bungle grievously in fixing the limits of the appropriate general theorem. But though he may conclude rightly, he never, properly speaking, knows whether he has done so or not; he has not tested his reasoning. Now, this is precisely what forms of reasoning do for us. We do not need them to enable us to reason, but to enable us to know whether we reason correctly.

In still further answer to the objection, it may be added that—even when the test has been applied, and the sufficiency of the evidence recognised—if it is sufficient to support the general proposition, it is sufficient also to support an inference from particulars to particulars without passing through the general proposition. The inquirer who has logically satisfied himself that the conditions of legitimate induction were realized in the cases A, B, C, would be as much justified in concluding directly to the Duke of Wellington as in concluding to all men. The general conclusion is never legitimate, unless the particular one would be so too; and in no sense, intelligible to me, can the particular conclusion be said to be drawn from the general one. Whenever there is ground for drawing any conclusion at all from particular instances, there is ground for a general conclusion; but that this general conclusion should be actually drawn, however useful, cannot be an indispensable condition of the validity of the inference in the particular case. A man gives away sixpence by the same power by which he disposes of his whole fortune; but it is not necessary to the legality of the smaller act, that he should make a formal assertion of his right to *f* the greater one.

Some additional remarks, in reply to minor objections, are appended.*ᵃ

*[62] A writer in the *British Quarterly Review* (August, 1846), in a review of this treatise, endeavours to show that there is no *petitio principii* in the syllogism, by denying *g*that the proposition. All men are mortal, asserts or assumes that Socrates is mortal. In support of this denial, he argues that we may, and in fact do, admit the general proposition that all men are mortal, without having particularly examined the case of Socrates, and even without knowing whether the individual so named is a man or something else. But this of course was never denied. That we can and do draw conclusions concerning cases specifically unknown to us, is the datum from which all who discuss this subject must set out. The question is, in what terms the evidence, or ground, on which we draw these conclusions,

*f*62, 65   do
*g–g*208[*also in* 51, 56 *at the end of* §7; *see* p. 203ᵉ *above, and see also* Appendix B, *where the other variants are given*]

^a§ 9. [*Of Formal Logic, and its relation to the Logic of Truth*] The pre-
ceding considerations enable us to understand the true nature of what is
termed, by recent writers, Formal Logic, and the relation between it and
Logic in the widest sense. Logic, as I conceive it, is the entire theory of the
ascertainment of reasoned or inferred truth. Formal Logic, therefore, which
Sir William Hamilton from his own point of view, and Archbishop Whately
from his, have represented as the whole of Logic properly so called, is really
a very subordinate part of it, not being directly concerned with the process
of Reasoning or Inference in the sense in which that process is a part of the
Investigation of Truth. What, then, is Formal Logic? The name seems to be

---

may best be designated—whether it is most correct to say, that the unknown
case is proved by known cases, or that it is proved by a general proposition including both sets of cases, the unknown and the known? I contend for the former
mode of expression. I hold it an abuse of language to say, that the proof that
Socrates is mortal, is that all men are mortal. Turn it in what way we will, this
seems to me to be asserting that a thing is the proof of itself. Whoever pronounces the words, All men are mortal, has affirmed that Socrates is mortal,
though he may never have heard of Socrates; for since Socrates, whether known
to be so or not, really is a man, he is included in the words, All men, and in every
assertion of which they are the subject. If the reviewer does not see that there is
a difficulty here, I can only advise him to reconsider the subject until he does: after
which he will be a better judge of the success or failure of an attempt to remove
the difficulty. That he had reflected very little on the point when he wrote his
remarks, is shown by his oversight respecting the *dictum de omni et nullo.* He
acknowledges [p. 27] that this maxim as commonly expressed,—"Whatever is
true of a class, is true of everything included in the class," is a mere identical
proposition, since the class *is* nothing but the things included in it. But he thinks
this defect would be cured by wording the maxim thus,—"Whatever is true of a
class, is true of everything which *can be shown* to be a member of the class:" as
if a thing could "be shown" to be a member of the class without being one. If a
class means the sum of all the things included in the class, the things which can
"be shown" to be included in it are part of the sum, and the *dictum* is as much an
identical proposition with respect to them as to the rest. One would almost
imagine that, in the reviewer's opinion, things are not members of a class until
they are called up publicly to take their place in it—that so long, in fact, as
Socrates is not known to be a man, he *is not* a man, and any assertion which can
be made concerning men does not at all regard him, nor is affected as to its truth
or falsity by anything in which he is concerned.
    The difference between the reviewer's theory and mine may be thus stated.
Both admit that when we say, All men are mortal, we make an assertion reaching
beyond the sphere of our knowledge of individual cases; and that when a new
individual, Socrates, is brought within the field of our knowledge by means of the
minor premise, we learn that we have already made an assertion respecting
Socrates without knowing it: our own general formula being, to that extent, for
the first time *interpreted* to us. But according to the reviewer's theory, the smaller

a—a208+65, 68, 72

properly applied to all that portion of doctrine which relates to the equivalence of different modes of expression; the rules for determining when assertions in a given form imply or suppose the truth or falsity of other assertions. This includes the theory of the Import of Propositions, and of their Conversion, Æquipollence, and Opposition; of those falsely called Inductions

---

assertion is proved by the larger: while I contend, that both assertions are proved together, by the same evidence, namely, the grounds of experience on which the general assertion was made, and by which it must be justified.

The reviewer says [p. 22], that if the major premise included the conclusion, "we should be able to affirm the conclusion without the intervention of the minor premise; but every one sees that that is impossible." A similar argument is urged by Mr. De Morgan (*Formal Logic*, p. 259): "The whole objection tacitly assumes the superfluity of the minor; that is, tacitly assumes we know Socrates* to be a man as soon as we know him to be Socrates." The objection would be well grounded if the assertion that the major premise includes the conclusion, meant that it individually specifies all it includes. As however the only indication it gives is a description by marks, we have still to compare any new individual with the marks; and to show that this comparison has been made, is the office of the minor. But since, by supposition, the new individual has the marks, whether we have ascertained him to have them or not; if we have affirmed the major premise, we have asserted him to be mortal. Now my position is that this assertion cannot be a necessary part of the argument. It cannot be a necessary condition of reasoning that we should begin by making an assertion, which is afterwards to be employed in proving a part of itself. I can conceive only one way out of this difficulty, viz. that what really forms the proof is *the other* part of the assertion; the portion of it, the truth of which has been ascertained previously: and that the unproved part is bound up in one formula with the proved part in mere anticipation, and as a memorandum of the nature of the conclusions which we are prepared to prove.

With respect to the minor premise in its formal shape, the minor as it stands in the syllogism, predicating of Socrates a definite class name, I readily admit that it is no more a necessary part of reasoning than the major. When there is a major, doing its work by means of a class name, minors are needed to interpret it: but reasoning can be carried on without either the one or the other. They are not the conditions of reasoning, but a precaution against erroneous reasoning. The only minor premise necessary to reasoning in the example under consideration, is, Socrates is *like* A, B, C, and the other individuals who are known to have died. And this is the only universal type of that step in the reasoning process which is represented by the minor. Experience, however, of the uncertainty of this loose mode of inference, teaches the expediency of determining beforehand what *kind* of likeness to the cases observed, is necessary to bring an unobserved case within the same predicate; and the answer to this question is the major. *h*The minor then identifies the precise kind of likeness possessed by Socrates, as being the kind required by the formula.*h* Thus the syllogistic major and the syllogistic

---

*[56] Mr. De Morgan says "Plato," but to prevent confusion I have kept to my own *exemplum*.

h–h+72

(to be hereafter spoken of*), in which the apparent generalization is a mere abridged statement of cases known individually; and finally, of the syllogism: while the theory of Naming, and *b*of (what is inseparably connected with it)*b* Definition, though belonging still more to the other and larger kind of logic than to this, is a necessary preliminary to this. The end aimed at by Formal Logic, and attained by the observance of its precepts, is not truth, but consistency. It has been seen that this is the only direct purpose of the rules of the syllogism; the intention and effect of which is simply to keep our inferences or conclusions in complete consistency with our general formulæ or directions for drawing them. The Logic of Consistency is a necessary auxiliary to the logic of truth, not only because what is inconsistent with itself or with other truths cannot be true, but also because truth can only be successfully pursued by drawing inferences from experience, which, if warrantable at all, admit of being generalized, and, to test their warrantableness, require to be exhibited in a generalized form; after which the correctness of their application to particular cases is a question which specially concerns the Logic of Consistency. This Logic, not requiring any preliminary knowledge of the processes or conclusions of the various sciences, may be studied with benefit in a much earlier stage of education than the Logic of Truth: and the practice which has empirically obtained of teaching it apart, through elementary treatises which do not attempt to include anything else, though the reasons assigned for the practice are in general very far from philosophical, admits of *c* philosophical justification.*a*

---

minor start into existence together, and are called forth by the same exigency. When we conclude from personal experience without referring to any record—to any general theorems, either written, or traditional, or mentally registered by ourselves as conclusions of our own drawing—we do not use, in our thoughts, either a major or a minor, such as the syllogism puts into words. When, however, we revise this rough inference from particulars to particulars, and substitute a careful one, the revision consists in selecting two syllogistic premises. But this neither alters nor adds to the evidence we had before; it only puts us in a better position for judging whether our inference from particulars to particulars is well grounded.*g*

*Infra, Bk. III, Chap. ii [pp. 288ff.].

*b–b*65   (what . . . it) of
*c*65, 68   a

CHAPTER IV

Of Trains of Reasoning, and Deductive Sciences

§ 1. [*For what purpose trains of reasoning exist*] In our analysis of the syllogism, it appeared that the minor premise always affirms a resemblance between a new case and some cases previously known; while the major premise asserts something which, having been found true of those known cases, we consider ourselves warranted in holding true of any other case resembling the former in certain given particulars.

If all ratiocinations resembled, as to the minor premise, the examples which ªwereª exclusively employed in the preceding chapter; if the resemblance, which that premise asserts, were obvious to the senses, as in the proposition "Socrates is a man," or were at once ascertainable by direct observation; there would be no necessity for trains of reasoning, and Deductive or Ratiocinative Sciences would not exist. Trains of reasoning exist only for the sake of extending an induction founded, as all inductions must be, on observed cases, to other cases in which we not only cannot directly observe ᵇthe fact whichᵇ is to be proved, but cannot directly observe even the mark which is to prove it.

§ 2. [*A train of reasoning is a series of inductive inferences*] Suppose the syllogism to be, All cows ruminate, the animal which is before me is a cow, therefore it ruminates. The minor, if true at all, is obviously so: the only premise the establishment of which requires any anterior process of inquiry, is the major; and provided the induction of which that premise is the expression was correctly performed, the conclusion respecting the animal now present will be instantly drawn; because, as soon as she is compared with the formula, she will be identified as being included in it. But suppose the syllogism to be the following:—All arsenic is poisonous, the substance which is before me is arsenic, therefore it is poisonous. The truth of the minor may not here be obvious at first sight; it may not be intuitively evident, but may itself be known only by inference. It may be the conclusion of another argu-

ª⁻ªMS, 43, 46   we
ᵇ⁻ᵇMS, 43, 46, 51, 56, 62, 65, 68   what

ment, which, thrown into the syllogistic form, would stand thus:—Whatever
*a*when lighted produces a dark spot on a piece of white porcelain held in the
flame, which spot is soluble in *b*hypochloride*b* of calcium*a*, is arsenic; the
substance before me conforms to this condition; therefore it is arsenic. To
establish, therefore, the ultimate conclusion, The substance before me is
poisonous, requires a process, which, in order to be syllogistically expressed,
stands in need of two syllogisms; and we have a Train of Reasoning.

When, however, we thus add syllogism to syllogism, we are really adding
induction to induction. Two separate inductions must have taken place to
render this chain of inference possible; inductions founded, probably, on
different sets of individual instances, but which converge in their results, so
that the instance which is the subject of inquiry comes within the range of
them both. The record of these inductions is contained in the majors of the
two syllogisms. First, we, or others *c*for*c* us, have examined various objects
which yielded under the given circumstances *d*a dark spot with the given
property*d*, and found that they possessed the properties connoted by the
word arsenic; they were metallic, volatile, their vapour had a smell of garlic,
and so forth. Next, we, or others *e*for*e* us, have examined various specimens
which possessed this metallic and volatile character, whose vapour had this
smell, &c., and have invariably found that they were poisonous. The first
observation we judge that we may extend to all substances whatever which
yield *f*that particular kind of dark spot*f*; the second, to all metallic and
volatile substances resembling those we examined; and consequently, not to
those only which are seen to be such, but to those which are concluded to be
such by the prior induction. The substance before us is only seen to come
within one of these inductions; but by means of this one, it is brought within
the other. We are still, as before, concluding from particulars to particulars;
but we are now concluding from particulars observed, to other particulars
which are not, as in the *g*simple*g* case, *seen* to resemble them in *h* material
points, but *inferred* to do so, because resembling them in something else,
which we have been led by quite a different set of instances to consider as a
mark of the former resemblance.

This first example of a train of reasoning is still extremely simple, the series
consisting of only two syllogisms. The following is somewhat more compli-

---

*a–a*MS, 43, 46, 51, 56, 62, 65   forms a compound with hydrogen, which yields a
black precipitate with nitrate of silver
*b–b*68   hypochlorite [*printer's error?*]
*c–c*MS, 43   before
*d–d*MS, 43, 46, 51, 56, 62, 65   the given precipitate
*e–e*MS, 43   before
*f–f*MS, 43, 46, 51, 56, 62, 65   the precipitate
*g–g*MS   simpler
*h*MS, 43, 46, 51, 56, 62, 65, 68   the

cated:—No government, which earnestly seeks the good of its subjects, is
*i*likely to be overthrown; some particular government earnestly seeks the
good of its subjects, therefore it is not likely to be overthrown*i*. The major
premise in this argument we shall suppose not to be derived from considerations *à priori*, but to be a generalization from history, which, whether correct
or erroneous, must have been founded on observation of governments concerning whose desire of the good of their subjects there was no doubt. It has
been found, or thought to be found, that these were not *j*easily overthrown*j*,
and it has been deemed that those instances warranted an extension of the
same predicate to any and every government which resembles them in the
attribute of desiring earnestly the good of its subjects. But *does* the *k*government in question*k* thus resemble them? This may be debated *pro* and *con* by
many arguments, and must, in any case, be proved by another induction; for
we cannot directly observe the sentiments and desires of the persons who
*l*carry on the government*l*. To prove the minor, therefore, we require an
argument in this form: Every government which acts in a certain manner,
desires the good of its subjects; the *m*supposed*m* government acts in that
particular manner, therefore it desires the good of its subjects. But is it true
that the *n* government acts in the manner supposed? This minor also may require proof; still another induction, as thus:—What is asserted by *o*intelligent
and disinterested witnesses, may*o* be believed to be true; that the *p* government acts in this manner, is asserted by *q*such witnesses, therefore it may*q* be
believed to be true. The argument hence consists of three steps. Having the
evidence of our senses that the case of the *r*government under consideration*r*
resembles a number of former cases, in the circumstance of having something
asserted respecting it by *s*intelligent and*s* disinterested witnesses, we infer,
first, that, as in those former instances, so in this instance, the assertion is
true. Secondly, what was asserted of the *t* government being that it acts in a
particular manner, and other governments or persons having been observed
to act in the same manner, the *u*government in question*u* is brought into

*i–i*MS, 43, 46   liable to revolution; the Prussian government earnestly seeks the
good of its subjects, therefore it is not in danger of revolution
*j–j*MS, 43, 46   liable to revolution]   51, 56   likely to be overthrown
*k–k*MS, 43, 46   Prussian government
*l–l*MS, 43, 46   conduct the government of that country
*m–m*MS, 43, 46   Prussian
*n*MS, 43, 46   Prussian
*o–o*MS, 43, 46   many disinterested witnesses, must
*p*MS, 43, 46   Prussian
*q–q*MS, 43, 46   many disinterested witnesses, therefore it must
*r–r*MS, 43, 46   Prussian government
*s–s*MS, 43, 46   many
*t*MS, 43, 46   Prussian
*u–u*MS, 43, 46   Prussian government

known resemblance with those other governments or persons; and since they were known to desire the good of the people, *v*it is thereupon, by a second induction, inferred that the particular government spoken of,*v* desires the good of the people. This brings that government into known resemblance with the other governments which were *w*thought likely*w* to escape revolution, and thence, by a third induction, *x*it is *v*concluded*v* that this particular government is also likely to*x* escape. *z*This is*z* still reasoning from particulars to particulars, but we now reason to the new instance from three distinct sets of former instances: to one only of those sets of instances do we directly perceive the new one to be similar; but from that similarity we inductively infer that it has the attribute by which it is assimilated to the next set, and brought within the corresponding induction; *a*after which*a* by a repetition of the same operation we infer it to be similar to the third set, and *b*hence*b* a third induction conducts us to the ultimate conclusion.

§ 3. [*A train of reasoning is a series of inductive inferences from particulars to particulars through marks of marks*] Notwithstanding the superior complication of these examples, compared with those by which in the preceding chapter we illustrated the general theory of reasoning, every doctrine which we then laid down holds equally true in these more intricate cases. The successive general propositions are not steps in the reasoning, are not intermediate links in the chain of inference, between the particulars observed and those to which we apply the observation. If we had sufficiently capacious memories, and a sufficient power of maintaining order among a huge mass of details, the reasoning could go on without any general propositions; they are mere formulæ for inferring particulars from particulars. The principle of general reasoning is (as before explained), that if, from observation of certain known particulars, what was seen to be true of them can be inferred to be true of any others, it may be inferred of all others which are of a certain description. And in order that we may never fail to draw this conclusion in a new case when it can be drawn correctly, and may avoid drawing it when it

*v–v*MS, 43, 46   we thereupon, by a second induction, infer that the Prussian government

*w–w*MS, 43, 46   observed

*x–x*MS, 43, 46   we predict that the Prussian government will in like manner

*v–v*51, 56, 62   predicted]   65   predicated [*printer's error?*]

*z–z*MS, 43, 46   And thus we are enabled to reason from the well-intentioned governments which we historically know as having escaped revolution, to other governments which, when we made the induction, we may have known nothing about: yet if the induction was good, and therefore applicable to all governments of which we know the intentions but do not know the fortunes, it must be no less applicable to those whose intentions we do not know, but can only infer, provided this inference also rests upon a good induction. We are

*a–a*MS, 43   when

*b–b*MS   thence

cannot, we determine once for all what are the distinguishing marks by which such cases may be recognised. The subsequent process is merely that of identifying an object, and ascertaining it to have those marks; whether we identify it by the very marks themselves, or by others which we have ascertained (through another and a similar process) to be marks of those marks. The real inference is always from particulars to particulars, from the observed instances to an unobserved one: but in drawing this inference, we conform to a formula which we have adopted for our guidance in such operations, and which is a record of the criteria by which we thought we had ascertained that we might distinguish when the inference could, and when it could not, be drawn. The real premises are the individual observations, even though they may have been forgotten, or, being the observations of others and not of ourselves, may, to us, never have been known: but we have before us proof that we or others once thought them sufficient for an induction, and we have marks to show whether any new case is one of those to which, if then known, the induction would have been deemed to extend. These marks we either recognise at once, or by the aid of other marks, which by another previous induction we collected to be marks of ᵃthe firstᵃ. Even these marks of marks may only be recognised through a third set of marks; and we may have a train of reasoning, of any length, to bring a new case within the scope of an induction grounded on particulars its similarity to which is only ascertained in this indirect manner.

Thus, in the ᵇpreceding exampleᵇ, the ultimate inductive inference was, that ᶜa certain government was not likely to be overthrownᶜ; this inference was drawn according to a formula in which desire of the public good was set down as a mark of not being ᵈlikely to be overthrownᵈ; a mark of this mark was, acting in a particular manner; and a mark of acting in that manner was, being asserted to do so by ᵉintelligent andᵉ disinterested witnesses: this mark, the ᶠgovernment under discussionᶠ was recognised by the senses as possessing. Hence that government fell within the last induction, and by it was brought within all the others. The perceived resemblance of the case to one set of observed particular cases, brought it into known resemblance with another set, and that with a third.

In the more complex branches of knowledge, the deductions seldom consist, as in the examples hitherto exhibited, of a single chain, a a mark of b, b of c, c of d, therefore a a mark of d. They consist (to carry on the same metaphor) of several chains united at the extremity, as thus: a a mark of d,

ᵃ⁻ᵃMS, 43, 46, 51, 56, 62 *them*
ᵇ⁻ᵇMS, 43, 46 argument concerning the Prussian government
ᶜ⁻ᶜMS, 43, 46 it was not liable to revolution
ᵈ⁻ᵈMS, 43, 46 liable to revolution
ᵉ⁻ᵉMS, 43, 46 many
ᶠ⁻ᶠMS, 43, 46 Prussian government

b of *e*, *c* of *f*, *d e f* of *n*, therefore *a b c* a mark of *n*. Suppose, for example, the following combination of circumstances; 1st, rays of light impinging on a reflecting surface; 2nd, that surface parabolic; 3rd, those rays parallel to each other and to the axis of the surface. It is to be proved that the concourse of these three circumstances is a mark that the reflected rays will pass through the focus of the parabolic surface. Now, each of the three circumstances is singly a mark of something material to the case. Rays of light impinging on a reflecting surface are a mark that those rays will be reflected at an angle equal to the angle of incidence. The parabolic form of the surface, is a mark that, from any point of it, a line drawn to the focus and a line parallel to the axis will make equal angles with the surface. And finally, the parallelism of the rays to the axis is a mark that their angle of incidence coincides with one of these equal angles. The three marks taken together are therefore a mark of all these three things united. But the three united are evidently a mark that the angle of reflection must coincide with the other of the two equal angles, that formed by a line drawn to the focus; and this again, by the fundamental axiom concerning straight lines, is a mark that the reflected rays pass through the focus. Most chains of physical deduction are of this more complicated type; and even in mathematics such are abundant, as in all propositions where the hypothesis includes numerous conditions: "*If* a circle be taken, and *if* within that circle a point be taken, not the centre, and *if* straight lines be drawn from that point to the circumference, then," &c.

§ 4. [*Why there are deductive sciences*] The considerations now stated remove a serious difficulty from the view we have taken of reasoning; which *a*view*a* might otherwise have seemed not easily reconcilable with the fact that there are Deductive or Ratiocinative Sciences. It might seem to follow, if all reasoning be induction, that the difficulties of philosophical investigation must lie in the inductions exclusively, and that when these were easy, and susceptible of no doubt or hesitation, there could be no science, or, at least, no difficulties in science. The existence, for example, of an extensive Science of Mathematics, requiring the highest scientific genius in those who contributed to its creation, and calling for a most continued and vigorous exertion of intellect in order to appropriate it when created, may seem hard to be accounted for on the foregoing theory. But the considerations more recently adduced remove the mystery, by showing, that even when the inductions themselves are obvious, there may be much difficulty in finding whether the particular case which is the subject of inquiry comes within them; and ample room for scientific ingenuity in so combining various inductions, as, by means of one within which the case evidently falls, to bring it within others in which it cannot be directly seen to be included.

a–a+43, 46, 51, 56, 62, 65, 68, 72

When the more obvious of the inductions which can be made in any science from direct *observations*, have been made, and general formulas have been framed, determining the limits within which these inductions are applicable; as often as a new case can be at once seen to come within one of the formulas, the induction is applied to the new case, and the business is ended. But new cases are continually arising, which do not obviously come within any formula whereby the *question* we want solved in respect *of* them could be answered. Let us take an instance from geometry: and as it is taken only for illustration, let the reader concede to us for the present, what we shall endeavour to prove in the next chapter, that the first principles of geometry are results of induction. Our example shall be the fifth proposition of the first book of Euclid. The inquiry is, Are the angles at the base of an isosceles triangle equal or unequal? The first thing to be considered is, what inductions we have, from which we can infer equality or inequality. For inferring equality we have the following formulæ:—Things which being applied to each other coincide, are equals. Things which are equal to the same thing are equals. A whole and the sum of its parts are equals. The sums of equal things are equals. The differences of equal things are equals. There are no other *original* formulæ to prove equality. For inferring inequality we have the following: A whole and its *parts* are unequals. The sums of equal things and unequal things are unequals. The differences of equal things and unequal things are unequals. In all, eight formulæ. The angles at the base of an isosceles triangle do not obviously come within any of these. The formulæ specify certain marks of equality and of inequality, but the angles cannot be perceived intuitively to have any of those marks. *g* On examination it appears that they have; and we ultimately succeed in bringing them within *the* formula, "The differences of equal things are equal." Whence *comes* the difficulty *of* recognising these angles as the differences of equal things? Because each of them is the difference not of one pair only, but of innumerable pairs of angles; and out of these we had to imagine and select two, which could either be intuitively perceived to be equals, or possessed some of the marks of equality set down in the various formulæ. By an exercise of ingenuity, which, on the part of the first inventor, deserves to be regarded as considerable, two pairs of angles were hit upon, which united these requisites. First, it could be perceived intuitively that their differences were the angles at the base; and, secondly, they possessed one of the marks of equality,

b–bMS observation   c–cMS, 43, 46   questions
d–dMS to   e–e+68, 72
f–fMS part
gMS, 43, 46, 51 We can, however, examine whether they have properties which, in any other formulæ, are set down as marks of those marks.
h–hMS, 43, 46, 51, 56, 62, 65 this   i–iMS came
j–jMS, 43, 46, 51 in

namely, coincidence when applied to one another. This coincidence, how-ever, was not perceived intuitively, but inferred, in conformity to another formula.

[k]For greater clearness, I[k] subjoin an analysis of the demonstration. Euclid, it will be remembered, demonstrates his fifth proposition by means of the fourth.[*] This it is not allowable for us to do, because we are undertaking to trace deductive truths not to prior deductions, but to their original inductive foundation. We must therefore use the premises of the fourth proposition instead of its conclusion, and prove the fifth directly from first principles. To do so requires six formulas. (We must begin, as in Euclid, by prolonging the equal sides AB, AC, to equal distances, and joining the extremities BE, DC.)

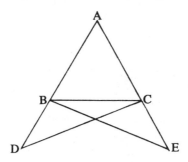

FIRST FORMULA. *The sums of equals are equal.*

AD and AE are sums of equals by the supposition. Having that mark of equality, they are concluded by this formula to be equal.

SECOND FORMULA. *Equal straight lines [l]or angles,[l] being applied to one another, coincide.*

AC, AB, are within this formula by supposition; AD, AE, have been brought within it by the preceding step. [m]The angle at A considered as an angle of the triangle ABE, and the same angle considered as an angle of the triangle ACD, are of course within the formula. All these pairs therefore possess the property which, according to the second formula, is a mark that when applied to one another they will coincide. Conceive them, then, applied to one another, by turning over the triangle ABE, and laying it on the triangle ACD in such a manner that AB of the one shall lie upon AC of the other.

[*See Playfair, *Elements of Geometry*, pp. 26–7.]

[k–k]MS, 43, 46   To make all clear, we
[l–l]+72
[m–m]MS, 43, 46, 51, 56, 62, 65, 68   Both these pairs of straight lines have the prop-erty of equality; which, according to the second formula, is a mark that, if applied to each other, they will coincide. Coinciding altogether means coinciding in every part

Then, by the equality of the angles, AE will lie on AD. But AB and AC, AE and AD are equals; therefore they will coincide altogether[m], and of course at their extremities, D, E, and B, C.

THIRD FORMULA. *Straight lines, having their extremities coincident, coincide.*

BE and [n]CD[n] have been brought within this formula by the preceding induction; they will, therefore, coincide.

FOURTH FORMULA. *Angles, having their sides coincident, coincide.*

[o]The third induction having shown that BE and CD coincide, and the second that AB, AC[o], coincide, the angles ABE and ACD are thereby brought within the fourth formula, and accordingly coincide.

FIFTH FORMULA. *Things which coincide are equal.*

The angles ABE and ACD are brought within this formula by the induction immediately preceding. This train of reasoning being also applicable, *mutatis mutandis*, to the angles EBC, DCB, these also are brought within the fifth formula. And, finally,

SIXTH FORMULA. *The differences of equals are equal.*

The angle ABC being the difference of ABE, CBE, and the angle ACB being the difference of ACD, DCB; which have been proved to be equals; ABC and ACB are brought within the last formula by the whole of the previous process.

The difficulty here encountered is chiefly that of figuring to ourselves the two angles at the base of the triangle ABC as remainders made by cutting one pair of angles out of another, while each pair shall be corresponding angles of triangles which have two sides and the intervening angle equal. It is by this happy contrivance that so many different inductions are brought to bear upon the same particular case. And this not being at all an obvious [p]thought[p], it may be seen from an example so near the threshold of mathematics, how much scope there may well be for scientific dexterity in the higher branches of that and other sciences, in order so to combine a few simple inductions, as to bring within each of them innumerable cases which are not obviously included in it; and how long, and numerous, and compli-

---

[n-n]MS, 43   DC
[o-o]MS, 43   The two previous inductions having shown that BE and DC coincide, and that AD, AE
[p-p]MS, 43, 46, 51, 56   idea

cated may be the processes necessary for bringing the inductions together, even when each induction may itself be very easy and simple. All the inductions involved in all geometry are comprised in those simple ones, the formulæ of which are the Axioms, and a few of the so-called Definitions. The remainder of the science is made up of the processes employed for bringing unforeseen cases within these inductions; or (in syllogistic language) for proving the minors necessary to complete the syllogisms; the majors being the definitions and axioms. In those definitions and axioms are laid down the whole of the marks, by an artful combination of which *it has been found possible* to discover and prove all that is proved in geometry. The marks being so few, and the inductions which furnish them being so obvious and familiar; the connecting of several of them together, which constitutes Deductions, or Trains of Reasoning, forms the whole difficulty of the science, and with a trifling exception, its whole bulk; and hence Geometry is a Deductive Science.

§ 5. [*Why* other sciences still remain experimental] It will be seen hereafter* that there are weighty scientific reasons for giving to every science as much of the character of a Deductive Science as possible; for endeavouring to construct the science from the fewest and the simplest possible inductions, and to make these, by any combinations however complicated, suffice for proving even such truths, relating to complex cases, as could be proved, if we chose, by inductions from specific experience. Every branch of natural philosophy was originally experimental; each generalization rested on a special induction, and was derived from its own distinct set of observations and experiments. From being sciences of pure experiment, as the phrase is, or, to speak more correctly, sciences in which the reasonings *mostly* consist of no more than one step, and are expressed by single syllogisms, all these sciences have become to some extent, and some of them in nearly the whole of their extent, sciences of pure reasoning; whereby multitudes of truths, already known by induction from as many different sets of experiments, have come to be exhibited as deductions or corollaries from inductive propositions of a simpler and more universal character. Thus mechanics, hydrostatics, optics, acoustics, *c* thermology, have successively been rendered mathematical; and astronomy was brought by Newton within the laws of general mechanics. Why it is that the substitution of this circuitous mode of proceeding for a process apparently much easier and more natural, is held, and justly, to be the greatest triumph of the investigation of nature, we are not, in this stage of our inquiry, prepared to examine. But it is necessary to remark, that al-

*[62] Infra, Bk. III, Chap. iv, §3, [pp. 320–2,] and elsewhere.

q–qMS, 43, 46   men have been able   a–aMS, 43, 46   *And why*
b–b+51, 56, 62, 65, 68, 72   c43, 46, 51, 56, 62   and

though, by this progressive transformation, all sciences tend to become more and more Deductive, they are not, therefore, the less Inductive; every step in the Deduction is still an Induction. The opposition is not between the terms Deductive and Inductive, but between Deductive and Experimental. A science is experimental, in proportion as every new case, which presents any peculiar features, stands in need of a new set of observations and experiments —a fresh induction. It is deductive, in proportion as it can draw conclusions, respecting cases of a new kind, by processes which bring those cases under old inductions; by ascertaining that cases which cannot be observed to have the requisite marks, have, however, marks of those marks.

We can now, therefore, perceive what is the generic distinction between sciences which can be made Deductive, and those which must as yet remain Experimental. The difference consists in our having been able, or not yet able, to discover marks of marks. If by our various inductions we have been able to proceed no further than to such propositions as these, a a mark of b, or a and b marks of one another, c a mark of d, or c and d marks of one another, without anything to connect a or b with c or d; we have a science of detached and mutually independent generalizations, such as these, that acids redden vegetable blues, and that alkalies colour them green; from neither of which propositions could we, directly or indirectly, infer the other: and a science, so far as it is composed of such propositions, is purely experimental. Chemistry, in the present state of our knowledge, has not yet thrown off this character. There are other sciences, however, of which the propositions are of this kind: a a mark of b, b a mark of c, c of d, d of e, &c. In these sciences we can mount the ladder from a to e by a process of ratiocination; we can conclude that a is a mark of e, and that every object which has the mark a has the property e, although, perhaps, we never were able to observe a and e together, and although even d, our only direct mark of e, may ^{d}not be^d perceptible in those objects, but only inferrible. Or, varying the first metaphor, we may be said to get from a to e underground: the marks b, c, d, which indicate the route, must all be possessed somewhere by the objects concerning which we are inquiring; but they are below the surface: a is the only mark that is visible, and by it we are able to trace in succession all the rest.

§ 6. [*Experimental sciences may become deductive by the progress of experiment*] We can now understand how an experimental ^{a}may transform^a itself into a deductive science by the mere progress of experiment. In an experimental science, the inductions, as we have said, lie detached, as, a a mark of b, c a mark of d, e a mark of f, and so on: now, a new set of instances, and a consequent new induction, may at any time bridge over the

$^{d-d}$MS, 43, 46, 51   be not
$^{a-a}$MS, 43   transforms

interval between two of these unconnected arches; b, for example, may be ascertained to be a mark of c, which enables us thenceforth to prove deductively that a is a mark of c. Or, as sometimes happens, some [b] comprehensive induction may raise an arch high in the air, which bridges over hosts of them at once: b, d, f, and all the rest, turning out to be marks of some one thing, or of things between which a connexion has already been traced. As when Newton discovered that the motions, whether regular or apparently anomalous, of all the bodies of the solar system, (each of which motions had been inferred by a separate logical operation, from separate marks,) were all marks of moving round a common centre, with a centripetal force varying directly as the mass, and inversely as the square of the distance from that centre.[*] This is the greatest example which has yet occurred of the transformation, at one stroke, of a science which was still to a great degree merely experimental, into a deductive science.

Transformations of the same nature, but on a smaller scale, continually take place in the less advanced branches of physical knowledge, without enabling them to throw off the character of experimental sciences. Thus with regard to the two unconnected propositions before cited, namely, Acids redden vegetable blues, Alkalies make them green; it is remarked by Liebig, that all blue colouring matters which are reddened by acids (as well as, reciprocally, all red colouring matters which are rendered blue by alkalies) contain nitrogen:[†] and it is quite possible [c] that this circumstance may one day furnish a bond of connexion between the two propositions in question, by showing that the [d]antagonistic[d] action of acids and alkalies in producing or destroying the colour blue, is the result of some one, more general, law. Although this connecting of detached generalizations is so much gain, it tends but little to give a deductive character to any science as a whole; because the new courses of observation and experiment, which thus enable us to connect together a few general truths, usually make known to us a still greater number of unconnected new ones. Hence chemistry, though similar extensions and simplifications of its generalizations are continually taking place, is still in the main an experimental science; and is likely so to continue unless some comprehensive induction should be hereafter arrived at, which, like Newton's, shall connect a vast number of the smaller known inductions

[*Isaac Newton. *Philosophiæ naturalis principia mathematica* (1687). In *Opera quae exstant omnia*. Ed. Samuel Horsely. 5 vols. London: Nichols, 1779–85, Vols. II–III.]

[†Justus von Liebig. *Organic Chemistry in its Applications to Agriculture and Physiology*. Ed. Lyon Playfair. London: Taylor and Walton, 1840, p. 71.]

[b]MS, 43, 46   grand
[c]MS, 43, 46   to conceive
[d–d]MS, 43, 46, 51, 56, 62   antagonist

together, and change the whole method of the science at once. Chemistry has already one great generalization, which, though relating to one of the subordinate aspects of chemical phenomena, possesses within its limited sphere this comprehensive character; the principle of Dalton, called the atomic theory, or the doctrine of chemical equivalents: which by enabling us to a certain extent to foresee the proportions in which two substances will combine, before the experiment has been tried, constitutes undoubtedly a source of new chemical truths obtainable by deduction, as well as a connecting principle for all truths of the same description previously obtained by experiment.

§ 7. [*In what manner this change from experimental to deductive usually takes place*] The discoveries which change the method of a science from experimental to deductive, mostly consist in establishing, either by deduction or by direct experiment, that the varieties of a particular phenomenon uniformly accompany the varieties of some other phenomenon better known. Thus the science of sound, which previously stood in the lowest rank of merely experimental science, became deductive when it was proved by experiment that every variety of sound was consequent on, and therefore a mark of, a distinct and definable variety of oscillatory motion among the particles of the transmitting medium. When this was ascertained, it followed that every relation of succession or coexistence which obtained between phenomena of the more known class, obtained also between the phenomena which *a*correspond*a* to them in the other class. Every sound, being a mark of a particular oscillatory motion, became a mark of everything which, by the laws of dynamics, was known to be inferrible from that motion; and everything which by those same laws was a mark of any oscillatory motion *b*among the particles of an elastic medium*b*, became a mark of the corresponding sound. And thus many truths, not before suspected, concerning sound, *c*become*c* deducible from the known laws of the propagation of motion through an elastic medium; while facts already empirically known respecting sound, *d*become*d* an indication of corresponding properties of vibrating bodies, previously undiscovered.

But the grand agent for transforming experimental into deductive sciences, is the science of number. The properties of *e*number*e*, alone among all known phenomena, are, in the most rigorous sense, properties of all things whatever. All things are not coloured, or ponderable, or even extended; but all things are numerable. And if we consider this science in its whole extent, from

*a–a*MS, 43, 46, 51, 56, 62, 65, 68   corresponded
b–b+51, 56, 62, 65, 68, 72
*c–c*MS, 43, 46   became
*d–d*MS, 43, 46   became
*e–e*MS, 43, 46, 51, 56, 62, 65, 68   numbers [*printer's error?*]

common arithmetic up to the calculus of variations, the truths already ascertained seem all but infinite, and admit of indefinite extension.

f These truths, though affirmable of all things whatever, of course apply to them only in respect of their quantity. But if it comes to be discovered that variations of quality in any class of phenomena, correspond regularly to variations of quantity either in those same or in some other phenomena; every formula of mathematics applicable to quantities which vary in that particular manner, becomes a mark of a corresponding general truth respecting the variations in quality which accompany them: and the science of quantity being (as far as any science can be) altogether deductive, the theory of that particular kind of qualities becomes, to this extent, deductive likewise.

The most striking instance in point which history affords (though not an example of an experimental science rendered deductive, but of an unparalleled extension given to the deductive process in a science which was deductive already), is the revolution in geometry which originated with *g* Descartes, and was completed by Clairaut. These *h*great mathematicians pointed out the importance of the fact*h*, that to every variety of position in points, direction in lines, or form in curves or surfaces (all of which are Qualities), there corresponds a peculiar relation of quantity between either two or three rectilineal co-ordinates; insomuch that if the law were known according to which those co-ordinates vary relatively to one another, every other geometrical property of the line or surface in question, whether relating to quantity or *i*quality*i*, would be capable of being inferred. Hence it followed that every geometrical question could be solved, if the corresponding algebraical one could; and geometry received an accession (actual or potential) of new truths, corresponding to every property of numbers which the progress of the calculus had brought, or might in future bring, to light. In the same general manner, mechanics, astronomy, and in a less degree, every branch of natural philosophy commonly so called, have been made algebraical. The varieties of physical phenomena with which those sciences are conversant, have been found to answer to determinable varieties in the quantity of some circumstance or other; or at least to varieties of form or position, for which corresponding equations of quantity had already been, or were susceptible of being, discovered by geometers.

In these various transformations, the propositions of the science of number do but fulfil the function proper to all propositions forming a train of reasoning, viz. that of enabling us to arrive in an indirect method, by marks of marks, at such of the properties of objects as we cannot directly ascertain

*f*MS [*no paragraph*]
*g*MS, 43   the illustrious
*h–h*MS, 43, 46   philosophers remarked
*i–i*MS   not

(or not so conveniently) by experiment. We travel from a given visible or tangible fact, through the truths of numbers, to the *facts* sought. The given fact is a mark that a certain relation subsists between the quantities of some of the elements concerned; while the fact sought presupposes a certain relation between the quantities of some other elements: now, if these last quantities are dependent in some known manner upon the former, or *vice versâ*, we can argue from the numerical relation between the one set of quantities, to determine that which subsists between the other set; the theorems of the calculus affording the intermediate links. And thus *k* one of the two physical facts becomes a mark of the other, by being a mark of a mark of a mark of it.

*j–j*MS, 43, 46, 51, 56, 62, 65   fact
*k*MS, 43, 46   the

CHAPTER V

Of Demonstration, and Necessary Truths

§ 1. [*The Theorems of geometry are* ^a*necessary truths only*^a *in the sense of necessarily following from hypotheses*] If, as laid down in the two preceding chapters, the foundation of all sciences, even deductive or demonstrative sciences, is Induction; if every step in the ratiocinations even of geometry is an act of induction; and if a train of reasoning is but bringing many inductions to bear upon the same subject of inquiry, and drawing a case within one induction by means of another; wherein lies the peculiar certainty always ascribed to the sciences which are entirely, or almost entirely, deductive? Why are they called the Exact Sciences? Why are mathematical certainty, and the evidence of demonstration, common phrases to express the very highest degree of assurance attainable by reason? Why are mathematics by almost all philosophers, and (by ^bsome^b) even those branches of natural philosophy which, through the medium of mathematics, have been converted into deductive sciences, considered to be independent of the evidence of experience and observation, and characterized as systems of Necessary Truth?

The answer I conceive to be, that this character of necessity, ascribed to the truths of mathematics, and even (with some reservations to be hereafter made) the peculiar certainty attributed to them, is an illusion; in order to sustain which, it is necessary to suppose that those truths relate to, and express the properties of, purely imaginary objects. It is acknowledged that the conclusions of geometry are deduced, partly at least, from the so-called Definitions, and that those definitions are assumed to be correct ^crepresentations^c, as far as they go, of the objects with which geometry is conversant. Now we have pointed out that, from a definition as such, no proposition, unless it be one concerning the meaning of a word, can ever follow; and that what apparently follows from a definition, follows in reality from an implied assumption that there exists a real thing conformable thereto. This assump-

^{a–a}MS, 43   *only necessary truths*
^{b–b}MS, 43, 46, 51   many
^{c–c}MS, 43, 46, 51, 56, 62, 65   descriptions

tion, in the case of the definitions of geometry, is *d*not strictly true*d*: there exist no real things exactly conformable to the definitions. There exist no points without magnitude; no lines without breadth, nor perfectly straight; no circles with all their radii exactly equal, nor squares with all their angles perfectly right. It will perhaps be said that the assumption does not extend to the actual, but only to the possible, existence of such things. I answer that, according to any test we have of possibility, they are not even possible. Their existence, so far as we can form any judgment, would seem to be inconsistent with the physical constitution of our planet at least, if not of the universe. To get rid of this difficulty, and at the same time to save the credit of the supposed *e*system*e* of necessary truth, it is customary to say that the points, lines, circles, and squares which are the subject of geometry, exist in our conceptions merely, and are part of our minds; which minds, by working on their own materials, construct an *à priori* science, the evidence of which is purely mental, and has nothing whatever to do with outward experience. By howsoever high authorities this doctrine may have been sanctioned, it appears to me psychologically incorrect. The points, lines, circles, and squares which any one has in his mind, are (I apprehend) simply copies of the points, lines, circles, and squares which he has known in his experience. *f*Our idea of a point, I apprehend to be simply our idea of the *minimum visible*, the smallest portion of surface which we can see.*f* A line, as defined by geometers, is wholly inconceivable. We can reason about a line as if it had no breadth; because we have a power, which is the foundation of all the control we can exercise over the operations of our minds; the power, when a perception is present to our senses, or a conception to our intellects, of *attending* to a part only of that perception or conception, instead of the whole. But we cannot *conceive* a line without breadth; we can form no mental picture of such a line: all the lines which we have in our minds are lines possessing breadth. If any one doubts this, we may refer him to his own experience. I much question if any one who fancies that he can conceive what is called a mathematical line, thinks so from the evidence of his consciousness: I suspect it is rather because he supposes that unless such a conception were possible, mathematics could not exist as a science: a supposition which there will be no difficulty in showing to be entirely groundless.

Since, then, neither in nature, nor in the human mind, do there exist any objects exactly corresponding to the definitions of geometry, while yet that science cannot be supposed to be conversant about non-entities; nothing remains but to consider geometry as conversant with such lines, angles, and figures, as really exist; and the definitions, as they are called, must be regarded

---

*d–d*MS, 43, 46, 51, 56, 62, 65, 68   false
*e–e*MS, 43, 46   systems
f–f+51, 56, 62, 65, 68, 72

as some of our first and most obvious generalizations concerning those natural objects. The correctness of *those* generalizations, *as* generalizations, is without a flaw: the equality of all the radii of a circle is true of all circles, so far as it is true of any one: but it is not exactly true of any circle; it is only nearly true; so nearly that no error of any importance in practice will be incurred by feigning it to be exactly true. When we have occasion to extend these inductions, or their consequences, to cases in which the error would be appreciable—to lines of perceptible breadth or thickness, parallels which deviate sensibly from equidistance, and the like—we correct our conclusions, by combining with them a fresh set of propositions relating to the aberration; just as we also take in propositions relating to the physical or chemical properties of the material, if those properties happen to introduce any modification into the result; which they easily may, even with respect to figure and magnitude, as in the case, for instance, of expansion by heat. So long, however, as there exists no practical necessity for attending to any of the properties of the object except its geometrical properties, or to any of the natural irregularities in those, it is convenient to neglect the consideration of the other properties and of the irregularities, and to reason as if these did not exist: accordingly, we formally announce in the definitions, that we intend to proceed on this plan. But it is an error to suppose, because we resolve to confine our attention to a certain number of the properties of an object, that we therefore conceive, or have an idea of, the object, denuded of its other properties. We are thinking, all the time, of precisely such objects as we have seen and touched, and with all the properties which naturally belong to them; but, for scientific convenience, we feign them to be divested of all properties, except those *which are material to our purpose, and* in regard to which we design to consider them.

The peculiar accuracy, supposed to be characteristic of the first principles of geometry, thus appears to be fictitious. The assertions on which the reasonings of the science are founded, do not, any more than in other sciences, exactly correspond with the fact; but we suppose that they do so, for the sake of tracing the consequences which follow from the supposition. The opinion of Dugald Stewart[*] respecting the foundations of geometry, is, I conceive, substantially correct; that it is built on hypotheses; that it owes to this alone the peculiar certainty supposed to distinguish it; and that in any science whatever, by reasoning from a set of hypotheses, we may obtain a body of conclusions as certain as those of geometry, that is, as strictly in

[*See *Elements of the Philosophy of the Human Mind*, Vol. I, pp. 28ff., Chap. i, sect. 1.]

*g-g*MS   these [*printer's error?*]
h-h+51, 56, 62, 65, 68, 72

accordance with the hypotheses, and as irresistibly compelling assent, *on condition* that those hypotheses are true.*

When, therefore, it is affirmed that the conclusions of geometry are necessary truths, the necessity consists in reality only in this, that they *i*correctly*i* follow from the suppositions from which they are deduced. Those suppositions are so far from being necessary, that they are not even true; they purposely depart, more or less widely, from the truth. The only sense in which necessity can be ascribed to the conclusions of any scientific investigation, is that of *j*legitimately*j* following from some assumption, which, by the conditions of the inquiry, is not to be questioned. In this relation, of course, the derivative truths of *k*every*k* deductive science must stand to the inductions, or assumptions, on which the science is founded, and which, whether true or untrue, certain or doubtful in themselves, are always supposed certain for the purposes of the particular science. And therefore the conclusions of all deductive sciences were said by the ancients to be necessary propositions. We have observed already that to be predicated necessarily was characteristic of the predicable Proprium, and that a proprium was any property of a thing which could be deduced from its essence, that is, from the properties included in its definition.

§ 2. [*Those hypotheses are real facts with some of their circumstances* *a*exaggerated or*a* omitted] The important doctrine of Dugald Stewart, which I have endeavoured to enforce, has been contested by *b*Dr.*b* Whewell, both in

*[72] It is justly remarked by Professor Bain (*Logic*, Pt. II, p. 134) that the word Hypothesis is here used in a somewhat peculiar sense. An hypothesis, in science, usually means a supposition not proved to be true, but surmised to be so, because if true it would account for certain known facts; and the final result of the speculation may be to prove its truth. The hypotheses spoken of in the text are of a different character; they are known not to be literally true, while as much of them as is true is not hypothetical, but certain. The two cases, however, resemble in the circumstance that in both we reason, not from a truth, but from an assumption, and the truth therefore of the conclusions is conditional, not categorical. This suffices to justify, in point of logical propriety, Stewart's use of the term. It is of course needful to bear in mind that the hypothetical element in the definitions of geometry is the assumption that what is very nearly true is exactly so. This unreal exactitude might be called a fiction, as properly as an hypothesis; but that appellation, still more than the other, would fail to point out the close relation which exists between the fictitious point or line and the points and lines of which we have experience.

*i–i*MS, 43, 46, 51, 56, 62   necessarily
*j–j*MS, 43, 46, 51, 56, 62   necessarily
*k–k*MS   any
a–a+56, 62, 65, 68, 72
*b–b*MS, 43, 46   a living philosopher, Mr.

the dissertation appended to his excellent *Mechanical Euclid,*[*] and in his *c* elaborate work on the *Philosophy of the Inductive Sciences*; in which last he also replies to an article in the *Edinburgh Review*, (ascribed to a writer of great scientific eminence),[†] in which Stewart's opinion was defended against his former strictures. *d*The supposed refutation of Stewart consists in proving*d* against him (as has also been done in this work) that the premises of geometry are not definitions, but assumptions of the real existence of things corresponding to those definitions. This, however, is doing little for Dr. Whewell's purpose; for it is these very assumptions which *e*are asserted to be*e* hypotheses, and which he, if he denies that geometry is founded on hypotheses, must show to be absolute truths. All he does, however, is to observe, that they at any rate, are not *arbitrary* hypotheses; that we should not be at liberty to substitute other hypotheses for them; that not only "a definition, to be admissible, must necessarily refer to and agree with some conception which we can distinctly frame in our thoughts," but that the straight lines, for instance, which we define, must be "those by which angles are contained, those by which triangles are bounded, those of which parallelism may be predicated, and the like."* And this is true; but this has never been contradicted. Those who say that the premises of geometry are hypotheses, are not bound to maintain them to be hypotheses which have no relation whatever to fact. Since an hypothesis framed for the purpose of scientific inquiry must relate to something which has real existence, (for there can be no science respecting non-entities,) it follows that any hypothesis we make respecting an object, to facilitate our study of it, must not involve anything which is distinctly false, and repugnant to its real nature: we must not ascribe to the thing any property which it has not; our liberty extends only to *f*slightly exaggerating some of those which it has, *g*(by assuming it to be completely what it really is very nearly,)*g* and suppressing others*f*, under the indispensable obligation of restoring them whenever, and in as far as, their presence or absence would make any material difference in the truth of our conclusions. Of this nature, accordingly, are the first principles involved in the

[*"Remarks on Mathematical Reasoning, and on the Logic of Induction," *Mechanical Euclid.* Cambridge: Deighton, 1837, pp. 143–82.]

[†Thomas F. Ellis, "Whewell's *Mechanical Euclid,*" *Edinburgh Review*, LXVII (April, 1838), pp. 81–102. (JSM may have been misled into ascribing the article to Sir David Brewster; see p. 1194 below.) Whewell, *Philosophy of the Inductive Sciences*, Vol. I, pp. 92–3, 98–107.]

Mechanical Euclid, p. 149.

*c*MS, 43, 46, 51, 56, 62, 65   more recent
*d–d*MS, 43   Mr. Whewell's mode of refuting Stewart is to prove
*e–e*MS, 43, 46   we say are
*f–f*MS, 43, 46, 51   suppressing some of those which it has
g–g+62, 65, 68, 72

definitions of geometry. *ʰ* That the hypotheses should be of this particular character, is however no further necessary, than inasmuch as no others could enable us to deduce conclusions which, with due corrections, would be true of real objects: and in fact, when our aim is only to illustrate truths, and not to investigate them, we are not under any such restriction. We might suppose an imaginary animal, and work out by deduction, from the known laws of physiology, its natural history; or an imaginary commonwealth, and from the elements composing it, might argue what would be its fate. And the conclusions which we might thus draw from purely arbitrary hypotheses, might form a highly useful intellectual exercise: but as they could only teach us what *would* be the properties of objects which do not really exist, they would not constitute any addition to our knowledge ⁱof natureⁱ: while on the contrary, if the hypothesis merely divests a real object of some portion of its properties, without clothing it in false ones, the conclusions will always express, under known liability to correction, actual truth.

§ 3. [*Some of the first principles of geometry are axioms, and these are not hypothetical*] But though Dr. Whewell has not shaken Stewart's doctrine as to the hypothetical character of that portion of the first principles of geometry which are involved in the so-called definitions, he has, I conceive, greatly the advantage of Stewart on another important point in the theory of geometrical reasoning; the necessity of admitting, among those first principles, axioms as well as definitions. Some of the axioms of Euclid might, no doubt, be exhibited in the form of definitions, or might be deduced, by reasoning, from propositions similar to what are so called. Thus, if instead of the axiom, Magnitudes which can be made to coincide are equal,[*] we introduce a definition, "Equal magnitudes are those which may be so applied to one another as to coincide;" the three axioms which follow (Magnitudes which are equal to the same are equal to one another—If equals are added to equals the sums are equal—If equals are taken from equals the remainders are equal,) may be proved by an imaginary superposition, resembling that by which the fourth proposition of the first book of Euclid is demonstrated. But though these and several others may be struck out of the list of first principles, because, though not requiring demonstration, they are susceptible of it; there will be found in the list of axioms two or three fundamental truths, not capable of being demonstrated: among which ᵃmust be reckonedᵃ the proposition that two straight lines cannot inclose a space, (or its equivalent,

[*See Euclid, Bk. I, Axiom 8; Playfair, *Elements of Geometry*, pp. 21–2.]

ʰMS, 43, 46, 51 In their positive part they are observed facts; it is only in their negative part that they are hypothetical.
ⁱ⁻ⁱ+51, 56, 62, 65, 68, 72
ᵃ⁻ᵃMS, 43 I agree with Mr. Whewell in placing

Straight lines which coincide in two points coincide altogether,)[*] and some property of parallel lines, other than that which constitutes their definition: *one of the most suitable for the purpose* being that selected by Professor Playfair:[†] "Two straight lines which intersect each other cannot both of them be parallel to a third straight line."*

The axioms, as well those which are indemonstrable as those which admit of being demonstrated, differ from that other class of fundamental principles which are involved in the definitions, in this, that they are true without any mixture of hypothesis. That things which are equal to the same thing are equal to one another, is as true of the lines and figures in nature, as it would be of the imaginary ones assumed in the definitions. In this respect, however, mathematics are only on a par with most other sciences. In almost all sciences there are some general propositions which are exactly true, while the greater part are only more or less distant approximations to the truth. Thus in mechanics, the first law of motion (the continuance of a movement once impressed, until stopped or slackened by some resisting force) is true without *qualification or error*. The rotation of the earth in twenty-four hours, of the same length as in our time, has gone on since the first accurate observations, without the increase or diminution of one second in all that period. These are inductions which require no fiction to make them be received as accurately true: but along with them there are others, as for instance the propositions respecting the figure of the earth, which are but approximations to the truth; and in order to use them for the further advancement of our knowledge, we must feign that they are exactly true, though they really want something of being so.

[*Ibid., Axiom 11; Playfair substitutes (p. 22) the definition cited below.]
[†Ibid.]
*We might, it is true, *insert* this property into the definition of parallel lines, framing the definition so as to require, both that when produced indefinitely they shall never meet, and also that any straight line which intersects one of them shall, if prolonged, meet the other. But by doing this we by no means get rid of the assumption; we are still obliged to take for granted the geometrical truth, that all straight lines in the same plane, which have the former of these properties, have also the latter. For if it were possible that they should not, that is, if any straight lines *in the same plane,* other than those which are parallel according to the definition, had the property of never meeting although indefinitely produced, the demonstrations of the subsequent portions of the theory of parallels could not be maintained.

*b-b*MS, 43, 46, 51, 56   the most suitable, perhaps,
*c-c*MS   foist
d-d+72
*e-e*MS   a particle of qualification or error; it is not affected by the frictions, and rigidities, and miscellaneous disturbing causes, which qualify, for example, the theories of the lever and of the pulley]   43, 46   *as* MS . . . frictions, rigidities . . . *as* MS

§ 4. [*Those first principles of geometry that are axioms are experimental truths*] It remains to inquire, what is the ground of our belief in axioms—what is the evidence on which they rest? I answer, they are experimental truths; generalizations from observation. The proposition, Two straight lines cannot inclose a space—or in other words, Two straight lines which have once met, do not meet again, but continue to diverge—is an induction from the evidence of our senses.

This opinion runs counter to a *scientific* prejudice of long standing and great strength, and there is probably no *b* proposition enunciated in this work for which *a more unfavourable* reception is to be expected. It is, however, no new opinion; and even if it were so, would be entitled to be judged, not by its novelty, but by the strength of the arguments by which it can be supported. I consider it very fortunate that so eminent a champion of the contrary opinion as Dr. Whewell, has *d* found occasion for a most elaborate treatment of the whole theory of axioms, in attempting to construct the philosophy of the mathematical and physical sciences on the basis of the doctrine against which I now contend. Whoever is anxious that a discussion should go to the bottom of the subject, must rejoice to see the opposite side of the question worthily represented. If what is said by *Dr.* Whewell, in support of an opinion which he has made the foundation of a systematic work, can be shown not to be conclusive, enough will have been done, without going *else-where in quest of* stronger arguments and a more powerful adversary.

It is not necessary to show that the truths which we call axioms are originally *suggested* by observation, and that we should never have known that two straight lines cannot inclose a space if we had never seen a straight line: thus much being admitted by Dr. Whewell, and by all, in recent times, who have *taken* his view of the subject. But they contend, that it is not experience which *proves* the axiom; but that its truth is perceived à *priori*, by the constitution of the mind itself, from the first moment when the meaning of the proposition is apprehended; and without any necessity for verifying it by repeated trials, as is requisite in the case of truths really ascertained by observation.

They cannot, however, but allow that the truth of the axiom, Two straight lines cannot inclose a space, even if evident independently of experience, is also evident from experience. Whether the axiom needs confirmation or not, it receives confirmation in almost every instant of our lives; since we cannot

*a–a*MS, 43, 46   philosophic
*b*MS, 43, 46, 51, 56   one
*c–c*MS   so unfavourable a
*d*MS, 43, 46, 51, 56, 62, 65   recently
*e–e*MS, 43   such a man as Mr.]   46   Mr.
*f–f*MS, 43, 46, 51, 56, 62, 65   further to seek]   68   further in quest of
*g–g*MS, 43, 46   adopted

look at any two straight lines which intersect one another, without seeing that from that point they continue to diverge more and more. Experimental proof crowds in upon us in such endless profusion, and without one instance in which there can be even a suspicion of an exception to the rule, that we should soon have [h] stronger ground for believing the axiom, even as an experimental truth, than we have for almost any of the general truths which we confessedly learn from the evidence of our senses. Independently of à priori evidence, we should certainly believe it with an intensity of conviction far greater than we accord to any ordinary physical truth: and this too at a time of life much earlier than that from which we date almost any part of our acquired knowledge, and much too early to admit of our retaining any recollection of the history of our intellectual operations at that period. Where then is the necessity for assuming that our recognition of these truths has a different origin from the rest of our knowledge, when its existence is perfectly accounted for by supposing its origin to be the same? when the causes which produce belief in all other instances, exist in this instance, and in a degree of strength as much superior to what exists in other cases, as the intensity of the belief itself is superior? The burden of proof lies on the advocates of the contrary opinion: it is for them to point out some fact, inconsistent with the supposition that this part of our knowledge of nature is derived from the same sources as every other part.*

*[65] Some persons find themselves prevented from believing that the axiom, Two straight lines cannot inclose a space, could ever become known to us through experience, by a difficulty which may be stated as follows. If the straight lines spoken of are those contemplated in the definition—lines absolutely without breadth and absolutely straight;—that such are incapable of inclosing a space is not proved by experience, for lines such as these do not present themselves in our experience. If, on the other hand, the lines meant are such straight lines as we do meet with in experience, lines straight enough for practical purposes, but in reality slightly zigzag, and with some, however trifling, breadth; as applied to these lines the axiom is not true, for two of them may, and sometimes do, inclose a small portion of space. In neither case, therefore, does experience prove the axiom.

Those who employ this argument to show that geometrical axioms cannot be proved by induction, show themselves unfamiliar with a common and perfectly valid mode of inductive proof; proof by approximation. Though experience furnishes us with no lines so unimpeachably straight that two of them are incapable of inclosing the smallest space, it presents us with gradations of lines possessing less and less either of breadth or of flexure, of which series the straight line of the definition is the ideal limit. And observation shows that just as much, and as nearly, as the straight lines of experience approximate to having no breadth or flexure, so much and so nearly does the space-inclosing power of any two of them approach to zero. The inference that if they had no breadth or flexure at all, they would inclose no space at all, is a correct inductive inference from

[h]MS, 43, 46, 51, 56   a

This, for instance, they would be able to do, if they could prove chronologically that we *had* the conviction (at least practically) so early in infancy as to be anterior to those impressions on the senses, upon which, on the other theory, the conviction is founded. This, however, cannot be proved: the point being too far back to be within the reach of memory, and too obscure for external observation. The advocates of the *à priori* theory are obliged to have recourse to other arguments. These are reducible to two, which I shall endeavour to state as clearly and as forcibly as possible.

§ 5. [*An objection answered*] In the first place it is said, that if our assent to the proposition that two straight lines cannot inclose a space, were derived from the senses, we could only be convinced of its truth by actual trial, that is, by seeing or feeling the straight lines; whereas in fact it is seen to be true by merely thinking of them. That a stone thrown into water goes to the bottom, may be perceived by our senses, but mere thinking of a stone thrown into the water *would never have led* us to that conclusion: not so, however, with the axioms relating to straight lines: if I could be made to conceive what a straight line is, *b* without having seen one, I should at once recognise that two such lines cannot inclose a space. Intuition is "imaginary looking;"* but experience must be real looking: if we see a property of straight lines to be true by merely fancying ourselves to be looking at them, the ground of our belief cannot be the senses, or experience; it must be something mental.

To this argument it might be added in the case of this particular axiom, (for the assertion would not be true of all axioms,) that the evidence of it from actual ocular inspection is not only unnecessary, but unattainable. What says the axiom? That two straight lines *cannot* inclose a space; that after having once intersected, if they are prolonged to infinity they do not meet, but continue to diverge from one another. How can this, in any single case, be proved by actual observation? We may follow the lines to any distance we please; but we cannot follow them to infinity: for aught our senses can testify, they may, immediately beyond the farthest point to which we have traced them, begin to approach, and at last meet. Unless, therefore, we had some other proof of the impossibility than observation affords us, we should have no ground for believing the axiom at all.

---

these facts, conformable to one of the four Inductive Methods hereinafter characterized, the Method of Concomitant Variations; of which the mathematical Doctrine of Limits presents the extreme case.

*Whewell's *History of Scientific Ideas* [2 vols. London: Parker, 1858], Vol. I, p. 140.

*ᵗ⁻ᵗ*MS, 43, 46   have
*ᵃ⁻ᵃ*MS, 43, 46   will never lead
*ᵇ*MS   even

To these arguments, which I trust I cannot be accused of understating, a satisfactory answer will, I conceive, be found, if we advert to one of the characteristic properties of geometrical forms—their capacity of being painted in the imagination with a distinctness equal to reality: in other words, the exact resemblance of our ideas of form to the sensations which suggest them. This, in the first place, enables us to make (at least with a little practice) mental pictures of all possible combinations of lines and angles, which resemble the realities quite as well as any which we could make on paper; and in the next place, ^cmake^c those pictures just as fit subjects of geometrical experimentation as the realities themselves; inasmuch as pictures, if sufficiently accurate, exhibit of course all the properties which would be manifested by the realities at one given instant, and on simple inspection: and in geometry we are concerned only with such properties, and not with that which pictures could not exhibit, the mutual action of bodies one upon another. The foundations of geometry would therefore be laid in direct experience, even if the experiments (which in this case consist merely in attentive contemplation) were practised solely upon what we call our ideas, that is, upon the diagrams in our minds, and not upon outward objects. For in all systems of experimentation we take some objects to serve as representatives of all which resemble them; and in the present case the conditions which qualify a real object to be the representative of its class, are completely fulfilled by an object existing only in our fancy. Without denying, therefore, the possibility of satisfying ourselves that two straight lines cannot inclose a space, by merely thinking of straight lines without actually looking at them; I contend, that we do not believe this truth on the ground of the imaginary intuition simply, but because we know that the imaginary lines exactly resemble real ones, and that we may conclude from them to real ones with quite as much certainty as we could conclude from one real line to another. The conclusion, therefore, is still an induction from observation. And we should not be authorized to substitute observation of the image in our mind, for observation of the reality, if we had not learnt by long-continued experience that ^d the properties of the reality are faithfully represented in the image; just as we should be scientifically warranted in describing ^e an animal which we ^fhave^f never seen, from a ^g picture made of it with a daguerreotype; but not until we had learnt by ample experience, that observation of such a picture is precisely equivalent to observation of the original.

These considerations also remove the objection arising from the impossibility of ocularly following the lines in their prolongation to infinity. For though, in order actually to see that two given lines never meet, it would be

^{c–c}MS, 43, 46, 51   makes   ^dMS, 43, 46   all
^eMS, 43   the shape and colour of   ^{f–f}MS, 43, 46, 51, 56, 62   had
^gMS, 43   photogenic

necessary to follow them to infinity; yet without doing so we may know that if they ever do meet, or [h] if, after diverging from one another, they begin again to approach, this must take place not at an infinite, but at a finite distance. Supposing, therefore, such to be the case, we can transport ourselves thither in imagination, and can frame a mental image of the appearance which one or both of the lines must present at that point, which we may rely on as being precisely similar to the reality. Now, whether we fix our contemplation upon this imaginary picture, or call to mind the generalizations we have had occasion to make from former ocular observation, we [i]learn by the evidence of experience[i], that a line which, after diverging from another straight line, begins to approach to it, produces the impression on our senses which we describe by the expression, "a bent line," not by the expression, "a straight line."*

*[51] Dr. Whewell (*Philosophy of Discovery*, p. 289) thinks it unreasonable to contend that we know by experience, that our idea of a line exactly resembles a real line. "It does not appear," he says, "how we can compare our ideas with the realities, since we know the realities only by our ideas." We know the realities [j]by our sensations[j]. Dr. Whewell surely does not hold the "doctrine of perception by means of ideas," which Reid gave himself so much trouble to refute.

[k]If Dr. Whewell doubts whether we compare our ideas with the corresponding sensations, and assume that they resemble, let me ask on what evidence do we judge that a portrait of a person not present is like the original. Surely because it is like our idea, or mental image of the person, and because our idea is like the man himself.[k]

Dr. Whewell also says, [*ibid.*,] that it does not appear why this resemblance of ideas to the sensations of which they are copies, should be spoken of as if it were a peculiarity of one class of ideas, those of space. My reply is, that I do not so speak of it. The peculiarity I contend for is only one of degree. All our ideas of sensation of course resemble the corresponding sensations, but they do so with very different degrees of exactness and of reliability. No one, I presume, can recall in imagination a colour or an odour with the same distinctness and accuracy with which almost every one can mentally reproduce an image of a straight line or a triangle. To the extent, however, of their capabilities of accuracy, our recollections of colours or of odours may serve as subjects of experimentation, as well as those of lines and spaces, and may yield conclusions which will be true of their external prototypes. A person in whom, either from natural gift or from cultivation, the impressions of colour were peculiarly vivid and distinct, if asked which of two blue flowers was of the darkest tinge, though he might never have compared the two, or even looked at them together, might be able to give a confident answer on the faith of his distinct recollection of the colours; that is, he might examine his mental pictures, and find there a property of the outward objects. But in hardly any case except that of simple geometrical forms, could this be done by mankind generally, with a degree of assurance equal to that which is given by

[h]MS, 43, 46   indeed
[i-i]MS, 43, 46   shall either way be equally satisfied
[j-j]51, 56   (I conceive) by our eyes]   62, 65, 68   *as* 51 . . . our senses
[k-k]+62, 65, 68, 72

*m*The preceding argument, which is, to my mind unanswerable, merges, however, in a still more comprehensive one, which is stated most clearly and conclusively by Professor Bain. The psychological reason why axioms, and indeed many propositions not ordinarily classed as such, may be learnt from the idea only without referring to the fact, is that in the process of acquiring the idea we have learnt the fact. The proposition is assented to as soon as the terms are understood, because in learning to understand the terms we have acquired the experience which proves the proposition to be true. "We required," says Mr. Bain,* "concrete experience in the first instance, to attain to the notion of whole and part; but the notion, once arrived at, implies that the whole is greater. In fact, we could not have the notion without an experience tantamount to this conclusion. . . . When we have mastered the notion of straightness, we have also mastered that aspect of it expressed by the affirmation that two straight lines cannot inclose a space. No intuitive or innate powers or perceptions are needed in such cases. . . . We cannot have the full meaning of Straightness, without going through a comparison of straight objects among themselves, and with their opposites, bent or crooked objects. The result of this comparison is, *inter alia,* that straightness in two lines is seen to be incompatible with inclosing a space; the inclosure of space involves crookedness in at least one of the lines." And similarly, in the case of every first principle,† "the same knowledge that makes it understood, suffices to verify it." The more this observation is considered the more (I am convinced) it will be felt to go to the very root of the controversy.*m*

§ 6. [*Dr. Whewell's opinions on axioms examined*] The first of the two *a* arguments in support of the theory that axioms are *à priori* truths, having, I think, been sufficiently answered; I proceed to the second, *b*which is usually the most relied on*b*. Axioms (it is asserted) are conceived by us not only as

a contemplation of the objects themselves. Persons differ most widely in the precision of their recollection, even of forms: one person, when he has looked any one in the face for half a minute, can draw an accurate likeness of him from memory; another may have seen him every day for six months, and hardly know whether his nose is long or short. But everybody has a perfectly distinct mental image of a straight line, a circle, or a rectangle. And every one concludes confidently from these mental images to the corresponding outward things. *l*The truth is, that we may, and continually do, study nature in our recollections, when the objects themselves are absent; and in the case of geometrical forms we can perfectly, but in most other cases only imperfectly, trust our recollections.*l*

*[72] *Logic*, Pt. I, pp. 222–3.
†[72] *Ibid.*, p. 226.

l–l+56, 62, 65, 68, 72   *m–m*+72
*a*MS, 43, 46   great
*b–b*MS, 43   on which most stress is usually laid, and which is chiefly insisted upon by Mr. Whewell

true, but as universally and necessarily true. Now, experience cannot possibly give to any proposition this character. I may have seen snow a hundred times, and may have seen that it was white, but this cannot give me entire assurance even that all snow is white; much less that snow *must* be white.

However many instances we may have observed of the truth of a proposition, there is nothing to assure us that the next case shall not be an exception to the rule. If it be strictly true that every ruminant animal yet known has cloven hoofs, we still cannot be sure that some creature will not hereafter be discovered which has the first of these attributes, without having the other. . . . Experience must always consist of a limited number of observations; and, however numerous these may be, they can show nothing with regard to the infinite number of cases in which the experiment has not been made.

Besides, Axioms are not only universal, they are also necessary. Now

experience cannot offer the smallest ground for the necessity of a proposition. She can observe and record what has happened; but she cannot find, in any case, or in any accumulation of cases, any reason for what *must* happen. She may see objects side by side; but she cannot see a reason why they must ever be side by side. She finds certain events to occur in succession; but the succession supplies, in its occurrence, no reason for its recurrence. She contemplates external objects; but she cannot detect any internal bond, which indissolubly connects the future with the past, the possible with the real. To learn a proposition by experience, and to see it to be necessarily true, are two altogether different processes of thought.*

And Dr. Whewell adds, "If any one does not clearly comprehend this distinction of necessary and contingent truths, he will not be able to go along with us in our researches into the foundations of human knowledge; nor, indeed, to pursue with success any speculation on the subject."†

In the following passage, we are told what the distinction is, the non-recognition of which incurs this denunciation *e*.

Necessary truths are those in which we not only learn that the proposition *is* true, but see that it *must be* true; in which the negation of the truth is not only false, but impossible; in which we cannot, even by an effort of imagination, or in a supposition, conceive the reverse of that which is asserted. That there are such truths cannot be doubted. We may take, for example, all relations of number. Three and Two added together make Five. We cannot conceive it to be otherwise. We cannot, by any freak of thought, imagine Three and Two to make Seven.‡

Although Dr. Whewell has naturally and properly employed a variety of phrases to bring his meaning more forcibly home, he *would*, I presume,

---

*History of Scientific Ideas, Vol. I, pp. 65–7.
†*Ibid.*, p. 60. ‡*Ibid.*, pp. 58 9.

c–cMS, 43, 46 Moreover d–dMS, 43 In order to learn
eMS, 43 , let us refer again to Mr. Whewell
f–fMS, 43, 46, 51, 56, 62, 65 will

allow that they are all equivalent; and that what he means by a necessary truth, would be sufficiently defined, *g* a proposition the negation of which is not only false but inconceivable. I am unable to find in any of *h*his*h* expressions, turn them what way you will, a meaning beyond this, and I do not believe he would contend that they mean anything more.

This, therefore, is the principle asserted: that propositions, the negation of which is inconceivable, or in other words, which we cannot figure to ourselves as being false, must rest on evidence of a higher and more cogent description than any which experience can afford. *i*

Now I cannot but wonder that so much stress should be laid on *j*the*j* circumstance of inconceivableness, when there is such ample experience to show, that our capacity or incapacity of conceiving a thing has very little to do with the possibility of the thing in itself; but is in truth very much an affair of accident, and depends on the past history and habits of our own minds. There is no more generally acknowledged fact in human nature, than the extreme difficulty at first felt in conceiving anything as possible, which is in contradiction to long established and familiar experience; or even to old *k* familiar habits of thought. And this difficulty is a necessary result of the fundamental laws of the human mind. When we have often seen and thought of two things together, and have never in any one instance either seen or thought of them separately, there is by the primary law of association an increasing difficulty, which *l*may in the end become*l* insuperable, of conceiving the two things apart. This is most of all conspicuous in uneducated persons, who are in general utterly unable to separate any two ideas which have once become firmly associated in their minds; and if persons of cultivated intellect have any advantage on the point, it is only because, having seen and heard and read more, and being more accustomed to exercise their imagination, they have experienced their sensations and thoughts in more varied combinations, and have been prevented from forming many of these inseparable associations. But this advantage has necessarily its limits. The *m* most practised intellect is not exempt from the universal laws of our conceptive faculty. If daily habit presents to *n*any one*n* for a long period two facts in combination, and *o*if*o* he is not led during that period either by accident or *p*by his voluntary mental operations*p* to think of them apart, he will *q*probably*q* in time become incapable of doing so even by the strongest effort;

---

*g*MS as

*h–h*MS, 43 Mr. Whewell's

*i*MS, 43, 46, 51 And we have next to consider whether there is any ground for this assertion.

*j–j*MS this

*l–l*MS, 43, 46 in the end becomes

*n–n*MS, 43, 46 him

*p–p*MS, 43, 46 intention

*k*MS, 43, 46 and

*m*MS, 43, 46 man of the

o–o+43, 46, 51, 56, 62, 65, 68, 72

q–q+51, 56, 62, 65, 68, 72

and the supposition that the two facts can be separated in nature, will at last present itself to his mind with all the characters of an inconceivable phenomenon.* There are remarkable instances of this in the history of science: instances in which the ʳmost instructedʳ men rejected as impossible, because inconceivable, things which their posterity, by earlier practice and longer perseverance in the attempt, found it quite easy to conceive, and which everybody now knows to be true. There was a time when men of the most cultivated intellects, and the most emancipated from the dominion of early prejudice, could not credit the existence of antipodes; were unable to conceive, in opposition to old association, the force of gravity acting upwards instead of downwards. The Cartesians long rejected the Newtonian doctrine of the gravitation of all bodies towards one another, on the faith of a general proposition, the reverse of which seemed to them to be inconceivable—the proposition that a body cannot act where it is not. All the cumbrous machinery of imaginary vortices, assumed without the smallest particle of evidence, appeared to these philosophers a more rational mode of explaining the heavenly motions, than one which involved what seemed to them so great an absurdity.† And they no doubt found it as impossible to conceive that a body should act upon the earth ᵛfromᵛ the distance of the sun or moon, as we find it to conceive an end to space or time, or two straight lines inclosing a space. Newton himself had not been able to realize the conception, or we should not have had his hypothesis of a subtle ether, the occult cause of

*[51] "If all mankind had spoken one language, we cannot doubt that there would have been a powerful, perhaps a universal, school of philosophers, who would have believed in the inherent connexion between names and things, who would have taken the sound *man* to be the mode of agitating the air which is essentially communicative of the ideas of reason, cookery, bipedality, &c." De Morgan, *Formal Logic*, p. 246.

†It would be difficult to name a man more remarkable at once for the greatness and the ˢwide rangeˢ of his ᵗmental accomplishmentsᵗ, than Leibnitz. Yet this ᵘeminentᵘ man gave as a reason for rejecting Newton's scheme of the solar system, that God *could not* make a body revolve round a distant centre, unless either by some impelling mechanism, or by miracle:—"Tout ce qui n'est pas explicable" says he in a letter to the Abbé Conti, "par la nature des créatures, est miraculeux. Il ne suffit pas de dire: Dieu a fait une telle loi de nature; donc la chose est naturelle. Il faut que la loi soit exécutable par les natures des créatures. Si Dieu donnait cette loi, par exemple, à un corps libre, de tourner à l'entour d'un certain centre, *il faudrait ou qu'il y joignît d'autres corps qui par leur impulsion l'obligeassent de rester toujours dans son orbite circulaire, ou qu'il mît un ange à ses trousses, ou enfin il faudrait qu'il y concourût extraordinairement*; car naturellement il s'écartera par la tangente." *Works of Leibnitz* [*Opera Omnia*], ed Dutens [Geneva. Fratres de Tournes, 1768], Vol. III, p. 446. [JSM's italics.]

ʳ⁻ʳMS, 43, 46 wisest
ᵗ⁻ᵗMS, 43, 46 intellectual powers
ᵛ⁻ᵛMS, 43, 46, 51, 56, 62, 65, 68 at

ˢ⁻ˢMS, 43 universality
ᵘ⁻ᵘMS, 43 great

gravitation; and his writings prove, that though he deemed the particular nature of the intermediate agency a matter of conjecture, the necessity of *some* such agency appeared to him indubitable. *w*

If, then, it be so natural to the human mind, even in *a high* state of culture, to be incapable of conceiving, and on that ground to believe impossible, what is afterwards not only found to be conceivable but proved to be true; what wonder if in cases where the association is still older, more confirmed, and more familiar, and in which nothing ever occurs to shake our conviction, or even suggest to us any conception at variance with the association, the acquired incapacity should continue, and be mistaken for a natural incapacity? It is true, our experience of the varieties in nature enables us, within certain limits, to conceive other varieties analogous to them. We can conceive the sun or moon falling; for though we never saw them fall, nor ever perhaps imagined them falling, we have seen so many other things fall, that we have innumerable familiar analogies to assist the conception; which, after all, we should probably have some difficulty in framing, were we not well accustomed to see the sun and moon move (or appear to move,) so that we are only called upon to conceive a slight change in the direction of motion, a circumstance familiar to our experience. But when experience affords no model on which to shape the new conception, how is it possible for us to form it? How, for example, can we imagine an end to space or time? We never saw any object without something beyond it, nor experienced any feeling without something following it. When, therefore, we attempt to conceive the last point of space, we have the idea irresistibly raised of other points beyond it. When we try to imagine the last instant of time, we cannot help conceiving another instant after it. Nor is there any necessity to assume, as is done by *v*a modern school of metaphysicians*v*, a peculiar fundamental law of the mind to account for the feeling of infinity inherent in our conceptions of space and time; that apparent infinity is sufficiently accounted for by simpler and universally acknowledged laws.

Now, in the case of a geometrical axiom, such, for example, as that two straight lines cannot inclose a space,—a truth which is testified to us by our very earliest impressions of the external world,—how is it possible (whether those external impressions be or be not the ground of our belief) that the reverse of the proposition *z could z* be otherwise than inconceivable to us? What analogy have we, what similar order of facts in any other branch of

_____

*w*MS, 43, 46, 51, 56, 62, 65, 68   It would seem that even now the majority of scientific men have not completely got over this very difficulty; for though they have at last learnt to conceive the sun *attracting* the earth without any intervening fluid, they cannot yet conceive the sun *illuminating* the earth without some such medium.
    *x–x*MS, 43, 46   its highest
    *v–v*MS, 43   the school to which Mr. Whewell belongs
    *z–z*MS, 43   can

our experience, to facilitate to us the conception of two straight lines inclosing a space? Nor is even this all. I have already called attention to the peculiar property of our impressions of form, that the ideas or mental images exactly resemble their prototypes, and adequately represent them for the purposes of scientific observation. From this, and from the intuitive character of the observation, which in this case reduces itself to simple inspection, we cannot so much as call up in our imagination two straight lines, in order to attempt to conceive them inclosing a space, without by that very act repeating the *scientific* experiment which establishes the contrary. Will it really be contended that the inconceivableness of the thing, *in* such circumstances, proves anything against the experimental origin of the conviction? Is it not clear that in whichever mode our belief in the proposition may have originated, the impossibility of our conceiving the negative of it must, *on* either hypothesis, be the same? As, then, Dr. Whewell exhorts those who have any difficulty in recognising the distinction held by him between necessary and contingent truths, to study geometry,—a condition which I can assure him I have conscientiously fulfilled,—I, in return, with equal confidence, exhort those who agree with *him*, to study the *general* laws of association; being convinced that nothing more is requisite than a moderate familiarity with those laws, to dispel the illusion which ascribes a peculiar necessity to our earliest inductions from experience, and measures the possibility of things in themselves, by the human capacity of conceiving them.

I hope to be pardoned for adding, that Dr. Whewell himself has both confirmed by his testimony the effect of habitual association in giving to an experimental truth the appearance of a necessary one, and afforded a striking instance of that remarkable law in his own person. In his *Novum Organon Renovatum*[*] he continually asserts, that propositions which not only are not self-evident, but which we know to have been discovered gradually, and by great efforts of genius and patience, have, when once established, appeared so self-evident that, but for historical *proof*, it would have been impossible to conceive that they had not been recognised from the first by all persons in a sound state of their faculties.

We now despise those who, in the Copernican controversy, could not conceive the apparent motion of the sun on the heliocentric hypothesis; or those who, in opposition to Galileo, thought that a uniform force might be that which generated a velocity proportional to the space; or those who held there was something absurd in Newton's doctrine of the different refrangibility of differently coloured rays; or those who imagined that when elements combine, their sensible qualities

[*London: Parker, 1858.]

*a–a*MS, 43   philosophic   *b–b*MS, 43, 46   under
*c–c*MS, 43, 46   under   *d–d*MS, 43   Mr. Whewell
*e–e*MS, 43, 46, 51, 56   elementary   *f–f*MS, 43, 46   evidence

must be manifest in the compound; or those who were reluctant to give up the distinction of vegetables into herbs, shrubs, and trees. We cannot help thinking that men must have been singularly dull of comprehension, to find a difficulty in admitting what is to us so plain and simple. We have a latent persuasion that we in their place should have been wiser and more clear-sighted; that we should have taken the right side, and given our assent at once to the truth. Yet in reality such a persuasion is a mere delusion. The persons who, in such instances as the above, were on the losing side, were very far, in most cases, from being persons more prejudiced, or stupid, or narrow-minded, than the greater part of mankind now are; and the cause for which they fought was far from being a manifestly bad one, till it had been so decided by the result of the war. . . . So complete has been the victory of truth in most of these instances, that at present we can hardly imagine the struggle to have been necessary. *The very essence of these triumphs is, that they lead us to regard the views we reject as not only false but inconceivable.**

This last proposition is precisely what I contend for; and I ask no more, in order to overthrow the whole theory of *g*its author*g* on the nature of the evidence of axioms. For what is that theory? That the truth of axioms cannot have been learnt from experience, because their falsity is inconceivable. But Dr. Whewell himself says, that we are continually led, by the natural progress of thought, to regard as inconceivable what our forefathers not only conceived but believed, nay even (he might have added) were unable to conceive the *h*reverse*h* of. *i*He*i* cannot intend to justify this mode of thought: he cannot mean to say, that we can be right in regarding as inconceivable what others have conceived, and as self-evident what to others did not appear evident at all. After so complete an admission that inconceivableness is an accidental thing, not inherent in the phenomenon itself, but dependent on the mental history of the person who tries to conceive it, how can he ever call upon us to reject a proposition as impossible on no other ground than its inconceivableness? Yet he not only does so, but has unintentionally afforded some of the most remarkable examples which can be cited of the very illusion which he has himself so clearly pointed out. *j*I*j* select as specimens, his remarks on the evidence of the three laws of motion, and of the atomic theory.

With respect to the laws of motion, Dr. Whewell says: "No one can doubt that, in historical fact, these laws were collected from experience. That such is the case, is no matter of conjecture. We know the time, the persons, the circumstances, belonging to each step of each discovery."† After *k*this*k* testimony, to adduce evidence of the fact would be superfluous. And not only

---

**Novum Organon Renovatum*, pp. 33, 32–3. [JSM's italics. For Newton see *Optics* in *Opera*, ed. Horsley, Vol. IV.]

†*History of Scientific Ideas*, Vol. I, p. 264.

*g–g*MS, 43, 46 Mr. Whewell	*h–h*MS, 43, 46, 51 contrary
*i–i*MS, 43 Mr. Whewell	*j–j*MS, 43, 46 We
*k–k*MS, 43 such a	

were these laws by no means intuitively evident, but some of them were originally paradoxes. The first law was especially so. That a body, once in motion, would continue for ever to move in the same direction with undiminished velocity unless acted upon by some new force, was a proposition which mankind found for a long time the greatest difficulty in crediting. It stood opposed to apparent experience of the most familiar kind, which taught that it was the nature of motion to abate gradually, and at last terminate of itself. Yet when once the contrary doctrine was firmly established, mathematicians, as Dr. Whewell observes, speedily began to believe that laws, thus contradictory to first appearances, and which, even after full proof had been obtained, it had required generations to render familiar to the minds of the scientific world, were under "a demonstrable necessity, compelling them to be such as they are and no other;" and *he himself, though not venturing "absolutely* to pronounce" that *all* these laws "can be rigorously traced to an absolute necessity in the nature of things,"* does actually *so think* of the law just mentioned; of which he says: "Though the discovery of the first law of motion was made, historically speaking, by means of experiment, we have now attained a point of view in which we see that it might have been certainly known to be true, independently of experience."† Can there be a more striking exemplification than is here afforded, of the effect of association which we have described? Philosophers, for generations, have the most extraordinary difficulty in putting certain ideas together; they at last succeed in doing so; and after a sufficient repetition of the process, they first fancy a natural bond between the ideas, then experience a growing difficulty, which at last, by the continuation of the same progress, becomes an impossibility, of severing them from one another. If such be the progress of an experimental conviction of which the date is of yesterday, and which is in opposition to first appearances, how must it fare with those which are conformable to appearances familiar from the first dawn of intelligence, and of the conclusiveness of which, from the earliest records of human thought, no sceptic has suggested even a momentary doubt?

The other instance which *I* shall quote is a truly astonishing one, and may be called the *reductio ad absurdum* of the theory of inconceivableness. Speaking of the laws of chemical composition, Dr. Whewell says:‡

That they could never have been clearly understood, and therefore never firmly established, without laborious and exact experiments, is certain; but yet we may

Ibid., p. 263.
†*Ibid.*, p. 240.
‡*Ibid.*, Vol. II, pp. 25–6 [JSM's italics].

*l–l*MS, 43 Mr. Whewell, though he has "not ventured absolutely
*m–m*MS, 43, 46, 51 think in that manner
*n–n*MS, 43, 46 we

venture to say, that being once known, they possess an evidence beyond that of mere experiment. *For how in fact can we conceive combinations, otherwise than as definite in kind and quantity?* If we were to suppose each element ready to combine with any other indifferently, and indifferently in any quantity, we should have a world in which all would be confusion and indefiniteness. There would be no fixed kinds of bodies. Salts, and stones, and ores, would approach to and graduate into each other by insensible degrees. Instead of this, we know that the world consists of bodies distinguishable from each other by definite differences, capable of being classified and named, and of having general propositions asserted concerning them. And as *we cannot conceive a world in which this should not be the case*, it would appear that we cannot conceive a state of things in which the laws of the combination of elements should not be of that definite and measured kind which we have above asserted. *o*

That a philosopher of Dr. Whewell's eminence should gravely assert that we cannot conceive a world in which the simple elements *p*should*p* combine in other than definite proportions; that by dint of meditating on a scientific truth, the original discoverer of which *q*was*q* still living, he should have rendered the association in his own mind between the idea of combination and that of constant proportions so familiar and intimate as to be unable to conceive the one fact without the other; is so signal an instance of the *r*mental law*r* for which I am contending, that one word more in illustration must be *s*superfluous.*s*

*t*In the latest and most complete elaboration of his metaphysical system

---

*o*51 [*footnote:*] *In his recent pamphlet [*Of Induction,*] (p. 81) [*Philosophy of Discovery*, p. 287], Dr. Whewell greatly attenuates the opinion here quoted, reducing it to a surmise "that if we could conceive the composition of bodies distinctly, we might be able to see that it is necessary that the modes of their composition be definite." The passage in the text asserts that we already see, or may and ought to see, this necessity; giving as the reason, that no other mode of combination is conceivable. That Dr. Whewell should ever have made this statement, is enough for the purposes of my illustration. To what he now says I have nothing to object. Undoubtedly, if we understood the ultimate molecular composition of bodies, we might find that their combining with one another in definite proportions is, in the present order of nature, a *necessary consequence* of that molecular composition; and has thus the only kind of necessity of which, in my view of the subject, any law of nature is susceptible. But in that case, the doctrine would be taken out of the class of axioms altogether. It would be no longer an ultimate principle, but a mere derivative law; regarded as necessary, not because self-evident, but because demonstrable.] 56 In his pamphlet "On Induction" (p. 81), . . . *as* 51

*p–p*MS   could]   43, 46, 51   would [*printer's error in 43?*]

*q–q*MS, 43   is

*r–r*MS, 43, 46   law of human nature

*s–s*MS, 43, 46   quite superfluous. I shall only, therefore, express my satisfaction that so long as the progress of scientific instruction has not rendered this association as indissoluble in the minds of most people as Mr. Whewell finds it, the majority of mankind will be fairly able to judge, from this example, of the value of the evidence which he deems sufficient to prove that a scientific proposition might be known to be true independently of experience.* [*footnote is that found in* 72 *on* pp. 248ff.]

*t–t*248+62, 65, 68, 72

(the *Philosophy of Discovery*), as well as in the earlier discourse on the *Fundamental Antithesis of Philosophy*, reprinted as an appendix to that work,[*] Dr. Whewell, while very candidly admitting that his language was open to misconception, disclaims having intended to say that mankind in general can *now* perceive the law of definite proportions in chemical combination to be a necessary truth. All he meant was that philosophical chemists in a future generation may possibly see this. "Some truths may be seen by intuition, but yet the intuition of them may be a rare and ᵘaᵘ difficult attainment."* And he explains that the inconceivableness which, accordingly to his theory, is the test of axioms,

depends entirely upon the clearness of the Ideas which the axioms involve. So long as those ideas are vague and indistinct, the contrary of an axiom may be assented to, though it cannot be distinctly conceived. It may be assented to, not because it is possible, but because we do not see clearly what is possible. To a person who is only beginning to think geometrically, there may appear nothing absurd in the assertion, that two straight lines may inclose a space. And in the same manner, to a person who is only beginning to think of mechanical truths, it may not appear to be absurd, that in mechanical processes, Reaction should be greater or less than Action; and so, again, to a person who has not thought steadily about Substance, it may not appear inconceivable, that by chemical operations, we should generate new matter, or destroy matter which already exists.†

Necessary truths, therefore, are not those of which we cannot conceive, but "those of which we cannot *distinctly* conceive, the contrary."‡ So long as our ideas are indistinct altogether, we do not know what is or is not capable of being distinctly conceived; but, by the ever increasing distinctness with which scientific men apprehend the general conceptions of science, they in time come to perceive that there are certain laws of nature, which, though historically and as a matter of fact they were learnt from experience, we cannot, now that we know them, distinctly conceive to be other than they are.

The account which I should give of this progress of the scientific mind is somewhat different. After a general law of nature has been ascertained, men's minds do not at first acquire a complete facility of familiarly representing to themselves the phenomena of nature in the character which that law assigns to them. The habit which constitutes the scientific cast of mind, that of conceiving facts of all descriptions conformably to the laws which regulate

[*"On the Fundamental Antithesis of Philosophy," *Philosophy of Discovery*, Appendix E, pp. 462–81; reprinted from *Transactions of the Cambridge Philosophical Society*, VIII, Part II (1844), pp. 170–81.]

*[62] *Philosophy of Discovery*, p. 339.

†[62] *Ibid.*, p. 338.

‡[62] *Ibid.*, p. 463.

ᵘ⁻ᵘ+65, 68, 72 [Source *as* 72]

them—phenomena of all descriptions according to the relations which have been ascertained really to exist between them; this habit, in the case of newly discovered relations, comes only by degrees. So long as it is not thoroughly formed, no necessary character is ascribed to the new truth. But in time, the philosopher attains a state of mind in which his mental picture of nature spontaneously represents to him all the phenomena with which the new theory is concerned, in the exact light in which the theory regards them: all images or conceptions derived from any other theory, or from the confused view of the facts which is anterior to any theory, having entirely disappeared from his mind. The mode of representing facts which results from the theory, has now become, to his faculties, the only natural mode of conceiving them. It is a known truth, that a prolonged habit of arranging phenomena in certain groups, and explaining them by means of certain principles, makes any other arrangement or explanation of these facts be felt as unnatural: and it may at last become as difficult to him to represent the facts to himself in any other mode, as it often was, originally, to represent them in that mode.

But, further, (if the theory is true, as we are supposing it to be,) any other mode in which he tries, or in which he was formerly accustomed, to represent the phenomena, will be seen by him to be inconsistent with the facts that suggested the new theory—facts which now form a part of his mental picture of nature. And since a contradiction is always inconceivable, his imagination rejects these false theories, and declares itself incapable of conceiving them. Their inconceivableness to him does not, however, result from anything in the theories themselves, intrinsically and à priori repugnant to the human faculties; it results from the repugnance between them and a portion of the facts; which facts as long as he did not know, or did not distinctly realize in his mental representations, the false theory did not appear other than conceivable; it becomes inconceivable, merely from the fact that contradictory elements cannot be combined in the same conception. Although, then, his real reason for rejecting theories at variance with the true one, is no other than that they clash with his experience, he easily falls into the belief, that he rejects them because they are inconceivable, and ᵛthat heᵛ adopts the true theory because it is self-evident, and does not need the evidence of experience at all.

This I take to be the real and sufficient explanation of the paradoxical truth, on which so much stress is laid by Dr. Whewell, that a scientifically cultivated mind is actually, in virtue of that cultivation, unable to conceive suppositions which a common man conceives without the smallest difficulty. For there is nothing inconceivable in the suppositions themselves; the impossibility is in combining them with facts inconsistent with them, as part of the same mental picture; an obstacle of course only felt by those who know

ᵛ⁻ᵛ+65, 68, 72

the facts, and are able to perceive the inconsistency. As far as the suppositions themselves are concerned, in the case of many of Dr. Whewell's necessary truths the negative of the axiom is, and probably will be as long as the human race lasts, as easily conceivable as the affirmative. There is no axiom (for example) to which Dr. Whewell ascribes a more thorough character of necessity and self-evidence, than that of the indestructibility of matter.[*] That this is a true law of nature I fully admit; but I imagine there is no human being to whom the opposite supposition is inconceivable—who has any difficulty in imagining a portion of matter annihilated: inasmuch as its apparent annihilation, in no respect distinguishable from real by our unassisted senses, takes place every time that water dries up, or fuel is consumed. Again, the law that bodies combine chemically in definite proportions is undeniably true; but few besides Dr. Whewell have reached the point which he seems personally to have arrived at, (though he only dares prophesy similar success to the multitude after the lapse of generations,) that of being unable to conceive a world in which the elements are ready to combine with one another "indifferently in any quantity;"[†] nor is it likely that we shall ever rise to this sublime height of inability, so long as all the mechanical mixtures in our planet, whether solid, liquid, or aëriform, exhibit to our daily observation the very phenomenon declared to be inconceivable.

According to Dr. Whewell, these and similar laws of nature cannot be drawn from experience, inasmuch as they are, on the contrary, assumed in the interpretation of experience. Our inability to "add to or diminish the quantity of matter in the world," is a truth which "neither is nor can be derived from experience; for the experiments which we make to verify it presuppose its truth. . . . When men began to use the balance in chemical analysis, they did not prove by trial, but took for granted, as self-evident, that the weight of the whole must be found in the aggregate weight of the elements."* True, it is assumed; but, I apprehend, no otherwise than as all experimental inquiry assumes provisionally some theory or hypothesis, which is to be finally held true or not, according as the experiments decide. The hypothesis chosen for this purpose will naturally be one which groups together some considerable number of facts already known. The proposition that the material of the world, as estimated by weight, is neither increased nor diminished by any of the processes of nature or art, had many appearances in its favour to begin with. It expressed truly a great number of familiar facts. There were other facts which it had the appearance of conflicting with, and which made its truth, as an universal law of nature, at first doubtful. Because it was doubtful, experiments were devised to verify it. Men assumed

[*See *Philosophy of Discovery*, pp. 472ff.]
[†*History of Scientific Ideas*, Vol. II, p. 25; see above, p. 244.]
Philosophy of Discovery, pp. 472–3.

its truth hypothetically, and proceeded to try whether, on more careful examination, the phenomena which apparently pointed to a different conclusion, would not be found to be consistent with it. This turned out to be the case; and from that time the doctrine took its place as an universal truth, but as one proved to be such by experience. That the theory itself preceded the proof of its truth—that it had to be conceived before it could be proved, and in order that it might be proved—does not imply that it was self-evident, and did not need proof. Otherwise all the true theories in the sciences are necessary and self-evident; for no one knows better than Dr. Whewell that they all began by being assumed, for the purpose of connecting them by deductions with those facts of experience on which, as evidence, they now confessedly rest.[t]*

* [w] The *Quarterly Review* [LXVIII,] for June 1841, [x]contained[x] an article of great ability on Dr. Whewell's two great works [y](since acknowledged and reprinted in Sir John Herschel's *Essays* [London: Longmans, 1857])[y] which maintains, on the subject of axioms, the doctrine advanced in the text, that they are generalizations from experience, and supports that opinion by a line of argument strikingly coinciding with mine. When I state that the whole of the present chapter [z](except the last four pages, added in the [a]fifth[a] edition)[z] was written before I had seen the article, (the greater part, indeed, before it was published,) it is not my object to occupy the reader's attention with a matter so unimportant as the degree of originality which may or may not belong to any portion of my own speculations, but to obtain for an opinion which is opposed to reigning doctrines, the recommendation derived from a striking concurrence of sentiment between two inquirers entirely independent of one another. I [b]embrace the opportunity of[b] citing from a writer of [c]the[c] extensive acquirements in physical and metaphysical knowledge and [d]the[d] capacity of systematic thought [e]which[e] the article evinces, passages so remarkably in unison with my own views as the following:

"The truths of geometry are summed up and embodied in its definitions and axioms. . . . Let us turn to the axioms, and what do we find? A string of propositions concerning magnitude in the abstract, which are equally true of space, time, force, number, and every other magnitude susceptible of aggregation and subdivision. Such propositions, where they are not mere definitions, as some of them are, carry their inductive origin on the face of their enunciation. . . . Those which declare that two straight lines cannot inclose a space, and that two straight lines which cut one another cannot both be parallel to a third, are in reality the only ones which express characteristic properties of space, and these it will be worth while to consider more nearly. Now the only clear notion we can form of straightness is uniformity of direction, for space in its ultimate analysis is nothing but an assemblage of distances and directions. And (not to dwell on the notion of

[w]MS, 43, 46 [*footnote occurs at p. 244 above; see 244[s-s]*] 51, 56 [*footnote to* superfluous *on* p. 244 *above; see* 244[s-s]]

[x-x]MS, 43, 46, 51, 56 contains   [y-y]MS, 43, 46, 51, 56   , the writer of
[z-z]+62, 65, 68, 72
[a-a]62 present   [b-b]MS, 43 have much pleasure in
[c-c]MS such   [d-d]MS such a
[e-e]MS , as

continued contemplation, *i.e.*, mental experience, as included in the very idea of uniformity; nor on that of transfer of the contemplating being from point to point, and of experience, during such transfer, of the homogeneity of the interval passed over) we cannot even propose the proposition in an intelligible form to any one whose experience ever since he was born has not assured him of the fact. The unity of direction, or that we cannot march from a given point by more than one path direct to the same object, is matter of practical experience long before it can by possibility become matter of abstract thought. *We cannot attempt mentally to exemplify the conditions of the assertion in an imaginary case opposed to it, without violating our habitual recollection of this experience, and defacing our mental picture of space as grounded on it.* What but experience, we may ask, can possibly assure us of the homogeneity of the parts of distance, time, force, and measurable aggregates in general, on which the truth of the other axioms depends? As regards the latter axiom, after what has been said it must be clear that the very same course of remarks equally applies to its case, and that its truth is quite as much forced on the mind as that of the former by daily and hourly experience, . . . *including always, be it observed, in our notion of experience, that which is gained by contemplation of the inward picture which the mind forms to itself in any proposed case, or which it arbitrarily selects as an example—such picture, in virtue of the extreme simplicity of these primary relations, being called up by the imagination with as much vividness and clearness as could be done by any external impression, which is the only meaning we can attach to the word intuition, as applied to such relations.*" ["Whewell on the Inductive Sciences," *Essays*, pp. 198–200, 206. JSM's italics.]

And again, of the axioms of mechanics: "As we admit no such propositions, other than as truths inductively collected from observation, even in geometry itself, it can hardly be expected that, in a science of obviously contingent relations, we should acquiesce in a contrary view. Let us take one of these axioms and examine its evidence: for instance, that equal forces perpendicularly applied at the opposite ends of equal arms of a straight lever will balance each other. What but experience, we may ask, in the first place, can possibly inform us that a force so applied will have any tendency to turn the lever on its centre at all? or that force can be so transmitted along a rigid line perpendicular to its direction, as to act elsewhere in space than along its own line of action? Surely this is so far from being self-evident that it has even a paradoxical appearance, which is only to be removed by giving our lever thickness, material composition, and molecular powers. Again, we conclude, that the two forces, being equal and applied under precisely similar circumstances, must, if they exert any effort at all to turn the lever, exert equal and opposite efforts: but what *à priori* reasoning can possibly assure us that they *do* act under precisely similar circumstances? that points which differ in place *are* similarly circumstanced as regards the exertion of force? that universal space may not have relations to universal force—or, at all events, that the organization of the material universe may not be such as to place that portion of space occupied by it in such relations to the forces exerted in it, as may invalidate the absolute similarity of circumstances assumed? Or we may argue, what have we to do with the notion of angular movement in the lever at all? The case is one of rest, and of quiescent destruction of force by force. Now how is this destruction effected? Assuredly by the counter-pressure which supports the fulcrum. But would not this destruction equally arise, and by the same amount of counter-acting force, if each force simply pressed its own half of the lever against the fulcrum? And what can assure us that it is not so, except removal of one or other force, and consequent tilting of the lever? The other fundamental axiom of statics, that the pressure on the point of support is the sum of the weights . . . is merely a scientific transformation and more refined mode of stating a coarse and obvious result of universal experience, viz. that the weight of a rigid body is the same, handle it or suspend it in what position or by what point we will, and that whatever sustains it sustains its total weight. Assuredly, as Mr. Whewell justly remarks, 'No one probably ever made a trial for the purpose of showing that the pressure on the support is equal to the sum of the weights.' [*History of Scientific Ideas*, Vol. I, p. 217.] . . . But it is precisely because in every action of his life from earliest infancy he has been continually making the trial, and seeing it made by every other living being about him, that he never dreams of staking its result on one additional attempt made with scientific accuracy. This would be as if a man should resolve to decide by experiment whether his eyes were useful for the purpose of seeing, by hermetically sealing himself up for half an hour in a metal case." [Herschel, "Whewell," pp. 216–19.]

On the "paradox of universal propositions obtained by experience," [Whewell, *History of Scientific Ideas*, Vol. I, p. 263 (title of Chap. viii),] the same writer says: "If there be necessary and universal truths expressible in propositions of axiomatic simplicity and obviousness, and having for their subject-matter the elements of all our experience and all our knowledge, surely these are the truths which, if experience suggest to us any truths at all, it ought to suggest most readily, clearly, and unceasingly. If it were a truth, universal and necessary, that a net is spread over the whole surface of every planetary globe, we should not travel far on our own without getting entangled in its meshes, and making the necessity of some means of extrication an axiom of locomotion. . . . There is, therefore, nothing paradoxical, but the reverse, in our being led by observation to a recognition of such truths, as *general* propositions, coextensive at least with all human experience. That they pervade all the objects of experience, must ensure their continual suggestion *by* experience; that they are true, must ensure that consistency of suggestion, that iteration of uncontradicted assertion, which commands implicit assent, and removes all occasion of exception; that they are simple, and admit of no misunderstanding, must secure their admission by every mind." [*Ibid.*, pp. 220–1.]

"A truth, necessary and universal, relative to any object of our knowledge, must verify itself in every instance where that object is before our contemplation, and if at the same time it be simple and intelligible, its verification must be obvious. *The sentiment of such a truth cannot, therefore, but be present to our minds whenever that object is contemplated, and must therefore make a part of the mental picture or idea of that object which we may on any occasion summon before our imagination. . . . All propositions, therefore, become not only untrue but inconceivable,* if . . . axioms be violated in their enunciation." [*Ibid.*, pp. 222–3.] [1]

---

[1]MS, 43, 46, 51, 56 [*paragraph*] Another high authority (if indeed it be another authority) may be cited in favour of the doctrine that axioms rest on the evidence of induction. "The axioms of geometry themselves may be regarded as in some sort an appeal to experience, not corporeal, but mental. When we say, the whole is greater than its part, we announce a general fact, which rests, it is true, on our ideas of whole and part; but, in abstracting these notions, we begin by considering them as subsisting in space, and time, and body, and again, in linear, and superficial, and solid space. Again,

*g*Another eminent mathematician had previously sanctioned by his authority the doctrine of the origin of geometrical axioms in experience. "Geometry is thus founded likewise on observation; but of a kind so familiar and obvious, that the primary notions which it furnishes might seem intuitive." Sir John Leslie [*Rudiments of Plane Geometry*. Edinburgh: Oliver and Boyd, 1828, p. 18], quoted by Sir William Hamilton, *Discussions*, p. 272.*g*

---

when we say, the equals of equals are equal, we mentally make comparisons, in equal spaces, equal times, &c., so that these axioms, however self-evident, are still general propositions so far of the inductive kind, that, independently of experience, they would not present themselves to the mind. The only difference between these and axioms obtained from extensive induction is this, that, in raising the axioms of geometry, the instances offer themselves spontaneously, and without the trouble of search, and are few and simple; in raising those of nature, they are infinitely numerous, complicated, and remote, so that the most diligent research and the utmost acuteness are required to unravel their web and place their meaning in evidence." Sir J. Herschel's [*A Preliminary*] *Discourse on the Study of Natural Philosophy* [London: Longman, 1831], pp. 95–6.

g–g+56, 62, 65, 68, 72

CHAPTER VI

The Same Subject Continued

§ 1. [*All deductive sciences are inductive*] In the examination which formed the subject of the last chapter, into the nature of the evidence of those deductive sciences which are commonly represented to be systems of necessary truth, we have been led to the following conclusions. *The* results of those sciences are indeed necessary, in the sense of necessarily following from certain first principles, commonly called axioms and definitions; *that is,* of being certainly true if those axioms and definitions are so *; for the word necessity, even in this acceptation of it, means no more than certainty*. But their claim to the character of necessity in any sense beyond this, as implying an evidence independent of and superior to observation and experience, must depend on the previous establishment of such a claim in favour of the definitions and axioms themselves. With regard to axioms, we found that, considered as experimental truths, they rest on superabundant and obvious evidence. We inquired, whether, since this is the case, it be *imperative* to suppose any other evidence of those truths than experimental evidence, any other origin for our belief of them than an experimental origin. We decided, that the burden of proof lies with those who maintain the affirmative, and we examined, at considerable length, such arguments as they have produced. The examination having led to the rejection of those arguments, we have thought ourselves warranted in concluding that axioms are but a class, the *most universal* class, of inductions from experience; the simplest and easiest cases of generalization from the facts furnished to us by our senses or by our internal consciousness.

While the axioms of demonstrative sciences thus appeared to be experimental truths, the definitions, as they are incorrectly called, *in* those sciences, were found by us to be generalizations from experience which are not even, accurately speaking, truths; being propositions in which, while we assert of some kind óf object, some property or properties which observation shows to belong to it, we at the same time deny that it possesses any other properties, though in truth other properties do in every individual instance

*a–a*MS That the   *b–b*+56, 62, 65, 68, 72
c–c+56, 62, 65, 68, 72   *d–d*MS, 43, 46, 51, 56, 62 necessary
*e–e*MS, 43, 46, 51, 56 highest   *f–f*MS, 43 of

accompany, and in *almost* all instances modify, the property thus exclusively predicated. The denial, therefore, is a mere fiction, or supposition, made for the purpose of excluding the consideration of those modifying circumstances, when their influence is of too trifling amount to be worth considering, or adjourning it, when important, to a more convenient moment.

From these considerations it would appear that Deductive or Demonstrative Sciences are all, without exception, Inductive Sciences; that their evidence is that of experience; but that they are also, in virtue of the peculiar character of one indispensable portion of the general formulæ according to which their inductions are made, Hypothetical Sciences. Their conclusions are only true on certain suppositions, which are, or ought to be, approximations to the truth, but are seldom, if ever, exactly true; and to this hypothetical character is to be ascribed the peculiar certainty, which is supposed to be inherent in demonstration.

What we have now asserted, however, cannot be received as universally true of Deductive or Demonstrative Sciences, until verified by being applied to the most remarkable of all those sciences, that of Numbers; the theory of the Calculus; Arithmetic and Algebra. It is harder to believe of the doctrines of this science than of any other, either that they are not truths *à priori*, but experimental truths, or that their peculiar certainty is owing to their being not absolute but only conditional truths. This, therefore, is a case which merits examination apart; and the more so, because on this subject we have a double set of doctrines to contend with; that of [h] the *à priori* philosophers on one side; and on the other, a [i] theory the most opposite to theirs, which was at one time very generally received, and is still far from being altogether exploded, among metaphysicians.

§ 2. [*The propositions of the science of number are not verbal, but generalizations from experience*] This theory attempts to solve the difficulty apparently inherent in the case, by representing the propositions of the science of numbers as merely verbal, and its processes as simple transformations of language, substitutions of one expression for another. The proposition, Two and one *is* equal to three, according to these *writers*, is not a truth, is not the assertion of a really existing fact, but a definition of the word three; a statement that mankind have agreed to use the name three as a sign exactly equivalent to two and one; to call by the former name whatever is called by the other more clumsy phrase. According to this doctrine, the longest process in algebra is but a succession of changes in terminology, by which equivalent expressions are substituted one for another; a series of

*g–g*MS, 43   most or even in   *h*MS, 43   Mr. Whewell and
*i*MS, 43, 46   philosophical
*a–a*MS, 43, 46, 51, 56, 62, 65, 68   are   *b–b*MS, 43, 46   philosophers

translations of the same fact, from one into another language; though how, after such a series of translations, the fact itself comes out changed (as when we demonstrate a new geometrical theorem by algebra,) they have not explained; and it is a difficulty which is fatal to their theory.

It must be acknowledged that there are peculiarities in the processes of arithmetic and algebra which render the ᶜtheory in questionᶜ very plausible, and have not unnaturally made those sciences the stronghold of Nominalism. The doctrine that we can discover facts, detect the hidden processes of nature, by an artful manipulation of language, is so contrary to common sense, that a person must have made some advances in philosophy to believe it: men fly to so paradoxical a belief to avoid, as they think, some even greater difficulty, which the vulgar do not see. What has led ᵈ many to believe that reasoning is a mere verbal process, is, that no other theory seemed reconcileable with the nature of the Science of Numbers. For we do not carry any ideas along with us when we use the symbols of arithmetic or of algebra. In a geometrical demonstration we have a mental diagram, if not one on paper; AB, AC, are present to our imagination as lines, intersecting other lines, forming an angle with one another, and the like; but not so *a* and *b*. These may represent lines or any other magnitudes, but those magnitudes are never thought of; nothing is realized in our imagination but *a* and *b*. The ideas which, on the particular occasion, they happen to represent, are banished from the mind during every intermediate part of the process, between the beginning, when the premises are translated from things into signs, and the end, when the conclusion is translated back from signs into things. Nothing, then, being in the reasoner's mind but the symbols, what can seem more inadmissible than to ᵉcontendᵉ that the reasoning process has to do with anything more? We seem to have come to one of ᶠ Bacon's Prerogative Instances;[*] an *experimentum crucis*[†] on the nature of reasoning itself.

Nevertheless, it will appear on consideration, that this apparently so decisive instance is no instance at all; that there is in every step of an arithmetical or algebraical calculation a real induction, a real inference of facts from facts; and that what disguises the induction is simply its comprehensive nature, and the consequent extreme generality of the language. All numbers must be numbers of something: there are no such things as numbers in the abstract. *Ten* must mean ten bodies, or ten sounds, or ten beatings of the pulse. But though numbers must be numbers of something, they may be

[*See Francis Bacon, *Novum Organum*. In *Works*, Vol. I, pp. 268ff.]
[†See Robert Hooke, *Micrographia*. London, 1663, p. 54. Though "*experimentum crucis*" is usually attributed to Bacon, his term is actually "*instantia crucis*"; see *Novum Organum*, p. 294.]

ᶜ⁻ᶜMS, 43, 46 above theory   ᵈMS so
ᶠ⁻ᶠMS, 43, 46 pretend   ᶠMS Lord

numbers of anything. Propositions, therefore, concerning numbers, have the remarkable peculiarity that they are propositions concerning all things whatever; all objects, all existences of every kind, known to our experience. All things possess quantity; consist of parts which can be numbered; and in that character possess all the properties which are called properties of numbers. That half of four is two, must be true whatever the word four represents, whether four ᵍhoursᵍ, four miles, or four pounds weight. We need only conceive a thing divided into four equal parts, (and all things may be conceived as so divided,) to be able to predicate of it every property of the number four, that is, every arithmetical proposition in which the number four stands on one side of the equation. Algebra extends the generalization still farther: every number represents that particular number of all things without distinction, but every algebraical symbol does more, it represents all numbers without distinction. As soon as we conceive a thing divided into equal parts, without knowing into what number of parts, we may call it a or x, and apply to it, without danger of error, every algebraical formula in the books. The proposition, $2 (a + b) = 2 a + 2 b$, is a truth co-extensive with ʰall natureʰ. Since then algebraical truths are true of all things whatever, and not, like those of geometry, true of lines only or ⁱofⁱ angles only, it is no wonder that the symbols should not excite in our minds ideas of any things in particular. When we demonstrate the forty-seventh proposition of Euclid,[*] it is not necessary that the words should raise in us an image of all right-angled triangles, but only of some one right-angled triangle: so in algebra we need not, under the symbol a, picture to ourselves all things whatever, but only some one thing; why not, then, the letter itself? The mere written characters, a, b, x, y, z, serve as well for representatives of Things in general, as any more complex and apparently more concrete conception. That we are conscious of them however in their character of things, and not of mere signs, is evident from the fact that our whole process of reasoning is carried on by predicating of them the properties of things. In resolving an algebraic equation, by what rules do we proceed? By applying at each step to a, b, and x, the proposition that equals added to equals make equals; that equals taken from equals leave equals; and other propositions founded on these two. These are not properties of language, or of signs as such, but of magnitudes, which is as much as to say, of all things. The inferences, therefore, which are successively drawn, are inferences concerning things, not symbols; though as any Things whatever will serve the turn, there is no necessity for keeping the idea of the Thing at all distinct, and consequently the process of thought may, in this case, be allowed without danger to do what all processes of thought,

[*Bk. I; Playfair, *Elements of Geometry*, pp. 61–2.]

ᵍ⁻ᵍMS, 43, 46, 51, 56, 62   men
ʰ⁻ʰMS, 43, 46   the creation   ⁱ⁻ⁱ+72

when they have been performed often, will do if permitted, namely, to become entirely mechanical. Hence the general language of algebra comes to be used familiarly without exciting ideas, as all other general language is prone to do from mere habit, though in no other case than this can it be done with complete safety. But when we look back to see from whence the probative force of the process is derived, we find that at every single step, unless we suppose ourselves to be thinking and talking of the things, and not the mere symbols, the evidence fails.

There is another circumstance, which, still more than that which we have now mentioned, gives plausibility to the notion that the propositions of arithmetic and algebra are merely verbal. *That* is, that when considered as propositions respecting Things, they *all have the appearance of being* identical propositions. The assertion, Two and one *is* equal to three, considered as an assertion respecting objects, *as* for instance "Two pebbles and one pebble are equal to three pebbles," does not affirm equality between two collections of pebbles, but absolute identity. It affirms that if we put one pebble to two pebbles, those very pebbles are three. The objects, therefore, being the very same, and the mere assertion that "objects are themselves" being insignificant, it seems but natural to consider the proposition, Two and one *is* equal to three, as asserting mere identity of signification between the two names.

This, however, though it looks so plausible, will not *bear* examination. The expression "two pebbles and one pebble," and the expression, "three pebbles," stand indeed for the same aggregation of objects, but they by no means stand for the same physical fact. They are names of the same objects, but of those objects in two different states: though they *de*note the same things, their *con*notation is different. Three pebbles in two separate parcels, and three pebbles in one parcel, do not make the same impression on our senses; and the assertion that the very same pebbles may by an alteration of place and arrangement be made to produce either the one set of sensations or the other, though *p* a very familiar proposition, is not an identical one. It is a truth known to us by early and constant experience: an inductive truth; and such truths are the foundation of the science of Number. The fundamental truths of that science all rest on the evidence of sense; they are proved by showing to our eyes and our fingers that any given number of objects, ten balls for example, may by separation and re-arrangement exhibit to our senses all the different sets of numbers the sum of which is equal to ten. All the improved methods of teaching arithmetic to children proceed on a knowledge of this fact. All who wish to carry the child's *mind* along with them in

*j–j*MS, 43, 46, 51, 56   This
*k–k*MS   have the appearance of being all
*l–l*MS, 43, 46, 51, 56, 62, 65, 68   are
m–m+43, 46, 51, 56, 62, 65, 68, 72   *n–n*MS, 43, 46, 51, 56, 62, 65, 68   are
*o–o*MS, 43, 46   stand   *p*MS, 43, 46   it is

learning arithmetic; all who *q* wish to teach numbers, and not mere ciphers—now teach it through the evidence of the senses, in the manner we have described. *r*

We may, if we please, call the proposition, "Three is two and one," a definition of the number three, and assert that arithmetic, as it has been asserted that geometry, is a science founded on definitions. But they are definitions in the geometrical sense, not the logical; asserting not the meaning of a term only, but along with it an observed matter of fact. The proposition, "A circle is a figure bounded by a line which has all its points equally distant from a point within it," is called the definition of a circle; but the proposition from which so many consequences follow, and which is really a first principle *s*in*s* geometry, is, that figures answering to this description exist. And thus we may call "Three is two and one" a definition of three; but the calculations which depend on that proposition do not follow from the definition itself, but from an arithmetical theorem presupposed in it, namely, that collections of objects exist, which while they impress the senses thus, °₀°, may be separated into two parts, thus, ᵒᵒ °. This proposition being granted, we term all such parcels Threes, after which the enunciation of the above mentioned physical fact will serve also for a definition of the word Three.

The Science of Number is thus no exception to the conclusion we previously arrived at, that the processes even of deductive sciences are altogether inductive, and that their first principles are generalizations from experience. It remains to be examined whether this science resembles geometry in the further circumstance, that some of its inductions are not exactly true; and that the peculiar certainty ascribed to it, on account of which its propositions are called Necessary Truths, is fictitious and hypothetical, being true in no other sense than that those propositions *t*legitimately*t* follow from the hypothesis of the truth of premises which are avowedly mere approximations to truth.

---

*q*MS, 43 (as Dr. Biber in his remarkable *Lectures on Education* expresses it) [George Edward Biber. *Christian Education*. London: Effingham Wilson, 1830, p. 163.]

*r*MS, 43, 46 [*footnote:*] *See, for illustrations of various sorts, Professor Leslie's *Philosophy of Arithmetic* [Edinburgh: Constable, 1817]; and see also two of the most efficient books ever written for training the infant intellect, Mr. Horace Grant's *Arithmetic for Young Children* [London: Knight, 1835], and his *Second Stage of Arithmetic* [new ed., London, 1861], both published by the Society for the Diffusion of Useful Knowledge.

"Number," says the reviewer of Mr. Whewell, already cited, "we cannot help regarding as an abstraction, and consequently its general properties or its axioms to be of necessity inductively concluded from the consideration of particular cases. And surely this is the way in which children do acquire their knowledge of number, and in which they learn its axioms. The apples and the marbles are put in requisition, and through the multitude of gingerbread nuts their ideas acquire clearness, precision, and generality." [Herschel, "Whewell on the Inductive Sciences," p. 205.]

*s–s*MS, 43, 46 of

*t–t*MS, 43, 46, 51, 56, 62 necessarily

§ 3. [*In what sense the propositions of the science of number are hypothetical*] The inductions of arithmetic are of two sorts: first, those which we have just expounded, such as One and one are two, Two and one are three, &c., which may be called the definitions of the various numbers, in the improper or geometrical sense of the word Definition; and secondly, the two following axioms: The sums of equals are equal, *a* The differences of equals are equal. These two are sufficient; for the corresponding propositions respecting unequals may be proved from these, by *b*a*b* *reductio ad absurdum*.

These axioms, and likewise the so-called definitions, are, as *c*has already been said*c*, results of induction; true of all objects whatever, and, as it may seem, exactly true, without *d*the*d* hypothetical assumption of unqualified truth where an approximation to it is all that exists. The conclusions, therefore, it will naturally be inferred, are exactly true, and the science of number is an exception to other demonstrative sciences in this, that the *e*categorical*e* certainty which is predicable of its demonstrations is independent of all hypothesis.

On more accurate investigation, however, it will be found that, even in this case, there is one hypothetical element in the ratiocination. In all propositions concerning numbers, a condition is implied, without which none of them would be true; and that condition is an assumption which may be false. The condition, is that $1 = 1$; that all the numbers are numbers of the same or of equal units. Let this be doubtful, and not one of the propositions of arithmetic will hold true. How can we know that one pound and one pound make two pounds, if one of the pounds may be troy, and the other avoirdupois? They may not make two pounds of either, or of any weight. How can we know that a forty-horse power is always equal to itself, unless we assume that all horses are of equal strength? It is certain that 1 is always equal in *number* to 1; and where the mere number of objects, or of the parts of an object, without supposing them to be equivalent in any other respect, is all that is material, the conclusions of arithmetic, so far as they go to that alone, are true without mixture of hypothesis. There are *f*such cases in statistics*f*; as, for instance, an inquiry into the amount of *g*the*g* population of any country. It is indifferent to that inquiry whether they are grown people or children, strong or weak, tall or short; the only thing we want to ascertain is their number. But whenever, from equality or inequality of number, equality or inequality in any other respect is to be inferred, arithmetic carried into

---

*a*MS &,
*b–b*MS, 43, 46   the process well known to mathematicians under the name of
*c–c*MS, 43, 46, 51, 56, 62, 65   already shown
*d–d*MS, 43   any
*e–e*MS, 43, 46, 51, 56, 62, 65   absolute
*f–f*MS, 43, 46, 51, 56, 62, 65, 68   a few such cases
g–g+MS, 51, 56, 62, 65, 68, 72   [*printer's error?*]

such inquiries becomes as hypothetical a science as geometry. All units must be assumed to be equal in that other respect; and this is never *accurately* true, for one *actual* pound weight is not exactly equal to another, nor one *measured* mile's length to another; a nicer balance, or more accurate measuring instruments, would always detect some difference.

What is commonly called mathematical certainty, therefore, which comprises the twofold conception of unconditional truth and perfect accuracy, is not an attribute of all mathematical truths, but of those only which relate to pure Number, as distinguished from Quantity in the more enlarged sense; and only so long as we abstain from supposing that the numbers are a precise index to actual quantities. The certainty usually ascribed to the conclusions of geometry, and even to those of mechanics, is nothing whatever but certainty of inference. We can have full assurance of particular results under particular suppositions, but we cannot have the same assurance that these suppositions are accurately true, nor that they include all the data which may exercise an influence over the result in any given instance.

§ 4. [*The characteristic property of demonstrative science is to be hypothetical*] It appears, therefore, that the method of all Deductive Sciences is hypothetical. They proceed by tracing the consequences of certain assumptions; leaving for separate consideration whether the assumptions are true or not, and if not exactly true, whether they are a sufficiently near approximation to the truth. The reason is obvious. Since it is only in questions of pure number that the assumptions are exactly true, and even there, only so long as no conclusions except purely numerical ones are to be founded on them; it must, in all other cases of deductive investigation, form a part of the inquiry, to determine how much the assumptions want of being exactly true in the case in hand. This is generally a matter of observation, to be repeated in every fresh case; or if it has to be settled by argument instead of observation, may require in every different case different evidence, and present every degree of difficulty, from the lowest to the highest. But the other part of the process—namely, to determine what else may be concluded if we find, and in proportion as we find, the assumptions to be true—may be performed once for all, and the results held ready to be employed as the occasions turn up for use. We thus do all beforehand that can be so done, and leave the least possible work to be performed when cases arise and press for a decision. This inquiry into the inferences which can be drawn from assumptions, is what properly constitutes Demonstrative Science.

It is of course quite as practicable to arrive at new conclusions from facts

*ʰ⁻ʰ*MS, 43, 46 precisely] 51 practically
ⁱ⁻ⁱ+46, 51, 56, 62, 65, 68, 72
ʲ⁻ʲ+68, 72

assumed, as from facts observed; from fictitious, as from real, inductions. Deduction, as we have seen, consists of a series of inferences in this form—*a* is a mark of *b*, *b* of *c*, *c* of *d*, therefore *a* is a mark of *d*, which last may be a truth inaccessible to direct observation. In like manner it is allowable to say, *suppose* that *a* were a mark of *b*, *b* of *c*, and *c* of *d*, *a* would be a mark of *d*, which last conclusion was not thought of by those who laid down the premises. A system of propositions as complicated as geometry might be deduced from assumptions which are false; as was done by Ptolemy, Descartes, and others, in their attempts to explain synthetically the phenomena of the solar system on the supposition that the apparent motions of the heavenly bodies were the real motions, or were produced in some way more or less different from the true one. Sometimes the same thing is knowingly done, for the purpose of showing the falsity of the assumption; which is called a *reductio ad absurdum*. In such cases, the reasoning is as follows: *a* is a mark of *b*, and *b* of *c*; now if *c* were also a mark of *d*, *a* would be a mark of *d*; but *d* is known to be a mark of the absence of *a*; consequently *a* would be a mark of its own absence, which is a contradiction; therefore *c* is not a mark of *d*.

§ 5. [*Definition of demonstrative evidence* [a]] It has even been held by some [b]writers[b], that all ratiocination rests in the last resort on a *reductio ad absurdum*; since the way to enforce assent to it, in case of obscurity, would be to show that if the conclusion be denied we must deny some one at least of the premises, which, as they are all supposed true, would be a contradiction. And in accordance with this, many have thought that the peculiar nature of the evidence of ratiocination consisted in the impossibility of admitting the premises and rejecting the conclusion without a contradiction in terms. This theory, however, is [c] inadmissible as an explanation of the grounds on which ratiocination itself rests. If any one denies the conclusion notwithstanding his admission of the premises, he is not involved in any direct and express contradiction until he is compelled to deny some premise; and he can only be forced to do this by a *reductio ad absurdum*, that is, by another ratiocination: now, if he denies the validity of the reasoning process itself, he can no more be forced to assent to the second syllogism than to the first. In truth, therefore, no one is ever forced to a contradiction in terms: he can only be forced to a contradiction (or rather an infringement) of the fundamental maxim of ratiocination, namely, that whatever has a mark, has what it is a mark of; or, (in the case of universal propositions,) that whatever is a mark of [d]anything[d], is a mark of whatever else that thing is a mark of.

[a]MS, 43, 46, 51   , *and of logical necessity*
[b–b]MS, 43, 46   philosophers
[c]MS, 43, 46   quite
[d–d]MS, 43, 46   a thing

For in the case of every correct argument, as soon as thrown into the syllogistic form, it is evident without the aid of any other syllogism, that he who, admitting the premises, fails to draw the conclusion, does not conform to the above axiom. *e*

f We have now proceeded as far in the theory of Deduction as we can advance in the present stage of our inquiry. Any further insight into the subject requires that the foundation shall have been laid of the philosophic theory of Induction itself; in which theory that of Deduction, as a mode of Induction, which we have now shown it to be, will assume spontaneously the place which belongs to it, and will receive its share of whatever light may be thrown upon the great intellectual operation of which it forms so important a part. *g*

*e*MS, 43, 46 [*paragraph*] Without attaching exaggerated importance to the distinction now drawn, I think it enables us to characterize in a more accurate manner than is usually done, the nature of demonstrative evidence and of logical necessity. That is necessary, from which to withhold our assent would be to violate the above axiom. And since the axiom can only be violated by assenting to premisses and rejecting a legitimate conclusion from them, nothing is necessary, except the connexion between a conclusion and premisses; of which doctrine, the whole of this and the preceding chapter are submitted as the proof.] 51 *as* MS . . . withhold assent . . . *as* MS

*f*MS §6. [*this section is not indicated or titled in the* MS *Table of Contents*]

*g*MS, 43, 46, 51 [*paragraph*] We here, therefore, close the Second Book. The theory of Induction, in the most comprehensive sense of the term, will form the subject of the Third. [cf. p. 279.14–16]

CHAPTER VII

Examination of Some Opinions
Opposed to the Preceding Doctrines

§ 1. [*Doctrine of the Universal Postulate*] Polemical discussion is foreign to the plan of this work. But an opinion which stands in need of much illustration, can often receive it most effectually, and least tediously, in the form of a defence against objections. And on subjects concerning which speculative minds are still divided, a writer does but half his duty by stating his own doctrine, if he does not also examine, and to the best of his ability judge, those of other thinkers.

In *the* dissertation which Mr. Herbert Spencer has prefixed to his, in many respects, highly philosophical treatise *on the Mind*,* he criticises some of the doctrines of the two preceding chapters, and propounds a theory of his own on the subject of first principles. Mr. Spencer agrees with me in considering axioms to be "simply our earliest inductions from experience." But he differs from me "widely as to the worth of the test of inconceivableness."[*] He thinks that it is the ultimate test of all beliefs. He arrives at this conclusion by two steps. First, we never can have any stronger ground for believing anything, than that the belief of it "invariably exists."[†] Whenever any fact or proposition is invariably believed; that is, if I understand Mr. Spencer rightly, believed by all persons, and by oneself at all times; it is entitled to be received as one of the primitive truths, or original premises of our knowledge. Secondly, the criterion by which we decide whether anything is invariably believed to be true, is our inability to conceive it as false. "The inconceivability of its negation is the test by which we ascertain whether a given belief invariably exists or not."[†] "For our primary beliefs, the fact of invariable existence, tested by an abortive effort to cause their non-existence, is the only reason assignable."[§] He thinks this the sole ground of our belief

---

*[62] *Principles of Psychology* [1st ed., 1855].
[*Ibid., p. 19.]   [†Ibid., e.g., p. 26.]
[‡Ibid.]   [§Ibid., p. 27.]

a–a279+56, 62, 65, 68, 72
b–b56   what I cannot but think the very unphilosophical]   62   what I venture to think the very unphilosophical
c–c+62, 65, 68, 72

in our own sensations. If I believe that I feel cold, I only receive this as true because I cannot conceive that I am not feeling cold. "While the proposition remains true, the negation of it remains inconceivable."[*] There are numerous other beliefs which Mr. Spencer considers to rest on the same basis; being chiefly those, or a part of those, which the metaphysicians of the Reid and Stewart school consider as truths of immediate intuition. That there exists a material world; that this is the very world which we directly and immediately perceive, and not merely the hidden cause of our perceptions; that Space, Time, Force, Extension, Figure, are not modes of our consciousness, but objective realities; are regarded by Mr. Spencer as truths known by the inconceivableness of their negatives. We cannot, he says, by any effort, conceive these objects of thought as mere states of our mind; as not having an existence external to us. Their real existence is, therefore, as certain as our sensations themselves. The truths which are the subject of direct knowledge, being, according to this doctrine, known to be truths only by the inconceivability of their negation; and the truths which are not the *object* of direct knowledge, being known as inferences from those which are; and those inferences being believed to follow from the premises, only because we cannot conceive them not to follow; inconceivability is thus the ultimate ground of all assured beliefs.

Thus far, there is no very wide difference between Mr. Spencer's doctrine and the ordinary one of philosophers of the intuitive school, from Descartes to Dr. Whewell; but at this point Mr. Spencer diverges from them. For he does not, like them, set up the test of inconceivability as infallible. On the contrary, he holds that it may be fallacious, not from any fault in the test itself, but because "men have mistaken for inconceivable things, some things which were not inconceivable."[†] And he himself, in this very book, denies not a few propositions usually regarded as among the most marked examples of truths whose negations are inconceivable. But occasional failure, he says, is incident to all tests. If such failure vitiates "the test of inconceivableness," it

must similarly vitiate all tests whatever. We consider an inference logically drawn from established premises to be true. Yet in millions of cases men have been wrong in the inferences they have thought thus drawn. Do we therefore argue that it is absurd to consider an inference true on no other ground than that it is logically drawn from established premises? No: we say that though men may have taken for logical inferences, inferences that were not logical, there nevertheless *are* logical inferences, and that we are justified in assuming the truth of what seem to us such, until better instructed. Similarly, though men may have thought some things inconceivable which were not so, there may still be inconceivable things; and the inability to conceive the negation of a thing, may still be our best warrant for believing it. . . . Though occasionally it may prove an imperfect test, yet, as our most certain beliefs are capable of no better, to doubt

[*Ibid., p. 28.]   [†Ibid., p. 20.]

*a–a*56, 62, 65   subject

any one belief because we have no higher guarantee for it, is really to doubt all beliefs.[*]

Mr. Spencer's doctrine, therefore, does not erect the curable, but only the incurable limitations of the human conceptive faculty, into laws of the outward universe.

§ 2. [*The test of inconceivability does not represent the aggregate of past experience*] The doctrine, that "a belief which is proved by the inconceivableness of its negation to invariably exist, is true,"[†] Mr. Spencer enforces by two arguments, one of which may be distinguished as positive, and the other as negative.

The positive argument is, that every such belief represents the aggregate of all past experience. "Conceding the entire truth of" the

position, that during any phase of human progress, the ability or inability to form a specific conception wholly depends on the experiences men have had; and that, by a widening of their experiences, they may, by and by, be enabled to conceive things before inconceivable to them, it may still be argued that as, at any time, the best warrant men can have for a belief is the perfect agreement of all pre-existing experience in support of it, it follows that, at any time, the inconceivableness of its negation is the deepest test any belief admits of. . . . Objective facts are ever impressing themselves upon us; our experience is a register of these objective facts; and the inconceivableness of a thing implies that it is wholly at variance with the register. Even were this all, it is not clear how, if every truth is primarily inductive, any better test of truth could exist. But it must be remembered that whilst many of these facts, impressing themselves upon us, are occasional; whilst others again are very general; some are universal and unchanging. These universal and unchanging facts are, by the hypothesis, certain to establish beliefs of which the negations are inconceivable; whilst the others are not certain to do this; and if they do, subsequent facts will reverse their action. Hence if, after an immense accumulation of experiences, there remain beliefs of which the negations are still inconceivable, most, if not all of them, must correspond to universal objective facts. If there be . . . certain absolute uniformities in nature; if these uniformities produce, as they must, absolute uniformities in our experience; and if . . . these absolute uniformities in our experience disable us from conceiving the negations of them; then answering to each absolute uniformity in nature which we can cognize, there must exist in us a belief of which the negation is inconceivable, and which is absolutely true. In this wide range of cases subjective inconceivableness must correspond to objective impossibility. Further experience will produce correspondence where it may not yet exist; and we may expect the correspondence to become ultimately complete. In nearly all cases this test of inconceivableness must be valid now; [I wish I could think we were so nearly arrived at omniscience] and where it is not, it still expresses the net result of our experience up to the present time; which is the most that any test can do.[‡]

[*Ibid., pp. 20–1.]   [†Ibid., p. 31.]
[‡Ibid., pp. 21–3; JSM's comment in square brackets.]

^aTo this I answer, first, that it is by no means true that the inconceivability, by us, of the negative of a proposition proves all, or even any, "pre-existing experience" to be in favour of the affirmative. There may have been no such pre-existing experiences, but only a mistaken supposition of experience. How did the inconceivability of antipodes prove that experience had given any testimony against their possibility? How did the incapacity men felt of conceiving sunset otherwise than as a motion of the sun, represent any "net result" of experience in support of its being the sun and not the earth that moves? It is not experience that is represented, it is only a superficial semblance of experience. The only thing proved with regard to real experience, is the negative fact, that men have *not had* it of the kind which would have made the inconceivable proposition conceivable.

Next:^a ^b Even if it were true that inconceivableness represents the net result of all past experience, why should we stop at the representative when we can get at the thing represented? If our incapacity to conceive the negation of a given supposition is proof of its truth, because proving that our experience has hitherto been uniform in its favour, the real evidence for the supposition is not the inconceivableness, but the uniformity of experience. Now this, which is the substantial and only proof, is directly accessible. We are not obliged to presume it from an incidental consequence. If all past experience is in favour of a belief, let this be stated, and the belief openly rested on that ground: after which the question arises, what that fact may be worth as evidence of its truth? For uniformity of experience is evidence in very different degrees: in some cases it is strong evidence, in others weak, in others it scarcely amounts to evidence at all. That all metals sink in water, was an uniform experience, from the origin of the human race to the discovery of potassium in the present century by Sir Humphry Davy. That all swans are white, was an uniform experience down to the discovery of Australia. In the few cases in which uniformity of experience does amount to the strongest possible proof, as with such propositions as these, Two straight lines cannot inclose a space, Every event has a cause, it is not because their negations are inconceivable, which is not always the fact; but because the experience, which has been thus uniform, pervades all nature. It will be shown in the following Book that none of the conclusions either of induction or of deduction can be considered certain, except ^cas^c far as their truth is shown to be inseparably bound up with truths of this class.

I maintain then, first, that uniformity of past experience is very far from being universally a criterion of truth. But secondly, inconceivableness is still farther from being a test even of that test. Uniformity of contrary experience is only one of many causes of inconceivability. Tradition handed down from a period of more limited knowledge, is one of the commonest. The mere familiarity of one mode of production of a phenomenon, often suffices to make every other mode appear inconceivable. Whatever connects two ideas by a strong association may, and continually does, render their separation in thought impossible; as Mr. Spencer, in other parts of his speculations, frequently recognises. It was not for want of experience that the Cartesians were unable to conceive that one body could produce motion in another without contact. They had as much experience of other modes of producing motion, as they had of that mode. The planets had revolved, and heavy bodies had fallen, every hour of their lives. But they fancied these phenomena to be produced by a hidden machinery which they did not see, because without it they were unable to conceive what they did see. The inconceivableness, instead of representing their experience, dominated and overrode their experience. *d*Without dwelling farther on what I have termed the positive argument of Mr. Spencer in support of his criterion of truth,*d* I pass to his negative argument, on which he lays more stress.

§ 3. [*Nor is the test of inconceivability implied in every process of thought*] The negative argument is, that, whether inconceivability be good evidence or bad, no stronger evidence is to be obtained. That what is inconceivable cannot be true, is postulated in every act of thought. It is the foundation of all our original premises. Still more *a*it is*a* assumed in all conclusions from those premises. The invariability of belief, tested by the inconceivableness of its negation, "is our sole warrant for every demonstration. Logic is simply a systematization of the process by which we indirectly obtain this warrant for beliefs that do not directly possess it. To gain the strongest conviction possible respecting any complex fact, we either analytically descend from it by successive steps, each of which we unconsciously test by the inconceivableness of its negation, until we reach some axiom or truth which we have similarly tested; or we synthetically ascend from such axiom or truth by such steps. In either case we connect some isolated belief, with a belief which invariably exists, by a series of intermediate beliefs which invariably exist."[*] The following passage sums up the *b* theory:

When we perceive that the negation of the belief is inconceivable, we have all possible warrant for asserting the invariability of its existence: and in asserting this, we express alike our logical justification of it, and the inexorable necessity we are under of holding it. . . . We have seen that this is the assumption on which every conclusion whatever ultimately rests. We have no other guarantee for the

[*Spencer, *Principles of Psychology*, 1st ed., pp. 28–9.]

*d–d*56, 62, 65, 68   It is needless to dwell farther . . . truth.
*a–a*56, 62   is it
*b*56, 62, 65, 68   whole

reality of consciousness, of sensations, of personal existence; we have no other guarantee for any axiom; we have no other guarantee for any step in a demonstration. Hence, as being taken for granted in every act of the understanding, it must be regarded as the Universal Postulate.[*]

But as this postulate which we are under an "inexorable necessity" of holding true, is sometimes false; as "beliefs that once were shown by the inconceivableness of their negations to invariably exist, have since been found untrue," and as "beliefs that now possess this character may some day share the same fate;"[†] the canon of belief laid down by Mr. Spencer is, that "the most certain conclusion" is that "which involves the postulate the fewest times."[‡] Reasoning, therefore, never ought to prevail against one of the immediate beliefs (the belief in Matter, in the outward reality of Extension, Space, and the like), because each of these involves the postulate only once; while an argument, besides involving it in the premises, involves it again in every step of the ratiocination, no one of the successive acts of inference being recognised as valid except because we cannot conceive the conclusion not to follow from the premises.

It will be convenient to take the last part of this argument first. In every reasoning, according to Mr. Spencer, the assumption of the postulate is renewed at every step. At each inference we judge that the conclusion follows from the premises, our sole warrant for that judgment being that we cannot conceive it not to follow. Consequently if the postulate is fallible, the conclusions of reasoning are more vitiated by that uncertainty than direct intuitions; and the disproportion is greater, the more numerous the steps of the argument.

To test this doctrine, let us first suppose an argument consisting only of a single step, which would be represented by one syllogism. This argument does rest on an assumption, and we have seen in the preceding chapters what the assumption is. It is, that whatever has a mark, has what it is a mark of. The evidence of this axiom I shall not consider at present;* let us suppose it (with Mr. Spencer) to be the inconceivableness of its reverse.

Let us now add a second step to the argument: we require, what? Another assumption? No: the same assumption a second time; and so on to a third, and a fourth. I confess I do not see how, on Mr. Spencer's own principles, the repetition of the assumption at all weakens the force of the argument. If it were necessary the second time to assume some other axiom, the argument

[*Ibid., p. 31.]
[†Ibid.]
[‡Ibid., p. 33.]
*[56] Mr. Spencer is mistaken in supposing me to claim any peculiar "necessity" for this axiom as compared with others. [See Principles of Psychology, pp. 24–5.] I have corrected the expressions which led him into that misapprehension of my meaning. [See Textual Introduction, xci above.]

would no doubt be weakened, since it would be necessary to its validity that both axioms should be true, and it might happen that one was true and not the other: making two chances of error instead of one. But since it is the *same* axiom, if it is true once it is true every time; and if the argument, being of a hundred links, assumed the axiom a hundred times, these hundred assumptions would make but one chance of error among them all. It is satisfactory that we are not obliged to suppose the deductions of pure mathematics to be among the most uncertain of argumentative processes, which on Mr. Spencer's theory they could hardly fail to be, since they are the longest. But the number of steps in an argument does not subtract from its reliableness, if no new *premises*, of an uncertain character, are taken up by the way.*

*[72] Mr. Spencer, in recently returning to the subject (*Principles of Psychology*, new edition [2nd ed. 2 vols. London: Williams and Norgate, 1870, 1872], Chap. xii, "The Test of Relative Validity,") makes two answers to the preceding remarks. One is:

"Were an argument formed by repeating the same proposition over and over again, it would be true that any intrinsic fallibility of the postulate would not make the conclusion more untrustworthy than the first step. But an argument consists of unlike propositions. Now since Mr. Mill's criticism on the Universal Postulate is that in some cases, which he names, it has proved to be an untrustworthy test; it follows that in any argument consisting of heterogeneous propositions, there is a risk, increasing as the number of propositions increases, that some one of them belongs to this class of cases, and is wrongly accepted because of the inconceivableness of its negation." [Vol. II, p. 433.]

No doubt: but this supposes new *premises* to be taken in. The point we are discussing is the fallibility not of the premises, but of the reasoning, as distinguished from the premises. Now the validity of the reasoning depends always upon the same axiom, repeated (in thought) "over and over again," viz. that whatever has a mark, has what it is a mark of. Even, therefore, on the assumption that this axiom rests ultimately on the Universal Postulate, and that, the Postulate not being wholly trustworthy, the axiom may be one of the cases of its failure; all the risk there is of this is incurred at the very first step of the reasoning, and is not added to, however long may be the series of subsequent steps.

I am here arguing, of course, from Mr. Spencer's point of view. From my own the case is still clearer; for, in my view, the truth that whatever has a mark has what it is a mark of, is wholly trustworthy, and derives none of its evidence from so very untrustworthy a test as the inconceivability of the negative.

Mr. Spencer's second answer is valid up to a certain point; it is, that every prolongation of the process involves additional chances of casual error, from carelessness in the reasoning operation. This is an important consideration in the private speculations of an individual reasoner; and even with respect to mankind at large, it must be admitted that, though mere oversights in the syllogistic process, like errors of addition in an account, are special to the individual, and seldom escape detection, confusion of thought produced (for example) by ambiguous terms has led whole nations or ages to accept fallacious reasoning as valid. But this very fact points to causes of error so much more dangerous than the mere

To speak next of the premises. Our assurance of their truth, whether they be generalities or individual facts, is grounded, in Mr. Spencer's opinion, on the inconceivableness of their being false. It is necessary to advert to a double meaning of the word inconceivable, which Mr. Spencer is aware of, and would sincerely disclaim founding an argument upon, but from which his case derives no little advantage notwithstanding. By inconceivableness is sometimes meant, inability to form or get rid of an *idea*; sometimes, inability to form or get rid of a *belief*. The former meaning is the most conformable to the analogy of language; for a conception always means an idea, and never a belief. The wrong meaning of "inconceivable" is, however, fully as frequent in philosophical discussion as the right meaning, and the intuitive school of metaphysicians could not well do without either. To illustrate the difference, we will take two contrasted examples. The early physical speculators considered antipodes incredible, because inconceivable. But antipodes were not inconceivable in the primitive sense of the word. An idea of them could be formed without difficulty: they could be completely pictured to the mental eye. What was difficult, and as it then seemed, impossible, was to apprehend them as believable. The idea could be put together, of men sticking on by their feet to the under side of the earth; but the belief *would* follow, that they must fall off. Antipodes were not unimaginable, but they were unbelievable.

On the other hand, when I endeavour to conceive an end to extension, the two ideas refuse to come together. When I attempt to form a conception of the last point of space, I cannot help figuring to myself a vast space beyond that last point. The combination is, under the conditions of our experience, unimaginable. This double meaning of inconceivable it is very important to bear in mind, for the argument from inconceivableness almost always turns on the alternate substitution of *c*each*c* of those meanings for the other.

*d*In which of these two senses does Mr. Spencer employ the term, when he makes it a test of the truth of a proposition that its negation is inconceivable? Until Mr. Spencer expressly stated the contrary, I inferred from the course of his argument, that he meant unbelievable. He has, however, in a paper published in the fifth number of the *Fortnightly Review*, disclaimed this meaning, and declared that by an inconceivable proposition he means, now and always, "one of which the terms cannot, by any effort, be brought before

---

length of the process, as quite to vitiate the doctrine that the "test of the relative validities of conflicting conclusions" [*ibid*., p. 435,] is the number of times the fundamental postulate is involved. On the contrary, the subjects on which the trains of reasoning are longest, and the assumption, therefore, oftenest repeated, are in general those which are best fortified against the really formidable causes of fallacy; as in the example already given of mathematics.

*c–c*56   one
*d–d*270 56, 62   Mr. Spencer leaves us in no doubt which of the two senses he intends, when . . . its negation is inconceivable. He means unbelievable.

consciousness in that relation which the proposition asserts between them—a proposition of which the subject and predicate offer an insurmountable resistance to union in thought."[*] We now, therefore, know positively that Mr. Spencer always endeavours to use the word inconceivable in this, its proper, sense: but it may yet be questioned whether his endeavour is always successful; whether the other, and popular use of the word does not sometimes creep in with its associations, and prevent him from maintaining a clear separation between the two. When, for example, he says, that when I feel cold, I cannot conceive that I am not feeling cold,[†] this expression cannot be translated into "I cannot conceive myself not feeling cold," for it is evident that I can: the word conceive, therefore, is here used to express the recognition of a matter of fact—the perception of truth or falsehood; which I apprehend to be exactly the meaning of an act of belief, as distinguished from simple conception. Again, Mr. Spencer calls the attempt to conceive something which is inconceivable, "an abortive effort to cause the non-existence"[‡] not of a conception or mental representation, but of a belief. There is need, therefore, to revise a considerable part of Mr. Spencer's language, if it is to be kept always consistent with his definition of inconceivability. But in truth the point is of little importance; since inconceivability, in Mr. Spencer's theory, is only a test of truth, inasmuch as it is a test of believability. The inconceivableness of a supposition is the extreme case of its unbelievability.[d] This is the very foundation of [e]Mr. Spencer's[e] doctrine. The invariability of the belief is with him the real guarantee. The attempt to conceive the negative, is made in order to test the inevitableness of the belief. It should be called, an attempt to *believe* the negative. When Mr. Spencer says that while looking at the sun a man cannot conceive that he is looking into darkness,[§] he [f]should have said that[f] a man cannot *believe* that he is doing so. For [g]it is surely[g] possible, in broad daylight, to *imagine* oneself looking into darkness.* As [h]Mr. Spencer himself[h] says, speaking of the belief of our own existence: "That he *might* not exist, he can conceive well enough; but that he *does* not

[*Herbert Spencer, "Mill *versus* Hamilton—The Test of Truth," *Fortnightly Review*, I (15 July, 1865), pp. 534–5.]

[†See *Principles of Psychology*, 1st ed., p. 28.]

[‡*Ibid.*, p. 27.]

[§*Ibid.*, p. 28.]

*[68] Mr. Spencer makes a distinction between conceiving myself looking into darkness, and conceiving *that I am* then and there looking into darkness. [See letter to Mill (11 Oct., 1865), in David Duncan, *The Life and Letters of Herbert Spencer*. London: Methuen, 1908, p. 121.] To me it seems that this change of the expression to the form *I am*, just marks the transition from conception to belief, and that the phrase "to conceive that *I am*," or "that anything *is*," is not consistent with using the word conceive in its rigorous sense.

[e–e]56, 62   his   [f–f]56, 62, 65   means,
[g–g]56, 62, 65   he is aware that it is   [h–h]56, 62, 65   he

exist, he finds it impossible to conceive,"[*] *i.e.* to believe. So that the statement resolves itself into this: That I exist, and that I have sensations, I believe, because I cannot believe otherwise. And in this case every one will admit that the *impossibility* is real. Any one's present sensations, or other states of subjective consciousness, that one person inevitably believes. They are facts known *per se*: it is impossible to ascend beyond them. Their negative is really unbelievable, and therefore there is never any question about believing it. Mr. Spencer's theory is not needed for these truths.

But according to Mr. Spencer there are other beliefs, relating to other things than our own subjective feelings, for which we have the same guarantee—which are, in a similar manner, invariable and necessary. With regard to these other beliefs, they cannot be necessary, since they do not always exist. There have been, and are, many persons who do not believe the reality of an external world, still less the reality of extension and figure as the forms of that external world; who do not believe that space and time have an existence independent of the mind—nor any other of Mr. Spencer's objective intuitions. The negations of these alleged invariable beliefs are not unbelievable, for they are believed *j*. It may be maintained, without obvious*j* error, that we cannot *imagine* tangible objects as mere states of our own and other people's consciousness; that the perception of them irresistibly suggests to us the *idea* of something external to ourselves: and I am not in a condition to say that this is not the fact (though I do not think any one is entitled to affirm it of any person besides himself). But many thinkers have believed, whether they could conceive it or not, that what we represent to ourselves as material objects, are mere modifications of consciousness; complex feelings of touch and of muscular action. Mr. Spencer may think the inference correct from the unimaginable to the unbelievable, because he holds that belief itself is but the persistence of an idea, and that what we can succeed in imagining we cannot at the moment help apprehending as believable. But of what consequence is it what we apprehend at the moment, if the moment is in contradiction to the permanent state of our mind? A person who has been frightened when an infant by stories of ghosts, though he disbelieves them in after years (and perhaps *k*never believed them*k*), may be unable all his life to be in a dark place, in circumstances stimulating to the imagination, without mental discomposure. The idea of ghosts, with all its attendant terrors, is irresistibly called up in his mind by the outward circumstances. Mr.

[**Principles of Psychology*, 1st ed., p. 19]

*i-i*56, 62, 65, 68   necessity
*j-j*56, 62   : and the only colour which Mr. Spencer has for representing them as inconceivable, is derived from the other meaning of the word. He *may* maintain, without being obviously in
*k-k*56, 62, 65, 68   disbelieved them at first

Spencer may say, that while he is under the influence of this terror he does not disbelieve in ghosts, but has a temporary and uncontrollable belief in them. Be it so; but allowing it to be so, which would it be truest to say of this man on the whole—that he believes in ghosts, or that he does not believe in them? Assuredly that he does not believe in them. The case is similar with those who disbelieve a material world. Though they cannot get rid of the idea; though while looking at a solid object they cannot help having the conception, and therefore, according to Mr. Spencer's metaphysics, the momentary belief, of its externality; even at that moment they would sincerely deny holding that belief: and it would be *incorrect* to call them other than disbelievers of the doctrine. The belief therefore is not invariable; and the test of inconceivableness fails in the only cases to which there could ever be any occasion to apply it.

That a thing may be perfectly believable, and yet may not have become conceivable, and that we may habitually believe one side of an alternative, and conceive only in the other, is familiarly exemplified in the state of mind of educated persons respecting sunrise and sunset. All educated persons either know by investigation, or believe on the authority of science, that it is the earth and not the sun which moves: but there are probably few who habitually *conceive* the phenomenon otherwise than as the ascent or descent of the sun. Assuredly no one can do so without a prolonged trial; and it is probably not easier now than in the first generation after Copernicus. Mr. Spencer does not say, "In looking at sunrise it is impossible not to conceive that it is the sun which moves, therefore this is what everybody believes, and we have all the evidence for it that we can have for any truth." Yet this would be an exact parallel to his doctrine about the belief in matter.

The existence of matter, and other Noumena, as distinguished from the phenomenal world, remains a question of argument, as it was before; and the very general, but neither necessary nor universal, belief in them, stands as a psychological phenomenon to be explained, either on the hypothesis of its truth, or on some other. The belief is not a conclusive proof of its own truth, unless there are no such things as *idola tribûs*;[*] but, being a fact, it calls on antagonists to show, from what except the real existence of the thing believed, so general and apparently spontaneous a belief can have originated. And its opponents have never hesitated to accept this challenge.* The amount of their success in meeting it will probably determine the ultimate verdict of philosophers on the question.

[*See Bacon, *Novum Organum*, pp. 163–4 (Bk. I, Aph. xli).]

*[65] I have *myself* accepted the contest, and fought it out on this battle-ground, in the eleventh chapter of *An Examination of Sir William Hamilton's Philosophy.*

l–l56 false   m–m+68, 72

*§ 4. [*Objections answered*] In a revision, or rather reconstruction, of his *Principles of Psychology*, as one of the stages or platforms in the imposing structure of his System of Philosophy, Mr. Spencer has resumed what he justly terms* the "amicable controversy that has been long pending between us;" expressing at the same time a regret, which I cordially share, that "this lengthened exposition of a single point of difference, unaccompanied by an exposition of the numerous points of concurrence, unavoidably produces an appearance of dissent very far greater than that which exists." I believe, with Mr. Spencer, that the difference between us, if measured by our conclusions, is "superficial rather than substantial;" and the value I attach to so great an amount of agreement, in the field of analytic psychology, with a thinker of his force and depth, is such as I can hardly overstate. But I also agree with him that the difference which exists in our premises is one of "profound importance, philosophically considered;" and not to be dismissed while any part of the case of either of us has not been fully examined and discussed.

In his present statement of the Universal Postulate, Mr. Spencer has exchanged his former expression, "beliefs which invariably exist,"[*] for the following: "cognitions of which the predicates invariably exist along with their subjects." And he says that "an abortive effort to conceive the negation of a proposition, shows that the cognition expressed is one of which the predicate invariably exists along with its subject; and the discovery that the predicate invariably exists along with its subject, is the discovery that this cognition is one we are compelled to accept."[†] Both these premises of Mr. Spencer's syllogism I am able to assent to, but in different senses of the middle term. If the invariable existence of the predicate along with its subject, is to be understood in the most obvious meaning, as an existence in actual Nature, or in other words, in our objective, or sensational, experience, I of course admit that this, once ascertained, compels us to accept the proposition: but then I do not admit that the failure of an attempt to conceive the negative, proves the predicate to be always coexistent with the subject in actual Nature. If, on the other hand (which I believe to be Mr. Spencer's meaning) the invariable existence of the predicate along with the subject is to be understood only of our conceptive faculty, *i.e.* that the one is inseparable from the other in our thoughts; then, indeed, the inability to separate the two ideas proves their inseparable conjunction, here and now, in the mind which has failed in the attempt; but this inseparability in thought does

---

*[72] [2nd ed.,] Chap. xi [Vol. II, p. 406n–407n]. [The passage quoted also appears in Spencer's "Mill *versus* Hamilton," p. 550.]

[*Principles of Psychology*, 1st ed., p. 29.]

[†*Ibid.*, 2nd ed., Vol. II, p. 425.]

*a–a*276+72

not prove a corresponding inseparability in fact; nor even in the thoughts of other people, or of the same person in a possible future.

"That some propositions have been wrongly accepted as true, because their negations were supposed inconceivable when they were not," does not, in Mr. Spencer's opinion, "disprove the validity of the test;" not only because any test whatever "is liable to yield untrue results, either from incapacity or from carelessness in those who use it," but because the propositions in question "were complex propositions, not to be established by a test applicable to propositions no further decomposable."[*] "A test legitimately applicable to a simple proposition, the subject and predicate of which are in direct relation, cannot be legitimately applied to a complex proposition, the subject and predicate of which are indirectly related through the many simple propositions implied."[†] "That things which are equal to the same thing are equal to one another, is a fact which can be known by direct comparison of actual or ideal relations. . . . But that the square of the hypothenuse of a right angled triangle equals the sum of the squares of the other two sides, cannot be known immediately by comparison of two states of consciousness: here the truth can be reached only mediately, through a series of simple judgments respecting the likenesses or unlikenesses of certain relations."[‡] Moreover, even when the proposition admits of being tested by immediate consciousness, people often neglect to do it. A schoolboy, in adding up a column of figures, will say "35 and 9 are 46," though this is contrary to the verdict which consciousness gives when 35 and 9 are really called up before it; but this is not done. And not only schoolboys, but men and thinkers, do not always "distinctly translate into their equivalent states of consciousness the words they use."[§]

It is but just to give Mr. Spencer's doctrine the benefit of the limitation he claims—viz. that it is only applicable to propositions which are assented to on simple inspection, without any intervening media of proof. But this limitation does not exclude some of the most marked instances of propositions now known to be false or groundless, but whose negative was once found inconceivable: such as, that in sunrise and sunset it is the sun which moves; that gravitation may exist without an intervening medium; and even the case of antipodes. The distinction drawn by Mr. Spencer is real; but, in the case of the propositions classed by him as complex, consciousness, until the media of proof are supplied, gives no verdict at all: it neither declares the equality of the square of the hypothenuse with the sum of the squares of the sides to be inconceivable, nor their inequality to be inconceivable. But in all the three

[*Ibid.]
[†Ibid., p. 410.]
[‡Ibid., pp. 411–12.]
[§Ibid., p. 413; the illustration is Spencer's.]

cases which I have just cited, the inconceivability seems to be apprehended directly; no train of argument was needed, as in the case of the square of the hypothenuse, to obtain the verdict of consciousness on the point. Neither is any of the three a case like that of the schoolboy's mistake, in which the mind was never really brought into contact with the proposition. They are cases in which one of two opposite predicates, *mero adspectu*, seemed to be incompatible with the subject, and the other, therefore, to be proved always to exist with it.*

As now limited by Mr. Spencer, the ultimate cognitions fit to be submitted to his test are only those of so universal and elementary a character as to be represented in the earliest and most unvarying experience, or apparent experience, of all mankind. In such cases the inconceivability of the negative, if real, is accounted for by the experience: and why (I have asked) should the truth be tested by the inconceivability, when we can go further back for proof—namely, to the experience itself? To this Mr. Spencer answers, that the experiences cannot be all recalled to mind, and if recalled, would be of unmanageable multitude. To test a proposition by experience seems to him to mean that "before accepting as certain the proposition that any rectilineal figure must have as many angles as it has sides," I have "to think of every triangle, square, pentagon, hexagon, &c., which I have ever seen, and to verify the asserted relation in each case."[*] I can only say, with surprise, that I do not understand this to be the meaning of an appeal to experience. It is enough to know that one has been seeing the fact all one's life, and has never remarked any instance to the contrary, and that other people, with every opportunity of observation, unanimously declare the same thing. It is

*[72] In one of the three cases, Mr. Spencer, to my no small surprise, thinks that the belief of mankind "cannot be rightly said to have undergone" the change I allege. Mr. Spencer himself still thinks we are unable to conceive gravitation acting through empty space. "If an astronomer avowed that he could conceive gravitative force as exercised through space absolutely void, my private opinion would be that he mistook the nature of conception. Conception implies representation. Here the elements of the representation are the two bodies and an agency by which either affects the other. To conceive this agency is to represent it in some terms derived from our experiences—that is, from our sensations. As this agency gives us no sensations, we are obliged (if we try to conceive it) to use symbols idealized from our sensations—imponderable units forming a medium." [*Ibid.*, p. 409n.]

If Mr. Spencer means that the action of gravitation gives us no sensations, the assertion is one than which I have not seen, in the writings of philosophers, many more startling. What other sensation do we need than the sensation of one body moving towards another? "The elements of the representation" are not two bodies and an "agency," but two bodies and an effect; viz. the fact of their approaching one another. If we are able to conceive a vacuum, is there any difficulty in conceiving a body falling to the earth through it?

[*Ibid., p. 417.]

true, even this experience may be insufficient, and so it might be even if I could recal to mind every instance of it; but its insufficiency, instead of being brought to light, is disguised, if instead of sifting the experience itself, I appeal to a test which bears no relation to the sufficiency of the experience, but, at the most, only to its familiarity. These remarks do not lose their force even if we believe, with Mr. Spencer, that mental tendencies originally derived from experience impress themselves permanently on the cerebral structure and are transmitted by inheritance, so that modes of thinking which are acquired by the race become innate and *à priori* in the individual, thus representing, in Mr. Spencer's opinion, the experience of his progenitors, in addition to his own. All that would follow from this is, that a conviction might be really innate, *i.e.* prior to individual experience, and yet not be true, since the inherited tendency to accept it may have been originally the result of other causes than its truth.

Mr. Spencer would have a much stronger case, if he could really show that the evidence of Reasoning rests on the Postulate, or, in other words, that we believe that a conclusion follows from premises only because we cannot conceive it not to follow. But this statement seems to me to be of the same kind as one I have previously commented on, viz. that I believe I see light, because I cannot, while the sensation remains, conceive that I am looking into darkness. Both these statements seem to me incompatible with the meaning (as very rightly limited by Mr. Spencer) of the verb to conceive. To say that when I apprehend that A is B and that B is C, I cannot conceive that A is not C, is to my mind merely to say that I am compelled to *believe* that A is C. If to conceive be taken in its proper meaning, viz. to form a mental representation, I *may* be able to conceive A as not being C. After assenting, with full understanding, to the Copernican proof that it is the earth and not the sun that moves, I not only can conceive, or represent to myself, sunset as a motion of the sun, but almost every one finds this conception of sunset easier to form, than that which they nevertheless know to be the true one.[a]

[a]§ 5.[a] [*Hamilton's opinion on the Principles of Contradiction and Excluded Middle*] Sir William Hamilton holds as I do, that inconceivability is no criterion of impossibility. "There is no ground for inferring a certain fact to be impossible, merely from our inability to conceive its possibility." "Things there are which *may*, nay *must*, be true, of which the understanding is wholly unable to construe to itself the possibility."* Sir William Hamilton is however a firm believer in the *à priori* character of many axioms, and of the sciences deduced from them; and is so far from considering those axioms to rest on the evidence of experience, that he declares certain of them to be

*[56] *Discussions*, p. 624.

[a–a]56, 62, 65, 68   §4.

true even of Noumena—of the Unconditioned—of which it is one of the principal aims of his philosophy to prove that the nature of our faculties debars us from having any knowledge. The axioms to which he attributes this exceptional emancipation from the limits which confine all our other possibilities of knowledge; the chinks through which, as he represents, one ray of light finds its way to us from behind the curtain which veils from us the mysterious world of Things in themselves,—are the two principles, which he terms, after the schoolmen, the Principle of Contradiction, and the Principle of Excluded Middle: the first, that two contradictory propositions cannot both be true; the second, that they cannot both be false. Armed with these logical weapons, we may boldly face Things in themselves, and tender to them the double alternative, sure that they must absolutely elect one or the other side, though we *may be* for ever precluded from discovering which. To take his favourite example, we cannot conceive the infinite divisibility of matter, and we cannot conceive a minimum, or end to divisibility: yet one or the other must be true.

As I have hitherto said nothing of the two axioms in question, those of Contradiction and of Excluded Middle, it is not unseasonable to consider them here. The former asserts that an affirmative proposition and the corresponding negative proposition cannot both be true; which has generally been held to be intuitively evident. Sir William Hamilton and the Germans consider it to be the statement in words of a form or law of our thinking faculty. Other philosophers, not less deserving of consideration, deem it to be an identical proposition; an assertion involved in the meaning of terms; a mode of defining Negation, and the word Not.

I am able to go one step with these last. An affirmative assertion and its negative are not two independent assertions, connected with each other only as mutually incompatible. That if the negative be true, the affirmative must be false, really is a mere identical proposition; for the negative proposition asserts nothing but the falsity of the affirmative, and has no other sense or meaning whatever. The Principium Contradictionis should therefore put off the ambitious phraseology which gives it the air of a fundamental antithesis pervading nature, and should be enunciated in the simpler form, that the same proposition cannot at the same time be false and true. But I can go no farther with the Nominalists; for I cannot look upon this last as a merely verbal proposition. I consider it to be, like other axioms, one of our first and most familiar generalizations from experience. The *original foundation* of it I take to be, that Belief and Disbelief are two different mental states, excluding one another. This we know by the simplest observation of our own minds. And if we carry our observation outwards, we also find that light and darkness, sound and silence, motion and quiescence, equality and inequality,

*b–b*56, 62, 65 are   *c–c*56 meaning

preceding and following, succession and simultaneousness, any positive phenomenon whatever and its negative, are distinct phenomena, pointedly contrasted, and the one always absent where the other is present. I consider the maxim in question to be a generalization from all these facts.

In like manner as the Principle of Contradiction (that one of two contradictories must be false) means that an assertion cannot be *both* true and false, so the Principle of Excluded Middle, or that one of two contradictories must be true, means that an assertion must be *either* true or false: either the affirmative is true, or otherwise the negative is true, which means that the affirmative is false. I cannot help thinking this principle a surprising specimen of a so-called necessity of Thought, since it is not even true, unless with a large qualification. A proposition must be either true or false, *provided* that the predicate be one which can in any intelligible sense be attributed to the subject; (and as this is always assumed to be the case in treatises on logic, the axiom is always laid down there as of absolute truth). "Abracadabra is a second intention" is neither true nor false. Between the true and the false there is a third possibility, the Unmeaning: and this alternative is fatal to Sir William Hamilton's extension of the maxim to Noumena. That Matter must either have a minimum of divisibility or be infinitely divisible, is more than we can ever know. For in the first place, Matter, in any other than the phenomenal sense of the term, may not exist: and it will scarcely be said that a non-entity must be either infinitely or finitely divisible. *d* In the second place, though matter, considered as the occult cause of our sensations, do really exist, yet what we call divisibility may be an attribute only of our sensations of sight and touch, and not of their uncognizable cause. Divisibility may not be predicable at all, in any intelligible sense, of Things in themselves, nor therefore of Matter in itself; and the assumed necessity of being either infinitely or finitely divisible, may be an inapplicable alternative.

*e*On this question I am happy to have the full concurrence of Mr. Herbert Spencer, from whose paper in the *Fortnightly Review* I extract the following passage.[*] The germ of an idea identical with that of Mr. Spencer may be found in the present chapter, about a page back, but in Mr. Spencer it is not an undeveloped thought, but a philosophical theory.

When remembering a certain thing as in a certain place, the place and the thing are mentally represented together; while to think of the non-existence of the thing in that place implies a consciousness in which the place is represented, but

[*"Mill *versus Hamilton*," p. 533.]

*d*56, 62, 65, 68　[*footnote:*] *If it be said that the *existence* of matter is among the things proved by the principle of Excluded Middle, that principle must prove also the existence of dragons and hippogriffs, because they must be either scaly or not scaly, creeping or not creeping, and so forth.
e-e+65, 68, 72

not the thing. Similarly, if instead of thinking of an object as colourless, we think of its having colour, the change consists in the addition to the concept of an element that was before absent from it—the object cannot be thought of first as red and then as not red, without one component of the thought being totally expelled from the mind by another. The law of the Excluded Middle, then, is simply a generalization of the universal experience that some mental states are directly destructive of other states. It formulates a certain absolutely constant law, that the appearance of any positive mode of consciousness cannot occur without excluding a correlative negative mode; and that the negative mode cannot occur without excluding the correlative positive mode: the antithesis of positive and negative being, indeed, merely an expression of this experience. Hence it follows that if consciousness is not in one of the two modes it must be in the other.[e]*

I must here close this supplementary chapter, and with it the Second Book. The theory of Induction, in the most comprehensive sense of the term, will form the subject of the Third.[a]

*[65] [f]Professor Bain (*Logic*, Pt. I, p. 16) identifies the Principle of Contradiction with his Law of Relativity, viz., that "everything that can be thought of, every affirmation that can be made, has an opposite or counter notion or affirmation;" a proposition which is one of the general results of the whole body of human experience.[f] For further considerations respecting the axioms of Contradiction and Excluded Middle, see the twenty-first chapter of *An Examination of Sir William Hamilton's Philosophy.*

[f]–[f]+72

BOOK III

OF INDUCTION

"According to the doctrine now stated, the highest, or rather the only proper object of physics, is to ascertain those established conjunctions of successive events, which constitute the order of the universe; to record the phenomena which it exhibits to our observations, or which it discloses to our experiments; and to refer these phenomena to their general laws." D. Stewart, *Elements of the Philosophy of the Human Mind*, Vol. II, [p. 321,] Chap. iv, sect. 1.

CHAPTER I

Preliminary Observations on Induction in General

§ 1. [*Importance of an inductive logic*] The portion of *the present*[a] inquiry upon which we are now about to enter, may be considered as the principal, both from its surpassing in intricacy all the other branches, and because it relates to a process which has been shown in the preceding Book to be that in which the investigation of nature essentially consists. We have found that all Inference, consequently all Proof, and all discovery of truths not self-evident, consists of inductions, and the interpretation of inductions: that all our knowledge, not intuitive, comes to us exclusively from that source. What Induction is, therefore, and what conditions render it legitimate, cannot but be deemed the main question of the science of logic—the question which includes all others. It is, however, one which professed writers on logic have almost entirely passed over. The generalities of the subject have not been altogether neglected by metaphysicians; but, for want of sufficient acquaintance with the processes by which science has actually succeeded in establishing general truths, their analysis of the inductive operation, even when unexceptionable as to correctness, has not been specific enough to be made the foundation of practical rules, which might be for induction itself what the rules of the syllogism are for the interpretation of induction: while those by whom physical science has been carried to its present [b] state of improvement—and who, to arrive at a complete theory of the process, needed only to generalize, and adapt to all varieties of problems, the methods which they themselves employed in their habitual pursuits—never until very lately made any serious attempt to philosophize on the subject, nor regarded the mode in which they arrived at their conclusions as deserving of study, independently of the conclusions themselves. [c]

*a–a*MS our
*b*MS, 43, 46 high
*c*MS Although, for these reasons, there is not yet extant a body of Inductive Logic, scientifically constructed; the materials for its construction exist, widely scattered, but abundant: and the selection and arrangement of those materials is a task with which intellects of the highest order, possessed of the necessary acquirements, have at length consented to occupy themselves. Within a few years three writers, profoundly versed

§ 2. [*The logic of science is also that of business and life*] For the purposes of the present inquiry, Induction may be defined, the operation of discovering and proving general propositions. It is true that (as already shown) the process of indirectly ascertaining individual facts, is as truly inductive as that by which we establish general truths. But it is not a different kind of induction; it is ᵃaᵃ form of the ᵇveryᵇ same process: since, on the one hand, generals are but collections of particulars, definite in kind but indefinite in number; and on the other hand, whenever the evidence ᶜwhich we deriveᶜ from observation of known cases justifies us in drawing an inference respecting even one unknown case, we should on the same evidence be justified in drawing a similar inference with respect to a whole class of cases. The inference either does not hold at all, or it holds in all cases of a certain description; in all cases which, in certain definable respects, resemble those we have observed.

If these remarks are just; if the principles and rules of inference are the same whether we infer general propositions or individual facts; it follows that a complete logic of the sciences would be also a complete logic of practical business and common life. Since there is no case of legitimate inference from experience, in which the conclusion may not legitimately be a general proposition; an analysis of the process by which general truths are arrived at, is virtually an analysis of all induction whatever. Whether we are inquiring into a scientific principle or into an individual fact, and whether we proceed by experiment or by ratiocination, every step in the train of inferences is essentially inductive, and the legitimacy of the induction depends in both cases on the same conditions.

---

in every branch of physical science, and not unaccustomed to carry their speculations into still higher regions of knowledge, have made attempts, of unequal but all of very great merit, towards the creation of a Philosophy of Induction: Sir John Herschel, in his *Discourse on the Study of Natural Philosophy*; Mr. Whewell, in his *History* and *Philosophy of the Inductive Sciences*; and, greatest of all, M. Auguste Comte, in his *Cours de Philosophie Positive* [6 vols. Paris: Bachelier, 1830–42], a work which only requires to be better known, to place its author in the very highest class of European thinkers. That the present writer does not consider any of these philosophers, or even all of them together, to have entirely accomplished this important work, is implied in his attempting to supply the deficiency; but with his comparatively imperfect knowledge of the various physical sciences, the attempt would have been desperate unless the materials had been brought together, and had undergone a partial elaboration, by their more competent hands; even if he could have dispensed with the many important logical ideas and principles, for the first suggestion of which he has been indebted to one or other of those writers.]   43 *as* MS . . . attempting to contribute something farther towards its achievement; but . . . *as* MS]   46 *as* MS . . . intellects of a high order, possessed . . . *as* MS . . . M. Auguste Comte, in his *Cours de Philosophie Positive*. That . . . *as* 43

ᵃ⁻ᵃMS, 43, 46, 51   another
ᵇ⁻ᵇ+43, 46, 51, 56, 62, 65, 68, 72
ᶜ⁻ᶜMS   we possess, derived

True it is that in the case of the practical inquirer, who is endeavouring to ascertain facts not for the purposes of science but for those of business, such for instance as the advocate or the judge, the chief difficulty is one in which the principles of induction will afford him no assistance. It lies not in making his inductions, but in the selection of them; in choosing from among all general propositions ascertained to be true, those which furnish *d* marks by which he may trace whether the given subject possesses or not the predicate in question. In arguing a doubtful question of fact before a jury, the general propositions or principles to which the advocate appeals are mostly, in themselves, sufficiently trite, and assented to as soon as stated: his skill lies in bringing his case under those propositions or principles; in calling to mind such of the known or *ereceived*e maxims of probability as admit of application to the case in hand, and selecting from among them those best adapted to his object. Success is here dependent on natural or acquired sagacity, aided by knowledge of the particular subject, and of subjects allied with it. Invention, though it can be cultivated, cannot be reduced to rule; there is no science which will enable a man to bethink himself of that which will suit his purpose.

But when he *has* thought of something, science can tell him whether that which he has thought of will suit his purpose or not. The inquirer or arguer must be guided by his own knowledge and sagacity in *fthe*f choice of the inductions out of which he will construct his argument. But the validity of the argument when constructed, depends on principles and must be tried by tests which are the same for all descriptions of inquiries, whether the result be to give A an estate, or to enrich science with a new general truth. In the one case and in the other, the senses, or testimony, must decide on the individual facts; the rules of the syllogism will determine whether, those facts being supposed correct, the case really falls within the formulæ of the different inductions under which it has been successively brought; and finally, the legitimacy of the inductions themselves must be decided by other rules, and these it is now our purpose to investigate. If this third part of the operation be, in many of the questions of practical life, not the most, but the least arduous portion of it, we have seen that this is also the case in some great departments of the field of science; in all those which are principally deductive, and most of all in mathematics; where the inductions themselves are few in number, and so obvious and elementary that they seem to stand in no need of the evidence of experience *g*, while*g* to combine them so as to prove a given theorem or solve a problem, may call for the *hutmost*h powers of invention and contrivance with which our species is gifted.

*d*MS, 43, 46   him with
*e–e*MS, 43, 46   recognised
*g–g*MS   ; but

*f–f*MS, 43, 46   his
*h–h*MS, 43   highest

If the identity of the logical processes which prove particular facts and those which establish general scientific truths, required any additional confirmation, it would be sufficient to consider that in many branches of science, single facts have to be proved, as well as principles; facts as completely individual as any that are debated in a court of justice; but which are proved in the same manner as the other truths of the science, and without disturbing in any degree the homogeneity of its method. A remarkable example of this is afforded by astronomy. The individual facts on which that science grounds its ᶦmost important deductionsᶦ, such facts as the magnitudes of the bodies of the solar system, their distances from one another, the figure of the earth, and its rotation, are scarcely any of them accessible to our means of direct observation: they are proved indirectly, by the aid of inductions founded on other facts which we can more easily reach. For example, the distance of the moon from the earth was determined by a very circuitous process. The share which direct observation had in the work consisted in ascertaining, at one and the same instant, the zenith distances of the moon, as seen from two points very remote from one another on the earth's surface. The ascertainment of these angular distances ascertained their supplements; and since the angle at the earth's centre subtended by the distance between the two places of observation was deducible by spherical trigonometry from the latitude and longitude of those places, the angle at the moon subtended by the same line became the fourth angle of a quadrilateral of which the other three angles were known. The four angles being thus ascertained, and two sides of the quadrilateral being radii of the earth; the two remaining sides and the diagonal, or in other words, the moon's distance from the two places of observation and from the centre of the earth, could be ascertained, at least in terms of the earth's radius, from elementary theorems of geometry. At each step in this demonstration ʲa new induction is taken inʲ, represented in the aggregate of its results by a general proposition.

Not only is the process by which an individual astronomical fact was thus ascertained, exactly similar to those by which the same science establishes its general truths, but ᵏalsoᵏ (as we have shown to be the case in all legitimate reasoning) a general proposition might have been concluded instead of a single fact. In strictness, indeed, the result of the reasoning *is* a general proposition; a theorem respecting the distance, not of the moon in particular, but of any inaccessible object; showing in what relation that distance stands to certain other quantities. And although the moon is almost the only heavenly body the distance of which from the earth can really be thus ascertained, this is merely owing to the accidental circumstances of the other

---

ᶦ⁻ᶦMS   highest inductions
ʲ⁻ʲMS, 43, 46, 51, 56, 62, 65, 68   we take in a new induction
ᵏ⁻ᵏMS, 43, 46   moreover

heavenly bodies, which render them incapable of affording such data as the application of the theorem requires; for the theorem itself is as true of them as it is of the moon.*

We shall fall into no error, then, if in treating of Induction, we limit our attention to the establishment of general propositions. The principles and rules of Induction as directed to this end, are the principles and rules of all Induction; and the logic of Science is the universal Logic, applicable to all inquiries in which man can engage [1].

*[51] Dr. Whewell thinks it improper to apply the term Induction to any operation not terminating in the establishment of a general truth. Induction, he says (*Philosophy of Discovery*, p. 245), "is not the same thing as experience and observation. Induction is experience or observation *consciously* looked at in a *general* form. This consciousness and generality are necessary parts of that knowledge which is science." And he objects (p. 241) to the mode in which the word Induction is employed in this work, as an undue extension of that term "not only to the cases in which the general induction is consciously applied to a particular instance, but to the cases in which the particular instance is dealt with by means of experience in that rude sense in which experience can be asserted of brutes, and in which of course we can in no way imagine that the law is possessed or understood as a general proposition." This use of the term he deems a "confusion of knowledge with practical tendencies."

I disclaim, as strongly as Dr. Whewell can do, the application of such terms as induction, inference, or reasoning, to operations performed by mere instinct, that is, from an animal impulse, without the exertion of any intelligence. But I perceive no ground for confining the use of those terms to cases in which the inference is drawn in the forms and with the precautions required by scientific propriety. To the idea of Science, an express recognition and distinct apprehension of general laws as such, is essential: but nine-tenths of the conclusions drawn from experience in the course of practical life, are drawn without any such recognition: they are direct inferences from known cases, to a case supposed to be similar. I have endeavoured to show that this is not only as legitimate an operation, but substantially the same operation, as that of ascending from known cases to a general proposition; except that the latter process has one great security for correctness which the former does not possess. In science, the inference must necessarily pass through the intermediate stage of a general proposition, because Science wants its conclusions for record, and not for instantaneous use. But the inferences drawn for the guidance of practical affairs, by persons who would often be quite incapable of expressing in unexceptionable terms the corresponding generalizations, may and frequently do exhibit intellectual powers quite equal to any which have ever been displayed in science: and if these inferences are not inductive, what are they? The limitation imposed on the term by Dr. Whewell seems perfectly arbitrary; neither justified by any fundamental distinction between what he includes and what he desires to exclude, nor sanctioned by usage, at least from the time of Reid and Stewart, the principal legislators (as far as the English language is concerned) of modern metaphysical terminology.

[1]MS   , and the test of all the conclusions at which he can arrive]   43, 46   *as* MS
. . . arrive by inference

CHAPTER II

Of Inductions Improperly So Called

§ 1. [*Inductions distinguished from verbal transformations*] Induction, then, is that operation of the mind, by which we infer that what we know to be true in a particular case or cases, will be true in all cases which resemble the former in certain assignable respects. In other words, Induction is the process by which we conclude that what is true of certain individuals of a class is true of the whole class, or that what is true at certain times will be true *a*in*a* similar circumstances at all times.

This definition excludes from the meaning of the term Induction, various logical operations, to which it is not unusual to apply that name.

Induction, as above defined, is a process of inference; it proceeds from the known to the unknown; and any operation involving no inference, any process in which what seems the conclusion is no wider than the premises from which it is drawn, does not fall within the meaning of the term. Yet in the common books of Logic we find this laid down as the most perfect, indeed the only quite perfect, form of induction. In those books, every process which sets out from a less general and terminates in a more general expression,— which admits of being stated in the form, "This and that A are B, therefore every A is B,"—is called an induction, whether anything be really concluded or not: and the induction is asserted *b*not to be*b* perfect, unless every single individual of the class A is included in the antecedent, or premise: that is, unless what we affirm of the class has already been ascertained to be true of every individual in it, so that the nominal conclusion is not really a conclusion, but a mere reassertion of the premises. If we were to say, All the planets shine by the sun's light, from observation of each separate planet, or All the Apostles were Jews, because this is true of Peter, Paul, John, and every other apostle,—these, and such as these, would, in the phraseology in question, be called perfect, and the only perfect, Inductions. This, however, is a totally different kind of induction from ours; it is *c*not an*c* inference from facts known to facts unknown, but a mere short-hand registration of facts known. The two simulated arguments which we have quoted, are not generalizations;

*a–a*MS, 43, 46   under
*b–b*MS, 43, 46, 51   to be not
*c–c*MS, 43, 46, 51   no

the propositions purporting to be conclusions from them, are not really general propositions. A general proposition is one in which the predicate is affirmed or denied of an unlimited number of individuals; namely, all, whether few or many, existing or capable of existing, which possess the properties connoted by the subject of the proposition. "All men are mortal" does not mean all now living, but all men past, present, and to come. When the signification of the term is limited so as to render it a name not for any and every individual falling under a certain general description, but only for each of a number of individuals designated as such, and as it were counted off individually, the proposition, though it may be general in its language, is no general proposition, but merely that number of singular propositions, written in an abridged character. The operation may be very useful, as most forms of abridged notation are; but it is no part of the investigation of truth, though often bearing an important part in the preparation of the materials for that investigation.

[d]As we may sum up a definite number of singular propositions in one proposition, which will be apparently, but not really, general, so we may sum up a definite number of general propositions in one proposition, which will be apparently, but not really, more general. If by a separate induction applied to every distinct species of animals, it has been established that each possesses a nervous system, and we affirm thereupon that all animals have a nervous system; this looks like a generalization, though as the conclusion merely affirms of all what has already been affirmed of each, it seems to tell us nothing but what we knew before. A distinction however must be made. If in concluding that all animals have a nervous system, we mean the same thing and no more as if we had said "all known animals," the proposition is not general, and the process by which it is arrived at is not induction. But if our meaning is that the observations made of the various species of animals have discovered to us a law of animal nature, and that we are in a condition to say that a nervous system will be found even in animals yet undiscovered, this indeed is an induction; but in this case the general proposition contains more than the sum of the special propositions from which it is inferred. The distinction is still more forcibly brought out when we consider, that if this real generalization be legitimate at all, its legitimacy probably does not require that we should have examined without exception every known species. It is the number and nature of the instances, and not their being the whole of those which happen to be known, that makes them sufficient evidence to prove a general law: while the more limited assertion, which stops at all known animals, cannot be made unless we have rigorously verified it in every species. In like manner (to return to a former example) we might have inferred, not that all *the* planets, but that all *planets*, shine by reflected light:

[d]–[d]290+56, 62, 65, 68, 72

the former is no induction; the latter is an induction, and a bad one, being disproved by the case of double stars—self-luminous bodies which are properly planets, since they revolve round a centre.[d]

§ 2. [*Inductions distinguished from inductions, falsely so called, in mathemathics*] [a]There are several processes used in mathematics which require to be distinguished from Induction, being not unfrequently called by that name, and being so far similar to Induction properly so called, that the propositions they lead[a] to are really general propositions. For example, when we have proved with respect to the circle, that a straight line cannot meet it in more than two points, and when the same thing has been successively proved of the ellipse, the parabola, and the hyperbola, it may be laid down as an universal property of the sections of the cone. [b]The distinction drawn in the two previous examples can have no place here, there being no difference between all *known* sections of the cone and *all* sections, since a cone demonstrably cannot be intersected by a plane except in one of these four lines. It would be difficult, therefore, to refuse to the proposition arrived at, the name of a generalization, since there is no room for any generalization beyond it. But[b] there is no induction, because there is no inference: the conclusion is a mere summing up of what [c]was[c] asserted in the various propositions from which it is drawn. A case somewhat, though not altogether, similar, is the proof of a geometrical theorem by means of a diagram. Whether the diagram be on paper or only in the imagination, the demonstration (as [d] formerly observed*) does not prove directly the general theorem; it proves only that the conclusion, which the theorem asserts generally, is true of the particular triangle or circle exhibited in the diagram; but since we perceive that in the same way in which we have proved it of that circle, it might also be proved of any other circle, we gather up into one general expression all the singular propositions susceptible of being thus proved, and embody them in an universal proposition. Having shown that the three angles of the triangle ABC are together equal to two right angles, we conclude that this is true of every other triangle, not because it is true of ABC, but for the same reason which proved it to be true of ABC. If this were to be called Induction, an appropriate name for it would be, induction by parity of reasoning. But the term cannot properly belong to it; the characteristic quality of Induction is want-

*Supra, p. 191.

[a–a]MS, 43, 46, 51   A second process which requires to be distinguished from Induction, is one to which mathematicians sometimes give that name: and which so far resembles Induction properly so called, that the propositions it leads
[b–b]MS, 43, 46, 51   In this example
[c–c]MS   is
[d]MS, 43   we

ing, since the truth obtained, though really general, is not believed on the evidence of particular instances. We do not conclude that all triangles have the property because some triangles have, but from the ulterior demonstrative evidence which was the ground of our conviction in the particular instances.

There are nevertheless, in mathematics, some examples of so-called Induction, in which the conclusion does bear the appearance of a generalization grounded on some of the particular cases included in it. A mathematician, when he has calculated a sufficient number of the terms of an algebraical or arithmetical series to have ascertained what is called the *law* of the series, does not hesitate to fill up any number of the succeeding terms without repeating the calculations. But I apprehend he only does so when it is apparent from *à priori* considerations (which might be exhibited in the form of demonstration) that the mode of formation of the subsequent terms, each from that which preceded it, must be similar to the formation of the terms which have been already calculated. And when the attempt has been hazarded without the sanction of such general considerations, there are instances on record in which it has led to false results.

It is said that Newton discovered the binomial theorem by induction; by raising a binomial successively to a certain number of powers, and comparing those powers with one another until he detected the relation in which the algebraic formula of each power stands to the exponent of that power, and to the two terms of the binomial. The fact is not improbable: but a *e*mathematician like Newton, who*e* seemed to arrive *per saltum* at principles and conclusions that ordinary mathematicians only reached by a succession of steps, certainly could not have performed the comparison in question without being led by it to the *à priori* ground of the law; since any one who understands sufficiently the nature of multiplication to venture upon multiplying several lines of *f* symbols at one operation, cannot but perceive that in raising a binomial to a power, the coefficients must depend on the laws of permutation and combination: and as soon as this is recognised, the theorem is demonstrated. Indeed, when once it was seen that the law prevailed in a few of the lower powers, its identity with the law of permutation would at once suggest the considerations which prove it to obtain universally. Even, therefore, such cases as these, are but examples of what I have called Induction by parity of reasoning, that is, not really Induction, because not involving *g* inference of a general proposition from particular instances. *h*

*e-e*MS, 43   mind like Newton's, which
*f*MS, 43, 46   figures or   *g*MS, 43   any
*h*MS, 43   [*footnote:*] *I am happy to be able to refer, in confirmation of this view of what is called induction in mathematics, to the highest English authority on the philosophy of algebra, Mr. Peacock. See pp. 107–8 of his profound *Treatise on Algebra* [Cambridge: Deighton, 1830].]   46   I may refer . . . *as* MS . . . *Algebra*, (1st ed.).

§ 3. [*Inductions distinguished from descriptions*] There remains a third improper use of the term Induction, which it is of real importance to clear up, because the theory of Induction has been, *in* no ordinary degree, confused by it, and because the confusion is exemplified in the most recent and *b* elaborate treatise on *the* inductive philosophy which exists in our language. The error in question is that of confounding a mere description *d*, by general terms,*d* of a set of observed phenomena, with an induction from them.

Suppose that a phenomenon consists of parts, and that these parts are only capable of being observed separately, and as it were piecemeal. When the observations have been made, there is a convenience (amounting for many purposes to a necessity) in obtaining a representation of the phenomenon as a whole, by combining, or as we may say, piecing these detached fragments together. A navigator sailing in the midst of the ocean discovers land: he cannot at first, or by any one observation, determine whether it is a continent or an island; but he coasts along it, and after a few days finds himself to have sailed completely round it: he then pronounces it an island. Now there was no particular time or place of observation at which he could perceive that this land was entirely surrounded by water: he ascertained the fact by a succession of partial observations, and then selected a general expression which summed up in two or three words the whole of what he so observed. But is there anything of the nature of an induction in this process? Did he infer anything that had not been observed, from something else which had? Certainly not. *He had observed the whole of what the proposition asserts.* That the land in question is an island, is not an inference from the partial facts which the navigator saw in the course of his circumnavigation; it is the facts themselves; it is a summary of those facts; the description of a complex fact, to which those simpler ones are as the parts of a whole.

Now there is *f*, I conceive,*f* no difference in kind between this simple operation, and that by which Kepler ascertained the nature of the planetary orbits: and Kepler's operation, all at least that was characteristic in it, was not more an inductive act than that of our supposed navigator.

The object of Kepler was to determine the real path described by each of the planets, or let us say *by* the planet Mars (*since it was of that body that he first established the two of his three laws which did not require a comparison of planets*). To do this there was no other mode than that of direct

*a–a*MS, 43   to
*b*MS, 43, 46, 51   most
c–c+43, 46, 51, 56, 62, 65, 68, 72
d–d+65, 68, 72
e–e+51, 56, 62, 65, 68, 72
f–f+51, 56, 62, 65, 68, 72
g–g+MS, 51, 56, 62, 65, 68 [*printer's error?*]
*h–h*MS, 43, 46, 51   for it was of that body that he first established two of the three great astronomical truths which bear his name

observation: and all which observation could do was to ascertain a great number of the successive places of the planet; or rather, of its apparent places. That the planet occupied successively all these positions, or at all events, positions which produced the same impressions on the eye, and that it passed from one of these to another insensibly, and without any apparent breach of continuity; thus much the senses, with the aid of the proper instruments, could ascertain. What Kepler did more than this, was to find what sort of a curve these different points would make, supposing them to be all joined together. He expressed the whole series of the observed places of Mars by what Dr. Whewell calls the general conception of an ellipse.[*] This operation was far from being as easy as that of the navigator who expressed the series of his observations on successive points of the coast by the general conception of an island. But it is the very same sort of operation; and if the one is not an induction but a description, this must also be true of the other.

*i*The only real induction concerned in the case, consisted in inferring*i* that because the observed places of Mars were correctly represented by points in an imaginary ellipse, therefore Mars would continue to revolve in that same ellipse; and *j*in concluding (before the gap had been filled up by further observations) that the positions*j* of the planet during the time which intervened between two observations, must have coincided with the intermediate points of the curve. *k*For these were facts which had not been directly observed. They were inferences from the observations; facts inferred, as distinguished from facts seen. But these inferences were so far from being a part of Kepler's philosophical operation, that they had been drawn long before he was born. Astronomers had long known that the planets periodically returned to the same places. When this had been ascertained, there was no induction left for Kepler to make, nor did he make any further induction. He merely applied his new conception to the facts inferred, as he did to the facts observed. Knowing already that the planets continued to move in the same paths; when he found that an ellipse correctly represented the past

[*See *Novum Organon Renovatum*, pp. 72ff.]

*i-i*MS, 43, 46, 51   To avoid misapprehension, we must remark that Kepler, in one respect, performed a real act of induction; namely, in concluding
*j-j*MS, 43, 46, 51   even in concluding that the position]   56 *as* 72 . . . the position
*k-k*294MS, 43, 46   But this really inductive operation requires to be carefully distinguished from the mere act of bringing the facts actually observed under a general description. So distinct are these two operations, that the one might have been performed without the other. Men might and did make correct inductions concerning the heavenly motions, before they had obtained correct general descriptions of them. It was known that the planets always moved in the same paths, long before it had been ascertained that those paths were ellipses. Men early remarked that the same set of apparent positions returned periodically. When they obtained a new description of the phenomenon, they did not necessarily make any further induction, nor (which is the true test of a new general truth) add anything to the power of prediction which they already possessed.]   51 *as* MS . . . ellipses. Astronomers early . . . *as* MS

path, he knew that it would represent the future path. In finding a compendious expression for the one set of facts, he found one for the other: but he found the expression only, not the inference; nor did he (which is the true test of a general truth) add anything to the power of prediction already possessed.[k]

§ 4. [*Examination of Whewell's theory of Induction*] The descriptive operation which enables a number of details to be summed up in a single proposition, Dr. Whewell, by an aptly chosen expression, has termed the Colligation of Facts. [a] In most of his observations concerning that mental process I fully agree, and would gladly transfer all that portion of his book into my own pages. I only think him mistaken in setting up this kind of operation, which according to the old and received meaning of the term, is not induction at all, as the type of induction generally; and laying down, throughout his work, as principles of induction, the principles of mere colligation.

Dr. Whewell [b]maintains[b] that the general proposition which binds together the particular facts, and makes them, as it were, one fact, is not the mere sum of those facts, but something more, since there is introduced a conception of the mind, which did not exist in the facts themselves.

The particular facts, [says he,*] are not merely brought together, but there is a new element added to the combination by the very act of thought by which they are combined. . . . When the Greeks, after long observing the motions of the planets, saw that these motions might be rightly considered as produced by the motion of one wheel revolving in the inside of another wheel, these wheels were creations of their minds, added to the facts which they perceived by sense. And even if the wheels were no longer supposed to be material, but were reduced to mere geometrical spheres or circles, they were not the less products of the mind alone,—something additional to the facts observed. The same is the case in all other discoveries. The facts are known, but they are insulated and unconnected, till the discoverer supplies from his own [c]store[c] a principle of connexion. The pearls are there, but they will not hang together till some one provides the string.

[d]Let me first remark that Dr. Whewell, in this passage, blends together, indiscriminately, examples of both the processes which I am endeavouring to

---

*Novum Organon Renovatum, pp. 72–3.

[a]43, 46, 51, 56 [*footnote:*] *Philosophy of the Inductive Sciences*, Vol. II, pp. 213–14.
   [b-b]MS insists
   [c-c]Source, MS stores
   [d-d]MS, 43 That a conception of the mind is introduced is indeed most certain, and Mr. Whewell has rightly stated elsewhere, that to hit upon the right conception is often a far more difficult and more meritorious achievement, than to prove its applicability when obtained. [See, e.g., *History of the Inductive Sciences*, 1st ed., Vol. I, pp. 7ff.] But a] 46 *as* MS . . . most certain, and I willingly concede, that to hit . . . *as* MS] 51 *as* MS . . . indeed undeniable, and . . . *as* 46

distinguish from one another. When the Greeks abandoned the supposition that the planetary motions were produced by the revolution of material wheels, and fell back upon the idea of "mere geometrical spheres or circles," there was more in this change of opinion than the mere substitution of an ideal curve for a physical one. There was the abandonment of a theory, and the replacement of it by a mere description. No one would think of calling the doctrine of material wheels a mere description. That doctrine was an attempt to point out the force by which the planets were acted upon, and compelled to move in their orbits. But when, by a great step in philosophy, the materiality of the wheels was discarded, and the geometrical forms alone retained, the attempt to account for the motions was given up, and what was left of the theory was a mere description of the orbits. The assertion that the planets were carried round by wheels revolving in the inside of other wheels, gave place to the proposition, that they moved in the same lines which would be traced by bodies so carried: which was a mere mode of representing the sum of the observed facts; as Kepler's was another and a better mode of representing the same observations.

It is true that for these simply descriptive operations, as well as for the erroneous inductive one, a conception of the mind was required. The conception of an ellipse must have presented itself to Kepler's mind, before he could identify the planetary orbits with it. According to Dr. Whewell, the conception was something added to the facts. He expresses himself as if Kepler had put something into the facts by his mode of conceiving them. But Kepler did no such thing. The ellipse was in the facts before Kepler recognised it; just as the island was an island before it had been sailed round. Kepler did not *put* what he had conceived into the facts, but *saw* it in them. A[d] conception implies, and corresponds to, something conceived: and though the conception itself is not in the facts, but in our mind, [e]yet if it is to convey any knowledge relating to them,[e] it must be a conception *of* something which really is in the facts, some property which they actually possess, and which they would manifest to our senses, if our senses were able to take cognizance of [f]it[f]. If, for instance, the planet left behind it in space a visible track, and if the observer were in a fixed position at such a distance [g]from[g] the plane of the orbit as would enable him to see the whole of it at once, he would see it to be an ellipse; and if gifted with appropriate instruments and powers of locomotion, he could prove it to be such by measuring its different dimensions. [h]Nay, further: if the track were visible, and he were so placed that he could see all parts of it in succession, but not all of them at once, he might be able,

[e]–[e]+56, 62, 65, 68, 72

[f]–[f]MS, 43, 46, 51   them

[g]–[g]MS, 43, 46, 51   above

[h]–[h]296MS, 43, 46, 51   These things are indeed impossible to us, but not impossible in themselves; if they were so, Kepler's law could not be true.

by piecing together his successive observations, to discover both that it was an ellipse and that the planet moved in it. The case would then exactly resemble that of the navigator who discovers the land to be an island by sailing round it. If the path was visible, no one I think would dispute that to identify it with an ellipse is to describe it: and I cannot see why any difference should be made by its not being directly an object of sense, when every point in it is as exactly ascertained as if it were so.[h]

Subject to the indispensable condition which has just been stated, I [i]do not conceive[i] that the part which conceptions have in the operation of studying facts, has ever been overlooked or undervalued [j] . No one ever disputed that in order to reason about anything we must have a conception of it; or that when we include a multitude of things under a general expression, there is implied in the expression a conception of something common to those things. But it by no means follows that the conception is necessarily preexistent, or constructed by the mind out of its own materials. If the facts are rightly classed under the conception, it is because there is in the facts themselves something of which the conception is itself a copy; and which if we cannot directly perceive, it is because of the limited power of our organs, and not because the thing itself is not there. The conception itself is often obtained by abstraction from the very facts which, in Dr. Whewell's language, it is afterwards called in to connect. This [k]he[k] himself admits, when he observes, (which he does on several occasions,) how great a service would be rendered to the science of physiology by the philosopher "who should establish a precise, tenable, and consistent conception of life."* Such a conception can only be abstracted from the phenomena of life itself; from the very facts which it is put in requisition to connect. In other cases, no doubt, instead of collecting the conception from the very phenomena which we are attempting to colligate, we select it from among those which have been previously collected by abstraction from other facts. In the instance of Kepler's laws, the latter was the case. The facts being out of the reach of being observed, in any such manner as would have enabled the senses to identify directly the path of the planet, the conception requisite for framing a general description of that path could not be collected by abstraction from the observations themselves; the mind had to supply hypothetically, from among the conceptions it had obtained from other portions of its experience, some one which would correctly represent the series of the observed facts. It had to frame a supposition respecting the general course of the phenomenon, and ask itself, If this be the general description, what will the details be? and then compare

*Novum Organon Renovatum, p. 32.

[i-i]MS, 43, 46, 51, 56, 62   cannot perceive]   65, 68   cannot conceive
[j]MS, 43   as Mr. Whewell supposes it has
[k-k]MS, 43   , Mr. Whewell

these with the details actually observed. If they agreed, the hypothesis would serve for a description of the phenomenon: if not, it was necessarily abandoned, and another tried. It is such a case as this which gives ⌐rise⌐ to the doctrine that the mind, in framing the description, adds something of its own which it does not find in the facts.

Yet it is a fact surely, that the planet does describe an ellipse; and a fact which we could see, if we had adequate visual organs and a suitable position. Not having these advantages, but possessing the conception of an ellipse, or (to express the meaning in less technical language) knowing what an ellipse was, Kepler tried whether the observed places of the planet were consistent with such a path. He found they were so; and he, consequently, asserted as a fact that the planet moved in an ellipse. But this fact, which Kepler did not add to, but found in, the motions of the planet, namely, that it occupied in succession the various points in the circumference of a given ellipse, was the very fact, the separate parts of which had been separately observed; it was the sum of the different observations. ᵐ

Having stated this fundamental difference between my ⁿopinion and that of Dr.ⁿ Whewell, I must add, that his account of the manner in which a conception is selected, suitable to express the facts, appears to me perfectly just. The experience of all thinkers will, I believe, testify that the process is tentative; that it consists of a succession of guesses; many being rejected, until one at last occurs fit to be chosen. We know from Kepler himself that before hitting upon the "conception" of an ellipse, he tried nineteen other imaginary paths, which, finding them inconsistent with the observations, he was obliged to reject. But as Dr. Whewell truly says, the successful hypothesis, though a guess, ought ᵒgenerally to be called, notᵒ a lucky, but a skilful guess.[*] The guesses which serve to give mental unity and wholeness to a chaos of scattered particulars, are accidents which ᵖrarely occur to anyᵖ minds but those abounding in knowledge and disciplined in ᑫintellectualᑫ combinations.

How far this tentative method, so indispensable as a means to the colligation of facts for purposes of description, admits of application to Induction itself, and what functions belong to it in that department, will be considered

[*See *Novum Organon Renovatum*, pp. 46ff., 78ff.]

ˡ⁻ˡMS, 43, 46   colour
ᵐMS, 43, 46   It superadded nothing to the particular facts which it served to bind together: except, indeed, the knowledge that a resemblance existed between the planetary orbit and other ellipses; an accession the nature and amount of which will be fully considered hereafter*. [*footnote:*] *Vide infra, Bk. IV, Chap. i [pp 647–8].
ⁿ⁻ⁿMS, 43, 46   views and those of Mr.
ᵒ⁻ᵒMS, 43, 46   not to be called
ᵖ⁻ᵖMS, 43, 46   occur to no
ᑫ⁻ᑫMS, 43, 46   scientific

in the chapter of the present Book which relates to Hypotheses. On the present occasion we have chiefly to distinguish this process of Colligation from Induction properly so called; and that the distinction may be made clearer, it is well to advert to a curious and interesting remark [r], which is as strikingly true of the former operation, as it [s]appears to me[s] unequivocally false of the latter.

In different stages of the progress of knowledge, philosophers have employed, for the colligation of the same order of facts, different conceptions. The early [t] rude observations of the heavenly bodies, in which minute precision was neither attained nor sought, presented nothing inconsistent with the representation of the path of a planet as an exact circle, having the earth for its centre. As observations increased in accuracy, [u] facts were disclosed which were not reconcileable with this simple supposition: for the colligation of those additional facts, the supposition was varied; and varied again and again as facts became more numerous and precise. The earth was removed from the centre to some other point within the circle; the planet was supposed to revolve in a smaller circle called an epicycle, round an imaginary point which revolved in a circle round the earth: in proportion as observation elicited fresh facts contradictory to these representations, other epicycles and other excentrics were added, producing additional complication; until at last Kepler swept all these circles away, and substituted the conception of an exact ellipse. Even this is found not to represent with complete correctness the accurate observations of the present day, which disclose many slight deviations from an orbit exactly elliptical. Now Dr. Whewell has remarked that these successive general expressions, though apparently so conflicting, were all correct: they all answered the purpose of colligation; they all enabled the mind to represent to itself with facility, and by a simultaneous glance, the whole body of facts at [v]the[v] time ascertained: each in its turn served as a correct description of the phenomena, so far as the senses had up to that time taken cognizance of them.[*] If a necessity afterwards arose for discarding one of these general descriptions of the planet's orbit, and framing a different imaginary line, by which to express the series of observed positions, it was because a number of new facts had now been added, which it was necessary to combine with the old facts into one general description. But this did not affect the correctness of the former expression, considered as a general statement of the only facts which it was intended to represent. And so true is this, that, as is well remarked by M. Comte, these ancient generalizations, even the rudest and most imperfect of them, that of uniform move-

[*See, e.g., *ibid.*, pp. 71ff.]

[r]MS, 43   of Mr. Whewell
[s-s]MS, 43, 46   is   [t]MS, 43, 46   and
[u]MS, 43, 46, 51, 56, 62, 65, 68   and   [v-v]MS, 43, 46, 51   that

ment in a circle, are so far from being entirely false, that they are even now habitually employed by astronomers when only a rough approximation to correctness is required.

L'astronomie moderne, en détruisant sans retour les hypothèses primitives, envisagées comme lois réelles du monde, a soigneusement maintenu leur valeur positive et permanente, la propriété de représenter commodément les phénomènes quand il s'agit d'une première ébauche. Nos ressources à cet égard sont même bien plus étendues, précisément à cause que nous ne nous faisons aucune illusion sur la réalité des hypothèses; ce qui nous permet d'employer sans scrupule, en chaque cas, celle que nous jugeons la plus avantageuse.*

Dr. Whewell's remark, therefore, is *w*philosophically correct*w*. Successive expressions for the colligation of observed facts, or in other words, successive descriptions of a phenomenon as a whole, which has been observed only in parts, may, though conflicting, be all correct as far as they go. But it would surely be absurd to assert this of conflicting inductions.

The *x*scientific*x* study of facts may be undertaken for three different purposes: the simple description of the facts; their explanation; or their prediction: meaning by prediction, the determination of the conditions under which similar facts may be expected again to occur. To the first of these three operations the name of Induction does not properly belong: to the other two it does. Now, Dr. Whewell's observation is true of the first alone. Considered as a mere description, the circular theory of the heavenly motions represents perfectly well their general features: and by adding epicycles without limit, those motions, even as now known to us, might be expressed with any degree of accuracy that might be required. The *y*elliptical theory, as a mere description, would have a great advantage in point of simplicity, and in the consequent facility of conceiving it and reasoning about it; but*y* it would not really be more true than the other. Different descriptions, therefore, may be all true: but not, surely, different explanations. The doctrine that the heavenly bodies moved by a virtue inherent in their celestial nature; the doctrine that they were moved by impact, (which led to the hypothesis of vortices as the only impelling force capable of whirling bodies in circles,) and the Newtonian doctrine, that they are moved by the composition of a centripetal with an original projectile force; all these are explanations, collected by real induction from supposed parallel cases; and they were all successively received by philosophers, as scientific truths on the subject of the heavenly bodies. Can it be said of these, as *z*was*z* said of the different

Cours de Philosophie Positive, Vol. II, p. 202.

*w–w*MS, 43   as just as it is interesting
*x–x*MS, 43, 46   philosophic
*y–y*MS, 43, 46   only real advantage of the elliptical . . . would be its simplicity, and the consequent . . . about it:
*z–z*MS, 43   we

descriptions, that they are all true as far as they go? Is it not clear that *only one* can be true in any degree, and the other two must be altogether false? So much for explanations: let us now compare different predictions: the first, that eclipses will occur *when* one planet or satellite is so situated as to cast its shadow upon another; the second, that they will occur *when* some great calamity is impending over mankind. Do these two doctrines only differ in the degree of their truth, as expressing real facts with unequal degrees of accuracy? Assuredly the one is true, and the other absolutely false.*

*[51] Dr. Whewell, in his reply, contests the distinction here drawn, and maintains, that not only different descriptions, but different explanations of a phenomenon, may all be true. Of the three theories respecting the motions of the heavenly bodies, he says (*Philosophy of Discovery*, pp. 251–2): "Undoubtedly all these explanations may be true and consistent with each other, and would be so if each had been followed out so as to show in what manner it could be made consistent with the facts. And this was, in reality, in a great measure done. The doctrine that the heavenly bodies were moved by vortices was successively modified, so that it came to coincide in its results with the doctrine of an inverse-quadratic centripetal force . . . . When this point was reached, the vortex was merely a machinery, well or ill devised, for producing such a centripetal force, and therefore did not contradict the doctrine of a centripetal force. Newton himself does not appear to have been averse to explaining gravity by impulse. So little is it true that if one theory be true the other must be false. The attempt to explain gravity by the impulse of streams of particles flowing through the universe in all directions, which I have mentioned in the *Philosophy*, is so far from being inconsistent with the Newtonian theory, that it is founded entirely upon it. And even with regard to the doctrine, that the heavenly bodies move by an inherent virtue; if this doctrine had been maintained in any such way that it was brought to agree with the facts, the inherent virtue must have had its laws determined; and then it would have been found that the virtue had a reference to the central body; and so, the 'inherent virtue' must have coincided in its effect with the Newtonian force; and then, the two explanations would agree, except so far as the word 'inherent' was concerned. And if such a part of an earlier theory as this word *inherent* indicates, is found to be untenable, it is of course rejected in the transition to later and more exact theories, in Inductions of this kind, as well as in what Mr. Mill calls Descriptions. There is, therefore, still no validity discoverable in the distinction which Mr. Mill attempts to draw between descriptions like Kepler's law of elliptical orbits, and other examples of induction."

If the doctrine of vortices had meant, not that vortices existed, but only that the planets moved *in the same manner* as if they had been whirled by vortices; if the hypothesis had been merely a mode of representing the facts, not an attempt to account for them; if, in short, it had been only a Description; it would, no doubt, have been reconcileable with the Newtonian theory. The vortices, however, were not a mere aid to conceiving the motions of the planets, but a supposed physical agent, actively impelling them; a material fact, which might be true or not true, but could not be both true and not true. According to Descartes' theory it was true, according to Newton's it was not true. Dr. Whewell probably means that since the phrases, centripetal and projectile force, do not declare the

In every way, therefore, it is evident that *to explain induction as the colligation of facts by means of appropriate conceptions, that is, conceptions which will really express them, is to confound mere description of the observed facts with inference from those facts, and ascribe* to the latter what is a characteristic property of the former.

---

nature but only the direction of the forces, the Newtonian theory does not absolutely contradict any hypothesis which may be framed respecting the mode of their production. The Newtonian theory, regarded as a mere *description* of the planetary motions, does not; but the Newtonian theory as an *explanation* of them does. For in what does the explanation consist? In ascribing those motions to a general law which obtains between all particles of matter, and in identifying this with the law by which bodies fall to the ground *d*. If the planets are kept in their orbits by a force which draws the particles composing them towards every other particle of matter in the solar system, they are not kept in those orbits by the impulsive force of certain streams of matter which whirl them round. The one explanation*d* absolutely excludes the other. Either the planets are not moved by vortices, or they do not move by *e*a law common to all matter*e*. It is impossible that both opinions can be true. As well might it be said that there is no contradiction between the assertions, that a man died because somebody killed him, and that he died a natural death.

So, again, the theory that the planets move by a virtue inherent in their celestial nature, is incompatible with either of the two others: either that of their being moved by vortices, or that which regards them as moving by a property which they have in common with the earth and all terrestrial bodies. Dr. Whewell says that the theory of an inherent virtue agrees with Newton's when the word inherent is left out, which of course it would be (he says) if "found to be untenable." But leave that out, and where is the theory? The word inherent *is* the theory. When that is omitted, there remains nothing except that the heavenly bodies move *f*"by a*f* virtue," *i.e.* by a power of some sort *g*; or by virtue of their celestial nature, which directly contradicts the doctrine that terrestrial bodies fall by the same law*g*.

If Dr. Whewell is not yet satisfied, any other subject will serve equally well to test his doctrine. He will hardly say that there is no contradiction between the emission theory and the undulatory theory of light; or that there can be both one and two electricities; or that the hypothesis of the production of the higher organic forms by development from the lower, and the supposition of separate and successive acts of creation, are quite reconcileable; or that the theory that volcanoes are fed from a central fire, and the doctrines which ascribe them to chemical action at a comparatively small depth below the earth's surface, are consistent with one another, and all true as far as they go.

If different explanations of the same fact cannot both be true, still less, surely, can different predictions. Dr. Whewell quarrels (on what ground it is not necessary *h*here*h* to consider) with the example I had chosen on this point, and thinks

---

*d–d*51   ; a kind of motion which the vortices did not, and as it was rectilineal, could not, explain. The one explanation, therefore,

*e–e*51   the law by which heavy bodies fall

*f–f*51, 56, 62, 65, 68   by "a

g–g+56, 62, 65, 68, 72   *h–h*+56, 62, 65, 68, 72

*i–i*MS, 43   when Mr. Whewell explains induction . . . them, he confounds mere . . . and ascribes

There is, however, between Colligation and Induction, a real correlation, which it is important to conceive correctly. Colligation is not always induction; but induction is always colligation. The assertion that the planets move in ellipses, was but a mode of representing observed facts; it was but a colligation; while the assertion that they are drawn, or tend, towards the sun, was the statement of a new fact, inferred by induction. But the induction, once made, accomplishes the purposes of colligation likewise. It brings the same facts, which Kepler had connected by his conception of an ellipse, under the additional conception of bodies acted upon by a central force, and serves therefore as a new bond of connexion for those facts; a new principle for their classification.

*j*Further, the descriptions which are improperly confounded with induction, are*j* nevertheless a necessary preparation for induction; no less necessary than correct observation of the facts themselves. Without the previous colligation of detached observations by means of one general conception, we could never have obtained any basis for an induction, except in the case of phenomena of *k* very limited compass. We should not be able to affirm any predicates at all, of a subject incapable of being observed otherwise than piecemeal: much less could we extend those predicates by induction to other similar subjects. Induction, therefore, always presupposes, not only that the necessary observations are made with the necessary accuracy, but also that the results of these observations are, so far as practicable, connected together by general descriptions, enabling the mind to represent to itself as *l*wholes*l* whatever phenomena are capable of being so represented. *m*

---

an objection to an illustration a sufficient answer to a theory. Examples not liable to his objection are easily found, if the proposition that conflicting predictions cannot both be true, can be made clearer by any examples. Suppose the phenomenon to be a newly-discovered comet, and that one astronomer predicts its return once in every 300 years—another once in every 400: can they both be right? When Columbus predicted that by sailing constantly westward he should in time return to the point from which he set out, while others asserted that he could never do so except by turning back, were both he and his opponents true prophets? Were the predictions which foretold the wonders of railways and steamships, and those which averred that the Atlantic could never be crossed by steam navigation, nor a railway train propelled ten miles an hour, both (in Dr. Whewell's words) "true, and consistent with one another"?

Dr. Whewell sees no distinction between holding contradictory opinions on a question of fact, and merely employing different analogies to facilitate the conception of the same fact. The case of different Inductions belongs to the former class, that of different Descriptions to the latter.

*j–j*MS, 43, 46   Moreover, that general description, which is improperly confounded with induction, is]   51   Further, that general description . . . *as* MS
*k*MS   a
*l–l*MS   a whole
*m*MS   [*paragraph*] To suppose, however, that nothing more is required from the

*§ 5. [*Further illustration of the preceding remarks*] Dr. Whewell has replied at some length to the preceding observations, re-stating his opinions, but without (as far as I can perceive) adding anything *material* to his former arguments.[*] Since, however, mine have not had the good fortune to make any impression upon him, I will subjoin a few remarks, tending to show more clearly in what our difference of opinion consists, as well as, in some measure, to account for it.

Nearly all the definitions of induction, by writers of authority, make it consist in drawing inferences from known cases to unknown; affirming of a class, a predicate which has been found true of some cases belonging to the class; concluding because some things have a certain property, that other things which resemble them have the same property—or because a thing has manifested a property at a certain time, that it has and will have that property at other times.

It will scarcely be contended that Kepler's operation was an Induction in this sense of the term. The statement, that Mars moves in an elliptical orbit, was no generalization from individual cases to a class of cases. Neither was it an extension to all time, of what had been found true at some particular time. The whole amount of generalization which the case admitted of, was already completed, or might have been so. Long before the elliptic theory was thought of, it had been ascertained that the planets returned periodically to the same apparent places; the series of these places was, or might have been, completely determined, and the apparent course of each planet marked out on the celestial globe in an uninterrupted line. Kepler did not extend an observed truth to other cases than those in which it had been observed: he did not widen the *subject* of the proposition which expressed the observed facts. *The* alteration he made was in the predicate. Instead of saying, the successive places of Mars are so and so, he summed them up in the statement, that the successive places of Mars are points in an ellipse. It is true, this statement, as Dr. Whewell says, was not the sum of the observations

[*See *Of Induction* (1849), reprinted as Chap. xxii of *On the Philosophy of Discovery* (1860).]

conception than that it shall serve to connect the observations, would be to substitute hypothesis for theory and imagination for proof. The connecting link must be some character which *really exists* in the facts themselves, and which would manifest itself therein if the conditions could be realized which our organs of sense require.

And hence (as will be seen hereafter) the principle of connexion must not be sought in any hypothesis respecting the cause, or mode of production of the phenomena; it must restrict itself within the bounds of a mere Description.

What more . . . [*see* 305*j–j* below]]   43, 46   *as* MS . . . sense require. [*paragraph*]
What more . . . *as* MS
*a–a*305+51, 56, 62, 65, 68, 72
b–b+56, 62, 65, 68, 72
*c–c*51, 56   All   *d–d*51   He left the subject as it was; the

merely; it was the sum of the observations *seen under a new point of view.**
But it was not the sum of *more* than the observations, as a real induction is.
It took in no cases but those which had been actually observed, or which
could have been inferred from the observations before the new point of view
presented itself. There was not that transition from known cases to unknown,
which constitutes Induction in the original and acknowledged meaning of
the term.

Old definitions, it is true, cannot prevail against new knowledge: and if
the Keplerian operation, as a logical process, *ebe* really identical with what
takes place in acknowledged induction, the definition of induction ought to
be so widened as to take it in; since scientific language ought to adapt itself
to the true relations which subsist between the things it is employed to designate. Here then it is that I *am at* issue with Dr. Whewell. He does think the
operations identical. He allows of no logical process in any case of induction,
other than what there was in Kepler's case, namely, guessing until a guess is
found which tallies with the facts; and accordingly, as we shall see hereafter,
he rejects all canons of induction, because it is not by means of them that we
guess. Dr. Whewell's theory of the logic of science would be very perfect if
it did not pass over altogether the question of Proof. But in my apprehension
there is such a thing as proof, and inductions differ altogether from descriptions in their relation to that element. Induction is proof; it is inferring
something unobserved from something observed: it requires, therefore, an
appropriate test of proof; and to provide that test, is the special purpose of
inductive logic. When, on the contrary, we merely collate known observations, and, in Dr. Whewell's phraseology, connect them by means of a new
conception; if the conception does *g* serve to connect the observations, we
have all we want. As the proposition in which it is embodied pretends to no
other truth than what it may share with many other modes of representing
the same facts, to be consistent with the facts is all it requires: it neither
needs nor admits of proof; though it may serve to prove other things, inasmuch as, by placing the facts in mental connexion with other facts, not
previously seen to resemble them, it assimilates the case to another class of
phenomena, concerning which real Inductions have already been made. Thus
Kepler's so-called law brought the orbit of Mars into the class ellipse, and by
doing so, proved all the properties of an ellipse to be true of the orbit: but in
this proof Kepler's law supplied the minor premise, and not (as is the case
with real Inductions) the major.

*h*Dr. Whewell calls nothing Induction where there is not a new mental

---

**Philosophy of Discovery*, pp. 256–7.

*e–e*51 were   *f–f*51 join   *g*51 but
h–h+56, 62, 65, 68, 72

conception introduced, and everything induction where there is.[*] But this is to confound two very different things, Invention and Proof. The introduction of a new conception belongs to Invention: and invention may be required in any operation, but is the essence of none. A new conception may be introduced for descriptive purposes, and so it may for inductive purposes. But it is so far from constituting induction, that induction does not necessarily stand in need of it. Most inductions require no conception but what was present in every one of the particular instances on which the induction is grounded. That all men are mortal is surely an inductive conclusion; yet no new conception is introduced by it. Whoever knows that any man has died, has all the conceptions involved in the inductive generalization. But Dr. Whewell considers the process of invention which consists in framing a new conception consistent with the facts, to be not merely a necessary part of all induction, but the whole of it.[h]

The mental operation which extracts from a number of detached observations certain general characters in which the observed phenomena resemble one another, or resemble other known facts, is what Bacon, Locke, and most subsequent metaphysicians, have understood by the word Abstraction. A general expression obtained by abstraction, connecting known facts by means of common characters, but without concluding from them to unknown, may, I think, with strict logical correctness, be termed a Description; nor do I know in what other way things can ever be described. My position, however, does not depend on the employment of that particular word; I am quite content to use Dr. Whewell's term Colligation, [i]or the more general phrases, "mode of representing, or of expressing, phenomena:"[i] provided it be clearly seen that the process is not Induction, but something radically different.

[j]What more may [k]usefully be[k] said on the subject of Colligation, or of the correlative expression invented by Dr. Whewell, the Explication of Conceptions,[†] and generally on the subject of ideas and mental representations as connected with the study of facts, will find a more appropriate place in the Fourth Book, on the Operations Subsidiary to Induction: to which [l]I must refer the reader[l] for the removal of any difficulty which the present discussion may have left.[ja]

[*See *Philosophy of Discovery*, pp. 253ff.]
[†*Novum Organon Renovatum*, title of Bk. II, Chap. ii.]

[i–i]+62, 65, 68, 72
[j–j]MS, 43, 46   [*appears at end of §4; see* 302[m] *above*]
[k–k]MS, 43, 46   be usefully
[l–l]MS, 43, 46, 51, 56, 62, 65   the reader must refer

CHAPTER III

Of the Ground of Induction

§ 1. [*Axiom of the uniformity of the course of nature*] Induction properly so called, as distinguished from those mental operations, sometimes though improperly designated by the name, which I have attempted in the preceding chapter to characterize, may, then, be summarily defined as Generalization from Experience. It consists in inferring from some individual instances in which a phenomenon is observed to occur, that it occurs in all instances of a certain class; namely, in all which *resemble* the former, in what are regarded as the material circumstances.

In what way the material circumstances are to be distinguished from those which are immaterial, or why some of the circumstances are material and others not so, we are not yet ready to point out. We must first observe, that there is a principle implied in the very statement of what Induction is; an assumption with regard to the course of nature and the order of the universe; namely, that there are such things in nature as parallel cases; that what happens once, will, under a sufficient degree of similarity of circumstances, happen again, and not only again, but ᵃas often as the same circumstances recurᵃ. This, I say, is an assumption, involved in every case of induction. And, if we consult the actual course of nature, we find that the assumption is warranted ᵇ. The universe, ᶜso far as known to usᶜ, is so constituted, that whatever is true in any one case, is true in all cases of a certain description; the only difficulty is, to find what description.

This universal fact, which is our warrant for all ᵈinferencesᵈ from experience, has been described by different philosophers in different forms of language: that the course of nature is uniform; that the universe is governed by general laws; and the like. One of the most usual of these modes of expression, but also one of the most inadequate, is that which has been brought into familiar use by the metaphysicians of the school of Reid and Stewart. The disposition of the human mind to generalize from experience,—a propensity considered by these philosophers as an instinct of our nature,—they usually describe under ᵉsome such name asᵉ "our intuitive conviction that the

---

a–aMS, 43, 46   always   bMS, 43, 46   ; the fact is so
c–cMS, 43, 46, 51   we find   d–dMS, 43, 46   inference
e–eMS, 43, 46   the name of

future will resemble the past." Now it has been well pointed out *by Mr. Bailey,* that* (whether the tendency be or not an original and ultimate element of our nature), Time, in its modifications of past, present, and future, has no concern either with the belief itself, or with the grounds of it. We believe that fire will burn to-morrow, because it burned to-day and yesterday; but we believe, on precisely the same grounds, that it burned before we were born, and that it burns this very day in Cochin-China. It is not from the past to the future, as past and future, that we infer, but from the known to the unknown; from facts observed to facts unobserved; from what we have perceived, or been directly conscious of, to what has not come within our experience. In this last predicament is the whole region of the future; but also the vastly greater portion of the present and of the past.

Whatever be the most proper mode of expressing it, the proposition that the course of nature is uniform, is the fundamental principle, or general axiom, of Induction. It would yet be a great error to offer this large generalization as any explanation of the inductive process. On the contrary, I hold it to be itself an instance of induction, and induction by no means of the most obvious kind. Far from being the first induction we make, it is one of the last, or at all events one of those which are latest in attaining strict philosophical accuracy. As a general maxim, indeed, it has scarcely entered into the minds of any but philosophers; nor even by them, as we shall have many opportunities of remarking, have its extent and limits been always very justly conceived. *The truth is, that this great generalization is itself founded on prior generalizations. The obscurer laws of nature were discovered by means of it, but the more obvious ones must have been understood and assented to as general truths before it was ever heard of. We should never have thought of affirming that all phenomena take place according to general laws, if we had not first arrived, in the case of a great multitude of phenomena, at some knowledge of the laws themselves; which could be done no otherwise than by induction. In what sense, then, can a principle, which is so far from being our earliest induction, be regarded as our warrant for all the others? In the only sense, in which (as we have already seen)* the general propositions which we place at the head of our reasonings when we throw them into syllogisms, ever really contribute to their validity. *As Archbishop Whately

Essays on the Pursuit of Truth [London: Hunter, 1829].

*f-f*MS   by a deservedly popular writer,* that [*footnote:* *Mr. Samuel Bailey, in his *Essays on the Pursuit of Truth.*]]   51, 56   , that [*i.e., reference to Bailey and footnote deleted*]

*g-g*MS, 43, 46   Yet this principle, though so far from being our earliest induction, must be considered as our warrant for all the others, in this sense, that unless it were true, all other inductions would be fallacious. And this, as we have already seen, is the sole mode in which

*h-h*MS, 43   Archbishop Whately has well remarked, that

remarks,[*] every induction is a syllogism with the major premise suppressed; or (as I prefer expressing it) ⁱ every induction may be thrown into the form of a syllogism, by supplying a major premise. If this be actually done, the principle which we are now considering, that of the uniformity of the course of nature, will appear as the ultimate major premise of all inductions, and will, therefore, stand to all inductions in the relation in which, as has been shown at so much length, the major proposition of a syllogism always stands to the conclusion; not contributing at all to prove it, but being a necessary condition of its being proved; since no conclusion is proved, for which there cannot be found a true major premise.*

[*Elements of Logic, p. 233.]

*[62] ʲIn the first edition a note was appended at this place, containing some criticism on Archbishop Whately's mode of conceiving the relation between Syllogism and Induction. In a subsequent issue of his Logic, the Archbishop made a reply to the criticism, which induced me to cancel part of the note, incorporating the remainder in the text. In a still later edition, the Archbishop observes in a tone of something like disapprobation, that the objections, "doubtless from their being fully answered and found untenable, were silently suppressed," and that hence he might appear to some of his readers to be combating a shadow. On this latter point, the Archbishop need give himself no uneasiness. His readers, I make bold to say, will fully credit his mere affirmation that the objections have actually been made.

But as he seems to think that what he terms the suppression of the objections ought not to have been made "silently," I now break that silence, and state

ⁱMS, 43   that

ʲ–ʲMS   From the fact, that every induction may be expressed in the form of a syllogism, Archbishop Whately concludes that Induction itself is but a peculiar case of ratiocination, and that the universal type of all Inference, or Reasoning, is the Syllogism. Our own inquiries have led us to a directly opposite result. Instead of resolving Induction into Ratiocination, it has appeared to us that Ratiocination is itself resolvable into Induction. The Archbishop's theory, may, I think, be shown to be fallacious by following out his own train of thought. The induction, "John, Peter, Thomas, &c., are mortal, therefore all mankind are mortal," may, as he justly says, be thrown into a syllogism by prefixing as a major premiss (what is at any rate a necessary condition of the validity of the argument) namely, that whatever is true of John, Peter, Thomas, &c., is true of all mankind. So far the case is made out; and Archbishop Whately (who, endowed with a penetrating and active rather than a patient and persevering intellect, seldom fails to cast his sounding line to a greater depth than his predecessors, and when he has done this, scarcely seems to care whether he reaches the bottom or not) omitted to ask himself the further question, How we come by the major premiss? It is not self-evident; nay, in all cases of unwarranted generalization, it is not true. How, then, is it arrived at? Necessarily either by induction or ratiocination; and if by induction, then, on the Archbishop's principles, it is by ratiocination still, that is, by a previous syllogism. This previous syllogism it is, therefore, necessary to construct. There is, in the long run, only one possible construction: the real proof that whatever is true of John, Peter, &c., is true of all mankind, can only be, that a different supposition would be inconsistent with the uniformity which we know to exist in the course of nature. Whether there would be this inconsistency or not, may be a matter of long and delicate inquiry; but unless there would, we have no sufficient ground for the major of the inductive syllogism. It hence appears, that if we throw the whole course

*j*The statement, that the uniformity of the course of nature is the ultimate major premise in all cases of induction, may be thought to require some explanation. The immediate major premise in every inductive argument, it certainly is not. Of that, Archbishop Whately's must be held to be the correct

---

exactly what it is that I suppressed, and why. I suppressed that alone which might be regarded as personal criticism on the Archbishop. I had imputed to him the having omitted to ask himself a particular question. I found that he had asked himself the question, and could give it an answer consistent with his own theory. I had also, within the compass of a parenthesis, hazarded some remarks on certain general characteristics of Archbishop Whately as a philosopher. These remarks, though their tone, I hope, was neither disrespectful nor arrogant, I felt, on reconsideration, that I was hardly entitled to make; least of all, when the instance which I had regarded as an illustration of them, failed, as I now saw, to bear them out. The real matter at the bottom of the whole dispute, the different view we take of the function of the major premise, remains exactly where it was; and so far was I from thinking that my opinion had been fully "answered" and was "untenable," that in the same edition in which I cancelled the note, I not only enforced the opinion by further arguments, but answered (though without naming him) those of the Archbishop.

For not having made this statement before, I do not think it needful to apologize. It would be attaching very great importance to one's smallest sayings, to think a formal retractation requisite every time that one *k*falls into*k* an error. Nor is Archbishop Whately's well-earned fame of so tender a quality as to require that in withdrawing a slight criticism on him I should have been bound to offer a public *amende* for having made it.*j*

---

of any inductive argument into a series of syllogisms, we shall arrive by more or fewer steps at an ultimate syllogism, which will have for its major premiss the principle, or axiom, of the uniformity of the course of nature. Having reached this point, we have the whole field of induction laid out in syllogisms, and every instance of inference from experience exhibited as the conclusion of a ratiocination, except one; but that one, unhappily, includes all the rest. Whence came the universal major? What proves to us that nature is governed by general laws? Where are the premisses of the syllogism of which that is the conclusion? Here, at least, is a case of induction which cannot be resolved into syllogism. And undoubtedly it would be the ideal perfection of Inductive Philosophy if all other general truths could be exhibited as conclusions deduced from that widest generalization of all. But such a mode of presenting them, however useful in giving coherence and systematic unity to our thoughts, would be an inversion of the real order of proof. This great generalization must itself have been founded on prior generalizations: the obscurer laws of nature were discovered by means of it, but the more obvious ones must have been understood and assented to as general truths before it was ever heard of. We should never have dared to affirm that all phenomena take place according to general laws, if we had not first arrived, in the case of a great multitude of phenomena, at some knowledge of the laws themselves; which could be done no otherwise than by induction. Archbishop Whately's theory, therefore, implying, as it does, the consequence that we never could have had a single well-grounded induction unless we had already reached that highest generalization, must, I conceive, be regarded as untenable.] 43 *as* MS . . . into syllogism. [*paragraph*] And undoubtedly . . . *as* MS] 46 *as* MS . . . then, on his principles, it is . . . *as* 43 . . . We should never have presumed to . . . *as* MS] 51, 56 [*no footnote*]
*k–k*62, 65, 68 commits
*j–j*310+51, 56, 62, 65, 68, 72 [MS, 43, 46 *partly in note; see following variants*]

account. ᵐThe induction, "John, Peter, ⁿ &c. are mortal, therefore all mankind are mortal," may, as he justly says, be thrown into a syllogism by prefixing as a major premise (what is at any rate a necessary condition of the validity of the argument) namely, that ᵒwhat is true of John, Peter,ᵒ &c. is true of all mankind.ᵐ But ᵖᑫhow came we by thisᑫ major premise? It is not self-evident; nay, in all cases of unwarranted generalization, it is not true. How, then, is it arrived at? Necessarily either by induction or ratiocination; and if by induction,ᵖ the process, like all other inductive arguments, may be thrown into the form of a syllogism. ʳThis previous syllogism it is, therefore, necessary to construct. There is, in the long run, only one possible construction. The real proof that ˢwhatˢ is true of John, Peter, &c. is true of all mankind, can only be, that a different supposition would be inconsistent with the uniformity which we know to exist in the course of nature. Whether there would be this inconsistency or not, may be a matter of long and delicate inquiry; but unless there would, we have no sufficient ground for the major of the inductive syllogism. It hence appears, that if we throw the whole course of any inductive argument into a series of syllogisms, we shall arrive by more or fewer steps at an ultimate syllogism, which will have for its major premise the principle, or axiom, of the uniformity of the course of nature.ʳˡ*

*[51] But though it is a condition of the validity of every induction that there be uniformity in the course of nature, it is not a necessary condition that the uniformity should pervade all nature. It is enough that it pervades the particular class of phenomena to which the induction relates. An induction concerning the motions of the planets, or the properties of the magnet, would not be vitiated though we were to suppose that wind and weather are the sport of chance, provided it be assumed that astronomical and magnetic phenomena are under the dominion of general laws. Otherwise the early experience of mankind would have rested on a very weak foundation; for in the infancy of science it could not be ᵗ known that *all* phenomena are regular in their course.

Neither would it be correct to say that every induction by which we infer any truth, implies the general fact of uniformity *as foreknown*, even in reference to the kind of phenomena concerned. It implies, *either* that this general fact is already known, *or* that we may now know it: as the conclusion, the Duke of Wellington is mortal, drawn from the instances A, B, and C, implies either that we have already concluded all men to be mortal, or that we are now entitled to do so from the same evidence. A vast amount of confusion and paralogism respecting the grounds of Induction would be dispelled by keeping in view these simple considerations.

ᵐ⁻ᵐMS, 43, 46 [*in footnote; see* 308ʲ⁻ʲ]
ⁿMS, 43, 46 Thomas, [*in footnote; see* 308ʲ⁻ʲ]
ᵒ⁻ᵒMS, 43, 46 whatever is true of John, Peter, Thomas, [*in footnote; see* 308ʲ⁻ʲ]
ᵖ⁻ᵖMS, 43, 46 [*in footnote; see* 308ʲ⁻ʲ]
ᑫ⁻ᑫMS, 43, 46 How we come by the [*in footnote; see* 308ʲ⁻ʲ]] 51, 56, 62 how come we by this
ʳ⁻ʳMS, 43, 46 [*in footnote; see* 308ʲ⁻ʲ]
ˢ⁻ˢMS, 43, 46 whatever [*in footnote; see* 308ʲ⁻ʲ]
ᵗ51 said to be

It was not to be expected that in the case of this axiom, any more than of other axioms, there should be unanimity among "thinkers" with respect to the grounds on which it is to be received as true. I have already stated that I regard it as itself a generalization from experience. Others hold it to be a principle which, antecedently to any verification by experience, we are compelled by the constitution of our thinking faculty to assume as true. Having so recently, and at so much length, combated a similar doctrine as applied to the axioms of mathematics, by arguments which are in a great measure applicable to the present case, I shall defer the more particular discussion of this controverted point in regard to the fundamental axiom of induction, until a more advanced period of our inquiry.* At present it is of more importance to understand thoroughly the import of the axiom itself. For the proposition, that the course of nature is uniform, possesses rather the brevity suitable to popular, than the precision requisite in philosophical language: its terms require to be explained, and a stricter than their ordinary signification given to them, before the truth of the assertion can be admitted.

§ 2. [*Axiom of the uniformity of nature not true in every sense. Induction per enumerationem simplicem*] Every person's consciousness assures him that he does not always expect uniformity in the course of events; he does not always believe that the unknown will be similar to the known, that the future will resemble the past. Nobody believes that the succession of rain and fine weather will be the same in every future year as in the present. Nobody expects to have the same dreams repeated every night. On the contrary, everybody mentions it as something extraordinary, if the course of nature is constant, and resembles itself, in these particulars. To look for constancy where constancy is not to be expected, as for instance that a day which has once brought good fortune will always be a fortunate day, is justly accounted superstition.

The course of nature, in truth, is not only uniform, it is also infinitely various. Some phenomena are always seen to recur in the very same combinations in which we met with them at first; others seem altogether capricious; while some, which we had been accustomed to regard as bound down exclusively to a particular set of combinations, we unexpectedly find detached from some of the elements with which we had hitherto found them conjoined, and united to others of quite a contrary description. To an inhabitant of Central Africa, fifty years ago, no fact probably appeared to rest on more uniform experience than this, that all human beings are black. To Europeans, not many years ago, the proposition, All swans are white, appeared an equally unequivocal instance of uniformity in the course of nature. Further experience has proved to both that they were mistaken; but they had

*Infra, Chap. xxi [pp. 562ff.].

u–uMS, 43, 46 philosophers

to wait fifty centuries for this experience. During that long time, mankind believed in an uniformity of the course of nature where no such uniformity really existed.

According to the notion which the ancients entertained of induction, the foregoing were cases of as legitimate inference as any inductions whatever. In these two instances, in which, the conclusion being false, the ground of inference must have been insufficient, there was, nevertheless, as much ground for it as this conception of induction admitted of. The induction of the ancients has been well described by Bacon, under the name of "Inductio per enumerationem simplicem, ubi non reperitur instantia contradictoria."[*] It consists in ascribing the character of general truths to all propositions which are true in every instance that we happen to know of. This is the kind of induction ^{a} which is natural to the mind when unaccustomed to scientific methods. The tendency, which some call an instinct, and which others account for by association, to infer the future from the past, the known from the unknown, is simply a habit of expecting that what has been found true once or several times, and never yet found false, will be found true again. Whether the instances are few or many, conclusive or inconclusive, does not much affect the matter: these are considerations which occur only on reflection; the unprompted tendency of the mind is to generalize its experience, provided this points all in one direction; provided no other experience of a conflicting character comes unsought. The notion of seeking it, of experimenting for it, of *interrogating* nature (to use Bacon's expression)[†] is of much later growth. The observation of nature, by uncultivated intellects, is purely passive: they ^{b}accept^b the facts which present themselves, without taking the trouble of searching for more: it is a superior mind only which asks itself what facts are needed to enable it to come to a ^{c}safe^c conclusion, and then looks out for these.

But though we have always a propensity to generalize from unvarying experience, we are not always warranted in doing so. Before we can be at liberty to conclude that something is universally true because we have never known an instance to the contrary, ^{d}we must have reason to believe^d that if there were in nature any instances to the contrary, we should have known of them. This assurance, in the great majority of cases, we cannot have, or can have only in a very moderate degree. The possibility of having it, is the foundation on which we shall see hereafter that induction by simple enumeration may in some remarkable cases amount ^{e}practically to^e proof.* No such

[*See *De Augmentis*, p. 620; cf. *Novum Organum*, Bk. I, Aph. 105, p. 205.]
[†See, e.g., *De Augmentis*, p. 635.]
*[43] Infra, Chaps. xxi, xxii [pp. 562ff.].

^{a}MS, 43, 46 , if it deserves the name,
$^{b-b}$MS, 43 take $^{c-c}$MS, 43, 46, 51, 56, 62   sure
$^{d-d}$MS, 43, 46   it must be proved to us $^{e-e}$MS, 43, 46   to full

assurance, however, can be had, on any of the ordinary subjects of scientific inquiry. Popular notions are usually founded on induction by simple enumeration; in science it carries us but a little way. We are forced to begin with it; we must often rely on it provisionally, in the absence of means of more searching investigation. But, for the accurate study of nature, we require a surer and a more potent instrument.

It was, above all, by pointing out the insufficiency of this rude and loose conception of Induction, that Bacon merited the title so generally awarded to him, of Founder of the Inductive Philosophy. The value of his own contributions to a more philosophical theory of the subject has certainly been exaggerated. Although (along with some fundamental errors) his writings contain, more or less fully developed, several of the most important principles of the Inductive Method, physical investigation has now far outgrown the Baconian conception of Induction. Moral and political inquiry, indeed, are as yet far behind that conception. The current and approved modes of reasoning on these subjects are still of the same vicious description against which Bacon protested; the method almost exclusively employed by those professing to treat such matters inductively, is the very *inductio per enumerationem simplicem* which he condemns; and the experience which we hear so confidently appealed to by all sects, parties, and interests, is still, in his own emphatic words, *mera palpatio*.[*]

§ 3. [*The question of Inductive Logic stated*] In order to a better understanding of the problem which the logician must solve if he would establish a scientific theory of Induction, let us compare a few cases of incorrect inductions with others which are acknowledged to be legitimate. Some, we know, which were believed for centuries to be correct, were nevertheless incorrect. That all swans are white, cannot have been a good induction, since the conclusion has turned out erroneous. The experience, however, on which the conclusion rested, was genuine. From the earliest records, the testimony of *a* the inhabitants of the known world was unanimous on the point. The uniform experience, therefore, of the inhabitants of the known world, agreeing in a common result, without one known instance of deviation from that result, is not always sufficient to establish a general conclusion.

But let us now turn to an instance apparently not very dissimilar to this. Mankind were wrong, it seems, in concluding that all swans were white: are we also wrong, when we conclude that all men's heads grow above their shoulders, and never below, in spite of the conflicting testimony of the naturalist Pliny?[†] As there were black swans, though civilized *b*people*b* had

[*Novum Organum*, Bk. I, Aph. 82, p. 189.]
[†Natural History. Ed. H. Rackham. 10 vols. London: Heinemann, 1938–1942, Vol. II, p. 520 (Bk. VII, Chap. ii).]
*a*MS, 43, 46   all   *b-b*MS, 43, 46   men

existed for three thousand years on the earth without meeting with them, may there not also be "men whose heads do grow beneath their shoulders,"[*] notwithstanding a rather less perfect unanimity of negative testimony from ^{o} observers? Most persons would answer No; it was more credible that a bird should vary in its colour, than that ^{d}men should vary in the relative position of their^d principal organs. And there is no doubt that in so saying they would be right: but to say why they are right, would be impossible, without entering more deeply than is usually done, into the true theory of Induction.

Again, there are cases in which we reckon with the most unfailing confidence upon uniformity, and other cases in which we do not count upon it at all. In some we feel complete assurance that the future will resemble the past, the unknown be precisely similar to the known. In others, however invariable may be the result obtained from the instances which ^{e}have been^e observed, we draw from them no more than a very feeble presumption that the like result will hold in all other cases. That a straight line is the shortest distance between two points, we do not doubt to be true even in the region of the fixed stars.* When a chemist announces the existence and properties of a newly-discovered substance, if we confide in his accuracy, we feel assured that the conclusions he has arrived at will hold universally, though the induction be founded but on a single instance. We do not withhold our assent, waiting for a repetition of the experiment; or if we do, it is from a doubt whether the one experiment was properly made, not whether if properly made it would be conclusive. Here, then, is a general law of nature, inferred without hesitation from a single instance; an universal proposition from a singular one. Now mark another case, and contrast it with this. Not all the instances which have been observed since the beginning of the world, in support of the general proposition that all crows are black, would be deemed a sufficient presumption of the truth of the proposition, to outweigh the testimony of one unexceptionable witness who should affirm that in some region of the earth not fully explored, he had caught and examined a crow, and had found it to be grey.

Why is a single instance, in some cases, sufficient for a complete induction, while in others, myriads of concurring instances, without a single exception known or presumed, go such a very little way towards establishing an universal proposition? Whoever can answer this question knows more of the philosophy of logic than the wisest of the ancients, and has solved the ^{f} problem of induction.

[*William Shakespeare. *Othello* (ed. Furness), I, iii, 167–8.]
*[72] In strictness, wherever the present constitution of space exists; which we have ample reason to believe that it does in the region of the fixed stars.

^{o}MS, 43, 46   all $^{d-d}$MS, 43, 46   man should . . . of his
$^{e-e}$MS, 43, 46   we have ^{f}MS, 43, 46   great

CHAPTER IV

Of Laws of Nature

§ 1. [*The general regularity in nature is a tissue of partial regularities, called laws*] In the contemplation of that uniformity in the course of nature, which is assumed in every inference from experience, one of the first observations that present themselves is, that the uniformity in question is not properly uniformity, but uniformities. The general regularity results from the co-existence of partial regularities. The course of nature in general is constant, because the course of each of the various phenomena that compose it is so. A certain fact invariably occurs whenever certain circumstances are present, and does not occur when they are absent; the like is true of another fact; and so on. From these separate threads of connexion between parts of the great whole which we term nature, a general tissue of connexion unavoidably weaves itself, by which the whole is held together. If A is always accompanied by D, B by E, and C by F, it follows that A B is accompanied by D E, A C by D F, B C by E F, and finally A B C by D E F; and thus the general character of regularity is produced, which, along with and in the midst of infinite diversity, pervades all nature.

The first point, therefore, to be noted in regard to what is called the uniformity of the course of nature, is, that it is itself a complex fact, compounded of all the separate uniformities which exist in respect to single phenomena. These various uniformities, when ascertained by what is regarded as a sufficient induction, we call in common parlance, Laws of Nature. Scientifically speaking, that title is employed in a more restricted sense, to designate the uniformities when reduced to their most simple expression. Thus in the illustration already employed, there were seven uniformities; all of which, if considered sufficiently certain, would, in the more lax application of the term, be called laws of nature. But of the seven, three alone are properly distinct and independent: these being pre-supposed, the others follow of course. The three first, therefore, according to the stricter acceptation, are called laws of nature; the remainder not; because they are in truth mere *cases* of the three first; virtually included in them; said, therefore, to *result* from them: whoever affirms those three has already affirmed all the rest.

To substitute real examples for symbolical ones, the following are three uniformities, or call them laws of nature: the law that air has weight, the law that pressure on a fluid is propagated equally in all directions, and the law that pressure in one direction, not opposed by [a] equal pressure in the contrary direction, produces motion, which does not cease until equilibrium is restored. From these three uniformities we should be able to predict another uniformity, namely, the rise of the mercury in the Torricellian tube. This, in the stricter use of the phrase, is not a law of nature. It is [b]the[b] result of laws of nature. It is a *case* of each and every one of the three laws: and is the only occurrence by which they could all be fulfilled. If the mercury were not sustained in the [c]barometer[c], and sustained at such a height that the column of mercury were equal in weight to a column of the atmosphere of the same diameter; here would be a case, either of the air not pressing upon the surface of the mercury with the force which is called its weight, or of the downward pressure on the mercury not being propagated equally in an upward direction, or of a body pressed in one direction and not in the direction opposite, either not moving in the direction in which it is pressed, or stopping before it had attained equilibrium. If we knew, therefore, the three simple laws, but had never tried the Torricellian experiment, we might *deduce* its result from those laws. The known weight of the air, combined with the position of the apparatus, would bring the mercury within the first of the three inductions; the first induction would bring it within the second, and the second within the third, in the manner which we [d]characterized[d] in treating of Ratiocination. We should thus come to know the more complex uniformity, independently of specific experience, through our knowledge of the simpler ones from which it results; though, for reasons which will appear hereafter, *verification* by specific experience would still be desirable, and might possibly be indispensable.

Complex uniformities which, like this, are mere cases of simpler ones, and have, therefore, been virtually [e]affirmed[e] in affirming those, may with propriety be called *laws*, but can scarcely, in the strictness of scientific speech, be termed Laws of Nature. It is the custom [f]in science, wherever regularity of any kind can be traced[f], to call the general proposition which expresses the nature of that regularity, a law; as when, in mathematics, we speak of the law of decrease of the successive terms of a converging series. But the expression *law of nature* [g]has generally been employed[g] with a sort of tacit reference to

[a]MS, 43, 46   an   [b-b]MS, 43, 46, 51, 56, 62, 65   a
[c-c]MS   tube   [d-d]MS, 43, 46   so fully illustrated
[c-c]MS, 43   inferred [*printer's error?*]
[f-f]MS, 43, 46   of philosophers, wherever they can trace regularity of any kind
[g-g]MS, 43   is generally employed by scientific men]   46   is generally employed in science

the original sense of the word law, namely, the expression of the will of a superior [h] . When, therefore, it appeared that any of the uniformities which were observed in nature, would result spontaneously from certain other uniformities, [i]no separate act of creative will being supposed necessary for the production of the derivative uniformities, these[i] have not usually been spoken of as laws of nature. According to [j]one mode of expression[j], the question, What are the laws of nature? may be stated thus:—What are the fewest and simplest [k]assumptions, which being granted, the whole existing order of nature would result[k]? Another mode of stating it would be thus: What are the fewest general propositions from which all the uniformities which exist in the universe might be deductively inferred?

[l]Every[l] great advance which marks an epoch in the progress of science, has consisted in a step made towards the solution of this problem. Even a simple colligation of inductions already made, without any fresh extension of the inductive inference, is already an advance in that direction. When Kepler expressed the regularity which exists in the observed motions of the heavenly bodies, by the three general [m]propositions[m] called his laws, he, in so doing, pointed out three simple [n]suppositions[n] which, instead of a much greater number, [o]would suffice to construct the whole scheme of the heavenly motions, so far as it was known up to that time[o]. A similar and still greater step was made when these laws, which at first did not seem to be included in any more general truths, were discovered to be cases of the three laws of motion, as obtaining among bodies which mutually tend towards one another with a certain force, and have had a certain instantaneous impulse originally impressed upon them. After this great discovery, Kepler's three propositions, though still called laws, would [p]hardly[p], by any person accustomed to use language with precision, be termed laws of nature: that phrase would be reserved for the simpler [q]and more general[q] laws into which Newton [r]is said to have[r] resolved them.

[h]MS, 43, 46   ; the superior, in this instance, being the Ruler of the universe
[i–i]MS, 43, 46   without any separate act of creative will, the former
[j–j]MS   this view of the subject]   43, 46, 51, 56, 62, 65   another mode of expression
[k–k]MS   volitions by which creative power could have produced the whole scheme of the universe
[l–l]MS, 43, 46   As has already been hinted, (and will be more fully discussed here-after,) every
[m–m]MS   descriptions
[n–n]MS, 43, 46   volitions, by
[o–o]MS   it appeared that the whole scheme of the heavenly motions, so far as yet observed, might have been produced by creative power]   43, 46   as MS . . . might be conceived to have been produced
[p–p]MS   not
[q–q]+62, 65, 68, 72
[r–r]MS, 43, 46   , as the expression is,

According to this language, every well-grounded inductive generalization is either a law of nature, or a result of laws of nature, capable, if those laws are known, of being predicted from them. And the problem of Inductive Logic may be summed up in two questions: how to ascertain the laws of nature; and how, after having ascertained them, to follow them into their results. On the other hand, we must not suffer ourselves to imagine that this mode of statement amounts to a real analysis, or to anything but a mere verbal transformation of the problem; for the expression, Laws of Nature, *means* nothing but the uniformities which exist among natural phenomena (or, in other words, the results of induction), when reduced to their simplest expression. It is, however, something to have advanced so far, as to see that the study of nature is the study of laws, not *a* law; of uniformities, in the plural number: that the different natural phenomena have their separate rules or modes of taking place, which, though much intermixed and entangled with one another, may, to a certain extent, be studied apart: that (to resume our former metaphor) the regularity which exists in nature is a web composed of distinct threads, and only to be understood by tracing each of the threads separately; for which purpose it is often necessary to unravel some portion of the web, and exhibit the fibres apart. The rules of experimental inquiry are the contrivances for unravelling the web.

§ 2. [*Scientific induction must be grounded on previous spontaneous inductions*] In thus attempting to ascertain the general order of nature by ascertaining the particular order of the occurrence of each one of the phenomena of nature, the most scientific proceeding can be no more than an improved form of that which was primitively pursued by the human understanding, *a*while*a* undirected by science. When *b*mankind*b* first formed the idea of studying phenomena according to a stricter and surer method than that which they had in the first instance spontaneously adopted, they did not, conformably to the well-meant but impracticable precept of Descartes, set out from the supposition that nothing had been already ascertained. Many of the uniformities existing among phenomena are so constant, and so open to observation, as to force themselves upon *c* involuntary recognition. Some facts are so perpetually and familiarly accompanied by certain others, that mankind learnt, as children *d* learn, to expect the one where they found the other, long before they knew how to put their expectation into words by asserting, in a proposition, the existence of a connexion between those phenomena. No science was needed to teach *e* that food nourishes, that water drowns, or quenches thirst, that the sun gives light and heat, that bodies fall to the ground. The first scientific inquirers assumed these and the like as

---

known truths, and set out from them to discover others which were unknown: nor were they wrong in so doing, subject, however, as they afterwards began to see, to an ulterior revision of these spontaneous generalizations themselves, when the progress of knowledge pointed out limits to them, or showed their truth to be contingent on some *f* circumstance not originally attended to. It will appear, I think, from the subsequent part of our inquiry, that there is no logical fallacy in this mode of proceeding; but we may see already that any other mode is rigorously impracticable: since it is impossible to frame any scientific method of induction, or test of the correctness of inductions, unless on the hypothesis that some inductions *g*deserving of reliance*g* have been already made.

Let us revert, for instance, to one of our former illustrations, and consider why it is that, with exactly the same amount of evidence, both negative and positive, we did not reject the assertion that there are black swans, while we should refuse credence to any testimony which asserted that there were men wearing their heads underneath their shoulders. The first assertion was more credible than the latter. But why more credible? So long as neither phenomenon had been actually witnessed, what reason was there for finding the one harder to be believed than the other? Apparently because there is less constancy in the colours of animals, than in the general structure of their *h* anatomy. But how do we know this? Doubtless, from experience. It appears, then, that we need experience to inform us, in what *i*degree, and in what cases, or*i* *j*sorts*j* of cases, experience is to be relied on. Experience must be consulted in order to learn from it under what circumstances arguments from it will be valid. We have no ulterior test to which we subject experience in general; but we make experience its own test. Experience testifies, that among the uniformities which it exhibits or seems to exhibit, some are more to be relied on than others; and uniformity, therefore, may be presumed, from any given number of instances, with a greater degree of assurance, in proportion as the case belongs to a class in which the uniformities have hitherto been found more uniform.

This mode of correcting one generalization by means of another, a narrower generalization by a wider, which common sense suggests and adopts in practice, is the real type of scientific Induction. All that art can do is but to give accuracy and precision to this process, and adapt it to all varieties of cases, without any essential alteration in its principle.

There are of course no means of applying such a test as that above described, unless we already possess a general knowledge of the prevalent

*f*MS, 43, 46, 51, 56   other
*g-g*MS, 43, 46   of unquestionable certainty
*h*MS, 43, 46, 51, 56   internal
*i-i*MS, 43, 46   cases, or in what
*j-j*65, 68   sort

character of the uniformities existing throughout nature. The indispensable foundation, therefore, of a scientific formula of induction, must be a survey of the inductions to which mankind have been conducted in unscientific practice; with the special purpose of ascertaining what kinds of uniformities have been found perfectly invariable, pervading all nature, and what are those which have been found to vary with difference of time, place, or other changeable circumstances.

§ 3. [*Are there any inductions fitted to be a test of all others?*] The necessity of such a survey is confirmed by the consideration, that the stronger inductions are the touchstone to which we always endeavour to bring the weaker. If we find any means of deducing one of the less strong inductions from stronger ones, it acquires, at once, all the strength of those from which it is deduced; and even adds to that strength; since the independent experience on which the weaker induction previously rested, becomes additional evidence of the truth of the better established law in which it is now found to be included. We may have inferred, from historical evidence, that the uncontrolled *power of a monarch*, of an aristocracy, or of the majority, will *often be abused*: but we are entitled to rely on this generalization with much greater assurance when it is shown to be a corollary from still better established *facts; the very low degree of elevation of character ever yet attained by the average of mankind, and the little efficacy, for the most part, of the modes of education hitherto practised, in maintaining the predominance of reason and conscience over the selfish propensities*. It is at the same time obvious that even these *more general facts* derive an accession of evidence from the testimony which history bears to the effects of despotism. The strong induction becomes still stronger when a weaker one has been bound up with it.

On the other hand, if an induction conflicts with stronger inductions, or with conclusions capable of being correctly deduced from them, then, unless on reconsideration it should appear that some of the stronger inductions have been *expressed with greater universality than their evidence warrants*, the weaker one must give way. The opinion so long prevalent that a comet, or any other unusual appearance in the heavenly regions, was the precursor of

*a–a*MS [*no section division; presumably added in proof, as given in* MS *Table of Contents*]

*b–b*MS, 43, 46   government of a monarchy

*c–c*MS, 43, 46   commonly be a tyranny

*d–d*MS, 43, 46   truths; the infirmity of human nature, and the impossibility of maintaining the predominance of reason and conscience over the selfish propensities by any means except such as the supposition of absolute power necessarily excludes

*e–e*MS, 43, 46   great facts in human nature

*f–f*MS, 43, 46   stretched too far

calamities to mankind, or to those *at least* who witnessed it; the belief in the veracity of the oracles of Delphi or Dodona; the reliance on astrology, or on the weather-prophecies in almanacks, were doubtless inductions supposed to be grounded on experience:* and faith in such delusions seems quite capable of holding out against a great multitude of failures, provided it be nourished by a reasonable number of casual coincidences between the prediction and the event. What has really put an end to these insufficient inductions, is their inconsistency with the stronger inductions subsequently obtained by scientific inquiry, respecting the causes on which terrestrial events really depend; and where those scientific truths have not yet penetrated, the same or similar delusions still prevail.

It may be affirmed as a general principle, that all inductions, whether strong or weak, which can be connected *by* ratiocination, are confirmatory of one another; while any which lead deductively to consequences that are incompatible, become mutually each other's test, showing that one or other

---

*[51] Dr. Whewell (*Philosophy of Discovery*, p. 246) will not allow these and similar erroneous *judgments* to be called inductions; inasmuch as such superstitious fancies "were not collected from the facts by seeking a law of their occurrence, but were suggested by an imagination of the anger of superior powers, shown by such deviations from the ordinary course of nature." I conceive the question to be, not in what manner these notions were at first suggested, but by what evidence they have, from time to time, been supposed to be substantiated. If the believers in these erroneous opinions had been put on their defence, they would have referred to experience: to the comet which preceded the assassination of Julius Cæsar, or to oracles and other prophecies known to have been fulfilled. It is by such appeals to facts that all analogous superstitions, even in our day, attempt to justify themselves; the supposed evidence of experience is *necessary to* their hold on the mind. I quite admit that the influence of such coincidences would not be what it is, if strength were not lent to it by an antecedent presumption; but this is not peculiar to such cases; preconceived notions of probability form part of the explanation of many other cases of belief on insufficient evidence. The *à priori* prejudice does not prevent the erroneous opinion from being sincerely regarded as a legitimate conclusion from experience; *though it improperly* predisposes the mind to that interpretation of experience.

Thus much in defence of the sort of examples objected to. But it would be easy to produce instances, equally adapted to the purpose, and in which no antecedent prejudice is at all concerned. "For many ages," says Archbishop Whately, "all farmers and gardeners were firmly convinced—and convinced of their knowing it by experience—that the crops would never turn out good unless the seed were sown during the increase of the moon." This was induction, but bad induction; just as a vicious syllogism is reasoning, but bad reasoning.

g–g+43, 46, 51, 56, 62, 65, 68, 72
*h–h*51, 56   opinions
*i–i*51, 56, 62, 65   what really gives them
*j–j*51, 56   but is, on the contrary, the very thing which
*k–k*MS, 43   together by a]   46, 51   by a

must be given up, or at least more guardedly expressed. In the case of inductions which confirm each other, the one which becomes a conclusion from ratiocination rises to at least the level of certainty of the weakest of those from which it is deduced; while in general all are more or less increased in certainty. Thus the Torricellian experiment, though a mere case of three more general laws, not only strengthened greatly the evidence on which those laws rested, but converted one of them (the weight of the atmosphere) from a *still* doubtful generalization into *a completely established doctrine*.

If, then, a survey of the uniformities which have been ascertained to exist in nature, should point out some which, as far as any human purpose requires certainty, may be considered *quite certain and quite* universal; then by means of these uniformities we may be able to raise multitudes of other inductions to the same point in the scale. For if we can show, with respect to any *inductive inference*, that either it must be true, or one of these certain and universal inductions must admit of an exception; the former generalization will attain the same *p* certainty, and indefeasibleness within the bounds assigned to it, which are the attributes of the latter. It will be proved to be a law; and if not a result of other and simpler laws, it will be a law of nature.

There are such certain and universal inductions; and it is because there are such, that a Logic of Induction is possible.

l–l+72
*m–m*MS, 43, 46, 51, 56   one of the best-established doctrines in the range of physical science
   *n–n*MS, 43, 46   as absolutely certain and absolutely] 51   as quite certain and quite
   *o–o*MS, 43, 46, 51, 56, 62, 65   induction
   *p*MS, 43, 46   absolute

CHAPTER V

Of the Law of Universal Causation

§ 1. [*The universal law of successive phenomena is the Law of Causation*]
The phenomena of nature exist in two distinct relations to one another; that
of simultaneity, and that of succession. Every phenomenon is *ᵃrelated, in an
uniform manner, to some phenomena that coexist with it, and toᵃ* some that
have preceded *ᵇandᵇ* will follow it.

Of the uniformities which exist among synchronous phenomena, the most
important, on every account, are the laws of number; and next to them those
of space, or, in other words, of extension and figure. The laws of number are
common to synchronous and successive phenomena. That two and two make
four, is equally true whether the second two follow the first two or accompany them. It is as true of days and years as of feet and inches. The laws of
extension and figure (in other words, the theorems of geometry, from its
lowest to its highest branches) are, on the contrary, laws of simultaneous
phenomena only. The various parts of space, and of the objects which are
said to fill space, coexist; and the unvarying laws which are the subject of the
science of geometry, are an expression of the mode of their coexistence.

ᶜ This is a class of laws, or in other words, of uniformities, for the comprehension and proof of which it is not necessary to suppose any lapse of time,
any variety of facts or events succeeding one another. *ᵈThe propositions of
geometry are independent of the succession of events.ᵈ* All things which
possess extension, or, in other words, which fill space, are subject to geometrical laws. Possessing extension, they possess figure; possessing figure,
they must possess some figure in particular, and have all the properties which
geometry assigns to that figure. If one body be a sphere and *ᵉanotherᵉ* a
cylinder, of equal height and diameter, the one will be exactly two-thirds of
the other, let the nature and quality of the material be what it will. Again,

---

*ᵃ⁻ᵃ*MS   connected, in . . . manner, with . . . and with
*ᵇ⁻ᵇ*MS, 43, 46, 51   or
*ᶜ*MS   [*no paragraph*]
*ᵈ⁻ᵈ*MS, 43, 46, 51, 56, 62, 65, 68   If all the objects in the universe were unchange-
ably fixed, and had remained in that condition from eternity, the propositions of
geometry would still be true of those objects.
*ᵉ⁻ᵉ*MS, 43   the other

each body, and each point of a body, must occupy some place or position among other bodies; and the position of two bodies relatively to each other, of whatever nature the bodies be, may be unerringly inferred from the position of each of them relatively to any third body.

In the laws of number, then, and in those of space, we recognise in the most unqualified manner, the rigorous universality of which we are in quest. Those laws have been in all ages the type of certainty, the standard of comparison for all inferior degrees of evidence. Their invariability is so perfect, that *it renders us* unable even to conceive any exception to them; and philosophers have been led, though (as I have endeavoured to show) erroneously, to consider their evidence as lying not in experience, but in the original constitution of the *ᵍ* intellect. If, therefore, from the laws of space and number, we were able to deduce uniformities of any other description, this would be conclusive evidence to us that those other uniformities possessed the same *ʰ* rigorous certainty. But this we cannot do. From laws of space and number alone, nothing can be deduced but laws of space and number.

Of all truths relating to phenomena, the most valuable to us are those which relate to the order of their succession. On a knowledge of these is founded every reasonable anticipation of future facts, and whatever power we possess of influencing *those facts* to our advantage. Even the laws of geometry are chiefly of practical importance to us as being a portion of the premises from which the order of the succession of phenomena may be inferred. *ʲ* Inasmuch as the *ᵏmotionᵏ* of bodies, the action of forces, and the propagation of influences of all sorts, take place in certain lines and over definite spaces, the properties of those lines and spaces are an important part of the laws to which those phenomena are themselves subject. *ˡAgainˡ*, motions, forces, or other influences, and times, are numerable quantities; and the properties of number are applicable to them as to all other things. *ᵐ* But though the laws of number and space are important elements in the ascertainment of uniformities of succession, they can do nothing towards it when taken by themselves. They can only be made instrumental to that purpose when we combine with them additional premises, expressive of uniformities of succession already known. By taking, for instance, as premises these propositions, that bodies acted upon by an instantaneous force move with uniform velocity in straight lines; that bodies acted upon by a continuous force move with accelerated velocity in straight lines; and that bodies acted upon by two forces in different directions move in the diagonal of a parallelo-

---

*f–f*MS, 43, 46, 51   we are
*ʰ*MS, 43, 46, 51, 56   degree of
*ʲ*43, 46   [*paragraph*]
*ˡ–ˡ*MS, 43, 46   Moreover

*ᵍ*MS, 43, 46   human
*i–i*MS   them
*k–k*MS   motions
*ᵐ*MS   [*paragraph*]

gram, whose sides represent the direction and quantity of those forces; we may by combining these truths with propositions relating to the properties of straight lines and of parallelograms, (as that a triangle is half [n] a parallelogram of the same base and altitude,) deduce another important uniformity of succession, viz., that a body moving round a centre of force describes areas proportional to the times. But unless there had been laws of succession in our premises, there could have been no truths of succession in our conclusions. A similar remark might be extended to every other class of phenomena really peculiar; and, had it been attended to, would have prevented many chimerical attempts at demonstrations of the indemonstrable, and explanations [o]which do not explain[o].

It is not, therefore, enough for us that the laws of space, which are only laws of simultaneous phenomena, and the laws of number, which though true of successive phenomena do not relate to their succession, possess [p]the[p] rigorous certainty and universality of which we are in search. We must endeavour to find some law of succession which has those same attributes, and is therefore fit to be made the foundation of processes for discovering, and of a test for verifying, all other uniformities of succession. This fundamental law must resemble the truths of geometry in their most remarkable peculiarity, that of never being, in any instance whatever, defeated or suspended by any change of circumstances.

[q] Now among all those uniformities in the succession of phenomena, which common observation is sufficient to bring to light, there are very few which have any, even apparent, pretension to this rigorous indefeasibility: and of those few, one only has been found capable of completely sustaining it. In that one, however, we recognise a law which is universal also in another sense; it is coextensive with the entire field of successive phenomena, all instances whatever of succession being examples of it. This law is the Law of Causation. [r]The truth that every fact which has a beginning has a cause, is coextensive with human experience.[r]

This generalization may appear to some minds not to amount to much, since after all it asserts only this: "it is a law, that every event depends on some [s]law:" "it is a law, that there is a law for everything."[s] We must not, however, conclude that the generality of the principle is merely verbal; it will be found on inspection to be no vague or unmeaning assertion, but a most important and really fundamental truth.

[n]MS, 43, 46, 51, 56, 62   of
[o-o]MS, 43, 46   of what cannot be explained
[p-p]MS, 43, 46   that
[q]MS   §2.
[r-r]MS, 43, 46   It is an universal truth that every fact which has a beginning has a cause.
[s-s]MS, 43, 46, 51   law."

§ 2. [*That is, the universal law of successive phenomena is the law that every consequent has an invariable antecedent*] The notion of Cause being the root of the whole theory of Induction, it is indispensable that this idea should, at the very outset of our inquiry, be, with the utmost practicable degree of precision, fixed and determined. If, indeed, it were necessary for the *purpose* of inductive logic that the strife should be quelled, which has so long raged among the different schools of metaphysicians, respecting the origin and analysis of our idea of causation; the promulgation, or at least the general reception, of a true theory of induction, might be considered desperate for a long time to come. But *ᶜ* the science of the Investigation of Truth by means of Evidence, *ᵈ*is happily independent of many of the controversies which perplex the science of the ultimate constitution of the human mind, and is under no necessity of pushing the analysis of mental phenomena to that extreme limit which alone ought to satisfy a metaphysician*ᵈ*.

I premise, then, that when in the course of this inquiry I speak of the cause of any phenomenon, I do not mean a cause which is not itself a phenomenon; I make no research into the ultimate or ontological cause of anything. To adopt a distinction familiar in the writings of the Scotch metaphysicians, and especially of Reid, the causes with which I concern myself are not *efficient*, but *physical* causes. They are causes in that sense alone, in which one physical fact *ᵉ*is*ᵉ* said to be the cause of another. Of the efficient causes of phenomena, or whether any such causes exist at all, I am not called upon to give an opinion. The notion of causation is deemed, by the schools of metaphysics most in vogue at the present moment, to imply a mysterious and most powerful tie, such as cannot, or at least does not, exist between any physical fact and that other physical fact on which it is invariably consequent, and which is popularly termed its cause: and thence is deduced the supposed necessity of ascending higher, into the essences and inherent constitution of things, to find the true cause, *ᶠthe cause*ᶠ which is not only followed by, but actually produces, the effect. No such necessity exists for the purposes of the present inquiry, nor will any such doctrine be found in the following pages. *ᵍ* The only notion of a cause, which the theory of induction requires, is such a notion as can be gained from experience. The Law of Causation, the recog-

---

*a–a*MS [*no section division*]

*b–b*MS, 43, 46   purposes

*c*MS, 43, 46   in this as in most other respects,

*d–d*MS, 43, 46   has no need to borrow any premisses from the science of the ultimate constitution of the human mind, except such as have at last, though often after long controversy, been incorporated into all the existing systems of mental philosophy, or all but such as may be regarded as essentially effete

*e–e*MS, 43   may be

f–f+43, 46, 51, 56, 62, 65, 68, 72

*g*MS, 43, 46, 51   But neither will there be found anything incompatible with it. We are in no way concerned in the question.

nition of which is the main pillar of inductive [h]science[h], is but the familiar truth, that invariability of succession is found by observation to obtain between every fact in nature and some other fact which has preceded it; independently of all [i]considerations[i] respecting the ultimate mode of production of phenomena, and of every other question regarding the nature of "Things in themselves."

Between the phenomena, then, which exist at any instant, and the phenomena which exist at the succeeding instant, there is an invariable order of succession; and, as we said in speaking of the general uniformity of the course of nature, this web is composed of separate fibres; this collective order is made up of particular sequences, obtaining invariably among the separate parts. To certain facts, certain [j] facts always do, and, as we believe, [k]will continue to[k], succeed. The invariable antecedent is termed the cause; the invariable consequent, the effect. And the universality of the law of causation consists in this, that every consequent is connected in this manner with some particular antecedent, or set of antecedents. Let the fact be what it may, if it has begun to exist, it was preceded by some fact or facts, with which it is invariably connected. For every event there exists some combination of objects or events, some given concurrence of circumstances, positive and negative, the occurrence of which [l]is always[l] followed by that phenomenon. We may not have found out what this concurrence of circumstances may be; but we never doubt that there is such a one, and that it never occurs without having the phenomenon in question as its effect or consequence. On the universality of this truth depends the possibility of reducing the inductive process to rules. The undoubted assurance we have that there is a law to be found if we only knew how to find it, will be seen presently to be the source from which the canons of the Inductive Logic derive their validity.

§ 3. [*The cause of a phenomenon is the assemblage of its conditions*] It is seldom, if ever, between a consequent and [a]a[a] single antecedent, that this invariable sequence subsists. It is usually between a consequent and the sum of several antecedents; the concurrence of [b]all of them[b] being requisite to produce, that is, to be certain of being followed by, the consequent. In such cases it is very common to single out one only of the antecedents under the denomination of Cause, calling the others merely Conditions. Thus, if a [c]person[c] eats of a particular dish, and dies in consequence, that is, would not have died if he had not eaten of it, people would be apt to say that eating of that dish was the cause of his death. There needs not, however, be any in-

[h–h]MS, 43, 46 philosophy
[i–i]MS, 43, 46, 51, 56, 62, 65, 68 consideration
[j]MS other
[l–l]MS, 43, 46 will always be
[b–b]MS, 43 them all
[k–k]MS, 43, 46 always will
[a–a]MS, 43, 46 one
[c–c]MS, 43, 46 man

variable connexion between eating of the dish and death; but there certainly is, among the circumstances which took place, some combination or other on which death is invariably consequent: as, for instance, the act of eating of the dish, combined with a particular bodily constitution, a particular state of present health, and perhaps even a certain state of the atmosphere; the whole of which circumstances perhaps constituted in this particular case the *conditions* of the phenomenon, or, in other words, the set of antecedents which determined it, and but for which it would not have happened. The real Cause, is the whole of these antecedents; and we have, philosophically speaking, no right to give the name of cause to one of them, exclusively of the others. What, in the case we have supposed, disguises the incorrectness of the expression, is this: that the various conditions, except the single one of eating the food, were not *events* (that is, instantaneous changes, or successions of instantaneous changes) but *states*, possessing more or less of permanency; and might therefore have preceded the effect by an indefinite length of duration, for want of the event which was requisite to complete the required concurrence of conditions: while as soon as that event, eating the food, occurs, no other cause is waited for, but the effect begins immediately to take place: and hence the appearance is presented of a more immediate and ᵈcloseᵈ connexion between the effect and that one antecedent, than between the effect and the remaining conditions. But though we may think proper to give the name of cause to that one condition, the fulfilment of which completes the tale, and brings about the effect without further delay; this condition has really no closer relation to the effect than any of the other conditions has. ᵉAll the conditions were equally indispensable to the production of the consequent; and theᵉ statement of the cause is incomplete, unless in some shape or other we introduce ᶠthem allᶠ. A man takes mercury, goes out of doors, and catches cold. We say, perhaps, that the cause of his taking cold was exposure to the air. It is clear, however, that his having taken mercury may have been a necessary condition ᵍof hisᵍ catching cold; and though it might consist with usage to say that the cause of his attack was exposure to the air, to be accurate we ought to say that the cause was exposure to the air while under the effect of mercury.

ʰ If we do not, when aiming at accuracy, enumerate all the conditions, it is only because some of them will in most cases be understood without being expressed, or because for the purpose in view they may without detriment be

ᵈ⁻ᵈMS, 43, 46   closer
ᵉ⁻ᵉMS, 43, 46, 51, 56, 62, 65, 68   The production of the consequent required that they should all *exist* immediately previous, though not that they should all *begin* to exist immediately previous. The
ᶠ⁻ᶠMS, 43, 46, 51, 56, 62, 65, 68   all the conditions
ᵍ⁻ᵍ56, 62, 65, 68   of
ʰMS [*no paragraph*]

overlooked. For example, when we say, the cause of a man's death was that his foot slipped in climbing a ladder, we omit as a thing unnecessary to be stated the circumstance of his weight, though quite as indispensable a condition of the effect which took place. When we say that the assent of the crown to a bill makes it law, we mean that the assent, being never given until all the other conditions are fulfilled, makes up the sum of the conditions, though no one now regards it as the principal one. When the decision of a legislative assembly has been determined by the casting vote of the chairman, we *sometimes* say that this one person was the cause of all the effects which resulted from the enactment. Yet we do not really suppose that his single vote contributed more to the result than that of any other person who voted in the affirmative; but, for the purpose we have in view, which is *to insist on his individual responsibility, the part which any other person had* in the transaction is not material.

In all these instances the fact which was dignified *with* the name of cause, was the one condition which came last into existence. But it must not be supposed that in the employment of the term this or any other rule is always adhered to. Nothing can better show the absence of any scientific ground for the distinction between the cause of a phenomenon and its conditions, than the capricious manner in which we select from among the conditions that which we choose to denominate the cause. However numerous the conditions may be, there is hardly any of them which may not, according to the purpose of our immediate discourse, obtain that nominal pre-eminence. This will be seen by analysing the conditions of some one familiar phenomenon. For example, a stone thrown into water falls to the bottom. What are the conditions of this event? In the first place there must be a stone, and water, and the stone must be thrown into the water; but these suppositions forming part of the enunciation of the phenomenon itself, to include them *also among the conditions* would be a vicious tautology; and this class of conditions, therefore, have never received the name of cause from any but *the Aristotelians*, by whom they were called the *material* cause, *causa materialis*. The next condition is, there must be an earth: and accordingly it is often said, that the fall of a stone is caused by the earth; or by a power or property of the earth, or a force exerted by the earth, all of which are merely roundabout ways of saying that it is caused by the earth; or, lastly, the earth's attraction; which also is only a technical mode of saying that the earth causes the motion,

*−*MS, 43, 46   often

*−*MS, 43, 46   that of fixing him with the responsibility, the share which any other person took]   51, 56   to insist on his share of the responsibility, the part which any other person had

*−*MS, 43, 46, 51, 56   by

*−*MS   among the conditions also

*−*MS, 43, 46, 51, 56   the schoolmen]   62   Aristotelians

with the additional particularity that the motion is towards the earth, which is not a character of the cause, but of the effect. Let us now pass to another condition. It is not enough that the earth should exist; the body must be within that distance from it, in which the earth's attraction preponderates over that of any other body. Accordingly we may say, and the expression would be confessedly correct, that the cause of the stone's falling is its being *within the sphere* of the earth's attraction. We proceed to a further condition. The stone is immersed in water: it is therefore a condition of its reaching the ground, that its specific gravity exceed that of the surrounding fluid, or in other words that it surpass in weight an equal volume of water. Accordingly any one would be acknowledged to speak correctly who said, that the cause of the stone's going to the bottom is its exceeding in specific gravity the fluid in which it is immersed.

ⁿ Thus we see that each and every condition of the phenomenon may be taken in its turn, and, with equal propriety in common parlance, but with equal impropriety in scientific discourse, may be spoken of as if it were the entire cause. And in practice, that particular condition is usually styled the cause, whose share in the matter is superficially the most conspicuous, or whose requisiteness to the production of the effect we happen to be insisting on at the moment. So great is the force of this last consideration, that it °sometimes° induces us to give the name of cause even to one of the negative conditions. We say, for example, The ᵖarmy was surprised because the sentinel wasᵖ off his post. But since the sentinel's absence was not what created the enemy, or ᑫput the soldiersᑫ asleep, how did it cause them to be surprised? All that is really meant is, that ʳthe event would not have happened if he had been at his dutyʳ. His being off his post was no producing cause, but the mere absence of a preventing cause: it was simply equivalent to his non-existence. From nothing, from a mere negation, no consequences can proceed. All effects are connected, by the law of causation, with some set of *positive* conditions; negative ones, it is true, being almost always required in addition. In other words, every fact or phenomenon which has a beginning, invariably arises when some certain combination of positive facts exists, provided certain other positive facts do not ˢexistˢ.

ᵗ There is, no doubt, a tendency (which our first example, that of death

---

ⁿMS [*no paragraph*]

°⁻°MS, 43, 46   often

ᵖ⁻ᵖMS, 43, 46   cause of the army's being surprised was the sentinel's being

ᑫ⁻ᑫMS, 43   made the soldiers to be]   46   made the soldiers be

ʳ⁻ʳMS   they would not have been so if he had been present

ˢ⁻ˢ+43, 46, 51, 56, 62, 65, 68, 72

ᵗMS, 43, 46   Since, then, mankind are accustomed, with acknowledged propriety so far as the ordinances of language are concerned, to give the name of cause to almost any one of the conditions of a phenomenon, or any portion of the whole number,

from taking a particular food, *sufficiently illustrates*) to associate the idea of causation with the proximate antecedent *event*, rather than with any of the antecedent *states*, or permanent facts, which may happen also to be conditions of the phenomenon; the reason being that the event not only exists, but begins to exist immediately previous; while the other conditions may have pre-existed for an indefinite time. And this tendency shows itself very visibly in the different logical fictions which are resorted to, even by *men of science*, to avoid the necessity of giving the name of cause to anything which had existed for an indeterminate length of time before the effect. Thus, rather than say that the earth causes the fall of bodies, they *w* ascribe it to a *force* exerted by the earth, or an *attraction* by the earth, abstractions which they can represent to themselves as exhausted by each effort, and therefore constituting at each successive instant a fresh fact, simultaneous with, or only immediately preceding, the effect. Inasmuch as the coming of the circumstance which completes the assemblage of conditions, is a change or event, it thence happens that an event is always the antecedent in closest apparent proximity to the consequent: and this may account for the illusion which disposes us to look upon the proximate event as standing more peculiarly in the position of a cause than any of the antecedent states. But even this peculiarity, of being in closer proximity to the effect than any other of its conditions, is, as we have already seen, far from being necessary to the common notion of a cause; with which notion, on the contrary, any one of the conditions, either positive or negative, is found, on occasion, completely to accord.*

*[51] The assertion, that any and every one of the conditions of a phenomenon may be and is, on some occasions and for some purposes, spoken of as the cause, has been disputed by an intelligent reviewer of this work *in the *Prospective Review* (the predecessor of the justly esteemed *National Review*),* who maintains that "we always apply the word cause rather to that element in the antecedents which exercises *force*, and which would *tend* at all times to produce the same or a similar effect to that which, under certain conditions, it would actually produce." [R. H. Hutton, "Mill and Whewell on the Logic of Induction," *Prospective Review*, VI (Feb., 1850), p. 104.] And he says, that "every one would feel" the expression, that the cause of a surprise was the sentinel's being off his post, to be incorrect; but that the "allurement or force which *drew* him off his post, might be so called, because in doing so it removed a resisting power which would have prevented the surprise." [P. 105.] I cannot think that it would be wrong to

arbitrarily selected, without excepting even those conditions which are purely negative, and in themselves incapable of causing anything; it will probably be admitted without longer discussion, that no one of the conditions has more claim to that title than another, and that the real cause of the phenomenon is the assemblage of all its conditions.

*u–u*MS   has sufficiently illustrated
*v–v*MS, 43, 46   philosophers   *w*MS   will
*x–x*51, 56   , (*Prospective Review* for February 1850,)

The cause, then, philosophically speaking, is the sum total of the conditions, positive and negative taken together; the whole of the contingencies of every description, which being realized, the consequent invariably follows. The negative conditions, however, of any phenomenon, a special enumeration of which would generally be very prolix, may be all summed up under one head, namely, the absence of preventing or counteracting causes. The

---

say, that the event took place because the sentinel was absent, and yet right to say that it took place because he was bribed to be absent. Since the only direct effect of the bribe was his absence, the bribe could be called the remote cause of the surprise, only on the supposition that the absence was the proximate cause; nor does it seem to me that any one (who had not a theory to support) would use the one expression and reject the other.

The reviewer observes, that when a person dies of poison, his possession of bodily organs is a necessary condition, but that no one would ever speak of it as the cause. I admit the fact; but I believe the reason to be, that the occasion could never arise for so speaking of it; for when in the inaccuracy of common discourse we are led to speak of some one condition of a phenomenon as its cause, the condition so spoken of is always one which it is at least possible that the hearer may require to be informed of. The possession of bodily organs is a known condition, and to give that as the answer, when asked the cause of a person's death, would not supply the information sought. Once conceive that a doubt could exist as to his having bodily organs, or that he were to be compared with some being who had them not, and cases may be imagined in which it might be said that his possession of them was the cause of his death. If Faust and Mephistopheles together took poison, it might be said that Faust died because he was a human being, and had a body, while Mephistopheles survived because he was a spirit.

It is for the same reason that no one (as the reviewer remarks) "calls the cause of a leap, the muscles or sinews of the body, though they are necessary conditions; nor the cause of a self-sacrifice, the knowledge which was necessary for it; nor the cause of writing a book, that a man has time for it, which is a necessary condition." [P. 106.] These conditions (besides that they are antecedent *states*, and not proximate antecedent *events*, and are therefore never the conditions in closest apparent proximity to the effect) are all of them so obviously implied, that it is hardly possible *ᵛ* there should exist that necessity for insisting on them, which alone gives occasion for speaking of a single condition as if it were the cause. Wherever this necessity exists in regard to some one condition, and does not exist in regard to any other, I conceive that it is consistent with usage, when scientific accuracy is not aimed at, to apply the name cause to that one condition. If the only condition which can be supposed to be unknown is a negative condition, the negative condition may be spoken of as the cause. It might be said that a person died for want of medical advice: though this would not be likely to be said, unless the person was already understood to be ill, and in order to indicate that this negative circumstance was what made the illness fatal, and not the weakness of his constitution, or the original virulence of the disease. It might be said that a person was drowned because he could not swim; the positive condition, namely, that he fell into the water, being already implied in the word

*ᵛ56   that

convenience of this mode of expression is *mainly grounded* on the fact, that the effects of any cause in counteracting another cause may in most cases be, with strict scientific exactness, regarded as a mere extension of its own proper and separate effects. If gravity retards the upward motion of a projectile, and deflects it into a parabolic trajectory, it produces, in so doing, the very same kind of effect, and even (as mathematicians know) the same quantity

---

drowned. And here let me remark, that his falling into the water is in this case the only positive condition: all the conditions not expressly or virtually included in this (as that he could not swim, that nobody helped him, and so forth) are negative. Yet, if it were simply said that the cause of a man's death was falling into the water, there would be quite as great a sense of impropriety in the expression, as there would be if it were said that the cause was his inability to swim; because, though the one condition is positive and the other negative, it would be felt that neither of them was sufficient, without the other, to produce death.

With regard to the assertion that nothing is termed the cause, except the element which exerts active force; I waive the question as to the meaning of active force, and accepting the phrase in its popular sense, I revert to a former example, and I ask, would it be more agreeable to custom to say that a man fell because his foot slipped in climbing a ladder, or that he fell because of his weight? for his weight, and not the motion of his foot, was the active force which determined his fall. If a person walking out in a frosty day, stumbled and fell, it might be said that he stumbled because the ground was slippery, or because he was not sufficiently careful; but few people, I suppose, would say, that he stumbled because he walked. Yet the only active force concerned was that which he exerted in walking: the others were mere negative conditions; but they happened to be the only ones which there could be any necessity to state; for he walked, most likely, in exactly his usual manner, and the negative conditions made all the difference. Again, if a person were asked why the army of Xerxes defeated that of Leonidas, he would probably say, because they were a thousand times the number; but I do not think he would say, it was because they fought, though that was the element of active force. *To borrow another example, used by Mr. Grove [William R. Grove. *On the Correlation of Physical Forces.* London: London Institution, 1846, p. 6,] and by Mr. Baden Powell [see *Essays on the Spirit of the Inductive Philosophy, The Unity of Worlds, and The Philosophy of Creation.* London: Longman, 1855, p. 120], the opening of floodgates is said to be the cause of the flow of water; yet the active force is exerted by the water itself, and opening the floodgates merely supplies a negative condition.* The reviewer adds, "there are some conditions absolutely passive, and yet absolutely necessary to physical phenomena, viz. the relations of space and time; and to these no one ever applies the word cause without being immediately arrested by those who hear him." ["Mill and Whewell, p. 105.] Even from this statement I am compelled to dissent. Few persons would feel it incongruous to say (for example) that a secret became known because it was spoken of when A. B. was within hearing; which is a condition of space: or that the cause why one of two particular trees is taller than the other, is that it has been longer planted; which is a condition of time.

z–z+56, 62, 65, 68, 72
*a–a*MS, 43, 46   grounded mainly

of effect, as it does in its ordinary operation of causing the fall of bodies when simply deprived of their support. If an alkaline solution mixed with an acid destroys its sourness, and prevents it from reddening vegetable blues, it is because the specific effect of the alkali is to combine with the acid, and form a compound with totally different qualities. This property, which causes of all descriptions possess, of preventing the effects of other causes by virtue (for the most part) of the same laws according to which they produce their own,* enables us, by establishing the general axiom that all causes are liable to be counteracted in their effects by one another, to dispense with the consideration of negative conditions entirely, and limit the notion of cause to the assemblage of the positive conditions of the phenomenon: one negative condition invariably understood, and the same in all instances (namely, the absence of ^{d} counteracting causes) being sufficient, along with the sum of the positive conditions, to make up the whole set of circumstances on which the phenomenon is dependent.

§ 4. [*The distinction of agent and patient illusory*] Among the positive conditions, as we have seen that there are some to which, in common parlance, the term cause is more readily and frequently awarded, so there are others to which it is, in ordinary circumstances, refused. In most cases of causation a distinction is commonly drawn between something which acts, and some other thing which is acted upon; between an *agent* and a *patient*. Both of these, it would be universally allowed, are conditions of the phenomenon; but it would be thought absurd to call the latter the cause, that title being reserved for the former. The distinction, however, vanishes on examination, or rather is found to be only verbal; arising from an incident of

---

*There are a few exceptions; for there are some properties of objects which seem to be purely preventive; as the property of opaque bodies, by which they intercept the passage of light. This, ^{b}as^b far as we are able to understand it, appears an instance not of one cause counteracting another by the same law whereby it produces its own effects, but of an agency which manifests itself in no other way than in defeating the effects of another agency. If we knew on what other relations to light, or on what peculiarities of structure, opacity depends, we might find that this is only an apparent, not a real, exception to the general proposition in the text. In any case it needs not affect the practical application. The formula which includes all the negative conditions of an effect in the single one of the absence of counteracting causes, is not violated by such cases as this; though, if all counteracting agencies were of this description, there would be no purpose served by employing the formula ^{c} .

$^{b-b}$MS so
^{c}MS, 43, 46, 51, 56, 62, 65, 68   , since we should still have to enumerate specially the negative conditions of each phenomenon, instead of regarding them as implicitly contained in the positive laws of the various other agencies in nature
^{d}MS, 43, 46, 51   all

mere expression, namely, that the object said to be acted upon, and which is considered as the scene in which the effect takes place, is commonly included in the phrase by which the effect is spoken of, so that if it were also reckoned as part of the cause, the seeming incongruity would arise of its being supposed to cause itself. In the instance which we have already had, of falling bodies, the question was thus put: What is the cause which makes a stone fall? and if the answer had been "the stone itself," the expression would have been in apparent contradiction to the meaning of the word cause. The stone, therefore, is conceived as the patient, and the earth (or, according to the common and most unphilosophical practice, *an* occult quality of the earth) is represented as the agent or cause. But that there is nothing fundamental in the distinction may be seen from this, that *it is quite possible to conceive the stone as causing its own fall, provided the language employed be such as to save the mere verbal incongruity. We might say that the stone moves towards the earth by the properties of the matter composing it; and according to this mode of presenting the phenomenon, the stone itself might without impropriety be called the agent*; though, to save the established doctrine of the inactivity of matter, men usually prefer here also to ascribe the effect to an occult quality, and say that the cause is not the stone itself, but the *weight* or *gravitation* of the stone.

Those who have contended for a radical distinction between agent and patient, have generally conceived the agent as that which causes some state of, or some change in the state of, another object which is called the patient. But a little reflection will show that the licence we assume of speaking of phenomena as *states* of the various objects which take part in them, (an artifice of which so much use has been made by some philosophers, Brown in particular, for the apparent explanation of phenomena,) is simply a sort of logical fiction, useful sometimes as one among several modes of expression, but which should never be supposed to be the *enunciation* of a *scientific truth. Even those* attributes of an object which might seem with greatest propriety to be called states of the object itself, its sensible qualities, its colour, hardness, shape, and the like, are in reality (as no one has pointed out more clearly than Brown himself) phenomena of causation, in which the substance is distinctly the agent, or producing cause, the patient being our own organs, and those of other sentient beings. What we call *e* states of

---

*a–a*MS, 43, 46, 51, 56, 62, 65, 68   some
*b–b*MS, 43, 46   if we do but alter the mere wording of the question, and express it thus, What is the cause which produces vertical motion towards the earth? we might now, without any incongruity, speak of the stone or other heavy body as the agent, which, by virtue of its own laws or properties, commences moving towards the earth
*c–c*MS, 43, 46, 51, 56   statement
*d–d*MS, 43, 46   philosophical truth. Even those of the
*e*MS, 43, 46   the

objects, are always sequences into which *the* objects enter, generally as antecedents or causes; and things are never more active than in the production of those phenomena in which they are said to be acted upon. Thus, in the *example of a stone falling to the earth, according to the theory of gravitation the stone is as much an agent as the earth, which not only attracts, but is itself attracted by, the stone. In the case of a sensation produced in our organs, the laws of our organization, and even those of our minds, are as directly operative in determining the effect produced, as the laws of the outward object.* Though we call prussic acid the agent of a *person's death, the whole of the vital and organic properties of the patient are as actively instrumental as the poison, in the chain of effects which so rapidly terminates his sentient existence.* In the process of education, we may call the teacher the agent, and the scholar only the material acted upon; yet in truth all the facts which pre-existed in the scholar's mind exert either co-operating or counteracting agencies in relation to the teacher's efforts. It is not light alone which is the agent in vision, but light coupled with the active properties of the eye and brain, and with those of the visible object. The distinction between agent and patient is merely verbal: patients are always agents; in a great proportion, indeed, of all natural phenomena, they are so to such a degree as to react *forcibly on the causes which acted upon them: and even when this is not the case, they contribute, in the same manner as any of the other conditions, to the production of the effect of which they are vulgarly treated as the mere theatre. All the positive conditions of a phenomenon are alike agents, alike active; and in any expression of the cause which professes to be *complete*, none of them can with reason be excluded, except such as have already been implied in the words used for describing the effect; nor by including even these would there be incurred any but a merely verbal *impropriety*.

*§ 5. [*Case in which the effect consists in giving a property to an object*] There is a case of causation which calls for separate notice, as it possesses a peculiar feature, and presents a greater degree of complexity than the common case. It often happens that the effect, or one of the effects, of a cause, is, not to produce of itself a certain phenomenon, but to fit something else for producing it. In other words, there is a case of causation in which the effect

---

*f–f*MS, 43, 46, 51   those
*g–g*MS, 43, 46   last example, that of a sensation produced in our organs, are not the laws . . . minds as directly . . . object?
*h–h*MS, 43, 46   man's death, are not the whole . . . patient as actively . . . existence?
*i*MS, 43, 46   most
*j–j*MS, 43, 46, 51, 56   a complete one
*k–k*MS, 43, 46, 51, 56, 62   inconsistency
*a–a*338+72

is to invest an object with a certain property. When sulphur, charcoal, and nitre are put together in certain proportions and in a certain manner, the effect is, not an explosion, but that the mixture acquires a property by which, in given circumstances, it will explode. The various causes, natural and artificial, which educate the human body or the human mind, have for their principal effect, not to make the body or mind immediately do anything, but to endow it with certain properties—in other words, to give assurance that in given circumstances certain results will take place in it, or as consequences of it. Physiological agencies often have for the chief part of their operation to *predispose* the constitution to some mode of action. To take a simpler instance than all these: putting a coat of white paint upon a wall does not merely produce in those who see it done, the sensation of white; it confers on the wall the permanent property of giving that kind of sensation. Regarded in reference to the sensation, the putting on of the paint is a condition of a condition; it is a condition of the wall's causing that particular fact. The wall may have been painted years ago, but it has acquired a property which has lasted till now and will last longer; the antecedent condition necessary to enable the wall to become in its turn a condition, has been fulfilled once for all. In a case like this, where the immediate consequent in the sequence is a property produced in an object, no one now supposes the property to be a substantive entity "inherent" in the object. What has been produced is what, in other language, may be called a state of preparation in an object for producing an effect. The ingredients of the gunpowder have been brought into a state of preparation for exploding as soon as the other conditions of an explosion shall have occurred. In the case of the gunpowder, this state of preparation consists in a certain collocation of its particles relatively to one another. In the example of the wall, it consists in a new collocation of two things relatively to each other—the wall and the paint. In the example of the moulding influences on the human mind, its being a collocation at all is only conjectural: for, even on the materialistic hypothesis, it would remain to be proved that the increased facility with which the brain sums up a column of figures when it has been long trained to calculation, is the result of a permanent new arrangement of some of its material particles. We must, therefore, content ourselves with what we know, and must include among the effects of causes, the capacities given to objects of being causes of other effects. This capacity is not a real thing existing in the objects; it is but a name for our conviction that they will act in a particular manner when certain new circumstances arise. We may invest this assurance of future events with a fictitious objective existence, by calling it a *state* of the object. But unless the state consists, as in the case of the gunpowder it does, in a collocation of particles, it expresses no present fact; it is but the contingent future fact brought back under another name.

It may be thought that this form of causation requires us to admit an exception to the doctrine that the conditions of a phenomenon—the antecedents required for calling it into existence—must all be found among the facts immediately, not remotely, preceding its commencement. But what we have arrived at is not a correction, it is only an explanation, of that doctrine. In the enumeration of the conditions required for the occurrence of any phenomenon, it always has to be included that objects must be present, possessed of given properties. It is a condition of the phenomenon explosion that an object should be present, of one or other of certain kinds, which for that reason are called explosive. The presence of one of these objects is a condition immediately precedent to the explosion. The condition which is not immediately precedent is the cause which produced, not the explosion, but the explosive property. The conditions of the explosion itself were all present immediately before it took place, and the general law, therefore, remains intact.[a]

[a]§ 6.[a] [*The cause is not the invariable antecedent, but the* unconditional *invariable antecedent*] It now remains to advert to a distinction which is of first-rate importance both for clearing up the notion of cause, and for obviating a very specious objection often made against the view which we have taken of the subject.

When we define the cause of anything (in the only sense in which the present inquiry has any concern with causes) to be "the antecedent which it invariably follows," we do not use this phrase as exactly synonymous with "the antecedent which it invariably *has* followed in our past experience." Such a mode of [b]conceiving[b] causation would be liable to the objection very plausibly urged by Dr. Reid, namely, that according to this doctrine night must be the cause of day, and day the cause of night; since these phenomena have invariably succeeded one another from the beginning of the world.[*] But it is necessary to our using the word cause, that we should believe not only that the antecedent always *has* been followed by the consequent, but that, as long as the present constitution of things* endures, it always *will* be so. And this would not be true of day and night. We do not believe that night

[*See Thomas Reid. *Essays on the Intellectual Powers of Man.* In *The Works of Thomas Reid.* Ed. William Hamilton. Edinburgh: Maclachlan and Stewart, 1846, p. 253 (Essay II, Chap. iv).]

*[56] I mean by this expression, the ultimate laws of nature (whatever they may be) as distinguished from the derivative laws and from the collocations. The diurnal revolution of the earth (for example) is not a part of the constitution of things, because nothing can be so called which might possibly be terminated or altered by natural causes.

[a-a]MS, 43, 46, 51, 56, 62, 65, 68   §5.
[b-b]MS, 43, 46   viewing

will be followed by day under *all* imaginable circumstances, but only that it will be so *provided* the sun rises above the horizon. If the sun ceased to rise, which, for aught we know, may be perfectly compatible with the general laws of matter, night would be, or might be, eternal. On the other hand, if the sun is above the horizon, his light not extinct, and no opaque body between us and him, we believe firmly that unless a change takes place in the properties of matter, this combination of antecedents will be followed by the consequent, day; that if the combination of antecedents could be indefinitely prolonged, it would be always day; and *that* if the same combination had always existed, it would always have been day, quite independently of night as a previous condition. Therefore is it that we do not call night the cause, nor even a condition, of day. The existence of the sun (or some such luminous body), and there being no opaque medium in a straight line* between that body and the part of the earth where we are situated, are the sole conditions; and the union of these, without the addition of any superfluous circumstance, constitutes the cause. This is what writers mean when they say that the notion of cause involves the idea of necessity. If there be any meaning which confessedly belongs to the term necessity, it is *unconditionalness*. That which is necessary, that which *must* be, means that which will be, whatever supposition we may make in regard to all other things. The succession of day and night evidently is not necessary in this sense. It is conditional on the occurrence of other antecedents. That which *will be* followed by a given consequent when, and only when, some third circumstance also exists, is not the cause, even though no case should *ever have* occurred in which the phenomenon took place without it.

Invariable sequence, therefore, is not synonymous with causation, unless the sequence, besides being invariable, is unconditional. There are sequences, as uniform in past experience as any others whatever, which yet we do not regard as cases of causation, but as conjunctions in some sort accidental. Such, to *an accurate thinker*, is that of day and night. The one might have existed for any length of time, and the other not have followed the sooner for its existence; it follows only if certain other antecedents exist; and where those antecedents existed, it would follow in any case. No one, probably, ever called night the cause of day; mankind must so soon have arrived at the very

---

*I use the words "straight line" for brevity and simplicity. In reality the line in question is not exactly straight, for, from the *effect* of refraction, we actually see the sun for a short interval during which the opaque mass of the earth is interposed in a direct line between the sun and our eyes; thus realizing, though but to a limited extent, the coveted desideratum of seeing round a corner.

*c–c*MS, 43, 46 any	*d–d*+43, 46, 51, 56, 62, 65, 68, 72
*e–e*MS, 43, 46 effects	*f–f*MS is
*g–g*MS, 43, 46, 51, 56 have ever	*h–h*MS, 43, 46 a philosopher

obvious generalization, that the state of general illumination which we call day would follow *from* the presence of a sufficiently luminous body, whether darkness had preceded or not.

We may define, therefore, the cause of a phenomenon, to be the antecedent, or *the* concurrence of antecedents, on which it is invariably and *unconditionally* consequent. Or if we adopt the convenient modification of the meaning of the word cause, which confines it to the assemblage of positive conditions without the negative, then instead of "unconditionally," we must say, "subject to no other than negative conditions."

To some it may appear, that the sequence between night and day being invariable in our experience, we have as much ground in this case as experience can give in any case, for recognising the two phenomena as cause and effect; and that to say that more is necessary—to require a belief that the succession is unconditional, or in other words that it would be invariable under all changes of circumstances, is to acknowledge in causation an element of belief not derived from experience. The answer to this is, that it is experience itself which teaches us that one uniformity of sequence is conditional and another unconditional. When we judge that the succession of night and day is a derivative sequence, depending on something else, we proceed on grounds of experience. It is the evidence of experience which convinces us that day could equally exist without being followed by night, and that night could equally exist without being followed by day. To say that these beliefs are "not generated by our mere observation of sequence," is to forget that twice in every twenty-four hours, when the sky is clear, we have an *experimentum crucis* that the cause of day is the sun. We have an experimental knowledge of the sun which justifies us on experimental grounds in concluding, that if the sun were always above the horizon there would be day, though there had been no night, and that if the sun were always below the horizon there would be night, though there had been no day. We thus know from experience that the succession of night and day is not unconditional. Let me add, that the antecedent which is only conditionally invariable, is not the invariable antecedent. Though a fact may, in experience, have always been followed by another fact, yet if the remainder of our experience teaches us that it might not always be so followed, or if the experience itself is such as leaves room for a possibility that the known cases may not correctly represent all possible cases, the hitherto invariable antecedent is not accounted the cause; but why? Because we are not sure that it *is* the invariable antecedent.

*[56] [*Theism.*] *Second Burnett Prize Essay* [Edinburgh: Blackwood, 1855], by *Principal* Tulloch, p. 25.

i–i+62, 65, 68, 72   *j–j*+43, 46, 51, 56, 62, 65, 68, 72
k–k+56, 62, 65, 68, 72   *l–l*56, 62, 65   the Rev. John

Such cases of sequence as that of day and night not only do not contradict the doctrine which resolves causation into invariable sequence, but are necessarily implied in that doctrine.[k] [m] It is evident, that from a limited number of unconditional sequences, there will result a much greater number of conditional ones. Certain causes being given, that is, certain antecedents which are unconditionally followed by certain consequents; the mere co-existence of these causes will give rise to an unlimited number of additional uniformities. If two causes exist together, the effects of both will exist together; and if many causes coexist, these causes (by what we shall term hereafter the intermixture of their laws) will give rise to new effects, accompanying or succeeding one another in some particular order, which order will be invariable while the causes continue to coexist, but no longer. The motion of the earth in a given orbit round the sun, is a series of changes which follow one another as antecedents and consequents, and will continue to do so while the sun's attraction, and the force with which the earth tends to advance in a direct line through space, continue to coexist in the same quantities as at present. But vary either of these causes, and [n]this particular[n] succession of motions would cease to take place. The series of the earth's motions, therefore, though a case of sequence invariable within the limits of human experience, is not a case of causation. It is not unconditional.

[o]This distinction between the relations of succession which so far as we know are unconditional, and those relations, whether of succession or of coexistence, which, like the earth's motions, or the succession of day and night, depend on the existence or on the coexistence of other antecedent facts—corresponds to the great division which Dr. Whewell and other writers have made of the field of science, into the investigation of what they term the Laws of Phenomena, and the investigation of causes; a phraseology, as I conceive, not philosophically sustainable, inasmuch as the ascertainment of causes, such causes as the human faculties can ascertain, namely, causes which are themselves phenomena, is, therefore, merely the ascertainment of other and more universal Laws of Phenomena. [p]And let me here observe, that Dr. Whewell, and in some degree even Sir John Herschel, seem to have misunderstood the meaning of those writers who, like M. Comte, limit the

[m]MS, 43, 46, 51 [paragraph]
[n-n]MS, 43, 46, 51, 56, 62, 65   the unvarying
[o-o]342MS   To distinguish these conditionally uniform sequences from those which are uniform unconditionally; to ascertain whether an apparently invariable antecedent of some consequent is really one of its conditions, or whether, in the absence of that antecedent, the effect would equally have followed from some other portion of the circumstances which are present whenever it occurs; is a principal part of the great problem of Induction; and is one of those questions, the solution of which will, it is to be hoped, result from the inquiry we have undertaken.]   43, 46   as MS . . . questions, the principles of the solution . . . as MS
[p-p]342 51, 56   Yet the distinction

sphere of scientific investigation to Laws of Phenomena, and speak of the inquiry into causes as vain and futile. The causes which M. Comte designates as inaccessible, are efficient causes. The investigation of physical, as opposed to efficient, causes (including the study of all the active forces in Nature, considered as facts of observation) is as important a part of M. Comte's conception of science as of Dr. Whewell's. His objection to the *word* cause is a mere matter of nomenclature, in which, as a matter of nomenclature, I consider him to be entirely wrong. "Those," it is justly remarked by Mr. Bailey,* "who, like M. Comte, object to designate *events* as causes, are objecting without any real ground to a mere but extremely convenient generalization, to a very useful common name, the employment of which involves, or needs involve, no particular theory." To which it may be added, that by rejecting this form of expression, M. Comte leaves himself without any term for marking a distinction which^p, however incorrectly expressed, is not only real, but is one of the fundamental distinctions in science; indeed it is on this alone, as we shall hereafter find, that the possibility rests of framing a rigorous Canon of Induction. ^{q}And as things left without a name are apt to be forgotten, a Canon of that description is not one of the many benefits which the philosophy of Induction has received from M. Comte's great powers.^{qo}

^{a}§ 7.^{a} [*Can a cause be simultaneous with its effect?*] Does a cause always stand with its effect in the relation of antecedent and consequent? Do we not often say of two simultaneous facts that they are cause and effect—as when we say that fire is the cause of warmth, the sun and moisture the cause of vegetation, and the like? ^{b}Since^b a cause does not necessarily perish because its effect has been produced, the two ^{c}things^c do very generally coexist; and there are some appearances, and some common expressions, seeming to imply not only that causes may, but that they must, be contemporaneous with their effects. *Cessante causâ cessat et effectus*, has been a dogma of the schools: the necessity for the continued existence of the cause in order to the continuance of the effect, seems to have been once a ^{d}generally received doctrine^d. ^{e} Kepler's numerous attempts to account for the ^{f}motions^f of the heavenly bodies on mechanical principles, were rendered abortive by his

*[62] *Letters on the Philosophy of the Human Mind*, First Series, p. 219.

$^{q-q}$+62, 65, 68, 72
$^{a-a}$MS, 43, 46, 51, 56, 62, 65, 68   §6.
$^{b-b}$MS, 43, 46   It is certain that
$^{c-c}$MS, 43, 46   , therefore,
$^{d-d}$MS, 43, 46   general doctrine among philosophers
^{e}MS, 43   Mr. Whewell observes [*History of the Inductive Sciences*, 1st ed., Vol. I, pp. 408–9] that
$^{f-f}$MS, 43, 46   motion

always supposing that the *agency* which set those bodies in motion must continue to operate in order to keep up the motion which it at first produced. Yet there were at all times many familiar instances *of the continuance of effects, long after their causes had ceased*. A *coup de soleil* gives a *person* brain fever: will the fever go off as soon as he is moved out of the sunshine? A sword is run through his body: must the sword remain in his body in order that he may continue dead? A ploughshare once made, remains a ploughshare, without any continuance of heating and hammering, and even after the man who heated and hammered it has been gathered to his fathers. On the other hand, the pressure which forces up the mercury in an exhausted tube must be continued in order to sustain it in the tube. This (it may be *replied*) is because another force is acting without intermission, the force of gravity, which would restore it to its level, unless counterpoised by a force equally constant. But again: a tight bandage causes pain, which pain will sometimes go off as soon as the bandage is removed. The illumination which the sun diffuses over the earth ceases when the sun goes down.

There is, therefore, a distinction to be drawn. The conditions which are necessary for the first production of a phenomenon, are occasionally also necessary for its continuance; *though* more commonly its continuance requires no condition except negative ones. Most things, once produced, continue as they are, until something changes or destroys them; but some require the permanent presence of the agencies which produced them at first. These may *, if we please,* be considered as instantaneous phenomena, requiring to be renewed at each instant by the cause by which they were at first generated. Accordingly, the illumination of any given point of space has always been looked upon as an instantaneous fact, which perishes and is perpetually renewed as long as the necessary conditions subsist. If we adopt this language we *avoid the necessity of* admitting that the continuance of the cause is ever required to maintain the effect. We may say, it is not required to maintain, but to reproduce, the effect, or else to counteract some force tending to destroy it. And this may be a convenient phraseology. But it is only a phraseology. The fact remains, that in some cases (though *those* are a minority) the continuance of the conditions which produced an effect is necessary to the continuance of the effect.

*g–g*MS, 43, 46, 51, 56, 62   force
*h–h*MS, 43, 46   in open contradiction to this supposed axiom
*i–i*MS, 43, 46   man a]   51, 56, 62, 65, 68   person a
*j–j*MS   said
*k–k*MS, 43   The solution of these difficulties will be found in a very simple distinction.
*l–l*MS, 43, 46, 51   but
*m–m*MS   conveniently
*n–n*MS, 43, 46   are enabled to avoid
*o–o*MS, 43, 46, 51, 56, 62, 65, 68   these

As to the ulterior question, whether it is strictly necessary that the cause, or assemblage of conditions, should precede, by ever so short an instant, the production of the effect, (a question raised and argued with much ingenuity by *p*Sir John Herschel in an Essay already quoted,*) the inquiry is of no consequence for our present purpose*p*. There certainly are cases in which the effect follows without any interval perceptible *r*by*r* our faculties; and when there is an interval, we cannot tell by how many intermediate links imperceptible to us that interval may really be filled up. But even granting that an effect may commence simultaneously with its cause, *s*the view I have taken*s* of causation is in no way practically affected. Whether the cause and its effect be necessarily successive or not, *t*the beginning of a phenomenon is what implies a cause, and causation is*t* the law of the succession of phenomena. *u*If these axioms*u* be granted *v*, we can afford, though *w*I*w* see no necessity for doing so, to drop the words antecedent and consequent as applied to cause and effect. *x*I*x* have no objection to define a cause, the assemblage of phenomena, which occurring, some other phenomenon invariably commences, or has its origin. Whether the effect coincides in point of time with, or immediately follows, the hindmost of its conditions, is immaterial. At all events it does not precede it; and when we are in doubt, between two co-existent phenomena, which is cause and which effect, we rightly deem the question solved if we can ascertain which of them preceded the other.

a§ 8.*a* [*Idea of a Permanent Cause, or original natural agent*] It continually happens that several different phenomena, which are not in the slightest degree dependent or conditional on one another, are found all to depend, as the phrase is, on one and the same agent; in other words, one and the same phenomenon is seen to be followed by several sorts of effects quite heterogeneous, but which go on simultaneously one with another; provided, of course, that all other conditions requisite for each of them also exist. Thus,

---

*q*Essays, pp. 206–8.*q*

*p–p*MS, 43   a writer from whom we have quoted,*) we think the inquiry an unimportant one]   46, 51   *as* MS . . . whom I have quoted,*) I think . . . *as* MS]   56   *as* 46 . . . quoted,*) the . . . *as* 72

*q–q*MS, 43, 46, 51, 56   The reviewer of Dr. Whewell in the *Quarterly Review.*

*r–r*MS, 43, 46   to

*s–s*MS   our view

*t–t*MS, 43, 46, 51   causation is still

*u–u*MS, 43, 46, 51   Everything which begins to exist must have a cause; what does not begin to exist does not need a cause; what causation has to account for is the origin of phenomena, and all the successions of phenomena must be resolvable into causation. These are the axioms of our doctrine. If these

*v*MS   us

*w–w*MS   we

*x–x*MS   We

*a–a*MS, 43, 46, 51, 56, 62, 65, 68   §7.

the sun produces the celestial motions, it produces daylight, and it produces heat. The earth causes the fall of heavy bodies, and it also, in its capacity of ^{b}a great^b magnet, causes the phenomena of the magnetic needle. A crystal of galena causes the sensations of hardness, of weight, of cubical form, of grey colour, and many others between which we can trace no interdependence. The purpose to which the phraseology of Properties and Powers is specially adapted, is the expression of this sort of cases. When the same phenomenon is followed (either subject or not to the presence of other conditions) by effects of different and dissimilar orders, it is usual to say that each different sort of effect is produced by a different property of the cause. Thus we distinguish the attractive or gravitative property of the earth, and its magnetic property: the gravitative, luminiferous, and calorific properties of the sun: the colour, shape, weight, and hardness of ^{c}a^c crystal. These are mere phrases, which explain nothing, and add nothing to our knowledge of the subject; but, considered as abstract names denoting the connexion between the different effects produced and the object which produces them, they are a very powerful instrument of abridgment, and of that acceleration of the process of thought which abridgment accomplishes.

This class of considerations leads ^{d} to a conception which we shall find ^{e}to be of great importance^e, that of a Permanent Cause, or original natural agent. There exist in nature a number of permanent causes, which have subsisted ever since the human race has been in existence, and for an indefinite and probably ^{f}an^f enormous length of time previous. The sun, the earth, and planets, with their various constituents, air, water, and ^{g} other distinguishable substances, whether simple or compound, of which nature is made up, are such Permanent Causes. These have existed, and the effects or consequences which they were fitted to produce have taken place (as often as the other conditions of the production met,) from the very beginning of our experience. But we can give ^{h} no account of the origin of the Permanent Causes themselves. Why these particular natural agents existed originally and no others, or why they are commingled in such and such proportions, and distributed in such and such a manner throughout space, is a question we cannot answer. More than this: we can discover nothing regular in the distribution itself; we can reduce it to no uniformity, to no law. There are no means by which, from the distribution of these causes or agents in one part of space, we could conjecture whether a similar distribution prevails in another. The

$^{b-b}$MS, 43, 46, 51, 56   an immense
$^{c-c}$MS, 43, 46   the
^{d}MS, 43, 46   us
$^{e-e}$MS, 43, 46   of great importance in the interpretation of nature
$^{f-f}$+51, 56, 62, 65, 68, 72
^{g}MS, 43, 46, 51   the
^{h}MS   , humanly speaking,]   43, 46   , scientifically speaking,

coexistence, therefore, of Primeval Causes, ranks, to us, among merely casual concurrences: and all those sequences or coexistences among the effects of several such causes, which, though invariable while those causes coexist, would, if the coexistence terminated, terminate along with it, we do not class as cases of causation, or laws of nature: we can only calculate on finding *these sequences or coexistences* where we know by direct evidence, that the natural agents on the properties of which they ultimately depend, are distributed in the requisite manner. These Permanent Causes are not always objects; they are sometimes events, that is to say, periodical cycles of events, that being the only mode in which events can possess the property of permanence. Not only, for instance, is the earth itself a permanent cause, or primitive natural agent, but the earth's rotation is so too: it is a cause which has produced, from the earliest period, (by the aid of other necessary conditions,) the succession of day and night, the ebb and flow of the sea, and many other effects, while, as we can assign no cause (except conjecturally) for the rotation itself, it is entitled to be ranked as a primeval cause. It is, however, only the *origin* of the rotation which is mysterious to us: once begun, its continuance is accounted for by the first law of motion (that of the permanence of *rectilinear* motion once impressed) combined with the gravitation of the parts of the earth towards one another.

All phenomena without exception which begin to exist, that is, all except the primeval causes, are effects either immediate or remote of those primitive facts, or of some combination of them. There is no Thing produced, no event happening, in the *known* universe, which is not connected by an uniformity, or invariable sequence, with some one or more of the phenomena which preceded it; insomuch that it will happen again as often as those phenomena occur again, and as no other phenomenon *having the character* of a counteracting cause shall coexist. These antecedent phenomena, again, were connected in a similar manner with some that preceded them; and so on, until we reach, as the ultimate step *attainable by us*, either the properties of some one primeval cause, or the conjunction of several. The whole of the phenomena of nature were therefore the necessary, or in other words, the unconditional, consequences of *some former* collocation of the Permanent Causes.

The state of the whole universe at any instant, we believe to be the consequence of its state at the previous instant; insomuch that *one who* knew all the agents which exist at the present moment, their collocation in space, and *all* their properties, in other words, the laws of their agency, could predict

*–*MS them
*j–j*MS, 43, 46   rectilineal   *k–k*+51, 56, 62, 65, 68, 72
*l–l*MS of the nature   *m–m*+51, 56, 62, 65, 68, 72
*n–n*MS, 43, 46   the original   *o–o*MS, 43, 46   if we
p–p+56, 62, 65, 68, 72   *q*MS, 43, 46   we

the whole subsequent history of the universe, at least ʳunlessʳ some new volition of a power capable of controlling the universe should supervene.* And if any particular state of the entire universe ʷcould ever recur a second time,ʷ all subsequent states would return too, and history would, like a circulating decimal of many figures, periodically repeat itself:

> Jam redit et virgo, redeunt Saturnia regna. . . .
> Alter erit tum Tiphys, et altera quæ vehat Argo
> Delectos heroas; erunt quoque altera bella,
> Atque iterum ad Trojam magnus mittetur Achilles.[*]

And though things do not really revolve in this eternal round, the whole series of events in the history of the universe, past and future, is not the less capable, in its own nature, of being constructed *à priori* by any one whom we can suppose acquainted with the original distribution of all natural agents, and with the whole of their properties, that is, the laws of succession existing between them and their effects: saving ˣthe farˣ more than human powers of

*To the universality which mankind are agreed in ascribing to the Law of Causation, there is one claim of exception, one disputed case, that of the Human Will; the determinations of which, a large class of metaphysicians are not willing to regard as following the causes called motives, according to as strict laws as those which they suppose to exist in the world of mere matter. This controverted point will undergo a special examination when we come to treat particularly of the Logic of the Moral Sciences (Bk. VI, chap. ii). In the meantime I may remark that these metaphysicians, who, it must be observed, ground the main part of their objection on the supposed repugnance of the doctrine in question to our consciousness, seem to me to mistake the fact which consciousness testifies against. What is really in contradiction to consciousness, they would, I think, on strict self-examination, find to be, the application to human actions and volitions of the ideas involved in the common use of the term Necessity; which I agree with them in ˢobjecting toˢ. But if they would consider that by saying that a ᵗperson'sᵗ actions *necessarily* follow from his character, all that is really meant (ᵘforᵘ no more is meant in any case whatever of causation) is that he invariably *does* act in conformity to his character, and that any one who thoroughly knew his character ᵛcouldᵛ certainly predict how he would act in any supposable case; they probably would not find this doctrine either contrary to their experience or revolting to their feelings. And no more than this is contended for by any one but an Asiatic fatalist.

[*Virgil, *Eclogue* IV, ll. 6, 34–6. In *P. Virgilius Maro Varietate lectionis et perpetua annotatione illustratus a C. G. Heyne.* 4 vols. London: Priestley, 1821, Vol. I, pp. 65, 70.]

ʳ⁻ʳMS until
ˢ⁻ˢMS, 43, 46 thinking highly objectionable
ᵗ⁻ᵗMS, 43, 46 man's
ᵘ⁻ᵘ+43, 46, 51, 56, 62, 65, 68, 72 ᵛ⁻ᵛ68 would
ʷ⁻ʷMS, 43, 46 should ever recur a second time, (which, however, all experience combines to assure us will never happen,)
ˣ⁻ˣMS, 43, 46 the infinitely] 51, 56 the

combination and calculation which would be required, even in one possessing the data, for the actual performance of the task.

[a]§ 9.[a] [*Uniformities of co-existence between effects of different permanent causes, are not laws*] Since everything which occurs [b] is determined by laws of causation and collocations of the original causes, it follows that the co-existences which are observable among effects cannot be themselves the subject of any [c]similar[c] set of laws, distinct from laws of causation. Uniformities there are, as well of coexistence as of succession, among [d] effects; but these must in all cases be a mere result either of the identity or of the coexistence of their causes: if the causes did not coexist, neither could the effects. And these causes being also effects of prior causes, and these of others, until we reach the primeval causes, it follows that (except in the case of effects which can be traced immediately or remotely to one and the same cause) the coexistences of phenomena can in no case be universal, unless the coexistences of the primeval causes to which the effects are ultimately traceable, can be reduced to an universal law: but we have seen that they cannot. There are, accordingly, no original and independent, in other words no unconditional, uniformities of coexistence, between effects of different causes; if they coexist, it is only because the causes have casually coexisted. The only independent and unconditional coexistences which are sufficiently invariable to have any claim to the character of laws, are between different and mutually independent effects of the same cause; in other words, between different properties of the same natural agent. This portion of the Laws of Nature will be treated of in the latter part of the present Book, under the name of the Specific Properties of Kinds. [e]

[a]§ 10. [*Theory of the Conservation of Force*] Since the first publication of the present treatise, the sciences of physical nature have made a great advance in generalization, through the doctrine known as the Conservation or Persistence of Force. This imposing edifice of theory, the building and laying out of which has for some time been the principal occupation of the most systematic minds among physical enquirers, consists of two stages: one, of ascertained fact, the other containing a large element of hypothesis.

To begin with the first. It is proved by numerous facts, both natural and of artificial production, that agencies which had been regarded as distinct and independent sources of force—heat, electricity, chemical action, nervous and muscular action, momentum of moving bodies—are interchangeable, in definite and fixed quantities, with one another. It had long been known that

[a-a]MS, 43, 46, 51, 56, 62, 65, 68   §8.   [b]MS, 43, 46   in the universe
[c-c]MS   peculiar [*printer's error?*]   [d]MS, 43, 46   the
[e][*see* Appendix C *for* §9 *in* MS, 43, 46]   a-a353+72

these dissimilar phenomena had the power, under certain conditions, of producing one another: what is new in the theory is a more accurate estimation of what this production consists in. What happens is, that the whole or part of the one kind of phenomena disappears, and is replaced by phenomena of one of the other descriptions, and that there is an equivalence in quantity between the phenomena that have disappeared and those which have been produced, insomuch that if the process be reversed, the very same quantity which had disappeared will reappear, without increase or diminution. Thus, the amount of heat which will raise the temperature of a pound of water one degree of the thermometer, will, if expended, say in the expansion of steam, lift a weight of 772 pounds one foot, or a weight of one pound 772 feet: and the same exact quantity of heat can, by certain means, be recovered, through the expenditure of exactly that amount of mechanical motion.

The establishment of this comprehensive law has led to a change in the language in which the scientific world had been accustomed to speak of what are called the Forces of nature. Before this correlation between phenomena most unlike one another had been ascertained, their unlikeness had caused them to be referred to so many distinct forces. Now that they are known to be convertible into one another without loss, they are spoken of as all of them results of one and the same force, manifesting itself in different modes. This force (it is said) can only produce a limited and definite quantity of effect, but always does produce that definite quantity; and produces it, according to circumstances, in one or another of the forms, or divides it among several, but so as (according to a scale of numerical equivalents established by experiment) always to make up the same sum: and no one of the manifestations can be produced, save by the disappearance of the equivalent quantity of another, which in its turn, in appropriate circumstances, will reappear undiminished. This mutual interchangeability of the forces of nature, according to fixed numerical equivalents, is the part of the new doctrine which rests on irrefragable fact.

To make the statement true, however, it is necessary to add, that an indefinite and perhaps immense interval of time may elapse between the disappearance of the force in one form and its reappearance in another. A stone thrown up into the air with a given force, and falling back immediately, will, by the time it reaches the earth, recover the exact amount of mechanical momentum which was expended in throwing it up, deduction being made of a small portion of motion which has been communicated to the air. But if the stone has lodged on a height, it may not fall back for years, or perhaps ages, and until it does, the force expended in raising it is temporarily lost, being represented only by what, in the language of the new theory, is called potential energy. The coal imbedded in the earth is considered by the theory as a vast reservoir of force, which has remained dormant for many geological periods, and will so remain until, by being burnt, it gives out the stored-up force in the form of heat. Yet it is not supposed that this force is a material thing which can be confined by bounds, as used to be thought of latent heat when that important phenomenon was first discovered. What is meant is that when the coal does at last, by combustion, generate a quantity of heat (transformable like all other heat into mechanical momentum, and the other forms of force), this extrication of heat is the reappearance of a force derived from the sun's rays, expended myriads of ages ago in the vegetation of the organic substances which were the material of the coal.

Let us now pass to the higher stage of the theory of Conservation of Force; the part which is no longer a generalization of proved fact, but a combination of fact and hypothesis. Stated in few words, it is as follows: That the Conservation of Force is really the Conservation of Motion; that in the various interchanges between the forms of force, it is always motion that is transformed into motion. To establish this, it is necessary to assume motions which are hypothetical. The supposition is, that there are motions which manifest themselves to our senses only as heat, electricity, &c., being molecular motions; oscillations, invisible to us, among the minute particles of bodies; and that these molecular motions are transmutable into molar motions (motions of masses), and molar motions into molecular. Now there is a real basis of fact for this supposition: we have positive evidence of the existence of molecular motion in these manifestations of force. In the case of chemical action, for instance, the particles separate and form new combinations, often with a great visible disturbance of the mass. In the case of heat, the evidence is equally conclusive, since heat expands bodies (that is, causes their particles to move *from* one another); and if of sufficient amount, changes their mode of aggregation from solid to liquid, or from liquid to gaseous. Again, the mechanical actions which produce heat—friction, and the collision of bodies—must from the nature of the case produce a shock, that is, an internal motion of particles, which indeed, we find, is often so violent as to break them permanently asunder. Such facts are thought to warrant the inference, that it is not, as was supposed, heat that causes the motion of particles, but the motion of particles that causes heat; the original cause of both being the previous motion (whether molar or molecular—collision of bodies or combustion of fuel) which formed the heating agency. This inference already contains hypothesis: but at least the supposed cause, the intestine motion of molecules, is a *vera causa*. But in order to reduce the Conservation of Force to Conservation of Motion, it was necessary to attribute to motion the heat propagated, through apparently empty space, from the sun. This required the supposition (already made for the explanation of the laws of light) of a subtle ether pervading space, which, though impalpable to us, must have the property which constitutes matter, that of resistance, since waves are propagated through it by an impulse from a given point. The ether must be supposed (a supposition not required by the theory of light) to penetrate into the minute interstices of all bodies. The vibratory motion supposed to be taking place in the heated mass of the sun, is considered as imparted from that mass to the particles of the surrounding ether, and through them to the particles of the same ether in the interstices of terrestrial bodies; and this, too, with a sufficient mechanical force to throw the particles of those bodies into a state of similar vibration, producing the expansion of their mass, and the sensation of heat in sentient creatures. All this is hypothesis, though, of its legitimacy as hypothesis, I do not mean to express any doubt. It would seem to follow as a consequence from this theory, that Force may and should be defined, matter in motion. This definition, however, will not stand, for, as has already been seen, the matter needs not be in *actual* motion. It is not necessary to suppose that the motion afterwards manifested, is actually taking place among the molecules of the coal during its sojourn in the earth;* certainly not in the stone which is at rest on the eminence to which it has been raised. The true definition of Force must be, not motion, but Potentiality of Motion; and what the doctrine, if established, amounts to, is, not that there is at all times the same quantity of actual motion in the universe; but that the possibilities of motion are limited to a definite quantity, which cannot be added to, but which cannot be exhausted; and that all actual motion which takes place in Nature is a draft upon this limited stock. It needs not all of it have ever existed as actual motion. There is a vast amount of potential motion in the universe in the form of gravitation, which it would be a great abuse of hypothesis to suppose to have been stored up by the expenditure of an equal amount of actual motion in some former state of the universe. Nor does the motion produced by gravity take place, so far as we know, at the expense of any other motion, either molar or molecular.

It is proper to consider whether the adoption of this theory as a scientific truth, involving as it does a change in the conception hitherto entertained of the most general physical agencies, requires any modification in the view I have taken of Causation as a law of nature. As it appears to me, none whatever. The manifestations which the theory regards as modes of motion, are as much distinct and separate phenomena when referred to a single force, as when attributed to several. Whether the phenomenon is called a transformation of force or the generation of one, it has its own set or sets of antecedents,

---

*[72] I believe, however, the accredited authorities do suppose that molecular motion, equivalent in amount to that which will be manifested in the combustion of the coal, is actually taking place during the whole of the long interval, if not in the coal, yet in the oxygen which will then combine with it. But how purely hypothetical this supposition is, need hardly be remarked; I venture to say, unnecessarily and extravagantly hypothetical.

with which it is connected by invariable and unconditional sequence; and that set, or those sets, of antecedents, are its cause. The relation of the Conservation theory to the principle of Causation is discussed in much detail, and very instructively, by Professor Bain, in the second volume of his *Logic*.[*] The chief practical conclusion drawn by him, bearing on Causation, is, that we must distinguish in the assemblage of conditions which constitutes the Cause of a phenomenon, two elements: one, the presence of a force; the other, the collocation or position of objects which is required in order that the force may undergo the particular transmutation which constitutes the phenomenon. Now, it might always have been said with acknowledged correctness, that a force and a collocation were both of them necessary to produce any phenomenon. The law of causation is, that change can only be produced by change. Along with any number of stationary antecedents, which are collocations, there must be at least one changing antecedent, which is a force. To produce a bonfire, there must not only be fuel, and air, and a spark, which are collocations, but chemical action between the air and the materials, which is a force. To grind corn, there must be a certain collocation of the parts composing a mill, relatively to one another and to the corn; but there must also be the gravitation of water, or the motion of wind, to supply a force. But as the force in these cases was regarded as a property of the objects in which it is embodied, it seemed tautology to say that there must be the collocation *and* the force. As the collocation must be a collocation of objects possessing the force-giving property, the collocation, so understood, included the force.

How, then, shall we have to express these facts, if the theory be finally substantiated that all Force is reducible to a previous Motion? We shall have to say, that one of the conditions of every phenomenon is an antecedent Motion. But it will have to be explained that this needs not be *actual* motion. The coal which supplies the force exerted in combustion is not shown to have been exerting that force in the form of molecular motion in the pit; it was not even exerting pressure. The stone on the eminence *is* exerting a pressure, but only equivalent to its weight, not to the additional momentum it would acquire by falling. The antecedent, therefore, is not a force in action; and we can still only call it a property of the objects, by which they would exert a force on the occurrence of a fresh collocation. The collocation, therefore still includes the force. The force said to be stored up, is simply a particular property which the object has acquired. The cause we are in search of, is a collocation of objects possessing that particular property. When indeed we inquire further into the cause from which they derive that property, the new conception introduced by the Conservation theory comes in: the property is itself an effect, and its cause, according to the theory, is a former motion of exactly equivalent amount, which has been impressed on the

[*See Pt. II, pp. 20ff.]

particles of the body, perhaps at some very distant period. But the case is simply one of those we have already considered, in which the efficacy of a cause consists in its investing an object with a property. The force said to be laid up, and merely potential, is no more a really existing thing than any other properties of objects are really existing things. The expression is a mere artifice of language, convenient for describing the phenomena: it is unnecessary to suppose that any thing has been in continuous existence except an abstract potentiality. A force suspended in its operation, neither manifesting itself by motion nor by pressure, is not an existing fact, but a name for our conviction that in appropriate circumstances a fact would take place. We know that a pound weight, were it to fall from the earth into the sun, would acquire in falling a momentum equal to millions of pounds; but we do not credit the pound weight with more of actually existing force than is equal to the pressure it is now exerting on the earth, and that is exactly a pound. We might as well say that a force of millions of pounds exists in a pound, as that the force which will manifest itself when the coal is burnt is a real thing existing in the coal. What is fixed in the coal is only a certain property: it has become fit to be the antecedent of an effect called combustion, which partly consists in giving out, under certain conditions, a given definite quantity of heat.

We thus see that no new general conception of Causation is introduced by the Conservation theory. The indestructibility of Force no more interferes with the theory of Causation than the indestructibility of Matter, meaning by matter, the element of resistance in the sensible world. It only enables us to understand better than before the nature and laws of some of the sequences.

This better understanding, however, enables us, with Mr. Bain,[*] to admit, as one of the tests for distinguishing causation from mere concomitance, the expenditure or transfer of energy. If the effect, or any part of the effect, to be accounted for, consists in putting matter in motion, then any of the objects present which has lost motion has contributed to the effect; and this is the true meaning of the proposition that the cause is that one of the antecedents which exerts active force.[a]

[ab]§ 11.[b] [*Doctrine that volition is an efficient cause, examined*] It is proper in this place to advert to a [c]rather ancient doctrine respecting causation,[c] which has been revived during the last few years in [d]many[d] quarters,

[*See *Logic*, Pt. II, pp. 23–4.]

[a–a]363+51, 56, 62, 65, 68, 72
[b–b]51, 56, 62, 65, 68 §9.
[c–c]51 doctrine at least as old as Dr. Reid, though propounded by him not as certain but as probable; [See Thomas Reid. *Essays on the Active Powers of Man*. In *The Works of Thomas Reid*. Ed. William Hamilton. Edinburgh: Maclachlan and Stewart, 1846, pp. 522ff. (Essay I, Chap. v), pp. 605ff. (Essay IV, Chap. iii).]
[d–d]51, 56 several

and at present gives more signs of life than any other theory of causation at variance with that set forth in the preceding pages.

According to the theory in question, Mind, or to speak more precisely, Will, is the only cause of phenomena. The type of Causation, as well as the exclusive source from which we derive the idea, is our own voluntary agency. Here, and here only (it is said) we have direct evidence of causation. We know that we can move our bodies. Respecting the phenomena of inanimate nature, we have no other direct knowledge than that of antecedence and sequence. But in the case of our voluntary actions, it is affirmed that we are conscious of power before we have experience of results. An act of volition, whether followed by an effect or not, is accompanied by a consciousness of effort, "of force exerted, of power in action, which is necessarily causal, or causative."[*] This feeling of energy or force, inherent in an act of will, is knowledge *à priori*; assurance, prior to experience, that we have the power of causing effects. Volition, therefore, it is asserted, is something more than an unconditional antecedent; it is a cause, in a different sense from that in which physical phenomena are said to cause one another: it is an Efficient Cause. From this the transition is easy to the further doctrine, that Volition is the *sole* Efficient Cause of all phenomena. "It is inconceivable that dead force could continue unsupported for a moment beyond its creation. We cannot even conceive of change or phenomena without the energy of a mind."[†] "The word *action*" itself, says another writer of the same school, "has no real significance except when applied to the doings of an intelligent agent. Let any one conceive, if he can, of any power, energy, or force, inherent in a lump of matter."[‡] Phenomena may have the semblance of being produced by physical causes, but they are in reality produced, say these writers, by the immediate agency of mind. All things which do not proceed from a human (or, I suppose, an animal) will, proceed, they say, directly from divine will. The earth is not moved by the combination of a centripetal and a projectile force; this is but a mode of speaking, which serves to facilitate our conceptions. It is moved by the direct volition of an omnipotent Being, in a path coinciding with that which we deduce from the hypothesis of these two forces.

As I have so often observed, the general question of the existence of Efficient Causes does not fall within the limits of our subject: but a theory which represents them as capable of being subjects of human knowledge, and

[*Francis Bowen, *Lowell Lectures, on the Application of Metaphysical and Ethical Science to the Evidences of Religion.* Boston: Little and Brown, 1849, p. 84.]

[†R. H. Hutton, "Mill and Whewell on the Logic of Induction," *Prospective Review*, VI (Feb., 1850), p. 87.]

[‡Bowen, *Lowell Lectures*, p. 88.]

which passes off as efficient causes what are only physical or phenomenal causes, belongs as much to Logic as to Metaphysics, and is a fit subject for discussion here.

To my apprehension, a volition is not an efficient, but simply a physical cause. Our will causes our bodily actions in the same sense, and in no other, in which cold causes ice, or a spark causes an explosion of gunpowder. The volition, a state of our mind, is the antecedent; the motion of our limbs in conformity to the volition, is the consequent. This sequence I conceive to be not a subject of direct consciousness, in the sense intended by the theory. The antecedent, indeed, and the consequent, are subjects of consciousness. But the connexion between them is a subject of experience. I cannot admit that our consciousness of the volition contains in itself any *à priori* knowledge that the muscular motion will follow. If our nerves of motion were paralysed, or our muscles stiff and inflexible, and had been so all our lives, I do not see the slightest ground for supposing that we should ever (unless by information from other people) have known anything of volition as a physical power, or been conscious of any tendency in feelings of our mind to produce motions of our body, or of other bodies. I will not undertake to say whether we should in that case have had the physical feeling which I suppose is meant when these writers speak of "consciousness of effort:" I see no reason why we should not; since that physical feeling is probably a state of nervous sensation beginning and ending in the brain, without involving the motory apparatus: but we certainly should not have designated it by any term equivalent to effort, since effort implies consciously aiming at an end, which we should not only in that case have had no reason to do, but could not even have had the idea of doing. If conscious at all of this peculiar sensation, we should have been conscious of it, I conceive, only as a kind of uneasiness, accompanying our feelings of desire.

*e*It is well argued by Sir William Hamilton against the theory in question, that it

is refuted by the consideration that between the overt fact of corporeal movement of which we are cognisant, and the internal act of mental determination of which we are also cognisant, there intervenes a numerous series of intermediate agencies of which we have no knowledge; and, consequently, that we can have no consciousness of any causal connexion between the extreme links of this chain, the volition to move and the limb moving, as this hypothesis asserts. No one is immediately conscious, for example, of moving his arm through his volition. Previously to this ultimate movement, muscles, nerves, a multitude of solid and fluid parts, must be set in motion by the will, but of this motion we know, from consciousness, absolutely nothing. A person struck with paralysis is conscious of no inability in his limb to fulfil the determinations of his will; and it is only after having willed, and finding that his limbs do not obey his volition, that he

*e–e*356+62, 65, 68, 72

learns by this experience, that the external movement does not follow the internal act. But as the paralytic learns after the volition that his limbs do not obey his mind; so it is only after volition that the man in health learns, that his limbs do obey the mandates of his will.*e

Those against whom I am contending have never produced, and do not pretend to produce, any positive evidence† that the power of our will to move our bodies would be known to us independently of experience. What they have to say on the subject is, that the production of physical events by a will seems to carry its own explanation with it, while the action of matter upon matter seems to require something else to explain it; and is even, according to them, "inconceivable" on any other supposition than that some will intervenes between the apparent cause and its apparent effect. They thus rest their case on an appeal to the inherent laws of our conceptive faculty; mistaking, as I apprehend, for the laws of that faculty its acquired habits, grounded on the spontaneous tendencies of its uncultured state. The succes-

---

*[62] *Lectures on Metaphysics* [*and Logic*], Vol. II, Lect. xxxix, pp. 391–2.
I regret that I cannot invoke the authority of Sir William Hamilton in favour of my own opinions on Causation, as I can against the particular theory which I am now combating. But that acute thinker has a theory of Causation peculiar to himself, which has never yet, as far as I know, been analytically examined, but which, I venture to think, admits of as complete refutation as any one of the false or insufficient psychological theories which strew the ground in such numbers under his potent metaphysical scythe. ʲ(Since examined and controverted in the sixteenth chapter of *An Examination of Sir William Hamilton's Philosophy*.)ʲ

†[51] Unless we are to consider as such the following statement, by one of the writers quoted in the text: "In the case of mental exertion, the result to be accomplished is *preconsidered* or meditated, and is therefore known *à priori*, or before experience." (Bowen's *Lowell Lectures on the Application of Metaphysical and Ethical Science to the Evidence of Religion*, Boston, 1849 [p. 85].) This is merely saying that when we will a thing we have an idea of it. But to have an idea of what we wish to happen, does not imply a prophetic knowledge that it will happen. Perhaps it will be said that the *first time* we exerted our will, when we had of course no experience of any of the powers residing in us, we nevertheless must already have known that we possessed them, since we cannot will that which we do not believe to be in our power. But the impossibility is perhaps in the words only, and not in the facts; for we may *desire* what we do not know to be in our power; and finding by experience that our bodies move according to our *desire*, we may then, and only then, pass into the more complicated mental state which is termed will.
After all, even if we had an instinctive knowledge that our actions would follow our will, this, as Brown remarks, would prove nothing as to the nature of Causation. [See *Inquiry into the Relation of Cause and Effect*, pp. 44ff.] Our knowing, previous to experience, that an antecedent will be followed by a certain consequence, would not prove the relation between them to be anything more than antecedent and consequence.

ʲ–ʲ+65, 68, 72

sion between the will to move a limb and the actual motion is one of the most direct and instantaneous of all sequences which come under our observation, and is familiar to every moment's experience from our earliest infancy; more familiar than any succession of events exterior to our bodies, and especially more so than any other case of the apparent origination (as distinguished from the mere communication) of motion. Now, it is the natural tendency of the mind to be always attempting to facilitate its conception of unfamiliar facts by assimilating them to others which are familiar. Accordingly, our voluntary acts, being the most familiar to us of all cases of causation, are, in the infancy and early youth of the human race, spontaneously taken as the type of causation in general, and all phenomena are supposed to be directly produced by the will of some sentient being. This original Fetichism I shall not characterize in the words of Hume, or of any follower of Hume, but in those of a religious metaphysician, Dr. Reid, in order more effectually to show the unanimity which exists on the subject among all competent thinkers.

When we turn our attention to external objects, and begin to exercise our rational faculties about them, we find that there are some motions and changes in them which we have power to produce, and that there are many which must have some other cause. Either the objects must have life and active power, as we have, or they must be moved or changed by something that has life and active power, as external objects are moved by us.
Our first thoughts seem to be, that the objects in which we perceive such motion have understanding and active power as we have. 'Savages,' says the Abbé Raynal, 'wherever they see motion which they cannot account for, there they suppose a soul.'[*] All men may be considered as savages in this respect, until they are capable of instruction, and of using their faculties in a more perfect manner than savages do.

The Abbé Raynal's observation is sufficiently confirmed, both from fact, and from the structure of all languages.
Rude nations do really believe sun, moon, and stars, earth, sea, and air, fountains, and lakes, to have understanding and active power. To pay homage to them, and implore their favour, is a kind of idolatry natural to savages.
All languages carry in their structure the marks of their being formed when this belief prevailed. The distinction of verbs and participles into active and passive, which is found in all languages, must have been originally intended to distinguish what is really active from what is merely passive; and in all languages, we find active verbs applied to those objects, in which, according to the Abbé Raynal's observation, savages suppose a soul.
Thus we say the sun rises and sets, and comes to the meridian, the moon changes, the sea ebbs and flows, the winds blow. Languages were formed by men who believed these objects to have life and active power in themselves. It was

[*Guillaume Thomas François Raynal. *Histoire philosophique et politique des etablissemens et du commerce des Européens dans les deux Indes.* Geneva: Pellet, 1780, Vol. VIII, p. 50.]

therefore proper and natural to express their motions and changes by active verbs.

There is no surer way of tracing the sentiments of nations before they have records, than by the structure of their language, which, notwithstanding the changes produced in it by time, will always retain some signatures of the thoughts of those by whom it was invented. When we find the same sentiments indicated in the structure of all languages, those sentiments must have been common to the human species when languages were invented.

When a few, of superior intellectual abilities, find leisure for speculation, they begin to philosophize, and soon discover, that many of those objects which at first they believed to be intelligent and active are really lifeless and passive. This is a very important discovery. It elevates the mind, emancipates from many vulgar superstitions, and invites to further discoveries of the same kind.

As philosophy advances, life and activity in natural objects retires, and leaves them dead and inactive. Instead of moving voluntarily, we find them to be moved necessarily; instead of acting, we find them to be acted upon; and Nature appears as one great machine, where one wheel is turned by another, that by a third; and how far this necessary succession may reach, the philosopher does not know.*

There is, then, a spontaneous tendency of the intellect to account to itself for all cases of causation by assimilating them to the intentional acts of voluntary agents like itself. This is the instinctive philosophy of the human mind in its earliest stage, before it has become familiar with any other invariable sequences than those between its own volitions ᵍor those of other human beings and theirᵍ voluntary acts. As the notion of fixed laws of succession among external phenomena gradually establishes itself, the propensity to refer all phenomena to voluntary agency slowly gives way before it. The suggestions, however, of daily life continuing to be more powerful than those of scientific thought, the original instinctive philosophy maintains its ground in the mind, underneath the growths obtained by cultivation, and keeps up a constant resistance to their throwing their roots deep into the soil. The theory against which I am contending derives its nourishment from that substratum. Its strength does not lie in argument, but in its affinity to an obstinate tendency of the infancy of the human mind.

That this tendency, however, is not the result of an inherent mental law, is proved by superabundant evidence. The history of science, from its earliest dawn, shows that mankind have not been unanimous in thinking either that the action of matter upon matter was not conceivable, or that the action of mind upon matter was. To some thinkers, and some schools of thinkers, both in ancient and in modern times, this last has appeared much more inconceivable than the former. Sequences entirely physical and material, as soon as they had become sufficiently familiar to the human mind, came to be

*[51] Reid's *Essays on the Active Powers*, Essay IV, Chap. iii [*Works*, p. 605].

ᵍ⁻ᵍ51, 56, 62, 65   and its

thought perfectly natural, and were regarded not only as needing no explanation themselves, but as being capable of affording it to others, and even of serving as the ultimate explanation of things in general.

One of the *ablest* recent supporters of the Volitional theory has furnished an explanation, at once historically true and philosophically acute, of the failure of the Greek philosophers in physical inquiry, in which, as I conceive, he unconsciously depicts his own state of mind.

Their stumbling-block was one as to the nature of the evidence they had to expect for their conviction. . . . They had not seized the idea that they must not expect to understand the processes of outward causes, but only their results: and consequently, the whole physical philosophy of the Greeks was an attempt to identify mentally the effect with its cause, to feel after some not only necessary but natural connexion, where they meant by natural that which would *per se* carry some presumption to their own mind. . . . They wanted to see some *reason* why the physical antecedent should produce this particular consequent, and their only attempts were in directions where they could find such reasons.*

In other words, they were not content merely to know that one phenomenon was always followed by another; they thought that they had not attained the true aim of science, unless they could perceive something in the nature of the one phenomenon from which it might have been known or presumed *previous to trial* that it would be followed by the other: just what the writer, who has so clearly pointed out their error, thinks that he perceives in the nature of the phenomenon Volition. And to complete the statement of the case, he should have added that these early speculators not only made this their aim, but were quite satisfied with their success in it; not only sought for causes which should carry in their mere statement evidence of their efficiency, but fully believed that they had found such causes. The reviewer can see plainly that this was an error, because *he* does not believe that there exist any relations between material phenomena which can account for their producing one another: but the very fact of the persistency of the Greeks in this error, shows that their minds were in a very different state: they were able to derive from the assimilation of physical facts to other physical facts, the kind of mental satisfaction which we connect with the word explanation, and which the reviewer would have us think can only be found in referring phenomena to a will. When Thales and Hippo held that moisture was the universal cause, and *external* element, of which all other things were but the infinitely various sensible manifestations; when Anaximenes predicated the same thing of air, Pythagoras of numbers, and the like, they all thought that they had found a

*[51] [Hutton, "Mill and Whewell,"] *Prospective Review* for February 1850 [VI, pp. 108–9].

*h–h*51, 56   most
*i–i*51, 56, 62   eternal [*printer's error?*]

real explanation; and were content to rest in this explanation as ultimate. The ordinary sequences of the external universe appeared to them, no less than to their critic, to be inconceivable without the supposition of some universal agency to connect the antecedents with the consequents; but they did not think that Volition, exerted by minds, was the only agency which fulfilled this requirement. Moisture, or air, or numbers, carried to their minds a precisely similar impression of making *intelligible what* was otherwise inconceivable, and gave the same full satisfaction to the demands of their conceptive faculty.

It was not the Greeks alone, who "wanted to see some reason why the physical antecedent should produce this particular consequent," some connexion "which would *per se* carry some presumption to their own mind." Among modern philosophers, Leibnitz laid it down as a self-evident principle that all physical causes without exception must contain in their own nature something which makes it intelligible that they should be able to produce the effects which they do produce. Far from admitting Volition as the only kind of cause which carried internal evidence of its own power, and as the real bond of connexion between physical antecedents and their consequents, he demanded some naturally and *per se* efficient physical antecedent as the bond of connexion between Volition itself and its effects. He distinctly refused to admit the will of *k* God as a sufficient explanation of anything except miracles; and insisted upon finding something that would account *better* for the phenomena of nature than a mere reference to divine volition.*

Again, and conversely, the action of mind upon matter (which, we are now told, not only needs no explanation itself, but is the explanation of all other effects), has appeared to some thinkers to be itself the grand inconceivability. It was to get over this very difficulty that the Cartesians invented the system of Occasional Causes. They could not conceive that thoughts in a mind could produce movements in a body, or that bodily movements could produce thoughts. They could see no necessary connexion, no relation *à priori*, between a motion and a thought. And as the Cartesians, more than any other school of philosophical speculation before or since, made their own minds the measure of all things, and refused, on principle, to believe that Nature had done what they were unable to see any reason why she must do, they affirmed it to be impossible that a material and a mental fact could be causes one of another. They regarded them as mere Occasions on which the real agent, God, thought fit to exert his power as a Cause. When a man wills to move his foot, it is not his will that moves it, but God (they said) moves it on the occasion of his will. God, according to this system, is the only

*[51] Vide supra, p. 239n.

*j–j*51, 56, 62, 65   that intelligible which
*k*51   a [*printer's error?*]

efficient cause, not *quâ* mind, or *quâ* endowed with volition, but *quâ* omnipotent. This hypothesis was, as I said, originally suggested by the supposed inconceivability of any real mutual action between Mind and Matter: but it was afterwards extended to the action of Matter upon Matter, for on a nicer examination they found this inconceivable too, and therefore, according to their logic, impossible. The *deus ex machinâ* was ultimately called in to produce a spark on the occasion of a flint and steel coming together, or to break an egg on the occasion of its falling on the ground.

All this, undoubtedly, shows that it is the disposition of mankind in general, not to be satisfied with knowing that one fact is invariably antecedent and another consequent, but to look out for something which may seem to explain their being so [1]. But we also see that this demand may be completely satisfied by an agency purely physical, provided it be much more familiar than that which it is invoked to explain. To Thales and Anaximenes, it appeared inconceivable that the antecedents which we see in nature, should produce the consequents; but perfectly natural that water, or air, should produce them. The writers whom I oppose declare this inconceivable, but can conceive that mind, or volition, is *per se* an efficient cause: while the Cartesians could not conceive even that, but peremptorily declared that no mode of production of any fact whatever was conceivable, except the direct agency of an omnipotent being. Thus giving additional proof of what finds new confirmation in every stage of the history of science: that both what persons can, and what they cannot, conceive, is very much an affair of accident, and depends altogether on their experience, and their habits of thought; that by cultivating the requisite associations of ideas, people may make themselves unable to conceive any given thing; and may make themselves able to conceive most things, however inconceivable these may at first appear: and the same facts in each person's mental history which determine what is or is not conceivable to him, determine also which among the various sequences in nature will appear to him so natural and plausible, as to need no other proof of their existence; to be evident by their own light, independent equally of experience and of explanation.

By what rule is any one to decide between one theory of this description and another? The theorists do not direct us to any external evidence; they appeal each to his own subjective feelings. One says, the succession C, B, appears to me more natural, conceivable, and credible *per se*, than the succession A, B; you are therefore mistaken in thinking that B depends upon A; I am certain, though I can give no other evidence of it, that C comes in between A and B, and is the real and only cause of B. The other answers— the successions C, B, and A, B, appear to me equally natural and conceivable,

[1] 51, 56, 62 —something ἄνευ οὗ τὸ αἴτιον οὐκ ἄν ποτ' εἴη αἴτιον [Plato, *Phaedo*, 99b (see Jowett, *Dialogues of Plato*, Vol. I, p. 392)]

or the latter more so than the former: A is quite capable of producing B without any other intervention. A third agrees with the first in being unable to conceive that A can produce B, but finds the sequence D, B, still more natural than C, B, or of nearer kin to the subject matter, and prefers his D theory to the C theory. It is plain that there is no universal law operating here, except the law that each person's conceptions are governed and limited by his individual *experiences* and habits of thought. We are warranted in saying of all three, what each of them already believes of the other two, namely, that they exalt into an original law of the human intellect and of outward nature, one particular sequence of phenomena, which appears to them more natural and more conceivable than other sequences, only because it is more familiar. And from this judgment I am unable to except the theory, that Volition is an Efficient Cause.

I am unwilling to leave the subject without adverting to the additional fallacy contained in the corollary from this theory; in the inference that because Volition is an efficient cause, therefore it is the only cause, and the direct agent in producing even what is apparently produced by something else. Volitions are not known to produce anything directly except nervous action, for the will influences even the muscles only through the nerves. Though it were granted, then, that every phenomenon has an efficient, and not merely a phenomenal cause, and that volition, in the case of the peculiar phenomena which are known to be produced by it, is that efficient cause; are we therefore to say, with these writers, that since we know of no other efficient cause, and ought not to assume one without evidence, there *is* no other, and volition is the direct cause of all phenomena? A more outrageous stretch of inference could hardly be made. Because among the infinite variety of the phenomena of nature there is one, namely, a particular mode of action of certain nerves, which has for its cause, and as we are now supposing for its efficient cause, a state of our mind; and because this is the only efficient cause of which we are conscious, being the only one of which in the nature of the case we *can* be conscious, since it is the only one which exists within ourselves; does this justify us in concluding that all other phenomena must have the same kind of efficient cause with that one eminently special, narrow, and peculiarly human or animal, phenomenon? *The nearest parallel to this specimen of generalization *is suggested by* the recently revived controversy on the old subject of Plurality of Worlds, in which the contending parties have been so conspicuously successful in overthrowing one another. Here also we have experience only of a single case, that of the world in which we live, but that this is inhabited we know absolutely, and without *p* possibility

---

*m–m*51, 56, 62, 65, 68   experience
*o–o*56   may be found in

n–n+56, 62, 65, 68, 72
*p*56, 62, 65   even the

of doubt. Now if on this evidence any one were to infer that every heavenly body without exception, sun, planet, satellite, comet, fixed star or nebula, is inhabited, and must be so from the inherent constitution of things, his inference would exactly resemble that of the writers who conclude that because volition is the efficient cause of our own bodily motions, it must be the efficient cause of everything else in the universe.[n] It is true there are cases in which, with acknowledged propriety, we generalize from a single instance to a multitude of instances. But they must be instances which resemble the one known instance, and not such as have no circumstance in common with it except that of being instances. I have, for example, no direct evidence that any creature is alive except myself: yet I attribute, with full assurance, life and sensation to other human beings and animals. But I do not conclude that all other things are alive merely because I am. I ascribe to certain other creatures a life like my own, because they manifest it by the same sort of indications by which mine is manifested. I find that their phenomena and mine conform to the same laws, and it is for this reason that I believe both to arise from a similar cause. Accordingly I do not extend the conclusion beyond the grounds for it. Earth, fire, mountains, trees, are remarkable agencies, but their phenomena do not conform to the same laws as my actions do, and I therefore do not believe earth or fire, mountains or trees, to possess animal life. But the supporters of the Volition Theory ask us to infer that volition causes everything, for no reason except that it causes one particular thing; although that one phenomenon, far from being a type of all natural phenomena, is eminently peculiar; its laws bearing scarcely any resemblance to those of any other phenomenon, whether of inorganic or of organic nature. [qa]

[a]NOTE SUPPLEMENTARY TO THE PRECEDING CHAPTER

The author of the Second Burnett Prize Essay [*Theism*] (Dr. Tulloch), who has employed a considerable number of pages in controverting the doctrines of the preceding chapter, has somewhat surprised me by denying a fact, which I imagined too well known to require proof—that there have been philosophers who found in physical explanations of phenomena the

[q]51 [*footnote:*] *In combating the theory, that Volition is the universal cause, I have purposely abstained from one of the strongest positive arguments against it— that volitions themselves obey causes, and even external causes, namely, the inducements, or motives, which determine the will to act; because an objector might say that to employ this argument would be begging the question against the freedom of the will. Though it is not begging the question to affirm a doctrine, referring elsewhere for the proof of it, I am unwilling without necessity to build any part of my reasoning on a proposition which I am aware that those opposed to me in the present discussion do not admit.

[n]—[n]369+56, 62, 65, 68, 72

same complete mental satisfaction which we are told is only given by volitional explanation, and others who denied the Volitional Theory on the same ground of inconceivability on which it is defended. The assertion of the Essayist is countersigned still more positively by an able reviewer of the Essay:* "Two illustrations," says the reviewer, "are advanced by Mr. Mill: the case of Thales and Anaximenes, stated by him to have maintained, the one Moisture and the other Air to be the origin of all things; and that of Descartes and Leibnitz, whom he asserts to have found the action of Mind upon Matter the grand inconceivability. In counterstatement as to the first of these cases the author shows—what we believe now hardly admits of doubt—that the Greek philosophers distinctly recognised as beyond and above their primal material source, the νοῦς, or Divine Intelligence, as the efficient and originating Source of all: and as to the second, by proof that it was the *mode*, not the *fact*, of that action on matter, which was represented as inconceivable."

A greater quantity of historical error has seldom been comprised in a single sentence. With regard to Thales, the assertion that he considered water as a mere material in the hands of νοῦς rests on a passage of Cicero *de Naturâ Deorum*: and whoever will refer to any of the accurate historians of philosophy, will find that they treat this as a mere fancy of Cicero, resting on no authority, opposed to all the evidence; and make surmises as to the manner in which Cicero may have been led into the error. (See [Heinrich] Ritter [*Geschichte der Philosophie alter Zeit*. Hamburg: Perthes, 1836], Vol. I, p. 211n., 2nd ed.; [Christian] Brandis, [*Handbuch der Geschichte der Griechisch-Römischen Philosophie*. Berlin: Reimer, 1835,] Vol. I, pp. 118–19, 1st ed.; [Ludwig] Preller, *Historia Philosophiæ Græco-Romanæ* [Hamburg, Perthes, 1838], p. 10. "Schiefe Ansicht, durchaus zu verwerfen;" "augenscheinlich folgernd statt zu berichten;" "quibus vera sententia Thaletis plane detorquetur;" are the expressions of these writers.) As for Anaximenes, he even according to Cicero, maintained, not that air was the material out of which God made the world, but that the air was a god: "Anaximenes aëra deum statuit:" [*De natura deorum*. Ed. H. Rackham. London: Heinemann, 1933, p. 28 (Bk. I, Chap. x)] or according to St. Augustine [*De civitate Dei*, Bk. VIII, Chap. ii], that it was the material out of which the gods were made; "non tamen ab ipsis [Diis] aërem factum, sed ipsos ex aëre ortos credidit." Those who are not familiar with the metaphysical terminology of antiquity, must not be misled [b] by finding it stated that Anaximenes attributed ψυχή (translated *soul*, or *life*) to his universal element, the air. The Greek philosophers acknowledged several kinds of ψυχή, the nutritive, the sensi-

*[56] [Anon., "Theism,"] *Westminster Review* [LXIV,] for October 1855 [p. 328].

[b]56, 62, 65   (as Dr. Tulloch is)

tive, and the intellective.* Even the moderns, with admitted correctness, attribute life to plants. As far as we can make out the meaning of Anaximenes, he made choice of Air as the universal agent, on the ground that it is perpetually in motion, without any apparent cause external to itself: so that he conceived it as exercising spontaneous force, and as the principle of life and activity in all things, men and gods inclusive. If this be not representing it as the Efficient Cause, the dispute altogether has no meaning.

If either Anaximenes, or Thales, or any of their ᶜcotemporariesᶜ, had held the doctrine that νοῦς was the Efficient Cause, that doctrine could not have been reputed, as it was throughout antiquity, to have originated with Anaxagoras. The testimony of Aristotle, in the first book of his Metaphysics,[*] is perfectly decisive with respect to these early speculations. After enumerating four kinds of causes, or rather four different meanings of the word Cause, viz. the Essence of a thing, the Matter of it, the Origin of Motion (Efficient Cause), and the End or Final Cause, he proceeds to say, that most of the early philosophers recognised only the second kind of Cause, the Matter of a thing, τὰς ἐν ὕλης εἴδει μόνας ᾠήθησαν ἀρχὰς εἶναι πάντων [983ᵇ 7–8]. As his first example he specifies Thales, whom he describes as taking the lead in this view of the subject, ὁ τῆς τοιαύτης ἀρχηγὸς φιλοσοφίας [983ᵇ 20–1], and goes on to Hippon, Anaximenes, Diogenes (of Apollonia), Hippasus of Metapontum, Heraclitus, and Empedocles. Anaxagoras, however, (he proceeds to say,) taught a different doctrine, as we know, and it is alleged that Hermotimus of Clazomenæ taught it before him. Anaxagoras represented, that even if these various theories of the universal material were true, there would be need of some other cause to account for the transformations of the material, since the material cannot originate its own changes: οὐ γὰρ δὴ τό γε ὑποκείμενον αὐτὸ ποιεῖ μεταβάλλειν ἑαυτὸ· λέγω δ' οἷον οὔτε τὸ ξύλον οὔτε ὁ χαλκὸς αἴτιος τοῦ μεταβάλλειν ἑκάτερον αὐτῶν, οὐδὲ ποιεῖ τὸ μὲν ξύλον κλίνην ὁ δὲ χαλκὸς ἀνδριάντα, ἀλλ' ἕτερόν τι τῆς μεταβολῆς αἴτιον [984ᵃ 21–5], viz., the other kind of cause, ὅθεν ἡ ἀρχὴ τῆς κινήσεως—an Efficient Cause [983ᵃ 30]. Aristotle expresses great approbation of this doctrine (which he says made its author appear the only sober man among persons raving, οἷον νήφων ἐφάνη παρ' εἰκῆ λέγοντας τοὺς πρότερον) [984ᵇ 17–18]; but while describing the influence which it exercised over subsequent speculation, he remarks that the philosophers against whom this, as he thinks, insuperable difficulty was urged, had not felt it to be any difficulty: οὐδὲν ἐδυσχέραναν ἐν ἑαυτοῖς [984ᵃ

---

*[56] See the whole doctrine in Aristotle de Anima: where the θρεπτικὴ ψυχὴ is treated as exactly equivalent to θρεπτικὴ δύναμις [415ᵃ 23ff. In tr., R. D. Hicks. Cambridge: Cambridge University Press, 1907, p. 63].

[*Tr. McMahon, pp. 12ff. (Bk. I, Chap. iii); references to the Greek text are given following each quotation below.]

ᶜ⁻ᶜ56 contemporaries

29]. It is surely unnecessary to say more in proof of the matter of fact which Dr. Tulloch and his reviewer ^ddisbelieve^d.

Having pointed out what he thinks the error of these early speculators in not recognising the need of an efficient cause, Aristotle goes on to mention two other efficient causes to which they might have had recourse, instead of intelligence: τύχη, chance, and τὸ αὐτόματον, spontaneity. He indeed puts these aside as not sufficiently worthy causes for the order in the universe, οὐδ' αὖ τῷ αὐτομάτῳ καὶ τῇ τύχῃ τοσοῦτον ἐπιτρέψαι πρᾶγμα καλῶς εἶχεν [984^b 14–15]: but he does not reject them as incapable of producing *any* effect, but only as incapable of producing *that* effect. He himself recognises τύχη and τὸ αὐτόματον as coordinate agents with Mind in producing the phenomena of the universe; the department allotted to them being composed of all the classes of phenomena which are not supposed to follow any uniform law. By thus including Chance among efficient causes, Aristotle fell into an error which philosophy has now outgrown, but which is by no means so alien to the spirit even of modern speculation as it may at first sight appear. Up to ^equite a^e recent period philosophers went on ascribing, and many of them have not yet ceased to ascribe, a real existence to the results of abstraction. Chance could make out as good a title to that dignity as many other of the mind's abstract creations: it had had a name given to it, and why should it not be a reality? As for τὸ αὐτόματον, it is recognised even yet as one of the modes of origination of phenomena, by all those thinkers who maintain what is called the Freedom of the Will. The same self-determining power which that doctrine attributes to volitions, was supposed by the ancients to be possessed also by some other natural phenomena: a circumstance which throws considerable light on more than one of the supposed invincible necessities of belief. I have introduced it here, because this belief of Aristotle, or rather of the Greek philosophers generally, is as fatal as the doctrines of Thales and the Ionic school, to the theory that the human mind is compelled by its constitution to conceive volition as the origin of all force, and the efficient cause of all phenomena.*

*[56] It deserves notice that the parts of nature which Aristotle regards as presenting evidence of design, are the Uniformities: the phenomena in so far as reducible to law. Τύχη and τὸ αὐτόματον satisfy him as explanations of the variable element in phenomena, but their occurring according to a fixed rule can only, to his conceptions, be accounted for by an Intelligent Will. The common, or what may be called the instinctive, religious interpretation of nature, is the reverse of this. The events in which men spontaneously see the hand of a supernatural being, are those which cannot, as they think, be reduced to a physical law. What they can distinctly connect with physical causes, and especially what they can predict, though of course ascribed to an Author of Nature if they al-

^{d–d}56, 62, 65, 68   deny
^{e–e}56, 62   a quite

With regard to the modern philosophers (Leibnitz and the Cartesians) whom I had cited as having maintained that the action of mind upon matter, so far from being the only conceivable origin of material phenomena, is itself inconceivable; the attempt to rebut this argument by asserting that the mode, not the fact, of the action of mind on matter was represented as inconceivable, is an abuse of the privilege of writing confidently about authors without reading them: for any knowledge whatever of Leibnitz would have taught those who thus speak of him, that the inconceivability of the mode, and the impossibility of the thing, were in his mind convertible expressions. What was his famous Principle of the Sufficient Reason, the very corner stone of his Philosophy, from which the Preestablished Harmony, the doctrine of Monads, and all the opinions most characteristic of Leibnitz, were corollaries? It was, that nothing exists, the existence of which is not capable of being proved and explained à priori; the proof and explanation in the case of contingent facts being derived from the nature of their causes; which could not be the causes unless there was something in their nature showing them to be capable of producing those particular effects. And this "something" which accounts for the production of physical effects, he was able to find in many physical causes, but could not find it in any finite minds, which therefore he unhesitatingly asserted to be incapable of producing any physical

---

ready recognise such an author, might be conceived, they think, to arise from a blind fatality, and in any case do not appear to them to bear so obviously the mark of a divine will. And this distinction has been countenanced by eminent writers on Natural Theology, in particular by Dr. Chalmers: who thinks that though design is present everywhere, the irresistible evidence of it is to be found not in the *laws* of nature but in the collocations, *i.e.* in the part of nature in which it is impossible to trace any law. [See Thomas Chalmers. *On the Power Wisdom and Goodness of God as Manifested in the Adaptation of External Nature to the Moral and Intellectual Constitution of Man.* 2 vols. London: Pickering, 1833, Vol. I, p. 20.] A few properties of dead matter might, he thinks, conceivably account for the regular and invariable succession of effects and causes; but that the different kinds of matter have been so placed as to promote beneficent ends, is what he regards as the proof of a Divine Providence. Mr. Baden Powell, in his Essay entitled "Philosophy of Creation," has returned to the point of view of Aristotle and the ancients, and vigorously reasserts the doctrine that the indication of design in the universe is not special adaptations, but Uniformity and Law, these being the evidences of mind, and not what appears to us to be a provision for our uses. While I decline to express any opinion here on this *vexata quæstio*, I ought not to mention Mr. Powell's volume [*Essays on the Spirit of the Inductive Philosophy, the Unity of Worlds, and the Philosophy of Creation.* London: Longman, 1855] without the acknowledgment due to the philosophic spirit which pervades generally the three Essays composing it, forming in the case of one of them (the "Unity of Worlds") an honourable contrast with the other dissertations, so far as they have come under my notice, which have appeared on either side of that controversy.

effects whatever. "On ne saurait concevoir," he says, "une action réciproque de la matière et de l'intelligence l'une sur l'autre," and there is therefore (he contends) no choice but between the Occasional Causes of the Cartesians, and his own Preestablished Harmony, according to which there is no more connexion between our volitions and our muscular actions than there is between two clocks which are wound up to strike at the same instant. But he felt no similar difficulty as to physical causes: and throughout his speculations, as in the passage I have already cited respecting gravitation, he distinctly refuses to consider as part of the order of nature any fact which is not explicable from the nature of its physical cause.

With regard to the Cartesians (not Descartes; I did not make that mistake, though the reviewer of Dr. Tulloch's Essay attributes it to me)[*] I take a passage almost at random from Malebranche, who is the best known of the Cartesians, and, though not the inventor of the system of Occasional Causes, is its principal expositor. In Part 2, chap. 3, of his Sixth Book [of *Recherche de la vérité, Oeuvres*. Paris: Charpentier, 1842, Vol. II, pp. 503–4], having first said that matter cannot have the power of moving itself, he proceeds to argue that neither can mind have the power of moving it. "Quand on examine l'idée que l'on a de tous les esprits finis, on ne voit point de liaison nécessaire entre leur volonté et le mouvement de quelque corps que ce soit, on voit au contraire qu'il n'y en a point, et qu'il n'y en peut avoir;" (there is nothing in the idea of finite mind which can account for its causing the motion of a body;) "on doit aussi conclure, si on veut raisonner selon ses lumières, qu'il n'y a aucun esprit créé qui puisse remuer quelque corps que ce soit comme cause véritable ou principale, de même que l'on a dit qu'aucun corps ne se pouvait remuer soi-même:" thus the idea of Mind is according to him as incompatible as the idea of Matter with the exercise of active force. But when, he continues, we consider not a created but a Divine Mind, the case is altered; for the idea of a Divine Mind includes omnipotence; and the idea of omnipotence does contain the idea of being able to move bodies. Thus it is the nature of omnipotence which renders the motion of bodies even by the divine mind credible or conceivable, while, so far as depended on the mere nature of mind, it would have been inconceivable and incredible. If Malebranche had not believed in an omnipotent being, he would have held all action of mind on body to be a demonstrated impossibility.*

[*See p. 364 above.]

*[56] In the words of Fontenelle, another celebrated Cartesian, "les philosophes aussi bien que le peuple avaient cru que l'âme et le corps agissaient réellement et physiquement l'un sur l'autre. Descartes vint, qui prouva que leur nature ne permettait point cette sorte de communication véritable, et qu'ils n'en pouvaient avoir qu'une apparente, dont Dieu était le Médiateur." (["Eloge de Mon-

A doctrine more precisely the reverse of the Volitional theory of causation cannot well be imagined. The Volitional theory is, that we know by intuition or by direct experience the action of our own mental volitions on matter; that we may hence infer all other action upon matter to be that of volition, and might thus know, without any other evidence, that matter is under the government of a divine mind. Leibnitz and the Cartesians, on the contrary, maintain that our volitions do not and cannot act upon matter, and that it is only the existence of an all-governing Being, and that Being omnipotent, which can account for the sequence between our volitions and our bodily actions. When we consider that each of these two theories, which, as theories of causation, stand at the opposite extremes of possible divergence from one another, invokes not only as its evidence, but as its sole evidence, the absolute inconceivability of any theory but itself, we are enabled to measure the worth of this kind of evidence: and when we find the Volitional theory entirely built upon the assertion that by our mental constitution we are compelled to recognise our volitions as efficient causes, and then find other thinkers maintaining that we know that they are not and cannot be such causes, and cannot conceive them to be so, I think we have a right to say, that this supposed law of our mental constitution does not exist.

Dr. Tulloch [*Theism*] (pp. 45–7) thinks it a sufficient answer to this, [f] that Leibnitz and the Cartesians were Theists, and believed the will of God to be an efficient cause. Doubtless they did, and the Cartesians even believed (though Leibnitz did not) that it is the only such cause. Dr. Tulloch [g] mistakes the nature of the question. I was not writing on Theism, as Dr. Tulloch is, but against a particular theory of causation, which, if it be unfounded, can give no effective support to Theism or to anything else. I found it asserted that volition is the only efficient cause, on the ground that no other efficient cause is conceivable. To this assertion I [h]oppose[h] the instances of Leibnitz and of the Cartesians, who affirmed with equal positiveness that volition as an efficient cause is itself not conceivable, and that omnipotence, which renders all things conceivable, can alone take away the impossibility. This I thought, and think, a conclusive answer to the argument on which this theory of causation avowedly depends. But I certainly did not imagine that Theism was bound up with that theory; nor expected to be charged with denying Leibnitz and the Cartesians to be Theists because I denied that they held the theory.[a]

---

sieur Leibnitz,"] *Œuvres de Fontenelle* [New ed. Paris: Brunet, 1758–61,] Vol. V, p. 534.)

[f]56, 62, 65   to say (as if any one had denied it)
[g]56, 62, 65   entirely
[h-h]56, 62   opposed

CHAPTER VI

ᵃOnᵃ the Composition of Causes

§ 1. [*Two modes of the conjunct action of causes, the mechanical and the chemical*] To complete the general notion of causation on which the rules of experimental inquiry into the laws of nature must be founded, one distinction still remains to be pointed out: a distinction so ᵇradicalᵇ, and of so much importance, as to require a chapter to itself.

The preceding discussions have rendered us familiar with the case in which several agents, or causes, concur as conditions to the production of an effect; a case, in truth, almost universal, there being very few effects to the production of which no more than one agent contributes. Suppose, then, that two different agents, operating jointly, are followed, under a certain set of collateral conditions, by a given effect. If either of these agents, instead of being joined with the other, had operated alone, under the same set of conditions in all other respects, some effect would probably have followed; which would have been different from the joint effect of the two, and more or less dissimilar to it. Now, if we happen to know what would be the ᶜeffectᶜ of each cause when acting separately from the other, we are often able to arrive deductively, or *à priori*, at a correct ᵈpredictionᵈ of what will arise from their conjunct agency. To ᵉrender this possibleᵉ, it is only necessary that the same law which expresses the effect of each cause acting by itself, shall also correctly express the part due to that cause, of the effect which follows from the two together. This condition is realized in the extensive and important class of phenomena commonly called mechanical, ᶠnamelyᶠ the phenomena of the communication of motion (or of pressure, which is tendency to motion) from one body to another. In this important class of cases of causation, one cause never, properly speaking, defeats or frustrates another; both have their full effect. If a body is propelled in two directions by two forces, one tending to drive it to the north and the other to the east, it is caused to move in a given time exactly as far in both directions as the two forces would separately have

ᵃ⁻ᵃMS, 43, 46, 51, 56, 62, 65   Of
ᵇ⁻ᵇMS, 43   fundamental
ᶜ⁻ᶜ43, 46, 51, 56, 62   effects [*printer's error; s cancelled in* MS]
ᵈ⁻ᵈMS   judgment
ᵉ⁻ᵉMS, 43, 46, 51, 56, 62, 65, 68   enable us to do this
ᶠ⁻ᶠMS   which consists of

carried it; and is left precisely where it would have arrived if it had been acted upon first by one of the two forces, and afterwards by the other. This law of nature is called, in $g$dynamics$g$, the principle of the Composition of Forces: and in imitation of that well-chosen expression, I shall give the name of the Composition of Causes to the principle $h$which is$h$ exemplified in all cases in which the joint effect of $i$several$i$ causes is identical with the sum of their separate effects.

This principle, however, by no means prevails in all departments of the field of nature. The chemical combination of two substances produces, as is well known, a third substance with properties j different from those of either of the two substances separately, or $k$of both$k$ of them taken together. Not a trace of the properties of hydrogen or of oxygen is observable in those of their compound, water. The taste of sugar of lead is not the sum of the tastes of its component elements, acetic acid and lead or its oxide; nor is the colour of $l$blue$l$ vitriol a mixture of the colours of sulphuric acid and copper. This explains why mechanics is a deductive or demonstrative science, and chemistry not. In the one, we can compute the effects of m combinations of causes, whether real or hypothetical, from the laws which we know to govern those causes when acting separately; because they continue to observe the same laws when in combination which they observed when separate: whatever would have happened in consequence of each cause taken by itself, happens when they are together, and we have only to $n$cast up$n$ the results. Not so in the phenomena which are the peculiar subject of the science of chemistry. There, most of the uniformities to which the causes conformed when separate, cease altogether when they are conjoined; and we are not, at least in the present state of our knowledge, able to foresee what result will follow from any new combination, until we have tried $o$the$o$ specific experiment.

If this be true of chemical combinations, it is still more true of those far more complex combinations of elements which constitute organized bodies; and in which those extraordinary new uniformities arise, which are called the laws of life. All organized bodies are composed of parts similar to those composing inorganic nature, and which have even themselves existed in an inorganic state; but the phenomena of life, which result from the juxtaposition of those parts in a certain manner, bear no analogy to any of the effects which would be produced by the action of the component substances considered as mere physical agents. To whatever degree we might imagine our knowledge of the properties of the several ingredients of a living body to be extended and perfected, it is certain that no mere summing up of the

g–gMS, 43, 46   mechanical philosophy
h–h+43, 46, 51, 56, 62, 65, 68, 72
jMS, 43, 46, 51, 56, 62, 65, 68   entirely
l–lMS, 43, 46, 51, 56, 62   green
n–nMS   add together

i–iMS   a plurality of
k–k51, 56, 62, 65, 68   both
mMS, 43, 46, 51, 56, 62, 65, 68   all
o–oMS, 43, 46   it by

separate actions of those elements will ever amount to the action of the living body itself. The tongue, for instance, is, like all *other* parts of the animal frame, composed of gelatine, fibrin, and other products of the chemistry of digestion, but from no knowledge of the properties of those substances could we ever predict that it could taste, unless gelatine or fibrin could themselves taste; for no elementary fact can be in the conclusion, which was not *q* in the premises.

There are thus two different modes of the conjunct action of causes; from which arise two modes of conflict, or mutual interference, between laws of nature. Suppose, at a given point of time and space, two or more causes, which, if they acted separately, would produce effects contrary, or at least conflicting with each other; one of them tending to undo, wholly or partially, what the other tends to do. Thus, the expansive force of the gases generated by the ignition of gunpowder tends to project a bullet towards the sky, while its gravity tends to make it fall to the ground. A stream running into a reservoir at one end tends to fill it higher and higher, while a drain at the other extremity tends to empty it. Now, in such cases as these, even if the two causes which are in joint action exactly annul one another, still the laws of both are fulfilled; the effect is the same as if the drain had been open for half an hour first,* and the stream had flowed in for as long afterwards. Each agent produced the same amount of effect as if it had acted separately, though the contrary effect which was taking place during the same time obliterated it as fast as it was produced. Here then *are* two causes, producing by their joint operation an effect which at first seems quite dissimilar to those which they produce separately, but which on examination proves to be really the sum of those separate effects. It will be noticed that we here enlarge the idea of the sum of two effects, so as to include what is commonly called their difference, but which is in reality the result of the addition of opposites; a conception to which *w* mankind are indebted for that admirable extension of the algebraical calculus, which has so vastly increased its powers as an instrument of discovery, by introducing into its reasonings (with the sign of subtraction prefixed, and under the name of Negative Quantities) every description whatever of positive phenomena, provided they are of such a

---

*I omit, for simplicity, to take into account the effect, in this latter case, of the *diminution of* pressure, in diminishing the flow of *s* water through the drain; which evidently in no way affects the truth or applicability of the principle *t*, since *when the two causes act simultaneously* the conditions of that diminution of pressure do not arise *t*.

*p–p*MS   the   *q*MS, 43, 46, 51, 56   first
*r–r*MS   diminished   *s*MS, 43, 46   the
t–t+56, 62, 65, 68, 72   *u–u*+62, 65, 68, 72
*v–v*MS, 43, 46   we have   *w*MS, 43, 46   , as is well known,

quality in reference to those previously introduced, that to add the one is equivalent to subtracting an equal quantity of the other.

There is, then, one mode of the mutual interference of laws of nature, in which, even when the concurrent causes annihilate each other's effects, each exerts its full efficacy according to its own law, its law as a separate agent. But in the other description of cases, the *y* agencies which are brought together cease entirely, and a totally different set of phenomena arise: as in the experiment of two liquids which, when mixed in certain proportions, instantly become *z*, not a larger amount of liquid, but a solid mass*z*.

§ 2. [*The composition of causes the general rule; the other case exceptional*] This difference between the case in which the joint effect of causes is the sum of their separate effects, and the case in which it is heterogeneous to them; between laws which work together without alteration, and laws which, when called upon to work together, cease and give place to others; is one of the fundamental distinctions in nature. The former case, that of the Composition of Causes, is the general one; the other is always special and exceptional. There are no objects which do not, as to some of their phenomena, obey the principle of the Composition of Causes; none that have not some laws which are rigidly fulfilled in every combination into which the objects enter. The weight of a body, for instance, is a property which it retains in all the combinations in which it is placed. The weight of a chemical compound, or of an organized body, is equal to the sum of the weights of the elements which compose it. The weight either of the elements or of the compound will vary, if they be carried farther from their centre of attraction, or brought nearer to it; but whatever affects the one affects the other. They always remain precisely equal. So again, the component parts of a vegetable or animal substance do not lose their mechanical and chemical properties as separate agents, when, by a peculiar mode of juxtaposition, they, as an aggregate whole, acquire physiological or vital properties in addition. Those bodies continue, as before, to obey mechanical and chemical laws, *a*in*a* so far as the operation of those laws is not counteracted by the new laws which govern them as organized beings. When, in short, a concurrence of causes takes place which calls into action new laws bearing no analogy to any that we can trace in the separate operation of the causes, the new laws *b*, while they supersede one portion of the previous laws, may*b* coexist with another portion, and may even compound the effect of those previous laws with their own.

ª *ª*MS   This therefore is
*y*MS, 43, 46   two
*z–z*MS, 43, 46, 51   a solid mass, instead of merely a larger amount of liquid
a–a+43, 46, 51, 56, 62, 65, 68, 72
*b–b*MS, 43, 46   may supersede one . . . laws but

Again, laws which were themselves generated in the second mode, may generate others in the first. Though there ^{c}are^c laws which, like those of chemistry and physiology, owe their existence to a breach of the principle of Composition of Causes, it does not follow that these peculiar, or as they might be termed, *heteropathic* laws, are not capable of composition with one another. The causes which by one combination have had their laws altered, may carry their new laws with them unaltered into their ulterior combinations. And hence there is no reason to despair of ultimately raising chemistry and physiology to the condition of deductive sciences; for though it is impossible to deduce all chemical and physiological truths from the laws or properties of simple substances or elementary agents, they may ^{d}possibly^d be deducible from laws which commence when ^{e}these^e elementary agents are brought together into some moderate number of not very complex combinations. The Laws of Life will never be deducible from the mere laws of the ingredients, but the prodigiously complex Facts of Life may all be deducible from comparatively simple laws of life; which laws (depending indeed on combinations, but on comparatively simple combinations, of antecedents) may, in more complex circumstances, be strictly compounded with one another, and with the physical and chemical laws of the ingredients. The details of ^{f}the^f vital phenomena, even now, afford innumerable exemplifications of the Composition of Causes; and in proportion as ^{g}these^g phenomena are more accurately studied, there appears more ^{h} reason to believe that the same laws which operate in the simpler combinations of circumstances do, in fact, continue to be observed in the more complex. ^{i} This will be found equally true in the phenomena of mind; and even in social and political phenomena,

---

$^{c-c}$MS, 43, 46, 51, 56 be

$^{e-e}$MS those [*printer's error?*]

$^{g-g}$MS those [*printer's error?*]

$^{d-d}$MS, 43 probably

$^{f-f}$+43, 46, 51, 56, 62, 65, 68, 72

^{h}MS, 43, 46 and more

^{i}MS [*footnote:*] *For illustrations of this remark, I may be permitted to refer to an author, whose works are well deserving the attention of any reader, desirous of finding in a moderate compass the highest generalizations which the science of life has yet reached, and the best modern conception of that science as a whole, exhibited in a manner equally perspicuous and philosophical. I allude to the writings of Dr. W. B. Carpenter of Bristol, & especially his admirable treatise on General Physiology. On the details of such a treatise the present writer would be an incompetent witness; these however have been sufficiently vouched for by some of the highest living authorities; while of the genuinely scientific spirit which pervades it, those may be permitted to express an opinion, in whom it would be presumption to offer to a work on such a subject, any other praise.] 43 [*footnote:*] *For abundant illustrations of this remark, I may refer to the writings of Dr. W. B. Carpenter, of Bristol, and especially his treatise on *General Physiology*, in which the highest . . . *as* MS . . . a whole, are exhibited . . . *as* MS . . . philosophical. On the details . . . *as* MS . . . an opinion, who would not be entitled to offer . . . *as* MS] 46 *as* 43 . . . may refer the reader to Dr. Carpenter's two treatises on General and Human Physiology, in which . . . *as* 43 . . . and philosophical. [William Benjamin Carpenter. *Principles of General and Comparative Physiology*. London: Churchill, 1839; *Principles of Human Physiology*. London: Churchill, 1842.]

the ^{j}results^j of the laws of mind. It is in the case of chemical phenomena that the least progress has yet been made in bringing the special laws under general ones from which they may be deduced; but there are even in chemistry many circumstances to encourage the hope that such general laws will ^{k}hereafter^k be discovered. The different actions of a chemical compound will never, undoubtedly, be found to be the ^{l}sums^l of the actions of its separate elements; but there may exist, between the properties of the compound and those of its elements, some constant relation, which, if discoverable by a sufficient induction, would enable us to foresee the sort of compound which will result from a new combination before we have actually tried it, and to judge of what sort of elements some new substance is compounded before we have analysed it ^{m} . The ^{n} law of definite proportions, first discovered in its full generality by Dalton, is a complete solution of this problem in one ^{o}, though but a secondary aspect,^{o} that of quantity: and in respect to quality, we have already some partial generalizations, sufficient to indicate the possibility of ultimately proceeding ^{p}farther^p. We can predicate ^{q}some^q common properties of the kind of compounds which result from the combination, in each of the small number of possible proportions, of any acid whatever with any base. We have also the ^{r} curious law, discovered by Berthollet, that two soluble salts mutually decompose one another whenever the new combinations which result produce an insoluble compound, or one less soluble than the two former. Another uniformity ^{s}is that^s called the law of isomorphism; the identity of the crystalline forms of substances which possess in common certain peculiarities of chemical composition.* Thus it appears that even heteropathic laws, such laws of combined agency as are not compounded of the laws of the separate agencies, are yet, at least in some cases, derived from them according to a fixed principle. There may, therefore, be laws of the generation of laws from others dissimilar to them; and in chemistry, these

---

*[72] Professor Bain adds several other well-established chemical generalizations: "The laws that simple substances exhibit the strongest affinities; that compounds are more fusible than their elements; that combination tends to a lower state of matter from gas down to solid;" and some general propositions concerning the circumstances which facilitate or resist chemical combination. (*Logic*, Pt. II, p. 254.)

$^{j-j}$MS, 43, 46, 51, 56, 62, 65   result

$^{k-k}$MS   one day

$^{l-l}$MS, 43, 46   sum

^{m}MS, 43   : a problem, the solution of which has been propounded by M. Comte as the ideal aim and purpose of chemical speculation [see, e.g., *Cours*, Vol. III, p. 20]

^{n}MS, 43, 46   great

$^{o-o}$MS, 43, 46   single aspect, (of secondary importance it is true,)

$^{p-p}$MS, 43, 46   further

$^{q-q}$MS, 43, 46   many

^{r}MS, 43, 46   very

$^{s-s}$MS, 43, 46   has been observed, commonly

undiscovered laws of the dependence of the properties of the compound on the properties of its elements, may, together with the laws of the elements themselves, furnish the premises by which the science is *perhaps* destined one day to be rendered deductive.

It would seem, therefore, that there is no class of phenomena in which the Composition of Causes does not obtain: that as a general rule, causes in combination produce exactly the same effects as when acting singly: but that this rule, though general, is not universal: that in some instances, at some particular points in the transition from separate to united action, the laws change, and an entirely new set of effects are either added to, or take the place of, those which arise from the separate agency of the same causes: the laws of these new effects being again susceptible of composition, to an indefinite extent, like the laws which they superseded.

§ 3. [*Are effects proportional to their causes?*] That effects are proportional to their causes is laid down by some writers as an axiom in the theory of causation; and great use is sometimes made of this principle in reasonings respecting the laws of nature, though it is encumbered with many difficulties and apparent exceptions, which much ingenuity has been expended in showing not to be real ones. This proposition, in so far as it is true, enters as a particular case into the general principle of the Composition of Causes; the causes compounded being, in this instance, homogeneous; in which case, if in any, their joint effect might be expected to be identical with the sum of their separate effects. If a force equal to one hundred weight will raise a certain body along an inclined plane, a force equal to two hundred weight will *a* raise two bodies exactly similar, and thus the effect is proportional to the cause. But does not a force equal to two hundred weight actually contain in itself two forces each equal to one hundred weight, which, if employed apart, would separately raise the two bodies in question? The fact, therefore, that when exerted jointly they raise both bodies at once, results from the Composition of Causes, and is a mere instance of the general fact that mechanical forces are subject to the law of Composition. And so in every other case which can be supposed. For the doctrine of the proportionality of effects to their causes cannot of course be applicable to cases in which the augmentation of the cause alters the *kind* of effect; that is, in which the surplus quantity superadded to the cause does not become compounded with it, but the two together generate an altogether new phenomenon. Suppose that the application of a certain quantity of heat to a body merely increases its bulk, that a double quantity melts it, and a triple quantity decomposes it: these three effects being heterogeneous, no ratio, whether corresponding or

t–t+51, 56, 62, 65, 68, 72
*a*MS, 43, 46   , we know,

not to that of the quantities of heat applied, can be established between them. Thus [b] the supposed axiom of the proportionality of effects to their causes fails at the precise point where the principle of the Composition of Causes also fails; [c]viz. where[c] the concurrence of causes is such as to determine a change in the properties of the body generally, and render it subject to new laws, more or less dissimilar to those to which it conformed in its previous state [d]. The recognition, therefore, of any such law of proportionality, is superseded by the more comprehensive principle, in which as much of it as is true is implicitly asserted.*

The general remarks on causation, which seemed necessary as an introduction to the theory of the inductive process, may here terminate. That process is essentially an inquiry into cases of causation. All the uniformities which exist in the succession of phenomena, and most of [e]the uniformities[e] in their co-existence, are either, as we have seen, themselves laws of causation, or consequences resulting from, and corollaries capable of being deduced from, such laws. If we could determine what causes are correctly assigned to what effects, and what effects to what causes, we should be virtually ac-

---

*[72] Professor Bain (*Logic*, Pt. II, p. 39) points out a class of cases, other than that spoken of in the text, which he thinks must be regarded as an exception to the Composition of Causes. "Causes that merely make good the collocation for bringing a prime mover into action, or that release a potential force, do not follow any such rule. One man may direct a gun upon a fort as well as three: two sparks are not more effectual than one in exploding a barrel of gunpowder. In medicine there is a certain dose that answers the end; and adding to it does no more good."

I am not sure that these cases are really exceptions. The law of Composition of Causes, I think, is really fulfilled, and the appearance to the contrary is produced by attending to the remote instead of the immediate effect of the causes. In the cases mentioned, the immediate effect of the causes in action is a collocation, and the duplication of the cause does double the quantity of collocation. Two men could raise the gun to the required angle twice as quickly as one, though one is enough. Two sparks put two sets of particles of the gunpowder into the state of intestine motion which makes them explode, though one is sufficient. It is the collocation itself that does not, by being doubled, always double the effect; because in many cases a certain collocation, once obtained, is all that is required for the production of the whole amount of effect which can be produced at all at the given time and place. Doubling the collocation with difference of time and place, as by pointing two guns, or exploding a second barrel after the first, does double the effect. This remark applies still more to Mr. Bain's third example, that of a double dose of medicine: for a double dose of an aperient does purge more violently, and a double dose of laudanum does produce longer and sounder sleep. But a double purging, or a double amount of narcotism, may have remote effects different in kind from the effect of the smaller amount, reducing the case to that of heteropathic laws, discussed in the text.

---

[b]MS, 43, 46 we see that
[d]MS, 43, 46 of existence

[c–c]MS the point at which
[e–e]MS, 43, 46 those which prevail

quainted with the whole course of nature. All those uniformities which are mere results of causation might then be explained and accounted for; and every individual fact or event might be predicted, provided we had the requisite data, that is, the requisite knowledge of the circumstances which, in the particular instance, preceded it.

To ascertain, therefore, what are the laws of causation which exist in nature; to determine the *effect* of every cause, and the causes of all effects,— is the main business of Induction; and to point out how this is done is the chief object of Inductive Logic.

*f–f*MS, 43, 46, 51, 56, 62, 65   effects

CHAPTER VII

Of Observation and Experiment

§ 1. [*The first step of inductive inquiry is a mental analysis of complex phenomena into their elements*] It results from the preceding exposition, that the process of ascertaining what consequents, in nature, are invariably connected with what antecedents, or in other words what phenomena are related to each other as causes and effects, is in some sort a process of analysis. That every fact which begins to exist has a cause, and that this cause must be found *a*in some fact or concourse of*a* facts which immediately preceded *b*the*b* occurrence, may be taken for certain. The whole of the present facts are the infallible result of all past facts, and more immediately of all the facts which existed at the moment previous. Here, then, is a great sequence, which we know to be uniform. If the whole prior state of the entire universe could again recur, it would again be followed by the *c* present state. The question is, how to resolve this complex uniformity into the simpler uniformities which compose it, and assign to each portion of the vast antecedent *d*the*d* portion of the consequent which is attendant on it.

This operation, which we have called analytical, inasmuch as it is the resolution of a complex whole into the component elements, is more than a merely mental analysis. No mere contemplation of the phenomena, and partition of them by the intellect alone, will of itself accomplish the end we have now in view. Nevertheless, such a mental partition is an indispensable first step. The order of nature, as perceived at a first glance, presents at every instant a chaos followed by another chaos. We must decompose each chaos into single facts. We must learn to see in the chaotic antecedent a multitude of distinct antecedents, in the chaotic consequent a multitude of distinct consequents. This, supposing it done, will not of itself tell us on which of the antecedents each consequent is invariably attendant. To determine that point, we must endeavour to effect a separation of the *e*facts*e* from one another, not in our minds only, but in nature. The mental analysis, however, must take place first. And every one knows that in the mode of performing it, one intellect differs immensely from another. It is the essence of the act of observ-

---

*a–a*MS, 43, 46, 51, 56, 62, 65, 68   somewhere among the
*b–b*MS, 43, 46   its   *c*MS, 43, 46   whole
*d–d*MS, 43, 46   that   *e–e*MS   parts [*printer's error?*]

ing; for the observer is not he who merely sees the thing which is before his eyes, but he who sees what parts that thing is composed of. To do this well is a rare talent. One person, from inattention, or attending only in the wrong place, overlooks half of what he sees; another sets down much more than he sees, confounding it with what he imagines, or with what he infers; another takes note of the *kind* of all the circumstances, but being inexpert in estimating their degree, leaves the quantity of each vague and uncertain; another sees indeed the whole, but makes such an awkward division of it into parts, throwing things into one mass which require to be separated, and separating others which might more conveniently be considered as one, that the result is much the same, sometimes even worse, than if no analysis had been attempted at all. It would be possible to point out what qualities of mind, and modes of mental culture, fit a person for being a good observer: that, however, is a question not of Logic, but of the Theory of Education, in the most enlarged sense of the term. There is not properly an Art of Observing. *There* may be rules for observing. But these, like rules for inventing, are properly instructions for the preparation of one's own mind; for putting it into the state in which it will be most fitted to observe, or most likely to invent. They are, therefore, essentially rules of self-education, which is a different thing from Logic. They do not teach how to do the thing, but how to make ourselves capable of doing it. They are an art of strengthening the limbs, not an art of using them.

The extent and minuteness of observation which may be requisite, and the degree of decomposition to which it may be necessary to carry the mental analysis, depend on the particular purpose in view. To ascertain the state of the whole universe at any particular moment is impossible, but would also be useless. In making chemical experiments, we *do* not think it necessary to note the position of the planets; because experience has shown, as a very superficial experience is sufficient to show, that in such cases that circumstance is not material to the result: and accordingly, in the *ages* when men believed in the occult influences of the heavenly bodies, it might have been unphilosophical to omit ascertaining the precise condition of those bodies at the moment of the experiment. As to the degree of minuteness of the mental subdivision, if we were obliged to break down what we observe into its very simplest elements, that is, literally into single facts, it would be difficult to say where we should find them: we can hardly ever affirm that our divisions of any kind have reached the ultimate unit. But this, too, is fortunately unnecessary. The only object of the mental separation is to suggest the requisite

<hr>

*f–f*MS   "How to observe," generally means only *what* to observe; that is, what facts are worth observing. I do not attempt to deny that there
*g–g*MS, 43   should
*h–h*MS, 43, 46   age

physical separation, so that we may either accomplish it ourselves, or seek for it in nature; and we have done enough when we have carried the subdivision as far as the point at which we are able to see what observations or experiments we require. It is only essential, at whatever point our mental decomposition of facts may for the present have stopped, that we should hold ourselves ready and able to carry it farther as occasion requires, and should not allow the freedom of our discriminating faculty to be imprisoned by the swathes and bands of ordinary classification; as was the case with all early speculative inquirers, not excepting the Greeks, to whom it *seldom* occurred that what was called by one abstract name might, in reality, be several phenomena, or that there was a possibility of decomposing the facts of the universe into any elements but those which ordinary language already recognised.

§ 2. [*The next step of inductive inquiry is an actual separation of those elements of complex phenomena*] The different antecedents and consequents, being, then, supposed to be, so far as the case requires, ascertained and discriminated from one another; we are to inquire which is connected with which. In every instance which comes under our observation, there are many antecedents and many consequents. If those antecedents could not be severed from one another except in thought, or if those consequents never were found apart, it would be impossible for us to distinguish (*à posteriori* at least) the real laws, or to assign to any cause its effect, or to any effect its cause. To do so, we must be able to meet with some of the antecedents apart from the rest, and observe what follows from them; or some of the consequents, and observe by what they are preceded. We must, in short, follow the Baconian rule of *varying the circumstances*.[*] This is, indeed, only the first rule of physical inquiry, and not, as some have thought, the sole rule; but it is the foundation of all the rest.

For the purpose of varying the circumstances, we may have recourse (according to a distinction commonly made) either to observation or to experiment; we may either *find* an instance in nature suited to our purposes, or, by an artificial arrangement of circumstances, *make* one. The value of the instance depends on what it is in itself, not on the mode in which it is obtained: its employment for the purposes of induction depends on the same principles in the one case and in the other; as the uses of money are the same whether it is inherited or acquired. There is, in short, no difference in kind, no real logical distinction, between the two processes of investigation. There are, however, practical distinctions to which it is of considerable importance to advert.

[*See, e.g., *De Augmentis Scientiarum*, pp. 624ff. (Bk. V.)]
i–iMS, 43, 46, 51, 56, 62, 65   hardly ever

§ 3. [*Advantages of experiment over observation*] The first and most obvious distinction between Observation and Experiment is, that the latter is an immense extension of the former. It not only enables us to produce a much greater number of variations in the circumstances than nature spontaneously offers, but *also*, in thousands of cases, to produce the precise *sort* of variation which we are in want of for discovering the law of the phenomenon; a service which nature, being constructed on a quite different scheme from that of facilitating our studies, is seldom so friendly as to bestow upon us. For example, in order to ascertain what principle in the atmosphere enables it to sustain life, the variation we require is that a living animal should be immersed in each component element of the atmosphere separately. But nature does not supply either oxygen or azote in a separate state. We are indebted to artificial experiment for our knowledge that it is the former, and not the latter, which supports respiration; and *b* for our knowledge of the very existence of the two ingredients.

Thus far the advantage of experimentation over simple observation is universally recognised: all are aware that it enables us to obtain innumerable combinations of circumstances which are not to be found in nature, and so add to nature's experiments a multitude of experiments of our own. But there is another superiority (or, as Bacon would have expressed it, another prerogative) of instances artificially obtained over spontaneous instances,—of our own experiments over even the same experiments when made by nature, —which is not of less importance, and which is far from being felt and acknowledged in the same degree.

When we can produce a phenomenon artificially, we can take it, as it were, home with us, and observe it in the midst of circumstances with which in all other respects we are accurately acquainted. If we desire to know what are the effects of the cause A, and are able to produce A by *means* at our disposal, we can generally determine at our own discretion, so far as is compatible with the nature of the phenomenon A, the whole of the circumstances which shall be present along with it: and thus, knowing exactly the simultaneous state of everything else which is within the reach of A's influence, we have only to observe what alteration is made in that state by the presence of A.

For example, by the *electric* machine we can produce, in the midst of known circumstances, the phenomena which nature exhibits on a grander scale *in* the form of lightning and thunder. Now let any one consider what amount of knowledge of the effects and laws of electric agency mankind

a–aMS, 43, 46   , moreover
bMS, 43, 46   even
c–cMS, 43   any means] 46   means which are
d–dMS, 43, 46   electrical
e–eMS, 43, 46   under

could *f* have obtained from the mere observation of thunderstorms, and compare it with that which they have gained, and may expect to gain, from electrical and galvanic experiments. This example is the more striking, now that we have reason to believe that electric action is of all natural phenomena *g*(except heat)*g* the most pervading and universal, which, therefore, it might antecedently have been supposed could stand least in need of artificial means of production to enable it to be studied; while the fact is so much the contrary, that without the electric machine, the *h*Leyden jar, and the voltaic battery*h*, we *i*probably*i* should never have suspected the existence of electricity as one of the great agents in nature; the few electric phenomena we should have known of would have continued to be regarded either as supernatural, or as a sort of anomalies and eccentricities in the order of the universe.

When we have succeeded in insulating the phenomenon which is the subject of inquiry, by placing it among known circumstances, we may produce further variations of circumstances to any extent, and of such kinds as we think best calculated to bring the laws of the phenomenon into a clear light. By introducing one well-defined circumstance after another into the experiment, we obtain assurance of the manner in which the phenomenon behaves under an indefinite variety of possible circumstances. *j*Thus,*j* chemists, after having obtained some newly-discovered substance in a pure state (that is, having made sure that there is nothing present which can interfere with and modify its agency,) introduce various other substances, one by one, to ascertain whether it will combine with them, or decompose them, and with what result; and also apply heat, or electricity, or pressure, to discover what will happen to *k*the substance*k* under each of these circumstances.

But if, on the other hand, it is out of our power to produce the phenomenon, and we have to seek for instances in which nature produces it, the task before us is *l*very different*l*.

m Instead of being able to *n*choose*n* what the concomitant circumstances shall be, we now have to discover what they are; which, when we go beyond the simplest and most accessible cases, it is next to impossible to do, with any precision and completeness. Let us take, as an exemplification of a phenomenon which we have no means of *o*fabricating artificially*o*, a human mind. Nature produces many; but the consequence of our not being able to produce

*f*MS, 43, 46   ever
g-g+43, 46, 51, 56, 62, 65, 68, 72
*h-h*MS, 43, 46, 51, 56   voltaic battery, and the Leyden jar
i-i+51, 56, 62, 65, 68, 72
*j-j*MS   As when
*k-k*MS   it
*l-l*MS, 43, 46   one of quite another kind
*m*MS, 43, 46, 51, 56, 62, 65, 68   [*no paragraph*]
*n-n*MS   determine
*o-o*MS   producing

them by art is, that in every instance in which we see a human mind developing itself, or acting upon other things, we see it surrounded and obscured by an indefinite multitude of unascertainable circumstances, rendering the use of the common experimental methods almost delusive. We may conceive to what extent *this is true,* if we consider, among other things, that whenever nature produces a human mind, she produces, in close connexion with it, *r* a body; that is, a vast complication of physical facts, in no two cases perhaps exactly similar, and most of which (except the mere structure, which we can examine in a sort of coarse way after it has ceased to act), are radically out of the reach of our means of exploration. If, instead of a human mind, we suppose the subject of investigation to be a human society or State, all the same difficulties recur in a greatly augmented degree.

We have thus already come within sight of a conclusion, which the progress of the inquiry will, I think, bring before us with the clearest evidence: namely, that in the sciences which deal with phenomena in which artificial experiments are impossible (as in the case of astronomy), or in which they have a very limited range (as in *mental philosophy, social science, and even physiology*) induction from direct experience is practised at a disadvantage *in most cases* equivalent to impracticability: from which it follows that the methods of those sciences, in order to accomplish anything worthy of attainment, must be to a great extent, if not principally, deductive. This is already known to be the case with the first of the sciences we have mentioned, astronomy; that it is not generally recognised as true of the others, is probably one of the reasons why they are *not in a more advanced state.*

§ 4. [*Advantages of observation over experiment*] If what is called pure observation *a* is at so great a disadvantage, compared with artificial experimentation, in one department of the direct exploration of phenomena, there is another branch in which the advantage is all on the side of the former.

Inductive inquiry having for its object to ascertain what causes are connected with what effects, we may begin this search at either end of the road which leads from the one point to the other: we may either inquire into the effects of a given cause, or into the causes of a given effect. The fact that light blackens chloride of silver might have been discovered either by experiments on light, trying what effect it would produce on various substances, or

*p-p*MS, 43, 46, 51, 56   it

q-q+43, 46, 51, 56, 62, 65, 68, 72

*r*MS, 43, 46, 51, 56   also

*s-s*MS, 43, 46, 51, 56   physiology, mental philosophy, and the social science,]   62, 65   *as* MS . . . and social science

*t-t*MS, 43, 46, 51, 56, 62, 65   generally

*u-u*MS, 43, 46   still in their infancy. But any further notice of this topic would at present be premature.]   51, 56, 62, 65   still in their infancy.

*a*MS   , as distinguished from Experiment,

by observing that portions of the chloride had repeatedly become black, and inquiring into the circumstances. The effect of the urali poison might have become known either by administering it to animals, or by examining how it happened that the wounds which the Indians of Guiana inflict with their arrows prove so uniformly mortal. Now it is manifest from the mere statement of the examples, without any theoretical discussion, that artificial experimentation is applicable only to the former of these modes of investigation. We can take a cause, and try what it will produce: but we cannot take an effect, and try what it will be produced by. We can only watch till we see it produced, or are enabled to produce it by accident.

This would be of little importance, if it always depended on our choice from which of the two ends of the sequence we would undertake our inquiries. But we have seldom any option. As we can only travel from the known to the unknown, we are obliged to commence at whichever end we are best acquainted with. If the agent is more familiar to us than its effects, we watch for, or contrive, instances of the agent, under such varieties of circumstances as are open to us, and observe the result. If, on the contrary, the conditions on which a phenomenon depends are obscure, but the phenomenon itself familiar, we must commence our inquiry from the effect. If we are struck with the fact that chloride of silver has been blackened, and have no suspicion of the cause, we have no resource but to compare instances in which the fact has chanced to occur, until by that comparison we discover that in all those instances the ^{b}substances^b had been exposed to ^{c} light. If we knew nothing of the Indian arrows but their fatal effect, accident alone could turn our attention to experiments on the urali; in the regular course of investigation, we could only ^{d}inquire, or try to observe,^{d} what had been done to the arrows in particular instances.

Wherever, having nothing to guide us to the cause, we are obliged to set out from the effect, and to apply the rule of varying the circumstances to the consequents, not the antecedents, we are necessarily destitute of the resource of artificial experimentation. We cannot, at our choice, obtain consequents, as we can antecedents, under any set of circumstances compatible with their nature. There are no means of producing effects but through their causes, and by the supposition the causes of the effect in question are not known to us. We have, therefore, no expedient but to study it where it offers itself spontaneously. If nature happens to present us with instances sufficiently varied in their circumstances, and if we are able to discover, either among the proximate antecedents or among some other order of antecedents, something which is always found when the effect is found, however various the circum-

$^{b-b}$MS, 43, 46, 51, 56 substance
^{c}MS, 43, 46 the
$^{d-d}$MS try to observe or enquire

stances, and never found when it is not; we may discover, by mere observation without experiment, a real uniformity in nature.

But though this is certainly the most favourable case for sciences of pure observation, as contrasted with those in which artificial experiments are possible, there is in reality no case which more strikingly illustrates the inherent imperfection of direct induction when not founded on experimentation. Suppose that, by a comparison of cases of the effect, we have found an antecedent which appears to be, and perhaps is, invariably connected with it: we have not yet proved that antecedent to be the cause, until we have reversed the process, and produced the effect by means of that antecedent. If we can produce the antecedent artificially, and if, when we do so, the effect follows, the induction is complete; that antecedent is the cause of that consequent.* But we *have then* added the evidence of experiment to that of simple observation. Until we had done so, we had only proved *invariable* antecedence *within the limits of experience*, but not *unconditional* antecedence, or causation. Until it had been shown by the actual production of the antecedent under known circumstances, and the occurrence thereupon of the consequent, that the antecedent was really the condition on which it depended; the uniformity of succession which was proved to exist between them might, for aught we knew, be (like the succession of day and night) *not a* case of causation at all; both antecedent and consequent might be successive stages of the effect of an ulterior cause. Observation, in short, without experiment (*supposing no* aid from deduction) can ascertain *sequences and coexistences*, but cannot prove causation.

In order to see these remarks verified by the actual state of the sciences, we have only to think of the condition of natural history. In zoology, for example, there is an immense number of uniformities ascertained, some of coexistence, others of succession, to many of which, notwithstanding considerable variations of the attendant circumstances, we know not any exception: but the antecedents, for the most part, are such as we cannot artificially produce; or if we can, it is only by setting in motion the exact process by which nature produces them; and this being to us a mysterious process, of which the main circumstances are not only unknown but unobservable, *we

---

*Unless, indeed, the consequent was generated, not by the antecedent, but by the means *e* employed to produce the antecedent *f*. As, however,*f* these means are under our power, there is so far a probability that they are also sufficiently within our knowledge, to enable us to judge whether that could be the case or not.

*e*MS, 43, 46, 51, 56, 62, 65   we
*g–g*MS, 43, 46   then have
*i–i*MS, 43, 46, 51, 56, 62, 65   no
*k–k*MS, 43, 46   uniformities
*f–f*MS   ; but as
h–h+56, 62, 65, 68, 72
*j–j*MS, 43, 46   and without any
*l–l*MS, 43, 46, 51, 56   the name of experimentation would here be completely misapplied. Such are the facts: and what

do not succeed in obtaining the antecedents under known circumstances. What[l] is the result? That on this vast subject, which affords so much and such varied scope for observation, we have [m]made most scanty progress in ascertaining any laws of causation[m]. We know not [n]with certainty, in the case of most[n] of the phenomena that we find conjoined, which is the condition of the other; which is cause, and which effect, or whether either of them is so, or they are not rather [o] conjunct effects of causes yet to be discovered, complex results of laws hitherto unknown.

Although some of the foregoing [p]observations[p] may be, in technical strictness of arrangement, premature in this place, it seemed that a few general [q]remarks[q] on the difference between sciences of mere observation and sciences of experimentation, and the extreme disadvantage under which directly inductive inquiry is necessarily carried on in the former, were the best preparation for discussing the methods of direct induction; a preparation rendering superfluous much that must otherwise have been introduced, with some inconvenience, into the heart of that discussion. To the consideration of these methods we now proceed.

[m-m]MS, 43, 46, 51, 56, 62, 65   not, properly speaking, ascertained a single cause, a single unconditional uniformity
[n-n]MS, 43, 46   , in the case of almost any]   51, 56, 62   , in the case of most
[o]MS, 43, 46   all of them
[p-p]MS   remarks
[q-q]MS   observations

CHAPTER VIII

Of the Four Methods of Experimental Inquiry

§ 1. [*Method of Agreement*] The simplest and most obvious modes of singling out from among the circumstances which precede or follow a phenomenon, those with which it is really connected by an invariable law, are two in number. One is, by comparing together different instances in which the phenomenon occurs. The other is, by comparing instances in which the phenomenon does occur, with instances in other respects similar in which it does not. These two methods may be respectively denominated, the Method of Agreement, and the Method of Difference.

In illustrating these methods, it will be necessary to bear in mind the two-fold character of inquiries into the laws of phenomena; which may be either inquiries into the cause of a given effect, or into the effects or properties of a given cause. We shall consider the methods in their application to either order of investigation, and shall draw our examples equally from both.

We shall denote antecedents by the large letters of the alphabet, and the consequents corresponding to them by the small. Let A, then, be an agent or cause, and let the object of our inquiry be to ascertain what are the effects of this cause. If we can either find, or produce, the agent A in such varieties of circumstances, that the different cases have no circumstance in common except A; then whatever effect we find to be produced in all our trials [a], is indicated as[a] the effect of A. Suppose, for example, that A is tried along with B and C, and that the effect is *a b c*; and suppose that A is next tried with D and E, but without B and C; and that the effect is *a d e*. Then we may reason thus: *b* and *c* are not effects of A, for they were not produced by it in the second experiment; nor are *d* and *e*, for they were not produced in the first. Whatever is really the effect of A must have been produced in both instances; now this condition is fulfilled by no circumstance except *a*. The phenomenon *a* cannot have been the effect of B or C, since it was produced where they were not; nor of D or E, since it was produced where they were not. Therefore it is the effect of A.

[a]-[a]MS, 43   must, it would seem, be

For example, let the antecedent A be the contact of an alkaline substance and an oil. This combination being tried under several varieties of [b]circumstances[b], [c]resembling each other[c] in nothing else, the results agree in the production of a greasy and detersive or saponaceous substance: it is therefore concluded that the combination of an oil and an alkali causes the production of a soap. [d]It is thus we inquire, by the Method of Agreement, into[d] the effect of a given cause.

In a similar manner we may [e]inquire into[e] the cause of a given effect. Let *a* be the effect. Here, as [f]shown in the last chapter[f], we have only the resource of observation without experiment: we cannot take a phenomenon of which we know not the origin, and try to find its mode of production by producing it: if we succeeded in such a random [g]trial[g] it could only be by accident. But if we can observe *a* in two different combinations, *a b c* and *a d e*; and if we know, or can discover, that the antecedent circumstances in these cases respectively were A B C and A D E; we may conclude by a reasoning similar to that in the preceding example, that A is the antecedent connected with the consequent *a* by a law of causation. B and C, we may say, cannot be causes of *a*, since on its second occurrence they were not present; nor are D and E, for they were not present on its first occurrence. A, alone of the five circumstances, was found among the antecedents of *a* in both instances.

For example, let the effect *a* be crystallization. We compare instances in which bodies are known to assume crystalline structure, but which have no other point of agreement; and we find them to have one, and as far as we can observe, only one, antecedent in common: the deposition of solid matter from a liquid state, either a state of fusion or of solution. We conclude, therefore, that the solidification of a substance from a liquid state is an invariable antecedent of its crystallization.

In this example we may go farther, and say, it is not only the invariable antecedent but the cause[h]; or at least the proximate event which completes the cause[h]. For in this case we are able, after detecting the antecedent A, to produce it artificially, and by finding that *a* follows it, verify the result of our induction. The importance of thus reversing the proof was [i]strikingly manifested[i] when by keeping a phial of water charged with siliceous particles undisturbed for years, a chemist (I believe Dr. Wollaston) succeeded in obtaining crystals of quartz; [j]and[j] in the equally interesting experiment in which Sir James Hall produced artificial marble by the cooling of its materials

---

[b-b] MS, 43, 46, 51   circumstance
[g] [e] MS   agreeing
[d-d] MS   And thus we have ascertained, by the Method of Agreement,
[e-e] MS   ascertain   [f-f] MS   already shewn
[g-g] MS   guess   [h-h] +51, 56, 62, 65, 68, 72
[i-i] MS, 43, 46   never more strikingly manifested than
[j-j] MS   or

from fusion under immense pressure: two admirable examples of the light which may be thrown upon the most secret processes of nature by well-contrived interrogation of her.

[k] But if we cannot artificially produce the phenomenon A, the conclusion that it is the cause of *a* remains subject to very considerable doubt. Though an invariable, it may not be the unconditional antecedent of *a*, but may precede it as day precedes night or night day. This uncertainty arises from the impossibility of assuring ourselves that A is the *only* immediate antecedent common to both the instances. If we could be certain of having ascertained all the invariable antecedents, we might be sure that the unconditional invariable antecedent, or cause, must be found somewhere among them. Unfortunately it is hardly ever possible to ascertain all the antecedents, unless the phenomenon is one which we can produce artificially. Even then, the difficulty is merely lightened, not removed: men knew how to raise water in pumps long before they adverted to what was really the operating circumstance in the means they employed, namely, the pressure of the atmosphere on the open surface of the water. It is, however, much easier to analyse completely a set of arrangements made by ourselves, than the whole complex mass of the agencies which nature happens to be exerting at the moment [l]of the production of a[l] given phenomenon. We may overlook some of the material circumstances in an experiment with an electrical machine; but we shall, at the worst, be better acquainted with them than with those of a thunder-storm.

The mode of discovering and proving laws of nature, which we have now examined, proceeds on the following axiom: Whatever circumstance can be excluded, without prejudice to the phenomenon, or can be absent notwithstanding its presence, is not connected with it in the way of causation. The casual circumstances being thus eliminated, if only one remains, that one is the cause which we are in search of: if more than one, they either are, or contain among them, the cause; and so, *mutatis mutandis*, of the effect. As this method proceeds by comparing different instances to ascertain in what they agree, I have termed it the Method of Agreement: and we may adopt as its regulating principle the following canon:

FIRST CANON

If two or more instances of the phenomenon under investigation have only one circumstance in common, the circumstance in which alone all the instances agree, is the cause (or effect) of the given phenomenon.

Quitting for the present the Method of Agreement, to which we shall almost immediately return, we proceed to a still more potent instrument of the investigation of nature, the Method of Difference.

[k]MS [*no paragraph*]   [l–l]MS, 43, 46 when she produces any

§ 2. [*Method of Difference*] In the Method of Agreement, we endeavoured to obtain instances which agreed in the given circumstance but differed in every other: in the present method we require, on the contrary, two instances resembling one another in every other respect, but differing in the presence or absence of the phenomenon we wish to study. If our object be to discover the effects of an agent A, we must procure A in some set of ascertained circumstances, as A B C, and having noted the effects produced, compare them with the effect of the remaining circumstances B C, when A is absent. If the effect of A B C is *a b c*, and the effect of B C, *b c*, it is evident that the effect of A is *a*. So again, if we begin at the other end, and desire to investigate the cause of an effect *a*, we must select an instance, as *a b c*, in which the effect occurs, and in which the antecedents were A B C, and we must look out for another instance in which the remaining circumstances, *b c*, occur without *a*. If the antecedents, in that instance, are B C, we know that the cause of *a* must be A: either A alone, or A in conjunction with some of the other circumstances present.

It is scarcely necessary to give examples of a logical process to which we owe almost all the inductive conclusions we draw in daily life. When a man is shot through the heart, it is by this method we know that it was the gunshot which killed him: for he was in the fulness of life immediately before, all circumstances being the same, except the wound.

The axioms *a*implied*a* in this method are evidently the following. Whatever antecedent cannot be excluded without preventing the phenomenon, is the cause, or a condition, of that phenomenon *b*: Whatever*b* consequent can be excluded, with no other difference in the antecedents than the absence of a particular one, is the effect of that *c*one*c*. Instead of comparing different instances of a phenomenon, to discover in what they agree, this method compares an instance of its occurrence with an instance of its non-occurrence, to discover in what they differ. The canon which is the regulating principle of the Method of Difference may be expressed as follows:

SECOND CANON

If an instance in which the phenomenon under investigation occurs, and an instance in which it does not occur, have every circumstance ᵈin common save oneᵈ, that one occurring only in the former; the circumstance in which alone the two instances differ, is the effect, or ᵉtheᵉ cause, or ᶠan indispensableᶠ part of the cause, of the phenomenon.

ᵃ⁻ᵃMS, 43, 46   which are taken for granted
ᵇ⁻ᵇMS   , & whatever
ᶜ⁻ᶜMS   antecedent
ᵈ⁻ᵈMS, 43   *save one in common*
ᵉ⁻ᵉ+56, 62, 65, 68, 72
ᶠ⁻ᶠMS, 43, 46, 51, 56   *a necessary*

§ 3. [*Mutual relation of the Methods of Agreement and Difference*] The two methods which we have now stated have many features of resemblance, but there are also many distinctions between them. Both are methods of *elimination*. This term ([a] employed in the theory of equations to denote the process by which one after another of the elements of a question is excluded, and the solution made to depend on the relation between the remaining elements only) is well suited to express the operation, analogous to this, which has been understood since the time of Bacon to be the foundation of experimental inquiry: namely, the successive exclusion of the various circumstances which are found to accompany a phenomenon in a given instance, in order to ascertain what are those among them which can be absent consistently with the existence of the phenomenon. The Method of Agreement stands on the ground that whatever can be eliminated, is not connected with the phenomenon by any law. The Method of Difference has for its foundation, that whatever cannot be eliminated, is connected with the phenomenon by a law.

Of these methods, that of Difference is more particularly a method of artificial experiment; while that of Agreement is more especially the resource [b]employed[b] where experimentation is impossible. A few reflections will prove the fact, and point out the reason of it.

It is inherent in the peculiar character of the Method of Difference, that the nature of the combinations which it requires is much more strictly defined than in the Method of Agreement. The two instances which are to be compared with one another must be exactly similar, in all circumstances except the one which we are attempting to investigate: they must be in the relation of A B C and B C, or of *a b c* and *b c*. It is true that this similarity of circumstances needs not extend to such as are already known to be immaterial to the result. And in the case of most phenomena we learn at once, from the [c]commonest[c] experience, that most of the coexistent phenomena of the universe may be either present or absent without affecting the given phenomenon; or, if present, are present indifferently when the phenomenon does not happen and when it does. Still, even limiting the identity which is required between the two instances, A B C and B C, to such circumstances as are not already known to be indifferent; it is very seldom that nature affords two instances, of which we can be assured that they stand in this precise relation to one another. In the spontaneous operations of nature there is generally such complication and such obscurity, they are mostly either on so overwhelmingly large or on so inaccessibly minute a scale, we are so ignorant of a great part of the facts which really take place, and even those of which we are not ignorant are so multitudinous, and therefore so seldom exactly alike in any two cases, that a spontaneous experiment, of the kind required by the

[a]MS, 43, 46   which is
[b–b]MS, 43, 46   we employ   [c–c]MS, 43   most ordinary

Method of Difference, is ^dcommonly not^d to be found. When, on the contrary, we obtain a phenomenon by an artificial experiment, a pair of instances such as the method requires is obtained almost as a matter of course, provided the process does not last a long time. A certain state of surrounding circumstances existed before we commenced the experiment; this is B C. We then introduce A; say, for instance, by merely bringing an object from another part of the room, before there has been time for any change in the other elements. It is, in short (as M. Comte observes), the very nature of an experiment, to introduce into the pre-existing state of circumstances a change perfectly definite.[*] We choose a previous state of things ^ewith which we are well acquainted^e, so that no unforeseen alteration in that state is likely to pass unobserved; and into this we introduce, as rapidly as possible, the phenomenon which we wish to study; so that ^fin general we^f are entitled to feel complete assurance that the pre-existing state, and the state which we have produced, differ in nothing except ^g the presence or absence of that phenomenon. If a bird is taken from a cage, and instantly plunged into carbonic acid gas, the experimentalist may be fully assured (at all events after one or two repetitions) that no circumstance capable of causing suffocation had supervened in the interim, except the change from immersion in the atmosphere to immersion in carbonic acid gas. There is one doubt, indeed, which may remain in some cases of this description; the effect may have been produced not by the change, but by the means ^h employed to produce the change. The possibility, however, of this last supposition generally admits of being conclusively tested by other experiments. It thus appears that in the study of the various kinds of phenomena which we can, by our voluntary agency, modify or control, we can in general satisfy the requisitions of the Method of Difference; but that by the spontaneous operations of nature those requisitions are seldom fulfilled.

The reverse of this is the case with the Method of Agreement. We do not here require instances of so special and determinate a kind. Any instances whatever, in which nature presents us with a phenomenon, may be examined for the purposes of this method; and if all such instances agree in anything, a conclusion of considerable value is already attained. We can seldom, indeed, be sure that ⁱtheⁱ one point of agreement is the only one; but ^jthis^j ignorance does not, as in the Method of Difference, vitiate the conclusion; the certainty of the result, as far as it goes, is not affected. We have ascertained one invariable antecedent or consequent, however many other invariable ante-

[*See, e.g., *Cours*, Vol. III, p. 321.]

^{d–d}MS scarcely ever
^{e–e}MS which we exactly know
^gMS, 43 in
^{i–i}MS, 43, 46 this

^{f–f}MS, 43, 46 we in general
^hMS, 43, 46 we
^{j–j}MS, 43, 46 our

cedents or consequents may still remain unascertained. If A B C, A D E, A F G, are all equally followed by a, then a is an invariable consequent of A. If $a\ b\ c,\ a\ d\ e,\ a\ f\ g$, all number A among their antecedents, then A is connected as an antecedent, by some invariable law, with a. But to determine whether this invariable antecedent is a cause, or this invariable consequent an effect, we must be able, in addition, to produce the one by means of the other; or, at least, to obtain that which alone constitutes our assurance of having produced anything, namely, an instance in which the effect, a, has come into existence, with no other change in the pre-existing circumstances than the addition of A. And this, if we can do it, is an application of the Method of Difference, not of the Method of Agreement.

It thus appears to be by the Method of Difference alone that we can ever, in the way of direct experience, arrive ᵏwith certaintyᵏ at causes. The Method of Agreement leads only to laws of phenomena ˡ(as some writers call them, but improperly, since laws of causation are also laws of phenomena): that is, to uniformities, which either are not laws of causation, orˡ in which the question of causation must for the present remain undecided. The Method of Agreement is chiefly to be resorted to, as a means of suggesting applications of the Method of Difference (as in the last example the comparison of A B C, A D E, A F G, suggested that A was the antecedent on which to try the experiment whether it could produce a); or as an inferior resource, in case the Method of Difference is impracticable; which, as we before showed, generally arises from the impossibility of artificially producing the phenomena. And hence it is that the Method of Agreement, though applicable in principle to either case, is more emphatically the method of investigation on those subjects where artificial experimentation is impossible: because on those it is, generally, our only resource of a directly inductive nature; while, in the phenomena which we can produce at pleasure, the Method of Difference generally affords a more efficacious process, which will ascertain causes as well as mere laws.

§ 4. [*Joint Method of Agreement and Difference*] ᵃThere are, however,ᵃ many cases in which, though our power of producing the phenomenon is complete, the Method of Difference either cannot be made available at all, or not without a previous employment of the Method of Agreement. This occurs when the agency by which we can produce the phenomenon is not that of one single antecedent, but ᵇ a combination of antecedents, which we

ᵏ⁻ᵏ+43, 46, 51, 56, 62, 65, 68, 72

ˡ⁻ˡMS, 43   , as Mr. Whewell calls them [*Philosophy of the Inductive Sciences*, Vol. II, pp. 260ff.], but which (since laws of causation are also laws of phenomena) I prefer to designate as uniformities] 46   , as some writers call them . . . *as* MS

ᵃ⁻ᵃMS, 43, 46 Our next remark shall be, that there are

ᵇ51   of

have no power of separating from each other, and exhibiting apart. For instance, suppose the subject of inquiry to be the cause of the double refraction of light. We can produce this phenomenon at pleasure, by employing any one of the many substances which are known to refract light in that peculiar manner. But if, taking one of those substances, as Iceland spar for example, we wish to determine on which of the properties of Iceland spar this remarkable phenomenon depends, we can make no use, for that purpose, of the Method of Difference; for we cannot find another substance precisely resembling Iceland spar except in some one property. The only mode, therefore, of prosecuting this inquiry is that afforded by the Method of Agreement; by which, in fact, through a comparison of all the known substances which *have* the property of doubly refracting light, it was ascertained that they *agree in the* circumstance of being crystalline substances; and though the converse does not hold, though all crystalline substances have not the property of double refraction, it was concluded, with reason, that there is a real connexion between these two properties; that either crystalline structure, or the cause which gives rise to that structure, is one of the conditions of double refraction.

Out of this employment of the Method of Agreement arises a peculiar modification of that method, which is sometimes of great avail in the investigation of nature. In cases similar to the above, in which it is not possible to obtain the precise pair of instances which our second canon requires— instances agreeing in every antecedent except A, or in every consequent except *a*; we may yet be able, by a double employment of the Method of Agreement, to discover in what the instances which contain A or *a*, differ from those which do not.

If we compare various instances in which *a* occurs, and find that they all have in common the circumstance A, and (as far as can be observed) no other circumstance, the Method of Agreement, so far, bears testimony to a connexion between A and *a*. In order to convert this *evidence* of connexion into proof of causation by the direct Method of Difference, we ought to be able, in some one of these instances, as for example A B C, to leave out A, and observe whether by doing so, *a* is prevented. Now supposing (what is often the case) that we are not able to try this decisive experiment; yet, provided we can by any means discover what would be its result if we could try it, the advantage will be the same. Suppose, then, that as we previously examined a variety of instances in which *a* occurred, and found them to agree in containing A, so we now observe a variety of instances in which *a* does not occur, and find them agree in not containing A; which establishes, by the

*c-c*MS, 43, 46   had
*d-d*MS, 43, 46   agreed in the single
*e-e*MS, 43   proof

Method of Agreement, the same connexion between the absence of A and the absence of *a*, which was before established between their presence. As, then, it had been shown that whenever A is present *a* is present, so it being now shown that when A is taken away *a* is removed along with it, we have by the one proposition A B C, *a b c*, by the other B C, *b c*, the positive and negative *ʲinstancesʲ* which the Method of Difference requires. *ᵍ*

This method may be called the Indirect Method of Difference, or the Joint Method of Agreement and Difference; and consists in a double employment of the Method of Agreement, each proof being independent of the other, and corroborating it. But it is not equivalent to a proof by the direct Method of Difference. For the requisitions of the Method of Difference are not satisfied, unless we can be quite sure either that the instances affirmative of *a*, agree in no antecedent whatever but A, or that the instances negative of *a* agree in nothing but the negation of A. Now if it were possible, which it never is, to have this assurance, we should not need the joint method; for either of the two sets of instances separately, would then be sufficient to prove causation. This indirect method, therefore, can only be ʰregardedʰ as a great extension and improvement of the Method of Agreement, but not as participating in the more cogent nature of the Method of Difference. The following may be stated as its canon:

THIRD CANON

If two or more instances in which the phenomenon occurs have only one circumstance in common, while two or more instances in which it does not occur have nothing in common save the absence of that circumstance; the circumstance in which alone the two sets of instances differ, is the effect, or ⁱtheⁱ cause, or ʲan indispensableʲ part of the cause, of the phenomenon.

We shall presently ᵏseeᵏ that the Joint Method of Agreement and Difference constitutes, in another respect not yet adverted to, an improvement upon the common Method of Agreement, namely, in being unaffected by a characteristic imperfection of that method, the nature of which still remains to be pointed out. But as we cannot enter into this exposition without introducing

---

*ʲ–ʲ*MS   instance
*ᵍ*MS, 43, 46   Thus, if it be true that all animals which have a well-developed respiratory system, and therefore aërate the blood perfectly, agree in being warm-blooded, while those whose respiratory system is imperfect, do not maintain a temperature much exceeding that of the surrounding medium, we may argue from this twofold experience, that the change which takes place in the blood by respiration is the cause of animal heat.
*ʰ–ʰ*MS, 43, 46   viewed
ⁱ–ⁱ+56, 62, 65, 68, 72
*ʲ–ʲ*MS, 43, 46, 51, 56   *a necessary*
*ᵏ–ᵏ*MS, 43   show

a new element of complexity into ¹this long and intricate discussion¹, I shall postpone it to ᵐa subsequentᵐ chapter, and shall at once proceed to ⁿaⁿ statement of two other methods, which will complete the enumeration of the means which mankind possess for exploring the laws of nature by specific observation and experience.

§ 5. [*Method of Residues*] The first of these has been aptly denominated the Method of Residues.[*] Its principle is very simple. Subducting from any given phenomenon all the portions which, by virtue of preceding inductions, can be assigned to known causes, the remainder will be the effect of the antecedents which had been overlooked, or of which the effect was as yet an unknown quantity.

Suppose, as before, that we have the antecedents A B C, followed by the consequents *a b c*, and that by previous inductions (founded, we will suppose, on the Method of Difference) we have ascertained the causes of some of these effects, or the effects of some of these causes; and are ᵃthenceᵃ apprised that the effect of A is *a*, and that the effect of B is *b*. Subtracting the sum of these effects from the total phenomenon, there remains *c*, which now, without any fresh ᵇexperimentsᵇ, we may know to be the effect of C. This Method of Residues is in truth a peculiar modification of the Method of Difference. If the instance A B C, *a b c*, could have been compared with a single instance A B, *a b*, we should have proved C to be the cause of *c*, by the common process of the Method of Difference. In the present case, however, instead of a single instance A B, we have had to study separately the causes A and B, and to infer from the effects which they produce separately, what effect they must produce in the case A B C where they act together. Of the two instances, therefore, which the Method of Difference requires,—the one positive, the other negative,—the negative one, or that in which the given phenomenon is absent, is not the direct result of observation and experiment, but has been arrived at by deduction. As one of the forms of the Method of Difference, the Method of Residues partakes of its rigorous certainty, provided the previous inductions, those which gave the effects of A and B, were obtained by the same infallible method, and provided we are certain that C is the *only* antecedent to which the residual phenomenon *c* can be referred; the only agent of which we had not already calculated and subducted the

[*See Whewell, *Novum Organon Renovatum*, p. 216. *JSM cancelled in* MS *a simple reference to Whewell.*]

ˡ⁻ˡMS   a discussion already, I fear, sufficiently fatiguing to the reader
ᵐ⁻ᵐMS, 43, 46   the next
ⁿ⁻ⁿMS, 43, 46, 51, 56   the
ᵃ⁻ᵃMS, 43, 46, 51   by this means
ᵇ⁻ᵇMS, 43, 46, 51, 56, 62   experiment

effect. But as we can never be quite certain of this, the evidence derived from the Method of Residues is not complete unless we can obtain C artificially and try it separately, or unless its agency, when once suggested, can be accounted for, and proved deductively, from known laws.

Even with these reservations, the Method of Residues is one of the most important among our instruments of discovery. Of all the methods of investigating laws of nature, this is the most fertile in unexpected results: often informing us of sequences in which neither the cause nor the effect were sufficiently conspicuous to attract of themselves the attention of observers. The agent C may be an obscure circumstance, not likely to have been perceived unless sought for, nor likely to have been sought for until attention had been awakened by the insufficiency of the obvious causes to account for the whole of the effect. And *c* may be so disguised by its intermixture with *a* and *b*, that it would scarcely have presented itself spontaneously as a subject of separate study. Of these uses of the method, we shall presently cite some remarkable examples. The canon of the Method of Residues is as follows:

FOURTH CANON

Subduct from any phenomenon such part as is known by previous inductions to be the effect of certain antecedents, and the residue of the phenomenon is the effect of the remaining antecedents.

§ 6. [*Method of Concomitant Variations*] There remains a class of laws which it is impracticable to ascertain by any of the three methods which *ª*I*ª* have attempted to characterize; namely, the laws of those Permanent Causes, or indestructible natural agents, which it is impossible either to exclude or to isolate; which we can neither hinder from being present, nor contrive that they shall be present alone. It would appear at first sight that we could by no means separate the effects of these agents from the effects of those other phenomena with which they cannot be prevented from coexisting. In respect, indeed, to most of the permanent causes, no such difficulty exists; since though we cannot eliminate them as coexisting facts, we can eliminate them as influencing agents, by simply trying our experiment in a local situation beyond the limits of their influence. The pendulum, for example, has its oscillations disturbed by the vicinity of a mountain: we remove the pendulum to a sufficient distance from the mountain, and the disturbance ceases: from these data we can determine by the Method of Difference, the amount of effect *ᵇ* due to the mountain; and beyond a certain distance everything goes on precisely as it would do if the mountain exercised no influence whatever, which, accordingly, we, with sufficient reason, conclude to be the fact.

*ª–ª*MS   we
*ᵇ*MS, 43, 46   really

The difficulty, therefore, in applying the methods already treated of to determine the effects of Permanent Causes, is confined to thc cases in which it is impossible for us to get out of the local limits of their influence. The pendulum can be removed from the influence of the mountain, but it cannot be removed from the influence of the earth: we cannot take away the earth from the pendulum, nor the pendulum from the earth, to ascertain whether it would continue to vibrate if the action which the earth exerts upon it were withdrawn. On what evidence, then, do we ascribe its vibrations to the earth's influence? Not on any sanctioned by the Method of Difference; for one of the two instances, the negative instance, is wanting. Nor by the Method of Agreement; for though all pendulums agree in this, that during their oscillations the earth is always present, why may we not as well ascribe the phenomenon to the sun, which is equally a coexistent fact in all the experiments? It is evident that to establish even so simple a fact of causation as this, there was required some method over and above those which we have yet examined.

As another example, let us take the phenomenon Heat. Independently of all hypothesis as to the real nature of the agency so called, this fact is certain, that we are unable to exhaust any body of the whole of its heat. It is equally certain, that no one ever perceived heat not emanating from a body. Being unable, then, to separate Body and Heat, we cannot effect such a variation of circumstances as the foregoing three methods require; we cannot ascertain, by those methods, what portion of the phenomena exhibited by any body ^{c}is^c due to the heat contained in it. If we could observe a body with its heat, and the same body entirely divested of heat, the Method of Difference would show the effect due to the heat, apart from that due to the body. If we could observe heat under circumstances agreeing in nothing but heat, and therefore not characterized also by the presence of a body, we could ascertain the effects of heat, from an instance of heat with a body and an instance of heat without a body, by the Method of Agreement; or ^{d} we could determine by the Method of Difference what effect was due to the body, when the remainder which was due to the heat would be given by the Method of Residues. But we can do ^{e}none^e of these things; and without them the application of any of the three methods to the solution of this problem would be illusory. It would be idle, for instance, to attempt to ascertain the effect of heat by subtracting from the phenomena exhibited by a body, all that is due to its other properties; for as we have never been able to observe any bodies without a portion of heat in them, ^{f} effects due to that heat ^{g}might^g form a part of

$^{v-v}$MS, 43, 46, 51, 56   are
^{d}MS, 43, 46   , if we pleased,
$^{e-e}$MS   neither
^{f}MS, 43, 46, 51, 56   the
$^{g-g}$MS, 43, 46   may

the very results, which we *were affecting* to subtract in order that the effect of heat *might* be shown by the residue.

If, therefore, there were no other methods of experimental investigation than these three, we should be *j* unable to determine the effects due to heat as a cause. But we have still a resource. Though we cannot exclude an antecedent altogether, we may be able to produce, or nature may produce for us, some modification in it. By a modification is here meant, a change in it, not amounting to its total removal. If some modification in the antecedent A is always followed by a change in the consequent *a*, the other consequents *b* and *c* remaining the same; or *vice versâ*, if every change in *a* is found to have been preceded by some modification in A, none being observable in any of the other antecedents; we may safely conclude that *a* is, wholly or in part, an effect traceable to A, or at least in some way connected with it through causation. For example, in the case of heat, though we cannot expel it altogether from any body, we can modify it in quantity, we can increase or diminish it; and doing so, we find by the various methods of experimentation or observation already treated of, that such increase or diminution of heat is followed by expansion or contraction of the body. In this manner we arrive at the conclusion, otherwise unattainable by us, that one of the effects of heat is to enlarge the dimensions of bodies; or what is the same thing in other words, to widen the distances between their particles.

A change in a thing, not amounting to its total removal, that is, a change which leaves it still the same thing it was, must be a change either in its quantity, or in some of its *variable* relations to other things, of which *variable* relations the principal is its position in space. In the previous example, the modification which was produced in the antecedent was an alteration in its quantity. Let us now suppose the question to be, what influence the moon exerts on the surface of the earth. We cannot try an experiment in the absence of the moon, so as to observe what terrestrial phenomena her annihilation would put an end to; but when we find that all the variations in the *position* of the moon are followed by corresponding variations in the time and place of high water, the place being always either *the part* of the earth which is nearest to, or *n* that which is most remote from, the moon, we have ample evidence that the moon is, wholly or partially, the cause which determines the tides. It very commonly happens, as it does in this instance, that the variations of an effect are correspondent, or analogous, to those of its cause; as the moon moves *farther* towards the east, the high water point does the same: but this is not an indispensable condition; as may be seen in

*h–h*MS, 43, 46   affect   *i–i*MS, 43, 46   may
*j*MS, 43, 46   for ever   *k–k*+62, 65, 68, 72
l–l+62, 65, 68, 72   *m–m*MS, 43, 46   on the side
*n*MS, 43, 46   on   *o–o*43, 46, 51   further [*printer's error?*]

the same example, for along with that high water point there is at the same instant another high water point diametrically opposite to it, and which, therefore, of necessity, moves towards the west, as the moon, followed by the nearer of the tide waves, advances towards the east: and yet both these motions are equally effects of the moon's motion.

That the oscillations of the pendulum are caused by the earth, is proved by similar evidence. Those oscillations take place between equidistant points on the two sides of a line, which, being perpendicular to the earth, varies with every variation in the earth's position, either in space or relatively to the object. Speaking accurately, we only know by the method now characterized, that all terrestrial bodies tend to the earth, and not to some unknown fixed point lying in the same direction. In every twenty-four hours, by the earth's rotation, the line drawn from the body at right angles to the earth coincides successively with all the radii of a circle, and in the course of six months the place of that circle varies by nearly two hundred millions of miles; yet in all these changes of the earth's position, the line in which bodies tend to fall continues to be directed towards it: which proves that terrestrial gravity is directed to the earth, and not, as was once fancied by some, to a fixed point of space.

The method by which these results were obtained, may be termed the Method of Concomitant Variations: it is regulated by the following canon:

FIFTH CANON
Whatever phenomenon varies in any manner whenever another pheno-menon varies in some particular manner, is either a cause or an effect of that phenomenon, or is connected with it through some fact of causation.

The last clause is subjoined, because it by no means follows when two phenomena accompany each other in their variations, that the one is cause and the other effect. The same thing may, and indeed must happen, supposing them to be two different effects of a common cause: and by this method alone it would never be possible to ascertain which of the *ᵖ* suppositions is the true one. The only way to solve the doubt would be that which we have so often adverted to, viz. by endeavouring to ascertain whether we can produce the one set of variations by means of the other. In the case of heat, for example, by increasing the temperature of a body we increase its bulk, but by increasing its bulk we do not increase its temperature; on the contrary, (as in the rare-faction of air under the receiver of an air-pump,) we generally diminish it: therefore heat is not an effect, but a cause, of increase of bulk. If we cannot ourselves produce the variations, we must endeavour, though it is an attempt

ᵖMS, 43, 46   two

which is seldom successful, to find them produced by nature in some case in which the pre-existing circumstances are perfectly known to us.

It is scarcely necessary to say, that in order to ascertain the uniform concomitance of variations in the effect with variations in the cause, the same precautions must be used as in any other case of the determination of an invariable sequence. We must endeavour to retain all the other antecedents unchanged, while that particular one is subjected to the requisite series of variations; or in other words, that we may be warranted in inferring causation from concomitance of variations, the concomitance itself must be proved by the Method of Difference.

It might at first appear that the Method of Concomitant Variations assumes a new axiom, or law of causation in general, namely, that every modification of the cause is followed by a change in the effect. And it does usually happen that when a phenomenon A causes a phenomenon *a*, any variation in the quantity or in the various relations of A, is uniformly followed by a variation in the quantity or relations of *a*. To take a familiar instance, that of gravitation. The sun causes a certain tendency to motion in the earth; here we have cause and effect; but that tendency is *towards* the sun, and therefore varies in direction as the sun varies in the relation of position; and moreover the tendency varies in intensity, in a certain numerical qcorrespondenceq to the sun's distance from the earth, that is, according to another relation of the sun. Thus we see that there is not only an invariable connexion between the sun and the earth's gravitation, but that two of the relations of the sun, its position with respect to the earth and its distance from the earth, are invariably connected as antecedents with the quantity and direction of the earth's gravitation. The cause of the earth's gravitating at all, is simply the sun; but the cause of ritsr gravitating with a given intensity and in a given direction, is the existence of the sun in a given direction and at a given distance. It is not strange that a modified cause, which is in truth a different cause, should produce a different effect. [s]

Although it is for the most part true that a modification of the cause is followed by a modification of the effect, the Method of Concomitant Variations does not, however, presuppose this as an axiom. It only requires the converse proposition; that anything on whose modifications, modifications of an effect are invariably consequent, must be the cause (or connected with the cause) of that effect; a proposition, the truth of which is evident; for if the thing itself had no influence on the effect, neither could the modifications of the thing have any influence. If the stars have no power over the fortunes

q–qMS, 43, 46, 51   ratio
r–rMS, 43, 46   her
[s]MS, 43   But as the cause is only different in its quantity, or in some of its relations, it usually happens that the effect also is only changed in its quantity or its relations.

of *mankind*, it is implied in the very terms, that the conjunctions or oppositions of different stars can have no such power.

Although the most striking applications of the Method of Concomitant Variations take place in the cases in which the Method of Difference, strictly so called, is impossible, its use is not confined to those cases; it may often usefully follow after the Method of Difference, to give additional precision to a solution which that has *found*. When by the Method of Difference it has first been ascertained that a certain object produces a certain effect, the Method of Concomitant Variations may be usefully called in, to determine according to what law the quantity or the different relations of the effect follow those of the cause.

§ 7. [*Limitations of the Method of Concomitant Variations*] The case in which this method admits of the most extensive employment, is that in which the variations of the cause are variations of quantity. Of such variations we may in general affirm with safety, that they will be attended not only with variations, but with similar variations, of the effect: the proposition, that more of the cause is followed by more of the effect, being a corollary from the principle of the Composition of Causes, which, as we have seen, is the general rule of causation; cases of the opposite description, in which causes change their properties on being conjoined with one another, being, on the contrary, special and exceptional. Suppose, then, that when A changes in quantity, *a* also changes in quantity, and in such a manner that we can trace the numerical relation which the changes of the one bear to such changes of the other as take place within our limits of observation. We may then, with certain precautions, safely conclude that the same numerical relation will hold beyond those limits. If, for instance, we find that when A is double, *a* is double; that when A is treble or quadruple, *a* is treble or quadruple; we may conclude that if A were a half or a third, *a* would be a half or a third, and finally, that if A were annihilated, *a* would be annihilated; and that *a* is wholly the effect of A, or wholly the effect of the same cause with A. And so with any other numerical relation according to which A and *a* would vanish simultaneously; as, for instance, if *a* were proportional to the square of A. If, on the other hand, *a* is not wholly the effect of A, but yet varies when A varies, it is probably *a mathematical* function not of A alone, but of A and *something else*: its changes *, for example, may* be such as would occur if part of it remained constant, or varied on some other principle, and the remainder varied in some numerical relation to the variations of A. In that

*t–t*MS, 43, 46   men
*u–u*MS   given
*a–a*MS, 43, 46   (to use a mathematical phrase) a
*b–b*MS   some other quantity
*c–c*MS, 43, 46   will

case, when A diminishes, a will ᵈbe seenᵈ to approach not towards zero, but towards some other limit: and when the series of variations is such as to indicate what that limit is, if constant, or the law of its variation if variable, the limit will exactly measure how much of a is the effect of some other and independent cause, and the remainder will be the effect of A (or of the cause of A).

These conclusions, however, must not be drawn without certain precautions. In the first place, the possibility of drawing them at all, manifestly supposes that we are acquainted not only with the variations, but with the absolute quantities both of A and a. If we do not know the total quantities, we cannot, of course, determine the real numerical relation according to which those quantities vary. It is therefore an error to conclude, as some have concluded, that because increase of heat expands bodies, that is, increases the distance between their particles, therefore ᵉtheᵉ distance is wholly the effect of heat, and that if we could entirely exhaust the body of its heat, the particles would be in complete contact. This ᶠis noᶠ more than a guess, and of the most hazardous sort, not a legitimate induction: for since we neither know how much heat there is in any body, nor what is the real distance between any two of its particles, we cannot judge whether the contraction of the distance does or does not follow the diminution of the quantity of heat according to such a numerical relation that the two quantities would vanish simultaneously.

In contrast with this, let us consider a case in which the absolute quantities are known; the case contemplated in the first law of motion; viz. that all bodies in motion continue to move in a straight line with uniform velocity until acted upon by some new force. This assertion is in open opposition to first appearances; all terrestrial objects, when in motion, gradually abate their velocity and at last stop; which accordingly the ancients, with their *inductio per enumerationem simplicem*, imagined to be the law. Every moving body, however, encounters various obstacles, as friction, the resistance of the atmosphere, &c., which we know by daily experience to be causes capable of destroying motion. It was suggested that the whole of the retardation might be owing to these causes. How was this inquired into? If the obstacles could have been entirely removed, the case would have been amenable to the Method of Difference. They could not be removed, they could only be diminished, and the case, therefore, admitted only of the Method of Concomitant Variations. This accordingly being employed, it was found that every diminution of the obstacles diminished the retardation of the motion: and inasmuch as in this case (unlike the case of heat) the total quantities

d–ᵈMS, 43, 46, 51   seem
e–ᵉMS, 43   that
f–ᶠMS, 43, 46   can never be

both of the antecedent and of the consequent were known; it was practicable to estimate, with an approach to accuracy, both the amount of the retardation and the amount of the retarding causes, or resistances, and to judge how near they both were to being exhausted; and it appeared that the effect dwindled as rapidly, and at each step was as far on the road towards annihilation, as the cause was. The simple oscillation of a weight suspended from a fixed point, and moved a little out of the perpendicular, which in ordinary circumstances lasts but a few minutes, was prolonged in Borda's experiments to more than thirty hours, by diminishing as much as possible the friction at the point of suspension, and by making the body oscillate in a space exhausted as nearly as possible of its air. There could therefore be no hesitation in assigning the whole of the retardation of motion to the influence of the obstacles; and since, after subducting this retardation from the total phenomenon, the remainder was an uniform velocity, the result was *g*the proposition known as*g* the first law of motion.

There is also another characteristic uncertainty affecting the inference that the law of variation which the quantities observe within our limits of observation, will hold beyond those limits. There is of course, in the first instance, the possibility that beyond the limits, and in circumstances therefore of which we have no direct experience, some counteracting cause might develop itself; either a new agent, or a new property of the agents concerned, which lies dormant in the circumstances we are able to observe. This is an element of uncertainty which enters largely into all our predictions of effects; but it is not peculiarly applicable to the Method of Concomitant Variations. The uncertainty, however, of which I am about to speak, is characteristic of that method; especially in the cases in which the extreme limits of our *h*observation*h* are very narrow, in comparison with the possible variations in the quantities of the phenomena. Any one who has the slightest acquaintance with mathematics, is aware that very different laws of variation may produce numerical results which differ but slightly from one another within narrow limits; and it is often only when the absolute amounts of variation are considerable, that the difference between the results given by one law and by another becomes appreciable. When, therefore, such variations in the quantity of the antecedents as we have the means of observing, are *i* small in comparison with the total quantities, there is much danger lest we should mistake the numerical law, and be led *j* to miscalculate the variations which would take place beyond the limits; a miscalculation which would vitiate any conclusion respecting the dependence of the effect upon the cause, *k*that*k* could

g–g+43, 46, 51, 56, 62, 65, 68, 72
*h–h*MS   observations
*i*MS, 43, 46   but
*j*MS, 43, 46   quite
*k–k*MS, 43   which

be founded on those variations. Examples are not wanting of such mistakes. "The formulæ," says Sir John Herschel,* "which have been empirically deduced for the elasticity of steam, (till very recently,) and those for the resistance of fluids, and other similar subjects," when relied on beyond the limits of the observations from which they were deduced, "have almost invariably failed to support the theoretical structures which have been erected on them."

ᶦInᶦ this uncertainty, the conclusion we may draw from the concomitant variations of a and A, to the existence of an invariable and exclusive connexion between them, or to the permanency of the same numerical relation between their variations when the quantities are much greater or smaller than those which we have had the means of observing, cannot be considered to rest on a complete induction. All that in such a case can be regarded as proved on the subject of causation is, that there is some connexion between the two phenomena; that A, or something which can influence A, must be *one* of the causes which collectively determine a. We may, however, feel assured that the relation which we have observed to exist between the variations of A and a, will hold true in all cases which fall between the same extreme limits; that is, wherever the utmost increase or diminution in which the result has been found by observation to coincide with the law, is not exceeded.

The four methods which it has now been attempted to describe, are the only possible modes of experimental inquiry—of direct induction *à posteriori*, as distinguished from deduction: at least, I know not, nor am able to ᵐimagineᵐ, any others. And even of these, the Method of Residues, as we have seen, is not independent of deduction; though, as it ⁿalsoⁿ requires specific experience ᵒ, it may, without impropriety, be included among methods of direct observation and experiment.

These, then, with such assistance as can be obtained from Deduction, compose the available resources of the human mind for ascertaining the laws of the succession of phenomena. Before proceeding to point out certain circumstances, by which the employment of these methods is subjected to an immense increase of complication and of difficulty, it is expedient to illustrate the use of the methods, by suitable examples drawn from actual physical investigations. These, accordingly, will form the subject of the succeeding chapter.

*Discourse on the Study of Natural Philosophy, p. 179.

ᶦ⁻ᶦMS, 43   Under
ᵐ⁻ᵐMS, 43, 46   conceive
ⁿ⁻ⁿ+51, 56, 62, 65, 68, 72
ᵒMS, 43, 46   in addition

CHAPTER IX

Miscellaneous Examples of the Four Methods

§ 1. [*Liebig's theory of metallic poisons*] I shall select, as ^{a}a^a first example, an interesting speculation of one of the most eminent ^{b}of theoretical chemists, Baron^b Liebig.[*] The object in view, is to ascertain the immediate cause of the death produced by metallic poisons.

^{c} Arsenious acid, and the salts of lead, bismuth, copper, and mercury, if introduced into the animal organism, except in the smallest doses, destroy life. These facts have long been known, as insulated truths of the lowest order of generalization; but it was reserved for Liebig, by an apt employment of the first two of our methods of experimental inquiry, to connect these truths together by a higher induction, pointing out what property, common to all these deleterious substances, is the really operating cause of their fatal effect.

When solutions of these substances are placed in sufficiently close contact with many animal products, albumen, milk, muscular fibre, and animal membranes, the acid or salt leaves the water in which it was dissolved, and enters into combination with the animal substance: which substance, ^{d}after^d being thus acted upon, is found to have lost its tendency to spontaneous decomposition, or putrefaction.

Observation also shows, in cases where death has been produced by these poisons, that the parts of the body with which the poisonous substances have been brought into contact, do not afterwards putrefy.

And, finally, when the poison has been supplied in too small a quantity to destroy life, eschars are produced, that is, certain superficial portions of the tissues are destroyed, which are afterwards thrown off by the reparative process taking place in the healthy parts.

These three sets of instances admit of being treated according to the

[**Organic Chemistry*, pp. 335ff.]

$^{a-a}$MS, 43, 46   my
$^{b-b}$MS, 43, 46   theoretical chemists of the present or any age, Dr.]   51, 56, 62   *as*
72 . . . chemists, Professor
^{c}MS   [*no paragraph*]
$^{d-d}$+43, 46, 51, 56, 62, 65, 68, 72

Method of Agreement. In all of them the metallic compounds are brought into contact with the substances which compose the human or animal body; and the instances do not seem to agree in any other circumstance. The remaining antecedents are as different, and even opposite, as they could possibly be made; for in some the animal substances exposed to the action of the poisons are in a state of life, in others only in a state of organization, in others not even in that. And what is the result which follows in all the cases? The conversion of the animal substance (by combination with the poison) into a chemical compound, held together by so powerful a force as to resist the subsequent action of the ordinary causes of decomposition. Now, organic life (the necessary condition of sensitive life) consisting in a continual state of decomposition and recomposition of the different organs and tissues; whatever incapacitates them for this decomposition destroys life. And thus the proximate cause of the death produced by this description of poisons, is ascertained, as far as the Method of Agreement can ascertain it.

Let us now bring our conclusion to the test of the Method of Difference. Setting out from the cases already mentioned, in which the antecedent is the presence of substances forming with the tissues a compound incapable of putrefaction, (and à fortiori incapable of the chemical actions which constitute life,) and the consequent is death, either of the whole organism, or of some portion of it; let us compare with these cases other cases, as much resembling them as possible, but in which that effect is not produced. And, first *e* , "many insoluble basic salts of arsenious acid are known not to be poisonous. The substance called alkargen, discovered by Bunsen, which contains a very large quantity of arsenic, and approaches very closely in composition to the organic arsenious compounds found in the body, has not the slightest injurious action upon the organism."[*] Now when these substances are brought into contact with the tissues in any way, they do not combine with them; they do not arrest their progress to decomposition. As far, therefore, as these instances go, it appears that when the effect is absent, it is by reason of the absence of that antecedent which we had already good ground for considering as the proximate cause.

But the rigorous conditions of the Method of Difference are not yet satisfied; for we cannot be sure that these unpoisonous bodies agree with the poisonous substances in every property, except the particular one, of entering into a difficultly decomposable compound with the animal tissues. To render the method strictly applicable, we need an instance, not of a different substance, but of one of the very same substances, *f*in*f* circumstances which would prevent it from forming, with the tissues, the sort of compound in

[*Ibid., p. 338.]

*e*MS, 43, 46   of all   *f–f*MS, 43, 46   under question; and then, if death does not follow, our case is made out. Now such instances are afforded by the antidotes to these poisons. For example, in case of poisoning by arsenious acid, if hydrated peroxide of iron is administered, the destructive agency is instantly checked. Now this peroxide is known to combine with the acid, and form a compound, which, being insoluble, cannot act at all on animal tissues. So, again, sugar is a well-known antidote to poisoning by salts of copper; and sugar reduces those salts either into metallic copper, or into the red suboxide, neither of which enters into combination with animal matter. The disease called painter's colic, so common in manufactories of white lead, is unknown where the workmen are accustomed to take, as a preservative, sulphuric acid lemonade (a solution of sugar rendered acid by sulphuric acid). Now diluted sulphuric acid has the property of decomposing all compounds of lead with organic matter, *or* of preventing them from being formed.

There is another class of instances, of the nature required by the Method of *Difference*, which seem at first sight to conflict with the theory. Soluble salts of silver, such for instance as the nitrate, have the same stiffening antiseptic effect on decomposing animal substances, as corrosive sublimate and the most deadly metallic poisons; and when applied to the external parts of the body, the nitrate is a powerful caustic, depriving those parts of all active vitality, and causing them to be thrown off by the neighbouring living structures, in the form of an eschar. The nitrate and the other salts of silver ought, then, it would seem, if the theory be correct, to be poisonous; yet they may be administered internally with perfect impunity. From this apparent exception arises the strongest confirmation which *the theory* has yet received. Nitrate of silver, in spite of its chemical properties, does not poison when introduced into the stomach; but in the stomach, as in all animal liquids, there is common salt; and in the stomach there is also free muriatic acid. These substances operate as natural antidotes, combining with the nitrate, and if its quantity is not too great, immediately converting it into chloride of silver; a substance very slightly soluble, and therefore incapable of combining with the tissues, although to the extent of its solubility it has a medicinal influence, through an entirely different class of organic actions.

*The preceding instances have afforded an induction of a high order of conclusiveness, illustrative of the two simplest of our four methods; though not rising to the maximum of certainty which the Method of Difference, in its most perfect exemplification, is capable of affording. For (let us not forget) the positive instance and the negative one which the rigour of that

*g–g*MS, 43, 46   and (of course)
*h–h*MS   Differences
*i–i*MS, 43   this theory of Liebig
*j*MS, 43, 46   §2. [—*how far a perfect example*]

method requires, ought to differ only in the presence or absence of one single circumstance. Now, in the preceding argument, they differ in the presence or absence not of a single *circumstance*, but of a single *substance*: and as every substance has innumerable properties, there is no knowing what number of real differences are involved in what is nominally and apparently only one difference. It is conceivable that the antidote, the peroxide of iron for example, may counteract the poison through some other of its properties than that of forming an insoluble compound with it; and if so, the theory would fall to the ground, so far as it is supported by that instance. This source of uncertainty, which is a serious hindrance to all extensive generalizations in chemistry, is however reduced in the present case to almost the lowest degree possible, when we find that not only one substance, but many substances, possess the capacity of acting as antidotes to metallic poisons, and that all these agree in the property of forming insoluble compounds with the poisons, while they cannot be ascertained to agree in any other property whatsoever. We have thus, in favour of the theory, all the evidence which can be obtained by what we termed the Indirect Method of Difference, or the Joint Method of Agreement and Difference; the evidence of which, though it never can amount to that of the Method of Difference properly so called, may approach indefinitely near to it. [k]

[a]§ 2.[a] [*Theory of induced electricity* [b]] Let the object be* to ascertain the law of what is termed *induced* electricity; to find under what conditions any electrified body, whether positively or negatively electrified, gives rise to a contrary electric state in some other body adjacent to it.

*[51] For this speculation [c], as for many other of my scientific illustrations,[c] I am indebted to [d]Professor Bain, whose subsequent treatise on Logic abounds with apt illustrations of all the inductive methods[d].

[k]MS [*paragraph*] No similar defect of completeness in proof will be found in the following original investigation, for which I am indebted to Mr. Alexander Bain, at present Lecturer on Moral Philosophy in Marischal College in Aberdeen; one of the men from whom science and philosophy have most to hope, and who has permitted me to lay his extensive knowledge of every department of physical inquiry freely under contribution, for the purpose of exemplifying and illustrating the doctrines of this work.] 43, 46 *as* MS . . . College, Aberdeen . . . *as* MS [*cf. footnote above, added in* 51]

    [a–a]MS, 43, 46 §3.   [b]MS   , *by Mr. Alexander Bain*

    [c–c]+65, 68, 72

    [d–d]51 Mr. Alexander Bain] 56 Mr. Alexander Bain, who has since, in his treatise entitled *The Senses and the Intellect*, carried the analytic investigation of the mental phenomena according to the methods of physical science, to the most advanced point which it has yet reached, and has worthily inscribed his name among the successive constructors of an edifice to which Hartley, Brown, and James Mill had each contributed their part] 62, 65, 68 Professor Bain, of Aberdeen, who has since, in his profound treatises entitled *The Senses and the Intellect*, and *The Emotions and the Will*, carried . . . *as* 56

The most familiar exemplification of the phenomenon to be investigated is the following. Around the prime conductors of an electrical machine, the atmosphere to some distance, or any conducting surface suspended in that atmosphere, is found to be in an electric condition opposite to that of the prime conductor itself. Near and around the positive prime conductor there is negative electricity, and near and around the negative prime conductor there is positive electricity. When pith balls are brought near to either of the conductors, they become electrified with the opposite electricity to it; either receiving a share from the already electrified atmosphere by conduction, or acted upon by the direct inductive influence of the conductor itself: they are then attracted by the conductor to which they are in opposition; or, if withdrawn in their electrified state, they will be attracted by any other oppositely charged body. In like manner the hand, if brought near enough to the conductor, receives or gives an electric discharge; now we have no evidence that a charged conductor can be suddenly discharged unless by the approach of a body oppositely electrified. In the case, therefore, of the ^{e}electric^e machine, it appears that the accumulation of electricity in an insulated conductor is always accompanied by the excitement of the contrary electricity in the surrounding atmosphere, and in every conductor placed near the former conductor. It does not seem possible, in this case, to produce one electricity by itself.

Let us now examine all the other instances which we can obtain, resembling this instance in the given consequent, namely, the evolution of an opposite electricity in the neighbourhood of an electrified body. As one remarkable instance we have the Leyden jar; and after the splendid experiments of Faraday in complete and final establishment of the substantial identity of magnetism and electricity, we may cite the magnet, both the natural and the electro-magnet, in neither of which ^{f}it is^f possible to produce one kind of electricity by itself, or to charge one pole without charging an opposite pole with the contrary electricity at the same time. We cannot have a magnet with one pole: if we break a natural loadstone into a thousand pieces, each piece will have its two oppositely electrified poles complete within itself. In the voltaic circuit ^{g}, again,^{g} we cannot have one current without its opposite. In the ordinary electric machine, the glass cylinder or plate, and the rubber, acquire opposite electricities.

From all these instances, treated by the Method of Agreement, a general law appears to result. The instances embrace all the known modes in which a body can become charged with electricity; and in all of them there is found, as a concomitant or consequent, the excitement of the opposite electric state

$e-e$MS, 43, 46, 51, 56 electrical
$f-f$MS, 43, 46, 51 is it
$g-g+$43, 46, 51, 56, 62, 65, 68, 72

in some other body or bodies. It seems to follow that the two facts are invariably connected, and that the excitement of electricity in any body has for one of its necessary conditions the possibility of a simultaneous excitement of the opposite electricity in some neighbouring body.

[h]As the two contrary electricities can only be produced together, so they can only cease together. This may be shown by an application of the Method of Difference to the example of the Leyden jar. It needs scarcely be here remarked that in[h] the Leyden jar, electricity can be accumulated and retained in considerable quantity, by the contrivance of having two conducting surfaces of equal extent, and parallel to each other through the whole of that extent, with a non-conducting substance such as glass between them. When one side of the jar is charged positively, the other is charged negatively, and it was by virtue of this fact that the Leyden jar served just now as an instance in our employment of the Method of Agreement. [i]Now it is impossible to discharge one of the coatings unless the other can be discharged at the same time. A conductor held to the positive side cannot convey away any electricity unless an equal quantity be allowed to pass from the negative side: if one coating be perfectly insulated, the charge is safe. The dissipation of one must proceed[i] *pari passu* with [j]that of[j] the other. [k]

[l]The law thus strongly indicated admits of corroboration[l] by the Method of Concomitant Variations. The Leyden jar is capable of receiving a much higher charge than can ordinarily be given to the conductor of an electrical machine. Now in the case of the Leyden jar, the metallic surface which receives the induced electricity is a conductor exactly similar to that which receives the primary charge, and is therefore as susceptible of receiving and retaining the one electricity, as the opposite surface of receiving and retaining the other; but in the machine, the neighbouring body which is to be oppositely electrified is the surrounding atmosphere, or any body casually brought near to the conductor; and as these are generally much inferior in their capacity of becoming electrified, to the conductor itself, their limited power imposes a corresponding limit to the capacity of the conductor for being charged. As the capacity of the neighbouring body for supporting the opposition in-

[h-h]MS   This law, suggested by the Method of Agreement, will be found on a minuter examination of the example of the Leyden jar, to have the sanction also of the Method of Difference. In

[i-i]MS   [*paragraph*] But the instance goes much further; for if the negative charging is not permitted; if the negative electricity is carried off as fast as it is produced, the positive charge on the neighbouring surface cannot proceed; the one must take place

[j-j]+51, 56, 62, 65, 68, 72

[k]MS   This is a clear case under the Method of Difference. We had first the one circumstance always accompanied by the other; we now have the former circumstance removed & the other thereby prevented. There seems therefore to be conclusive indication of a general law, that there can be no electric excitement unless an opposite excitement in a neighbouring body is possible.

[l-l]MS   A comparison of instances will afford a corroboration of this law,

creases, a higher charge becomes possible: and to this appears to be owing the great superiority of the Leyden jar.

A further and most decisive confirmation by the Method of Difference, is to be found in one of Faraday's experiments in the course of his researches on the subject of Induced Electricity.[*]

Since common or machine electricity, and voltaic electricity, may be considered for the present purpose to be identical, Faraday wished to know whether, as the prime conductor developes opposite electricity upon a conductor in its vicinity, so a voltaic current running along a wire would induce an opposite current upon another wire laid parallel to it at a short distance. Now this case is similar to the cases previously examined, in every circumstance except the one to which we have ascribed the effect. We found in the former instances that whenever electricity of one kind was excited in one body, electricity of the opposite kind must be excited in a neighbouring body [m]. But in Faraday's experiment this indispensable opposition exists within the wire itself. From the nature of a voltaic charge, the two opposite currents necessary to the existence of each other are both accommodated in one wire; and there is no need of another wire placed beside it to contain one of them, in the same way as the Leyden jar must have a positive and a negative surface. The exciting cause can and does produce all the effect which its laws require, independently of any electric excitement of a neighbouring body. Now the result of [n]the[n] experiment with the second wire was, that no opposite current was produced. There was an instantaneous effect at the closing and breaking of the voltaic circuit; electric inductions appeared when the two wires were moved to and from one another; but these are phenomena of a different class. There was no induced electricity in the sense in which this is predicated of the Leyden jar; there was no sustained current running up the one wire while an opposite current ran down the neighbouring wire; and this alone would have been a true parallel case to the other.

It thus appears by the combined evidence of the Method of Agreement, the Method of Concomitant Variations, and the most rigorous form of the Method of Difference, that neither of the two kinds of electricity can be excited without an equal excitement of the other and opposite kind: that both are effects of the same cause; that the possibility of the one is a condition of the possibility of the other, and the quantity of the one an impassable limit to the quantity of the other. A scientific result of considerable interest in

[*See Michael Faraday. *Experimental Researches in Electricity.* London: Taylor, 1839, Series 1, §1.]

[m]MS, 43   ; and the interpretation of this, in the language of cause and effect, is, that all causes which can excite the one kind of electricity, have the property of simultaneously exciting an equal amount of the other
[n–n]MS, 43   Faraday's

itself, and illustrating those three methods in a manner both characteristic and easily intelligible.*

^a§ 3.^a [*Wells' theory of dew*] Our third example shall be extracted from Sir John Herschel's *Discourse on the Study of Natural Philosophy*, a work replete with ^bhappily-selected^b exemplifications of inductive processes from almost every department of physical science, and in which alone, of all books which I have met with, the four methods of induction are ^cdistinctly recognised, though not so clearly characterized and defined, nor their correlation so fully shown,^c as has appeared to me desirable. The present example is ^d described by Sir John Herschel as "one of the most beautiful specimens" which can be cited "of inductive experimental inquiry lying within a moderate compass;"[*] the theory of dew, first promulgated by the late Dr. Wells,[†] and now universally adopted by scientific ^eauthorities^e. ^f The passages in inverted commas are extracted verbatim from ^gthe *Discourse*.†^g

"Suppose *dew* were the phenomenon proposed, whose cause we would know. In the first place" we must determine precisely what we mean by dew: what the fact really is, whose cause we desire to investigate. "We must separate dew from rain, and the moisture of fogs, and limit the application

---

*[51] This view of the necessary coexistence of opposite excitements involves a great extension of the original doctrine of two electricities. The early theorists assumed that, when amber was rubbed, the amber was made positive and the rubber negative to the same degree; but it never occurred to them to suppose that the existence of the amber charge was dependent on an opposite charge in the bodies with which the amber was contiguous, while the existence of the negative charge on the rubber was equally dependent on a contrary state of the surfaces that might accidentally be confronted with it; that, in fact, in a case of electrical excitement by friction, four charges were the minimum that could exist. But this double electrical action is essentially implied in the explanation now universally adopted in regard to the phenomena of the common electric machine.
[*Discourse*, p. 163.]
[†See William Charles Wells. *An Essay on Dew, and Several Appearances connected with it*. London: Taylor and Hessey, 1814.]
†*Discourse*, pp. 159–62.

^{a–a}MS, 43, 46   §4.
^{b–b}MS, 43   admirably-selected
^{c–c}MS, 43   recognised, although not characterised and defined, nor their correlation shown, so distinctly
^dMS, 43, 46   justly
^{e–e}MS, 43   men
^f43, 46   [*paragraph*] [*printer's error?*]
^{g–g}MS, 43   Sir John Herschel*, but to those who possess his work I would strongly recommend to read the entire passage in the original, and fully possess themselves of the purport of the speculation as a whole, before applying themselves, with me, to the logical analysis of the different steps of the argument.]   46   the *Discourse*,* but . . . *as* MS . . . possess that work . . . *as* MS . . . entire discussion in . . . *as* MS . . . fully impress themselves with the . . . *as* MS

of the term to what is really meant, which is the spontaneous appearance of moisture on substances exposed in the open air when no rain or *visible* wet is falling." This answers to a preliminary operation which will be characterized in the ensuing book, treating of operations subsidiary to induction.* [h]

"Now, here we have analogous phenomena in the moisture which bedews a cold metal or stone when we breathe upon it; that which appears on a glass of water fresh from the well in hot weather; that which appears on the inside of windows when sudden rain or hail chills the external air; that which runs down our walls when, after a long frost, a warm moist thaw comes on." Comparing these cases, we find that they all contain the phenomenon which was proposed as the subject of investigation. Now "all these instances agree in one point, the coldness of the object dewed, in comparison with the air in contact with it." But there still remains the most important case of all, that of nocturnal dew: does the same circumstance exist in this case? "Is it a fact that the object dewed *is* colder than the air? Certainly not, one would at first be inclined to say; for what is to *make* it so? But . . . the experiment is easy: we have only to lay a thermometer in contact with the dewed substance, and hang one at a little distance above it, out of reach of its influence. The experiment has been therefore made, the question has been asked, and the answer has been invariably in the affirmative. Whenever an object contracts dew, it *is* colder than the air."

Here then is a complete application of the Method of Agreement, establishing the fact of an invariable connexion between the deposition of dew on a surface, and the coldness of that surface compared with the external air. But which of these is cause, and which effect? or are they both effects of something else? On this subject the Method of Agreement can afford us no light: we must call in a more potent method. [i]"We must[i] collect more facts, or, which comes to the same thing, vary the circumstances; since every instance in which the circumstances differ is a fresh fact: and especially, we must note the contrary or negative cases, *i.e.* where no dew is produced:" [j] a comparison between instances of dew and instances of no dew, [k]being[k] the condition necessary to bring the Method of Difference into play.

"Now, first, no dew is produced on the surface of polished metals, but it *is* very copiously on glass, both exposed with their faces upwards, and in some

---

*Infra, Bk. IV, Chap. ii, On Abstraction.

[h]MS, 43, 46, 51, 56, 62   The state of the question being fixed, we come to the solution.
[i] [i]MS, 43, 46 [*paragraph*] "That dews are accompanied with a chill is a common remark; but vulgar prejudice would make the cold the effect rather than the cause. We must therefore
[j]MS, 43, 46 for we are aware that]   51   for
[k–k]MS, 43, 46, 51   is

cases the under side of a horizontal plate of glass is also dewed." [1] Here is an instance in which the effect is produced, and another instance in which it is not produced; but we cannot yet pronounce, as the canon of the Method of Difference requires, that the latter instance agrees with the former in all its circumstances except one; for the differences between glass and polished metals are manifold, and the only thing we can as yet be sure of is, that the cause of dew will be found among the circumstances by which the former substance is distinguished from the latter. But if we could be sure that glass, and the various other substances on which dew is deposited, have only one quality in common, and that polished metals and the other substances on which dew is not deposited have also nothing in common but *the one circumstance,* of not having the one quality which the others have; the requisitions of the Method of Difference would be completely satisfied, and we should recognise, in that quality of the substances, the cause of dew. This, accordingly, is the path of inquiry which is next to be pursued.

"In the cases of polished metal and polished glass, the contrast shows evidently that the *substance* has much to do with the phenomenon; therefore let the substance *alone* be diversified as much as possible, by exposing polished surfaces of various kinds. This done, a *scale of intensity* becomes obvious. Those polished substances are found to be most strongly dewed which conduct heat worst; while those which conduct well, resist dew most effectually." The complication increases; here is the Method of Concomitant Variations called to our assistance; and no other method was practicable on this occasion; for the quality of conducting heat could not be excluded, since all substances conduct heat in some degree. The conclusion obtained is, that *cæteris paribus* the deposition of dew is in some proportion to the power which the body possesses of resisting the passage of heat; and that this, therefore, (or something connected with this,) must be at least one of the causes which assist in producing the deposition of dew on the surface.

"But if we expose rough surfaces instead of polished, we sometimes find this law interfered with. Thus, roughened iron, especially if painted over or blackened, becomes dewed sooner than varnished paper; the kind of *surface,* therefore, has a great influence. Expose, then, the *same* material in very diversified states as to surface," (that is, employ the Method of Difference to ascertain concomitance of variations,) "and another scale of intensity be-

---

[1]MS, 43 [*footnote:*] *This last circumstance (adds Sir John Herschel) "excludes the *fall* of moisture from the sky in an invisible form, which would naturally suggest itself as a cause." I have omitted this passage in the text, as not pertinent to the purpose in hand, the argument which it contains being deductive and *à priori.* The fall of moisture is rejected as a cause, because from its laws previously known, we infer that it *could* not have produced the particular phenomenon last mentioned.] 46   *This last circumstance "excludes . . . *as* MS
*m–m*MS   one circumstance, that

comes at once apparent; those *surfaces* which *part with their heat* most readily by radiation, are found to contract dew most copiously." Here, therefore, are the requisites for a second employment of the Method of Concomitant Variations; which in this case also is the only method available, since all substances radiate heat in some degree or other. The conclusion obtained by this new application of the method is, that *cæteris paribus* the deposition of dew is also in some proportion to the power of radiating heat; and that the quality of doing this abundantly (or some cause on which that quality depends) is another of the causes which promote the deposition of dew on the substance.

"Again, the influence ascertained to exist of *substance* and *surface* leads us to consider that of *texture*: and here, again, we are presented on trial with remarkable differences, and with a third scale of intensity, pointing out substances of a close firm texture, such as stones, metals, &c., as unfavourable, but those of a loose one, as cloth, "velvet, wool," eider-down, cotton, &c., as eminently favourable to the contraction of dew." The Method of Concomitant Variations is here, for the third time, had recourse to; and, as before, from necessity, since the texture of no substance is absolutely firm or absolutely loose. Looseness of texture, therefore, or something which is the cause of that quality, is another circumstance which promotes the deposition of dew; but this third cause resolves itself into the first, viz. the quality of resisting the passage of heat: for substances of loose texture "are precisely those which are best adapted for clothing, or for impeding the free passage of heat from the skin into the air, so as to allow their outer surfaces to be very cold, while they remain warm within;" and this last is, therefore, an induction (from fresh instances) simply *corroborative* of a former induction.

It thus appears that the instances in which much dew is deposited, [o] which are very various, agree in this, and, so far as we are able to observe, in this only, that they either radiate heat rapidly or conduct it slowly: qualities between which there is no other circumstance of agreement, than that by virtue of either, the body tends to lose heat from the surface more rapidly than it can be restored from within. The instances, on the contrary, in which no dew, or but a small quantity of it, is formed, and which are also extremely various, agree ([p]as[p] far as we can observe) in nothing except in *not* having this same property. We seem, therefore, to have detected the [q]characteristic[q] difference between the substances on which dew is produced, and those on which it is not produced. And thus have been realized the requisitions of what we have termed the Indirect Method of Difference, or the Joint Method

---

[n] [n]Source, MS, 43, 46   wool, velvet
[o]MS   and
[p]–[p]MS, 43, 46, 51   so
[q]–[q]MS, 43, 46   sole

of Agreement and Difference. The example afforded of this indirect method, and of the manner in which the data are prepared for it by the Methods of Agreement and of Concomitant Variations, is the most important of all the illustrations of induction afforded by this [r] interesting speculation.

We might now consider the question, on what the deposition of dew depends, to be completely solved, if we could be quite sure that the substances on which dew is produced differ from those on which it is not, in *nothing* but in the property of losing heat from the surface faster than the loss can be repaired from within. And though we never can have that complete certainty, this is not of so much importance as might at first be supposed; for we have, at all events, ascertained that even if there be any other quality hitherto unobserved which is present in all the substances which contract dew, and absent in those which do not, this other property must be one which, in all that great number of substances, is present or absent exactly where the property of being a better radiator than conductor is present or absent; an extent of coincidence which affords [s]a strong[s] presumption of a community of cause, and a consequent invariable coexistence between the two properties; so that the property of being a better radiator than conductor, if not itself the cause, almost certainly always accompanies the cause, and, for purposes of prediction, no error [t]is likely to[t] be committed by treating it as if it were really such.

Reverting now to an earlier stage of the inquiry, let us remember that we had ascertained that, in every instance where dew is formed, there is actual coldness of the surface below the temperature of the surrounding air; but we were not sure whether this coldness was the cause of dew, or its effect. This doubt we are now able to resolve. We have found that, in every such instance, the substance [u]is[u] one which, by its own properties or laws, would, if exposed in the night, become colder than the surrounding air. [v]The coldness therefore being accounted for independently of the dew, while it is proved that there is a connexion between the two, it must be the dew which depends on the coldness; or in other words, the coldness is the cause of the dew.[v]

[r]MS, 43   most
[s]–[s]MS, 43, 46   the strongest·
[t]–[t]MS, 43, 46   will
[u]–[u]MS, 43, 46, 51   must be
[v]–[v]MS, 43, 46   But if the dew were the *cause* of the coldness, that effect would be produced in other substances, and not solely in those whose own laws suffice to produce it whether there were dew or no. That supposition, therefore, is repelled. But there were only three suppositions possible; the dew is the cause of the coldness; both are caused by some third circumstance; or the coldness is the cause of the dew. The first is refuted. The second is inapplicable: the cause of the coldness is a known cause; a radiation from the surface greater than can be supplied by conduction; now this, by its known laws, can produce no direct effect except coldness. There remains only the third supposition, that the coldness is the cause of the dew: which, therefore, may be considered as completely made out.

This law of causation, already so amply established, admits, however, of [w] efficient additional corroboration in no less than three ways. First, by deduction from the known laws of aqueous vapour when diffused through air or any other gas; and though we have not yet come to the Deductive Method, we will not omit what is necessary to render this speculation complete. It is known by direct experiment that only a limited quantity [x]of water[x] can remain suspended in the state of vapour at each degree of temperature, and that this maximum grows less and less as the temperature diminishes. From this it follows, deductively, that if there is already as much vapour suspended as the air will contain at its existing temperature, any lowering of that temperature will cause a portion of the vapour to be condensed, and become water. But, again, we know deductively, from the laws of heat, that the contact of the air with a body colder than itself, will necessarily lower the temperature of the stratum of air immediately applied to its surface; and will therefore cause it to part with a portion of its water, which accordingly will, by the ordinary laws of gravitation or cohesion, attach itself to the surface of the body [y], thereby constituting dew[y]. This deductive proof, it will have been seen, has the advantage of [z]at once proving[z] causation as well as coexistence; and it has the additional advantage that it also accounts for the exceptions to the occurrence of the phenomenon, the cases in which, although the body is colder than the air, yet no dew is deposited; by showing that this will necessarily be the case when the air is so under-supplied with aqueous vapour, comparatively to its temperature, that even when somewhat cooled by the contact of the colder body, it can still continue to hold in suspension all the vapour which was previously suspended in it: thus in a very dry summer there are no dews, in a very dry winter no hoar frost. Here, therefore, is an additional condition of the production of dew, which the methods we previously made use of failed to detect, and which might have remained [a]still[a] undetected, if recourse had not been had to the plan of deducing the effect from the ascertained properties of the agents known to be present.

The second corroboration of the theory is by direct experiment, according to the canon of the Method of Difference. We can, by cooling the surface of any body, find in all cases some temperature, (more or less inferior to that of the surrounding air, according to its hygrometric condition,) at which dew will begin to be deposited. Here, too, therefore, the causation is directly proved. We can, it is true, accomplish this only on a small scale; but we have ample reason to conclude that the same operation, if conducted in Nature's great laboratory, would equally produce the effect.

[w]MS, 43, 46   most
[x-x]+43, 46, 51, 56, 62, 65, 68, 72
[y] y+43, 46, 51, 56, 62, 65, 68, 72
[z-z]MS, 43, 46, 51, 56, 62, 65   proving at once
[a-a]MS   long

And, finally, even on that great scale we are able to verify the result. The case is one of those rare cases, as we have shown them to be, in which nature works the experiment for us in the same manner in which we ourselves perform it; introducing into the previous state of things a single and perfectly definite new circumstance, and manifesting the effect so rapidly that there is not time for any other material change in the pre-existing circumstances. [b] "It is observed that dew is never copiously deposited in situations much screened from the open sky, and not at all in a cloudy night; but *if the clouds withdraw even for a few minutes, and leave a clear opening, a deposition of dew presently begins,* and goes on increasing. . . . Dew formed in clear intervals will often even evaporate again when the sky becomes thickly overcast."[*] The proof, therefore, is complete, that the presence or absence of an uninterrupted communication with the sky causes the deposition or non-deposition of dew. Now, since a clear sky is nothing but the absence of clouds, and it is a known property of clouds, as of all other bodies between which and any given object nothing intervenes but an elastic fluid, that they tend to raise or keep up the superficial temperature of the object by radiating heat to it, we see at once that the disappearance of clouds will cause the surface to cool; so that Nature, in this case, produces a change in the antecedent by definite and known means, and the consequent follows accordingly: a natural experiment which satisfies the requisitions of the Method of Difference.*

   [*Herschel, *Discourse,* p. 162; *JSM's italics.*]
*I must, however, remark, that this example, which seems to militate against the assertion we made of the comparative inapplicability of the Method of Difference to cases of pure observation, is really one of those exceptions which, according to a proverbial expression, prove the general rule. For [c] in this case, in which Nature, in her experiment, seems to have imitated the type of the experiments made by man, she has only succeeded in producing the likeness of man's most imperfect experiments; namely, those in which, though he succeeds in producing the phenomenon, [d]he does so[d] by employing complex means, which he is unable perfectly to analyse, and can form therefore no sufficient judgment what portion of the effects may be due, not to the supposed cause, but to some unknown agency of the means by which that cause was produced. In the natural experiment which we are speaking of, the means used was the clearing off a canopy of clouds; and we certainly do not know sufficiently in what this process consists, or on what it depends, to be certain *à priori* that it might not operate upon the deposition of dew independently of any thermometric effect at the earth's surface. Even, therefore, in a case so favourable as this to Nature's experimental talents, her experiment is of little value except in corroboration of a conclusion already attained through other means.

   [b]MS, 43 Let us quote again Sir John Herschel:
   [c]MS, 43, 46   , be it observed,
   [d-d]MS   it is

The accumulated proof of which the Theory of Dew has been found susceptible, is a striking *instance* of the fulness of assurance which the inductive evidence of laws of causation may attain, in cases in which the invariable sequence is by no means obvious to a superficial view. [f]

*§ 4. [*Brown-Séquard's theory of cadaveric rigidity*] The admirable physiological investigations of Dr. Brown-Séquard afford brilliant examples of the application of the Inductive Methods to a class of inquiries in which, for reasons which will presently be given, direct induction takes place under peculiar difficulties and disadvantages. As one of the most apt instances, I select his speculation (in the *Proceedings of the Royal Society* for May 16, 1861) on the relations between muscular irritability, cadaveric rigidity, and putrefaction.

The law which Dr. Brown-Séquard's investigation tends to establish, is the following: "The greater the degree of muscular irritability at the time of death, the later the cadaveric rigidity sets in, and the longer it lasts, and the later also putrefaction appears, and the slower it progresses."[*] [b]One would say at first sight that[b] the method here required must be that of Concomitant Variations. But this is a delusive appearance, arising from the circumstance that the conclusion to be tested is itself a fact of concomitant [c]variations[c]. For the establishment of that fact any of the Methods may be put in requisition, and it will be found that the fourth Method, though really employed, has only a subordinate place in this particular investigation.

The evidences by which Dr. Brown-Séquard establishes the law may be enumerated as follows:

1st. Paralysed muscles have greater irritability than healthy muscles. Now, paralysed muscles are later in assuming the cadaveric rigidity than healthy muscles, the rigidity lasts longer, and putrefaction sets in later, and proceeds more slowly.

Both these propositions had to be proved by experiment; and for the experiments which prove them, science is also indebted to Dr. Brown-Séquard. The former of the two—that paralysed muscles have greater irrit-

[*Charles E. Brown-Séquard, "On the Relations between Muscular Irritability, Cadaveric Rigidity, and Putrefaction," *Proceedings of the Royal Society*, XI (1860–62), p. 204.]

[e]-[e]MS, 43   example
[f]MS It is unnecessary to subjoin Sir John Herschel's summary of the result, as it does not contain all the proofs which we have given, and our more detailed analysis of each step of the process renders such a recapitulation unnecessary.] 43 *as* MS . . . which I have . . . *as* MS
[a] [a]1120+65, 68, 72
[b]-[b]65 According to first appearances,
[c]-[c]65, 68 variation [*printer's error?*]

ability than healthy muscles—he ascertained in various ways, but most decisively by "comparing the duration of irritability in a paralysed muscle and in the corresponding healthy one of the opposite side, while they are both submitted to the same excitation."[*] He "often found in experimenting in that way, that the paralysed muscle remained irritable twice, three times, or even four times as long as the healthy one."[†] This is a case of induction by the Method of Difference. The two limbs, being those of the same animal, were presumed to differ in no circumstance material to the case except the paralysis, to the presence and absence of which, therefore, the difference in the muscular irritability was to be attributed. This assumption of complete resemblance in all material circumstances save one, evidently could not be safely made in any one pair of experiments, because the two legs of any given animal might be accidentally in very different pathological conditions; but if, besides taking pains to avoid any such difference, the experiment was repeated sufficiently often in different animals to exclude the supposition that any abnormal circumstance could be present in them all, the conditions of the Method of Difference were adequately secured.

In the same manner in which Dr. Brown-Séquard proved that paralysed muscles have greater irritability, he also proved the correlative proposition respecting cadaveric rigidity and putrefaction.[‡] Having, by section of the roots of the sciatic nerve, and again of a lateral half of the spinal cord, produced paralysis in one hind leg of an animal while the other remained healthy, he found that not only did muscular irritability last much longer in the paralysed limb, but rigidity set in later and ended later, and putrefaction began later and was less rapid than on the healthy side. This is a common case of the Method of Difference, requiring no comment. A further and very important corroboration was obtained by the same method. When the animal was killed, not shortly after the section of the nerve, but a month later, the effect was reversed; rigidity set in sooner, and lasted a shorter time, than in the healthy muscles. But after this lapse of time, the paralysed muscles, having been kept by the paralysis in a state of rest, had lost a great part of their irritability, and instead of more, had become less irritable than those on the healthy side. This gives the A B C, a b c, and B C, b c, of the Method of Difference. One antecedent, increased irritability, being changed, and the other circumstances being the same, the consequence did not follow; and moreover, when a new antecedent, contrary to the first, was supplied, it was followed by a contrary consequent. This instance is attended with the special advantage, of proving that the retardation and prolongation of the rigidity do not depend directly on the paralysis, since that was the same in both the

[*Ibid., p. 205.]
[†Ibid.]
[‡Ibid., pp. 206–7.]

instances; but specifically on one effect of the paralysis, namely, the increased irritability; since they ceased when it ceased, and were reversed when it was reversed.

2ndly. Diminution of the temperature of muscles before death increases their irritability. But diminution of their temperature also retards cadaveric rigidity and putrefaction.

Both these truths were first made known by Dr. Brown-Séquard himself,[*] through experiments which conclude according to the Method of Difference. There is nothing in the nature of the process requiring specific analysis.

3rdly. Muscular exercise, prolonged to exhaustion, diminishes the muscular irritability.[†] This is a well-known truth, dependent on the most general laws of muscular action, and proved by experiments under the Method of Difference, constantly repeated. Now it has been shown by observation that overdriven cattle, if killed before recovery from their fatigue, become rigid and putrefy in a surprisingly short time. A similar fact has been observed in the case of animals hunted to death; cocks killed during or shortly after a fight; and soldiers slain in the field of battle. These various cases agree in no circumstance, directly connected with the muscles, except that these have just been subjected to exhausting exercise. Under the canon, therefore, of the Method of Agreement, it may be inferred that there is a connexion between the two facts. The Method of Agreement, indeed, as has been shown, is not competent to prove causation. The present case, however, is already known to be a case of causation, it being certain that the state of the body after death must somehow depend upon its state at the time of death. We are therefore warranted in concluding that the single circumstance in which all the instances agree, is the part of the antecedent which is the cause of that particular consequent.

4thly. In proportion as the nutrition of muscles is in a good state, their irritability is high.[†] This fact also rests on the general evidence of the laws of physiology, grounded on many familiar applications of the Method of Difference. Now, in the case of those who die from accident or violence, with their muscles in a good state of nutrition, the muscular irritability continues long after death, rigidity sets in late, and persists long without the putrefactive change. On the contrary, in cases of disease in which nutrition has been diminished for a long time before death, all these effects are reversed. These are the conditions of the Joint Method of Agreement and Difference. The cases of retarded and long continued rigidity here in question, agree only in being preceded by a high state of nutrition of the muscles; the cases of rapid

[*Ibid., pp. 207–8.]
[†Ibid., pp. 210–11.]
[‡Ibid., pp. 211–12.]

and brief rigidity agree only in being preceded by a low state of muscular nutrition; a connexion is therefore inductively proved between the degree of the nutrition, and the slowness and prolongation of the rigidity.

5thly. Convulsions, like exhausting exercise, but in a still greater degree, diminish the muscular irritability. Now, when death follows violent and prolonged convulsions, as in tetanus, hydrophobia, some cases of cholera, and certain poisons, rigidity sets in very rapidly, and after a very brief duration, gives place to putrefaction. This is another example of the Method of Agreement, of the same character with No. 3.

6thly. The series of instances which we shall take last, is of a more complex character, and requires a more minute analysis.

It has long been observed that in some cases of death by lightning, cadaveric rigidity either does not take place at all, or is of such extremely brief duration as to escape notice, and that in these cases putrefaction is very rapid. In other cases, however, the usual cadaveric rigidity appears. There must be some difference in the cause, to account for this difference in the effect. Now "death by lightning may be the result of, 1st, a syncope by fright, or in consequence of a direct or reflex influence of lightning on the par vagum; 2ndly, hemorrhage in or around the brain, or in the lungs, the pericardium, &c.; 3rdly, concussion, or some other alteration in the brain;"[*] none of which phenomena have any known property capable of accounting for the suppression, or almost suppression, of the cadaveric rigidity. But the cause of death may also be that the lightning produces "a violent convulsion of every muscle in the body," of which, if of sufficient intensity, the known effect would be that "muscular irritability ceases almost at once."[†] If Dr. Brown-Séquard's generalization is a true law, these will be the very cases in which rigidity is so much abridged as to escape notice; and the cases in which, on the contrary, rigidity takes place as usual, will be those in which the stroke of lightning operates in some of the other modes which have been enumerated. How, then, is this brought to the test? By experiments not on lightning, which cannot be commanded at pleasure, but on the same natural agency in a manageable form, that of artificial galvanism. Dr. Brown-Séquard galvanized the entire bodies of animals immediately after death. Galvanism cannot operate in any of the modes in which the stroke of lightning may have operated, except the single one of producing muscular convulsions. If, therefore, after the bodies have been galvanized, the duration of rigidity is much shortened and putrefaction much accelerated, it is reasonable to ascribe the same effects when produced by lightning, to the property which galvanism shares with lightning, and not to those which it does not. Now this Dr. Brown-Séquard found to be the fact. The galvanic experiment was tried with

[*Ibid., p. 208.]
[†Ibid.]

charges of very various degrees of strength; and the more powerful the charge, the shorter was found to be the duration of rigidity, and the more speedy and rapid the putrefaction. In the experiment in which the charge was strongest, and the muscular irritability most promptly destroyed, the rigidity only lasted fifteen minutes.[*] On the principle, therefore, of the Method of Concomitant Variations, it may be inferred that the duration of the rigidity depends on the degree of the irritability; and that if the charge had been as much stronger than Dr. Brown-Séquard's strongest, as a stroke of lightning must be stronger than any electric shock which we can produce artificially, the rigidity would have been shortened in a corresponding ratio, and might have disappeared altogether. This conclusion having been arrived at, the case of an electric shock, whether natural or artificial, becomes an instance in addition to all those already ascertained, of correspondence between the irritability of the muscle and the duration of rigidity.

All these instances are summed up in the following statement: "That when the degree of muscular irritability at the time of death is considerable, either in consequence of a good state of nutrition, as in persons who die in full health from an accidental cause, or in consequence of rest, as in cases of paralysis, or on account of the influence of cold, cadaveric rigidity in all these cases sets in late and lasts long, and putrefaction appears late, and progresses slowly:" but "that when the degree of muscular irritability at the time of death is slight, either in consequence of a bad state of nutrition, or of exhaustion from over-exertion, or from convulsions caused by disease or poison, cadaveric rigidity sets in and ceases soon, and putrefaction appears and progresses quickly."[†] These facts present, in all their completeness, the conditions of the Joint Method of Agreement and Difference. Early and brief rigidity takes place in cases which agree only in the circumstance of a low state of muscular irritability. Rigidity begins late and lasts long in cases which agree only in the contrary circumstance, of a muscular irritability high and unusually prolonged. It follows that there is a connexion through causation between the degree of muscular irritability after death, and the tardiness and prolongation of the cadaveric rigidity.

᷎ This investigation places in a strong light the value and efficacy of the Joint Method. For, as we have already seen, the defect of that Method is, that like the Method of Agreement, of which it is only an improved form, it cannot prove causation. But in the present case (as in one of the steps in the argument which led up to it) causation is already proved; since there could never be any doubt that the rigidity altogether, and the putrefaction which follows it, are caused by the fact of death: the observations and experiments

[*Ibid., pp. 209–10.]
[†Ibid., pp. 213–14.]
᷎65, 68 [no paragraph]

on which this rests are too familiar to need analysis, and fall under the Method of Difference. It being, therefore, beyond doubt that the aggregate antecedent, the death, is the actual cause of the whole train of consequents, whatever of the circumstances attending the death can be shown to be followed in all its variations by variations in the effect under investigation, must be the particular feature of the fact of death on which that effect depends. The degree of muscular irritability at the time of death fulfils this condition. The only point that could be brought into question, would be whether the effect depended on the irritability itself, or on something which always accompanied the irritability: and this doubt is set at rest by establishing, as the instances do, that by whatever cause the high or low irritability is produced, the effect equally follows; and cannot, therefore, depend upon the causes of irritability, nor upon the other effects of those causes, which are as various as the causes themselves; but upon the irritability, solely.[a]

[a]§ 5.[a] [*Examples of the Method of Residues*] [b]The last two examples will have conveyed to any one by whom they have[b] been duly followed, so clear a conception of the use and practical management of three of the four methods of experimental inquiry, as to supersede the necessity of any further exemplification of them. The remaining method, that of Residues, not having found [c]a place in any of the[c] preceding investigations, I shall [d]quote[d] from Sir John Herschel some examples of that method, with the remarks by which they are introduced.

It is by this process, in fact, that science, in its present advanced state, is chiefly promoted. Most of the phenomena which Nature presents are very complicated; and when the effects of all known causes are estimated with exactness, and subducted, the residual facts are constantly appearing in the form of phenomena altogether new, and leading to the most important conclusions.

For example: the return of the comet predicted by Professor Encke, a great many times in succession, and the general good agreement of its calculated with its observed place during any one of its periods of visibility, would lead us to say that its gravitation towards the sun and planets is the sole and sufficient cause of all the phenomena of its orbital motion; but when the effect of this cause is strictly calculated and subducted from the observed motion, there is found to remain behind a *residual phenomenon*, which would never have been otherwise ascertained to exist, which is a small anticipation of the time of its reappearance, or a diminution of its periodic time, which cannot be accounted for by gravity, and whose cause is therefore to be inquired into. Such an anticipation would be caused by the resistance of a medium disseminated through the celestial regions;

[a–a]51, 56, 62   §4.
[b–b]MS, 43, 46   This admirable example will . . . whom it has]   51, 56, 62   The last example . . . *as* MS
[c–c]MS, 43, 46, 51, 56, 62   any place either in this or in the two
[d–d]MS, 43, 46, 51, 56   extract

and as there are other good reasons for believing this to be a *vera causa*, [an actually existing antecedent,] it has therefore been ascribed to such a resistance.*

M. Arago, having suspended a magnetic needle by a silk thread, and set it in vibration, observed, that it came much sooner to a state of rest when suspended over a plate of copper, than when no such plate was beneath it. Now, in both cases there were two *veræ causæ* [antecedents known to exist] why it *should* come at length to rest, viz. the resistance of the air, which opposes, and at length destroys, all motions performed in it; and the want of perfect mobility in the silk thread. But the effect of these causes being exactly known by the observation made in the absence of the copper, and being thus allowed for and subducted, a residual phenomenon appeared, in the fact that a retarding influence was exerted by the copper itself; and this fact, once ascertained, speedily led to the knowledge of an entirely new and unexpected class of relations.[*]

This example belongs, however, not to the Method of Residues but to the Method of Difference, the law being ascertained by a direct comparison of the results of two experiments, which differed in nothing but the presence or absence of the plate of copper. To have made it exemplify the Method of Residues, the effect of the resistance of the air and that of the rigidity of the silk should have been calculated *à priori*, from the laws obtained by separate and foregone experiments.

Unexpected and peculiarly striking confirmations of inductive laws frequently occur in the form of residual phenomena, in the course of investigations of a widely different nature from those which gave rise to the inductions themselves. A very elegant example may be cited in the unexpected confirmation of the law of the development of heat in elastic fluids by compression, which is afforded by the phenomena of sound. The inquiry into the cause of sound had led to conclusions respecting its mode of propagation, from which its velocity in the air could be precisely calculated. The calculations were performed; but, when compared with fact, though the agreement was quite sufficient to show the general correctness of the cause and mode of propagation assigned, yet the *whole* velocity could not be shown to arise from this theory. There was still a residual velocity to be accounted for, which placed dynamical philosophers for a long time in a great dilemma. At length Laplace struck on the happy idea, that this might arise from the *heat* developed in the act of that condensation which necessarily takes place at every vibration by which sound is conveyed. The matter was subjected to exact calculation, and the result was at once the complete explanation of the residual phenomenon, and a striking confirmation of the general law of the development of heat by compression, under circumstances beyond artificial imitation.[†]

Many of the new elements of chemistry have been detected in the investigation of residual phenomena. Thus Arfwedson discovered lithia by perceiving an excess of weight in the sulphate produced from a small portion of what he con-

*[65] In his subsequent work, *Outlines of Astronomy* (§570), Sir John Herschel suggests another possible explanation of the acceleration of the revolution of a comet. [See 5th ed. London: Longman, 1858, pp. 383–4.]

[*Herschel, *Discourse*, pp. 156–7.]

[†*Ibid.*, pp. 171–2.]

sidered as magnesia present in a mineral he had analysed. It is on this principle, too, that the small concentrated residues of great operations in the arts are almost sure to be the lurking places of new chemical ingredients: witness iodine, brome, selenium, and the new metals accompanying platina in the experiments of Wollaston and Tennant. It was a happy thought of Glauber to examine what everybody else threw away.*

[e]Almost all the greatest discoveries in Astronomy, [says the same author,][†] have resulted from the consideration of residual phenomena of a quantitative or numerical kind. . . . It was thus that the grand discovery of the precession of the equinoxes resulted as a residual phenomenon, from the imperfect explanation of the return of the seasons by the return of the sun to the same apparent place among the fixed stars. Thus, also, aberration and nutation resulted as residual phenomena from that portion of the changes of the apparent places of the fixed stars which was left unaccounted for by precession. And thus again the apparent proper motions of the stars are the observed residues of their apparent movements outstanding and unaccounted for by strict calculation of the effects of precession, nutation, and aberration. The nearest approach which human theories can make to perfection is to diminish this residue, this *caput mortuum* of observation, as it may be considered, as much as practicable, and, if possible, to reduce it to nothing, either by showing that something has been neglected in our estimation of known causes, or by reasoning upon it as a new fact, and on the principle of the inductive philosophy ascending from the effect to its cause or causes.[e]

The disturbing effects mutually produced by the earth and planets upon each other's motions were first brought to light as residual phenomena, by the difference which appeared between the observed places of those bodies, and the places calculated on a consideration solely of their gravitation towards the sun. It was this which determined [f]astronomers[f] to consider the law of gravitation as obtaining between all bodies whatever, and therefore between all particles of matter; their first tendency having been to regard it as a force acting only between each planet or satellite and the central body to whose system it belonged. Again, the catastrophists, in geology, be their opinion right or wrong, support it on the plea, that after the effect of all causes now in operation has been allowed for, there remains in the existing constitution of the earth a large residue of facts, proving the existence at former periods either of other forces, or of the same forces in a much greater degree of intensity. To add one more example: [g]those who assert, what no one has shown any real ground for believing[g], that there is in one human indivi-

Ibid., p. 158.
†[51] *Outlines of Astronomy* [London: Longman, 1849], §856 [p. 584; 5th ed., p. 626].

[e]–[e]+51, 56, 62, 65, 68, 72   [f]–[f]MS, 43, 46   philosophers
[g]–[g]MS, 43   if it be possible to establish, what is generally rather assumed than proved]   46   *as* 72 . . . has ever succeeded in proving]   51, 56, 62, 65   *as* 72 . . . has ever shown . . . *as* 72

dual, one sex, or one race of mankind over another, an inherent and inexplicable superiority in mental faculties, [h]could only substantiate their proposition[h] by subtracting from the differences of intellect which we in fact see, all that can be traced by known laws either to the ascertained differences of physical organization, or to the differences which have existed in the outward circumstances in which the subjects of the comparison have hitherto been placed. What these causes might fail to account for, would constitute a residual phenomenon, which and which alone would be evidence of an ulterior original distinction, and the measure of its amount. But the [i]assertors of such supposed differences have not provided[i] themselves with these [j] necessary logical conditions of the establishment of their doctrine.

The spirit of the Method of Residues being, it is hoped, sufficiently intelligible from these examples, and the other three methods having [k]already been so fully exemplified[k], we may here close our exposition of the four methods, considered as employed in the investigation of the simpler and more elementary order of the combinations of phenomena.

[ab]§ 6.[b] [*Whewell's objections to the Four Methods*] Dr. Whewell [c]has expressed[c] a very unfavourable opinion of the utility of the Four Methods, as well as of the aptness of the examples by which I have attempted to illustrate them. His words are these:*

Upon these methods, the obvious thing to remark is, that they take for granted the very thing which is most difficult to discover, the reduction of the phenomena to formulæ such as are here presented to us. When we have any set of complex facts offered to us; for instance, those which were offered in the cases of discovery which I have mentioned,—the facts of the planetary paths, of falling bodies, of refracted rays, of cosmical motions, of chemical analysis; and when, in any of these cases, we would discover the law of nature which governs them, or, if any one chooses so to term it, the feature in which all the cases agree, where are we to look for our A, B, C, and a, b, c? Nature does not present to us the cases in this form; and how are we to reduce them to this form? You say, *when* we find the combination of A B C with *a b c* and A B D with *a b d*, then we may draw our inference. Granted; but when and where are we to find such combinations? Even now that the discoveries are made, who will point out to us what

*[62] *Philosophy of Discovery*, pp. 263–4.

[h-h]MS, 43   this must be proved
[i-i]MS, 43, 46   strongest assertors of such supposed differences have hitherto been very negligent of providing
[j]MS   the
[k-k]MS, 43, 46, 51, 56, 62   been so aptly exemplified in the inductive processes which produced the Theory of Dew
[a-a]43[+51, 56, 62, 65, 68, 72   [*in* 51, 56 *this section (including* 433[i-i] *in* 56) *appears as a note at the end of the preceding section*]
[b-b]62   §5.
[c-c]51, 56   , in his reply, expresses

are the A, B, C, and *a, b, c* elements of the cases which have just been enumerated? Who will tell us which of the methods of inquiry those historically real and successful inquiries exemplify? Who will carry these formulæ through the history of the sciences, as they have really grown up; and show us that these four methods have been operative in their formation; or that any light is thrown upon the steps of their progress by reference to these formulæ?

He adds that, in this work, the methods have not been applied "to a large body of conspicuous and undoubted examples of discovery, extending along the whole history of science;" which ought to have been done in order that the methods might be shown to possess the "advantage" (which he claims as belonging to his own) of being those "by which all great discoveries in science have really been made." (Pp. 264, 277.)

There is a striking similarity between the objections here made against Canons of Induction, and what was alleged, in the last century, by as able men as Dr. Whewell, against the acknowledged Canon of Ratiocination. Those who protested against the Aristotelian Logic said of the Syllogism, what Dr. Whewell says of the Inductive Methods, that it "takes for granted the very thing which is most difficult to discover, the reduction of the argument to formulæ such as are here presented to us." The grand difficulty, they said, is to obtain your syllogism, not to judge of its correctness when obtained. On the matter of fact, both they and Dr. Whewell are right. The greatest difficulty in both cases is first that of obtaining the evidence, and next, of reducing it to the form which tests its conclusiveness. But if we try [d] to reduce it without knowing [e]what it is to be reduced to[e], we are not likely to make much progress. It is a more difficult thing to solve a geometrical problem, than to judge whether a proposed solution is correct: but if people were not able to judge of the solution when found, they would have little chance of finding it. And it cannot be pretended that to judge of an induction when found, is perfectly easy, is a thing for which aids and instruments are superfluous; for erroneous inductions, false inferences from experience, are quite as common, on some subjects much commoner, than true ones. The business of Inductive Logic is to provide rules and models (such as the Syllogism and its rules are for ratiocination) to which if inductive arguments conform, those arguments are conclusive, and not otherwise. This is what the Four Methods profess to be, and what I believe they are universally considered to be by experimental philosophers, who had practised all of them long before any one sought to reduce the practice to theory.

The assailants of the Syllogism had also anticipated Dr. Whewell in the other branch of his argument. They said that no discoveries were ever made by syllogism; and Dr. Whewell says, or seems to say, that none were ever

[d]51   so
[e-e]51, 56, 62, 65, 68   *to what*

made by the four Methods of Induction. To the former objectors, Archbishop Whately very pertinently answered, that their argument, if good at all, was good against the reasoning process altogether; for whatever cannot be reduced to syllogism, is not reasoning. And Dr. Whewell's argument, if good at all, is good against all inferences from experience. In saying that no discoveries were ever made by the four Methods, he affirms that none were ever made by observation and experiment; for assuredly if any were, it was by *processes reducible to* one or other of those methods.

This difference between us accounts for the dissatisfaction which my examples give him; for I did not select them with a view to satisfy any one who required to be convinced that observation and experiment are modes of acquiring knowledge: I confess that in the choice of them I thought only of illustration, and of facilitating the *conception* of the Methods by concrete instances. If it had been my object to justify the processes themselves as means of investigation, there would have been no need to look far off, or make use of recondite or complicated instances. As a specimen of a truth ascertained by the Method of Agreement, I might have chosen the proposition "Dogs bark." This dog, and that dog, and the other dog, answer to A B C, A D E, A F G. The circumstance of being a dog, answers to A. Barking answers to *a*. As a truth made known by the Method of Difference, "Fire burns" might have sufficed. Before I touch the fire I am not burnt; this is B C; I touch it, and am burnt; this is A B C, *a* B C.

Such familiar experimental processes are not regarded as inductions by Dr. Whewell; but they are perfectly homogeneous with those by which, even on his own showing, the pyramid of science is supplied with its base. In vain he attempts to escape from this *conclusion* by laying the most arbitrary restrictions on the choice of examples admissible as instances of Induction: they must neither be such as are still matter of discussion (p. 265), nor must any of them be drawn from mental and social subjects (p. 269), nor from ordinary observation and practical life (pp. 241–7). They must be taken exclusively from the generalizations by which scientific thinkers have ascended to great and comprehensive laws of natural phenomena. Now it is seldom possible, in these complicated inquiries, to go much beyond the initial steps, without calling in the instrument of Deduction, and the temporary aid of hypotheses; as I myself, in common with Dr. Whewell, have maintained against the purely empirical school. Since therefore such cases could not conveniently be selected to illustrate the principles of mere observation and experiment, Dr. Whewell *is misled by their absence into representing* the Experimental Methods as serving no purpose in scientific

---

f–f+65, 68, 72
*g–g*51, 56, 62, 65   truth
*h–h*51, 56, 62   takes advantage of their absence to represent

investigation; forgetting that if those methods had not supplied the first generalizations, there would have been no materials for his own conception of Induction to work upon.

His challenge, however, to point out which of the four methods are exemplified in certain important cases of scientific inquiry,[*] is easily answered. "The planetary paths," as far as they are a case of induction at all,* fall under the Method of Agreement. The law of "falling bodies," namely that they describe spaces proportional to the squares of the times, was historically a deduction from the first law of motion; but the experiments by which it was verified, and by which it might have been discovered, were examples of the Method of Agreement; and the apparent variation from the true law, caused by the resistance of the air, was cleared up by experiments *in vacuo*, constituting an application of the Method of Difference. The law of "refracted rays" (the constancy of the ratio between the sines of incidence and of refraction for each refracting substance) was ascertained by direct measurement, and therefore by the Method of Agreement. The "cosmical motions" were determined by highly complex processes of thought, in which Deduction was predominant, but the Methods of Agreement and of Concomitant Variations had a large part in establishing the empirical laws. Every case without exception of "chemical analysis" constitutes a well-marked example of the Method of Difference. To any one acquainted with the subjects—to Dr. Whewell himself, there would not be the smallest difficulty in setting out "the A B C and *a b c* elements" of these cases.

If discoveries are ever made by observation and experiment without Deduction, the four methods are methods of discovery: but even if they were not methods of discovery, it would not be the less true that they are the sole methods of Proof; and in that character, even the results of deduction are amenable to them. The great generalizations which begin as Hypotheses, must end by being proved, and are in reality (as will be shown hereafter) proved, by the Four Methods. Now it is with Proof, as such, that Logic is principally concerned. This distinction has indeed no chance of finding favour with Dr. Whewell; for it is the peculiarity of his system, not to recognise, in cases of Induction, any necessity for proof. If, after assuming an hypothesis and carefully collating it with facts, nothing is brought to light inconsistent with it, that is, if experience does not *dis*prove it, he is content: at least until a simpler hypothesis, equally consistent with experience, presents itself. If this be Induction, doubtless there is no necessity for the four methods. But to suppose that it is so, appears to me a radical misconception of the nature of the evidence of physical truths.[a]

[*Philosophy of Discovery, p. 263; see pp. 429–30 above.]
*See, on this point, the second chapter of the present Book [pp. 292ff.]

*So real and practical is the need of a test for induction, similar to the syllogistic test of ratiocination, that inferences which bid defiance to the most elementary notions of inductive logic are put forth without misgiving by persons eminent in physical science, as soon as they are off the ground on which they are conversant with the facts, and not reduced to judge only by the arguments; and as for educated persons in general, it may be doubted if they are better judges of a good or a bad induction than they were before Bacon wrote. The improvement in the results of thinking has seldom extended to the processes; or has reached, if any process, that of investigation only, not that of proof. A knowledge of many laws of nature has doubtless been arrived at, by framing hypotheses and finding that the facts corresponded to them; and many errors have been got rid of by coming to a knowledge of facts which were inconsistent with them, but not by discovering that the mode of thought which led to the errors was itself faulty, and might have been known to be such independently of the facts which disproved the specific conclusion. Hence it is, that while the thoughts of mankind have on many subjects worked themselves practically right, the thinking power remains as weak as ever: and on all subjects on which the facts which would check the result are not accessible, as in what relates to the invisible world, and even, as has been seen lately, to the visible world of the planetary regions, men of the greatest scientific acquirements argue as pitiably as the merest ignoramus. For though they have made many *sound* inductions, they have not learnt from them (and Dr. Whewell thinks there is no necessity that they should learn) the principles of inductive *evidence.*

–+56, 62, 65, 68, 72
*–*56, 62   good

CHAPTER X

Of Plurality of Causes; and of the Intermixture of Effects

§ 1. [*One effect may have many causes*] In the preceding exposition of the four methods of observation and experiment, by which we contrive to distinguish among a mass of coexistent phenomena the particular effect due to a given cause, or the particular cause which gave birth to a given effect; it has been necessary to suppose, in the first instance, for the sake of simplification, that this analytical operation is encumbered by no other difficulties than what are essentially inherent in its nature; and to represent to ourselves, therefore, every effect, on the one hand as connected exclusively with a single cause, and on the other hand as incapable of being mixed and confounded with any other coexistent effect. We have regarded *a b c d e*, the aggregate of the phenomena existing at any moment, as consisting of dissimilar *ª*facts*ª*, *a, b, c, d,* and *e,* for each of which one, and only one, cause needs be sought; the difficulty being only that of singling out this one cause from the multitude of antecedent circumstances, A, B, C, D, and E. *ᵇ*The cause indeed may not be simple; it may consist of an assemblage of conditions; but we have supposed that there was only one possible assemblage of conditions, from which the given effect could result.*ᵇ*

If such were the fact, it would be comparatively an easy task to investigate the laws of nature. But the supposition does not hold, in either of its parts. In the first place, it is not true that the same phenomenon is always produced by the same cause: the effect *a* may sometimes arise from A, sometimes from B. And, secondly, the effects of different causes are often not dissimilar, but homogeneous, and marked out by no assignable boundaries from one another: A and B may produce not *a* and *b,* but different portions of an effect *a.* The obscurity and difficulty of the investigation of the laws of phenomena is singularly increased by the necessity of adverting to these two circumstances; Intermixture of Effects, and Plurality of Causes. To the latter, being the simpler of the two considerations, we shall first direct our attention.

It is not true, then, that one effect must be connected with only one cause, or assemblage of conditions; that each phenomenon can be produced only in one way. There are often several independent modes in which the same phenomenon could have originated. One fact may be the consequent in several invariable sequences; it may follow, with equal uniformity, any one of several antecedents, or collections of antecedents. Many causes may produce *mechanical* motion: many causes may produce some kinds of sensation: many causes may produce death. A given effect may really be produced by a certain cause, and yet be perfectly capable of being produced without it.

§ 2. [*Plurality of causes is the source of a characteristic imperfection of the Method of Agreement*] One of the principal consequences of this fact of Plurality of Causes is, to render the first of *the* inductive methods, that of Agreement, uncertain. To illustrate that method, we supposed two instances, A B C followed by *a b c*, and A D E followed by *a d e*. From these instances it might *apparently* be concluded that A is an invariable antecedent of *a*, and even that it is the unconditional invariable antecedent, or cause, if we could be sure that there is no other antecedent common to the two cases. That this difficulty may not stand in the way, let us suppose the two cases positively ascertained to have no antecedent in common except A. The moment, however, that we let in the possibility of a plurality of causes, the conclusion fails. For it involves a tacit supposition, that *a* must have been produced in both instances by the same cause. If there can possibly have been two causes, those two may, for example, be C and E: the one may have been the cause of *a* in the former of the instances, the other in the latter, A having no influence in either case.

Suppose *, for example,* that two great artists, or great philosophers, that two extremely selfish, or extremely generous characters, were compared together as to the circumstances of their education and history, and the two cases were found to agree only in one circumstance: would it follow that this one circumstance was the cause of the quality which characterized both those individuals? Not at all; for the causes *which may produce any* type of character are *very numerous*; and the two persons might equally have agreed in their character, though there had been no manner of resemblance in their previous history.

This, therefore, is a characteristic imperfection of the Method of Agreement; from which imperfection the Method of Difference is free. For if we

c–c+72
*a–a*MS, 43, 46   our
b–b+62, 65, 68, 72
c–c+43, 46, 51, 56, 62, 65, 68, 72
*d–d*MS, 43, 46   at work to produce any given
*e–e*MS, 43, 46, 51, 56, 62, 65, 68   innumerable

have two instances, A B C and B C, of which B C gives *b c*, and A being added converts it into *a b c*, it is certain that in this instance at least, A was *f*either the cause of *a*, or*f* an indispensable portion of its cause, even though the cause which produces it in other instances may be altogether different. Plurality of Causes, therefore, not only does not diminish the reliance due to the Method of Difference, but does not even render a greater number of observations or experiments necessary: two instances, the one positive and the other negative, are still sufficient for the most complete and rigorous induction. Not so, however, with the Method of Agreement. The conclusions which that yields, when the number of instances compared is small, are of no real value, except as, in the character of suggestions, they may lead either to experiments bringing them to the test of the Method of Difference, or to reasonings which may explain and verify them deductively.

It is only when the instances, being indefinitely multiplied and varied, continue to suggest the same result, that this result acquires any high degree of independent value. If there are but two instances, A B C and A D E, though these instances have no antecedent in common except A, yet as the effect may possibly have been produced in the two cases by different causes, the result is at most only a slight probability in favour of A; there may be causation, but it is almost equally probable that there was only *g* a coincidence. But the oftener we repeat the observation, varying the circumstances, the more we advance towards a solution of this doubt. For if we try A F G, A H K, &c., all *h* unlike one another except in containing the circumstance A, and if we find the effect *a* entering into the result in all these cases, we must suppose one of two things, either that it is caused by A, or that it has as many different causes as there are instances. With each addition, therefore, to the number of instances, the presumption is strengthened in favour of A. The inquirer, of course, will not neglect, if an opportunity present itself, to exclude A from some one of these combinations, from A H K for instance, and by trying H K separately, appeal to the Method of Difference in aid of the Method of Agreement. By the *i*Method of Difference*i* alone can it be ascertained that A is the cause of *a*; but that it is either the cause, or another effect of the same cause, may be placed beyond any reasonable doubt by the Method of Agreement, provided the instances are very numerous as well as sufficiently various.

After how great a multiplication, then, of varied instances, all agreeing in no other antecedent except A, is the supposition of a plurality of causes sufficiently rebutted, and the conclusion that *a* is *j*connected with*j* A divested of the characteristic imperfection, and reduced to a virtual certainty? This is

---

*f–f*MS   the cause of *a*, or at least   *g*MS, 43, 46   , as the expression is,
*h*MS, 43, 46   entirely   *i–i*MS, 43   former method
*j–j*MS, 43, 46, 51, 56   the effect of

a question which we cannot be exempted from answering: but the consideration of it belongs to what is called the Theory of Probability, which will form the subject of a chapter hereafter. It is seen, however, at once, that the conclusion does amount to a practical certainty after a sufficient number of instances, and that the method, therefore, is not radically vitiated by the characteristic imperfection. The result of these considerations is only, in the first place, to point out a new source of inferiority in the Method of Agreement as compared with other modes of investigation, and new reasons for never resting contented with the results obtained by it, without attempting to confirm them either by the Method of Difference, or by connecting them deductively with some law or laws already ascertained by that superior method. And, in the second place, we learn from this the true theory of the value of mere *number* of instances in inductive inquiry. *k*The Plurality of Causes is the only reason why mere number is of any importance.*k* The tendency of unscientific inquirers is to rely too much on number, without analysing the instances; without looking closely enough into their nature, to ascertain what circumstances are or are not eliminated by means of them. Most people hold their conclusions with a degree of assurance proportioned to the mere *mass* of the experience on which they appear to rest; not considering that by the addition of instances to instances, all of the same kind, that is, differing from one another only in points already recognised as immaterial, nothing whatever is added to the evidence of the conclusion. A single instance eliminating some antecedent which existed in all the other cases, is of more value than the greatest multitude of instances which are reckoned by their number alone. It is necessary, no doubt, to assure ourselves, by *l* repetition of the observation or experiment, that no error has been committed concerning the individual facts observed; and until we have assured ourselves of this, instead of varying the circumstances, we cannot too scrupulously repeat the same experiment or observation without any change. But when once this assurance has been obtained, the multiplication of instances which do not exclude any more circumstances *m*is entirely useless, provided there have been already enough to exclude the supposition of*m* Plurality of Causes.

It is of importance to remark, that the peculiar modification of the Method of Agreement, which, as partaking in some degree of the nature of the Method of Difference, I have called the Joint Method of Agreement and Difference, is not affected by the characteristic imperfection now pointed out. For, in the joint method, it is supposed not only that the instances in which *a* is, agree only in containing A, but also that the instances in which *a* is not,

k–k+46, 51, 56, 62, 65, 68, 72
*l*MS, 43, 46, 51, 56, 62 a
*m–m*MS, 43, 46, 51 would be entirely useless, were it not for the

agree only in not containing A. Now, if this be so, A must be not only the cause of *a*, but the only possible cause: for if there were another, as for example B, then in the instances in which *a* is not, B must have been absent as well as A, and it would not be true that "these" instances agree *only* in not containing A. This, therefore, constitutes an immense advantage of the joint method over the simple Method of Agreement. It may seem, indeed, that the advantage does not belong so much to the joint method, as to one of its two premises, (if they may be so called,) the negative premise. The Method of Agreement, when applied to negative instances, or those in which a phenomenon does *not* take place, is certainly free from the characteristic imperfection which affects it in the affirmative case. The negative premise, it might therefore be supposed, could be worked as a simple case of the Method of Agreement, without requiring an affirmative premise to be joined with it. But though this is true in principle, it is generally altogether impossible to work the Method of Agreement by negative instances without positive ones: it is so much more difficult to exhaust the field of negation than that of affirmation. For instance, let the question be, what is the cause of the transparency of bodies; with what prospect of success could we set ourselves to inquire directly in what the multifarious substances which are *not* transparent, agree? But we might hope much sooner to seize some point of resemblance °among° the comparatively few and definite species of objects which *are* transparent; and this being attained, we should quite naturally be put upon examining whether the *absence* of this one circumstance be not precisely the point in which all opaque substances will be found to resemble.

The Joint Method of Agreement and Difference, therefore, or, as I have otherwise called it, the Indirect Method of Difference (because, like the Method of Difference properly so called, it proceeds by ascertaining how and in what the cases where the phenomenon is present, differ from those in which it is absent) is, after the Direct Method of Difference, the most powerful of the remaining instruments of inductive investigation; and in the sciences which depend on pure observation, with little or no aid from experiment, this method, so well exemplified in the *p* speculation on the cause of dew, is the primary resource, so far as direct appeals to experience are concerned.

§ 3. [*Plurality of causes, how ascertained*] We have thus far treated Plurality of Causes only as a possible supposition, which, until removed, renders our inductions uncertain; and have only considered by what means,

*n–n*MS   those [*printer's error?*]
*o–o*MS   in
*p*MS, 43   beautiful

where the plurality does not really exist, we may be enabled to disprove it. But we must also consider it as a case actually occurring in nature, and which, as often as it does occur, our methods of induction ought to be capable of ascertaining and establishing. For this, however, there is required no peculiar method. When an effect is really producible by two or more causes, the process for detecting them is in no way different from that by which we discover single causes. They may [a](first)[a] be discovered as separate sequences, by separate sets of instances. One set of observations or experiments shows that the sun is a cause of heat, another that friction is a source of it, another that percussion, another that electricity, another that chemical action is such a source. Or [b](secondly)[b] the plurality may come to light in the course of collating a number of instances, when we attempt to find some circumstance in which they all agree, and fail in doing so. We find it impossible to trace, in all the cases in which the effect is met with, any common circumstance. We find that we can eliminate *all* the antecedents; that no one of them is present in all the instances, no one of them [c] indispensable to the effect. On closer scrutiny, however, it appears that though no one is always present, one or other of several always is. If, on further analysis, we can detect in these any common element, we may be able to ascend from them to some one cause which is the really operative circumstance in them all. Thus it [d]is now thought[d] that in the production of heat by friction, percussion, chemical action, &c., the ultimate source is one and the same. But if (as continually happens) we cannot take this ulterior step, the different antecedents must be set down [e]provisionally[e] as distinct causes, each sufficient of itself to produce the effect.

We [f] here close our remarks on the Plurality of Causes, and proceed to the still more peculiar and more complex case of the Intermixture of Effects, and the interference of causes with one another: a case constituting the principal part of the complication and difficulty of the study of nature; and with which the four only possible methods of directly inductive investigation by observation and experiment, are for the most part, as will appear presently, quite unequal to cope. The instrument of Deduction alone is adequate to unravel the complexities proceeding from this source; and the four methods have little more in their power than to supply premises for [g], and a verification of,[g] our deductions.

[a-a]+43, 46, 51, 56, 62, 65, 68, 72
[b-b]+43, 46, 51, 56, 62, 65, 68, 72
[c]MS is
[d-d]MS, 43, 46, 51, 56, 62 might, and perhaps will, be discovered,
[e-e]+51, 56, 62, 65, 68, 72
[f]MS, 43 may
[g-g]+51, 56, 62, 65, 68, 72

§ 4. [*Concurrence of causes which do not compound their effects*] A concurrence of two or more causes, not separately producing each its own effect, but interfering with or modifying the effects of one another, takes place, as has already been explained, in two different ways. In the one [a], which is exemplified by the joint operation of different forces in mechanics, the separate effects of all the causes continue to be produced, but are compounded with one another, and disappear in one total. In the other [b], illustrated by the case of chemical action, the separate effects cease entirely, and are succeeded by phenomena altogether different, and governed by different laws.

Of these cases the former is by far the more frequent, and this case it is which, for the most part, eludes the grasp of our experimental methods. The other and exceptional case is essentially amenable to them. When the laws of the original agents cease entirely, and a phenomenon makes its appearance, which, with reference to those laws, is quite heterogeneous; when, for example, two gaseous substances, hydrogen and oxygen, on being brought together, throw off their peculiar properties, and produce the substance called water; in such cases the new fact may be subjected to experimental inquiry, like any other phenomenon; and the elements which are said to compose it may be considered as the mere agents of its production; the conditions on which it depends, the facts which make up its cause.

The *effects* of the new phenomenon, the *properties* of water, for instance, are as easily found by experiment as the effects of any other cause. But to discover the *cause* of it, that is, the particular conjunction of agents from which it results, is often difficult enough. In the first place, the origin and actual production of the phenomenon [c]are[c] most frequently inaccessible to our observation. If we could not have learned the composition of water until we found instances in which it was actually produced from oxygen and hydrogen, we should have been forced to wait until the casual thought struck some one of passing an electric spark through a mixture of the two gases, or inserting a lighted taper into it, merely to try what would happen. [d]Besides, many substances, though they can be analysed, cannot by any known artificial means be recompounded.[d] Further, even if we could have ascertained, by the Method of Agreement, that oxygen and hydrogen were both present when water is produced, no experimentation on oxygen and hydrogen separately, no knowledge of their laws, could have enabled us deductively to infer that they would produce water. We require a specific experiment on the two combined.

Under these difficulties, we should generally have been indebted for our knowledge of the causes of this class of effects, not to any inquiry directed

<hr>

[a]MS, 43   case
[c–c]MS, 43   , is

[b]MS, 43   case
[d–d]+56, 62, 65, 68, 72

specifically towards that end, but either to accident, or to the gradual progress of experimentation on the different combinations of which the producing agents are susceptible; if it were not for a peculiarity belonging to effects of this description, that they often, under some particular combination of circumstances, reproduce their causes. If water results from the juxtaposition of hydrogen and oxygen whenever this can be made sufficiently close and intimate, so, on the other hand, if water itself be placed in certain situations, hydrogen and oxygen are reproduced from it: an abrupt termination is put to the new laws, and the agents reappear separately with their own properties as at first. What is called chemical analysis is the process of searching for the causes of a phenomenon among its effects, or rather among the effects produced by the action of some other ^{e}causes^e upon it.

Lavoisier, by heating mercury to a high temperature in a close vessel containing air, found that the mercury increased in weight, and became what was then called red precipitate, while the air, on being examined after the experiment, proved to have lost weight, and to have become incapable of supporting life or combustion. When red precipitate was exposed to a still greater heat, it became mercury again, and gave off a gas which did support life and flame. Thus the agents which by their combination produced red precipitate, namely the mercury and the gas, reappear as effects resulting from that precipitate when acted upon by heat. So, if we decompose water by means of iron filings, we produce two effects, rust and hydrogen: now rust is already known by experiments upon the component substances, to be an effect of the union of iron and oxygen: the iron we ourselves supplied, but the oxygen must have been produced from the water. The result therefore is that ^{f} water has disappeared, and hydrogen and oxygen have appeared in its stead: or in other words, the original laws of these gaseous agents, which had been suspended by the superinduction of the new laws called the properties of water, have again started into existence, and the causes of water are found among its effects.

Where two phenomena, between the laws or properties of which considered in themselves no connexion can be traced, are thus reciprocally cause and effect, each capable in its turn of being produced from the other, and each, when it produces the other, ceasing itself to exist (as water is produced from oxygen and hydrogen, and oxygen and hydrogen are reproduced from water); this causation of the two phenomena by one another, each ^{g} being generated by the other's destruction, is properly transformation. The idea of chemical composition is an idea of transformation, but of a transformation which is incomplete; since we consider the oxygen and hydrogen to be present in the water *as* oxygen and hydrogen, and capable of being discovered

$^{e-e}$MS cause $\qquad$ ^{f}MS, 43, 46 the
^{g}MS, 43, 46 of them

in it if our senses were sufficiently keen: a supposition (for it is no more) grounded solely on the fact, that the weight of the water is the sum of the separate weights of the two ingredients. If there had not been this exception to the entire disappearance, in the compound, of the laws of the separate ingredients; if the combined agents had not, in this one particular of weight, preserved their own laws, and produced a joint result equal to the sum of their separate results; we should never, probably, have had the notion now implied by the words chemical composition: and, in the *h*facts*h* of water produced from hydrogen and oxygen, and hydrogen and oxygen produced from water, as the transformation would have been complete, we should have seen only a transformation. *i*

In these cases, *j*where*j* the heteropathic effect (as we called it in a former chapter)* is but a transformation of its cause, or in other words, *k*where*k* the effect and its cause are reciprocally such, and mutually convertible into each other; the problem of finding the cause resolves itself into the far easier one of finding an effect, which is the kind of inquiry that admits of being prose-cuted by direct experiment. But there are other cases of heteropathic effects to which this mode of investigation is not applicable. Take, for instance, the heteropathic laws of mind; that portion of the phenomena of our mental nature which are analogous to chemical rather than to dynamical phenomena; as when a complex passion is formed by the coalition of several elementary impulses, or a complex emotion by several simple pleasures or pains, of which it is the result without being the aggregate, or in any respect homo-geneous with them. The product, in these cases, is generated by its various factors; but the factors cannot be reproduced from the product; just as a youth can grow into an old man, but an old man cannot grow into a youth. We cannot ascertain from what simple feelings any of our complex states of mind *l*are*l* generated, as we ascertain the ingredients of a chemical com-pound, by making it, in its turn, generate them. We can only, therefore, dis-cover these laws by the slow process of studying the simple feelings them-selves, and ascertaining synthetically, by experimenting on the various com-binations of which they are susceptible, what they, by their mutual action upon one another, are capable of generating.

§ 5. [*Difficulties of the investigation, when causes compound their effects*] It might have been supposed that the other, and apparently simpler variety

---

*[51] Ante, Chap. vi, §2 [p. 374].

*h–h*MS, 43, 46, 51   fact
i[*see* Appendix D *for* 56, 62, 65, 68 *variants in a passage added in 56 and deleted in* 72]
*j–j*MS, 43, 46, 51   then, when
*k–k*MS, 43, 46, 51   when
*l–l*MS   is

of the mutual interference of causes, where each cause continues to produce its own proper effect according to the same laws to which it conforms in its separate state, would have presented fewer difficulties to the inductive inquirer than that of which we have just finished the consideration. It presents, however, so far as direct induction apart from deduction is concerned, infinitely greater difficulties. When a concurrence of causes gives rise to a new effect, bearing no relation to the separate effects of those causes, the resulting phenomenon [a] stands forth undisguised, inviting attention to its peculiarity, and presenting no obstacle to our recognising its presence or absence among any number of surrounding phenomena. It admits therefore of being easily brought under the canons of Induction, provided instances can be obtained such as those canons require: and the non-occurrence of such instances, or the want of means to produce them artificially, is the real and only difficulty in such investigations; a difficulty not logical, but in some sort physical. It is otherwise with cases of what, in a preceding chapter, has been denominated the Composition of Causes. There, the effects of the separate causes do not terminate and give place to others, thereby ceasing to form any part of the phenomenon to be investigated; on the contrary, they still take place, but are intermingled with, and disguised by, the homogeneous and closely allied effects of other causes. They are no longer a, b, c, d, e, existing side by side, and continuing to be separately discernible; they are $+ a$, $- a$, $\frac{1}{2} b$, $- b$, $2 b$, &c.; some of which cancel one another, while many others do not appear distinguishably, but merge in one sum: forming altogether a result, between which and the causes whereby it was produced there is often an insurmountable difficulty in tracing by observation any fixed relation whatever.

The general idea of the Composition of Causes has been seen to be, that though two or more laws interfere with one another, and apparently frustrate or modify one another's operation, yet in reality all are fulfilled, the collective effect being the exact sum [b] of the effects of the causes taken separately. A familiar instance is that of a body kept in equilibrium by two equal and contrary forces. One of the forces if acting alone would carry [c]the body in a given time a certain distance[c] to the west, the other if acting alone would carry it exactly as far towards the east; and the result is the same as if it had been first carried to the west as far as the one force would carry it, and then back towards the east as far as the other would carry it, that is, precisely the same distance; being ultimately left where it was found at first.

All laws of causation are liable to be in this manner counteracted, and seemingly frustrated, by coming into conflict with other laws, the separate result of which is opposite to theirs, or more or less inconsistent with it. And

[a]MS, 43, 46 at least
[b]MS, 43, 46 total
[c]–[c]MS, 43, 46 it so far] 51, 56 it in . . . *as* 72

hence, with almost every law, many instances in which it really is entirely fulfilled, do not, at first sight, appear to be cases of its operation at all. It is so in the example just adduced: a force, in mechanics, means neither more nor less than a cause of motion, yet the sum of the effects of two causes of motion may be rest. Again, a body solicited by two forces in directions making an angle with one another, moves in the diagonal; and it seems a paradox to say that motion in the diagonal is the sum of two motions in two other lines. Motion, however, is but change of place, and at every instant the body is in the exact place it would have been in if the forces had acted during alternate instants instead of acting in the same instant; (saving that if we suppose ^{d}two^d forces to act successively which are in truth simultaneous, we must of course allow them double the time.) It is evident, therefore, that each force has had, during each instant, all the effect which belonged to it; and that the modifying influence which one of two concurrent causes is said to exercise with respect to the other, may be considered as exerted not over the action of the cause itself, but over the effect after it is completed. For all purposes of predicting, calculating, or explaining their joint result, causes which compound their effects may be treated as if they produced simultaneously each of them its own effect, and all these effects coexisted visibly.

Since the laws of causes are as really fulfilled when the causes are said to be counteracted by opposing causes, as when they are left to their own undisturbed action, we must be cautious not to express the laws in such terms as would render the assertion of their being fulfilled in those cases a contradiction. If, for instance, it ^{e}were^e stated as a law of nature that a body to which a force is applied moves in the direction of the force, with a velocity proportioned to the force directly, and to its own mass inversely; when in point of fact some bodies to which a force is applied do not move at all, and those which do move ^{f}(at least in the region of our earth)^f are, from the very first, retarded by the action of gravity and other resisting forces, and at last stopped altogether; it is clear that the general proposition, though it would be true under a certain hypothesis, ^{g}would^g not express the facts as they actually occur. To accommodate the expression of the law to the real phenomena, we must say, not that the object moves, but that it *tends* to move, in the direction and with the velocity specified. We might, indeed, guard our expression in a different mode, by saying that the body moves in that manner unless prevented, or except in so far as prevented, by some counteracting cause. But the body does not only move in that manner unless counteracted; it *tends* to move in that manner even when counteracted; it still exerts, in the original direction, the same energy of movement as if its first impulse had been undisturbed, and produces, by that energy, an exactly

$^{d-d}$+43, 46, 51, 56, 62, 65, 68, 72 $^{e-e}$MS   be
$^{f-f}$+65, 68, 72 $^{g-g}$MS   does

equivalent quantity of effect. This is true even when the force leaves the body as it found it, in a state of absolute rest; as when we attempt to raise a body of three tons weight with a force equal to one ton. For if, while we are applying this force, [h] wind or water or any other agent supplies an additional force just exceeding two tons, the body will be raised; thus proving that the force we applied exerted its full effect, by neutralizing an equivalent portion of the weight which it was insufficient altogether to overcome. And if while we are exerting this force of one ton upon the object in a direction contrary to that of gravity, it be put into a scale and weighed, it will be found to have lost a ton of its weight, or in other words, to press downwards with a force only equal to the difference of the two forces.

These facts are correctly indicated by the expression *tendency*. All laws of causation, in consequence of their liability to be counteracted, require to be stated in words affirmative of tendencies only, and not of actual results. In those sciences of causation which have an accurate nomenclature, there are special words which signify a tendency to the particular effect with which the science is conversant; thus *pressure*, in mechanics, is synonymous with tendency to motion, and forces are not reasoned on as causing actual motion, but as exerting pressure. A similar improvement in terminology would be very salutary in many other branches of science.

The habit of neglecting this necessary element in the precise expression of the laws of nature, has given birth to the popular prejudice that all general truths have exceptions; and much unmerited distrust has thence accrued to the conclusions of [i]science[i], when they have been submitted to the judgment of [j]minds insufficiently disciplined and cultivated[j]. The rough generalizations suggested by common observation usually have exceptions; but [k]principles of science, or in other words,[k] laws of causation, have not. "What is thought to be an exception to a principle," (to quote words used on a different occasion,)

is always some other and distinct principle cutting into the former; some other force which impinges* against the first force, and deflects it from its direction. There are not a law and an exception to that law, the law acting in ninety-nine cases, and the exception in one. There are two laws, each possibly acting in the whole hundred cases, and bringing about a common effect by their conjunct operation. If the force which, being the less conspicuous of the two, is called the

*[51] It seems hardly necessary to say that the word *impinges*, as a general term to express collision of forces, [l]is[l] here used by a figure of speech, and not as expressive of any theory respecting the nature of force.

[h]MS, 43   the
[i-i]MS, 43, 46   philosophy
[j-j]MS, 43, 46   persons who were not philosophers
[k-k]MS, 43, 46   the principles . . . words, the
[l-l]51   was

disturbing force, prevails sufficiently over the other force in some one case, to constitute that case what is commonly called an exception, the same disturbing force probably acts as a modifying cause in many other cases which no one will call exceptions.

Thus if it were stated to be a law of nature that all heavy bodies fall to the ground, it would probably be said that the resistance of the atmosphere, which prevents a balloon from falling, constitutes the balloon an exception to that pretended law of nature. But the real law is, that all heavy bodies *tend* to fall; and to this there is no exception, not even the sun and moon; for even they, as every astronomer knows, tend towards the earth, with a force exactly equal to that with which the earth tends towards them. The resistance of the atmosphere might, in the particular case of the balloon, from a misapprehension of what the law of gravitation is, be said to *prevail over* the law; but its disturbing effect is quite as real in every other case, since though it does not prevent, it retards the fall of all bodies whatever. The rule, and the so-called exception, do not divide the cases between them; each of them is a comprehensive rule extending to all cases. To call one of these concurrent principles an exception to the other, is superficial, and contrary to the correct principles of nomenclature and arrangement. An effect of precisely the same kind, and arising from the same cause, ought not to be placed in two different categories, merely as there does or does not exist another cause preponderating over it.*

a§ 6.*a* [*Three modes of investigating the laws of complex effects*] We have now to consider according to what method these complex effects, compounded of the effects of many causes, are to be studied; how we are enabled to trace each effect to the concurrence of causes in which it originated, and ascertain the conditions of its recurrence—the circumstances in which it may be expected again to occur. *b* The conditions of a phenomenon which arises from *c*a*c* composition of causes, may be investigated either deductively or experimentally.

The case, it is evident, is naturally susceptible of the deductive mode of investigation. The law of an effect of this description is a result of the laws of the separate causes on the combination of which it depends, and is therefore in itself capable of being deduced from *d*these*d* laws. This is called the method *à priori*. The other, or *à posteriori* method, professes to proceed according to the canons of experimental inquiry. Considering the whole assemblage of concurrent causes which produced the phenomenon, as one single cause, it attempts to ascertain *e*the*e* cause in the ordinary manner, by a comparison of instances. This second method subdivides itself into two different varieties. If

*[51] *Essays on some Unsettled Questions of Political Economy* [London: Parker, 1844], Essay V ["On the Definition of Political Economy," pp. 162–3. In *Essays on Economics and Society, Collected Works*, Vol. IV. Toronto: University of Toronto Press, 1967, pp. 337–8].

*a–a*MS [*no section division*]   *b*MS §5. [*sic; should read* §6.]
*c–c*MS the   *d–d*MS those
*e–e*MS, 43, 46, 51, 56   that

it merely collates instances of the effect, it is a method of pure observation. If it operates upon the causes, and tries different combinations of them, in hopes of ultimately hitting the precise combination which will produce the given total effect, it is a method of experiment.

In order more completely to clear up the nature of each of these three methods, and determine which of them deserves the preference, it will be expedient (conformably to a favourite maxim of Lord Chancellor Eldon, to which, though it has often incurred philosophical ridicule, a deeper philosophy will not refuse its sanction) to "clothe them in circumstances." We shall select for this purpose a case which as yet furnishes no very brilliant example of the success of any of the three methods, but which is all the more suited to illustrate the difficulties inherent in them. Let the subject of inquiry be, the conditions of health and disease in the human body; or (for greater simplicity) the conditions of recovery from a given disease; and in order to narrow the question still more, let it be limited, in the first instance, to this one inquiry: Is, or is not some particular medicament (mercury, for instance) a remedy for *the given* disease.

Now, the deductive method would set out from known properties of mercury, and known laws of the human body, and by reasoning from these, would attempt to discover whether mercury will act upon the body when in the morbid condition supposed, in such a manner as *would tend* to restore health. The experimental method would simply administer mercury in as many cases as possible, noting the age, sex, temperament, and other peculiarities of bodily constitution, the particular form or variety of the disease, the particular stage of its progress, &c., remarking in which of these cases it *was attended with* a salutary effect, and with what circumstances it was on those occasions combined. The method of simple observation would compare instances of recovery, to find whether they agreed in having been preceded by the administration of mercury; or would compare instances of recovery with instances of failure, to find cases which, agreeing in all other respects, differed only in the fact that mercury had been administered, or that it had not.

§ 7. [*The method of simple observation inapplicable to the case of complex effects*] That the last of these three modes of investigation is applicable to the case, no one has ever seriously contended. No conclusions of value on a subject of such intricacy, ever were obtained in that way. The utmost that could result would be a vague general impression for or against

---

*f–f*MS, 43, 46, 51, 56, 62   that
g–g+72
*h–h*MS, 43, 46, 51, 56, 62, 65, 68   produced
*a–a*MS   §6. [*sic; should read* §7.]

the efficacy of mercury, of no [b] avail for guidance unless confirmed by one of the other two methods. Not that the results, which this method strives to obtain, would not be of the utmost possible value if they could be obtained. If all the cases of recovery which presented themselves, in an examination extending to a great number of instances, were cases in which mercury had been administered, we might generalize with confidence from this experience, and should have obtained a conclusion of real value. But no such basis for generalization can we, in a case of this description, hope to obtain. The reason is that which we have [c] spoken of as constituting the characteristic imperfection of the Method of Agreement; Plurality of Causes. Supposing even that mercury does tend to cure the disease, so many other causes, both natural and artificial, also tend to cure it, that there are sure to be abundant instances of recovery in which mercury has not been administered: unless, indeed, the practice be to administer it in all cases; on which supposition it will equally be found in the cases of failure.

When an effect results from the union of many causes, the share which each has in the determination of the effect cannot in general be great: and the effect is not likely, even in its presence or absence, still less in its variations, to follow [d], even approximately,[d] any one of the causes. Recovery from a disease is an event to which, in every case, many influences must concur. Mercury may be one such influence; but from the very fact that there are many other such, it will necessarily happen that although mercury is administered, the patient, for want of other concurring influences, will often not recover, and that he often will recover when it is not administered, the other favourable influences being sufficiently powerful without it. Neither, therefore, will the instances of recovery agree in the administration of mercury, nor will the instances of failure agree in [e]its non-administration[e]. It is much if, by multiplied and accurate returns from hospitals and the like, we can collect that there are rather more recoveries and rather fewer failures when mercury is administered than when it is not; a result of very secondary value even as a guide to practice, and almost worthless as a contribution to the theory of the subject.*

*[72] It is justly remarked by Professor Bain, that though the Methods of Agreement and Difference are not applicable to these cases, they are not wholly inaccessible to the Method of Concomitant Variations. "If a cause happens to vary alone, the effect will also vary alone: a cause and effect may be thus singled out under the greatest complications. Thus, when the appetite for food increases with the cold, we have a strong evidence of connexion between these two facts, although other circumstances may operate in the same direction. The assigning

[b]MS, 43, 46   real
[c]MS, 43, 46, 51   so often
[d-d]MS, 43   very exactly] 46, 51   , even approximatively,
[e-e]MS, 43, 46   the non-administration of it

ª§ 8.ª [The purely experimental method inapplicable to the case of complex effects] The inapplicability of the method of simple observation to ascertain the conditions of effects dependent on many concurring causes, being thus recognised; we shall next inquire whether any greater benefit can be expected from the other branch of the *à posteriori* method, that which proceeds by directly trying different combinations of causes, either artificially produced or found in nature, and taking notice what is their effect: as, for example, by actually trying the effect of mercury, in as many different circumstances as possible. This method differs from the one which we have just examined, in turning our attention directly to the causes or agents, instead of turning it to the effect, recovery from the disease. And since, as a general rule, the effects of causes are far more accessible to our study than the causes of effects, it is natural to think that this method *ᵇhas a much better chance of proving successful than the formerᵇ*.

The method now under consideration is called the Empirical Method; and in order to estimate it fairly, we must suppose it to be completely, not incompletely, empirical. We must exclude from it everything which partakes of the nature not of an experimental but of a deductive operation. If for instance we try experiments with mercury upon a person in health, in order to ascertain the general laws of its action upon the human body, and then reason from these laws to determine how it will act upon persons affected with a particular disease, this may be a really effectual method, but this is deduction. The experimental method does not derive the law of a complex case from the simpler laws which conspire to produce it, but makes its experiments directly upon the complex case. We must make entire abstraction of all knowledge of the simpler tendencies, the *ᶜmodiᶜ* operandi of mercury in detail. Our experi-

---

of the respective parts of the sun and moon in the action of the tides, may be effected, to a certain degree of exactness, by the variations of the amount according to the positions of the two attractive bodies. By a series of experiments of Concomitant Variations, directed to ascertain the elimination of nitrogen from the human body under varieties of muscular exercise, Dr. Parkes obtained the remarkable conclusion, that a muscle grows during exercise, and loses bulk during the subsequent rest." (*Logic*, Pt. II, p. 83.)

It is, no doubt, often possible to single out the influencing causes from among a great number of mere concomitants, by noting what are the antecedents, a variation in which is followed by a variation in the effect. But when there are many influencing causes, no one of them greatly predominating over the rest, and especially when some of these are continually changing, it is scarcely ever possible to trace such a relation between the variations of the effect and those of any one cause, as would enable us to assign to that cause its real share in the production of the effect.

*a–a*MS §7. [*sic; should read* §8.]
*b–b*MS, 43 may be successful although the former must necessarily fail
*c–c*MS *modus*

mentation must aim at obtaining a direct answer to the specific question, Does or does not mercury tend to cure the particular disease?

Let us see, therefore, how far ^{d}the^d case admits of the observance of those rules of experimentation, which it is found necessary to observe in other cases. When we devise an experiment to ascertain the effect of a given agent, there are certain precautions which we never, if we can help it, omit. In the first place, we introduce the agent into the midst of a set of circumstances which we have exactly ascertained. It needs hardly be remarked how far this condition is from being realized in any case connected with the phenomena of life; how far we are from knowing what are all the circumstances which pre-exist in any instance in which mercury is administered to a living being. This difficulty, however, though insuperable in most cases, may not be so in all; there are sometimes ^{e} concurrences of many causes, in which we yet know accurately what the causes are. ^{f}Moreover, the difficulty may be attenuated by sufficient multiplication of experiments, in circumstances rendering it improbable that any of the unknown causes should exist in them all.^{f} But when we have got clear of this obstacle, we encounter another still more serious. In other cases, when we intend to try an experiment, we do not reckon it enough that there be no circumstance in the case the presence of which is unknown to us. We require also that none of the circumstances which we do know^g, shall have effects susceptible of being confounded with those of the ^{h}agents^h whose properties we wish to study. We take the utmost pains to exclude all causes capable of composition with the given cause; or if forced to let in any such causes, we take care to make them such that we can compute and allow for their influence, so that the effect of the given cause may, after the subduction of those other effects, be apparent as a residual phenomenon.

These precautions are inapplicable to such cases as we are now considering. The mercury of our experiment being tried with an unknown multitude (or even let it be a known multitude) of other influencing circumstances, the mere fact of their being influencing circumstances implies that they disguise the effect of the mercury, and preclude us from knowing whether it has any effect or ^{i}not^i. Unless we already knew what and how much is owing to every other circumstance, (that is, unless we suppose the very problem solved which we are considering the means of solving,) we cannot tell that those other circumstances may not have produced the whole of the effect, independently or even in spite of the mercury. The Method of Difference, in

$^{d-d}$MS, 43   this
^{e}MS, 43, 46, 51, 56, 62   (though I should think never in physiology)
$^{f-f}$+65, 68, 72
^{g}MS, 43, 46   of
$^{h-h}$MS, 43, 46, 51, 56, 62, 65, 68   agent
$^{i-i}$MS, 43, 46, 51   no

the ordinary mode of its use, namely, by comparing the state of things following the experiment with the state which preceded it, is thus, in the case of intermixture of effects, entirely unavailing; because other causes than that whose effect we are seeking to determine, have been operating during the transition. As for the other mode of employing the Method of Difference, namely by comparing, not the same case at two different periods, but different cases, this in the present instance is quite chimerical. In phenomena so complicated it is questionable if two cases, similar in all respects but one, ever occurred; and were they to occur, we could not possibly know that they were so exactly similar.

Anything like a scientific use of the method of experiment, in these complicated cases, is therefore out of the question. We can *generally, even* in the most favourable cases, only discover by a succession of trials, that a certain cause is *very often* followed by a certain effect. For, in one of these conjunct effects, the portion which is determined by any one of the influencing agents, is *usually*, as we before remarked, but small; and it must be a more potent cause than most, if even the tendency which it really exerts is not thwarted by other tendencies in nearly as many cases as it is fulfilled. *Some causes indeed there are which are more potent than any counteracting causes to which they are commonly exposed; and accordingly there are some truths in medicine which are sufficiently proved by direct experiment. Of these the most familiar are those that relate to the efficacy of the substances known as Specifics for particular diseases; "quinine, colchicum, lime juice, cod liver oil,"* and a few others. Even these are not invariably followed by success; but they succeed in so large a proportion of cases, and against such powerful obstacles, that their *tendency* to restore health in the disorders for which they are prescribed may be regarded as an experimental truth.†*

If so little can be done by the experimental method to determine the conditions of an effect of many combined causes, in the case of medical science; still less is this method applicable to a class of phenomena more

*[72] Bain's *Logic*, Pt. II, p. 360.

†[72] What is said in the text on the inapplicability of the experimental methods to resolve particular questions of medical treatment, does not detract from their efficacy in ascertaining the general laws of the animal or human system. The functions, for example, of the different classes of nerves have been discovered, and probably could only have been discovered, by experiments on living animals. Observation and experiment are the ultimate basis of all knowledge: from them we obtain the elementary laws of life, as we obtain all other elementary truths. It is in dealing with the complex combinations that the experimental methods are for the most part illusory, and the deductive mode of investigation must be invoked to disentangle the complexity.

j–j+72
*k–k*MS, 43, 46, 51, 56, 62, 65, 68   generally
l–l+72

complicated than even those of physiology, the phenomena of politics and history. There, Plurality of Causes exists in almost boundless excess, and [m] effects are, for the most part, inextricably interwoven with one another. To add to the embarrassment, most of the inquiries in political science relate to the production of effects of a most comprehensive description, such as the public wealth, public security, public morality, and the like: results liable to be affected directly or indirectly either in *plus* or in *minus* by nearly every fact which exists, or event which occurs, in human society. The vulgar notion, that the safe methods on political subjects are those of Baconian induction—that the true guide is not general reasoning, but specific experience —will one day be quoted as among the most unequivocal marks of a low state of the speculative faculties in any age in which it is accredited. [n]Nothing[n] can be more ludicrous than the sort of parodies on experimental reasoning which one is accustomed to meet with, not in popular discussion only, but in grave treatises, when the affairs of nations are the theme. "How," it is asked, "can an institution be bad, when the country has prospered under it?" "How can such or such causes have contributed to the prosperity of one country, when another has prospered without them?" Whoever makes use of an argument of this kind, not intending to deceive, should be sent back to learn the elements of some one of the more easy physical sciences. Such reasoners ignore the fact of Plurality of Causes in the very case which affords the most signal example of it. So little could be concluded, in such a case, from any possible collation of individual instances, that even the impossibility, in social phenomena, of making artificial experiments, a circumstance otherwise so prejudicial to directly inductive inquiry, hardly affords, in this case, additional reason of regret. For even if we could try experiments upon a nation or upon the human race, with as little scruple as M. Magendie [o]tried[o] them on dogs [p]and[p] rabbits, we should never succeed in making two instances identical in every respect except the presence or absence of some one definite circumstance. The nearest approach to an experiment in the philosophical sense, which takes place in politics, is the introduction of a new operative element into national affairs by some special and assignable measure of government, such as the enactment or repeal of a particular law. But where there are so many influences at work, it requires some time for the influence of any new cause upon national phenomena to become apparent; and as the causes operating in so extensive a sphere are not only infinitely numerous, but in a state of perpetual alteration, it is always certain that before the effect of the new cause becomes conspicuous enough to be a

---

[m]MS, 43, 46, 51, 56, 62, 65   the
[n–n]MS, 43, 46   What
[o–o]MS, 43, 46, 51, 56   tries
[p–p]MS, 43, 46, 51, 56, 62   or

subject of induction, so many of the other influencing circumstances will have changed as to vitiate the experiment.*

Two, therefore, of the three possible methods for the study of phenomena resulting from the composition of many causes, being, from the very nature of the case, inefficient and illusory, there remains only the third,—that which considers the causes separately, and ᵍinfersᵍ the effect from the balance of the different tendencies which produce it: in short, the deductive, or à priori method. The more particular consideration of this intellectual process requires a chapter to itself.

*[72] Professor Bain, though concurring generally in the views expressed in this chapter, seems to estimate more highly than I do the scope for specific experimental evidence in politics. (*Logic*, Pt. II, pp. 333–7.) There are, it is true, as he remarks (p. 336) some cases "when an agent suddenly introduced is almost instantaneously followed by some other changes, as when the announcement of a diplomatic rupture between two nations is followed the same day by a derangement of the money-market." But this experiment would be quite inconclusive merely as an experiment. It can only serve, as any experiment may, to verify the conclusion of a deduction. Unless we already knew by our knowledge of the motives which act on business men, that the prospect of war *tends* to derange the money-market, we should never have been able to prove a connexion between the two facts, unless after having ascertained historically that the one followed the other in too great a number of instances to be consistent with their having been recorded with due precautions. Whoever has carefully examined any of the attempts continually made to prove economic doctrines by such a recital of instances, knows well how futile they are. It always turns out that the circumstances of scarcely any of the cases have been fully stated; and that cases, in equal or greater numbers, have been omitted, which would have tended to an opposite conclusion.

ᵍ–ᵍMS, 43, 46, 51, 56, 62   computes

CHAPTER XI

Of the Deductive Method

§ 1. [*First stage; ascertainment of the laws of the separate causes by direct induction*] The mode of investigation which, from the proved inapplicability of direct methods of observation and experiment, remains to us as the main source of the knowledge we possess or can acquire respecting the conditions, and laws of recurrence, of the more complex phenomena, is called, in its most general expression, the Deductive Method; and consists of three operations: the first, one of direct induction; the second, of ratiocination; *a* the third, of verification.

I call the first step in the process an inductive operation, because there must be a direct induction as the basis of the whole; though in many particular investigations the place of the induction may be supplied by a prior deduction; but the premises of this prior deduction must have been derived from induction.

The problem of the Deductive Method is, to find the law of an effect, from the laws of the different tendencies of which it is the joint result. The first requisite, therefore, is to know the laws of those tendencies; the law of each of the concurrent causes: and this supposes a previous process of observation or experiment upon each cause separately; or else a previous deduction, which also must depend for its ultimate premises on observation or experiment. Thus, if the subject be social or historical phenomena, the premises of the Deductive Method must be the laws of the causes which determine that class of phenomena; and those causes are human actions, together with the general outward circumstances under the *b*influence*b* of which mankind are placed, and which constitute man's position *c*on the earth*c*. The Deductive Method, applied to social phenomena, must begin, therefore, by investigating, or must suppose to have been already investigated, the laws of human action, and those properties of outward things by which the actions of human beings in society are determined. Some of these general truths will naturally be obtained by observation and experiment, others by deduction: the more complex laws of human action, for example, may be deduced from the

*a*MS, 43, 46, 51, 56 and
*b–b*MS, 43 dominion
*c–c*MS, 43, 46 in this world

simpler ones; but the simple or elementary laws will always, and necessarily, have been obtained by a directly inductive process.

To ascertain, then, the laws of each separate cause which takes a share in producing the effect, is the first desideratum of the Deductive Method. To know what the causes are, which must be subjected to this process of study, may or may not be difficult. In the case last mentioned, this first condition is of easy fulfilment. That social phenomena *depend* on the acts and mental impressions of human beings, never could have been a matter of any doubt, however imperfectly it may have been known either by what laws those impressions and actions are governed, or to what social consequences their laws naturally lead. Neither, again, after physical science had attained a certain development, could there be any real doubt where to look for the laws on which the phenomena of life depend, since they must be the mechanical and chemical laws of the solid and fluid substances composing the organized body and the medium in which it subsists, together with the peculiar vital laws of the different tissues constituting the organic structure. In other cases, really far more simple than these, it was much less obvious in what quarter the causes were to be looked for: as in the *e* case of the celestial phenomena. Until, by combining the laws of certain causes, it was found that those laws explained all the facts which experience had proved concerning the heavenly motions, and led to predictions which it always verified, mankind never knew that those *were* the causes. But whether we are able to put the question before, or not until after, we have become capable of answering it, in either case it must be answered; the laws of the different causes must be ascertained, before we can proceed to deduce from them the conditions of the effect.

The mode of ascertaining *those* laws neither is, nor can be, any other than the fourfold method of experimental inquiry, already discussed. A few remarks on the application of that method to cases of the Composition of Causes, are all that is requisite.

It is obvious that we cannot expect to find the law of a tendency, by an induction from cases in which the tendency is counteracted. The laws of motion could never have been brought to light from the observation of bodies kept at rest by the equilibrium of opposing forces. Even where the tendency is not, in the ordinary sense of the word, counteracted, but only modified, by having its *effects* compounded with the effects arising from some other tendency or tendencies, we are still in an unfavourable position for tracing, by means of such cases, the law of the tendency itself. It would have been *scarcely possible* to discover the law that every body in motion tends to continue moving in a straight line, by an induction from instances in

*d–d*MS, 43, 46   depended   *e*MS, 43, 46   great
*f–f*MS, 43, 46   these   *g–g*MS   effect
*h–h*MS, 43, 46, 51, 56   difficult

which the motion is deflected into a curve, by being compounded with the effect of an accelerating force. Notwithstanding the resources afforded in this description of cases by the Method of Concomitant Variations, the principles of a judicious experimentation prescribe that the law of each of the tendencies should be studied, if possible, in cases in which that tendency operates alone, or in combination with no agencies but those of which the effect can, from previous knowledge, be calculated and allowed for.

Accordingly, in the cases, *unfortunately* very numerous and important, in which the causes do not suffer themselves to be separated and observed apart, there is much difficulty in laying down with due certainty the inductive foundation necessary to support the deductive method. This difficulty is most *jof all* conspicuous in the case of physiological phenomena; it being *kseldom possible* to separate the different agencies which collectively compose an organized body, without destroying the very phenomena which it is our object to investigate:

—following life, in creatures we dissect,
We lose it, in the moment we detect.[*]

And for this reason I am *linclined* to the opinion, that physiology *m(greatly and rapidly progressive as it now is)m* is embarrassed by greater natural difficulties, and is probably susceptible of a less degree of ultimate perfection, than *neven* the social science; inasmuch as it is possible to study the laws *oand operations of one human mind apart from other minds*, much less imperfectly than we can study the laws of one organ or tissue of the human body apart from the other organs or tissues.

It *phas been judiciously remarkedp* that pathological facts, or, to speak in common language, diseases in their different forms and degrees, afford in the case of physiological investigation the *qmost valuableq* equivalent to experimentation properly so called; inasmuch as they often exhibit to us a definite disturbance in some one organ or organic function, the remaining organs and functions being, in the first instance at least, unaffected. It is true that

[*Alexander Pope, *Moral Essays*, Epistle I, ll. 29–30; in *Works*. New ed. Ed. Joseph Warton, *et al*. London: Priestley, 1822, Vol. III, p. 178.]

*i–i*MS, 43, 46   unhappily
j–j+51, 56, 62, 65, 68, 72
*k–k*MS, 43, 46, 51, 56, 62, 65   impossible
*l–l*MS, 43   not quite prepared to agree with M. Comte, in deeming the science of society and government intrinsically a more difficult study than the science of organic and animal life. [See, e.g., *Cours*, Vol. IV, pp. 471ff.] I cannot but incline
m–m+68, 72
n–n+46, 51, 56, 62, 65, 68, 72
*o–o*MS, 43, 46   of one man's mind and actions apart from other men
*p–p*MS, 43   is profoundly remarked by M. Comte, [see *Cours*, Vol. III, p. 333]
*q–q*MS, 43   nearest]   46, 51, 56, 62, 65   most available [*printer's error?*]

from the perpetual actions and reactions which are going on among all [r] parts of the organic economy, there can be no prolonged disturbance in any one function without ultimately involving many of the others; and when once it has done so, the experiment for the most part loses its scientific value. All depends on observing the early stages of the derangement; which, unfortunately, are of necessity the least marked. If, however, the organs and functions not disturbed in the first instance, become affected in a fixed order of succession, some light is thereby thrown upon the action which one organ exercises over another: and we occasionally obtain a series of effects which we can refer with some confidence to the original local derangement; but for this it is necessary that we should know that the original derangement *was* local. If it was what is termed constitutional, that is, if we do not know in what part of the animal economy it took its rise, or the precise nature of the disturbance which took place in that part, we are unable to determine which of the various derangements was cause and which effect; which of them were produced by one another, and which by the direct, though perhaps tardy, action of the original cause.

Besides [s] natural pathological facts, we can produce pathological facts artificially; we can try experiments, even in the popular sense of the term, by subjecting the living being to some external agent, such as the mercury of our former example [t], or the section of a nerve to ascertain the functions of different parts of the nervous system[t]. As this experimentation is not intended to obtain a direct solution of any practical question, but to discover general laws, from which afterwards the conditions of any particular effect may be obtained by deduction; the best cases to select are those of which the circumstances can be best ascertained: and such are generally not those in which there is any practical object in view. The experiments are best tried, not in a state of disease, which is essentially a changeable state, but in the condition of health, comparatively a fixed state. In the one, unusual agencies are at work, the results of which we have no means of predicting; in the other, the course of the accustomed physiological phenomena would, it may generally be presumed, remain undisturbed, were it not for the disturbing cause which we introduce.

Such, with the occasional aid of the Method of [u]Concomitant[u] Variations, (the latter not less incumbered than the more elementary methods by the peculiar difficulties of the subject,) are our inductive resources for ascertaining the laws of the causes considered separately, when we have it not in our power to make trial of them in a state of actual separation. The insufficiency

---

[r]MS, 43, 46 the
[s]MS the
[t–t]+65, 68, 72
[u–u]MS Comparative [*slip of the pen?*]

of these resources is so glaring, that no one can be surprised at the backward state of the science of physiology; in which indeed our knowledge of causes is so imperfect, that we can neither explain, nor could without specific experience have predicted, many of the facts which are certified to us by the most ordinary observation. Fortunately, we are much better informed as to the empirical laws of the phenomena, that is, the uniformities respecting which we cannot yet decide whether they are cases of causation, or mere results of it. Not only has the order in which the facts of organization and life successively manifest themselves, from the first germ of existence to death, been found to be uniform, and very accurately ascertainable; but, *v* by a great application of the Method of Concomitant Variations to the entire facts of comparative anatomy and physiology, the *w*characteristic organic structure corresponding to each class of functions has*w* been determined with considerable precision. *x* Whether these organic conditions are the whole of the conditions, and *y*in many cases whether they are*y* conditions at all, or mere collateral effects of some common cause, we are quite ignorant; nor are we ever likely to know, unless we could construct an organized body, and try whether it would live.

Under such disadvantages do we, in cases of this description, attempt the initial, or inductive step, in the application of the Deductive Method to complex phenomena. But such, fortunately, is not the common case. In general, the laws of the causes on which the effect depends may be obtained by an induction from comparatively simple instances, or, at the worst, by deduction from the laws of simpler causes, so obtained. By simple instances are meant, of course, those in which the action of each cause was not intermixed or interfered with, or not to any great extent, by other causes whose laws were unknown. And only when the induction which furnished the premises to the Deductive Method rested on such instances, has the application of such a method to the ascertainment of the laws of a complex effect, been attended with brilliant results.

§ 2. [*Second stage; ratiocination from the simple laws *a*of*a* the complex cases*] When the laws of the causes have been ascertained, and the first stage of the great logical operation now under discussion satisfactorily accomplished, the second part follows; that of determining from the laws of the causes, what effect any given combination of those causes will produce. This is a process of calculation, in the wider sense of the term; and very often

*v*MS, 43, 46   moreover,
*w-w*MS, 43, 46, 51, 56, 62, 65   conditions of organic . . . functions have
*x*MS, 43   [*footnote:*] *This great philosophical operation has been admirably characterized in the third volume of M. Comte's truly encyclopedical work.
*y-y*MS, 43, 46   whether they be]   51, 56, 62, 65   indeed whether they are
*a-a*MS, 43, 46, 51   to

involves processes of calculation in the narrowest sense. It is a ratiocination; and when our knowledge of the causes is so perfect, as to extend to the exact numerical laws which they observe in producing their effects, the ratiocination may reckon among its premises the theorems of the science of number, in the whole immense extent of that science. Not only are the *b*most advanced*b* truths of mathematics often required to enable us to compute an effect, the numerical law of which we already know; but, even by the aid of those *c*most advanced*c* truths, we can go but a little way. In so simple a case as the *d*common*d* problem of three bodies gravitating towards one another, with a force directly as their mass and inversely as the square of the distance, all the resources of the calculus have not hitherto sufficed to obtain *e*any general solution but an approximate one*e*. In a case a little more complex, but still one of the simplest which arise in practice, that of the motion of a projectile, the causes which affect the velocity and range (for example) of a cannon-ball may be all known and estimated; the force of the gunpowder, the angle of elevation, the density of the air, the strength and direction of the *f*wind*f*; but it is one of the most difficult of *g* mathematical problems to combine all these, so as to determine the effect resulting from their collective action.

Besides the theorems of number, those of geometry also come in as premises, where the effects take place in space, and involve motion and extension, as in mechanics, optics, acoustics, astronomy. But when the complication increases, and the effects are under the influence of so many and such shifting causes as to give no room either for fixed numbers, or for straight lines and regular curves, (as in the case of physiological, to say nothing of mental and social phenomena,) the laws of number and extension are applicable, if at all, only on that large scale on which precision of details becomes *h*unimportant. Although*h* these laws play a conspicuous part in the most striking examples of the investigation of nature by the Deductive Method, as for example in the Newtonian theory of the celestial motions, they are by no means an indispensable part of every such process. All that is essential in it is *i*reasoning from a general law to a particular case, that is, determining*i* by means of the particular circumstances of that case, what result is required in that instance to fulfil the law. Thus in the Torricellian experiment, if the fact that air *j*has*j* weight had been previously known, it

*b–b*MS, 43, 46, 51   highest
*c–c*MS, 43, 46, 51   highest
*d–d*MS, 43, 46   celebrated
*e–e*MS, 43   anything more than an approximate general solution
*f–f*43   sound [*printer's error?*]
*g*MS, 43, 46   all
*h–h*MS, 43, 46, 51, 56, 62, 65   unimportant; and although
*i–i*MS, 43, 46   the ratiocination from . . . is, the determination,
*j–j*MS, 43, 46   had

would have been easy, without any numerical data, to deduce from the general law of equilibrium, that the mercury would stand in the tube at such a height that the column of mercury would exactly balance a column of the atmosphere of equal diameter; because, otherwise, equilibrium would not exist.

By such ratiocinations from the separate laws of the causes, we may, to a certain extent, succeed in answering either of the following questions: Given a certain combination of causes, what effect will follow? ^{k}and^k, What combination of causes, if it existed, would produce a given effect? In the one case, we determine the effect to be expected in any complex circumstances of which the different elements are known: in the other case we learn, according to what law—under what antecedent conditions—a given complex effect will ^{l}occur^l.

§ 3. [*Third stage; verification by specific experience*] But (it may here be asked) are not the same arguments by which the methods of direct observation and experiment were set aside as illusory when applied to the laws of complex phenomena, applicable with equal force against the Method of Deduction? When in every single instance a multitude, often an unknown multitude, of agencies, are clashing and combining, what security have we that in our computation *à priori* we have taken all these into our reckoning? How many must we not generally be ignorant of? Among those which we know, how probable that some have been overlooked; and, even were all included, how vain the pretence of summing up the effects of many causes, unless we know accurately the numerical law of each,—a condition in most cases not to be fulfilled; and even when ^{a}it is^a fulfilled, to make the calculation transcends, in any but very simple cases, the utmost power of mathematical science with ^{b}all^b its most modern improvements.

These objections ^{c}have real^c weight, and would be altogether unanswerable, if there were no test by which, when we employ the Deductive Method, we might judge whether an error of any of the above descriptions had been committed or ^{d}not^d. Such a test however there is: and its application forms, under the name of Verification, the third essential component part of the Deductive Method; without which all the results it can give have little other value than that of ^{e}conjecture^e. To warrant reliance on the general conclusions arrived at by deduction, ^{f}these^f conclusions must be found, on ^{g} careful comparison, to accord with the results of direct observation wherever it can be had. If, when we have experience to compare with them, this experience

$^{k-k}$MS   or $^{l-l}$MS, 43, 46   recur
$^{a-a}$+72 $^{b-b}$+62, 65, 68, 72
$^{c-c}$MS, 43, 46   truly have much $^{d-d}$MS, 43, 46   no
$^{e-e}$MS, 43, 46, 51, 56, 62, 65   guess-work
$^{f-f}$MS   those [*printer's error?*] ^{g}MS, 43, 46   a

confirms them, we may safely trust to them in other cases of which our specific experience is yet to come. But if our deductions have led to the conclusion that from a particular combination of causes a given effect would result, then in all known cases where that combination can be shown to have existed, and where the effect has not followed, we must be able to show (or at least *h*to make a probable*h* surmise) what frustrated it: if we cannot, the theory is imperfect, and not yet to be relied upon. Nor is the verification complete, unless some of the cases in which the theory is borne out by the observed result, are of at least equal complexity with any other cases in which its application could be called for.

*i*If*i* direct observation and collation of instances have furnished us with any empirical laws of the effect (whether true in all observed cases, or only true for the most part), the most effectual verification of which the theory could be susceptible would be, that it led deductively to those empirical laws; that the uniformities, whether complete or incomplete, which were observed to exist among the phenomena, were accounted for by the laws of the causes— were such as could not but exist if those be really the causes by which the phenomena are produced. Thus it was very reasonably deemed an essential requisite of any true theory of the causes of the celestial motions, that it should lead by deduction to Kepler's laws: which, accordingly, the Newtonian theory did.

In order, therefore, to facilitate the verification of theories obtained by deduction, it is important that as many as possible of the empirical laws of the phenomena should be ascertained, by a comparison of instances, conformably to the Method of Agreement: as well as (it must be added) that the phenomena themselves should be described, in the most comprehensive as well as accurate manner possible; by collecting from the observation of parts, the simplest possible correct *j*expressions*j* for the corresponding wholes: as when the series of the observed places of a planet was first expressed *k*by a circle, then*k* by a system of epicycles, and subsequently by an ellipse.

It is worth remarking, that complex instances which would have been of no use for the discovery of the simple laws into which we ultimately analyse their phenomena, nevertheless, when they have served to verify the analysis, become additional evidence of the laws themselves. Although we could not have got at the law from complex cases, still when the law, got at otherwise, is found to be in accordance with the result of a complex case, that case becomes a new experiment on the law, and helps to confirm what it did not

h *h*MS , probably
*i–i*MS We need scarcely observe that if] 43, 46, 51, 56 It needs scarcely be observed, that,—if
*j–j*MS, 43 expression [*printer's error?*]
k–k+51, 56, 62, 65, 68, 72

assist [1] to discover. It is a new trial of the principle in a different set of circumstances; and occasionally serves to eliminate some circumstance not previously excluded, and [m] the exclusion of which might require an experiment impossible to be executed. This was strikingly conspicuous in [n]the[n] example formerly quoted, in which the difference between the observed and the calculated velocity of sound was ascertained to result from the heat extricated by the condensation which takes place in each sonorous vibration. This was a trial, in new circumstances, of the law of the development of heat by compression; and it [o] added materially to the proof of the universality of that law. Accordingly any law of nature is deemed to have gained in point of certainty, by being found to explain some complex case which had not previously been thought of in connexion with it; and this indeed is a consideration to which it is the habit of scientific [p]inquirers[p] to attach rather too much value than too little.

To the Deductive Method, thus characterized in its three constituent parts, Induction, Ratiocination, and Verification, the human mind is indebted for its most [q]conspicuous[q] triumphs in the investigation of nature. To it we owe all the theories by which vast and complicated phenomena are embraced under a few simple laws, which, considered as the laws of those great phenomena, could never have been detected by their direct study. We may form some conception of what the method has done for us, from the case of the celestial motions; one of the simplest among the greater instances of the Composition of Causes, since (except in a few cases not of primary importance) each of the heavenly bodies may be considered, without material inaccuracy, to be never at one time influenced by the attraction of more than two bodies, the sun and one other planet or satellite; making, with the reaction of the body itself, and the [r]force generated by the body's own motion and acting in the direction of the tangent[r], only four different agents on the concurrence of which the motions of that body depend; a much smaller number, no doubt, than that by which any other of the great phenomena of nature is determined or modified. Yet how could we ever have ascertained the combination of forces on which the motions of the earth and planets are dependent, by merely comparing the orbits or velocities of different planets, or the different velocities or positions of the same planet? Notwithstanding

[l]MS, 43, 46   us
[m]MS, 43, 46   to effect
[n-n]56   an
[o]MS, 43, 46   certainly
[p-p]MS, 43, 46   men
[q-q]MS, 43, 46   glorious
[r-r]MS, 43, 46   tangential force] 51, 56, 62, 65   tangential force (as I see no objection to calling the force generated . . . as 72 . . . tangent*) [footnote:] *There is no danger of confounding this acceptation of the term with the peculiar employment of the phrase "tangential force" in the theory of the planetary perturbations.

the regularity which manifests itself in those motions, in a degree so rare among the effects of [s] concurrence of causes; [t]and[t] although the periodical recurrence of exactly the same effect, affords positive proof that all the combinations of causes which occur at all, recur periodically; we should [u]not[u] have known what the causes were, if the existence of agencies precisely similar on our own earth had not, fortunately, brought the causes themselves within the reach of experimentation under simple circumstances. As we shall have occasion to analyse, further on, this great example of the Method of Deduction, we shall not occupy any time with it here, but shall proceed to that secondary application of the Deductive Method, the result of which is not to prove laws of phenomena, but to explain them.

[s]MS, 43, 46, 51, 56, 62, 65, 68   a
[t]–[t]+68, 72
[u]–[u]MS, 43, 46   never

CHAPTER XII

Of the Explanation of Laws
of Nature

§ 1. [*Explanation defined*] The deductive operation by which we derive the law of an effect from the laws of the causes, *ᵃ*the concurrence of which*ᵃ* gives rise to it, may be undertaken either for the purpose of discovering the law, or of explaining a law already discovered. The word *explanation* occurs so continually and holds so important a place in philosophy, that a little time spent in fixing the meaning of it will be profitably employed.

An individual fact is said to be explained, by pointing out its cause, that is, by stating the law or laws of causation, of which its production is an instance. Thus a conflagration is explained, when it is proved to have arisen from a spark falling into the midst of a heap of combustibles. And in a similar manner, a law or uniformity in nature is said to be explained, when another law or laws are pointed out, of which that law itself is but a case, and from which it could be deduced.

§ 2. [*First mode of explanation, by resolving the law of a complex effect into the laws of the concurrent causes and the fact of their coexistence*] There are three distinguishable sets of circumstances in which a law of causation may be explained from, or, as it also is often expressed, resolved into, other laws.

The first is the case already so fully considered; an intermixture of laws, producing a joint effect equal to the sum of the effects of the causes taken separately. The law of the complex *ᵃ*effect*ᵃ* is explained, by being resolved into the separate laws of the causes which contribute to it. Thus, the law of the motion of a planet is resolved into the law of the *ᵇ*acquired*ᵇ* force, which tends to produce an uniform motion in the tangent, and the law of the centripetal force which tends to produce an accelerating motion towards the sun; the real motion being a compound of the two.

ᵃ⁻ᵃMS, 43, 46, 51   of which the concurrence
ᵃ⁻ᵃ51, 56   effects [*printer's error?*]
ᵇ⁻ᵇMS, 43, 46, 51, 56, 62, 65   tangential

It is necessary here to remark, that in this resolution of the law of a complex effect, the laws of which it is compounded are not the only elements. It is resolved into the laws of the separate causes, together with the fact of their coexistence. The one is as essential an ingredient as the other; whether the object be to discover the law of the effect, or only to explain it. To deduce the laws of the heavenly motions, we require not only to know the law of a rectilineal and that of a gravitative force, but the existence of both °these° forces in the celestial regions, and even their relative amount. The complex laws of causation are thus resolved into two distinct kinds of elements: the one, simpler laws of causation, the other (in the aptly selected ᵈexpressionᵈ of Dr. Chalmers) collocations;[*] the collocations consisting in the existence of certain agents or powers, in certain circumstances of place and time. We shall hereafter have occasion to return to this distinction, and to dwell on it at such ᵉ length as dispenses with the necessity of further insisting on it here. The first mode, then, of the explanation of Laws of Causation, is when the law of an effect is resolved into the various tendencies of which it is the result, ᶠtogether withᶠ the laws of those tendencies.

§ 3. [*Second mode of explanation, by the detection of an intermediate link in the sequence*] A second case is when, between what seemed the cause and what was supposed to be its effect, further observation detects an intermediate link; a fact caused by the antecedent, and in its turn causing the consequent; so that the cause at first assigned is but the remote cause, operating through the intermediate phenomenon. A seemed the cause of C, but it subsequently appeared that A was only the cause of B, and that it is B which was the cause of C. For example: mankind were aware that the act of touching an outward object caused a sensation. It was ᵃsubsequentlyᵃ discovered, that after we have touched the object, and before we experience the sensation, some change takes place in a kind of thread called a nerve, which extends from our outward organs to the brain. Touching the object, therefore, is only the remote cause of our sensation; that is, not the cause, properly speaking, but the cause of the cause;—the real cause of the sensation is the change in the state of the nerve. Future experience may not only give us more knowledge than we now have of the particular nature of this change, but may also interpolate another link: between the contact (for example) of the object with our outward organs, and the production of the change of state in the nerve, there may take place some electric phenomenon ᵇ; or some phenomenon of a nature not resembling the effects of any known agencyᵇ. Hitherto,

[*On the Power Wisdom and Goodness of God, Vol. I, p. 20.]

c–cMS those [*printer's error?*]
ᵉMS, 43, 46, 51 a
ᵃ–ᵃMS, 43, 46, 51 , however, at last

ᵈ–ᵈMS, 43, 46, 51, 56, 62, 65 language
ᶠ–ᶠMS, 43, 46, 51, 56, 62 and into
ᵇ–ᵇ+51, 56, 62, 65, 68, 72

however, no such intermediate ^{c}link^c has been discovered; and the touch of the object must be considered, provisionally ^{d} , as the proximate cause of the affection of the nerve. The sequence, therefore, of a sensation of touch on contact with an object, is ascertained not to be an ultimate law; ^{e}it^e is resolved, as the phrase is, into two other laws,—the law that contact with an object produces an affection of the nerve; and the law, that an affection of the nerve produces sensation.

To take another example: the more powerful acids corrode or blacken organic compounds. This is a case of causation, but of remote causation; and is said to be explained when it is shown that there is an intermediate link, namely, the separation of some of the chemical elements of the organic structure from the rest, and their entering into combination with the acid. The acid causes this separation of the elements, and the separation of the elements causes the disorganization, and often the charring of the structure. So, again, chlorine extracts colouring matters (whence its efficacy in bleaching) and purifies the air from infection. This law is resolved into the two following laws. Chlorine has a powerful affinity for bases of all kinds, particularly metallic bases and hydrogen. Such bases are essential elements of colouring matters and contagious compounds: which substances, therefore, are decomposed and destroyed by chlorine.

§ 4. [*Laws are always resolved into laws more general than themselves*] It is of importance to remark, that when a sequence of phenomena is thus resolved into other laws, they are always laws more general than itself. The law that A is followed by C, is less general than either of the laws which connect B with C and A with B. This will appear from very simple considerations.

All laws of causation are liable to be counteracted or frustrated, by the non-fulfilment of some negative condition: the tendency, therefore, of B to produce C may be defeated. Now the law that A produces B, is equally fulfilled whether B is followed by C or not; but the law that A produces C by means of B, is of course only fulfilled when B is really followed by C, and is therefore less general than the law that A produces B. It is also less general than the law that B produces C. For B may have other causes besides A; and as A produces C only by means of B, while B produces C whether it has itself been produced by A or by anything else, the second law embraces a greater number of instances, covers as it were a greater space of ground, than the first.

Thus, in our former example, the law that the contact of an object causes

$^{c-c}$MS, 43, 46   agency
^{d}MS, 43, 46, 51   at least
$^{e-e}$+51, 56, 62, 65, 68, 72

a change in the state of the nerve, is more general than the law that contact with an object causes sensation, since, for aught we know, the change in the nerve may equally take place when, from a counteracting cause, as, for instance, strong mental excitement, the sensation does not follow; as in a battle, where wounds are *sometimes* received without any consciousness of receiving them. And again, the law that change in the state of a nerve produces sensation, is more general than the law that contact with an object produces sensation; since the sensation equally follows the change in the nerve when not produced by contact with an object, but by some other cause; as in the well-known case, when a person who has lost a limb, feels the *same* sensation which he has been accustomed to call a pain in the limb.

Not only are the laws of more immediate sequence into which the law of a remote sequence is resolved, laws of greater generality than that law is, but (as a consequence of, or rather as implied in, their greater generality) they are more to be relied on; there are fewer chances of their being ultimately found not to be universally true. From the moment when the sequence of A and C is shown not to be immediate, but to depend on an intervening phenomenon, then, however constant and invariable the sequence of A and C has hitherto been found, possibilities arise of its failure, exceeding those which can affect either of the more immediate sequences, A, B, and B, C. The tendency of A to produce C may be defeated by whatever is capable of defeating either the tendency of A to produce B, or the tendency of B to produce C; it is therefore twice as liable to failure as either of those more elementary tendencies; and the generalization that A is always followed by C, is *just* twice as likely to be found erroneous. And so of the converse generalization, that C is always preceded and caused by A; which will be erroneous not only if there should happen to be a second immediate mode of production of C itself, but moreover if there be a second mode of production of B, the immediate antecedent of C in the sequence.

The resolution of the one generalization into the other two, not only shows that there are possible limitations of the former, from which its two elements are exempt, but *shows* also where these are to be looked for. As soon as we know that B intervenes between A and C, we also know that if there be cases in which the sequence of A and C does not hold, these are most likely to be found by studying the effects *or* the conditions of the phenomenon B.

It appears, then, that in the second of the three modes in which a law may be resolved into other laws, the latter are more general, that is, extend to more cases, and are also less likely to require limitation from subsequent experience, than the law which they serve to explain. They are more nearly

a–aMS, 43, 46, 51, 56, 62, 65   often   b–bMS, 43, 46   very
cMS   just   d–d+43, 46, 51, 56, 62, 65, 68, 72
e–eMS, 43, 46   and

unconditional; they are defeated by fewer contingencies; they are a nearer approach to the universal truth of nature. The same observations are still more evidently true with regard to the first of the three modes of resolution. When the law of an effect of combined ꟾforcesꟾ is resolved into the separate laws of the causes, the nature of the case implies that the law of the effect is less general than the law of any of the causes, since it only holds when they are combined; while the law of any one of the causes holds good both then, and also when that cause acts apart from the rest. It is also manifest that the complex law is liable to be oftener unfulfilled than any one of the simpler laws of which it is the result, since every contingency which defeats any of the laws prevents so much of the effect as depends on it, and thereby defeats the complex law. The mere rusting, for example, of some small part of a great machine, often suffices entirely to prevent the effect which ought to result from the joint action of all the parts. The law of the effect of a combination of causes is always subject to the whole of the negative conditions which attach to the action of all the causes severally.

There is another and ᵍan equally strongᵍ reason why the law of a complex effect must be less general than the laws of the causes which conspire to produce it. The same causes, acting according to the same laws, and differing only in the proportions in which they are combined, often produce effects which differ not merely in quantity, but in kind. The combination of a ʰcentripetal with a projectileʰ force, in the proportions which obtain in all the planets and satellites of our solar system, gives rise to an elliptical motion; but if the ratio of the two forces to each other were slightly altered, it is ⁱdemonstratedⁱ that the motion produced would be in a circle, or a parabola, or an hyperbola: and it ʲis thoughtʲ that in the case of some comets ᵏone of theseᵏ is ˡprobablyˡ the fact. Yet the law of the parabolic motion would be resolvable into the very same simple laws into which that of the elliptical motion is resolved, namely, the law of the permanence of rectilineal motion, and the law of ᵐgravitationᵐ. If, therefore, in the course of ages, some circumstance were to manifest itself which, without defeating the law of either of those forces, should merely alter their proportion to one another, (such as the shock of ⁿsome solid bodyⁿ, or even the accumulating effect of the resistance of the medium in which astronomers have been led to surmise that the motions of the heavenly bodies take place,) the elliptical motion might be

ꟾ–ꟾMS, 43, 46, 51, 56, 62, 65, 68   causes
ᵍ–ᵍMS, 43, 46, 51, 56   a still stronger
ʰ–ʰMS, 43, 46   tangential with a centripetal
ⁱ–ⁱMS, 43, 46, 51   demonstrable
ʲ–ʲMS, 43   has been supposed]   46, 51, 56   has been surmised
ᵏ–ᵏMS   such
ˡ–ˡMS, 43, 46, 51, 56   really
ᵐ–ᵐMS, 43, 46   an uniform centripetal force
ⁿ–ⁿMS, 43, 46, 51, 56   a comet

changed into a motion in some other °conic section°; and the complex law, ᵖthat the planetary motions take place in ellipsesᵖ, would be deprived of its universality, though the discovery would not at all detract from the universality of the simpler laws into which that complex law is resolved. The law, in short, of each of the concurrent causes remains the same, however their collocations may vary; but the law of their joint effect varies with every difference in the collocations. There needs no more to show how much more general the elementary laws must be, than any of the complex laws which are derived from them.

§ 5. [*Third mode of explanation; the subsumption of less general laws under a more general one*] Besides the two modes which have been treated of, there is a third mode in which laws are resolved into one another; and in this it is self-evident that they are resolved into laws more general than themselves. This third mode is the *subsumption* (as it has been called) of one law under another: or (what comes to the same thing) the gathering up of several laws into one more general law which includes them all. The most splendid example of this operation was when terrestrial gravity and the central force of the solar system were brought together under the general law of gravitation. It had been proved antecedently that the earth and the other planets ᵃtendᵃ to the sun; and it had been known from the earliest times that ᵇ terrestrial bodies tend towards the earth. These were similar phenomena; and to enable them both to be subsumed under one law, it was only necessary to prove that, as the effects were similar in quality, so also they, as to quantity, conform to the same rules. This was first shown to be true of the moon, which agreed with terrestrial objects not only in tending to a centre, but in the fact that this centre was the earth. The tendency of the moon ᶜtowardsᶜ the earth ᵈbeing ascertained to vary as the inverse square of the distance,ᵈ it was deduced from this, by direct calculation, that if the moon were as near to the earth as terrestrial objects are, and the ᵉacquired force in the direction of the tangentᵉ were suspended, the moon would fall towards the earth through exactly as many feet in a second as those objects do by virtue of their weight. ᶠHenceᶠ the inference was irresistible, that the moon also tends to the earth by virtue of its weight: and that the two phenomena, the tendency of the moon to the earth and the tendency of terrestrial objects to the earth, being

°–°MS, 43   curve
ᵖ–ᵖMS, 43   of the heavenly motions, as at present understood]   46, 51, 56, 62   that the heavenly motions . . . as 72
ᵃ–ᵃMS, 43, 46   tended
ᵇMS, 43, 46   all
ᶜ–ᶜMS, 43, 46   to
ᵈ–ᵈMS, 43   was already known to vary . . . distance, and
ᵉ–ᵉMS, 43, 46, 51, 56, 62, 65   tangential force
ᶠ–ᶠMS   Thence

not only similar in quality, but, when ^{g}in^g the same circumstances, identical in quantity, are cases of one and the same law of causation. But the tendency of the moon to the earth, and the tendency of the earth and planets to the sun, were already known to be cases of the same law of causation: and thus the law of all these tendencies, and the law of terrestrial gravity, were recognised as identical, ^{h}and^h were subsumed under one general law, that of gravitation.

In a similar manner, the laws of magnetic phenomena have ^{i}more^i recently been subsumed under known laws of electricity. It is thus that the most general laws of nature are usually arrived at: we mount to them by successive steps. For, to arrive by correct induction at laws which hold under such an immense variety of circumstances, laws so general as to be independent of any varieties of space or time which we are able to observe, requires for the most part many distinct sets of experiments or observations, conducted at different times and by different people. One part of the law is first ascertained, afterwards another part: one set of observations teaches us that the law holds good under some conditions, another ^{j} that it holds good under other conditions, by combining which observations we find that it holds good under conditions much more general, or even universally. The general law, in this case, is literally the sum of all the partial ones; it is ^{k}a^k recognition of the same sequence in different sets of instances; and may, in fact, be regarded as merely one step in the process of elimination. ^{l}The^l tendency of bodies towards one another, which we now call gravity, had at first been observed only on the earth's surface, where it manifested itself only as a tendency of all bodies towards the earth, and might, therefore, be ascribed to a peculiar property of the earth itself: one of the circumstances, namely, the proximity of the earth, had not been eliminated. To eliminate this circumstance required a fresh set of instances in other parts of the universe: these we could not ourselves create; and though nature had created them for us, we were placed in very unfavourable circumstances for observing them. To make these observations, fell naturally to the lot of a different set of persons from those who studied terrestrial phenomena; and had, indeed, been a matter of great interest at a time when the idea of explaining celestial facts by terrestrial laws was looked upon as the confounding of an indefeasible distinction. When, however, the celestial motions were accurately ascertained, and the deductive processes performed, from which it appeared that their laws and those of terrestrial gravity corresponded, those celestial observations became a set of instances which exactly eliminated the circumstance of proximity to the earth; and proved that in the original case, that of terrestrial objects, it was

---

$^{g-g}$MS, 43   under
$^{i-i}$+65, 68, 72
$^{k-k}$MS, 43, 46, 51, 56, 62, 65, 68   the

$^{h-h}$MS, 43, 46, 51   or in other words,
^{j}MS   set
$^{l-l}$MS, 43, 46, 51, 56, 62, 65, 68   That

not the earth, as such, that caused the motion or the pressure, but the circumstance common to that case with the celestial instances, namely, the presence of some great body within certain limits of distance.

§ 6. [*What the explanation of a law of nature amounts to*] There are, then, three modes of explaining laws of causation, or, which is the same thing, resolving them into other laws. First, when the law of an effect of combined causes is resolved into the separate laws of the causes, together with the fact of their combination. Secondly, when the law which connects any two links, not proximate, in a chain of causation, is resolved into the laws which connect each with the intermediate links. Both of these are cases of resolving one law into two or more; in the third, two or more are resolved into one: when, after the law has been shown to hold good in several different classes of cases, we decide that what is true in each of these classes of cases, is true under some more general supposition, consisting of what all those classes of cases have in common. We may here remark that this last operation involves none of the uncertainties attendant on induction by the Method of Agreement, since we need not suppose the result to be extended by way of inference to any new class of cases, different from those by the comparison of which it was engendered.

In all these three processes, laws are, as we have seen, resolved into laws more general than themselves; laws extending to all the cases which the former *ᵃextendedᵃ* to, and others besides. In the first two modes they are also resolved into laws more certain, in other words, more universally true than themselves; they are, in fact, proved not to be themselves laws of nature, the character of which is to be universally true, but *results* of laws of nature, which may be only true conditionally, and for the most part. No difference of this sort exists in the third case; since here the partial laws are, in fact, the very same law as the general one, and any exception to them would be an exception to it too.

By all the three processes, the range of deductive science is extended; since the laws, thus resolved, may be thenceforth deduced demonstratively from the laws into which they are resolved. As already remarked, the same deductive process which proves a law or fact of causation if unknown, serves to explain it when known.

The word explanation is here used in *ᵇits philosophicalᵇ* sense. What is called explaining one law of nature by another, is but substituting one mystery for another; and does nothing to render the general course of nature other than mysterious: we can no more assign a *why* for the more extensive laws than for the partial ones. The explanation may substitute a mystery which

ᵃ⁻ᵃMS, 43, 46, 51, 56   extend
ᵇ⁻ᵇMS, 43, 46   a somewhat peculiar

has become familiar, and has grown to *seem* not mysterious, for one which is still strange. And this is the meaning of explanation, in common parlance. But the process with which we are here concerned often does the very contrary: it resolves a phenomenon with which we are familiar, into one of which we previously knew little or nothing; as when the common fact of the fall of heavy bodies *was* resolved into *the* tendency of all particles of matter towards one another. It must be kept constantly in view, therefore, that *in science, those who speak of explaining any phenomenon mean (or should mean)* pointing out not some more familiar, but merely some more general, phenomenon, of which it is a partial exemplification; or some laws of causation which produce it by their joint or successive action, and from which, therefore, its conditions may be determined deductively. Every such operation brings us a step nearer towards answering the question which was stated *in a previous chapter* as comprehending the whole problem of the investigation of nature, viz. What are the fewest *assumptions, which being granted, the order of nature as it exists would be the result? What are* the fewest general propositions from which all the uniformities existing in nature could be deduced?

The laws, thus explained or resolved, are sometimes said to be *accounted for*; but the expression is incorrect, if taken to mean anything more than what has been already stated. In minds not habituated to accurate thinking, there is often a confused notion that the general laws are the *causes* of the partial ones; that the law of general gravitation, for example, causes the phenomenon of the fall of bodies to the earth. But to assert this, would be a misuse of the word cause: terrestrial gravity is not an effect of general gravitation, but a *case* of it; that is, one kind of the particular instances in which that general law obtains. To account for a law of nature means, and can mean, *nothing* more than to assign other laws more general, together with collocations, which laws and collocations being supposed, the partial law follows without any additional supposition.

*c–c*MS, 43, 46, 51, 56, 62   is

*d–d*MS, 43, 46, 51, 56   a

*e–e*MS, 43, 46   when philosophers speak of explaining any of the phenomena of nature, they always mean,

*f–f*MS, 43   some time ago

*g–g*MS   volitions of a creative power, by which the order of nature as it exists could have been brought into existence; What

*h–h*MS, 43, 46   no more

CHAPTER XIII

Miscellaneous Examples of the Explanation of Laws of Nature

a§ 1. [*The general theories of the sciences*] The most striking example which the history of science presents, of the explanation of laws of causation and other uniformities of sequence among special phenomena, by resolving them into laws of greater simplicity and generality, is the great Newtonian generalization: respecting which typical instance so much having already been said, it is sufficient to call attention to the great number and variety of the special observed uniformities which are in this case accounted for, either as particular cases, or as consequences, of one very simple law of universal nature. The simple fact of a tendency of every particle of matter towards every other particle, varying inversely as the square of the distance, explains the fall of bodies to the earth, the revolutions of the planets and satellites, the motions (so far as known) of comets, and all the various regularities which have been observed in these special phenomena; such as the elliptical orbits, and the variations from exact ellipses; the relation between the solar distances of the planets and the duration of their revolutions; the precession of the equinoxes; the tides, and a vast number of minor astronomical truths.

Mention has also been made in the preceding chapter of the explanation of the phenomena of magnetism from laws of electricity; the special laws of magnetic agency having been affiliated by deduction to observed laws of electric action, in which they have ever since been considered to be included as special cases. An example not so complete in itself, but even more fertile in consequences, having been the starting point of the really scientific study of physiology, is the affiliation, commenced by Bichat, and carried on by subsequent biologists, of the properties of the bodily organs, to the elementary properties of the tissues into which they are anatomically decomposed.

Another striking instance is afforded by Dalton's generalization, commonly known as the atomic theory. It had been known from the very commencement of accurate chemical observation, that any two bodies combine chemi-

*a–a*477[*see* Appendix E *for* §§1–3 *in* MS, 43, 46, 51, 56, 62]

cally with one another in only a certain number of proportions; but those proportions were in each case expressed by a percentage—so many parts (by weight) of each ingredient, in 100 of the compound; (say 35 and a fraction of one element, 64 and a fraction of the other): in which mode of statement no relation was perceived between the proportion in which a given element combines with one substance, and that in which it combines with others. The great step made by Dalton consisted in perceiving, that a unit of weight might be established for each substance, such that by supposing the substance to enter into all its combinations in the ratio either of that unit, or of some low multiple of that unit, all the different proportions, previously expressed by percentages, were found to result. Thus 1 being assumed as the unit of hydrogen, if 8 were then taken as that of oxygen, the combination of one unit of hydrogen with one unit of oxygen would produce the exact proportion of weight between the two substances which is known to exist in water; the combination of one unit of hydrogen with two units of oxygen would produce the proportion which exists in the other compound of the same two elements, called peroxide of hydrogen; and the combinations of hydrogen and of oxygen with all other substances, would correspond with the supposition that those elements enter into combination by single units, or twos, or threes, of the numbers assigned to them, 1 and 8, and the other substances by ones or twos or threes of other determinate numbers proper to each. The result is that a table of the equivalent numbers, or, as they are called, atomic weights, of all the elementary substances, comprises in itself, and scientifically explains, all the proportions in which any substance, elementary or compound, is found capable of entering into chemical combination with any other substance whatever.

§ 2. [*Examples from chemical speculations*] Some interesting cases of the explanation of old uniformities by newly ascertained laws are afforded by the researches of Professor Graham. That eminent chemist was the first who drew attention to the distinction which may be made of all substances into two classes, termed by him crystalloids and colloids; or rather, of all states of matter into the crystalloid and the colloidal states, for many substances are capable of existing in either. When in the colloidal state, their sensible properties are very different from those of the same substance when crystallized, or when in a state easily susceptible of crystallization. Colloid substances pass with extreme difficulty and slowness into the crystalline state, and are extremely inert in all the ordinary chemical relations. Substances in the colloid state are almost always, when combined with water, more or less viscous or gelatinous. The most prominent examples of the state are certain animal and vegetable substances, particularly gelatine, albumen, starch, the gums, caramel, tannin, and some others. Among substances not of organic origin, the most notable instances are hydrated silicic acid, and hydrated alumina, with other metallic peroxides of the aluminous class.

Now it is found, that while colloidal substances are easily penetrated by water, and by the solutions of crystalloid substances, they are very little penetrable by one another: which enabled Professor Graham to introduce a highly effective process (termed dialysis) for separating the crystalloid substances contained in any liquid mixture, by passing them through a thin septum of colloidal matter, which does not suffer anything colloidal to pass, or suffers it only in very minute quantity. This property of colloids enabled Mr. Graham to account for a number of special results of observation, not previously explained.

For instance, "while soluble crystalloids are always highly sapid, soluble colloids are singularly insipid," as might be expected; for, as the sentient extremities of the nerves of the palate "are probably protected by a colloidal membrane," impermeable to other colloids, a colloid, when tasted, probably never reaches those nerves. Again, "it has been observed that vegetable gum is not digested in the stomach; the coats of that organ dialyse the soluble food, absorbing crystalloids, and rejecting all colloids." One of the mysterious processes accompanying digestion, the secretion of free muriatic acid by the coats of the stomach, obtains a probable hypothetical explanation through the same law. Fir ally, much light is thrown upon the observed phenomena of osmose (the passage of fluids outward and inward through animal membranes) by the fact that the membranes are colloidal. In consequence, the water and saline solutions contained in the animal body pass easily and rapidly through the membranes, while the substances directly applicable to nutrition, which are mostly colloidal, are detained by them.*

[a]The property which salt possesses of preserving animal substances from putrefaction is [b]resolved by Liebig[b] into two more general laws, the strong attraction of salt for water, and the necessity of the presence of water as a condition of putrefaction.[*] The intermediate phenomenon which is interpolated between the remote cause and the effect, can here be not merely inferred but seen; for it is a familiar fact, that flesh upon which salt has been thrown is speedily found swimming in brine.

*[65] *Vide* Memoir by Thomas Graham, F.R.S., Master of the Mint, "On ʟiquid Diffusion Applied to Analysis," in the *Philosophical Transactions* [*of the Royal Society*, Vol. CLI, p. 220,] for 1861, reprinted in the *Journal of the Chemical Society* [Vol. XV (1862)], and also separately as a pamphlet.

[*See *Organic Chemistry*, pp. 333–4.]

[a]–[a]476MS, 43, 46, 51, 56, 62   [*appears as opening paragraphs of §3; see* Appendix E, 1138–9 *below*]
[b]–[b]46   resolved

The second of the two factors (as they may be termed) into which the preceding law has been resolved, the necessity of water to putrefaction, itself affords an additional example of the Resolution of Laws. The law itself is proved by the Method of Difference, since flesh completely dried and kept in a dry atmosphere does not putrefy; as we see in the case of dried provisions, and human bodies in very dry climates. A deductive explanation of this same law results from Liebig's speculations. The putrefaction of animal and other azotised bodies is a chemical process, by which they are gradually dissipated in a gaseous form, chiefly in that of carbonic acid and ammonia; now to convert the carbon of the animal substance into carbonic acid requires oxygen, and to convert the azote into ammonia requires hydrogen, which are the elements of water. The extreme rapidity of the putrefaction of azotised substances, compared with the gradual decay of non-azotised bodies (such as wood and the like) by the action of oxygen alone, ᶜhe explainsᶜ from the general law that substances are much more easily decomposed by the action of two different affinities upon two of their elements, than by the action of only one.ᵃ

§ 3. [*Example from Brown-Séquard's researches on the nervous system*] Among the many important properties of the nervous system which have either been first discovered or strikingly illustrated by Dr. Brown-Séquard, I select the reflex influence of the nervous system on nutrition and secretion. By reflex nervous action is meant, action which one part of the nervous system exerts over another part, without any intermediate action on the brain, and consequently without consciousness; or which, if it does pass through the brain, at least produces its effects independently of the will. There are many experiments which prove that irritation of a nerve in one part of the body may in this manner excite powerful action in another part; for example, food injected into the stomach through a divided œsophagus, nevertheless produces secretion of saliva; warm water injected into the bowels, and various other irritations of the lower intestines, have been found to excite secretion of the gastric juice, and so forth. The reality of the power being thus proved, its agency explains a great variety of apparently anomalous phenomena; of which I select the following from Dr. Brown-Séquard's *Lectures on the Nervous System*:[*]

The production of tears by irritation of the eye, or of the mucous membrane of the nose:

The secretions of the eye and nose increased by exposure of other parts of the body to cold:

[*Charles Brown-Séquard, *Course of Lectures on the Physiology and Pathology of the Central Nervous System*. Philadelphia: Collins, 1860, pp. 154ff.]

ᶜ⁻ᶜMS, 43   is explained by Liebig

Inflammation of the eye, especially when of traumatic origin, very frequently excites a similar affection in the other eye, which may be cured by section of the intervening nerve:

Loss of sight sometimes produced by neuralgia; and has been known to be at once cured by the extirpation (for instance) of a carious tooth:

Even cataract has been produced in a healthy eye by cataract in the other eye, or by neuralgia, or by a wound of the frontal nerve:

The well-known phenomenon of a sudden stoppage of the heart's action, and consequent death, produced by irritation of some of the nervous extremities: e.g., by drinking very cold water; or by a blow on the abdomen, or other sudden excitation of the abdominal sympathetic nerve; though this nerve may be irritated to any extent without stopping the heart's action, if a section be made of the communicating nerves:

The extraordinary effects produced on the internal organs by an extensive burn on the surface of the body; consisting in violent inflammation of the tissues of the abdomen, chest, or head: which, when death ensues from this kind of injury, is one of the most frequent causes of it:

Paralysis and anæsthesia of one part of the body from neuralgia in another part; and muscular atrophy from neuralgia, even when there is no paralysis:

Tetanus produced by the lesion of a nerve; Dr. Brown-Séquard thinks it highly probable that hydrophobia is a phenomenon of a similar nature:

Morbid changes in the nutrition of the brain and spinal cord, manifesting themselves by epilepsy, chorea, hysteria, and other diseases, occasioned by lesion of some of the nervous extremities in remote places, as by worms, calculi, tumours, carious bones, and in some cases even by very slight irritations of the skin.[a]

§ 4. [*Examples of following newly-discovered laws into their complex manifestations*] From the foregoing and similar instances, we may see the importance, when a law of nature previously unknown has been brought to light, or when new light has been thrown upon a known law by experiment, of examining all cases which present the conditions necessary for bringing that law into action; a process [a] fertile in demonstrations of special laws previously unsuspected, and explanations of others already empirically known.

For instance, Faraday discovered by experiment, that voltaic electricity could be evolved from a natural magnet, provided a conducting body were set in motion at right angles to the direction of the magnet: and this he found to hold not only of small magnets, but of that great magnet, the earth.[*] The law being thus established experimentally, that electricity is evolved, by a

[*Experimental Researches in Electricity, Series 2, pp. 42ff.]
[a]MS, 43, 46   necessarily

magnet, and a conductor moving at right angles to the direction of its poles, we may now look out for fresh instances in which these conditions meet. Wherever a conductor moves or revolves at right angles to the direction of the earth's magnetic poles, there we may expect an evolution of electricity. In the northern regions, where the polar direction is nearly perpendicular to the horizon, all horizontal motions of conductors will produce electricity; horizontal wheels, for example, made of metal; *likewise* all running streams will evolve a current of electricity, which will circulate round them; and the air thus charged with electricity may be one of the causes of the Aurora Borealis. In the equatorial regions, on the contrary, upright wheels placed parallel to the equator will originate a voltaic circuit, and waterfalls will naturally become electric.

For a second example; it has *been proved*, chiefly by the researches of Professor Graham,[*] that gases have a strong tendency to permeate animal membranes, and diffuse themselves through the spaces which such membranes inclose, notwithstanding the presence of other gases in those spaces. Proceeding from this general law, and reviewing a variety of cases in which gases lie contiguous to membranes, we are enabled to demonstrate or to explain the following more special laws: 1st. The human or animal body, when surrounded with any gas not already contained within the body, absorbs it rapidly; such, for instance, as the gases of putrefying matters: which helps to explain malaria. 2nd. The carbonic acid gas of effervescing drinks, evolved in the stomach, permeates its membranes, and rapidly spreads through the system *d*. 3rd. Alcohol taken into the stomach *e* passes into vapour and spreads through the system with great rapidity; *(which, combined with the high combustibility of alcohol, or in other words its ready combination with oxygen, may perhaps help to explain the bodily warmth immediately consequent on drinking spirituous liquors.)* 4th. In any state of the body in which peculiar gases are formed within it, these will rapidly exhale through all parts of the body; and hence the rapidity with which, in certain states of disease, the surrounding atmosphere becomes tainted. 5th. The putrefaction of the interior parts of a carcase will proceed as rapidly as that of the exterior,

---

[*See, e.g., "Notice of the Singular Inflation of a Bladder," in his *Chemical and Physical Researches*. Edinburgh: Constable, 1876 (paper first published in 1829).]

*b–b*MS and

*c–c*MS, 43, 46, 51, 56 recently been found

*d*MS, 43, 46, 51, 56, 62 , where, as suggested in a former note, it probably combines with the iron contained in the blood

*e*MS, 43, 46 (the temperature of the stomach is above the boiling-point of pure alcohol)

*f–f*MS which helps to explain the spontaneous combustion of spirit-drinkers, & many other phenomena.

from the ready passage outwards of the gaseous products. 6th. The exchange of oxygen and carbonic acid in the lungs is not prevented, but rather promoted, by the intervention of the membrane of the lungs and the coats of the blood-vessels between the blood and the air. It is necessary, however, that there should be a substance in the blood with which the oxygen of the air may immediately combine; otherwise instead of passing into the blood, it would permeate the whole organism: and it is necessary that the carbonic acid, as it is formed in the capillaries, should also find a substance in the blood with which it can combine; otherwise it would leave the body at all points, instead of being discharged through the lungs.

§ 5. [*Examples of empirical generalizations, afterwards confirmed and explained deductively*] The following is a deduction which confirms, by explaining, the [a] empirical generalization, that soda powders weaken the human system. These powders, consisting of a mixture of tartaric acid with bicarbonate of soda, from which the carbonic acid is set free, must pass into the stomach as tartrate of soda. Now, neutral tartrates, citrates, and acetates of the alkalis are found, in their passage through the system, to be changed into carbonates; and to convert a tartrate into a carbonate requires an additional quantity of oxygen, the abstraction of which must lessen the oxygen destined for assimilation with the blood, [b]on[b] the quantity of which the vigorous action of the human system [c]partly depends[c].

The instances of new theories agreeing with and explaining old empiricisms, are innumerable. All the just remarks made by experienced persons on human character and conduct, are so many special laws, which the general laws of the human mind explain and resolve. The empirical generalizations on which the operations of the arts have usually been founded, are continually justified and confirmed on the one hand, or [d]corrected[d] and improved on the other, by the discovery of the simpler scientific laws on which the efficacy of those operations depends. The effects of the rotation of crops, of the various manures, and [e] other processes of improved agriculture, have been for the first time resolved in our own day into known laws of chemical and organic action, by Davy [f], Liebig, and others[f]. The processes of the [g]medical[g] art are even now mostly empirical: their efficacy is concluded, in each instance, from a special and most precarious experimental generalization: but as science advances in discovering the simple laws of chemistry and physiology, progress is made in ascertaining the intermediate links in the [h]series of[h] phenomena, and the more general laws on which they depend; and thus, while the

[a]MS, 43, 46, 51, 56, 62, 65, 68   old but not undisputed
[b-b]MS, 43   and to]   46   and on
[c-c]MS, 43   is proportional
[e]MS, 43, 46   the
[g-g]MS, 43, 46   healing

[d-d]MS, 43, 46   rectified
[f-f]MS, 43, 46, 51, 56   and Liebig
[h-h]+43, 46, 51, 56, 62, 65, 68, 72

old processes are either exploded, or their efficacy, in so far as real, explained, 'better' processes, founded on the knowledge of proximate causes, are continually suggested and brought into use.* Many even of the truths of geometry were generalizations from experience before they were deduced from first principles. The quadrature of the cycloid "is said to have been" first effected by measurement, or rather by weighing a cycloidal card, and comparing its weight with that of a piece of similar card of known dimensions.

§ 6. [*Example from mental science*] To the foregoing examples from physical science, let us add another from mental. The following is one of the simple laws of mind: Ideas of a pleasurable or painful character form associations more easily and strongly than other ideas, that is, they become associated after fewer repetitions, and the association is more durable. This is an experimental law, grounded on the Method of Difference. By deduction from this law, many of the more special laws which experience shows to exist among particular mental phenomena may be demonstrated and explained:— the ease and rapidity, for instance, with which thoughts connected with our passions or our more cherished interests are excited, and the firm hold which the facts relating to them have on our memory; the vivid recollection we retain of minute circumstances which accompanied any object or event that deeply interested us, and of the times and places in which we have been very happy or very miserable; the horror with which we view the accidental instrument of any occurrence which shocked us, or the locality where it took place, and the pleasure we derive from any memorial of past enjoyment; all these effects being proportional to the sensibility of the individual mind, and ^{a}to^a the consequent intensity of the pain or pleasure from which the associa-

---

*It was an old generalization in surgery, that tight bandaging ^{j}had^j a tendency to prevent or dissipate local ^{k}inflammation^k. This sequence, being, in the progress of physiological knowledge, resolved into more general laws, led to the important surgical invention ^{l}made^l by Dr. Arnott, ^{m} the treatment of local inflammation and tumours by means of an equable pressure, produced by a bladder partially filled with air. The pressure, by keeping back the blood from the part, prevents the inflammation, or the tumour, from being nourished: in the case of inflammation, it removes the stimulus, which the organ is unfit to receive; in the case of tumours, by keeping back the nutritive fluid, it causes the absorption of matter to exceed the supply, and the diseased mass is gradually absorbed and disappears.

$^{i-i}$MS, 43, 46　improved
$^{j-j}$MS　has
$^{k-k}$MS, 43, 46　inflammations
$^{l-l}$MS　recently promulgated]　43, 46　recently made
^{m}MS　to whose scientific knowledge & inventive genius mankind have been so often indebted:
$^{n-n}$MS, 43, 46　was
$^{a-a}$+43, 46, 51, 56, 62, 65, 68, 72

tion originated. It has been suggested by *b*the able writer of a biographical sketch of Dr. Priestley in *c*a monthly periodical*cb*,* that the same elementary law of our mental constitution, suitably followed out, would explain a variety of mental phenomena *d*previously*d* inexplicable, and in particular some of the fundamental diversities of human character and genius. *e*Associations*e* being of two sorts, either between synchronous, or between successive impressions; and the influence of the law which renders associations stronger in proportion to the pleasurable or painful character of the impressions, being felt with peculiar force in the synchronous class of associations; *f*it is remarked by the writer referred to*f*, that in minds of strong organic sensibility synchronous associations will be likely to predominate, producing a tendency to conceive things in pictures and in the concrete, *g*richly clothed in*g* attributes and circumstances, a mental habit which is commonly called Imagination, and is one of the peculiarities of the painter and the poet; while persons of more moderate susceptibility to pleasure and pain will have a tendency to associate facts chiefly in the order of their succession, and *h*such persons,*h* if they possess mental superiority, will addict themselves to history or science rather than to creative art. This interesting speculation the author of the present work has endeavoured, on another occasion, to pursue *i*farther*i*, and to *j*examine how far it will avail towards explaining the*j* peculiarities of the poetical temperament.† It is at least an example which may serve, instead of many others, to show the extensive scope which exists for deductive investigation in the important and *k*hitherto so*k* imperfect Science of Mind.

§ 7. [*a*Tendency of all the sciences to become deductive*a*] The copiousness with which *b* the discovery and explanation of special laws of pheno-

*[56] Since acknowledged and reprinted in Mr. Martineau's *Miscellanies*. [Boston: Crosby and Nichols, 1852, pp. 1–55. Originally published as "On the Life, Character, and Works of Dr. Priestley," *Monthly Repository*, n.s. VII (Jan., Feb., Apr., 1833); the reference is to pp. 239–41.]

†[62] ["Thoughts on Poetry and its Varieties,"] *Dissertations and Discussions*, Vol. I, fourth paper [pp. 63–94].

*b–b*MS   one of the few original thinkers, in this department of science, whom England now possesses, the Rev. James Martineau
*c–c*43, 46   one of our monthly periodicals
*d–d*MS, 43, 46, 51, 56   hitherto
*e–e*MS, 43, 46   Our associations
*f–f*MS   Mr. Martineau remarked
*g–g*MS, 43, 46   clothed in all their
h–h+51, 56, 62, 65, 68, 72
*i–i*MS   further [*printer's error?*]
*j–j*MS, 43, 46   explain, by means of it, the leading
*k–k*MS, 43, 46   so eminently
*a–a*MS, 43, 46   *The deductive method henceforth the main instrument of scientific inquiry*
*b*MS, 43, 46, 51   I have exemplified

mena by deduction from simpler and more general ones *has here been exemplified*, was prompted by a desire to characterize clearly, and place in its due position of importance, the Deductive Method; which, in the present state of knowledge, is destined *henceforth irrevocably to predominate in the course of scientific investigation*. A revolution is peaceably and progressively effecting itself in philosophy, the reverse of that to which Bacon has attached his name. That great man changed the *method of the sciences* from deductive to experimental, and it is now rapidly reverting from experimental to deductive. But the deductions which Bacon abolished were from premises hastily snatched up, or arbitrarily assumed. The principles were neither established by legitimate canons of experimental inquiry, nor the results tested by that indispensable element of a rational Deductive Method, verification by specific experience. Between the primitive method of Deduction and that which I have attempted to *characterize*, there is all the difference which exists between the Aristotelian physics and the Newtonian theory of the heavens.

*It would, however, be a mistake to expect that those great generalizations, from which the subordinate truths of the more backward sciences will probably at some future period be deduced by reasoning (as the truths of astronomy are deduced from the generalities of the Newtonian theory), will be found, in all, or even in most cases, among truths now known and admitted. We may rest assured, that many of the most general laws of nature are as yet entirely unthought of; and that many others, destined hereafter to assume the same character, are known, if at all, only as laws or properties of some limited class of phenomena; just as electricity, now recognised as one of the most universal of natural agencies, was once known only as a curious property which certain substances acquired by friction, of first attracting and then repelling light bodies. If the theories of heat, cohesion, crystallization, and chemical action, are destined, as there can be little doubt that they are,

c–c+56, 62, 65, 68, 72

*d–d*MS, 43, 46   irrevocably ... investigation from this time forward

*e–e*MS   Methods of Science

*f–f*MS, 43, 46   define

*g–g*MS, 43, 46   That the advances henceforth to be expected even in physical, and still more in mental and social science, will be chiefly the result of deduction, is evident from the general considerations already adduced. Among subjects really accessible to our faculties, those which still remain in a state of dimness and uncertainty (the succession of their phenomena not having yet been brought under fixed and recognisable laws) are mostly those of a very complex character, in which many agents are at work together, and their effects in a constant state of blending and intermixture. The disentangling of these crossing threads is a task attended with difficulties which, as we have already shown, are susceptible of solution by the instrument of deduction alone. Deduction is the great scientific work of the present and of future ages. The portion henceforth reserved for specific experience in the achievements of science, is mainly that of suggesting hints to be followed up by the deductive inquirer, and of confirming or checking his conclusions.

to become deductive, the truths which will then be regarded as the *principia* of those sciences would probably, if now announced, appear quite as novel* as the law of gravitation appeared to the cotemporaries of Newton; possibly even more so, since Newton's law, after all, was but an extension of the law of weight—that is, of a generalization familiar from of old, and which already comprehended a not inconsiderable body of natural phenomena. The general laws of a similarly commanding character, which we still look forward to the discovery of, may not always find so much of their foundations already laid.

These general truths will doubtless make their first appearance in the character of hypotheses; not proved, nor even admitting of proof, in the first instance, but assumed as premises for the purpose of deducing from them the known laws of concrete phenomena. But this, though their initial, cannot be their final state. To entitle an hypothesis to be received as one of the truths of nature, and not as a mere technical help to the human faculties, it must be capable of being tested by the canons of legitimate induction, and must actually have been submitted to that test. When this shall have been done, and done successfully, premises will have been obtained from which all the other propositions of the science will thenceforth be presented as conclusions, and the science will, by means of a new and unexpected Induction, be rendered Deductive.*

*[65] Written before the rise of the new views respecting the relation of heat to mechanical force; but confirmed rather than contradicted by them.

CHAPTER XIV

*Of*ᵃ the Limits to the Explanation of Laws of Nature; and of Hypotheses

§ 1. [*Can all the sequences in nature be resolvable into one law?*] The preceding considerations have led us to recognise a distinction between two kinds of laws, or observed uniformities in nature: ultimate laws, and what may be termed derivative laws. Derivative laws are such as are deducible from, and may, in any of the modes which we have pointed out, be resolved into, other and more general ones. Ultimate laws are those which cannot. We are not sure that any of the uniformities ᵇwith which we are yet acquaintedᵇ are ultimate laws; but we know that there must be ultimate laws; and that every resolution of a derivative law into more general laws, brings us nearer to them.

Since we are continually discovering that uniformities, not previously known to be other than ultimate, are derivative, and resolvable into more general laws; since (in other words) we are continually discovering ᶜtheᶜ explanation of some sequence which was previously known only as a fact; it becomes an interesting question whether there are any necessary limits to this philosophical operation, or whether it may proceed until all the uniform sequences in nature are resolved into some one universal law. For this seems, at first sight, to be the ultimatum towards which the progress of induction, by the Deductive Method resting on a basis of observation and experiment, is ᵈ tending. Projects of this kind were universal in the infancy of philosophy;

[*In all editions in Mill's lifetime, Volume II commenced with this chapter, which was preceded by the following epigraph: "In such cases the inductive and deductive methods of inquiry may be said to go hand in hand, the one verifying the conclusions deduced by the other; and the combination of experiment and theory, which may thus be brought to bear in such cases, forms an engine of discovery infinitely more powerful than either taken separately. This state of any department of science is perhaps of all others the most interesting, and that which promises the most to research." Sir J. Herschel, *Discourse on the Study of Natural Philosophy* [p. 181].]

ᵃ⁻ᵃ56, 62, 65   On
ᵇ⁻ᵇMS, 43, 46   which we are yet acquainted with
ᶜ⁻ᶜMS, 43, 46   an   ᵈMS, 43, 46   progressively

any speculations which held out a less brilliant prospect, being in those early times deemed not worth pursuing. And the idea receives so much apparent countenance from the nature of the most *remarkable* achievements of modern science, that speculators are even now *frequently appearing,* who profess either to have solved the problem, or to suggest modes in which it may one day be solved. Even where pretensions of this magnitude are not made, the character of the solutions which are given or sought of particular classes of phenomena, often involves such conceptions of what constitutes explanation, as would render the notion of explaining all phenomena whatever by means of some one cause or law, perfectly admissible.

§ 2. [*Ultimate laws cannot be less numerous than the distinguishable feelings of our nature*] It is therefore useful to remark, that the ultimate Laws of Nature cannot possibly be less numerous than the distinguishable sensations or other feelings of our nature;—those, I mean, which are distinguishable from one another in quality, and not merely in quantity or degree. For example; since there is a phenomenon *sui generis*, called colour, which our consciousness testifies to be not a particular degree of some other phenomenon, as heat or odour or motion, but intrinsically unlike all others, it follows that there are ultimate laws of colour; that though the facts of colour may admit of explanation, they never can be explained from laws of heat or odour alone, or of motion alone, but that however far the explanation may be carried, there will always remain in it a law of colour. I do not mean that it might not possibly be shown that some other phenomenon, some chemical or mechanical action for example, invariably precedes, and is the cause of, every phenomenon of colour. But though this, if proved, would be an important extension of our knowledge of nature, it would not explain how or why a motion, or a chemical action, *can* produce a sensation of colour; and however diligent might be our scrutiny of the phenomena, whatever number of hidden links we might detect in the chain of causation terminating in the colour, the last link would still be a law of colour, not a law of motion, nor of any other phenomenon whatever. Nor does this observation apply only to colour, as compared with any other of the great classes of sensations; it applies to every particular colour, as compared with others. White colour can in no manner be explained exclusively by the laws of the production of red colour. In any attempt to explain it, we cannot but introduce, as one element of the explanation, the proposition that some antecedent or other produces the sensation of white.

---

*e–e*MS   memorable
*f–f*MS, 43, 46   constantly rising up (more often on the Continent of Europe than in this island)
*a–a*MS, 43, 46   should

The ideal limit, therefore, of the explanation of natural phenomena (towards which as towards other ideal limits we are constantly tending, without the prospect of ever completely attaining it) would be to show that each distinguishable variety of our sensations, or other states of consciousness, has only one sort of cause; that, for example, whenever we perceive a white colour, there is some one condition or set of conditions which is always present, and the presence of which always produces in us that sensation. As long as there are several known modes of production of a phenomenon (several different substances, for instance, which have the property of whiteness, and between which we cannot trace any other resemblance) so long it is not impossible that one of these modes of production may be resolved into another, or that all of them may be resolved into some more general mode of production, not hitherto recognised. But when the modes of production are reduced to one, we cannot, in point of simplification, go any further. This one may not, after all, be the ultimate mode; there may be other links to be discovered between the supposed cause and the effect; but we can only further resolve the known law, by introducing some other law hitherto unknown; which will not diminish the number of ultimate laws.

In what cases, accordingly, has science been most successful in explaining phenomena, by resolving their complex laws into laws of greater simplicity and generality? Hitherto chiefly in cases of the propagation of various phenomena through space: and, first and principally, the most extensive and important of all facts of that description, _b_mechanical_b_ motion. Now this is _c_exactly_c_ what might be expected from the principles _d_here_d_ laid down. Not only is motion one of the most universal of all phenomena, it is also (as might be expected from _e_that_e_ circumstance) one of those which, apparently at least, are produced in the greatest number of ways; but the phenomenon itself is always, to our sensations, the same in every respect but degree. Differences of duration, or of velocity, are evidently differences in degree only; and differences of direction in space, which alone has any semblance of being a distinction in kind, entirely disappear (so far as our sensations are concerned) by a change in our own position; indeed the very same motion appears to us, according to our position, to take place in every variety of direction, and motions in every different direction to take place in the same. And again, motion in a straight line _f_and_f_ in a curve are no otherwise distinct than that the one is motion continuing in the same direction, the other is motion which at each instant changes its direction. There is, therefore, according to the _g_principles_g_ I have stated, no absurdity in supposing that all

---

_b–b_MS, 43, 46, 51, 56, 62, 65, 68   the fact of
_c–c_MS, 43, 46   entirely   _d–d_MS, 43, 46   which I have
_e–e_MS, 43, 46, 51   the former   _f–f_MS   or [_printer's error?_]
_g–g_MS   views which]   43, 46   views

motion may be produced in one and the same way; by the same kind of cause. Accordingly, the greatest achievements in physical science have consisted in resolving one observed law of the production of motion into the laws of other known modes of production, or the laws of several such modes into one more general mode; as when the fall of bodies to the earth, and the motions of the planets, were brought under the one law of the mutual attraction of all particles of matter; when the motions said to be produced by magnetism were shown to be produced by electricity; when the motions of fluids in a lateral direction, or even contrary to the direction of gravity, were shown to be produced by gravity; and *h*the like*h*. There is an abundance of distinct causes of motion still unresolved into one another; gravitation, heat, electricity, chemical action, nervous action, and so forth; but *i*whether the efforts of the present generation of savans to resolve all these different modes of production into one, are ultimately successful or not*i*, the attempt so to resolve them is perfectly legitimate. For though these various causes produce, in other respects, sensations intrinsically different, and are not, therefore, capable of being resolved into one another, yet in so far as they all produce motion, it is quite possible that the immediate antecedent of the motion may in all these different cases be the same; *j*nor is it impossible that these various agencies themselves may *k*, as the new doctrines assert,*k* all of them have for their own immediate antecedent, modes of molecular motion*j*.

We need not extend our illustration to other cases, as for instance to the propagation of light, sound, heat, electricity, &c. through space, or any of the other phenomena which have been found susceptible of explanation by the resolution of their observed laws into more general laws. Enough has been said to display the difference between the kind of explanation and resolution of laws which is chimerical, and that of which the accomplishment is the great aim of *l*science*l*; and to show into what sort of elements the resolution must be effected, if at all.*

*[72] As is well remarked by Professor Bain, in the very valuable chapter of his *Logic* which treats of this subject (Pt. II, pp. 121–2) "scientific explanation and inductive generalization being the same thing, the limits of Explanation are the limits of Induction," and "the limits to inductive generalization are the limits to the agreement or community of facts. Induction supposes similarity among phenomena; and when such similarity is discovered, it reduces the phenomena

*h–h*MS   so forth
*i–i*MS, 43, 46, 51, 56, 62   however improbable it may be that these different modes of production of motion should ever actually be resolved into one
*j–j*MS, 43, 46, 51, 56   that the other causes may produce motion through the intermediate agency of heat, for instance, or of electricity, or of some common medium yet to be discovered]   62   *as* MS . . . agency of some one of their number, or of some agency different from all, and still remaining to be discovered
k–k+68, 72
*l–l*MS, 43, 46   philosophy

§ 3. [*In what sense ultimate facts can be explained*] As, however, there is scarcely any *ᵃone*ᵃ of the principles of a true method of philosophizing which does not require to be guarded against errors on both sides, I must enter a caveat against another misapprehension, of a kind directly contrary to the preceding *ᵇ*. M. Comteᵇ, among other occasions on which he has condemned, with some asperity, any attempt to explain phenomena which are "evidently primordial," (meaning, apparently, no more than that every *ᶜpeculiar*ᶜ phenomenon must have at least one peculiar and *ᵈtherefore*ᵈ inexplicable

---

under a common statement. The similarity of terrestrial gravity to celestial attraction enables the two to be expressed as one phenomenon. The similarity between capillary attraction, solution, the operation of cements, &c., leads to their being regarded not as a plurality, but as a unity, a single causative link, the operation of a single agency. . . . If it be asked whether we can merge gravity itself in some still higher law, the answer must depend upon the facts. Are there any other forces, at present held distinct from gravity, that we may hope to make fraternize with it, so as to join in constituting a higher unity? Gravity is an attractive force; and another great attractive force is cohesion, or the force that binds together the atoms of solid matter. Might we then join these two in a still higher unity, expressed under a more comprehensive law? Certainly we might, but not to any advantage. The two kinds of force agree in the one point, attraction, but they agree in no other; indeed, in the manner of the attraction, they differ widely; so widely that we should have to state totally distinct laws for each. Gravity is common to all matter, and equal in amount in equal masses of matter, whatever be the kind; it follows the law of the diffusion of space from a point (the inverse square of the distance); it extends to distances unlimited; it is indestructible and invariable. Cohesion is special for each separate substance; it decreases according to distance much more rapidly than the inverse square, vanishing entirely at very small distances. Two such forces have not sufficient kindred to be generalized into one force; the generalization is only illusory; the statement of the difference would still make two forces; while the consideration of one would not in any way simplify the phenomena of the other, as happened in the generalization of gravity itself."

To the impassable limit of the explanation of laws of nature, set forth in the text, must therefore be added a further limitation. Although, when the phenomena to be explained are not, in their own nature, generically distinct, the attempt to refer them to the same cause is scientifically legitimate; yet to the success of the attempt it is indispensable that the cause should be shown to be capable of producing them according to the same law. Otherwise the unity of cause is a mere guess, and the generalization only a nominal one, which, even if admitted, would not diminish the number of ultimate laws of nature.

ᵃ⁻ᵃ+46, 51, 56, 62, 65, 68, 72

ᵇ⁻ᵇMS, 43   , and against which there is the more necessity to be on our guard, as it has the appearance of being countenanced (for I am persuaded that it is only the appearance) by so great a thinker as M. Auguste Comte. That philosopher]   46   ; which receives a certain degree of apparent countenance from some expressions of M. Auguste Comte. That philosopher

ᶜ⁻ᶜMS, 43, 46   such

ᵈ⁻ᵈ+51, 56, 62, 65, 68, 72

law,) has spoken of the attempt to furnish any explanation of the colour belonging to each substance, "la couleur élémentaire propre à chaque substance," as essentially illusory. "No one," says he, "in our time attempts to explain the particular specific gravity of each substance or of each structure. Why should it be otherwise as to the specific colour, the notion of which is undoubtedly no less primordial?"*

Now although, as *he* elsewhere observes,[*] a colour must always remain a different thing from a weight or a sound, *f* varieties of colour might nevertheless follow, or correspond to, given varieties of weight, or sound, or some other phenomenon as different as these are from colour itself. It is one question what a thing is, and another what it depends on; and though to ascertain the conditions of an elementary phenomenon is not to obtain any new insight into the nature of the phenomenon itself, that is no reason against attempting to discover the conditions. *gThe*g interdict against endeavouring to reduce distinctions of colour to any common principle, would have held equally good against a like attempt on the subject of distinctions of sound; which nevertheless have been found to be immediately preceded and caused by distinguishable varieties in the vibrations of elastic bodies: though a sound, no doubt, is quite as different as a colour is from any motion of particles, vibratory or otherwise. We might add, that, in the case of colours, there are strong positive indications that they are not ultimate properties of the different kinds of substances, but depend on conditions capable of being superinduced upon all substances; since there is no substance which cannot, according to the kind of light thrown upon it, be made to assume *h*almost any colour*h*; and since almost every change in the mode of aggregation of the particles of the same substance, is attended with alterations in its colour, and *i*in*i* its optical properties generally.

The *j*really weak point*j* in the attempts which have been made to account for colours by the vibrations of a fluid, is not that the attempt itself is unphilosophical, but that the existence of the fluid, and the fact of its vibratory motion, are not proved; but are assumed, on no other ground than the facility they are supposed to afford of explaining the phenomena. And *k*this consideration leads*k* to the important question of the proper use of scientific

*Cours de Philosophie Positive, Vol. II, pp. 655–7.
[*Ibid., p. 648.]

e–eMS, 43   M. Comte
fMS, 43   it ought not to be forgotten, and notwithstanding these expressions, cannot possibly be forgotten by M. Comte, that]   46   he will admit that
g–gMS, 43   M. Comte's
h–hMS, 43, 46, 51, 56, 62, 65   any colour we think fit
i–i+43, 46, 51, 56, 62, 65, 68, 72
j–jMS, 43, 46, 51, 56, 62, 65, 68   real defect
k–kMS, 43, 46   these considerations lead us

hypotheses; *the connexion of which with the subject* of the explanation of the phenomena of nature, and of the necessary limits to that explanation, needs not be pointed out.

§ 4. [*The proper use of scientific hypotheses*] An hypothesis is any supposition which we make (either without actual evidence, or on evidence avowedly insufficient) in order to endeavour to deduce from it conclusions in accordance with facts which are known to be real; under the idea that if the conclusions to which the hypothesis leads are known truths, the hypothesis itself either must be, or at least is likely to be, true. If the hypothesis relates to the cause, or mode of production of a phenomenon, it will serve, if admitted, to explain such facts as are found capable of being deduced from it. And this explanation is the purpose of many, if not most, hypotheses. Since explaining, in the scientific sense, means resolving an uniformity which is not a law of causation, into the laws of causation from which it results, or a complex law of causation into simpler and more general ones from which it is capable of being deductively inferred; if there do not exist any known laws which fulfil this requirement, we may feign or imagine some which would fulfil it; and this is making an hypothesis.

An hypothesis being a mere supposition, there are no other limits to hypotheses than those of the human imagination; we may, if we please, imagine, by way of accounting for an effect, some cause of a kind utterly unknown, and acting according to a law altogether fictitious. But as hypotheses of this sort would not have any of the plausibility belonging to those which ally themselves by analogy with known laws of nature, and besides would not supply the want which arbitrary hypotheses are generally invented to satisfy, by enabling the imagination to represent to itself an obscure phenomenon in a familiar light; there is probably no hypothesis in the history of science in which both the agent itself and the law of its operation were fictitious. Either the phenomenon assigned as the cause is real, but the law according to which it acts, merely supposed; or the cause is fictitious, but is supposed to produce its effects according to laws similar to those of some known class of phenomena. An instance of the first kind is afforded by the different suppositions *made* respecting the law of the planetary central force, anterior to the discovery of the true law, that the force varies as the inverse square of the distance; which *also suggested itself to* Newton, in the first instance, as an hypothesis, and was verified by proving that it led deductively to Kepler's laws. Hypotheses of the second kind are such as the vortices of Descartes, which were fictitious, but were supposed to obey the known laws of rotatory

---

*l–l*MS, 43, 46   a subject the connexion of which with that
a–a+51, 56, 62, 65, 68, 72
*b–b*MS, 43, 46, 51, 56, 62   was itself suggested by

motion; or the two rival hypotheses respecting the nature of light, the one ascribing the phenomena to a fluid emitted from all luminous bodies, the other (now *c* generally received) attributing them to vibratory motions among the particles of an ether pervading all space. Of the existence of either fluid there is no evidence, save the explanation they are calculated to afford of some of the phenomena; but they are supposed to produce their effects according to known laws; the ordinary laws of continued locomotion in the one case, and in the other, those of the propagation of undulatory movements among the particles of an elastic fluid.

According to the foregoing remarks, hypotheses are invented to enable the Deductive Method to be earlier applied to phenomena. But* in order to discover the cause of any *d*phenomenon*d* by the Deductive Method, the process must consist of three parts; induction, ratiocination, and verification. Induction, (the place of which, however, may be supplied by a prior deduction,) to ascertain the laws of the causes; ratiocination, to compute from those laws, how the causes will operate in the particular combination known to exist in the case in hand; verification, by comparing this calculated effect with the actual phenomenon. No one of these three parts of the process can be dispensed with. In the *e* deduction which proves the identity of gravity *f*with*f* the central force of the solar system, all the three are found. First, it is proved from the moon's motions, that the earth attracts her with a force varying as the inverse square of the distance. This (though partly dependent on prior deductions) corresponds to the first, or purely inductive, step, the ascertainment of the law of the cause. Secondly, from this law, and from the knowledge previously obtained of the moon's mean distance from the earth, and of the actual amount of her deflection from the tangent, it is ascertained with what rapidity the earth's attraction would cause *g*the moon*g* to fall, if she were no further off, and no more acted upon by extraneous forces, than terrestrial bodies are: *h*that*h* is the second step, the ratiocination. Finally, this calculated velocity being compared with the observed velocity with which all heavy bodies fall, by mere gravity, towards the surface of the earth, (*i* sixteen feet in the first second, forty-eight in the second, and so forth, in the ratio of the odd numbers, 1, 3, 5, &c.,) the two quantities *j*are*j* found to agree. The order in which *k*the steps are here presented, was not that*k* of their discovery; but it is their correct logical order, as portions of the proof that the same

*Vide supra, Bk. III, Chap. xi [pp. 454ff.].

*c*MS, 43, 46, 51, 56, 62, 65   more
*d–d*43, 46   phenomena [*printer's error?*]
*e*MS, 43, 46   great
g *g*MS, 43, 46   her
*i*MS, 43, 46   namely
*k–k*MS, 43, 46   I have here presented the three steps was not the exact order

*f–f*MS, 43, 46   and
*h–h*MS, 43, 46, 51, 56   this
*j–j*MS, 43, 46, 51   were

attraction of the earth which causes the moon's motion, causes also the fall of heavy bodies to the earth: a proof which is thus complete in all its parts.

Now, the Hypothetical Method suppresses the first of the three steps, the induction to ascertain the law; and contents itself with the other two operations, ratiocination and verification; the law which is reasoned from, being assumed, instead of proved.

This process may evidently be legitimate on one supposition, namely, if the nature of the case be such that the final step, the verification, shall amount to, and fulfil the conditions of, a complete induction. We want to be assured that the law we have hypothetically assumed is a true one; and its leading deductively to true results will afford this assurance, provided the case be such that a false law cannot lead to a true result; provided no law, except the very one which we have assumed, can lead deductively to the same conclusions which that leads to. And this proviso is *l* often realized. For example, in *m*the very complete*m* specimen of deduction which we just cited, the original major premise of the ratiocination, the law of the attractive force, was ascertained in this *n* mode; by this legitimate employment of the Hypothetical Method. Newton began by an assumption, that the force which at each instant deflects a planet from its rectilineal course, and makes it describe a curve round the sun, is a force tending directly towards the sun. He then proved that if this be so, the planet will describe, as we know by Kepler's first law that it does describe, equal areas in equal times; and, lastly, he proved that if the force acted in any other direction whatever, the planet would not describe equal areas in equal times. It being thus shown that no other hypothesis *o*would*o* accord with the facts, the assumption was proved; the hypothesis became *p*an inductive truth*p*. Not only did Newton ascertain by this hypothetical process the direction of the deflecting force; he proceeded in exactly the same manner to ascertain the law of variation of the quantity of that force. He assumed that the force varied inversely as the square of the distance; showed that from this assumption the remaining two of Kepler's laws might be deduced; and finally, that any other law of variation would give results inconsistent with those laws, and inconsistent, therefore, with the real motions of the planets, of which Kepler's laws were known to be a correct expression.

*q*I have said that in this case the verification fulfils the conditions of an induction: but an induction of what sort? On examination we find that it conforms to the canon of the Method of Difference. It affords the two in-

*l*MS, 43, 46   very
*m–m*MS, 43, 46   that perfect
*n*MS, 43, 46   very
*o–o*MS, 43, 46   could
*p–p*MS, 43, 46   a law, established by the Method of Difference
q–q+51, 56, 62, 65, 68, 72

stances, A B C, *a b c*, and B C, *b c*. A represents central force; A B C, the planets *plus* a central force; B C, the planets [r]apart from[r] a central force. The planets with a central force give *a*, areas proportional to the times; the planets without a central force give *b c* (a set of motions) without *a*, or with something else instead of *a*. This is the Method of Difference in all its strictness. It is true, the two instances which the method requires are obtained in this case, not by experiment, but by a prior deduction. But that is of no consequence. It is immaterial what is the nature of the evidence from which we derive the assurance that A B C will produce *a b c*, and B C only *b c*; it is enough that we have that assurance. In the present case, a process of reasoning furnished Newton with the very instances, which, if the nature of the case had admitted of it, he would have sought by experiment.[q]

It is thus perfectly possible, and indeed is a very common occurrence, that what [s]was[s] an hypothesis at the beginning of the inquiry, becomes a proved law of nature before its close. But [t]in order that this should happen, we must be able, either by deduction or experiment, to obtain *both* the instances which the Method of Difference requires. That we are able from the hypothesis to deduce the known facts, gives only the affirmative instance, A B C, *a b c*. It is equally necessary that we should be able to obtain, as Newton did, the negative instance B C, *b c*; by showing that no antecedent, except the one assumed in the hypothesis, would in conjunction with B C produce *a*.

Now it appears to me that this assurance cannot be obtained, when the cause assumed in the hypothesis is an unknown cause, imagined solely to account for *a*. When we are only seeking to determine the precise law of a cause already ascertained, or to distinguish the particular agent which is in fact the cause, among several agents of the same kind, one or other of which it is already known to be, we may then obtain the negative instance. An inquiry, which of the bodies of the solar system causes by its attraction some particular irregularity in the orbit or periodic time of some satellite or comet, would be a case of the second description. Newton's was a case of the first.[t] If it had not been [u]previously[u] known that the planets were hindered from moving in straight lines by some force tending towards the interior of their orbit, though the exact direction was doubtful; or if it had not been known that the force increased in some proportion or other as the distance diminished, and diminished as it increased; Newton's argument would not have proved his conclusion. These facts, however, being already certain, the range of admissible suppositions was limited to the various possible directions of a line, and the various possible numerical relations between the variations of

r–r51 as they would be without

s–sMS, 43, 46 is

t–tMS, 43, 46 this can only happen when the inquiry has for its object, not to detect an unknown cause, but to determine the precise law of a cause already ascertained.

u–uMS, 43, 46 already

the distance, and the variations of the attractive force: now among these it was easily shown that different suppositions could not lead to identical consequences.

Accordingly, Newton could not have performed his second great ᵛscientific ᵛ operation, that of identifying terrestrial gravity with the central force of the solar system, by the same hypothetical method. When the law of the moon's attraction had been proved from the data of the moon itself, then on finding the same law to accord with the phenomena of terrestrial gravity, he was warranted in adopting it as the law of those phenomena likewise; but it would not have been allowable for him, without any lunar data, to assume that the moon was attracted towards the earth with a force as the inverse square of the distance, merely because that ratio would enable him to account for ʷterrestrial gravityʷ: for it would have been impossible for him to prove that the observed law of the fall of heavy bodies to the earth could not result from any force, save one extending to the moon, and proportional to the inverse square.

It appears, then, to be a condition of ˣthe mostˣ genuinely scientific hypothesis, that it be not destined always to remain an hypothesis, but be ʸof such a nature asʸ to be either proved or disproved by ᶻcomparison with observed facts. This condition is fulfilled when the effect isᶻ already known to depend on the very cause supposed, and the hypothesis ᵃrelatesᵃ only to the precise mode of dependence; the law of the variation of the effect according to the variations in the quantity or ᵇin theᵇ relations of the cause. With these ᶜmayᶜ be classed the hypotheses which do not make any supposition with regard to causation, but only with regard to the law of correspondence between facts which accompany each other in their variations, though there may be no relation of cause and effect between them. Such ᵈwereᵈ the different false hypotheses which Kepler made respecting the law of the refraction of light. It was known that the direction of the line of refraction varied with every variation in the direction of the line of incidence, but it was not known how; that is, what changes of the one corresponded to the different changes of the other. In this case any law, different from the true one, must have led to false results. And, lastly, we must add to these, all hypothetical modes of

ᵛ⁻ᵛMS, 43, 46   philosophical

ʷ⁻ʷMS, 43, 46   gravity by a similar attraction]   51   gravity

ˣ⁻ˣMS, 43, 46, 51, 56, 62, 65, 68   a

ʸ⁻ʸMS, 43, 46   certain

ᶻ⁻ᶻMS, 43, 46   that comparison with observed facts which is termed Verification. In hypotheses of this character, if they relate to causation at all, the effect must be] 51, 56, 62   *as* MS . . . Verification. This . . . *as* 72

ᵃ⁻ᵃMS, 43, 46   must relate

ᵇ⁻ᵇ+43, 46, 51, 56, 62, 65, 68, 72

ᶜ⁻ᶜMS   must

ᵈ⁻ᵈMS, 43, 46   are

merely *representing, or* describing, phenomena; such as the hypothesis of the ancient astronomers that the heavenly bodies moved in circles; the various hypotheses of excentrics, deferents, and epicycles, which were added to that original hypothesis; the nineteen false hypotheses which Kepler made and abandoned respecting the form of the planetary orbits; and even the *f* doctrine in which he finally rested, that those orbits are ellipses, which was but an hypothesis like the rest until verified by facts.

In all these cases, verification is proof; if the supposition accords with the phenomena there needs no other evidence of it. But in order that this may be the case, *g*I conceive it to be*g* necessary, when the hypothesis relates to causation, that the supposed cause should not only be a real phenomenon, something actually existing in nature, but should be already known to *h*exercise, or at least to be capable of exercising, an influence of some sort over the effect*h*. In any other case, it is no *i*sufficient*i* evidence of the truth of the hypothesis that we are able to deduce the real phenomena from it.

Is it, then, never allowable, in a scientific hypothesis, to assume a cause; but only to ascribe an assumed law to a known cause? I do not assert this. I only say, that in the latter case alone can the hypothesis be received as true merely because it explains the phenomena. In the former case it *j*may be very*j* useful by suggesting a line of investigation which may possibly terminate in obtaining real proof. *k*But, for*k* this purpose, as is justly remarked by M. *l* Comte, *m* it is indispensable that the cause suggested by the hypothesis should be in its own nature susceptible of being proved by other evidence. This seems to be the philosophical import of Newton's maxim, (so often cited with approbation by subsequent writers,) that the cause assigned for any phenomenon must not only be such as if admitted would explain the phenomenon, but must also be a *vera causa*.[*] What he meant by a *vera causa* Newton did not indeed very explicitly define; and Dr. Whewell, who dissents from the propriety of any such restriction upon the latitude of framing hypotheses, has had little difficulty in showing* that his conception of it was neither precise nor consistent with itself: accordingly his optical theory was a signal instance

[*"Regulæ philosophandi," *Principia*, Vol. III, p. 2 (Bk. III, Regula 1).]
Philosophy of Discovery, pp. 185 et seqq.

e–e+62, 65, 68, 72
*f*MS, 43, 46   true
*g–g*MS, 43, 46   it is (as we have seen)
*h–h*MS, 43, 46   have some influence upon the supposed effect; the precise degree and manner of the influence being the only point undetermined
i–i | 72
*j–j*MS, 43, 46, 51, 56, 62, 65, 68   is only
*k–k*MS, 43, 46, 51, 56, 62, 65, 68   For
*l*MS   Auguste
*m*MS, 43   (who of all philosophers seems to me to have approached the nearest to a sound view of this important subject,)]   46   (who seems to me . . . *as* MS

of the violation of his own rule. *n*It is certainly not*n* necessary that the cause assigned should be a cause already known; *o*otherwise we should sacrifice our best opportunities of becoming acquainted with new causes.*o* But what is true in the maxim is, that the cause, though not known previously, should be capable of being known thereafter; that its existence should be capable of being detected, and its connexion with the effect ascribed to *p*it should be*p* susceptible of being proved, by independent evidence. The hypothesis, by suggesting observations and experiments, puts us on the road to that independent evidence if it be really attainable; and till it be attained, the hypothesis ought *q*only to count for a more or less plausible conjecture*q*.

§ 5. [*The indispensableness of scientific hypotheses*] This function, however, of hypotheses, is one which must be reckoned absolutely indispensable in science. When Newton said, "Hypotheses non fingo,"[*] he did not mean that he deprived himself of the facilities of investigation afforded by assuming in the first instance what he hoped ultimately to be able to prove. Without such assumptions, science could never have attained its present state: they are necessary steps in the progress to something more certain; and nearly everything which is now theory was once hypothesis. Even in purely experimental science, some inducement is necessary for trying one experiment rather than another; and though it is abstractedly possible that all the experiments which have been tried, might have been produced by the mere desire to ascertain what would happen in certain circumstances, without any previous conjecture as to the result; yet, in point of fact, those unobvious, delicate, and often cumbrous and tedious processes of experiment, which have thrown most light upon the general constitution of nature, would hardly ever have been undertaken by the persons or at the time they were, unless it had seemed to depend on them whether some general doctrine or theory which had been suggested, but not yet proved, should be admitted or not. If this be true even of merely experimental inquiry, the conversion of experimental into deductive truths could still less have been effected without large temporary assistance from hypotheses. The process of tracing regularity in any complicated, and at first sight confused set of appearances, is necessarily tentative: we begin by making any supposition, even a false one, to see what consequences will follow from it; and by observing how these differ from the real phenomena, we learn what corrections to make in our assumption. The

[*"Scholium Generale," *Principia*, Vol. III, p. 174.]

*n-n*MS, 43   And Mr. Whewell is clearly right in denying it to be]   46   And those are clearly right who deny it to be
*o-o*MS, 43, 46, 51, 56, 62, 65, 68   else how could we ever become acquainted with any new cause?
*p-p*MS, 43, 46   it,
*q-q*MS, 43, 46, 51   not to count for more than a suspicion]   56, 62, 65, 68   *as* MS . . . than a conjecture

simplest supposition which accords with *the more* obvious facts, is the best to begin with; because its consequences are the most easily traced. This rude hypothesis is then rudely corrected, and the operation repeated; and the comparison of the consequences deducible from the corrected hypothesis, with the observed facts, suggests still further correction, until the deductive results are at last made to tally with the phenomena. "Some fact *b* is as yet little understood, or some law is unknown: we frame on the subject an hypothesis as accordant as possible with the whole of the data already possessed; and the science, being thus enabled to move forward freely, always ends by leading to new consequences capable of observation, which either confirm or refute, unequivocally, the first supposition." Neither induction nor deduction *c* would enable us to understand even the simplest phenomena, "if we did not often commence by anticipating on the results; by making a provisional supposition, at first essentially conjectural, as to some of the very notions which constitute the final object of the inquiry."* Let any one watch the manner in which he himself unravels *d*a*d* complicated mass of evidence; let him observe how, for instance, he elicits the true history of any occurrence from the involved statements of one or of many witnesses: he will find that he does not take all the items of evidence into his mind at once, and attempt to weave them together: *e* he extemporises, from a few of the particulars, a first rude theory of the mode in which the facts took place, and then looks at the other statements one by one, to try whether they can be reconciled with that provisional theory, or what *f*alterations*f* or additions it requires to make it square with them. In this way, which *g*has been justly compared*g* to the Methods of Approximation of mathematicians, we arrive, by means of hypotheses, at conclusions not hypothetical.†

*Comte, *Philosophie Positive*, Vol. II, pp. 437–8, 434.

†As an example of *h* legitimate hypothesis according to the test here laid down, *i*has been justly cited*i* that of Broussais, who, proceeding on the very rational principle that every disease must originate in some definite part or other of the organism, boldly assumed that certain fevers, which not being known to be local were called constitutional, had their origin in the mucous membrane of the alimentary canal. The supposition was indeed, as *j*is now generally admitted*j*, erroneous; but he was justified in making it, since by deducing the consequences of the supposition, and comparing them with the facts of those maladies, he might

a–aMS, 43, 46, 51, 56   any of the most
bMS, 43   ," says M. Comte*, " [*footnote:*] **Cours de Philosophie Positive*, Vol. II, p. 437.
cMS, 43   , he justly remarks, [*Ibid.*, p. 434.]
d dMS, 43, 46   any
eMS, 43, 46   the human faculties are not equal to such an undertaking:
f–fMS, 43, 46   corrections
g–gMS, 43   , as M. Comte remarks, has some resemblance
hMS, 43, 46, 51, 56   a
i–iMS, 43   M. Comte cites [*Cours*, Vol. III, p. 409.]
j–jMS, 43, 46   there is strong ground to believe] 51   is now generally believed

§ 6. [*The two degrees of legitimacy in hypotheses*] It is perfectly consistent with the spirit of the method, to assume in this provisional manner not only an hypothesis respecting the law of what we already know to be the cause, but an hypothesis respecting the cause itself. It is allowable, useful, and often even necessary, to begin by asking ourselves what cause *may* have produced the effect, in order that we may know in what direction to look out

----

be certain of disproving his hypothesis [k]if[k] it was ill founded, and might expect that the comparison would materially aid him in framing another more conformable to the phenomena.

The doctrine now universally received, that the earth is a [l]natural magnet[l], was originally an hypothesis of the celebrated Gilbert.

Another hypothesis, to the legitimacy of which no objection can lie, and [m] which is well calculated to light the path of scientific inquiry, is that suggested [n]by several recent writers[n], that the brain is a voltaic pile, and that each of its pulsations is a discharge of electricity through the system. It has been remarked that the sensation felt by the hand from the beating of a brain, [o] bears a strong resemblance to a voltaic shock. And the hypothesis, if followed to its consequences, [p]might[p] afford a plausible explanation of many physiological facts, while there is nothing to discourage the hope that we may in time sufficiently understand the conditions of voltaic phenomena to render the truth of the hypothesis amenable to observation and experiment.

The attempt to localize, in different regions of the brain, the physical organs of our different mental faculties and propensities, was, on the part of its original author, a [q] legitimate example of a scientific hypothesis; and we ought not, therefore, to blame him for the extremely slight grounds on which he often proceeded, in an operation which could only be tentative, though we may regret that materials barely sufficient for a first rude hypothesis should have been hastily worked up [r] into the vain semblance of a science. [s]If there be really a[s] connexion between the scale of mental endowments and the various degrees of complication in the cerebral system [t], the nature of that connexion[t] was in no other way so likely to be brought to light as by framing, in the first instance, an hypothesis similar to that of Gall. But the verification of any such hypothesis is attended, from the peculiar nature of the phenomena, with difficulties which phrenologists have not [u] shown themselves even competent to appreciate, much less to overcome.

[v]Mr. Darwin's remarkable speculation on the Origin of Species is another un-

----

[k-k]MS, 43, 46   in case
[l-l]MS, 43, 46   great natural magnet with two poles
[m]MS, 43, 46, 51   one
[n-n]MS, 43   both by Dr. Arnott and Sir John Herschel
[o]MS, 43, 46   or even of the great arteries,
[p-p]MS   would
[q]MS, 43, 46   strictly
[r]MS, 43, 46, 51, 56, 62, 65   by his successors
[s-s]MS, 43, 46   Whatever there may be of reality in the
[t-t]MS, 43   (and that there is some such connexion comparative anatomy seems strongly to indicate,) it]   46   *as* MS . . . seems in some degree to indicate,) it
[u]MS, 43, 46   hitherto
[v-v]+62, 65, 68, 72
[a-a]MS, 43, 46, 51, 56, 62, 65, 68   *Legitimate, how distinguished from illegitimate hypotheses*

for evidence to determine whether it actually *did*. The vortices of Descartes would have been a perfectly legitimate hypothesis, if it had been possible, by any mode of exploration which we could entertain the hope of ever possessing, to bring the *b*reality of the vortices, as a fact in nature, conclusively to the test of observation*b*. The *c*vice of the hypothesis was that*c* it could not lead to any course of investigation capable of converting it from an hypothesis into a proved fact. *d*It might chance to be *dis*proved, either by some want of correspondence with the phenomena it purported to explain, or (as actually happened) by some extraneous fact. "The free passage of comets through the spaces in which these vortices should have been, convinced men that these vortices did not exist."* But the hypothesis would have been false, though no such direct evidence of its falsity had been procurable. Direct evidence of its truth there could not be.*d*

e The prevailing hypothesis of a luminiferous ether *f*, in other respects not without analogy to that of Descartes, is not in its own nature entirely cut off from the possibility of direct evidence in its favour. It is well known that the difference between the calculated and the observed times of the periodical return of Encke's comet, has led to a conjecture that a medium capable of opposing resistance to motion is diffused through space. If this surmise should be confirmed, in the course of ages, by the gradual accumulation of a similar variance in the case of the other bodies of the solar system, the luminiferous ether would have made a considerable advance towards the character of a *vera causa*, since the existence would have been ascertained of a great

---

impeachable example of a legitimate hypothesis. What he terms "natural selection" is not only a *vera causa*, but one proved to be capable of producing effects of the same kind with those which the hypothesis ascribes to it: the question of possibility is entirely one of degree. [See Charles Darwin. *On the Origin of Species*. London: Murray, 1859.] It is unreasonable to accuse Mr. Darwin (as has been done) of violating the rules of Induction. The rules of Induction are concerned with the conditions of Proof. Mr. Darwin has never pretended that his doctrine was proved. He was not bound by the rules of Induction, but by those of Hypothesis. And these last have seldom been more completely fulfilled. He has opened a path of inquiry full of promise, the results of which none can foresee. And is it not a wonderful feat of scientific knowledge and ingenuity to have rendered so bold a suggestion, which the first impulse of every one was to reject at once, admissible and discussable, even as a conjecture?*v*

*[51] Whewell's *Philosophy of Discovery*, pp. 275–6.

*b-b*MS, 43, 46   question, whether such vortices exist or not, within the reach of our observing faculties
*c-c*MS, 43, 46, 51, 56, 62, 65, 68   hypothesis was vicious, simply because
d-d+51, 56, 62, 65, 68, 72
*e*MS, 43, 46   [*no paragraph*]
*f-f*500MS, 43, 46   I cannot but consider, with M. Comte [*Cours*, Vol. II, p. 639], to be tainted with the same vice. It can never be brought to the test of observation, because the ether is supposed wanting in all the properties by means of which our senses take cognizance of external phenomena. It can neither be seen, heard, smelt, tasted, nor touched. The

cosmical agent, possessing some of the attributes which the hypothesis assumes· though there would still remain many difficulties, and the identification of the ether with the resisting medium would even, I imagine, give rise to new ones. At present, however, this supposition cannot be looked upon as more than a conjecture; the existence of the ether still rests on the[f] possibility of deducing from its [g]assumed[g] laws a considerable number of [h]actual phenomena; and this evidence I cannot regard as conclusive[h], because we cannot have, in the case of such an hypothesis, the assurance that if the hypothesis be false it must lead to results at variance with the true facts.

Accordingly, most thinkers of any degree of sobriety allow, that an hypothesis of this kind is not to be received as probably true because it accounts for all the known phenomena; since this is a condition [i]sometimes fulfilled tolerably[i] well by two conflicting hypotheses;[j] while there are probably [k]many others[k] which are equally possible, but which, for want of anything analogous in our experience, our minds are unfitted to conceive. But it seems to be thought that an hypothesis of the sort in question is entitled to a more favourable reception, if, besides accounting for all the facts previously known, it has led to the anticipation and prediction of others which experience afterwards verified; as the undulatory theory of light led to the prediction, subsequently realized by experiment, that two luminous rays might meet each other in such a manner as to produce darkness. Such predictions and their fulfilment are, indeed, well calculated to [l]impress the uninformed[l], whose faith in science rests solely on similar coincidences between its prophecies and what comes to pass. But it is strange that any considerable stress should be laid upon such a coincidence by [m]persons of scientific attainments[m]. If the laws of the propagation of light accord with those of the vibrations of an elastic fluid in as many respects as is necessary to make the hypothesis [n]afford a correct expression[n] of all or most of the phenomena known at the time, it is nothing strange that they should accord with each other in one respect more. Though twenty such coincidences should occur, they would not prove the reality of the undulatory ether; it would not follow that the phenomena of light were results of the laws of elastic fluids, but at

[g-g]MS, 43, 46   supposed
[h-h]MS, 43, 46   the phenomena of light, is the sole evidence of its existence that we have ever to hope for; and this evidence cannot be of the smallest value]   51, 56   the phenomena of light: and to this evidence I can attach no importance]   62, 65, 68   the phenomena of light; and this evidence . . . as 72
[i-i]MS, 43, 46, 51, 56, 62   often fulfilled equally]   65   often fulfilled tolerably
[j]MS, 43, 46   and if we give ourselves the licence of inventing the causes themselves as well as their laws, a person of fertile imagination might devise a hundred modes of accounting for any given fact,
[k-k]MS, 43, 46, 51, 56, 62, 65, 68   a thousand more
[l-l]MS, 43, 46   strike the ignorant vulgar
[m-m]MS, 43, 46   scientific thinkers
[n-n]MS, 43, 46   a plausible explanation

most that they are governed by laws [o]partially identical with[o] these; which, we may observe, is already certain, from the fact that the hypothesis in question could be for a moment tenable.* [q]Cases may be cited, even in our imperfect acquaintance with nature, where agencies that we have good reason to consider as radically distinct, produce their effects, or some of their effects, according to laws which are identical. The law, for example, of the inverse square of the distance, is the measure of the intensity [r]not only of gravitation, but (it is believed)[r] of illumination, and of heat diffused from a centre. Yet no one looks upon this identity as proving similarity in the mechanism by which the three kinds of phenomena are produced.

According to Dr. Whewell, the coincidence of [s]results[s] predicted from an hypothesis, with facts afterwards observed, amounts to a conclusive proof of the truth of the theory. "If I copy a long series of letters, of which the last half dozen are concealed, and if I guess these aright, as is found to be the case when they are afterwards uncovered, this must be because I have made out the import of the inscription. To say, that because I have copied all that I could see, it is nothing strange that I should guess those which I cannot see, would be absurd, without supposing such a ground for guessing."† If any one, from examining the greater part of a long inscription, can interpret the characters so that the inscription gives a rational meaning in a known language, there is a strong presumption that his interpretation is correct; but I do not think the presumption much increased by his being able to guess the

*[46] What has most contributed to accredit the hypothesis of a physical medium for the conveyance of light, is the certain fact that light *travels*, (which cannot be proved of gravitation,) that its communication is not instantaneous, but requires time, and that it is intercepted (which gravitation is not) by intervening objects. These are analogies between its phenomena and those of the mechanical motion of a solid or fluid substance. But we [p]are not entitled[p] to assume that mechanical motion is the only power in nature capable of exhibiting those attributes.

†[51] *Philosophy of Discovery*, p. 274.

[o-o]MS, 43, 46 in some measure analogous to

[p-p]46, 51, 56 have no reason

[q-q503]MS There are many such harmonies running through the laws of phenomena in other respects radically distinct. The remarkable resemblance between the laws of light and many of the laws of heat (while others are as remarkably different) is a case in point. There is an extraordinary similarity running through the properties, considered generally, of certain substances, as chlorine, iodine, and brome, or sulphur and phosphorus; so much so that when chemists discover any new property of the one, they not only are not surprised, but expect, to find that the other or others have a property analogous to it. But the hypothesis that chlorine, iodine, and brome, or that sulphur and phosphorus, are the same substance, would, no doubt, be quite inadmissible.] 43, 46 *as* MS . . . same substances, would . . . *as* MS [MS, 43, 46 *continue with the passage commencing with* 504[b-b] *below*]

[r-r]51, 56, 62 of gravitation,

[s-s]56 result [*printer's error?*]

few remaining letters without seeing them: for we should naturally expect (when the nature of the case excludes chance) that even an erroneous interpretation which accorded with all the visible *parts* of the inscription would accord also with the small remainder; as would be the case, for example, if the inscription had been designedly so contrived as to admit of a double sense. I assume that the uncovered characters afford an amount of coincidence too great to be merely casual: otherwise the illustration is not a fair one. No one supposes the agreement of the phenomena of light with the theory of undulations to be merely fortuitous. It must arise from the actual identity of some of the laws of undulations with some of those of light: and if there be that identity, it is reasonable to suppose that its consequences would not end with the phenomena which first suggested the identification, nor be even confined to such phenomena as were known at the time. But it does not follow, because some of the laws agree with those of undulations, that there are any actual undulations; no more than it followed because some (though not so many) of the same laws agreed with those of the projection of particles, that there was actual emission of particles. Even the undulatory hypothesis does not account for all the phenomena of light. The natural colours of objects, the compound nature of the solar ray, the absorption of light, and its chemical and vital action, the hypothesis leaves as mysterious as it found them; and some of these facts are, at least apparently, more reconcileable with the emission theory than with that of Young and Fresnel. Who knows but that some third hypothesis, including all these phenomena, may in time leave the undulatory theory as far behind as that has left the theory of Newton and his successors?

To the statement, that the condition of accounting for all the known phenomena is often fulfilled equally well by two conflicting hypotheses, Dr. Whewell makes answer that he knows "of no such case in the history of science, where the phenomena are at all numerous and complicated."* Such an affirmation, by a writer of Dr. Whewell's minute acquaintance with the history of science, would carry great authority, if he had not, a few pages before, taken pains to refute it,† by maintaining that even the exploded scientific hypotheses might always, or almost always, have been so modified as to make them correct representations of the phenomena. The hypothesis of vortices, he tells us, was, by successive *modifications*, brought to coincide in its results with the Newtonian theory and with the facts. The vortices did not indeed explain all the phenomena which the Newtonian theory was

---

*[51] P. 271.

†[51] P. 251 and the whole of Appendix G ["On the Transformation of Hypotheses in the History of Science," pp. 492–503].

*t–t*51, 56   part
*u–u*51, 56, 62, 65   modification

ultimately found to account for, such as the precession of the equinoxes; but this phenomenon was not, at the time, in the contemplation of either party, as one of the facts to be accounted for. All the facts which they did contemplate, we may believe on Dr. Whewell's authority to have accorded as accurately with the Cartesian hypothesis, in its finally improved state, as with Newton's.

But it is not, I conceive, a valid reason for accepting any given hypothesis, that we are unable to imagine any other which will account for the facts. There is no necessity for supposing that the true explanation must be one which, with only our present experience, we could imagine. Among the natural agents with which we are acquainted, the vibrations of an elastic fluid may be the only one whose laws bear a close resemblance to those of light; but we cannot tell that there does not exist an unknown cause, other than an elastic ether diffused through space, yet producing effects identical in some respects with those which would result from the undulations of such an ether. To assume that no such cause can exist, appears to me an extreme case of assumption without evidence.[q] [v]And at the risk of being charged with want of modesty, I cannot help expressing astonishment that a philosopher of [w]Dr. Whewell's abilities and attainments[w] should have written an elaborate treatise on the philosophy of induction, in which he recognises absolutely no mode of induction except that of trying hypothesis after hypothesis until one is found which fits the phenomena; which one, when found, is to be assumed as true, with no other reservation than that if on re-examination it should appear to assume more than is needful for explaining the phenomena, the superfluous part of the assumption should be cut off. [x] And this without the slightest distinction between the cases in which it may be known beforehand that two different hypotheses cannot lead to the same result, and those in which, for aught we can ever know, the range of suppositions, all equally consistent with the phenomena, may be infinite.[v]*

*[62] [y] In Dr. Whewell's latest version of his theory (*Philosophy of Discovery*, p. 331) he makes a concession respecting the medium of the transmission of light, which, taken in conjunction with the rest of his doctrine on the subject, is not, I confess, very intelligible to me, but which goes far towards removing, if it does not actually remove, the whole of the difference between us. He is contending, against Sir William Hamilton, that all matter has weight. Sir William, in proof of the contrary, cited the luminiferous ether, and the calorific and electric fluids,

[v-v]MS, 43, 46, 51, 56, 62, 65, 68   [*passage occurs at the end of that indicated by variant c-c below, and concludes §6.*]

[w-w]MS, 43   the extraordinary attainments of Mr. Whewell

[x]MS, 43   It is no exaggeration to say that the process which we have described in these few words, is the beginning, middle, and end of the philosophy of induction as Mr. Whewell conceives it.]   46   *as MS . . . which I have . . . as MS*

[y]62, 65, 68   [*this note appears, as does the passage to which it is appended, at the end of §6.*]

^{b}Nevertheless, I do not agree with M. Comte[*] in condemning^b those who employ themselves in working out into detail ^{c}the application of these hypotheses to the explanation of ascertained facts; provided they bear in mind that the utmost they can prove is, not that the hypothesis *is*, but that it *may* be true. The ether hypothesis has a very strong claim to be so followed out, a claim greatly strengthened since it has been shown to afford a mechanism

---

"which," he said, "we can neither denude of their character of substance, nor clothe with the attribute of weight." ["Note D," in William Hamilton, ed. *The Works of Thomas Reid*. Edinburgh: Maclachlan and Stewart, 1846, p. 854n.] "To which," continues Dr. Whewell, "my reply is, that precisely because I cannot clothe these agents with the attribute of Weight, I *do* denude them of the character of Substance. They are not substances, but agencies. These Imponderable Agents, are not properly called Imponderable Fluids. This I conceive that I have proved." Nothing can be more philosophical. But if the luminiferous ether is not matter, and fluid matter too, what is the meaning of its undulations? Can an agency undulate? Can there be alternate motion forward and backward of the particles of an agency? And does not the whole mathematical theory of the undulations imply them to be material? Is it not a series of deductions from the known properties of elastic fluids? *This* opinion of Dr. Whewell reduces the undulations to a figure of speech, and the ^{z}undulatory^z theory to the proposition which all must admit, that the transmission of light takes place according to laws which present a very striking and remarkable agreement with those of undulations. If Dr. Whewell is prepared to stand by this doctrine, I have no difference with him on the subject. ^{a}
[*See *Cours*, Vol. II, p. 639.]

$^{z-z}$62 undulating
^{a}65, 68 [*paragraph*] Since this chapter was written, the hypothesis of the luminiferous ether has acquired a great accession of apparent strength, by being adopted into the new doctrine of the Conservation of Force, as affording a mechanism by which to explain the mode of production not of light only, but of heat, and probably of all the other so-called imponderable agencies. In the present immature stage of the great speculation in question, I would not undertake to define the ultimate relation of the hypothetical fluid to it; but I must remark that the essential part of the new theory, the reciprocal convertibility and interchangeability of these great cosmic agencies, is quite independent of the molecular motions which have been imagined as the immediate causes of those different manifestations and of their substitutions for one another; and the former doctrine by no means necessarily carries the latter with it. I confess that the entire theory of the vibrations of the ether, and the movements which these vibrations are supposed to communicate to the particles of solid bodies, seems to me at present the weakest part of the new system, tending rather to weigh down than to prop up those of its doctrines which rest on real scientific induction.
$^{b-b}$MS, 43   I do not, like M. Comte, altogether condemn]   46, 51, 56, 62, 65, 68   I do not mean to condemn
$^{c-c}$505MS   this sort of hypotheses; it is useful to ascertain what are the known phenomena, to the laws of which those of the subject of inquiry bear the greatest, or even a great analogy, since it may suggest (as in the case of the luminiferous ether it actually did) experiments to determine whether the analogy which goes so far does not extend still further. But that, in doing this, men should imagine themselves to be seriously inquiring whether the hypothesis of an ether, an electric fluid, or the like, is true; that they should fancy it possible to obtain the assurance that the phenomena are produced in that way and no other; seems to me, I confess, as unworthy of the present

which would explain the mode of production not of light only, but also of heat. Indeed the speculation has a smaller element of hypothesis in its application to heat, than in the case for which it was originally framed. We have proof by our senses of the existence of molecular movement among the particles of all heated bodies; while we have no similar experience in the case of light. When, therefore, heat is communicated from the sun to the earth across apparently empty space, the chain of causation has molecular motion both at the beginning and end. The hypothesis only makes the motion continuous, by extending it to the middle. Now motion in a body is known to be capable of being imparted to another body contiguous to it; and the intervention of a hypothetical elastic fluid occupying the space between the sun and the earth, supplies the contiguity which is the only condition wanting, and which can be supplied by no supposition but that of an intervening medium. The supposition, notwithstanding, is at best a probable conjecture, not a proved truth. For there is no proof that contiguity is absolutely required for the communication of motion from one body to another. Contiguity does not always exist, to our senses at least, in the cases in which motion produces motion. The forces which go under the name of attraction, especially the greatest of all, gravitation, are examples of motion producing motion without apparent contiguity. When a planet moves, its distant satellites accompany its motion. The sun carries the whole solar system along with it in the progress which it is ascertained to be executing through space. And even if we were to accept as conclusive the geometrical reasonings (strikingly similar to those by which the Cartesians defended their vortices) by which it has been attempted to show that the motions of the ether may account for gravitation itself, even then it would only have been proved that the supposed mode of production may be, but not that no other mode can be, the true one.[c]

§ 7. [*Some inquiries apparently hypothetical are really inductive*] It is necessary, before quitting the subject of hypotheses, to guard against the appearance of reflecting upon the [a]scientific value[a] of several branches of physical inquiry, which, though only in their infancy, I hold to be strictly inductive. There is a great difference between inventing [b]agencies[b] to account for classes of phenomena, and [c] endeavouring, in conformity with known

---

improved conceptions of the methods of physical science, as it does to M. Comte.]   43
as MS . . . analogy, since this may . . . *as* MS]   46, 51, 56   *as* 43 . . . I confess, unworthy of the present improved conceptions of the methods of physical science.]   62, 65, 68   *as* 43 . . . in doing this, we should imagine ourselves to be . . . *as* MS . . . true; that we should . . . *as* 46 [MS, 43, 46, 51, 56, 62, 65, 68   *continue with the passage indicated by variant v–v above*]
[a–a]MS, 43, 46   philosophical certainty
[b–b]MS, 43, 46   laws of nature
[c]MS, 43, 46   merely

laws, to conjecture what ^dformer collocations of known agents^d may have given birth to individual facts still in existence. The latter is the ^e legitimate operation of inferring from an observed effect, the existence, in time past, of a cause similar to that by which we know it to be produced in all cases in which we have actual experience of its origin. This, for example, is the scope of the inquiries of geology; and they are no more illogical or visionary than judicial inquiries, which also aim at discovering a past event by inference from those of its effects which still subsist. As we can ascertain whether a man was murdered or died a natural death, from the indications exhibited by the corpse, the presence or absence of signs of struggling on the ground or on the adjacent objects, the marks of blood, the footsteps of the supposed murderers, and so on, proceeding throughout on uniformities ascertained by a perfect induction without any mixture of hypothesis; so if we find, on and beneath the surface of our planet, masses exactly similar to deposits from water, or to results of the cooling of matter melted by fire, we may justly conclude that such has been their origin; and if the effects, though similar in kind, are on a far larger scale than any which are ^fnow produced^f, we may rationally, and without hypothesis, conclude ^geither^g that the causes existed formerly with greater intensity ^h, or that they have operated during an enormous length of time^h. Further than this no geologist of authority has, since the rise of the present enlightened school of geological speculation, attempted to go.

In many geological inquiries it doubtless happens that though the laws to which the phenomena are ascribed are known laws, and the agents known agents, those agents are not known to have been present in the particular case. ⁱInⁱ the speculation respecting the igneous origin of trap or granite, the fact does not admit of direct proof, that those substances have been actually subjected to intense heat. But the same thing might be said of all judicial inquiries which proceed on circumstantial evidence. We can conclude that a man was murdered, though it is not proved by the testimony of eye-witnesses that ^jsome person^j who had the intention of murdering him was present on the spot. It is enough ^k, for most purposes,^k if no other known cause could have generated the effects shown to have been produced. ^l

^{d–d}MS, 43, 46   collocations, now gone by,
^eMS, 43, 46   strictly   ^{f–f}MS, 43, 46   produced now
^{g–g}+62, 65, 68, 72
^{h–h}+62, 65, 68, 72
^{i–i}MS, 43, 46, 51, 56, 62   Thus in
^{j–j}MS, 43, 46   a man
^{k–k}+51, 56, 62, 65, 68, 72
^lMS, 43, 46   And so, in geology, it is enough that no other known agent than heat could, according to any known law, have produced the unstratified rocks, while there is the strongest reason to believe that any terrestrial agent capable of operating on so large a scale would not have remained unknown.

The celebrated speculation of Laplace [m] concerning the origin of the earth and planets, participates essentially in the [n] inductive character of modern geological theory.[*] The speculation is, that the atmosphere of the sun originally extended to the present limits of the solar system; from which, by the process of cooling, it has contracted to its present dimensions; and since, by the general principles of mechanics, the rotation of the sun and of its accompanying atmosphere must increase in rapidity as its volume diminishes, the increased centrifugal force generated by the more rapid rotation, over-balancing the action of gravitation, [o]has caused[o] the sun to abandon succes-sive rings of vaporous matter, which are supposed to have condensed by cooling, and to have become [p]the[p] planets. There is in this theory no unknown substance introduced on supposition, nor any unknown property or law ascribed to a known substance. The known laws of matter authorize us to suppose that a body which is constantly giving out so large an amount of heat as the sun is, must be progressively cooling, and that, by the process of cooling, it must contract; if, therefore, we endeavour, from the present state of that luminary, to infer its state in a time long past, we must necessarily suppose that its atmosphere extended much farther than at present, and we are entitled to suppose that it extended as far as we can trace [q]effects such as it might[q] naturally leave behind it on retiring; and such the planets are. These suppositions being made, it follows from known laws that successive zones of the solar atmosphere [r]might[r] be abandoned; that these would continue to revolve round the sun with the same velocity as when they formed part of [s]its substance; and that they would cool down, long before the sun itself[s], to any given temperature, and consequently to that at which the greater part of the vaporous matter of which they consisted would become liquid or solid. The known law of gravitation would then cause them to agglomerate in masses, which would assume the shape our planets actually exhibit; would acquire, each [t]about[t] its own axis, a rotatory movement; and would in that state revolve, as the planets actually do, about the sun, in the same direction with the sun's rotation, but with less velocity, [u]because[u] in the [v] same periodic

[*See Pierre Simon de Laplace. *Exposition du système du monde.* 2 vols. Paris: Cercle-Social, 1796, Vol. II, pp. 301ff.]

[m]MS, 43, 46 , now very generally received as probable by astronomers,
[n]MS, 43, 46, 51, 56, 62   strictly
[o]–[o]MS, 43   would cause
[p]–[p]MS, 43, 46   our
[q]–[q]MS, 43   those effects which it would
[r]–[r]MS, 43   would
[s]–[s]MS, 43, 46   his substance . . . sun himself
[t]–[t]MS, 43, 46   round
[u]–[u]MS, 43   and each of them
[v]MS   very

time which the sun's rotation occupied when his atmosphere extended to that point *w* . There is thus, in Laplace's theory, nothing *x*, strictly speaking,*x* hypothetical: it is an example of legitimate reasoning from a present effect to *y*a possible past cause, according to the known laws of that cause*y*. The theory therefore is, as I have said, of a similar character to the theories of geologists; *za*but considerably inferior to them in point of evidence*a*. Even if it were proved (which it is not) that the conditions necessary for determining the breaking off of successive rings would certainly occur; there would still be a much greater chance of error in assuming that the existing laws of nature are the same which existed at the origin of the solar system, than in merely presuming (with geologists) that those laws have lasted through a few revolutions and transformations of a single one among the bodies of which that system is composed.*z*

---

*w*MS, 43 ; and this also M. Comte has, by the necessary calculations, ascertained to be true, within certain small limits of error* [*footnote:*] *Cours de Philosophie Positive*, Vol. II, pp. 378–83.

x–x+51, 56, 62, 65, 68, 72

*y–y*MS, 43 its past cause . . . cause; it assumes nothing more than that objects which really exist, obey the laws which are known to be obeyed by all terrestrial objects resembling them

*z–z*MS inferior to them in certainty, in about the same ratio as those are inferior to facts conclusively established by a judicial inquiry. For, the uncertainty whether the laws of nature which prevail on our earth prevail in the whole solar system, is about equal to the uncertainty whether the laws which prevail in our earth to-day, prevailed there a thousand ages ago. Laplace's theory requires both these assumptions, geology the latter only, and judicial inquiries require neither*. [*footnote:*] *See, for an interesting exposition of this theory of Laplace, the *Architecture of the Heavens*, by Professor Nichol, of Glasgow; a work professedly popular rather than scientific, but the production of a thinker who, both in this and in other departments, is capable of much more than merely expounding the speculations of his predecessors. [John Pringle Nichol. *Views of the Architecture of the Heavens*. Edinburgh: Tait, 1837, pp. 177–80.]]

43 *as* MS . . . Glasgow; a book professedly . . . *as* MS

*a–a*46 though I am far from comparing it with them in point of certainty

CHAPTER XV

Of Progressive Effects; and of the Continued Action of Causes

§ 1. [*How a progressive effect results from the simple continuance of the cause*] In the last four chapters we have traced the general outlines of the theory of the generation of derivative laws from ultimate ones. In the present chapter our attention will be directed to a particular case of the derivation of laws from other laws, but a case so general, and so important, as not only to repay, but to require, a separate examination. This is, the case of a complex phenomenon resulting from one simple law, by the continual addition of an effect to itself.

There are some phenomena, some bodily sensations for example, which are essentially instantaneous, and whose existence can only be prolonged by the prolongation of the existence of the cause by which they are produced. But most phenomena are in their own nature permanent; *having begun to exist, they*[a] would exist for ever unless some cause intervened having a tendency to alter or destroy them. Such, for example, are all the facts or phenomena which we call bodies. Water, once produced, will not of itself relapse into *a*[b] state of hydrogen and oxygen; such a change requires some agent having the power of decomposing the compound. Such, again, are the positions in space, and the movements, of bodies. No object at rest alters its position without the intervention of some conditions extraneous to itself; and when once in motion, no object returns to a state of rest, or alters either its direction or its velocity, unless some new external conditions are superinduced. It, therefore, perpetually happens that a temporary cause gives rise to a permanent effect. The contact of iron with moist air for a few hours, produces a rust which may endure for centuries; or a projectile force which launches a cannon ball into space, produces a motion which would continue for ever unless some other force counteracted it.

Between the two examples which we have here given, there is a difference worth pointing out. In the former (in which the phenomenon produced is a

*a–a*MS &, having begun to exist
*b–b*MS, 43, 46 the

substance, and not a motion of a substance), since the rust remains for ever and unaltered unless some new cause supervenes, we may speak of the contact of air a hundred years ago as even the proximate cause of the rust which has existed from that time until now. But when the effect is motion, which is itself a change, we must use a different language. The permanency of the effect is now only the permanency of a series of changes. The second foot, or inch, or mile of motion, is not the mere prolonged duration of the first foot, or inch, or mile, but another fact which succeeds ^{c} , and which may in some respects be very unlike the former, since it carries the body through a different region of space. Now, the original projectile force which set the body moving is the remote cause of all its motion, however long continued, but the proximate cause of no motion except that which took place at the first instant. The motion at any subsequent instant is proximately caused by the motion which took place at the instant preceding. It is on that, and not on the original moving cause, that the motion at any given moment depends. For, suppose that the body passes through some resisting medium, which partially counteracts the effect of the original impulse, and ^{d} retards the motion: this counteraction (it ^{e}need^e scarcely here be repeated) is as strict an example of obedience to the law of the impulse, as if the body had gone on moving with its original velocity; but the motion which results is different, being now a compound of the effects of two causes acting in contrary directions, instead of the ^{f}single^f effect of one cause. Now, what cause does the body obey in its subsequent motion? The original cause of motion, or the actual motion at the preceding instant? The latter: for when the object issues from the resisting medium, it continues moving, not with its original, but with its retarded velocity. The motion having once been diminished, all that which follows is diminished. The effect changes, because the cause which it really obeys, the proximate cause, the real cause in fact, has changed. This principle is recognised by mathematicians when they enumerate among the causes by which the motion of a body is at any instant determined, the *force generated* by the previous motion; an expression which would be absurd if taken to imply that this "force" was an intermediate link between the cause and the effect, but which really means only the previous motion itself, considered as a cause of further motion. We must, therefore, if we would speak with perfect precision, consider each link in the succession of motions as the effect of the link preceding it. But if, for the convenience of discourse, we speak of the whole series as one effect, it must be as an effect produced by the original impelling force; a permanent effect produced by an instantaneous cause, and possessing the property of self-perpetuation.

^{c}MS   it ^{d}MS, 43, 46   by so doing
$^{c-c}$MS, 43, 46, 51, 56, 62, 65, 68   needs
$^{f-f}$MS, 43, 46   one

Let us now suppose that the original agent or cause, instead of being instantaneous, is permanent. Whatever effect has been produced up to a given time, would (unless prevented by the intervention of some new cause) subsist permanently, even if the cause were to perish. Since, however, the cause does not perish, but continues to exist and to operate, it must go on producing more and more of the effect; and instead of an uniform effect, we have a progressive series of effects, arising from the accumulated influence of a permanent cause. Thus, the contact of iron with the atmosphere causes a portion of it to rust; and if the cause ceased, the effect already produced would be permanent, but no further effect would be added. If, however, the cause, namely, exposure to moist air, continues, more and more of the iron becomes rusted, until *all which is exposed is* converted into a red powder, when one of the conditions of the production of rust, namely, the presence of unoxidized iron, has ceased, and the effect cannot any longer be produced. Again, the earth causes bodies to fall towards it, that is, the existence of the earth at a given instant, causes an unsupported body to move towards it at the succeeding instant: and if the earth were *h* annihilated, as much of the effect as is already produced would continue; the object would go on moving in the same direction, with its acquired velocity, until intercepted by some body or deflected by some other force. The earth, however, not being annihilated, goes on producing in the second instant an effect similar and of equal amount *with* the first, which two effects being added together, there results an accelerated velocity; and this operation being repeated at each successive instant, the mere permanence of the cause, though without increase, gives rise to a constant progressive increase of the effect, so long as all the conditions, negative and positive, of the production of that effect, continue to be realized.

It *is* obvious that this state of things is merely a case of the Composition of Causes. A cause which continues in action, must on a strict analysis be considered as a number of causes exactly similar, successively introduced, and producing by their combination the sum of the effects which they would severally produce if they acted singly. The progressive rusting of the iron is in strictness the sum of the effects of many particles of air acting in succession upon corresponding particles of iron. The continued action of the earth upon a falling body is equivalent to a series of forces, applied in successive instants, each tending to produce a certain constant quantity of motion; and the motion at each instant is the sum of the effects of the new force applied at the preceding instant, and *k* the motion already acquired. In each instant, a fresh effect, of which gravity is the proximate cause, is added to the effect of which

*g–g*MS, 43, 46 it is all
*i–i*MS, 43, 46, 51 to
*k*MS, 43, 46 of

*h*MS, 43, 46 instantly
*j–j*MS, 43, 46, 51, 56 must be

it was the remote cause: or (to express the same thing in another manner) the effect produced by the earth's influence at the instant last elapsed, is added to the sum of the effects of which the remote causes were the influences exerted by the earth at all the previous instants since the motion began. The case, therefore, comes under the principle of a concurrence of causes producing an effect equal to the sum of their separate effects. But as the causes come into play not all at once, but successively, and as the effect at each instant is the sum of the effects of those causes only which have come into action up to that instant, the result assumes the form of an ascending series; a succession of sums, each greater than that which preceded it; and we have thus a progressive effect from the continued action of a cause.

Since the continuance of the cause influences the effect only by adding to its quantity, and since the addition takes place according to a fixed law (equal quantities in equal times), the result is capable of being computed on mathematical principles. In fact, this case, being that of infinitesimal increments, is precisely the case which the differential calculus was invented to meet. The questions, what effect will result from the continual addition of a given cause to itself, and what amount of the cause, being continually added to itself, will produce a given amount of the effect, are evidently mathematical questions, and to be treated, therefore, deductively. If, as we have seen, cases of the Composition of Causes are seldom adapted for any other than deductive investigation, this is especially true in the case now examined, the continual composition of a cause with its own previous effects; since such a case is peculiarly amenable to the deductive method, while the undistinguishable manner in which the effects are blended with one another and with the causes, must make the treatment of such an instance experimentally, still more chimerical than in any other case.

§ 2. [*And how a progressive effect results from the progressiveness of the cause*] We shall next advert to a rather more intricate operation of the same principle, namely, when the cause does not merely continue in action, but undergoes, during the same time, a progressive change in those of its circumstances which contribute to determine the effect. In this case, as in the former, the total effect goes on accumulating by the continual addition of a fresh effect to that already produced, but it is no longer by the addition of equal quantities in equal times; the quantities added are unequal, and even the quality may now be different. If the change in the state of the permanent cause be progressive, the effect will go through a double series of changes, arising partly from the accumulated action of the cause, and partly from the *a*changes*a* in its action. The effect is still a progressive effect, produced however, not by the mere continuance of a cause, but by its continuance and its progressiveness combined.

*a–a*MS   change [*printer's error? s cancelled in* MS]

A familiar example is afforded by the increase of the temperature as summer advances, that is, as the sun draws nearer to a vertical position, and remains a greater number of hours above the horizon. This instance exemplifies in a very interesting manner the twofold operation on the effect, arising from the continuance of the cause, and from its progressive change. When once the sun has come near enough to the zenith, and remains above the horizon long enough, to give more warmth during one diurnal rotation than the counteracting cause, the earth's radiation, can carry off, the mere continuance of the cause would progressively increase the effect, even if the sun came no nearer and the days grew no longer; but in addition to this, a change takes place in the accidents of the cause (its series of diurnal positions), tending to increase the quantity of the effect. When the summer solstice has passed, the progressive change in the cause begins to take place the reverse way; but, for some time, the accumulating effect of the mere continuance of the cause exceeds the effect of the changes in it, and the temperature continues to increase.

Again, the *b*motion of a planet is*b* a progressive effect, produced by causes at once permanent and progressive. The orbit of a planet is determined (omitting perturbations) by two causes: first, the action of the central body, a permanent cause, which alternately increases and diminishes as the planet draws nearer to or goes further from its perihelion, and which acts *c* at every point in a different direction; and, secondly, the tendency of the planet to continue moving in the direction and with the velocity which it has already acquired. This force also grows greater as the planet draws nearer to its perihelion, because as it does so its velocity increases; and less, as it recedes from its perihelion: and this force as well as the other acts at each point in a different direction, because at every point the action of the central force, by deflecting the planet from its previous direction, alters the line in which it tends to continue moving. The motion at each instant is determined by the amount and direction of the motion, and the amount and direction of the sun's action, at the previous instant: and if we speak of the entire revolution of the planet as one phenomenon (which, as it is periodical and similar to itself, we often find it convenient to do,) that phenomenon is the progressive effect of two permanent and progressive causes, the central force and the acquired motion. Those causes happening to be progressive in the particular way which is called periodical, the effect necessarily is so too; because the quantities to be added together returning in a regular order, the same sums must also regularly return.

This example is *d* worthy of consideration also in another respect. Though the causes themselves are permanent, and independent of all conditions known to us, the changes which take place in the quantities and relations of

b–bMS, 43, 46   motions of a planet are
cMS, 43, 46   moreover   dMS, 43, 46   well

the causes are actually caused by the periodical changes in the effects. The causes, as they exist at any moment, having produced a certain motion, that motion, becoming itself a cause, reacts upon the causes, and produces a change in them. By altering the distance and direction of the central body relatively to the planet, and the direction and quantity of the *force in the direction of the tangent*, it alters the elements which determine the motion at the next succeeding instant. This change renders the next motion somewhat different; and this difference, by a fresh reaction upon the causes, renders the next motion *again* different, and so on. The original state of the causes might have been such, that this series of actions modified by reactions would not have been periodical. The sun's action, and the original impelling force, might have been in such a ratio to one another, that the reaction of the effect would have been such as to alter the causes more and more, without ever bringing them back to what they were at any former time. The planet would then have moved in a parabola, or an hyperbola, curves not returning into themselves. The quantities of the two forces were, however, originally such, that the successive reactions of the effect bring back the causes, after a certain time, to what they were before; and from that time all the variations continue to recur again and again in the same periodical order, and must so continue while the causes subsist and are not counteracted.

§ 3. [*Derivative laws generated from a single ultimate law*] In all cases of progressive effects, whether arising from the accumulation of *a* unchanging or of changing elements, there is an uniformity of succession not merely between the cause and the effect, but between the first stages of the effect and its subsequent stages. That a body *in vacuo* falls sixteen feet in the first second, forty-eight in the second, and so on in the ratio of the odd numbers, *b* is as much an uniform sequence as that when the supports are removed the body falls. The sequence of spring and summer is as regular and invariable as that of the approach of the sun and spring: but we do not consider spring to be the cause of summer; it is *c* evident that *d*both are successive effects of the heat received from the sun, and that, considered merely in itself*d*, spring might continue for ever, without having the slightest tendency to produce summer. As we have so often remarked, not the conditional, but the unconditional invariable antecedent is termed the cause. That which would not be followed by the effect unless something else had preceded, *e*and which if

*e–e*MS, 43, 46, 51, 56, 62, 65   tangential force
*f–f*MS, 43   still more
*a*MS, 43   an   *b*MS, 43, 46   one, three, five, &c.,
*c*MS   so
*d–d*MS, 43, 46   they are both effects of the increased heat received from the sun, and that if that cause did not exist
e–e+72

that something else had preceded, would not have been required,[e] is not the cause, however invariable the sequence may in fact be.

It is in this way that most of [f]those[f] uniformities of succession are generated, which are not cases of causation. When a phenomenon goes on increasing, or periodically increases and diminishes, or goes through any continued and unceasing process of variation reducible to an uniform rule or law of succession, we do not on this account presume that any two successive terms of the series are cause and effect. We presume the contrary; we expect to find that the whole series originates either from the continued action of fixed causes, or from causes which go through a corresponding process of continuous change. A tree grows from half an inch high to a hundred feet; and some trees will generally grow to that height, unless prevented by some counteracting cause. But we do not call the seedling the cause of the full-grown tree; the invariable antecedent it certainly is, and we know very imperfectly on what other antecedents the sequence is contingent, but we are convinced that it is contingent on something; because the homogeneousness of the antecedent with the consequent, the [g] close resemblance of the seedling to the tree in all respects except magnitude, and the graduality of the growth, so exactly resembling the progressively accumulating effect produced by the long action of some one cause, [h]leave no[h] possibility of doubting that the seedling and the tree are [i] two terms in a series of that description, the first term of which is yet to seek. The conclusion is further confirmed by this, that we are able to prove by strict induction the dependence of the growth of the tree, and even of the continuance of its existence, upon the continued repetition of certain processes of nutrition, the rise of the sap, the absorptions and exhalations by the leaves, &c.; and the same experiments would probably prove to us that the growth of the tree is the accumulated sum of the effects of these continued processes, were we not, for want of sufficiently microscopic eyes, unable to observe correctly and in detail what those effects are.

[j]This supposition by no means requires that the effect should not, during its progress, undergo many modifications besides those of quantity, or that it should not sometimes appear to undergo a very marked change of character. This may be either because the unknown cause consists of several component elements or agents, whose effects, accumulating according to different laws, are compounded in different proportions at different periods in the existence of the organized being; or because, at certain points in its progress, fresh causes or agencies come in, or are evolved, which intermix their laws with those of the prime agent.[j]

[f-f]43   these [*printer's error?*]   [g]MS   very
[h-h]MS   leaves scarcely a]   43, 46   leave scarcely a
[i]MS, 43, 46   really   [j-j]+51, 56, 62, 65, 68, 72

CHAPTER XVI

Of Empirical Laws

§ 1. [*Definition of an empirical law*] [a]Scientific inquirers[a] give the name of Empirical Laws to those uniformities which observation or experiment has shown to exist, but on which they hesitate to rely in cases varying much from those which have been actually observed, for want of seeing any reason *why* such a law should exist. It is implied, therefore, in the notion of an empirical law, that it is not an ultimate law; that if true at all, its truth is capable of being, and requires to be, accounted for. It is a derivative law, the derivation of which is not yet known. To state the explanation, the *why*, of the empirical law, would be to state the laws from which it is derived; the ultimate causes on which it is contingent. And if we knew [b]these[b], we should also know what are its limits; under what conditions it would cease to be fulfilled.

The periodical return of eclipses, as originally ascertained by the persevering observation of the early eastern astronomers, was an empirical law, until the general laws of the celestial motions had accounted for it. The following are empirical laws still waiting to be resolved into the simpler laws from which they are derived. The local laws of the flux and reflux of the tides in different places: the succession of certain kinds of weather to certain appearances of sky: the apparent exceptions to the almost universal truth that bodies expand by increase of temperature: the law that breeds, both animal and vegetable, are improved by crossing: that gases have a strong tendency to permeate animal membranes: [c] that substances containing a very high proportion of nitrogen (such as hydrocyanic acid and morphia) are powerful poisons: that when different metals are fused together, the alloy is harder than the various elements: that the number of atoms of acid required to neutralize one atom of any base, is equal to the number of atoms of oxygen in the base: that the solubility of substances in one another, depends* (at least in some degree) on the similarity of their elements.

*Thus, water, of which eight-ninths in weight are oxygen, dissolves most bodies which contain a high proportion of oxygen, such as all the nitrates, (which have more oxygen than any others of the common salts,) most of the sulphates, many

[a]–[a]MS, 43, 46   Experimental philosophers usually
[b]–[b]MS   this
[c]MS, 43, 46   that opium and alcohol intoxicate:

An empirical law, then, is an observed uniformity, presumed to be resolvable into simpler laws, but not yet resolved into them. The ascertainment of the empirical laws of phenomena often precedes by a long interval the explanation of those laws by the Deductive Method; and the verification of a deduction usually consists in the comparison of its results with empirical laws previously ascertained.

§ 2. [*Derivative laws commonly depend on collocations*] From a limited number of ultimate laws of causation, there are necessarily generated a vast number of derivative uniformities, both of succession and of coexistence. Some are laws of succession or of coexistence between different effects of the same cause: of *a*these*a* we had *b* examples in the last chapter. Some are laws of succession between effects and their remote causes; resolvable into the laws which connect each with the intermediate link. Thirdly, when causes act together and compound their effects, the laws of those causes generate the fundamental law of the effect, namely, that it depends on the coexistence of those causes. And, finally, the order of succession or of coexistence which obtains among effects, necessarily depends on their causes. If they are effects of the same cause, it depends on the laws of that cause; if of different causes, it depends on the laws of those causes severally, and on the circumstances which determine their coexistence. If we inquire further when and how the causes will coexist, that, again, depends on *their* causes: and we may thus trace back the phenomena higher and higher, until the different series of effects meet in a point, and the whole is shown to have depended ultimately on some common cause; or until, instead of converging to one point, they terminate in different points, and the order of the effects is proved to have arisen from the *c* collocation of some of the primeval causes, or natural agents. For example, the order of succession and of coexistence among the heavenly motions, which is expressed by Kepler's laws, is derived from the coexistence of two primeval causes, the sun, and the original impulse or projectile force *d*belonging to*d* each planet.* Kepler's laws are resolved into the laws of these causes and the fact of their coexistence.

---

of the carbonates, &c. Again, bodies largely composed of combustible elements, like hydrogen and carbon, are soluble in bodies of similar composition; rosin, for instance, will dissolve in alcohol, tar in oil of turpentine. This empirical generalization is far from being universally true; no doubt because it is a remote, and therefore easily defeated, result of general laws too deep for us at present to penetrate; but it will probably in time suggest processes of inquiry, leading to the discovery of *d*those*d* laws.

*Or (according to Laplace's theory) the sun and the sun's rotation.

*d–d*43   these [*printer's error?*]
*a–a*MS   the former kind   *b*MS, 43, 46, 51, 56   abundant
*c*MS, 43, 46   original   *d–d*MS, 43, 46   impressed upon

Derivative laws, therefore, do not depend solely on the ultimate laws into which they are resolvable: they mostly depend on those ultimate laws, and an ultimate fact; namely, the mode of coexistence of some of the *component* elements of the universe. The ultimate laws of causation might be the same as at present, and yet the derivative laws completely different, if the causes coexisted in different proportions, or with any difference in those of their relations by which the effects are influenced. If, for example, the sun's attraction, and the original projectile force, had existed in some other ratio to one another than they did (and we know of no reason why this should not have been the case), the derivative laws of the heavenly motions might have been quite different from what they are. The proportions which exist happen to be such as to produce regular elliptical motions; any other proportions would have produced different ellipses, or circular, or parabolic, or hyperbolic motions, but still regular ones; because the effects of each of the agents accumulate according to an uniform law; and two regular series of quantities, when their corresponding terms are added, must produce a regular series of some sort, whatever the quantities themselves are.

§ 3. [*The collocations of the permanent causes are not reducible to any law*] Now this last-mentioned element in the resolution of a derivative law, the element which is not a law of causation, but a collocation of causes, cannot itself be reduced to any law. There is (as formerly remarked*) no uniformity, no *norma*, principle, or rule, perceivable in the distribution of the primeval natural agents through the universe. The *different* substances composing the earth, the powers that pervade the universe, stand in no constant relation to one another. One substance is more abundant than others, one power acts through a larger extent of space than others, without any pervading analogy that we can discover. We not only do not know of any reason why the sun's attraction and the *force in the direction of the tangent* coexist in the exact proportion they do, but we can trace no coincidence between it and the proportions in which any other elementary powers in the universe are intermingled. The utmost disorder is apparent in the combination of the causes; which is consistent with the most *regular* order in their effects; for when each agent carries on its own operations according to an uniform law, even the most capricious combination of agencies will generate a regularity of some sort; as we see in the kaleidoscope, where any casual arrangement of coloured bits of glass produces by the laws of reflection a beautiful regularity in the effect.

*Supra, Bk. III, Chap. v, §8 [pp. 344ff.].

e–eMS, 43, 46   original
a–a+43, 46, 51, 56, 62, 65, 68, 72
b–bMS, 43, 46, 51, 56, 62, 65   tangential force
c–cMS, 43, 46   perfect

§ 4. [*Hence* empirical laws cannot be relied on beyond the limits of actual experience] In the above considerations lies the justification of the limited degree of reliance which *scientific inquirers* are accustomed to place in empirical laws.

A derivative law which results wholly from the operation of some one cause, will be as universally true as the laws of the cause itself; that is, it will always be true except where some one of those effects of the cause, on which the derivative law depends, is defeated by a counteracting cause. But when the derivative law results not from different effects of one cause, but from effects of several causes, we cannot be certain that it will be true under any variation in the mode of coexistence of those causes, or of the primitive natural agents on which the causes ultimately depend. The proposition that coal beds rest on certain descriptions of strata exclusively, though true on the earth so far as our observation has reached, cannot be extended to the moon or the other planets, supposing coal to exist there; because we cannot be assured that the original constitution of any other planet was such as to produce the different depositions in the same order as in our globe. The derivative law in this case depends not solely on laws, but on a collocation; and collocations cannot be reduced to any law.

Now it is the very nature of a derivative law which has not yet been resolved into its elements, in other words, an empirical law, that we do not know whether it results from the different effects of one cause, or from effects of different causes. We cannot tell whether it depends wholly on laws, or partly on laws and partly on a collocation. If it depends on a collocation, it will be true in all the cases in which that particular collocation exists. But, since we are entirely ignorant, in case of its depending on a collocation, what the collocation is, we are not safe in extending the law beyond the limits of time and place in which we have actual experience of its truth. Since within those limits the law has always been found true, we have evidence that the collocations, whatever they are, on which it depends, do really exist within those limits. But, knowing of no rule or principle to which the collocations themselves conform, we cannot conclude that because a collocation is proved to exist within certain limits of place or time, it will exist beyond those limits. Empirical laws, therefore, can only be *received as* true within the limits of time and place in which they have been found true by observation: and not merely the limits of time and place, but of time, place, and circumstance: for since it is the very meaning of an empirical law that we do not know the ultimate laws of causation on which it is dependent, we cannot foresee, without actual trial, in what manner or to what extent the introduction of any new circumstance may affect it.

*a–a*MS, 43, 46   *And hence*
*b–b*MS, 43, 46   philosophers
*c–c*MS, 43, 46   held

§ 5. [*Generalizations which rest only on the Method of Agreement can only be received as empirical laws*] But how are we to know that an uniformity, ascertained by experience, is only an empirical law? Since, by the supposition, we have not been able to resolve it into ^aany other^a laws, how do we know that it is not an ultimate law of causation?

I answer, that no generalization amounts to more than an empirical law when the only proof on which it rests is that of the Method of Agreement. For it has been seen that by that method alone we never can arrive at causes. ^bThe utmost^b that the Method of Agreement can do is, to ascertain the whole of the circumstances common to all cases in which a phenomenon is produced: and this ^caggregate^c includes not only the cause of the phenomenon, but all phenomena with which it is connected by any derivative uniformity, whether as being collateral effects of the same cause, or effects of any other cause which, in all the instances we have been able to observe, coexisted with it. The method affords no means of determining which of these uniformities are laws of causation, and which are merely derivative laws, resulting from those laws of causation and from the collocation of the causes. None of them, therefore, can be received in any other character than that of derivative laws, the derivation of which has not been traced; in other words, empirical laws: in which light, all results obtained by the Method of Agreement (and therefore almost all ^d truths obtained by simple observation without experiment) must be considered, until either confirmed by the Method of Difference, or explained deductively, in other words accounted for *à priori*.

These empirical laws may be of greater or ^e less authority, according as there is reason to presume that they are resolvable into laws only, or into laws and collocations together. The sequences which we observe in the production and subsequent life of an animal or a vegetable, resting on the Method of Agreement only, are mere empirical laws; but though the antecedents in those sequences may not be the causes of the consequents, both the one and the other are ^fdoubtless^f, in the main, successive stages of a progressive effect originating in a common cause, and therefore independent of collocations. The uniformities, on the other hand, in the order of superposition of strata on the earth, are empirical laws of a much weaker kind, since they ^gnot only are^g not laws of causation, but there is no reason to believe that they depend on any common cause: all appearances are in favour of their depending on the particular collocation of natural agents which ^hat some time or other^h existed on our globe, and from which no inference can be drawn as to the collocation which exists or has existed in any other portion of the universe.

^{a–a}MS, 43, 46 higher	^{b–b}MS, 43, 46, 51, 56, 62, 65 All
^{c–c}MS, 43, 46, 51, 56 of course	^dMS, 43, 46 the
^eMS, 43, 46 of	^{f–f}MS, 43, 46 probably
^{g–g}43, 46 are not only	^{h–h}MS, 43, 46 primitively

§ 6. [*Signs from which an observed uniformity of sequence may be presumed to be resolvable*] Our definition of an empirical law including not only those uniformities which are not known to be laws of causation, but also those which are, provided there be reason to presume that they are not ultimate laws; this is the proper place to consider by what signs we may judge that even if an observed uniformity be a law of causation, it is not an ultimate but a derivative law.

The first sign is, if between the antecedent *a* and the consequent *b* there be evidence of some intermediate link; some phenomenon of which we can *surmise* the existence, though from the imperfection of our senses or of our instruments we are unable to ascertain its precise nature and laws. If there be such a phenomenon (which may be denoted by the letter *x*), it follows that even if *a* be the cause of *b*, it is but the remote cause, and that the law, *a* causes *b*, is resolvable into at least two laws, *a* causes *x*, and *x* causes *b*. This is a very frequent case, since the operations of nature mostly take place on so minute a scale, that many of the successive steps are either imperceptible, or very indistinctly perceived.

Take, for example, the laws of the chemical composition of substances; as that hydrogen and oxygen being combined, water is produced. All we see of the process is, that the two gases being mixed in certain proportions, and heat or electricity being applied, an explosion takes place, the gases disappear, and water remains. There is no doubt about the law, or about its being a law of causation. But between the antecedent (the gases in a state of mechanical mixture, heated or electrified), and the consequent (the production of water), there must be an intermediate process which we do not see. For if we take any portion whatever of the water, and subject it to analysis, we find that it always contains *hydrogen and* oxygen; nay, the very same proportions of them, namely, two thirds, in volume, of hydrogen, and one third oxygen. This is true of a single drop; it is true of the minutest portion which our instruments are capable of appreciating. Since, then, the smallest perceptible portion of the water contains both those substances, portions of hydrogen and oxygen smaller than the smallest perceptible must have come together in every such minute portion of space; must have come closer together than when the gases were in a state of mechanical mixture, since (to mention no other reasons) the water occupies far less space than the gases. Now, as we cannot see this contact or close approach of the minute particles, we cannot observe with what circumstances it is attended, or according to what laws it produces its effects. The production of water, that is, of the sensible phenomena which characterize the compound, may be a very remote effect of those laws. There may be innumerable intervening links; and we are sure that there must be some. Having full proof that corpuscular action of

*a–a*MS, 43, 46   collect
*b–b*MS, 43, 46, 51, 56, 62, 65   some hydrogen and some

some kind takes place previous to any of the great transformations in the sensible properties of substances, we can have no doubt that the laws of chemical action, as at present known, are not ultimate but derivative laws; however ignorant we may be, and even though we should for ever remain ignorant, of the nature of the laws of corpuscular action from which they are derived.

In like manner, all the processes of vegetative life, whether in the vegetable properly so called or in the animal body, are corpuscular processes. Nutrition is the addition of particles to one another, ^{c}sometimes merely replacing other particles separated and excreted, sometimes^c occasioning an increase of bulk or weight, so gradual, that only after a long continuance does it become perceptible. Various organs, by means of peculiar vessels, secrete from the blood, fluids, the component particles of which must have been in the blood, but which differ from it most widely both in mechanical properties and in chemical composition. Here, then, are abundance of unknown links to be filled up; and there can be no doubt that the laws of the phenomena of vegetative or organic life are derivative laws, dependent on properties of the corpuscles, and of those elementary tissues which are comparatively simple combinations of corpuscles.

The first sign, then, from which a law of causation, though hitherto unresolved, may be inferred to be a derivative law, is any indication of the existence of an intermediate link or links between the antecedent and the consequent. The second is, when the antecedent is an extremely complex phenomenon, and its effects therefore, probably, in part at least, compounded of the effects of its different elements; since we know that the case in which the effect of the whole is not made up of the effects of its parts, is exceptional, the Composition of Causes being by far the more ordinary case.

We will illustrate this by two examples, in one of which the antecedent is the sum of many homogeneous, in the other of heterogeneous, parts. The weight of a body is made up of the weights of its minute particles: a truth which astronomers express in its most general terms, when they say that bodies, at equal distances, gravitate to one another in proportion to their quantity of matter. All true propositions, therefore, which can be made concerning gravity, are derivative laws; the ultimate law into which they are all resolvable being, that every particle of matter attracts every other. As our second example, we may take any of the sequences observed in meteorology: for instance, ^{d} a diminution of the pressure of the atmosphere (indicated by a fall of the barometer) is followed by rain. The antecedent is here a complex phenomenon, made up of heterogeneous elements; the column of the atmosphere over any particular place consisting of two parts, a column of air, and a column of aqueous vapour mixed with it; and the change in the two together manifested by a fall of the barometer, and followed by rain, must be either a change in one of these, or in the other, or in both. We might, then, even in the absence of any other evidence, form a reasonable presumption, from the invariable presence of both *these* elements in the antecedent, that the sequence is probably not an ultimate law, but a result of the laws of the two different agents; a presumption only to be destroyed when we had made ourselves so well acquainted with the laws of both, as to be able to affirm that those laws could not by themselves produce the observed result.

f There are but few known cases of succession from very complex antecedents, which have not either been actually accounted for from simpler laws, or inferred with great probability (from the ascertained existence of intermediate links of causation not yet understood) to be capable of being so accounted for. It is, therefore, highly probable that all sequences from complex antecedents are thus resolvable, and that ultimate laws are in all cases comparatively simple. If there were not the other reasons already mentioned for believing that the laws of organized nature are resolvable into simpler laws, it would be almost a sufficient reason that the antecedents in most of the sequences are so very complex. *g*

*e–e*MS   those [*printer's error?*]

*f*MS, 43, 46   §7. [*Most, if not all, cases of sequence from very complex antecedents, are resolvable*]

*g*MS   [*paragraph*] There are appearances strongly favouring the suspicion, that these phenomena are really resolvable into much simpler laws than might at first be expected. The growth of an animal from infancy to maturity, of a plant from infancy till death, and even that process of decay which is but a slow death, bear a most striking resemblance to the progressive effect of the continued action of some cause, proceeding until it meets agencies which overpower it, or until its accumulated effect gives rise to conditions inconsistent with its own existence. This supposition by no means requires that the effect should not, during its progress, undergo many modifications besides those of quantity, or that it should not sometimes appear to undergo a very marked change of character. This may be, either because the unknown cause consists of several component elements or agents, whose effects, accumulating according to different laws, are compounded in different proportions at different periods in the existence of the organized being; or it may be because, at certain points in its progress, fresh causes or agencies come in, or are evolved, which intermix their laws with those of the prime agent.

This great problem, the most difficult in all physics, the ascertainment of the ultimate laws of organized nature, is one which natural science in its progress seems now at least to have fairly come up to; and a beginning has been made at the point where the phenomena appear most accessible to experiment, namely, in separating the effects of partial from those of general causes. The result, as far as it goes, fully accords with the above surmise. I allude to the new and infant science of morphology, created with respect to animals by the genius of Cuvier and St. Hilaire, and with respect to vegetables by that of the illustrious Goethe, to whom the world owes so much in quite a different field of intellect, and whose researches on the *Metamorphoses of Plants* [*Versuch die Metamorphose der Pflanzen*. In *Werke*. Stuttgart: Cotta, 1828, Vol. III, pp. 92ff.] have met with a more favourable reception from the scientific world than his speculations on colours. It seems to be now considered by natural philosophers as sufficiently established, that plants and animals, in the process of growing up from their

§ 7. [*Two kinds of empirical laws*] In the preceding discussion we have recognised two kinds of empirical laws: those known to be laws of causation, but presumed to be resolvable into simpler laws; and those not known to be laws of causation at all. Both these kinds of laws agree in the demand which they make for being explained by deduction, and agree in being the appropriate means of verifying such deduction, since they represent the experience with which the result of the deduction must be compared. They agree, further, in this, that until explained, and connected with the ultimate laws from which they result, they have not attained the highest degree of certainty of which laws are susceptible. It has been shown on a former occasion that laws of causation which are derivative, and compounded of simpler laws, are not only, as the nature of the case implies, less general, but even less certain, than the simpler laws from which they result; not *b*in the same degree*b* to be relied on as universally true. The inferiority of evidence, however, which attaches to this class of laws, is trifling, compared with that which is inherent in uniformities not known to be laws of causation at all. So long as these are unresolved, we cannot tell on how many collocations, as well as laws, their truth may be dependent; *c*we*c* can never, therefore, extend them with *d*any*d* confidence to cases in which we have not assured ourselves, by trial, that the necessary collocation of causes, whatever it may be, exists. It is to this class of laws alone that the property, which philosophers usually consider as characteristic of empirical laws, belongs in all its strictness; the property of being unfit to be relied on beyond the limits of time, place, and circumstance, in which the observations have been made. These are empirical laws in a more emphatic sense; and when I employ that term (except where the context manifestly indicates the reverse) I shall generally mean to designate those uniformities only, whether of succession or of coexistence, which are not known to be laws of causation.

---

germs, have a tendency to develop themselves in a much more uniform manner than they in fact do; that the differences, for example, of leaf, flower, and fruit, are mere modifications of one general phenomenon; or (which is only another expression for the same idea) joint results of one common tendency and of several partial causes combining with it.]   43, 46   *as* MS . . . accumulated effects give rise . . . *as* MS . . . being; or because, at certain . . . *as* MS

*a–a*MS, 43, 46   §8.
*b–b*MS, 43, 46   so positively
*c–c*MS, 43, 46, 51, 56   and
*d–d*MS, 43, 46   perfect

CHAPTER XVII

Of Chance and Its Elimination

§ 1. [*The proof of empirical laws depends on the theory of chance*] Considering then as empirical laws only those observed uniformities respecting which the question whether they are laws of causation must remain undecided until they can be explained deductively, or until some means are found of applying the Method of Difference to the case; it has been shown in the preceding chapter, that until an uniformity can, in one or the other of these modes, be taken out of the class of empirical laws, and brought either into that of laws of causation or of the demonstrated results of laws of causation, it cannot with any assurance be pronounced true beyond the local and other limits within which it has been found so by actual observation. It remains to consider how we are to assure ourselves of its truth even within those limits; after what quantity of experience a generalization which rests solely on the Method of Agreement, can be considered sufficiently established, even as an empirical law. In a former chapter, when treating of the Methods of Direct Induction, we expressly reserved this question,* and the time is now come for endeavouring to solve it.

We found that the Method of Agreement has the defect of not proving causation, and can therefore only be employed for the ascertainment of empirical laws. But we *also found* that besides this deficiency, it labours under a characteristic imperfection, tending to render uncertain even such conclusions as it is in itself adapted to prove. This imperfection arises from Plurality of Causes. Although two or more cases in which the phenomenon *a* has been met with, may have no common antecedent except A, this does not prove that there is any connexion between *a* and A, since *a* may have many causes, and may have been produced, in these different instances, not by anything which the instances had in common, but by some of those elements in them which were different. We nevertheless observed, that in proportion to the multiplication of instances pointing to A as the antecedent, the characteristic uncertainty of the method diminishes, and the existence of a law of connexion between A and *a* more nearly approaches to certainty. It is now

*Supra, Bk. III, Chap. x, §2 [pp. 436–7].

*a–a*MS, 43, 46   found, moreover,

to be determined, after what amount of experience this certainty may be deemed to be practically attained, and the connexion between A and *a* may be received as an empirical law.

This question may be otherwise stated in more familiar terms:—After how many and what sort of instances may it be concluded, that an observed coincidence between two phenomena is not the effect of chance?

It is of the utmost importance for understanding the logic of induction, that we should form a distinct conception of what is meant by chance, and how the phenomena which common language ascribes to that abstraction are really produced.

§ 2. [*Chance defined and characterized*] Chance is usually spoken of in direct antithesis to law; whatever (it is supposed) cannot be ascribed to any law, is attributed to chance. It is, however, certain, that whatever happens is the result of some law; is an effect of causes, and could have been predicted from a knowledge of the existence of those causes, and from their laws. If I turn up a particular card, that is a consequence of its place in the pack. Its place in the pack was a consequence of the manner in which the cards were shuffled, or of the order in which they were played in the last game; which, again, were *a* effects of prior causes. At every stage, if we had possessed an accurate knowledge of the causes in existence, it would have been abstractedly possible to foretell the effect.

An event occurring by chance, may be *b*better*b* described as a coincidence from which we have no ground to infer an uniformity: the occurrence of a phenomenon in certain circumstances, without our having reason on that account to infer that it will happen again in those circumstances. This, however, when looked closely into, implies that the enumeration of the circumstances is not complete. Whatever the fact be, since it has occurred once, we may be sure that if *all* the same circumstances were repeated, it would occur again; and not only if all, but there is some particular portion of those circumstances, on which the phenomenon is invariably consequent. With most of them, however, it is not connected in any permanent manner: its conjunction with those is said to be the effect of chance, to be merely casual. Facts casually conjoined are separately the effects of causes, and therefore of laws; but of different causes, and causes not connected by any law.

It is incorrect, then, to say that any phenomenon is produced by chance; but we may say that two or more phenomena are conjoined by chance, that they coexist or succeed one another only by chance; meaning that they are in no way related through causation; that they are neither cause and effect, nor effects of the same cause, nor effects of causes between which there subsists

*a*MS, 43, 46   the
b–b+51, 56, 62, 65, 68, 72

any law of coexistence, nor even effects of the same ^{c} collocation of primeval causes.

If the same casual coincidence never occurred a second time, we should have an easy test for distinguishing such from the coincidences which are ^{d}the^d results of a law. As long as the phenomena had been found together only once, so long, unless we knew some more general laws from which the coincidence might have resulted, we could not distinguish it from a casual one; but if it occurred twice, we should know that the phenomena so conjoined must be in some way connected through their causes.

There is, however, no such test. A coincidence may occur again and again, and yet be only casual. Nay, it would be inconsistent with what we know of the order of nature, to doubt that every casual coincidence will sooner or later be repeated, as long as the phenomena between which it occurred do not cease to exist, or to be ^{e}reproduced^e. The recurrence, therefore, of the same coincidence more than once, or even its frequent recurrence, does not prove that it is an instance of any law; does not prove that it is not casual, or, in common language, the effect of chance.

And yet, when a coincidence cannot be deduced from known laws, nor proved by experiment to be itself a case of causation, the frequency of its occurrence is the only evidence from which we can infer that it is the result of a law. Not, however, its absolute frequency. The question is not whether the coincidence occurs often or seldom, in the ordinary sense of those terms; but whether it occurs more often than chance will account for; more often than might rationally be expected if the coincidence were casual. We have to decide, therefore, what degree of frequency in a coincidence, chance will account for. And to this there can be no general answer. We can only state the principle by which the answer must be determined: the answer itself will be different in every different case.

Suppose that one of the phenomena, A, exists always, and the other phenomenon, B, only occasionally: it follows that every instance of B will be an instance of its coincidence with A, and yet the coincidence will be merely casual, not the result of any connexion between them. The fixed stars have been constantly in existence since the beginning of human experience, and all phenomena that have come under human observation have, in every single instance, coexisted with them; yet this coincidence, though equally invariable with that which exists between any of those phenomena and its own cause, does not prove that the stars are its cause, nor that they are in anywise connected with it. As strong a case of coincidence, therefore, as can possibly exist, and a much stronger one in point of mere frequency than most of those

^{c}MS, 43, 46   original
$^{d-d}$+56, 62, 65, 68, 72
$^{e-e}$MS, 43, 46   produced

which prove laws, does not here prove a law: why? because, since the stars exist always, they *must* coexist with every other phenomenon, whether connected with them by causation or not. The uniformity, great though it be, is no greater than would occur on the supposition that no such connexion exists.

On the other hand, suppose that we were inquiring whether there be any connexion between rain and any particular wind. Rain, we know, occasionally occurs with every wind; therefore the connexion, if it exists, cannot be an actual law: but still, rain may be connected with some particular wind through causation; that is, though they cannot be always effects of the same cause (for if so they would *regularly* coexist), there may be some causes common to the two, so that in so far as either is produced by those common causes, they will, from the laws of the causes, be found to coexist. How, then, shall we ascertain this? The obvious answer is, by observing whether rain occurs with one wind more frequently than with any other. That, however, is not enough; for perhaps that one wind blows more frequently than any other; so that its blowing more frequently in rainy weather is no more than would happen, although it had no connexion with the causes of rain, provided it were not connected with causes adverse to rain. In England, westerly winds blow during about twice as great a portion of the year as easterly. If, therefore, it rains only twice as often with a westerly, as with an easterly wind, we have no reason to infer that any law of nature is concerned in the coincidence. If it rains more than twice as often, we may be sure that some law is concerned; either there is some cause in nature *which, in this climate, tends* to produce both rain and a westerly wind, or a westerly wind has itself some tendency to produce rain. But if it rains less than twice as often, we may draw a directly opposite inference: the one, instead of being a cause, or connected with causes, of the other, must be connected with causes adverse to it, or with the absence of some cause which produces it; and though it may still rain much oftener with a westerly wind than with an easterly, so far would this be from proving any connexion between the phenomena, that the connexion proved would be between rain and an easterly wind, *h* to which, in mere frequency of coincidence, it is *less* allied.

Here, then, are two examples: in one, the greatest possible frequency of coincidence, with no instance whatever to the contrary, does not prove that there is any law; in the other, a much less frequency of coincidence, even when non-coincidence is still more frequent, does prove that there is a law. In both cases the principle is the same. In both we consider the positive frequency of the phenomena themselves, and how great frequency of coincidence that must of itself bring about, without supposing any connexion between them, provided there be no repugnance; provided neither be con-

*f–f*MS, 43, 46   always
*h*MS, 43, 46   the wind

*g–g*MS, 43, 46   tending
*i–i*MS, 43, 46   least

nected with any cause tending to frustrate the other. If we find a greater frequency of coincidence than this, we conclude that there is some connexion; if a less frequency, that there is some repugnance. In the former case, *j*we conclude*j* that one of the phenomena can under some circumstances cause the other, or that there exists something capable of causing them both; in the latter, that one of them, or some cause which produces one of them, is capable of counteracting the production of the other. We have thus to deduct from the observed frequency of coincidence, as much as may be the effect of chance, that is, of the mere frequency of the phenomena themselves; and if anything remains, what does remain is the residual fact which proves the existence of a law.

The frequency of the phenomena can only be ascertained within definite limits of space and time; depending as it does on the quantity and distribution of the primeval natural agents, of which we can know nothing beyond the boundaries of human observation, since no law, no regularity, can be traced in it, enabling us to infer the unknown from the known. But for the present purpose this is no disadvantage, the question being confined within the same limits as the data. The coincidences occurred in certain places and times, and within those we can estimate the frequency with which such coincidences would be produced by chance. If, then, we find from observation that A exists in one case out of every two, and B in one case out of every three; then if there be neither connexion nor repugnance between them, or between any of their causes, the instances in which A and B will both exist, that is to say will coexist, will be one case in every six. For A exists in three cases out of six: and B, existing in one case out of every three without regard to the presence or absence of A, will exist in one case out of those three. There will therefore be, of the whole number of cases, two in which A exists without B; one case of B without A; two in which neither B nor A exists, and one case out of six in which they both exist. If then, in point of fact, they are found to coexist oftener than in one case out of six; and, consequently, A does not exist without B so often as twice in three times, nor B without A so often as once in every twice; there is some cause in existence which tends to produce a conjunction between A and B.

Generalizing the result, we may say, that if A occurs in a larger proportion of the cases where B is, than of the cases where B is not; then will B also occur in a larger proportion of the cases where A is, than of the cases where A is not; and there is some connexion, through causation, between A and B. If we could ascend to the causes of the two phenomena, we should find, at some stage, either proximate or remote, some cause or causes common to both; and if we could ascertain what these are, we could frame a generalization which would be true without restriction of place or time; but until we

j–j+43, 46, 51, 56, 62, 65, 68, 72

can do so, the fact of a connexion between the two phenomena remains an empirical law.

§ 3. [*The elimination of chance*] Having considered in what manner it may be determined whether any given conjunction of phenomena is casual, or the result of some law; to complete the theory of chance, it is necessary that we should now consider those effects which are partly the result of chance and partly of law, or, in other words, in which the effects of casual conjunctions of causes are habitually blended in one result with the effects of a constant cause.

This is a case of Composition of Causes; and the peculiarity of it is, that instead of two or more causes intermixing their effects in a regular manner with those of one another, we have now one constant cause, producing an effect which is successively modified by a series of variable causes. Thus, as summer advances, the approach of the sun to a vertical position tends to produce a constant increase of temperature; but with this effect of a constant cause, there are blended the effects of many variable causes, winds, clouds, evaporation, electric agencies and the like, so that the temperature ^{a}of^a any given day depends in part on these fleeting causes, and only in part on the constant cause. If the effect of the constant cause is always accompanied and disguised by effects of variable causes, it is impossible to ascertain the law of the constant cause in the ordinary manner, by separating it from all other causes and observing it apart. Hence arises the necessity of an additional rule of experimental inquiry.

When the action of a cause A is liable to be interfered with, not steadily by the same cause or causes, but by different causes at different times, and when these are so frequent, or so indeterminate, that we cannot possibly exclude all of them from any experiment, though we may vary them; our resource is, to endeavour to ascertain what is the effect of all the variable causes taken together. In order to do this, we make as many trials as possible, preserving A invariable. The results of these different trials will naturally be different, since the indeterminate modifying causes are different in each; if, then, we do not find these results to be progressive, but, on the contrary, to oscillate about a certain point, one experiment giving a result a little greater, another a little less, one a result tending a little more in one direction, another a little more in the contrary direction; while the average or middle point does not vary, but different sets of experiments (taken ^{b}in^b as great a variety of circumstances as possible) yield the same mean, provided only they be sufficiently numerous; then that mean or average result, is the part, in each experiment, which is due to the cause A, and is the effect which would have been obtained if A

$a-a$MS, 43, 46, 51, 56, 62   on
$b-b$MS, 43, 46   under

could have acted alone: the variable remainder is the effect of chance, that is, of causes the coexistence of which with the cause A was merely casual. The test of the sufficiency of the induction in this case is, when any increase of the number of trials from which the average is struck, does not materially alter the average.

This kind of elimination, in which we do not eliminate any one assignable cause, but the multitude of *floating* unassignable ones, may be termed the Elimination of Chance. We afford an example of it when we repeat an experiment, in order, by taking the mean of different results, to get rid of the effects of the unavoidable errors of each individual experiment. When there is no permanent cause such as would produce a tendency to error peculiarly in one direction, we are warranted by experience in assuming that the errors on one side will, in a certain number of experiments, about balance the errors on the contrary side. We *therefore* repeat the experiment, until any change which is produced in the average of the whole by further repetition, falls within limits of error consistent with the degree of accuracy required by the purpose we have in view.*

§ 4. [*Discovery of residual phenomena by eliminating chance*] In the supposition hitherto made, the effect of the constant cause A has been assumed to form so great and conspicuous a part of the general result, that its existence never could be a matter of uncertainty, and the object of the eliminating process was only to ascertain *how much* is attributable to that cause; what is its exact law. Cases, however, occur in which the effect of a constant cause is so small, compared with that of some of the changeable

*[62] In the preceding discussion, the *mean* is spoken of as if it were exactly the same thing with the *average*. But the mean for purposes of inductive inquiry, is not the average, or arithmetical mean, though in a familiar illustration of the theory the difference may be disregarded. If the deviations on one side of the average are much more numerous than those on the other (these last being fewer but greater), the effect due to the invariable cause, as distinct from the variable ones, will not coincide with the average, but will be either below or above the average, *the deviation being towards* the side on which the greatest number of the instances are found. This follows from a truth, ascertained both inductively and deductively, that small deviations from the true central point are greatly more frequent than large ones. The mathematical law is, "that the most probable determination of one or more invariable elements from observation is that in which the *sum of the squares* of the individual aberations," or deviations, "*shall be the least possible*." See this principle stated, and its grounds popularly explained, by Sir John Herschel, in his review of Quetelet on Probabilities, *Essays*, pp. 395 *et seq.*

*c–c*MS   fleeting [*printer's error?*]
*d–d*MS, 43, 46   have, therefore, to
*e–e*62, 65, 68   whichever be
*a–a*MS   [*no section division*]

causes with which it is liable to be casually conjoined, that of itself it escapes notice, and the very existence of any effect arising from a constant cause is first learnt, by the process which in general serves only for ascertaining the quantity of that effect. This case of induction may be characterized as follows. A given effect is known to be chiefly, and not known not to be wholly, determined by changeable causes. If it be wholly so produced, then if the aggregate be taken of a sufficient number of instances, the effects of these different causes will cancel one another. If, therefore, we do not find this to be the case, but, on the contrary, after such a number of trials has been made that no further increase alters the average result, we find that average to be, not zero, but some other quantity, *about* which, though small in comparison with the total effect, the effect nevertheless oscillates, and which is the middle point in its oscillation; we may conclude this to be the effect of some constant cause: which cause, by some of the methods already treated of, we may hope to detect. This may be called *the discovery of a residual phenomenon by eliminating the *effects* of chance*.

It is in this manner, for example, that *loaded dice may be discovered*. Of course no dice are so clumsily loaded that they must always throw certain numbers; otherwise the fraud would be instantly detected. The loading, a constant cause, mingles with the changeable causes which determine what cast will be thrown in each individual instance. If the dice were not loaded, and the throw were left to depend entirely on the changeable causes, these in a sufficient number of instances would balance one another, and there would be no preponderant number of throws of any one kind. If, therefore, after such a number of trials that no further increase of their number has any material effect upon the average, we find a preponderance in favour of a particular throw; we may conclude with assurance that there is some constant cause acting in favour of that throw, or in other words, that the dice are not fair; and *e* the exact amount of the unfairness. In a similar manner, what is called the diurnal variation of the barometer, which is very small compared with the variations arising from the irregular changes in the state of the atmosphere, was discovered by comparing the average height of the barometer at different hours of the day. When this comparison was made, it was found that there was a small difference, which on the average was constant, however the absolute quantities might vary, and which difference, therefore, must be the effect of a constant cause. This cause was afterwards ascertained, deductively, to be the rarefaction of the air, occasioned by the increase of temperature as the day advances.

*b–b*MS, 43, 46, 51   around]   56, 62   round
*c–c*MS, 43, 46   *effect*
*d–d*MS   we may discover loaded dice
*e*MS, 43, 46   moreover

§ 5. [*The doctrine of chances*] After these general remarks on the nature of chance, we are prepared to consider in what manner assurance may be obtained that a conjunction between two phenomena, which has been observed a certain number of times, is not casual, but a result of causation, and to be received therefore as one of the uniformities *of* nature, though (until accounted for *à priori*) only as an empirical law.

We will suppose the strongest case, namely, that the phenomenon B has never been observed except in conjunction with A. Even then, the probability that they are connected is not measured by the total number of instances in which they have been found together, but by the excess of that number above the number due to the absolute frequency of A. If, for example, A exists always, and therefore coexists with everything, no number of instances of its coexistence with B would prove a connexion; as in our example of the fixed stars. If A be a fact of such common occurrence that it may be presumed to be present in half of all the cases that occur, and therefore in half the cases in which B occurs, it is only the proportional excess above half, that *is* to be reckoned as evidence towards proving a connexion between A and B.

In addition to the question, What is the number of coincidences which, on an average of a great multitude of trials, may be expected to arise from chance alone? there is also another question, namely, Of what extent of deviation from that average is the occurrence credible, from chance alone, in some number of instances smaller than that *required for striking* a fair average? It is not only to be considered what is the general result of the chances in the long run, but also what are the extreme limits of variation from *the* general result, which may occasionally be expected as the result of some smaller number of instances.

The consideration of the latter question, and any consideration of the former beyond that already given to it, belong to what mathematicians term the doctrine of chances, or, in a phrase of greater pretension, the Theory of Probabilities. *f*

*a–a*MS §4.
*b–b*MS, 43, 46, 51, 56 in
*c–c*MS, 43, 46, 51, 56 are
*d–d*MS, 43, 46 which constitutes
*e–e*MS, 43, 46, 51, 56, 62 that
*f*MS, 43, 46 An attempt at a philosophical appreciation of that doctrine is, therefore, a necessary portion of our task.

CHAPTER XVIII

Of the Calculation of Chances

§ 1. [*Foundation of the doctrine of chances, as taught by mathematics*] [a]"Probability," says Laplace,*

has reference partly to our ignorance, partly to our knowledge. We know that among three or more events, one, and only one, must happen; but there is nothing leading us to believe that any one of them will happen rather than the others. In this state of indecision, it is impossible for us to pronounce with certainty on their occurrence. It is, however, probable that any one of these events, selected at pleasure, will not take place; because we perceive several cases, all equally possible, which exclude its occurrence, and only one which favours it.

The theory of chances consists in reducing all events of the same kind to a certain number of cases equally possible, that is, such that we are *equally undecided* as to their existence; and in determining the number of these cases which are favourable to the event of which the probability is sought. The ratio of that number to the number of all the possible cases, is the measure of the probability; which is thus a fraction, having for its numerator the number of cases favourable to the event, and for its denominator the number of all the cases which are possible.

To a calculation of chances, then, according to Laplace, two things are necessary: we must know that of several events some one will certainly happen, and no more than one; and we must not know, nor have any reason to expect, that it will be one of these events rather than another. [b]It has been contended[b] that these are not the only requisites, and that Laplace has overlooked, in [c]the[c] general theoretical statement, a necessary part of the foundation of the doctrine of chances. To be able (it has been said) to pronounce two events equally probable, it is not enough that we should know that one or the other must happen, and should have no [d]grounds[d] for conjecturing which. Experience must have shown that the two events are of equally frequent occurrence. Why, in tossing up a halfpenny, do we reckon it equally

---

Essai Philosophique sur les Probalités, fifth Paris Edition [Bachelier, 1825], p. 7.

[a]–[a]547[*for* MS, 43 *versions of this chapter, see* Appendix F; *in passages that persisted through all versions, however, the* MS, 43 *variants are also given here*]
[b]–[b]MS, 43 I contend] 46 It has, however, been contended
[c]–[c]MS, 43, 46, 51, 56, 62 this
[d]–[d]MS, 43, 46, 51, 56, 62 ground

probable that we shall throw cross or pile? Because we know that in any great number of throws, cross and pile are thrown about equally often; and that the more throws we make, the more nearly the equality is perfect. We may know this if we please by actual experiment; or by the daily experience which life affords of events of the same general character; or deductively, from the effect of mechanical laws on a symmetrical body acted upon by forces varying indefinitely in quantity and direction. We may know it, in short, either by specific experience, or on the evidence of our general knowledge of nature. But, in one way or the other, we must know it, to justify us in calling the two events equally probable; and if we knew it not, we should proceed as much at haphazard in staking equal sums on the result, as in laying odds.

This view of the subject was taken in the first edition of the present work: but I have since *become convinced*, that the theory of chances, as conceived by Laplace and by mathematicians generally, has not the fundamental fallacy which I had ascribed to it.

We must remember that the probability of an event is not a quality of the event itself, but a mere name for the degree of *ground which* we, or some one else, have for expecting it. The probability of an event to one person is a different thing from the probability of the same event to another, or to the same person after he has acquired additional evidence. The probability to me, that an individual of whom I know nothing but his name, will die within *the* year, is totally altered by my being told, the next minute, that he is in the last stage of a consumption. Yet this makes no difference in the event itself, nor in any of the causes on which it depends. Every event is in itself certain, not probable: if we knew all, we should either know positively that it will happen, or positively that it will not. But its probability to us means the degree of expectation of its occurrence, which we are warranted in entertaining by our present evidence.

Bearing this in mind, I think it must be admitted, that even when we have no knowledge whatever to guide our expectations, except the knowledge that what happens must be some one of a certain number of possibilities, we may still reasonably judge, that one supposition is more probable *to us* than another supposition; and if we have any interest at stake, we shall best provide for it by acting conformably to that judgment.

§ 2. [*The doctrine of chances tenable*] Suppose that we are required to take a ball from a box, of which we only know that it contains balls both black and white, and none of any other colour. We know that the ball we

*e–e*46 seen reason to think
*f–f*46 reason
*g–g*46, 51 a

select will be either a black or a white ball; but we have no ground ^a for expecting black rather than white, or white rather than black. In that case, if we are obliged to make a choice, and to stake ^bsomething on^b one or the other supposition, it will, as a question of prudence, be perfectly indifferent which; and we shall act precisely as we should have acted if we had known beforehand that the box contained an equal number of black and ^c white balls. But though our conduct would be the same, it would not be founded on any surmise that the balls were in fact thus equally divided; for we might, on the contrary, know, by ^dauthentic^d information, that the box contained ninety-nine balls of one colour, and only one of the other; still, if we are not told which colour has only one, and which has ninety-nine, the drawing of a white and of a black ball will be equally probable to us; we shall have no reason for staking anything on the one event rather than on the other; the option between the two will be a matter of indifference; in other words it will be an even chance.

But let it now be supposed that instead of two there are three colours—white, black, and red; and that we are entirely ignorant of the proportion in which they are mingled. We should then have no reason for expecting one more than another, and if obliged to bet, should venture our stake on red, white, or black, with equal indifference. But should we be indifferent whether we betted for or against some one colour, as, for instance, white? Surely not. From the very fact that black and red are each of them separately equally probable to us with white, the two together must be twice as probable. We should in this case expect not-white rather than white, and so much rather, that we would lay two to one upon it. It is true, there might for aught we knew be more white balls than black and red together; and if so, our bet would, if we knew more, be seen to be a disadvantageous one. But so also, for aught we ^eknew, might^e there be more red balls than black and white, or more black balls than white and red, and in such case the effect of additional knowledge would be to prove to us that our bet was more advantageous than we had supposed it to be. There is in the existing state of our knowledge a rational probability of two to one against white; a probability fit to be made a basis of conduct. No reasonable person would lay an even wager in favour of white, against black and red; though against black alone, or red alone, he might do so without imprudence.

The common theory, therefore, of the calculation of chances, appears ^f to be tenable. Even when we know nothing except the number of the possible and mutually excluding contingencies, and are entirely ignorant of their comparative frequency, we may have grounds, and grounds numerically ap-

^a46   whatever   ^{b–b}46   some interest of ours upon
^c46, 51, 56, 62   of   ^{d–d}46   credible
^{e–e}46   know, may   ^f46   to me

preciable, for acting on one supposition rather than on another; and this is the meaning of Probability.

§ 3. [*On what foundation the doctrine of chances really rests*] The principle, however, on which *ª*the*ª* reasoning proceeds, is sufficiently evident. It is the obvious one, that when the cases which exist are shared among several kinds, it is impossible that *each* of those kinds should be a majority of the whole: on the contrary, there must be a majority against each kind, except one at most; and if any kind has more than its share in proportion to the total number, *ᵇ*the others collectively*ᵇ* must have less. Granting this axiom, and assuming that we have no ground for selecting any one kind as more likely than the rest to surpass the average proportion, it follows that we cannot rationally presume this of any; which we should do, if we were to bet in favour of it, receiving less odds than in the ratio of the *ᶜ* number of the other kinds. Even, therefore, in this extreme case of the calculation of probabilities, which does not rest on special experience at all, the logical ground of the process is our knowledge, such knowledge as we then have, of the laws governing the frequency of occurrence of the different cases; but in this case the knowledge is limited to that which, being universal and axiomatic, does not require reference to specific experience, or to any considerations arising out of the special nature of the problem under discussion.

Except, however, in such cases as games of chance, where the very purpose in view requires ignorance instead of knowledge, I can conceive no case in which we ought to be satisfied with such an estimate of chances as this; an estimate founded on the absolute minimum of knowledge respecting the subject. It is plain that, in the case of the coloured balls, a very slight ground of surmise that the white balls were really more numerous than either of the other colours, would suffice to *ᵈ* vitiate the whole of the calculations made in our previous state of indifference. It would place us in that position of more advanced knowledge, in which the probabilities, to us, would be different from what they were before; and in estimating these new probabilities we should have to proceed on a totally different set of data, furnished no longer by mere counting of possible suppositions, but by specific knowledge of facts. Such data it should always be our endeavour to obtain; and in all inquiries, unless on subjects equally beyond the range of our means of knowledge and our practical uses, they may be obtained, if not good, at least better than none at all.*

*[46] It even appears to me that the calculation of chances, where there are no data grounded either on special experience or on special inference, must, in an immense majority of cases, break down, from sheer impossibility of assigning any

It is obvious, too, that even when the probabilities are derived from observation and experiment, a very slight improvement in the data, by better observations, or by taking into fuller consideration the special circumstances of the case, is of more use than the most elaborate application of the calculus to probabilities founded on the data in their previous state of inferiority. The neglect of this obvious reflection has given rise to misapplications of the calculus of probabilities which have made it the real opprobrium of mathematics. It is sufficient to refer to the applications made of it to *e*the credibility of witnesses, and to*e* the correctness of the verdicts of juries. In regard to the first, common sense would dictate that it is impossible to strike a general average of the veracity, and other qualifications for true testimony, of mankind, or of any class of them; and *f*even if it were possible, the employment of it for such a purpose implies a misapprehension of the use of averages: which serve indeed to protect those whose interest is at stake, against mistaking the general result of large masses of instances, but are of extremely small value as grounds of expectation in any one individual instance, unless the case be one of those in which the great majority of individual instances do not differ much from the average. In the case of a*f* witness, persons of common sense would draw their conclusions from the degree of consistency of his statements, his conduct under cross-examination, and the relation of the case itself to his interests, his partialities, and his mental capacity, instead of applying so rude a standard (even if it were capable of being verified) as the ratio between the number of *g*true and the number of erroneous statements which he may be supposed to make in the course of his*g* life.

---

principle by which to be guided in setting out the list of possibilities. In the case of the coloured balls we have no difficulty in making the enumeration, because we ourselves determine what the possibilities shall be. But suppose a case more analogous to those which occur in nature: instead of three colours, let there be in the box all possible colours: we being supposed ignorant of the comparative frequency with which different colours occur in nature, or in the productions of art. How is the list of cases to be made out? Is every distinct shade to count as a colour? If so, is the test to be a common eye, or an educated eye, a painter's for instance? On the answer to these questions would depend whether the chances against some particular colour would be estimated at ten, twenty, or perhaps five hundred to one. While if we knew from experience that the particular colour occurs on an average a certain number of times in every hundred or thousand, we should not require to know anything either of the frequency or of the number of the other possibilities.

   *e–e*46   the estimation of the credibility of witnesses, and of
   *f–f*46, 51, 56, 62, 65   if it were possible, such an average would be no guide, the credibility of almost every witness being either below or above the average. And even in the case of an individual
   *g–g*46   truths and of falsehoods which he may be supposed to tell in the course of his daily

Again, on the subject of juries, or other tribunals, some mathematicians have set out from the proposition that the judgment of any one judge, or juryman, is, at least in some small degree, more likely to be right than wrong, and have concluded that the chance of a number of persons concurring in a wrong verdict is diminished, the more the number is increased; so that if the judges are only made sufficiently numerous, the correctness of the judgment may *h*be reduced almost*h* to certainty. I say nothing of the disregard shown to the effect produced on the moral position of the judges by multiplying their numbers; the virtual destruction of their individual responsibility, and weakening of the application of their minds to the subject. I remark only the fallacy of reasoning from a wide average, to cases necessarily differing greatly from any average. It may be true that taking all causes one with another, the opinion of any one of the judges would be oftener right than wrong; but the argument forgets that in all *i*but *j*the more*j* simple cases, in all*i* cases in which it is really of much consequence what the tribunal is, the proposition might probably be reversed; besides which, the cause of error, whether arising from the intricacy of the case or from *k*some common prejudice or mental infirmity*k*, if it acted upon one judge, would be extremely likely to affect all the others in the same manner, or at least a majority, and thus render a wrong instead of a right decision more probable, the more the number was increased.

These are but samples of the errors frequently committed by men who, having *l*made themselves familiar with*l* the difficult formulæ which algebra affords for the estimation of chances under suppositions of a complex character, like better to employ those formulæ in computing what are the probabilities to a person half informed about a case, than to look out for means of being better informed. Before applying the doctrine of chances to any scientific purpose, the foundation must be laid for an evaluation of the chances, by possessing ourselves of the utmost attainable amount of positive knowledge. The knowledge required is that of the comparative frequency with which the different events in fact occur. For the purposes, therefore, of the present work, it is allowable to suppose, that conclusions respecting the probability of a fact of a particular kind, rest on our knowledge of the proportion between the cases in which facts of that kind occur, and those in which they do not occur: this knowledge being either derived from specific experiment, or deduced from our knowledge of the causes in operation which tend to produce, compared with those which tend to prevent, the fact in question.

*h–h*46   almost be reduced
*i–i*46   the
*j–j*51, 56   very
*k–k*46   the prejudices or infirmities common to human nature
*l–l*46, 51, 56   mastered

Such [m]calculation of chances is grounded on an induction; and to render the calculation legitimate, the induction must be a valid one. It is not less an induction, though it does not prove that the event occurs in all cases of a given description, but only that out of a given number of such cases, it occurs in about so many. The fraction which mathematicians use to designate the probability of an event, is the ratio of these two numbers; the ascertained proportion between the number of cases in which the event occurs, and the sum of all the cases, those in which it occurs and in which it does not occur taken together. In playing at cross and pile, the description of cases concerned are throws, and the probability of cross is one-half, because [n] if we throw often enough, cross is thrown about once in every two throws [o]. In the cast of a die, the probability of ace is one-sixth; not simply because there are six possible throws, of which ace is one, and because we do not know any reason why one should turn up rather than another; though I have admitted the validity of this ground in default of a better; but [p]because we do actually know, either by reasoning or[p] by experience, that in a hundred, or a million of throws, ace [q]is[q] thrown [r]in[r] about one-sixth of that number, or once in six times.[m]

[a]§ 4. [*The ultimate dependence of the doctrine of chances on causation*] I say, "either by reasoning or by experience;" meaning specific experience. But in estimating probabilities, it is not a matter of indifference from which of these two sources we derive our assurance. The probability of events as calculated from their mere frequency in past experience, affords a less secure basis for practical guidance, than their probability as deduced from an equally accurate knowledge of the frequency of occurrence of their causes.

The generalization, that an event occurs in ten out of every hundred cases of a given description, is as real an induction as if the generalization were that it occurs in all cases. But when we arrive at the conclusion by merely counting instances in actual experience, and comparing the number of cases in which A has been present with the number in which it has been absent, the evidence is only that of the Method of Agreement, and the conclusion amounts only to an empirical law. We can make a step beyond this when we can ascend to the causes on which the occurrence of A or its non-occurrence will depend, and form an estimate of the comparative frequency of the causes favourable and

[m–m][*this passage was transferred from another context in* MS, 43; *see* App. F, 1142–3]
[n]MS, 43, 46 it is found that
[o]MS, 43, 46 ; and because this induction is made under circumstances justifying the belief that the proportion will be the same in other cases as in the cases examined
[p–p]46 we now have a better, namely, our knowledge, obtained
[q–q]MS, 43, 46 will be
[r–r]+72
[a–a542]+51, 56, 62, 65, 68, 72

of those unfavourable to the occurrence. These are data of a higher order, by which the empirical law derived from a mere numerical comparison of affirmative and negative instances will be either corrected or confirmed, and in either case we shall obtain a more correct measure of probability than is given by that numerical comparison. It has been well remarked that in the kind of examples by which the doctrine of chances is usually illustrated, that of balls in a box, the estimate of probabilities is supported by reasons of causation, stronger than specific experience. "What is the reason that in a box where there are nine black balls and one white, we expect to draw a black ball nine times as much (in other words, nine times as often, frequency being the gauge of intensity in expectation) as a white? Obviously because the local conditions are nine times as favourable, because the hand may alight in nine places and get a black ball, while it can only alight in one place and find a white ball; just for the same reason that we do not expect to succeed in finding a friend in a crowd, the conditions in order that we and he should come together being many and difficult. This of course would not hold to the same extent were the white balls of smaller size than the black, neither would the probability remain the same: the larger ball would be much more likely to meet the hand."*

It is, in fact, evident, that when once causation is admitted as an universal law, our expectation of events can only be rationally grounded on that law. To a person who recognises that every event depends on causes, a thing's having happened once is a reason for expecting it to happen again, only because proving that there exists, or is liable to exist, a cause adequate to produce it.† The frequency of the particular event, apart from all surmise

*[51] ["Mill and Whewell,"] *Prospective Review* for February, 1850 [VI, p. 100].

†[51] "If this be not so, why do we feel so much more probability added by the first instance, than by any single subsequent instance? Why, except that the first instance gives us its possibility (a cause *adequate* to it), while every other only gives us the frequency of its conditions? If no reference to a cause be supposed, possibility would have no meaning; yet it is clear, that, antecedent to its happening, we might have supposed the event impossible, *i.e.*, have believed that there was no physical energy really existing in the world equal to producing it. . . . After the first time of happening, which is, then, more important to the whole probability than any other single instance (because proving the possibility), the *number* of times becomes important as an index to the intensity or extent of the cause, and its independence of any particular time. If we took the case of a tremendous leap, for instance, and wished to form an estimate of the probability of its succeeding a certain number of times; the first instance, by showing its possibility (before doubtful) is of the most importance; but every succeeding leap shows the power to be more perfectly under control, greater and more invariable, and so increases the probability; and no one would think of reasoning in this case straight from one instance to the next, without referring to the physical energy which each leap indicated. Is it not then clear that we do not ever" (let us rather say, that we do

respecting its cause, can give rise to no other induction than that *per enumerationem simplicem*; and the precarious inferences derived from this, are
superseded, and disappear from the field, as soon as the principle of causation
makes its appearance there.

Notwithstanding, however, the abstract superiority of an estimate of
probability grounded on causes, it is a fact that in almost all cases in which
chances admit of estimation sufficiently precise to render their numerical
appreciation of any practical value, the numerical data are not drawn from
knowledge of the causes, but from experience of the events themselves. *b*The
probabilities of life at different ages, or in different climates; the probabilities
of recovery from a particular disease; the chances of the birth of male or
female offspring; the chances of the destruction of houses or other property
by fire; the chances of the loss of a ship in a particular voyage; are deduced
from bills of mortality, returns from hospitals, registers of births, of shipwrecks, &c., that is, from the observed frequency not of the causes, but of the
effects.*b* The reason is, that in all these classes of facts, the causes are either
not amenable to direct observation at all, or not with the requisite precision,
and we have no means of judging of their frequency except from the empirical
law afforded by the frequency of the effects. The inference does not the less
depend on causation alone. We reason from an effect to a similar effect by
passing through the cause. If the actuary of an insurance office infers from
his tables that among a hundred persons now living, of a particular age, five
on the average will attain the age of seventy, his inference is legitimate, not
for the simple reason that this is the proportion who have lived till seventy in
times past, but because the fact of their having so lived shows that this is the
proportion existing, at that place and time, between the causes which prolong
life to the age of seventy, and those tending to bring it to an earlier close.*a*

---

not in an advanced state of our knowledge) "conclude directly from the happening of an event to the probability of its happening again; but that we refer to
the cause, regarding the past cases as an index to the cause, and the cause as our
guide to the future?" *Ibid.* [pp. 101–2.]

*[51] The writer last quoted says that the valuation of chances by comparing
the number of cases in which the event occurs with the number in which it does
not occur, "would generally be wholly erroneous," and "is not the true theory of
probability." It is at least that which forms the foundation of insurance, and of
all those calculations of chances in the business of life which experience so
abundantly verifies. The reason which the reviewer gives for rejecting the theory,
is that it "would regard an event as certain which had hitherto never failed; which
is exceedingly far from the truth, even for a very large number of constant suc-
cesses." ["Mill and Whewell," pp. 102n–103n.] This is not a defect in a particular
theory, but in any theory of chances. No principle of evaluation can provide for
such a case as that which the reviewer supposes. If an event has never once failed,
in a number of trials sufficient to eliminate chance, it really has all the certainty

b–b[cf. 544*i* below]

§ 5. [*Theorem of the doctrine of chances which relates to the cause of a given event*] From *the preceding principles* it is easy to deduce the demonstration of that theorem of the doctrine of probabilities, which is the foundation of its *c* application to *d* inquiries for ascertaining the occurrence of a given event, or the reality of an individual fact. The signs or evidences by which a fact is usually proved, are some of its consequences: and the inquiry hinges upon determining what cause is most likely to have produced a given effect. The theorem applicable to such investigations is the Sixth Principle in Laplace's *Essai Philosophique sur les Probabilités*, which is described by him as *e*the "fundamental*e* principle of that branch of the Analysis of Chances, which consists in ascending from events to their causes."*

Given an effect to be accounted for, and there being several causes which might have produced it, but of the presence of which in the particular case nothing is known; the probability that the effect was produced by any one of these causes *is as the antecedent probability of the cause, multiplied by the probability that the cause, if it existed, would have produced the given effect.*

Let M be the effect, and A, B, two causes, by either of which it might have been produced. To find the probability that it was produced by the one and not by the other, ascertain which of the two is most likely to have existed, and which of them, if it did exist, was most likely to produce the effect M: the probability sought is a compound of these two probabilities.

CASE I. Let the causes be both alike in the second respect; either A or B, when it exists, being supposed equally likely (or equally certain) to produce M; but let A be in itself twice as likely as B to exist, that is, twice as frequent a phenomenon. Then it is twice as likely to have existed in this case, and to have been the cause which produced M.

For, since A exists in nature twice as often as B; in any 300 cases in which one or other existed, A has existed 200 times and B 100. But either A or B must have existed wherever M is produced: therefore in 300 times that M is produced, A was the producing cause 200 times, B only 100, that is, in the

---

which can be given by an empirical law: it *is* certain during the continuance of the same collocation of causes which existed during the observations. If it ever fails, it is in consequence of some change in that collocation. Now, no theory of chances will enable us to infer the future probability of an event from the past, if the causes in operation, capable of influencing the event, have intermediately undergone a change.

*Pp. 18–19. The theorem is not stated by Laplace in the exact terms in which I have stated it; but the identity of import of the two modes of expression is easily demonstrable.

*a–a*MS, 43 §3.] 46 §4.
*b–b*MS, 43 these principles] 46 this principle
*c*MS, 43, 46 principal
*d*MS, 43, 46, 51, 56 judicial or other
*e–e*MS, 43, 46, 51, 56 "the fundamental

ratio of 2 to 1. Thus, then, if the causes are alike in their capacity of producing the effect, the probability as to which actually produced it, is in the ratio of their antecedent probabilities.

CASE II. Reversing the last hypothesis, let us suppose that the causes are equally frequent, equally likely to have existed, but not equally likely, if they did exist, to produce M: that in three times in which A occurs, it produces that effect twice, while B, in three times, produces it only once. Since the two causes are equally frequent in their occurrence; in every six times that either one or the other exists, A exists three times and B three times. A, of its three times, produces M in two; B, of its three times, produces M in one. Thus, in the whole six times, M is only produced thrice; but of that thrice it is produced twice by A, once only by B. Consequently, when the antecedent probabilities of the causes are equal, the chances that the effect was produced by them are in the ratio of the probabilities that if they did exist they would produce the effect.

CASE III. The third case, that in which the causes are unlike in both respects, is solved by what has preceded. For, when a quantity depends on two other quantities, in such a manner that while either of them remains constant it is proportional to the other, it must necessarily be proportional to the product of the two quantities, the product being the only function of the two which obeys that [f] law of variation. Therefore, the probability that M was produced by either cause, is as the antecedent probability of the cause, multiplied by the probability that if it existed it would produce M. Which was to be demonstrated.

Or we may prove the third case as we proved the first and second. Let A be twice as frequent as B; and let them also be unequally likely, when they exist, to produce M: let A produce it twice in four times, B thrice in four times. The antecedent probability of A is to that of B as 2 to 1; the probabilities of their producing M are as 2 to 3; the product of these ratios is the ratio of 4 to 3 [g]: and this[g] will be the ratio of the probabilities that A or B was the producing cause in the given instance. [h] For, since A is twice as frequent as B, out of twelve cases in which one or other exists, A exists in 8 and B in 4. But of its eight cases, A, by the supposition, produces M in only 4, while B of its four cases produces M in 3. M, therefore, is only produced at all in seven of the twelve cases; but in four of these it is produced by A, in three by B; hence, the probabilities of its being produced by A and by B are as 4 to 3, and are expressed by the fractions $\frac{4}{7}$ and $\frac{3}{7}$. Which was to be demonstrated. [i]

[f]MS, 43, 46   particular
[g-g]MS, 43, 46   , which therefore, if the theorem be true,
[h]MS, 43, 46   And such will that ratio really be.
[i]46   §5. [*In what cases the doctrine is practically applicable*] From the preceding view of the foundation of the doctrine of chances, its general principles may be seen to

ª§ 6.ª [*How the doctrine of chances is applicable to the elimination of chance*] It remains to examine the bearing of the doctrine of chances on the peculiar problem *ᵇwhich occupied us in the preceding chapterᵇ*, namely, how to distinguish coincidences which are casual from those which are the result of law; from those in which the facts which accompany or follow one another are somehow connected through causation.

ᶜ The doctrine of chances affords means by which, if we knew the *average* number of coincidences to be looked for between two phenomena connected only casually, we could determine how often any given deviation from that average will occur by chance. If the probability of any casual coincidence, considered in itself, be $1/m$, the probability that the same coincidence will be repeated n times in succession is $1/m^n$. For example, in one throw of a die the probability of ace being $1/6$; the probability of throwing ace twice in succession will be 1 divided by the square of 6, or $1/36$. For ace is thrown at the first throw once in six, or six in thirty-six times, and of those six, the die being cast again, ace will be thrown but once; being altogether once in thirty-six times. The chance of the same cast three times successively is, by a similar reasoning, $1/6^3$ or $1/216$: that is, the event will happen, on a large average, only once in two hundred and sixteen throws.

We have thus a rule by which to estimate the probability that any given series of coincidences arises from chance; provided we can measure correctly the probability of a single coincidence. If we *ᵈcanᵈ* obtain an equally precise expression for the probability that the same series of coincidences arises from causation, we should only have to compare the numbers. This, however, can rarely be done. Let us see what degree of approximation can practically be made to the necessary precision.

---

be applicable in a rough way to many subjects which are by no means amenable to its precise calculations. To render these applicable, there must be numerical data, derived from the observation of a very large number of instances. The probabilities of life at different ages, or in different climates; the probabilities of recovery fom a particular disease; the chances of the birth of male or female offspring; the chances of the loss of a vessel in a particular voyage; all these admit of estimation sufficiently precise to render the numerical appreciation of their amount a thing of practical value; because there are bills of mortality, returns from hospitals, registers of births, of shipwrecks, &c., founded on cases sufficiently numerous to afford average proportions which do not materially vary from year to year, or from ten years to ten years. But where observation and experiment have not afforded a set of instances sufficiently numerous to eliminate chance, and sufficiently various to eliminate all non-essential specialities of circumstance, to attempt to calculate chances is to convert mere ignorance into dangerous error by clothing it in the garb of knowledge. [*this paragraph also appears in* MS, 43; *see* App. F, pp. 1147–8. *Part retained in later editions; cf.* 542*ᵇ⁻ᵇ above*]
   *ª⁻ª*MS, 43, 46 [*no section division*]
   *ᵇ⁻ᵇ*MS, 43, 46 for the sake of which we have on this occasion adverted to it
   *ᶜ*MS, 43 §5.] 46 §6.
   *ᵈ⁻ᵈ*MS, 43, 46, 51, 56, 62, 65 could

The question falls within Laplace's sixth principle, *just demonstrated*. The given fact, that is to say, the series of coincidences, may have originated either in a casual conjunction of causes, or in a law of nature. The probabilities, therefore, that the fact originated in these two modes, are as their antecedent probabilities, multiplied by the probabilities that if they existed they would produce the effect. But the particular combination of chances, if it occurred, or the law of nature if real, would certainly produce the series of coincidences. The probabilities, therefore, that the coincidences are produced by the two causes in question, are as the antecedent probabilities of the causes. One of these, the antecedent probability of the combination of mere chances which would produce the given result, is an appreciable quantity. The antecedent probability of the other supposition may be susceptible of a more or less exact estimation, according to the nature of the case.

In some cases, the coincidence, supposing it to be the result of causation at all, must be the result of a known cause: as the succession of aces, if not accidental, must arise from the loading of the die. In such cases we may be able to form a conjecture as to the antecedent probability of such a circumstance, from the characters of the parties concerned, or other such evidence; but it would *f* be impossible to estimate that probability with anything like numerical precision. The counter-probability, however, that of the accidental origin of the coincidence, dwindling so rapidly as it does at each new trial; the stage is soon reached at which the chance of unfairness in the die, however small in itself, must be greater than that of a casual coincidence: and on this ground, a practical decision can generally be come to without much hesitation, if there be the power of repeating the experiment.

When, however, the coincidence is one which cannot be accounted for by any known cause, and the connexion between the two phenomena, if produced by causation, must be the result of some law of nature hitherto unknown; which is the case we had in view in the last chapter; then, though the probability of a casual coincidence may be capable of appreciation, that of the counter-supposition, the existence of an undiscovered law of nature, is clearly unsusceptible of even an approximate *ᵍvaluationᵍ*. In order to have the data which such a case would require, it would be necessary to know what proportion of all the individual sequences or coexistences occurring in nature are the result of law, and what proportion are *ʰmere casual coincidencesʰ*. It being evident that we cannot form any plausible conjecture as to this proportion, much less appreciate it numerically, we cannot attempt any precise estimation of the comparative probabilities. But of this we are sure, that the

---

*ᶜ⁻ᶜ*MS, 43 of which, a short distance back, we gave the demonstration] 46 *as* 43
. . . a demonstration
*ᶠ*MS, 43, 46 clearly
*ᵍ⁻ᵍ*MS, 43, 46 evaluation
*ʰ⁻ʰ*MS, 43, 46 the result of chance

detection of an unknown law of nature—of some previously unrecognised constancy of conjunction among phenomena—is no uncommon event. If, therefore, the number of instances in which a coincidence is observed, over and above that which would arise on the average from the mere concurrence of chances, be such that so great an amount of coincidences from accident alone would be an extremely uncommon event; we have reason to conclude that the coincidence is the effect of causation, and may be received (subject to correction from further experience) as an empirical law. Further than this, in point of precision, we cannot go; nor, in most cases, is greater precision required, for the solution of any practical doubt.*[a]

*[68] For a fuller treatment of the many interesting questions raised by the theory of probabilities, I may now refer to a recent work by Mr. Venn, Fellow of Caius College, Cambridge, *The Logic of Chance* [London: Macmillan, 1866]; one of the most thoughtful and philosophical treatises on any subject connected with Logic and Evidence, which have been produced[i], to my knowledge,[i] for many years. Some criticisms contained in it have been very useful to me in revising the corresponding chapters of the present work. In several of Mr. Venn's opinions, however, I do not agree. What these are will be obvious to any reader of Mr. Venn's work who is also a reader of this.

[i-i]68 in this or any other country

^aOf^a the Extension of Derivative Laws to Adjacent Cases

§ 1. [*Derivative laws, when not causal, are almost always contingent on collocations*] We have had frequent occasion to notice the inferior generality of derivative laws, compared with the ultimate laws from which they are derived. This inferiority, which affects not only the extent of the propositions themselves, but their degree of certainty within that extent, is most conspicuous in the uniformities of coexistence and sequence obtaining between effects which depend ultimately on different primeval causes. Such uniformities will only obtain where there exists the same collocation of those primeval causes. If the collocation varies, though the laws themselves remain the same, a totally different set of derivative uniformities may, and generally will, be the result.

Even where the derivative uniformity is between different effects of the same cause, it will by no means obtain as universally as the law of the cause itself. If *a* and *b* accompany or succeed one another as effects of the cause A, it by no means follows that A is the only cause which can produce them, or that if there be another cause, as B, capable of producing *a*, it must produce *b* likewise. The conjunction therefore of *a* and *b* perhaps does not hold universally, but only in the instances in which *a* arises from A. When it is produced by a cause other than A, *a* and *b* may be dissevered. Day (for example) is always in our experience followed by night; but day is not the cause of night; both are successive effects of a common cause, the periodical passage ^bof the spectator^b into and out of the earth's shadow, consequent on the earth's rotation, and on the illuminating property of the sun. If, therefore, day is ever produced by a different cause or set of causes from this, day will not, or at least may not, be followed by night. On the sun's own surface, for instance, this may be the case.

Finally, even when the derivative uniformity is itself a law of causation (resulting from the combination of several causes), it is not altogether independent of collocations. If a cause supervenes, capable of wholly or partially counteracting the effect of any one of the conjoined causes, the effect will no longer conform to the derivative law. While, therefore, each ultimate law is only liable to frustration from one set of counteracting causes, the derivative law is liable to it from several. Now, the possibility of the occurrence of counteracting causes which do not arise from any of the conditions involved in the law itself, depends on the original collocations.

It is true that (as we formerly remarked) laws of causation, whether ultimate or derivative, are, in most cases, fulfilled even when counteracted; the cause produces its effect, though that effect is destroyed by something else. That the effect may be frustrated, is, therefore, no objection to the universality of *laws* of causation. But it is *fatal* to the universality of the sequences or coexistences of effects, which compose the greater part of the derivative laws flowing from laws of causation. When, from the law of a certain combination of causes, there results a certain order in the effects; as from the combination of a single sun with the rotation of an opaque body round its axis, there results, on the whole surface of that opaque body, an alternation of day and night; then if we suppose one of the combined causes counteracted, the rotation stopped, the sun extinguished, or a second sun superadded, the truth of that particular law of causation is in no way affected; it is still true that one sun shining on an opaque revolving body will alternately produce day and night; but since the sun no longer does shine on such a body, the derivative uniformity, the succession of day and night on the given planet, is no longer true. Those derivative uniformities, therefore, which are not laws of causation, are (except in the rare case of their depending on one cause alone, not on a combination of causes,) always more or less contingent on collocations; and are hence subject to the characteristic infirmity of empirical laws, that of being admissible only where the collocations are known by experience to be such as are requisite for the truth of the law, that is, only within the conditions of time and place confirmed by actual observation.

§ 2. [*On what grounds derivative laws can be extended to cases beyond the bounds of actual experience*] This principle, when stated in general terms, seems clear and indisputable; yet many of the ordinary judgments of mankind, the propriety of which is not questioned, have at least the semblance of being inconsistent with it. On what grounds, it may be asked, do we expect that the sun will rise to-morrow? *To-morrow is beyond the limits of time comprehended in our observations.* They have extended over some thousands of years past, but *they do not include the future.* Yet we infer with

c–cMS, 43, 46   the law
d–dMS, 43   an objection
a–aMS, 43, 46   Is to-morrow within the limits of time comprehended in our observations?
b–bMS, 43, 46   do they include the future?

confidence that the sun will rise to-morrow; and nobody doubts that we are entitled to do so. Let us consider what is the warrant for this confidence.

In the example in question, we know the causes on which the derivative uniformity depends. They are, the sun giving out light, the earth in a state of rotation and intercepting light. The induction which shows these to be the real causes, and not merely prior effects of a common cause, being complete [e]; the only circumstances which could defeat the derivative law are such as would destroy or counteract one or other of the combined causes. While the causes exist, and are not counteracted, the effect will continue. If they exist and are not counteracted to-morrow, the sun will rise to-morrow.

Since the causes, namely the sun and the earth, the one in the state of giving out light, the other in a state of rotation, will exist until something destroys them; all depends on the probabilities of their destruction, [d]or[d] of their counteraction. We know by observation (omitting the inferential proofs of an existence for thousands of ages anterior), that these phenomena have continued for [e](say)[e] five thousand years. Within that time there has existed no cause sufficient to diminish them appreciably; nor which has counteracted their effect in any appreciable degree. The chance, therefore, that the sun may not rise to-morrow, amounts to the chance that some cause, which has not manifested itself in the smallest degree during five thousand years, will exist to-morrow in such intensity as to destroy the sun or the earth, the sun's light or the earth's rotation, or to produce an immense disturbance in the effect resulting from those causes.

Now, if such a cause will exist to-morrow, or at any future time, some cause, proximate or remote, of that cause must exist now, and must have existed during the whole of the five thousand years. If, therefore, the sun do not rise to-morrow, it will be because some cause has existed, the effects of which though during five thousand years they have not amounted to a perceptible quantity, will in one day become overwhelming. Since this cause has not been recognised during such an interval of time, by observers stationed on our earth, it must, if it [f]be a single agent, be either one[f] whose effects develop themselves gradually and very slowly, or one which existed in regions beyond our observation, and is now on the point of arriving in our part of the universe. Now all causes which we have experience of, act according to laws incompatible with the supposition that their [g]effects[g], after accumulating so slowly as to be imperceptible for five thousand years, should start into immensity in a single day. No mathematical law of proportion between an effect and the quantity or relations of its cause, could produce

[c]MS, 43   and irrefragable
[d-d]MS, 43, 46, 51, 56, 62, 65   and on those
[e-e]+65, 68, 72
[f-f]MS, 43, 46, 51, 56, 62, 65, 68   exist, be either some agent
[g-g]MS   effect

such contradictory results. The sudden development of an effect of which there was no previous trace, always arises from the coming together of several distinct causes, not previously conjoined; but if such sudden conjunction is destined to take place, the causes, or *their* causes, must have existed during the entire five thousand years; and their not having once come together during that period, shows how rare that particular combination is. We have, therefore, the warrant of a rigid induction for considering it probable, in a degree undistinguishable from certainty, that the known conditions requisite for the sun's rising will exist to-morrow.

§ 3. [*Cases beyond the bounds of actual experience to which derivative laws can be extended must be adjacent cases*] But this extension of derivative laws, not causative, beyond the limits of observation, can only be to *adjacent* cases. If instead of to-morrow we had said this day twenty thousand years, the inductions would have been anything but conclusive. That a cause which, in opposition to very powerful causes, produced no perceptible effect during five thousand years, should produce a very considerable one by the end of twenty thousand, has nothing in it which is not in conformity with our experience of causes. We know many agents, the effect of which in a short period does not amount to a perceptible quantity, but by accumulating for a much longer period becomes considerable. Besides, looking at the immense multitude of the heavenly bodies, their vast distances, and the rapidity of the motion of such of them as are known to move, it is a supposition not at all contradictory to experience that some body may be in motion towards us, or we towards it, within the limits of whose influence we have not come during five thousand years, but which in twenty thousand more may be producing effects upon us of the most extraordinary kind. Or the fact which is capable of preventing sunrise may be, not the cumulative effect of one cause, but some new combination of causes; and the chances favourable to that combination, though they have not produced it once in five thousand years, may produce it once in twenty thousand. So that the inductions which authorize us to expect future events, grow weaker and weaker the further we look into the future, and at length become inappreciable.

We have considered the probabilities of the sun's rising to-morrow, as derived from the real laws, that is, from the laws of the causes on which that uniformity is dependent. Let us now consider how the matter would have stood if the uniformity had been known only as an empirical law; if we had not been aware that the sun's light, and the earth's rotation (or the sun's motion), were the causes on which the periodical occurrence of *a*daylight*a* depends. We could have extended this empirical law to cases adjacent in time, though not to so great a distance of time as we can now. Having

*a–a*MS, 43   sunrise

evidence that the effects had remained unaltered and been punctually con-joined for five thousand years, we could infer that the unknown causes on which the conjunction is dependent had existed undiminished and uncounter-acted during the same period. The same conclusions, therefore, would follow as in the preceding case; except that we should only know that during five thousand years nothing had occurred to defeat perceptibly this particular effect; while, when we know the causes, we have the additional assurance, that during that interval no such change has been noticeable in the causes themselves, as by any degree of multiplication or length of continuance could defeat the effect.

To this must be added, that when we know the causes, we may be able to judge whether there exists any known cause capable of counteracting them; *while as long as* they are unknown, we cannot be sure but that if we did know them, we could predict their destruction from causes actually in exist-ence. A bedridden savage, who had never seen the cataract of Niagara, but who lived within hearing of it, might imagine that the sound he heard would endure for ever; but if he knew it to be the effect of a rush of waters over a barrier of rock which is progressively wearing away, he would know that within a number of ages which may be calculated, it will be heard no more. In proportion, therefore, to our ignorance of the causes on which the em-pirical law depends, we can be less assured that it will continue to hold good; and the *farther* we look into futurity, the less improbable is it that some one of the causes, whose coexistence gives rise to the derivative uniformity, may be destroyed or counteracted. With every prolongation of time, the chances multiply of such an event, that is to say, its non-occurrence hitherto becomes a less guarantee of its not occurring within the given time. If, then, it is only to cases which in point of time are adjacent (or nearly adjacent) to those which we have actually observed, that *any* derivative law, not of causation, can be extended with an assurance equivalent to certainty, much more is this true of a merely empirical law. Happily, for the purposes of life it is to such cases alone that we can almost ever have occasion to extend them.

In respect of place, it might seem that a merely empirical law could not be extended even to adjacent cases; that we *could* have no assurance of its being true in any place where it has not been specially observed. The past duration of a cause is a guarantee for its future existence, unless something occurs to destroy it; but the existence of a cause in one or any number of places, is no guarantee for its existence in any other place, since there is no uniformity in the collocations of primeval causes. When, therefore, an empirical law is extended beyond the local limits within which it has been found true by observation, the cases to which it is thus extended must be

---

such as are presumably within the influence of the same individual agents. If we ᵉdiscoverᵉ a new planet within the known bounds of the solar system (or even beyond those bounds, but indicating its connexion with the system by revolving round the sun), we ᶠmayᶠ conclude, with great probability, that it revolves on its axis. For all the known planets do so; and this uniformity points to some common cause, antecedent to the first records of astronomical observation: and though the nature of this cause can only be matter of conjecture, yet if it be, as is not unlikely, ᵍand as Laplace's theory supposes, not merely the same kind of cause, but the same individual cause (such as an impulse given to all the bodies at once)ᵍ, that cause, acting at the extreme points of the space occupied by the sun and planets, ʰis likely, unless defeated by some counteracting cause, toʰ have acted at every intermediate point, and probably somewhat beyond; and therefore acted, in all probability, upon the supposed newly discovered planet.

When, therefore, effects which are always found conjoined, can be traced with any probability to an identical (and not merely a similar) origin, we may with ⁱthe sameⁱ probability extend the empirical law of their conjunction to all places within the extreme local boundaries within which the fact has been observed; subject to the possibility of counteracting causes in some portion of the field. Still more confidently may we do so when the law is not merely empirical; when the phenomena ʲwhichʲ we find conjoined are effects of ascertained causes, from the laws of which the conjunction of their effects is deducible. In that case, we may both extend the derivative uniformity over a larger space, and with less ᵏabatementᵏ for the chance of counteracting causes. The first, because instead of the local boundaries of our observation of the fact itself, we may include the extreme boundaries of the ascertained influence of its causes. Thus the succession of day and night, we know, holds true of all the bodies of the solar system except the sun ˡitselfˡ; but we know this only because we are acquainted with the causes: if we were not, we could not extend the proposition beyond the orbits of the earth and moon, at both extremities of which we have the evidence of observation for its truth. With respect to the probability of counteracting causes, it has been seen that this calls for a greater abatement of confidence, in proportion to our ignorance of the causes on which the phenomena depend. On both accounts, therefore, a derivative law which we know how to resolve, is susceptible of a greater extension to cases adjacent in place, than a merely empirical law.

ᵉ⁻ᵉMS, 43, 46   discovered
ᶠ⁻ᶠMS, 43, 46   might
ᵍ⁻ᵍMS, 43   (and as Laplace's theory suggests,) one and the same individual impulse given to all the bodies at once]   46   *as* 43 . . . theory supposes,) . . . *as* 43
ʰ⁻ʰMS, 43, 46   must, unless . . . cause,
ⁱ⁻ⁱMS, 43, 46   great   ʲ⁻ʲ+43, 46, 51, 56, 62, 65, 68, 72
ᵏ⁻ᵏMS, 43, 46   deduction   ˡ⁻ˡMS, 43, 46   himself

CHAPTER XX

Of Analogy

§ 1. [*Various senses of the word analogy*] The word Analogy, as the name of a mode of reasoning, is generally taken for some kind of argument supposed to be of an inductive nature, but not amounting to a complete induction. There is no word, however, which is used more loosely, or in a greater variety of senses, than Analogy. It sometimes stands for arguments which may be examples of the most *rigorous* Induction. Archbishop Whately, for instance, following Ferguson and other writers, defines Analogy conformably to its primitive acceptation, that which was given to it by mathematicians, Resemblance of Relations.[*] In this sense, when a country which has sent out colonies is termed the mother country, the expression is analogical, signifying that the colonies of a country stand in the same *relation* to her in which children stand to their parents. And if any inference be drawn from this resemblance of relations, as, for instance, that *obedience or affection is due from colonies to the mother country*, this is called reasoning by analogy. Or if it be argued that a nation is most beneficially governed by an assembly elected by the people, from the admitted fact that other associations for a common purpose, such as joint-stock companies, are best managed by a committee chosen by the parties interested; this *, too,* is an argument from analogy in *the preceding* sense, because its foundation is, not that a nation is like a joint-stock company, or Parliament like a board of directors, but that Parliament stands in the same *relation* to the nation in which a board of directors stands to a joint-stock company. Now, in an argument of this nature, there is no inherent inferiority of conclusiveness. Like other arguments from resemblance, it may amount to nothing, or it may be a perfect and conclusive induction. The circumstance in which the two cases resemble, may be capable of being shown to be the *material* circumstance; to be that on which all the consequences, necessary to be taken into account in the parti-

[*Elements of Logic, p. 186.]

a–aMS, 43, 46, 51, 56, 62   rigid
b–bMS, 43, 46   the same obedience . . . country which is due from children to a parent
c–c+46, 51, 56, 62, 65, 68, 72
d–dMS, 43   Archbishop Whately's

cular discussion, depend. In the *example last given*, the resemblance is one of relation; the *fundamentum relationis* being the management by a few persons, of affairs in which a much greater number are interested along with them. Now, some may contend that this circumstance which is common to the two cases, and the various consequences which follow from it, have the chief share in determining all *the* effects which make up what we term good or bad administration. If they can establish this, their argument has the force of a *rigorous* induction; if they cannot, they are said to have failed in proving the analogy between the two cases; a mode of speech which implies that when the analogy can be proved, the argument founded on it cannot be resisted.

§ 2. [*Nature of analogical evidence*] It is on the whole more usual, however, to extend the name of analogical evidence to arguments from any sort of resemblance, provided they do not amount to a complete induction: without peculiarly distinguishing resemblance of relations. Analogical reasoning, in this sense, may be reduced to the following formula:—Two things resemble each other in one or more respects; a certain proposition is true of the one; therefore it is true of the other. But we have *nothing here* by which to discriminate analogy from induction, since this type will serve for all reasoning from experience. In the *strictest* induction, equally with the faintest analogy, we conclude because A resembles B in one or more properties, that it does so in a certain other property. The difference is, that in the case of a *complete* induction it has been previously shown, by due comparison of instances, that there is an invariable conjunction between the former *property or* properties and the latter property; but in what is called analogical reasoning, no such conjunction has been made out. There have been no opportunities of putting in practice the Method of Difference, or even the Method of Agreement; but we conclude (and that is all which the argument of analogy amounts to) that a fact m, known to be true of A, is more likely to be true of B if B agrees with A in some of its properties (even though no connexion is known to exist between m and those properties), than if no resemblance at all could be traced between B and any other thing known to possess the attribute m.

To this argument it is of course requisite, that the properties common to A with B shall be merely not known to be connected with m; they must not be properties known to be unconnected with it. If, either by processes of elimination, or by deduction from previous knowledge of the laws of the

*e–e*MS, 43, 46, 51, 56   case in question
*f–f*MS, 43, 46, 51, 56   those
*a–a*MS, 43, 46   here nothing
*c–c*MS, 43, 46, 51, 56   real

*g–g*MS, 43, 46, 51, 56, 62   rigid
*b–b*MS, 43, 46, 51, 56, 62   most rigid
d–d+43, 46, 51, 56, 62, 65, 68, 72

properties in question, it can be concluded that they have nothing to do with
m, the argument of analogy is put out of court. The supposition must be that
m is an effect really dependent on some property of A, but we know not on
which. We cannot point out any of the properties of A, which is the cause of
m, or united with it by any law. After rejecting all which we know to have
nothing to do with it, there remain several ^{e}between^e which we are unable to
decide: of which remaining properties, B possesses one or more. This accordingly, we consider as affording grounds, of more or less ^{f}strength^f, for concluding by analogy that B possesses the attribute m.

There can be no doubt that every such resemblance which can be pointed
out between B and A, affords some degree of probability, beyond what would
otherwise exist, in favour of the conclusion drawn from it. If B resembled A
in all its ultimate properties, its possessing the attribute m would be a certainty, not a probability: and every resemblance which can be shown to exist
between them, places it by so much the nearer to that point. If the resemblance be in an ultimate property, there will be resemblance in all the
derivative properties dependent on that ultimate property, and of these m
may be one. If the resemblance be in a derivative property, there is reason to
expect resemblance in the ultimate property on which it depends, and in the
other derivative properties dependent on the same ultimate property. Every
resemblance which can be shown to exist, affords ground for expecting an
indefinite number of other resemblances: the particular resemblance sought
will, therefore, be oftener found among things thus known to resemble, than
among things between which we know of no resemblance. ^{g}

For example, I might infer that there are probably inhabitants in the
moon, because there are inhabitants on the earth, in the sea, and in the air:
and this is the evidence of analogy. The circumstance of having inhabitants
is here assumed not to be an ultimate property, but (as ^{h} is reasonable to

---

$^{e-e}$MS   , among $^{f-f}$MS, 43, 46   weight
^{g}MS [*footnote:*] *There was no greater foundation than this for Newton's celebrated conjecture that the diamond was combustible. [See *Optics*, Vol. IV, pp. 174–5
(Pt. III, Prop. x).] He grounded his guess on the very high refracting power of the
diamond, comparatively to its density; a peculiarity which had been observed in combustible substances; and on similar grounds he conjectured that water, though not combustible, contained a combustible ingredient.
Experiment having subsequently shown that in both instances he guessed right, the
prophecy is considered to have done great honour to his scientific sagacity; but it is to
this day uncertain whether the praise was merited; whether the guess was, in truth, what
there are so many examples of in the history of science, a farsighted anticipation of a
law afterwards to be discovered. The progress of science has not hitherto shown ground
for believing that there is any real connexion between combustibility and a high refracting power.]   43, 46   *as* MS . . . observed to exist in . . . *as* MS . . . ingredient. [*no
paragraph*] Experiment . . . *as* MS]   51, 56, 62, 65   *as* 43 . . . day uncertain whether
the guess was, in truth . . . *as* 43]   68   There was no greater foundation for this than
for . . . *as* 51
^{h}43, 46   it

suppose) a consequence of other properties; and depending, therefore, in the case of *the* earth, on some of its properties as a portion of the universe, but on which of those properties we know not. Now the moon resembles the earth in being a solid, opaque, nearly spherical substance *j*, appearing to contain, or to have contained,*j* active volcanoes; receiving heat and light from the sun, in about the same quantity as our earth; revolving on its axis; *k*composed of materials which gravitate, and obeying*k* all the various laws resulting from that property. And I think no one will deny that if this were all that was known of the moon, the existence of inhabitants in that luminary would derive from these various resemblances to the earth, a greater degree of probability than it would otherwise have: though the amount of the augmentation it would be *l*useless*l* to attempt to estimate.

If, however, every resemblance proved between B and A, in any point not known to be immaterial with respect to *m*, forms some additional reason for presuming that B has the attribute *m*; it is clear, *è contra*, that every dissimilarity which can be proved between them, furnishes a counter-probability of the same nature on the other side. It is not indeed *m*unusual that different ultimate properties should*m*, in some particular instances, produce the same derivative property; but on the whole it is certain that things which differ in their ultimate properties, will differ at least as much in the aggregate of their derivative properties, and that the differences which are unknown will on the average of cases bear some proportion to those which are known. There will, therefore, be a competition between the known points of agreement and the known points of difference in A and B; and according as the one or the other *n*may be*n* deemed to preponderate, the probability derived from analogy will be for or against B's having the property *m*. The moon, for instance, agrees with the earth in the circumstances already mentioned; but differs in being smaller, in having its surface more unequal, and apparently volcanic throughout, in having *o*, at least on the side next the earth,*o* no atmosphere sufficient to refract light, no clouds, and *p*(it is therefore concluded)*p* no water. These differences, considered merely as such, might perhaps balance the resemblances, so that analogy would afford no presumption either way. But considering that some of the circumstances which are wanting on the moon are among those which, on *q*the*q* earth, are found to be indispensable conditions

*i–i*MS, 43, 46   our
*j–j*MS, 43   ; containing]   46   ; containing, or having contained,
*k–k*MS, 43, 46   whose materials gravitate, and which obeys
l *l*MS, 43, 46   ridiculous
*m–m*MS, 43, 46, 51, 56   impossible that different ultimate properties may
*n–n*MS, 43, 46   are
o–o+62, 65, 68, 72
*p–p*MS, 43, 46   therefore (it is inferentially concluded)]   51   therefore (it is concluded)
*q–q*MS, 43, 46   our

of animal life, we may conclude that if that phenomenon does exist in the moon, ^{r}(or at all events on the nearer side,)^r it must be as ^{s}an^s effect of causes totally different from those on which it depends here; as a consequence, therefore, of the moon's differences from the earth, not of ^{t}the^t points of agreement. Viewed in this light, all the resemblances which exist become presumptions against, not in favour of, ^{u}the moon's^u being inhabited. Since life cannot exist there in the manner in which it exists here, the greater the resemblance of the lunar world to the terrestrial in ^{v} other respects, the less reason we have to believe that it can contain life.

There are, however, other bodies in our system, between which and the earth there is a much closer resemblance; which possess an atmosphere, clouds, consequently water (or some fluid analogous to it), and even give strong indications of snow in their polar regions; while the cold, or heat, though differing greatly on the average from ours, is, in some parts at least of those planets, possibly not more extreme than in some regions of our own which are habitable. To balance these agreements, the ascertained differences are chiefly in the average light and heat, velocity of rotation, ^{w}density of material,^{w} intensity of gravity, and similar circumstances of a secondary kind. With regard to these planets, therefore, the argument of analogy gives a decided preponderance in favour of their resembling the earth in any of its derivative properties, such as that of having inhabitants; though, when we consider how immeasurably multitudinous are those of their properties which we are entirely ignorant of, compared with the few which we know, we ^{x}can attach but^x trifling weight to any considerations of resemblance in which the known elements bear so inconsiderable a proportion to the unknown.

Besides the competition between analogy and diversity, there may be a competition of conflicting analogies. The new case may be similar in some of its circumstances to cases in which the fact m exists, but in others to cases in which it is known not to exist. Amber has some properties in common with vegetable, others with mineral products. A painting of unknown origin, may resemble, in certain of its characters, known works of a particular master, but in others it may as strikingly resemble ^{v}those of some other painter^v. A vase may bear some analogy to works of Grecian, and some to those of Etruscan, or Egyptian art. We are of course supposing that it does not possess any quality which has been ascertained, by a sufficient induction, to be a conclusive mark either of the one or of the other.

$^{r-r}$+62, 65, 68, 72 $^{s-s}$MS, 43, 46   the
$^{t-t}$MS, 43, 46   their
$^{u-u}$MS, 43, 46   her
^{v}MS, 43, 46, 51   all
$^{w-w}$+56, 62, 65, 68, 72
$^{x-x}$MS, 43, 46   cannot attach more than a very
$^{v-v}$MS, 43, 46, 51, 56   productions known not to be his

§ 3. [*On what circumstances the value of analogical evidence depends*]
Since the value of an analogical argument inferring one resemblance from
other resemblances without any antecedent evidence of a connexion between
them, depends on the extent of ascertained resemblance, compared first with
the amount of ascertained difference, and next with the extent of the unexplored region of unascertained properties; it follows that where the
resemblance is very great, the ascertained difference very small, and our
knowledge of the subject-matter tolerably extensive, the argument from
analogy may approach in strength very near to a valid induction. If, after
much observation of B, we find that it agrees with A in nine out of ten of its
known properties, we may conclude with a probability of nine to one, that it
will possess any given derivative property of A. If we discover, for example,
an unknown animal or plant, resembling closely some known one in the
greater number of the properties we observe in it, but differing in some few,
we may reasonably expect to find in the unobserved remainder of its properties, a general agreement with those of the former; but also a difference
corresponding *proportionately*[a] to the amount of observed diversity.

It thus appears that the conclusions derived from analogy are only of any
considerable value, when the case to which we reason is an adjacent case;
adjacent, not as before, in place or time, but in circumstances. In the case of
effects of which the causes are imperfectly or not at all known, when consequently the observed order of their occurrence amounts only to an empirical
law, it often happens that the conditions which have coexisted whenever the
effect was observed, have been very numerous. Now if a new case presents
itself, in which all these conditions do not exist, but the far greater part of
them do, some one or a few only being wanting, the inference that the effect
will occur, notwithstanding this deficiency of complete resemblance to the
cases in which it has been observed, may, though of the nature of analogy,
possess a high degree of probability. It is hardly necessary to add that, however considerable this probability may be, no competent inquirer into nature
will rest satisfied with it when [b]a complete induction is attainable[b]; but will
consider the analogy as a mere guide-post, pointing out the direction in which
more rigorous investigations should be prosecuted.

It is in this last respect that considerations of analogy have the highest
[c]scientific[c] value. The cases in which analogical evidence affords in itself any
very high degree of probability, are, as we have [d] observed, only those in
which the resemblance is very close and extensive; but there is no analogy,
however faint, which may not be of the utmost value in suggesting experi-

[a–a]MS, 43, 46, 51, 56   proportionally
[b–b]MS, 43, 46   it is possible to obtain a complete induction
[c–c]MS, 43, 46   philosophical
[d]MS, 43, 46   just

ments or observations that may lead to more positive conclusions. When the agents and their effects are out of the reach of further observation and experiment, as in the speculations already alluded to respecting the moon and planets, such slight probabilities are no more than an interesting theme for the pleasant exercise of imagination; but any suspicion, however slight, that sets an ingenious person at work to contrive an experiment, or *e* affords a reason for trying one experiment rather than another, may be of *f*the greatest benefit to science*f*.

On this ground, *g*though I cannot accept as positive *h*truths*h* any of those scientific hypotheses*g* which are unsusceptible of being ultimately brought to the test of actual induction, such, for instance, as the two theories of light, the emission theory of the last century, and the undulatory theory which predominates in the present, I am yet unable to agree with *i*those who consider such*i* hypotheses to be worthy of entire disregard. As is well said by Hartley (and concurred in by a *j*thinker*j* in general so diametrically opposed to Hartley's *k*opinions*k* as Dugald Stewart), "any hypothesis *l*which*l* has so much plausibility as to explain a considerable number of facts, helps us to digest these facts in proper order, to bring new ones to light, and make *experimenta crucis* for the sake of future inquirers."* If an hypothesis *m*both explains known facts, and*m* has led to the prediction of others previously unknown, and since verified by experience, the laws of the phenomenon which is the subject of inquiry must bear at least a great similarity to those of the class of phenomena to which the hypothesis assimilates it; and since the analogy which extends so far may probably extend *n*farther*n*, nothing is more likely to suggest experiments tending to throw light upon the real properties of the phenomenon, than the following out such an hypothesis. But to this end it is by no means necessary that the hypothesis be mistaken for a scientific truth. On the contrary, that illusion is in this respect, as in every other, an

---

*Hartley's *Observations on Man* [London: Hitch and Austen, 1749], Vol. I, p. 16. The passage is not in Priestley's curtailed edition. [Joseph Priestley, *Hartley's Theory of the Human Mind*. London: Johnson, 1775.]

*e*MS, 43, 46, 51   that
*f-f*MS, 43, 46   eminent service to philosophy
*g-g*MS, 43   notwithstanding the unfavourable judgment which I have concurred with M. Comte in passing upon those scientific hypotheses (when considered as positive doctrines)
*h-h*46, 51, 56, 62, 65, 68   doctrines
*i-i*MS, 43   M. Comte in considering those]   46   those philosophers who consider such
*j-j*MS, 43, 46   philosopher
*k-k*MS, 43, 46   views
*l-l*Source, MS, 43, 46   that
*m-m*MS, 43, 46   not only explains known facts, but
*n-n*MS, 43, 46   further

impediment to the progress of real knowledge, by leading °inquirers° to restrict themselves arbitrarily to the particular hypothesis which is most accredited at the time, instead of looking out for every class of phenomena between the laws of which and those of the given phenomenon any analogy exists, and trying all such experiments as may tend to the discovery of ulterior analogies pointing in the same direction.

°–°MS, 43, 46   men

CHAPTER XXI

Of the Evidence of the Law of Universal Causation

§ 1. [*The law of causality* *ᵃdoes not rest on an instinctᵃ*] We have now completed our review of the logical processes by which the laws, or uniformities, of the *ᵇsequenceᵇ* of phenomena, and those uniformities in their coexistence which depend on the laws of their sequence, are ascertained *ᶜor testedᶜ*. As we recognised in the commencement, and have been enabled to see more clearly in the progress of the investigation, the basis of all these logical operations is *ᵈ* the law of causation. The validity of all the Inductive Methods depends on the assumption that every event, or the beginning of every phenomenon, must have some cause; some antecedent, on the existence of which it is invariably and unconditionally consequent. In the Method of Agreement this is obvious; that method avowedly proceeding on the supposition that we have found the true cause *ᵉasᵉ* soon as we have negatived every other. The assertion is equally true of the Method of Difference. That method authorizes us to infer a general law from two instances; one, in which A exists together with a multitude of other circumstances, and B follows; another, in which, A being removed, and all other circumstances remaining the same, B is prevented. What, however, does this prove? It proves that *ᶠB, in the particular instance, cannot have had any other cause than Aᶠ*; but to conclude from this that A was the cause, or that A will on other occasions be followed by B, is only allowable on the assumption that B must have some cause; that among its antecedents in any single instance in which it occurs, there must be one which has the capacity of producing it at other times *ᵍ*. This*ᵍ* being admitted, it is seen that in the case in question that antecedent can be no other than A; but, that if it be no other than A it must be A, is not proved, by these instances at least, but taken for granted. There is no need to

---

ᵃ⁻ᵃMS, 43, 46   *rests upon an induction by simple enumeration* [*cf. title of* §2. *in* 51, 56, 62, 65, 68, 72, *and* §2ᵃ⁻ᵃ]
ᵇ⁻ᵇMS, 43, 46, 51, 56, 62, 65   sequences
ᶜ⁻ᶜ+51, 56, 62, 65, 68, 72
ᵈMS, 43, 46   the universality of   ᵉ⁻ᵉMS, 43, 46, 51, 56, 62   so
ᶠ⁻ᶠMS, 43, 46   A, in . . . than B   ᵍ⁻ᵍMS   ; which

spend time in proving that the same thing is true of the other Inductive Methods. The universality of the law of causation is assumed in them all.

But is this assumption warranted? Doubtless (it may be said) *most* phenomena are connected as effects with some antecedent or cause, that is, are never produced unless some assignable fact has preceded them; but the very circumstance that complicated processes of induction are sometimes necessary, shows that cases exist in which this regular order of succession is not apparent to our *unaided* apprehension. If, then, the processes which bring these cases within the same category with the rest, require that we should assume the universality of the very law which they do not at first sight appear to exemplify, is not this a *petitio principii*? Can we prove a proposition, by an argument which takes it for granted? And if not so proved, on what evidence does it rest?

For this difficulty, which I have purposely stated in the strongest terms it *will* admit of, the school of metaphysicians who have long predominated in this country find a ready salvo. They affirm, that the universality of causation is a truth which we cannot help believing; that the belief in it is an instinct, one of the laws of our believing faculty. As the proof of this, they say, and they have nothing else to say, that everybody does believe it; and they number it among the propositions, rather numerous in their catalogue, which may be logically argued against, and perhaps cannot be logically proved, but which are of higher authority than logic, and *so essentially inherent in the human mind, that even he who denies them* in speculation, shows by his habitual practice that his arguments make no impression upon himself.

*Into the merits of this question, considered as one of psychology, it would be foreign to my purpose to enter *here*: but I must protest against adducing, as evidence of the truth of a fact in external nature, the disposition, however strong or however general, of the human mind to believe it. Belief is not proof, and does not dispense with the necessity of proof. I am aware,

*h–h*MS, 43, 46, 51, 56   first and simplest   *i*MS, 43, 46   real
*j–j*MS, 43, 46, 51, 56, 62, 65   would
*k–k*MS, 43, 46   which even he who denies
*l–l*565MS, 43, 46   I have no intention of entering into the merits of this question, as a problem of transcendental metaphysics. But I must renew my protest against adducing as evidence of the truth of a fact in external nature, any necessity which the human mind may be conceived to be under of believing it. It is the business of human intellect to adapt itself to the realities of things, and not to measure those realities by its own capacities of comprehension. The same quality which fits mankind for the offices and purposes of their own little life, the tendency of their belief to follow their experience, incapacitates them for judging of what lies beyond. Not only what man can know, but what he can conceive, depends upon what he has experienced. Whatever forms a part of all his experience, forms a part also of all his conceptions, and appears to him universal and necessary, though really, for aught he knows, having no existence beyond certain narrow limits. The habit, however,
m–m+68, 72

that to ask for evidence of a proposition which we are supposed to believe instinctively, is to expose oneself to the charge of rejecting the authority of the human faculties; which of course no one can consistently do, since the human faculties are all which any one has to judge by: and inasmuch as the meaning of the word evidence is supposed to be, something which when laid before the mind, induces it to believe; to demand evidence when the belief is ensured by the mind's own laws, is supposed to be appealing to the intellect against the intellect. But this, I apprehend, is a misunderstanding of the nature of evidence. By evidence is not meant anything and everything which produces belief. There are many things which generate belief besides evidence. A mere strong association of ideas often causes a belief so intense as to be unshakeable by experience or argument. Evidence is not that which the mind does or must yield to, but that which it ought to yield to, namely, that, by yielding to which, its belief is kept conformable to fact. There is no appeal from the human faculties generally, but there is an appeal from one human faculty to another; from the judging faculty, to those which take cognizance of fact, the faculties of sense and consciousness. *The legitimacy of this appeal is admitted whenever it is allowed that our judgments ought to be conformable to fact.* To say that belief suffices for its own justification is making opinion the test of opinion; it is denying the existence of any outward standard, the conformity of an opinion to which constitutes its truth. We call one mode of forming opinions right and another wrong, because the one does, and the other does not, tend to make the opinion agree with the fact— to make people believe what really is, and expect what really will be. Now a mere disposition to believe, even if supposed instinctive, is no guarantee for the truth of the thing believed. If, indeed, the belief ever amounted to an irresistible necessity, there would then be no *use* in appealing from it, because there would be no possibility of altering it. But even then the truth of the belief would not follow; it would only follow that mankind were under a permanent necessity of believing what might possibly not be true; *in other words, that a case might occur in which our senses or consciousness, if they could be appealed to, might testify one thing, and our reason believe another*. But in fact there is no such permanent necessity. There is no proposition of which it can be asserted that every human mind must eternally and irrevocably believe it. Many of the propositions of which this is most confidently *stated*, great numbers of human beings have disbelieved. The things which it has been supposed that nobody could possibly help believing, are innumerable; but no two generations would make out the same catalogue of

---

n–n+62, 65, 68, 72

*o–o*51, 56 just as they were under a temporary necessity (quite as irresistible while it lasted) of believing that the heavens moved and the earth stood still

*p–p*51 asserted

them. One age or nation believes implicitly what to another seems incredible and inconceivable; one individual has not a vestige of a belief which another qdeemsq to be absolutely inherent in humanity. There is not one of these supposed instinctive beliefs which is really rinevitabler. It is in the power of every one to cultivate habits of thought which make him independent of them. The habitt of philosophical analysis, s(of which it is the surest effect to enable the mind to command, instead of being commanded by, the laws of the merely passive part of its own nature,) by showing to us that things are not necessarily connected in fact because their ideas are connected in our minds, is able to loosen innumerable associations which reign despotically over the undisciplined tort early-prejudiced mind. Ands this habit is not without power even over those associations which the u school of which I have been speaking regard as connate and instinctive. I am convinced that any one accustomed to abstraction and analysis, who will fairly exert his faculties for the purpose, will, when his imagination has once learnt to entertain the notion, find no difficulty in conceiving that in some one, for instance, of the many firmaments into which sidereal astronomy now divides the universe, events may succeed one another at random, without any fixed law; nor can anything in our experience, or in our mental nature, constitute a sufficient, or indeed any, reason for believing that this is nowhere the case. v

wWere we to suppose (what xit isx perfectly possible to imagine) that the present order of the universe were brought to an end, and ythaty a chaos succeeded in which there was no fixed succession of events, and the past gave no assurance of the future; z if a human being were miraculously kept alive to witness this change, he surely would soon cease to believe in any uniformity, the uniformity itself no longer existing. If this be admitted, the belief in

q–q51, 56   holds
r–r51   universal
s–sMS, 43   of . . . nature, and which, by showing . . . undisciplined mind;]   46   (of . . . as 43 . . . mind);
t–t51   and the
uMS, 43, 46   philosophical
vMS   The grounds, therefore, which warrant us in rejecting such a supposition with respect to any of the phenomena within our ken, must be sought elsewhere than in any supposed necessity of our intellectual faculties.]   43, 46   as MS . . . phenomena of which we have experience, must . . . as MS]   51   as 43 . . . faculties.* [footnote:] *There have . . . as in MS text (see 5th sentence of §3 in 570i–i below) . . . causation. [paragraph] Were we . . . as 72 text (see w–w below) . . . and a chaos . . . future; and if . . . as 72 text . . . knowledge. [paragraph] The justification of our belief that the future will resemble the past, is that the future does resemble the past: and the logician is bound to demand this outward evidence, and not to accept, as a substitute for it, a supposed internal necessity.
w–w56B+51 (in footnote; see v above), 56, 62, 65, 68, 72
x–x56   is [printer's error?]
y–y+62, 65, 68, 72   [cf. 51 in v above]
z–z51, 56   and [cf. 51 in v above]

uniformity either is not an instinct, or it is an instinct conquerable, like all other instincts, by acquired knowledge.[w]

[a]But there is no need to speculate on what might be, when we have positive and certain knowledge of what has been. It is not true as a matter of fact, that mankind have always believed that all the successions of events were uniform and according to fixed laws. The Greek philosophers, not even excepting Aristotle, recognised Chance and Spontaneity (τύχη and τὸ αὐτομάτον) as among the agents in nature; in other words, they believed that to that extent there was no guarantee that the past had been similar to itself, or that the future would resemble the past. Even now a full half of the philosophical world, including the very same metaphysicians who contend most for the instinctive character of the belief in uniformity, consider one important class of phenomena, volitions, to be an exception to the uniformity, and not governed by a fixed law.[a]*

*[56] I am happy to be able to quote the following excellent passage from Mr. Baden Powell's "Essay on the Inductive Philosophy," in confirmation, both in regard to history and to doctrine, of the [b]statement[b] made in the text. Speaking of the "conviction of the universal and permanent uniformity of nature," Mr. Powell says (pp. 98–100),

"We may remark that this idea, in its proper extent, is by no means one of popular acceptance or natural growth. Just so far as the daily experience of every one goes, so far indeed he comes to embrace a certain persuasion of this kind, but merely to this limited extent, that what is going on around him at present, in his own narrow sphere of observation, will go on in like manner in future. The peasant believes that the sun which rose to-day will rise again to-morrow; that the seed put into the ground will be followed in due time by the harvest this year as it was last year, and the like; but has no notion of such inferences in subjects beyond his immediate observation. And it should be observed that each class of persons, in admitting this belief within the limited range of his own experience, though he doubt or deny it in everything beyond, is, in fact, bearing unconscious testimony to its universal truth. Nor, again, is it only among the *most* ignorant that this limitation is put upon the truth. There is a very general propensity to believe that everything beyond common experience, or especially ascertained laws of nature, is left to the dominion of chance or fate or arbitrary intervention; and even to object to any attempted explanation by physical causes, if conjecturally thrown out for an apparently unaccountable phenomenon.

The precise doctrine of the *generalization* of this idea of the uniformity of nature, so far from being obvious, natural, or intuitive, is utterly beyond the attainment of the many. In all the extent of its universality it is characteristic of the philosopher. It is clearly the result of philosophic cultivation and training, and by no means the spontaneous offspring of any primary principle naturally inherent in the mind, as some seem to believe. It is no mere vague persuasion taken up without examination, as a common prepossession to which we are always accustomed; on the contrary, all common prejudices and associations are against it. It is pre-eminently *an acquired idea*. It is not attained without deep

[a]–[a]+56, 62, 65, 68, 72   [*cf. final sentence with first paragraph of §3 in 570*[i]–[i] *below*]
[b]–[b]56, 62   statements

§ 2. *[The law of causality rests on an induction by simple enumeration]*
As was observed in a former place,* the belief we entertain in the universality,
throughout nature, of the law of cause and effect, is itself an instance of
induction; and by no means one of the earliest which any of us, or which
mankind in general, can have made. We arrive at this universal law, by
generalization from many laws of inferior generality. *We should never have
had the notion of causation (in the philosophical meaning of the term) as a
condition of all phenomena, unless* many cases of causation, or in other
words, many partial uniformities of sequence, had *previously* become
familiar. The more obvious of the particular uniformities suggest, and *give
evidence of, the general uniformity, and the* general uniformity, once established, enables us to prove the remainder of the particular uniformities of
which it is made up. As, however, all rigorous processes of induction presuppose the general uniformity, our knowledge of the particular uniformities
from which it was first inferred was not, of course, derived from *rigorous*
induction, but from the loose and uncertain mode of induction *per enumerationem simplicem*; and the law of universal causation, being collected from
results so obtained, cannot itself rest on any better foundation.

*It would seem, therefore, that induction *per enumerationem simplicem*
not only is not necessarily an illicit logical process, but is in reality the only
kind of induction possible; since the more elaborate process depends for its
validity on a law, itself obtained in that inartificial mode. Is there not then an
inconsistency in contrasting the looseness of one method with the rigidity of
another, when that other is indebted to the looser method for its own foundation?

The inconsistency, however, is only apparent. Assuredly, if induction by

---

study and reflection. The best informed philosopher is the man who most firmly
believes it, even in opposition to received notions; its acceptance depends on the
extent and profoundness of his inductive studies."
*Supra, Bk. III, Chap. iii, § 1 [pp. 306ff.].

*a–a*MS, 43, 46 [*no section division*]
*b–b*MS, 43, 46   The generalizing propensity, which, instinctive or not, is one of the
most powerful principles of our nature, does not indeed wait for the period when such
a generalization becomes strictly legitimate. The mere unreasoning propensity to expect
what has been often experienced, doubtless led men to believe that everything had a
cause, before they could have conclusive evidence of that truth. But even this cannot be
supposed to have happened until
c–c+51, 56, 62, 65, 68, 72
*d–d*MS, 43, 46   prove the general uniformity, and that
*e–e*MS, 43, 46, 51, 56, 62   rigid
*f–f*56⁹MS, 43, 46   §2. [*In what cases such induction is allowable*] This opens to us a
consideration of very great importance; namely, that induction by simple enumeration,
or, in other words, generalization of an observed fact from the mere absence of any
known instances to the contrary, is by no means the illicit logical process in all cases
which it is in most. It

simple enumeration were an invalid process, no process grounded on it could be valid; just as no reliance could be placed on telescopes, if we could not trust our eyes. But though a valid process, it is a fallible one, and fallible in very different degrees: if therefore we can substitute for the more fallible forms of the process, an operation grounded on the same process in a less fallible form, we shall have effected a very material improvement. And this is what scientific induction does.

A mode of concluding from experience must be pronounced untrustworthy, when subsequent experience refuses to confirm it. According to this criterion, induction by simple enumeration—in other words, generalization of an observed fact from the mere absence of any known instance to the contrary—affords in general a precarious and unsafe ground of assurance; for such generalizations are incessantly discovered, on further experience, to be false. Still, however, it affords some assurance, sufficient, in many cases, for the ordinary guidance of conduct. It would be absurd to say, that the generalizations arrived at by mankind in the outset of their experience, such as these, Food nourishes, Fire burns, Water drowns, were unworthy of reliance.* There is a scale of trustworthiness in the results of the original unscientific Induction; and on this diversity (as observed in the fourth chapter of the present book) depend the rules for the improvement of the process. The improvement consists in correcting one of these *h*inartificial*h* generalizations by means of another. As has been already pointed out, this is all that art can do. To test a generalization, by showing that it either follows from, or conflicts with, some stronger induction, some generalization resting on a broader foundation of experience, is the beginning and end of the logic of Induction.

*[51] It deserves remark, that these early generalizations did not, like scientific *g*inductions*g*, presuppose causation. What they did presuppose, was *uniformity* in physical facts. But the observers were as ready to presume uniformity in the coexistences of facts as in the sequences. On the other hand, they never thought of assuming that this uniformity was a principle pervading all nature: their generalizations did not imply that there was uniformity in everything, but only that as much uniformity as existed within their observation, existed also beyond it. The induction, Fire burns, does not require for its validity that all nature should observe uniform laws, but only that there should be uniformity in one particular class of natural phenomena; the effects of fire on the senses and on combustible substances. And uniformity to this extent was not assumed, anterior to the experience, but proved by the experience. The same observed instances which proved the narrower truth, proved as much of the wider one as corresponded to it. It is from losing sight of this fact, and considering the law of causation in its full extent as necessarily presupposed in the very earliest generalizations, that persons have been led into the belief that the law of causation is known *à priori*, and is not itself a conclusion from experience.

*g–g*51, 56 induction   *h–h*51 unartificial [*printer's error?*]

ᵃ§ 3.ᵃ [In what cases induction by simple enumeration is allowable] Now
the precariousness of the method of simple enumeration is in an inverse ratio
to the largeness of the generalization. The processᶠ is delusive and insufficient,
exactly in proportion as the subject-matter of the observation is special and
limited in extent. As the sphere widens, this unscientific method becomes less
and less liable to mislead; and the most universal class of truths, the law of
causation for instance, and the principles of number and of geometry, are
duly and satisfactorily proved by that method alone, nor are they susceptible
of any other proof.

With respect to ᵇthe wholeᵇ class of generalizations of which we have
recently treated, the uniformities which depend on causation, the truth of the
remark just made follows by obvious inference from the principles laid down
in the preceding chapters. When a fact has been observed a certain number of
times to be true, and is not in any instance known to be false; if we at once
affirm that fact as an universal truth or law of nature, without ᶜeither testing
it by any of the four methods of induction, orᶜ deducing it ᵈ from other known
laws, we shall in general err grossly: but we are perfectly justified in affirming
it as an empirical law, true within certain limits of time, place, and circumstance, provided the number of coincidences ᵉbeᵉ greater than can with any
probability be ascribed to chance. The reason for not extending it beyond
those limits is, that the fact of its holding true within them may be a consequence of collocations, which cannot be concluded to exist in one place
because they exist in another; or may be dependent on the accidental absence
of counteracting agencies, which ᶠanyᶠ variation of time, or the smallest
change of circumstances, may possibly bring into play. If we suppose, then,
the subject-matter of any generalization to be so widely diffused that there is
no time, no place, and no combination of circumstances, but must afford an
example either of its truth or of its falsity, and if it be never found otherwise
than true, its truth cannot ᵍbe contingentᵍ on any collocations, unless such as
exist at all times and places: nor can it be frustrated by any counteracting
agencies, unless by such as never actually occur. It is, therefore, an empirical
law coextensive with all human experience; at which point the distinction
between empirical laws and laws of nature vanishes, and the proposition
takes its place ʰamong the most firmly established as well as largestʰ truths
accessible to science.

ᵃ⁻ᵃMS, 43, 46 [no section division; see §2ᶠ⁻ᶠ above, and §3ⁱ⁻ⁱ below]
ᵇ⁻ᵇMS, 43   all the
ᶜ⁻ᶜMS, 43, 46, 51, 56, 62, 65, 68   testing . . . induction, nor
ᵈMS, 43, 46   by reasoning
ᵉ⁻ᵉMS, 43, 46   is
ᶠ⁻ᶠ+43, 46, 51, 56, 62, 65, 68, 72
ᵍ⁻ᵍMS, 43, 46, 51, 56, 62, 65, 68   depend
ʰ⁻ʰMS, 43, 46   in the highest order of

ᵗNow, the most extensive in its subject-matter of all generalizations which experience warrants, respecting the sequences and coexistences of phenomena, is the law of causation. It stands at the head of all observed uniformities, in point of universality, and therefore (if the preceding observations are correct) in point of certainty. And if we consider, not what mankind would have been justified in believing in the infancy of their knowledge, but what may rationally be believed in its present more advanced state, we shall find ourselves warranted in considering this fundamental law, though itself obtained by induction from particular laws of causation, as not less certain, but on the contrary, more so, than any of those from which it was drawn. It adds to them as much proof as it receives from them. For there is probably no one even of the best established laws of causation which is not sometimes counteracted, and to which, therefore, apparent exceptions do not present themselves, which would have necessarily and justly shaken the confidence of mankind in the universality of those laws, if inductive processes founded on the universal law had not enabled us to refer those exceptions to the agency of counteracting causes, and thereby reconcile them with the law with which they apparently conflict. Errors, moreover, may have slipped into the statement of any one of the special laws, through inattention to some material circumstance: and instead of the true proposition, another may have been

---

ᵗ⁻⁴⁵⁷³MS [no paragraph] Such a character strictly belongs to the law of universal causation, and to the ultimate principles of mathematics. The induction by which they are established is of that kind which can establish nothing but empirical laws: an empirical law, however, of which the truth is exemplified at every moment of time and in every variety of place or circumstance, has an evidence which surpasses that of the most rigid induction, even if the foundation of scientific induction were not itself laid (as we have seen that it is) in a generalization of this very description.

§3. [*The universal prevalence of the law of causality may once have been doubtful*] With respect to the general law of causation, it does appear that there must have been a time when the universal prevalence of that law throughout nature could not have been affirmed in the same confident and unqualified manner as at present. There was a time when many of the phenomena of nature must have appeared altogether capricious and irregular, not governed by any laws, nor steadily consequent upon any causes. Such phenomena, indeed, were commonly, in that early stage of human knowledge, ascribed to the direct intervention of the will of some supernatural being, and therefore still to a cause. This shows the strong tendency of the human mind to ascribe every phenomenon to some cause or other; but it shows also that experience had not, at that time, pointed out any regular order in the occurrence of those particular phenomena, nor proved them to be, as we now know that they are, dependent upon prior phenomena as their proximate causes. There have been sects of philosophers who have admitted what they termed Chance as one of the agents in the order of nature, by which certain classes of events were entirely regulated; which could only mean that those events did not occur in any fixed order, or depend upon uniform laws of causation. Finally, there is one class of phenomena which, even in our own day, at least one-half of the speculative world do not admit to be governed by causes; I mean human volitions. These are believed, by the metaphysicians who espouse the free-will doctrine, to be self-determining, self-causing; that is, not caused by anything external to themselves, not determined by any prior fact. [*Cf. last two sentences with* 566ᵃ⁻ᵃ *above.*] It is true that the real

enunciated, false as an universal law, though leading, in all cases hitherto observed, to the same result. To the law of causation, on the contrary, we not only do not know of any exception, but the exceptions which limit or apparently invalidate the special laws, are so far from contradicting the universal one, that they confirm it; since in all cases which are sufficiently open to our observation, we are able to trace the difference of result, either to the absence of a cause which had been present in ordinary cases, or to the presence of one which had been absent.

The law of cause and effect, being thus certain, is capable of imparting its certainty to all other inductive propositions which can be deduced from it; and the narrower inductions may be regarded as receiving their ultimate sanction from that law, since there is no one of them which is not rendered more certain than it was before, when we are able to connect it with that larger induction, and to show that it cannot be denied, consistently with the law that everything which begins to exist has a cause. And hence we are justified in the seeming inconsistency, of holding induction by simple enumeration to be good for proving this general truth, the foundation of scientific induction, and yet refusing to rely on it for any of the narrower inductions. I fully admit that if the law of causation were unknown, generalization in the

opinion of these philosophers does not go quite so far as their words seem to imply; they do not in reality claim for this class of phenomena much more than the absence of that mystical tie which the word *necessity* seems to involve, and the existence of which, even in the case of inorganic matter, is but an illusion produced by language. But their system of philosophy does not the less prove that the existence of phenomena which are not rigorously consequent upon any antecedents, does not necessarily, even in the present state of our experience, appear an inadmissible paradox.

The truth is, as M. Comte has well pointed out [see, e.g., *Cours*, Vol. I, Leçon i], that although the generalizing propensity must have prompted mankind from almost the beginning of their experience to ascribe all events to some cause more or less mysterious, the conviction that phenomena have invariable laws, and follow with regularity certain antecedent *phenomena*, was only acquired gradually; and extended as knowledge advanced, from one order of phenomena to another, beginning with those whose laws were most accessible to observation. This progress has not yet attained its ultimate point; there being still, as before observed, one class of phenomena, the subjection of which to invariable laws is not yet universally recognised. So long as any doubt hung over this fundamental principle, the various Methods of Induction which took that principle for granted could only afford results which were admissible conditionally; as showing what law the phenomenon under investigation must follow if it followed any fixed law at all. As, however, when the rules of correct induction had been conformed to, the result obtained never failed to be verified by all subsequent experience; every such inductive operation had the effect of extending the acknowledged dominion of general laws, and bringing an additional portion of the experience of mankind to strengthen the evidence of the universality of the law of causation: until now at length we are fully warranted in considering that law, as applied to all phenomena within the range of human observation, to stand on an equal footing in respect to evidence with the axioms of geometry itself.

§4. [*Ground of its present certainty*] I apprehend that the considerations which] 43 *as* MS . . . gradually; and extended itself, as knowledge . . . *as* MS] 46 *as* MS . . . The truth is, that although . . . *as* 43 . . . §4. [*Grounds* . . . *as* MS

more obvious cases of uniformity in phenomena would nevertheless be possible, and though in all cases more or less precarious, and in some extremely so, would suffice to constitute a certain measure of probability: but what the amount of this probability might be, we are dispensed from estimating, since it never could amount to the degree of assurance which the proposition acquires, when, by the application to it of the Four Methods, the supposition of its falsity is shown to be inconsistent with the Law of Causation. We are therefore logically entitled, and, by the necessities of scientific Induction, required, to disregard the probabilities derived from the early rude method of generalizing, and to consider no minor generalization as proved except so far as the law of causation confirms it, nor probable except so far as it may reasonably be expected to be so confirmed.

§ 4. [*The universal prevalence of the law of causality, on what grounds admissible*] [a]The assertion, that our inductive processes assume the law of causation, while the law of causation is itself a case of induction, is a paradox, only on the old theory of reasoning, which supposes the universal truth, or major premise, in a ratiocination, to be the real proof of the particular truths which are ostensibly inferred from it. According to the doctrine maintained in the present treatise,* the major premise is not the proof of the conclusion, but is itself proved, along with the conclusion from the same evidence. "All men are mortal" is not the proof that Lord Palmerston is mortal; but our past experience of mortality authorizes us to infer *both* the general truth and the particular fact, and the one with exactly the same degree of assurance as the other. The mortality of Lord Palmerston is not an inference from the mortality of all men, but from the experience which proves the mortality of all men; and is a correct inference from experience, if that general truth is so too. This relation between our general beliefs and their particular applications holds equally true in the more comprehensive case which we are now discussing. Any new fact of causation inferred by induction, is rightly inferred, if no other objection can be made to the inference than can be made to the general truth that every event has a cause. The utmost certainty which can be given to a conclusion arrived at in the way of inference, stops at this point. When we have ascertained that the particular conclusion must stand or fall with the general uniformity of the laws of nature—that it is liable to no doubt except the doubt whether every event has a cause—we have done

*[65] Bk. II, Chap. iii [pp. 183ff.].

[a-a]51, 56, 62 For the justification of the scientific method of induction as against the unscientific, notwithstanding that the scientific ultimately rests on the unscientific, the preceding considerations may suffice. All that is requisite to support the Canons of Induction is, that the generalization which gives the Law of Universal causation should be

all that can be done for it. The strongest assurance we can obtain of any theory respecting the cause of a given phenomenon, is that the phenomenon has either that cause or none.

The latter supposition might have been an admissible one in a very early period of our study of nature. But we have been able to perceive that in the stage which mankind have now reached, the generalization which gives the Law of Universal Causation has grown into[a] a stronger and better induction, one deserving of greater reliance, than any of the subordinate generalizations. [b]We may even[b], I think, go a step further than this, and regard the certainty of that great induction as not merely comparative, but, for all practical purposes, [c]complete[c].

The considerations, which, as I apprehend,[i] give, at the present day, to the proof of the law of uniformity of succession as true of all phenomena without exception, this character of completeness and conclusiveness, are the following:—First, that we now know it directly to be true of far the greatest number of phenomena; that there are none of which we know it not to be true, the utmost that can be said being, that of some we cannot positively from direct evidence affirm its truth; [d]while[d] phenomenon after phenomenon, as they become better known to us, are constantly passing from the latter class into the former; and in all cases in which that transition has not yet taken place, the absence of direct proof is accounted for by the rarity or the obscurity of the phenomena, our deficient means of observing them, or the logical difficulties arising from the complication of the circumstances in which they occur; insomuch that, notwithstanding as rigid a dependence on given conditions as exists in the case of any other phenomenon, it was not likely that we should be better acquainted with those conditions than we are. Besides this first class of considerations, there is a second, which still further corroborates the conclusion [e] . Although there are phenomena the production and changes of which elude all our attempts to reduce them universally to any ascertained law; yet in every such case, the phenomenon, or the objects concerned in it, are found in some instances to obey the known laws of nature. The wind, for example, is the type of uncertainty and caprice, yet we find it in some cases obeying with as much constancy as any phenomenon in nature the law of the tendency of fluids to distribute themselves so as to equalize the pressure on every side of each of their particles; as in the case of the trade winds, and the monsoons. Lightning might once have been supposed to obey no laws; but [f] since it has been ascertained to be identical with electricity, we know that the very same phenomenon in [g]some of its[g] manifestations is implicitly

b–b51, 56, 62   But we may   c–c51, 56, 62, 65, 68   absolute
d–dMS   that
eMS, 43, 46   , and from the recognition of which the complete establishment of the universal law may reasonably be dated
fMS   ever   g–gMS   its other

obedient to the action of fixed causes. I do not believe that there is now one object or event in all our experience of nature, within the bounds of the solar system at least, which has not either been ascertained by direct observation to follow laws of its own, or been proved to be [h]closely[h] similar to objects and events which, in more familiar manifestations, or on a more limited scale, follow strict laws: our inability to trace the same laws on [i]a[i] larger scale and in the more recondite instances, being accounted for by the number and complication of the modifying causes, or by their inaccessibility to observation.

The progress of experience, therefore, has dissipated the doubt which [j]must[j] have rested on the universality of the law of causation while there were phenomena which seemed to be *sui generis*, not subject to the same laws with any other class of phenomena, and [k]not[k] as yet ascertained to have peculiar laws of their own. This great generalization, however, might reasonably have been, as it in fact was [l], acted on as a probability of the highest order, before there were sufficient grounds for receiving it as a certainty. [m]In matters of evidence, as in all other human things, we neither require, nor can attain, the absolute. We must hold even our strongest convictions with an opening left in our minds for the reception of facts which contradict them; and only when we have taken this precaution, have we earned the right to act upon our convictions with complete confidence when no such contradiction appears.[m] [n]Whatever[n] has been found true in innumerable instances, and never found to be false after due examination in any, we are safe in acting on as universal provisionally, until an undoubted exception appears; provided the nature of the case be such that a real exception could scarcely have escaped [o] notice. When every phenomenon that we ever knew sufficiently well to be able to answer the question, had a cause on which it was invariably consequent, it was more rational to suppose that our inability to assign the causes of other phenomena arose from our ignorance, than that there were phenomena which were uncaused, and which happened [p] to be exactly those which we [q]had hitherto[q] had no sufficient opportunity of studying.

[r] It must, at the same time, be remarked, that the reasons for this reliance do not hold in circumstances unknown to us, and beyond the possible range of our experience. In distant parts of the stellar regions, where the phenomena may be entirely unlike those with which we are acquainted, it would

[h-h]MS, 43, 46   exactly
[j-j]MS   may
[l]MS, 43, 46   by all great thinkers
[n-n]MS, 43, 46, 51, 56, 62, 65, 68   For, whatever
[o]MS, 43, 46, 51, 56, 62, 65, 68   our
[p]MS, 43, 46   accidentally
[r]MS, 43, 46   §5. [*Limits of the reliance due to it*]

[i-i]MS, 43, 46, 51, 56   the
[k-k]MS   which had not been
[m-m]+72

[q-q]MS   have

be folly to affirm confidently that this general law prevails, any more than those special ones which we have found to hold universally on our own planet. The uniformity in the succession of events, otherwise called the law of causation, must be received not as a law of the universe, but of that portion of it only which is within the range of our means of sure observation, with a reasonable degree of extension to adjacent cases. To extend it further is to make a supposition without evidence, and to which, in the absence of any ground from experience for estimating its degree of probability, it would be *idle to attempt* to assign any.* *t*

*[62] One of the most rising thinkers of the new generation in France, M. Taine (who has given, in the *Revue des Deux Mondes* [1e ser., XXXII (1 March, 1861), pp. 44–82], the most masterly analysis, at least in one point of view, ever made of the present work), though he rejects, on this and similar points of psychology, the intuition theory in its ordinary form, nevertheless assigns to the law of causation, and to some other of the most universal laws, that certainty beyond the bounds of human experience, which I have not been able to accord to them. He does this on the faith of our faculty of abstraction, in which he seems to recognise an independent source of evidence, not indeed disclosing truths not contained in our experience, but affording an assurance which experience cannot give, of the universality of those which it does contain. By abstraction M. Taine seems to think that we are able, not merely to analyse that part of nature which we see, and exhibit apart the elements which pervade it, but to distinguish such of them as are elements of the system of nature considered as a whole, not incidents belonging to our limited terrestrial experience. I am not sure that I fully enter into M. Taine's meaning; but I confess I do not see how any mere abstract conception, elicited by our minds from our experience, can be evidence of an objective fact in universal Nature, beyond what the experience itself bears witness of; or how, in the process of interpreting in general language the testimony of experience, the limitations of the testimony itself can be cast off.

uDr. Ward, in an able article in the *Dublin Review* [n.s. XVII,] for October

s–sMS, 43, 46   ridiculous to affect
tMS, 43, 46 [*paragraph*] But, on the other hand, within the bounds of human experience, this fundamental law, though itself obtained by induction from particular laws of causation, cannot be deemed less certain, but on the contrary more so, than any of those from which it was drawn. It adds to them as much proof as it receives from them. For there is probably no one even of the best established laws of causation which is not sometimes counteracted, and to which, therefore, apparent exceptions do not present themselves, which would have necessarily and justly shaken the confidence of mankind in the universality of those laws, if inductive processes founded on the universal law had not enabled us to refer those exceptions to the agency of counteracting causes, and thereby reconcile them with the law with which they apparently conflict. Errors, moreover, may have slipped into the statement of any one of the special laws, through inattention to some material circumstance; and instead of the true proposition, another may have been enunciated, false as an universal law, though leading, in all cases hitherto observed, to the same result. But the general law of causation would remain unaffected by any such error. The law of cause and effect is therefore, not without reason, placed, in point of certainty, at the head of all our inductions; on a level with the first principles of mathematics, which rest, as we shall see presently, upon much the same species of induction as itself.
u–u577+72

1871, [p. 311,] contends that the uniformity of Nature cannot be proved from experience, but from "transcendental considerations" only, and that, consequently, all physical science would be deprived of its basis, if such transcendental proof were impossible.

When physical science is said to depend on the assumption that the course of nature is invariable, all that is meant is that the conclusions of physical science are not known as *absolute* truths: the truth of them is *conditional* on the uniformity of the course of nature; and all that the most conclusive observations and experiments can prove, is that the result arrived at will be true if, and as long as, the present laws of nature are valid. But this is all the assurance we require for the guidance of our conduct. Dr. Ward himself does not think that his transcendental proofs make it practically greater; for he believes, as a Catholic, that the course of nature not only has been, but frequently and even daily is, suspended by supernatural intervention.

But though this conditional conclusiveness of the evidence of experience, which is sufficient for the purposes of life, is all that I was necessarily concerned to prove, I have given reasons for thinking that the uniformity, as itself a part of experience, is sufficiently proved to justify undoubting reliance on it. This, Dr. Ward contests, for the following reasons:—

First (p. 315), supposing it true that there has hitherto been no well authenticated case of a breach in the uniformity of nature; "the number of natural agents constantly at work is incalculably large; and the observed cases of uniformity in their action must be immeasurably fewer than one thousandth of the whole. Scientific men, we assume for the moment, have discovered that in a certain proportion of instances—immeasurably fewer than one thousandth of the whole—a certain fact has prevailed; the fact of uniformity; and they have not found a single instance in which that fact does *not* prevail. Are they justified, we ask, in inferring from these premises that the fact is universal? Surely the question answers itself. Let us make a very grotesque supposition, in which, however, the conclusion would really be tried according to the arguments adduced. In some desert of Africa there is an enormous connected edifice, surrounding some vast space, in which dwell certain reasonable beings, who are unable to leave the enclosure. In this edifice are more than a thousand chambers, which some years ago were entirely locked up, and the keys no one knew where. By constant diligence twenty-five keys have been found, out of the whole number; and the corresponding chambers, situated promiscuously throughout the edifice, have been opened. Each chamber, when examined, is found to be in the precise shape of a dodecahedron. Are the inhabitants justified on that account in holding with certitude that the remaining 975 chambers are built on the same plan?"

Not with perfect certitude, but (if the chambers to which the keys have been found are really "situated promiscuously") with so high a degree of probability that they would be justified in acting upon the presumption until an exception appeared.

Dr. Ward's argument, however, does not touch mine as it stands in the text. My argument is grounded on the fact that the uniformity of the course of nature as a whole, is constituted by the uniform sequences of special effects from special natural agencies; that the number of these natural agencies in the part of the universe known to us is not incalculable, nor even extremely great; that we have now reason to think that at least the far greater number of them, if not separately, at least in some of the combinations into which they enter, have been made sufficiently amenable to observation, to have enabled us actually to ascertain some of their fixed laws; and that this amount of experience justifies the same degree of assurance that the course of nature is uniform throughout, which we previously had of the uniformity of sequence among the phenomena best known to us. This view of the subject, if correct, destroys the force of Dr. Ward's first argument.

His second argument is, that many or most persons, both scientific and unscientific, believe that there *are* well authenticated cases of breach in the uniformity of nature, namely miracles. [Pp. 315–16.] Neither does this consideration touch what I have said in the text. I admit no other uniformity in the events of nature than the law of Causation; and (as I have explained in the chapter of this volume which treats of the Grounds of Disbelief) a miracle is no exception to that law. In every case of alleged miracle, a *new antecedent* is affirmed to exist; a *counteracting cause*, namely the volition of a supernatural being. To all, therefore, to whom beings with superhuman power over nature are a *vera causa*, a miracle is a *case* of the Law of Universal Causation, not a deviation from it.

Dr. Ward's last, and as he says, strongest argument, is the familiar one of Reid, Stewart, and their followers—that whatever knowledge experience gives us of the past and present, it gives us none of the future. [Pp. 316–17.] I confess that I see no force whatever in this argument. Wherein does a future fact differ from a present or a past fact, except in their merely momentary relation to the human beings at present in existence? The answer made by Priestley, in his *Examination of Reid* [London: Johnson, 1774, pp. 85–6], seems to me sufficient, viz. that though we have had no experience of what *is* future, we have had abundant experience of what *was* future. The "leap in the dark" (as Professor Bain calls it) [see *Logic*, Pt. I, p. 273; Pt. II, p. 2] from the past to the future, is exactly as much in the dark and no more, as the leap from a past which we have personally observed, to a past which we have not. I agree with Mr. Bain in the opinion that the resemblance of what we have not experienced to what we have, is, by a law of our nature, presumed through the mere energy of the idea, before experience has proved it. This *psychological* truth, however, is not, as Dr. Ward [pp. 311–12] when criticizing Mr. Bain appears to think, inconsistent with the *logical* truth that experience does prove it. The proof comes after the presumption, and consists in its invariable *verification* by experience when the experience arrives. The fact which while it was future could not be observed, having as yet no existence, is always, when it becomes present and *can* be observed, found conformable to the past.

Dr. M'Cosh maintains (*Examination of Mr. J. S. Mill's Philosophy*, [London: Macmillan, 1866,] p. 257) that the uniformity of the course of nature is a different thing from the law of causation; and while he allows that the former is only proved by a long continuance of experience, and that it is not inconceivable nor necessarily incredible that there may be worlds in which it does not prevail, he considers the law of causation to be known intuitively. There is, however, no other uniformity in the events of nature than that which arises from the law of causation: so long therefore as there remained any doubt that the course of nature was uniform throughout, at least when not modified by the intervention of a new (supernatural) cause, a doubt was necessarily implied, not indeed of the reality of causation, but of its universality. If the uniformity of the course of nature has any exceptions—if any events succeed one another without fixed laws —to that extent the law of causation fails; there are events which do not depend on causes.[u]

CHAPTER XXII

Of Uniformities of Coexistence not Dependent on Causation

§ 1. [*ᵃUniformitiesᵃ of coexistence which result from laws of sequence*] The order of the occurrence of phenomena in time, is either successive or simultaneous; the uniformities, therefore, which obtain in their occurrence, are either uniformities of succession or of coexistence. Uniformities of succession are all comprehended under the law of causation and its consequences. Every phenomenon has a cause, which it invariably follows; and from this are derived other invariable sequences among the successive stages of the same effect, as well as between the effects resulting from causes which invariably succeed one another.

In the same manner with these derivative uniformities of succession, a great variety of uniformities of coexistence also take their rise. Coordinate effects of the same cause naturally coexist with one another. High water at any point on the earth's surface, and high water at the point diametrically opposite to it, are effects uniformly simultaneous, resulting from the direction in which the combined ᵇattractionsᵇ of the sun and moon act upon the waters of the ocean. An eclipse of the sun to us, and an eclipse of the earth to a spectator situated in the moon, are in like manner phenomena invariably coexistent; and their coexistence can equally be deduced from the laws of their production.

It is ᶜan obviousᶜ question, therefore, whether all the uniformities of coexistence among phenomena may not be accounted for in this manner. And it cannot be doubted that between phenomena which are themselves effects, the coexistences must necessarily depend on the causes of those phenomena. If they are effects immediately or remotely of the same cause, they cannot coexist except by virtue of some laws or properties of that cause: if they are effects of different causes, they cannot coexist unless it be because their causes coexist; and the uniformity of coexistence, if such there be, between the effects, proves that ᵈ those particular causes, within the limits of our observation, have uniformly been coexistent.

ᵃ⁻ᵃMS, 43, 46 *The uniformities*   ᵇ⁻ᵇMS, 43   attraction
ᶜ⁻ᶜMS   a natural   ᵈMS, 43, 46   in the original collocation

§ 2. [*The properties of Kinds are uniformities of coexistence*] But these same considerations compel us to recognise that there must be one class of coexistences which cannot depend on causation; the coexistences between the ultimate properties of ᵃthings—thoseᵃ properties which are the causes of all phenomena, but are not themselves caused by any phenomenon, and ᵇa cause for which could only be sought by ascendingᵇ to the origin of all things. Yet among these ultimate properties there are not only coexistences, but uniformities of coexistence. General propositions may be, and are, formed, which assert that whenever certain properties are found, certain others are found along with them. We perceive an object; say, for instance, water. We recognise it to be water, of course by certain of its properties. Having recognised it, we are able to affirm of it innumerable other properties; which we could not do unless it were a general truth, a law or uniformity in nature, that the set of properties by which we identify the substance as water, always have those other properties conjoined with them.

In a ᶜformer placeᶜ,* it has been explained in some detail what is meant by the Kinds of objects; those classes which differ from one another not by a limited and definite, but by an indefinite and unknown, number of distinctions. To this we have now to add, that every proposition by which anything is asserted of a Kind, affirms an uniformity of coexistence. Since we know nothing of Kinds but their properties, the Kind, to us, *is* the set of properties by which it is identified, and which must of course be sufficient to distinguish it from every other Kind.† In affirming anything, therefore, of a Kind, we are affirming something to be uniformly coexistent with the properties by which the Kind is recognised; and that is the sole meaning of the assertion.

Among the uniformities of coexistence which exist in nature, may hence be numbered all the properties of Kinds. The whole of these, however, are

*Book I, Chap. vii [pp. 122ff.]. ᵈ

†In some cases, a Kind is sufficiently identified by some one remarkable property: but most commonly several are required; each property considered singly, being a joint property of that and of other Kinds. The ᵉ colour and brightness of the diamond are common to it with the paste from which false diamonds are made; ᶠits octohedral form is common to it with alum, and magnetic iron oreᶠ; but the colour and brightness and the ᵍformᵍ together, identify its Kind; that is, are a mark to us that it is combustible; that when burnt it produces carbonic acid; that it cannot be cut with any known substance; together with many other ascertained properties, and the fact that there exist an indefinite number still unascertained.

ᵃ⁻ᵃMS, 43, 46, 51, 56, 62 things: between those
ᵇ⁻ᵇMS, 43, 46 to find a cause for which, we must ascend
ᶜ⁻ᶜMS, 43, 46, 51, 56 chapter of a former book
ᵈMS, 43, 46 [*footnote to* objects *in next line*]
ᵉMS, 43, 46 mere
ᶠ⁻ᶠMS, 43, 46, 51, 56 the double refraction is common to it with Iceland spar, and many other stones
ᵍ⁻ᵍMS, 43, 46, 51, 56 double refraction

not independent of causation, but only a portion of them. Some are ultimate properties, others derivative; of some, no cause can be assigned, but others are manifestly dependent on causes. Thus, *h*pure oxygen gas*h* is a Kind, and one of its most unequivocal properties is its gaseous form: this property, however, has for its cause the presence of a certain quantity of latent heat; and if that heat could be taken away (as has been done from so many gases in *i* Faraday's experiments),[*] the gaseous form would doubtless disappear, together with numerous other properties which depend on, or are caused by, that property.

In regard to all substances which are chemical compounds, and which therefore may be regarded as products of the juxtaposition of substances different in Kind from themselves, there is considerable reason to presume that the specific properties of the compound are consequent, as effects, on some of the properties of the elements, though *j* little progress has yet been made in tracing any invariable relation between the latter and the former. Still more strongly will a similar presumption exist, when the object itself, as in the case of organized beings, is no primeval agent, but an effect, which depends on a cause or causes for its very existence. The Kinds therefore which are called in chemistry simple substances, or elementary natural agents, are the only ones, any of whose properties can with certainty be considered ultimate; and of these the ultimate properties are probably much more numerous than we at present recognise, since every successful instance of the resolution of the properties of their compounds into simpler laws, generally leads to the recognition of properties in the elements distinct from any previously known. The resolution of the laws of the heavenly motions, established the previously unknown ultimate property of a mutual attraction between all bodies: the resolution, so far as it has yet proceeded, of the laws of crystallization, of chemical composition, electricity, magnetism, &c. points to various polarities, ultimately inherent in the particles of which bodies are composed; the comparative atomic weights of different kinds of bodies were ascertained by resolving, into more general laws, the uniformities observed in the proportions in which substances *k*combine*k* with one another; and so forth. Thus although every resolution of a complex uniformity into simpler and more elementary laws has an apparent tendency to diminish the number of the ultimate properties, and really does remove many properties from the list; yet, (since the result of this simplifying process is to trace up an ever greater variety of different effects to the same agents,) the *l*farther*l* we ad-

[*See Michael Faraday. "On the Condensation of Several Gases into Liquids." In his *Experimental Researches in Chemistry and Physics*. London: Taylor, 1859, pp. 89–95.]

*h–h*MS, 43, 46   atmospheric air]   51, 56, 62, 65, 68   pure atmospheric air
*i*MS, 43, 46   Mr.]   51   Professor   *j*MS, 43, 46   but
*k–k*43, 46   combined [*printer's error?*]   *l–l*MS, 43, 46, 51, 56, 62, 65, 68   further

vance in this direction, the greater number of distinct properties we are forced to recognise in one and the same object: the coexistences of which properties must accordingly be ranked among the ultimate generalities of nature.

§ 3. [*Some properties of Kinds are derivative, others ultimate*] There are, therefore, only two kinds of propositions which assert *a* uniformity of co-existence between properties. Either the properties depend on causes, or they do not. If they do, the proposition which affirms them to be coexistent is a derivative law of coexistence between effects, and until resolved into the laws of causation on which it depends, is an empirical law, and to be tried by the principles of induction to which such laws are amenable. If, on the other hand, the properties do not depend on causes, but are ultimate properties; then if it be true that they invariably coexist, they must *b*all*b* be ultimate properties of one and the same Kind; and it is of these only that the co-existences can be classed as a peculiar sort of laws of nature.

When we affirm that all crows are black, or that all negroes have woolly hair, we assert an uniformity of coexistence. We assert that the property of blackness, or of having woolly hair, invariably coexists with the properties which, in common language, or in the scientific classification that we adopt, are taken to constitute the class crow, or the class negro. Now, supposing blackness to be an ultimate property of black objects, or woolly hair an ultimate property of the animals which possess it; supposing that these properties are not results of causation, are not connected with antecedent phenomena by any law; then if all crows are black, and all negroes have woolly hair, *c*these*c* must be ultimate properties of the Kind *crow*, or *negro*, or of some Kind which includes them. If, on the contrary, blackness or woolly hair be an effect depending on causes, these general propositions are mani-festly empirical laws; and all that has already been said respecting that class of generalizations may be applied without modification to these.

Now, we have seen that in the case of all compounds—of all things, in short, except the elementary substances and primary powers of nature—the presumption is, that the properties do really depend upon causes; and it is impossible in any case whatever to be certain that they do not. We therefore should not be safe in claiming for any generalization respecting the co-existence of properties, a degree of certainty to which, if the properties should happen to be the result of causes, it would have no claim. A generalization respecting coexistence, or in other words respecting the properties of Kinds, may be an ultimate truth, but it may, also, be merely a derivative one; and since, if so, it is one of those derivative laws which are neither laws of

*a*MS, 43, 46   an
*b–b*MS, 43, 46   both
*c–c*MS, 43, 46   those

causation, nor have been resolved into the laws of causation on which they depend, it can possess no higher degree of evidence than belongs to an empirical law.

§ 4. [*No universal axiom of coexistence*] This conclusion will be confirmed by the consideration of one great deficiency, which precludes the application to the ultimate uniformities of coexistence, of a system of rigorous *a* scientific induction, such as the uniformities in the succession of phenomena have been found *b*to admit*b* of. The basis of such a system is wanting: there is no general axiom, standing in the same relation to the uniformities of coexistence as the law of causation does to those of succession. The Methods of Induction applicable to the ascertainment of causes and effects, are grounded on the principle that everything which has a beginning must have some cause or other; that among the circumstances which actually existed at the time of its commencement, there is certainly some one *c*combination*c*, on which the effect in question is unconditionally consequent, and on the repetition of which it would certainly again recur. But in an inquiry whether some kind (as crow) universally possesses a certain property (as blackness), there is no room for any assumption analogous to this. We have no previous certainty that the property must have something which constantly coexists with it; must have an invariable coexistent, in the same manner as an event must have an invariable antecedent. When we feel pain, we must be in some circumstances under which if exactly repeated we should always feel pain. But when we are conscious of blackness, it does not follow that there is something *d*else*d* present of which blackness is a constant accompaniment. There is, therefore, no room for elimination; no Method of Agreement or Difference, or of Concomitant Variations (which is but a modification either of the Method of Agreement or of the Method of Difference). We cannot conclude that the blackness we see in crows must be an invariable property of crows, merely because there is nothing else present of which it can be an invariable property. We therefore inquire into the truth of a proposition like "All crows are black," under the same disadvantage as if, in our inquiries into causation, we were compelled to let in, as one of the possibilities, that the effect may in that particular instance have arisen without any cause at all.

To overlook this grand distinction was, as it seems to me, the capital error in Bacon's view of inductive philosophy. The principle of elimination, that great logical instrument which he had the immense merit of first bringing into general use, he deemed applicable in the same sense, and in as un-

*a*MS, 43, 46   and
*b–b*MS, 43   to be susceptible]   46   susceptible
*c–c*MS, 43   or more
d–d+65, 68, 72

qualified a manner, to the investigation of the coexistences, as to that of the successions of phenomena. He seems to have thought that as every event has a cause, or invariable antecedent, so every property of an object has an invariable coexistent, which he called its Form: and the examples he chiefly selected for the application and illustration of his method, were inquiries into such Forms; attempts to determine in what else all those objects resembled, which agreed in some one general property, as hardness or softness, dryness or moistness, heat or coldness. Such inquiries could lead to no result. The objects seldom have any such *circumstances*[e] in common. They usually agree in the one point inquired into, and in nothing else. A great proportion of the properties which, so far as we can conjecture, are the likeliest to be really ultimate, would seem to be inherently properties of many different Kinds of things, not allied in any other respect. And as for the properties which, being effects of causes, we are able to give some account of, they have generally nothing to do with the ultimate resemblances or diversities in the objects themselves, but depend on some outward circumstances, under the influence of which any objects whatever are capable of manifesting those properties; as is emphatically the case with those favourite subjects of Bacon's scientific inquiries, hotness and coldness; as well as with hardness and softness, solidity and fluidity, and many other [f] conspicuous qualities.

In the absence, then, of any universal law of coexistence, similar to the universal law of causation which regulates sequence, we are thrown back upon the unscientific induction of the ancients, *per enumerationem simplicem, ubi non reperitur instantia contradictoria.* The reason we have for believing that all crows are black, is simply that we have seen and heard of many black crows, and never one of any other colour. It remains to be considered how far this evidence can reach, and how we are to measure its strength in any given case.

§ 5. [*The evidence of uniformities of coexistence, how measured*] It sometimes happens that a mere change in the mode of verbally enunciating a question, though nothing is really added to the meaning expressed, is of itself a considerable step towards its solution. This, I think, happens in the present instance. The degree of certainty of any generalization which rests on no other evidence than the agreement, so far as it goes, of all past observation, is but another phrase for the degree of improbability that an exception, if *any*[a] existed, could have hitherto remained unobserved. The reason for believing that all crows are black, is measured by the improbability that crows of any other colour should have existed to the present time without

e—eMS, 43, 46, 51, 56, 62   circumstance
fMS, 43, 46   very
a—aMS, 43, 46   it

our being aware of it. Let us state the question in this last mode, and consider what is implied in the supposition that there may be crows which are not black, and under what conditions we can be justified in regarding this as incredible.

If there really exist crows which are not black, one of two things must be the fact. Either the circumstance of blackness, in all crows hitherto observed, must be, as it were, an accident, not connected with any distinction of Kind; or if it be a property of Kind, the crows which are not black must be a new Kind, a Kind hitherto overlooked, though coming under the same general description by which crows have hitherto been characterized. The first sup-position *would be proved true* if we were to discover casually a white crow among black ones, or if it were found that black crows sometimes turn white. The second would be shown to be the fact if in Australia or Central Africa a species or a race of white or grey crows were found to *exist*.

§ 6. [*When uniformities of coexistence are derivative, their evidence is that of empirical laws*] The former of these suppositions necessarily implies that the colour is an effect of causation. If blackness, in the crows in which it has been observed, be not a property of Kind, but can be present or absent without any difference generally in the properties of the object; then it is not an ultimate fact in the individuals themselves, but is certainly dependent on a cause. There are, no doubt, many properties which vary from individual to individual of the same Kind, even the same *infima species*, or lowest Kind. *Some flowers* may be either white or red, without differing in any other respect. But these properties are not ultimate; they depend on causes. So far as the properties of a thing belong to its own nature, and do not arise from some cause extrinsic to it, they are always the same in the same Kind. *ᵇ* Take, for instance, all simple substances and elementary powers; the only things of which we are certain that some at least of *their* properties are really ulti-mate. Colour is generally esteemed the most variable of all properties: yet we do not find that sulphur is sometimes yellow and sometimes white, or that it varies in colour at all, except so far as colour is the effect of some extrinsic cause, as of the sort of light thrown upon it, the mechanical arrangement of the particles *ᵈ(as after fusion) &c.ᵈ* We do not find that iron is sometimes fluid and sometimes solid at the same temperature; gold sometimes malleable

ᵇMS   is what would be proved

ᶜ⁻ᶜMS, 43, 46   prevail

ᵃ⁻ᵃMS, 43, 46, 51, 56   A flower

ᵇMS, 43, 46, 51, 56, 62   [*footnote:*] *I do not here include among properties the accidents of quantity and local position. Every one is aware that no distinctions of Kind can be grounded upon these; and that they are incident equally to things of different Kinds and to things of the same.

ᶜ⁻ᶜMS, 43, 46   the

ᵈ⁻ᵈ43, 46, 51, 56, 62, 65   &c. (as after fusion) [*printer's error?*]

and sometimes brittle; that hydrogen will sometimes combine with oxygen and sometimes not; or the like. If from simple substances we pass to any of their definite compounds, as water, lime, or sulphuric acid, there is the same constancy in their properties. When properties vary from individual to individual, it is either in the case of miscellaneous aggregations, such as atmospheric air or rock, composed of heterogeneous substances, and not constituting or belonging to any real Kind,* or it is in the case of organic beings. In them, indeed, there is variability in a high degree. Animals of the same species and race, human beings of the same age, sex, and country, will be most different, for example, in face and figure. But organized beings (from the extreme complication of the laws by which they are regulated) being more eminently modifiable, that is, liable to be influenced by a greater number and variety of causes, than any other phenomena whatever; having ᵉalsoᵉ themselves had a beginning, and therefore a cause; there is reason to believe that none of their properties are ultimate, but all of them derivative, and produced by causation. And the presumption is confirmed, by the fact that the properties which vary from one individual to another, also generally vary more or less at different times in the same individual; which variation, like any other event, supposes a cause, and implies, consequently, that the properties are not independent of causation.

If, therefore, blackness be merely accidental in crows, and capable of varying while the Kind remains the same, its presence or absence is doubtless no ultimate fact, but the effect of some unknown cause: and in that case the universality of the experience that all crows are black is sufficient proof of a common cause, and establishes the generalization as an empirical law. Since there are innumerable instances in the affirmative, and hitherto none at all in the negative, the causes on which the property depends must exist everywhere in the limits of the observations which have been made; and the proposition may be received as universal within those limits, and with the allowable degree of extension to adjacent cases.

§ 7. [*So also, when uniformities of coexistence are ultimate, their evidence is that of empirical laws*] If, in the second place, the property, in the instances in which it has been observed, is not an effect of causation, ᵃ it is a property of Kind; and in that case the generalization can only be set aside by the discovery of a new Kind of crow. That, however, a peculiar Kind, not hitherto discovered, should exist in nature, is a supposition so often realized,

*[65] This doctrine of course assumes that the allotropic forms of what is chemically the same substance are so many different Kinds; and such, in the sense in which the word Kind is used in this treatise, they really are.

ᵉ⁻ᵉMS, 43, 46 , moreover,
ᵃMS not accidental,

that it cannot be considered at all improbable. We have nothing to authorize us in attempting to limit the Kinds of things which exist in nature. The only unlikelihood would be that a new Kind should be discovered in localities which there was previously reason to believe had been thoroughly explored; and even this improbability depends on the degree of conspicuousness of the difference between the newly-discovered Kind and all others, since new Kinds of minerals, plants, and even animals, previously overlooked or confounded with known species, are still continually detected in the most frequented situations. On this second ground, therefore, as well as on the first, the observed uniformity of coexistence can only hold good as an empirical law, within the limits not only of actual observation, but of an observation as accurate as the nature of the case required. And hence it is that (as remarked in an early chapter of the present Book) we so often give up generalizations of this class at the first summons. If any credible witness stated that he had seen a white crow, under circumstances which made it not incredible that it should have escaped notice previously, we should give full credence to the statement.

It appears, then, that the uniformities which obtain in the coexistence of phenomena,—those which we have reason to consider as ultimate, no less than those which arise from the laws of causes yet undetected—are entitled to reception only as empirical laws; are not to be presumed true except *within* the limits of time, place, and circumstance, in which the observations were made, or except in cases strictly adjacent.

§ 8. [*The evidence of empirical laws is stronger in proportion as the law is more general*] We have seen in the last chapter that there is a point of generality at which empirical laws become as certain as laws of nature, or rather, at which there is no longer any distinction between empirical laws and laws of nature. As empirical laws approach this point, in other words, as they rise in their degree of generality, they become more certain; their universality may be more strongly relied on. For, in the first place, if they are results of causation (which, even in the class of uniformities treated of in the present chapter, we never can be certain that they are not) the more general they are, the greater is proved to be the space over which the necessary collocations prevail, and within which no causes exist capable of counteracting the unknown causes on which the empirical law depends. To say that anything is an invariable property of some very limited class of objects, is to say that it invariably accompanies some very numerous and complex group of distinguishing properties; which, if causation be at all concerned in the matter, argues a combination of many causes, and therefore a *great liability

*b–b*MS, 43, 46, 51, 56   in
*a*MS, 43, 46   very

to counteraction; while the comparatively narrow range of the observations renders it impossible to predict to what extent unknown counteracting causes may be distributed throughout nature. But when a generalization has been found to hold good of a very large proportion of all things whatever, it is already proved that nearly all the causes which exist in nature have no power over it; that very few changes in the combination of causes can affect it; since the greater number of possible combinations must have already existed in some one or other of the instances in which it has been found true. If, therefore, any empirical law is a result of causation, the more general it is, the more it may be depended on. And even if it be no result of causation, but an ultimate coexistence, the more general it is, the greater amount of experience it is derived from, and the greater therefore is the probability that if exceptions had existed, some would already have presented themselves.

For these reasons, it requires much more evidence to establish an exception to one of the more general empirical laws than to the more special ones. We should not have any difficulty in believing that there might be a new Kind of crow; or a *new* kind of bird resembling a crow in the properties hitherto considered distinctive of that Kind. But it would require stronger proof to convince us of the existence of a Kind of crow having properties at variance with any generally recognised universal property of birds; and a still higher degree if the properties conflict with any recognised universal property of animals. And this is conformable to the mode of judgment recommended by the common sense and general practice of mankind, who are more incredulous as to any novelties in nature, according to the degree of generality of the experience which these novelties seem to contradict.

§ 9. [*Every distinct Kind must be examined*] *It is conceivable that the alleged properties might conflict with some recognised universal property of all matter. In that case their improbability would be at the highest, but would not even then amount to incredibility. There are only two known properties common to all matter; in other words, there is but one known uniformity of coexistence of properties, coextensive with all physical nature: namely, that whatever opposes resistance to movement, gravitates; or, as Professor Bain expresses it, Inertia and Gravity are coexistent through all matter, and proportionate in their amount.[*] These properties, as he truly says, are not mutually implicated; from neither of them could we, on grounds of causation, presume the other. But, for this very reason, we are never certain that a Kind may not be discovered possessing one of the properties without the other. The hypothetical ether, if it exists, may be such a Kind. Our senses

[*Logic, Pt. II, p. 13.]

b–b+46, 51, 56, 62, 65, 68, 72
a–a588+72

cannot recognise in it either resistance or gravity: but if the reality of a resisting medium should eventually be proved (by alteration, for example, in the times of revolution of periodic comets, combined with the evidences afforded by the phenomena of light and heat), it would be rash to conclude from this alone, without other proofs, that it must gravitate.[a]

[b]For even the[b] greater generalizations, which embrace comprehensive Kinds containing under them a great number and variety of *infimæ species*, are only empirical laws, resting on induction by simple enumeration merely, and not on any process of elimination, a process wholly inapplicable to [c]this sort[c] of case. Such generalizations, therefore, ought to be grounded on an examination of all the *infimæ species* comprehended in them, and not of a portion only. We cannot conclude [d](where causation is not concerned),[d] because a proposition is true of a number of things resembling one another only in being animals, that it is therefore true of all animals. If, indeed, anything be true of species which differ more from one another than either differs from a third, (especially if that third species occupies in most of its known properties a position between the two former,) there is some probability that the same thing will also be true of that intermediate species; for it is often, though by no means universally, found, that there is a sort of parallelism in the properties of different Kinds, and that their degree of unlikeness in one respect bears some proportion to their unlikeness in others. We see this parallelism in the properties of the different metals; in those of sulphur, phosphorus, and carbon; of [e] chlorine, iodine, and [f]bromine[f]; in the natural orders of plants and animals, &c. But there are innumerable anomalies and exceptions to this sort of conformity [g]; if indeed the conformity itself be anything[g] but an anomaly and an exception in nature.

Universal propositions, therefore, respecting the properties of superior Kinds, unless grounded on proved or presumed connexion by causation, ought not to be hazarded except after separately examining every known sub-kind included in the larger Kind. And even then such generalizations must be held in readiness to be given up on the occurrence of some new anomaly, which, when the uniformity is not derived from causation, can never, even in the case of the most general of these empirical laws, be considered very improbable. Thus, all the universal propositions which it has been attempted to lay down respecting simple substances, or concerning any of the classes which have been formed among simple substances, (and the attempt has been often made,) have, with the progress of experience, either

b–bMS, 43, 46, 51, 56, 62, 65, 68   Still, however, even these
c–cMS, 43, 46, 51, 56, 62   the kind
d–dMS, 43, 46, 51   , merely
eMS, 43, 46   oxygen,
f–fMS, 43, 46, 51   brome
g–gMS, 43   , or rather the conformity itself is

faded into inanity, or been proved to be erroneous; and each Kind of simple substance remains with its own collection of properties apart from the rest, saving a certain parallelism with a few other Kinds, the most similar to itself. In organized beings, indeed, there are abundance of propositions ascertained to be universally true of superior genera, to many of which the discovery hereafter of any exceptions must be regarded as *h*extremely*h* improbable. But these, as already observed, are, we have every reason to believe, *i*properties*i* dependent on causation.*

Uniformities of coexistence, then, not only when they are consequences of laws of succession, but also when they are ultimate truths, must be ranked, for the *j*purpose*j* of logic, among empirical laws; and are amenable in every respect to the same rules with those unresolved uniformities which are known to be dependent on causation.†

*[72] Professor Bain (*Logic*, Pt. II, p. 13), mentions two empirical laws, which he considers to be, with the exception of the law connecting Gravity with Resistance to motion, "the two most widely operating laws as yet discovered whereby two distinct properties are conjoined throughout substances generally." The first is, "a law connecting Atomic Weight and Specific Heat by an inverse proportion. For equal weights of the simple bodies, the atomic weight multiplied by a number expressing the specific heat, gives a nearly uniform product. The products, for all the elements, are near the constant number 6." The other is a law which obtains "between the specific gravity of substances in the gaseous state, and the atomic weights. The relationship of the two numbers is in some instances equality; in other instances the one is a multiple of the other."

Neither of these generalizations has the smallest appearance of being an ultimate law. They point unmistakeably to higher laws. Since the heat necessary to raise to a given temperature the same weight of different substances (called their specific heat) is inversely as their atomic weight, that is, directly as the number of atoms in a given weight of the substance, it follows that a single atom of every substance requires the same amount of heat to raise it to a given temperature: a most interesting and important law, but a law of causation. The other law mentioned by Mr. Bain points to the conclusion, that in the gaseous state all substances contain, in the same space, the same number of atoms; which, as the gaseous state suspends all cohesive force, might naturally be expected, though it could not have been positively assumed. This law may also be a result of the mode of action of causes, namely, of molecular motions. The cases in which one of the numbers is not identical with the other, but a multiple of it, may be explained on the nowise unlikely supposition, that in our present estimate of the atomic weights of some substances, we mistake two, or three, atoms for one, or one for several.

†[72] Dr. M'Cosh (p. 324 of his book) considers the laws of the chemical composition of bodies as not coming under the principle of Causation; and thinks it an omission in this work not to have provided special Canons for their investigation and proof. But every case of chemical composition is, as I have explained, a case of causation. When it is said that water is composed of hydrogen and oxygen,

*h–h*MS, 43, 46, 51   supremely
*i–i*MS, 43, 46   truths
*j–j*MS, 43, 46, 51, 56   purposes

the affirmation is that hydrogen and oxygen, by the action on one another which they exert under certain conditions, *generate* the properties of water. The Canons of Induction, therefore, as laid down in this treatise, are applicable to the case. Such special adaptations as the Inductive methods may require in their application to chemistry, or any other science, are a proper subject for any one who treats of the logic of the special sciences, as Professor Bain has done in the latter part of his work; but they do not appertain to General Logic.

Dr. M'Cosh also complains (p. 325) that I have given no canons for those sciences in which "the end sought is not the discovery of Causes or of Composition, but of Classes; that is, Natural Classes." Such canons could be no other than the principles and rules of Natural Classification, which I certainly thought that I had expounded at considerable length. But this is far from the only instance in which Dr. M'Cosh does not appear to be aware of the contents of the books he is criticizing.

CHAPTER XXIII

Of Approximate Generalizations, and Probable Evidence

§ 1. [*The inferences called probable, rest on approximate generalizations*] In our inquiries into the nature of the inductive process, we *must not confine* our notice to such generalizations from experience as profess to be universally true. *There is a class of inductive truths* avowedly not universal; in which it is not pretended that the predicate is always true of the subject; but the value of which, as generalizations, is nevertheless extremely great. An important portion of the field of inductive knowledge does not consist of universal truths, but of approximations to such truths; and when a conclusion is said to rest on probable evidence, the premises it is drawn from are usually generalizations of this sort.

As every certain inference respecting a particular case, implies that there is ground for a general proposition, of the form, Every A is B; so does every probable inference suppose that there is ground for a proposition of the form, Most A are B: and the degree of probability of the inference in an average case, will depend on the proportion between the number of instances existing in nature which accord with the generalization, and the number of those which conflict with it.

§ 2. [*Approximate generalizations less useful in science than in life*] Propositions in the form, Most A are B, are of a very different degree of importance in science, and in the practice of life. To the scientific inquirer they are valuable chiefly as materials for, and steps towards, universal truths. The discovery of these is the proper end of science: its work is not done if it stops at the proposition that a majority of A are B, without circumscribing

---

*a–a*MS, 43, 46 have hitherto confined
*b–b*MS, 43, 46 We indeed recognised a distinction between generalizations which are certain and those which are only probable: but the propositions themselves, though they differed in being more or less doubtful in the one case, and not at all doubtful in the other, were always of the form, Every A is B; they claimed nothing less than universality, whatever might be the completeness or the incompleteness of our assurance of their truth. There remain, however, a class of propositions

that majority by some common character, *fitted to distinguish* them from the minority. Independently of the inferior precision of such imperfect generalizations, and the inferior assurance with which they can be applied to individual cases, it is plain that, compared with exact generalizations, they are almost useless as means of discovering ulterior truths by way of deduction. We may, it is true, by combining the proposition Most A are B, with an universal proposition, Every B is C, arrive at the conclusion that Most A are C. But when a second proposition of the approximate kind is introduced,— or even when there is but one, if that one be the major premise,—nothing can *in general* be positively concluded. When the major is Most B are D, then, even if the minor be Every A is B, we cannot infer that most A are D, or with any certainty that even some A are D. Though the majority of the class B have the attribute signified by D, the whole of the sub-class A may belong to the minority.*

Though so little use can be made, in science, of approximate generalizations, except as a stage on the road to something better, for practical guidance they are often all we have to rely on. Even when science has really determined the universal laws of any phenomenon, not only are those laws generally too much encumbered with conditions to be adapted for every-day use, but the cases which present themselves in life are too complicated, and our decisions require to be taken too rapidly, to admit of waiting till the existence of a phenomenon can be proved by what have been scientifically ascertained to be universal marks of it. To be indecisive and reluctant to act, because we have not evidence of a perfectly conclusive character to act on, is a defect sometimes incident to scientific minds, but which, *wherever* it exists, renders them unfit for practical emergencies. If we would succeed in action, we must judge by indications which, though they do not generally mislead us, sometimes do; and *must* make up, as far as possible, for the incomplete conclusiveness of any one indication, by obtaining others to corroborate it. The principles of induction applicable to approximate generalization are therefore a not less important subject of inquiry, than the rules for the investigation of universal truths; and might reasonably be expected to detain us almost as long, were it not that these principles are mere corollaries from those which have been already treated of.

*[51] Mr. De Morgan, in his *Formal Logic*, [p. 139,] makes the just remark, that from two such premises as Most A are B, and Most A are C, we may infer with certainty that some B are C. But this is the utmost limit of the conclusions which can be drawn from two approximate generalizations, when the precise degree of their approximation to universality is unknown or undefined.

a–aMS   that distinguishes   b–b+51, 56, 62, 65, 68, 72
c–cMS   whenever [*printer's error?*]   d–d+43, 46, 51, 56, 62, 65, 68, 72

§ 3. [*In what cases approximate generalizations* ^{a}*may*^{a} *be resorted to*]
There are two sorts of cases in which we are forced to guide ourselves by
generalizations of the imperfect form, Most A are B. The first is, when we
have no others; when we have not been able to carry our investigation of the
laws of the phenomena any farther: as in the following propositions: Most
dark-eyed persons have dark hair; Most springs contain mineral substances;
Most stratified formations contain fossils. The importance of this class of
generalizations is not very great; for, though it frequently happens that we
see no reason why that which is true of most individuals of a class is not true
of the remainder, nor are able to bring the former under any general description which can distinguish them from the latter, yet if we are willing to be
satisfied with propositions of a less degree of generality, and to break down
the class A into sub-classes, we may generally obtain a collection of propositions exactly true. We do not know why most wood is lighter than water,
nor can we point out any general property which discriminates wood that is
lighter than water from that which is heavier. But we know exactly what
species are the one and what the other. And if we meet with a specimen not
conformable to any known species (the only case in which our previous
knowledge affords no other guidance than the approximate generalization),
we can generally make a specific experiment, ^{b}which is a surer^b resource.

It ^{c}often^c happens, however, that the proposition, Most A are B, is not the
ultimatum of our scientific ^{d}attainments^d, though the knowledge we possess
beyond it cannot conveniently be brought to bear upon the particular instance. ^{e}We may^e know well enough what circumstances ^{f} distinguish the
portion of A which ^{g}has the attribute B from the portion which has^g it not,
but ^{h}may have no means, or may not have^h time, to examine whether those
characteristic circumstances exist or not in the individual case. This is ^{i}the
situation we are generally^i in when the inquiry is of the kind called moral, that
is, of the kind which ^{j}has^j in view to predict human actions. To enable us to
affirm anything universally concerning the actions of classes of ^{k}human
beings^k, the classification must be grounded on the circumstances of their
mental culture and habits, which in an individual case are seldom exactly

$^{a-a}$MS, 43, 46 *must*
$^{b-b}$MS always a safer] 43, 46 which is always a safer] 51, 56 which is a safer
$^{c-c}$MS, 43, 46, 51, 56, 62 oftener
$^{d-d}$MS, 43, 46, 51, 56, 62, 65, 68 progress
$^{e-e}$MS, 43, 46, 51, 56, 62, 65, 68 In such a case we
^{f}MS, 43, 46 really
$^{g-g}$MS, 43, 46, 51, 56 have the . . . which have [*sic*]
$^{h-h}$MS, 43, 46, 51 have no means, or no] 56, 62, 65, 68 have no means, or have
not
$^{i-i}$MS, 43, 46 generally the situation we are
$^{j-j}$MS, 43, 46 have
$^{k-k}$MS, 43, 46 men

known; and classes grounded on these distinctions would never precisely accord with those into which mankind are [l] divided for social purposes. All propositions which can be framed respecting the actions of [m]human beings[m] as ordinarily classified, or as classified according to any kind of outward indications, are merely approximate. We can only say, Most [n]persons[n] of a particular age, profession, country, or rank in society, have such and such qualities; or, Most persons when placed in certain circumstances act in such and such a way. Not that we do not [o]often[o] know well enough on what causes the qualities depend, or what sort of persons they are who act in that particular way; but we have seldom the means of knowing whether any individual person has been under the influence of those causes, or is a person of that particular sort. We could replace the approximate generalizations by propositions universally true; but these would hardly ever be capable of being applied to practice. We should be sure of our majors, but we should not be able to get minors [p]to fit[p]: we are forced, therefore, to draw our conclusions from coarser and more fallible indications.

§ 4. [*In what manner approximate generalizations are proved*] Proceeding now to consider, what is to be regarded as sufficient evidence of an approximate generalization; we can have no difficulty in at once recognising that when admissible at all, it is admissible only as an empirical law. Propositions of the form, Every A is B, are not necessarily laws of causation, or ultimate uniformities of coexistence; propositions like Most A are B, *cannot* be so. Propositions hitherto found true in every observed instance, may yet be no necessary [a]consequence[a] of laws of causation, or of ultimate uniformities, and unless they are so, may, for aught we know, be false beyond the limits of actual observation: still more evidently must this be the case with propositions which are only true in a mere majority of the observed instances.

There is some difference, however, in the degree of certainty of the proposition, Most A are B, according as that approximate generalization composes the whole of our knowledge of the subject, or not. Suppose, first, that the former is the case. We know only that most A are B, not why they are so, nor in what respect those which are, differ from those which are not. How then did we learn that most A are B? Precisely in the manner in which we should have learnt, had such happened to be the fact, that all A are B. We collected a number of instances sufficient to eliminate chance, and having done so, compared the number of instances in the affirmative with the number in the negative. The result, like other unresolved derivative laws, can be relied on solely within the limits not only of place and time, but also of

[l]MS, 43, 46   necessarily   [m–m]MS, 43, 46   men
[n–n]MS, 43, 46   men   [o–o]MS, 43, 46   in general
[p–p]MS, 43, 46, 51, 56, 62, 65   corresponding to them
[a–a]51, 56, 62, 65   consequences

circumstance, under which its truth has been actually observed; for as we are supposed to be ignorant of the causes which make the proposition true, we cannot tell in what manner any new circumstance might perhaps affect it. The proposition, Most judges are inaccessible to bribes, would *probably* be found true of Englishmen, Frenchmen, Germans, North Americans, and so forth; but if on this evidence alone we extended the assertion to Orientals, we should step beyond the limits, not only of place but of circumstance, within which the fact had been observed, and *should* let in possibilities of the absence of the determining causes, or *d* the presence of counteracting ones, which might be fatal to the approximate generalization.

In the case where the approximate proposition is not the ultimatum of our scientific knowledge, but only the most available form of it for *e* practical guidance; where we know, not only that most A have the attribute B, but also the causes of B, or some properties by which the portion of A which has that attribute is distinguished from the portion which has it not; we are rather more favourably situated than in the preceding case. For we have now a double mode of ascertaining whether it be true that most A are B; the direct mode, as before, and an indirect one, that of examining whether the proposition admits of being deduced from the known cause, or from *any* known criterion, of B. Let the question, for example, be whether most Scotchmen can read? We may not have observed, or received the testimony of others respecting, a sufficient number and variety of Scotchmen to ascertain this fact; but when we consider that the cause of being able to read is the having been taught it, another mode of determining the question presents itself, namely, by inquiring whether most Scotchmen have been sent to schools where reading is effectually taught. Of these two modes, sometimes one and sometimes the other is the more available. In some cases, the frequency of the effect is the more accessible to that extensive and varied observation which is indispensable to the establishment of an empirical law; at other times, the frequency of the causes, or of some collateral indications. It commonly happens that neither is susceptible of so satisfactory an induction as could be desired, and that the grounds on which the conclusion is received are compounded of both. Thus a *person* may believe that most Scotchmen can read, because, so far as his information extends, most Scotchmen have been sent to school, and most Scotch schools teach reading effectually; and also because most of the Scotchmen whom he has known or heard of, could read; though *neither of these two sets of observations* may by itself fulfil the necessary conditions of extent and variety.

Although the approximate generalization may in most cases be indispens-

b–b+72

*d*MS of

*f–f*MS, 43, 46   the

*h–h*MS   of these two sets of observations neither

c–c+43, 46, 51, 56, 62, 65, 68, 72

*e*MS, 43, 46   our

*g–g*MS, 43, 46   man

able for our guidance, even when we know the cause, or some certain mark, of the attribute predicated; it needs hardly be observed that we may always replace the uncertain indication by a certain one, in any case in which we can actually recognise the existence of the cause or mark. For example, an assertion is made by a witness, and the question is, whether to believe it. If we do not look to any of the individual circumstances of the case, we have nothing to direct us but the approximate generalization, that truth is more common than falsehood, or, in other words, that most persons, on most occasions, speak truth. But if we consider in what circumstances the cases *where* truth is spoken differ from those in which it is not, we find, for instance, the following: the witness's being an honest *person* or not; his being an accurate observer or not; his having an interest to serve in the matter or not. Now, not only may we be able to obtain other approximate generalizations respecting the degree of frequency of these various possibilities, but we may know which of them is positively realized in the individual case. That the witness has or has not an interest to serve, we *perhaps* know directly; and the other two points indirectly, by means of marks; as, for example, from his conduct on some former occasion; or from his reputation, which, though *a very uncertain* mark, affords an approximate generalization (as, for instance, Most persons who are *believed to be* honest by those with whom they have had frequent dealings, are really so) which approaches nearer to an universal truth than the approximate general proposition with which we set out, viz. Most persons on most occasions speak truth.

As it seems unnecessary to dwell *n* further on the question of the evidence of approximate generalizations, we shall proceed to a not less important topic, that of the cautions to be observed in arguing from these incompletely universal propositions to particular cases.

§ 5. [*With what precautions approximate generalizations may be employed*] So far as regards the direct application of an approximate generalization to an individual instance, this question presents no difficulty. If the proposition, Most A are B, has been established, by a sufficient induction, as an empirical law, we may conclude that any particular A is B with a probability proportioned to the preponderance of the number of affirmative instances over the number of exceptions. If it has been found practicable to attain numerical precision in the data, a corresponding degree of precision may be given to the evaluation of the chances of error in the conclusion. If it can be established as an empirical law that nine out of every ten A are B, there will be one chance in ten of error in assuming that any A, not indivi-

---

*i-i*MS, 43, 46, 51   when
*k-k*MS, 43, 46   may
*m-m*MS, 43, 46   reputed

*j-j*MS, 43   man
*l-l*MS, 43, 46   not a sure
*n*MS, 43, 46   any

dually known to us, is a B: but this of course holds only within the limits of time, place, and circumstance, embraced in the observations, and therefore cannot be counted on for any sub-class or variety of A (or for A in any set of external circumstances) which were not included in the average. It must be added, that we can *a*guide ourselves by the proposition, Nine out of every ten A are B, only*a* in cases of which we know nothing except that they fall within the class A. For if we know, of any particular instance *i*, not only that it falls under A, but to what species or variety of A it belongs, we shall generally err in applying to *i* the average struck for the whole genus, from which the average corresponding to that species alone would, in all probability, materially differ. And so if *i*, instead of being a particular sort of instance, is an instance known to be under the influence of a particular set of circumstances. The presumption drawn from the numerical proportions in the whole genus would probably, in such a case, only mislead. A general average should only be applied to *b*cases which are neither known, nor can be presumed, to be other than average cases*b*. Such averages, therefore, are commonly of little use for the practical guidance of any affairs but those which concern large numbers. Tables of the chances of life are useful to insurance offices, but they go a very little way towards informing any one of the chances of his own life, or any other life in which he is interested, since almost every life is either better or worse than the average. Such averages can only be considered as supplying the first term in a series of approximations; the subsequent terms proceeding on an appreciation of the circumstances belonging to the particular case.

§ 6. [*The two modes of combining probabilities*] From the application of a single approximate generalization to individual cases, we proceed to the application of two or more of them together to the same case.

When a judgment applied to an individual instance is grounded on two approximate generalizations taken in conjunction, the propositions may co-operate towards the result in two different ways. In the one, each proposition is separately applicable to the case in hand, and our object in combining them is to give to the conclusion in that particular case the double probability arising from the two propositions separately. This may be called joining two probabilities by way of Addition; and the result is a probability greater than either. The other mode is, when only one of the propositions is directly applicable to the case, the second being only applicable to it by virtue of the application of the first. This is joining two probabilities by way of *a*Ratiocination or*a* Deduction; the result of which is a less probability than either.

a–aMS, 43, 46   only guide . . . B,
b–bMS, 43, 46   a case which is neither . . . than an average case
a–a+56, 62, 65, 68, 72

The type of the first argument is, Most A are B; most C are B; this thing is both an A and a C; therefore it is probably a B. The type of the second is, Most A are B; most C are A; this is a C; therefore it is probably an A, therefore it is probably a B. The first is exemplified when we prove a fact by the testimony of two unconnected witnesses; the second, when we adduce only the testimony of one witness that he has heard the thing asserted by another. Or again, in the first mode it may be argued that the accused committed the crime, because he concealed himself, and because his clothes were stained with blood; in the second, that he committed it because he *washed or destroyed* his clothes, which is supposed to render it probable that they were stained with blood. Instead of only two links, as in these instances, we may suppose chains of any length. A chain of the former kind was termed by *Bentham** a self-corroborative chain of evidence; the second, a self-infirmative chain.

When approximate generalizations are joined by way of addition, *we may deduce* from the theory of probabilities laid down in a former chapter, in what manner each of them adds to the probability of a conclusion which has the warrant of them all.

*If *, on an average,* two of every three *As are Bs, and three of every four Cs are Bs*, the probability that something which is both an A and a C is a B, will be more than two in three, or than three in four. Of every twelve things which are As, all except four are Bs by the supposition; and if the whole twelve, and consequently those four, have the characters of C likewise, three *of these* will be Bs on that ground. Therefore, out of twelve which are both As and Cs, eleven are Bs. To state the argument in another way; a thing which is both *an A and a C, but which is not a* B, is found in only one of three sections of the class A, and in only one of four sections of the class C; but this fourth of C being spread over the whole of A indiscriminately, only one-third part of it (or one-twelfth of the whole number) belongs to the third section of A; therefore a thing which is not *a* B occurs only once, among

Rationale of Judicial Evidence [ed. J. S. Mill. 5 vols. London: Hunt and Clarke, 1827], Vol. III, p. 224n.

*b−b*MS burnt] 43 washed or burnt
*c*MS, 43, 46 Mr.
*d−d*MS, 43, 46, 51, 56, 62 it is easily seen
*e*MS, 43, 46, 51, 56, 62 [*no paragraph*]] 65 [*paragraph*] In the former editions of this treatise, the joint probability arising from the sum of two independent probabilities was estimated in the following manner.] 68 [*paragraph*] In the early editions . . . *as* 65
f−f+46, 51, 56, 62, 65, 68, 72
*g−g*MS, 43, 46, 51, 56, 62 A are B, and three of every four C are B [*throughout this paragraph* MS, 43, 46, 51, 56, 62 *read* A, B, *and* C *for* As, Bs, *and* Cs]
*h−h*MS, 43 more
*i−i*MS, 43, 46, 51, 56, 62 A and C, but which is not
j−j+65, 68, 72

twelve things which are both As and Cs. The argument would in the language of the doctrine of chances, be thus expressed: the chance that an A is not ^{k}a^k B is ⅓, the chance that a C is not ^{l}a^l B is ¼; hence if the thing be both an A and a C, the chance is ⅓ of ¼ $= \frac{1}{12}$.* ^{n}

*[72] ^{m}The evaluation of the chances in this statement has been objected to by a mathematical friend [G. C. De Morgan]. The correct mode, in his opinion, of setting out the possibilities is as follows. If the thing (let us call it T) which is both an A and a C, is a B, something is true which is only true twice in every thrice, and something else which is only true thrice in every four times. The first fact being true eight times in twelve, and the second being true six times in every eight, and consequently six times in those eight; both facts will be true only six times in twelve. On the other hand if T, although it is both an A and a C, is not a B, something is true which is only true once in every thrice, and something else which is only true once in every four times. The former being true four times out of twelve, and the latter once in every four, and therefore once in those four; both are only true in one case out of twelve. So that T is a B six times in twelve, and T is not a B, only once: making the comparative probabilities, not eleven to one, as I had previously made them, but six to one.^{m}

In the last edition I accepted this reasoning as conclusive. More attentive consideration however has convinced me that it contains a fallacy.

The objector argues, that the fact of A's being a B is true eight times in twelve, and the fact of C's being a B six times in eight, and consequently six times in those eight; both facts therefore are true only six times in every twelve. That is, he concludes that because among As taken indiscriminately only eight out of twelve are Bs and the remaining four are not, it must equally hold that four out of twelve are not Bs when the twelve are taken from the select portion of As which are also Cs. And by this assumption he arrives at the strange result, that there are fewer Bs among things which are both As and Cs than there are among either As or Cs taken indiscriminately; so that a thing which has both chances of being a B, is less likely to be so than if it had only the one chance or only the other.

The objector (as has been acutely remarked by another correspondent) applies to the problem under consideration, a mode of calculation only suited to the

$^{k-k}$+65, 68, 72
$^{l-l}$+65, 68, 72
$^{m-m}$65, 68   [see variant ^{n} below]
^{n}65, 68   [paragraph] It has, however, been pointed out to me by a mathematical friend, that in this statement the evaluation of the chances is erroneous. The correct mode of setting . . . as in 72 footnote above . . . six to one.

It may be asked, what happens in the remaining cases? since in this calculation seven out of twelve cases seem to have exhausted the possibilities. If T is a B in only six cases of every twelve, and a not-B in only one, what is it in the other five? The only supposition remaining for those cases is that it is neither a B nor not a B, which is impossible. But this impossibility merely proves that the state of things supposed in the hypothesis does not exist in those cases. They are cases that do not furnish anything which is both an A and a C.

To make this intelligible, we will substitute for our symbols a concrete case. Let there be two witnesses, M and N, whose probabilities of veracity correspond with the ratios of the preceding example: M speaks truth twice in every thrice, N thrice in every four times. The question is, what is the probability that a statement, in which they both concur, will be true. The cases may be classed as follows. Both the witnesses will speak truly

In this computation it is of course supposed that the probabilities arising from A and C are independent of *each other*. There must not be any such connexion between A and C, that when a thing belongs to the one class it will therefore belong to the other, or even have a greater chance of doing so. *Otherwise the not-Bs which are Cs may be, most or even all of them, identi-

---

reverse problem. Had the question been—If two of every three Bs are As and three out of every four Bs are Cs, how many Bs will be both As and Cs, his reasoning would have been correct. For the Bs that are both As and Cs must be fewer than either the Bs that are As or the Bs that are Cs, and to find their number we must abate either of these numbers in the ratio due to the other. But when the problem is to find, not how many Bs are both As and Cs, but how many things that are both As and Cs are Bs, it is evident that among these the proportion of Bs must be not less, but greater, than among things which are only A, or among things which are only B.

The true theory of the chances is best found by going back to the scientific grounds on which the proportions rest. The degree of frequency of a coincidence depends on, and is a measure of, the frequency, combined with the efficacy, of the causes in operation that are favourable to it. If out of every twelve As taken indiscriminately eight are Bs and four are not, it is implied that there are causes operating on A which tend to make it a B, and that these causes are sufficiently constant and sufficiently powerful to succeed in eight out of twelve cases, but fail in the remaining four. So if of twelve Cs, nine are Bs and three are not, there must be causes of the same tendency operating on C, which succeed in nine cases and fail in three. Now suppose twelve cases which are both As and Cs. The whole twelve are now under the operation of both sets of causes. One set is sufficient to prevail in eight of the twelve cases, the other in nine. The analysis of the cases shews that six of the twelve will be Bs through the operation of both sets of causes; two more in virtue of the causes operating on A; and three more through those operating on C, and that there will be only one case in which all the causes will be inoperative. The total number therefore which are Bs will be eleven in twelve, and the evaluation in the text is correct.

---

six in every twelve times; both falsely once in twelve times. Therefore, if they both agree in an assertion, it will be true six times, for once that it will be false. What happens in the remaining cases is here evident; there will be five cases in every twelve in which the witnesses will not agree. M will speak truth and N falsehood in two cases of every twelve; N will speak truth and M falsehood in three cases, making in all five. In these cases, however, the witnesses will not agree in their testimony. But disagreement between them is excluded by the supposition. There are, therefore, only seven cases which are within the conditions of the hypothesis; of which seven, veracity exists in six, and falsehood in one. Resuming our former symbols, in five cases out of twelve T is not both an A and a C, but an A only, or a C only. The cases in which it is both are only seven, in six of which it is a B, in one not a B, making the chance six to one, or $\frac{6}{7}$ and $\frac{1}{7}$ respectively.

*–*MS, 43, 46, 51, 56, 62   This argument presupposes (as the reader will doubtless have remarked)]   65, 68   In this correct, as in the former incorrect computation, it is of course presupposed

*–*MS, 43, 46   one another

*–*MS, 43, 46, 51, 56, 62   Else the fourth section of C, instead of being equally dis-

cal with the not-Bs which are As^q; in which last case the probability arising from A and C together ^{r}will^r be no greater than that arising from A alone.

When approximate generalizations are joined together in the other mode, that of deduction, the degree of probability of the inference, instead of increasing, diminishes at each step. From two such premises as Most A are B, Most B are C, we cannot with certainty conclude that even a single A is C; for the whole of the portion of A which in any way falls under B, may perhaps be comprised in the exceptional part of it. Still, the two propositions in question afford an appreciable probability that any given A is C, provided the average on which the second proposition is grounded, was taken fairly with reference to the first; provided the proposition, Most B are C, was arrived at in a manner leaving no suspicion that the probability arising from it is otherwise than fairly distributed over the section of B which belongs to A. For though the instances which are A *may* be all in the minority, they may, also, be all in the majority; and the one possibility is to be set against the other. On the whole, the probability arising from the two propositions taken together, will be correctly measured by the probability arising from the one, abated in the ratio of that arising from the other. If nine out of ten Swedes have light hair, and eight out of nine inhabitants of Stockholm are Swedes, the probability arising from these two propositions, that any given inhabitant of Stockholm is light-haired, will amount to eight in ten; though it is rigorously possible ^{s} that the whole Swedish population of Stockholm ^{t}might^t belong to that tenth section of the people of Sweden who are an exception to the rest.

If the premises are known to be true not of a bare majority, but of nearly the whole, of their respective subjects, we may go on joining one such proposition to another for several steps, before we reach a conclusion not presumably true even of a majority. The error of the conclusion will amount to the aggregate of the errors of all the premises. Let the proposition, Most A are B, be true of nine in ten; Most B are C, of eight in nine: then not only will one A in ten not be C, because not B, but even of the nine-tenths which are B, only eight-ninths will be C: that is, the cases of A which are C will be only $\frac{8}{9}$ of $\frac{9}{10}$, or four-fifths. Let us now add Most C are D, and suppose this to be true of seven cases out of eight; the proportion of A which is D will be only $\frac{7}{8}$ of $\frac{8}{9}$ of $\frac{9}{10}$, or $\frac{7}{10}$. Thus the probability progressively dwindles. The experience, however, on which our approximate generalizations are grounded, has so rarely been subjected to, or admits of, accurate numerical estimation, that we cannot in general apply any measurement to the diminution of prob-

tributed over the three sections of A, might be comprised in greater proportion, or even wholly, in the third section
$^{r-r}$MS, 43, 46, 51, 56, 62   would ^{s}MS, 43   (however improbable)
$^{t-t}$MS, 43   may

ability which takes place at each illation; but must be content with remembering that it does diminish at every step, and that unless the premises approach very nearly indeed to being *universally true*, the conclusion after a very few steps is worth nothing. A hearsay of a hearsay, or an argument from presumptive evidence depending not on immediate marks but on marks of marks, is worthless at a very few removes from the first stage.

§ 7. [*How approximate generalizations may be converted into accurate generalizations equivalent to them*] There are, however, two cases in which reasonings depending on approximate generalizations may be carried to any length we please with as much assurance, and are as strictly scientific, as if they were composed of universal laws of nature. *But* these cases are exceptions of the sort which are currently said to prove the rule. The approximate generalizations are as suitable, in the cases in question, for purposes of ratiocination, as if they were complete generalizations, because they are *capable of being* transformed into complete generalizations exactly equivalent.

First: If the approximate generalization is of the class in which *our reason for stopping at the approximation is not the impossibility, but only* the inconvenience, of going further; if we are cognizant of the character which distinguishes the cases that accord with the generalization from those which are exceptions to it; we may then substitute for the approximate proposition, an universal proposition with a proviso. The proposition, Most persons who have uncontrolled power employ it ill, is a generalization of this class, and may be transformed into the following:—All persons who have uncontrolled power employ it ill, provided they are not persons of unusual strength of judgment *and rectitude of purpose*. The proposition, carrying the hypothesis or proviso with it, may then be dealt with no longer as an approximate, but as an universal proposition; and to whatever number of steps the reasoning may reach, the hypothesis, being carried forward to the conclusion, will exactly indicate how far that conclusion is from being applicable universally. If in the course of the argument other approximate generalizations are introduced, each of them being in like manner expressed as an universal proposition with a condition annexed, the sum of all the conditions will appear at the end as the sum of all the errors which affect the conclusion. Thus, to the proposition last cited, let us add the following:—All absolute monarchs have uncontrolled power, unless their position is such that they need the active support of their subjects (as was the case with Queen

*u–u*MS, 43, 46   universal truths   *a–a*MS, 43, 46, 51   Both
b–b+43, 46, 51, 56, 62, 65, 68, 72
*c–c*MS   we stop at the approximation not from the impossibility but only from
*d–d*MS, 43, 46   and will, and confirmed habits of virtue]   51   , goodness of heart, and rectitude of purpose

Elizabeth, Frederick of Prussia, and others). Combining these two propositions, we can deduce from them an universal conclusion, which will be subject to both the hypotheses in the premises; All absolute monarchs employ their power ill, unless their position makes them need the active support of their subjects, or unless they are persons of unusual strength of judgment *and rectitude of purpose*. It is of no consequence how rapidly the errors in our premises accumulate, if we are able in this manner to record each error, and keep an account of the aggregate as it swells up.

Secondly: there is a case in which approximate propositions, even without our taking note of the conditions under which they are not true of individual cases, are yet, for the purposes of science, universal ones; namely, in the *f* inquiries which relate to the properties not of individuals, but of multitudes. The principal of these is the science of politics, or of human society. This science is principally concerned with the actions not of solitary individuals, but of masses; with the fortunes not of single persons, but of communities. For the statesman, therefore, it is generally enough to know that *most* persons act or are acted upon in a particular way; since his speculations and his practical arrangements refer almost exclusively to cases in which the whole community, or some large portion of it, is acted upon at once, and in which, therefore, what is done or felt by *most* persons determines the result produced by or upon the body at large. He can get on well enough with approximate generalizations on human nature, since what is true approximately of all individuals is true absolutely of all masses. And even when the operations of individual men have a part to play in his deductions, as when he is reasoning of kings, or other single rulers, still, as he is providing for indefinite duration, involving an indefinite succession of such individuals, he must in general both reason and act as if what is true of most persons were true of all.

The two kinds of considerations above adduced are a sufficient refutation of the popular error, that speculations on society and government, as resting on merely probable evidence, must be inferior in certainty and scientific accuracy to the conclusions of what are called the exact sciences, and less to be relied on in practice. There are reasons enough why the moral sciences must remain inferior to at least the more perfect of the physical: why the laws of their more complicated phenomena cannot be so completely deciphered, nor the phenomena predicted with the same degree of assurance. But though we cannot attain to so many truths, there is no reason that those we can attain should deserve less reliance, or have less of a scientific character. Of this topic, however, *gIg* shall treat more systematically in the concluding Book, to which place any further consideration of it must be deferred.

---

*e–e*MS, 43, 46   and will, and confirmed habits of virtue]   51   , goodness of heart, and rectitude of purpose
*f*MS, 43, 46   scientific   *g–g*MS, 43, 46   we

CHAPTER XXIV

Of the Remaining Laws of Nature

§ 1. [*Propositions which assert mere existence*] In the First Book, we found that all the assertions which can be conveyed by language, express some one or more of five different things: Existence; Order in Place; Order in Time; Causation; and Resemblance.* Of these, Causation, in our view of the subject, not being fundamentally different from Order in Time, the five species of possible assertions are reduced to four. The propositions which affirm Order in Time, in either of its two modes, Coexistence and Succession, have formed, thus far, the subject of the present Book. And we have now concluded the exposition, so far as it falls within the limits assigned to this work, of the nature of the evidence on which these propositions rest, and the processes of investigation by which they are ^aascertained^a and proved. There remain three classes of facts: Existence, Order in Place, and Resemblance; in regard to which the same questions are now to be resolved.

Regarding the first of these, very little needs be said. Existence in general, is a subject not for our science, but for ^b metaphysics. To determine what things can be recognised as really existing, independently of our own sensible or other impressions, and in what meaning the term is, in that case, predicated of them, belongs to the consideration of "Things in themselves," from which, throughout this work, we have as much as possible kept aloof. Existence, so far as Logic is concerned about it, has reference only to phenomena; to actual, or possible, states of external or internal consciousness, in ourselves or others. Feelings of sensitive beings, or possibilities of having such feelings, are the only things the existence of which can be a subject of logical induction, because the only things of which the existence in individual cases can be a subject of experience.

It is true that a thing is said by us to exist, even when it is absent, and therefore is not and cannot be perceived. But even then, its existence is to us only another word for our conviction that we should perceive it on a certain supposition; ^cnamely, if we were^c in the needful circumstances of time and

*Supra, Bk. I, Chap. v [pp. 99ff.].

^{a–a}MS, 43, 46   discovered   ^bMS, 43, 46   the higher
^{c–c}MS, 43, 46   if we were placed

place, and endowed with the needful perfection of organs. My belief that the Emperor of China exists, is simply my belief that if I were transported to the imperial palace or some other locality in Pekin, I should see him. My belief that Julius Cæsar existed, is my belief that I should have seen him if I had been present in the field of Pharsalia, or in the senate-house at Rome. When I believe that stars exist beyond the utmost range of my vision, though assisted by the most powerful telescopes yet invented, my belief, philosophically expressed, is, that with still better telescopes, if such existed, I could see them, or that they may be perceived by beings less remote from them in space, or whose capacities of perception are superior to mine.

The existence, therefore, of a phenomenon, is but another word for its being perceived, or for the inferred possibility of perceiving it. When the phenomenon is within the range of present observation, by present observation we assure ourselves of its existence; when it is beyond that range, and is therefore said to be absent, we infer its existence from marks or evidences. But what can these evidences be? Other phenomena; ascertained by induction to be connected with the given phenomenon, either in the way of succession or of coexistence. The simple existence, therefore, of an individual phenomenon, when not directly perceived, is inferred from some inductive law of succession or coexistence: and is consequently not amenable to any peculiar inductive principles. We prove the existence of a thing, by proving that it is connected by succession or coexistence with some known thing.

With respect to *general* propositions of this class, that is, which affirm the bare fact of existence, they have a peculiarity which renders the logical treatment of them a very easy matter; they are generalizations which are sufficiently proved by a single instance. That ghosts, or unicorns, or sea-serpents exist, would be fully established if it could be ascertained positively that such things had been even once seen. Whatever has once happened, is capable of happening again; the only question relates to the conditions under which it happens.

So far, therefore, as relates to simple existence, the Inductive Logic has no knots to untie. And we may proceed to the remaining two of the great classes into which facts have been divided; Resemblance, and Order in *d*Place*d*.

§ 2. [*Resemblance, considered as a subject of science*] Resemblance and its opposite, except in the case in which they assume the names of Equality and Inequality, are seldom regarded as subjects of science; they are supposed to be perceived by simple apprehension; by merely applying our senses or directing our attention to the two objects at once, or in immediate succession. And this simultaneous, or virtually simultaneous, application of our faculties

*d–d*MS, 43, 46, 51, 56, 62, 65, 68   Space

to the two things which are to be compared, does necessarily constitute the ultimate appeal, wherever such application is practicable. But, in most cases, it is not practicable: the objects cannot be brought so *close* together that the feeling of their resemblance (at least a complete feeling of it) directly arises in the mind. We can only compare each of them with some third object, capable of being transported from one to the other. And besides, even when the objects can be brought into immediate juxtaposition, their resemblance or difference is but imperfectly known to us, unless we have compared them minutely, part by part. Until this has been done, things in reality very dissimilar often appear undistinguishably alike. Two lines of very unequal length will appear about equal when lying in different directions; but place them parallel with their farther extremities even, and if *we* look at the nearer extremities, their inequality becomes a matter of direct perception.

To ascertain whether, and in what, two phenomena resemble or differ, is not always, therefore, so easy a thing as it might at first appear. When the two cannot be brought into juxtaposition, or not so that the observer is able to compare their several parts in detail, he must employ the indirect means of reasoning and general propositions. When we cannot bring two straight lines together, to determine whether they are equal, we do it by the physical aid of a foot rule applied first to one and then to the other, and the logical aid of the general proposition or formula, "Things which are equal to the same thing are equal to one another." The comparison of two things through the intervention of a third thing, when their direct comparison is impossible, is the appropriate scientific process for ascertaining resemblances and dissimilarities, and is the sum total of what Logic has to teach on the subject.

An undue extension of *this remark* induced Locke to consider reasoning itself as nothing but the comparison of two ideas through the medium of a third, and knowledge as the perception of the agreement or disagreement of two ideas: doctrines which the Condillac school blindly adopted, without the qualifications and distinctions with which they were studiously guarded by their illustrious author. Where, indeed, the agreement or disagreement (otherwise called resemblance or dissimilarity) of any two things is the very matter to be determined, as is the case particularly in the sciences of quantity and extension; there, the process by which a solution, if not attainable by direct perception, must be indirectly sought, consists in comparing these two things through the medium of a third. But this is far from being true of all inquiries. The knowledge that bodies fall to the ground is not a perception of agreement or disagreement, but of a series of physical occurrences, a succession of sensations. Locke's definitions of knowledge and of reasoning required

*a–a*MS, 43, 46, 51, 56, 62, 65   closely
*b–b*MS, 43, 46   you
*c–c*MS, 43, 46   these views

to be limited to our knowledge of, and reasoning about, resemblances. Nor, even when thus restricted, are the propositions strictly correct; since the comparison is not made, as he represents, between the ideas of the two phenomena, but between the phenomena themselves. This mistake has been pointed out in an earlier part of our inquiry,* and we traced it to an imperfect conception of what takes place in mathematics, where very often the comparison is really made between the ideas, without any appeal to the outward senses; only, however, because in mathematics a comparison of the ideas is strictly equivalent to a comparison of the phenomena themselves. Where, as in the case of numbers, lines, and figures, our idea of an object is a complete picture of the object, so far as respects the matter in hand; we can, of course, learn from the picture, whatever could be learnt from the object itself by mere contemplation of it as it exists at the particular instant when the picture is taken. No mere contemplation of gunpowder would ever teach us that a spark would make it explode, nor, consequently, would the contemplation of the idea of gunpowder do so: but the mere contemplation of a straight line shows that it cannot inclose a space: accordingly the contemplation of the idea of it will show the same. What takes place in mathematics is thus no argument that the comparison is between the ideas only. It is always, either indirectly or directly, a comparison of the phenomena.

In cases in which we cannot bring the phenomena to the test of direct inspection at all, or not in a manner sufficiently precise, but must judge of their resemblance by inference from other resemblances or dissimilarities more accessible to observation, we of course require, as in all cases of ratiocination, generalizations or formulæ applicable to the subject. We must reason from laws of nature; from the uniformities which are observable in the fact of likeness or unlikeness.

§ 3. [*The axioms and theorems of mathematics comprise the principal laws of resemblance*] Of these laws or uniformities, the most comprehensive are those supplied by mathematics; the axioms relating to equality, inequality, and proportionality, and the various theorems thereon founded. And these are the only Laws of Resemblance which require to be, or which can be, treated apart. It is true there are innumerable other theorems which affirm resemblances among phenomena; as that the angle of the reflection of light is *equal* to its angle of incidence (equality being merely exact resemblance in magnitude). Again, that the heavenly bodies describe *equal* areas in equal times; and that their periods of revolution are *proportional* (another species of resemblance) to the sesquiplicate powers of their distances from the centre of force. These and similar propositions affirm resemblances, of the same nature with those asserted in the theorems of mathematics; but the distinction

*Supra, Bk. I, Chap. v, §1 [pp. 87ff.], and Bk. II, Chap. v, §5 [pp. 233ff.].

is, that the propositions of mathematics are true of all phenomena whatever, or at least without distinction of origin; while the truths in question are affirmed only of special phenomena, which originate in a certain way; and the equalities, proportionalities, or other resemblances, which exist between such phenomena, must necessarily be either derived from, or identical with, the law of their origin—the law of causation on which they depend. The equality of the areas described *in equal times* by the planets, is *derived* from the laws of the causes; and, until its derivation was shown, it was an empirical law. The equality of the angles of reflexion and incidence is *identical* with the law of the cause; for the cause is the incidence of a ray of light upon a reflecting surface, and the equality in question is the very law according to which that cause produces its effects. This class, therefore, of *the* uniformities of resemblance between phenomena, are inseparable, in fact and in thought, from the laws of the production of those phenomena: and the principles of induction applicable to them are no other than those of which we have treated in the preceding chapters of this Book.

It is otherwise with the truths of mathematics. The laws of equality and inequality between spaces, or between numbers, have no connexion with laws of causation. That the angle of reflexion is equal to the angle of incidence, is a statement of the mode of action of a particular cause; but that when two straight lines intersect each other the opposite angles are equal, is true of all such lines and angles, by whatever cause produced. That the squares of the periodic times of the planets are proportional to the cubes of their distances from the sun, is an uniformity derived from the laws of the causes *(or forces) which produce the planetary motions*; but that the square of any number is four times the square of half the number, is true independently of any cause. The only laws of resemblance, therefore, which we are called upon to consider independently of causation, belong to the province of mathematics.

§ 4. [*The axioms and theorems of mathematics also comprise the principal laws of order in space, and rest on induction by simple enumeration*] The same thing is evident with respect to the only *one remaining* of our five categories, Order in Place. The order in place, of the effects of a cause, is (like everything else belonging to the effects) a consequence of the laws of that cause. The order in place, or, as we have termed it, the collocation, of the primeval causes, is (as well as their resemblance) in each instance an ultimate fact, in which no laws or uniformities are traceable. The only re-

---

a–a+51, 56, 62, 65, 68, 72
b–b+43, 46, 51, 56, 62, 65, 68, 72
*c–c*MS, 43, 46, 51, 56, 62, 65   which produce the planetary motions, namely, the central and the tangential force
*a–a*MS, 43   remaining one

maining general propositions respecting order in place, and the only ones which have nothing to do with causation, are [b]some[b] of the truths of geometry; laws through which we are able, from the order in place of certain points, lines, or spaces, to infer the order in place of others which are connected with the former in some known mode; quite independently of the particular nature of those points, lines, or spaces, in any other respect than position or magnitude, as well as independently of the physical cause from which in any particular case they happen to derive their origin.

It thus appears that mathematics is the only department of science into the methods of which it still remains to inquire. And there is the less necessity that this inquiry should occupy us long, as we have already, in the Second Book, made considerable progress in it. We there remarked, that the directly inductive truths of mathematics are few in number; consisting of the axioms, together with certain propositions concerning existence, tacitly involved in most of the so-called definitions. And we [c]gave what appeared conclusive reasons for affirming[c] that these original premises, from which the remaining truths of the science are deduced, are, notwithstanding all appearances to the contrary, results of observation and experience; founded, in short, on the evidence of the senses. That things equal to the same thing are equal to [d]one another, and[d] that two straight lines which have once intersected [e] one another continue to diverge, are inductive truths; resting, indeed, like the law of universal causation, only on induction *per enumerationem simplicem*; on the fact that they have been perpetually [f]perceived to be true, and never once found to be[f] false. But, as we have seen in a recent chapter that this evidence, in the case of a law so completely universal as the law of causation, amounts to the fullest proof[g], so is this even more evidently true of the general propositions to which we are now adverting; because, as a perception of their truth in any individual case whatever, requires only the simple act of looking at the objects in a proper position, there never could have been in their case (what, for a long period, [h]there were in the case of the law of causation[h]) instances which were apparently, though not really, exceptions to them. Their infallible truth was recognised from the very dawn of speculation; and as their extreme familiarity made it impossible for the mind to conceive the objects under any other law, they were, and still are, generally considered as truths recognised by their own evidence, or by instinct.

[b-b]MS certain

[c-c]MS, 43, 46 proved, at such length as makes any return to the subject altogether superfluous,

[d-d]MS, 43, 46, 51, 56 another, or

[e]43, 46, 51, 56 with

[f-f]MS, 43, 46 found true and never once

[g]MS, 43, 46 attainable by the human faculties

[h-h]MS, 43, 46 in the case of the law of causation, there were

§ 5. [*The propositions of arithmetic affirm the modes of formation of some given number*] There is something which seems to require explanation, in the fact that the immense multitude of truths (a multitude still as far from being exhausted as ever) comprised in the mathematical sciences, can be elicited from so small a number of elementary laws. One sees not, at first, how it is that there can be room for such an infinite variety of true propositions, on subjects apparently so limited.

To begin with the science of number. The elementary or ultimate truths of this science are the common axioms concerning equality, namely, "Things which are equal to the same thing are equal to one another," and "Equals added to equals make equal sums," (no other axioms are *required*,*) together with the definitions of the various numbers. Like other so-called definitions, these are composed of two things, the explanation of a name, and the assertion of a fact: of which the latter alone can form a first principle or premise of a science. The fact asserted in the definition of a number is a physical fact. Each of the numbers two, three, four, &c., denotes physical phenomena, and connotes a physical property of those phenomena. Two, for instance, denotes all pairs of things, and twelve all dozens of things, connoting what makes them pairs, or dozens; and that which makes them so is something physical; since it cannot be denied that two apples are physically distinguishable from three apples, two horses from one horse, and so forth: that they are a different visible and tangible phenomenon. I am not undertaking to say what the difference is; it is enough that there is a difference of which the senses can take cognizance. And although a hundred and two horses are not so easily distinguished from a hundred and three, as two horses are from three—though in most positions the senses do not perceive any difference—yet they may be so placed that a difference will be perceptible, or else we should never have distinguished them, and given them different

---

*The axiom, "Equals subtracted from equals leave equal differences," may be demonstrated from the two axioms in the text. If $A = a$ and $B = b$, $A - B = a - b$. For if not, let $A - B = a - b + c$. Then since $B = b$, adding equals to equals, $A = a + c$. But $A = a$. Therefore $a = a + c$, which is *impossible*.

This proposition having been demonstrated, we may, by means of it, demonstrate the following: "If equals be added to unequals, the sums are unequal." If $A = a$ and B not $= b$, $A + B$ is not $= a + b$. For suppose it to be so. Then, since $A = a$ and $A + B = a + b$, subtracting equals from equals, $B = b$; which is contrary to the hypothesis.

So again, it may be proved that two things, one of which is equal and the other unequal to a third thing, are unequal to one another. If $A = a$ and A not $= B$, neither is $a = B$. For suppose it to be equal. Then since $A = a$ and $a = B$, and since things equal to the same thing are equal to one another, $A = B$: which is contrary to the hypothesis.

*ᵃ⁻ᵃ*MS, 43, 46   necessary
*ᵇ⁻ᵇ*MS, 43, 46, 51   absurd

names. Weight is confessedly a physical property of things; yet small differences between great weights are as imperceptible to the senses in most situations, as small differences between great numbers; and are only put in evidence by placing the two objects in a peculiar position—namely, in the opposite scales of a delicate balance.

What, then, is that which is connoted by a name of number? Of course, some property belonging to the agglomeration of things which we call by the name; and that property is, the characteristic manner in which the agglomeration is made up of, and may be separated into, parts. *I* will endeavour to make this more intelligible by a few explanations.

When we call a collection of objects *two*, *three*, or *four*, they are not two, three, or four in the abstract; they are two, three, or four things of some particular kind; pebbles, horses, inches, pounds weight. What the name of number connotes is, the manner in which single objects of the given kind must be put together, in order to produce that particular aggregate. If the aggregate be of pebbles, and we call it *two*, the name implies that, to compose the aggregate, one pebble must be joined to one pebble. If we call it *three*, *one and one and one pebble must be brought together to produce it, or else* one pebble must be joined to an aggregate of the kind called *two*, already existing. The aggregate which we call *four*, has a still greater number of characteristic modes of formation. One and one and one and one pebble may be brought together; or two aggregates of the kind called *two* may be united; or one pebble may be added to an aggregate of the kind called *three*. Every succeeding number in the ascending series, may be formed by the junction of smaller numbers in a progressively greater variety of ways. Even limiting the parts to two, the number may be formed, and consequently may be divided, in as many different ways as there are numbers smaller than itself; and, if we admit of threes, fours, &c., in a still greater variety. Other modes of arriving at the same aggregate present themselves, not by the union of smaller, but by the dismemberment of larger aggregates. Thus, *three pebbles* may be formed by taking away one pebble from an aggregate of four; *two pebbles*, by an equal division of a similar aggregate; and so on.

Every arithmetical proposition; every statement of the result of an arithmetical operation; is a statement of one of the modes of *e* formation of a given number. It affirms that a certain aggregate might have been formed by putting together certain other aggregates, or by withdrawing certain portions of some aggregate; and that, by consequence, we might reproduce those aggregates from it, by reversing the process.

Thus, when we say that the cube of 12 is 1728, what we affirm is this:

c–cMS, 43, 46 We
d–dMS, 43, 46, 51, 56, 62 we mean that one . . . else that
eMS, 43, 46, 51, 56, 62 the

that if, having a sufficient number of pebbles or of any other objects, we put them together *into* the particular sort of parcels or aggregates called twelves; and put together these twelves again into similar collections; and, finally, make up twelve of these largest parcels; the aggregate thus formed will be such a one as we call 1728; namely, that which (to take the most familiar of its modes of formation) may be made by joining the parcel called a thousand pebbles, the parcel called seven hundred pebbles, the parcel called twenty pebbles, and the parcel called eight pebbles.

g The converse proposition, that the cube root of 1728 is 12, asserts that this large aggregate may again be decomposed into the twelve twelves of twelves of pebbles which it consists of.

The modes of formation of any number are innumerable; but when we know one mode of formation of each, all the rest may be determined deductively. If we know that a is formed from b and c, b from *a* and e, c from d and f, and so forth, until we have included all the numbers of any scale we choose to select, (taking care that for each number the mode of formation *be* really a distinct one, not bringing us round again to the former numbers, but introducing a new number,) we have a set of propositions from which we may reason to all the other modes of formation of those numbers from one another. Having established a chain of inductive truths connecting together all the numbers of the scale, we can ascertain the formation of any one of those numbers from any other by merely travelling from *j* one to the other along the chain. Suppose that we know only the following modes of formation: $6 = 4 + 2$, $4 = 7 - 3$, $7 = 5 + 2$, $5 = 9 - 4$. We *could* determine how 6 may be formed from 9. For $6 = 4 + 2 = 7 - 3 + 2 = 5 + 2 - 3 + 2 = 9 - 4 + 2 - 3 + 2$. It may *therefore* be formed by taking away 4 and 3, and adding 2 and 2. If we know besides that $2 + 2 = 4$, we obtain 6 from 9 in a simpler mode, by merely taking away 3.

It is sufficient, therefore, to select one of the various modes of formation of each number, as a means of ascertaining all the rest. And since things which are uniform, and therefore simple, are most easily received and retained by the understanding, there is an obvious advantage in selecting a mode of formation which shall be alike for all; in fixing the connotation of names of number on one uniform principle. The mode in which our existing numerical nomenclature is contrived possesses this advantage, with the additional one, that it happily conveys to the mind two of the modes of formation of every number. Each number is considered as formed by the addition of an unit to the number next below it in magnitude, and this mode

*f–f*MS, 43, 46   in
*g*MS, 43, 46   [*no paragraph; printer's error in 51?*]
*h–h*MS, 43   d   *i–i*MS, 43, 46   is
*j*MS, 43, 46, 51   the   *k–k*MS   can
l–l+43, 46, 51, 56, 62, 65, 68, 72

of formation is conveyed by the place which it occupies in the series. And
[m]each[m] is also considered as formed by the addition of a number of units less
than ten, and a number of aggregates each equal to one of the successive
powers of ten; and this mode of its formation is expressed by its spoken
name, and by its [n]numerical[n] character.

What renders arithmetic [o]the type of[o] a deductive science, is the fortunate
applicability to it of a law so comprehensive as "The sums of equals are
equals:" or (to express the same principle in less familiar but more characteristic language), Whatever is made up of parts, is made up of the parts of
those parts. This truth, obvious to the senses in all cases which can be fairly
referred to their decision, and so general as to be coextensive with nature
itself, being true of all sorts of phenomena, (for all admit of being numbered,) must be considered an inductive truth, or law of nature, of the highest
order. And every arithmetical operation is an application of this law, or of
other laws capable of being deduced from it. This is our warrant for all
calculations. We believe that five and two are equal to seven, on the evidence
of this inductive law, combined with the definitions of those numbers. We
arrive at that conclusion (as all know who remember how they first learned
it) by adding a single unit at a time: $5 + 1 = 6$, therefore $5 + 1 + 1 = 6 +
1 = 7$: and again $2 = 1 + 1$, therefore $5 + 2 = 5 + 1 + 1 = 7$.

§ 6. [*The propositions of algebra affirm the equivalence of different modes
of formation of numbers generally*] Innumerable as are the true propositions
which can be formed concerning particular numbers, no adequate conception
could be gained, from these alone, of the extent of the truths composing the
science of number. Such propositions as we have spoken of are the least
general of all numerical truths. It is true that even these are coextensive with
all nature: the properties of the number four are true of all objects that are
divisible into four equal parts, and all objects are either actually or ideally so
divisible. But the propositions which compose the science of algebra are true,
not of a particular number, but of all numbers; not of all things under the
condition of being divided in a particular way, but of all things under the
condition of being divided in any way—of being designated by a number
at all.

Since it is impossible for different numbers to have any of their modes of
formation completely in common, it [a]is a kind of[a] paradox to say, that all
propositions which can be made concerning numbers relate to their modes
of formation from other numbers, and yet that there are propositions which
are true of all numbers. But this very paradox leads to the real principle of

[m]-[m]MS   it
[n]-[n]MS   numeral   [o]-[o]+51, 56, 62, 65, 68, 72
[a]-[a]MS, 43, 46, 51, 56   looks like a

generalization concerning the properties of numbers. Two different numbers cannot be formed in the same manner from the same numbers; but they may be formed in the same manner from different numbers; as nine is formed from three by multiplying it into itself, and sixteen is formed from four by the same process. Thus there arises a classification of modes of formation, or in the language commonly used by mathematicians, a classification of Functions. Any number, considered as formed from any other number, is called a function of it; and there are as many kinds of functions as there are modes of formation. The simple functions are by no means numerous, most functions being formed by the combination of several of the operations which form simple functions, or by successive repetitions of some one of those operations. The simple functions of any number x are all reducible to the following forms: $x + a$, $x - a$, $a x$, x/a, x^a, $^a\sqrt{x}$, log. x (to the base a), and the same expressions varied by putting x for a and a for x, wherever that substitution would alter the value: to which perhaps ^{b}ought to be added^b sin x, and arc (sin $= x$). All other functions of x are formed by putting some one or more of the simple functions in the place of x or a, and subjecting them to the same elementary operations.

In order to carry on general reasonings on the subject of Functions, we require a nomenclature enabling us to express any two numbers by names which, without specifying what particular numbers they are, shall show what function each is of the other; or, in other words, shall put in evidence their mode of formation from one another. The system of general language called algebraical notation does this. The expressions a and $a^2 + 3a$ denote, the one any number, the other the number formed from it in a particular manner. The expressions a, b, n, and $(a + b)^n$, denote any three numbers, and a fourth which is formed from them in a certain mode.

The following may be stated as the general problem of the algebraical calculus: F being a certain function of a given number, to find what function F will be of any function of that number. For example, a binomial $a + b$ is a function of its two parts a and b, and the parts are, in their turn, functions of $a + b$: now $(a + b)^n$, is a certain function of the binomial; what function will this be of a and b, the two parts? The answer to this question is the binomial theorem. The formula $(a + b)^n = a^n + \dfrac{n}{1} a^{n-1}b + \dfrac{n.n - 1}{1.2} a^{n-2}b^2 +$ &c., shows in what manner the number which is formed by multiplying $a + b$ into itself n times, might be formed without that process, directly from a, b, and n. And of this nature are all the theorems of the science of number. They assert the identity of the result of different modes of formation. They affirm that some mode of formation from x, and some mode of formation from a certain function of x, produce the same number.

$^{b-b}$MS, 43   we ought to add (with M. Comte) [*Cours*, Vol. I, p. 173]

Besides these general theorems or formulæ, what remains in the algebraical calculus is the resolution of equations. But the resolution of an equation is also a theorem. If the equation be $x^2 + ax = b$, the resolution of this equation, viz. $x = -\frac{1}{2} a \pm \sqrt{\frac{1}{4} a^2 + b}$, is a general proposition, which may be regarded as an answer to the question, If b is a certain function of x and a (namely $x^2 + ax$), what function is x of b and a? The resolution of equations is, therefore, a mere variety of the general problem as above stated. The problem is—Given a function, what function is it of some other function? And in the resolution of an equation, the question is, to find what function of one of its own functions the number itself is.

Such as above described, is the aim and end of the calculus. As for its processes, every one knows that they are simply deductive. In demonstrating an algebraical theorem, or in resolving an equation, we travel from the *datum* to the *quæsitum* by pure ratiocination; in which the only premises introduced, besides the original hypotheses, are the fundamental axioms already mentioned—that things equal to the same thing are equal to one another, and that the sums of equal things are equal. At each step in the demonstration or in the calculation, we apply one or other of these truths, or truths ^{c}deducible^c from them, as, that the differences, products, &c., of equal numbers are equal.

It would be inconsistent with the scale of this work, and not necessary to its design, to carry the analysis of the truths and processes of algebra any farther; which is ^{d}also the less needful, as the task has been, to a very great extent,^{d} performed by other writers. ^{e} Peacock's *Algebra*, and Dr. Whewell's *Doctrine of Limits*,[*] ^{f}are full of instruction on the subject. The profound treatises of a truly philosophical mathematician, Professor De Morgan,^{f} should be studied by every one who desires to comprehend the evidence of mathematical truths, and the meaning of the obscurer processes of the calculus;[†] ^{g}and the speculations of M. Comte, in his *Cours de Philosophie*

[*Cambridge: Deighton, 1838.]

[†See, e.g., Augustus De Morgan. *The Elements of Algebra*. London: Taylor, 1835; *The Differential and Integral Calculus*. London: Baldwin and Cradock, 1842.]

$^{c-c}$MS, 43, 46, 51 deduced
$^{d-d}$MS, 43, 46 moreover the less needful, as the task has been recently and thoroughly
^{e}MS, 43, 46, 51, 56 Professor $^{f-f}$+65, 68, 72
$^{g-g}$616MS, 43 while, even after mastering these treatises, the student will have much to learn on the subject from M. Comte, of whose admirable work one of the most admirable portions is that in which he may truly be said to have created the philosophy of the higher mathematics [i.e., Vol. I, Leçons iii ff.]*. [*footnote:*] *In the concluding pages of his *Cours de Philosophie Positive*, of which the final volume has but recently appeared, M. Comte announces the intention of hereafter producing a special and systematic work on the Philosophy of Mathematics. [Vol. VI, pp. 889–90; *the first volume of the planned two-volume work appeared as* Synthèse subjective, ou Système universel

Positive, on the philosophy of the higher branches of mathematics, are among the *h*many*h* valuable gifts for which philosophy is indebted to that eminent thinker.*g*

§ 7. [*The propositions of geometry are laws of outward nature*] If the extreme generality, and remoteness not so much from sense as from the visual and tactual imagination, of the laws of number, renders it a somewhat difficult effort of abstraction to conceive those laws as being in reality physical truths obtained by observation; the same difficulty does not exist with regard to the laws of extension. The facts of which those laws are *a*expressions*a*, are of a kind peculiarly accessible to the *b*senses*b*, and suggesting eminently distinct images to the fancy. That geometry is a strictly physical science would doubtless have been recognised in all ages, had it not been for the illusions produced by two *c*circumstances*c*. One of these is the characteristic property, already noticed, of the facts of geometry, that they may be collected from our ideas or mental pictures of objects as effectually as from the objects themselves. The other is, the demonstrative character of geometrical truths; which was at one time supposed to constitute a radical distinction between them and physical truths, the latter, as resting on merely probable evidence, being deemed essentially uncertain and unprecise. The advance of knowledge has, however, made it manifest that physical science, in its better understood branches, is quite as demonstrative as geometry. The task of deducing its details from a few comparatively simple principles *d*is found to be anything but the impossibility it was once supposed to be; and the notion of the superior certainty of geometry is*d* an illusion, arising from the ancient prejudice which, in that science, mistakes the ideal data from which we reason, for a peculiar class of realities, while the corresponding ideal data of any deductive physical science are recognised as what they really are, *e* hypotheses.

Every theorem in geometry is a law of external nature, and might have been ascertained by generalizing from observation and experiment, which in this case resolve themselves into comparison and measurement. But it was found practicable, and being practicable, was desirable, to deduce these

---

des conceptions propres à l'état normal de l'humanité. Paris: Comte, Dalmont, 1856.] All competent judges who are acquainted with what M. Comte has already accomplished in that great department of the philosophy of the sciences, will look with the highest expectations to this promised treatise.] 46 *as* MS . . . from M. Comte, to whose speculations the philosophy of the higher mathematics is more indebted than to those of any other writer.] 51, 56, 62 *as* 46 . . . higher branches of mathematics . . . *as* 46 . . . writer I am acquainted with.

*h–h*65 most
*b–b*MS, 43, 46 sense
*d–d*MS, 43, 46, 51, 56 being found . . . geometry being
*e*MS, 43, 46, 51, 56, 62, 65, 68 mere

*a–a*MS the expression
*c–c*MS, 43, 46, 51 causes

truths by ratiocination from a small number of general laws of nature, the certainty and universality of which ʲareʲ obvious to the most careless observer, and which compose the first principles and ultimate premises of the science. Among these general laws must be included the same two which we have noticed as ultimate principles of the Science of Number also, and which are applicable to every description of quantity; viz. The sums of equals are equal, and Things which are equal to the same thing are equal to one another; the latter of which may be expressed in a manner more suggestive of the inexhaustible multitude of its consequences, by the following terms: Whatever is equal to any one of a number of equal magnitudes, is equal to any other of them. To these two must be added, in geometry, a third law of equality, namely, that lines, surfaces, or solid spaces, which can be so applied to one another as to coincide, are equal. Some writers have asserted that this law of nature is a mere verbal definition; that the expression "equal magnitudes" *means* nothing but magnitudes which can be so applied to one another as to coincide. But in this opinion I cannot agree. The equality of two geometrical magnitudes cannot differ fundamentally in its nature from the equality of two weights, two degrees of heat, or two portions of duration, to none of which would this ᵍ definition of equality be suitable. None of these things can be so applied to one another as to coincide, yet we perfectly understand what we mean when we call them equal. Things are equal in magnitude, as things are equal in weight, when they are felt to be exactly similar in respect of the attribute in which we compare them: and the application of the objects to each other in the one case, like the balancing them with a pair of scales in the other, is but a mode of bringing them into a position in which our senses can recognise deficiencies of exact resemblance that would otherwise escape our notice.

Along with these three general principles or axioms, the remainder of the premises of geometry ʰconsistsʰ of the so-called definitions: that is to say, propositions asserting the real existence of the various objects therein designated, together with some one property of each. In some cases more than one property is commonly assumed, but in no case is more than one necessary. It is assumed that there are such things in nature as straight lines, and that any two of them setting out from the same point, diverge more and more without limit. This assumption, (which includes and goes beyond Euclid's axiom that two straight lines cannot inclose a space,) [*] is as indispensable in geometry, and as evident, resting on as simple, familiar, and universal observation, as

[*See Bk. I, Axiom 11; Playfair, *Elements of Geometry*, p. 22; and pp. 230ff. above.]

ʲ⁻ʲMS, 43, 46, 51   was]   56, 62, 65   were
ᵍMS, 43, 46, 51, 56, 62, 65, 68   pretended
ʰ⁻ʰMS, 43, 46, 51, 56, 62, 65   consist

any of the other axioms. It is also assumed that straight lines diverge from one another in different degrees; in other words, that there are such things as angles, and that they are capable of being equal or unequal. It is assumed that there is such a thing as a circle, and that all its radii are equal; such things as ellipses, and that the sums of the focal distances are equal for every point in an ellipse; such things as parallel lines, and that those lines are everywhere equally distant.*

§ 8. [*Why geometry is almost entirely deductive*] It is a matter of [*a*] more than curiosity to consider, to what peculiarity of the physical truths which are the subject of geometry, it is owing that they can all be deduced from so small a number of original premises: why it is that we can set out from only one characteristic property of each kind of phenomenon, and with that and two or three general truths relating to equality, can travel from mark to mark until we obtain a vast body of derivative truths, to all appearance extremely unlike those elementary ones.

The explanation of this remarkable fact seems to lie in the following circumstances. In the first place, all questions of position and figure may be resolved into questions of magnitude. The position and figure of any object [*b*]are[*b*] determined by determining the position of a sufficient number of points in it; and the position of any point may be determined by the magnitude of three rectangular co-ordinates, that is, of the perpendiculars drawn from the

---

*Geometers have usually preferred to define parallel lines by the property of being in the same plane and never meeting. This, however, has rendered it necessary for them to assume, as an additional axiom, some other property of parallel lines; and the unsatisfactory manner in which properties for that purpose have been selected by Euclid and others has always been deemed the opprobrium of elementary geometry. Even as a verbal definition, equidistance is a fitter property to characterize parallels by, since it is the attribute really involved in the signification of the name. If to be in the same plane and never to meet were all that is meant by being parallel, we should feel no incongruity in speaking of a curve as parallel to its asymptote. The meaning of parallel lines is, lines which pursue exactly the same direction, and which, therefore, neither [*i*]draw[*i*] nearer nor go farther from one another; a conception suggested at once by the contemplation of nature. That the lines will never meet is of course [*j*]included[*j*] in the more comprehensive proposition that they are everywhere equally distant. And that any straight lines which are in the same plane and not equidistant will certainly meet, may be demonstrated in the most [*k*]rigorous[*k*] manner from the fundamental property of straight lines assumed in the text, viz. that if they set out from the same point, they diverge more and more without limit.

[*i–i*]MS, 43, 46, 51, 56, 62 approach   [*j–j*]MS, 43, 46 implied
[*k–k*]MS, 43, 46, 51, 56, 62 rigid
[*a*]MS, 43, 46, 51, 56, 62 something   [*b–b*]MS, 43, 46 is

point to three *planes* at right angles to one another, arbitrarily selected. By this transformation of all questions of quality into questions only of quantity, geometry is reduced to the single problem of the measurement of magnitudes, that is, the ascertainment of the equalities which exist between them. Now when we consider that by one of the general axioms, any equality, when ascertained, is proof of as many other equalities as there are other things equal to either of the two equals; and that by another of those axioms, any ascertained equality is proof of the equality of as many pairs of magnitudes as can be formed by the numerous operations which resolve themselves into the addition of the equals to themselves or to other equals; we cease to wonder that in proportion as a science is conversant about equality, it should afford a more copious supply of marks of marks; and that the sciences of number and extension, which are conversant with little else than equality, should be the most deductive of all the sciences.

There are *also* two or three of the principal laws of space or extension which are unusually fitted for rendering one position or magnitude a mark of another, and thereby contributing to render the science largely deductive. First; the magnitudes of inclosed spaces, whether superficial or solid, are completely determined by the magnitudes of the lines and angles which bound them. Secondly, the length of any line, whether straight or curve, is measured (certain other things being given) by the angle which it subtends, and *vice versâ*. Lastly, the angle which any two straight lines make with each other at an inaccessible point, is measured by the angles they severally make with any third line we choose to select. By means of these general laws, the measurement of all lines, angles, and spaces whatsoever might be accomplished *e* by measuring a single straight line and a sufficient number of angles; which is *f* the plan actually pursued in the trigonometrical survey of a country; and fortunate it is that this is practicable, the exact measurement of *long straight lines being always difficult, and often impossible*, but that of angles very easy. Three such generalizations as the foregoing afford such facilities for the indirect measurement of magnitudes, (by supplying us with known lines or angles which are marks of the magnitude of unknown ones, and thereby of the spaces which they inclose,) that it is easily *intelligible* how from a few data we can go on to ascertain the magnitude of an indefinite multitude of lines, angles, and spaces, which we could not easily, or could not at all, measure by any more direct process.

c–cMS, 43, 46, 51, 56, 62   axes
d–dMS, 43, 46   , moreover,
eMS, 43   (to borrow an observation from M. Comte) [*Cours*, Vol. I, p. 129]
fMS, 43, 46, 51, 56, 62   , indeed,
g–gMS, 43, 46, 51, 56, 62   straight lines being difficult
h–hMS, 43, 46, 51, 56, 62   conceivable

§ 9. [*Function of mathematical truths in the other sciences, and limits of that function*] Such are the *a*remarks which it seems*a* necessary to make in this place, respecting the laws of nature which are the peculiar subject of the sciences of number and extension. The immense part which those laws take in giving a deductive character to the other departments of physical science, is well known; and is not surprising, when we consider that all causes operate according to mathematical laws. The effect is always dependent on, or *b* is a function of, the quantity of the agent; and generally of its position also. We cannot, therefore, reason respecting causation, without introducing considerations of quantity and extension at every step; and if the nature of the phenomena admits of our obtaining numerical data of sufficient accuracy, the laws of quantity become the grand *c*instrument*c* for calculating forward to an effect, or backward to a cause. That in all other sciences, as well as in geometry, questions of quality are scarcely ever independent of questions of quantity, may be seen from the most familiar phenomena. Even when several colours are mixed on a painter's palette, the comparative quantity of each entirely determines the colour of the mixture.

With this mere suggestion of the general causes which render mathematical principles and processes so predominant in those deductive sciences which afford precise numerical data, I must, on the present occasion, content myself: referring the reader who desires a *d*more thorough acquaintance with the*d* subject, to the first two volumes of M. Comte's systematic work.

In the same work, and more particularly in the third volume, are also fully discussed the *e* limits of the applicability of mathematical principles to the improvement of other sciences. Such principles are manifestly inapplicable, where the causes on which any class of phenomena depend are so imperfectly accessible to our observation, that we cannot ascertain, by a proper induction, their numerical laws; or where the causes are so numerous, and intermixed in so complex a manner with one another, that even supposing their laws known, the computation of the aggregate effect transcends the powers of the calculus as it is, or *f*is*f* likely to be; or lastly, where the causes themselves are in a state of perpetual fluctuation; as in physiology, and still more, if possible, in the social science. *g*The*g* mathematical solutions of physical questions become progressively more difficult and *h* imperfect, in proportion as the ques-

---

*a–a*MS, 43, 46, 62, 65, 68   few remarks which it seemed]   51, 56 *as* MS . . . it seems
*b*MS, 43, 46   , in mathematical language,
*c–c*MS, 43, 46, 51, 56   instruments
*d–d*MS, 43, 46   thorough acquaintance with this great
*e*MS, 43, 46   necessary
*f–f*MS, 43, 46   as it is ever
*g–g*MS, 43   As M. Comte* well observes, the [*footnote:*] *Cours de Philosophie Positive, Vol. III, pp. 414–16. [*cf.* 621n *below*]
*h*MS, 43, 46   more

tions divest themselves of their abstract and hypothetical character, and approach nearer to the degree of complication actually existing in nature; insomuch that beyond the limits of astronomical phenomena, and ‘of‘ those most nearly analogous to them, mathematical accuracy is generally obtained "at the expense of the reality of the inquiry:" while even in astronomical questions, "notwithstanding the admirable simplicity of their mathematical elements, our feeble intelligence becomes incapable of following out effectually the logical combinations of the laws on which the phenomena are dependent, as soon as we attempt to take into simultaneous consideration more than two or three essential influences."* Of this, the problem of the Three Bodies has already been cited [k], more than once, as a remarkable instance; the complete solution of so comparatively simple a question having vainly tried the skill of the most profound mathematicians. We may conceive, then, how chimerical would be the hope that mathematical principles could [l] be advantageously applied to phenomena dependent on the mutual action of the innumerable minute particles of bodies, as those of chemistry, and still more, of physiology; and for similar reasons those principles [m]remain[m] inapplicable to the still more complex inquiries, the subjects of which are phenomena of society and government.

The value of mathematical instruction as a preparation for those more difficult investigations, consists in the applicability not of its doctrines, but of its method. Mathematics will ever remain the most perfect type of the Deductive Method in general; and the applications of mathematics to the [n]deductive[n] branches of physics, furnish the only school in which philosophers can effectually learn the most difficult and important portion of their art, the employment of the laws of simpler phenomena for explaining and predicting those of the more complex. These grounds are quite sufficient for deeming mathematical training an indispensable basis of real scientific education, and regarding [o](according to the *dictum* which an old but [p]unauthentic[p] tradition ascribes to Plato)[o] one who is [q]$\dot{\alpha}\gamma\epsilon\omega\mu\acute{\epsilon}\tau\rho\eta\tau o\varsigma$[q], as wanting in one of the most essential qualifications for the successful cultivation of the higher branches of philosophy.

*[46] *Philosophie Positive*, Vol. III, 414–16. [j]

[i–i]+43, 46, 51, 56, 62, 65, 68, 72
[j]MS, 43   [see variant g–g above]
[k]MS, 43, 46   by us
[l]MS, 43, 46   ever
[m–m]MS, 43, 46   must be for ever
[n–n]MS, 43, 46, 51   simpler]   56   similar [printer's error in 56?]
[o–o]MS, 43, 46, 51   , with Plato,
[p–p]56, 62   erroneous
[q–q]MS $\dot{\alpha}\gamma\epsilon\omega\mu\epsilon\tau\rho\eta\varsigma$ [sic]

CHAPTER XXV

Of the Grounds of Disbelief

§ 1. [*Improbability and impossibility*] The method of arriving at general truths, or general propositions fit to be believed, and the nature of the evidence on which they are grounded, have been discussed, as far as space and the writer's faculties permitted, in the twenty-four preceding chapters. But the result of the examination of evidence is not always belief, nor even suspension of judgment; it is sometimes disbelief. The philosophy, therefore, of induction and experimental inquiry is incomplete, unless the grounds not only of belief, but of disbelief, are treated of; and to this topic we shall devote one, and the final, chapter.

By disbelief is not here to be understood the mere absence of belief. The ground for abstaining from belief is simply the absence or insufficiency of proof; and in considering what is sufficient evidence to support any given conclusion, we have already, by implication, considered what evidence is not sufficient for the same purpose. By disbelief is here meant, not the state of mind in which we *form no opinion concerning* a subject, but that in which we are fully persuaded that some opinion is not true; insomuch that if evidence, even of great *apparent strength, (whether grounded on the testimony of others or on our own supposed* perceptions,) were produced in favour of the opinion, we should believe that the witnesses spoke falsely, or that they, or *we* ourselves if we were the direct percipients, were mistaken.

That there are such cases, no one is likely to dispute. Assertions for which there is abundant positive evidence are often disbelieved, on account of what is called their improbability, or impossibility. And the question for consideration is what, in the present case, these words mean, and how far and *in* what circumstances the properties which they express are sufficient grounds for disbelief.

§ 2. [*Examination of Hume's doctrine of miracles*] It is to be remarked in the first place, that the positive evidence produced in support of an asser-

---

$a-a$MS, 43, 46   are ignorant, and form no opinion upon
$b-b$MS, 43, 46   strength . . . own apparent
$c-c$+65, 68, 72
$d-d$MS, 43, 46   under

tion which is nevertheless rejected on the score of impossibility or improbability, is never such as amounts to full proof. It is always grounded on some approximate generalization. The fact may have been asserted by a hundred witnesses; but there are many exceptions to the universality of the generalization that what a hundred witnesses affirm is true. We may seem to ourselves to have actually seen the fact: but, that we really see what we think we see, is by no means an universal truth; our organs may have been in a morbid state; or we may have inferred something, and imagined that we perceived it. The evidence, then, in the affirmative being never more than an approximate generalization, all will depend on what the evidence in the negative is. If that also rests on an approximate generalization, it is a case for comparison of probabilities. If the approximate generalizations leading to the affirmative are, when added together, less strong, or in other words, *farther from being universal*, than the approximate generalizations which support the negative side of the question, the proposition is said to be improbable, and is to be disbelieved provisionally. If however *an alleged fact* be in contradiction, not to any number of approximate generalizations, but to a completed generalization grounded on a rigorous induction, it is said to be impossible, and is to be disbelieved totally.

This last principle, simple and evident as it appears, is the doctrine which, on the occasion of an attempt to apply it to the question of the credibility of miracles, excited so violent a controversy. Hume's celebrated *doctrine*, that nothing is credible which is contradictory to experience, or at variance with laws of nature,[*] is merely this very plain and harmless proposition, that whatever is *contradictory* to a complete induction is incredible. That such a maxim as this should either be accounted a dangerous heresy, or mistaken for a great and recondite truth, speaks ill for the state of philosophical speculation on such subjects.

But does not (it may be asked) the very statement of the proposition imply a contradiction? An alleged fact, according to this theory, is not to be believed if it contradict a complete induction. But it is essential to the completeness of an induction that it shall not contradict any known fact. Is it not then a *petitio principii* to say, that the fact ought to be disbelieved because the induction opposed to it is complete? How can we have a right to declare the induction complete, while facts, supported by credible evidence, present themselves in opposition to it?

[*See David Hume. "Of Miracles," *An Inquiry Concerning Human Understanding. In Essays and Treatises on Several Subjects.* 2 vols. Edinburgh: Cadell, 1793, Vol. II, pp. 124–47.]

*a–a*MS, 43, 46 further removed from universality
*b–b*MS a proposition   *c–c*MS, 43, 46, 51, 56 principle
*d–d*MS in contradiction

I answer, we have that right whenever the scientific canons of induction give it to us; that is, whenever the induction *can* be complete. We have it, for example, in a case of causation in which there has been an *experimentum crucis*. If an antecedent A, superadded to a set of antecedents in all other respects unaltered, is followed by an effect B which did not exist before, A is, in that instance at least, the cause of B, or *e*an indispensable part of its*e* cause; and if A be tried again with many totally different sets of antecedents and B still follows, then it is the whole cause. If these observations or experiments have been repeated so often, and by so many persons, as to exclude all supposition of error in the observer, a law of nature is established; and so long as this law is received as such, the assertion that on any particular occasion A took place, and yet B did not follow, *without any counteracting cause*, must be disbelieved. Such an assertion is not to be credited on any less evidence than what would suffice to overturn the law. The general truths, that whatever has a beginning has a cause, and that when none but the same causes exist, the same effects follow, rest on the strongest inductive evidence possible; the proposition that things affirmed by even a crowd of respectable witnesses are true, is but an approximate generalization; and—even if we fancy we actually saw or felt the fact which is in contradiction to the law— what a human being can see is no more than a set of appearances; from which the real nature of the phenomenon is merely an inference, and in this inference approximate generalizations usually have a large share. If, therefore, we make our election to hold by the law, no quantity of evidence whatever ought to persuade us that there has occurred anything in contradiction to it. If, indeed, the evidence produced is such that it is more likely that the set of observations and experiments on which the law rests should have been inaccurately performed or incorrectly interpreted, than that the evidence in question should be false, we may believe the evidence; but then we must abandon the law. And since the law was received on what seemed a complete induction, it can only be rejected on evidence equivalent; *f*namely,*f* as being inconsistent not with any number of approximate generalizations, but with some other and better established law of nature. This extreme case, of a conflict between two supposed laws of nature, has probably never actually occurred where, in the process of investigating both the laws, the true canons of scientific induction had been kept in view; but if it did occur, it must terminate in the total rejection of one of the supposed laws. It would prove that there must be a flaw in the logical process by which either one or the other was established: and if there be so, that supposed general truth is *g*no truth*g* at all. We cannot admit a proposition as a law of nature, and yet believe

e–*e*MS, 43, 46, 51, 56   a necessary part of that
f–*f*+43, 46, 51, 56, 62, 65, 68, 72
g–*g*MS   not true

a fact in real contradiction to it. We must disbelieve the alleged fact, or believe that we were mistaken in admitting the supposed law.

But in order that any alleged fact should be contradictory to a law of causation, the allegation must be, not simply that the cause existed without being followed by the effect, for that would be no uncommon occurrence; but that this happened in the absence of any adequate counteracting cause. Now in the case of an alleged miracle, the assertion is the exact opposite of this. It is, that the effect was defeated, not in the absence, but in consequence of a counteracting cause, namely, a direct interposition of an act of the will of some being who has power over nature; and in particular of a Being, whose will *h*being assumed to have*h* endowed all the causes with the powers by which they produce their effects, may well be supposed able to counteract them. A miracle (as was justly remarked by Brown*) is no contradiction to the law of cause and effect; it is a new effect, *i*supposed to be*j* produced by the introduction of a new cause. Of the adequacy of that cause, if *k*present*k*, there can be no doubt; and the only antecedent improbability which can be ascribed to the miracle, is the improbability that any such cause *l*existed*l*.

All, therefore, which Hume has made out, and this he must be considered to have made out, is, that *m*(at least in the imperfect state of our knowledge of natural agencies, which leaves it always possible that some *n* of the physical antecedents may have been hidden from us,)*m* no evidence can *o* prove a miracle to any one who did not previously believe the existence of a being or beings with supernatural power; or who *p*believes*p* himself to have full proof that the character of the Being whom he recognises, is inconsistent with his having seen fit to interfere on the occasion in question.

*q*If we do not already believe in supernatural agencies, no miracle can prove to us their existence. The miracle itself, considered merely as an extra-

---

*See the two *i* remarkable notes (A) and (F), appended to his *Inquiry into the Relation of Cause and Effect* [3rd ed. Edinburgh: Constable, 1818, pp. 493–7, 527–40].

*h–h*MS, 43, 46   having originally
j–j+43, 46, 51, 56, 62, 65, 68, 72
*l–l*MS, 43, 46   had existence in the case
m–m+46, 51, 56, 62, 65, 68, 72
*o*MS, 43   be sufficient to

*i*MS, 43, 46, 51, 56   very
*k–k*MS, 43, 46   it exist

*n*46   one or more
*p–p*MS, 43, 46, 51   believed

*q–q*626MS   [*no paragraph*]   The truth of this (however fatal to a school of theology which has recently been revived in this country, and which has the weakness to rest all the evidences of religion upon tradition and testimony) may be, and is, admitted by all defenders of revelation who have made much figure as such during the present century. It is now acknowledged by nearly all the ablest writers on the subject, that natural religion is the necessary basis of revealed; that the proofs of Christianity pre-suppose the being and moral attributes of God; and that it is the conformity of a religion to those attributes which determines whether credence ought to be given to its external evidences; that (as the proposition is sometimes expressed) the doctrine must prove the miracles, not the miracles the doctrine. It is hardly necessary to point out the complete

ordinary fact, may be satisfactorily certified by our senses or by testimony; but nothing can ever prove that it is a miracle: there is still another possible hypothesis, that of its being the result of some unknown natural cause: and this possibility cannot be so completely shut out, as to leave no alternative but that of admitting the existence and intervention of a being superior to nature. Those, however, who already believe in such a being, have two hypotheses to choose from, a supernatural and an unknown natural agency; and they have to judge which of the two is the most probable in the particular case. In forming this judgment, an important element of the question will be the conformity of the result to the laws of the supposed agent, that is, to the character of the Deity as they conceive it. But, with the knowledge which we now possess of the general uniformity of the course of nature, religion, following in the wake of science, has been compelled to acknowledge the government of the universe as being on the whole carried on by general laws, and not by special interpositions. To whoever holds this belief, there is a general presumption against any supposition of divine agency not operating through general laws, or in other words, there is an antecedent improbability in every miracle, which, in order to outweigh it, requires an extraordinary strength of antecedent probability derived from the special circumstances of the case.[q]

§ 3. [*The degrees of improbability correspond to differences in the nature of the generalization with which an assertion conflicts*] It appears from what has been said, that the assertion that a cause has been defeated of an effect [a]which is[a] connected with it by a completely ascertained law of causation, is

---

accordance of these views with the opinions which (not to mention other testimonies) the New Testament itself shows to have been generally prevalent in the apostolic age; when it was believed indeed that miracles were necessary as credentials, and that whoever was sent by God must have the power of working them; but no one dreamed that such power sufficed by itself as proof of a divine mission, and St. Paul expressly warned the churches, if any one came to them working miracles, to observe what he taught, and unless he preached "Christ, and him crucified," not to listen to the teaching. [See I Corinthians, 2:2 and 1:23.] There is no reason, therefore, that timid Christians should shrink from accepting the logical canon of the Grounds of Disbelief. And it is not hazarding much to predict that a school which peremptorily rejects all evidences of religion, except such as, when relied upon exclusively, the canon in question irreversibly condemns; which denies to mankind the right to judge of religious doctrine, and bids them depend on miracles as their sole guide; must, in the present state of the human mind, inevitably fail in its attempt to put itself at the head of the religious feelings and convictions of this country: by whatever learning, argumentative skill, and even, in many respects, comprehensive views of human affairs, their peculiar doctrines may be recommended to the acceptance of thinkers.]   43   *as* MS . . . human affairs, its peculiar doctrines . . . *as* MS]   46   [*no paragraph*] The truth of this (however fatal to those schools of theology which have the weakness . . . *as* MS . . . It is now laid down by nearly . . . *as* MS . . . the Grounds of Disbelief.
     [a–a]+43, 46, 51, 56, 62, 65, 68, 72

to be disbelieved or not, according to the probability or improbability that there existed in the particular instance an adequate counteracting cause. To form an estimate of this, is not more difficult than of *other probabilities*. With regard to all *known* causes capable of counteracting the given causes, we have generally some previous knowledge of the frequency or rarity of their occurrence, from which we may draw an inference as to the antecedent improbability of their having been present in any particular case. And neither in respect to known *nor* unknown causes are we required to pronounce on the probability of their existing in nature, but only of their having existed at the *time* and place at which the transaction is alleged to have happened. We are seldom, therefore, without the means (when the circumstances of the case are at all known to us) of judging how far it is likely that such a cause should have existed at that time and place without manifesting its presence by some other marks, and (in the case of an unknown cause) without having hitherto manifested its existence in any other instance. According as this circumstance, or the falsity of the testimony, appears more improbable, that is, conflicts with an approximate generalization of a higher order, we believe the testimony, or disbelieve it; with a stronger or a weaker degree of conviction, according to the preponderance: at least until we have sifted the matter further.

So much, then, for the case in which the alleged fact conflicts, or appears to conflict, with a real law of causation. But a more common case, perhaps, is that of its conflicting with uniformities of mere coexistence, not proved to be dependent on causation: in other words, with the properties of Kinds. It is with these uniformities principally, that the marvellous stories related by travellers are apt to be at variance: as of men with tails, or with wings, and (until confirmed by experience) of flying fish; or of ice, in the celebrated anecdote of the Dutch travellers and the King of Siam. Facts of this description, facts previously unheard of but which could not from any known law of causation be pronounced impossible, are what Hume characterizes as not contrary to experience, but merely unconformable to it; and Bentham, in his treatise on Evidence, denominates them facts disconformable *in specie*, as distinguished from such as are disconformable *in toto* or in *degree*.[*]

In a case of this description, the fact asserted is the existence of a new Kind; which in itself is not in the slightest degree incredible, and only to be rejected if the improbability that any variety of object existing at the particular place and time should not have been discovered sooner, be greater than

[*Rationale of Judicial Evidence, ed. J. S. Mill, Vol. III, pp. 283–307; in a note to this passage, JSM cites Hume's "Of Miracles."]

*b–b*MS, 43, 46, 51, 56   any other probability
*c–c*62, 65, 68   or
*d*MS, 43, 46   precise

that of error or mendacity in the witnesses. Accordingly, such assertions, when made by credible persons, and of unexplored places, are not disbelieved, but at most regarded as requiring confirmation from subsequent observers; unless the alleged properties of the supposed new Kind are at variance with known properties of some larger Kind which includes it; or in other words, unless, in the new Kind which is asserted to exist, some properties are said to have been found disjoined from others which have always been known to accompany them; as in the case of Pliny's men, or any other kind of animal of a structure different from that which has always been found to coexist with animal life. On the mode of dealing with any such case, little needs be added to what has been said on the same topic in the twenty-second chapter.* When the uniformities of coexistence which the alleged fact would violate, are such as to raise a strong presumption of their being the result of causation, the fact which conflicts with them is to be disbelieved; at least provisionally, and subject to further investigation. When the presumption amounts to a virtual certainty, as in the case of the general structure of organized beings, the only question requiring consideration is whether, in phenomena so little *understood*, there may not be liabilities to counteraction from causes hitherto unknown; or whether the phenomena may not be capable of originating in some other way, which would produce a different set of derivative uniformities. Where (as in the case of the flying fish, or the ornithorhynchus) the generalization to which the alleged fact would be an exception is very special and of limited range, neither of the above suppositions can be deemed very improbable; and it is generally, in the case of such alleged anomalies, wise to suspend our judgment, pending the subsequent inquiries which will not fail to confirm the assertion if it be true. But when the generalization is very comprehensive, embracing a vast number and variety of observations, and covering a considerable province of the *domain* of nature; then, for reasons which have been fully explained, such an empirical law comes near to the certainty of an ascertained law of causation: and any alleged exception to it cannot be admitted, unless on the evidence of some law of causation proved by a still more complete induction.

Such uniformities in the course of nature as do not bear marks of being the results of causation, are, as we have already seen, admissible as universal truths with a degree of credence proportioned to their generality. Those which are true of all things whatever, or at least which are totally independent of the varieties of Kinds, namely, the laws of number and extension, to which we may add the law of causation itself, are probably the only ones, an exception to which is absolutely and *permanently* incredible. Accordingly, it is to

*Supra, pp. 585–6.

assertions supposed to be contradictory to these laws, or [h]to[h] some others coming near to them in generality, that the word impossibility (at least [i]total[i] impossibility) seems to be generally confined. Violations of other laws, of special laws of causation for instance, are said, by persons studious of accuracy in expression, to be impossible *in the circumstances of the case*; or impossible unless some cause had existed which did not exist in the particular case.* Of no assertion, not in contradiction to some of these very general laws, will more than improbability be asserted by any cautious person; and improbability not of the [m] highest degree, unless the time and place in which the fact is said to have occurred, render it almost certain that the anomaly, if real, could not have been overlooked by other observers. Suspension of judgment is in all other cases the resource of the judicious inquirer; provided the testimony in favour of the anomaly presents, when well sifted, no suspicious circumstances.

But the testimony is scarcely ever found to stand that test, in cases in which the anomaly is not real. In the instances on record in which a great number of witnesses, of good reputation and scientific acquirements, have testified to the truth of something which has turned out untrue, there have almost always been circumstances which, to a keen observer who had taken due pains to sift the matter, would have rendered the testimony untrust-

*[51] A writer to whom I have several times referred, gives as the definition of an impossibility, that which there exists in the world no cause adequate to produce. [Hutton, "Mill and Whewell on the Logic of Induction," pp. 101–2.] This definition does not take in such impossibilities as these—that two and two should make five; that two straight lines should inclose a space; or that anything should begin to exist without a cause. I can think of no definition of impossibility comprehensive enough to include all its varieties, except the one which I have given: viz. An impossibility is that, the truth of which would conflict with a complete induction, that is, with the most conclusive evidence which we possess of universal truth.

As to the [j]reputed impossibilities which rest on no other grounds[j] than our ignorance of any cause capable of producing [k]the supposed effects; very few of them are certainly impossible, or permanently incredible. The[k] facts of travelling seventy miles an hour, painless surgical operations, and conversing by instantaneous signals between London and [l]New York, held a high place, not many years ago, among such[l] impossibilities.

[h-h]+43, 62, 65, 68, 72
[i-i]MS, 43, 46, 51, 56 *absolute*
[j-j]51 impossibilities which are reputed such on no other ground] 56 *as* 51 . . . other grounds
[k-k]51 them; if impossibility means incredibility, very few of them are impossibilities at all. Otherwise, the] 56 them; very few of them are either impossible or incredible. The
[l-l]51 Paris, held a high place thirty years ago among absolute] 56 Constantinople, held . . . *as* 51 . . . among such] 62, 65 Constantinople, held . . . *as* 72
[m]MS, 43, 46 very

worthy. There have generally been means of accounting for the impression on the senses or minds of the alleged percipients, by fallacious appearances; or some epidemic delusion, propagated by the contagious influence of popular feeling, has been concerned in the case; or some strong interest has been implicated—religious zeal, party feeling, vanity, or at least the passion for the marvellous, in persons strongly susceptible of it. When none of these or similar circumstances exist to account for the apparent strength of the testimony; and where the assertion is not in contradiction either to those universal laws which know no counteraction or anomaly, or to the generalizations next in comprehensiveness to them, but would only amount, if admitted, to the existence of an unknown cause or an anomalous Kind, in circumstances not so thoroughly explored but that it is credible that things hitherto unknown may still come to light; a cautious person will neither admit nor reject the testimony, but will wait for confirmation at other times and from other unconnected sources. Such ought to have been the conduct of the King of Siam when the Dutch travellers affirmed to him the existence of ice. But an ignorant person is as obstinate in his contemptuous incredulity as he is unreasonably credulous. Anything unlike his own narrow experience he disbelieves, if it flatters no "propensity"; any °nursery° tale is swallowed implicitly by him if it does.

§ 4. [*A fact is not incredible because the chances are against it*] ªI shall now ª advert to a very serious misapprehension of the principles of the subject, which has been committed by some of the writers against Hume's Essay on Miracles, *b*and by Bishop Butler before them,*b*[*] in their anxiety to destroy what appeared to them a formidable weapon of assault against the Christian religion; and *c*the effect of which is*c* entirely to confound the doctrine of the Grounds of Disbelief. The mistake consists in overlooking the distinction between (what may be called) improbability before the fact, and improbability after it; *d*or (since, as Mr. Venn remarks,[†] the distinction of past and future is not the material circumstance) between the improbability of a mere guess being right, and the improbability of an alleged fact being true*d*.

[*See Joseph Butler. *The Analogy of Religion*. London: Knapton, 1736.]
[†*Logic of Chance*, pp. 129–31.]

*n–n*MS   passion
*o–o*MS   nurse's [*printer's error?*]
*a–a*MS, 43   Before concluding this inquiry, we must
b–b+68, 72
    *c–c*MS, 43   to which, with entirely different views on the religious question, Laplace, in his *Essay on Probabilities*, has been led to give his sanction; the effect in both cases being,
    *d–d*MS   two different properties, & the latter of which is always a ground of disbelief; the former is so or not, as it may happen]   43, 46   two different properties, the latter . . . *as* MS]   51, 56, 62, 65   *as* 43 . . . disbelief, the former not always

Many events are altogether improbable to us, before they have happened, or before we are informed of their happening, which are not in the least incredible when we are informed of them, because not contrary to any, even approximate, induction. In the cast of a perfectly fair die, the chances are five to one against throwing ace, that is, ace will be thrown on an average only once in six throws. But this is no reason against believing that ace was thrown on a given occasion, if any credible witness asserts it; since though ace is only thrown once in six times, *some* number which is only thrown once in six times must have been thrown if the die was thrown at all. The improbability, then, or in other words, the unusualness, of any fact, is no reason for disbelieving it, if the nature of the case renders it certain that either that or something equally improbable, that is, equally unusual, did happen. *Nor is this all: for even if the other five sides of the die were all twos, or all threes, yet as ace would still on the average come up once in every six throws, its coming up in a given throw would be not in any way contradictory to experience.* If we disbelieved all facts which had the chances against them beforehand, we should believe hardly anything. We are told that A. B. died yesterday: the moment before we were so told, the chances against his having died on that day may have been ten thousand to one; but since he was certain to die at some time or other, and when he died must necessarily die on some particular day, while the *preponderance of chances is very great* against every day in particular, experience affords no ground *g* for discrediting any testimony which may be produced to the event's having taken place on a given day.

Yet it has been considered, by Dr. Campbell[*] and others, *as* a complete answer to Hume's doctrine (that things are incredible which are *contrary* to the uniform course of experience), that we do not disbelieve, merely because the chances were against them, things in strict *conformity* to the uniform course of experience; that we do not disbelieve an alleged fact merely because the combination of causes on which it depends occurs only once in a certain number of times. It is evident that whatever is shown by *observation, or can be proved from laws of nature,* to occur in a certain proportion (however small) of the whole number of possible cases, is not contrary to experience; *though we are right in disbelieving it, if some other supposition respecting the matter in question involves on the whole a less departure from the ordin-

[*George Campbell. *A Dissertation on Miracles.* Edinburgh: Kincaid and Bell, 1762.]

e–e+68, 72
*f–f*MS, 43, 46, 51, 56 chances are innumerable
*g*MS, 43, 46 whatever   *h* *h*+43, 46, 51, 56, 62, 65, 68, 72
*i–i*MS, 43 experience
*j–j*MS, 43 (though . . . *as* 72 . . . in question would be true in a greater proportion of the whole number of cases.) What would really be contrary to experience, would be

ary course of events. Yet, on such grounds as this have able writers been led to the extraordinary conclusion, that nothing supported by credible testimony ought ever to be disbelieved.[j]

[a]§ 5. [*Are coincidences less credible than other facts?*] We have considered two species of events, commonly said to be improbable; one kind which are in no way extraordinary, but which, having an immense preponderance of chances against them, are improbable until they are affirmed, but no longer; another kind which, being contrary to some recognised law of nature, are incredible on any amount of testimony except such as would be sufficient to shake our belief in the law itself. But between these two classes of events, there is an intermediate class, consisting of what are commonly termed Coincidences: in other words, those combinations of chances which present some peculiar and unexpected regularity, assimilating them, in so far, to the results of law. As if, for example, in a lottery of a thousand tickets, the numbers should be drawn in the exact order of what are called the natural numbers, 1, 2, 3, &c. We have still to consider the principles of evidence applicable to this case: whether there is any difference between coincidences and ordinary events, in the amount of testimony or other evidence necessary to render them credible.

It is certain, that on every rational principle of expectation, a combination of this peculiar sort may be expected quite as often as any other given series of a thousand numbers; that with perfectly fair dice, sixes will be thrown twice, thrice, or any number of times in succession, quite as often in a thousand or a million throws, as any other succession of numbers fixed upon beforehand; and that no judicious player would give greater odds against the one series than against the other. Notwithstanding this, there is a general disposition to regard the one as much more improbable than the other, and as requiring much stronger evidence to make it credible. Such is the force of this impression, that it has led some [b]thinkers[b] to the conclusion, that nature has greater [c]difficulty[c] in producing regular combinations than irregular ones; or in other words, that there is some general tendency of things, some law, which prevents regular combinations from occurring, or at least from occurring so often as others. Among these [d]thinkers[d] may be numbered D'Alembert; who, in an Essay on Probabilities to be found in the fifth volume of his

---

the assertion that the event had happened more frequently in some large number of times, than the same combination had ever been known to occur in that number of times; and this alone it is which is improbable, in the sense of incredibility, or, as we have called it, improbability after the fact.

a—a634+46, 51, 56, 62, 65, 68, 72
b—b46   philosophers
c—c56   difficulties
d—d46   philosophers

Mélanges,[*] contends that regular combinations, though equally probable according to the mathematical theory with any others, are physically less probable. He appeals to common sense, or in other words, to common impressions; saying, if dice thrown repeatedly in our presence gave sixes every time, should we not, before the number of throws had reached ten, (not to speak of thousands ᵉofᵉ millions,) be ready to affirm, with the most positive conviction, that the dice were false?

The common and natural impression is in favour of D'Alembert: the regular series would be thought much more unlikely than an irregular. But this common impression is, I apprehend, ᶠmerely grounded on theᶠ fact, that scarcely anybody remembers to have ever seen one of these peculiar coincidences: the reason of which is simply that no one's experience extends to anything like the number of trials, within which that or any other given combination of events ᵍcan be expectedᵍ to happen. The chance of sixes on a single throw of two dice being ¹⁄₃₆, the chance of sixes ten times in succession is 1 divided by the tenth power of 36; in other words, such a concurrence is only likely to happen once in 3,656,158,440,062,976 trials, a number which no dice-player's experience comes up to a millionth part of. But if, instead of sixes ten times, any other given succession of ten throws had been fixed upon, it would have been exactly as unlikely that in any individual's experience that particular succession had ever occurred; although this does not *seem* equally improbable, because no one ʰwould be likely toʰ have remembered whether it had occurred or not, and because the comparison is tacitly made, not between sixes ten times and any one particular series of throws, but between all regular and all irregular successions taken together.

That (as D'Alembert says) if the succession of sixes was actually thrown before our eyes, we should ascribe it not to chance, but to unfairness in the dice, is unquestionably true. But this arises from a totally different principle. We should then be considering, not the probability of the fact in itself, but the comparative probability with which, when it is known to have happened, it may be referred to one or to another cause. The regular series is not at all less likely than the irregular one to be brought about by chance, but it is much more likely than the irregular one to be produced by design; or by some general cause operating through the structure of the dice. It is the nature of casual combinations to produce a repetition of the same event, as often and no oftener than any other series of events. But it is the nature of general causes to reproduce, in the same circumstances, always the same event.

[*Jean le Rond d'Alembert, "Doutes et questions sur le calcul des probabilités," in *Mélanges de littérature, d'histoire, et de philosophie*. 4th ed. 5 vols. Amsterdam: Chatelain, 1767, Vol. V, p. 284.]

ᵉ⁻ᵉ46   or [*printer's error?*]
ᵍ⁻ᵍ46, 51, 56, 62, 65   is likely

ᶠ⁻ᶠ46   grounded on the single
ʰ⁻ʰ46, 51, 56, 62, 65, 68   could possibly

Common sense and science alike dictate that, all other things being the same, we should rather attribute the effect to a cause which if real would be very likely to produce it, than to a cause which would be very unlikely to produce it. According to Laplace's sixth theorem, which we demonstrated in a former chapter, the difference of probability arising from the superior *efficacy* of the constant cause, unfairness in the dice, would after a very few throws far outweigh any antecedent probability which there could be against its existence.

D'Alembert should have put the question in another manner. He should have supposed that we had ourselves previously tried the dice, and knew by ample experience that they were fair. Another person then tries them in our absence, and assures us that he threw sixes ten times in succession. Is the assertion credible or not? Here the effect to be accounted for is not the occurrence itself, but the fact of the witness's asserting it. This may arise either from its having really happened, or from some other cause. What we have to estimate is the comparative probability of these two suppositions.

If the witness affirmed that he had thrown any other series of numbers, supposing him to be a person of veracity, and tolerable accuracy, and to profess that he took particular notice, we should *i* believe him. But the ten sixes are exactly as likely to have been really thrown as the other series. If, therefore, this assertion is less credible than the other, the reason must be, not that it is less likely than the other to be made truly, but that it is more likely than the other to be made falsely.

One reason obviously presents itself why what is called a coincidence, should be oftener asserted falsely than an ordinary combination. It excites wonder. It gratifies the love of the marvellous. The motives, therefore, to falsehood, one of the most frequent of which is the desire to astonish, operate more strongly in favour of this kind of assertion than of the other kind. Thus far there is evidently more reason for discrediting an alleged coincidence, than a statement in itself not more probable, but which if made would not be thought remarkable. There are cases, however, in which the presumption on this ground would be the other way. There are some witnesses who, the more extraordinary an occurrence might appear, would be the more anxious to verify it by the utmost *j* carefulness of observation before they would venture to believe it, and still more before they would assert it to others.*a*

a§ 6. [*An opinion of Laplace examined*] Independently, however, of any peculiar chances of mendacity arising from the nature of the assertion,

---

*i*46 fully
*j*46 possible
*a–a*638[*for MS, 43 versions of this section (§5 in those versions) see* Appendix G; *the second paragraph and the final paragraph appear, in modified wording, in all versions*]

Laplace contends, that merely on the general ground of the fallibility of testimony, a coincidence is not credible on the same amount of testimony on which we should be warranted in believing an ordinary combination of events. In order to do justice to his argument, it is necessary to illustrate it by the example chosen by himself.

If, says Laplace,[*] there were one thousand tickets in a box, and one only has been drawn out, then if an eye-witness affirms that the number drawn was 79, this, though the chances were 999 in 1000 against it, is not on that account the less credible; its credibility is equal to the antecedent probability of the witness's veracity. But if there were in the box 999 black balls and only one white, and the witness affirms that the white ball was drawn, the case according to Laplace is very different: the credibility of his assertion is *but a small fraction* of what it was in the former case; the reason of the difference being as follows.

The witnesses of whom we are speaking must, from the nature of the case, be of a kind whose credibility falls materially short of certainty: let us suppose, then, the credibility of the witness in the case in question to be 9/10; that is, let us suppose that in every ten statements *which* the witness makes, nine on an average are correct, and one incorrect. Let us now suppose that there *have* taken place a sufficient number of drawings to exhaust all the possible combinations, the witness deposing in every one. In one case out of every ten in all these drawings he will actually have made a false announcement. But in the case of the thousand tickets these false announcements will have been distributed impartially over all the numbers, and of the *999* cases in which No. 79 was not drawn, there will have been only one *case* in which it was announced. On the contrary, in the case of the thousand balls, (the announcement being always either "black" or "white,") if white was not drawn, and there was a false announcement, that false announcement *must* have been white; and since by the supposition there was a false announcement once in every ten times, white will have been announced falsely in one tenth part of all the cases in which it was not drawn, that is, in one tenth part of 999 cases out of every thousand. White, then, is drawn, on an average, exactly as often as No. 79, but it is announced, without having been really

[*Essai philosophique sur les probabilités, pp. 138ff.]

*b–b*46   only 1/999
*c–c*46   No witness's assertions are always true; every one makes, unintentionally if not designedly, in any great number of statements, some which are incorrect, and the average proportion of his incorrect to his correct statements measures the value of his testimony. Let us suppose this proportion
d–d+51, 56, 62, 65, 68, 72
*e–e*46   has
f–f+51, 56, 62, 65, 68, 72
*g–g*46   out of 999

drawn, 999 times as often as No. 79; the announcement therefore requires *a much greater amount of* testimony to render it credible.*

To make this argument valid it must of course be supposed, that the announcements made by the witness are average specimens of his general veracity and accuracy; or, at least, that they are *neither more nor less* so in the case of the black and white balls, *than* in the case of the thousand tickets *. This assumption, however, is not warranted. A person is far less likely to mistake, who has only one form of error to guard against, than if he had 999 different errors to avoid. For instance, in the example chosen, a messenger who might make a mistake once in ten times in reporting the number drawn in a lottery, might not err once in a thousand times if sent simply to observe whether a ball *was* black or white. Laplace's argument therefore is faulty even as applied to his own case. Still less can that case be received as completely representing all cases of coincidence. Laplace has so contrived his example,* that though black answers to 999 distinct possibilities, and white only to one, the witness has nevertheless no bias which can make him prefer black to white. * The witness did not know that there were 999 black balls in the box and only one white; or if he did, Laplace has taken care to make all the 999 cases so undistinguishably alike, that there is hardly a possibility of any cause of falsehood or error operating in favour of *any of* them, which would not operate in the same manner if there were only one. Alter this supposition, and the whole argument falls to the ground. Let the balls, for instance, be numbered, and let the white ball be No. 79. Considered

---

*[46] *Not, however, as might at first sight appear, 999 times as much. A complete analysis of the cases shows that (always assuming the veracity of the witness to be $9/10$) in 10,000 drawings, the drawing of No. 79 will occur nine times, and be announced incorrectly once; the credibility therefore of the announcement of No. 79 is $9/10$; while the drawing of a white ball will occur nine times, and be announced incorrectly 999 times. The credibility therefore of the announcement of white is $9/1008$, and the ratio of the two $1008:10$; the one announcement being thus only about a hundred times more credible than the other, instead of 999 times.*

*h–h*46   999 times as much [cf. *i–i* below]

*i–i*46   A complete analysis of the cases shows that (always assuming the veracity of the witness to be 9/10) the drawing of No. 79 will occur once in a thousand, and be announced incorrectly once in 10,000 times; while the drawing of a white ball will occur once in a thousand, and be announced incorrectly, 999 out of 10,000 times.

*j–j*46   This argument of Laplace's, though I formerly thought it fallacious, is irrefragable in the case which he supposes, and in all others which that case fairly represents. But I do not think his case a perfect representative of all cases of coincidence. To make his

*k–k*46   as likely to be

*l–l*46   as

*m–m*46   : insomuch

*n–n*51, 56   were

*o*46   Now this condition is fully provided for in Laplace's case.

p–p+51, 56, 62, 65, 68, 72

in respect of their colour, there are but two things which the witness can be interested in asserting, or can have dreamt or hallucinated, or has to choose from if he answers at random, viz. black and white: but considered in respect of the numbers attached to them, there are a thousand: and if his interest or error happens to be connected with the numbers, though the only assertion he makes is about the colour, the case becomes precisely assimilated to that of the thousand tickets. Or instead of the balls suppose a lottery, with 1000 tickets and but one prize, and that I hold No. 79, and being interested only in that, ask the witness not what was the number drawn, but whether it was 79 or some other. There are now only two cases, as in Laplace's example; yet he surely would not say that if the witness answered 79, the assertion would be ^{q}in an enormous proportion^q less credible, than if he made the same answer to the ^{r}same question asked in the other^r way. If, for instance, (to put a case supposed by Laplace himself,) he has staked a large sum on one of the chances, and thinks that by announcing its occurrence he shall increase his credit; he is equally likely to have betted on any one of the 999 numbers which are attached to black balls, and so far as the chances of mendacity from this cause are concerned, there will be 999 times as many chances of his announcing black falsely as white.

Or suppose a regiment of 1000 men, 999 Englishmen and one Frenchman, and that of these one man has been killed, and it is not known which. I ask the question, and the witness answers, the Frenchman. This was not only as improbable à priori, but is in itself as singular a circumstance, as remarkable a coincidence, as the drawing of the white ball: yet we should believe the statement as readily, as if the answer had been John Thompson. Because, though the 999 Englishmen were all alike in the point in which they differed from the Frenchman, they were not, like the 999 black balls, undistinguishable in every other respect; but being all different, they admitted as many chances of interest or error, as if each man had been of a different nation; and if a lie was told or a mistake made, the misstatement was as likely to fall on any Jones or Thompson of the set, as on the Frenchman.

The example of a coincidence selected by D'Alembert, that of sixes thrown on a pair of dice ten times in succession, belongs to this sort of cases rather than to such as Laplace's. The coincidence is here far more remarkable, because of far rarer occurrence, than the drawing of the white ball. But though the improbability of its really occurring is greater, the superior probability of its being announced falsely cannot be established with the same evidence. The announcement "black" represented 999 cases, but the witness may not have known this, and if he did, the 999 cases are so exactly alike, that there is really only one set of possible causes of mendacity cor-

$^{q-q}$46 999 times
$^{r-r}$46 question asked in a different

responding to *the whole*. The announcement "sixes *not* drawn ten times," represents, and is known by the witness to represent, a great multitude of contingencies, every one of which being unlike every other, there may be a different and a fresh set of *causes* of mendacity corresponding to each.

It appears to me, therefore, that Laplace's doctrine *is not strictly true of any coincidences, and is wholly inapplicable to most:* and that to know whether a coincidence does or does not require more evidence to render it credible than an ordinary event, we must refer, in every instance, to first principles, and estimate afresh what is the probability that the given testimony would have been *delivered* in that instance, supposing the fact which it asserts not to be true.

With these remarks we close the discussion of the Grounds of Disbelief; and along with it, such exposition as *space admits, and as the writer has* it in his power to furnish, of the Logic of Induction.*

*s–s*46   them all
*t–t*46   chances [*printer's error?*]
*u–u*46   does not hold true of all coincidences;
*v–v*46   given
*w–w*MS, 43, 46   our space admitted, and as the writer had